Real Property and Real People
Principles of Land Law

Real Property and Real People

Principles of Land Law

K. J. Gray
MA, PhD
Fellow of Trinity College Cambridge;
University Lecturer in Law,
University of Cambridge

P. D. Symes
BA
Research Fellow of Lucy Cavendish College, Cambridge

London
Butterworths
1981

England Butterworth & Co (Publishers) Ltd
88 Kingsway, London WC2B 6AB

Australia Butterworths Pty Ltd
271–273 Lane Cove Road, North Ryde
Sydney, NSW 2113
Also at Melbourne, Brisbane, Adelaide and Perth

Canada Butterworth & Co (Canada) Ltd
2265 Midland Avenue, Scarborough
Toronto, M1P 4S1

Butterworth & Co (Western Canada)
409 Granville Street, Ste 856
Vancouver BC, V6C 1T2

New Zealand Butterworths of New Zealand Ltd
33–35 Cumberland Place, Wellington

Singapore Butterworth & Co (Asia) Pte Ltd
Crawford Post Office Box 770, Singapore 9119

South Africa Butterworth Publishers (Pty) Ltd
Box No 792, Durban

USA Mason Publishing Co
Finch Building, 366 Wacouta Street
St Paul, Minnesota 55101

Butterworth (Legal Publishers) Inc
15014 NE 40th, Ste 205, Redmond, Washington 98052

Butterworth (Legal Publishers) Inc
381 Elliot Street, Newton, Upper Falls
Massachusetts 02164

ISBN Casebound 0 406 59110 5
Limp 0 406 59111 3

Reprinted *July 1983*

Limp cover illustration: *Cottages at Burghclere* by Stanley Spencer.

Printed and bound in Great Britain by
Thomson Litho Ltd, East Kilbride, Scotland

Preface

The ultimate objective of a university education in law is not the learning of rules but the critical perception of value. This means not only that the student should be taught to distinguish between a good argument and a bad one. It means also that he should be taught that law does not exist in a moral or social vacuum but is profoundly affected by the predominant values of the society in which he lives. The task of the teacher is in part to indicate the points at which the legal solutions are not predetermined by some logical system but are instead explicable only in terms of more fundamental value judgments. None of this is to argue that the learning of rules is irrelevant. On the contrary it provides the essential basis for any further inquiry into the function of law in society. As Otto Kahn-Freund said,

> legal education is at its best if the student learns to look at each concrete situation from two different angles . . . He should learn to look at it in a strictly and rigidly dogmatic way and he should also learn to look at it as a social situation requiring the solution of a social problem . . . A law student must go through the process of rigid deductive argument from the premiss set by statute or precedent. He must not be allowed to go around it by escaping into talk about policies, he must go through it. But he must go *through* it and not get stuck in it. Some of our American colleagues are inclined to allow the students to escape into 'policy' discussions before the dogmatic mechanism, the purported deductive reasoning from statute or precedent is fully displayed. In this country there is no such danger: the danger is that the discussion gets stuck in the perhaps intellectually very fascinating game of legal argument without ever condescending to the realities of the situation and to what for example a court wanted to achieve (probably without saying so) or in fact did achieve with its decision . . .

This book attempts to apply Kahn-Freund's approach to the learning of land law. It is absolutely essential that the student should go through what Kahn-Freund called 'the mill of rigorous argument of the traditional kind'. Hence the emphasis in this book upon the 'principles of land law' and upon the careful deduction of results from first principles. However, the land lawyer must reach beyond the technical mastery of his subject towards some vision of the social and economic dimension of the law of property. Land law is a reflection of one kind of distributive justice. The land lawyer's area of concern should extend to a curiosity about the criteria which govern the allocation of the rights and benefits to which we attach the label 'property'. The aim of this book is therefore to combine a technical understanding of complex legal phenomena with some critical awareness of the broader values and preferences which inform the law.

Throughout this book we shall examine the principles of real property law which apply to all forms of land, whether used for residential, commercial or investment purposes. However, it is often the case that the operation of land law principles is seen with greatest clarity in the context of residential property. We shall therefore relate land law, at least initially, to the setting which will be most familiar to the student—that which involves the domestic living arrangements of the ordinary citizen. All too often in the past land law has been taught as if it had no reference to real everyday life. Land law is in fact very much concerned with the way in which 'real people' live their lives. All of us—even the truly homeless—live somewhere, and each therefore stands in some relation to land as owner-occupier, tenant, licensee or squatter. Land law thus has something to say about each one of us. If the student can grasp the principles of land law in this more immediate and realistic context, he can easily apply these principles to land which is used for other than residential purposes. This primary focus upon residential property is made even more important for the land lawyer because it is in this area that the land law of the 1980s may diverge most significantly from the conventional rules of real property law. Changing times produce new needs, and one of the foremost claims of the present age is the demand for residential security. Recent developments have witnessed the recognition of what is virtually a modern concept of seisin—the idea that the possession of the actual occupier of land must be protected. This concept is being increasingly engrafted upon the existing structure of the law of real property, and much of this book is devoted to tracing this aspect of the evolving law.

This book seeks to deal with the law of real property in force in England and Wales as of June 1981. The material covered is essentially the material contained in the syllabus of the Land Law I course taught in the University of Cambridge. This explains the inclusion of the (now largely archaic) law of strict settlements and the virtual exclusion of such matters as the law relating to conveyancing, planning, compulsory purchase and priorities of mortgages. The teaching technique employed stems from two ideas. First, English land law is rooted in a limited number of axioms from which almost all other propositions may be derived by logical deduction. Second, most of the principles of land law are richly exemplified in a relatively small group of important cases. It is much more profitable for the student to have an excellent understanding of perhaps a dozen cases than that he should have a superficial acquaintance with the hundreds of cases which are normally served up before him in the traditional land law course. It is with these beliefs in mind that in this book we highlight certain significant decisions and work through them in close detail. The object of each extended analysis is to illuminate not only the actual decision under scrutiny but also the underlying thought processes which make our land law a coherent and systematic body of principles.

Cambridge
3rd June 1981

K.J.G.
P.D.S.

Contents

Chapter 3
The acquisition of title to land 78

PART II UNREGISTERED CONVEYANCING

Chapter 4
Land charges 111

Chapter 5
Strict settlements 154

Chapter 6
The rule against perpetuities 185

PART V MATRIMONIAL PROPERTY

Chapter 16
The matrimonial home 553

PART VI CONTROL OF LAND USE

Chapter 17
Easements and profits 577

Chapter 18
Covenants and the planning of land use 605

Index 637

Table of statutes

References in this table to 'Statutes' are to Halsbury's Statutes of England (Third Edition) showing the volume and page at which the annotated text of the Act will be found.

List of cases

PART I

General

CHAPTER 1

The idea of property

1. INTRODUCTION

Property is necessarily a central element in any system of rules concerned with the governance of human activity. It is difficult to envisage a society which recognises no right of property, for this concept is used by almost every social group for the expression of man's relationship with his fellow man and with the environment in which he lives. Indeed, some philosophers have perceived in the institution of property the vital prerequisite of civilised co-existence. David Hume was able to say, for instance, that

> No one can doubt that the convention for the distinction of property, and for the stability of possession, is of all circumstances the most necessary to the establishment of human society, and that after the agreement for the fixing and observing of this rule, there remains little or nothing to be done towards settling a perfect harmony and concord[1].

However, not all would share this view. For some social theorists the demarcation of property rights of any kind is a cause of profound regret[2]. For others it is a stimulus to radical change of the social order[3]. It is nevertheless undeniable that the concept of property now plays a vital part in the organisation of our social and economic life. We can no more contemplate a society without some conception of 'property' than we can imagine a society which has not yet discovered the institution of 'contract'. Indeed, it was John Locke who argued that the 'great and chief end ... of men's uniting into commonwealths, and putting themselves under government, is the preservation of their property[4].'

1 *A Treatise of Human Nature* (Everyman's Library edn., London 1911), Vol. II, p. 196f. (Book III, Part II).

2 'The first man who, having enclosed a piece of ground, bethought himself of saying "This is mine," and found people simple enough to believe him, was the real founder of civil society. From how many crimes, wars, and murders, from how many horrors and misfortunes might not anyone have saved mankind, by pulling up the stakes, or filling up the ditch, and crying to his fellows: "Beware of listening to this imposter, you are undone if you once forget that the fruits of the earth belong to us all, and the earth itself to nobody."' See J.-J. Rousseau, *Discourse on the Origin of Inequality*, in *The Social Contract and Discourses* (Everyman's Library edn., London 1913), p. 76.

3 This view is epitomised in Proudhon's often quoted remark that 'property is theft'. See *Qu'est-ce que la Propriété? Premier Memoir* (Paris 1840), 131.

4 *The Second Treatise of Civil Government* (ed. J. W. Gough, Oxford 1946), para. 124.

(1) The function of the law of property

The law of property provides the rules by which a necessary element of legitimacy is conferred upon the de facto possession of scarce goods and resources[5]. However, it is essential to note at the outset that there is a fundamental *unreality* in any search for 'the' owner of any particular 'thing'. The law of property is not so much concerned with 'things'; it is more concerned with the relationships between individuals in respect of 'things'. It is concerned with values, obligations and ideologies cast in sharp relief against the universe of 'things'. To embark upon a study of the law of property otherwise than in terms of this perspective is therefore to ignore the organic human dimension which makes the concept of property a central legal institution. It is also to condemn the student to the misconception that the law of property is an arid and unexciting subject, and to dim his vision of critically important contemporary developments in the realm of property which have an impact upon us all.

(2) A social view of land law

This book contains an outline of the English law of real property. However, it also incorporates a social view of property, for it is only in this context that the technical rules of property law and conveyancing practice can be seen in their full significance. As Alice Tay has emphasised[6],

> The concept of property, the way in which it is legally defined and the extent to which it is legally, socially and politically protected raise immediately the most fundamental problems of political philosophy and social life—the relationship between the individual and his social environment, between the citizen and the State and—in modern society—between the personal and the commercial.

Land law is that part of the general law which regulates the allocation of rights and obligations in relation to 'real' (or immoveable) property. Land provides the physical substratum for social and economic life, and land law has thus become an instrument of social engineering. All of us—even the truly homeless—live somewhere, and each therefore stands in some relation to land as owner-occupier, tenant, licensee or squatter. In this way land law impinges upon a vast area of social orderings and expectations, and exerts a fundamental influence upon the lifestyles of ordinary people. It was Karl Renner who recognised that the institution of property leads automatically to an organisation similar to the state: 'Power over matter begets personal power[7].' Ultimately, as

5 Goods and resources which are not scarce are not traditionally subjected to rules of property law (e.g., air and water). However, the property perspective may enter where environmentalists begin to stress the importance of clean air and unpolluted water, p. 19, post.

6 'Property and Law in the Society of Mass Production, Mass Consumption and Mass Allocation', p. 19, in *A Revolution in our Age: The Transformation of Law, Justice and Morals* (Canberra Seminars in the History of Ideas 1975).

7 *The Institutions of Private Law and their Social Functions* (ed. O. Kahn-Freund, London and Boston 1949), p. 107.

Professor C. B. Macpherson has more recently observed, 'property is a political *relation* between persons[8].'

Irrespective of political viewpoint, it is undeniable that the law of property embodies a broad range of value judgments. These value judgments reflect the body of cultural norms, the social ethic—and also necessarily the political economy[9]—prevailing in any given community. It is inevitable that property law should thus serve as a vehicle for ideology, for 'property' has commonly been the epithet used to identify that which people most greatly value.

(3) Property, dependence and personality

Not only does 'property' identify resources of value. The label 'property' indicates something even more subtle, for it exposes relationships of dependence: dependence is the inescapable outcome of an unequal distribution of that which is valued. Viewed in this way, the terms 'property' and 'dependence' are positive and negative descriptions respectively of any existing distribution of socially valued resources.

This appears clearly in the following example. The most obvious kind of 'dependant' is, of course, an infant or minor. Significantly, English law declares that a legal estate in land cannot be owned by any person below the age of 18 years[10]. Thus, starting from the premise of the infant's physical and mental immaturity, a technical legal rule has evolved which in turn confirms and reinforces a more general cultural image of the infant's incompleteness as a legal and social personality. More pernicious, however, is the way in which for centuries a similar process of reasoning resulted in the legal and social disadvantages suffered by married women[11]. Only relatively recently has the law moved on from the position described by Blackstone, according to whom

8 'The Meaning of Property', in C. B. Macpherson (ed.), *Property: Mainstream and Critical Positions* (Toronto, Buffalo and London 1978), p. 4.

9 It was Maitland who described 'feudalism' as a state of society in which 'all or a great part of public rights and duties are inextricably interwoven with the tenure of land, in which the whole governmental system—financial, military, judicial—is part of the law of private property ... [I]t is still utterly impossible to speak of our medieval constitution except in terms of our medieval land law.' See F. W. Maitland, *The Constitutional History of England* (London 1908), p. 23f.

10 'A legal estate is not capable of ... being held by an infant' (Law of Property Act 1925, s. 1(6)). The age of majority was lowered to 18 by the Family Law Reform Act 1969, s. 1(1).

11 Starting from a similar premise—the temporary physiological and economic incapacity imposed by motherhood—the law effectively denied the married woman sufficient legal personality to hold property in her own name. Almost all her property vested in her husband upon marriage. Only with the enactment of the Married Women's Property Acts of 1870 and 1882 did the married woman regain the capacity to own property in her own right, and full recognition of her legal personality did not come until the passing of the Law Reform (Married Women and Tortfeasors) Act 1935. In this sense, the laws governing the property rights of husband and wife have comprised a substantial portion of the secular definition of the institution of marriage, and the evolution of matrimonial property law over the past century provides an unfailing index of changing social relations between the sexes. Yet, although the sex-based discrimination contained in the legal norms has now largely disappeared, the wider cultural inheritance of women's dependence (in terms of social and economic disability) is still very much with us.

'the very being or legal existence of the woman is suspended during the marriage[12].'

This abrogation of legal personality is the more unacceptable because of the pervasive association which exists between a man's material substance and his integrity as an individual[13]. Alice Tay has pointed out that 'property' is inherently linked with some notion in the common law of an area of personal inviolability. This notion is reflected in the origins of the action of trespass (both to person and to land) as the earliest and most important action at common law[14], and is rooted in an even older Anglo-Saxon and Norse concept of 'seisin' which arguably occupies a central position in the development of democracy in northwestern Europe[15]. In the analysis of Professor Tay[16],

> Property is that which a man has a right to use and enjoy without interference; it is what makes him as a person and guarantees his independence and security. It includes his person, his name, his reputation, his chattels, the land that he owns and works, the house he builds and lives in and so on. These things are seen as his property in early law because they are seen as the reification of his will, as the tangible, physical manifestation of his work and his personality[17].

If 'property' connotes 'independence and security', it follows that the absence of 'property' is inevitably linked with some degree of dependence and insecurity. Herein lies the significance of the law of property, since it isolates and identifies those who shall enjoy the socially valued assets of independence and material well-being.

12 W. Blackstone, *Commentaries on the Laws of England* (1st edn. London 1765), p. 430. Of course, Blackstone was able to argue that the merger of the wife's legal personality with that of her husband was a most benevolent form of indulgence: 'we may observe that even the disabilities which the wife lies under are for the most part intended for her protection and benefit. So great a favourite is the female sex of the laws of England.' For an excellent, and more sanguine, account of the legal emancipation of the married woman, see O. Kahn-Freund (1970) 33 MLR 601: 'Recent Legislation on Matrimonial Property'; (1971) 4 Human Rights Journal 493: 'Matrimonial Property and Equality before the Law: Some Sceptical Reflections'. See also Chapter 16, p. 553, post.

13 This association is, of course, a commonplace in literature. See, for instance, John Galsworthy, *The Forsyte Saga, Vol. 1: The Man Of Property* (London 1906), p. 44f.: 'In his great chair with the book-rest sat old Jolyon, the figurehead of his family and class and creed, with his white head and dome-like forehead, the representative of moderation, and order, and love of property.'

14 See J. G. Fleming, *An Introduction to the Law of Torts* (Oxford 1967), p. 2f.; *The Law of Torts* (5th edn. Sydney 1977), p. 14ff.

15 See Alice Tay's interesting account of the significance of the concept of 'seisin' in 'Property and Law in the Society of Mass Production, Mass Consumption and Mass Allocation', loc. cit., p. 7ff. It was Charles Reich who said that 'the institution called property guards the troubled boundary between individual man and the state. It is not the only guardian; many other institutions, laws, and practices serve as well. But in a society that chiefly values material well-being, the power to control a particular portion of that well-being is the very foundation of individuality' (see (1964) 73 Yale LJ 733: 'The New Property').

16 'Law, the citizen and the state', in E. Kamenka, R. Brown and A. E.-S. Tay (ed.), *Law and Society* (London 1978), p. 10.

17 Although the word 'man' is of course being used here in its generic sense, a not unreasonable suspicion is that the dignifying concept of property here referred to has never really been extended to the woman.

(4) The purpose of this book

In this book we set out to explore the broader connotation of 'property' within the strict context of the rules of English land law. We shall examine the way in which the land lawyer uses and manipulates the technical concepts of real property in order to describe the manner in which we all live, work, and accumulate wealth and security. We shall look particularly closely at the underlying ideology of property law and at its interaction with key issues of priority and efficiency. Above all, we shall see that 'property' is essentially a relation between individuals or groups which expresses certain social values and provides certain forms of social utility. Property law is ultimately that body of rules which governs the distribution of utility in socially valued resources.

2. THE MEANING OF PROPERTY

(1) Property is not a 'thing' but a 'relationship'

It is important at this stage to dispel one common lay notion concerning 'property'. Non-lawyers (and sometimes even lawyers) speak loosely of property as the *thing* which is owned. While this usage is harmless enough in day-to-day speech, it does obscure certain salient features of property as a legal phenomenon, for, semantically, 'property' is the condition of being 'proper' to (or belonging to) a particular person[18]. Thus, originally, it was the relationship between the thing (or 'object') and the person (or 'subject') which provided the key to the definition of 'property'.

This is not an easy idea to grasp. It was the philosopher, Jeremy Bentham, who had to remind lawyers that property is not a thing but a relationship:

> It is to be observed that in common speech in the phrase *the object of a man's property*, the words *the object of* are commonly left out; and by an ellipsis, which, violent as it is, is now become more familiar than the phrase at length, they have made that part of it which consists of the words *a man's property* perform the office of the whole[19].

Professor Macpherson has pointed to the way in which, in the transition from the pre-capitalist world to the world of the exchange economy, the distinction between a right to a thing (i.e., the legal relation) and the thing itself, became blurred. 'The thing itself became, in common parlance, the property[20].' In truth, however, as even lawyers have sometimes conceded,

18 'The condition of being owned by or belonging to some person or persons' (*Oxford English Dictionary*, Vol. VIII, p. 1471). The sense conveyed here is similar to that in which reference to a 'proper thing' meant, in archaic usage, 'one's own thing'. The Oxford English Dictionary gives the instance, under the heading 'proper', of Tindale who in 1538 wrote that 'Some call themselues poore, wythout hauyng ony thynge proper'. Similarly, an even earlier reference (dating from 1400) records that 'With his own propre Swerd he was slayn.'

19 *An Introduction to the Principles of Morals and Legislation* (ed. W. Harrison, Oxford 1948), p. 337, note 1 (Chapter XVI, section 26).

20 'Capitalism and the Changing Concept of Property', in E. Kamenka and R. S. Neale (ed.), *Feudalism, Capitalism and Beyond* (Canberra 1975), p. 111.

The term 'property' may be defined to be the interest which can be acquired in external objects or things. The things themselves are not, in a true sense, property, but they constitute its foundation and material, and the idea of property springs out of the connection, or control, or interest which, according to law, may be acquired in them, or over them[1].

'Property' is therefore, at one level of analysis, the relation between the owner and the thing (i.e., between a 'subject' and an 'object'). However, as we have already suggested, it is unreal to think simply in terms of 'the' owner of any particular thing, for the reality of the matter is of course more complex. Because it is possible for conflicting claims to be brought by two or more 'subjects' in respect of the same 'object', the property lawyer is necessarily concerned with the merits of *relative* claims. In order to establish what belongs to, or is 'proper' to, any particular 'subject', he must first analyse the legal relations between a number of competing subjects vis à vis the same object. A further level of complexity arises because any particular 'object' of property may itself be capable of sustaining a variety of different (but not necessarily conflicting) claims. This is demonstrated most clearly in the case of land. Land may, for instance, be the object of a multiplicity of claims made simultaneously by an owner-occupier, a tenant, a building society, a neighbour who enjoys a right of way or restrictive covenant, or even by a spouse who has certain rights not to be evicted from the property.

Thus, for the lawyer, the law of property is concerned with the network of legal relationships prevailing between individuals in respect of things. This may be illustrated diagrammatically. In *Fig.* 1, the dotted lines represent various kinds of claim made by a number of 'subjects' (A, B, C, D, E, . . .) in respect of a particular 'object'. The 'property' with which we shall be concerned is

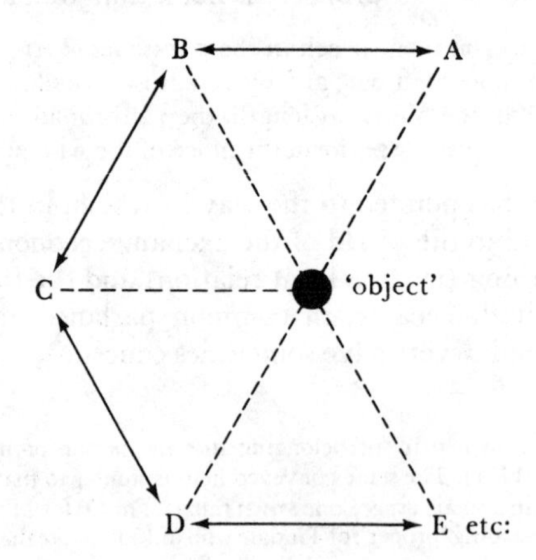

Fig. 1

1 See C. R. Noyes, *The Institution of Property* (New York and Toronto 1936), p. 357.

represented by the unbroken lines which depict, in part, the network of mutual relations between the 'subjects'[2].

Seen in this way, 'property' comprises bundles of mutual rights and obligations between 'subjects' in respect of certain 'objects', and the study of the law of property becomes an inquiry into a variety of socially defined relationships and morally conditioned obligations. Of course, the student must begin by mastering the technical structures and concepts of property law, albeit that these are in themselves mechanical and value-free. It is, however, the social, ethical and economic dimension of property as a 'relationship' which gives the law of property both direction and substance. To confine property law to its mechanical aspects and to ignore the inevitable infusion of extra-legal factors, is to impoverish legal study by forcing it into a moral and social vacuum. It is therefore vital that the student should approach the technical rules of property law with some awareness of their much wider significance.

This relation-based view, when applied to the law of land, highlights those characteristics of property which are essential to any real understanding of property law in general. These features are perhaps best summed up in the words of Professor Bruce Ackerman[3]:

I think it fair to say that one of the main points of the first-year Property course is to disabuse entering law students of their primitive lay notions regarding ownership. They learn that only the ignorant think it meaningful to talk about owning things free and clear of further obligation. Instead of defining the relationship between a person and 'his' things, property law discusses the relationships that arise *between people* with respect to things. More precisely, the law of property considers the way rights to use things may be parceled out amongst a host of competing resource users. Each resource user is conceived as holding a bundle of rights vis à vis other potential users; . . . the ways in which user rights may be legally packaged and distributed are wondrously diverse. And it is probably never true that the law assigns to any single person the right to use any thing in absolutely *any* way he pleases. Hence, it risks serious confusion to identify any single individual as *the* owner of any particular thing. At best, this locution may sometimes serve as identifying the holder of that bundle of rights which contains a range of entitlements more numerous or more valuable than the bundle held by any other person with respect to the thing in question. Yet, like all shorthands, talk about 'the' property owner invites the fallacy of misplaced concreteness, of reification. Once one begins to think sloppily, it is all too easy to start thinking that 'the' property owner, by virtue of being 'the' property owner, must *necessarily* own a particular bundle of rights over a thing. And this is to commit the error that separates layman from lawyer. For the fact (or is it the law?) of the matter is that property is not a thing, but a set of legal relations between persons governing the use of things.

In this book we shall approach 'property' as a relationship between people in respect of things. The structural features of the law of property are perhaps most clearly and most intelligibly manifested in the law relating to residential property. We shall therefore use this particular area of land law in order to open

2 To be comprehensive, *Fig.* 1 should contain a number of criss-crossing unbroken lines linking A with C, D and E, B with D and E, and so on. However the diagram is already sufficiently complex to illustrate the point being made.

3 *Private Property and the Constitution* (New Haven and London 1977), p. 26f.

up an avenue to a more general understanding of the law of real property—which of course extends far beyond land destined for merely residential use.

(2) Property is a dynamic relationship

If property is a relationship, it is a dynamic relationship. In other words, the content of the relationship is liable to change. The 'subjects' of property may be differently determined in one social era as compared with another. The 'objects' of property are likewise liable to fluctuate with the passage of time and the emergence of new economic conditions. Above all, the ideology of property is profoundly influenced by much wider factors of social, political and economic philosophy.

(a) *The changing 'subjects' of property*

An element of social control is exercised over the property relation in every society, in that each social group to a greater or lesser extent determines for itself the categories of person who may be recognised as the potential 'subjects' of property. In some societies of the past various classes of labourer or serf (e.g., slaves) have been excluded from legal competence as the 'subjects' of property. Even until relatively recently in England, the married woman was precluded from the legal capacity to hold property in her own name[4]. We have already seen that at the present day a minor (i.e., a person under 18 years of age) is still precluded from holding a legal estate in land.

The definition of the potential 'subjects' of property has, of course, an important political significance precisely because the delineation of potential right-holders fundamentally affects both the balance of power and the distribution of goods within a society. It is symptomatic of the more collectivist times in which we live that in England today few classes of person are explicitly excluded from holding property in their own name. As Lord Diplock once pointed out, we have seen in recent years the 'emergence of a property-owning, particularly a real-property-mortgaged-to-a-building-society-owning, democracy[5].' The years of greater affluence following the World Wars have brought about, in the words of Lord Wilberforce[6], 'the extension, beyond the paterfamilias, of rights of ownership, itself following from the diffusion of property and earning capacity.' It should, however, be noted that the diffusion of property among ever increasing segments of the population only serves to accentuate the demand that certain social rights should be recognised as 'proprietary' rights on behalf of those social groups which are *not* advantaged in the same degree[7]. Those, for instance, who are not owner-occupiers (even on the strength of mortgage finance) may be particularly anxious to claim that their occupation rights (e.g., as tenants) have secured for them a proprietary status equivalent to that of the owner-occupier.

4 See p. 5, ante.
5 *Pettitt v Pettitt* [1970] AC 777 at 824.
6 *Williams & Glyn's Bank Ltd v Boland* [1980] 3 WLR 138 at 147.
7 See p. 417, post.

(b) *The changing 'objects' of property*

If the 'objects' of property are those resources to which social or economic value is generally attached, it is inevitable that variations of social interest and concern should alter the emphasis of the property relationship with the passage of time. There was, for instance, an age in which both wives and slaves were regarded as the 'objects' of property. In medieval England, the husband was viewed as enjoying proprietary rights in relation to his wife, her domestic services and her productive capacity[8]. Much of the concern which generated this assessment of the spousal relationship was itself brought about by the supposed paramountcy of the need to ensure the devolution of property within a dynastic line of legitimate issue. However, the 'objects' of property are continually redefined by reason of changes in the social ethics practised by the society in which we live. It is today no longer acceptable that either wives or certain classes of labourer should be regarded as 'objects' of a proprietary relation.

The 'objects' of property can, however, change in more subtle degrees. For centuries the most highly prized 'object' of property in the common law world was land. In the 19th century and early 20th century the phenomenon of the company share came close to dislodging land as the pre-eminent 'object' of commercial value, at a time when the bulk of ordinary men and women owned little of value themselves other than perhaps the clothes which they wore. In the modern post-industrial society, however, with the diffusion of property among classes never before entitled, the traditional concept of a man's wealth has undergone yet another transformation. His material substance is now no longer even particularly related to the 'ownership' of tangible assets designed for enjoyment and consumption, but is nowadays more readily expressed in terms of intangible, non-assignable, and often non-survivable, claims of a largely personal nature. The things which are today of real value to the man in the street are assets like his job, his pension, and the right to undisturbed possession of his home. On the fringes of these new categories of property lie certain less well defined rights such as the right to education, the right to health and the right to a wholesome environment.

This changing picture of a man's wealth in the modern world was classically described by Professor Charles Reich in a seminal law review article in 1964[9]. Reich drew attention to the dramatic changes taking place in the nature and forms of wealth in industrial democratic societies. In particular, he pointed to the way in which government operates today as a major distributor of wealth in the form of welfare payments, salaries for those in public service, pensions for those who have retired from employment, and many other forms of licence, franchise, subsidy and fiscal benefit. As Reich indicated, 'today's distribution of largesse is on a vast, imperial scale.' Reich went on to argue that the principal forms of wealth for most people in our society are comprised in their employment or profession (and in various work-related benefits such as pensions) or in their dependency claims upon government (in the guise of social security payments).

8 See p. 555, post.
9 (1964) 73 Yale LJ 733: 'The New Property'.

These forms of wealth, which for Reich were concerned essentially with income security, have become in fact the 'new property', and Reich's major thesis was that this 'new property' should be accorded the same standard of legal protection as has been accorded in the past to more traditional entitlements of private property. In his view, the goal of future development in this area must be to

> try to build an economic basis for liberty today—a Homestead Act for rootless twentieth century man. We must create a new property[10].

The call for legal recognition of and protection for the 'new property' has intensified during the years since the publication of Reich's major article. In 1970, in its fundamentally significant decision in *Goldberg v Kelly*[11], the Supreme Court of the United States acknowledged the 'new property' to be deserving of constitutional protection. In the years following this decision, the prominence of the 'new property' has been accentuated by developments in other fields of law.

As Professor Mary Ann Glendon has observed, the emergence of the 'new property' can be placed in the historical context of a more general shift in the relative importance of family, work and government as determinants of social status and as sources of economic security[12]. Today, in an age of liberal divorce and increasingly attenuated family ties, the primary source of economic security for the individual is no longer the family but rather the individual's employment or his dependency relationship with government. Glendon thus correlates the developments which have taken place during the last century in the areas of family law and employment law. Whereas a hundred years ago marriage and family life were subject to onerous legal regulation (particularly with respect to the legal termination of the marriage relationship), the employment relationship was dominated by the relatively unrestrained power of the master to engage and dismiss his servants. Legal developments in these cognate fields since then have led today to an almost total reversal of the conceptual starting-points relevant to the law of work and family respectively. As Glendon notes, the 'relationships that, unlike marriage and contract, are relatively hard to enter and leave today are the preferred sorts of new property—good jobs with good fringe benefits[13].' Glendon goes on to say

> If it is true that decreasing state regulation of legal marriage is to some degree a reflection of change in the economic order and in the economic importance of the family, it should not be surprising to find *increased* legal regulation of whatever relation is competing with the family as a determinant of wealth, standing, and security for the majority of people. This is indeed what we do see, not only in the increased regulation and protection of the individual's interest in her job, but also in the increased legal control and protection that is crystallizing around other 'new property', such as pension rights and governmental entitlements[14].

It is plain therefore that important changes have occurred (and continue to occur) in the legal bonding of the individual, his family, his work and his

10 (1964) 73 Yale LJ 733 at 787.
11 397 US 254 (1970).
12 See M. A. Glendon (1979) 53 Tulane LR 697: 'The New Family and the New Property'.
13 (1979) 53 Tulane LR 697 at 708.
14 See also M. A. Glendon and E. R. Lev (1979) 20 Boston College LR 457: 'Changes in the Bonding of the Employment Relationship: An Essay on the New Property'.

relationship with government. The law increasingly recognises the significance of the relationship which secures the individual's job, with its attendant benefits and privileges, and which (as Glendon astutely adds) even more subtly ties him to his job[15]. Thus, while marriage is today terminable more or less at will, the employment relationship is not normally terminable by the employer save on exceptionally clear and convincing grounds.

The jurisprudence of the 'new property' has arisen so far largely in connection with the individual's rights in the fields of employment and social security. However, an object which lies more immediately within the ambit of a 'Homestead Act for rootless twentieth century man' is the general provision of security in the enjoyment of residential accommodation. The contemporary emphasis upon the need for residential security is profoundly linked with the fact that we seem to be living in an age of great *insecurity*. In times which are characterised by housing shortage, economic recession and an unprecedented rate of family breakdown, it becomes increasingly important to have a secure domestic base. There is a very real sense in which the right to live in a house or flat free from the threat of arbitrary eviction, free from the unrestricted impact of normal market forces, has itself become a new form of proprietary right. It matters not that the residential occupier has no legal title to the property which he occupies. His position is secure so long as the courts are prepared to recognise that he enjoys a 'status of irremovability'. Protected de facto possession of residential property has become an informal version of title. Entitlement to the 'use value' of property has become more important than entitlement to the 'exchange value' on the freehold market. To be sure, property is still bought and sold in the residential sector with an eye to possible profit, but the increasing significance of the 'use value', quite divorced from title, should not be underestimated.

We shall see throughout this book the ways in which our land law is beginning to recognise various forms of claim to the protection of residential security. In effect it is coming to be acknowledged that the enjoyment of residential protection in circumstances of adequate housing is an essential condition for a life of dignity and purpose. The recognition that the residential occupier may be entitled to a certain 'status of irremovability' appeared first in the context of the law of landlord and tenant. However, a notion equivalent to 'security of tenure' has also emerged in other areas of land law, where for reasons which are basically social in origin, residential protection has been conferred upon defined classes of deserving citizen. Slowly but surely the law is moving towards a realisation of the idea that the interest of residential security is itself an integral component of the 'new property'. The creation and vindication of protective rights in the area of housing law have in this way done much to widen the social distribution of the 'goods of life'.

(c) *The changing ideology of property*

The 'subjects' and 'objects' of property are thus constantly on the move, and in a subtle relation of cause and effect the entire ideology of property moves with

15 (1979) 53 Tulane LR 697 at 705.

them. The ideological shift is gradual and indeed scarcely perceptible. However, when history is viewed in the larger perspective of the last six or seven centuries—which is roughly the life span of the common law of England—it may be possible to point to three major phases in the development of our conceptual approach to the institution of property.

(i) *The age of feudal solidarity* Deeply buried in the mentality of lawyers of both the common law and the civil law traditions is a memory of a past age in which life styles and property were organically linked. In this lost world, as Otto Kahn-Freund once wrote,

> The conception of ownership was the mirror of a society in which wealth mainly consisted of tangible things, things which formed a functional unit: the house containing workshop and tools, dwelling room and furniture, the self-contained entity of the farm. They were held together by their common dedication to one single economic objective: to safeguard a livelihood to the owner and to his family. The 'own and patrimony' assisted the *dominus* in filling his place in the process of production and of distribution, and it served as the principal basis of consumption. Legal and economic property coincided: the notion of ownership applied to, and was the corollary of, a functional microcosm, a *universitas rerum*[16].

In this *universitas rerum*, the 'house connoted man as well as matter, the family was nothing but that aspect of the house which was concerned with reproduction of the species and with consumption[17].' The community of goods enjoyed by the household centred around an ownership vested firmly in the *paterfamilias*, who exercised patriarchal power over all members of his house. All members of this household other than the *paterfamilias* were subject in some degree to legal disability in the ownership and administration of the patrimonial property. Wives and infants were excluded from the capacity (and the need) to hold property and to make contracts, for their dealings with the external world were mediated by the *paterfamilias* and their rights within the household unit were governed by the emanations of patriarchal power. In the system of simple commodity production practised by the family, the law of inheritance provided the only legal regulation required to ensure the uninterrupted working of the social mechanism from one generation to another.

The world which we have just described reflects with varying degrees of accuracy the archetypal images generated by the medieval family or household. In this world, the *universitas rerum* of the house served as a microcosm of tangible objects and therefore as the 'substratum of the property norm[18].' The property of the household fulfilled the 'functions of providing an order of goods, and, in part, an order of power[19].' The things which a man 'owned' were held together by a common economic function and provided the base for an effective form of family government. This form of household organisation and the property

16 'Introduction' to K. Renner, *The Institutions of Private Law and Their Social Functions* (London and Boston 1949), p. 24f.
17 K Renner, op. cit., p. 227.
18 O. Kahn-Freund, loc. cit., p. 27.
19 O. Kahn-Freund, loc. cit., p. 26.

concept which it created were to last until the end of the 15th century, disintegrating only with the gradual break-up of the order of simple commodity production and the removal of the locus of production from the home to some external workplace.

The shorthand term in which these images of social relationship have been summed up in traditional sociological theory is the term *Gemeinschaft*[20]. A *Gemeinschaft* is a community or association of a particular kind. The term describes an association which is internal and organic, private and spontaneous—an organic merger of individuals bound together by a common purpose. The term was first used as a tool of sociological inquiry in the classic work of Ferdinand Tönnies, *Gemeinschaft und Gesellschaft*, published in 1887[1]. For Tönnies, the key to an understanding of the *Gemeinschaft* lay in the household and in the concept of kinship. The *Gemeinschaft* epitomised an essentially religious and essentially traditional perception of the proper relation between man and his fellow man. This perception found its highest expression in the organic unity of the medieval agrarian household. Here dealings between individuals were mediated by principles of love and duty and were guided by a common understanding of a shared purpose. Priorities within this household were arranged in accordance with religious teaching and the inherited folkways of the community. The concept of 'status' was the central organising principle in the regulation of personal relationships. Rights and duties within the household were ordered in accordance with the relative status of individuals within the unit, and the unit itself often marked the boundaries of the individual's world. In short, the *Gemeinschaft* was based upon a community of 'blood and soil' and expressed above all an integrative vision of man and his social relations. It was a family-oriented, status-dependent form of association which elevated the importance of the values of affection, loyalty, voluntarily assumed obligation and community-based solidarity.

This is, of course, an idealised picture of human association. There is general agreement among social theorists that the *Gemeinschaft* never existed in any pure form. However, the abstraction is useful because it symbolises certain ideological features which clearly were more deeply rooted in communities of the past than perhaps in the society of the present day. As our study of land law proceeds, we shall see that the law of property is founded upon principles which are the entire antithesis of the values of the *Gemeinschaft*.

(ii) *The age of commercialism* The system of simple commodity production began to break up with the transfer of productive labour to a workplace outside the home, a movement which in England was brought about initially by the growing influence of public guild law and the law of free employment and which was, of course, accelerated by the process of the industrial revolution of the 18th and 19th centuries.

This revolution in production destroyed the *universitas rerum* comprised within

20 See the roughly equivalent use of the term 'integry' by J. Bernard, *Women, Wives, Mothers: Values and Options* (Chicago 1975), p. 267ff.

1 See F. Tönnies, *Community and Association* (London 1955).

the household. The advent of wage labour on a vast scale, organised through the complementary institution of contract, tore asunder the common productive function of the family. The things which a man 'owned' were no longer held together by a common economic purpose. Things which had once constituted the elements of a functional entity were now, in the Marxist sense, 'expropriated'. In the words of Otto Kahn-Freund,

> the bulk of all the things which are privately owned have no intrinsic connection with the proprietor at all. They happen to belong to him—legally—, they would function just as well if they belonged to someone else. From his point of view their sole object is to be a title, a title to profits, a title to interest, a title to rent. It does not matter what the thing is: it may be a block of flats, an agricultural estate, a factory, or so many South African gold shares. The property object has become 'capital'[2].

The property object had indeed become capital. In the age dominated by this new economic ethos, property was no longer seen as providing merely the material substratum of an integrated communal life based upon shared economic functions. Property came to be seen as both the tool and the object of commerce. The 'exchange value' of property was elevated far above its 'use value'. The main purpose to be served by property was the provision of a base for capitalist enterprise. The highest purpose which the law could achieve was that property should be freely alienable and therefore productive of income and conducive to profit.

The impact of these developments upon the ideology and the reality of social relationships was profound. The integrative vision of the *Gemeinschaft* was replaced by what Tönnies was to term the *Gesellschaft*. The *Gesellschaft* represents, in social terms, an atomistic world of self-determining individuals locked in remorseless competition. It reflects an impersonal, contract-based society in which each individual strives to maximise his own material interests. The aggressive pursuit of self-interest must, so runs the theory, conduce to the common good—a belief which attained its clearest expression in the era of the free market laisser faire philosophy which came to dominate the laws of economic relations in the late 19th century. This philosophy gave priority to the institution of contract as the pre-eminent determining factor in the distribution of the material advantages of life, a view which was brought to the fore not least by Henry Sumner Maine's classic analysis of 1861 that 'the movement of the progressive societies has hitherto been a movement from *Status to Contract*[3].' As Lord Simon of Glaisdale more recently observed,

> It was natural for Maine, writing in the middle of the 19th century, to discern such a movement. The laisser-faire laisser-aller ideology was dominant. Human felicity, it was argued, was best promoted by leaving to every person to seek his own advantage in competition with his fellows. A free market would ensure that the individual's effort was directed to anticipating and satisfying with maximum efficiency the wants of his fellows. The most powerful motive force in the universe—man's pursuit of his own interest—would thus be harnessed to drive a whole society forward. 'Man's selfishness is God's

2 Loc. cit., p. 27f.
3 *Ancient Law* (1861, Everyman's Library edn., London 1917), p. 100.

providence,' they said. The general development of the law, as so often, reflected the dominant ideology. Freedom and sanctity of contract tended to be considered as pre-eminent legal values[4].

The social ethic of the *Gesellschaft* was the maximisation of private profit—a result which was achieved with the aid of a legally recognised freedom to compete and exploit. The 'integry' had indeed been monetised[5]. The moral basis of the *Gemeinschaft* was replaced by an ideology which

finds its paradigmatic expression in the relationship to money, to property that is expressed as credit or debit in a ledger, to goods and commodities that one acquires with no other aim but to be rid of them, as quickly as possible, at a profit. Its ultimate consummation is the commercial *share*, which can be held by a man who has never even seen the property it confers on him and has no interest in it whatsoever except as an item of credit. It is in such relationships that joy and sorrow, satisfaction and dissatisfaction are sharply differentiated; profit is *plus*, joy, satisfaction; loss is *minus*, sorrow, dissatisfaction. Everything is abstracted, torn out of its living context, subsumed under an inviolable end[6].

This new mode of relationship was characterised by rational calculation and purposive economic self-interest. The primary vision of society was that of 'a collection of isolated and isolable windowless monads that come into collision only externally and as a departure from the norm[7].' The idea that the property relation might serve a higher end of social obligation not rewarded by immediate and tangible profit was ideologically somewhat distant. In the world of the *Gesellschaft*, the law of property has no moral dimension. Its only function is to serve as a value-neutral medium of exploitation and exchange.

It was in this ideological climate that the property legislation currently in force in this country was brought into being. The keystone of the edifice is the body of enactments passed by Parliament in 1925, which effectively consolidated the judge-made law and legislation of the late 19th century, and it is this corpus of property law which in the main provides the subject-matter of this book.

(iii) *The age of social welfare* It is not difficult to appreciate that the social ethic of the *Gesellschaft* has come under heavy attack during the present century. Even towards the end of the 19th century the ideology of laisser faire was beginning to be questioned. The priority accorded to the claim of freedom of contract was challenged by the new ethic of social welfare. It was contended that

society's objective should be not wealth but welfare (with the implication that the pursuit and achievement of wealth were destructive of welfare), which was best promoted by the direct intervention of the organs of the state and could not be left to the bargain of the marketplace. 'Competition' came to have the cliché 'cut-throat' attached to it. Others, more subtly, argued that, for the laisser-faire system to work felicitously as claimed, there must be a genuinely free, open and abundant market in which there is equality of

4 *Johnson v Moreton* [1980] AC 37 at 65f.
5 See J. Bernard, op. cit., p. 272 (see note 20, p. 15).
6 E. Kamenka (1965) 16 Political Science 3, 5: 'Gemeinschaft and Gesellschaft'.
7 See A. E.-S. Tay, 'Beyond Bourgeois Individualism: the Contemporary Crisis in Law and Legal Ideology', in E. Kamenka and R. S. Neale (ed.), op. cit., p. 133.

bargaining power—equality of knowledge of the market and of staying-power in holding out for a bargain: this called for at least a limited intervention by the state to prevent or counteract rigging of the market by monopolies or oligopolies and to redress inequalities of bargaining power. And consonantly, even in the 19th century, the law began to back-pedal . . . it was apparently no longer accepted by the law that freedom and sanctity of contract were conclusive of the public interest[8].

Within the present century the claims of social welfare have been increasingly recognised both by the enactment of protective legislation and by the activist interpretation of existing law by the judges. Legislation has gone some distance towards ensuring a more equitable distribution of the 'goods of life', essentially by giving legal force to certain kinds of 'security claim'. These claims cover broadly the interests to which we have already referred as the 'new property'. Thus the claim to security in employment is recognised, at least to some extent, by legislation which protects the individual employee from 'unfair dismissal'[9]; the claim to residential security, by the Rent Acts and other statutory means; the claim to income security, by the vast range of legislation which underpins the social security system[10]. Inherent in all these measures is a quite remarkable return to the idea of a 'status'. The individual receives the benefits of protective legislation, not because he has in any sense contracted or bargained to receive them, but because he enjoys a defined 'status' which entitles him to some appropriate form of 'security'[11].

Seen in this way, the 'new property' operates as an agent of distributive justice. By operating in this way, the 'new property' begins to re-define the ideology of property itself, for the age of social welfare has introduced what seems to be an entirely new dimension into the property concept. In past times the concept of the property relation has been essentially negative and exclusory. The traditional concept of a right of property comprises the right to exclude all others from the use or enjoyment of some thing[12]. However, the 'new property' by contrast comprises various kinds of claim *not* to be excluded from the use or enjoyment of some thing. Thus the idea of property is gradually being broadened to include a 'right to a kind of society or set of power relations which will enable the individual to live a fully human life[13].' This perspective indicates, at least in some incipient form, an intellectual shift away from the idea that property is a private right to exclude from personally owned resources towards a conception that property is a public right of access to socially valued resources.

According to the new view, the law of property is ultimately concerned to secure to the individual citizen 'that kind of society which is instrumental to a full and free life . . . and [to the] development of one's human capacities[14].' It is, however, prudent to remember that 'there is no new thing under the sun . . . it

8 *Johnson v Moreton* [1980] AC 37 at 66 per Lord Simon of Glaisdale.
9 See Employment Protection (Consolidation) Act 1978, ss. 54ff.
10 See D. S. Pearl and K. J. Gray, *Social Welfare Law* (London 1981), p. 79ff.
11 See *Johnson v Moreton* [1980] AC 37 at 67 per Lord Simon of Glaisdale.
12 See C. B. Macpherson, in E. Kamenka and R. S. Neale (ed.), op. cit., p. 116ff.
13 Ibid., p. 120.
14 Ibid., p. 121.

hath been already of old time, which was before us[15].' There are perfectly good historical antecedents for the claims presented by the 'new property', and indeed for the view that those claims may be the 'object' of 'property'. One need look no further than the 17th century to find political philosophers who entertained a similarly broad concept of property. In speaking unrestrainedly of 'things held in propriety', Thomas Hobbes observed that

> those that are dearest to a man are his own life, and limbs; and in the next degree, in most men, those that concern conjugal affection; and after them, riches and means of living[16].

The same latitude was exercised by John Locke, who did perhaps more than any other philosopher to make explicit the connection between property and political society. Locke referred in the same liberal manner to the idea that 'property' comprises a man's 'life, liberty and estate'[17], making it quite clear that in his terms 'property' included 'that property which men have in their persons as well as their goods[18].'

It is no novel idea, then, that in the interests of social justice every man should enjoy access to the 'goods of life.' It may well be that our concept of property is undergoing a subtle transformation and is in the process of becoming more a *right of access* than a *right of exclusion.* In this sense, access becomes something independent of 'ownership' and the social demand for access becomes opposable to the assertion of 'ownership'. The political implications of this development cannot be over-estimated. Some contemporary writers have even suggested that the modern decline in respect for private property is substantially attributable to the fact that claims to access are increasingly regarded as maintainable in derogation of claims to 'ownership'[19]. Alice Tay has, for instance, warned of the dangers implicit in a new version of the law of property, in which the state allocates to individual citizens a variety of 'status-claims' which are graded and distributed on the basis of an inscrutable calculus of social and administrative considerations. In her view, the traditional adjudicative system of justice is threatened by the advent of a regime of 'bureaucratic-administrative regulation.' Under such a regime, the law of property would become merely

> a bureaucratic-administrative, regulatory and even confiscatory resources-allocation concern, in which the state stands above property owners as the representative of a general 'socio-political' interest[20].

Whether such fears will ever become reality it is still too early to judge. It is, however, not without significance that the 'new property' comprises many kinds of 'status-claim' in respect of the wholesome and fulfilled life. It is increasingly contended, for example, that the 'new property' recognises that citizens have a proprietary right to clean and unpolluted air in their cities or to certain standards of health care and education. However, the 'new property' may be

15 *Ecclesiastes*, i: 9, 10.
16 *Leviathan* (Collins/Fontana edn., London 1978), p. 300.
17 *The Second Treatise of Civil Government* (ed. J. W. Gough, Oxford 1946), para. 87.
18 Ibid., para. 173.
19 See p. 418, post.
20 'Law, the citizen and the state', in E. Kamenka, R. Brown and A. E.-S. Tay (ed.), op. cit., p. 13.

even more extensive than this. It has been said that it comprises not merely rights of access to 'the accumulated means of labour' but also rights of access to political power. Looking far (or perhaps not so far?) into the future, Professor C. B. Macpherson has said that we may anticipate

a change from property as a right of access to the means of labour, to property as a right to the means of a fully human life. This seems to move us back through the centuries, to bring us back again to the idea that property in the means of life (a 'good' life) is the main form of property, as it was for the earliest theorists, for example Aristotle, before emphasis shifted to property in land and capital (the means of producing the means of life). So it does, but the outcome is not the same. For, in the assumed circumstances of greatly increased productivity, the crucial question will no longer be how to provide a sufficient flow of the material means of life: it will be a question of getting the quality and kinds of things wanted for a full life, and, beyond that, of the quality of life itself. And both of these matters will require a property in the control of the mass of productive resources. If one envisages the extreme of an automated society in which nobody has to labour in order to produce the material means of life, the property in the massed productive resources of the whole society becomes of utmost importance. The property that would then be most important to the individual would no longer be the right of access to the means of labour; it would be instead, the right to a share in the control of the massed productive resources. That right would presumably have to be exercised politically. Political power then becomes the most important kind of property. Property, as an individual right, becomes essentially the individual's share in political power. This becomes *the* important form of property, not only because it is the individual's guarantee of sharing equitably in the flow of consumables, in some part of which he will of course still need a property in the sense of an exclusive right. It becomes important also because only by sharing the control can he be assured of the means of the good or commodious or free life, which would then be seen to consist of more than a flow of consumables[1].

Whether the demand for access to political power may not ultimately destroy the democracy to which Macpherson refers is one of the major questions of our time. The 'new property' is not without its share of dangers for the body politic. However, none of this should blind us to the fact that the 'new property' does assert the legitimacy of some 'security-claims' which are undeniably intrinsic to the achievement of social justice in the age in which we live. In effect, basic human rights are expressed in terms of property.

In this book we will examine some of these 'security-claims' which have special relevance for land lawyers. However, we must for the moment turn our attention to one of the great influences upon our existing law of property—the institution of the trust. Perhaps more than any other institution, the trust concept has moulded and directed our law of property. The trust idea pervades our understanding of property, and for this reason it is essential that we should trace something of its origins and functions. We shall also see in due course that the concept of the trust and the ideology of the 'new property' are not entirely unrelated. It may be that an extension of the private trust will provide the means by which the equitable impulse of the 'new property' may attain its truest expression.

1 'Capitalism and the Changing Concept of Property', in E. Kamenka and R. S. Neale (ed.), op. cit., p. 120f.

3. THE INSTITUTION OF THE TRUST

The great codes of continental law follow Roman Law in defining 'property' as the right to enjoy a thing and to dispose of it in the most absolute manner, i.e., as the right to deal with that thing as one pleases and to exclude strangers from interference[2]. Property or ownership thus expresses itself as an absolute relationship between a person and a thing. The *dominium* of Roman Law comprises both the legal title and the right of actual beneficial enjoyment. In other words, *dominium* regarded as conceptually inseparable the owner's right to use, dispose of, and exclude others from, his property. The idea that *dominium* might be fragmented between a number of owners, each with a separate proprietary right to some aspect of *dominium*, was, and still is, unacceptable to Romanist legal thought. *Dominium* is an indivisible unity.

This rather stolid conception of property and ownership has made it difficult for continental systems of law to accommodate the fragmentation of rights of title, use and enjoyment which is integral to the economic reality of property in the complex world in which we live. These problems have, however, been avoided in English law and in most legal systems derived from the common law tradition. English law has been able to develop a concept of property which accords more faithfully with modern economic reality because deeply grounded in the English lawyer's tradition is the institution of the trust, as developed by the courts of equity. Otto Kahn-Freund reminded us that, in developing the trust, 'in some ways its most original contribution to jurisprudence', the English legal mind has made it 'unnecessary and impossible for itself to search for a definition of property in the continental sense[3].' Maitland, one of the greatest of our lawyers, was able to say[4]

> Of all the exploits of Equity the largest and the most important is the invention and development of the Trust. It is an 'institute' of great elasticity and generality; as elastic, as general as contract. This perhaps forms the most distinctive achievement of English lawyers. It seems to us almost essential to civilisation, and yet there is nothing quite like it in foreign law[5].

It is therefore at the institution of the trust that we must now look.

(1) Definition of 'trust'

Many attempts have been made to define the notion of a 'trust'. The essence of a 'trust' is the idea that the trustee is the nominal owner of property but that the real or beneficial owner of that property is the 'beneficiary' or 'cestui que trust.' Since the notion of 'trust' is integral to the structure and development of land law, we must explore this matter of definition further.

The essential feature of a trust is that the formal or 'titular' interest in property is vested in a nominee (or 'trustee') whose duty it is to deflect the

2 See French Civil Code, art. 544; German Civil Code, para. 903; Swiss Civil Code, art. 641.
3 Op. cit., p. 23.
4 *Equity* (2nd edn., London 1936), p. 23.
5 See S. Bolgár (1953) 2 AJCL 204: 'Why No Trusts in the Civil Law?'

beneficial enjoyment of the property to those who hold the 'equitable interests' under the trust. In its classical form, the trust is a device which is created expressly for a specific purpose. A trust is in effect an obligation arising out of a confidence reposed in the trustee, or person who has the legal title to property conveyed to him, that he will faithfully apply the property according to the confidence reposed in him, i.e., in accordance with the wishes of the creator of the trust. This may be represented diagrammatically as follows, where A, the owner of property, conveys that property to T as trustee, in order that T may hold 'on trust for' B, a named beneficiary:

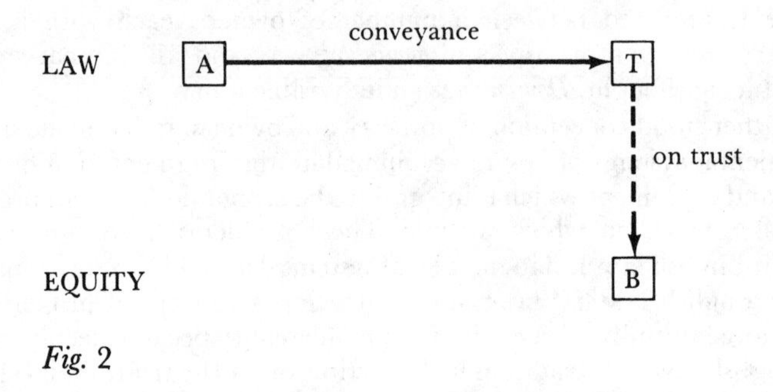

Fig. 2

Once the trust has been created, its author, A, has no further part to play. The legal title in the trust property is held thereafter by T, who as title-holder is invested with the administrative powers of 'management and disposition' with respect to that property. In other words, T is charged with the fiduciary responsibility of managing the trust property in such manner as to render it productive of income or other use value, subject always to the duty to divert the benefit (whether in the form of income or actual enjoyment) to the beneficiary or beneficiaries nominated by A. T must never profit himself by reason of his office of trust: this is one of the cardinal principles of trust law. His task is simply one of decision-making in the performance of the administrative duties connected with the trust. He manages the trust property and ultimately exercises the power of disposition over that property. However, even the latter function is purely administrative, since a disposition of the trust property simply converts that property into cash which is still governed by the terms of the trust and which therefore requires to be reinvested in another form for the benefit of the person or persons entitled in equity.

(2) The relationship between law and equity

It is easily seen that the fundamental feature of a trust is that it separates the functions of administration and enjoyment which were so inseparably combined in the Roman law concept of *dominium.* Although the trustee is invested with the legal title (which, by definition, carries the administrative powers of management and disposition), his ownership is nominal and purely formal. The legal title is a 'paper title'; the trustee, a mere 'paper owner'. The substance of beneficial enjoyment is reserved at all times for the beneficiary. Here we see another important feature of the trust. The legal title is a matter of *form*; the rights of beneficiaries represent the *substance*. However, the common law of England was from its earliest days concerned only with form[6]. If a court of common law were asked to determine the ownership of land, it would declare simply that full rights of ownership were vested in the person indicated by the paper title, i.e., the person whose name appeared on the deed of conveyance. The common law steadfastly refused to take cognisance of the moral obligation which the author of a trust had fastened upon the conscience of the transferee of the paper title. The courts of common law regarded the formal title as conclusive of any question relating to use, benefit or enjoyment.

It was left to a jurisdiction founded upon conscience to remedy the defects of the common law. It was in the court of the Chancellor, and only in his court, that the moral obligations imposed upon the trustee were capable of enforcement. The court of the Chancellor, or the Court of the Chancery, as it came to be called, developed a body of rules which supplemented the rules of common law in the interest of achieving a greater equity in the dealings of men. This body of rules became known as 'equity', and it was by virtue of equity that the beneficiary of a trust could secure the enforcement of the trust which had been reposed in his trustee. From the 14th century the Chancellors, although never denying that the trustee was the legal owner of the trust property, nevertheless began to give to the beneficiary a remedy denied him by the courts of common law. The courts of equity insisted that the terms of the trust be observed and that the trust property be dealt with for the benefit of those persons named as beneficiaries or, as it came to be said, for the benefit of those persons 'entitled in equity'.

Immense volumes have been written in description of the emergence of the Court of Chancery and the development of the principles of equity. Here it must suffice to say that the courts of common law and equity diverged fundamentally in the approach adopted in relation to trust property. The courts of common law would afford a remedy only to the legal owner (the trustee). The courts of equitable jurisdiction gave a remedy to the beneficiary. The courts of law and equity therefore came into conflict. By the 17th century it had been decided that legal supremacy was vested in the Court of Chancery, but the mutual antagonism of the courts of law and equity was not finally resolved until late in the 19th century. The Supreme Court of Judicature Acts of 1873–1875 established that the rules of law and equity should be administered by all the courts of the land, so that the remedy obtained should no longer depend upon the precise court in which the plaintiff brought his action. Furthermore, in cases of conflict between law and equity, it was enacted that the rules of equity should prevail[7].

In the orthodox analysis, the changes of the late 19th century brought about a fusion merely of administration in respect of law and equity. 'The two streams of jurisdiction, though they run in the same channel, run side by side and do not

6 See A. E.-S. Tay, 'The sense of justice in the Common Law', in E. Kamenka and A. E.-S. Tay (ed.), *Justice* (London 1979), p. 79.
7 Supreme Court of Judicature Act 1873, s. 25(11), p. 399, post.

mingle their waters[8].' Although all courts may now grant legal and equitable remedies, the principles upon which those remedies are granted remain distinct. There is a further distinction which is particularly important for land law. The characteristic remedy of the common law is the award of damages. The range of equitable remedies extends much more widely, embracing forms of relief which act *in personam* (e.g., decrees of specific performance, injunctions and orders for rectification). However, whereas the common law remedy of damages is available as of right once the plaintiff's case has been proved[9], the equitable remedies are always discretionary. Even if the plaintiff has proved his case, he may be denied equitable relief on the ground, for instance, that he has not come to court 'with clean hands'[10]. That is, he may be precluded from relief simply because he has forfeited any claim to the assistance of equity by reason of his own inequitable or unconscionable conduct[11].

(3) The origin and types of trust

The modern trust developed from the ancient 'use', and it is interesting to enquire briefly into the etymology and the function of the 'use'.

Maitland tells us that the derivation of the term 'use' lies not in the Latin *usus* but in the Latin *opus*[12]. In the vulgar or barbarous Latin of the 7th and 8th centuries, the phrase *ad opus* had already acquired the meaning of 'on behalf of'. Thus, if Coemgenus held land *ad opus Johannis*, this meant that Coemgenus held land *on behalf of* Johannes. *Ad opus* became in time *ad oeps* or *ad eops*, emerging later in the form of the law-french *a son oes* and finally as the English 'to the use of'. A might hold lands 'to the use of' B.

But why might a situation arise where A held lands 'to the use of' B? Once again Maitland gives us the answer. The device of the use arose because of the restraints imposed by feudal law upon the owner of land. The owner of land could not leave his land by will. Every germ of testamentary power in respect of land had been ruthlessly stamped out in the 12th century. Yet the calls of lineage and the need for spiritual solace were strong. As Maitland explains[13],

> the Englishman would like to leave his land by will. He would like to provide for the weal of his sinful soul, and he would like to provide for his daughters and younger sons. That is the root of the matter. But further, it is to be observed that the law is hard upon him at the hour of death, more especially if he is one of the great. If he leaves an heir of full age, there is a relevium to be paid to the lord. If he leaves an heir under age, the lord may take

8 *Ashburner's Principles of Equity* (2nd edn. by D. Browne, London 1933), p. 18. See, however, *United Scientific Holdings Ltd v Burnley Borough Council* [1978] AC 904 at 925 per Lord Diplock. Compare P. H. Pettit, *Equity and the Law of Trusts* (4th edn. London 1979), p. 9.

9 The quantum of the damages awarded remains, however, a matter to be decided within the discretion of the court.

10 See *Snell's Principles of Equity* (27th edn. R. E. Megarry and P. V. Baker, London 1973), p. 32f.; R. P. Meagher, W. M. C. Gummow and J. R. F. Lehane, *Equity: Doctrines and Remedies* (Sydney, Melbourne, Brisbane and Perth 1975), p. 67f.

11 See pp. 85, 397, post.

12 Op. cit., p. 24.

13 *The Collected Papers of Frederic William Maitland* (ed. H. A. L. Fisher, Cambridge 1911), Vol. III, p. 335.

the profits of the land, perhaps for twenty years, and may sell the marriage of the heir. And then if there is no heir, the land falls back ('escheats') to the lord for good and all.

In the face of these difficulties, recourse is had to the institution of the 'use'. The landowner conveys his land to some friends, who are instructed to hold it 'to his use'. They are directed to allow him to enjoy the land during his lifetime, and he can give further instructions detailing what they shall do with the land on his death. It may be that they are directed to hold the land 'to the use of' other members of the landowner's family or 'to the use of' the Church. The latter form of use had the two-fold consequence of evading the Statutes of Mortmain, which prohibited the conveyance of lands to the Church[14], and securing eternal rest for the soul of the 'feoffor to uses'.

Thus the 'feoffment to uses' became a most flexible device. A conveyance (or 'feoffment') of land might be made on terms which would prove highly beneficial to the 'feoffor'. Provided the 'feoffees' survived the 'feoffor', they could hold land to the uses indicated by the 'feoffor'. The utility of this scheme was so extensive, and the scheme itself became so commonplace, that in time it became standard practice to enfeoff a purely fictitious 'feoffee', so that a man of straw held land 'to the use of' each beneficiary (or 'cestui que use')[15].

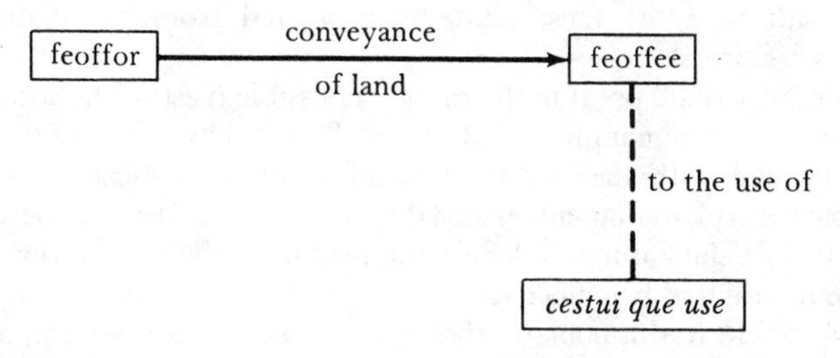

Fig. 3

Although, as we have seen, the courts of common law looked only to the feoffee as the owner of the land, it was the Chancellor who by the 14th century had begun to enforce the use. It was natural, of course, that restrictions should later be imposed on the use, and in 1535 the Statute of Uses effectively abolished the power to create a use by will. However, within the next two centuries the foundations had been laid for an alternative device which was to perform most of the functions earlier discharged by the use. This device was the trust. From the late 17th century onwards the courts of equity began to fashion the principles which were to harden into the bleak and inflexible body of rules known as 'equity'—rules which were primarily (but not exclusively) concerned with the internal administration and external consequences of trusts of both real and personal property.

The trust has since become as essential a legal device as is the institution of contract. The trust may appear in a multiplicity of forms and may be directed

14 See p. 188, post.
15 C. R. Noyes, *The Institution of Property* (New York, Toronto and London 1936), p. 320.

towards a multiplicity of purposes. In this book we shall examine several of the forms which the trust device may assume, but it may be helpful to outline here some of the manifestations which are possible.

We have seen that a trust is essentially a medium by which the administrative and enjoyment functions pertaining to property may be separated and vested in different persons. Trusts may be distinguished one from another on the basis of the precise allocation of function which they express. The degree of control vested in trustee and beneficiary respectively varies according to the kind of trust.

At one end of the range is the *bare trust,* in which the trustee's control over the trust property is minimal and the beneficiary's control is paramount. The trustee of a bare trust has no active duty to perform: he is merely the depository of the naked or 'bare' title. Although he is technically empowered to dispose of the legal title in the trust property, he must at all times comply with the directions as to disposition given by his beneficiary[16].

At the other end of the range of possible trusts is the *spendthrift* or *protective trust,* under which the beneficiary has no alienable interest and therefore no control over the trust property. Such trusts are frequently used to confer upon a beneficiary an interest which is terminable automatically upon his insolvency, with the result that the trust estate is protected from the claims of the beneficiary's creditors.

At some intermediate point in the range of possible trusts is the *active* or *special trust*—perhaps the most common of all types of trust. This is a trust in which the trustee is charged with the performance of active and substantial duties in respect of the control, management and disposition of the trust property, subject always to the fiduciary duty to deflect the benefit derived from that property towards the nominated beneficiaries.

At various points in this book we shall refer to other types of trust, such as the *trust for sale,* the *resulting trust* and the *constructive trust.* However, these are best left to be explained within the context in which they arise.

(4) The effect of the trust on third parties

As we have seen, a trust is a fiduciary relationship with respect to property. The trustee holds the legal title to the trust property, together with the appropriate powers of management and disposition. The beneficiary or 'cestui que trust' has an essentially personal right against his trustee to ensure that the latter carries out the terms of his trust. As Maitland points out[17], the liability of the trustee is almost certainly of contractual origin. He is bound by the terms of his trust because he has bound himself: he has agreed with the author of the trust that he will faithfully observe the conditions upon which the trust property was transferred to himself. The right of the cestui que trust is the benefit of an obligation—a right which can be enforced by appeal to the equitable jurisdiction of the courts. The cestui may apply for a court order directing his trustee to act

16 See p. 160, post.
17 *Equity,* p. 110f.

conformably with the terms of his trust, or he may recover damages in respect of any breach of trust which has already occurred.

When stated in this way, it is apparent that the fiduciary relationship of the trust should in principle affect only the rights and obligations of the trustee, the author of the trust and the cestui que trust. Other third parties should not be subjected to the onerous liability undertaken voluntarily by the trustee. However, a proper understanding of the rights enjoyed by the cestui que trust begins with the realisation that equity, being a jurisdiction of conscience, gradually extended the ramifications of the private trust, thereby affecting many categories of person other than those already mentioned. We must now trace the conceptual or doctrinal process by which the trust came to exert an impact upon third parties. The persons who might be affected by a transfer of title in the trust property are detailed in the following diagram.

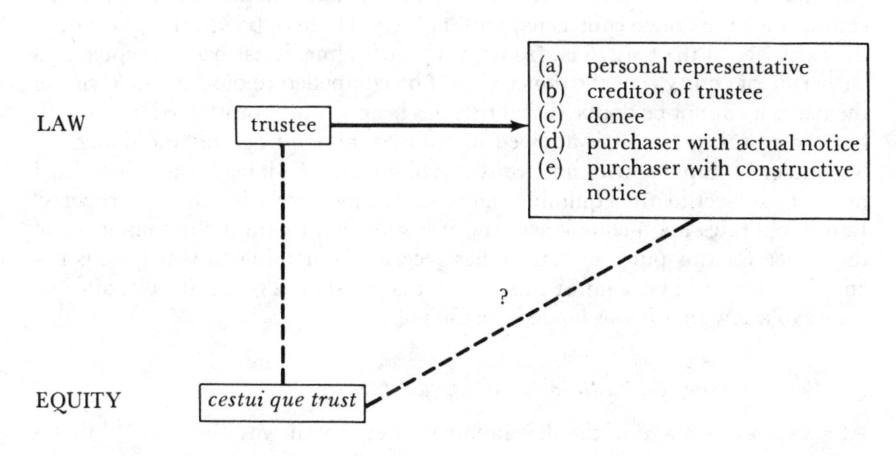

Fig. 4

(a) *Persons who succeed to the rights of the trustee*

The cestui que trust may enforce the trust against his original trustee. It was but a short step for equity to declare that the cestui que trust may also enforce the terms of the trust against all persons who by succession on the death of the trustee fill the place of that trustee. Thus he may enforce the trust against such persons as the trustee's personal representatives (i.e., 'executors' in the case where the trustee dies testate, and 'administrators' in the case of death intestate). These persons are regarded as 'sustaining wholly or partially the *persona* of the original trustee and being bound by his obligations as regards the proprietary rights to which they have succeeded[18].'

18 *Equity*, p. 112.

(b) *Creditors of the trustee*

The next step is to allow the cestui que trust to enforce the trust against the trustee's creditors[19]. The creditors may not claim the trust property in satisfaction of debts owed by the trustee, for the trust property is that to which the trustee is only nominally entitled as a paper owner. The benefit derived from the trust property belongs to the cestui que trust[20].

(c) *Donees of the trustee*

Grave problems arise if the trustee, in breach of his trust, gives the trust property to a third party without receiving valuable consideration. Here there is presented a difficult question of social, ethical and economic priority. Both the donee and the cestui que trust are entirely innocent, yet only one can prevail. It cannot be said that the donee is under any form of contractual liability in favour of the cestui, since the donee contracted with nobody. He may be utterly ignorant of the existence of the trust. Yet, from a very early time, it has been accepted as a clear rule of equity that the donee should be compelled to observe the terms of the trust. It cannot be doubted that title has been validly transferred by the gift, but the cestui que trust is allowed to enforce the trust against the donee (or 'volunteer'). 'Equity will not assist a volunteer.' A donee takes the gifted property subject to any equitable claims subsisting in relation to that property. Equity operates upon conscience, and it is sufficient to affect the conscience of the donee for this purpose that he has received something to which he is not entitled[1]. It would be 'against conscience' that he should retain the gift after he comes to know that it was made in breach of trust.

(d) *Purchasers from the trustee with actual notice of the trust*

At a very early stage in the development of equity, it was also decided that a cestui que trust may enforce the trust against one who purchases the trust property with actual knowledge of the existence of the trust. The ground of liability in the third party is something akin to fraud. It is unconscientious—'against conscience'—to buy what one knows to be held on trust for another. The purchaser is liable *ex delicto vel quasi*[2]. The basis for this conclusion is to be found in the beautiful and poignant language of the law-french of 1471:

Si mon feoffee de trust etc. enfeoffe un autre, que conust bien que le feoffor rien ad forsque a mon use, subpoena girra vers ambideux: scil. auxibien vers le feoffee come vers le feoffor . . . pur ceo que en conscience il purchase ma terre[3].

19 See *Finch v Earl of Winchelsea* (1715) 1 P Wms 277, 24 ER 387.
20 See p. 482, post.
1 See *Re Diplock* [1948] Ch 465 at 503.
2 Maitland, *Equity*, p. 113.
3 YB 11 Edw IV, fol. 8: 'If my trustee conveys the land to a third person who well knows that the trustee holds for my use, I shall have a remedy in the Chancery against both of them: as well against the buyer as against the trustee: for in conscience he buys my land' (see Maitland, *Collected Papers*, Vol. III, p. 345).

Thus the claims of equity operated upon the guilty conscience. If a third party knowingly bought land held on trust, he did what was unconscientious and must now be regarded as holding on trust for me, for *en conscience il purchase ma terre.*

(e) *Purchasers from the trustee with constructive notice of the trust*

If equity had stopped there and gone no further, it would have been possible that third party purchasers would take care to ensure that their consciences were not affected by actual notice of any trust. They would simply have 'shut their eyes' to the possible existence of a trust, and would have relied upon the absence of actual notice as their ground of immunity from the obligation of the trust. To prevent such a result, equity developed the further rule that, in order to take the trust property free of the trust, the purchaser must not only be honest: he must also be diligent. He must have made all such investigation of the vendor's title as a prudent purchaser would have made, and he is affected with 'constructive notice' of all equitable rights of which he would have acquired actual notice had he made the proper enquiries. The trust may be enforced against any purchaser who would have known of the trust had he behaved as prudent purchasers behave in the conduct of their affairs. Thus a standard of diligence has been elaborated by the courts in order to fasten upon the conscience of the unreasonable or disingenuous purchaser. If not actually guilty of *dolus*, such a purchaser is at least 'guilty of that sort of negligence which is equivalent to *dolus.* He had shut his eyes in order that he might not see[4].'

At this point the long arm of equity stopped. Equity recognised that if the purchaser who acquired ownership from the trustee was excusably ignorant of the rights of the cestui que trust, then he must be left to enjoy the ownership thus obtained. Since his conscience was unaffected, the Chancellor's equity had no hold upon him. The classic statement of this position is that of James LJ in *Pilcher v Rawlins*[5]:

> I propose simply to apply myself to the case of a purchaser for valuable consideration, without notice, obtaining, upon the occasion of his purchase, and by means of his purchase deed, some legal estate, some legal right, some legal advantage; and according to my view of the established law of this Court, such a purchaser's plea of a purchase for valuable consideration without notice is an absolute, unqualified, unanswerable defence, and an unanswerable plea to the jurisdiction of this Court. Such a purchaser may be interrogated and tested to any extent as to the valuable consideration which he has given in order to show the bona fides or mala fides of his purchase, and also the presence or the absence of notice; but when once he has gone through that ordeal, and has satisfied the terms of the plea of purchase for valuable consideration without notice, then this Court has no jurisdiction whatever to do anything more than to let him depart in possession of that legal estate, that legal right, that legal advantage which he has obtained. In such a case the purchaser is entitled to hold that which, without breach of duty, he has had conveyed to him.

4 Maitland, *Collected Papers*, Vol. III, p. 346.
5 (1872) 7 Ch App 259 at 268f.

As Maitland asks, with his characteristic acuity, 'How could it be otherwise?' A purchaser in good faith has obtained a legal right. In a court of law that right is his: the law of the land gives it to him. On what ground of equity may it be taken away from him? The purchaser has not himself undertaken any obligation; he does not participate in the *persona* of the trustee; he has done no wrong; he has acted honestly and with diligence. 'Equity cannot touch him, because . . . his conscience is unaffected by the trust[6].'

As Maitland points out, this result could be stated in either of two ways:

Formulation A

The cestui que trust may enforce his rights against
(i) the trustee, *and*
(ii) all who claim through the trustee as volunteers (personal representatives, devisees, donees), *and*
(iii) all those who acquire the trust property with actual or constructive notice of the trust.

Formulation B

The cestui que trust may enforce his rights against
all persons *except*
a *bona fide* purchaser of the legal title for valuable consideration without notice of the trust (whether actual or constructive).

Formulation B is now the more common means of stating the relevant proposition, and as such constitutes what is generally known as the *equitable doctrine of notice.* It is, however, a statement of a negative kind, and it is not without interest that Maitland himself preferred *Formulation A* 'because it puts us at what is historically the right point of view—the benefit of an obligation has been so treated that it has come to look rather like a true proprietary right[7].' Whether the 'benefit of an obligation' has *actually* become a true proprietary right is the question to which we must now turn.

(5) The nature of the interest of the cestui que trust

The debate concerning the nature of the rights of the cestui que trust has been conducted very largely in terms of the distinction between rights *in rem* and rights *in personam.*

(a) *Rights in rem and rights in personam*

A right *in personam* is a right to enforce the performance of an obligation undertaken by or imposed upon a specific person. Such an obligation arises

6 *Equity*, p. 115.
7 *Equity*, p. 115.

typically by reason of the law of contract, the law of torts, the law of trusts or, indeed, the law of property. The contractual promisee has rights *in personam* against his promisor. The victim of a tort has rights in personam against the tortfeasor. The cestui que trust has rights *in personam* against his trustee. It is possible to have rights in personam in respect of a thing. In each case, however, the rights concerned are rights enforceable only against the particular individual who incurs liability by virtue of some transaction in law (whether contract, tort, trust, or licence). The identity or *persona* of the individual against whom enforcement proceedings are brought is highly relevant to the success of those proceedings, because there is no point in A's attempting to enforce against C a contract which A has concluded with B[8]. There is no point in A's attempting to recover damages from E in respect of a tort committed by D[9].

A right *in rem*, however, is a right not against one person but against the entire world. The assertion of a right *in rem* is ultimately the assertion of some kind of ownership of a thing[10]. A right in rem is a right enforceable 'against the world' in respect of that thing: in a sense, it represents the summation of all possible rights *in personam*[11]. If, in respect of the 'thing' concerned, A is entitled to assert a right *in personam* against each and every individual in the world, the enforceability of his right is in no way dependent upon the precise identity of the individual against whom enforcement is sought (whether B, C, D, E, F, . . .). A's right *in personam* is equally enforceable against all, and the *persona* of the individual enforced against ceases to be a determinant of A's ability to vindicate his rights. The *persona* no longer represents a relevant variable in the equation which leads to enforcement of what were originally rights *in personam*. A's rights may just as comprehensively be described as rights against the thing itself, that is, as rights *in rem*.

Now the difference between rights *in rem* and rights *in personam* may seem academic. If rights are enforceable in any given situation, it matters not whether they are described as rights *in rem* or as rights *in personam*. However, the distinction between rights *in rem* and rights *in personam* will become important for us as we explore the law of land, because the borderline between these two categories of rights marks the boundaries of the 'proprietary right'. Only rights *in rem* are truly proprietary rights; only rights *in rem* properly come within the ambit of the law of property. Rights *in personam* are regarded as constituting purely personal rights which remain outside the realm of the law of property. Thus, according to Lord Wilberforce in *National Provincial Bank Ltd v Hastings Car Mart Ltd*[12],

before a right or interest can be admitted into the category of property, or a right

8 This is, of course, the doctrine of 'privity of contract'.

9 An exception to this proposition arises where E is D's employer and is therefore vicariously liable in respect of torts committed by D.

10 We must, as always, bear in mind that it is ultimately unreal to search for 'the' owner of any particular 'thing', p. 9, ante.

11 It has been said that a 'right *in rem* is a name for a large number of rights *in personam*, actual or potential. A violation of a right *in rem* is always a violation of a definite one of these rights *in personam*.' See W. W. Cook (1915) 15 Columbia LR 37 at 53: 'The Powers of Courts of Equity'.

12 [1965] AC 1175 at 1247f.

affecting property, it must be definable, identifiable by third parties, capable in its nature of assumption by third parties, and have some degree of permanence or stability.

The borderline between rights *in rem* and rights *in personam* is therefore crucial, for it expresses an important social judgment. The designation of a right as 'proprietary' is a kind of social accolade which signifies that great social importance is attached to the entitlement or interest in question. The right concerned is sufficiently important to merit public protection vis à vis not merely the participants in the private transaction which generated the right, but vis à vis the entire world. In the words of Professor F. R. Crane,

> The basic badge of a proprietary right—that is, of an interest in property—is that unlike a personal right it is enforceable against the relevant property in the hands of third parties[13].

The frontier between rights *in rem* and rights *in personam* has not yet been definitively settled. It is not impossible that a purely personal right may undergo a slow juristic metamorphosis, qualifying eventually for full recognition as a *proprietary* interest. Such an evolution is not unknown in the law of land, a prime example being the development which affected the law of restrictive covenants in the middle of the 19th century[14]. There are indications that a similar development is currently taking place in the law of contractual licences[15]. There has been a tendency in the recent case law to elevate the contractual licence from its orthodox status as a purely personal right affecting land to a new status as a proprietary right evincing all the characteristics attributed by Lord Wilberforce to proprietary rights in land.

One of the most intriguing doctrinal questions in this general context is whether a given right is enforced against third parties because it is a proprietary right, or whether a given right acquires proprietary status precisely because it is enforced against such parties. Is enforcement by the courts the cause or the effect of proprietary character? We shall see later that this question is deeply bound up with the way in which the courts conceptualise the underlying issues in the context of property. It may even be that the balance of cause and effect is undergoing a noticeable reversal in some areas of the law of property today, as increasingly the courts fashion proprietary rights in order to give effect to what are thought to be the 'legitimate' moral expectations of litigants or the demands of conscionable conduct in their dealings[16].

(b) *Is the right of the cestui que trust a right in rem or a right in personam?*

The debate concerning the precise nature of the rights of the cestui que trust has traditionally been conducted in terms of whether the cestui has a right *in rem* or merely a right *in personam*. We must look closely here at the relationship of the trustee and the cestui:

13 (1967) 31 Conv (NS) 332: 'Estoppel Interests in Land'.
14 See p. 614, post.
15 See p. 500, post.
16 See pp. 225, 488, post.

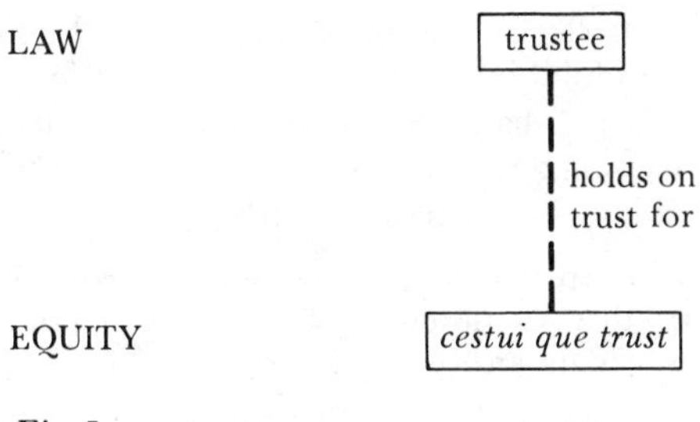

Fig. 5

It is tempting, on first analysis of this situation, to say that two different forms of ownership are recognised in relation to the property which forms the subject matter of the trust. At law the owner is the trustee; in equity the owner is the cestui que trust. However, this analysis has not received an unqualified imprimatur in the orthodox teaching on the nature of the rights of the cestui, for it seems to assert that the cestui has a right *in rem*, i.e., that he is the 'equitable owner' of the property held on trust. Conventional doctrine has us believe that the rights of the cestui are essentially and ultimately mere rights *in personam*.

(i) *The orthodox view* The more generally accepted view of the nature of beneficial rights is that once expressed by Professor J. B. Ames, who observed that

> A cestui que trust is frequently spoken of as an equitable owner of the land. This, though a convenient form of expression, is clearly inaccurate. The trustee is the owner of the land, and, of course, two persons with adverse interests cannot be owners of the same thing. What the cestui que trust really owns is the obligation of the trustee . . .[17]

Maitland went further in his efforts to maintain that equitable estates and interests are not rights in rem[18]. According to Maitland,

> The trustee is the owner, the full owner of the thing, while the cestui que trust has no rights in the thing[19].

Maitland thus found exception with the proposition that 'whereas the common law said that the trustee was the owner of the land, equity said that the cestui que trust was the owner.' For Maitland there was an absurdity in the statement that before 1875 there were two courts of co-ordinate jurisdiction, one of which said that A was the owner, the other that B was the owner, of Blackacre:

> That means civil war and utter anarchy . . . Equity did not say that the cestui que trust was the owner of the land, it said that the trustee was the owner of the land, but added that he was bound to hold the land for the benefit of the cestui que trust. There was no conflict here[20].

17 (1887) 1 Harvard LR 1 at 9: 'Purchase for Value without Notice'.

18 '. . . the thesis that I have to maintain is this, that equitable estates and interests are not *iura in rem*' (see *Equity*, p. 107).

19 *Equity*, p. 47.

20 *Equity*, p. 17. In this sense Equity was true to its maxim: 'Equity follows the law'. As Meagher,

In this way, Equity performed its historical purpose: 'Equity had not come to destroy the law, but to fulfil it. Every jot and every tittle of the law was to be obeyed, but when all this had been done something might yet be needful, something that equity would require.' But at every point equity presupposed the existence of common law. In Maitland's words,

It's of no use for Equity to say that A is a trustee of Blackacre for B, unless there can be some court that can say that A is the owner of Blackacre. Equity without common law would have been a castle in the air[1].

The Supreme Court of Judicature Acts 1873–1875 declared, of course, that in any case of variance the rules of equity should prevail over the rules of law, but as Maitland shrewdly pointed out this only served to show that there had not been any conflict before 1875 as to the identity of the 'owner' of land held on trust. Had there been a conflict, the legislation would have had the effect of abolishing the entire law of trusts by its confirmation of the supremacy of equitable rules: B would have been recognised, in a situation of conflict, as the only owner of Blackacre. Such a conclusion is, however, patently untenable: the institution of the trust remains alive and well to this day.

Thus, in the conventional view of the matter, the right of the cestui que trust is merely the benefit of an obligation—the obligation binding the trustee to observe and perform the duties of his trust. The right of a cestui is ultimately a right *in personam* against his trustee and all persons claiming through him to the extent that the trust is fastened upon their conscience[2].

(ii) *The wider view* To other jurists it has seemed plausible to maintain that ultimately the cestui que trust has more than merely rights *in personam*. This wider view attributes greater significance to substance than to form. It recognises that the legal estate of the trustee is in most cases a mere 'shadow' following the equitable estate 'which is the substance[3].' Support for this view may be found in the range of third parties against whom the cestui can enforce his rights. With the sole exception of the bona fide purchaser without notice, all third parties are bound by the trust, and in this sense the cestui is able to assert an 'equitable ownership' of the trust property against almost all the world. Thus for Salmond

If we have regard to the essence of the matter rather than to the form of it, a trustee is not an owner at all, but a mere agent, upon whom the law has conferred the power and

---

Gummow and Lehane have noted, '[e]quity can never say that what the common law recognises as a legal fee simple is not a legal fee simple. It can only prevent a legal owner from making an unconscientious use of his legal rights' (op. cit., para. 307). For a further explanation of this maxim, see later, p. 36, post.

1 *Equity*, p. 19.

2 This was essentially the reason why Maitland preferred 'an enumeration of the persons against whom the equitable rights are good to a general statement that they are good against all, followed by an exception of persons who obtain legal rights bona fide, for value and without notice.' See *Equity*, p. 115, p. 30, ante. It has been said that the insistence upon the 'in personam' nature of the *cestui's* right 'reached its apotheosis in *Maitland's Equity*, of which it is the warm and swelling leitmotif' (see R. P. Meagher, W. M. C. Gummow and J. R. F. Lehane, op. cit., para. 332).

3 See *Town of Cascade v Cascade Co* 75 Mont 304 at 311 (1925). This wider view was, of course, the view adopted by Lord Mansfield CJ, who stated quite clearly in *Burgess v Wheate* (1759) 1 Eden 177 at 217, that 'trusts are considered as real estates, as the real ownership of the land.'

imposed the duty of administering the property of another person. In legal theory, however, he is not a mere agent but an owner. He is a person to whom the property of some one else is fictitiously attributed by the law, to the extent that the rights and powers thus vested in a nominal owner shall be used by him on behalf of the real owner. As between trustee and beneficiary, the law recognises the truth of the matter; as between these two, the property belongs to the latter and not to the former. But as between the trustee and third persons, the fiction prevails. The trustee is clothed with the rights of his beneficiary, and is so enabled to personate or represent him in dealings with the world at large[4].

Even Maitland was prepared to concede that the cestui has 'rights which in many ways are treated as analogous to true proprietary rights, to *iura in rem*[5].' In his *Lectures on Equity*, he expressed the view that

The best answer may be that in history, and probably in ultimate analysis, it is *ius in personam*; but that it is so treated (and this for many important purposes) that it is very like *ius in rem.* A right primarily good against *certa persona*, viz. the trustee, but so treated as to be almost equivalent to a right good against all—a *dominium*, ownership, which however exists only in equity. And this is so from a remote time[6].

In his later writings it seems that Maitland mellowed even further towards a recognition that the cestui has rights which may be treated as ownership, or 'as some of those modalities of *Eigenthum* [ownership] in which our medieval law is so rich[7].' In considering the question whether the rights of the 'destinatory' (or cestui) are rights *in rem* (*dinglich*) or mere rights *in personam* (*obligatorisch*), Maitland made reference to the wide categories of third party whose conscience is bound by the trust, and concluded:

Thus we come by the idea of an 'equitable ownership' or 'ownership in equity.' Supposing that a man is in equity the owner ('tenant in fee simple') of a piece of land, it makes very little difference to him that he is not also 'owner at law' and that, as we say, 'the legal ownership is outstanding in trustees.' The only serious danger that he is incurring is that this 'legal ownership' may come to a person who acquires it bona fide, for value, and without actual or constructive notice of his rights. And that is an uncommon event. It is an event of which practical lawyers must often be thinking when they give advice or compose documents; but still it is an uncommon event. I believe that for the ordinary thought of Englishmen 'equitable ownership' is just ownership pure and simple, though it is subject to a peculiar, technical and not very intelligible rule in favour of bona fide purchasers. A professor of law will tell his pupils that they must not think, or at any rate must not begin by thinking, in this manner. He may tell them that the destinatory's rights are in history and in ultimate analysis not *dinglich* but *obligatorisch*: that they are valid only against those who for some special reason are bound to respect them. But let the Herr

4 *Jurisprudence* (12th edn. by P. J. Fitzgerald, London 1966), p. 256f.
5 *Equity*, p. 110.
6 *Equity*, p. 23.
7 *Collected Papers*, Vol. III, p. 343. In Maitland's day, juristic debate in the area of property law was conducted largely in German—a factor which was to influence much of Maitland's writing. Maitland clearly envied the greater expressive capacity of the German language: see, for instance, his remark that 'we have to envy our neighbours such a word as *Dinglichkeit*', a term which Maitland himself could render in English only in the rather ungainly form of 'thinglikeness' (Pollock and Maitland, *The History of English Law* (2nd edn., London 1968), Vol. 2, p. 125).

Professor say what he likes, so many persons are bound to respect these rights that practically they are almost as valuable as if they were *dominium*[8].

Later commentators have exposed the flaws in the position classically expounded in the earlier writings of Maitland. Meagher, Gummow and Lehane have pointed, for instance, to the hybrid nature of the cestui's rights and to the fact that it is widely acknowledged today that

an equitable right is not a *ius in personam* nor a *ius in rem* but a *ius in personam ad rem*: See *Smith v Layh* (1953) 90 CLR 102 at 109. This view demonstrated more gravity of expression than profundity of analysis. The epigram is soothing but not illuminating. The truth is that for most purposes Maitland's view is today wholly incorrect; equitable rights are, for most purposes, rights *in rem* in the sense that they are usually proprietary rather than contractual, assignable rather than personal, and capable of being inherited rather than perishing with their owner[9].

Ultimately the question whether a cestui que trust has rights *in rem* or rights *in personam* may simply be a matter of emphasis and perspective. However, it is important to notice that from the earliest times there has been a willingness to concede that the cestui holds at the very least the benefit of an obligation and that this benefit may well, in some sense, comprise a *form* of 'equitable ownership'. We shall see shortly that the 'equitable ownership' thus derived from the enforceability of the trustee's fiduciary obligation is strikingly similar to new forms of 'ownership' which are beginning to emerge in the contemporary law of property.

(6) Equity follows the law

It is one of the maxims of equity that 'equity follows the law[10].' By this is meant simply that equity generally endorses and reinforces the law except in those situations in which it diverges in order to give expression to some principle of conscience. For the most part, equity adopts the solutions and even the thought processes of the common law.

This has one interesting implication in the present context. We shall discover shortly that the common law never regarded the holder of land as owning the land itself. What he owned was an 'estate' in the land[11]. The common law thus interposed the abstract entity of the 'estate' between the man and the land, and the doctrine of estates was an integral part of the medieval scholasticism of land law. In any given case, the precise nature of the 'estate' determined (and still determines) the extent and duration of the man's rights over the land in question. The estate at common law may be an estate in fee simple, or in fee tail, or for life, or for a term of years[12]. When expressed diagrammatically, this relationship between the 'subject' and the 'object' of property spells out a distinctive pattern:

8 *Collected Papers*, Vol. III, p. 349f. In the words of Meagher, Gummow and Lehane (op. cit., para. 334), 'That the purity of Maitland's doctrine can no longer be maintained is almost universally recognised.'

9 R. P. Meagher, W. M. C. Gummow and J. R. F. Lehane, op. cit., para. 334.

10 See Snell's *Principles of Equity*, p. 29; R. P. Meagher, W. M. C. Gummow and J. R. F. Lehane, op. cit., paras. 307f.; p. 33, ante.

11 See p. 45, post.

12 See p. 46 ff., post.

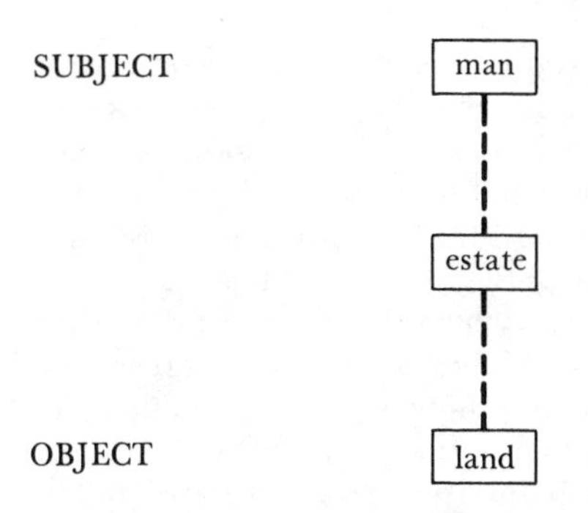

Fig. 6

When equity began to take cognisance of the institution of the trust, we find that this distinct pattern of relationship is duplicated. In the orthodox view, as Maitland explains, the cestui que trust enjoys 'the benefit of an obligation.' But, because equity follows the law, the Chancery adopted the rules of the common law as a model in its dealings with the rights of those for whom property was held in trust. The 'estates' of the common law found their analogue in equity, so that it could be said that the cestui had an estate in fee simple, or in fee tail, or for life, or for a term of years, as the case might be. In all such matters, 'the analogies of the common law prevailed; the Chancery moulded equitable estates and interests after the fashion of the common law estates and interests[13].' However, the estate held by the cestui could not be an estate in the land, since this was held by the trustee. Instead, says Maitland, the cestui 'has an "estate", not in the land, but in "the use"[14].' This idea, when represented diagrammatically, once again spells out the encoded pattern of relations between the 'subject' and the 'object' of property:

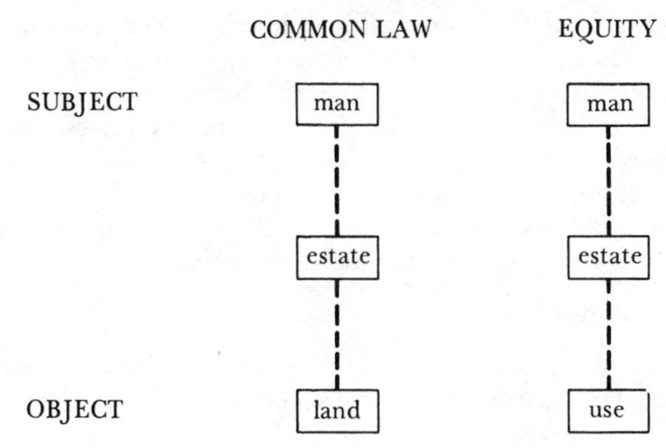

Fig. 7

Thus, in Maitland's terms, 'we might say that "the use" is turned into an incorporeal thing, an incorporeal piece of land; and in this incorporeal thing you may have all those rights, those "estates", which you could have in a real, tangible piece of land[15].' This reification of 'the use' is not without significance.

13 Maitland, *Equity*, p. 108.
14 *Collected Papers*, Vol. III, p. 343.
15 Ibid.

The realm of medieval law was 'rich with incorporeal things,' and as Pollock and Maitland were to point out, these incorporeal rights were, by virtue of their 'thinglikeness', regarded very much as a piece of land[16]. Even the corody—which was a form of personal annuity usually granted by a house of religion[17]—could be enforced through the assize of novel disseisin, which was a remedy peculiarly appropriate to the recovery of land[18].

In any event, the point which is of interest for us is the way in which equity, while substituting *the use* for *land* as the 'object' of property, interposed the 'estate' between the man and the thing which was valued. Just as the common law interposed the abstraction of the 'estate' between man and the valued resource (land), so equity likewise interposed the concept of the 'estate' between the cestui que trust and the 'thing' which was of value for him, i.e., the 'use' or moral obligation for giving effect to which his trustee was appointed. In one sense the cestui owned only the benefit of the trustee's obligation. But there was a further, and deeper, sense in which that benefit acquired a 'thinglikeness' which converted the rights of the cestui in equity into proprietary rights in land just as effectively as the landholder's rights were recognised, through the medium of the 'estate', as proprietary rights at common law.

Moreover, by adopting the traditional code of the proprietary relation—the doctrine of estates—equity quietly but effectively recognised that the 'thing' of value to the cestui is not whether his rights be considered rights *in rem* or merely rights *in personam*, but rather whether the obligation of the trust is performed. The true 'property' of the cestui is secure if, and for so long as, the terms of the trust are observed by the person who holds legal title. Herein lies an important lesson for the property lawyer. A man's 'property' is complete and effectual so long as he is entitled to the enjoyment of, or is guaranteed access to, some valued resource. It matters not how loudly or how long the theorists debate the precise status of his rights, for their nature (as 'proprietary' or 'personal') matters not at all so long as he can find a court which is prepared to enforce those rights on his behalf. Ultimately, his rights are 'proprietary' because they are enforced, and not vice versa. It is this reversal of the expected line of enquiry which makes it unprofitable to ask whether a given entitlement is or is not a 'proprietary' right. To ask *this* question is to ask merely a 'second order' question, for the real question in every case is whether the courts will sanction the use of the socially legitimated power vested in them to reinforce the supposed entitlement.

(7) The 'new property'[19]

In the light of the foregoing, it becomes relevant to ask how the 'new property' can be accommodated within the structure of the thought processes which have pervaded our law for over seven centuries.

16 Op. cit., Vol. 2, p. 124f.

17 A 'corody' was a benefit granted by a house of religion in consideration of services rendered. Alternatively a man might invest ready money in a corody in order to provide for his old age. A corody often took the form of an undertaking to supply the corodian with food, clothes and other commodities at stated intervals, and was in effect the medieval forerunner of our modern index-linked pension. See Pollock and Maitland, op. cit., Vol. 2, p. 134f. See also Lord Bowden of Chesterfield, Times, 4th June 1980.

18 See p. 49, post.

19 See p. 11f., ante.

The answer is that the institution and indeed the philosophy of the 'new property' are surprisingly amenable to the analysis which was imposed upon the proprietary concept by both the common lawyers and the equity lawyers. We have seen already that the 'new property' comprises essentially claims to security of various kinds. These forms of security are integrally bound up with the particular 'goods of life' which are nowadays commonly the object of much social striving.

Prominent in the attention of the modern land lawyer is the general social interest represented by *residential security*. The land law of today is increasingly concerned with the claim to security in the enjoyment of residential occupation—a claim which gathers force in times of economic insecurity and housing shortage. We shall discover, however, that this particular form of claim is often difficult to classify in terms of the orthodox canons of the law of property, and many of the difficulties of our present law flow from the attempt to place these new claims within forced categories.

Nevertheless when we analyse the general claim to security in the enjoyment of residential occupation, we find once again the distinctive historical pattern of the proprietary relationship. The essence of the claim to residential security is the assertion of a 'status of irremovability.' In other words, the residential occupier need not be particularly concerned with the legal title relevant to his home: his concern is merely that he be allowed to continue in the enjoyment of that property free from the intrusions of strangers. It matters not that he is excluded from the legal title: the right to continuing and unhindered de facto possession is far more valuable than any legal title. The desired 'good' is *irremovability*, and we find that many of the land law developments of recent decades recognise a status of irremovability vested in specified classes of residential occupier—the spouse in the matrimonial home, the licensee in the informal family arrangement, the tenant in his rented home. The orthodox property lawyer would find it difficult to describe these developments as conferring a 'proprietary' right upon the classes mentioned—indeed it is a badge of orthodoxy that the rights in question here should be firmly classified as merely 'personal'. But watch closely as the encoded message of the proprietary relationship is spelt out once again with inexorable exactitude:

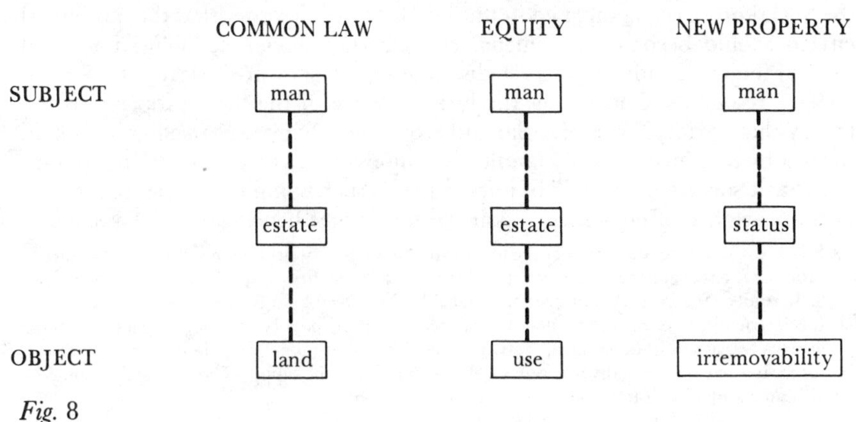

Fig. 8

Even the semantic link between 'status' and 'estate' serves merely to emphasise the structural integrity and historical consistency of the concept of the 'new property' in land. It becomes clear that, although the ideology of the 'new property' is as yet far from fully developed and although it is still far too early to point to a coherent body of 'new property law', the advent of a 'new property' is something with which the property lawyers of the next generation will increasingly have to deal.

It may be true to say that with the advent of the 'new property' we begin to see also the emergence of a 'new equity'[20]. It is ultimately this remarkable capacity for rejuvenation and regeneration which makes the law of property exciting, and ensures a continuing and fertile response to the ever changing universe of human needs and aspirations. The equity of the medieval Chancellors converted the benefit of a moral obligation into a recognisable proprietary right: the cestui was regarded as having an 'estate' in 'the use'. In just the same way, the 'new property' converts the benefit of a social obligation into a form of proprietary interest: in the context of land, the residential occupier is regarded as having, in certain circumstances, a 'status' of 'irremovability'. The conceptual structure remains the same—the man is given an 'estate' or 'status' in some 'object' of value—but the social purpose and the social impact of the law move on.

The variable in the structure is, of course, the precise 'object' to which value is attached. For the medieval common lawyer, with his blunt and pragmatic grasp of reality, the valued resource was land. For the equity lawyer, indelibly marked by his training in an ecclesiastical jurisdiction of conscience, the ultimate value was the faithful discharge of moral obligation. However, for the modern lawyer concerned with the 'new property', the paramount interest is the achievement of 'social justice' in a much more secular context. In terms of the underlying philosophy of the 'new property', there are certain limited resources (e.g., secure housing, purposeful employment, income security and adequate education) access to which is essential for the enjoyment of a wholesome life. Equity has for a long time fastened a trust upon the conscience of the legal owner of private property in order to give effect to the moral obligations owed to the cestui. In just the same way the 'new property' fastens a public trust upon the 'social property' comprised in the 'goods of life', in order that the individual citizen should become the beneficiary of certain socialised obligations, and thereby enjoy a more equitable distribution of certain critically important welfare resources. Underlying the jurisprudence of the 'new property' is the theory that various forms of social and economic advantage are effectively held in trust by nominees (e.g., by landlords, employers, fiscal authorities and so on), and that a 'social trust' should be imposed upon such nominees by the conferment of 'status-rights' of enjoyment upon the individual beneficiaries[1]. A socialised

20 It is not without significance that the judge who has done most in England in recent decades to promote the recognition of the 'new property' was also the first to speak of the emergence of a 'new equity'. See Lord Denning (1952) 5 CLP 1: 'The Need for a New Equity'.

1 It is instructive to bear in mind that, for vast sections of the population, the provision of income security already rests upon the operation of public or quasi-public trusts in the form of pension funds. It is not an essentially different kind of demand that the supply of housing stock should be allocated and administered on a similar principle of 'public trust'.

version of the 'constructive trust[2]' is thus established, without reference to the intentions of the nominees.

In the context of land law, the social rights which are given proprietary status under the broadly based 'trust' of the 'new property' are rights connected with the protection of that highly valuable resource of modern times—residential security. It is in this context that we must place the contemporary emergence of a 'status of irremovability'. Recent developments in our law mark a hesitant but nevertheless increasing recognition that the provision of adequate residential accommodation under conditions of reasonable security constitutes an elementary precondition of human dignity and purposeful achievement in life. As with equitable rights of the traditional mould, the 'social rights of property' created in the realm of the 'new property' may not be absolute. They are, however, sufficiently distinctive and important to become the focus of much of the land lawyer's attention during the last two decades of the 20th century.

Of course, much of our land law is unrelated to claims of residential security and the emergence of a 'new property'. We shall throughout this book examine the principles of real property which apply to all forms of land, whether used for residential, commercial or investment purposes. However, it is often the case that the operation of land law principles is seen with greatest clarity in the context of residential property, and for this reason the emphasis of the exposition contained in the following chapters will frequently be placed, at least initially, upon residential land.

2 See p. 476ff., post.

CHAPTER 2

An overall view

Professor F. H. Lawson once said of the English law of property that

> It is logical and orderly, its concepts are perfectly defined, and they stand in well recognised relations to one another. It is no longer easy to make any remarkable inventions, though new combinations of concepts are constantly being worked out. Above all, this part of the law is intensely abstract and has become a calculus remarkably similar to mathematics. The various concepts had, and still have, when properly understood, a very necessary relation to the economic facts of life, but once created and defined they seem to move among themselves according to the rules of a game which exists for its own purposes. So extreme are these various characteristics that they make of this part of the law something more logical and more abstract than anything that to my knowledge can be found in any other law in the world. More than anywhere else we seem to be moving in a world of pure ideas from which everything physical or material is entirely excluded[1].

It is the purpose of this chapter to introduce some of the basic notions of the English law of real property and to provide the reader with an overall view of areas of that law which will be examined in greater detail in the following chapters of this book.

1. FUNDAMENTAL CONCEPTS IN THE HISTORY OF LAND LAW

The English law of real property cannot be properly understood except in the light of its history[2]. The historical roots of our law of land are to be found in the doctrine of tenures, the doctrine of estates and the concept of seisin. All three elements played a fundamentally important role in the structuring of our law.

(1) The doctrine of tenures

The source of the medieval theory of land law was the Norman invasion of England in 1066. From this point onwards the King considered himself to be the owner of all land in England. Since the Normans had no written laws to bring with them to their newly conquered territory, what they created was effectively a system of landholding in return for the performance of services. Thus came

1 *The Rational Strength of the English Law* (London 1951), p. 79.

2 On the history of land law, see generally S. F. C. Milsom, *Historical Foundations of the Common Law* (London 1969), p. 88ff; A. W. B. Simpson, *An Introduction to the History of the Land Law* (London 1961); J. H. Baker, *An Introduction to English Legal History* (2nd edn., London 1979), p. 193ff.

into being the classic feudal structure. According to feudal theory, all land was owned by the Crown and was granted to subjects of the Crown only upon the continued fulfilment of certain conditions. Land was never granted by way of an actual transfer of ownership. As Pollock and Maitland were later to say,

> All land in England must be held of the king of England, otherwise he would not be the king of all England. To wish for an ownership of land that shall not be subject to royal rights is to wish for the state of nature[3].

It was a direct consequence of this theory that all occupiers of land were at best regarded as 'tenants', i.e., as holders of the land, who in return for their grants rendered services of some specified kind either to the King himself or to some immediate overlord who, in his turn, owed services ultimately to the Crown. In this way there emerged a feudal pyramid, with the King at its apex, and the doctrine of tenures defined the terms of grant on which each 'tenant' enjoyed his occupation of land.

(a) *The classification of tenures*

The feudal services rendered by 'tenants' were thus an integral part of early English land law, and in time became standardised and identifiable by the type of service exacted and performed. The different methods of landholding (differentiated according to the form of service required) were known as 'tenures', each tenure indicating the terms on which the land was held. The tenures were themselves subdivided by the common law into those tenures which were 'free' (and therefore formed part of the strict feudal framework) and those tenures which were 'unfree' (and appertained to tenants of lowly status who were *adscripti glebae*—effectively little better than slaves).

(i) *Unfree tenures* The common labourer or 'villein tenant' originally had no place on the feudal ladder at all. He merely occupied land on behalf of his lord, who was deemed by the common law to have seisin of the land thus occupied[4]. Villeinage (later called copyhold tenure), although an unfree tenure, came to enjoy increasing protection in practice. It retained its existence in fact until the enactment of the property legislation of 1922–1925.

(ii) *Free tenures* The kinds of service provided by those who enjoyed free tenure included, for instance, the provision of armed horsemen for battle (the tenure of 'knight's service') or the performance of some personal service for the King himself such as the bearing of high office at the King's court (the tenure of 'grand sergeanty'). These tenures were known as 'tenures in chivalry' and were distinct from the 'spiritual tenures' of 'frankalmoign' and 'divine service' (by which ecclesiastical lands were held in return for the performance of some sacred office) and the somewhat humbler 'tenures in socage' (which obliged the tenant to render agricultural service to his lord). With the passage of time, the

3 *The History of English Law* (2nd edn., London 1968), Vol. 2, 3.
4 See p. 48, post.

military and socage tenures were commuted for money payments, but all tenures carried with them 'incidents' (or privileges enjoyed by the lord) which were often more valuable than the services themselves. It was, however, only the free tenures which could be held by free tenants who occupied a place in the feudal hierarchy.

(b) *The feudal pyramid*

What emerged was a kind of feudal pyramid of free tenants, with the actual occupiers of the land (the 'tenants in demesne') forming the base, their overlords ('mesne lords') standing in the middle—both receiving services and rendering services in their turn, and with the King at the apex receiving services from his immediate tenants ('tenants in chief'). Pollock and Maitland described the system of tenures as a series of 'feudal ladders', citing one such real instance:

> In Edward I's day Roger of St German holds land at Paxton in Huntingdonshire of Robert of Bedford, who holds of Richard of Ilchester, who holds of Alan of Chartres, who holds of William le Boteler, who holds of Gilbert Neville, who holds of Devorguil Balliol, who holds of the king of Scotland, who holds of the king of England[5].

Pollock and Maitland indicated that a feudal ladder with as many rungs as this was 'uncommon', but added that

> theoretically there is no limit to the possible number of rungs, and practically . . . men have enjoyed a large power, not merely of adding new rungs to the bottom of the ladder, but of inserting new rungs in the middle of it.

This process of potentially infinite extension of the feudal ladder was known as 'subinfeudation': a new tenure could be created simply by adding another rung to the ladder. However, subinfeudation carried the disadvantage that it tended to make the feudal ladder long and cumbersome, and in time the process of alienation of land by 'substitution' became more common. By the process of substitution, the alienee of land assumed the rung on the feudal ladder previously occupied by the alienor, and the creation of a new and inferior rung was no longer necessary. By the end of the 13th century a more modern concept of land as freely alienable property was beginning to displace the restrictive feudal order, and this evolution culminated in the Statute Quia Emptores of 1290. This enactment was the pre-eminent expression of a new preference for freedom of alienation as a principle of public policy.

(c) *The Statute Quia Emptores*

The principal measure effected by the Statute Quia Emptores was the prohibition for the future of alienation by subinfeudation. Henceforth only the Crown could grant new tenures, and the existing network of tenures could only contract. Every conveyance of land simply *substituted* the grantee in the tenurial position formerly occupied by his grantor: no new relationship of lord and tenant was generated by the transfer. It is this statute which—quite unnoticed—

5 Op. cit., Vol. 1, p. 233. See also F. H. Lawson, *Introduction to the Law of Property* (London 1958), p. 62: 'Tenure is a relation which looks both ways, towards a parcel of land and towards a lord.'

still regulates the effect of every conveyance of land in fee simple today. Every such conveyance is merely a process of substitution of the purchaser in the shoes of the vendor, and the effect of the statute during the last seven centuries has been the gradual flattening of the feudal pyramid so that all tenants in fee simple today are presumed (in the absence of contrary evidence) to hold directly of the Crown as 'tenants in chief'.

(d) *The reduction in tenures*

The dismantling of the feudal order was later accelerated by more direct measures aimed at a reduction of the forms of tenure. Under the Tenures Abolition Act 1660, almost all free tenures were converted into 'free and common socage' or 'freehold tenure'. By 1925 the only tenures remaining which enjoyed any importance were socage tenure and copyhold tenure. The Law of Property Act 1922 (which came into force on 1 January 1926) enfranchised all copyhold tenure, converting it automatically into freehold (i.e., socage) tenure.

There is therefore only one surviving form of tenure—freehold tenure in socage—but the conceptual vestiges of the doctrine of tenures live on. It is still true that every parcel of land in England is held of some lord—almost invariably the Crown. It is still technically true that no one owns land except the Crown, and that all occupiers of land are merely—in the feudal sense—'tenants'. However, for all practical purposes the doctrine of tenures is now obsolete. Tenure of land for an estate in fee simple is now tantamount to absolute ownership of the land—or as close to total control of land as is possible today.

We must now turn to the doctrine of estates, which, although also having medieval origins, still enjoys a huge significance in our modern land law. Whereas the doctrine of tenures indicated the conditions on which a grant of land was held, the doctrine of estates defines the effective duration of that grant.

(2) The doctrine of estates

Fundamental to the classification of interests in our modern land law is the doctrine of estates. It followed from the medieval theory of land law that the only owner of land in England was the King. His subjects—be they ever so great—were merely tenants, occupying land on the terms of one or other form of tenure. What then did the tenant own (if indeed he owned anything)? The answer to this question has been provided by Professor F. H. Lawson:

> The solution adopted by English law was to create an abstract entity called the estate in the land and to interpose it between the tenant and the land. Since the estate was an abstract entity imagined to serve certain purposes, it could be made to conform to a specification, and the essential parts of the specification were that the estate should represent the temporal aspect of the land—as it were a fourth dimension—that it should be divisible within that dimension in respect of time according to a coherent set of rules, but that the whole of that dimension, the estate, should be regarded as existing at the present moment so that slices of the estate representing rights to successive holdings of the land should be regarded as present estates coexisting at the same time[6].

6 Op. cit., p. 66f.

As Professor Lawson said, with the doctrine of estates 'the law of property ceased to be earth-bound'. What the medieval 'tenant' and the modern proprietor alike own is not strictly the land itself, but rather an 'estate' in the land. That is, each owns an *interest in* the land which confers specific rights and powers according to the nature of the 'estate'. It is this concentration upon the rights and powers appertinent to differing kinds of 'estate' which so sharply distinguishes the common law view of real property from the continental emphasis on full ownership in the abstract sense (i.e., *dominium*). In the words of Otto Kahn-Freund,

Owing to its habit of looking at the powers and rights arising from ownership rather than at ownership in the abstract, English law has been able to introduce the time element into the property concept. The continental notion of property, like the dominium of Roman law, contains, as a matter of principle, the element of eternity . . .[7]

An 'estate' is therefore simply an interest in land which confers certain powers of management, enjoyment and disposition over the land *for a particular period of time.* In terms of the feudal conceptions which generated the earliest principles of our law, an 'estate' denoted the *duration* of a grant of land from a superior owner within the vertical power structure which emanated from the Crown; and no man could grant another any greater 'estate' than that which he himself owned (*nemo dat quod non habet*).

We must examine in closer detail the three freehold estates of the common law: the fee simple, the fee tail and the life estate. The theory of 'estates' has never been more accurately or more elegantly summarised than in the sixteenth century *Walsingham's* case[8]. Here the court declared of one, Wyat:

Wyat had the land, but the land itself is one thing, and the estate in the land is another thing, for an estate in the land is a time in the land, or land for a time, and there are diversities of estates, which are no more than diversities of time, for he who has a fee-simple in land has a time in the land without end, or the land for time without end, and he who has land in tail has a time in the land or the land for time as long as he has issue of his body, and he who has an estate in land for life has no time in it longer than for his own life, and so of him who has an estate in land for the life of another, or for years. Then when Wyat had but an estate in the land for a time as long as there was any issue of the body of his father, and after the failure of such issue the King had a time in the land without end, or the land for time without end, which is termed a fee-simple, the words of Wyat upon his livery could not take that away from the Crown, nor give it to Moulton, and the law does not measure the gift of Wyat according to his words, but according to his ability, and here he was disabled to give the land for a greater time than he had, for which reason no fee-simple could pass.

(a) *The estate in fee simple*

The estate in fee simple has always been the primary estate in land. It represents the amplest or largest right which a 'tenant' can have in or over land. Although

7 'Introduction' to K. Renner, *The Institutions of Private Law and their Social Functions* (London and Boston 1949), p. 23.

8 2 Plowden 547 at 555; 75 ER 805 at 816f.

in theory each 'tenant in fee simple' is still merely a tenant in chief of the Crown, the estate in fee simple is nowadays tantamount to absolute ownership of land[9]. If we adhere to the feudal fiction, an estate in fee simple denotes a grant of land from the Crown in perpetuity—a right of tenure of the land which endures for ever and which is capable, more or less indefinitely, of transfer inter vivos or of devolution on death. The owners of the estate in fee simple may come and go but the estate remains, for it is of infinite duration. Each new owner steps into the shoes of his predecessor as a tenant in chief of the Crown—the modern effect of the Statute Quia Emptores of 1290.

The owner of an estate in fee simple is sometimes called a 'freeholder'—the owner of a freehold estate. Although modern legislation often curtails the fee simple owner's rights of use and enjoyment (for environmental and planning purposes)[10], there are relatively few limitations upon his power to dispose of the estate in the land whether by will or by alienation inter vivos[11]. There is an important public policy which requires that land should be freely alienable in fee simple, since the unrestricted transferability of land is a vital precondition of a healthy and vibrant economy. Thus any grant or conveyance of an estate in fee simple subject to a condition which completely prohibits alienation by the grantee is in conflict with public policy, and the offending condition is declared void at common law[12]. The conveyance takes effect unconditionally.

An estate in fee simple may be 'absolute', 'determinable' or 'conditional', or may in some cases take the form of a 'base fee'[13]. We shall analyse these terms shortly, but first we must look at the two other freehold estates which could subsist before 1926. These were the fee tail and the life estate. Neither is very common today, and both must now exist, if at all, behind some form of trust. Since 1926 they have been referred to simply as an 'entailed interest' and a 'life interest' respectively.

(b) *The entailed interest*

An entailed interest endures so long as the original grantee (the 'tenant in tail') or any of his lineal descendants is alive. Historically the entail provided a form of landholding designed to retain land within the family. However, from the 16th century onwards, this purpose was commonly frustrated by the 'barring' of the entail by the tenant in possession—which usually had the effect of converting the entail into some form of fee simple[14]. The grantor's expressed

9 Once again the words of Otto Kahn-Freund (op. cit., p. 42) are instructive: 'Every student of English law is familiar with the survival of the names of former feudal realities as symbols for capitalist institutions. To borrow Bagehot's terminology, the term "fee simple" is merely a "dignified" and, therefore, deceptive nomenclature for ownership.'

10 See p. 635, post.

11 See however the Inheritance (Provision for Family and Dependants) Act 1975; Race Relations Act 1976, ss. 21f.

12 Coke upon Littleton (19th edn., 1832), 223a.

13 A 'base fee' was produced where an entail was barred by the process of 'levying a fine'. See R. E. Megarry and H. W. R. Wade, *The Law of Real Property* (4th edn., London 1975), p. 89.

14 See p. 66, post.

intention had thereby been subverted, but few tears are shed for this reason nowadays, partly because it is widely accepted that the 'dead hand' of the grantor should not prevail for ever and partly because an entailed interest generates an especially onerous liability to taxation.

(c) *The life interest*

A life interest is plainly coextensive and coterminous with the life of the grantee. If a life interest is sold to a third party, it becomes an interest *pur autre vie*, since it still endures only for the lifetime of the original grantee. Unlike an entailed interest, a life interest cannot be transformed into an interest of greater duration.

(d) *Words of limitation*

In accordance with the rules as to words of limitation now contained in section 60 of the Law of Property Act 1925,

> A conveyance of freehold land to any person without words of limitation, or any equivalent expression, shall pass to the grantee the fee simple or other the whole interest which the grantor had power to convey in such land, unless a contrary intention appears in the conveyance[15].

Thus a conveyance of freehold land without further reference to the estate or interest intended to be granted (e.g., Blackacre 'to X') is normally effective to invest the grantee with an estate in fee simple in the land. If the grantor wishes to dispose of a lesser estate in the land, he must actually employ words of limitation in his grant (e.g., Blackacre 'to X in tail' or 'to X for life')[16].

(3) The concept of seisin

The concept of seisin is a very early idea lying at the root of the development of the English law of real property. The notion of seisin marks the beginning of the common law tradition that proprietary rights in land are based upon physical possession rather than upon an abstract title[17]. In its original form seisin consisted essentially of the actual or de facto possession of land—quite irrespective of right. Seisin was fact not right, although the right might flow from the fact and be reinforced by the passage of time[18]. As Pollock and Maitland wrote[19],

> A man is in seisin of land when he is enjoying it or in a position to enjoy it.

Seisin thus expressed the organic element in the relationship between man and land and as such provided presumptive evidence of ownership within the

15 Law of Property Act 1925, s. 60(1).
16 Law of Property Act 1925, s. 60(4).
17 See A. E.-S. Tay, 'Property and Law in the Society of Mass Production, Mass Consumption and Mass Allocation', in *A Revolution in Our Age: The Transformation of Law, Justice and Morals* (Canberra Seminars in the History of Ideas, August 1975).
18 Ibid., p. 11ff.
19 Op. cit., Vol. 2, p. 34.

medieval framework of rights in land. Furthermore it was only the person seised of the land who could avail himself of an owner's rights in respect of the land. Since seisin was a matter of fact, even the thief could enjoy seisin and it is significant that he could be dispossessed only if the rightful owner brought against him the action of novel disseisin. In other words, it was the recovery of seisin which provided the first step towards recovery of full rights of ownership.

From the 15th Century onwards, as Lord Mansfield was later to state,

> Seisin is a technical term to denote the completion of that investiture by which the tenant was admitted into the tenure, and without which no freehold could be constituted or pass[20].

Indeed only the person seised could effect a feoffment (i.e., conveyance of freehold land) with 'livery of seisin' in the symbolic sense required by the common law. 'Livery of seisin' took the form of a solemn ceremony. The grantor and grantee entered upon the land conveyed and the feoffor, in the presence of witnesses, delivered the seisin to the feoffee either by some symbolic act, such as handing him a twig or sod of earth, or by expressing appropriate words of alienation and leaving him in possession of the land[1].

In its technical sense seisin is no longer of importance today. However, the emphasis which it placed upon possession rather than title continues to influence several areas of modern law. The pragmatic process of conveyancing rests largely upon the assumption that proof of continued de facto enjoyment of land by the vendor and his predecessors in title provides a good root of title for the purchaser[2]. The law of adverse possession likewise relies upon the significance of unhindered possession of land, insofar as uninterrupted enjoyment of land over a period of time stipulated by law generates title to the land concerned[3]. Moreover the pre-eminent position accorded de facto possession in English land law ensures that there is no such thing as 'absolute title' to land[4]. All title is ultimately relative: the title of the present possessor will be upheld unless and until a better claim is advanced on behalf of somebody else. As Cockburn CJ observed in *Asher v Whitlock*[5],

> I take it as clearly established, that possession is good against all the world except the person who can shew a good title: and it would be mischievous to change this established doctrine . . . All the old law on the doctrine of disseisin was founded on the principle that the disseisor's title was good against all but the disseisee.

Quite apart from these vestigial traces in the English law of real property, it has been said that the concept of seisin has laid an indelible mark upon the way in which the common lawyer thinks of land. Alice Tay has pointed out that

> it is because all proprietary and possessory rights ultimately stem from enjoyment that seisin lies at the very root of the development of the English law of property and of the

20 *Taylor dem. Atkyns v Horde* (1757) 1 Burr 60 at 107; 97 ER 190 at 216.

1 See R. E. Megarry and H. W. R. Wade, op. cit., p. 50; Pollock and Maitland, op. cit., Vol. 2, p. 85f.

2 See p. 87, post.

3 See p. 93ff., post.

4 See p. 101, post.

5 (1865) LR 1 QB 1 at 5.

Englishman's concept of freedom—of his home as his castle. The common law, then, begins with and long maintains a bias in favour of the factual situation—the citizen's actual behaviour and powers *against* the claims of privilege and authority as such . . . The role of the underlying seisin-possession concept in the common law is to recognise and protect those still important areas in which men live, work and plan as users–owners, to set out their rights and obligations, to give them an area of privacy in which they have a right to be free of state and community interference, to repel the unattractive neighbour, the busybody, the officious policeman, and to ensure that they allow their neighbours the same possibility of undisturbed enjoyment. Only in societies that do not have such protection do men realise how important this concept of personal security and inviolability is . . . It is also the base and shaper of the social sentiment that shrinks with distaste from the forcible eviction[6].

It is therefore not without significance that the organic dimension epitomised in the medieval notion of seisin finds a modern counterpart in the importance attached nowadays to the 'utility-based' aspects of ownership of land and to the role of the 'occupation interest'. We shall throughout this book trace the emergence of a contemporary emphasis upon the 'use value' of land as distinct from its 'exchange value', and in terms of English land law an important index of this development was provided, for instance, by the judgments of the Court of Appeal and House of Lords in *Williams & Glyn's Bank Ltd v Boland*[7]. In the Court of Appeal Lord Denning MR construed the pivotal statutory concept of 'actual occupation of the land[8]' in language reminiscent of the medieval concept of seisin:

'[A]ctual occupation' is matter of fact, not matter of law . . . It does not depend on title. A squatter is often in actual occupation . . .[9]

As Lord Wilberforce indicated in the House of Lords, the phrase 'actual occupation' emphasises 'that what is required is physical presence, not some entitlement in law[10].' However, just as in the context of seisin the fact was instrumental in establishing the right, similarly in *Boland's* case it was the fact of physical possession which ultimately conferred overriding status upon a legal entitlement.

At many other points in this book, we shall see comparable developments in the law of residential security which in some sense owe their origin to the historical function and significance of the concept of seisin.

2. THE MEANING OF 'LAND'

For the property lawyer, the word 'land' bears an extended meaning[11]. According to section 205(1)(ix) of the Law of Property Act 1925, 'land' includes

6 'Law, the citizen and the state', in E. Kamenka, R. Brown and A. E.-S. Tay (ed.), *Law and Society: The Crisis in Legal Ideals* (London 1978), p. 11f.
7 [1979] Ch 312, [1980] 3 WLR 138, p. 353, post.
8 See Land Registration Act 1925, s. 70(1)(g).
9 [1979] Ch 312 at 332.
10 [1980] 3 WLR 138 at 143.
11 See W. Blackstone, *Commentaries on the Laws of England* (Oxford 1766), Vol. II, p. 16; '*Land* comprehends all things of a permanent, substantial nature; being a word of a very extensive signification.'

land of any tenure, and mines and minerals, whether or not held apart from the surface, buildings or parts of buildings (whether the division is horizontal vertical or made in any other way) and other corporeal hereditaments; also a manor, an advowson, and a rent and other incorporeal hereditaments, and an easement, right, privilege, or benefit in, over, or derived from land; but not an undivided share in land . . .

It can therefore be seen that, for the purpose of the Law of Property Act 1925, 'land' includes not merely 'corporeal hereditaments' such as the physical clods of earth which make up the surface layer of land, mines and minerals beneath the surface, and buildings or parts of buildings erected on the surface. It includes also many kinds of intangible right or 'incorporeal hereditament'. An example of an 'incorporeal hereditament' is an 'easement'—a right over somebody else's land—typically a right of way.

It is a curious feature of the English land lawyer's mode of thought that certain of the intangible rights which A enjoys over the land of B are often conceptualised as becoming just as much a part of 'A's land' as the very soil on which A's house is built. The benefit of A's right of way over B's land is regarded as an integral piece of 'A's land', with the result that any future conveyance of 'A's land' to C will effectively transfer to C not only A's corporeal hereditaments—essentially ownership of the physical land—but also ownership of the right of way over B's land[12].

The extended significance of the term 'land' is sometimes more eloquently than accurately expressed by reference to two Latin maxims. *Cuius est solum eius est usque ad coelum et ad inferos*: he who owns the land owns everything extending to the very heavens and to the depths of the earth. This medieval brocard contains a measure of truth as far as English law is concerned. However, it is now subject to so many qualifications as to be virtually worthless as a statement of law. The land-owner has, for instance, no right to coal or oil[13] or treasure trove[14] discovered in his land: ownership of such commodities is vested in the state. Nor does the land-owner have unqualified rights over the air space above his land[15].

The other phrase which is occasionally invoked is the general rule that *quicquid plantatur solo, solo cedit*; whatever is attached to the ground becomes a part of it[16]. That is, of course, the source of the idea reflected in section 205(1)(ix) of the Law of Property Act 1925 that buildings constructed on the soil become part of the 'land'. Even the top floor of a high-rise block of flats comprises 'land' for this purpose.

The rule also implies that objects attached to the building in question become annexed to the realty with the result that they are regarded as 'fixtures'. Once annexed to the land, there are often legal restrictions on their removal or

12 See Law of Property Act 1925, s. 62(1), p. 595, post.

13 See Coal Industry Nationalisation Act 1946; Petroleum (Production) Act 1934.

14 'Treasure trove' applies only to objects of gold and silver (see *Attorney General of the Duchy of Lancaster v G. E. Overton (Farms) Ltd* [1980] 3 WLR 869). See generally N. E. Palmer (1981) 44 MLR 178: 'Treasure Trove and the Protection of Antiquities'.

15 See, for instance, *Bernstein v Skyviews & General Ltd* [1978] QB 479. See, however, *Grigsby v Melville* [1974] 1 WLR 80 (conveyance of void below dwelling-house).

16 See *Montague v Long* (1972) 24 P & CR 240.

severance from that realty. Whether a chattel (such as a bathroom cabinet or an overhead heater or an extractor fan) merges into 'land' by reason of attachment to a wall depends upon both the degree and the purpose of the annexation[17]. Similar considerations govern the question whether a statue or piece of machinery becomes part of the 'land' on which it stands[18].

Of course, there are circumstances in which the person who has attached a fixture to the land may nevertheless remove the object so affixed. An owner of the absolute interest in the land can always do so, since the removal of his own fixtures is simply part and parcel of his rights of ownership. But if he sells his interest in the land to a third party, the conveyance will obviously include all fixtures attached to the land at the time of the contract of sale, unless vendor and purchaser then agreed to the contrary[19]. Under certain conditions a tenant has a right as against his landlord at the termination of the tenancy to remove any fixtures attached by the tenant for trade[20], ornamental and domestic[1], or agricultural purposes[2].

3. LEGAL AND EQUITABLE RIGHTS

Having now some broad conception of the nature of 'estates' in 'land', we must look more closely at the classification of real property rights contained in the Law of Property Act 1925. What follows is very much a matter of gaining an acquaintance with the grammar of land law[3]. Once this is done, it is possible to analyse and construct land law statements which hitherto may have seemed like a foreign language.

We should expect something fairly basic about land law to appear in the first section of the Law of Property Act 1925. And indeed it does. Section 1 in its terms surveys the entire field of proprietary rights in land[4], and then drives

17 See *Holland v Hodgson* (1872) LR 7 CP 328 at 335. Here Blackburn J adverted to a useful but not conclusive guideline: 'When the article in question is not further attached to the land than by its own weight it is generally considered a mere chattel.'

18 See *D'Eyncourt v Gregory* (1866) LR 3 Eq 382 (ornamental statues); *Re De Falbe* [1901] 1 Ch 523 (tapestries), affirmed *sub nom. Leigh v Taylor* [1902] AC 157; *Reynolds v Ashby & Son* [1904] AC 466; *Hulme v Brigham* [1943] KB 152 (machines); *Berkley v Poulett* (1976) 242 Estates Gazette 39 (pictures and marble statue).

19 Additional rights of both a tangible and intangible nature are conferred by the conveyance. See Law of Property Act 1925, s. 62(1), p. 595, post.

20 *Climie v Wood* (1869) LR 4 Exch 328.

1 *Spyer v Phillipson* [1931] 2 Ch 183.

2 See Agricultural Holdings Act 1948, s. 13.

3 For an exciting intellectual challenge, see Professor Bernard Rudden's remarkable attempt to construct a 'grammar' of land law ([1980] Conv 325: 'Notes Towards a Grammar of Property').

4 For the distinction between 'proprietary' rights and 'personal' rights in land, see earlier, p. 30, ante. It is important to note that section 1 of the Law of Property Act 1925 says nothing about those categories of rights affecting land which are not truly proprietary rights as such but are merely personal rights in land. The difference between 'proprietary' and 'personal' rights in land is essentially that the former confer a 'stake' in the land itself, whereas the latter confer merely a personal and usually transient permission to live upon or do something on the land in question. 'Personal' rights in land affect only the immediate grantor and grantee: they are not normally regarded as capable of binding third parties.

home a distinction of fundamental importance. It fixes a wide gulf between those proprietary rights in land which are *legal* and those which are *equitable*. All proprietary rights in land fall within one or other of these major categories.

Some proprietary rights in land exist and have their being 'at law': they are 'legal' rights. Other proprietary rights in land may be created only 'in equity': they are 'equitable' rights. Of course, the distinction between legal and equitable rights derives from the days when legal rights were those rights which were recognised by the courts of common law, while equitable rights were enforced only by the courts of equity. The jurisdictions of law and equity have now been fused for more than a century[5], but legal and equitable rights (although recognised and enforced in all courts alike) still differ in one paramountly significant respect—in their impact upon third party purchasers of the land to which they relate.

It is for precisely this reason that section 1 of the Law of Property Act 1925 takes pains to provide a clear demarcation between legal and equitable proprietary rights. Legal proprietary rights may take the form of *estates* (section 1(1)), or the form of *interests or charges* (section 1(2)).

1.—(1) The only estates in land which are capable of subsisting or of being conveyed or created at law are—

(a) An estate in fee simple absolute in possession;

(b) A term of years absolute.

(2) The only interests or charges in or over land which are capable of subsisting or of being conveyed or created at law are—

(a) An easement, right, or privilege in or over land for an interest equivalent to an estate in fee simple absolute in possession or a term of years absolute;

(b) A rentcharge in possession issuing out of or charged on land being either perpetual or for a term of years absolute;

(c) A charge by way of legal mortgage;

(d) ... and any other similar charge on land which is not created by an instrument;

(e) Rights of entry exercisable over or in respect of a legal term of years absolute, or annexed, for any purpose, to a legal rentcharge.

(3) All other estates, interests, and charges in or over land take effect as equitable interests.

Section 1 thus distinguishes between, on the one hand, two legal *estates* (section 1(1)) and five legal *interests* or *charges* (section 1(2)) and, on the other hand, all other proprietary rights in land—which must necessarily by reason of their exclusion from the first two subsections be equitable only (section 1(3)). The distinction between legal and equitable proprietary rights in land is therefore both artificial and crude, but is none the less crystal clear. Whether an estate, interest or charge can ever be *legal* depends quite simply on whether we can find reference to it within one of the categories laid down in section 1(1), (2). If we can, then the right in question is indeed capable of existing at law[6]. If we cannot

5 See Supreme Court of Judicature Acts 1873–1875.

6 Note that section 1 of the Law of Property Act 1925 indicates only whether a given property right is 'capable' of existing at law. Whether, within a particular context, that proprietary right in fact constitutes a legal estate or interest usually depends upon whether certain formalities were observed at the time of its grant. These formalities normally require that the grant be expressed in the form of a deed, p. 88, post.

find reference to a particular proprietary right within section 1(1), (2), then that right can only be equitable[7].

4. THE CENTRAL QUESTION OF LAND LAW

The central question of land law relates to whether certain rights in land survive a transfer of the legal estate in that land to a purchaser, thereby remaining valid and enforceable against him. Since land law in practice means conveyancing—the quotidian business of buying and selling homes and other property—this question ranks as one of the utmost social importance. This is the more so because most people tend to make the largest investments of their lifetime savings in one or other form of real property right, and it becomes a matter of more than marginal social concern that the rights which they purchase should not be defeated before they run their due course.

At the same time, the purchaser of land has a legitimate interest in the question whether, after the purchase, the land remains subject to any rights vested in another. Any uncertainty as to the effect of land transactions upon various types of real property right would inhibit purchasers and stultify dealings in the land. No purchaser would risk his money in buying land if there were any palpable degree of danger that the land purchased might be subject to an encumbrance which rendered his own title effectively or substantially worthless. The social and economic implications involved here become even more acute if we bear in mind that for this purpose the term 'purchaser' includes not only one who buys land but also one who lends money on the security of land, i.e., a mortgagee[8]. In most instances the mortgagee is one of the large lending institutions or building societies which operate to finance home ownership. Any inhibition imposed upon the availability of mortgage facilities would radically alter the living patterns of millions. As Lord Upjohn observed in *National Provincial Bank Ltd v Hastings Car Mart Ltd*[9],

> It has been the policy of the law for over one hundred years to simplify and facilitate transactions in real property. It is of great importance that persons should be able freely and easily to raise money on the security of their property.

Thus it is of primary importance to ascertain the fate of proprietary rights in the event of transactions with third parties. The answer to this central question of land law depends ultimately upon the characterisation of those rights as either *legal* or *equitable*, although the importance of this distinction will in time be eroded by the gradual extension of the system of registration of title[10].

7 Moreover, it is equitable irrespective of its mode of creation.
8 A 'purchaser' is generally defined in the property legislation of 1925 as including a 'lessee, mortgagee or other person who for valuable consideration acquires an interest in property.' See Law of Property Act 1925, s. 205(1)(xxi); Land Registration Act 1925, s. 3(xxi); Settled Land Act 1925, s. 117(1)(xxi); Land Charges Act 1925, s. 20(8); Land Charges Act 1972, s. 17(1); Administration of Estates Act 1925, s. 55(1)(xviii). See also Law of Property Act 1925, s. 87(1), p. 533, post.
9 [1965] AC 1175 at 1233f.
10 See pp. 73, 319, post.

At this point we must introduce the two most basic axioms of English land law:

(i) *legal rights bind the world;*
(ii) *equitable rights bind all persons except a bona fide purchaser of a legal estate for value without notice of those equitable rights*[11].

5. LEGAL RIGHTS BIND THE WORLD

Land law is based upon a relatively small number of axioms, and of these the most important is the axiom that 'legal rights bind the world'. In other words, legal rights are binding *in rem*[12].

If B owns a legal right in or over land belonging to A, and A then sells any interest in his land to C, B's right is binding on and enforceable against C—irrespective of whether C previously knew of the existence of B's right. This result scarcely ever works injustice since almost all legal rights in or over land are recorded on the face of documents of title (or in the Land Register in the case of registered land[13]) which the third party purchaser automatically inspects before concluding his purchase. Thus it is that legal rights in the land transferred are normally absolutely secure vis à vis a third party purchaser, and, by the same token, that third party is quite clear as to what he is purchasing.

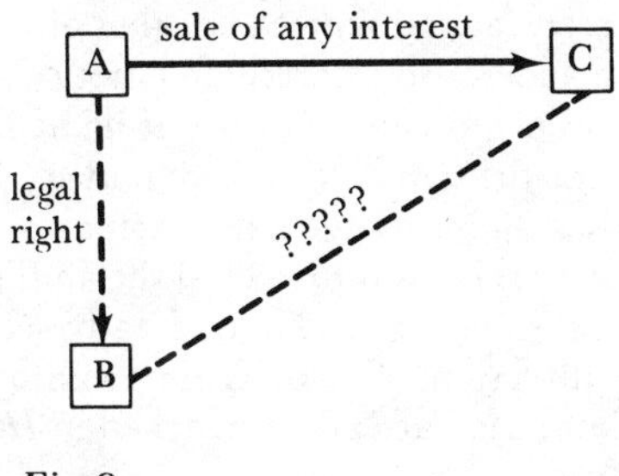

Fig. 9

6. EQUITABLE RIGHTS AND THE DOCTRINE OF NOTICE

By contrast with legal rights, equitable rights in or over land are binding on all persons *other than* the 'bona fide purchaser of a legal estate for value without notice of the equitable rights which affect the land.' This proposition incorporates the 'equitable doctrine of notice.' Equitable rights are subject to defeat upon the advent of a third party purchaser who has no knowledge of their existence. In *Midland Bank Trust Co Ltd v Green*[14] Lord Wilberforce related the equitable doctrine of notice to its origin in a jurisdiction of conscience:

11 See p. 30, ante.
12 See p. 31, ante.
13 See pp. 73, 319, post.
14 [1981] 2 WLR 28 at 32f.

The character in the law known as the bona fide (good faith) purchaser for value without notice was the creation of equity. In order to affect a purchaser for value of a legal estate with some equity or equitable interest, equity fastened upon his conscience and the composite expression was used to epitomise the circumstances in which equity would or rather would not do so. I think that it would generally be true to say that the words 'in good faith' related to the existence of notice. Equity, in other words, required not only absence of notice, but genuine and honest absence of notice. As the law developed, this requirement became crystallised in the doctrine of constructive notice which assumed a statutory form in the Conveyancing Act 1882, section 3. But . . . it would be a mistake to suppose that the requirement of good faith extended only to the matter of notice, or that when notice came to be regulated by statute, the requirement of good faith became obsolete. Equity still retained its interest in and power over the purchaser's conscience. The classic judgment of James LJ in *Pilcher v Rawlins* (1872) LR 7 Ch 259, 269 is clear authority that it did not: good faith there is stated as a separate test which may have to be passed even though absence of notice is proved.

The insecurity which the equitable doctrine of notice imposes upon equitable rights is made more acute by the fact that such rights commonly do not appear on the face of the documents of title inspected by the purchaser[15]. Thus in an impersonal and socially mobile urban community there is an ever increasing likelihood that a third party purchaser will be unaware of equitable rights concealed behind the title which he is buying. This is so even though the idea of 'notice', for the purpose of the doctrine of notice, bears an extended meaning. 'Notice' includes not merely 'actual notice', i.e., that of which the purchaser was consciously aware. It includes also 'constructive notice', i.e., that of which the purchaser would have been consciously aware if he had taken reasonable care to inspect both land and title, and 'imputed notice', i.e., that of which his counsel, solicitor or other agent as such had actual or constructive notice[16]. Nevertheless, the courts are reluctant to extend the ambit of constructive notice to any significant degree, since, as we have already seen, a persuasive policy element points in the direction of conferring maximum protection on the innocent purchaser of land. As Farwell J remarked in *Hunt v Luck*[17],

This doctrine of constructive notice, imputing as it does, knowledge which the person affected does not actually possess, is one which the courts of late years have been unwilling to extend.

Equitable rights are therefore insecure against 'Equity's Darling'—the bona fide purchaser of a legal estate for value without notice. Purchase of a legal estate by a third party who has no notice of equitable rights affecting that estate has the result of destroying the equitable rights concerned. They cannot thereafter revive even vis à vis a subsequent purchaser who *does* have notice of the fact that equitable rights once existed. The equitable rights have been destroyed for ever by the earlier transfer of the legal estate to a purchaser *without notice.* This

15 Of course, if those equitable rights do appear in the documentary title they are binding on a third party purchaser precisely because he *does* have notice of them. This is the position under the doctrine of notice in its pre-1926 form. We shall go on to modify this proposition in the light of the 1925 legislation, p. 74, post.
16 See Law of Property Act 1925, s. 199(1)(ii).
17 [1901] 1 Ch 45 at 48; aff. [1902] 1 Ch 428, CA.

operation of the doctrine of notice was exemplified in *Wilkes v Spooner*[18] (See *Fig.* 10). On the facts presented in this case, C takes free of B's equitable right, since in terms of the doctrine of notice C is a bona fide purchaser of A's legal estate for value without notice. D also takes free of B's equitable right, albeit that he does have notice of it, since the equitable right has already been destroyed by the earlier transfer of the legal estate to a purchaser *without* notice—i.e., to 'Equity's Darling'—the purchaser to whom the indulgence of equity is extended. B therefore has no rights *in rem*, i.e., rights in the land enforceable against the third parties, C and D. Such rights as he retains are rights *in personam*, in other words, rights against A alone deriving from the transaction which gave rise in the first place to B's ownership of an equitable interest in A's land.

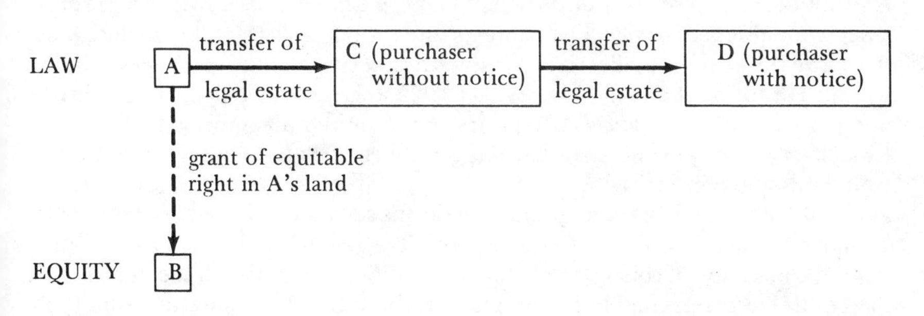

Fig. 10

7. LEGAL ESTATES

The implications of the doctrine of notice demonstrate quite clearly why section 1 of the Law of Property Act 1925 so firmly marks out two legal estates and five legal interests or charges, and then defines all other proprietary rights in land as necessarily equitable. We must now look more carefully at the two estates in land which are capable of existing at law. Section 1(1) provides that

> The only estates in land which are capable of subsisting or of being conveyed or created at law are—
> (a) An estate in fee simple absolute in possession;
> (b) A term of years absolute.

These legal estates are respectively the 'freehold' and 'leasehold' estates in land. According to section 1(6), such estates cannot be held by a minor, i.e., by a person who has not attained the age of 18 years. Section 1(2) proceeds to enumerate five categories of legal interest or charge in land. The rights referred to in section 1(1), (2) are alike *legal* in character. The distinction between estates, interests and charges consists in the fact that an 'estate' is a right in land owned or occupied by oneself, while an 'interest' or 'charge' tends to be a right acquired in or over property owned or occupied by someone else. However, this formal

18 [1911] 2 KB 473.

distinction should not obscure the fact that the estates, interests and charges referred to in section 1(1), (2) are all potentially *legal* rather than equitable[19].

(1) Fee simple absolute in possession

It is important to recognise the full significance of the phrase 'fee simple absolute in possession[20].'

(a) *'absolute'*

The term 'absolute' is used in contradistinction to 'determinable' or 'conditional'. A grant of Blackacre 'to A until King's College Chapel falls down' is a grant of a determinable fee simple. The estate granted is not in fee simple absolute, and therefore the grant is ineffective to convey a *legal* estate to the grantee A. Under section 1(3) of the Law of Property Act 1925, the right in Blackacre conferred upon A can only be *equitable.* By parity of reasoning, a conditional fee simple ('Blackacre to A on condition that King's College Chapel shall not fall down') would also confer upon A merely an equitable fee simple. However, an amendment to the 1925 Act specifically deems such a conditional fee simple to be 'for the purposes of this Act a fee simple absolute' and thus to be a legal estate[1]. Curiously, of course, there may be no difference between the duration of the equitable determinable fee simple and the legal conditional fee simple in these examples.

(b) *'in possession'*

The other element in the definition of the sole freehold estate which requires clarification is the phrase 'in possession'. This phrase is used in contradistinction to 'in remainder' and 'in reversion'. An interest 'in possession' confers an

19 In the legislation which was consolidated in the 1925 enactments legal estates interests and charges were in fact thrown together under *one* subsection rather than under the *two* subsections which appear as section 1(1), (2) of the Law of Property Act 1925 (see Law of Property Act 1922, s. 1(1)).

20 See p. 46, ante.

1 Law of Property Act 1925, s. 7(1), as amended by the Law of Property (Amendment) Act 1926, Schedule. The amendment is somewhat anomalous since it was intended primarily to confer legal character upon those owners who held a fee simple estate subject to a 'fee farm rent' or perpetual rentcharge. Such forms of landholding were common in Manchester and in the North of England, the purchaser of a fee simple paying not a capital sum by way of purchase price but rather an annual sum for non-payment of which the vendor of the fee simple reserved a right of entry. In other words, the purchaser held an estate in fee simple conditional upon the payment of the 'fee farm rent'. It would have been highly inconvenient that such a fee simple should only be equitable, for this would have introduced conveyancing difficulties and might even have brought the arrangement within the scope of the Settled Land Acts, p. 154, post. It was therefore to confirm the legal quality of the fee simple subject to a fee farm rent or perpetual rentcharge that section 7(1) of the Law of Property Act 1925 was amended in 1926. However, the amending provision appears to be sufficiently widely drafted to apply not merely to the Mancunian fee farm rents but to all forms of conditional fee simple. For a fuller account, see R. E. Megarry and H. W. R. Wade, *The Law of Real Property* (4th edn., London 1975), p. 138.

immediate right to occupation and enjoyment of the land from the effective date of the grant. An interest 'in remainder' is an interest which will 'fall into possession' on the expiry of some prior interest or interests. It is nevertheless important to realise that the grantee of an interest in remainder does indeed receive a proprietary right *at the date of the grant*: he receives a present right to future enjoyment. He is excluded from present enjoyment merely by the presence of a prior interest or prior interests[2]. An interest 'in reversion' is the interest retained throughout by a grantor who fails to exhaust the entire interest in the land in the terms of his grant. In other words, if a grantor fails to dispose of the fee simple absolute in his land, that fee simple reverts to him (or to his estate if he is dead) on the determination of the limited interests which he has granted away (e.g., a lease or a life interest).

All of this may be demonstrated by an analysis of a grant of Blackacre to A for life, then to B for life, then to C for life. If we examine each grantee's interest at the date of the grant, it is obvious that A has an interest in possession. B has an interest in remainder: it will fall into possession when A dies. Likewise, C has an interest in remainder, for he is excluded from possession by prior interests. All the while, the grantor holds the fee simple absolute in reversion, because he failed in the terms of the grant to divest himself of the fee simple estate in the land which formed the subject matter of the grant.

(2) Term of years absolute

The only other estate in land which is capable of subsisting or of being conveyed or created *at law* is the 'term of years absolute'. This estate is often called the leasehold estate and its owner a leaseholder as distinct from a freeholder. A term of years absolute denotes quite simply the relationship of landlord and tenant—of lessor and lessee[3]. The word 'absolute' in this context appears to have no special significance. In Great Britain approximately 46 per cent of dwelling houses are occupied by leaseholders and 54 per cent by freeholders[4].

The distinguishing characteristic of a term of years is that it confers a right to occupy and enjoy land for a period of fixed maximum duration. It matters not whether that period is one week or three thousand years: a term of years can exist in either case[5]. A term of years is thus a form of estate in land, and can itself be the subject matter of an 'assignment' (i.e., sale) or of a sub-lease.

Leases of land are exceedingly important in social and commercial terms. Historically the landlord, operating from a superior bargaining position, was able to impose oppressive rents and conditions upon the tenant. However, the Rent Act legislation of the last sixty years has done much to redress the balance

2 See p. 66, post.
3 See Chapters 12 and 13, pp. 389, 415, post.
4 *General Household Survey 1978* (Office of Population Censuses and Surveys, 1980), p. 31 (Table 3.1).
5 The longest lease on record seems to be one of 100,000 years. It is reported that part of the cattle market in Dublin was leased by John Jameson to Dublin City Corporation for 100,000 years expiring on 21 January A.D. 101,863 (see N. McWhirter (ed.), *Guinness Book of Records* (27th edn., Enfield, Middx. 1980), p. 190).

of power in the residential context, by affording substantial security of tenure and by establishing effective rent controls[6]. The effect of much of the recent legislation is the recognition that, in many cases, a tenancy of a privately owned dwelling-house (whatever its stipulated duration) is not determinable during the lifetime of the original tenant or indeed during the lifetime of some of the members of his family[7]. To this extent the social interest in residential security for the family has been allowed to override the right of the owner of land to dispose freely of his property in accordance with the nominal terms of the lease or tenancy. The extensive protection afforded under the Rent Acts has thus tended to inhibit the residential letting of private property in days when the national housing problem is becoming increasingly acute. The policy of the Rent Act legislation is, however, subject to political manipulation—as most recently demonstrated in the enactment of the Housing Act 1980[8]. Whether this legislation has the effect of increasing supply on the rental market remains to be seen. Nevertheless, it is clear that no study of land law can afford to ignore the implications of the tenant's protected status under such legislation.

(3) Formal creation

With certain exceptions no conveyance of land is effective to confer a legal estate on the grantee unless the conveyance is made by deed. According to section 52(1) of the Law of Property Act 1925,

> All conveyances of land or of any interest therein are void for the purpose of conveying or creating a legal estate unless made by deed[9].

A grant of a fee simple absolute (or, for that matter, a term of years absolute) which is contained merely in an unsealed form of writing operates to create an equitable interest only. It is therefore possible to hold an *equitable* fee simple absolute in possession or an *equitable* term of years absolute. Section 1(1) of the Law of Property Act 1925 merely provides that it is only these estates in land which have even the *potential* of legal existence.

The formalities of creation required in the case of legal estates in land are the subject of further discussion in Chapter 3[10].

8. LEGAL INTERESTS AND CHARGES

Section 1(2) of the Law of Property Act 1925 defines five categories of 'interest' or 'charge' which are capable of existence 'at law'. We must now look at each category in turn.

6 See Chapter 13, p. 415, post.
7 See p. 435ff., post.
8 See p. 449, post.
9 To this general principle there are certain exceptions, which are spelt out in section 52(2) of the Law of Property Act 1925. Of these the most important relate to assents by a personal representative (s. 52(2)(a)) and leases or tenancies or other assurances not required by law to be made in writing (s. 52(2)(d)). See also Law of Property Act 1925, s. 54(2), p. 392, post.
10 See p. 88, post.

(1) Easements, rights and privileges (s. 1(2)(a))

Section 1 (2) (a) refers to

An easement, right, or privilege in or over land for an interest equivalent to an estate in fee simple absolute in possession or a term of years absolute.

A typical easement is a right of way. Suppose that A, the owner of an estate in fee simple, by deed grants to his neighbour, B, a right of way in perpetuity over his (that is, A's) land. The right of way obtained by B is necessarily legal rather than equitable, since its duration is equivalent to that of an estate in fee simple absolute in possession and it has been granted by deed.

Now, for most practical purposes, the quality of B's right of way makes not the slightest difference to its enforceability as between the original grantor, A, and the original grantee, B. But it becomes profoundly important if either or both of A and B sell their land. Let us suppose that A sells his fee simple to C and B sells his fee simple to D:

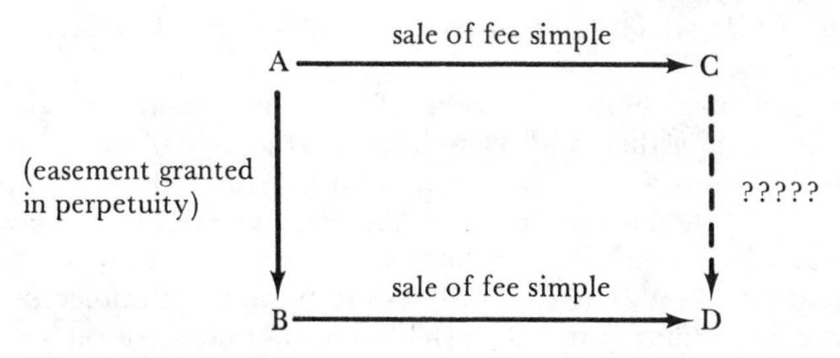

Fig. 11

May D exercise the right of way over the land which now belongs to C? The answer here is a very clear affirmative.

We must at this point be careful because in the eyes of the layman the exercise of a 'right' by one person necessarily implies a 'duty' of compliance in somebody else. However, the land lawyer approaches the question in an artificial manner which to the layman appears semantically confusing. The land lawyer reaches his conclusion as to the enforceability of a right of way by D against C by asking two supposedly unconnected questions concerning the respective status of D and C. First, does D enjoy the 'benefit' of the right of way? Second, is C subject to the 'burden' of that right of way? The land lawyer asks both questions in this apparently unconnected manner, although in reality of course D's enjoyment of 'benefit' is meaningless unless C is simultaneously subject to 'burden'. The slightly illogical approach of the property lawyer appears less puzzling, however, if the problem is addressed in the forensic terms which are naturally uppermost in the mind of the practising lawyer. Any action to enforce a right of way will succeed only if the plaintiff can be shown to have the 'benefit', and the defendant the 'burden', of the right of way in dispute. The equation which lies behind any successful enforcement proceeding involves a simultaneous attribution of 'benefit' and 'burden' (in the technical sense explained above) to plaintiff and defendant respectively. In other words, the land lawyer is concerned with ensuring that the plaintiff and defendant in any action are possessed of the *potential* benefit and burden respectively in relation to the interest in question.

Returning to *Fig.* 11 it is possible to analyse the problem as follows. The benefit of the right of way granted by A to B attached to B's land in such manner as to pass with any conveyance of B's land, e.g., to D[11]. Therefore D now enjoys the benefit of the easement. The second, and not less important, aspect of this problem relates to whether the burden of the easement has passed from A to C. Here the answer is that B's right of way was granted in perpetuity and by deed. Therefore, in accordance with section 1 (2) (a) of the Law of Property Act 1925, the interest acquired by B was legal. Legal rights bind the world. Therefore B's right of way, the benefit of which has now been transferred to D, is binding on and enforceable against C. All of this follows inexorably from the legal character of the easement granted by A to B. C's knowledge or ignorance of the right in question is completely irrelevant. The chances are, none the less, that C had notice of the existence of the grant to B from the face of the document or documents of title which he must have seen before purchasing the fee simple estate from A.

A precisely similar result would occur if by deed A grants B a right of way for ten years (or for three thousand years). Here too the right of way would be legal, being framed on an analogy with the term of years absolute referred to in section 1 (2) (a) of the Law of Property Act 1925. The right of way would then be enforceable by D against C for the duration of the term stipulated.

The position, however, is very different if in the first instance A grants B a right of way for the duration of B's own lifetime (or indeed for *any* indeterminate period short of perpetuity). The easement does not then fall within either of the categories of legal easement defined in section 1 (2) (a), and is therefore necessarily equitable even if granted by deed. The question arises whether B may continue to exercise this equitable right of way if A subsequently sells and conveys his land to a third party, C. Diagrammatically the problem looks like this:

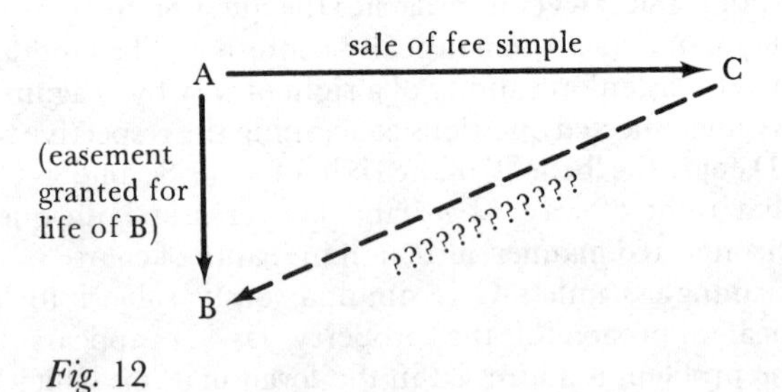

Fig. 12

The solution of this problem lies in the equitable doctrine of notice: equitable rights bind all persons other than a bona fide purchaser of a legal estate for value without notice. In our example, C is (we presume) bona fide; he is a purchaser

11 Law of Property Act 1925, s. 62(1), p. 51, ante and p. 595, post.

of a legal estate (a fee simple); we assume that in the normal course of things he gave value, i.e., he paid the purchase price. Therefore the enforceability of B's equitable right of way against C turns simply on whether C bought A's fee simple with or without notice (actual, constructive or imputed) of the existence of B's easement for life. If at the time of the purchase C *did* have notice, then he is bound by B's right of way and must suffer B to exercise it during B's lifetime. If at the time of the purchase C did *not* have notice of the easement, then he takes the land free of it. B's right of way is defeated and destroyed, and will never revitalise. B's only remedy at this point is a remedy *in personam* against A, who, after all, promised B that he could exercise the right of way throughout his lifetime, and in all probability sold this promise to B in return for a sum of money. B, however, has no rights *in rem*[12]. (It might be noticed that the reasoning used throughout this example is equally applicable to an easement which is equitable merely by reason of its informal creation, i.e., because it was granted not by deed but by unsealed writing or by word of mouth).

(2) **Rentcharges (s. 1(2)(b))**

Much the same approach can be applied under section 1(2)(b) of the Law of Property Act 1925 in order to distinguish between legal and equitable rentcharges. This provision refers to the potential legal character of

> A rentcharge in possession issuing out of or charged on land being either perpetual or for a term of years absolute.

A rentcharge is a right to a periodical payment of money secured upon land; it has nothing whatsoever to do with rent payable by a tenant to a landlord under a lease. A rentcharge arises for instance where A, the owner in fee simple, charges his own land with a payment of £100 per annum in favour of B. Such an arrangement may be brought about where A purchases an estate in fee simple from B but pays all or part of the purchase price in instalments secured upon A's land. A's fee simple is therefore conditional (but nevertheless legal[13]), and B can be said to own a rentcharge over A's land. The rentcharge is legal if it is 'either perpetual or for a term of years absolute,' and on this basis binds any subsequent purchaser irrespective of notice. However, a rentcharge created for the duration of B's lifetime (or any other indeterminate period) is necessarily equitable, and will not bind a bona fide purchaser for value of a legal estate in the land provided that the latter has no notice of the rentcharge.

Rentcharges are today fairly uncommon and, in any case, are being gradually phased out of existence under the terms of the Rentcharges Act 1977[14]. This legislation recognises the anomalous nature of rentcharges[15] in the modern context and provides that no new rentcharge may be created after 1977 'whether

12 See p. 31, ante.
13 See p. 58, ante.
14 See Law Commission, *Report on Rentcharges* (Law Com. No. 68, August 1975).
15 A 'rentcharge' is defined for the purpose of the Rentcharges Act 1977 as meaning 'any annual or other periodic sum charged on or issuing out of land, except—(a) rent reserved by a lease or tenancy, or (b) any sum payable by way of interest' (Rentcharges Act 1977, s. 1).

at law or in equity[16].' Any instrument which purports to create a new rentcharge is declared void[17], and all existing rentcharges are liable to be extinguished at the expiry of a period of sixty years beginning with the commencement of the 1977 Act or with the date on which the rentcharge in question first became payable, whichever is the later[18].

(3) Mortgages (s. 1(2)(c))

Section 1(2)(c) of the Law of Property Act 1925 indicates that another possible form of legal charge is a 'charge by way of legal mortgage.'

A mortgage is a charge on real property which is taken by a lender of money as security for the loan which he has advanced to the owner of that property[19]. Mortgage transactions have now become the primary means of financing home ownership in fee simple, the prospective home-owner often raising the bulk of the required purchase price by way of loan from an institutional mortgagee such as a bank, building society or local authority. The purchaser then acquires the fee simple in the property purchased, granting a charge by way of mortgage as security for the loan[20]. He retains ownership in fee simple throughout the loan term, although he is under an obligation gradually to repay both the capital amount of the loan and any interest which it bears. The home-owner—the mortgagor—is thereby enabled to acquire both a family base and a major capital asset by way of instalment purchase over a lengthy period (usually 20 or 25 years). Meanwhile the creditor—the mortgagee—is protected since the charge taken as security can always be realised by taking possession of the home if the mortgagor becomes unable to discharge his obligations under the terms of the loan.

A charge granted by way of legal mortgage is, in terms of section 1(2)(c) of the Law of Property Act 1925, a legal charge and therefore binds all who purchase the fee simple estate from the mortgagor. In effect, however, the mortgagor will be unable to sell the fee simple without first redeeming the existing charge, since the title deeds (or where appropriate the land certificate) relating to the property will usually be retained throughout the loan period either by the mortgagee or by the Land Registry.

(4) Miscellaneous charges (s. 1(2)(d))

Section 1(2)(d) of the Law of Property Act 1925 refers to a group of legal charges on property which are now anomalous. The charges included within

16 Rentcharges Act 1977, s. 2(1). This provision does not, however, prohibit the creation of a rentcharge which has the effect of making the land on which the rent is charged settled land by virtue of section 1(1)(v) of the Settled Land Act 1925, p. 160, post. See Rentcharges Act 1977, s. 2(3)(a).
17 Rentcharges Act 1977, s. 2(2).
18 Rentcharges Act 1977, s. 3(1).
19 See Chapter 15, p. 506, post.
20 Alternatively, the purchaser might acquire a term of years absolute (in the form of a long lease), granting a charge by way of legal mortgage as security for any loan used in raising the purchase price, p. 517, post.

the 'unrepealed remnant[1]' of this paragraph are statutory charges such as the now almost archaic tithe redemption annuity[2].

(5) Rights of entry (s. 1(2)(e))

Section 1(2)(e) of the Law of Property Act 1925 establishes the legal character of

> rights of entry exercisable over or in respect of a legal term of years absolute, or annexed, for any purpose, to a legal rentcharge.

A 'right of entry' has nothing to do with a 'right of way'. A right of entry is essentially a right to impose forfeiture of a lease upon an erring tenant or to penalise non-compliance with the terms of a rentcharge. Under section 1(2)(e), such a right of entry is legal if attached to a lease or rentcharge which is itself legal. Otherwise, the right of entry must be equitable.

9. EQUITABLE INTERESTS

All proprietary rights in land which are not referred to in section 1(1) or section 1(2) of the Law of Property Act 1925 must be equitable[3]. They cannot be legal.

10. ANALYSING INTERESTS IN LAND

There are three elements or variables which we can always identify in respect of any proprietary interest in land, and the process of identification is usually a salutary and constructive exercise. However tiresome it may seem at this stage, the ability to analyse correctly these various elements is an essential part of the land lawyer's skill. We can predicate
(1) the exact nature of the estate or interest in question;
(2) whether that estate or interest is legal or equitable; and
(3) whether that estate or interest is in possession, remainder or reversion.

Take, for instance, a grant of Blackacre in the following terms:

To A for life, then to B in tail, then to C in fee simple absolute.

This grant comprises what is known as a 'strict settlement' of land coming within the ambit of the Settled Land Act 1925[4]. It provides for successive entitlements in the land. We can now analyse the proprietary interest held by each grantee *at the date of the grant.*

(i) *A's interest*

(a) A's interest is a life interest.

1 See R. E. Megarry and H. W. R. Wade, op. cit., p. 143.
2 Tithe Act 1936, s. 3.
3 Law of Property Act 1925, s. 1(3), p. 53, ante.
4 See Chapter 5, p. 154, post.

(b) A life interest cannot be a *legal* estate or interest, since it is not included in the list of legal estates and legal interests contained in section 1(1), (2) of the Law of Property Act 1925.
(c) A life interest must therefore be equitable.
(d) A's interest is in possession since he is not excluded from immediate enjoyment of the land by the presence of prior interests. A is to occupy and enjoy the land from the moment of the grant.

Therefore: *A holds an equitable life interest in possession.*

(ii) *B's interest*

(a) B's interest is an entailed interest.
(b) An entailed interest cannot be a *legal* estate or interest since it is not included in the list of legal estates and legal interests contained in section 1(1), (2) of the Law of Property Act 1925.
(c) An entailed interest must therefore be equitable.
(d) B's interest is not in possession since B is excluded from immediate occupation and enjoyment of Blackacre by reason of A's prior (life) interest.
(e) B's interest is therefore in remainder at the date of the grant: it will fall into possession on A's death.

Therefore: *B holds an equitable entailed interest in remainder.*

(iii) *C's interest*

(a) C's interest is a fee simple absolute.
(b) A fee simple absolute can be a legal estate within section 1(1)(a) of the Law of Property Act 1925 if it is in possession.
(c) C's interest is not in possession at the date of the grant because C is excluded from immediate occupation and enjoyment of Blackacre by reason of two prior interests—those of A and B.
(d) C's interest is therefore in remainder.
(e) C's interest must therefore be equitable.

Therefore: *C holds an equitable fee simple absolute in remainder.*

Of course, when the prior interests of A and B have both determined (i.e., come to an end), C may ultimately acquire a legal fee simple absolute in possession. In all probability, however, this will never happen since it is highly likely that before C's equitable interest can vest in possession, B will 'bar' his entail, thereby enlarging his entailed interest into some form of fee simple. B may do this quite easily by means of a disentailing assurance, which is simply a declaration by deed that henceforth he holds a fee simple rather than an entailed interest[5]. Alternatively, he may bar his entail by will[6]. He does not need the consent of C for this purpose, although the barring of B's entail will have the effect of destroying C's interest: there cannot be a remainder following upon a fee simple absolute. This may appear to be monstrously unfair as far as C is

5 See R. E. Megarry and H. W. R. Wade, op. cit., p. 82ff.
6 Law of Property Act 1925, s. 176.

concerned, but this is not really the case. C's interest in terms of the grant was minimal in the first place: he had an interest subject to a prior entail. In this situation no great injustice is worked against C if a right which was initially almost worthless (in view of the possibility of the barring of the entail) is in fact rendered completely worthless (when that possibility materialises). The law did once permit the creation of unbarrable entails, but it is now thought desirable in policy terms (not least for reasons of tax liability) to lean in favour of sweeping limited interests such as entails off the land at the earliest possible opportunity.

11. ANALYSING THE STRICT SETTLEMENT

Let us return to our original grant of Blackacre to A for life, then to B in tail, then to C in fee simple. We have seen that the interest enjoyed by each grantee in terms of the grant is equitable. Here, we have in effect a series of equitable limitations or successive entitlements in the land. We have a typical strict settlement.

The more astute reader will, at this point, say something like this. If the interests of A, B and C are equitable, what happens to the legal fee simple absolute in possession at the date of the grant? Surely it does not go into abeyance for the duration of the strict settlement: it must vest in somebody. And of course that is correct. There cannot be a vacuum of the legal estate in the land.

The answer devised by the Settled Land Act 1925 is that the legal fee simple absolute in possession should, in so far as possible, vest in the person who at any given moment holds an equitable interest in possession[7]. It makes sense to vest the legal estate and the attendant powers of management and disposition in the man on the spot at any given time. No prospective third party purchaser wants to be told that the person with whom he will be dealing—with whom he must negotiate the price and from whom he must take a conveyance of the legal title—actually lives 500 miles away. Furthermore, it would be unlikely that such an owner has been able to exercise his powers of management effectively from that distance, and the settled estate may therefore have suffered from his neglect.

Under the Settled Land Act 1925 the equitable owner in possession is entitled to hold the full legal estate in the settled land for the duration of his equitable interest. In our example the legal fee simple absolute is vested initially in A, the owner of the equitable life interest in possession. When A dies, the legal estate will normally be transferred to the next equitable owner whose interest falls into possession, i.e., to B. And, in theory at any rate, when B's entail determines—when B and his lineal descendants cease to reproduce themselves—the legal fee simple absolute in possession will become united with C's equitable fee simple absolute which at this point has fallen into possession. C will then become the absolute owner at law and in equity, free of any settlement. This can be

7 See p. 161, post.

represented diagrammatically as follows, keeping firmly separate the legal and equitable rights which arise:

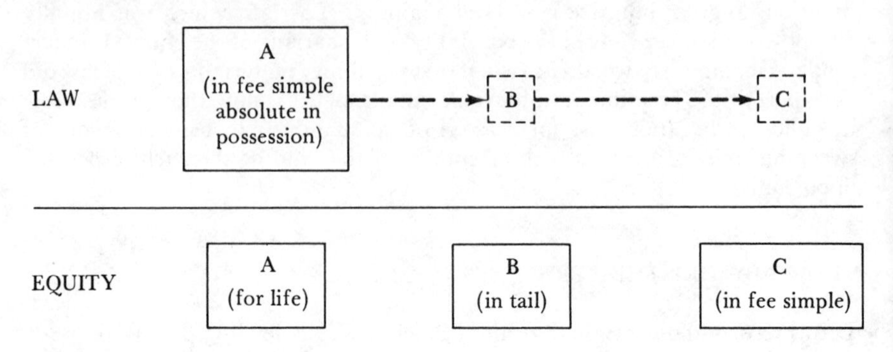

Fig. 13

Here we see, incidentally, the characteristic feature of the strict settlement—the duality of the position occupied by the equitable owner in possession. He holds both an *equitable* interest in possession and the full *legal* estate in fee simple in the settled land. Here emerges a point of paramount importance. The equitable owner in possession (the 'tenant for life'), although invested with the legal fee simple absolute in possession, derives no *benefit* from his ownership of the legal estate. He merely has, in respect of that legal estate, certain powers of management and disposition. He is, moreover, a fiduciary in respect of his exercise of these powers. It is only to the extent of his equitable life interest that A derives benefit as such: he is entitled to occupy and enjoy the land only during his lifetime. The benefit which he enjoys is strictly delimited by the quantum of his equitable interest. It is for this reason that A's equitable interest is sometimes known simply as his 'beneficial' interest. (The etymology is obvious: one *benefits* to the extent of one's *beneficial*, i.e., equitable, interest.) Ownership of the legal estate is merely nominal ownership. The legal fee simple absolute in possession is simply a paper title. 'A bare legal title,' said Lord Simon of Glaisdale, 'is a shell[8].' Its owner has, by reason of his ownership, merely administrative or decision-making powers and functions concerned with interim management and eventual disposition (the latter term including sale, lease and mortgage of the land).

If A does decide to dispose of the legal estate to a third party, the capital moneys arising are normally paid, not to him, but to independent trustees. Thus is maintained the strict distinction between nominal ownership at law and beneficial ownership in equity. It is this possibility of separating administration of property from enjoyment of property—the essential concept of a trust—which perhaps forms the most original contribution made by English jurisprudence[9].

8 *Hanlon v Law Society* [1980] 2 WLR 756 at 799.
9 See p. 21, ante.

12. FAMILY AND COMMERCIAL EQUITABLE INTERESTS

Having looked at some length at the slightly complex structure of the strict settlement we are now better able to understand a further and necessary subdivision of equitable interests in land. This is the distinction which may be drawn between 'family' equitable interests and 'commercial' equitable interests. The terms 'family' and 'commercial' have no statutory authority. Indeed the property legislation nowhere characterises equitable rights as having either a 'family' or a 'commercial' basis, but the distinction is nevertheless of considerable assistance to us at this point.

'Family' equitable interests are the kinds of equitable interest which usually arise within the family context. They are the kinds of interest which, in a bygone age, a paterfamilias would have endowed upon members of his own family. Such interests are conferred upon their recipients not because of commercial or monetary motivations but simply on the ground of family relationship.

'Commercial' equitable interests are those interests which usually arise in a commercial context between strangers (i.e., between persons not belonging to the same family) who are dealing with each other 'at arm's length'. The transactions of strangers are not motivated by the familial bonds of love and duty, but rather by the mercenary incentives of the world of the exchange economy. The commercial equitable interest is granted as part of an economic quid pro quo: normally money or other valuable consideration is paid over.

We have already come across one example of a commercial equitable interest. We looked previously at the results which flow if one estate-owner, A, grants his neighbour, B, a right of way over A's land during the lifetime of B[10]. Such a right of way is an equitable easement and is usually bought and sold for money or money's worth.

The paterfamilias referred to above would not, of course, confer upon a member of his own family a right of way over the ancestral home. The idea of conceptualising access and egress in this manner would never occur in the family context, and the very notion of extracting money from one's relatives in return for a right of way is somewhat bizarre. But the kind of property interest which the paterfamilias might indeed think of conferring upon members of his family is the kind which we have just considered in terms of the strict settlement. He might very well wish that upon his death his widow, A, should enjoy a life interest in the property, and that thereafter his eldest son, B, should enjoy an interest in tail, and that finally his favourite charity, C, should take the land in fee simple in the event that the family line fail.

The social pattern epitomised in the strict settlement is now, of course, archaic, but the model of the strict settlement nevertheless provides a cogent demonstration of the difference between 'family' and 'commercial' equitable interests. It is somewhat unlikely that a moribund testator would confer a right of way upon his widow, but he might well sell such a right to a neighbouring farmer. For our present purpose the strict settlement serves to distinguish

10 See p. 62, ante.

'family' and 'commercial' interests slightly more sharply than would be the case if we referred to the type of 'family' equitable interest which is much more common today—the equitable interest created behind a trust for sale. This will, however, be dealt with in due course[11].

13. ALIENABILITY OF LAND AND THE FRAGMENTATION OF BENEFIT

One of the most difficult problems faced in any system of property law is the need to reconcile the conflicting objectives of alienability of land and fragmentation of benefit.

On the one hand it is quite clear that land must be allowed to be freely alienable or commerciable. Transactions in respect of the legal estate in land (whether in the form of sale, lease or mortgage) must not be unduly restricted or hampered by law. Uninhibited alienability of land is essential to the effective functioning of an exchange economy. Land is a highly marketable resource, and it is vital that the market in land should not stagnate. We have already noted Lord Upjohn's assertion that it has been 'the policy of the law for over one hundred years to simplify and facilitate transactions in real property[12].' Moreover, insofar as the alienation of land may take the form of a mortgage transaction, the objective of alienability is no less vital for the provision of institutional loan facilities for the financing of home ownership or private commercial enterprise.

On the other hand it is highly desirable that the owner of a legal estate in land should be able to fragment, and thereby reallocate, the benefit which is derived from the land. It is for instance important that land should provide a convenient and flexible medium of endowment: the objective of endowment is the central motive behind the creation of 'family' equitable interests. The owner of the legal estate may well wish to grant limited interests in his land to members of his own family (e.g., a life interest to his widow, followed by an entailed interest to his eldest son—to adopt one possible form of the now archaic family settlement). He may want to grant land to children or relatives in equal (or other) shares, or he may simply want to share the equitable ownership of his home with his wife. Such is the nature of the flexibility required by the motive of endowment. Indeed the desideratum of endowment is recognised in any society which acknowledges both private ownership and the bonds of familial relationship, for endowment is integral to the intergenerational transfer of private wealth.

Alternatively, the owner of the legal estate in land may wish to fragment the benefit derived from the land not through the creation of 'family' equitable interests, but rather through the granting of 'commercial' equitable interests over the land to third parties. He may be persuaded to sell to a stranger a right of way or the benefit of a restrictive covenant over his own land, thus conferring upon that third party a portion of the utility which otherwise he himself would have retained in the land.

11 See Chapter 7, p. 212, post.
12 *National Provincial Bank Ltd v Hastings Car Mart Ltd* [1965] AC 1175 at 1233f., p. 54, ante.

The twin objectives of alienability of title and fragmentation of benefit are, in the first analysis, set against each other in irreconcilable opposition. If the legal title in land is to be freely alienable, how can rights in that land, when conferred upon 'family' or 'commercial' grantees, be other than transient and defeasible rights which perish upon the alienation of the legal title to a third party? The interest of the alienee in taking title to the land utterly free of conflicting rights militates directly against the objective of fragmentation of benefit. It seems to conflict with the creation, for familial or financial reasons, of durable rights in the land which do not lapse if and when the land is sold. Even the grantor of rights of endowment has a legitimate interest in ensuring that the land is capable of alienation to a third party free of the endowed interests if, at any future stage, market conditions or practical necessity should indicate the wisdom of such a transaction. Returning to our model of the strict settlement, the settlor/testator may well be concerned to ensure that the land settled upon his widow and eldest son should be freely alienable in the event that, for instance, some third party offers to purchase that land at more than twice the market value of the property.

Perhaps the most distinctive success of English land law lies in the way in which it resolves the inherent tension between the interests of alienation and fragmentation. The accommodation of these divergent objectives of the law is made possible by a series of provisions which simplify dealings with the legal estate in land. These provisions simultaneously ensure that fragments of benefit (which in the artificial schema of section 1 of the Law of Property Act 1925 are almost always equitable interests) are secured in such a way as to survive the alienation of the legal estate to a third party purchaser.

14. THE PROMOTION OF FREE ALIENATION OF LAND

Two factors, above all others, ensure that land is freely alienable. First, legal estates in land are now deliberately restricted to two in number—the fee simple absolute in possession and the term of years absolute[13]. Before 1926 it was possible for a legal estate in land to be held by many kinds of owner (e.g., by the owner of a life interest or fee tail). Even the fee simple could be fragmented between almost endless numbers of persons each holding a specific share or proportion of the legal estate. The task of an intending purchaser in investigating all the component parts of the legal title which he wished to purchase might be rendered quite horrifyingly complex and protracted. Since 1926 however the would-be purchaser knows that the only vendor competent to convey a freehold legal estate is the owner of an estate in fee simple absolute in possession and that it is therefore from such an owner that he must seek title. Alternatively, he knows that the only vendor competent to convey a leasehold legal estate is the owner of a term of years absolute. In either case the maximum number of persons who may hold the legal estate, and from whom title must be taken, is limited to four[14]. Even these four owners are now regarded as owners of one and

13 Law of Property Act 1925, s. 1(1), p. 53, ante.
14 Law of Property Act 1925, s. 34(2), (3); Trustee Act 1925, s. 34(2), p. 241, post.

the same estate, with the result that the purchaser need investigate only one title[15].

The other major factor which promotes the free alienability of land is the generous protection afforded a purchaser in respect of third party rights in the land which he purchases. Although he is bound by any legal interest affecting the land (e.g., a legal right of way), the existence of such an interest is almost sure to have been apparent from the face of the documentary title inspected by him before the purchase was completed. Of even more importance is the fact that according to the equitable doctrine of notice the purchaser takes free of any equitable interests affecting the land of which he had no notice at the time of the purchase.

Thus, as will emerge time and time again, the larger social interest that land be freely alienable is positively assisted by conferring various kinds of facility and protection upon third party purchasers. We must now examine how a corresponding security is achieved for those who own fragments of benefit in the land transferred.

15. THE PROTECTION OF EQUITABLE INTERESTS

It becomes increasingly obvious that if a right in real property is equitable rather than legal, it is, in the orthodox theory, exceedingly insecure vis à vis third party purchasers of a legal estate. Equitable rights are liable to be destroyed if the legal estate which they affect is transferred to a purchaser who has no notice of their existence. Because equitable rights are not normally referred to in the formal documents of title, there is a strong probability that a third party purchaser will not be fixed with notice and will accordingly take free of the equitable rights in question.

It may be highly inconvenient and quite unfair that equitable rights should be defeated in this capricious way, especially where—as in the case of 'commercial' equitable interests—the rights have been created for valuable consideration. No equitable owner will be able to sleep easily at night for fear that he may be confronted on the following day by a purchaser who appears from nowhere to announce that he has just bought the relevant legal estate without notice of any equitable rights affecting his title. Such uncertainty cannot be allowed to attach to equitable ownership, for indeed the vulnerability of equitable rights in such circumstances would represent the very antithesis of a law of property. It is for this reason that English land law takes positive measures to protect equitable rights against the possibility of destruction at the hands of 'Equity's Darling'—the bona fide purchaser of a legal estate for value without notice (actual, constructive or imputed) of the equitable rights concerned. This the law does essentially by mitigating or modifying the effect of the traditional doctrine of notice in certain situations.

At this point we reach our final major classification in land law terminology, although in a technical sense this classification is the primary classification in

15 See p. 239f., post.

land law. All land in England and Wales is held by way of either *registered title* or *unregistered title*. Where title is registered, the land is sometimes—slightly inelegantly—known as 'registered land.' Correspondingly, the term 'unregistered land' is used of that land title to which is not registered.

Where title is registered, almost all the pertinent details of ownership relating to that land are recorded on a central register at the Land Registry[16]. An intending purchaser need only consult that central register in order to discover the relevant legal information about the land which he proposes to buy. Where title to land is not registered, none of the details of ownership appears on any central register (with one exception relating to 'land charges', which are centrally recorded on the Land Charges Register[17]). Otherwise the purchaser of unregistered land must investigate the historical documents of title (the 'title deeds') in order to elicit the relevant legal information which he requires before he decides to purchase. Only if the would-be purchaser in this way establishes a chain of ownership over at least 15 years leading to his proposed vendor, will he finally complete the transaction and pay over his purchase money[18].

It may seem strange that there are two systems of land law operating side by side in this way. In fact the system of unregistered title is gradually being displaced by registration of title. At present registration of title applies to approximately half the conveyancing transactions carried out each year in England and Wales, but it will be some time yet before unregistered land disappears completely from the scene. For this reason, we must now translate into terms of registered and unregistered land that which has already been discussed—in slightly simplistic terms—in relation to equitable interests in land and their effect on third party purchasers.

(1) Unregistered land

The property legislation of 1925 introduced two major means of eliminating the insecurity of equitable interests vis à vis third party purchasers of a legal estate in unregistered land. First, it established a system of formal registration of land charges in respect of commercial equitable interests in land. Second, it provided that under certain conditions family equitable interests should be 'overreached' on a transfer of a legal estate to a third party, thereafter taking effect in the resulting proceeds of sale. These two methods of protecting equitable interests are mutually exclusive. Commercial rights are registrable as land charges; family rights are overreachable—and not vice versa. Each form of protection requires further explanation.

(a) *Registration of land charges*

Let us return to the equitable easement (e.g., a right of way for life) granted by A in favour of B[19]. Such an easement constituted a commercial equitable interest

16 See Chapter 10, p. 319, post.
17 See Chapter 4, p. 111, post.
18 See Chapter 3, p. 78, post.
19 See p. 62, ante.

owned by B over the land of A. We discovered that the bindingness of B's right as against C (a third party purchaser of A's legal estate) turned on whether C had notice of the existence of B's equitable interest. The Law of Property Act 1925 merely modifies this application of the traditional doctrine of notice, by providing that B's formal registration of a right of way in the Land Charges Register shall 'be deemed to constitute actual notice . . . to all persons and for all purposes' of the existence of that right[20]. Registration of commercial equitable interests is therefore advantageous both to the owner of any such equitable rights and to the purchaser of the land which may be affected by those rights. By registration of his rights the equitable incumbrancer effectively disables any subsequent purchaser from denying notice of his rights. At the same time the prospective purchaser is enabled, by a simple search of the Land Charges Register, to discover an exhaustive list of all commercial equitable interests affecting the land. Thus security for the equitable interests is combined with facility for the purchaser. The purchaser knows exactly what he is buying; the commercial equitable interest is preserved in the situation of third party transfer by being made absolutely binding on the purchaser through the artificial medium of notice provided by the register.

(b) *Overreaching*

When we turn to 'family' equitable interests, the last result which we would wish to bring about—whether by registration or otherwise—is that those equitable rights should be rendered binding on third party purchasers. In this context we may employ yet again our model of the strict settlement[1]. Here the prime object for the purchaser of the legal estate in the settled land is that he should take the land free from all such 'family' interests which previously attached to it.

The property legislation of 1925 now ensures that on a sale of settled land to a third party all family equitable interests are indeed swept off the land so that the purchaser may take a clear title. However, the equitable interests which existed in the settled land are not thereby destroyed. Although the purchaser of the legal estate is enabled to 'overreach' (or disregard) the equitable interests of the settlement, those interests are nevertheless preserved after sale by being diverted on to the resulting proceeds. In other words, the beneficiaries' interests in land under the terms of the strict settlement are translated into precisely equivalent interests in the proceeds of sale.

Let us take the example of our settlement of Blackacre upon A for life, with remainder to B in tail, with final remainder to C in fee simple. Suppose that a property developer, P, purchases the legal estate for £1 million. Provided that P pays the purchase money to two trustees (or to a trust corporation), he takes the legal fee simple absolute in possession free from the equitable interests of A, B and C. The interests of A, B and C are thus 'overreached', but are thereafter converted into money.

After the sale A takes an equivalent interest in the £1 million paid by P and

20 Law of Property Act 1925, s. 198(1), p. 113, post.
1 See p. 67, ante.

now held by the trustees. He formerly had the right to use the *land* for life: so he now has the right to use the *money* for life. He may therefore draw the income which will be derived from an investment of the capital proceeds of sale. He has no right to the capital itself—that is, to the £1 million. Similarly, when eventually the entailed interest falls into possession on A's death, B and his issue enjoy only rights in income, not capital. The capital fund is being reserved for C on the expiry of B's entail, because it was C who, in the terms of the original settlement of land, held the absolute interest—the fee simple absolute. Here again there is an optimal compromise between security for the equitable interests and facility for the purchaser. The rights of the beneficiaries under the settlement survive alienation of the land, being preserved thereafter in the form of money. There is now a settlement or trust of personalty. The purchaser is accommodated since the settled land interests are now swept off the land. He knows that he takes the legal title free of the claims of A, B and C, for their interests have been 'overreached'[2]. In terms of *Fig.* 13[3] what has happened is as follows:

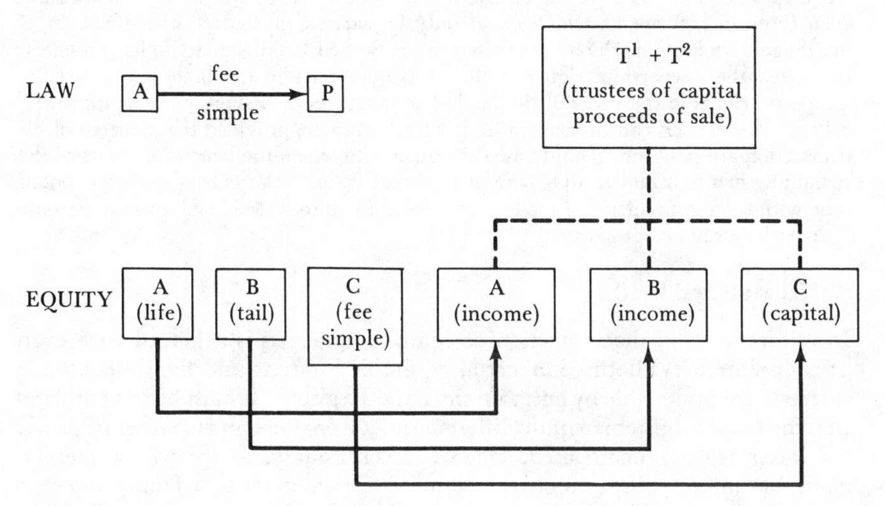

Fig. 14

It could of course be objected that A's exercise of the power to sell the settled land in this situation converts the beneficial interests behind the strict settlement somewhat involuntarily into money. It may be that the owners of the beneficial interests (i.e., the remaindermen) would have preferred that their interests should remain interests in the land which they might enjoy through occupation. Here emerges the major bias of the property legislation of 1925. Such was the predominant influence of the 'exchange value' concept of property over the 'use value' concept that the 1925 legislation quite happily makes the assumption that

2 Overreaching occurs in broadly the same way in relation to the equitable interests behind a trust for sale of land. See Chapter 7, p. 227ff., post.

3 See p. 68, ante.

a money interest is as good as an occupation interest[4]. This assumption confirms a 'capital investment' theory of property in preference to a 'utility-based' theory of property. The 'utility-based' theory is often linked with the requirements of family living, but in 1925, as Otto Kahn-Freund once indicated[5], the convertibility of land into money was peculiarly within the conception of the English common lawyer:

'Property' in a mere 'fund', a unit of values, is inconceivable to Romanist legal thought. English law, on the other hand, is perfectly capable of giving effect to the idea of 'floating' property, of a 'property' right which does not attach to any individualised asset, but to a 'value' which may, at any given moment, be represented either by land or by a bank account (i.e., a banker's debt) or by Government securities. It is very difficult indeed for a continental lawyer to understand the legislative technique which enabled English lawyers to adapt the institution of settled land to the needs of modern society. The rights of the members of the family other than the tenant in possession were originally 'property' rights in the sense that they attached to the land itself. The land was 'in fetters'. The multitude of rights of 'remainder men' whose concurrence was needed for any disposition over the land itself prevented its development for building purposes and even those improvements which could only be carried into effect with the help of mortgages. Legislation which culminated in the Settled Land Act, 1925, has, in effect, converted the 'ownership' rights of the remainder men in the land into beneficial 'property' rights in the value of the land. The tenant in possession, now, significantly, called 'estate owner' can (in certain limits) freely dispose, provided the proceeds of his transaction are paid into a fund vested in trustees to which the beneficial rights of the remainder men continue to attach. Family 'ownership' in the strict legal sense was out of tune with the requirements of modern society and had to be 'softened' so as to become . . . merely 'economic property'.

(2) **Registered land**

In registered land the protection of equitable interests is achieved with even greater simplicity. Both commercial equitable interests and family equitable interests are protectible by entry on the Land Register. (It must be remembered that the Land Register is a quite different thing from the Land Charges Register, the latter register being used, somewhat confusingly, to record commercial equitable interests in 'unregistered land'[6].) Commercial and family interests both rank as 'minor interests' in registered land, and may be entered as such in the appropriate subdivisions of the Land Register in respect of the title concerned. A purchaser of registered land is bound by all the interests thus registered[7], but he takes free of all minor interests which have not been protected by entry on the Register[8].

A commercial equitable interest should generally be entered on the Land Register by way of 'notice' or 'caution'[9]. A family equitable interest may be

4 See p. 221f., post.
5 'Introduction' to K. Renner, *The Institutions of Private Law and Their Social Functions* (London and Boston, 1949), pp. 20f.
6 See p. 73, ante, p. 111, post.
7 Land Registration Act 1925, s. 20(1)(a), p. 327, post.
8 Land Registration Act 1925, s. 59(6), p. 327, post.
9 See p. 326, post.

entered by way of a 'restriction'—a note against the title which puts any third party purchaser on notice that there is either a strict settlement or a trust for sale in respect of the land. In either case the purchaser then knows that he should pay the purchase money in a 'restricted' manner (i.e., to at least two trustees), whereupon the whole overreaching mechanism is activated and the equitable rights of beneficiaries are translated into equivalent interests in the proceeds of sale held by the trustees[10].

Thus, once again, the law strives towards a compromise between facility for the purchaser and security for the owners of equitable interests in registered land. The purchaser may see the relevant details of title on the face of the Land Register; the owners of equitable interests may safeguard their interests by entry on the Register. This at least is the position in theory. We shall see later that the registered land system (like unregistered land conveyancing) is not entirely free of problems in practice.

We shall in succeeding chapters examine the foregoing aspects of land law more closely. In the meantime, however, the following diagram summarises the principal classifications and subdivisions already introduced:

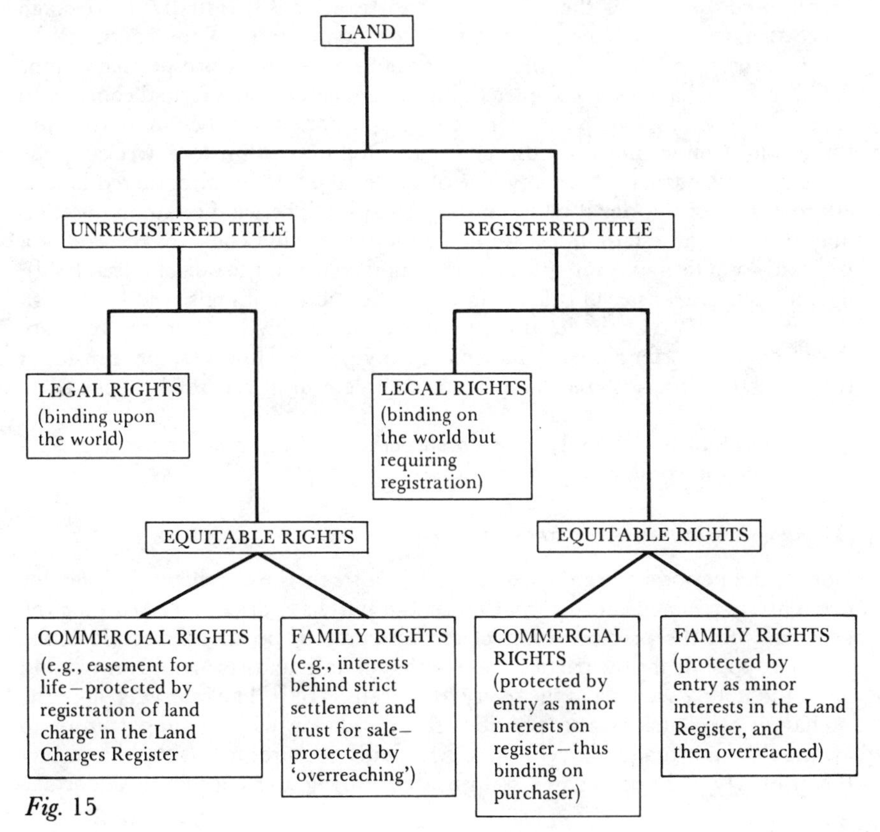

Fig. 15

10 See p. 326, post.

CHAPTER 3

The acquisition of title to land

In this chapter we examine two methods by which title to land may be acquired. In the first part of the chapter we look at the process of acquisition by purchase and transfer. In the second part we outline the rules of acquisition of title by means of adverse possession.

1. CONTRACT AND CONVEYANCE

In England and Wales the process of land transfer is essentially a two-stage process: first contract, then conveyance (or 'completion' of the contract). In other words, when the preliminary negotiations between the prospective vendor and purchaser have been completed, the parties enter into a formal contract to execute in favour of the purchaser a conveyance of the legal estate in the land to be sold. Conveyance or transfer usually follows within four weeks of the exchange of contracts. A conveyance of the legal estate in unregistered land is effective to vest that legal estate in the purchaser. The legal estate in question may be either an estate in fee simple (if the transaction concerns the sale of a freehold) or a term of years (if the transaction concerns the sale of a leasehold). The process of transfer of title is similar in the context of registered land, with the qualification that the legal estate in such land may be alienated by mere document of transfer rather than deed of conveyance. However, the transfer of the legal title in registered land is not complete until recorded in the Land Registry[1].

We must look more closely at certain aspects of the law relating to the process of contract and conveyance.

(1) Agreement 'subject to contract'

During the period before the exchange of contracts the purchaser and vendor negotiate agreement on such matters as the purchase price to be paid for the property and the precise extent of the property to be transferred. It is, for instance, possible for the parties to agree that certain fixtures and fittings should or should not pass as part of the realty to be transferred[2]. The interval before the exchange of contracts also provides the purchaser with an opportunity to arrange the mortgage finance which he usually requires to enable him to buy the property. The purchaser is also able during this period to undertake

1 See p. 324, post.
2 See p. 51f., ante.

'preliminary enquiries' which are addressed both to his vendor and to the appropriate local authority. These enquiries, usually made in standard form, attempt to elicit information about existing disputes relating to the property, the ownership of boundary walls, hedges and fences, the existence of main services to the property, rights of way, planning matters, compulsory purchase orders and the ownership and maintenance of roads serving the property[3]. The purchaser may also wish to commission a structural survey of the property, and any lending institution which helps to finance his purchase will certainly insist upon such a survey in order that the security offered for its loan be proved to be sound.

It is common that, while these negotiations and enquiries are taking place, the prospective vendor and purchaser will wish to express some kind of consensus ad idem in the matter of sale. It is invariable practice for vendor and purchaser at this stage to reach an agreement for sale 'subject to contract'. However, it is generally accepted that such an agreement, albeit in written form, is not contractually binding unless and until its terms are incorporated in a formal contract of sale signed and exchanged by the parties[4]. It is, of course, the lack of legal consequence attaching to agreements 'subject to contract' which fosters the practice of 'gazumping' at times when the property market becomes unstable and volatile. With total impunity the intending vendor can choose to disregard an existing agreement for sale 'subject to contract' if it emerges that a more favourable price can be extracted from another potential purchaser[5]. In a rising property market, the total absence of legal obligation until the exchange of formal contracts can lead to highly inequitable results, not least because it creates the setting for that most unseemly form of competition between would-be purchasers—the 'contract race'. There is something to be said in favour of the practice in Scots law which ensures that even informal agreements for the sale of land are contractually binding. Too often the 'gentleman's agreement' expressed in an agreement 'subject to contract' turns out to be merely, as Sachs J once said, 'a transaction in which each side hopes the other will act like a gentleman and neither intends so to act if it is against his material interests[6].'

In view of the inherent danger of inequity, judicial attempts have been made during recent years to place limitations upon the utility of the suspensive condition expressed in the phrase 'subject to contract'. In *Griffiths v Young*[7], the Court of Appeal was ready to hold that an agreement 'subject to contract' had been superseded by a subsequent unconditional offer and acceptance communicated by telephone. Likewise, in *Law v Jones*[8] the Court of Appeal decided by

3 An incorrect answer to a preliminary enquiry may found liability in negligence. See *Wilson v Bloomfield* (1979) 123 Sol Jo 860, [1980] Conv 401.
4 *Winn v Bull* (1877) 7 Ch D 29.
5 It has even been pointed out that 'the duty of trustees to sell only at the best price reasonably obtainable will override commercial morality, i.e., on receiving a higher offer before exchange, they must "gazump".' See J. T. Farrand, *Contract and Conveyance* (3rd edn., London 1980), 17; *Buttle v Saunders* [1950] WN 255.
6 See *Goding v Frazer* [1967] 1 WLR 286, 293.
7 [1970] Ch 675. See (1971) 35 Conv (NS) 55 (F. R. Crane).
8 [1974] Ch 112. See (1973) 32 Cambridge LJ 214 (C. T. Emery); (1973) 37 Conv (NS) 282 (F. R. Crane).

a majority that the unilateral use of the phrase 'subject to contract' in correspondence between vendor and purchaser could not derogate from any oral contract for sale which had already been concluded between the parties. Moreover, the Court seemed to hold that such 'subject to contract' correspondence can indeed provide the very written memorandum which is required under section 40(1) of the Law of Property Act 1925[9] in order to ensure the enforceability of the earlier oral contract.

These decisions caused much consternation in the world of conveyancers. As Lord Denning MR observed in *Tiverton Estates Ltd v Wearwell Ltd*[10], the decision in *Law v Jones* in particular falsified the belief of most practising solicitors in this country that they could, on a sale of land, protect their clients by writing their letters 'subject to contract'. To the minds of solicitors, said Lord Denning, 'it virtually repealed the Statute of Frauds.' The Master of the Rolls continued:

> *Law v Jones* has sounded an alarm bell in the offices of every solicitor in the land. And no wonder. It is everyday practice for a solicitor, who is instructed in a sale of land, to start the correspondence with a letter 'subject to contract' setting out the terms or enclosing a draft. He does it in the confidence that it protects his client. It means that the client is not bound by what has taken place in conversation. The reason is that, for over a hundred years, the courts have held that the effect of the words 'subject to contract' is that the matter remains in negotiation until a formal contract is executed: see *Eccles v Bryant and Pollock* [1948] Ch 93. But *Law v Jones* has taken away all protection from the client. The plaintiff can now assert an oral contract in conversation with the defendant *before* the solicitor wrote the letter and then rely on the letter as a writing to satisfy the statute, even though it was expressly 'subject to contract': or, alternatively, the plaintiff can assert that *after* the solicitor wrote the letter, he met the defendant and in conversation orally agreed to waive the words 'subject to contract.' If this is right, it means that the client is exposed to the full blast of 'frauds and perjuries' attendant on oral testimony. Even without fraud or perjury, he is exposed to honest difference of recollections leading to law suits, from which it was the very object of the statute to save him[11].

Thus, in *Tiverton Estates Ltd v Wearwell Ltd*, a differently constituted Court of Appeal decided that the insertion of the magical phrase 'subject to contract' effectively prevented correspondence from satisfying the requirement of a written memorandum under section 40(1) of the Law of Property Act 1925[12]. This decision is plainly in conflict with the Court's earlier decision in *Law v Jones*[13], and the point in issue awaits ultimate clarification by the House of Lords[14]. In the absence of such clarification, however, it is perhaps significant that the Council of the Law Society has expressed its view that the traditional view of the status of 'subject to contract' correspondence has been vindicated by the approach adopted in *Tiverton Estates Ltd v Wearwell Ltd*[15].

9 See p. 81, post.
10 [1975] Ch 146. See (1974) 38 Conv (NS) 127 (F. R. Crane); (1974) 33 Cambridge LJ 42 (C. T. Emery); (1974) 37 MLR 695 (J. W. Tinnion); (1974) 90 LQR 1.
11 [1975] Ch 146 at 159f.
12 See p. 82, post.
13 See *Daulia Ltd v Four Millbank Nominees Ltd* [1978] Ch 231 at 249f. per Buckley LJ. See also [1978] Conv 375 (F. R. Crane); (1979) 38 Cambridge LJ 31 (C. Harpum and D. L. Jones).
14 See J. T. Farrand, op. cit., p. 23.
15 See (1973) 70 Law Soc Gaz 2637: 'Council Statement: *Law v Jones*'.

In view of the uncertainty surrounding the status and propriety of agreements 'subject to contract', the Law Commission has examined the existing 'subject to contract' procedure for the sale of houses by private agreement. The Law Commission has now expressed its opinion that the law should not be changed to give legal effect to agreements 'subject to contract' or to impose any liability (civil or criminal) on any person who withdraws from such an agreement. In the Law Commission's view, although the 'subject to contract' procedure

> has drawbacks and is capable of being abused in certain circumstances, [it] is based on a sound concept, namely that the buyer should be free from binding commitment until he has had the opportunity of obtaining legal and other advice, arranging his finance and making the necessary inspections, searches and enquiries ... In the context of house purchase it is ... of paramount importance that the law should place no fetter on the freedom of each of the parties, and in particular, the buyer, to refrain from binding commitment if he so wishes[16].

It is, of course, the unenforceability of agreements 'subject to contract' which makes possible the practice of a 'contract race'. Such a practice occurs where a vendor deals 'subject to contract' with more than one prospective purchaser, with the intention of becoming contractually bound only to the first to reach the stage of formal exchange of contracts at the price required by the vendor. The Council of the Law Society has in fact taken steps to control, if not to condemn, the practice of the 'contract race'. In the face of increasing dissatisfaction with the inequity of this form of competition between would-be purchasers, the Law Society has laid down guidelines for the conduct of the vendor's solicitor in such a situation. The essence of the control imposed by the Law Society is that the vendor's solicitor must, by written communication, disclose the existence of a 'contract race' to the solicitors acting for each prospective purchaser[17].

(2) The exchange of contracts

When a binding contract of sale of land is eventually concluded, it may take any form. The agreement may be either oral or written, but certain rules govern the circumstances and implications of exchange of contracts.

(a) *The requirement of a written memorandum*

According to section 40(1) of the Law of Property Act 1925, no action may be brought upon any contract for the sale or other disposition of land or any interest in land

> unless the agreement upon which such action is brought, or some memorandum or note thereof, is in writing, and signed by the party to be charged or by some other person thereunto by him lawfully authorised.

16 Law Commission, *Report on 'Subject to Contract' Agreements* (Law Com No. 65, January 1975), paras. 4, 7.

17 See (1977) 74 Law Soc Gaz 834: 'Council Direction: Vendor's Solicitor Submitting Draft Contracts to more than one Prospective Purchaser'.

This provision derives from the Statute of Frauds 1677, and is designed to prevent dispute over oral dealings in land. Section 40(1) does not render void a purely oral contract for the sale of land: it merely provides that such a contract shall be unenforceable.

As we have already seen, it seems that the decision of the Court of Appeal in *Law v Jones*[18], which would have rendered oral contracts enforceable, no longer represents good law[19]. In *Law v Jones*, the Court of Appeal appeared to hold that subsequent 'subject to contract' correspondence might itself constitute the written memorandum required by section 40(1) of the Law of Property Act 1925. In the judgment of Buckley LJ, it is not necessary that the note or memorandum required by section 40(1) should acknowledge the existence of a contract: 'It is not the fact of agreement but the terms agreed upon that must be found recorded in writing[20].' However, in *Tiverton Estates Ltd v Wearwell Ltd*[1] a differently constituted Court of Appeal declined to follow *Law v Jones*, holding instead that for the purpose of section 40(1) a memorandum or note must not only state the terms of the contract concerned, but must also contain an acknowledgment or recognition by the signatory to the document that a contract had been entered into. The law in this area is, in respect of this point, in a state of considerable confusion[2].

In practice, however, there is little confusion as to whether section 40(1) has been satisfied by the provision of a written memorandum or note. Most contracts for the sale of land are in writing in any event. The contract of sale may be 'open', i.e., may provide expressly for nothing beyond the identity of the parties, the definition of the subject matter and the price to be paid. The rights and duties of vendor and purchaser under an 'open' contract are then determined with reference to the general law of property. More common than 'open' contracts for the sale of land are 'closed' contracts which incorporate a number of standardised conditions relevant to the generality of land transactions. The most commonly used standard terms are those contained in the National Conditions of Sale[3], the Law Society's Conditions of Sale[4] and the Conveyancing Lawyers' Conditions of Sale[5]. The use of standard term conditions of sale substantially aids the process of land transfer. The vendor, whose duty it is in any event to draw up the contract of sale, may adopt one or other set of standard clauses with such modifications as may appear appropriate to the circumstances of his particular sale.

Irrespective of non-compliance with the provisions of section 40(1) of the Law of Property Act 1925, a contract for the sale of land may be actionable, even in the absence of writing, if there has been part performance of the

18 [1974] Ch 112.
19 See p. 80, ante.
20 [1974] Ch 112 at 124.
1 [1975] Ch 146.
2 See J. T. Farrand, op. cit., p. 36f.; A. M. Prichard, (1974) 90 LQR 55: 'An Aspect of Contracts and their Terms'.
3 19th Edn.
4 1980 Edn. See [1980] Conv 404 (H. W. Wilkinson).
5 See J. T. Farrand, op. cit., p. 76.

obligations contained in it[6]. Part performance generally requires that the party seeking to enforce the contract has, in reliance upon that contract, undertaken some action to his own detriment or prejudice, e.g., by giving up secure accommodation elsewhere in order to enter into possession[7].

(b) *Manner of exchange of contracts*

Until recently the most common method of exchanging contracts for the sale of land, thereby rendering the contract in question legally binding, has consisted of a postal exchange of the two parts signed by vendor and purchaser respectively. The general rule in the law of contract is that a postal acceptance of a contractual offer is complete when the offeree actually posts his acceptance to the offeror[8]. There has always been some doubt whether this postal rule applies to the exchange of contracts for sale of land, since the security sought by both parties in a land transaction seems to require that acceptance be complete only at the point of actual delivery of the acceptance to the offeror[9]. The legal conundrum involved here is now commonly obviated by the fact that most standardised sets of contractual conditions of sale provide that where the exchange of contracts is effected by post, the contract is made when the last part is actually posted[10].

Just as the postal exchange of contracts has largely superseded any form of ceremonial exchange of contracts, so the postal mode of exchange is itself being gradually overtaken by telephonic exchange. In *Domb v Isoz*[11], the Court of Appeal recognised that the synchronised transactions which are required by the 'chain bargains' common today on the domestic property market cannot be secured either by physical exchange or by postal exchange. In a practical world, the practical realities of 'chain transactions' require that solicitors should be able to use the medium of the telephone for the purpose of exchanging contracts. Thus, in *Domb v Isoz*, Buckley LJ declared that

> Exchange of a written contract for sale is in my judgment effected so soon as each part of the contract, signed by the vendor or the purchaser as the case may be, is in the actual or constructive possession of the other party or of his solicitor. Such possession need not be actual or physical possession; possession by an agent of the party or of his solicitor, in such circumstances that the party or solicitor in question has control over the document and can at any time procure its actual physical possession will, in my opinion, suffice. In such a case the possession of the agent is the possession of the principal. A party's solicitor employed to act in respect of such a contract has, subject to express instructions, implied authority to effect exchange of contracts and so to make the bargain binding upon his

6 Law of Property Act 1925, s. 40(2). See *Maddison v Alderson* (1883) 8 App Cas 467 at 475 per Earl of Selborne LC; *Kingswood Estate Co Ltd v Anderson* [1963] 2 QB 169. The notion of 'part performance' was significantly extended by the House of Lords in *Steadman v Steadman* [1976] AC 536 (see (1974) 90 LQR 433 (H. W. R. Wade); (1974) 38 Conv (NS) 354 (F. R. Crane); (1974) 33 Cambridge LJ 205 (C. T. Emery)). See now *Re Gonin* [1979] Ch 16.
7 See, e.g., *Wakeham v Mackenzie* [1968] 1 WLR 1175.
8 See *Household Fire Insurance Co v Grant* (1879) 4 Ex D 216.
9 See *Eccles v Bryant and Pollock* [1948] Ch 93 at 99f. per Lord Greene MR.
10 See, e.g., The Law Society's Conditions of Sale (1980 Edn), 10(1).
11 [1980] Ch 548. See [1980] Conv 227 (H. W. Wilkinson).

client. This he can, in my judgment, do by any method which is effectual to constitute exchange[12].

Thus, held the Court of Appeal, telephonic exchange may be used where it appears both effectual and appropriate, the practice of telephonic exchange serving substantially to reduce the danger that any client may lose a bargain or be left without a home. It is clear, however, that exchange by telephone will be permitted only under certain fairly stringent conditions. As Templeman LJ said,

Exchange by telephone can only take place after both vendor and purchaser sign contracts in identical form (subject to the question of rectification, which can apply to any contract) so that there is no doubt about the terms of the contract. Exchange by telephone can only take place when a contract signed by a client is in the physical possession of his own solicitor or in the possession of the solicitor on the other side who has agreed to hold that part to the order of the despatching solicitor. It is said that there may be uncertainty about the terms and effect of a telephone conversation which creates an exchange of contracts by telephone. This is perhaps a reason why, as a matter of professional practice, exchange by telephone should only be carried out by a partner or proprietor of a firm of solicitors. It is a reason why, if two solicitors exchange by telephone, they should then and there agree and record identical attendance notes[13].

(c) *The vendor as constructive trustee*

There is one important feature of contracts for the sale of land which must be noted at this point. A contract for the sale of a legal estate in land is one in respect of which equity will generally grant specific performance. In other words, if the vendor fails to convey the legal estate according to the terms of the relevant contract, the remedy available to the frustrated purchaser will normally consist not of compensatory damages, but of a court decree that the vendor do that which he promised to do, i.e., execute the conveyance and thus transfer the legal estate to the contractual promisee. Specific performance is available in the discretion of equity on the ground that, since the subject matter of a sale of land is unique, breach of a contract for the sale of land cannot be compensated adequately by a mere award of money[14]. The end result is that once a contract for the sale of a legal estate in land has been concluded, the eventual conveyance of that estate is virtually inevitable. Either the vendor will duly convey according to his contract or the purchaser will enlist the aid of equity towards this end by means of a decree of specific performance[15]. The assistance of equity

12 [1980] Ch 548 at 557.
13 [1980] Ch 548 at 560f.
14 In the words of Professor Farrand, specific performance is 'available almost as of right' (op. cit., p. 208). See *Hall v Warren* (1804) 9 Ves 605 at 608; *Hexter v Pearce* [1900] 1 Ch 341 at 346; *Rudd v Lascelles* [1900] 1 Ch 815 at 817.
15 In the case of a failure to complete a contract for the sale of land, it is, of course, open to a contracting party to rescind the contract and seek monetary compensation instead of specific performance of the contract. A failure to complete on the contractual date is remediable in damages for breach of contract or in damages in lieu of a decree for specific performance under the Chancery Amendment Act 1858 (Lord Cairns' Act). However, no right to rescind arises

will normally be forthcoming in each case unless the purchaser has forfeited such help by reason of some unconscionable act or default[16] or specific performance would prejudice the rights of third parties[17].

The fact that conveyance of the legal estate according to contract is now generally inexorable itself activates the equitable maxim that 'Equity looks on that as done which ought to be done.' Since the contract for sale ought (by one means or another) to eventuate in a conveyance of an estate in the land governed by the contract, equity regards the estate as having passed with the contract—provided that the contract was one in relation to which equity would have granted the remedy of specific performance. Thus the contract is effective to transfer the equitable ownership of the estate to the prospective purchaser, whether that estate be a fee simple or a term of years absolute.

Let us take the example of a contract for the sale of a fee simple in Blackacre. The effect of contract and conveyance will look like this:

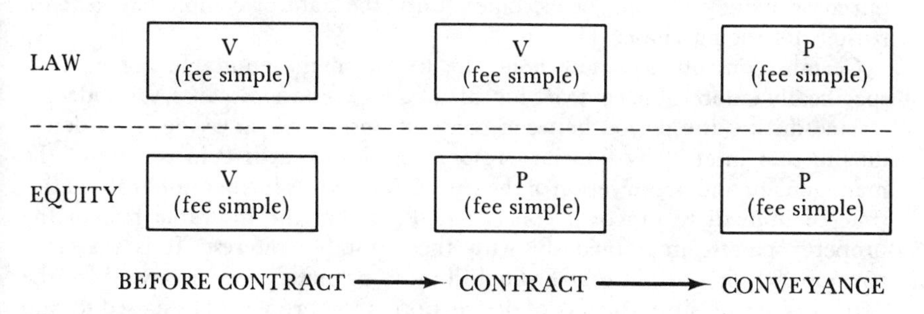

Fig. 16

Clearly the entire interest in Blackacre—both legal and equitable—is vested initially in the vendor V. However, from the moment when a specifically enforceable contract for sale is entered into with the purchaser, P, the fee simple is treated in equity as belonging to the latter. This is so even though the conveyance has not yet been executed and even though the purchase price has not yet been paid[18]. In effect, V holds the legal estate on trust for P[19]. The

---

until time becomes 'of the essence' by virtue of a notice to complete served by the party seeking completion or by virtue of unreasonable delay. See *Raineri v Miles* [1980] 2 WLR 847; (1980) 39 Cambridge LJ 21 (D. J. Hayton); (1981) 44 MLR 100 (A. Samuels). Where an aggrieved contracting party has treated another's repudiation or breach of contract as discharging the contract, or where an order for specific performance is not complied with, damages may be recovered not only for restitution and indemnity in respect of sums paid and expenses incurred, but also for loss of bargain. See *Johnson v Agnew* [1980] AC 367, overruling *Horsler v Zorro* [1975] Ch 302. See also A. J. Oakley (1980) 39 Cambridge LJ 58: 'Pecuniary Compensation for Failure to Complete a Contract for the Sale of Land'; M. Hetherington (1980) 96 LQR 403: 'Keeping the Plaintiff out of his Contractual Remedies: the Heresies that survive *Johnson v Agnew*'; (1979) 42 MLR 696 (G. Woodman); [1979] Conv 293 (F. R. Crane).

16 See *Coatsworth v Johnson* (1886) 55 LJQB 220, p. 397, post.

17 See *Warmington v Miller* [1973] QB 877.

18 It is normal for the purchaser to pay 10 per cent of the purchase price at the point of contract.

19 See *Lysaght v Edwards* (1876) 2 Ch D 499 at 506 per Jessel MR; *Howard v Miller* [1915] AC 318 at 326 per Lord Parker of Waddington.

particular type of trust which arises in this situation is often called a 'constructive trust'. When the conveyance of the legal estate is subsequently executed (or, in registered land parlance, the transfer of title is completed), the legal fee simple will be re-united with the equitable fee simple which passed with the contract[20].

It is, of course, only in a somewhat qualified sense that V may be said to be a 'constructive trustee' of the legal title for P during the interim between the conclusion of the specifically enforceable contract and the eventual legal transfer. He still enjoys a 'paramount right ... to protect his own interest as vendor of the property[1].' He still enjoys certain valuable rights in relation to the property. He has a right to remain in possession of the land until completion of the contract and payment of the purchase moneys[2], and is entitled to the rents and profits which accrue before the date of completion[3]. Moreover, if V parts with possession he enjoys in equity an 'unpaid vendor's lien' over the property until the purchase moneys are paid in full[4]. However, once V has received those purchase moneys in full, he becomes (until the date of completion) a 'bare trustee' for the purchaser, P[5].

Certain consequences flow none the less from the equitable impact of a specifically enforceable contract for sale of a legal estate. Because V is indeed a trustee during the period between contract and conveyance, he is burdened during that interim by fiduciary responsibilities towards P in respect of the management and preservation of the trust property[6]. A further implication, this time of immediate practical concern to P, is that the insurable risk in the property passes simultaneously with the equitable interest. It is therefore paramountly important that P should buy insurance cover effective from the date of contract, since the risk of destruction of the property has passed to him as the beneficial owner behind the trust of the legal estate. Even if, for instance, a building on the land to be conveyed is utterly destroyed by fire between contract and conveyance, P is still contractually bound to take the conveyance of the land and the charred remains and is required to pay the full purchase price named in the contract[7].

For our purposes, however, the most important implication of the foregoing is that, from the very moment of exchange of contracts, the purchaser of land acquires not merely a *contractual* right but also a *proprietary* right. In our example,

20 For further reference to the 'chameleonic changes of character' undergone by the vendor, see J. T. Farrand, op. cit., p. 168.

1 *Shaw v Foster* (1872) LR 5 HL 321 at 338 per Lord Cairns LC.

2 See *Gedye v Montrose* (1858) 26 Beav 45; *Phillips v Silvester* (1872) LR 8 Ch App 173.

3 See *Cuddon v Tite* (1858) 1 Giff 395. This differs from the 'inflexible rule' of equity that a trustee or fiduciary may never under any circumstances derive profit from his position of trust. See *Parker v McKenna* (1874) LR 10 Ch App 96 at 124 per James LJ; G. H. Jones (1968) 84 LQR 472: 'Unjust Enrichment and the Fiduciary's Duty of Loyalty.'

4 See *Winter v Lord Anson* (1827) 3 Russ 488; *Nives v Nives* (1880) 15 Ch D 649; *Re Birmingham, Savage v Stannard* [1959] Ch 523; *London and Cheshire Insurance Co Ltd v Laplagrene Property Co Ltd* [1971] Ch 499, p. 338, post.

5 See elsewhere for a definition of 'bare trust', p. 160, post. See also *Bridges v Mees* [1957] Ch 475, p. 333, post.

6 See *Clarke v Ramuz* [1891] 2 QB 456; *Phillips v Lamdin* [1949] 2 KB 33.

7 *Rayner v Preston* (1881) 18 Ch D 1.

he acquires the equitable fee simple absolute in the property. This helps to explain why one of the most significant categories of registrable land charge—the Class C (iv) estate contract—is designed to protect precisely such a right as that of the purchaser to require conveyance according to contract[8]. By virtue of the anticipatory effect of the equitable doctrine, the contractual right of the purchaser has been transformed into a right in real property and (like any other commercial equitable interest) requires protection against third parties.

The same doctrine of equity has application to a contract to convey a lease or term of years. The contract itself is effective (under the doctrine in *Walsh v Lonsdale*[9]) to invest the lessee or tenant with an equitable interest in the land, i.e., an equitable term of years. Furthermore, an imperfect conveyance of a leasehold interest (e.g., in writing instead of by deed) has a similar effect: the lessee holds an equitable term of years. Of course, in both cases the tenant can usually obtain specific performance of the lease by means of a court order that the landlord execute a legal lease in the proper form. However, the tenant often has no interest in seeking specific performance since in equity he is already regarded as holding a term of years on conditions identical to those contained in the original contract or imperfect lease[10]. Thus, in many instances, a contract for a lease may never eventuate in a valid conveyance of the leasehold. For our present purpose, however, the important point is that an equitable lease constitutes a commercial equitable interest requiring protection against the lessor as a Class C (iv) land charge either by registration under the Land Charges Act 1972 or by entry of a notice or caution under the Land Registration Act 1925.

(3) Completion

By virtue of the exchange of contracts, vendor and purchaser are legally committed to complete the transaction. However, as Lord Erskine observed in *Hiern v Mill*[11], 'no man in his senses would take an offer of a purchase from a man merely because he stood on the ground.' Mere possession by the vendor is not sufficient; the vendor must satisfy the purchaser that he has a good title to the property and that it is subject only to the adverse interests specified in the contract. If the title is unregistered, the vendor must supply an abstract of the title of the property which discloses dealings affecting the land during at least the past 15 years[12]. In the case of registered title, the purchaser is given authority

8 See p. 135ff., post.
9 (1882) 21 Ch D 9, p. 398, post.
10 See p. 400, post.
11 (1806) 13 Ves 114 at 122.
12 Law of Property Act 1969, s. 23. The maximum period in respect of which (in the absence of contrary contractual stipulation) the purchaser could insist on investigating title was originally fixed by common law as 60 years (see *Barnwell v Harris* (1809) 1 Taunt 430). The period was progressively reduced to 40 years (Vendor and Purchaser Act 1874, s. 1), 30 years (Law of Property Act 1925, s. 44(1)), and now 15 years, p. 127, post. Michael Joseph has said that the gradual restriction of the period of investigation of title is evidence that 'Parliament itself has acknowledged the fatuity of the procedure . . . Since the [Law of Property Act 1969] was passed . . . the purchaser's solicitor's task of investigating title has therefore been cut by half (without, curiously enough, any corresponding reduction of fees) . . . Yet no one seems any the worse for

to inspect the Land Register for entries in respect of the vendor's title[13]. If either the abstract of title or the register entries disclose apparent defects in the title, the purchaser may make 'requisitions' in order to clarify matters in doubt. When satisfied that the title is in order, the purchaser sends to the vendor a draft conveyance or, in the case of registered land, a draft form of transfer, for approval. When approved, the draft conveyance or transfer is engrossed (i.e., a fair copy is typed on durable paper). The purchaser makes a final search of the Land Charges Register or the Land Register, as is appropriate[14], in order to ensure that the property remains free of undisclosed adverse interests. On the day fixed for completion (which is usually four weeks after the exchange of contracts), the purchaser pays over the balance of the purchase moneys and the vendor hands over the appropriate title deeds or documents. The transaction is now complete, except that in the case of registered land the document of transfer must be sent to the Land Registry in order that the purchaser may be registered as the new proprietor[15].

The foregoing is a brief description of the process by which a title is investigated and title is finally transferred from vendor to purchaser. Certain aspects of the transaction require greater emphasis.

(a) *Formalities*

By contrast with the relative informality with which a contract for the sale of land may be concluded, certain stringent requirements must be satisfied in the transfer of a legal estate in land. According to section 52(1) of the Law of Property Act 1925,

> All conveyances of land or of any interest therein are void for the purpose of conveying or creating a legal estate unless made by deed.

There are a number of exceptions to this rule, the most important of which relate to assents by a personal representative[16] and leases which are expressly exempted by statute from the requirement of formality[17].

A deed is quite simply a document of transfer or conveyance which has been 'signed, sealed and delivered' by the party executing the same[18]. It used to be the case that 'no writing without a seal can be a deed'[19], but this proposition belonged to an age in which the general illiteracy of the population meant that a personal seal provided the only reliable means of authenticating a legal

this drastic measure ... So what is the magic in the period of 15 years? If the period can be satisfactorily cut from 30 years to 15 years, why not cut it still further to 10 or 5? Or simply require the vendor to produce the actual conveyance to himself, possession being nine tenths of ownership, with such conveyance making up the remaining tenth.' See *The Conveyancing Fraud* (London 1980), p. 55f.

13 See p. 323, post.

14 See pp. 127, 327, post.

15 See p. 324, post.

16 Law of Property Act 1925, s. 52(2)(a), p. 168, post.

17 Law of Property Act 1925, s. 52(2)(d), p. 392, post.

18 See *Goddard's case* (1584) 2 Co Rep 4b at 5a.

19 *Sheppard's Touchstone of Common Assurances* (8th edn. by E. G. Atherley, London 1826), p. 56.

document. Nowadays the grantor's signature has acquired greater practical significance than the seal in establishing the authenticity of the document concerned[20]. Section 73(1) of the Law of Property Act 1925 provides that where an individual executes a deed, he shall either sign or place his mark upon the same, and 'sealing alone shall not be deemed sufficient.' In any event, a seal today tends to be merely a mass-produced red adhesive paper disc which is attached to the bottom of the document concerned: the ceremony of sealing with the aid of sealing wax has almost entirely disappeared. Such is the diminishing mystique of the seal that in *First National Securities Ltd v Jones*[1] the Court of Appeal held that the requirement of a deed was satisfied by a signed document on which was printed a circle containing the letters 'LS'—representing *locus sigilli* (the place of a seal)[2]. Delivery of the signed and sealed document comprises any unilateral act or statement by the grantor adopting the deed as his own[3].

It is curious to reflect upon the importance attached historically to the requirement that a deed be signed, sealed and delivered by the grantor. Conveyancing, magic and sorcery are not wholly unconnected phenomena—witness the medieval ritual and symbolism of conveyances of freehold land in bygone times when a conveyance could be effected only by a 'feoffment with livery of seisin'[4]. It is an interesting feature of the social anthropology of land law that the talismanic effect of a little red wafer is such as to confer upon certain transactions a legal efficacy which they would not otherwise possess. The use of a deed is more than a mere sine qua non of actionability[5]. It is a condition precedent to the validity of the conveyance expressed on its face. However, even the residual importance of the seal is somewhat in decline in the present day, Goddard J noting as long ago as 1937 that 'a seal nowadays is very much in the nature of a legal fiction.'[6] It may be that the requirement of a seal may some day be altogether removed. In 1971, Lord Wilberforce, speaking extra-judicially in the House of Lords, castigated 'this medieval doctrine of the seal' and expressed the hope that 'we might have got rid of that mumbo-jumbo and aligned ourselves with most other civilised countries.'[7]

(b) *Criticism of present conveyancing practice*

The conveyancing process is normally conducted by the solicitors acting for the vendor and purchaser respectively. In their hands, the process is slow and costly.

20 As Danckwerts J once pointed out, 'with the spread of education, the signature became of importance for the authentication of documents.' See *Stromdale and Ball Ltd v Burden* [1952] Ch 223 at 230.
1 [1978] Ch 109.
2 See D. C. Hoath (1980) 43 MLR 415: 'The Sealing of Documents—Fact or Fiction?'
3 See D. E. C. Yale (1970) 28 Cambridge LJ 52: 'The Delivery of a Deed'.
4 See p. 49, ante.
5 Compare, in relation to contracts for the sale of land, Law of Property Act 1925, s. 40(1), p. 82, ante.
6 Sixth Interim Report of the Law Revision Committee on *Statute of Frauds and the Doctrine of Consideration* (Cmd 5449, 1937), p. 35.
7 *Parliamentary Debates, House of Lords, Official Report (1970–71)*, Vol. 315, Col. 1213 (25 February 1971).

Indeed, Buckley J once made mention, in a famous dictum, of 'the stately saraband which takes place between vendor and purchaser on the purchase of land.'[8] It is inevitable that, at a time of increased emphasis upon the rights of consumers, some question should arise as to whether solicitors give value for money. An average domestic sale and purchase may well cost the client £500 in solicitors' fees alone and may often take four or five months to complete. Furthermore, solicitors enjoy an extraordinary monopoly by virtue of statute, since section 22(1) of the Solicitors Act 1974 imposes criminal liability upon any 'unqualified person' who receives any 'fee, gain or reward' for the purpose of drawing or preparing any instrument of transfer or charge or any other instrument relating to real or personal estate. In this context, an 'unqualified person' is a person who is not qualified under section 1 of the Solicitors Act 1974 to act as a solicitor[9]. The 1974 Act imposes no restriction upon a lay person who merely wishes to do his own conveyancing; the prohibition strikes only at 'unqualified persons' who undertake conveyancing for a fee.

The conveyancing monopoly enjoyed by solicitors is one of the primary targets of recent criticism of the standard and range of legal services provided by the legal profession. It has been alleged that the monopoly serves only the interest of the profession and that the entire conveyancing process constitutes a massive fraud upon the public at large. According to Michael Joseph,

> The art of conveyancing, as practised by solicitors, is to relieve the house buyer and seller of as much money as possible for as little work as possible. This in itself does not amount to fraud. The fraud lies in the solicitors' claim that they *safeguard* the house buyer in the most important purchase of his life; whereas what they actually *do* is not only useless, it is worse than useless. It is useless because of the methods which solicitors employ to check that the house being bought has no quasi-legal defects[10].

Among the charges which Mr Joseph levels at professional conveyancers are the allegations that solicitors leave the crucial aspects of conveyancing to chance, that the bulk of conveyancing work is done not by solicitors but by unqualified and unsupervised solicitors' clerks, and that the remuneration received by solicitors is wholly disproportionate to the amount of work done[11]. In short, the entire business of conveyancing is a huge confidence trick practised upon an unsuspecting public by a profession with powerful vested interests in maintaining its lucrative monopoly. In the acerbic words of Mr Joseph,

> Mix ignorance and fear in roughly equal proportions—modern legislation and land law are so complicated, local authorities have such wide powers, there are so many things which can go wrong, there are so many legal problems which can arise—and then add the magic ingredient, and the result will be a philosopher's stone in the hands of every

8 *Re Stone and Saville's Contract* [1962] 1 WLR 460 at 465.

9 Solicitors Act 1974, s. 87(1). For a disastrous misquotation of s. 22(1) of the Solicitors Act 1974, see later, p. 400f., post.

10 *The Conveyancing Fraud* (London 1980), p. 1.

11 Scale charges for conveyancing were abolished in January 1973 on the initiative of the Lord Chancellor, following unfavourable reports emanating from the National Board for Prices and Incomes. It was anticipated that this relaxation might allow solicitors to make charges below the scale rates, but the change did not bring about any palpable reduction in the costs of conveyancing.

established solicitor. And the magic ingredient? The price of the house. The fact that the would-be house owner, who apart from his car has probably never previously made a purchase for more than £300, is now buying something which costs between £10,000 and £25,000. It is this fact more than any other which sends a man quivering into the comforting arms of a solicitor. Understandably, solicitors make the fullest use of it... The implication is that without professional advice a man might spend his life's savings, might sign his twenty five year mortgage, only to find that he had not got a house at all, but perhaps a chicken run or a coal scuttle; or even if he had succeeded in buying a house, the highway authority would as like as not be driving a major road through its sitting room on the morrow.

And then reassurance: we are the highly trained experts, the specialists, who know all about these terrifying Acts of Parliament and regulations which would trap you, but won't trap us; we know all about these complicated land laws with their jargon incomprehensible to you, but not to us. We'll make sure that nothing goes wrong; we'll look after you all the way along the line. Remember, you're spending £15,000. Surely its sensible to lay out another hundred or two in employing a solicitor?

The layman obligingly agrees. So bemused is he at the prospect of £15,000 passing through his hands that it will never occur to him that a transaction involving such a sum need be no more complicated than getting a passport. So respectful is he of the solicitors' mystique that it will never occur to him that buying a house for all practical purposes probably involves *less* law than buying a washing machine. And so stoical is he that it will never occur to him to wonder whether his solicitor, whom he will have paid between £100 and £350 for carrying out his conveyancing, has in fact done anything of any real value[12].

Mr Joseph has further startling things to say about the rate of remuneration received by solicitors for conveyancing work. He calculates that, even after making generous allowance for the amounts of time which could conceivably be spent by solicitors on the work involved in a normal conveyancing transaction[13], the average solicitor charges 'at a basic rate of about £80 an hour, and this is probably a minimum[14].' The underlying reason for the 'ritual dance' of the conveyancing process is therefore the need to conceal this remarkable rate of remuneration behind the needless verbiage of documents, a barrage of pointless enquiries and (above all) the expanse of time which customarily elapses between the beginning of a transaction and its eventual completion. According to Mr Joseph,

The indictment against solicitors therefore is not that they charge at the rate of £80 an hour (there is, after all, no reason why they should be untainted by the universal love of money); nor that they find out nothing useful about the houses their clients are buying (in the case of ninety nine out of a hundred houses there is nothing useful to find out anyway). The indictment against solicitors is that in order to conceal the fact that they charge at the rate of £80 an hour, and that they find out nothing useful, they—with the aid of the building societies—have foisted on the public a system of ludicrous inefficiency, which can and frequently does cause their clients frustration and misery[15].

12 Op. cit., p. 22f.
13 Mr Joseph even adds on an extra 10 minutes 'for nose-picking and drinking coffee' (op cit., p. 88f.).
14 Op. cit., p. 90.
15 Op. cit., p. 102.

Mr Joseph, who is himself a qualified solicitor, is understandably not an entirely popular member of his own profession. However, many of the criticisms which he expresses are borne out by Stephen Cretney, a fellow solicitor and now one of Her Majesty's Law Commissioners[16]. Mr Cretney too has spoken of 'the casual attitude' of conveyancers to potential defects in transacted titles. In his view, a purchaser is protected in many cases 'by little more than the honesty of his vendor[17].' Mr Cretney points in particular to the way in which existing conveyancing practice does little or nothing to eradicate the defects which flow from faulty plans and inadequate descriptions of boundaries and the defects which arise from 'double conveyancing[18].' In his view, although much criticism of the conveyancing system and its practitioners is misguided, the current popular campaign directed against solicitors 'produces an exaggerated reaction by solicitors who wish to preserve both proper standards and their own financial position[19].'

It was partly in response to the mounting condemnation of conveyancing practice that a Royal Commission was established in 1976 to examine the provision of legal services in England and Wales. The Commission reported in 1979, and its conclusions in the area of conveyancing law and practice emerged as a quite extraordinary vindication of the status quo. The Commission observed that, although land law and the process of registration had been substantially simplified by legislation, this progress had been offset by the increasing need for expert legal advice on 'matters ancillary to a conveyance, such as planning, taxation and matrimonial law[20].' The Commission took the view that a 'free-for-all' in which any person might offer conveyancing services without restriction was plainly undesirable, and that it was only by virtue of the 'positive control' currently exercised by the responsible professional body that high standards of competence and ethical conduct could be maintained. The Commission not only endorsed the conveyancing monopoly already conferred upon solicitors by statute, but proposed that the monopoly should be extended to cover *contracts* for the sale of land[1]. The Commission was, however, persuaded to recommend the introduction of a system of 'standard charges' for conveyancing transactions, a move which would reinstate a scheme similar to the scale rates of remuneration which prevailed until 1973[2]. Otherwise the Commission saw no reason to intervene in the affairs of practising conveyancers.

16 (1969) 32 MLR 477: 'Land Law and Conveyancing Reforms'.
17 (1969) 32 MLR 477, 494.
18 For a fierce condemnation of 'slapdash conveyancing' by solicitors see the judgment of Cumming-Bruce LJ in the Court of Appeal in *Scarfe v Adams* (1980) Times, 5th December.
19 (1969) 32 MLR 477, 498.
20 *Final Report of the Royal Commission on Legal Services* (Cmnd 7648, October 1979), Vol. 1, para. 21.60(b).
1 Ibid., para. 21.61, p. 400, post.
2 Ibid., paras. 21.92ff. The argument against scale charges is that they inhibit competition. Before 1973 there was even a professional rule of conduct which prohibited undercutting by solicitors (see Solicitors' Practice Rules 1936, r. 2). Under the scheme proposed by the Royal Commission, it would be open to solicitors to reduce their charges below the 'standard' charge if they so wished, but it would also be open to them to charge in excess of the 'standard' rate upon giving

Perhaps with justification the Report of the Royal Commission has been regarded by some as indicating an unnecessarily supine acceptance of self-serving submissions made by a profession which is desperately anxious to preserve its huge vested interest in the business of conveyancing. However, the underlying problems in this area are deep and possibly intractable. It is unfortunate that the Royal Commission did not address itself more clearly and more analytically to the fundamental criticisms which have been directed in recent years at conveyancing practice. Some indication of the thought-processes which conditioned the response made by the Royal Commission may, however, be gathered from the judgment of Templeman LJ in *Domb v Isoz*[3]. Here Templeman LJ (one of the members of the Royal Commission) expressed the view that

> Conveyancing is a complicated business. A chain of transactions is frequently involved where no vendor will sell until he can purchase and no purchaser will buy until he can sell. Each client as vendor and purchaser needs time to make up his mind and change his mind after studying surveys and legal reports and other relevant matters and each client expects everyone else to be ready when he is ready. Skilful conveyancers are required to forge the chain, to see that no bargain is lost and that no one is left without a home. Binding and enforceable undertakings between professional men play an essential part at different stages. Mistakes are bound to occur occasionally and each client must be protected by the insurance of his solicitor against financial loss, even though damages will never fully compensate a client for the loss of a bargain or the loss of a home. This appeal illustrates some of the difficulties which can arise and some of the reasons why the Royal Commission on Legal Services came to the conclusion that conveyancing should be confined to members of a trained and responsible profession, which should be improved rather than diluted or invaded.

2. ACQUISITION OF TITLE UNDER THE STATUTES OF LIMITATION[4]

The Statutes of Limitation provide a second means by which the title to land may be acquired. This mode of acquisition is quite different from acquisition by contract and conveyance or transfer, for its essence is that if the owner of property fails within a certain period to secure the eviction of a squatter or trespasser from his land, that owner is statutorily barred from recovering possession thereafter. The intruder acquires, by virtue of the Acts of Limitation, a title which enables him to remain in possession. In this sense, English land law gives effect to the pragmatic expectation, born no doubt in the more physical climate of earlier times, that a property owner will rise with rugged fortitude to assert his title against unlawful intruders. As Streatfield J observed in *RB Policies at Lloyd's v Butler*[5],

---

written notice to the client (see *Final Report*, para. 21.98). See H. W. Wilkinson [1980] Conv 12: 'Standard Conveyancing Charges after the Royal Commission'.

3 [1980] Ch 548 at 560f.

4 See generally C. H. S. Preston and G. H. Newsom, *Limitation of Actions* (3rd edn., London 1953); A. W. B. Simpson, *An Introduction to the History of the Land Law* (London 1961), p. 141ff.

5 [1950] 1 KB 76 at 81.

It is a policy of the Limitation Acts that those who go to sleep upon their claims should not be assisted by the courts recovering their property, but another, and, I think, equal policy behind these Acts, is that there shall be an end of litigation.

Thus the Limitation Acts are directed towards extinguishing the title which an owner has failed to protect within the period specified by statute, and instead indirectly permit third parties to set up new titles good against the world.

The policy promoted by the Limitation Acts derives ultimately from the importance attached in the common law to the 'seisin-possession' concept[6]. In *A'Court v Cross*[7], Best CJ stated that a Statute of Limitation is 'an Act of peace. Long dormant claims have often more of cruelty than of justice in them[8].' More recently a Law Reform Committee recognised in express terms that

certainty of title to land is a social need and occupation of land which has long been unchallenged should not be disturbed[9].

It has of course been questioned whether under modern conditions the law of acquisition by adverse possession still has any role to play. For the first time, the concept of 'theft' of land has become a real and workable concept by reason of the provisions of the Theft Act 1968[10]. However, it is not difficult to see that even today the acquisition of title by means of adverse possession may have a benign influence upon the social policy that security should be given to the long possessor of land. Increasingly, as the emphasis of the law turns to the protection of residential security, the law of adverse possession ensures that de facto possession does not diverge too markedly from de iure title. Furthermore, it is salutary to remember that the law of adverse possession is often the consumer's ultimate remedy for the deficiencies of modern conveyancing techniques. As Michael Goodman has said,

the doctrine of adverse possession has still a considerable and beneficial part to play in curing inadvertent defects in unregistered titles, and in making the title to land follow the physical occupation or the actual boundaries, rather than divorcing the 'paper title' from reality[11].

(1) The period of limitation

The broad principle of the law of adverse possession is that no action may be brought for the recovery of land after the expiration of a statutorily prescribed period of time running from the date when the right of action first accrued. The period prescribed differs according to the particular cause of action, but at the termination of the appropriate period the action for recovery becomes statute-barred.

6 See p. 48, ante.
7 (1825) 3 Bing 329 at 332.
8 The first statute of limitation was the Limitation Act 1623. The current statute is the Limitation Act 1980, which came into force on 1 May 1981.
9 Law Reform Committee, *Report on Acquisition of Easements and Profits by Prescription* (14th Report, Cmnd 3100, 1966), para. 36.
10 See Theft Act 1968, s. 4(1). See also J. C. Smith and B. Hogan, *Criminal Law* (4th edn., London 1978), 499.
11 (1970) 33 MLR 281 at 282f.: 'Adverse Possession of Land—Morality and Motive'.

The general rule is laid down in section 15(1) of the Limitation Act 1980:

> No action shall be brought by any person to recover any land after the expiration of twelve years from the date on which the right of action accrued to him or, if it first accrued to some person through whom he claims, to that person[12].

The period of limitation is thus generally twelve years. Other provisions in the Limitation Act 1980 deal specifically with the accrual of rights of action in relation to future interests, settled land and land held on trust for sale[13]. It should be noted that the limitation period appropriate to land held by way of periodic tenancy is stipulated in paragraph 5 of Schedule 1 of the Limitation Act 1980:

> (1) Subject to sub-paragraph (2) below, a tenancy from year to year or other period, without a lease in writing, shall for the purposes of this Act be treated as being determined at the expiration of the first year or other period; and accordingly the right of action of the person entitled to the land subject to the tenancy shall be treated as having accrued at the date on which in accordance with this sub-paragraph the tenancy is determined.
> (2) Where any rent has subsequently been received in respect of the tenancy, the right of action shall be treated as having accrued on the date of the last receipt of rent.

In order that a right of action should accrue, and therefore cause the period of limitation to begin to run, the land concerned must be 'in the possession of some person in whose favour the period of limitation can run[14].' The possession here referred to is commonly known as 'adverse possession'. Thus the limitation period begins to run from the date of the owner's dispossession by an adverse possessor[15] or from the date of the inception of adverse possession by a third party following a 'discontinuance' of possession by the original owner[16].

It is quite clear that the limitation period prescribed by statute may be established by a series of adverse possessors of land. In other words, if X is dispossessed of land by A who, in his turn, is dispossessed by B, B may claim the period of A's adverse possession as if it were his own in defence to any action for recovery brought by X[17]. B would, however, be vulnerable to an action for recovery brought against him by A at any point before the time when B's adverse possession has prevailed for the period prescribed by statute. If A abandons his adverse possession within the limitation period and, after an interval, B begins adversely to possess, B cannot add to his possession the period of adverse possession earlier established by A[18]. The limitation period begins to run only from the inception of B's adverse possession.

12 The limitation period is 30 years in respect of actions brought by the Crown and 60 years in respect of actions brought by the Crown to recover foreshore (Limitation Act 1980, Sch. 1, paras. 10, 11). For reference to a 'tenuous if picturesque' form of adverse possession, see A. R. Everton, (1971) 35 (Conv (NS) 249: 'Built in a Night . . .'.

13 Limitation Act 1980, s. 18, Sch. 1, para. 4.

14 Limitation Act 1980, Sch. 1, para. 8(1). Thus, the possession of a tenant cannot be considered adverse until the period covered by the last payment of rent has expired. See *Hayward v Chaloner* [1968] 1 QB 107 at 122 per Russell LJ.

15 Limitation Act 1980, Sch. 1, para. 1.

16 Limitation Act 1980, Sch. 1, para. 8(1).

17 Limitation Act 1980, s. 15(1).

18 Limitation Act 1980, Sch. 1, para. 8(2).

(2) Dispossession and discontinuance of possession

In *Treloar v Nute*[19], Sir John Pennycuick stated in the Court of Appeal that under the Limitation Act the person claiming land by possession must show either

(i) 'discontinuance by the paper owner followed by possession' or
(ii) 'dispossession' (or 'ouster') of the paper owner.

The second category of case is nowadays somewhat rare, and most of the difficulties in the law of adverse possession have arisen in the context of 'discontinuance' of possession by the paper owner followed by 'possession' on the part of an intruder. We must look more closely at the precise meaning of the terms 'discontinuance' and 'possession'.

(a) *'Discontinuance' of possession by the paper owner*

In the absence of evidence to the contrary, the owner of land with the 'paper title' is deemed to be in possession of that land, since he is the person who enjoys the prima facie right to possession. The law thus ascribes possession either to the paper owner or to persons who can establish a title as claiming through the paper owner[20].

It is usually not difficult to determine whether there has been a 'discontinuance' of possession by the paper owner. However, the case which is problematical is that in which the paper owner, although not technically in possession, has in mind some purpose to which he intends to put the land in the future. There is strong authority for the view that there is no 'discontinuance' of possession by the paper owner simply by reason of the fact that some other person enjoys physical occupation of the land during a period in which the paper owner retains the land with a view to its utilisation for some specific purpose at a later date[1]. As Lord Denning MR said in *Wallis's Cayton Bay Holiday Camp Ltd v Shell-Mex and BP Ltd*[2],

> The true owner must have discontinued possession or have been dispossessed and another must have taken it adversely to him. There must be something in the nature of an ouster of the true owner by the wrongful possessor. That is shown by a series of cases in this court which, on their very facts, show this proposition to be true. When the true owner of land intends to use it for a particular purpose in the future, but meanwhile has no immediate use for it, and so leaves it unoccupied, he does not lose his title to it simply because some other person enters on it and uses it for some temporary purpose, like stacking materials; or for some seasonal purpose, like growing vegetables. Not even if this temporary or seasonal purpose continues year after year for 12 years, or more.

(b) *The inception of 'possession' by a third party*

In cases of adverse possession arising otherwise than by 'ouster', it is essential to show not merely that there has been a 'discontinuance' of possession by the

19 [1976] 1 WLR 1295 at 1300.
20 See *Powell v McFarlane* (1977) 38 P & CR 452 at 470.
1 See *Leigh v Jack* (1879) 5 Ex D 264; *Williams Brothers Direct Supply Ltd v Raftery* [1958] 1 QB 159.
2 [1975] QB 94 at 103. See (1975) 39 Conv (NS) 57 (F. R. Crane); (1975) 34 Cambridge LJ 32 (D. Macintyre); (1975) 91 LQR 7 (J. L. Barton).

paper owner, but also that there has been an inception of 'possession' by an adverse occupier. For this purpose 'possession' is given a qualified meaning. In order that 'possession' should be attributed in law to a third party who can establish no paper title to possession, it must be shown that that third party has both factual possession and the requisite 'intention to possess' (*animus possidendi*)[3].

(i) *Factual possession* The requirement of factual possession signifies an appropriate degree of physical control of the land in question. It must involve a 'single and conclusive possession'[4] and in this sense must be 'adverse' to the possession otherwise enjoyed by the paper owner. Thus possession concurrent with the paper owner is insufficient[5], for what is required, as Bramwell LJ said in *Leigh v Jack*[6], are 'acts . . . which are inconsistent with [the paper owner's] enjoyment of the soil for the purposes for which he intended to use it.' The paper owner and the intruder cannot both be in possession at the same time[7].

The kinds of 'possession' required for the purpose of establishing exclusive physical control on the part of the adverse occupier must depend upon the circumstances of each case. In *Powell v McFarlane*[8], Slade J indicated that the question of 'possession' must be determined with particular reference to 'the nature of the land and the manner in which land of that nature is commonly used or enjoyed.' Thus, in Slade J's view,

> In the case of open land, absolute physical control is normally impracticable, if only because it is generally impossible to secure every part of a boundary so as to prevent intrusion . . . It is clearly settled that acts of possession done on parts of land to which a possessory title is sought may be evidence of possession of the whole.

In other cases it has been held, however, that 'possession' could be established by an adverse occupier who used the land for shooting[9], or erected fences[10], or used the land for grazing and for storage purposes[11]. In effect, it must be shown that 'the alleged possessor has been dealing with the land in question as an occupying owner might have been expected to deal with it and that no-one else has done so[12].' Trivial or equivocal acts by the adverse occupier will not be sufficient to prove 'possession'. In *Tecbild Ltd v Chamberlain*[13], for instance, the Court of Appeal declined to have regard to the fact that the adverse occupier's children had been accustomed to play on the disputed plots of land as and when they wished and that the family ponies had been tethered and exercised there[14].

3 See *Powell v McFarlane* (1977) 38 P & CR 452 at 470.
4 Ibid.
5 *Treloar v Nute* [1976] 1 WLR 1295 at 1300 per Sir John Pennycuick.
6 (1879) 5 Ex D 264 at 273.
7 *Powell v McFarlane* (1977) 38 P & CR 452 at 470.
8 (1977) 38 P & CR 452 at 471.
9 *Red House Farms (Thorndon) Ltd v Catchpole* (1977) 244 Estates Gazette 295, 121 Sol Jo 136.
10 *Seddon v Smith* (1877) 36 LT 168 at 169.
11 *Treloar v Nute* [1976] 1 WLR 1295.
12 *Powell v McFarlane* (1977) 38 P & CR 452 at 471.
13 (1969) 20 P & CR 633.
14 Compare *Powell v McFarlane* (1977) 38 P & CR 452, p. 99, post.

The courts used to apply a doctrine of 'implied licence' in determining whether a squatter could validly claim 'possession' of land left unoccupied by a paper owner who had no immediate use for that land. In *Wallis's Cayton Bay Holiday Camp Ltd v Shell-Mex and BP Ltd*[15], Ormrod LJ pointed out that

The overall impression created by the authorities is that the courts have always been reluctant to allow an incroacher or squatter to acquire a good title to land against the true owner, and have interpreted the word 'possession' in this context very narrowly.

Lord Denning MR led the majority in the Court of Appeal in holding that the occasional acts of user pleaded in this case as constituting 'adverse possession' by a trespasser were insufficient for the purpose. In the words of the Master of the Rolls,

The line between acts of user and acts of possession is too fine for words. The reason behind the decisions is because it does not lie in that other person's mouth to assert that he used the land of his own wrong as a trespasser. Rather his user is to be ascribed to the licence or permission of the true owner. By using the land, knowing that it does not belong to him, he impliedly assumes that the owner will permit it: and the owner, by not turning him off, impliedly gives permission. And it has been held many times in this court that acts done under licence or permitted by the owner do not give a licensee a title under the Limitation Act ... They do not amount to adverse possession[16].

Again, in *Gray v Wykeham Martin*[17], an area of land of between one-quarter and one-half an acre had been used by a stranger 'for temporary purposes in one sense, letting hens run there, keeping a few rabbits, drying her washing; and the like.' The alleged period of adverse possession began in 1948 when, in the view expressed by the Court of Appeal, 'any sensible and neighbourly person who exercised control over a piece of land and had not any particular use for it at the time would have given a licence to anybody who wanted to use it in the way the plaintiff did.' Lawton LJ thought therefore that the plaintiff must have realised that she was 'being allowed as of grace to carry on as before during these times of food shortage.'

In these cases the Court of Appeal applied a doctrine of implied licence as precluding *as a matter of law* the inception of any adverse possession by a stranger. In this respect the law of limitation has since been amended by the Limitation Amendment Act 1980, s. 4. This amendment, which now appears as paragraph 8(4) of Schedule 1 of the Limitation Act 1980, provides as follows:

For the purpose of determining whether a person occupying any land is in adverse possession of the land it shall not be assumed by implication of law that his occupation is by permission of the person entitled to the land merely by virtue of the fact that his occupation is not inconsistent with the latter's present or future enjoyment of the land[18].

This amendment may not, however, overturn the earlier decisions based

15 [1975] QB 94 at 114.
16 [1975] QB 94 at 103.
17 Court of Appeal Transcript No. 10A of 1977.
18 See Law Reform Committee 21st Report, *Final Report on Limitation of Actions* (Cmnd 6923, 1977), para 3.47ff.; (1977) 244 Estates Gazette 291, 375 (D. Brahams).

upon the concept of implied licence, since paragraph 8(4) goes on to state that

> This provision shall not be taken as prejudicing a finding to the effect that a person's occupation of any land is by implied permission of the person entitled to the land in any case where such a finding is justified on the actual facts of the case.

It is therefore open to the courts to reach similar conclusions in cases arising after 1980, based not upon an implication of law but upon a finding of fact[19].

(ii) *Intention to possess (animus possidendi)* The *animus possidendi* which is required to constitute 'possession' on the part of an adverse occupier was defined by Lindley MR in *Littledale v Liverpool College*[20] as the 'intention of excluding the owner as well as other people.' More recently, in *Powell v McFarlane*[1], Slade J indicated that *animus possidendi* involves

> the intention, in one's own name and on one's own behalf, to exclude the world at large, including the owner with the paper title if he be not himself the possessor, so far as is reasonably practicable and so far as the processes of the law will allow.

The paper owner or any other person with the right of possession of land will be readily assumed to have the requisite intention to possess unless the contrary is clearly proved. Thus even the slightest acts done by or on behalf of the paper owner will in practice be found to negative any supposed 'discontinuance' of his possession. But where the question arises whether a trespasser has acquired 'possession', it has been said that the courts will

> require clear and affirmative evidence that the trespasser, claiming that he has acquired possession, not only had the requisite intention to possess, but made such intention clear to the world. If his acts are open to more than one interpretation and he has not made it perfectly plain to the world at large by his actions or words that he has intended to exclude the owner as best he can, the courts will treat him as not having had the requisite *animus possidendi* and consequently as not having dispossessed the owner[2].

There are many cases in which the courts have rejected claims to possessory titles by trespassers on the ground that there was no sufficient evidence of the requisite intent[3]. Moreover, it is clear that when possession or dispossession has to be inferred from equivocal acts, the intention with which they are done becomes 'all-important'[4]. In *Powell v McFarlane*[5], Slade J confirmed that 'compelling evidence' of *animus* is required where a trespasser's user of land does not by itself clearly betoken an intention on his part to claim the land as his own to the exclusion of the true owner. In this case, Slade J declined to find the necessary *animus* proved on behalf of a plaintiff who, at the age of 14, had begun to use land for the purpose of grazing his cow.

19 See P. Jackson, (1980) 96 LQR 333 at 335f.; 'The Animus of Squatting'.
20 [1900] 1 Ch 19 at 23.
1 (1977) 38 P & CR 452 at 471f.
2 Ibid., 472.
3 See, e.g., *Littledale v Liverpool College* [1900] 1 Ch 19; *George Wimpey & Co Ltd v Sohn* [1967] Ch 487; *Tecbild Ltd v Chamberlain* (1969) 20 P & CR 633.
4 *Littledale v Liverpool College* [1900] 1 Ch 19 at 23 per Lindley MR.
5 (1977) 38 P & CR 452 at 476.

It has been said that in *Powell v McFarlane* Slade J imposed such onerous restrictions upon the notion of *animus possidendi* that 'few squatters, if any, could satisfy it.' Indeed, the heavy reliance upon a strict test of *animus* has allegedly emerged as 'yet another weapon in the armoury to be deployed against squatters[6].' It is this interface with the law of squatting which has made the determination of *animus possidendi* so crucial. As Slade J pointed out in *Powell v McFarlane*[7],

> The status of possession, after all, confers on the possessor valuable privileges *vis-à-vis* not only the world at large, but also the owner of the land concerned. It entitles him to maintain an action in trespass against anyone who enters the land without his consent, save only against a person having a better title to possession than himself. Furthermore it gives him one valuable element of protection even against the owner himself. Until the possession of land has actually passed to the trespasser, the owner may exercise the remedy of self-help against him. Once possession has passed to the trespasser, this remedy is not available to the owner, so that the intruder's position becomes that much more secure; if he will not then leave voluntarily, the owner will find himself obliged to bring proceedings for possession and for this purpose to prove his title.

A brief reference, in the context of *animus possidendi*, must be made to the question of proof of the requisite intent. It is generally irrelevant, in the absence of concealed fraud, that a paper owner is ignorant of the fact that he has been dispossessed[8]. However, in view of the drastic results of a change of possession, a person seeking to dispossess a paper owner must 'at least make his intentions sufficiently clear so that the owner, if present at the land, would clearly appreciate that the claimant is not merely a persistent trespasser, but is actually seeking to dispossess him[9].' Courts will attach 'very little evidential value' to retrospective assertions of the required *animus*, because 'they are obviously easily capable of being merely self-serving, while at the same time they may be very difficult for the paper owner positively to refute'[10]. For the same reason even contemporary declarations by an adverse occupier to the effect that he is intending to assert a claim to the land provide but little support for a claim of 'possession' at the relevant time unless they are specifically brought to the attention of the true owner[11]. In general, as Sachs LJ said in *Tecbild Ltd v Chamberlain*[12], 'intent has to be inferred from the acts themselves.'

The law of limitation was amended by the Limitation Amendment Act 1980 in order to cover the cases of fraud, concealment and mistake. This amendment has been consolidated in section 32(1) of the Limitation Act 1980, which provides that

> Subject to subsection (3) [of this section], where in the case of any action for which a period of limitation is prescribed by this Act, either—
> (*a*) the action is based upon the fraud of the defendant; or

6 P. Jackson (1980) 96 LQR 333 at 334.
7 (1977) 38 P & CR 452 at 476.
8 *Rains v Buxton* (1880) 14 Ch D 537.
9 *Powell v McFarlane* (1977) 38 P & CR 452 at 480.
10 Ibid., 476 per Slade J.
11 Ibid., 476 per Slade J.
12 (1969) 20 P & CR 633 at 643.

(*b*) any fact relevant to the plaintiff's right of action has been deliberately concealed from him by the defendant or
(*c*) the action is for relief from the consequences of a mistake;
the period of limitation shall not begin to run until the plaintiff has discovered the fraud, concealment or mistake (as the case may be) or could with reasonable diligence have discovered it[13].

(3) The effect of the Limitation Act 1980

The operation of the Limitation Act 1980 is negative in nature. The effluxion of the limitation period does not create a title in the adverse possessor; it merely prevents the paper owner from enforcing his own title. There is no *transfer* of title from the paper owner to the successful intruder, for the precise reason that the title of the paper owner is extinguished by the operation of the statute[14]. As the Court of Appeal made clear in *Tichborne v Weir*[15], the Limitation Act does not effect a 'parliamentary conveyance'. However, it is equally plain that the extinguishing effect of the Limitation Act and the positive effect of adverse possession, when placed in conjunction, have the consequence that the adverse possessor may claim a new estate of his own.

Title to land is always relative[16]. Title is secure only to the extent that no other person can assert any better claim. This brings about the consequence that if the paper owner whose title has been extinguished was a fee simple owner, the adverse possessor is by virtue of his long possession entitled to an estate in fee simple since nobody else can claim a better right than the paper owner whose right of recovery is now statute-barred and whose title is now extinguished. Thus, in the case of unregistered land, the adverse possessor is entitled to claim a legal estate in fee simple absolute.

In registered land, of course, it is not quite true to say that the title of the paper owner has been extinguished by the operation of the Limitation Act, because the paper owner remains registered as the proprietor in the Land Register. However, the Land Registration Act 1925 provides that where, if the land in question were not registered, the estate of the existing registered proprietor would have been extinguished, his estate in registered land shall be 'deemed to be held by the proprietor for the time being in trust for the person who, by virtue of the [Limitation] Acts, has acquired title against any proprietor[17].' Moreover, the adverse possessor of registered land may apply to be registered as proprietor of that land[18], and in the meantime his rights are regarded as an 'overriding interest' with reference to that land[19].

If the paper owner who has been dispossessed had merely a leasehold title rather than a freehold title in fee simple, the adverse possessor enjoys, by virtue

13 See Limitation Amendment Act 1980, s. 7. Protection is provided for innocent third parties who purchase property for valuable consideration (Limitation Act 1980, s. 32(3)).
14 Limitation Act 1980, s. 17.
15 (1892) 67 LT 735 at 737 per Lord Esher MR.
16 See p. 49, ante.
17 Land Registration Act 1925, s. 75(1).
18 Land Registration Act 1925, s. 75(2).
19 Land Registration Act 1925, s. 70(1)(f), p. 333, post.

of his long possession, a better claim than the leaseholder. After 12 years the leaseholder becomes statute-barred from recovering his land and his leasehold estate is extinguished. However, the adverse possessor's new estate is still inferior to that of the owner of the freehold reversion (i.e., the lessor of the land in question). The extinction of the lessee's title has no effect upon the lessor's title, since the lessor's right of action against the intruder does not accrue until the expiry of the term of the lease[20]. It is only at this point that the limitation period of 12 years begins to run against the paper owner of the freehold reversion as distinct from the paper owner of the leasehold title.

(4) The nature of possessory title

Precisely because there has been no transfer or assignment of title by the paper owner to the adverse possessor, the latter is not affected by certain rules of land law which would have impinged upon a transferee or assignee. Thus, for instance, a squatter (even after 12 years of adverse possession) cannot claim to take title free of equitable interests binding the land, because he can never establish status as a bona fide *purchaser* without notice. He has not *purchased* the land, but has taken title by operation of law. In this case, equitable interests such as restrictive covenants will be binding upon him[1], and this will be so regardless of whether those interests have been duly registered or protected by the incumbrancer[2]. Moreover, a squatter cannot be sued directly for rent or damages by a lessor on the ground of a breach of leasehold covenants, since he is not an *assignee* of any term of years and is therefore not covered by the doctrine of 'privity of estate[3]'. However, the adverse occupier may be subject to a right of re-entry exercisable by a landlord in respect of breach of covenant, and in this case the squatter cannot claim rights to relief against forfeiture[4].

Perhaps the most important feature of the adverse possessor's rights in the land which he occupies is indeed the fact that he acquires certain rights even before his possessory title has been completed. Even before the paper owner becomes statute-barred from recovery, the squatter acquires incipient rights in the land which are good against all the world except those persons who (like the paper owner) are meanwhile able to assert a better title. The squatter may assign his rights inter vivos or may dispose of them by will. Alternatively, his rights will devolve upon his next of kin if he dies intestate. An assignee from a squatter may count the period of possession by the squatter towards the period of 12 years of adverse possession which will be required to establish the completion of the limitation period in favour of the *assignee*[5].

20 Limitation Act 1980, Sch. 1, para. 4.
1 *Re Nisbet and Potts' Contract* [1906] 1 Ch 386. See F. W. Maitland, *Equity* (2nd edn., London 1936), p. 116.
2 See p. 620, post.
3 *Tichborne v Weir* (1892) 67 LT 735, p. 410, post.
4 *Tickner v Buzzacott* [1965] Ch 426, p. 408, post.
5 *Asher v Whitlock* (1865) LR 1 QB 1.

(5) Recovery of possession by the paper owner

Finally in this chapter we must deal briefly with the process by which the paper owner may attempt to assert his title in recovering land in respect of which a third party claims 'possession'. As we have seen, the law of limitation is such that any action for recovery may only be brought *before* the expiration of the limitation period. After the expiration of that period, the right of recovery becomes statute-barred and the title of the paper owner is extinguished.

The recovery of land by a paper owner has been rendered somewhat more controversial in an era when 'squatting' has become a common means of coercing political action or expressing political or other protest. The 'sit-in' has emerged as a standard non-violent method of demonstrating a particular viewpoint, whether the issue at stake be a proposed mass redundancy at the workplace, supposedly oppressive action taken by university authorities or the obscenity of empty office blocks at a time of severe homelessness. However, during recent years the judicial reaction to 'squatting' and 'sit-ins' has taken the form of a marked reinforcement of the legal power of the paper owner of the land concerned. The courts have not been prepared to endorse any social or political justification for the dispossession of a paper owner from 'his' property. The idea that the existing distribution of land may itself express or conceal inequity is not a notion which the courts have been ready to explore.

In *McPhail v Persons, Names Unknown*[6], a group of homeless persons secured entry to residential premises which had been left unoccupied and locked by the owner. The owner brought proceedings for the recovery of possession. In the Court of Appeal, Lord Denning MR defined a 'squatter' as 'one who, without any colour of right, enters upon an unoccupied house or land, intending to stay there as long as he can[7].' Lord Denning held that the Court could not entertain, by way of defence, a plea by a squatter that 'he was homeless and that this house or land was standing empty, doing nothing.' No such excuse could be of any avail in law, since, as Lord Denning himself had said in *Southwark London Borough Council v Williams*[8],

> If homelessness were once admitted as a defence to trespass, no one's house could be safe. . . . So the courts must, for the sake of law and order, take a firm stand. They must refuse to admit the plea of necessity to the hungry and the homeless: and trust that their distress will be relieved by the charitable and the good.

Indeed, far from being justifiable on grounds of a social or compassionate nature, the adverse occupation of residential premises is now made a criminal offence in certain circumstances by reason of the Criminal Law Act 1977. Under this Act, a criminal offence is committed by

> any person who is on any premises as a trespasser after having entered as such [and who] fails to leave those premises on being required to do so by or on behalf of—(a) a displaced

6 [1973] Ch 447. See A. M. Prichard, (1976) 40 Conv (NS) 255: 'Squatters—The Law and The Mythology'; (1973) 32 Cambridge LJ 220 (D. Macintyre).
7 [1973] Ch 447 at 456.
8 [1971] Ch 734 at 744.

residential occupier of the premises; or (b) an individual who is a protected intending occupier of the premises . . .[9]

Criminal trespass is punishable summarily by six months' imprisonment and/or a fine not exceeding £1,000[10].

There are three possible civil remedies available to a paper owner against persons who occupy his land.

(a) *The remedy of self-help*

It is quite clear that where strangers have taken over occupation of land belonging to a paper owner, that paper owner may exercise the remedy of self-help at any stage *before* the occupying strangers acquire 'possession' of the property in the sense required by the law of adverse possession. It is for precisely this reason that the inception of 'possession' by an intruder is so restrictively defined by the courts[11]. A householder who returns home from holiday to find his house occupied by squatters is entitled to throw the intruders out of his house without further ceremony. They were trespassers when they entered his house and they continued to be trespassers so long as they remained there awaiting the householder's return. The owner has not acquiesced in their presence in his house, and the vital consequence in law is that their occupation is not such as to enable them to allege that they ever gained 'possession' for the purpose of adverse possession[12]. In such a case, as Lord Denning observed in *McPhail v Persons, Names Unknown*[13],

> The owner is not obliged to go to the courts to obtain possession. He is entitled, if he so desires, to take the remedy into his own hands. He can go in himself and turn them out without the aid of the courts of law. This is not a course to be recommended because of the disturbance which might follow. But the legality of it is beyond question.

If the owner himself uses force to secure the eviction of the trespassers, he must not use more force than is reasonably necessary for the purpose. However, the exercise of self-help under these circumstances is subject to the important qualification that the owner must ensure that his actions are lawful under the Criminal Law Act 1977.

It is an offence under the Criminal Law Act 1977 for any person without lawful authority to use or threaten violence for the purpose of securing entry into any premises where, to his knowledge, there is someone present on those premises who is opposed to the entry[14]. This provision would apply, for instance,

9 Criminal Law Act 1977, s. 7(1). A 'protected intending occupier' is defined in s. 7(2). A 'displaced residential occupier' is defined in section 12(3), p. 105, post. See (1978) 37 Cambridge LJ 11.
10 Criminal Law Act 1977, s. 7(10).
11 See p. 100, ante.
12 'A trespasser may in any case be turned off land before he has gained possession and he does not gain possession until there has been something like acquiescence in the physical fact of his occupation on the part of the rightful owner' (Sir F. Pollock, *Torts* (15th edn., London 1951), p. 292).
13 [1973] Ch 447 at 456.
14 Criminal Law Act 1977, s. 6(1).

to a trespasser who breaks a door or window in order to secure entry, but not to one who merely forces a yale-type lock or window catch with a thin piece of metal[15]. However, a squatter who has entered premises by non-violent means may, by virtue simply of his de facto possession of the property, be entitled to resist trespass by others. His claims must, of course, give way in the face of the superior claim of the real owner to regain possession. The Criminal Law Act 1977 provides a defence to any charge of violent entry for any person who is kept out of his own living accommodation by trespassers. Such a person has a defence to a charge under section 6 of the Act if he can prove that he is a 'displaced residential occupier' seeking to secure access to residential premises from which he has been excluded by a trespasser[16]. Apart from the case where the displaced occupier is himself a trespasser[17], the status of 'displaced residential occupier' is defined as attaching to 'any person who was occupying any premises as a residence immediately before being excluded from occupation by anyone who entered those premises . . . as a trespasser'[18]. Such a person continues to rank as a 'displaced residential occupier' so long as he continues to be excluded from occupation of the premises by the original trespasser or by any subsequent trespasser.

It must never be forgotten that the 'possession' of a lawful occupier (e.g., a tenant or licensee) may not be terminated by recourse to the remedy of self-help, even where the interest granted to the occupier has duly expired. Once 'possession' has been enjoyed by a tenant or licensee the occupier cannot be evicted except by due process of law. In such cases a criminal offence is committed by any person who seeks to secure the eviction of the occupier by any means other than that of court order for possession[19].

(b) *The remedy by action for possession*

Although the law provides a displaced owner with the remedy of self-help in certain circumstances, this is not usually a course to be encouraged. As Lord Denning MR said in *McPhail v Persons, Names Unknown*[20],

> In a civilised society, the courts should themselves provide a remedy which is speedy and effective: and thus make self-help unnecessary. The courts of common law have done this for centuries. The owner is entitled to go to the court and obtain an order that the owner 'do recover' the land, and to issue a writ of possession immediately. That was the practice in the old action of ejectment which is well described by Sir William Blackstone in his *Commentaries*, 8th edn. (1778), vol. III, pp. 200–205 and Appendix No. II; and by Maitland in his *Equity* (1909), pp. 352–354. So far as I can discover, the courts of common law never suspended the order for possession.

The action for possession has thus become the traditional means by which a

15 See Law Commission, *Report on Conspiracy and Criminal Law Reform* (Law Com No. 76, 1976), para. 2.61.
16 Criminal Law Act 1977, s. 6(3).
17 Criminal Law Act 1977, s. 12(4).
18 Criminal Law Act 1977, s. 12(3).
19 See p. 470, post.
20 [1973] Ch 447 at 457.

displaced owner can dislodge trespassers from his property. However, it became obvious in decisions reached during the late 1960s and early 1970s that the conventional possession procedure was subject to certain disadvantages. The procedure was ineffective where the occupiers of premises were unidentifiable and were not therefore named as defendants in the possession proceedings[1]. Nor could a possession order be made if one squatter followed another in quick succession. These technical defects were remedied by a reformulation of the rules of court, a matter which is dealt with under the next heading.

(c) *The remedy by summons*

Under the amended rules of court, as introduced in 1970[2], the law now lends very substantial assistance to land-owners who are dispossessed by trespassers or squatters. The land-owner may invoke a speedy remedy by summons against any person who occupies his land without his consent. He may issue an originating summons claiming possession even though he cannot ascertain the identity of the squatter. This is known as the 'fast possession action' under RSC Ord. 113 (in the High Court) and under CCR Ord. 26 (in the county court). The court may make an order for possession seven days after the service of the summons, and even this period may be shortened in cases of urgency. The court has no discretion to withhold or suspend the order for possession once the case for possession has been established. As Lord Denning indicated in *McPhail v Persons, Names Unknown*[3],

> RSC Ord. 113, of the High Court and Ord. 26 in the county court are quite clear. A summons can be issued for possession against squatters even though they cannot be identified by name and even though, as one squatter goes, another comes in. Judgment can be obtained summarily. It is an order that the plaintiffs 'do recover' possession. That order can be enforced by a writ of possession immediately. It is an authority under which any one who is squatting on the premises can be turned out at once. There is no provision for giving any time. The court cannot give any time. It must, at the behest of the owner, make an order for recovery of possession. It is then for the owner to give such time as he thinks right to the squatters. They must make their appeal to his goodwill and consideration, and not to the courts.

It is clear, moreover, that the procedure by way of summons may be used to recover possession on the termination of an expired licence[4]. There was also a suggestion in 1980 that the summons procedure should be extended to the recovery of possession in respect of tenancies covered by the Rent Acts, but this proposal proved to be so controversial that it was eventually abandoned as politically unfeasible[5].

It has been established that an order for possession under the procedure by

1 See *Re Wykeham Terrace, Brighton, Sussex, Ex parte Territorial Auxiliary and Volunteer Reserve Association for the South East* [1971] Ch 204.
2 Summary Proceedings for Possession of Land; Rules of the Supreme Court (Amendment No. 2) 1970 (S.I. 1970/944).
3 [1973] Ch 447 at 458.
4 *Greater London Council v Jenkins* [1975] 1 WLR 155.
5 See (1980) LAG Bulletin 201.

way of summons may extend to a larger area of the owner's property than is adversely affected by the occupation in respect of which relief is sought. In *University of Essex v Djemal*[6], for instance, a group of university students occupied the university's administrative offices as a protest. Faced with a summons under RSC Ord. 113, they vacated the occupied premises but threatened to take further direct action if the university did not agree to their demands. The university continued with legal proceedings, and Walton J made an order for possession under RSC Ord. 113, but limited the order to that part of the university premises which had been occupied[7]. The Court of Appeal took the view that RSC Ord. 113 confers

> a jurisdiction directed to protecting the right of the owner of property to the possession of the whole of his property, uninterfered with by unauthorised adverse possession[8].

Because there was a threat that the students might occupy other parts of the university's premises, the Court of Appeal extended Walton J's possession order to cover the whole of the university's premises.

6 [1980] 1 WLR 1301.
7 The part last occupied had been Level 6 of the Social and Comparative Studies building.
8 [1980] 1 WLR 1301 at 1304 per Buckley LJ.

PART II

Unregistered conveyancing

CHAPTER 4

Land charges

In previous chapters we have established that proprietary rights in land may be classified as either legal or equitable rights. The primary rule of land law dictates that legal rights bind the world irrespective of notice[1]. Legal rights thus require no artificial protection against third party purchasers: their integrity is inviolable. The same, however, is not true of equitable rights in land. In the event of a transfer of the legal title of land, equitable rights in or over that land are subject to defeat at the hands of 'Equity's Darling'—the bona fide purchaser of a legal estate for value without notice of the rights in question.

In the context of unregistered land, the insecurity which therefore afflicts equitable rights would be quite intolerable were it not for the fact that the 1925 property legislation provides two important devices which are designed to preserve equitable rights precisely in the situation of transactions with third parties. We have already seen that 'family' equitable interests (e.g., the interests of beneficiaries behind a trust for sale or strict settlement) may be protected by the consequences of 'overreaching'[2]. In other words, the beneficiaries may regard the transfer of the legal title with indifference, since their equitable claims attach henceforth to the proceeds of that sale, rather than to the land itself and to the rents and profits derived from the land. In effect, all that has happened is that the nature of the investment—the character of the trust property—has undergone transformation. In reality (if not perhaps in legal theory[3]), the beneficiaries' rights are swept off the land and on to the capital proceeds of sale. The third party purchaser takes the legal estate in the land free of such rights. In this way, security for the equitable interests is coupled with facility for the purchaser.

Protection for 'commercial' equitable interests in unregistered land is provided by other means[4]. For this purpose the 1925 legislation adapts the traditional doctrine of notice, by ensuring that the only acceptable form of notice as far as a third party purchaser is concerned consists now of the formal registration of the 'commercial' equitable rights in question. This system of

1 In registered land, however, it is true that even legal rights require to be entered on the Land Register in order to be fully effective, p. 324, post.

2 See p. 74, ante.

3 See p. 220, post.

4 The protection available in respect of commercial equitable rights in *registered* land is discussed elsewhere, p. 326, post. The machinery of registration provided by the Land Charges Act 1972 is inapplicable to registered land (see Land Charges Act 1972, s. 14(1)), but, as we shall see, commercial equitable rights rank in registered land as protectible 'minor interests' and sometimes even as 'overriding interests', p. 345, post.

registration is known as registration of 'land charges'[5]. By registering his commercial equitable interest as a species of land charge, the equitable owner effectively utilises the element of publicity inherent in formal registration, thereby fixing the world with statutory notice of his right. He thus forecloses the possibility that any subsequent purchaser will ever claim to have bought the legal estate in the encumbered land *without* notice of his equitable interest. Once registered his equitable interest remains binding on the land into whosesoever hands the legal estate may pass.

Registration of land charges thus provides an ingenious means of combining security for various kinds of equitable owner with facility for third party purchasers. It is the task of this chapter to examine more closely the statutory machinery of land charge registration.

1. THE BASIC CONCEPT OF REGISTRATION

(1) The process of registration

The basic concept of land charge registration is simple. The owner of a commercial equitable interest falling within one of the classes of registrable interest under the Land Charges Act 1972 may register his interest in the Land Charges Register[6]. The interest must be registered 'in the name of the estate owner whose estate is intended to be affected[7].' Such registration of a 'land charge' is therefore possible only in relation to land of which the title is not registered—hence the apparent paradox that a land charge is registered in *unregistered* land.

It is vital, however, that registration of a land charge be entered in the name of 'the estate owner whose estate is intended to be affected'. This statutory requirement may cause difficulty for an incumbrancer who is unaware that he is dealing with a sub-vendor. Take, for example, the situation where A (the

5 Registration of 'land charges' must be carefully distinguished from registration of 'local land charges'. A register of local land charges (which usually relate to such public matters as planning permissions or local government activities affecting property) is maintained by the relevant local authority in respect of both registered and unregistered land situated within its area.

6 Throughout this chapter reference is made to the Land Charges Act 1972. However, at several crucial points, the provisions of the Land Charges Act 1972 are correlated with the equivalent sections in the Land Charges Act 1925, which still governs land charges matters arising before the commencement of the 1972 Act.

7 Land Charges Act 1972, s. 3(1). The function of the Registrar in registering land charges is, it has been said, 'purely ministerial' (see S. M. Cretney (1969) 32 MLR 477 at 486f.: 'Land Law and Conveyancing Reforms'). No inquiry is made at the time of registration into the validity of the charge registered, and there is no requirement that the estate owner concerned be informed of the registration (see, e.g., *Taylor v Taylor* [1968] 1 All ER 843). Land charge registration may therefore be used for tactical reasons in order to impose an apparent (but entirely fictitious) blot upon an owner's title. Such a registration may well delay or frustrate a sale of the property affected, and requires that the estate owner take positive action in securing a vacation of the entry on the register (see, e.g., *Georgiades v Edward Wolfe & Co Ltd* [1964] 3 All ER 433; *Rawlplug Co Ltd v Kamvale Properties Ltd* (1968) 20 P & CR 32; S. M. Cretney (1968) 118 NLJ 1167: 'Land Charges').

owner of a legal estate in fee simple in unregistered land) makes a contract to sell that estate to B. Before the appropriate conveyance is executed, B may contract (by way of sub-sale) to convey the same legal estate to C. There are here two registrable 'estate contracts' as defined in section 2(4) of the Land Charges Act 1972[8]. The first exists between A and B, and consists in the terms of section 2(4) of 'a contract by an estate owner . . . to convey . . . a legal estate . . .' The second exists between B and C, and consists, again in the terms of section 2(4), of 'a contract . . . by a person entitled at the date of the contract to have a legal estate conveyed to him to convey . . . a legal estate . . .' It is necessary that both estate contracts should be registered against the name of A, who remains 'the estate owner' throughout. If C, unaware that he is caught up in a sub-sale, registers *his* estate contract against B, that registration is a nullity and can be vacated. If in such a case A then duly conveys the legal estate to B, and B in breach of contract conveys that estate not to C but to X, C's only remedy is in damages payable by B in respect of breach of contract[9]. In other words, C's land charge cannot bind X, for C's remedy is *in personam* and not *in rem*[10].

(2) The effect of registration

Once a proper registration has been effected against the name of the appropriate estate owner, that registration is, in the terms of section 198(1) of the Law of Property Act 1925

> deemed to constitute actual notice . . . of the fact of such registration, to all persons and for all purposes connected with the land affected . . .

This provision has great force. It has even been held that it overrides, for instance, the protection apparently afforded a lessee by section 44(5) of the Law of Property Act 1925[11]. In *White v Bijou Mansions Ltd*[12], Simonds J took the view that, by virtue of section 198(1), a land charge registered by a stranger against the freehold title of a lessor is binding upon even a lessee or sublessee regardless of the fact that the latter are not entitled to investigate the superior title. By reason of the statutory fiction, the due registration of any land charge is deemed (in the widest terms possible) to constitute *actual notice* of the equitable interest concerned.

8 See p. 135, post.
9 See *Barrett v Hilton Developments Ltd* [1975] Ch 237; (1975) 39 Conv (NS) 65 (F. R. Crane).
10 There is, of course, no legal *duty* to register a land charge. It therefore follows that any damages recovered by C in respect of B's breach of contract will not be reduced in view of C's improper registration (see *Wright v Dean* [1948] Ch 686 at 696 per Wynn-Parry J).
11 Under section 44 of the Law of Property Act 1925, an intending lessee or assignee is not entitled to examine the title to the freehold or to a leasehold reversion connected with the interest which he proposes to purchase. However, section 44(5), overturning the rule established in *Patman v Harland* (1881) 17 Ch D 353, provides that such a lessee or assignee 'shall not . . . be deemed to be affected with notice of any matter or thing of which, if he had contracted that such title should be furnished, he might have had notice.'
12 [1937] Ch 610 at 619.

(3) The effect of non-registration

Just as the effect of registration is phrased in absolute terms in section 198(1) of the Law of Property Act 1925, so the effect of non-registration of a registrable interest is specified in similarly draconian language. The precise consequence of non-registration depends upon the category of land charge concerned, but the general effect of a failure to register a registrable land charge is that the registrable interest is rendered void against certain classes of purchaser.

A land charge of Class A, Class B, Class C (i), (ii) and (iii), or Class F is rendered 'void' for want of registration

> as against a purchaser of the land charged with it, or of any interest in such land . . .[13]

However, land charges of Class C (iv) and Class D are rendered void for want of registration against a somewhat narrower category of purchasers. Such a charge becomes 'void' in the event of non-registration merely

> as against a purchaser for money or money's worth of a legal estate in the land charged with it . . .[14]

Thus, non-registration renders a general equitable charge (which belongs to Class C (iii)) void as against a purchaser of *any* estate or interest—legal or equitable—in the land, but renders an estate contract (which belongs to Class C (iv)) void only as against a purchaser of a legal estate for money or money's worth. Unregistered land charges remain binding upon third party donees of the land affected (i.e., upon those persons who have not given any valuable consideration in respect of the transaction of transfer).

The statutory consequence of non-registration is therefore clearly spelt out. Furthermore, in all cases where a land charge is declared void by statute for non-registration, it is quite irrelevant that, at the date of the conveyance, the purchaser had from another source actual express knowledge of the existence of the registrable but unregistered interest. The rigour of the rules of land charge registration is thus maintained, as we shall see in the following section.

(4) The irrelevance of the doctrine of notice

It has always been a characteristic feature of the property lawyer's thinking that he should prefer certainty over justice in the ascertainment of proprietary rights. The property legislation of 1925 was heavily influenced by this policy preference—not least in the approach adopted in respect of land charge registration. The major objective of the 1925 legislation was the simplification of conveyancing, and this objective is, in the context of land charge registration, more effectively secured if the consequences of registration and non-registration are absolutely clear-cut and conclusive. It is for this reason that the traditional doctrine of notice is displaced in respect of land charges by the 1925 legislation—or, more accurately, is drastically adapted and modified.

13 Land Charges Act 1972, s. 4(2), (5), (8) [Land Charges Act 1925, s. 13(1)(2)(3)]. For reference to the Classes defined in the Land Charges Act, see later, p. 134ff., post.
14 Land Charges Act 1972, s. 4(6) [Land Charges Act 1925, s. 13(2)].

Under the Law of Property Act 1925 and the Land Charges Act 1925, the orthodox doctrine of notice suffered modification to the extent that registration of a land charge has now become the *only* recognised form of notice to third parties in respect of wide categories of commercial equitable interest. The law in this area thus tends (as generally in property law) towards ensuring certainty rather than achieving justice. A commercial equitable interest affecting unregistered land is *either* duly registered as a land charge and is therefore binding *or* is not so registered and is therefore void.

The overall efficiency of the system of land charge registration is further promoted by the rule that a purchaser is unaffected by notice of any registrable interest where that notice is obtained by him outside the register of land charges. Thus even actual express knowledge of a registrable but unregistered interest will not suffice to bind a purchaser. According to section 199(1)(i) of the Law of Property Act 1925,

> A purchaser shall not be prejudicially affected by notice of . . . any instrument or matter capable of registration under the Land Charges Act [1972] . . . which is void or not enforceable as against him under that Act . . . by reason of the non-registration thereof.

As Professor H. W. R. Wade once said[15],

> The policy of 1925 was to abandon the equitable principle of notice in favour of the mechanical principle of registration. This was a shift from a moral to an a-moral basis . . .

A dramatic illustration of the rigour with which actual knowledge of an unregistered charge is excluded from relevance is found in *Hollington Bros Ltd v Rhodes*[16]. Here L contracted to grant a lease to T; this contract was in fact an 'estate contract' registrable as a land charge of Class C (iv)[17]. T neglected to register the land charge. L then conveyed the legal estate in the property to P, expressly 'subject to and with the benefit of such tenancies as may affect the premises.'

Hollington Bros Ltd v Rhodes

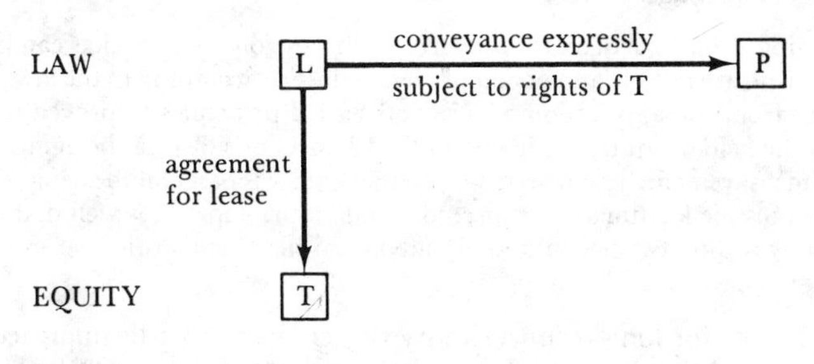

Fig. 17

Notwithstanding that P thus had actual express knowledge of the rights of T, P gave T notice to quit the premises and thereby forced T to negotiate a new lease.

15 (1956) 14 Cambridge LJ 216 at 227: 'Land Charges Registration Reviewed'.
16 [1951] 2 TLR 691.
17 See p. 135, post.

In proceedings subsequently brought by T, Harman J held that T's estate contract was void as against P by reason of its non-registration and that it was quite irrelevant that P had actual knowledge from another source of the existence of tenancies affecting the premises. According to Harman J,

> The fact is that it was the policy of the framers of the 1925 legislation to get rid of equitable rights of this sort unless registered . . . [A]s under [section 4 of the Land Charges Act 1972] . . . an unregistered estate contract is void, and under section 199 of the Law of Property Act 1925 the purchaser is not to be prejudicially affected by it, I do not see how that which is void and which is not to prejudice the purchaser can be validated by some equitable doctrine[18].

Thus it was that the purchaser in *Hollington Bros Ltd v Rhodes* was able to take his interest free of the adverse claims of the existing tenant. The result is indeed ethically unsatisfying. The price paid by the purchaser had been calculated with reference to the existing tenancy, but he was enabled to repudiate the tenancy and to force the tenant to re-negotiate the lease at an inflated rent.

Professor Wade has spoken of 'the defiance of ethics which occurs when a purchaser with *actual* notice is allowed to disregard a third party's rights.' In his view, such an outcome imposes 'an unreasonable penalty on the venial fault of non-registration[19].' Nevertheless the result in *Hollington Bros Ltd v Rhodes* at least makes the position clear-cut. No difficult enquiry is required into the state of mind of the individual purchaser in each transaction. Either the equitable owner registers his interest and makes it binding, or he fails to register—in which case his interest almost always becomes void as against a third party purchaser. Efficiency is bought at the expense of fairness, and this is a trade-off which commands the approval of most hard-headed property lawyers. The latter would argue in any event that certainty and justice are not independent and absolute but interactive and conditional. When viewed in the dimension of time, certainty may indeed be seen to be an intrinsic component of justice. The classical position of the property lawyer was clearly expressed in *Cowcher v Cowcher*[20], where Bagnall J observed that

> in determining rights, particularly property rights, the only justice that can be attained by mortals, who are fallible and not omniscient, is justice according to the law; the justice which flows from the application of sure and settled principles to proved or admitted facts. So in the field of equity the length of the Chancellor's foot has been measured or is capable of measurement. This does not mean that equity is past childbearing; simply that its progeny must be legitimate—by precedent out of principle. It is well that this should be so; otherwise no lawyer could safely advise on his client's title and every quarrel would lead to a law suit.

In its concern for long-term certainty rather than short-term justice, the law of property (and particularly the law relating to land charges) is thus largely indifferent to moral disparities between litigants. When viewed in terms of the

18 [1951] 2 TLR 691 at 696. See also *Coventry Permanent Economic Building Society v Jones* [1951] 1 All ER 901 at 904 per Harman J.
19 (1956) 14 Cambridge LJ 216 at 217.
20 [1972] 1 WLR 425 at 430.

Gesellschaft perspective[1], it is not necessarily bad faith to take advantage of the folly of one who neglects to protect an interest which is registrable under the Land Charges Act[2]. Nevertheless it is difficult to remain entirely indifferent to the ethical and practical aspects of the relationship of purchaser and equitable owner. Here, for a moment, we leave the law as it is in order to consider the law as it ought to be. Let us look briefly at two possible means of making the operation of the system of land charge registration more 'just'.

(a) *Protection for actual occupation*

It has been suggested that non-registration of a land charge should not have the effect of rendering void a registrable incumbrance belonging to a person who is *in actual occupation of the land.* Persons in actual possession of land may well have equitable interests of a fairly short-term nature in relation to which it is unrealistic to expect the vigilance of registration. The ageing widow who occupies property by virtue of an agreement for a lease has, in technical terms, a registrable estate contract. However, it seems unreasonable that the protection of her interest should depend on the registration of a Class C (iv) land charge—a registration which, in such circumstances and in the absence of legal advice, the lay person is highly unlikely to effect. It seems much more reasonable that such a person should be able to rely, for her protection, upon her actual occupation of the land. After all, as Professor Wade has pointed out[3], 'possession is the strongest possible title to security.' The fact of physical possession indicates to a purchaser just as effectively as the fact of registration that there is a possibility that the occupier has a proprietary interest of some kind in the land[4].

Under the law as it now stands, however, even the fact of actual occupation provides no protection for an incumbrancer who fails—albeit quite excusably—to register a land charge in respect of his interest. This is so even though section 14 of the Law of Property Act 1925 provides that

> This Part of this Act shall not prejudicially affect the interest of any person in possession or in actual occupation of land to which he may be entitled in right of such possession or occupation.

It was once thought that this provision enabled an incumbrancer in actual occupation to escape the consequences of non-registration[5], but it is now generally agreed that the section is 'too restricted in its effect to be of help[6].' Herein lies an irony, since the restriction which disables section 14 from giving assistance to the present problem is precisely the fact that it applies expressly

1 See p. 16, ante.
2 For discussion of the equivalent point in the context of registration of title, see later, p. 327, post.
3 (1956) 14 Cambridge LJ 216 at 228. For further reference to the importance of physical possession of land, see earlier, p. 48, ante.
4 This idea is effectively recognised, in the context of registration of title, in section 70(1)(g) of the Land Registration Act 1925, p. 334ff., post.
5 See, for instance, *Bendall v McWhirter* [1952] 2 QB 466 at 483 per Denning LJ.
6 H. W. R. Wade (1956) 14 Cambridge LJ 216 at 228. See also *Coventry Permanent Economic Building Society v Jones* [1951] 1 All ER 901 at 903f. per Harman J; R. E. Megarry (1952) 68 LQR 379, 385: 'The Deserted Wife's Right to Occupy the Matrimonial Home'.

only to Part I of the Law of Property Act 1925. The consequences of non-registration of land charges are spelt out in a separate statute—the Land Charges Act—and those consequences cannot therefore be muted by the saving provision contained in section 14 for the benefit of persons in possession.

The Law of Property Act 1925 is, of course, a consolidating statute: it consolidates the provisions contained in the Law of Property Act 1922. However, the 1922 Act was the historical source not merely of the provisions consolidated in the Law of Property Act 1925. It contained also the provisions which in 1925 were diverted into a separate statute—the Land Charges Act 1925, i.e., the provisions which established the effects of registration and non-registration of land charges. Thus, when section 33 of the Law of Property Act 1922 (which precisely foreshadows the terms of section 14 of the Law of Property Act 1925) provided that nothing in 'Part I' of the 1922 Act should 'prejudicially affect' the rights of actual occupiers, this saving provision clearly applied inter alia to the consequences of non-registration of land charges as laid down in section 3(5) of the 1922 Act. It seems that the formal restructuring of the 1922 property legislation, by diverting the land charges provisions into a separate statute in 1925, brought about a perhaps unintended substantive change in the law, by depriving the land charges provisions of the protection which was eventually incorporated as section 14 of the Law of Property Act 1925.

The substantive change has, however, occurred. It is now impossible to plead the Law of Property Act 1922 in support of the rights of actual occupiers of unregistered land who have failed to register their incumbrances as land charges. In terms of the law currently applicable, the fact of actual occupation of unregistered land is quite irrelevant to the fate of unregistered land charges. This is so even though the law of land charges thus discloses a 'glaring' anomaly when compared with the rules relating to land with registered title[7]. In the latter context, 'overriding' protection is given to

> the rights of every person in actual occupation of the land or in receipt of the rents and profits thereof, save where enquiry is made of such person and the rights are not disclosed[8].

(b) *Relevance of actual but not constructive notice*

Another possible means of making the operation of the land charges system more 'just' is found in the suggestion of Professor Wade that

> Between the two extremes of making all notice relevant, or all notice irrelevant, lies the middle road of making actual notice relevant, but not constructive notice. The benefits of registration can be obtained, and unconscionable results also avoided, by providing that an unregistered charge shall be void against a purchaser provided that he or his agent (acting as such and in the same transaction) had not actual notice of it[9].

7 According to Professor Wade, it is 'capricious to have two such radically differing principles for protecting owners of charges who are in possession.' See (1956) 14 Cambridge LJ 216 at 228.
8 Land Registration Act 1925, s. 70(1)(g), p. 334, post.
9 (1956) 14 Cambridge LJ 216 at 227. According to Professor Wade, the one case where even constructive notice ought to be respected occurs where the owner of the unregistered charge is in possession of the land.

This approach is not unknown in other systems of registration for legal purposes. We shall see[10] that, in one of the more controversial developments in the law of registered title, actual notice on the part of a purchaser has been held to disable that purchaser from relying on the non-registration of an equitable interest. The technique of according relevance to actual but not constructive notice has been adopted in other registration areas (e.g., in the law relating to the registration of rights in patents[11]). Yet, in the context of registration of land charges, a consensus has been reached that even actual express knowledge of an unregistered charge will not bind the purchaser. However, as R. J. Smith has said,

> it is clear that purchasers with actual notice pose real problems for registration systems ... Is the greater certainty and ease of conveyancing, resulting from protecting a purchaser with actual notice, sufficient to off-set any sense of injustice in the result in individual cases? The question is not an easy one, but it must be faced; it is submitted that the purchaser should be protected[12].

The issue concerned here was most recently discussed in *Midland Bank Trust Co Ltd v Green*[13] (see *Fig.* 18). Here W, who owned land in fee simple, granted his son, G, an option to purchase the land at a specified price amounting to a total expenditure of £22,500. G failed to register his option as an estate contract under Class C (iv) of the Land Charges Act. Six years later, in consequence of some family discord, W sought to revoke the option which he had earlier granted to G. Upon discovering that the option had not yet been registered by G, W conveyed the land (which was then worth £40,000) to his own wife, E, for a consideration of merely £500, with the clear intention of defeating the unregistered option. G, who had at all material times been a tenant in occupation of the land, then purported to exercise the option. His mother declined to sell the land in accordance with the option, and G began proceedings against his father

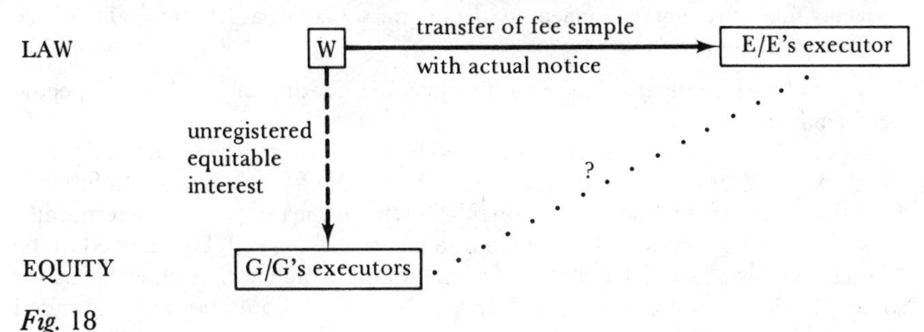

Fig. 18

10 See p. 328, post.

11 According to section 33(1) of the Patents Act 1977, a person who claims to have acquired the property in a patent takes priority over any person who claims to have acquired that property by virtue of an earlier transaction. However, he enjoys priority only if the earlier transaction was not registered in the register of patents *and* if, at the time of the later transaction, he 'did not know of the earlier transaction ...' Thus actual but not constructive notice is relevant in determining the issue of priority.

12 (1980) 96 LQR 8 at 11: 'Land Charges and Actual Notice: Justice More or Less Fanciful'.

13 [1980] Ch 590 CA; revsd. [1981] 2 WLR 28, HL.

and the executors of his mother's estate—his mother having meanwhile died—claiming a declaration that the option was binding on his mother's estate and an order of specific performance of the option. G then died and the action was continued by his executors, the plaintiff bank. E's executors pleaded in their defence that the conveyance to E had been a bona fide sale and that E had been a purchaser of a legal estate for money or money's worth for the purpose of what is now section 4(6) of the Land Charges Act 1972.

By the time the action reached the courts, the value of the land in dispute had inflated to over £400,000, a figure which, as Lord Denning MR pointed out in the Court of Appeal, represented a 'prize worth a fight'[14]. Large consequences flowed from the view to be taken by the courts, since a decision against E's executors would effectively enable G's widow and children to buy the land for £22,500 in accordance with the terms of the option (for which G had originally paid W the sum of £1). A decision in favour of E's executors would mean that the land would be sold and the proceeds of sale divided between the five children of W and E, with the result that G's widow and children would receive only 20% of the value of the land.

At first instance Oliver J held that the land charge unregistered by G was not binding upon the estate of E. In other words, Oliver J took the orthodox property lawyer's view that E was a purchaser of a legal estate for money or money's worth against whom G's unregistered option was statutorily void. Oliver J, in coming to this conclusion, stated:

> That there may have been some ulterior motive for the transaction does not . . . make the transaction other than it was. Obviously a substantial and indeed an almost overwhelming element of gift existed here but in my judgment that cannot matter . . . The conclusion I have reached . . . is one which I reach with regret, because as it seems to me [G] had a clear legal right which was deliberately frustrated by his parents in breach of the contract created by the option. Nevertheless I cannot, with the best will in the world, allow my subjective moral judgment to stand in the way of what I apprehend to be the clear meaning of the statutory provisions[15].

Oliver J therefore dismissed the claims for a declaration and decree of specific performance.

This decision was subsequently reversed by a majority in the Court of Appeal. Lord Denning MR, in giving judgment in favour of G's executors, refused to hold that E had given 'money or money's worth' for the purpose of the immunity now conferred by section 4(6) of the Land Charges Act 1972. He referred to the 'grotesquely small sum' of £500 paid by E for land which at that time was worth some £40,000, and stated his belief that the legislature could not have intended

> to protect a purchaser who paid far less than the land was worth in collusion with the vendor. If that were the case, it would open the door to fraud of the worst description. All that a man who had contracted to sell his land would have to do to get out of his bargain would be to convey it to his wife for a very small sum. I know that, in the ordinary law of contract, we never enquire into the adequacy of the consideration. But this is different.

14 [1980] Ch 590 at 623.
15 [1980] Ch 590 at 613.

'Money or money's worth' means a fair and reasonable value in money or money's worth: not an undervalue: particularly a gross undervalue as here[16].

However, Lord Denning MR was not prepared to decide the case simply on the ground that E had not been a 'purchaser of a legal estate for money or money's worth' within the statutory formula. He went further and held that the statutory immunity from an unregistered land charge can never protect a purchaser 'when the sale to him is done in fraud of the holder of the estate contract[17].' He quoted his own words in *Lazarus Estates Ltd v Beasley*[18]:

No court in this land will allow a person to keep an advantage which he has obtained by fraud... Fraud unravels everything.

In Lord Denning's view,

Fraud in this context covers any dishonest dealing done so as to deprive unwary innocents of their rightful dues. The marks of it are transactions done stealthily and speedily in secret for no sufficient consideration.

As the Master of the Rolls indicated, all the characteristics of 'fraud' so defined appeared in the conveyance made in this case by W to E. G's parents had 'hatched a plot... [of which] the predominant purpose was to damage [G].' An absurdly low price (one eightieth of the current market value) had been paid, and the deliberate object of the transaction had been to deprive G of the benefit of his option. Such a result would, said Lord Denning, have been 'most unfair to G, his widow and children, who have farmed [the land] all their lives, and ought in justice to be able to remain there[19].' A fraud had been perpetrated upon G, and in the view of Lord Denning neither E nor the executors of her estate could be allowed to take advantage of it to the prejudice of G, his widow or his children. Lord Denning therefore ruled that E's estate took the land subject to the option, albeit unregistered, and that her executors should honour it by transferring the disputed land to G's estate.

It is clear that Lord Denning's judgment gave weight to subjective perceptions of justice in terms of family sentiment and redistributive fairness as between family members. The Master of the Rolls effectively applied the land charges legislation as if it were an integral part of the general law of succession. He was therefore able to negate the effect of the conveyance by W to E on grounds of fairness towards other family members (i.e., G, his widow and his children) in much the same way as it is open to the courts under the Inheritance (Provision for Family and Dependants) Act 1975 to make provision for statutory

16 [1980] Ch 590 at 624. It was Sir Stanley Rees who pointed out (at 632) that 'in view of the powerful comments which have so properly been made about the inadequacy of the £500 actually paid by [E] for the farm, it is perhaps slightly ironic to observe that for the wholly nominal, and perhaps even illusory, sum of £1 [G] gained an option to buy [the land] for half of its true value which was then £40,000 and is now said to be worth ten times that sum. Yet the law of contract in relation to consideration is such that no one has argued that the option was a sham or on any ground unenforceable.'

17 [1980] Ch 590 at 624.

18 [1956] 1 QB 702 at 712.

19 [1980] Ch 590 at 622.

dependants in derogation of adverse testamentary dispositions by a deceased person[20]. In other words, Lord Denning dispensed family justice rather than the justice of the hard-nosed property lawyer who sees only the pragmatic commercial realities of the situation.

Like Lord Denning, Eveleigh LJ was prepared to accept that the consideration for W's conveyance to E was a sham. In his view,

The true transaction . . . was a gift coupled with a token of £500 sought to be included to meet the requirements of [section 4] of the Land Charges Act [1972]. . . In the present case I do not say that the conveyance was a deceptive form but I do think that the statement of the consideration was deceptive. Money would never have passed had it not been thought necessary in order to satisfy [section 4]. Its role in this transaction was simply a token. I do not regard the transaction as a conveyance following a contract of sale of the land. I regard it as a conveyance giving effect to a gift coupled with reference to a payment of £500 in an attempt to secure the advantage of [section 4][1].

In this way Eveleigh LJ ruled that E could not claim the immunity now contained in section 4(6) of the Land Charges Act 1972 on the ground that the disputed conveyance had not been made 'for' money or money's worth within the terms of that subsection. E could not therefore claim the protection conferred upon 'a purchaser of a legal estate for money or money's worth.'

Eveleigh LJ also declined to allow E's estate the benefit of section 199(1)(i) of the Law of Property Act 1925[2]. According to this provision, a 'purchaser' shall not be prejudicially affected by any charge registrable under the Land Charges Act 1972 which is void under that Act by reason of non-registration. Eveleigh LJ had regard to the fact that a 'purchaser' for this purpose is defined as 'a purchaser in good faith for valuable consideration. . .[3]' and that, furthermore, 'valuable consideration' is itself defined as not including 'a nominal consideration in money[4].' In Eveleigh LJ's judgment, E could not invoke section 199(1)(i) because she was not a purchaser in good faith and because the purchase price of £500 was only a nominal consideration[5].

The third judge in the Court of Appeal, Sir Stanley Rees, gave a dissenting judgment which illustrates clearly some of the elusive problems exposed by any enquiry into the intentions of parties in relation to transactions of this kind. Sir Stanley Rees agreed that it had been the deliberate object of W and E to frustrate the option earlier granted to G, but went on to say

The family background to the case as well as what was done with the farm in my

20 It appeared in *Midland Bank Trust Co Ltd v Green* that W had treated other members of the family more generously than G, a point which did not escape the notice of Lord Denning MR.

1 [1980] Ch 590 at 628. (References to the Land Charges Act 1925 amended to Land Charges Act 1972.)

2 See p. 115, ante.

3 Law of Property Act 1925, s. 205(1)(xxi).

4 Ibid.

5 [1980] Ch 590 at 629. Eveleigh LJ agreed, as did Sir Stanley Rees (at 635), that it is not permissible to import a definition section from the Law of Property Act 1925 in order to construe the term 'purchaser' under the Land Charges Act. That term is indeed defined in section 17(1) of the Land Charges Act 1972, but without any equivalent reference to 'good faith' or the adequacy of consideration.

judgment plainly gives rise to an inference that the motive of [W] and [E] was to redistribute their assets among the family in a manner which they considered justified in the family interest. Similarly, the evidence does support an inference that [W] and [E] were acting spitefully and deceitfully and without any just cause at all to deprive their eldest son [G] of his contractual right in the farm which he had worked since 1954. If the latter inference were established and the former disproved by the plaintiffs, that would clearly justify a finding of fraud. In my judgment, the evidence on a balance of probabilities is in favour of the inference that [W] and [E] acting as they believed fairly in the family's interest had just cause to act as they did. What they did would harm [G] by depriving him of his option and was a breach of contract committed by [W] and procured by [E]. But as Viscount Simon LC pointed out . . . in a family situation there may well be a justification for such action so that it would not amount to fraud. It is not, however, necessary in order to decide the issue of fraud to hold that the inference from the facts against fraud is stronger than the inference in favour of fraud. It is sufficient to say that the plaintiffs have not established their allegation of fraud to the standard required[6].

No fraud having been proved, Sir Stanley Rees refused to hold that the conveyance by W to E had been a 'sham'. Furthermore, he was satisfied that for the purpose of (what is now) section 4(6) of the Land Charges Act 1972 E had been a 'purchaser for money or money's worth'[7]. He thus reached the conclusion that

unless fraud is proved or unless the conveyance is a sham or unless the consideration is nominal or illusory then an unregistered estate contract is void against it. Were this not the case one would be departing from the sound ordinary rule in contract law that the court will not look into the adequacy of consideration and from what seemed to Harman J and seems to me the policy of the Land Charges Act [1972], namely to get rid of the equitable rights arising from unregistered estate contracts. Nevertheless the protection remains that 'Fraud unravels all'[8].

The Court of Appeal's judgments in *Midland Bank Trust Co Ltd v Green* thus exposed some of the difficulties inherent in any attempt to displace the crude but efficient rule that the only form of notice relevant in the land charges context is the notice constituted by due entry in the register.

6 [1980] Ch 590 at 632. The reference to Viscount Simon LC is a reference to his speech in *Crofter Hand Woven Harris Tweed Co Ltd v Veitch* [1942] AC 435 at 442f., where the Lord Chancellor stated that even where there is an inducement by one party to procure another to break a contract there may be a justification. The (rather interesting) example given was that of the father who persuades his daughter to break her engagement to marry a 'scoundrel'. Although the 'scoundrel' would have had an action against the daughter for breach of contract (in the days before the Law Reform (Miscellaneous Provisions) Act 1970, s. 1, which made agreements to marry unenforceable at law), the father would, in Viscount Simon's view, have been able to justify his own procurement of the breach of contract on the ground of his 'moral duty to urge his daughter that the contract should be repudiated.' The analogy drawn in *Green*'s case by Sir Stanley Rees (himself a Family Division judge) throws interesting light upon the family-based reasoning which pervades the judgments of the Court of Appeal.

7 [1980] Ch 590 at 635. Sir Stanley Rees was of the opinion that s. 199(1) of the Law of Property Act 1925 could not be read as 'giving rise to a valid argument that a purchaser who enters into a transaction with the deliberate intention of taking advantage of the provisions of the Land Charges Act [1972] is to be prejudicially affected by an unregistered estate contract.'

8 [1980] Ch 590 at 635.

It may well be that even greater difficulties are presented by any endeavour to hold a purchaser bound by actual (but not constructive) notice of an unregistered land charge. Apart from the point that it may sometimes be difficult to distinguish actual from constructive notice[9], such an approach would provide a clear incentive for a purchaser to remain wilfully blind in the face of facts which disclose the existence of an unregistered interest. It would, in this event, become necessary to elaborate the categories and gradations of knowledge which would render a purchaser bound by an unregistered charge. This problem has already arisen in other areas of the law. In determining, for instance, whether a third party should be fixed with liability as a constructive trustee on the ground of participation in the fraud perpetrated by a fiduciary, it is notorious that the courts have experienced the greatest difficulty in maintaining consistent and sensible distinctions between various states of mind in the third party ranging from actual knowledge through recklessness (i.e., a deliberate 'shutting of the eyes') to gross negligence and, finally, plain carelessness on his part[10].

In any event, the possibility that some distinction might be drawn in the land charges context between actual and constructive notice on the part of a purchaser has now been ruled out in conclusive terms by the decision of the House of Lords in *Midland Bank Trust Co Ltd v Green*[11]. Here the House of Lords unanimously reversed the decision of the majority in the Court of Appeal and re-asserted the strict conveyancer's view of the problem which arose on the facts of the case. The House decided that E had indeed been a purchaser of a legal estate for money and that she had therefore taken title to the land free of G's option, which was statutorily void for want of registration under the Land Charges Act.

Lord Wilberforce, in giving the only substantial speech in the House, fully endorsed the orthodox property view which had been adopted at first instance by Oliver J. According to Lord Wilberforce,

> The case is plain: the Act is clear and definite. Intended as it was to provide a simple and understandable system for the protection of title to land, it should not be read down or glossed: to do so would destroy the usefulness of the Act. Any temptation to remould the Act to meet the facts of the present case, on the supposition that it is a hard one and that justice requires it, is . . . removed by the consideration that the Act itself provides a simple and effective protection for persons in [G's] position—viz—by registration[12].

Lord Wilberforce went on to express a firm conviction that the omission from the land charges legislation of any requirement of good faith in a purchaser is entirely deliberate. He outlined the disadvantageous consequences which would flow from any other view[13]:

9 See R. J. Smith (1980) 96 LQR 8 at 11.
10 See *Barnes v Addy* (1874) LR 9 Ch App 244; *Selangor United Rubber Estates Ltd v Cradock (No. 3)* [1968] 1 WLR 1555; *Carl Zeiss Stiftung v Herbert Smith & Co (No. 2)* [1969] 2 Ch 276; *Nelson v Larholt* [1948] 1 KB 339; *Karak Rubber Co Ltd v Burden (No. 2)* [1972] 1 WLR 602; *Belmont Finance Corpn Ltd v Williams Furniture Ltd* [1979] Ch 250.
11 [1981] 2 WLR 28.
12 [1981] 2 WLR 28 at 32.
13 [1981] 2 WLR 28 at 34.

Addition of a requirement that the purchaser should be in good faith would bring with it the necessity of enquiring into the purchaser's motives and state of mind. The present case is a good example of the difficulties which would exist. If the position was simply that the purchaser had notice of the option, and decided nevertheless to buy the land, relying on the absence of notification, nobody could contend that she would be lacking in good faith.

It is of course possible to stop right there and disagree. There must be many to whom the conduct described by Lord Wilberforce would appear to be a fairly clear manifestation of bad faith. However, Lord Wilberforce justified his view in terms of the traditional approach of the law of property. This approach requires that the overwhelming emphasis of land law be placed upon the simple mechanics of contract and conveyance and that the morality of exchange be unquestioned. As Lord Wilberforce explained, the purchaser on his hypothesis

would merely be taking advantage of a situation, which the law has provided, and the addition of a profit motive could not create an absence of good faith. But suppose, and this is the respondents' argument, the purchaser's motive is to defeat the option, does this make any difference? Any advantage to oneself seems necessarily to involve a disadvantage for another: to make the validity of the purchase depend upon which aspect of the transaction was prevalent in the purchaser's mind seems to create distinctions equally difficult to analyse in law as to establish in fact: avarice and malice may be distinct sins, but in human conduct they are liable to be intertwined. The problem becomes even more acute if one supposes a mixture of motives. Suppose—and this may not be far from the truth—that the purchaser's motives were in part to take the farm from [G], and in part to distribute it between [G] and his brothers and sisters, but not at all to obtain any benefit for herself, is that acting in 'good faith' or not? Should family feeling be denied a protection afforded to simple greed? To eliminate the necessity for enquiries of this kind may well have been part of the legislative intention. Certainly there is here no argument for departing—violently—from the wording of the Act[14].

Lord Wilberforce thus ruled that the presence or absence of good faith was irrelevant to the issue to be decided in *Midland Bank Trust Co Ltd v Green.* This clearly disposed of one of the principal bases of Lord Denning MR's judgment in the Court of Appeal. Lord Wilberforce also rejected Lord Denning's view that the consideration provided by the purchaser must be 'adequate' before immunity from an unregistered charge can be secured. Lord Wilberforce condemned the notion of 'adequate consideration' in this context as 'an expression of transparent difficulty.' He pointed out that

The word 'purchaser', by definition ([section 17(1)]), means one who provides valuable consideration—a term of art which precludes any enquiry as to adequacy . . . [Section 4(6)] requires money or money's worth to be provided: the purpose of this being to exclude the consideration of marriage. There is nothing here which suggests, or admits of, the introduction of a further requirement that the money must not be nominal[15].

14 [1981] 2 WLR 28 at 34.
15 [1981] 2 WLR 28 at 35. Lord Wilberforce added that, had the decision been necessary, he would have had 'great difficulty' in holding that £500 is a 'nominal sum of money'. He indicated that 'nominal consideration' and a 'nominal sum' appeared to him, 'as terms of art, to refer to a sum or consideration which can be mentioned as consideration but is not necessarily paid. To equate nominal with inadequate or even grossly inadequate would embark the law upon enquiries which I cannot think were contemplated by Parliament' ([1981] 2 WLR 28 at 36).

Viewed within the broad context of the law of property, the decision of the House of Lords in *Midland Bank Trust Co Ltd v Green* represents a clear and concerted preference for efficiency rather than fairness[16]. By thus according priority to certainty over justice, the law of property may be seen by some to enshrine the *Gesellschaft* ideal of a world of bourgeois individualism in which all are presumed equal and competent to transact freely for the purpose of private gain[17]. In this sense, *Midland Bank Trust Co Ltd v Green* may be one of the most important property decisions of recent years. It reflects an extremely traditional view, according to which the primary purpose of the law of property is to provide clarity and procedural efficiency in the combined operation of bargain and exchange. It exemplifies the belief that the transaction concluded has no significant moral dimension, since the only ethic of the *Gesellschaft* is the freedom to compete and exploit. Yet this approach, in its relative amorality, incorporates the great merit which Pollock and Maitland once attributed to the medieval notion of land tenure:

> It has dealt rudely with the facts, it has neglected many a distinction of great social and economic importance, it has driven its trenchant dilemmas through the middle of natural classes and athwart some lines of customary morality; but it has been bold and strong and therefore simple[18].

There are no easy solutions to the moral dilemma which pervades many areas of property law. The law of property is not, and in a practical world never can be, a branch of moral philosophy. There is therefore much to be said in favour of trading off a little justice in return for enhanced security and certainty in commercial transactions, although this pragmatic approach to the crux of the moral issue will never satisfy all of the people all of the time. There will always be hard cases like *Midland Bank Trust Co Ltd v Green*, and as we all know 'hard cases make bad law.'

2. SEARCH OF THE LAND CHARGES REGISTER

(1) The timing of the search

In unregistered land conveyancing the investigation of title undertaken by the prospective purchaser begins in earnest only after the contract of sale has been concluded[19]. It is only at this stage that the vendor becomes subject to any duty to show title to the land over the requisite period of time. During the interim between contract and conveyance, the purchaser must satisfy himself that that

16 In *Midland Bank Trust Co Ltd v Green*, the House of Lords effectively left G's estate to such non-proprietary remedies as might be available. It must therefore be recorded that the 'unfairness' of the result achieved by the House of Lords was somewhat mitigated by the fact that G's estate was held, in different proceedings before Oliver J, to be entitled to recover damages for the tort of negligence from G's solicitor, who had failed to register G's Class C (iv) land charge. See *Midland Bank Trust Co Ltd v Hett, Stubbs and Kemp (A Firm)* [1979] Ch 384.

17 See p. 369, post.

18 *The History of English Law* (1968 edn.), Vol. 1, p. 406.

19 See p. 88, ante.

title is good. This he does by examining the deeds or documents of title relating to dispositions of the land during at least the past 15 years[20]. Investigation of title must commence with a 'good root of title', i.e., with the first deed of conveyance which is at least 15 years old. In any event it now becomes clear for our purpose that it is only *after* the purchaser has agreed to buy the land that he has the contractual right of access to the historical documents of title which will disclose the names of previous estate owners against whom land charges may have been registered. His right of access extends to all title deeds within the scope of the statutory 15 year period (or other agreed period), but does not extend back beyond the root of title.

(2) The process of search

Shortly before the projected date of completion, the purchaser searches the Register of Land Charges against the names of estate owners comprised within the relevant title. If the first conveyance relating to the property which is at least 15 years old was executed in 1930, then the relevant title commences in 1930.

Search may be personal[1], but most purchasers take advantage of the alternative 'official search' of the Register which is available upon application and the payment of a small fee. In the latter case the officials of the Land Registry provide a computerised check of the Land Charges Register for subsisting entries against the name of the estate owners included in the purchaser's requisition for search[2].

(3) The effect of an 'official search'

The principal advantage of an official search of the Land Charges Register consists in the fact that the result of the search is set out in a certificate issued to the intending purchaser. Then, according to section 10(4) of the Land Charges Act 1972,

> In favour of a purchaser or an intending purchaser . . . the certificate, according to its tenor, shall be conclusive, affirmatively or negatively, as the case may be[3].

Thus, even if the Registry mistakenly issues a clear or 'nil' certificate of official search in respect of a particular estate owner named in the relevant title, the certificate is *conclusive* according to its tenor. A land charge, albeit duly registered against such an estate owner, becomes utterly void[4]. The irrebuttable

20 Law of Property Act 1969, s. 23, p. 87, ante.
1 Land Charges Act 1972, s. 9(1).
2 Land Charges Act 1972, s. 10(1), (2).
3 See Land Charges Act 1925, s. 17(3).
4 The effect of a clear certificate issued in error must be to extinguish (and not merely to suspend) the registered charge. Otherwise, the recipient would be compelled to sell the land in his turn subject to the incumbrance, having bought the land free from the incumbrance on the strength of the clear certificate. Such a result would impose a palpable financial loss upon the recipient of the certificate and would not therefore constitute an outcome 'in favour of [the] purchaser' as is strictly required by the wording of section 10(4) of the Land Charges Act 1972. In other words, the purchaser armed with an erroneously issued clear certificate of official search is the

presumption contained in the statute thus coerces the facts to accord with the fiction contained on the face of the clear certificate. The purchaser can safely take the land free of the land charge in question, and the owner of the now destroyed charge is thrown back upon a remedy in damages against the Land Registry for the tort of negligence. A negligent misrepresentation by the Registry to the applicant for official search has caused loss to a third party, the owner of the previously subsisting land charge[5].

Once again it is clear that the underlying policy reflected in the statute tends to ensure both certainty and facility in land transactions and, incidentally, to discourage personal searches of the Register. The latter point was borne out in *Oak Co-operative Building Society v Blackburn*[6], where the Court of Appeal was concerned with the effect of a registration against an incorrect version of the name of the estate owner[7]. Russell LJ indicated that

> a personal searcher in the full correct name in the present case would, it seems, not have encountered the registration in the present case: he would not have had the benefit of an official certificate under [section 10(4)] and on the contrary would have been affected by a deemed actual notice of the estate contract under section 198 of the Law of Property Act 1925. But we think that anyone who nowadays is foolish enough to search personally deserves what he gets: and if the aim of the statute is to arrive at a sensible working system that aim is better furthered by upholding a registration such as this than by protecting a personal searcher from his folly[8].

The conclusive nature of a certificate of official search in effect provides the only instance in which a duly registered land charge can be defeated. The primary rule of land charge registration is that the fact of registration constitutes 'actual notice . . . to all persons for all purposes'[9]. This rule gives way only in the face of a clear certificate of official search[10].

(4) The consequence of discovering a registered charge

There used to be one other important situation in which the courts upheld the absolute nature of a land charge registration. This case concerned precisely the problem which arises when a prospective purchaser discovers that the Land

---

statutory equivalent of 'Equity's Darling'. His advent, like that of 'Equity's Darling', destroys existing incumbrances so that they cannot subsequently affect even a later purchaser with actual notice: see *Wilkes v Spooner* [1911] 2 KB 473, p. 57, ante.

5 See *Ministry of Housing and Local Government v Sharp* [1970] 2 QB 223 (dealing with the equivalent problem in the analogous area of local land charges). An ambivalent provision in section 10(6) of the Land Charges Act 1972 purports to protect officers and employees of the Registry from personal liability for any loss arising, except where that loss is caused by an act of fraud. The clear intention is that persons aggrieved by the negligence of an officer or employee of the Registry should be able to recover damages on the basis of the vicarious liability of the Registry. The Registry may more reasonably be expected to carry insurance against such eventualities than the individual clerk.

6 [1968] Ch 730.

7 See p. 130, post.

8 [1968] Ch 730 at 743f.

9 Law of Property Act 1925, s. 198(1).

10 Land Charges Act 1972, s. 10(4).

Charges Register does in fact contain an entry prejudicial to his intended use or enjoyment of the land. In the nature of things, as we have seen, such a discovery can usually be made only *after* vendor and purchaser have exchanged contracts for the purchase of the land. It was held in *Re Forsey and Hollebone's Contract*[11] that the unqualified terms of section 198(1) of the Law of Property Act 1925 were such that the purchaser must be deemed to have had 'actual notice' at the date of the contract of any subsisting registration disclosed later on search of the Register. This being so, the purchaser was obliged to complete the contract of sale and take a conveyance of the land notwithstanding that the sale was expressed to be 'free from encumbrances' and even though the land might well be valueless to him.

This 'indefensible' and quite inequitable rule[12] has now been displaced in respect of contracts entered into since 1969. Where search reveals the existence of a registered land charge unknown to the purchaser at the date of contract, that purchaser will now be able to plead his ignorance as a ground for declining to complete the contract. According to section 24(1) of the Law of Property Act 1969, the issue is no longer to be determined with reference to the fictitious notice imposed by section 198(1) of the Law of Property Act 1925:

> Where under a contract for the sale of other disposition of any estate or interest in land the title to which is not registered under the Land Registration Act 1925 . . . any question arises whether the purchaser had knowledge, at the time of entering into the estate contract, of a registered land charge, that question shall be determined by reference to his actual knowledge and without regard to the provisions of section 198 of the Law of Property Act 1925 (under which registration under the Land Charges Act [1972] . . . is deemed to constitute actual notice).

(5) Defective registration and defective search

To err is human. It is possible that mistakes (usually as to name[13]) may be made, either in the process of registration of a land charge or in the process of search or—in rare concatenations of error—in both registration and search. The possibility of error arises from the fact that the Register of Land Charges is a register against names rather than title numbers or plots of land—a point which will be taken up later[14].

The correct name against which a registration should be entered on the Land Charges Register is deemed to be the full name of the estate owner as recorded on his title deeds. If the incumbrancer registers against any other name, such registration will not bind any party who subsequently requisitions an official search against the full correct name. In *Diligent Finance Co Ltd v Alleyne*[15] the first defendant, Erskine Owen Alleyne, was the estate owner of a matrimonial home. He deserted his wife, who later registered her statutory rights of occupation in

11 [1927] 2 Ch 379.
12 See the criticisms advanced by H. W. R. Wade (1956) 14 Cambridge LJ 216 at 228ff.
13 For an ambiguity arising in relation to the precise plot of land concerned in an application for official search against a specific name, see *Du Sautoy v Symes* [1967] Ch 1146.
14 See p. 131, post.
15 (1971) 23 P & CR 346.

the matrimonial home as a Class F land charge against the name of 'Erskine Alleyne'. Two months after the registration the first defendant negotiated an increased mortgage loan from the plaintiff moneylender, which duly requisitioned an official search of the Land Charges Register before taking a new legal charge on the property and releasing the loan moneys. The plaintiff company requisitioned its search against the name of the first defendant as recorded on his title deeds, 'Erskine Owen Alleyne'. The official certificate of search made no reference to the Class F charge registered by the first defendant's wife. On receiving the increased advance, the first defendant left the country and the plaintiff company brought proceedings for possession of the house in question against the wife as second defendant[16]. Foster J held that in these circumstances the Class F registration against an incomplete version of the estate owner's name could not rank ahead of the plaintiff's legal charge where the plaintiff had obtained an official search certificate against the complete and correct version of that name.

It follows that a purchaser who requisitions an official search against an incorrect name must lose priority to an incumbrancer who has registered a land charge against the correct name of the estate owner as it appears on the title deeds. More difficult is the issue of priority arising where an incumbrancer has registered incorrectly, but the purchaser has requisitioned an official search against the wrong name.

This unlikely coincidence of error occurred in *Oak Co-operative Building Society v Blackburn*[17]. Here D[1] was an estate agent whose full name was 'Francis David Blackburn'. D[1] owned a dwelling-house in fee simple, and he entered into an agreement to sell the property to D[3]. D[3] was not legally represented; she agreed to pay a deposit of £100 and to pay the balance of the purchase price (£1,900) over a period of 15 years. D[3] subsequently registered this estate contract as a Class C (iv) land charge against the name of 'Frank David Blackburn', 'Frank' being the name by which D[1] was generally known in the locality. Several years later, D[1] obtained a mortgage advance of £1,300 from P on the security of the property. Before accepting a legal charge on the property, P instructed their solicitor to requisition an official search of the Land Charges Register. The solicitor mistakenly applied for an official search against the name 'Francis Davis Blackburn'[18]. The search certificate made no reference to the subsisting entry against 'Frank David Blackburn'. D[1] was subsequently adjudicated bankrupt and some time later, in the words of Russell LJ, P 'roused themselves from torpor' and brought proceedings against D[3] for possession of the house. The Court of Appeal had to decide an issue which ultimately turned on the relative gravity of two errors—an error in the initial registration and an error

16 Foster J acknowledged that it was 'unfortunate, to say the least, that the Class F registration was not made against the proper name Erskine Owen Alleyne but only against Erskine Alleyne, but that is a mistake which I for my part cannot unfortunately rectify.' The debt to the plaintiff credit company amounted to only £700.

17 [1968] Ch 730, on appeal from [1967] Ch 1169.

18 One of the hilarious features of this case is the fact that the solicitor who requisitioned the official search was himself called 'Davis' and appears, by error, to have transposed his own name into the application for search!

in the requisition of official search. Reversing the judgment of Ungoed-Thomas J at first instance, the Court of Appeal came to the conclusion that

> the registration on this occasion ought not to be regarded as a nullity simply because the formal name of Blackburn was Francis and not Frank, and notwithstanding that Frank as a name is not merely an abbreviation or version of Francis but also a name in its own right, as are also for example Harry and Willie . . . We take a broad view that so far as possible the system should be made to work in favour of those who seek to make use of it in a sensible and practical way. If a proposing purchaser had here requested a search in the correct full names he would have got a clean certificate and a clear title under [section 10(4) of the Land Charges Act 1972], and would have suffered no harm from the fact that the registration was not in such names: and a person registering who is not in a position to satisfy himself what are the correct full names runs that risk. But if there be registration in what may be fairly described as a version of the full names of the vendor, albeit not a version which is bound to be discovered on a search in the correct full names, we would not hold it a nullity against someone who does not search at all, or who (as here) searches in the wrong name[19].

3. THE BASIC FLAW OF THE SYSTEM

(1) The problem

As mentioned above, the basic flaw of the system of registration of land charges lies in the fact that registration is effected against the *name* of the estate owner whose estate is intended to be affected[20]. Names belong to people and, since people are mere mortals, their names are evanescent. As time passes, they disappear into the mists of history. The same is not true of land, which is immoveable[1].

The difficulty which unfolds itself is this. Suppose the following series of conveyances in fee simple of a plot of land, Blackacre:

A conveys to B in 1929
B conveys to C in 1958
C conveys to D in 1963
D conveys to E in 1981

19 [1968] Ch 730 at 743. See (1968) 32 Conv (NS) 284 (F. R. Crane). It is clear that the Court of Appeal had little patience with the Oak Co-operative Building Society. The Building Society was even informed by the Registry of earlier charges on the property against the name of 'Francis David Blackburn', but had not been moved to inquire further. Russell LJ indicated the temper of the Court when he remarked (at 744): 'We do not feel we need shed any tears for the plaintiffs, who could easily have protected themselves by a proper official search but which owing to the error of their solicitor they never made . . . [T]hey could without great trouble have caused somebody to visit the property in question, when they would have found the third defendant living there.'

20 Land Charges Act 1972, s. 3(1), p. 112, ante. It has been pointed out that name-registration is a perfectly suitable method of protecting land charges which have a limited expectation of life (e.g., estate contracts). However, other kinds of land charge (e.g., restrictive covenants) are commonly imposed in order to control the use of land over an indefinitely long period. See H. W. R. Wade (1956) 14 Cambridge LJ 216 at 222f.

1 See p. 322, post.

Suppose further that in 1936 B's neighbour, N, duly registered a restrictive covenant as a Class D (ii) land charge against the name of the current estate owner, B. It is almost certain that when E searches the Land Charges Register prior to completing his purchase in 1981, he will not discover the existence of N's incumbrance. In the normal case, E's investigation of the title to Blackacre will commence with the conveyance by C to D in 1963—that is, with the first conveyance which is at least 15 years old[2]. E will have no contractual right of access to earlier deeds of conveyance and will therefore never have heard of B (or A). Yet, according to the draconian terms of section 198(1) of the Law of Property Act 1925, N's registration against B constitutes 'actual notice' of N's equitable interest 'to all persons and for all purposes . . .'. E is thus fixed with actual notice of N's restrictive covenant. The fact that E has received a clear certificate of official search against the names of C and D is quite irrelevant. Through no fault of his own he has not obtained a certificate of search against the name of B—and that is all that matters here. He is inescapably bound by a land charge duly registered behind a root of title.

The problem disclosed is endemic in any system of name-registration operating within a conveyancing framework which is governed by the pragmatic assumption that those investigating title need not be concerned with events anterior to an artificial and arbitrarily defined 'root of title'. The difficulty was already sufficiently clear to the Lord Chancellor's Committee on Land Charges which reported in 1956, when the statutory period of investigation of title was still 30 years[3]. In its report[4], that Committee (which sat under the chairmanship of Roxburgh J) confessed itself unable to suggest any remedy appropriate to the grave defect exposed in the operation of the land charges system, which was by then already 30 years old. The Committee conjectured that the inherently flawed name-register had been instituted in 1925 in the belief that all land in England and Wales would be subsumed under a system of compulsory registration of title within the following 30 years. This goal remained woefully unrealised in 1956, and the Committee was forced to the conclusion that

> we are the inheritors of a transitory system which was bound to disclose this defect after 30 years of transition and it seems too late to disclaim our inheritance . . . The only policy which we can recommend is to press on as quickly as may be with the extension of the system of compulsory registration of title[5].

As Professor H. W. R. Wade observed of the draftsmen of the 1925 legislation,

> Lord Birkenhead and Sir Benjamin Cherry appear to have succeeded in creating the conveyancing equivalent of a Franckenstein's monster, which with the passing years would become not only more dangerous but also more difficult to kill[6].

2 Law of Property Act 1969, s. 23, p. 127, ante.
3 Law of Property Act 1925, s. 44(1), p. 87, ante.
4 Cmd 9825 (July 1956).
5 Ibid., para. 22.
6 (1956) 14 Cambridge LJ 216. As Professor Wade pointed out, it was 'quite impracticable' even in 1956 to convert the Land Charges Register from a name register to a register which identifies the land charged. The 'herculean labour' required to effect the transition of millions of charges already registered makes the task now utterly impossible.

The problem of the hidden registration still did not occasion widespread difficulty while the minimum statutory period of investigation of title remained 30 years. In the example which we have discussed[7], this period would have embraced the conveyance from B to C in 1958, thus revealing to E the name of B as an earlier estate owner of Blackacre. However, in 1969 the statutory period of investigation of title was reduced to a mere 15 years[8], and the problem became instantly more acute. It became much more likely that purchasers would be trapped by registrations concealed behind a good root of title of whose existence they had no conceivable means of discovery. A partial remedy was therefore enacted in the Law of Property Act 1969[9].

(2) A partial remedy

Section 25(1) of the Law of Property Act 1969 confers a right to compensation from public moneys on any purchaser of an estate or interest in land who suffers loss by reason of a registered land charge hidden behind a root of title. In other words, the legislative solution preferred in relation to the dilemma of the concealed charge is that the charge should remain binding under section 198(1) of the Law of Property Act 1925, but that the purchaser who suffers loss should receive financial compensation[10]. However, the compensation (to be paid by the Chief Land Registrar[11]) is subject to three conditions. *First*, the completion of the transaction which occasions the loss must be after the commencement date of the Law of Property Act 1969[12]. Thus the compensation provision applies only to conveyances effected on or after 1 January 1970. *Second*, the purchaser must have had no 'actual knowledge' of the charge at the date of completion of his purchase[13]. *Third*, the charge in question must have been

> registered against the name of an owner of an estate in the land who was not as owner of any such estate a party to any transaction, or concerned in any event, comprised in the relevant title[14].

In other words, the registration in respect of which compensation is sought must be truly concealed behind the root of title.

It has been said[15] that the problem of the unknown registered land charge is still 'an entirely academic creation.' In practice, registered land charges are

7 See p. 131, ante.
8 Law of Property Act 1969, s. 23, p. 127, ante.
9 See Law Commission, *Report on Land Charges affecting Unregistered Land* (Law Com. No. 18, 1969), para. 27.
10 'The solution adopted amounts merely to a worldly resort to money ...' See J. T. Farrand, *Contract And Conveyance* (3rd edn., London 1980), p. 97.
11 Law of Property Act 1969, s. 25(4).
12 Law of Property Act 1969, s. 25(1)(a).
13 Law of Property Act 1969, s. 25(1)(b). For this purpose, 'actual knowledge' is to be determined without regard to the provisions of section 198(1) of the Law of Property Act 1925 (see Law of Property Act 1969, s. 25(2)).
14 Law of Property Act 1969, s. 25(1)(c).
15 J. T. Farrand, op. cit., p. 98.

referred to in later title deeds so long as there remains any possibility that those charges are of effect. It is therefore a rare purchaser who can plead ignorance of a charge registered behind the root of title, but it is predictable that the day is fast coming when the compensation provisions of the Law of Property Act 1969 will assume a vital significance for the conveyancer.

4. THE CATEGORIES OF REGISTRABLE LAND CHARGE

We have now looked at the basic principles of land charge registration. It remains for us to outline the major categories of interest which are registrable as land charges. These categories are enumerated in section 2 of the Land Charges Act 1972, which has effectively duplicated most of the provisions previously contained in the Land Charges Act 1925. There are six classes of land charge registrable in unregistered land, of which the most important are Classes C, D and F.

(1) Class A

Class A charges comprise various kinds of charge derived ultimately from statute, which arise only on the making of some statutory application[16].

(2) Class B

Class B charges arise likewise by virtue of statute law, and include such charges as, for instance, the Law Society's charge on land recovered or preserved for a legally assisted client under the Legal Aid Act 1974 in respect of unpaid contributions to the legal aid fund[17]. Class B charges differ from Class A charges in that they originate directly in the statute concerned and do not arise merely upon the chargee's application.

(3) Class C

Class C charges fall under four heads:

(a) *Class C (i)*

This class comprises the 'puisne mortgage', i.e., a legal mortgage which is not protected by a deposit of documents relating to the legal estate affected. A puisne mortgage is therefore a second mortgage granted by a mortgagor who has already deposited his title deeds with the first mortgagee[18]. The second mortgagee, being unable to enjoy the security provided by retention of the title deeds, is offered the alternative security of being able to register his mortgage

16 See, for instance, Agricultural Holdings Act 1948, s. 82(2).
17 Legal Aid Act 1974, s. 9(6).
18 See p. 533, post.

interest even though it is *legal*. Class C (i) thus provides a rare example of a legal charge which is registrable under the Land Charges Act. Land charges are in principle commercial *equitable* rights in land which require protection against third parties. However, the puisne mortgage is included among the registrable categories simply for reasons of convenience and the security which registration confers upon a second mortgagee.

(b) *Class C (ii)*

This class comprises the 'limited owner's charge'. Such a charge arises where, for instance, a tenant for life of settled land discharges out of his own pocket a liability to taxation attracted by the settled estate as a whole. The limited owner's charge is therefore an equitable charge which, if registered, secures the right of the limited owner (i.e., the tenant for life) to reimbursement of the money paid by him to the Revenue.

(c) *Class C (iii)*

This class comprises the 'general equitable charge'. It includes effectively many kinds of equitable charge not otherwise registrable. The incumbrances registrable under Class C (iii) must not be secured by the deposit of documents relating to the legal estate affected. As such, the class therefore includes such charges as a rentcharge for life[19] (or 'equitable annuity'), an equitable mortgage of a legal estate[20], and an unpaid vendor's equitable lien upon the property sold. However, Class C (iii) does not include any equitable charge which arises or affects an interest arising under a trust for sale or settlement of land, nor any charge on the proceeds of sale of land (as distinct from a charge upon the land itself). Thus Class C (iii) cannot include an agreement to share the proceeds of sale of land[1] or an estate agent's charge on those proceeds for the purpose of securing his commission[2]. In these cases, the interest of the chargee is in effect an interest in money rather than an interest in land, and Class C (iii) is appropriate only to interests in land[3].

(d) *Class C (iv)*

This class comprises the 'estate contract' which is statutorily defined as

19 See pp. 63, ante and 160, post. 'Equitable annuities outside trusts for sale and settlements must be extremely rare, even if only because most kinds of annuity charged upon land make it settled land' (see H. W. R. Wade (1956) 14 Cambridge LJ 216 at 224).

20 See p. 519, post. Equitable mortgages of an equitable interest under a trust for sale or strict settlement of land are normally overreached on a conveyance of that land to a third party, thereafter being satisfied out of the proceeds of sale. See Law of Property Act 1925, s. 2(1)(i), (ii); Settled Land Act 1925, s. 72(2).

1 *Thomas v Rose* [1968] 1 WLR 1797.

2 *Georgiades v Edward Wolfe & Co Ltd* [1965] Ch 487.

3 In 1956 the Roxburgh Committee favoured the abolition of Class C (iii) with the exception of the category of mortgages (see *Report of the Committee on Land Charges*, para. 13). See also H. W. R. Wade (1956) 14 Cambridge LJ 216 at 224f.

a contract by an estate owner or by a person entitled at the date of the contract to have a legal estate conveyed to him to convey or create a legal estate, including a contract conferring either expressly or by statutory implication a valid option to purchase, a right of pre-emption or any other like right[4].

We have already seen[5] that it is integral to the process of conveyancing that, from the very moment of exchange of contracts, the purchaser of a legal estate in land acquires not merely a *contractual* right but also a *proprietary* right. It is for precisely this reason that the Class C (iv) land charge is designed to protect the purchaser's estate contract, i.e., the purchaser's right to require conveyance of the legal estate in accordance with the contract[6]. The purchaser's interest requires protection during the interim between contract and conveyance since there is, at least in theory, a possibility that the vendor may in breach of contract convey the legal estate to a third party who has no notice of the equitable rights created by the estate contract. It has been pointed out that estate contracts—which of their very nature create short-term interests in land—are peculiarly appropriate for protection under a system of name-registration such as the land charges scheme[7]. Paradoxically, however, estate contracts are rarely registered in practice by solicitors, being entered in the Land Charges Register only in cases of suspicion or delayed completion. Professor Wade has remarked:

Why it should be [the] collective practice [of conveyancing solicitors] to run this risk is a mystery, but the Land Registry must be grateful that they do not, for the volume of entries would be enormous, and 'dead wood' would accumulate in the registry as fast as contracts were completed[8].

Estate contracts include not merely contracts for the sale of an estate in fee simple. They include also contracts for a lease[9], contracts to create a mortgage of a legal estate, and certain kinds of option. An option to purchase a legal estate is registrable as a Class C (iv) land charge[10], as is an option of renewal in a lease[11]. The category of Class C (iv) charges also includes a right of pre-emption[12], a right to require a tenant to surrender (rather than assign) his leasehold term[13], and a tenant's notice to purchase the freehold reversion or to acquire an extended lease under the Leasehold Reform Act 1967[14].

It is more debatable whether Class C (iv) applies to a contract to create a contract in relation to land. In *Turley v Mackay*[15], Uthwatt J thought that Class C (iv) covered 'a contract under which one person is bound to a second person

4 Land Charges Act 1972, s. 2(4).
5 See p. 86, ante.
6 The legal estate may be either freehold or leasehold. On leaseholds see later, p. 401, post.
7 H. W. R. Wade (1956) 14 Cambridge LJ 216 at 222, p. 131, ante.
8 (1956) 14 Cambridge LJ 216 at 223.
9 See p. 396ff., post.
10 See, for instance, *Midland Bank Trust Co Ltd v Green* [1981] 2 WLR 28, p. 119, ante.
11 *Beesly v Hallwood Estates Ltd* [1960] 1 WLR 549. The Roxburgh Committee suggested that such options should cease to be registrable (*Report of the Committee on Land Charges,* para. 15).
12 See *Pritchard v Briggs* [1979] 3 WLR 868; see (1980) 39 Cambridge LJ 35 (C. Harpum).
13 *Greene v Church Commissioners for England* [1974] Ch 467.
14 Leasehold Reform Act 1967, s. 5(5), p. 404, post.
15 [1944] Ch 37 at 40f.

to create a legal estate in such a third person as the second person may direct.' Justifying this view, he said that the object of Class C (iv) is

to secure that obligations affecting land may be registered by persons who have a commercial interest in seeing that those obligations shall be carried out.

In *Thomas v Rose*[16], however, Megarry J entered certain qualifications upon the scope of this statement[17]. Megarry J agreed that Class C (iv) was sufficiently wide to cover (i) a contract by A and B whereby A agrees to grant a legal estate (e.g., a lease) to X—'it matters not that the contract is a contract to create a legal estate in favour of someone other than a contracting party'; (ii) a contract by A and B to convey or create a legal estate in favour of such persons as B shall direct. Here it matters not that the contract is not a firm contract in favour of a named person nor that B never in fact gives any direction. However, a contract by A and B conferring on B the power to accept 'any offer for the sale' of A's land would not, in the view of Megarry J, constitute an estate contract:

[A] contract providing for the making of a further contract to convey or create a legal estate is not itself a contract to convey or create a legal estate. I do not see how Class C (iv) can be read as embracing contracts at one remove. In my judgment, on the wording of the statute the only contracts that fall within Class C (iv) are those which themselves bind the estate owner (or other person entitled) to convey or create a legal estate. It is not enough for the contract merely to provide machinery whereby such an obligation may be created by some other transaction; the very contract itself must impose the obligation[18].

Thus Megarry J decided that a contract empowering B to accept 'any offer for the sale' of A's land constituted

at most an authority to do some further act which may or may not bring such a contract into being. In short, this agreement seems ... to be essentially an agency agreement regulating the disposal of the land and providing for payment of the agent out of the proceeds of sale, and not a contract for the conveyance or creation of a legal estate at all, even incidentally; and I do not think Class C (iv) applies to such agreements, either in the letter or in the spirit[19].

(4) Class D

Class D falls under three heads.

(a) *Class D (i)*

This class comprises an Inland Revenue charge for tax payable on death.

16 [1968] 1 WLR 1797.
17 Megarry J observed that 'as at present advised *Turley v Mackay* does not seem ... to be a case which ought to be extended in its ambit. The agents' real claim in that case was for damages, and it is possible to wonder whether their contractual rights fell within the spirit of Class C (iv).' [1968] 1 WLR 1797 at 1804.
18 [1968] 1 WLR 1797 at 1805.
19 [1968] 1 WLR 1797 at 1805.

(b) *Class D (ii)*

This class comprises the 'restrictive covenant'. For this purpose, a restrictive covenant is defined as

> a covenant or agreement (other than a covenant or agreement between a lessor and a lessee) restrictive of the user of land and entered into on or after 1 January 1926.

A restrictive covenant contained in a lease is governed by the ordinary rules as to the enforceability of leasehold covenants[20] where the restrictive covenant in question relates to the land demised (i.e., subject to the lease). However, where a restrictive covenant relates not to the user of the land demised but to the user of other land of the lessor, that covenant—although clearly not registrable as a Class D (ii) land charge—is governed by the equitable doctrine of notice[1].

Let us take as a typical restrictive covenant an agreement between two neighbouring freeholders A and B, to the effect that A shall not use his land, nor permit it to be used, for the purpose of any trade or business. In all probability B will have secured this agreement in return for a payment of money or for other valuable consideration. A's promise clearly has contractual force and, by curtailing the potential scope of A's activities on his own property, thereby promotes the amenity enjoyed by B on his property. A's contract precludes him from using his premises as a rag merchant, bookmaker or indeed music teacher. B has a *contractual* interest in the performance of A's promise.

If the legal analysis of the relationship between A and B stopped at this point, the agreement framed between A and B would have no enduring impact upon third parties. Only the contracting parties may enforce the benefit or be called upon to suffer the burden of contractual terms. No third party purchasing either A's land or B's land would be affected by a contract to which he was not privy. However, land law does not regard B's interest in the performance of A's promise as a purely contractual interest. Ever since the decision in *Tulk v Moxhay*[2], the covenantee of a restrictive covenant has been regarded as having, in some sense, a 'proprietary' interest in the covenantor's land to the extent that he enjoys a contractual right to control activities conducted on that land. In other words, as we saw in the case of the estate contract[3], the contractual right tends to enlarge into, and arrogate to itself the character of, a proprietary interest.

Since 1926 the proprietary interest thus acquired by the restrictive covenantee must take effect as an equitable interest because it is not included among the legal estates, interests and charges enumerated in section 1(1), (2) of the Law of Property Act 1925[4]. As such, the proprietary right—the 'restrictive covenant'—is fully subject to the equitable doctrine of notice. The burden of the restrictive covenant—the burden initially assumed by A—will bind all third party purchasers of A's land other than a bona fide purchaser of a legal estate for value

20 See p. 408ff., post.
1 *Dartstone v Cleveland Petroleum Co Ltd* [1969] 1 WLR 1807.
2 (1848) 2 Ph 774, p. 614, post.
3 See p. 136, ante.
4 See p. 53, ante.

without notice of the restrictive covenant. Today this doctrine still applies to restrictive covenants entered into by freeholders *before* 1926. In relation to restrictive covenants created by freeholders *after* 1925, the orthodox doctrine of notice has been modified to the extent that the only recognised form of notice of the covenantee's equitable interest is now the notice which is ensured by registration of a Class D (ii) land charge.

Let us suppose that A is the covenantor and B the covenantee in relation to a restrictive covenant which precludes trade or business on A's land. A then sells and conveys his legal estate in fee simple to C, and B sells and conveys his legal estate in fee simple to D. May D enforce the restrictive covenant against C?

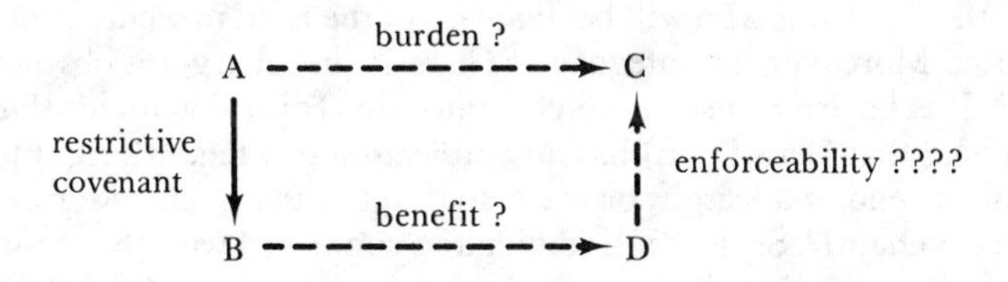

Fig. 19

The enforceability of the restrictive covenant as between C and D will turn upon whether an affirmative answer can be given to two quite distinct questions.

(i) *Has the burden of A's restrictive covenant been passed to C?* If the covenant was made after 1925 the only way in which the burden may 'run' with A's land is in consequence of the registration of a Class D (ii) land charge by B against the name of A. If such a registration was effected before A's conveyance of the fee simple to C, C cannot now deny that he has received 'actual notice' of the covenant[5]. If B failed to register the land charge, the restrictive covenant becomes void as against C[6].

(ii) *Has the benefit of the restrictive covenant been passed to D?* Unless the benefit of the restrictive covenant has indeed been passed to D, it will be entirely irrelevant that the land charge was duly registered against A[7]. The modes of transmission of the benefit of restrictive covenants are three in number: annexation, assignment and the creation of a 'scheme of development'. These methods of passing the benefit are discussed later[8], and for the moment it is sufficient simply to recognise that the restrictive covenant in question will be enforceable against C at the behest of D only if *both* benefit *and* burden have been duly transmitted to the appropriate persons.

(c) *Class D (iii)*

This class comprises the 'equitable easement', which is statutorily defined as

5 Law of Property Act 1925, s. 198(1), p. 113, ante.
6 Land Charges Act 1972, s. 4(6), p. 114, ante.
7 For a discussion of 'benefit' and 'burden' see earlier, p. 61, ante.
8 See p. 621ff., post.

an easement, right or privilege over or affecting land created or arising on or after 1 January 1926, and being merely an equitable interest[9].

We have already examined the distinction between legal and equitable easements[10]. Generally an equitable easement arises where a right in the nature of an easement has been created otherwise than by deed (e.g., by mere contract, unsealed writing or verbal grant) or has been created otherwise than for an interest equivalent to an estate in fee simple absolute in possession or a term of years absolute.

The Class D (iii) land charge has been the cause of much difficulty in practice. The very persons in whose favour such a charge may commonly arise are precisely those persons who will be unaware of the need to secure protection by registration. Moreover the category of Class D (iii) charges is obscure and ill-defined[11]. It is far from certain which rights are registrable under this head. It has been held that Class D (iii) has no application to a tenant's right to remove fixtures at the end of a lease[12], or to an equitable right of entry for breach of a leasehold covenant[13]. Such are the difficulties connected with the registration of equitable easements that the Roxburgh Committee proposed that Class D (iii) might be abolished altogether[14]. As Professor Wade has said[15],

> It has always been rather a mystery what equitable easements are . . . It would be more satisfactory to close the class, for it is just as objectionable on the score of vagueness as is that of general equitable charges.

These difficulties appear most clearly perhaps in the judgments of the Court of Appeal in *E. R. Ives Investment Ltd v High*[16]. Here the defendant, D, and X were neighbours. X began to construct on his property a block of flats the foundations of which marginally encroached on D's land. D agreed to ignore the unintentional incursion on condition that he be granted a right of way for his car across X's yard. This right of way was not granted by deed and constituted therefore a merely equitable easement. As such it was never registered by D as a Class D (iii) land charge against the name of X. X later conveyed the fee simple estate in his property to Y, who knew of the earlier agreement. Y also knew that D had more recently built a garage upon his own land accessible only across the yard. Moreover D contributed part of the cost of surfacing this yard. Y then sold the legal estate to the plaintiff, P, expressly subject to the right of way enjoyed by D across the yard. P brought an action against D for trespass to the yard, claiming that D's equitable easement should have been registered against X as a Class D (iii) charge. Since it had not been so registered, P

9 Land Charges Act 1972, s. 2(5).
10 See p. 62, ante.
11 See H. W. R. Wade (1956) 14 Cambridge LJ 216 at 225f.
12 *Poster v Slough Estates Ltd* [1968] 1 WLR 1515.
13 *Shiloh Spinners Ltd v Harding* [1973] AC 691; (1973) 32 Cambridge LJ 218 (P. B. Fairest). The enforceability of such a right of entry against a later purchaser of the land turned therefore on an application of the equitable doctrine of notice, pp. 313, 414, post.
14 *Report of the Committee on Land Charges*, para. 16.
15 (1956) 14 Cambridge LJ 216 at 225f.
16 [1967] 2 QB 379; (1967) 31 Conv (NS) 338 (F. R. Crane).

contended, the charge now became void notwithstanding the actual knowledge which P had received[17].

On the facts the merits of the case clearly pointed in favour of D. As an honest but uninformed layman, it had never occurred to him that the agreement informally reached with X—largely as an act of grace on D's part—required formal protection vis à vis third parties. In contrast the plaintiff was an investment company which had bought with full knowledge of the agreement and which was quite prepared to plead the statute in order to further its own unconscionable dealing. This being the ethical relationship of the parties, it is not surprising that the Court of Appeal strained to uphold the county court judgment at first instance in favour of D[18].

Danckwerts and Winn LJJ agreed that D's equitable right of way was rendered statutorily void against P for non-registration notwithstanding that P purchased with actual notice of D's rights[19]. However, both judges held that P was 'estopped' (or precluded) from pleading non-registration by D in view of the past history of acquiescence in D's expenditure on the building of a garage in a particular position and on the surfacing of the yard which now belonged to P. This acquiescence, together with the doctrine of 'mutual benefit and burden'[20], created an 'equity' in favour of D which bound all subsequent purchasers with actual notice[1]. The 'equity' thus raised was, unlike the equitable right of way, not registrable under the Land Charges Act and was therefore unaffected by D's failure to register his easement.

The third member of the Court of Appeal, Lord Denning MR, went even further. He held not merely that the estoppel prevented P from asserting a legally valid answer based on want of registration, but that D's equitable easement had not even been registrable in the first place. In the opinion of the Master of the Rolls, the 'equitable easement' which is registrable as a Class D (iii) land charge is

> a proprietary interest in land such as would before 1926 have been recognised as capable of being conveyed or created *at law*, but which since 1926 only takes effect as an equitable interest . . . [It does not] include a right, liberty or privilege arising in equity by reason of 'mutual benefit and burden', or arising out of acquiescence, or by reason of a contractual licence: because none of those before 1926 were proprietary interests such as were capable of being conveyed or created *at law*. They only subsisted *in equity*. They do

17 See p. 114, ante.
18 'Could anything be more monstrous and inequitable afterwards to deprive [D] of the benefit of what he has done?' ([1967] 2 QB 379 at 399 per Danckwerts LJ).
19 [1967] 2 QB 379 at 399, 403.
20 This doctrine prescribes that when adjoining owners of land make an agreement to secure continuing rights and benefits for each of them in or over the land of the other, neither of them can take the benefit of the agreement and throw over the burden of it. This applies not only to the original parties, but also to their successors. The successor who takes the continuing benefit must take it subject to the continuing burden. This principle has been applied, for instance, to neighbours who send their water into a common drainage system (see *Hopgood v Brown* [1955] 1 WLR 213) and to purchasers of houses on a building estate who had the benefit of using the roads on that estate and were subject to the burden of contributing to their upkeep (see *Halsall v Brizell* [1957] Ch 169).
1 See p. 498, post.

> not need to be registered as land charges, so as to bind successors, but take effect in equity without registration . . . The right of [D] to cross this yard was not a right such as could ever have been created or conveyed at law. It subsisted only in equity. It therefore still subsists in equity without being registered. Any other view would enable the owners of the flats to perpetrate the grossest injustice. They could block up [D's] access to the garage, whilst keeping their foundations in his land. That cannot be right[2].

P was therefore held bound by D's rights on the ground of purchase with actual notice[3]. As Lord Denning MR himself observed, the decision in *E. R. Ives Investment Ltd v High* illustrates the willingness of the courts to cut down the scope of interests registrable under Class D (iii)[4]. However, Lord Denning found this restrictive tendency 'not disturbing'[5], and moreover to be wholly in keeping with the Roxburgh Committee's proposal that Class D (iii) charges should be abandoned altogether.

The Court of Appeal's judgments in *E. R. Ives Investment Ltd v High* underscore the vagueness of the category of charges registrable under Class D (iii). However, perhaps the most profound difficulty raised by the decision is that it marks

> a definite stage in the evolution of one sort of licence as a proprietary interest in land, and makes it possible also pro tanto to discard the term licence and to speak of 'estoppel interests in land'[6].

Professor Crane has expressed the view that estoppel interests fall outside the 'necessarily tidy world of the conveyancer,' in that they tend to 'diminish both certainty of title and the availability of land on the market[7].' These are clearly serious problems, and we shall have cause later to examine more closely the difficulties involved[8].

(5) Class E

Class E land charges comprise annuities arising before 1926 but not registered until after the Land Charges Act 1925 came into force.

(6) Class F

Class F land charges comprise those charges in respect of spousal rights of

2 [1967] 2 QB 379 at 395f. See C. V. Davidge (1937) 53 LQR 259 at 260: 'Equitable Easements'.
3 See also P. V. Baker (1972) 88 LQR 336: 'Equitable Interests and Constructive Notice Today'; D. Yates (1974) 37 MLR 87: 'The Protection of Equitable Interests under the 1925 legislation'. For reasoning similar to that applied by Lord Denning MR in *E. R. Ives Investment Ltd v High*, see *Montague v Long* (1972) 24 P & CR 240 at 247f. per Graham J.
4 See also *Poster v Slough Estates Ltd* [1968] 1 WLR 1515; *Shiloh Spinners Ltd v Harding* [1973] AC 691.
5 [1967] 2 QB 379 at 396.
6 (1967) 31 Conv (NS) 332 (F. R. Crane).
7 (1967) 31 Conv (NS) 342. The Law Commission has recommended that in registered land an 'equity' of the kind raised in *E. R. Ives Investment Ltd v High* should be protectable by allowing the person entitled to apply for notice of the 'equity' to be entered on the register. See Law Commission, Published Working Paper No. 67: *Land Registration* (*Fourth Paper*) (April 1976), paras. 64ff.
8 See p. 497, post.

occupation which arise pursuant to the Matrimonial Homes Act 1967[9]. Since this enactment has been described as a 'statute which bristles with difficulties'[10], it is necessary to understand something of the background to the legislation.

(a) *The common law*

At common law a wife has a right to occupy the matrimonial home. This right is an integral part of her right to be maintained by her husband. If her common law right of occupation is threatened by an impending sale of the matrimonial home, such sale may be restrained by court injunction[11].

A more difficult problem arises if the husband owns the matrimonial home in his sole name and then sells and conveys that home to a third party without the knowledge or consent of his wife. The wife is then confronted with the claim of that third party to own and occupy the house. During the 1950s the Court of Appeal developed the doctrine of the 'deserted wife's equity', according to which there accrued to the wife at the date of desertion an 'equity' which she could successfully oppose against any third party purchaser from her husband who had notice of her rights[12].

This doctrine, although motivated by 'family considerations'[13], proved to be quite unacceptable in terms of orthodox property law. The 'deserted wife's equity' represented the nightmare of practising conveyancers—the unregistrable, non-overreachable incumbrance capable of binding purchasers on the basis of actual or even constructive notice. In effect an embarrassing onus of enquiry was imposed upon any third party entering into any transaction (e.g., sale, lease or mortgage) with a man who manifestly lived with a woman. The purchaser, in order to be safe, had to inquire, first, whether that woman was the wife of the vendor/lessor/mortgagor and, second, whether the marriage (if there was one) was happy and stable[14]. The problem of enquiry was far-reaching. As Megarry J later pointed out[15], it was

> intolerable if, when an overdraft was secured on the husband's house, the bank had to make inquiries as to the husband's matrimonial behaviour before honouring his cheques.

9 For good descriptions of the operation of this Act, see Law Commission, Published Working Paper No. 42: *Family Law: Family Property Law* (1971), paras. 1.3–1.5; *Third Report on Family Law: The Matrimonial Home (Co-ownership and Occupation Rights) and Household Goods* (Law Com No. 86, June 1978), paras. 2.1–2.50.

10 R. E. Megarry and H. W. R. Wade *The Law of Real Property* (4th edn., London 1975), p. 785.

11 *Lee v Lee* [1952] 2 QB 489.

12 For the development of this doctrine, see *Bendall v McWhirter* [1952] 2 QB 466; *Ferris v Weaven* [1952] 2 All ER 233; *Lee v Lee* [1952] 2 QB 489; *Jess B. Woodcock and Sons Ltd v Hobbs* [1955] 1 WLR 152; *Westminster Bank Ltd v Lee* [1956] Ch 7. See also F. R. Crane (1955) 19 Conv (NS) 343: 'The Deserted Wife's Licence'.

13 See p. 151, post.

14 See the criticisms expressed by property lawyers of the traditional mould in *Westminster Bank Ltd v Lee* [1956] Ch 7 at 22 per Upjohn J; *National Provincial Bank Ltd v Hastings Car Mart Ltd* [1964] Ch 665 at 699 per Russell LJ, [1965] AC 1175 at 1234 per Lord Upjohn, 1248f. per Lord Wilberforce. See also R. E. Megarry (1952) 68 LQR 379 at 383: 'The Deserted Wife's Right to Occupy the Matrimonial Home'.

15 *Wroth v Tyler* [1974] Ch 30 at 42.

The doctrine of the 'deserted wife's equity' was finally destroyed in *National Provincial Bank Ltd v Hastings Car Mart Ltd*[16]. Here the House of Lords conclusively rejected the idea that the deserted wife's rights were other than personal rights enforceable against her husband alone. Her common law rights of occupation could have no impact upon third parties.

(b) *The statutory 'rights of occupation'*

The remedy lay plainly in statutory intervention, and the Matrimonial Homes Act 1967 was enacted in order to fulfil some of the purposes previously served by the doctrine of the 'deserted wife's equity.' In terms which are entirely sex-neutral, the 1967 Act confers statutory 'rights of occupation' in the matrimonial home[17] upon certain categories of spouse.

The Act confers upon a qualifying spouse *first* a right, if that spouse is in occupation of the matrimonial home, 'not to be evicted or excluded from the dwelling house or any part thereof by the other spouse except with the leave of the court, and *second*, a right, if not in occupation, by leave of the court 'to enter into and occupy the dwelling house[18].' These rights are granted in any situation where

> one spouse is entitled to occupy a dwelling house by virtue of any estate or interest or contract or by virtue of any enactment giving him or her the right to remain in occupation, *and the other spouse is not so entitled*[19].

The Act thus confers benefit upon only those spouses who are denuded of any other kind of protection in their occupation of the matrimonial home—which meant initially that as a matter of social reality the statute operated primarily for the protection of 'the bare wife'[20]—the wife who had no rights (legal or equitable) in the matrimonial home. It follows then that, if A and B are married, B will enjoy the statutory 'rights of occupation' in situation (i) below (*Fig.* 20), where A is the sole owner of the matrimonial home both at law and in equity.

The protective scheme of the Matrimonial Homes Act 1967 was subsequently extended to confer the statutory 'rights of occupation' upon a spouse who owns an equitable but not a legal interest in the home[1]. This extension was brought about by section 38 of the Matrimonial Proceedings and Property Act 1970

16 [1965] AC 1175. For an excellent account of the significance of this decision, see O. Kahn-Freund (1970) 33 MLR 601 at 608ff.: 'Recent Legislation on Matrimonial Property'. See also F. R. Crane (1965) 29 Conv (NS) 254 at 464: 'After the Deserted Wife's Licence'.

17 Under section 1(8) of the Matrimonial Homes Act 1967, the Act has no application to a dwelling-house 'which has at no time been a matrimonial home of the spouses in question.' See for instance *Whittingham v Whittingham* [1979] Fam 9 at 16. The statutory rights of occupation may not be registered in respect of more than one matrimonial home at any one time (Matrimonial Homes Act 1967, s. 3).

18 Matrimonial Homes Act 1967, s. 1(1).

19 Emphasis supplied.

20 This graphic phrase is frequently used by Lord Denning MR. See *Gurasz v Gurasz* [1970] P 11 at 17; *Williams & Glyn's Bank Ltd v Boland* [1979] Ch 312 at 328.

1 For an examination of the circumstances which may give rise to beneficial co-ownership of this kind, see p. 256, post.

which inserted a new subsection (9) in section 1 of the Matrimonial Homes Act 1967. Section 38 contains a rather confusing fiction which was designed to preserve the framework of the parent statute. In order to qualify a beneficially owning spouse within section 1 of the 1967 Act, that beneficiary (i.e., the equitable but not legal owner) is

> to be treated for the purpose only of determining whether he or she has rights of occupation under [section 1] as not being entitled to occupy the dwelling house by virtue of [his beneficial interest].

The amendment thus confers statutory rights under the Matrimonial Homes Act 1967 by effectively removing existing rights. The equitable owner, by virtue of the statutory fiction, is denuded of any existing right of occupation and therefore qualifies for protection within section 1 of the 1967 Act[2]. Statutory 'rights of occupation' are, accordingly, enjoyed by B in situation (ii) below. However, the 1967 Act—even as amended—confers no statutory rights upon either A or B in situations (iii) and (iv) below, where A and B are jointly entitled to a legal estate in the matrimonial home and are, respectively, joint tenants and tenants in common of the equitable interest[3]. In both situations A and B are adequately protected by reason of their legal co-ownership, and the matrimonial home cannot be conveyed to a third party in either case without the co-operation of both spouses.

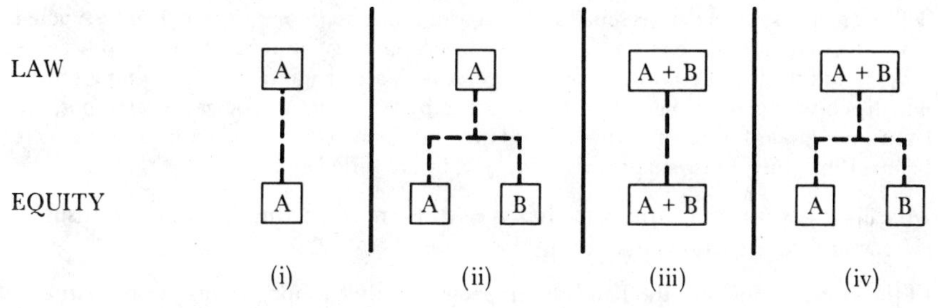

Fig. 20

It is vital to note that section 1 of the Matrimonial Homes Act 1967 confers purely personal rights of occupation. One spouse may apply to the court for an order controlling the exercise of those rights by the other spouse[4], but the rights granted by section 1 have no impact at all upon third parties. They do nothing

2 See p. 298, post.
3 See p. 251ff., post. See *Gurasz v Gurasz* [1970] P 11 at 17.
4 The court can, for instance, order one spouse to leave the home (Matrimonial Homes Act 1967, s. 1(2), (3), as amended by Domestic Violence and Matrimonial Proceedings Act 1976, s. 3). See S. M. Cretney, *Principles of Family Law* (3rd edn., London 1979), p. 208ff. Section 4 of the Domestic Violence and Matrimonial Proceedings Act 1976 gives the court jurisdiction to regulate occupation of the family home by joint tenants, even though those joint tenants do not enjoy the statutory 'rights of occupation' conferred by the Matrimonial Homes Act 1967. This extension of jurisdiction is, however, merely a recognition of the need for the courts to be able to intervene in cases of domestic violence or other domestic disruption.

to help the deserted wife in the situation of sale of the matrimonial home to a third party. The solution needed here is found in section 2 of the 1967 Act.

(c) *Registration*

The rights of occupation conferred by section 1 of the Matrimonial Homes Act 1967 are merely rights *in personam*: they are opposable against only the other spouse. However, the rights *in personam* secured by section 1 may be effectively transformed into rights *in rem* through the medium of registration. As Otto Kahn-Freund said[5], the 1967 Act 'uses the machinery of publicity in order to transform the internal right of enjoyment into a modification of title.' The statutory rights of occupation may, under section 2 of the Act, be registered as a Class F land charge (if title to the matrimonial home is unregistered[6]) or protected by a notice or caution (if title is registered[7]). In either case, the rights may be registered notwithstanding that the registering spouse is not currently in occupation (e.g., because he or she has been expelled from the home or has indeed left the home voluntarily)[8]. The registration can be effected quite unilaterally and, moreover, it is the 'positive practice' of the Registry *not* to serve notice of the application for registration upon the owner of the legal estate[9].

In *Wroth v Tyler*[10], Megarry J described the statutory entitlement of an occupying spouse in the following terms:

> The right is in essence a personal and non-assignable statutory right not to be evicted from the matrimonial home in question during marriage or until the court otherwise orders; and this right constitutes a charge on the estate or interest of the owning spouse which requires protection against third parties by registration. For various reasons, the right may be said to be one which readily fits into no category known to conveyancers before 1967; the phrase sui generis seems apt, but of little help.

Megarry J went on to indicate that the Matrimonial Homes Act 1967 ensured that 'spite' registrations may easily be made:

> [T]he Act has put into the hands of all spouses with statutory rights of occupation a weapon of great power and flexibility. Registration is a relatively simple, speedy and

5 (1970) 33 MLR 601 at 610.
6 Matrimonial Homes Act 1967, s. 2 (6).
7 Matrimonial Homes Act 1967, s. 2(7). The Law Commission has suggested that, in registered land, a spouse's rights of occupation should always be protected by entry of a 'notice', even though the consent of the registered proprietor may not be available. See Published Working Paper No. 67: *Land Registration (Fourth Paper)*, para. 60, p. 326, post.
8 *Watts v Waller* [1973] QB 153.
9 See *Wroth v Tyler* [1974] Ch 30 at 39 per Megarry J; T. B. F. Ruoff and R. B. Roper, *Law and Practice of Registered Conveyancing* (4th edn., London 1979), p. 747. Megarry J went on to say in *Wroth v Tyler* that 'A practice which warns a mortgagee of the registration of a charge over which his mortgage takes priority, but leaves unwarned the landowner, who may proceed to act to his detriment in ignorance of his wife's application, is a practice which seems to me (and I speak temperately) to deserve further consideration.' See, however, Law Commission, *Third Report on Family Property: The Matrimonial Home (Co-ownership and Occupation Rights) and Household Goods* (Law Com No. 86, June 1978), para. 2.85f.
10 [1974] Ch 30 at 46, p. 152, post.

secret process, as compared with the necessarily more complex, protracted and less private process of selling a house and carrying through the contract to completion. As this case illustrates, Parliament has made it possible for the protected spouse to go far towards having his or her way as to not moving from the matrimonial home, at the expense of the other spouse and innocent purchasers. No doubt, too, the protected spouse may, by registering the statutory charge, and particularly by registering it at an inconvenient moment, require the owning spouse to buy off the charge. In some cases this may be very proper; in others it may be less so: but the power to do it is a unilateral power, free from any restraints[11].

Considerations such as these led Megarry J to express severe criticism of the statutory charge as 'a companion in obloquy for what in *Keeves v Dean* ... Scrutton LJ stigmatised as monstrum horrendum informe ingens[12].' We shall look more closely at the defects of the 1967 Act in the following pages. However, we must first observe the consequences of registration.

(d) *The effect of registration*

Once registered, the statutory rights of occupation conferred by the 1967 Act become binding upon almost all third parties[13], with the exception of the trustee in bankruptcy of the spouse upon whose estate the registration was intended to constitute a charge[14]. This means that a deserted wife's statutory rights of occupation can still be defeated (despite registration) if her husband goes bankrupt under the financial strain involved in supporting two families: few men can afford successive polygamy. As we shall see again and again in land law, the commercial interest (as here represented by the husband's creditors) prevails over the family interest (as here represented by the deserted family's need of residential security)[15]. We do not in this country have the protective homestead legislation in force in parts of the Commonwealth and the United States, which preserves a portion of the bankrupt's estate intact for his family[16]. In fact, English law has always strongly resisted the idea that the property rights of husband and wife should be governed by any rules other than the ordinary principles of law and equity which regulate the property relations of strangers[17].

It is a telling commentary upon our pragmatic values that, in cases of conflict, the importance of the cash nexus consistently predominates over the less articulate values represented by the family as an organic social phenomenon.

11 [1974] Ch 30 at 46.
12 [1974] Ch 30 at 64, p. 434, post.
13 Law of Property Act 1925, s. 198(1), p. 113, ante.
14 Matrimonial Homes Act 1967, s. 2(5).
15 See pp. 282, 381, post.
16 See A. Milner (1959) 22 MLR 458: 'A Homestead Act for England?' New Zealand, for instance, has enjoyed some form of homestead legislation since the enactment of the Family Homes Protection Act 1895. On the purpose and implications of this legislation (now contained in the Joint Family Homes Act 1964), see *Sutherland v Sutherland* [1955] NZLR 689 at 691 per Turner J; *Official Assignee of Pannell v Pannell* [1966] NZLR 324 at 326.
17 See *Gissing v Gissing* [1971] AC 886 at 899 per Viscount Dilhorne; *Cowcher v Cowcher* [1972] 1 WLR 425 at 429. See also *Wirth v Wirth* (1956) 98 CLR 228 at 231f. per Dixon CJ; *Allen v Snyder* [1977] 2 NSWLR 685 at 689 per Glass JA.

The ethics of the *Gesellschaft* displace the sentiment of the *Gemeinschaft* no less firmly in the context of land charge registration than in any other area. A notable irony of legislative history is thus revealed: the judge-made doctrine of the 'deserted wife's equity' held that the deserted wife's right of occupation was opposable against even her husband's trustee in bankruptcy[18].

(e) *The consequence of non-registration*

It is a clear consequence of failure to register the statutory rights of occupation that those rights become 'void as against a purchaser of the land . . . or of any interest in such land . . .[19]'

Herein lies one curious feature concerning the registration of the spousal rights of occupation. In the case of all other land charges, the plain statutory expectation is that registration will be effected in all situations where registration is available, on pain of the dire penalty that an unregistered charge will be rendered void as against a third party purchaser[20]. It can hardly have been the case, however, that the legislature contemplated that there would be mass registrations in respect of all matrimonial homes, regardless of the stability of the marriage relationship. Such vigilance on the part of those who enjoy statutory rights of occupation would have the disastrous effect of swamping the Registry with literally millions of applications for registration. In *Wroth v Tyler*[1], Megarry J opined that in the case of the happy marriage

> it may well be that the expectation was that there would be no registration, and so no need for any release of the statutory rights or cancellation of the registration when the home was sold; for although the wife held a charge on the husband's estate in the house, that charge would be void against the purchaser . . . [I]t would not be surprising if in fact the Act in the main has been operating on a basis of the mass invalidation of the statutory charges for want of registration, with registration being effected only in cases of actual or impending disputes.

It seems strange that the operation of a statute of such vast social import should depend on the ignorance or apathy of the citizens whose protection it is designed to secure. The irony is that the registration of spousal rights of occupation is abused, for malicious purposes, by those who need protection least[2], but is frequently not effected by those who most clearly stand in need of the protection which registration provides. As Lord Denning MR pointed out in *Williams & Glyn's Bank Ltd v Boland*[3], the Matrimonial Homes Act 1967 gave the deserted wife

> a charge on the house: but it was subject to this severe restriction: it had to be registered as a Class F charge, and not all of the deserted wives had sufficient knowledge or advice to do this . . . [T]he Act was of precious little use to [the wife], at any rate when she was

18 See *Bendall v McWhirter* [1952] 2 QB 466.
19 Land Charges Act 1972, s. 4(8), p. 114, ante.
20 Land Charges Act 1972, s. 4, p. 114, ante.
1 [1974] Ch 30 at 46.
2 See the earlier reference to 'spite' registrations, p. 146, ante.
3 [1979] Ch 312 at 328.

living at home in peace with her husband. She would never have heard of a Class F charge: and she would not have understood it if she had.

In any event, as Ormrod LJ indicated in the same case[4],

the registration of Class F land charges or cautions is an essentially 'hostile' type of proceeding which is not well suited to couples who are living together on reasonably good terms. In these cases the remedy offered is usually 'too little and too late'.

(f) *Compulsory co-ownership of the matrimonial home*

There can be little doubt that the social purpose which the Matrimonial Homes Act 1967 seeks to achieve would be more easily attained through the statutory imposition of a rule of automatic co-ownership of the legal estate in all matrimonial homes[5]. Such a solution would mean that no disposition in relation to that legal estate (whether by way of conveyance, lease or mortgage) could occur without the active participation of both spouses. Both would have to sign any document of transfer or mortgage. Complete protection would be secured for the deserted wife without any necessity for a hostile registration during the difficult period when a marriage first threatens to break down. Automatic co-ownership would cut clean through the difficulties which have been exposed in the operation of the Matrimonial Homes Act 1967, but as yet no legislation to this effect has been enacted in this country[6].

In 1978 the Law Commission took the imaginative and innovative step of proposing a statutory scheme of co-ownership of the matrimonial home applicable to most dwelling-houses in which one or other spouse has an interest legal or equitable[7]. Where the statutory regime applied, the spouses would become joint tenants of the equitable interest in the matrimonial home behind a statutory trust for sale. The Law Commission's suggestions for realising this regime of co-ownership still relied heavily, however, upon the existing machinery of registration of rights in both registered and unregistered land.

The Commission correctly analysed the needs of spouses in respect of the

4 [1979] Ch 312 at 339.

5 See p. 303, post.

6 Compare the presumption of joint tenancy of the matrimonial home applied in the Marriage Act 1958 (Victoria), s. 161(4)(b), as amended by the Marriage (Property) Act 1962, s. 3. (See, e.g., *Hogben v Hogben* [1964] VR 468). It has been proposed that the Victorian model should serve as a basis upon which to build a new and comprehensive matrimonial property regime within the federal jurisdiction in Australia. In 1980 the Joint Select Committee on the Family Law Act recommended that the Family Law Act 1975 be amended to provide that during the subsistence of a marriage and on the breakdown of a marriage the parties to the marriage will be presumed to own the matrimonial home in equal shares. See Parliament of the Commonwealth of Australia, *Family Law in Australia* (Report of the Joint Select Committee on the Family Law Act, July 1980), Vol. 1, para. 5.158 (Recommendation 37)).

7 See Law Commission, *Third Report on Family Property: The Matrimonial Home (Co-ownership and Occupation Rights) and Household Goods* (Law Com No. 86, June 1978), para. 1.1. The scheme of statutory co-ownership was subject to a number of exceptions covering homes acquired before marriage, property interests given to a spouse by a third party, and exclusory agreements drawn up by the spouses themselves (see Law Com No. 86, paras. 1.104ff.).

matrimonial home as being essentially twofold. It considered[8] that each spouse should have

(a) a right to ensure that the property is not sold, mortgaged or otherwise disposed of without his or her consent (i.e., a 'right of control');
(b) a right to ensure that he or she is not deprived of his or her due share of money realised by any dealing which does take place (i.e., a 'money right').

Both of these rights are already enjoyed by spouses who hold the legal title to the matrimonial home as joint tenants (i.e., in situations (iii) and (iv) in *Fig.* 20[9]). However, neither right is effectively secured to a spouse who owns merely a beneficial interest in the home (situation (ii)) or who owns no interest at all (situation (i))[10].

It was to the latter two situations that the Law Commission directed its attention. These situations would normally, in the terms of the Commission's proposals, be covered by the scheme of 'statutory co-ownership'[11]. Effect would be given to that scheme by conferring upon the spouse who was *not* entitled at law the right to register a Class G land charge (in the case of unregistered land) or to enter a 'restriction' upon the title (in the case of registered land)[12]. If a Class G land charge were duly registered, such registration would constitute automatic notice to any purchaser of the registering spouse's beneficial interest in the property under the new scheme of statutory co-ownership. It would, moreover, constitute notice of that spouse's 'consent requirement' (if any) in respect of any proposed transaction[13]. The net result of the registration would be that no dealing with a matrimonial home could be effected without the consent of the registering spouse and the payment of any relevant capital money to two trustees (thereby ensuring that the registering spouse's beneficial entitlement survived in the proceeds of the transaction[14]). Any dealing with unregistered land subject to a Class G registration would be void unless the terms of the statute were fully observed[15]. A similar result would follow in the case of

8 Law Com No. 86, paras. 1.230f.

9 See p. 145, ante.

10 Law Com No. 86, paras. 1.234ff.

11 The Law Commission recognised that there would be no need for 'statutory co-ownership' in cases where the spouses had already imposed co-ownership on their home in express terms (i.e., by means of a conveyance of the home to themselves expressly as joint tenants of the legal estate). See Law Com No. 86, para. 1.3.

12 Law Com No. 86, paras. 1.318ff., 1.328ff.

13 Law Com No. 86, paras. 1.320f.

14 'The ... purchaser is automatically treated as having actual notice, by virtue of section 198(1) of the Law of Property Act 1925, of the registering spouse's beneficial interest under the trust. The existing law will apply on that basis and will ensure that the beneficial interest in question is not overreached unless the *two trustee rule* is complied with. The registration facility thus remedies, for relevant land, the unsatisfactory feature of the present law about the two trustee rule in relation to land which is unregistered: that there is no satisfactory way to ensure that a purchaser has notice of the circumstances which bring the rule into play' (see Law Com No. 86, para. 1.320). For an explanation of the 'two trustee rule', see later, p. 303, post.

15 According to the Law Commission, the registering spouse's beneficial interest would remain binding upon the purchaser if the latter failed to observe the two trustee rule. To this extent, the disposition to the purchaser would be valid but the purchaser would take an encumbered title.

registered land if the spousal rights were secured by restriction, because in this event no valid transaction could be effected in relation to that land[16].

The Law Commission's proposals were extremely complex. Perhaps the most acute difficulty raised by the entire scheme of statutory co-ownership turned on the fact that protection for a spouse depended effectively on some active step of land charge registration or formal entry in the Land Register. If a major problem with the existing Class F registration is precisely the fact that, for reasons of ignorance or sheer inertia, qualifying spouses neglect to register their rights, it seems scarcely likely that such spouses will be any more ready to register their Class G entitlements. Furthermore, the Law Commission left no doubt as to the consequence of non-registration. It made it quite clear that under the proposed statutory scheme a purchaser would take free of any unregistered Class G charge, 'no matter whether the purchaser has notice of the trust, or of the beneficial interest, in other ways or from other sources[17].'

Once again, as with the Matrimonial Homes Act 1967 itself, a worthwhile measure of reform was vitiated by the attempt to engraft family-based rights on to an existing system of registration of incumbrances governed by the general law of property. The problems which have arisen under the Matrimonial Homes Act are almost entirely attributable to the fact that this statute is not rooted unequivocally in 'family' considerations such as those which underlie the homestead legislation in force in other parts of the Commonwealth. It is perhaps inevitable that the security of spouses will be assured only when the 1967 legislation finally gives way to a rule of automatic co-ownership of the legal estate in the matrimonial home during marriage—a regime not brought about by the application of the commercialist principles of property law but resulting instead from the status of marriage.

The Law Commission's proposal for statutory co-ownership was presented before Parliament during the 1979–1980 session in the form of the Matrimonial Homes (Co-ownership) Bill. Put forward as a Private Member's Bill by Lord Simon of Glaisdale, it failed to pass through the necessary stages of parliamentary process before the end of the session and thus fell to the ground. However, the introduction of the Bill (flawed as it may have been) marked the closest approach yet made in English law towards achieving a specific regime for the governance of matrimonial property relations during the subsistence of marriage.

It may well be that, in default of ameliorating legislation, the problems exposed in the existing matrimonial homes legislation may in fact be relieved by a development of a quite different kind. There is evidence that in England and Wales there has occurred a remarkable and fairly rapid shift during the past

---

However, if the transaction were effected in the face of a 'consent requirement' on the part of the registering spouse, and that spouse did not consent to the disposition in question, the transaction would not even be effective at law. The disposition would be entirely void and no title would pass at all (see Law Com No. 86, para. 1.320).

16 See p. 326, post.

17 Law Com No. 86, para. 1.322. 'This is consistent with the principles of the existing law about registration, and in particular with section 199(1) of the Law of Property Act 1925 . . . Any other solution would involve purchasers in making the enquiries which we are anxious to avoid.'

decade towards a pattern of joint ownership of the matrimonial home on the part of young married couples[18]. This trend—doubtless influenced by the desire of lending institutions to fasten the mortgage commitment upon both wage-earners in the newly emerging dual-career family—may indeed remove much of the pressure generated by the difficulties uncovered in the Matrimonial Homes Act 1967. Moreover, the decision of the House of Lords in *Williams & Glyn's Bank Ltd v Boland*[19] will certainly hasten the movement towards de facto compulsory co-ownership of the matrimonial home in this country, simply because no bank or building society will now dare to lend money on the security of a family home without ensuring the participation of both spouses in the transaction.

(g) *Release and cancellation of registered Class F charges*

There is provision in the Matrimonial Homes Act 1967 for a written release of rights of occupation[20] and cancellation of any registration of those rights[1] in the event that, for instance, the marriage is stable and the estate owner simply wishes to transfer an unencumbered title to a third party purchaser. It is, moreover, a term of any contract for the sale of the legal title which guarantees vacant possession on completion that 'the vendor will before such completion procure the cancellation of the registration' of spousal rights of occupation[2]. Considerable problems ensue if the vendor cannot secure the release of his spouse's statutory rights of occupation and the cancellation of any existing registration.

In *Wroth v Tyler*[3], D and P exchanged contracts for the sale of the matrimonial home with vacant possession on completion. On the day following the exchange of contracts, D's wife entered on the Land Register a notice of her rights of occupation under the Matrimonial Homes Act 1967[4], being unwilling to move away from the district and the friends she had made in that area. D was unable to persuade his wife to remove her notice from the Register in order that completion be effected with vacant possession. P sued D for specific performance of the contract for sale. Megarry J, while declining to order specific performance, awarded P damages for breach of contract on the ground that D had proved unable to give vacant possession as agreed. The measure of contractual damages awarded was of the order of £5,500, a figure which represented the extraordinary inflation of house values during the period which intervened between the date of contract and the date of the court hearing. The irony of this outcome was, as Megarry J himself recognised, that the probable consequence of the wife's obstinacy in refusing to remove her notice was the bankruptcy of her husband—

18 See J. E. Todd and L. M. Jones *Matrimonial Property* (London 1972), p. 79ff.
19 [1980] 3 WLR 138, p. 370, post.
20 Matrimonial Homes Act 1967, s. 6(1).
1 Matrimonial Homes Act 1967, s. 6(2).
2 Matrimonial Homes Act 1967, s. 4(1).
3 [1974] Ch 30.
4 Although this problem arose in the context of land with registered title, exactly the same issue would have been raised by the registration of a Class F land charge in respect of unregistered land.

in which case the matrimonial home would be sold with vacant possession by the husband's trustee in bankruptcy free of any rights in the wife. Even registered rights are ineffective against a trustee in bankruptcy[5]. Being loathe to bring about this conclusion, Megarry J adjourned proceedings to allow the wife to reconsider her position, but she still refused to remove her notice and the court's award of damages took effect. As Megarry J observed, 'there should be displayed in every conveyancer's office the minatory legend Cave uxorem[6].'

5. FINAL ASSESSMENT OF THE LAND CHARGES SYSTEM

As we have seen, the land charges system abounds with difficulty. It is now freely admitted that the Land Charges Act 1925 was a great mistake. Professor Wade has described the land charges scheme of 1925 as 'over-ambitious as well as inherently defective[7].' Yet it should not be forgotten that, as Professor Wade pointed out,

> Public control of land is now the dominant subject, and searches for local land charges and inquiries from local authorities . . . are now of much greater practical importance than the pitfalls and refinements of private conveyancing[8].

This conclusion, reached in 1956, is certainly still valid today—but with the all-important rider that the Matrimonial Homes Act 1967 has introduced complexities which could not be envisaged then. It is chiefly in this respect that there must now be some measure of dissent from Professor Wade's assertion that none of the deficiencies of the land charges system 'seems to matter in real life[9].' The explosion of both the rate of owner-occupation of the matrimonial home and the incidence of marital breakdown which has occurred in recent years ensures that the private conveyancing implications of matrimonial home ownership are very much in the forefront of the property lawyer's mind when he deals with the registration of land charges.

5 Matrimonial Homes Act 1967, s. 2(5), p. 147, ante.

6 [1974] Ch 30 at 64. The Law Commission has, however, answered criticism of the difficulties exposed by *Wroth v Tyler* by asserting that a wife's exercise of her right to register a Class F charge is 'not rendered an abuse merely because it may interfere with smooth conveyancing. It is an essential step in protecting her substantive rights and we think that to introduce restrictions on that exercise would be contrary to the policy of the Act' (see Law Com No. 86, para. 2.83). See D. J. Hayton (1974) 38 Conv (NS) 110: 'The Femme Fatale in Conveyancing Practice'.

7 (1956) 14 Cambridge LJ 216 at 226.

8 (1956) 14 Cambridge LJ 216 at 234. See an earlier reference to local land charges, p. 112, ante.

9 (1956) 14 Cambridge LJ 216 at 234.

CHAPTER 5

Strict settlements

The term 'settlement' is a generic term which, when properly applied, covers all deliberately created trust arrangements which bring about a succession of interests in land or other property. Thus in this broad sense the term 'settlement' in land law includes not only a 'strict settlement' of land (which is governed by the provisions of the Settled Land Act 1925) but also a 'trust for sale' in relation to land (which is governed by a series of provisions found mainly in the Law of Property Act 1925). Both the strict settlement and the trust for sale involve an arrangement whereby the legal estate in land is held on trust, in order that the benefit derived from the land be deflected towards specified persons called 'beneficiaries'. The present chapter will deal with the law relating to strict settlements of land; the institution of the trust for sale will be discussed in chapters 7 and 8.

In order to understand the device of the strict settlement, it may be helpful to bear in mind the social milieu in which the strict settlement has characteristically operated. Although the strict settlement is today rarely used as a means of land ownership, in former days it epitomised the vertical power structure inherent in certain social relations. The strict settlement reflected the living arrangements ordained by a patriarchal family figure; it provided a medium for the conferment of family largesse. The settlement could be made to mirror a number of important and complex social evaluations within the family context, through the dispensing of differing grades of interest to differing kinds of family member[1]. Professor A. W. B. Simpson has spoken of

> the scheme of estates associated with *family* land-ownership: the life estate, the entail, conditional and determinable fees, and estates in remainder and reversion. All the elaboration here was the product of aristocratic dynastic family landholding. To the wealthy landed classes, real property was the essential endowment not of individuals but of the family, a continuing but constantly changing entity forming and reforming around the basic family events—birth, the attainment of majority, marriage and death—and rendered continuous by the concepts of blood and inheritance. Land was to be exploited in the interests of the family, not the individual, but the mechanism for its exploitation was, paradoxically, a subtle manipulation of individual property rights; the family was never treated as an entity capable of itself owning or possessing rights, nor on the other hand were patriarchal notions carried to the point at which only the father of the family enjoyed rights. In the complex history of the subject was expressed a continuous

1 'The evolution of the property object gives to property the power to create separate species within the genus homo, a power like that of an Egyptian king who establishes castes . . .' See K. Renner, *The Institutions of Private Law and Their Social Functions* (London and Boston 1949), p. 109.

tension between two strategies. According to one, the family endowment is best secured by permitting individuals, particularly the current head of the family, as little discretion and power of disposition over the family lands as possible. According to the other, the same end was better achieved by a flexible system under which the endowment can be reallocated so as to adapt to changes in the family, catering for personalities and uncovenanted family events. The compromise commonly employed in Blackstone's time, and evolved in the seventeenth century, was the strict settlement under which the land was managed by a succession of life tenants . . .[2]

Imagine the position of a wealthy but moribund member of the landed aristocracy of a previous social era. This paterfamilias owned the ancestral home and estate in fee simple, but wished to provide for the members of his family upon his imminent decease. What living arrangements could he fashion which might appropriately govern the land in his absence? How could he provide both for his widow and for his eldest son (the new representative of the proud family line)? The difficulty inherent in providing simultaneously for both was accentuated by the extremely important social fact that, if there were two persons whom a moribund testator did well not to trust, those persons were precisely his own widow and his prodigal son. The widow could not be entrusted with the fee simple absolute in the ancestral home—for several reasons. First, she might remarry, with the consequence that the ancestral homestead might pass into the hands of another family. Second, there was a common assumption that a widow, being a female, could be guaranteed to be quite incompetent in business matters, and would doubtless be prone to administer and dispose of the family estate in an irresponsible manner. Nor was the eldest son necessarily worthy of any greater confidence. It might be almost *de rigueur* for that son to waste his substance in riotous living at such institutions as the University of Cambridge!

The resolution of the dilemma disclosed in this slightly hyperbolic account of times past was achieved in the institution of the strict settlement. The obvious method by which all interests might be accommodated could be found in a type of landholding described earlier in this book[3]. The testator could draw up a strict settlement to take effect on his death, under which his widow would receive a life interest in the ancestral home and estate. His eldest son would receive an entailed interest in remainder—an interest which would of course fall into possession on the widow's death but which would never enable him to lay his hands on the capital investment represented by the land[4]. Thus, by making arrangements which conferred merely limited beneficial interests upon the widow and son, the testator could effectively ward off the possibility of

2 'Introduction' to W. Blackstone, *Commentaries on the Laws of England* (Facsimile edn., Chicago and London 1979), pp. x–xi.

3 See p. 67, ante.

4 In the course of time it became possible for a tenant in tail to 'bar' the entail, thus upgrading his interest to some form of estate in fee simple, p. 66f, ante. However, the real truth of the matter was often that the land was subject to resettlement every generation. As Professor A. W. B. Simpson has observed, the settlement was 'reconstituted each generation to ensure that no single individual ever acquired an unfettered power to appropriate the family capital for his individual purposes' (loc. cit., xi).

depredation against the family inheritance committed either through negligence or through over-weening self-interest.

The settled land limitations could be further calibrated. It was common to confer upon the widow a life interest *durante viduitate* (i.e., terminating on her remarriage). The restrictions imposed upon the prodigal son might be reinforced by providing that his entail should be contingent on his attaining the age of 21 or on his entering some 'respectable' profession (e.g., on being called to the Bar). Thereafter the interest given to the son could be made to devolve upon the male heirs of his body, thus ensuring that unless the entail were barred the ancestral home would necessarily remain within the family. In the event that the family line should terminate at some future date, the ultimate remainder in fee simple could be conferred upon, say, some charity. In this way, if and when all possible temporal benefit had been extracted from the land in favour of one's family, one could finally buy a little spiritual credit by leaving the property for the purposes of some charitable object.

These manifold motivations could be conveniently reconciled within the framework of a strict settlement which vested the bare legal title to the land in a nominee while ensuring that the intrinsic benefit to be derived from the land was diverted to the beneficiaries at the appropriate time and in the appropriate proportions:

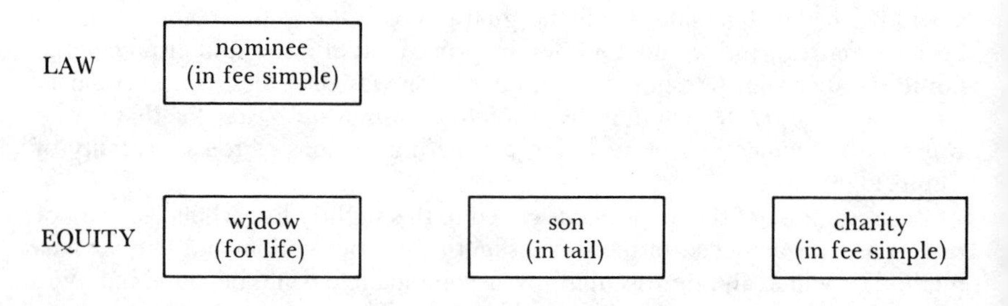

Fig. 21

The essence of this arrangement was that the paper title to the land (i.e., the legal estate) was vested in a nominee who was entrusted with purely administrative functions (powers of management and disposition) and who was bound by fiduciary duties in relation to those functions. However, the valuable as distinct from nominal ownership of the land vested in the beneficiaries behind the trust arrangement thus devised. The enjoyment function therefore devolved upon the beneficiaries in turn, and it became possible in this way to reconcile the conflicting objectives of commerciability and endowment.

Of course, the evolution of the strict settlement in its final form occurred over a long period of time, and the device of landholding described above contains some fairly sophisticated developments which were not perfected until the enactment of the Settled Land Act 1925. It is ironical that just as the strict settlement reached its zenith of refinement as a legal institution, other factors began to operate in such a way as to render the strict settlement an unsuitable (if not indeed fiscally disastrous) form of landholding. As we shall see later[5], the strict settlement has been all but displaced by the trust for sale as the legal model which more aptly expresses the kinds of living arrangement which are common nowadays. Moreover, the tax consequences which flow from the creation of a strict settlement are onerous in the extreme[6]. Today the fiscal implications of strict settlements are such that lawyers' ingenuity is more commonly invested in avoiding the creation of such arrangements in relation to land.

Nevertheless, although the strict settlement now represents a somewhat archaic institution, we shall look in a little detail at the law of settled land, which has much to teach us about both the trade of the land lawyer and the operation of trust and fiduciary arrangements.

1. WHAT CONSTITUTES A 'STRICT SETTLEMENT' WITHIN THE SETTLED LAND ACT 1925?

A 'settlement' is, in the correct sense of the word, a document or group of documents, but the term is commonly used to refer to the form of landholding expressed within those documents. Section 1 of the Settled Land Act 1925 provides that a strict settlement within the meaning of the Act arises in two kinds of situation: (1) where successive or limited beneficial interests are carved out of the ownership of land; (2) where an absolute (as distinct from limited) interest is conferred upon a grantee who is, in some sense, subject to disability or liability.

(1) Successive or limited beneficial interests

The first group of situations is described in section 1(1) of the Settled Land Act 1925. This group includes the straightforward case where land 'stands ... limited in trust for any persons by way of succession[7].' This case neatly catches the facts hypothesised in *Fig.* 21[8]. It would also apply, for instance, where land is granted to A for life, remainder to B for life, remainder to C for life, and so on. All these interests are equitable, and thus take effect successively in possession behind the trust arrangement known as the 'strict settlement'.

Section 1(1)(ii)(a) extends the definition of 'settlement' to cover the situation where land is 'limited in trust for any person in possession for an entailed interest...' This means that the Settled Land Act has application to the following case:

5 See p. 232, post.
6 The form of taxation once known as estate duty (now known as capital transfer tax) falls upon the full capital value of the settled estate on the termination of each successive interest. This form of taxation was introduced by the Finance Act 1894, and the wealth retrieved by the Revenue by means of this tax was to provide the basis of the great naval rearmament in this country which immediately preceded the First World War. See F. H. Lawson, *Introduction to the Law of Property* (London 1958), p. 94f.
7 Settled Land Act 1925, s. 1(1)(i).
8 See p. 156, ante.

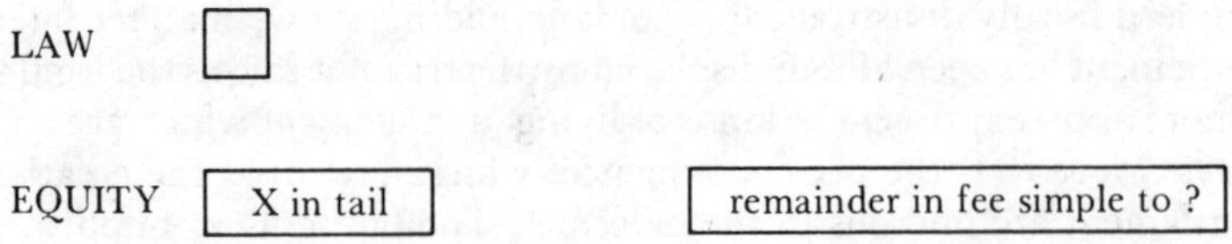

LAW		
EQUITY	X in tail	remainder in fee simple to ?

Fig. 22

Here the limited interest held beneficially by X means necessarily that there is some kind of successive interest which must fall into possession when X's interest determines. If the fee simple is not otherwise disposed of, it will revert to the original grantor or to his estate. It should be noted that, at this stage, the name of the owner of the legal estate (the fee simple absolute in possession) has been left blank. His identity will become obvious shortly[9].

Section 1(1)(ii)(b) refers to an unusual kind of limitation where land is granted to A in fee simple, subject to that interest divesting in favour of B in the event that some specified condition is or is not fulfilled as the case may be. A's interest is said to be subject to a 'condition subsequent', and B's interest is subject to a 'condition precedent'. An example could, for instance, take the form: 'Blackacre to A in fee simple, but if A joins the Labour Party, then to B in fee simple.' There would be a strict settlement here, the determinability of A's equitable interest providing the element of succession which is one characteristic of this form of landholding[10]:

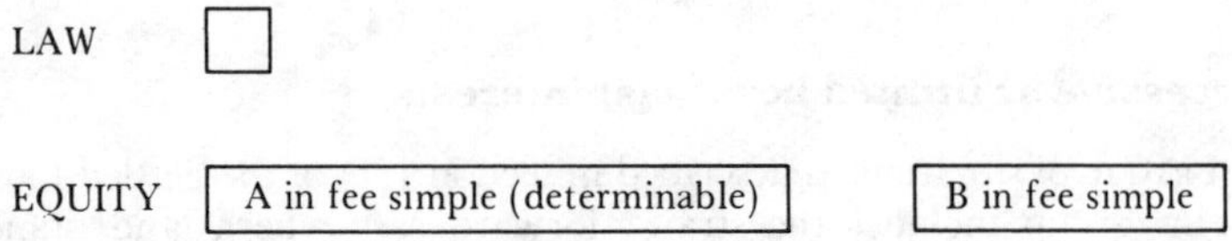

LAW		
EQUITY	A in fee simple (determinable)	B in fee simple

Fig. 23

Section 1(1)(iii) completes the first group of cases where a strict settlement arises by reason of successive limited entitlements[11]. The Settled Land Act applies where land is 'limited in trust for any person for an estate in fee simple . . . contingently on the happening of any event[12].' An example of such an

9 See p. 163, post.

10 *Fig.* 23 is a clear illustration of a 'shifting interest', i.e., an interest which may be divested in favour of another party in the event of some stipulated contingency. (Once again, the identity of the legal owner will be supplied later, p. 163, post). Note, however, that in this situation nothing 'shifts' except the right to 'possession' in the technical sense. No interest passes from A to B.

11 Section 1(1)(ii)(c) refers to base fees resulting from the barring of entailed interests and to other anomalous kinds of interest. This category of strict settlement situation is not particularly significant.

12 Section 1(1)(iii) also applies to the contingent grant of a leasehold interest. In either case, the reference here is to a 'springing interest', i.e., an interest which may or may not materialise at a future date.

interest could arise where land is granted to G in fee simple in the event that he should qualify as a barrister, or play rugby for England, and so on. G's fee simple is contingent upon his performing the qualifying condition. This arrangement in relation to land can be brought about only under the aegis of a strict settlement, since someone has to manage and administer the land until it becomes clear whether G will or will not satisfy the contingency[13]:

LAW	
EQUITY	G in fee simple (contingent)

Fig. 24

(2) Absolute interests granted to persons subject to disability or liability

All the foregoing situations have involved some element of succession or suspense, and are therefore—primarily for reasons of convenience—brought within the ambit of the Settled Land Act 1925. There is, however, a second group of situations which is also governed by the Act. These situations concern not the granting of limited interests by way of succession, but rather the conferment of an absolute beneficial interest in land upon a recipient who is, for some reason, subject to a disability or liability which precludes his holding the absolute interest at law.

The clearest example of this arrangement arises where land is granted in fee simple to an infant or minor (i.e., one who has not yet attained the age of 18). Under section 1 (6) of the Law of Property Act 1925, a minor is never competent to hold a legal estate in land. Thus the grant of a fee simple to a minor can confer only an equitable interest—there is no equivalent objection which prevents a minor from holding an equitable interest. But during the minority, the legal fee simple absolute in possession must be vested in an adult nominee who is entrusted with fiduciary powers of management and disposition. This arrangement must be effected behind a strict settlement, as is made clear in the terms of section 1 (1) (ii) (d) of the Settled Land Act 1925:

LAW	
EQUITY	M (minor) in fee simple

Fig. 25

13 Of course, if the contingency is never satisfied, the fee simple reverts to the settlor or (if he is dead) to his estate.

There is one other situation in which the Settled Land Act 1925 is applicable to the grant of an absolute interest in land. Where land is charged 'whether voluntarily or in consideration of marriage' with the payment of any rentcharge for the life of any person or any less period, the land is subjected to a strict settlement[14]. This would be the case, for instance, where a testator, T, left land to his eldest son, S, in fee simple subject to the payment of an annual income (derived from the rents and profits drawn from the land) to T's widow for the remainder of her life or until her remarriage[15]:

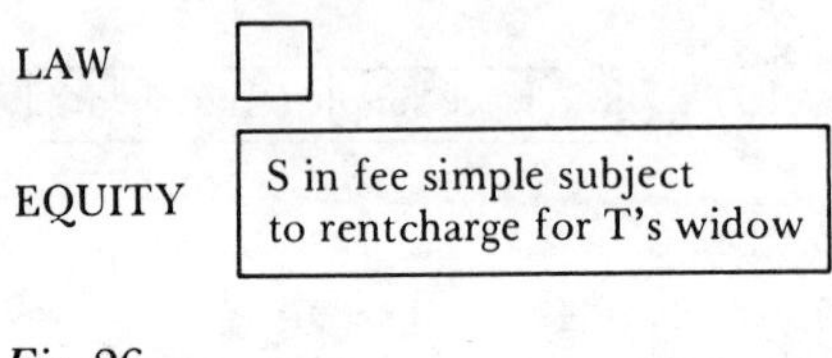

Fig. 26

It may be worthwhile to note that there are several situations which are quite clearly excluded from the ambit of the Settled Land Act 1925. First, the provisions governing strict settlements have no relevance to a 'bare trust'[16]. A bare trust arises where the legal estate in property is, at any time, vested in one person absolutely while simultaneously the entire equitable interest is held by another person absolutely:

LAW	A in fee simple
EQUITY	B in fee simple

Fig. 27

It is a principle of general application to bare trusts that, since A's interest comprises a purely nominal or 'paper' title, A must convey his estate in accordance with any directions given by B, who as owner of the absolute beneficial interest is the only person with any right to enjoy the property and derive value from it. Thus, if B is of full age and sound mind, he may direct A to convey the legal estate to himself, B. Such a conveyance would destroy the bare trust by constituting B the sole owner at law and in equity. This indeed is what should happen in the normal course of events, because a bare trust is

14 Settled Land Act 1925, s. 1(1)(v).

15 However, if S's fee simple were subject to the payment of a rentcharge which arose, not voluntarily or in consideration of marriage, but in return for money or money's worth, then the fee simple would rank technically as a conditional fee simple. Such an estate is deemed to be a legal estate and may, of course, exist without the necessity of creating a strict settlement, p. 58, ante.

16 See p. 26, ante.

intrinsically an anomalous and somewhat unstable arrangement in respect of property. A bare trust connotes a state of disequilibrium: the 'paper' title is for the time being vested in one who has no beneficial stake in the property. Thus equity favours a return to a state of equilibrium, and this is most easily achieved by means of a conveyance by the legal owner to the equitable owner[17].

For present purposes, it is sufficient to understand that a bare trust falls outside the scope of the Settled Land Act 1925, and, by way of corollary, that wherever settled land interests resolve themselves into the form of a bare trust, the land has ceased to be subject to a strict settlement and is no longer governed by the Act.

Another situation falls unequivocally outside the ambit of the strict settlement. Section 1(7) of the Settled Land Act 1925 provides that the Act has no application to 'land held on trust for sale'. The essential difference between a strict settlement and a trust for sale is the fact that under the latter form of landholding the legal estate is vested in trustees and the beneficial interests are normally concurrent and absolute rather than successive and limited[18].

2. IN WHOM IS THE LEGAL ESTATE VESTED UNDER A STRICT SETTLEMENT?

We have discovered that the situations described in *Figs.* 21 to 26 inclusive can exist only by way of a strict settlement under the Settled Land Act 1925. We were able to define the nature of the equitable or beneficial interests in each case, but the owner of the full legal estate in the settled land (i.e., of the legal fee simple absolute in possession) was at each point left unspecified. It is now possible to clarify the identity of the legal owner in each case, because there can be no vacuum in relation to the legal estate during the currency of a strict settlement.

It has already been emphasised that legal ownership relates only to a nominal or 'paper' title. It confers no benefit upon the holder of that title, merely fiduciary obligations of administration (in the form of certain powers of management and disposition of the trust property). This being so, it matters not greatly who holds the legal estate in settled land so long as he faithfully exercises his fiduciary responsibilities. Since the allocation of legal ownership is thus reduced to a question of convenience, it makes sense to vest the legal estate (with its attendant decision-making powers) in the 'man on the spot' at any given time—the beneficiary who currently enjoys an equitable interest in possession. This individual may reasonably be expected to discharge with some degree of care the day-to-day management of the settled property, since it is he who will derive the immediate and tangible benefit of his vigilance. Moreover, an

17 Of course, it is not impossible that the equitable owner B should direct that A convey the legal estate to a third party X. B's right so to direct is simply an application of the rule in *Saunders v Vautier* (1841) 4 Beav 115. However, such a conveyance would not destroy the existence of a bare trust. The transferee at law X would thenceforth hold on a bare trust for B, unless he took title as a bona fide purchaser for value without notice..

18 See p. 214, post.

argument of utility speaks strongly in favour of vesting the legal estate in him for the purpose of facilitating any eventual land transfer. Clearly, it will be more convenient for a purchaser of the settled land if the person living on the property has the requisite power of disposition and is competent to transact with him directly[19].

It was in the light of these considerations that the Settled Land Act 1925 confirmed the office or status of the 'tenant for life'. It is the tenant for life who, in the scheme of the Act, is competent to hold the legal estate and to exercise the concomitant powers of interim management and eventual disposition.

According to section 19(1) of the Settled Land Act 1925, the office of 'tenant for life' is conferred upon

> the person of full age who is for the time being beneficially entitled under a settlement to possession of settled land for his life.

Thus the person who holds an equitable life interest in possession qualifies under this provision as the tenant for life[20]. In *Fig.* 21[1], for instance, the widow is clearly entitled on this basis to hold the legal estate in the settled land. It is at this point that the duality of the tenant for life's interest in the land is most apparent: the tenant for life holds two distinct interests. His legal ownership however is purely nominal and fiduciary in nature. It is only to the extent of his equitable ownership that a tenant for life derives any benefit or value. As soon as the tenant for life enters a situation in which there arises any possibility that he may derive profit from his legal ownership[2], we shall see that independent 'trustees of the settlement' intervene to ensure that the tenant for life suffers no temptation to abandon his fiduciary role for the advancement of self-interest[3]. The intervention of the trustees of the settlement also ensures that the interests of the settled land beneficiaries are 'overreached' by a purchaser and are translated into the proceeds of sale paid over by him[4].

19 See p. 67, ante.

20 'Possession' bears the extended meaning discussed at p. 58f, ante. It is, of course, possible that there may be more than one tenant for life (see Settled Land Act 1925, s. 117(1)(xxviii)), e.g., where land is granted to A and B for their joint lives with remainder to the survivor for life. Both A and B, if of full age, occupy the position of tenant for life (Settled Land Act 1925, s. 19(2)). They are entitled to hold the legal estate as joint tenants, and in the exercise of their joint powers of management and disposition must act unanimously or not at all (see *Re 90 Thornhill Road, Tolworth, Barker v Addiscott* [1970] Ch 261). The survivor becomes, of course, a single tenant for life.

1 See p. 156, ante.

2 Such a situation arises, for instance, where in the exercise of his power of disposition (under section 38 of the Settled Land Act 1925) he sells the entire settled estate, whereupon the capital proceeds of sale are handed over.

3 See p. 184, post.

4 This functional analysis of the roles played by the tenant for life—whether before or after sale of the settled land—makes it plain that there is no inherent contradiction in the duality of the interests initially held by him under the characteristic strict settlement. Qua legal owner, the tenant for life is competent to administer interim management of the settled land and finally to put his signature to any deed of conveyance disposing of a legal estate in that land. Qua beneficial owner, the tenant for life is entitled to enjoy the settled land before sale (i.e., to live on

Section 19(1) thus confers the status and powers of the 'tenant for life' on any person who, at a given point in time, holds an equitable life interest in possession in settled land[5]. This description would not, however, be apt in relation to the beneficiaries referred to in *Figs.* 22 to 26 inclusive, none of whom held a life interest in possession. Here again, the pragmatic common sense of the Settled Land Act dictates that the legal estate and attendant powers be vested in the beneficiary currently in possession—albeit that he holds some beneficial interest other than a *life* interest. Section 20(1) thus confers the powers of the 'tenant for life' upon the holders of other limited interests in the settled land, subject only to the proviso that such persons must be of full age[6] and that the beneficial interest of each is in possession. By a gentle fiction, the office of 'tenant for life' is extended to cover any settled land beneficiary who can properly claim to be the 'man on the spot' at any given moment of time.

Thus X (the tenant in tail in *Fig.* 22) is invested with the powers of the tenant for life by reason of section 20(1)(i); A (in *Fig.* 23) by reason of section 20(1)(ii); S (in *Fig.* 26) by reason of section 20(1)(ix). All are, as it were, artificially invested with the legal estate in the settled land and thenceforth may exercise the appropriate powers of management and disposition in respect of that nominal or 'paper' title[7].

It will be noticed that no reference has yet been made in this context to *Figs.* 24 and 25. In fact section 20(1) does not contain any provision which extends the powers of the tenant for life either to G (in *Fig.* 24) or to M (in *Fig.* 25). The reason for these omissions is obvious. In *Fig.* 24, G was granted land in fee simple contingent upon the happening of some event. Until that event happens, the contingency to which G's interest is subject remains unfulfilled and G has no vested interest in the property at all. Therefore he cannot claim to be the 'man on the spot': he does not have a beneficial interest in possession. There is in this situation no more reason to allocate the legal estate in the settled land to G than there is to vest it in any randomly selected member of the public at large. Therefore, during the interim period, before it becomes clear whether or not G will satisfy the relevant contingency, the legal estate must be held by another nominee[8].

In *Fig.* 25, M was a minor to whom had been granted a fee simple absolute in possession. Section 20(1) does not extend the powers of the tenant for life to such a person, for the plain reason that a minor is incompetent to hold a legal estate

---

the property or receive rents and profits therefrom for the duration of his beneficial interest). That beneficial interest is converted, on sale of the legal estate, into the equivalent right to draw the periodic income from the invested capital proceeds of sale.

5 Exceedingly difficult problems are raised by an informal grant of rent-free occupation for life. See *Bannister v Bannister* [1948] 2 All ER 133; *Binions v Evans* [1972] Ch 359, p. 490, post.

6 See Law of Property Act 1925, s. 1(6).

7 However, it is provided by section 1 of the Law of Property (Amendment) Act 1926 that someone in the position of S (in *Fig.* 26) may convey the land subject to a prior interest 'as if the land had not been settled land'.

8 We shall discover shortly that, in the absence of a tenant for life duly qualified in terms of section 19(1) or section 20(1), the legal estate and the attendant powers are vested in the 'statutory owner' (which usually turns out to be the collective name given to the trustees of the settlement).

in land[9]. Here again is a case where a nominee must step in to hold the legal estate in the settled land until the beneficiary is relieved of his disability. During the minority of the grantee, the powers of the tenant for life are conferred either upon a personal representative of the settlor (in the case of a testamentary grant) or upon the trustees of the settlement[10]. When M attains the age of 18, the legal fee simple absolute must be conveyed to him, whereupon the strict settlement will come to an end[11].

We have seen that there can never be a vacuum in relation to the legal estate in settled land, and the 1925 Act confirms in order of priority certain categories of persons competent to hold the legal estate and to exercise the relevant powers. In default of any person qualified under sections 19 and 20, the powers of the tenant for life are usually conferred upon the 'statutory owner' pursuant to section 23(1). The 'statutory owner' is either the person of full age on whom such powers are expressly conferred by the terms of the strict settlement or, failing such a nomination, the trustees of the settlement.

3. WHO ARE THE TRUSTEES OF THE SETTLEMENT?

It will already be clear that the trustees of a strict settlement play an essentially residual role. They stand normally, as it were, in the wings and look on from a distance: they exercise a general supervision of the strict settlement from afar. They dash on stage only on those rare occasions when their presence is required, as, for instance, where there is no beneficiary qualified to hold the legal estate in the settled land, or where the settled estate is about to be sold and conveyed to a third party purchaser. In the normal course of events, the trustees play only a 'back-up role', and in this respect perform a quite different function from that of the trustees in a trust for sale, who are almost always intimately involved in everything that happens to the land held on trust. Trustees of a strict settlement are—to change the metaphor precipitately—the policemen of the settlement, constantly exercising a low-key surveillance of what goes on.

Thus, in creating a strict settlement of land, the settlor normally not only settles the land in favour of certain beneficiaries but also nominates quite separate trustees of the settlement to exercise a general overseeing role[12]. In the first instance, the settlement trustees will be those persons upon whom have been conferred, by the express terms of the settlement, the various powers and consents which are characteristic of the function of such trustees. Section 30(1) of the Settled Land Act 1925 contains, in a descending order of priority, a list of the categories of person who thus qualify for the trusteeship. If the settlement arises by way of will or intestacy, then, in default of a person or persons nominated within the terms of section 30(1), the personal representatives of the

9 Law of Property Act 1925, s. 1(6).
10 Settled Land Act 1925, s. 26(1).
11 Settled Land Act 1925, s. 7(5).
12 These trustees need not be, and commonly are not in fact, beneficially entitled under the settlement.

deceased (i.e., the executors or persons holding letters of administration) exercise for the time being the functions of the trustees of the settlement[13]. If, for whatever reason, no persons qualify as the settlement trustees within any of the categories enumerated in section 30, any beneficiary or any person otherwise interested in the settlement may apply to the court for the appointment of a fit person as trustee[14].

4. THE CREATION OF A STRICT SETTLEMENT

The basic principle with regard to the creation of strict settlements of land is that two documents are required to be executed. A settlement created by means of one document alone is imperfect—but not altogether ineffective, as will shortly appear.

The requirement of two documents makes good sense. One document is a 'vesting' document of some kind—a 'vesting deed' or a 'vesting instrument'. Its job is to ensure that the 'paper' title (i.e., the legal estate) and the administrative and decision-making functions connected with it are duly vested in the person or persons qualified to exercise the powers of the tenant for life for the purpose of the particular strict settlement. Thus the vesting document is, broadly speaking, a *conveyance* of the legal estate in the settled land to the person or persons entitled at LAW in *Figs.* 21 to 26. The second document is concerned, however, with the beneficial interests in the settled land—that is, the interests marked out in EQUITY in each of the same diagrams. This second document—the 'trust instrument'—lays out the details of the trust by specifying the beneficial equitable interests created under the strict settlement. Its function is entirely different from that of the vesting document.

The use of two quite separate documents is convenient as a matter of conveyancing practice, and indeed represents a highly significant component of the ultimate scheme of the Settled Land Act 1925. That scheme is designed to enable land which is the subject of a family settlement to be freely commerciable despite the existence of beneficial interests in the land. The old idea that settled land must be kept within the family had by 1925 given way to a recognition that somehow the preservation of family interests in the land (the interests of 'endowment') must be reconciled with the overall economic objective of making

13 Settled Land Act 1925, s. 30(3).

14 Settled Land Act 1925, s. 34(1). It is therefore plain that a strict settlement cannot fail for want of the correct dramatis personae. All the way down the line, there is built into the mechanism of the Settled Land Act a series of back-up provisions designed to ensure that the show will go on. A tenant for life must be found somewhere. If he does not appear within section 19, he may be found lurking in the interstices of section 20. Failing that, the statutory owner (i.e., the trustees of the settlement) can be drafted in to perform the role of the tenant for life (section 23). In default of trustees of the settlement, recourse may be had to the settlor's personal representatives if any (section 30(3)), and in the very last resort the court itself may appoint the missing persons (section 34). The artificial nature of these selections is insignificant since in every case the persons concerned perform purely administrative or overseeing functions and do not necessarily derive beneficial enjoyment from the property. The only criteria for selection are therefore good faith and the convenience of the settlement.

land freely marketable. We have already alluded to the fact that the 1925 legislation accommodates these conflicting objectives through the device of 'overreaching'[15]. The legal estate in settled land may be conveyed to a third party purchaser, but the beneficial entitlements—the real wealth in the settled property—survive that transfer inasmuch as after the sale they adhere not to the land but to the capital proceeds of sale.

It is intrinsic to this device that the purchaser takes the legal title to the land free of the equitable interests under the strict settlement. The beneficiaries' rights are swept off the land on to the proceeds of sale. The less the purchaser knows about them the better: his position is quite secure so long as overreaching takes place. He need not even inquire into the nature of the beneficiaries' rights: he is concerned only with the legal title.

These quite simple facts provide the rationale for the 'curtain principle' which appears at the culmination of the Settled Land Act 1925[16]. The 'curtain principle' drives a wedge between matters affecting the legal title to land and matters concerned with beneficial entitlement. On a sale of settled land, the third party purchaser need look only at the document which relates to the legal title. The trusts under the settlement—the beneficial interests—are kept off the title. They are concealed behind a 'curtain' and are not normally revealed to the purchaser. After all, he has no proper concern with the precise details of the family equitable interests dispensed by the original settlor. The operation of the 'curtain principle' is thus dependent on the use of two separate documents relating to the settled land, only one of which is inspected by the intending purchaser. Under section 110(2) of the Settled Land Act 1925, a purchaser of a legal estate in settled land normally 'shall not . . . be bound or entitled to call for the production of the trust instrument . . .' He is not even entitled, under normal circumstances, to investigate the details of the trust because overreaching will automatically sweep all beneficial interests off the land.

The Settled Land Act 1925 thus requires that an inter vivos settlement be effected by the use of two deeds[17]. If effected in any other way, the settlor will have failed to secure a proper vesting of the legal estate[18]. An inter vivos settlement can arise in two slightly different ways. If the settlor, S, wishes to settle Blackacre (which he owns in fee simple) upon A for life, with remainder to B in tail and further remainder to C in fee simple, he may simply execute a vesting deed conveying the legal fee simple absolute in Blackacre to A (the first tenant for life) on the trusts which are outlined in a second document. S simultaneously indicates in that second document (the trust instrument) the equitable interests to be enjoyed successively by A, B and C. Thus the position would be as follows:

15 See p. 74ff, ante.
16 See p. 184, post.
17 Settled Land Act 1925, s. 4(1).
18 A vesting deed must contain reference to those matters with which a future purchaser may justly be concerned. That deed must make it clear that the legal estate transferred is held on the trusts of a strict settlement (Settled Land Act 1925, s. 5(1)). It should also name the persons who are to be the trustees of the settlement. However the private details of those trusts are contained only in the trust instrument (Settled Land Act 1925, s. 4(3)). A minor error in the details required to be present in a vesting deed does not invalidate the deed (Settled Land Act 1925, s. 5(3)).

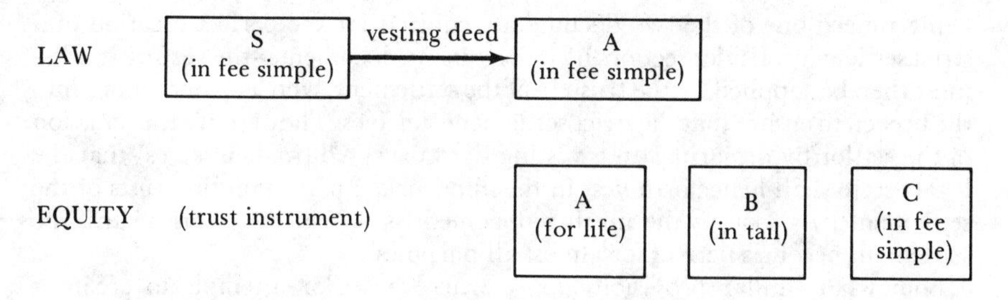

Fig. 28

Alternatively, since he proposes to settle Blackacre during his own lifetime, S may well wish to include himself among the beneficiaries of the strict settlement. In this case, he may settle Blackacre upon himself for life, with remainders to A, B and C successively as before[19]:

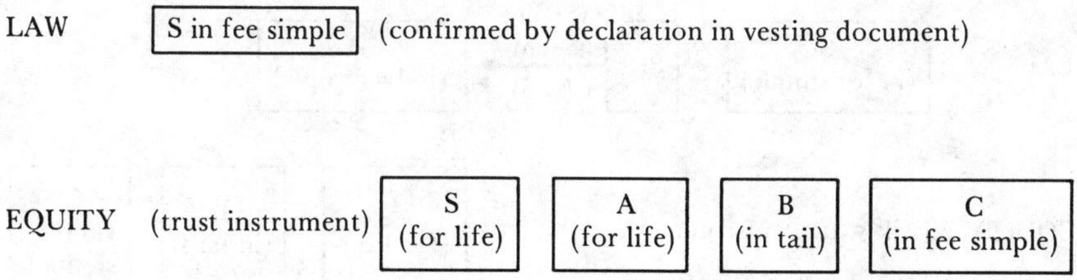

LAW S in fee simple (confirmed by declaration in vesting document)

EQUITY (trust instrument) S (for life) A (for life) B (in tail) C (in fee simple)

Fig. 29

Difficulties present themselves if, for instance, the settlor in *Fig.* 28 attempts to create a strict settlement by means of only one document. What happens if he signs a simple written statement granting Blackacre to A for life, with remainders over to B and C? In the absence of a vesting instrument the settlement is imperfect, but the Settled Land Act 1925 provides a remedy for the defect. Section 9(1) deems certain categories of document to be a 'trust instrument' for the purpose of the Act, and included among these categories is an

instrument inter vivos intended to create a settlement of a legal estate in land which . . . does not comply with the requirements of this Act with respect to the method of effecting such a settlement[20].

Thus the settlor's scrap of paper, which in its unsophisticated way spells out the beneficial entitlements just as would a proper trust instrument, is regarded as

19 The only difference from *Fig.* 28 is that no conveyance as such of the legal estate is required, since S (the first tenant for life) is already invested with the fee simple qua original owner. Here it is sufficient that the vesting document merely 'declares' that henceforth S is to hold the legal estate on the trusts of the strict settlement contained in the trust instrument (see Settled Land Act 1925, s. 4(2)).

20 Settled Land Act 1925, s. 9(1)(iii).

being indeed one of the two documents required for the perfect creation of a strict settlement. Under section 9(2), the missing document—the vesting deed—must then be supplied by the trustees of the settlement, who leap once more into the breach to ensure that the strict settlement survives. They rectify the omission of the settlor by declaring (in a vesting deed executed by themselves) that the legal estate shall henceforth vest in the appropriate person on the trusts of the settlement[1]. As soon as the missing document is provided by this means, the settlement becomes perfect for almost all purposes[2].

Somewhat similar provisions apply where a settlor attempts to create a settlement of land not inter vivos but by will. Under section 6 of the Settled Land Act 1925, the will is deemed to be the trust instrument—because it naturally spells out the interests in the land to be enjoyed by the various beneficiaries. The second document—the vesting document—is executed in favour of the appropriate tenant for life, this time by the testator/settlor's personal representatives[3]:

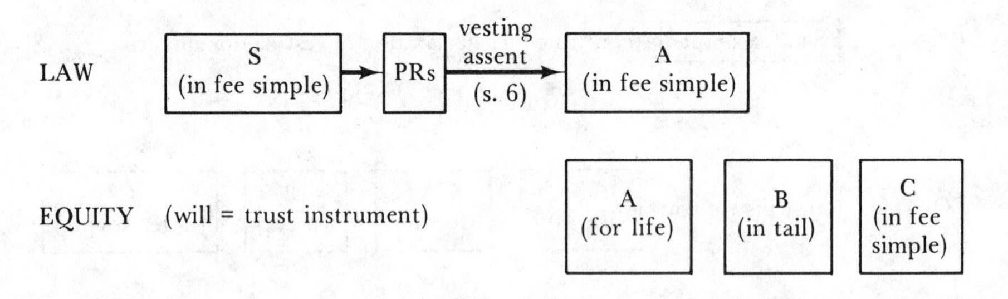

Fig. 30

There are other kinds of error or omission which may conceivably arise in the creation of a strict settlement, but the 1925 Act incorporates at almost every point of default the appropriate machinery for rectifying the initial error[4].

1 In *Fig.* 28, this person is A. If, in the situation depicted in *Fig.* 29, the settlor omitted to confirm by way of a vesting document that he himself henceforth held the legal estate subject to the trusts of the settlement, the trustees of the settlement would have a similar power to make the appropriate declaration on his behalf. If there exist no trustees of the settlement to perform these functions, the court may be asked to make a suitable appointment (Settled Land Act 1925, s. 9(3)).

2 See p. 184, post.

3 This makes sense because it is in these persons that the testator's legal estate automatically vests at the moment of his death. By means of a ministerial act of signature upon a 'vesting assent', they simply shuffle the nominal legal title on to the person entitled in terms of the settlor's will. It seems that a vesting document is still required even where that person is already invested with the full legal estate (e.g., as the survivor of the original personal representatives). See *In re King's WT* [1964] Ch 542. However, the vesting document used here need not be a 'vesting deed'; it may be a simple written statement or 'vesting assent' (Settled Land Act 1925, s. 8(1)).

4 See also section 27 of the Settled Land Act 1925, which uses the device of the settlement to deal with ineffective conveyances of the legal estate to a minor.

5. THE EFFECTS OF IMPERFECT AND PERFECT VESTING OF THE LEGAL ESTATE

The implications of imperfect and perfect vesting of the legal estate in settled land are contained in a notable pair of sections in the Settled Land Act 1925, sections 13 and 18. These two sections are mutually exclusive in their scope and operation. Section 18 takes over where section 13 has ceased to operate.

Section 13 relates to the situation in which a strict settlement is as yet imperfect for want of a second (i.e., vesting) document. The legal estate in the settled land has not been properly vested in the tenant for life: only the trustees of the settlement (in the case of an inter vivos settlement) or the testator's personal representatives (in the case of a settlement by will) are now competent to cure the initial defect. There is an awkward hiatus between the execution of the two documents which are essential to the full validity of the settlement. It may be questioned whether, during this period of limbo and before the second document is duly provided by the responsible persons, any dealings may take place in respect of the legal estate in the settled land. Here section 13 enters to provide unequivocally that, during the currency of an imperfect settlement,

> any purported disposition [of the legal estate] inter vivos by any person . . . shall operate only as a contract for valuable consideration to carry out the transaction after the requisite vesting instrument has been executed . . .

Section 13 allows certain exceptions, however, where a disposition of a legal estate in the settled land can, notwithstanding the imperfection, enjoy the full legal effect intended. The most important exception exists in favour of a purchaser of a legal estate who has no notice of the fact that the person with whom he is dealing is in reality entitled to have a vesting deed or assent executed in his favour. Thus section 13 honours the general principle which pervades English land law whereby the innocent purchaser of a legal estate in land receives maximum protection.

The effect of section 13 is otherwise to paralyse dealings with the legal estate for the duration of the imperfect settlement. However, it is not true that during this period transactions in relation to the legal estate have utterly no effect. The import of section 13 is simply that they usually cannot have the full effect originally intended (e.g., the effect of conveying the fee simple in the land to a third party). However, the transaction in question will enjoy a limited contractual effect in that it is deemed to constitute an agreement to carry out the original intention of the contracting parties if and when the settlement is rendered perfect by the execution of a proper vesting deed.

The operation of section 13 can most clearly be seen in the situation described in *Fig.* 29[5]. Suppose that S has not yet confirmed in any vesting document the fact that henceforth he holds the legal fee simple in Blackacre on the trusts of the settlement which he has created. Even in the absence of a declaration reciting the existence of the settlement trusts, S is of course entitled to continue to live on Blackacre, since his beneficial life interest is currently the only equitable interest

5 See p. 167, ante.

in possession. S, however, will still possess his original title deeds in respect of Blackacre, and those title deeds will show him to be the owner in fee simple without any reference to the as yet non-existent strict settlement. If S attempts to use *these* title deeds as the basis of any transaction with a third party, section 13 will come into play:

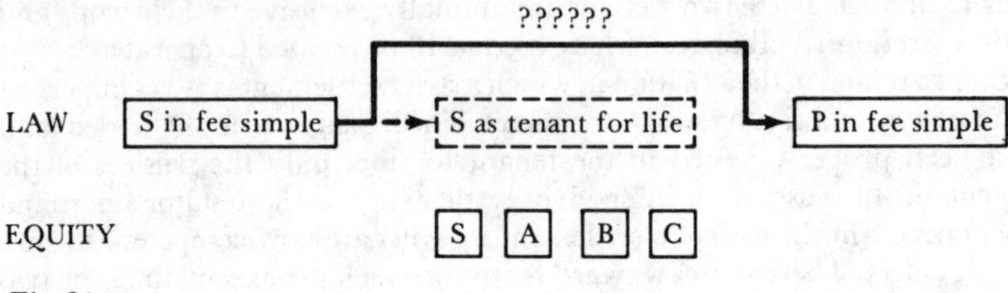

Fig. 31

S has attempted to sidestep the existence of the strict settlement (albeit imperfect), and has in effect tried to defraud the other settled land beneficiaries by selling the fee simple in his earlier role as absolute owner. If successful in this ploy, S would receive the capital proceeds of sale (paid over by the purchaser P) for himself absolutely. If he had sold qua tenant for life, his own beneficial interest would have been overreached (provided that the capital moneys were paid to the trustees of the settlement), and he would have received merely a life interest in the income from the proceeds of sale[6].

If, in this situation, P is a purchaser who has no knowledge of the existence of the strict settlement (still less of S's entitlement to a vesting instrument), then he will take the legal estate free of the settled land interests, in accordance with the principal exception embodied in section 13[7].

If, on the other hand, P were a purchaser who does not enjoy the immunity referred to within section 13 (e.g., where he knows of the existence of the imperfect settlement), then the result is somewhat different. At this point, section 13 would intervene to frustrate the conveyance of S's fee simple to P: the transaction has purely the effect of a contract by S to convey the legal estate to P at a later date when the settlement has been perfected by the provision of a vesting document—a document which would of course, by its very nature, compel S to convey as a tenant for life subject to the settlement trusts. A sale under these circumstances would overreach the beneficial interests under the settlement (provided again that the proceeds of sale were paid to the trustees of the settlement)[8].

6 See p. 74f, ante.
7 S, however, would be liable for breach of trust, and could therefore be forced to pay the settled land beneficiaries compensation out of the capital proceeds of sale which he has wrongfully received.
8 Pending the conveyance, P's contractual rights can be protected by the registration of a Class C(iv) land charge (in the case of unregistered land) or by a notice or caution upon the title (in the case of registered land). P's contractual right to call for a conveyance at the later point in time when the settlement is perfected is thereby protected as a form of estate contract (Settled Land Act 1925, s. 13). By the appropriate registration, P can effectively prevent S from conveying the legal estate under the perfected settlement to any other third party.

It appears that section 13 automatically ceases to have any application if the circumstances which in the first place raise the necessity for a strict settlement themselves cease to exist. For present purposes, the facts of *Re Alefounder's Will Trusts*[9] may be deemed to be identical to those expressed in *Fig.* 22. Here, however, the settlement was technically imperfect because the tenant in tail had never received a proper vesting in his favour qua tenant for life. The tenant in tail nevertheless barred his entail, thus converting his equitable interest into a fee simple interest and destroying any remainder over. He now wished to convey the fee simple to a third party purchaser, and claimed to be able to do so free of the fetters imposed by section 13. He happened quite fortuitously to possess title deeds which appeared to show him to be an absolute owner at law and in equity. Astbury J held that the situation had originally come within the four corners of the Settled Land Act 1925 by reason of the fact that an entailed interest can exist only behind a strict settlement[10]. From the moment the entail was barred, however, the land ceased to be settled land. By the act of disentailing, the tenant in tail had destroyed the very premise for the application of the Settled Land Act and was thus entirely free to convey the fee simple to a third party without first perfecting the imperfect settlement. Section 13 has no application if an imperfect settlement of land is demolished before its construction is complete.

Section 13 inhibits purported dispositions of the legal estate in settled land during that awkward period of limbo before an initially imperfect settlement is put on a proper footing by the execution of the requisite vesting instrument[11]. It is now time to turn to section 18, which operates in an entirely different context: it applies only where the strict settlement is indeed perfect (i.e., where the two necessary documents have been executed—whether belatedly or not).

Section 18(1)(a) provides that where

> land is the subject of a vesting instrument and the trustees of the settlement have not been discharged . . . then any disposition of a legal estate by the tenant for life or statutory owner . . . other than a disposition authorised by this Act or any other statute . . . shall be void.

In other words, where a strict settlement is perfect, the legal estate may be dealt with only in accordance with the terms laid down in the Act. Any irregular disposition of the legal estate is utterly void and ineffectual—a most draconian result[12].

The scope of authorised dealing with the legal estate in settled land is effectively circumscribed by section 18(1)(b), (c)[13]. Section 18(1)(b) provides that a conveyance of the legal estate to a purchaser shall be effective only if the

9 [1927] 1 Ch 360.

10 Settled Land Act 1925, s. 1(1)(ii)(a), see p. 157, ante.

11 A 'disposition' in this sense may include not only a conveyance on sale but also a lease or mortgage of the settled land (see Settled Land Act 1925, s. 117(1)(v)).

12 Section 18 has no application to dealings with an equitable interest—it strikes only at transactions related to the legal estate in the settled land. Other minor exceptions to section 18 are contained in section 18(2).

13 The ambit of authorised dealing with the legal estate may be widened by the express words of the vesting instrument.

capital proceeds of sale arising are paid to or by the direction of the trustees of the settlement or into court. Section 18(1)(c) provides imperatively that the capital money

> shall not, except where the trustee is a trust corporation, be paid to or by the direction of fewer persons than two as trustees of the settlement.

These vital provisions must be read in conjunction with section 2(1)(i) of the Law of Property Act 1925[14]. The last-mentioned subsection categorises those transactions in real property which are generally capable of having overreaching effect. Section 2(1)(i) makes it a clear precondition of overreaching in the settled land context that 'the statutory requirements respecting the payment of capital money arising under the settlement are complied with.' Thus, exceptional instances apart, no overreaching of the settled land interests ever takes place unless the capital money arising on the relevant disposition is paid to at least two trustees. The combined effect of these provisions is, of course, to nullify any purported disposition of the legal estate in the settled land which fails to safeguard the beneficiaries' interests. Once again, it will be noticed, the trustees of the settlement are called upon to play a vital role in preserving the settled land entitlements. Payment to at least two trustees minimises the possibility of self-serving fraud on the part of the tenant for life (even if he is also one of the trustees), and causes the settled land interests to attach henceforth to the proceeds of sale. The settlement trustees now stand in a fiduciary position in relation not to land but to a fund of money, and the beneficiaries' rights are converted automatically into the equivalent interests in that fund[15].

The best known application of section 18 of the Settled Land Act 1925 occurs in *Weston v Henshaw*[16]. Here a tenant for life under a perfect strict settlement fortuitously possessed (in addition to the vesting instrument) an old set of title deeds derived from an earlier transaction. These title deeds inaccurately made him appear to be a 'beneficial owner', i.e., to be absolutely entitled both at law and in equity without reference to any settlement or trust. The tenant for life wrongfully produced the earlier documents of title in order to persuade a third party to lend money on the security of an apparently unencumbered fee simple. The fraud succeeded, and the third party took a mortgage over the land as his security. Never suspecting for one moment the existence of the later deed of settlement, he paid the loan moneys to the tenant for life alone, who then proceeded to dissipate the amounts advanced. On the death of the tenant for life, the remainderman discovered the fraud and argued that the mortgage granted by the dishonest tenant for life was a void disposition under section 18(1) by reason of the fact that the capital moneys arising had not been paid to at least two trustees, but had been paid merely to one tenant for life (see *Fig.* 32).

On these facts Danckwerts J held that the mortgagee must indeed lose his security, since the mortgage had been unauthorised in the special sense used in the legislation and because, in the strict terms of section 18(1)(a), an unauthorised

14 See p. 314, post.
15 See p. 74f, ante.
16 [1950] Ch 510.

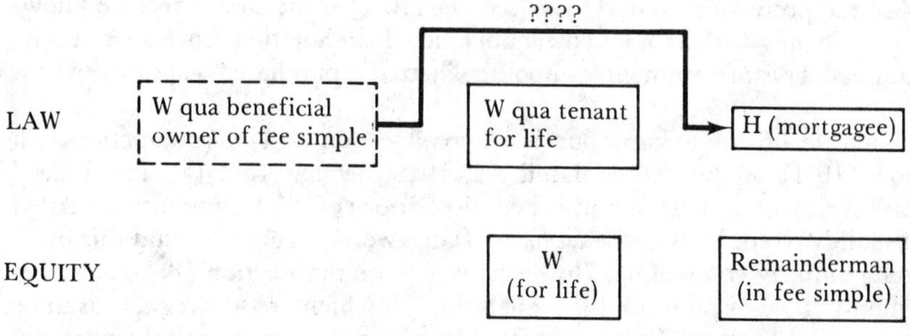

Fig. 32

disposition 'shall be void.' If this decision was correct, *Weston v Henshaw* represents a remarkable exception to the fundamental policy of English land law that the innocent purchaser should not be prejudiced or penalised[17].

Doubt has in fact been cast upon the correctness of the decision in *Weston v Henshaw*, reference being made to section 110(1) of the Settled Land Act 1925, which provides that in any transaction in which a purchaser deals 'in good faith with a tenant for life or statutory owner', that purchaser shall 'be conclusively taken . . . to have complied with all the requisitions of this Act.' In other words, it is argued, the purchaser must be irrebuttably presumed to have paid the capital money to at least two trustees in accordance with section 18(1)(c) even though he clearly did not do so. This argument was rejected by Danckwerts J, who thought that section 110(1) applied only in favour of a purchaser who actually knew that he was dealing with a tenant for life[18]. However, in *Re Morgan's Lease*[19] Ungoed-Thomas J was later to express the *obiter* view that section 110(1) is relevant irrespective of the knowledge of the purchaser[20]. This view has generally been preferred by the commentators to that put forward by Danckwerts J in *Weston v Henshaw*[1], not least because it introduces some common sense into the matter. The very situation in which the purchaser stands least in

17 We shall see (p. 286ff, post) that essentially the same conflict between commercial and family considerations arises in connection with the equivalent problem in respect of trusts for sale, where an innocent purchaser buys land entirely unaware of the fact that the land is held on trust for sale. In the latter context it will emerge that the courts have generally striven to protect the innocent purchaser. In commenting on *Weston v Henshaw*, G. A. Grove once pointed out: 'Had the borrower been instead of a tenant for life the last survivor of trustees for sale it would seem that the mortgagee would have acquired a good title as a bona fide purchaser of the legal estate without notice of the equitable interests. For the protection of purchasers it seems desirable that the law should be altered. Section 13, in avoiding dispositions of settled land made prior to the execution of a vesting instrument, expressly excludes dispositions made in favour of a purchaser of a legal estate without notice of any settlement' ((1961) 24 MLR 123 at 129: 'Conveyancing and the Property Acts of 1925').

18 [1950] Ch 510 at 519.

19 [1972] Ch 1 at 9.

20 Ungoed-Thomas J also noted that the earlier authority of the Court of Appeal in *Mogridge v Clapp* [1892] 3 Ch 382 had not been cited before Danckwerts J in *Weston v Henshaw*. See E. H. Scamell [1957] CLP 152 at 163: 'The Reform of the Settled Land Act 1925'.

1 See R. H. Maudsley (1973) 36 MLR 25 at 28f.: 'Bona Fide Purchasers of Registered Land'.

need of the protection conferred by section 110(1) is the case where he knows that he is dealing with a limited owner of land which is settled. Correspondingly, section 110(1) is pre-eminently apposite where the purchaser is *unaware* of that fact.

It is a little difficult to know how best to read section 18(1) in conjunction with section 110(1) of the Settled Land Act 1925. Section 18(1)(a) does indeed declare forthrightly that unauthorised dispositions of the legal estate in settled land shall be void. In *Weston v Henshaw*, Danckwerts J seemed to find this plain language utterly compelling. However, it may be that section 18(1)(a) strikes down only those dispositions by a tenant for life which are so irregular as to be ultra vires the Act itself. In *Weston v Henshaw*, not only was the capital money not paid to the trustees of the settlement, but the tenant for life acted ultra vires the Settled Land Act in using redundant title deeds for the fraudulent purpose of deceiving the mortgagee. The Settled Land Act gives the tenant for life no authority to cheat. Indeed, in *Weston v Henshaw* the mortgagor made no attempt at all to transact in his capacity as tenant for life; he purported to act, vis à vis the mortgagee, in the capacity of sole beneficial owner.

Accordingly, it is arguable that a purchaser takes a good title under the immunity given by section 110(1) where the tenant for life, while remaining intra vires the Act, violates some provision of the Act. Such would be the case, for instance, where a disposition by the tenant for life is within the authority conferred upon him by the Act (i.e., where he makes no attempt to act otherwise than qua tenant for life), but he fails to ensure that the capital moneys arising on the disposition are paid to the settlement trustees. This rationale derives some support from section 112(2) of the Settled Land Act 1925, which provides that any provision in the Settled Land Act (including presumably section 110(1)) which refers to 'sale, purchase, . . . mortgaging, . . . leasing, or other disposition or dealing' shall be construed as extending only to 'transactions under this Act.' Thus, it can be argued, the immunity granted by section 110(1) extends only to tenants for life or statutory owners who transact within the four corners of the Act. Conversely, as Danckwerts J indicated in *Weston v Henshaw*, section 18(1) is by its very essence concerned with 'transactions which are not in pursuance of the Act and which it therefore makes void[2].'

This rationale, although neat, still leaves some fundamental problems in its wake. In giving support to the decision in *Weston v Henshaw*, it produces a result in contravention of the principle which pervades English land law, i.e., the unspoken rule that innocent purchasers must be protected. The result is strange in view of the fact that it is where he is defrauded by a dishonest tenant for life that the purchaser most needs protection; and even stranger when it is borne in mind that it is for the default of his vendor that the innocent purchaser is being penalised. Even then it seems odd that, if the purchaser is disabled from pleading section 110(1) because his vendor has, as it were, committed a 'fundamental breach' of the Settled Land Act, the purchaser's title should be held void under another provision of that same Act, i.e., section 18(1)(a).

It may be that the confusion generated by sections 18(1)(a) and 110(1) can be

2 [1950] Ch 510 at 519.

relieved only by reference to their historical background. In its classical form, the strict settlement was essentially a *landholding* mechanism which was only gradually and with great ingenuity modified by statute in the late 19th and early 20th centuries to ensure the commerciability of the great landed estates. The strict settlement provided a structure whose overriding purpose was the protection of the interests of the beneficiaries and, ultimately, the protection of the dynastic impulse. For the settled land beneficiaries, the value of the land lay not in some supposed 'exchange value' but rather in the 'use value' or utility derived from physical occupation of the land. Accordingly the primary emphasis of the law of settled land was upon the need to safeguard the settlement from the prejudicial interventions of third parties and to preserve the remaindermen from an abuse of power by the beneficiary currently entitled in possession. So marked was this emphasis that the position of the tenant for life before 1926 was, as Professor Elliott has pointed out[3], 'essentially that of a donee of a power.' As a mere donee of a power, his transactions in respect of the legal estate were strictly controlled in the interest of protecting the remaindermen, and an invalid exercise of his power could result in his transactions being ineffective at law.

In 1926, however, the function of the tenant for life changed dramatically, in furtherance of the policy of the 1925 legislation to facilitate conveyancing. This objective was secured in the context of the strict settlement, not merely by concentrating administrative powers in the hands of the tenant for life but by investing him with the full legal estate in the settled land. In the light of this development, as Professor Elliott explains, the role of section 18 of the Settled Land Act 1925 is nevertheless to return the tenant for life to something approximating to his pre-1926 position:

> After 1925, he is made an estate owner. He has not merely a power, but the entire legal estate vested in him. It is true that there are regulations, similar to the pre-existing ones, which he must observe in passing the legal estate to anyone else, but in the absence of any further statutory provision, a failure to comply with these regulations would not prevent him from passing the legal estate which is in him. If his alienee were a bona fide purchaser for value there would be no way in which the remainderman or other beneficiaries could pursue the property thus irregularly conveyed. Hence section 18(1), which prevents this by providing that an unauthorised disposition is void, and puts the purchaser firmly back to rely on the 'defective execution' procedure in section 110(1) . . . Thus it appears that the object of section 18(1) was not to alter the position in favour of the remainderman, but to prevent it from being altered in prejudice of the remainderman. The legislature, having decided to simplify conveyancing by making the tenant for life an actual estate owner instead of a mere donee of a power, nevertheless balks at the logical implications of this change, and ends by making his position indistinguishable from a mere donee.

Having thus provided a more satisfactory account for the presence of section 18(1)(a), Professor Elliott proceeds to read down the scope of section 110(1). In his view, this provision is 'far from being a charter of immunity' for a purchaser in good faith[4]. Section 110(1) does not say that the purchaser receives a good

3 (1971) 87 LQR 338 at 341: 'Curing a Defective Lease granted by a Tenant for Life'.
4 (1971) 87 LQR 338 at 343.

title; it merely provides that he is to be conclusively taken to have complied with all the requisitions of the Act.

This historical excursus still does not reconcile sections 18(1) and 110(1) of the Settled Land Act 1925, nor does it make the plain wording of section 18(1)(a) any more conformable to the major bias in English land law towards protecting innocent purchasers. It does, however, make the apparent confusion in the 1925 legislation rather less baffling than might at first appear. The real difficulty underlying the entire problem discussed here is the way in which legislation has attempted to transform into a conveyancing device an institution whose essential object was not sale but the retention of land for family purposes. In this sense, the difficulties experienced here are the precise reverse of those encountered in the context of the trust for sale, where the general movement of the law in recent times has been away from the trust for sale as a conveyancing device towards the recognition of the trust for sale as a medium of landholding for family purposes[5].

6. THE POWERS OF THE TENANT FOR LIFE OR STATUTORY OWNER

We shall look at the powers of the tenant for life (or statutory owner, as the case may be) first in relation to his equitable or beneficial interest then in relation to the legal estate in the settled land.

(1) Powers in relation to equitable interests

The primary rule is that a tenant for life may deal as he wishes with his own equitable interest under the strict settlement, and that such dealings normally have no effect upon the ownership of the legal estate in the settled land[6]. Let us look again at our archetypal strict settlement.

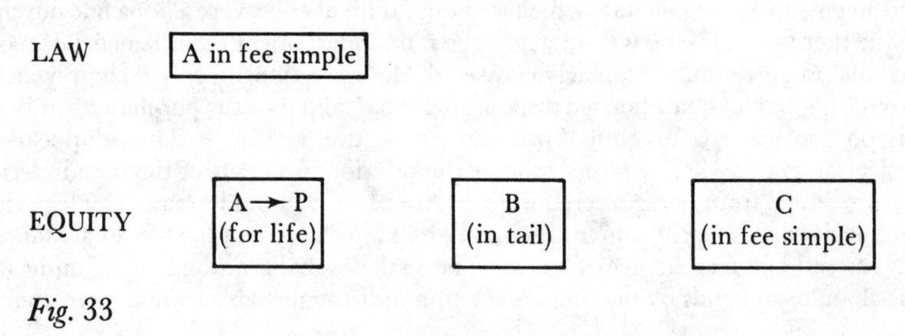

Fig. 33

Here A has sold his beneficial life interest to P. P simply takes A's place among the settled land beneficiaries, although it must be remembered that P's equitable interest will terminate on the death of *A*. P has simply bought that which A owned in equity, with the result that he now holds an estate *pur autre vie*. This is

5 See p. 217, post.
6 Settled Land Act 1925, s. 104(1).

clearly an imprudent purchase by P, since it represents an extremely incautious gamble on the longevity of A. However, the fact remains that A's dealing with his equitable interest does not in any way affect his holding of the legal fee simple absolute in the settled land. Notwithstanding that A has realised his beneficial share or stake in the property, he is still expected to exercise his fiduciary responsibilities in relation to the administration and disposition of the settled land: in this respect he is in the same position as any other fiduciary who holds property on trust without being entitled to enjoy the property beneficially[7].

There are several minor exceptions to the basic rule that equitable dealings have no automatic effect upon the legal title to settled land, and these exceptions are of a commonsense nature. If, in *Fig.* 33, A had not sold his beneficial life interest to P, but had instead surrendered that life interest to the next remainderman, B, ownership of the legal estate would indeed have been affected. Such a transaction accelerates the point at which B's equitable interest falls into possession, and it therefore makes sense that the nominal legal title should be shuffled on to B as the man now beneficially entitled in possession. Section 105(1) of the Settled Land Act 1925 provides accordingly that where there is an 'assurance' (or written declaration) by a tenant for life in favour of the next remainderman, with 'intent to extinguish' the tenant for life's interest under the settlement, then the statutory powers of the tenant for life

> shall ... cease to be exercisable by him and ... shall thenceforth become exercisable as if he were dead ...[8]

The corollary of section 105(1) appears in section 7(4), according to which

> if by reason of ... surrender ... the estate owner of any settled land ceases to have the statutory powers of a tenant for life and the land remains settled land, he shall be bound forthwith to convey the settled land to the person who under the trust instrument ... becomes the tenant for life ...

Thus, by means of a series of tightly interlocking provisions, the Settled Land Act ensures that, on A's abdicating his beneficial interest in favour of B, the legal title must also be passed along the line (see *Fig.* 34)[9]:

7 Of course, when a sale of the settled land eventually takes place, A carrying out the ministerial act of signing the conveyance, the equities which will on overreaching attach to the proceeds of sale will be those belonging to P (for A's life), B and C.

8 See also Settled Land Act 1925, s. 19(4).

9 It might be said that, even after A surrenders his life interest to B, the land still remains settled land for the purpose of section 7(4), simply by reason of the fact that there is a succession of beneficial entitlements which can exist only by way of a strict settlement (see Settled Land Act 1925, s. 1(1)(ii)(a) and *Fig.* 22, p.158, ante). Section 7(4) operates with similar effect wherever the estate owner of settled land ceases to have the statutory powers of the tenant for life for reasons other than surrender of his beneficial interest (e.g., in the case of forfeiture of the equitable interest or where that interest determines in accordance with the terms of the settlement). However, these instances concern not so much the tenant for life's dealings with his equitable interest, but rather the operation of extrinsic factors which bring the equitable interest to an end.

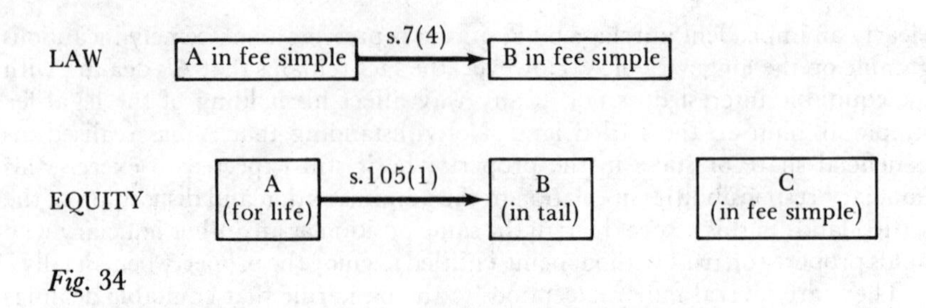

Fig. 34

The other occasion on which equitable dealings by a tenant for life impinge upon ownership of the legal estate occurs, for instance, in the situation depicted in *Fig.* 33[10]. If A, on disposing of his equitable life interest to P, then wilfully neglects to discharge his remaining fiduciary responsibilities in relation to the legal estate, section 24(1) of the Settled Land Act 1925 may be brought into play. It may be that A takes the view that, since he no longer has any beneficial stake in the property, there is no further incentive for him to devote any care to the administrative responsibilities connected with nominal legal ownership. In such a case section 24(1) provides that application may be made to the court for an order authorising the trustees of the settlement to exercise any of the statutory powers of the tenant for life in his name and on his behalf[11]. Once again, the settlement trustees intervene to ensure that the settlement continues unprejudiced.

(2) Powers in relation to the legal estate in settled land

The powers of the tenant for life in relation to the legal estate in settled land are contained in sections 38–75 of the Settled Land Act 1925. These powers include certain powers to sell, lease and mortgage the legal estate.

The tenant for life is, of course, a fiduciary in respect of his ownership of the legal estate and the exercise of the statutory powers of management and disposition[12]. He is subject to the draconian rule which affects all who act, in this broad sense, as trustees in relation to property, in that he is not permitted to derive any profit or personal advantage from his trusteeship[13]. Any improper exercise of the statutory powers conferred upon the tenant for life constitutes a breach of trust, in respect of which the settled land beneficiaries may seek damages or other remedies.

The tenant for life must at all times consult the interests of the beneficiaries, although difficulties may present themselves simply by virtue of the fact that the tenant for life is often himself one of the beneficiaries. It seems that a tenant for life may

10 See p. 176, ante.
11 See *Re Thornhill's Settlement* [1941] Ch 24. The court may order that any documents of title in the possession of the tenant for life be delivered to the trustees.
12 See Settled Land Act 1925, ss. 16(1)(i), 107(1).
13 See *Parker v McKenna* (1874) LR 10 Ch 96 at 124 per James LJ; *Bray v Ford* [1896] AC 44 at 51f. per Lord Herschell; *Meinhard v Salmon* 164 NE 545 at 546, (1928) per Cardozo CJ; *Phipps v Boardman* [1964] 1 WLR 993 at 1010 per Wilberforce J.

legitimately exercise his powers with some, but not of course, an exclusive regard for his own personal interests[14].

However, there must come a point beyond which the advancement of self-interest constitutes a violation of the tenant for life's fiduciary responsibilities, e.g., where, to the long-term detriment of the other beneficiaries, the tenant for life favours an immediate sale of the settled estate at a gross under-value, simply because short-run hedonism indicates an imperative need of ready cash[15].

Another situation in which the tenant for life may be tempted to exercise his statutory powers improperly arises where he proposes to sell the legal estate and the purchaser whom he has in mind is himself. There is a fairly stern rule of English law to the effect that a trustee is not allowed to 'self-deal' in this way[16]. A fiduciary may not normally purchase trust property since there is an obvious temptation for the fiduciary to offer himself exceptionally favourable terms of sale to the prejudice of the other beneficiaries. However, section 68 of the Settled Land Act 1925 permits the tenant for life to purchase the settled estate provided that the negotiations preceding sale (or other disposition) are conducted not by the tenant for life as vendor but by the trustees of the settlement[17].

The trustees of the settlement thus perform their protective role as the policemen of the settlement[18]. In general, however, the trustees have no power to control the tenant for life's decisions in effecting dispositions of the settled property[19]. The breadth of the discretion conferred on the tenant for life is further accentuated by section 106(1) of the Settled Land Act 1925, which renders 'void' any provision which purports to restrict or inhibit a tenant for life from exercising any statutory power vested in him. Section 106(1) may well be relevant where a settled land beneficiary is granted an interest determinable upon his ceasing to reside on the settled property. It has been held that if the beneficiary ceases to reside precisely because he has exercised the tenant for life's statutory power to sell the settled estate, the forfeiture clause is rendered void under section 106(1), and that beneficiary's interest endures in the capital proceeds of sale[20]. If, however, the cessation of residence is not attributable to the

14 *Re Boston's Will Trusts* [1956] Ch 395 at 405 per Vaisey J. For a discussion of Vaisey J's 'somewhat delphic answer', see (1956) 15 Cambridge LJ 174 (H. W. R. Wade).

15 See also *Wheelwright v Walker* (1883) 31 WR 912; *Re Earl Somers* (1895) 11 TLR 567; *Middlemas v Stevens* [1901] 1 Ch 574.

16 See *Wright v Morgan* [1926] AC 788; *Williams v Scott* [1900] AC 499; *Holder v Holder* [1968] Ch 353.

17 See *Re Pennant's Will Trusts* [1970] Ch 75.

18 This role is reinforced by the duty imposed on the tenant for life to give the trustees written notice of his intention to effect a sale, lease, mortgage or other disposition (Settled Land Act 1925, s. 101). Such a warning puts the trustees on notice that they must receive the capital money shortly to be paid over in order that the overreaching mechanism be activated and the beneficiaries' interests safeguarded.

19 Only in the case of a proposed sale of a 'principal mansion house' or the cutting of certain timber do the trustees have a requisite consent which must be obtained as a preliminary to action taken by the tenant for life (see Settled Land Act 1925, ss. 65, 66). Moreover, the tenant for life's statutory powers may be increased but not diminished by the express terms of the actual settlement (see Settled Land Act 1925, s. 109(1)).

20 See *Re Acklom* [1929] 1 Ch 195.

exercise of any statutory power by the tenant for life, the forfeiture clause is given its intended effect: the beneficial interest terminates. In this case, the beneficiary no longer in residence is not eligible to receive the rents and profits drawn from the land or to participate further in the beneficial enjoyment provided by the settlement[1].

7. THE FUNCTIONS OF THE TRUSTEES OF THE SETTLEMENT

The primary duty of the trustees of the strict settlement is to 'conserve the settled property[2].' We have seen that, although the trustees rarely hold the legal estate themselves, they constantly supervise the settlement from a distance. Their responsibilities are fiduciary and, for the most part, residual. They simply watch the settlement from afar in order to ensure fair dealing not only for the tenant for life but for all the settled land beneficiaries.

8. CONTINUATION AND TERMINATION OF A STRICT SETTLEMENT

As will already have been seen, the Settled Land Act 1925 is a quite remarkable piece of legislation. It resembles in many ways a well oiled piece of machinery in which all the component parts operate smoothly and efficiently to achieve the statutory objective. The legislative scheme was designed to *work*: it is dynamic not static. By and large it has worked successfully. Nowhere is the smooth functioning of the machinery more clearly visible than in the provisions regulating the continuation and determination of a strict settlement.

Let us return to our model strict settlement, in which the settlor has conferred a life interest upon A, with remainder to B in tail, and remainder thereafter to C in fee simple. Of course, when A dies, his life interest determines; B's entailed interest falls into possession. The land, however, continues to be settled land since there is still an element of beneficial succession between B and C sufficient to be caught by the terms of section 1(1) of the Settled Land Act 1925. As soon as A dies, the legal estate in the settled land must vest in somebody else, for dead people cannot hold legal estates. The scheme devised by the Settled Land Act ensures that where, on the determination of any interest by death, the land continues to be settled land, then the legal estate vests automatically in the deceased's 'special personal representatives'[3].

The next step is contained in section 7(1) of the Settled Land Act 1925. According to this provision,

1 See *Re Haynes* (1887) 37 Ch D 306.
2 *Re Boston's Will Trusts* [1956] Ch 395 at 405 per Vaisey J.
3 The settlor is normally deemed to have appointed as the 'special personal representatives' for this purpose the persons who are trustees of the settlement (see Administration of Estates Act 1925, s. 22(1)). Here again recourse is had to the settlement trustees—as distinct from the deceased's ordinary personal representatives, in whom is vested all property of the deceased other than the settled land—on the ground that the former group of persons will have a special concern for the interests of the settlement.

> If, on the death of the tenant for life ... the land remains settled land, his personal representatives shall hold the settled land on trust, if and when required so to do, to convey it to the person who ... becomes the tenant for life.

In our model settlement, B, the equitable tenant in tail in possession, now qualifies as the next tenant for life[4], and under section 7(1) he may require A's special personal representatives to vest the legal estate in the settled land in him[5]. The transition of ownership of the settled land interests from A to B has now been completed.

The next transition occurs (perhaps many years later) when B's equitable entailed interest determines—as would happen, for instance, if B died childless[6]. At this point C's equitable fee simple absolute will fall into possession—though it will still remain equitable. C will not become owner of the *legal* fee simple absolute until there has been a proper vesting of that estate in his favour. The legal estate vests from the moment of B's death in B's ordinary personal representatives rather than in his special personal representatives[7]. Section 7(5) now comes into play. This subsection provides that

> If any person of full age becomes absolutely entitled to the settled land (whether beneficially ... or otherwise) ... he shall be entitled to require the ... personal representatives ... to convey the land to him ...

If C invokes section 7(5), and B's personal representatives duly convey the legal estate in what was formerly settled land, absolute legal and equitable ownership will finally vest in a single person free of any settlement or trust:

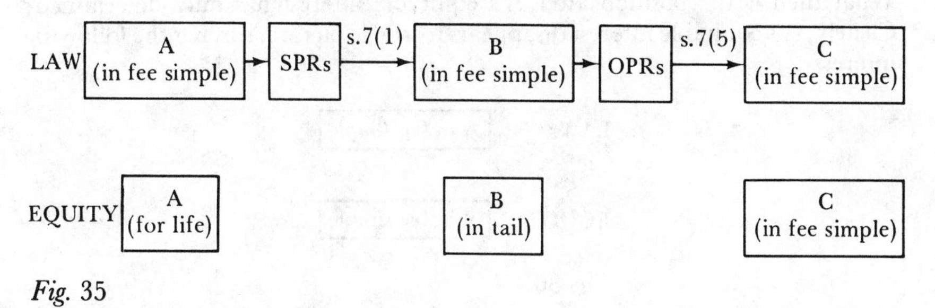

Fig. 35

9. THE CULMINATION OF THE SETTLED LAND ACT 1925

We have already seen that one of the major tasks before the draftsmen of the 1925 property legislation was to render land commerciable without thereby

4 Settled Land Act 1925, s. 20(1)(i).
5 The transfer may be effected by mere 'vesting assent', p. 168, ante.
6 We are, for this purpose, ignoring the possibility that B may have 'barred' his entail, p. 66f, ante.
7 See *Re Bridgett and Hayes' Contract* [1928] Ch 163. The distinction here is attributable to the fact that when B's equitable interest determines, the land ceases to be settled land: there is no longer any succession of equitable interests sufficient to bring the land within the ambit of section 1(1) of the Settled Land Act 1925.

destroying its utility as a medium of family endowment. The outstanding merit of that legislation is that it goes a long way towards achieving this objective. The device of overreaching ensures that the land is sold free of any interests contained behind a settlement or trust, while simultaneously those beneficial interests survive sale and endure as equitable interests in the proceeds of sale. Thus the culmination of the Settled Land Act 1925—the ultimate protection for both the third party purchaser and the settled land beneficiaries—lies in the overreaching effect of dispositions of the legal estate in the settled land.

Overreaching of settled land interests is, however, dependent upon certain conditions which are laid down in section 2(1)(i) of the Law of Property Act 1925. These conditions are three in number:

(1) The conveyance must be 'made under the powers conferred by the Settled Land Act 1925'

A conveyance of the legal estate in settled land will overreach the beneficial interests under the settlement only if, first, the conveyance is made under the powers conferred by the 1925 Act. Let us return to the settlement described in *Fig.* 23[8]. Initially A is invested with the legal estate in the land qua tenant for life by virtue of his holding an equitable determinable fee simple in possession. If A then joins the Labour Party, his equitable fee simple automatically determines, but he remains invested with the *legal* fee simple absolute in possession. This estate can leave A only if he dies or if he conveys it by deed to a third party. What then is the position after A's equitable interest has duly determined? Clearly, A's equitable interest disappears from the picture, leaving the following interests:

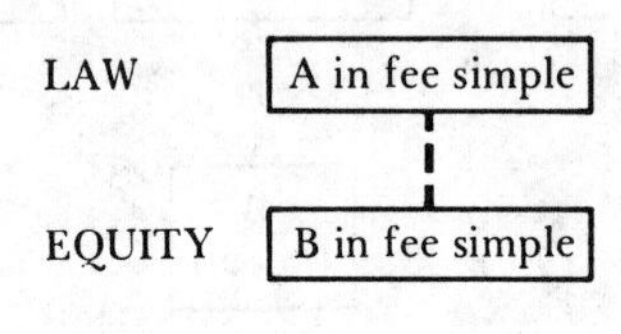

Fig. 36

The reader should not have too much difficulty in recognising this as a bare trust[9]. The strict settlement has in fact come to an end, because there is no longer a plurality of interests in equity. The strict settlement has quietly become a bare trust, and the situation no longer falls within the four corners of the Settled Land Act 1925. In this case, the normal rule is that A, the nominal owner, should convey the legal estate to or by the direction of the real owner, B. But suppose that A conveys the land instead to a third party purchaser, P, in order to defraud the beneficiary behind the bare trust (see *Fig.* 37)

It cannot be argued that this conveyance overreaches B's equitable interest by virtue of section 2(1)(i) of the Law of Property Act 1925, since the conveyance

8 See p. 158, ante.
9 If he does, he should perhaps look again at *Fig.* 27, p. 160, ante.

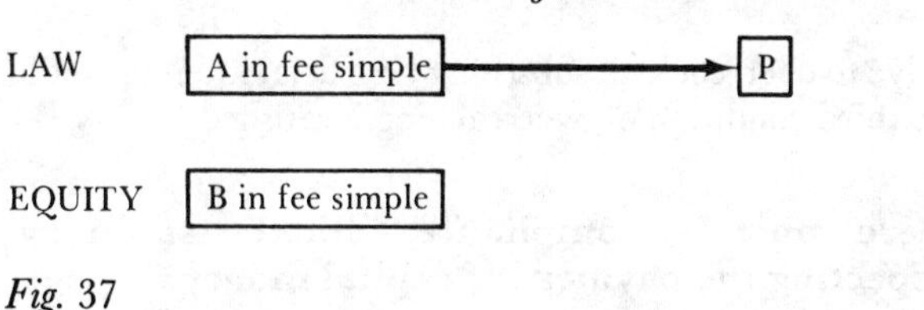

Fig. 37

here has not been effected 'under the powers conferred by the Settled Land Act 1925'[10]. A bare trustee cannot give an overreaching conveyance, and since there is no question of B's having had a commercial equitable interest capable of registration, the fate of B's equitable interest must be governed by the traditional doctrine of notice. In other words, B's equitable fee simple will bind P (again as a bare trustee) only if P bought the legal estate with notice—actual, constructive or imputed—of the existence of B's equity[11].

(2) The equitable interests must be 'capable of being overreached'

A second condition of overreaching is that the equitable interests in question must be 'capable of being overreached'. Commercial equitable interests are not normally capable of being overreached[12]. Overreaching is appropriate only in the case of family equitable interests. However, for reasons of convenience, the Settled Land Act 1925 does provide that a conveyance of a legal estate in settled land will be effective to overreach even certain categories of commercial equitable interest registered under the Land Charges Act 1925 or 1972[13]. The sale of settled land will not, of course, overreach existing *legal* rights over the settled estate already granted away to third parties (e.g., leases or mortgages)[14]. Such interests remain binding in their terms upon the new owner of the legal estate. Otherwise, however, the disposition of the legal estate in the settled land

10 By the same token, P cannot claim the protection of section 110(1), (2) of the Settled Land Act 1925 as a 'purchaser of a legal estate in settled land'.

11 See R. E. Megarry and H. W. R. Wade, *Law of Real Property* (4th edn., London 1975), p. 307. Clearly, if A as vendor had produced his vesting deed under the settlement for inspection by the purchaser P, P could not subsequently disclaim notice of beneficial interests existing behind the settlement. But it is just possible that A could have made his title as vendor on the basis of an old (and now redundant) set of title deeds—as in *Weston v Henshaw* [1950] Ch 510. (For another way in which the same possibility could arise, see *Fig.* 29, p. 167, ante). If this were the case, P could then claim the immunity of a bona fide purchaser of a legal estate for value without notice, and could thus take free of B's equitable interest. B's only remedy at this stage would lie in a claim against A for an undoubted breach of trust. One last word on this situation—it almost goes without saying that section 18 of the Settled Land Act 1925 has no application here. As soon as the settlement is ended by the determination of A's equitable interest (i.e., as soon as a bare trust arises), the situation is lifted right outside the ambit of the Settled Land Act 1925, and *Weston v Henshaw* has no relevance at all.

12 See p. 69, ante.

13 These interests comprise annuities, limited owner's charges and general equitable charges, all of which have a definite quantifiable money value and therefore might as well be paid out of the proceeds of sale arising and thus swept off the land at this convenient opportunity (see Settled Land Act 1925, s. 72(3)).

14 Settled Land Act 1925, s. 72(2).

is effective to overreach all subsisting beneficial interests in the land[15], provided that the third condition of overreaching is satisfied.

(3) There must be compliance with the statutory requirements respecting the payment of capital money

A disposition of the legal estate in settled land will have overreaching effect only if certain statutory requirements respecting the payment of capital money are complied with[16]. In general, this means that the capital proceeds of any disposition must be paid to at least two trustees of the settlement. If this does not happen, it may well be that the disposition is entirely void[17].

The purchaser of settled land is, however, quite safe if he pays the purchase money to at least two settlement trustees, who thereafter hold the money on a trust of personalty[18]. From the moment when the purchaser obtains his receipt from the settlement trustees, he is exonerated from any liability for loss or misapplication of the funds now in the hands of the trustees[19]. Further protection is heaped upon the purchaser by section 110(1) of the Settled Land Act 1925, under which he is conclusively deemed to have given the best price reasonably obtainable for the land and to have 'complied with all the requisitions of this Act.' This ample immunity is dependent only upon the purchaser having dealt 'in good faith with a tenant for life or statutory owner,' and as we have seen may well confer protection on the purchaser in some situations where he has innocently failed to pay the purchase money to at least two trustees[20].

The protection thus afforded the purchaser leads to the culmination of the Settled Land Act 1925—the operation of the 'curtain principle'[1]. In the normal case the purchaser is neither bound nor indeed entitled to call for the production of the trust instrument relating to the settled land[2]. The trusts of the settlement remain concealed from his view, and in this way the Act combines maximum facility for the purchaser with protection for the settled land beneficiaries. The purchaser takes a clear title and the beneficial interests are swept off the land by the device of overreaching[3].

15 Settled Land Act 1925, s. 72(1), (2).
16 See p. 172, ante.
17 Settled Land Act 1925, s. 18(1)(a).
18 As trustees they are of course under a duty to invest the capital prudently and to distribute income and capital in accordance with the terms of the original trust instrument.
19 Settled Land Act 1925, s. 95.
20 See *Re Morgan's Lease* [1972] Ch 1, p. 173, ante.
1 See p. 166, ante.
2 Settled Land Act 1925, s. 110(2), p. 166, ante.
3 The only occasions on which the purchaser may insist upon seeing the trust instrument relate to the exceptional cases in which an originally imperfect settlement has been rendered perfect under section 9 of the Settled Land Act 1925 (p. 167, ante). See the proviso to s. 110(2) of the Settled Land Act 1925.

CHAPTER 6

The rule against perpetuities

The subject of this chapter is the rule against perpetuities, which can sometimes invalidate gifts made by way of settlement. The classic statement of the rule is that given by John Chipman Gray:

> No interest is good unless it must vest, if at all, not later than twenty-one years after some life in being at the creation of the interest[1].

The mysteries of this rule have bemused and irritated whole generations of law students. Although it began life as a very flexible principle, the rule in due course became 'one of the most rigid and mathematical of all judge-made rules[2].' There is indeed high judicial authority for the proposition that, in view of the 'net which the Rule spreads for the unwary', a lawyer who omits to take account of the rule in drafting an instrument cannot be said, for the purpose of a claim in negligence, to have 'failed to use such skill, prudence and diligence as lawyers of ordinary skill and capacity commonly exercise[3].' Such indulgence, although commending itself to the Supreme Court of California, is unlikely to be extended to the law student by his examiners in land law—and very rightly not.

As Professors Morris and Leach once pointed out[4], the rule against perpetuities is

> one of those precepts of judge-made law which, in the interest of producing a workable and satisfactory law fashioned in the public interest, declares that certain intentions of a settlor or testator may not be carried out. In any system of private property a prohibitory rule is not lightly to be invoked. The prohibition should be imposed only upon interests the creation of which would offer a real threat to the public interest.

The rule against perpetuities is therefore a rule which, in the public interest, invalidates interests which vest too remotely. Although the most obvious cases in which this danger may materialise involve interests granted under a strict settlement, the rule against perpetuities strikes at many other kinds of interest in land. However, in view of its immediate reference to the context of settled land, it seems convenient to deal with the rule at this point in the book.

The rule against perpetuities was first formulated at common law, but has in recent years been substantially amended by statute. The rule is supposedly one of baffling complexity, epitomising the arid technicality of the law of real

1 *The Rule against Perpetuities* (4th edn., Boston 1942), s. 201.
2 J. H. C. Morris and W. B. Leach, *The Rule Against Perpetuities* (1st edn., London 1956), p. 12.
3 *Lucas v Hamm* 15 Cal Rptr 821 at 825, 364 P 2d 685 at 689 (1961) per Gibson CJ in the Supreme Court of California. See also (1965) 81 LQR 478 (REM).
4 Op. cit., p. 25f.

property. This grim (and quite inaccurate) analysis makes it all the more important to perceive and understand the policy which underlies the original rule. On closer examination, it will appear that the rule against perpetuities both reflects and expresses fascinating insights into the way in which society regards the institution of property.

1. THE POLICY BEHIND THE RULE AGAINST PERPETUITIES

The rule against perpetuities represents one of the most remarkable attempts made by the common law to give legal effect to a number of distinct (but not unrelated) elements of social and economic policy[5]. We shall look now at some of the concerns which gave rise to the rule.

(1) The policy against the withdrawal of property from commerce

The rule against perpetuities stems from the general policy of the law against the withdrawal of property from commerce. Part of the purpose of the rule is to ensure the full utilisation of land as a commerciable and therefore income-producing commodity. John Chipman Gray saw in the rule one of the 'modes adopted by the Common Law for forwarding the circulation of property[6].' In the words of Professor Lewis Simes,

> the Rule against Perpetuities furthers alienability; if it were not for this Rule, property would be unproductive and society would have less income[7].

This argument bears a little further explanation. It will be seen in due course that the rule against perpetuities developed as a rule restricting the grant of future interests in specific land, i.e., the grant of interests in land which might 'vest' at a future date on the fulfilment of some 'contingency' stipulated by the settlor. An example of a future interest occurs, for instance, where a settlor grants Blackacre 'to A in fee simple, but upon the condition that if all A's sons should die under the age of 30, then to B in fee simple[8].' In the latter case, A's interest vests immediately, but is liable to be determined by future events over which he has no control. B's interest is not vested at the date of grant, but remains contingent until the specified contingency is fulfilled (i.e., until it becomes clear that all of A's sons have died under the age of 30).

It is not difficult to perceive the rationale for the rule against perpetuities in the context of such a grant. The public policy expressed in the rule is violated by rendering specific things inalienable, for inalienability renders property less productive and thereby diminishes the national income. In the example given

5 See generally L. M. Simes (1953–54) 52 Michigan LR 179 at 190ff.: 'Is the Rule against Perpetuities Doomed?'; (1954–55) 103 University of Pennsylvania LR 707 'The Policy against Perpetuities'; *Public Policy and the Dead Hand* (Ann Arbor, Michigan 1955), p. 32ff.

6 Op. cit., p. 4.

7 (1954–55) 103 University of Pennsylvania LR 707 at 710.

8 The creation of this kind of determinable fee simple necessarily attracts the operation of the Settled Land Act 1925, p. 158, ante.

above, the possessory owner, A, may well decline to invest heavily in the cultivation or development of Blackacre because his ownership is liable to terminate on the happening of an uncertain event. The income derived from the property will therefore be diminished. Furthermore, although A's determinable fee simple is in theory alienable, no third party purchaser will want to buy it, since the interest alienated will remain defeasible upon the stipulated contingency. Any interest taken by the purchaser would, of course, determine automatically in that event in favour of the fee simple absolute vested in B. These simple facts of economic life bring about the result that A cannot even sell Blackacre to a third party who (unlike himself) may be willing and able to make the property productive, since the existence of B's future interest makes that property effectively unmarketable. This consequence is so contrary to the public interest that, as we shall see, the future interest granted to B is in fact struck down by the common law rule against perpetuities, and the fee simple vested in A is made absolute. In general, as Professor Simes wrote[9],

> In order to make a profit from land, one must have a type of ownership which insures enjoyment forever or for a fixed and determinate period of time. People who purchase land, whether for profit or for their own use and enjoyment, are not likely to buy unless they can secure either a fee simple absolute or a lease for a fixed term of years.

For these reasons, then, the rule against perpetuities restricts the creation of future interests in property. It holds a balance between those future interests which vest within the foreseeable future and those which do not, and declares the latter invalid on grounds of public policy. The mischief against which the rule inveighs was vividly described thus in 1841 in a leading treatise on the law of wills:

> The necessity of imposing some restraint on the power of protracting the acquisition of the absolute interest in, or dominion over, property will be obvious if we consider, for a moment, what would be the state of a community in which a considerable portion of the land and capital was locked up. That free and active circulation of property, which is one of the springs as well as the consequences of commerce, would be obstructed; the improvement of land checked; its acquisition rendered difficult; the capital of the country gradually withdrawn from trade; and the incentives to exertion in every branch of industry diminished. Indeed, such a state of things would be utterly inconsistent with national prosperity . . .[10]

(2) The policy against concentration of wealth in the hands of a few

The rule against perpetuities has not only ensured the alienability of land for the purpose of productivity. It has played an important part in countering what Professor Barton Leach called the 'urge to family aggrandisement[11].' The lawyers of the early common law era were deeply conscious of the threat to the public welfare posed by family dynasties founded either on great landed estates or on great capital wealth. Thus a vital component of the policy incorporated

9 (1954–55) 103 University of Pennsylvania LR 707 at 710.
10 T. Jarman, *A Treatise on Wills* (1st edn., London 1841), Vol. 1, p. 219.
11 (1952) 68 LQR 35 at 40: 'Perpetuities: Staying the Slaughter of the Innocents'.

in the rule against perpetuities was the desire to 'prevent the tying up of the soil of England in the hands of the great families[12].' In this sense, the rule was akin to the medieval Statutes of Mortmain which were designed to prevent an excessive amount of landed wealth from coming within the sole control of the Church. There was a clear social interest in curtailing the concentration of the basic resource of land in the hands of constricted social groups. The rule thus invalidated the creation of infinite series of contingent future interests for family members which had the effect of withdrawing land from commerce.

It may well be that the centrifugal force of the rule against perpetuities has played a more significant role in our social history than might on first reflection be imagined. As Morris and Leach have pointed out[13],

> It is interesting to reflect that the Rule against Perpetuities and its kindred succeeded in preventing enormous concentrations of land in the hands of a very few and thereby brought it about that England never suffered unbearably from those conditions which elsewhere have produced violent social revolution—land hunger, a class of servants or peons and widespread destitution.

(3) The policy in favour of the survival of the fittest

There is an interesting by-product of the argument that the rule against perpetuities strikes at the undue concentration of landed wealth in a few great families behind family settlements. It may be that all societies apply, perhaps quite unconsciously, rules of eugenic self-control. It has been suggested, for instance, that the origin of the rule against perpetuities gives effect to a social evolutionary principle in favour of the survival of the fittest[14]. In the terms of this argument, it is said to be socially undesirable that some members of society should have assured incomes and should thus be protected from the economic struggle for existence. The principle of the survival of the fittest should apply, so that those who are unable to maintain themselves in the economic struggle should not survive. According to this view, there is a strong social objection to the continuation of a line of weaklings, and the rule against perpetuities therefore represents an elementary expression of the impulse to preserve unfettered the operation of economic competition.

The American Law Institute, in issuing its *Restatement of the Law of Property*[15], endorsed the eugenic rationale of the rule against perpetuities:

> It is obvious that limitations unalterably effective over a long period of time would hamper the normal operation of the competitive struggle. Persons less fit, less keen in the social struggle, might be thereby enabled to retain property disproportionate to their skills in the competitive struggle.

The rule against perpetuities thus ensures that, while economic provision may be made for the unfit for one generation and during the minority of the next

12 J. H. C. Morris and W. B. Leach, op. cit., p. 11.
13 Ibid.
14 See L. M. Simes (1954–55) 103 University of Pennsylvania LR 707 at 722.
15 American Law Institute, *Restatement of the Law of Property* (St. Paul, Mo, 1944), p. 2132.

generation (i.e., during 'lives in being' plus 21 years), any attempt to continue that provision for further generations is rendered void.

(4) The policy against capricious gifts

It is sometimes said that the rule against perpetuities prevents effect being given to capricious or eccentric dispositions of property. In other words, the rule is a significant check upon gifts of property which might have anti-social consequences in sterilising the use of economically valuable resources or in dissipating the substance of existing wealth[16].

(5) The policy in favour of balancing the interests of the living and the dead

Another policy reflected in the common law rule against perpetuities has to do with the human aspiration for dispositive power over things. In this context there arises rather starkly the problem, both practical and philosophical, that the unhindered exercise of dispositive power by one generation may curtail or even destroy the dispositive power of succeeding generations. As Professor Simes observed,

> It is almost axiomatic that one of the most common human wants is the desire to distribute one's property at death without restriction in whatever manner he desires . . . The difficulty here is that, if we give free rein to the desires of one generation to create future interests, the members of succeeding generations will receive the property in a restricted state. They will thus be unable to create all the future interests they wish. Perhaps, they may not even be able to devise it at all. Hence, to come most nearly to satisfying the desires of peoples of all generations, we must strike a fair balance between unrestricted testamentary disposition of property by the present generation and unrestricted disposition by future generations[17].

The problem exposed here is that of imposing a necessary check upon the entirely natural human desire to provide for one's family in the foreseeable future. The liberty enjoyed by one generation may in fact curtail the liberty enjoyed by a succeeding generation. There is a sense in which the sovereign power of alienation attains its highest expression in a disposition which negates the dispositive power of the alienee. But this proposition, while it may have a certain existential poetry about it, as a statement of law remains hopelessly remote from the ordinary and practical concerns of the law of real property. As Morris and Leach pointed out,

> The dilemma is thus precisely what it has been throughout the history of English law, namely, how to prevent the power of alienation from being used to its own destruction[18].

16 See J. H. C. Morris and W. B. Leach, op. cit., p. 15.
17 (1954–55) 103 University of Pennsylvania LR 707 at 723.
18 Op. cit., p. 17. The dilemma described here is essentially the one which Henry Sidgwick defined as the 'dilemma of individualism'. See *The Elements of Politics* (4th edn., London 1919), p. 103, where Sidgwick wrote that 'it rather follows from the fundamental assumption of individualism, that any such posthumous restraint on the use of bequeathed wealth will tend to make it less

The resolution of this dilemma is provided, in part, by the common law rule against perpetuities which, in its terms, aims to strike a 'fair balance between the desires of members of the present generation, and similar desires of succeeding generations, to do what they wish with the property which they enjoy[19]'. It is in this compromise between two competing policies that Morris and Leach professed to find the 'best justification' for the modern operation of the rule against perpetuities[20].

(6) The policy in favour of limiting the control of 'the dead hand'

In the view of Professor Lewis Simes, the primary rationale for a rule against perpetuities is the consideration that it is 'socially desirable that the wealth of the world be controlled by its living members and not by the dead[1].' This view gives effect to the idea that, in an almost religious sense, the inhabitants of the earth are owners not of the fee simple but merely of a life interest. This idea was expressed thus by Thomas Jefferson, writing to James Madison:

> The earth belongs always to the living generation. They manage it then, and what proceeds from it, as they please, during their usufruct[2].

The creation of future interests in property may well result in the control of that property by the dead and not the living. The far-reaching hand of the testator may, by making rules for distant times, have the wholly deleterious effect of storing up economic stagnation for future generations. Thus, the theory maintains, the economic prosperity of a nation is dependent upon the dynamic interaction of trust capital and risk capital. Trust capital is, by definition, capital in relation to which the trustee is bound, in virtue of his fiduciary role, to take no substantial risk. The trustee cannot therefore invest the trust fund as freely as one who is unfettered by the obligations of fiduciary status. It is, however, a widely accepted premise of the capitalist economy that much of our social and economic advancement depends upon the free availability of risk investments. Without the practice of risk investment, the progress of commercial and technological development would be gravely diminished.

It is on the basis of this view of the national economy that the rule against perpetuities is alleged to be beneficial. By imposing mandatory limits upon the extent to which wealth can be locked up as trust capital behind settlements of future interests, the rule frees capital for risk investment and thereby militates against stagnation in the economy. Moreover, by striking down future interests

---

useful to the living, as it will interfere with their freedom in dealing with it. Individualism, in short, is in a dilemma . . . of this difficulty there is . . . no general theoretical solution: it can only be reduced by some practical compromise.' The problem in the context of property law is broadly comparable with the question whether, in the field of constitutional theory, a sovereign legislative body is competent to restrict its own sovereignty for the future by entrenching fundamental principles or rights in unrepealable legislation.

19 L. M. Simes (1954–55) 103 University of Pennsylvania LR 707 at 723.

20 Op. cit., p. 17.

1 (1954–55) 103 University of Pennsylvania LR 707 at 723f.

2 *Writings of Thomas Jefferson* (Ford edn. 1895), Vol. 5, p. 121.

for reasons of remoteness, the rule plays its part in ensuring that the norms of conduct and belief embraced by a long dead settlor are not arbitrarily foisted in wholly different social conditions upon beneficiaries of a different generation. Such, however, would be the result if the rule did not invalidate gifts which shift a beneficial entitlement from A to B in the event that A fails to conform to some code of behaviour or conscience deemed desirable by the settlor[3].

As with almost all the other rationales proffered for the common law rule against perpetuities, this last argument reflects a free market philosophy more reminiscent of the economic doctrines of Adam Smith than of the view prevalent in the mixed economy of a post-industrial age. We shall in due course have to examine the extent to which these rationales have any relevance under modern conditions. There can, however, be no doubt that each rationale played some part in the formulation and enforcement of the common law rule against perpetuities, and it is to the history and the application of that rule that we must now turn.

2. A BRIEF HISTORY OF THE RULE AGAINST PERPETUITIES

The history of the English law of real property relates the almost relentless struggle between forces which for economic reasons favour the free alienability of land and forces which for essentially familial reasons favour the restriction of the right to dispose. The early common law era began with what Pollock and Maitland were to call 'a strong bias in favour of free alienation[4].' This tendency towards freedom of alienation was then temporarily checked by the Statute *De Donis Conditionalibus* of 1285, which permitted the creation of unbarrable entailed interests in land[5]. However, by *Taltarum's* case in 1472[6] the courts had discovered a method of barring even such entails by the technique of 'common recovery'[7]. Landowners retaliated by using 'clauses of perpetuity' in deeds of grant in order to evade this result, but it was not until the 16th and 17th centuries that the threat posed by grants in perpetuity became substantial.

The real danger in relation to perpetuity arose in respect of executory interests in freehold and leasehold land[8]. So long as such interests were destructible as contingent remainders, they offered no threat of a 'perpetuity'[9]. However, from the early 17th century onwards, the Court of King's Bench began to uphold executory devises of freehold and leasehold land as immune from destruction[10]. These decisions made possible the creation of family settlements which brought about the equivalent of an unbarrable entail in specific parcels of land, and the

3 See p. 158, ante.
4 *The History of English Law* (2nd edn., London 1968), Vol. 2, p. 18f.
5 See p. 66f, ante. See J. H. C. Morris and W. B. Leach, op. cit., p. 3f.
6 (1472) YB 12 Edw IV Mich., fol 14, pl 16, fol 19, pl 25.
7 J. H. C. Morris and W. B. Leach, op. cit., p. 4.
8 An 'executory interest' is an interest which cuts off a previous interest instead of following it when it has terminated. See the example given earlier, *Fig.* 23, p. 158, ante.
9 See J. H. C. Morris and W. B. Leach, op. cit., p. 5ff.
10 See *Pells v Brown* (1620) Cro Jac 590.

dangers implicit in this development were to produce the judge-made rule against perpetuities.

The rule against perpetuities first emerged in the *Duke of Norfolk's* case[11] in 1683, but its development was to span 150 years until the decision in *Cadell v Palmer*[12] in 1833. In the *Duke of Norfolk's* case, Lord Nottingham LC made the classic statement that

> A perpetuity is the settlement of an estate or an interest in tail, with such remainders expectant upon it, as are in no sort in the power of the tenant in tail to dock by any recovery or assignment, but such remainders must continue as perpetual clogs upon the estate . . . and they are against the reason and policy of the law, and therefore not to be endured[13].

Initially a rule aimed at the restriction of unbarrable entails in land, the rule against perpetuities subsequently extended to apply not only to interests in land but also to a wide range of interests in personal property. Its vitality was consistent with the ethos of free enterprise which flourished at the end of the 19th century and beginning of the 20th century, in that the rule gave apt expression to the commonly accepted view of that time that 'restraints of trade are contrary to public policy . . .'[14].

With the passage of time and changes in social and economic conditions, the common law rule against perpetuities began to seem less attractive, and the last 50 years of the rule have witnessed a dramatic and quite remarkable retraction from the principle which so abhorred perpetuity. We shall trace this development, but first we must master the operation of the rule at common law.

3. THE COMMON LAW RULE AGAINST PERPETUITIES

(1) The rule itself

The rule against perpetuities is a rule which invalidates interests which vest too remotely. In its common law formulation[15], the rule declares that

> No interest is good unless it must vest, if at all, not later than twenty-one years after some life in being at the creation of the interest[16].

In other words, the rule against perpetuities renders void ab initio any limitation where it is possible that the interest of the grantee may vest outside the perpetuity period.

11 (1683) 3 Cas in Ch 1.
12 (1833) 1 Cl & F 372.
13 (1683) 3 Cas in Ch 1 at 31.
14 *In re Trustees of Hollis' Hospital and Hague's Contract* [1899] 2 Ch 540 at 553 per Byrne J, citing in support the judgment of the House of Lords in *Nordenfelt v Maxim Nordenfelt Guns & Ammunition Co* [1894] AC 535.
15 The common law formulation still governs gifts taking effect on or before 15 July 1964, and provides the base on which gifts taking effect thereafter are tested from the point of view of perpetuity, p. 205, post.
16 J. C. Gray, op. cit., s. 201.

The perpetuity period, measured from the date of the instrument (in the case of an inter vivos grant) and from the date of the testator's death (in the case of a testamentary disposition), comprises the artificial period of all the 'lives in being' at common law plus 21 years[17]. Only if it can be predicted with total certainty that an interest (if it is going to vest at all) must vest within the perpetuity period so defined, is that interest valid in terms of the rule. Moreover, it is not permitted in the application of the common law rule to 'wait and see' whether the interest in question does in fact vest within the time allowed[18]. The interest is struck down as void ab initio unless, at the effective date of grant, it can be predicted that a vesting within the permitted period is a matter of logical necessity. It will not save the interest that there is very little likelihood that it can in fact vest outside the period. Such is the rigour of the common law rule that the interest is invalidated if there is even the remotest possibility that the point of vesting may be postponed outside the perpetuity period. In such a case, the interest granted in violation of the rule either reverts to the original settlor or passes on a partial intestacy to his next of kin.

(2) The meaning of 'vesting'

The operation of the rule against perpetuities at common law turns upon the date of 'vesting'. Morris and Leach have described the significance of 'vesting' in the following terms:

(a) A remainder is 'vested' when the persons to take it are ascertained and there is no condition precedent attached to the remainder other than the termination of the prior estates.
(b) An executory interest (that is, an interest which cuts off a previous interest instead of following it when it has terminated) is not 'vested' until the time comes for taking possession.
(c) Most important of all, a class gift is not 'vested' until the exact membership of the class has been determined; or, to put it differently, a class gift is still contingent if any more persons can become members of the class or if any present members can drop out of the class[19].

This explanation may be amplified by pointing out that there is a vital distinction between interests which are
(i) 'vested in possession',
(ii) 'vested in interest', and
(iii) 'contingent'.
Let us examine the following example: Blackacre is settled upon A for life, with remainder to B for life and further remainder to C in fee simple on condition that he qualifies at the Bar.

At the date of grant A has an equitable life interest 'vested in possession': he

17 This period can be extended by a further period of gestation of 9 months in respect of a life in being or of a beneficiary in the event of the birth of a posthumous child. See *Duke of Norfolk's* case (1683) 3 Cas in Ch 1; *Thellusson v Woodford* (1805) 11 Ves 112 at 143.
18 The only case in which the common law permits the 'wait and see' principle to operate is the case of alternative contingencies. See *Re Curryer's Will Trust* [1938] Ch 952.
19 Op. cit., p. 1.

is not excluded from present possession by reason of any prior entitlement[20]. Again at the date of grant B has an equitable life interest 'vested in interest': he is excluded from present possession merely by reason of A's prior interest. B's interest is not, however, 'contingent' since it is not conditional upon his fulfilling any kind of qualification. His interest, if he receives it at all, is delayed merely as a matter of time and not as a matter of contingency. By contrast, C's equitable fee simple is delayed by more than merely a factor of time. It is truly 'contingent', in the sense that even if A and B were dead, C would still be required to perform the qualifying condition to which his entitlement is subject (i.e., he would still have to qualify at the Bar). Herein lies the nub of the rule against perpetuities: *the rule strikes only at contingent interests.* As soon as an interest vests (whether 'in interest' or 'in possession'), it is safe from the ambit of the rule.

A commonly used figure which in many ways neatly illustrates the common law rule is the idea of a queue. In a series of settled land limitations, for instance, the grantee who first enjoys possession stands at the head of the queue: his interest has already *vested in possession.* Those standing behind him in the queue hold interests *vested in interest*: their interests will eventually fall into possession as one by one they work their way to the head of the queue. However, their arrival at the head of the queue is only a matter of time: they are subject to no contingency, since the element of contingency consists effectively of *getting into* the queue. It is those who stand around outside the queue—in the hope of one day joining it—whose interests are *contingent.* The rule against perpetuities thus directs its narrow focus upon the point in time at which any given interest crosses the crucial borderline from contingency to vesting. If it is even remotely conceivable that a specified contingency may be fulfilled outside the artificially defined perpetuity period (i.e., that a grantee may take too long to join the queue), then the contingent interest is declared void ab initio at common law for reasons of public policy. The grantee is, in consequence of the rigour of the rule, deprived of even the bare opportunity of seeing whether he could in fact have satisfied the stipulated contingency within the permitted period.

(3) The perpetuity period at common law

The perpetuity period defined by common law is the period marked out by 'lives in being' plus 21 years. For the purpose of the common law rule, a 'life in being' is the life of any person[1] alive at the date of the grant who is either expressly or impliedly mentioned in the grant. A 'life in being' need not be related to any of the beneficiaries of the grant[2], although the question of perpetuity is of course

20 See p. 65f, ante.

1 A 'life in being' must be *human*: see *Re Dean* (1889) 41 Ch D 552; *Re Kelly* [1932] IR 255 at 260 per Meredith J: '"Lives" means human lives. It was suggested that the last of the dogs could in fact not outlive the testator by more than twenty-one years. I know nothing of that. The court does not enter into the question of a dog's expectation of life. In point of fact neighbours' dogs and cats are unpleasantly long-lived; but I have no knowledge of their precise expectation of life . . . [T]here can be no doubt that "lives" means lives of human beings, not of animals or trees in California.'

2 See, for instance, the common use of a 'royal lives' clause, i.e. a clause included in an instrument of gift which selects as the measuring lives for the purpose of the gift all the descendants of a

averted completely if a grantee is himself a 'life in being' for the purpose of the grant in question[3]. It must be possible to say of any candidate 'life in being' that his longevity may affect the point in time at which the interest under challenge will vest[4].

The clear purpose of the common law rule against perpetuities was to tie the perpetuity period to the life span of a group of existing persons to be selected by the settlor as the measuring yard-stick for his grant, and then to extend the period thus demarcated by a further 21 years. The rationale for this artificial period has been well explained by Professor Lewis Simes:

> Regarding the Rule as a fair compromise between the desires of the normal testator to create future interests and the desires of members of future generations to control the property which they enjoy, we may ask this question: What period will take care of the normal desires of the testator who makes a family settlement by way of testamentary trust? The answer is clear enough. It is lives in being and twenty-one years. The testator may well desire to give life estates to his wife and children; he may also wish to provide for unborn grandchildren during their minority[5].

The rule thus enabled the settlor/testator to use the attainment of majority as a condition precedent to entitlement under a family settlement[6].

If there are no relevant 'lives in being' at common law, the perpetuity period is simply a period 'in gross' of 21 years from the effective date of grant[7].

(4) Simple applications of the rule

Armed with the information outlined above, we are now in a position to apply the common law rule to several simple grants. For this purpose it must be borne in mind that a grant of a contingent interest in property can fail for two quite separate reasons. Such a grant may fail

either (i) because the grantee never satisfies the specified contingency,

or (ii) because, although the grantee satisfies the specified contingency, he does so at a point in time outside the perpetuity period.

The perpetuity question is a narrow inquiry. The focus of the rule is fixed only upon whether a contingency may be met outside the perpetuity period. If

---

named sovereign who are living at the effective date of gift. See *Re Villar* [1928] Ch 471, where a testator validly used as the 'period of restriction' the period 'ending at the expiration of 20 years from the day of the death of the last survivor of all the lineal descendants of Her late Majesty Queen Victoria who shall be living at the time of my death.' The formula contained in more recent 'royal lives' clauses has been amended to refer to King George V (see *Re Leverhulme (No. 2)* [1943] 2 All ER 274). See generally R. H. Maudsley, *The Modern Law of Perpetuities* (London 1979), p. 88ff.

3 An example would be a gift to 'my son Sam if he swims the Channel'.

4 'The proper question to ask is: Can I point to some person or persons now living and say that this interest will by the very terms of its creation be vested in an identified individual within twenty-one years after that person dies?' (See B. M. Sparks, (1955) 8 University of Florida LR 465 at 470: 'Perpetuities problems of the general practitioner'.)

5 (1954–55) 103 University of Pennsylvania LR 707 at 729f.

6 The age of majority was lowered from 21 to 18 years by s. 1(1) of the Family Law Reform Act 1969, but this has not affected the operation of the rule against perpetuities.

7 See *Palmer v Holford* (1828) 4 Russ 403.

there is any possibility that this may happen, the interest granted is immediately declared void at common law on the ground of perpetuity (i.e., for reason (ii) above). It is utterly irrelevant for the purpose of the rule against perpetuities that a grant may be destined to fail on the quite different ground that nobody qualifies in terms of the stipulated contingency (i.e., for reason (i) above). The fact that nobody qualifies simply means that the property in question remains unclaimed; it does *not* render the contingent interest void on the ground of perpetuity (i.e., for reason (ii) above).

(a) *'Blackacre to my first child to become a barrister'*

If this grant is contained in an inter vivos settlement, it is void at common law—unless of course at the date of grant one of the settlor's children has already qualified as a barrister (in which case his interest would be no longer *contingent* but *vested in possession*). However, if this grant is contained in a will it is perfectly valid under the rule against perpetuities.

(i) *Inter vivos grant* In applying the common law rule to the inter vivos grant, the technique is to set up the 'easy' case in which it is least likely that any violation of the spirit of the rule may arise. If even this case can be struck down for perpetuity, then all 'harder' cases must fall with it.

In the present context, the easiest case is that in which, at the effective date of grant, the settlor has *n* existing children all of whom are on the verge of being called to the Bar. It is, let us suppose, scarcely conceivable that within a very short period of time the stipulated contingency will not have been met by at least one of the settlor's children. Our next step is to inquire whether, adopting the most pessimistic prognosis possible, the 'easy' case thus constructed may be knocked down. Here it is possible—although admittedly unlikely—that the instant after the settlor signs the document of grant all the settlor's existing children may perish in some collective disaster. If this possibility were to materialise, the only life in being for the purpose of delimiting the perpetuity period at common law would be the life of the settlor himself. Any child who claimed the interest granted would necessarily be a future born child (i.e., not a life in being), and it is quite likely that such a child might not qualify at the Bar until more than 21 years after the death of the only life in being (i.e., that of the settlor). At common law, the mere logical possibility of such a conclusion is enough to render the grant void ab initio, thus overriding the extreme improbability that the settlor's expressed intentions should be so comprehensively and fatefully frustrated. The common law has regard only to possibilities not probabilities, and in the present instance it is *possible* that the interest granted may not vest (i.e., the contingency may not be satisfied) until after the perpetuity period has elapsed.

(ii) *Testamentary grant* If the grant of Blackacre 'to my first child to become a barrister' is contained in the will of a testator/settlor, it is perfectly valid under the rule against perpetuities. In such a case the testator's children (but not of course the testator) would be the relevant lives in being. Apart from the possible addition of a child *en ventre sa mère*—for which possibility the common law expressly makes allowance—the potential recipients of the interest granted are all in being and ascertainable at the effective date of the gift (i.e., the date of the testator's death). Thus their own lives become the measuring lives, with the result that the gift is clearly validated. It is not logically possible that anybody should practise posthumously at the Bar—however strenuously opponents of the profession may argue to the contrary!

(b) *'Blackacre to A (a bachelor) for life, remainder to any wife he may marry for life, and, upon their deaths, remainder to the eldest child of A then living'*

There are three quite distinct gifts involved here. The first two gifts are valid under the common law rule against perpetuities, but the third is void. It is irrelevant whether the gifts in question are inter vivos or testamentary, since there is no family relationship between the settlor and the recipients of the grant.

(i) '*. . . to A (a bachelor) for life . . .*' This first gift vests in possession immediately and clearly no question of perpetuity arises.

(ii) '*. . . to any wife he may marry for life . . .*' This second gift vests in interest on A's marriage, since at this point A's wife will have satisfied the contingency of becoming A's wife. A's marriage must occur (if at all) during A's lifetime and therefore well within the perpetuity period which here consists of A's life plus 21 years.

(iii) '*. . . to the eldest child of A then living*' The third gift is, however, subject to a contingency which may be satisfied outside the perpetuity period. The identity of 'the eldest child of A then living' can be determined only upon the deaths of A and his wife. It is possible that A may marry a woman who is not alive at the date of the settlement. Such an 'unborn spouse' cannot rank as a 'life in being' for the purpose of the common law rule. She might, however, outlive her husband by more than 21 years, with the result that the contingency which governs the gift is not resolved until more than 21 years after the death of the only person who does rank as a 'life in being' for the purpose of this gift (i.e., A). Because there is a slight *possibility* that the foregoing hypothetical developments may in due course materialise, this third gift—but not the first two gifts—must be struck down at the very outset for reasons of perpetuity[8].

(5) Applications of the rule to class gifts

We have so far examined the application of the common law rule against perpetuities to gifts to a single donee. However, a settlor may well gift his property not to a single donee in each instance but to an entire 'class'.

It is an intrinsic characteristic of any 'class gift' that the size of the share taken

8 *Re Frost* (1889) 43 Ch D 246.

by each donee is capable of variation in accordance with the numerical membership of the class. The difficulty inherent in applying the common law rule to class gifts is compounded by the principle that a class gift does not 'vest' until the exact membership of the class has been determined[9]. In other words, no class gift is valid under the rule unless it is possible at the effective date of grant to predict that as a matter of logical necessity the quantum (or at least the minimum size of each share) will have been ascertained at the latest by the end of the perpetuity period. A class gift is valid only if it can be predicted with total certainty that the interest to be taken by each and every class member will have vested in interest by the end of that period. If it is possible that the interest of even one class member may not vest in interest until after the expiry of the perpetuity period, the class gift is vitiated for all members. Remoteness which taints the interest of one taints the gift for all[10].

The rigour of this rule is mitigated only by the 'class-closing presumption' permitted by the decision in *Andrews v Partington*[11]. This presumption is a presumption of convenience (designed initially to facilitate the administration of estates) which often quite fortuitously enables a class gift to avoid the vice of perpetuity. In accordance with *Andrews v Partington*, the donor is *presumed*[12] to have intended that the class to whom a gift is made should *close* as soon as the first share vests in possession. In other words, as soon as the first share of any member of the class vests in possession, the class is artificially closed around the potential donees who are alive at that time. Only the potential donees who are within the class thus redefined may actually go on to attempt to satisfy the specified contingency (if any) and thereby qualify for their respective shares in possession. The operation of this 'class-closing presumption' has the effect that future-born class members are somewhat arbitrarily excluded from the class. However, it often happens—entirely fortuitously—that their exclusion saves the class gift as a whole from failure on the ground of perpetuity.

In order to demonstrate the application of the common law rule against perpetuities to class gifts, let us examine two instances of a class gift.

(a) *'Blackacre to such of the children of A as attain the age of 25'*

This gift is valid at common law, whether the gift is effected inter vivos or by will, so long as at the effective date of the gift one of A's children has already reached the age of 25. Otherwise, the gift is rendered void by the possibility that A may die leaving a child aged 1 who was not alive at the effective date of the gift. Such a child would not meet the contingency stipulated (i.e., the attainment of the age of 25) until three years after the end of the perpetuity period, which here consists of A's life plus 21 years.

We must examine more closely the reasons for these conclusions. If, however,

9 See p. 193, ante.
10 See *Leake v Robinson* (1817) 2 Mer 363.
11 (1791) 3 Bro CC 401.
12 On the circumstances required to rebut this presumption, see *Re Chapman's Settlement Trusts* [1977] 1 WLR 1163; [1978] Conv 73 (F. R. Crane).

one of A's children is aged 25 at the date of the gift, the presumption raised by *Andrews v Partington* comes into play in the absence of contrary intention expressed by the donor. Since the first share within the class (i.e., that of the 25 year-old) has already vested in possession, the class closes immediately at the date of the gift and includes only those children of A who are alive at that point. Since any existing children are in being and ascertainable at the date of the gift, they must themselves be the measuring lives for the purpose of the common law rule. There is no possibility that any member of this artificially reduced class can attain the age of 25 posthumously. Thus the class gift as a whole is valid. The consequence of applying the class-closing presumption has been to eliminate from the class of potential donees precisely those children of A (i.e., those born after the date of the gift) who, as we have just seen, would vitiate the entire class gift for reasons of perpetuity. Only the potential donees who remain within the class have an opportunity to satisfy the contingency and thereby qualify to receive their proportionate share of the gift. As and when each child of A within the class attains the age of 25, his aliquot share vests in possession.

(b) *'Blackacre to A for life, with remainder to A's grandchildren'*

The gift to A is perfectly valid since it vests immediately in possession. The class gift to A's grandchildren is valid at common law provided that at the effective date of the gift (whether inter vivos or testamentary) at least one of the grandchildren is alive.

The reasoning which underlies the validity of the class gift is as follows. If at the date on which the settlement takes effect A already has at least one grandchild, that grandchild has an interest vested in interest. He is excluded from immediate possession only by reason of A's prior life interest. That grandchild's interest must necessarily fall into possession on A's death since, even if the grandchild predeceases A, the grandchild's estate will call for his share in possession. This merely goes to demonstrate that an interest which is *vested in interest*—as distinct from an interest which is still only *contingent*—is a sufficiently substantial right of property to pass with a deceased's estate. Once again the borderline between contingency and vesting is crucial.

In the light of the foregoing, it can be predicted on the very day on which the settlement takes effect that at least one share within the class will *vest in possession* on A's death. It can therefore be predicted with total certainty that the class must, in accordance with *Andrews v Partington*, close well within the perpetuity period (which here consists of A's life plus 21 years). The class will then comprise all grandchildren of A who are alive at the date of A's death. The nature and quantum of their respective entitlements will be resolved entirely at that point—21 years before the perpetuity period ends. Once again, the operation of the class-closing presumption eliminates precisely those potential donees (i.e., grandchildren born after A's death) who would at common law vitiate the class gift even for those grandchildren born before A's death.

If the class gift just discussed had been made not simply to 'A's grandchildren', but to 'such of A's grandchildren as qualify at the Bar', the result would have been quite different. In this instance, the class would remain indefinitely open in the absence of a grandchild of A already fully qualified at the effective date of the gift. It could not be predicted with certainty that the class would close within the perpetuity period (i.e., that at least one of A's grandchildren would necessarily qualify at the Bar within 21 years of A's death), and in this case the whole class gift is void at common law.

4. THE REACTION AGAINST THE COMMON LAW RULE AGAINST PERPETUITIES

We have now examined some applications of the common law rule against perpetuities. That rule was, and still is, draconian in the extreme. Most of the cases decided under the rule have involved a harsh application of what has become a mechanical, over-technical and (for the layman) quite incomprehensible principle. The common law rule has no regard to probabilities, merely to possibilities. In defiance of the laws of nature and experience, it presumes things physically impossible to be legally feasible. The octogenarian woman is disingenuously deemed to be fertile[13]. In *Jee v Audley*[14], it was held that for the purpose of the rule a person should be deemed to be capable of having further children regardless of his or her age or physical condition[15]. The common law looks, moreover, only to the possibility that a gift may *not* vest in time. It is totally unmoved by the possibility—or even the probability—that a gift may indeed vest *within* the period allowed under the rule[16]. Contingent gifts are struck down if there is even the slightest possibility that they may offend the rule: it is not possible to 'wait and see' whether they do in fact offend.

The common law rule is therefore rigid and inflexible. Furthermore, the application of the rule in a given case often violates good sense. It was Professor Barton Leach who pointed out that

> Usually in our system of law when A violates a rule A is made to suffer in one way or another—by a criminal penalty or a civil judgment. But not under the Rule against Perpetuities. When A violates this Rule property is taken away from B and given to C.

13 As Professor W. B. Leach once pointed out, in the 'Never Never Land' of the common law rule against perpetuities, the cases on supposedly fertile octogenarians breed much more successfully than the octogenarians themselves. See (1952) 68 LQR 35 at 46. The oldest mother for whom there is authenticated evidence seems to have been a Mrs R. A. Kistler of Glendale, California, who gave birth to a child on 18 October 1956 at the age of 57 years 129 days. See *Guinness Book of Records* (27th edn., London 1980), p. 17.

14 (1787) 1 Cox Eq Cas 324.

15 In *Re Gaite's Will Trusts* [1949] 1 All ER 459, a gift was held valid on the ground that it was *legally* impossible, in view of the Age of Marriage Act 1929, that a five year-old child should produce legitimate issue (who would necessarily have vitiated the gift). The court was unwilling to base its decision upon a mere factual impossibility. See, however, W. B. Leach (1952) 68 LQR 35 at 47, for a well documented instance of birth given by a five year-old girl in Peru in 1939. The case was fully discussed in a report presented to the Academy of Medicine at Lima and published in *La Reforma Medica*, No. 306 (Lima, Peru, May 1939). In respect of dispositions taking effect after 1 January 1970, any reference to a child or other relative includes, in the absence of contrary intention, an illegitimate child and persons descended through illegitimate persons (see Family Law Reform Act 1969, s. 15).

16 See, e.g., *Re Wood* [1894] 2 Ch 310, [1894] 3 Ch 381.

The reason stated is that the gift to B might have vested too remotely and thus might have tied up property for too long a period, and C is the person (next-of-kin or residuary legatee) who would have taken the property if the invalid gift had not been made[17].

There is a further irony in this result. C is frequently the very person from whom the settlor wished to *divert* his estate in the event of his death. Yet the strict application of the common law rule against perpetuities has often led to a situation in which the person 'whom the testator clearly wished to restrict to a limited participation in his estate quitted the fray laden with the testator's money bags[18].'

Only one outcome could be worse than this—and it is that the testator's lawyer should make off laden with his money bags. But even this result is not unknown in litigation on perpetuities questions[19]. It was, again, Professor Leach who rather trenchantly indicated that

> Perpetuities cases that have arisen in the courts, English or American, in recent decades do not deal with testators and settlors who have long-term designs which press against the limits of the Rule against Perpetuities. Rather they deal with persons who, starting from reasonable plans for the support of their families, have run afoul of the Rule through the ignorance or oversight of the particular member of our profession to whom they have entrusted their affairs. I do not recall a single twentieth-century case, English or American, in which the will or trust could not have been so drafted as to carry out the client's essential desires within the limits of the Rule. This means that our courts in applying the Rule are not protecting the public welfare against the predatory rich but are imposing forfeitures upon some beneficiaries and awarding windfalls to others because some member of the legal profession has been inept[20].

The ineptitude of the lawyer who falls foul of the rule against perpetuities is indeed gross, for there is always one method by which the traps laid by the common law rule can be altogether avoided. It is obvious, after a moment's reflection, that no gift of property can possibly offend against the rule if into that gift is built the express rider that the gift itself shall not vest outside the relevant perpetuity period. No contingent interest can ever be struck down for perpetuity if part of the contingency specified is that the interest must vest in such a way as not to violate the rule against perpetuities. On this analysis, the failure of any gift at common law is ultimately attributable to a drafting defect of heinous proportions—that is, to a failure to include in the instrument of gift some simple phrase such as 'provided that this gift shall not vest outside the perpetuity period allowed by law[1].'

However, the disfavour with which the common law rule against perpetuities has come to be viewed in recent years is not entirely due to the fact that the

17 (1952) 68 LQR 35 at 49f. See, however, the statement made, with apparently unconscious irony, by Lord Dunedin in *Ward v Van der Loeff* [1924] AC 653 at 667, to the effect that a testator had framed a testamentary disposition in such manner as to offend the rule against perpetuities and 'I am afraid he must take the consequences.'

18 See W. B. Leach (1952) 68 LQR 35 at 36.

19 Ibid.

20 Ibid.

1 See, however, the disinclination of judges to uphold claims in negligence against the errant lawyer, p. 185, ante.

interests of non-culpable donees are sacrificed on an altar of inflexible principle in the midst of the faithful acolytes of the rule. The reaction which has overtaken the common law rule in most jurisdictions is much more a response to the fact that the underlying policy of that rule is no longer served by the rigid application of the rule. Let us look briefly at each of the rationales proposed earlier for the common law rule[2].

(1) The policy against the withdrawal of property from commerce[3]

It is scarcely possible under the changed conditions of the modern era to maintain with any accuracy the contention that contingent future interests render property unproductive and that the creation of such interests should therefore be restrained for reasons of public policy. Under the property legislation of 1925, for instance, all contingent future interests are automatically swept into equity. All such interests now take effect behind a trust of some kind (whether in the form of a strict settlement or a trust for sale). It cannot be argued that the presence of those contingent future interests makes the land to which they relate uncommerciable, for a major part of the purpose realised in the 1925 enactments was precisely to ensure the liquidity of land which is encumbered with equitable interests. The very essence of the Settled Land Act 1925 and the Law of Property Act 1925 is that there is always *some* person invested with the legal competence to market the land[4]. Moreover, that person (whether tenant for life or trustee for sale) is able, on compliance with certain statutory conditions, to give a conveyance of his title on sale which overreaches all equitable interests subsisting behind the 'curtain' of the trust[5]. Even if the land is never sold, one of the most important duties of the fiduciary owner (whether tenant for life or trustee for sale) is to make the trust property productive.

Thus it can be seen that contingent future interests in land are now, by virtue of the 1925 legislation, effectively interests in a 'revolving fund' in relation to which some fiduciary is bound by duties of competent management and productive investment. It was in this sense that Professor Lewis Simes detected that in England

> a remarkable compromise has been effected between the desire to tie up property in the family and the policy of free alienability. The old strict settlement, with its life estates and remainders in tail, can still be used in England. But if the life tenant has no ability or inclination to make the land productive, it will not lie idle. He can have it sold, and thereupon a fund will be substituted for the land. If no provision for trustees has been made in the settlement, trustees can be appointed by the court who will be competent to invest the proceeds of the sale and make them productive. Indeed, since 1925, future interests in England have become, actually or potentially, future interests in a fund which can always be productively invested[6].

2 See p. 186ff., ante.
3 See p. 186, ante.
4 See p. 161, ante.
5 See p. 74f, ante.
6 (1954–55) 103 University of Pennsylvania LR 707 at 717.

It cannot today be maintained with much conviction that the policy of free alienability of land requires the application of a rule against perpetuities, nor can it really be said that it is the rule against perpetuities which achieves alienability. Thus one of the principal rationales for the common law rule falls to the ground. If there is a rationale for a modern perpetuity principle, it is not that a rule is required to prevent inalienability, but rather that a rule is needed to prevent the remote vesting of interests in a shifting fund[7].

(2) The policy against concentration of wealth in the hands of a few[8]

While it is undeniable that this consideration played an important part in the formulation of the common law rule against perpetuities, it is also undeniable that undue concentrations of wealth in the modern world are more effectively restrained by the operation of the law of income and capital taxation.

(3) The policy in favour of the survival of the fittest[9]

The social policy which favours the survival of the fittest has become distinctly unfashionable in recent decades. The modern welfare state is founded upon an ideology of social relations which is almost the complete reverse of the brutal social evolutionary theory which may in part have animated the common law rule against perpetuities. In the post-industrial age of welfare capitalism there is no place for the 'social statics' of Herbert Spencer[10].

(4) The policy against capricious gifts[11]

If ever there were conclusive proof that the common law rule against perpetuities is powerless to prevent the valid creation of capricious, eccentric and anti-social interests in property, that proof lies in the fact that the famous disposition contained in the will of Peter Thellusson withstood challenge on the basis of the rule[12]. Peter Thellusson died in 1797, leaving a fortune valued then at £30 million. He left the residue of his estate to trustees upon trust to accumulate the rents and profits during the lives of all his sons, grandsons and great-grandsons living at his death or born in due time afterwards, to invest the rents and profits in the purchase of land, and on the death of the survivor to divide it into three lots, each of which was to be strictly settled on the eldest lineal male descendant then living of each of his three sons. Thus, as Morris and Leach so aptly describe,

7 See J. H. C. Morris and W. B. Leach, op. cit., p. 15.
8 See p. 187, ante.
9 See p. 188, ante.
10 According to Herbert Spencer, legal and social development was best left to evolve by a process of natural selection similar to that operating in the sphere of biology. See H. Spencer, *Social Statics* (London 1851).
11 See p. 189, ante.
12 See also the will made by Timothy Forsyte in Galsworthy's *The Forsyte Saga.* Timothy Forsyte is recorded as having died in 1920, leaving the residue of his estate 'in trust for that male lineal descendant of my father Jolyon Forsyte who after the decease of all lineal descendants of my said father in being at the time of my death shall last attain the age of twenty-one absolutely . . .'

Peter Thellusson 'locked his treasure in a mausoleum and flung the key to some remote descendant yet unborn, regardless of the claims which his wife and children might have had upon his bounty[13].' Yet the will was upheld by the House of Lords as valid under the rule against perpetuities[14]. A special Act of Parliament was required to prevent future exhibitions of similar posthumous greed, and the Thellusson litigation was to drag through the courts for another 50 years[15].

(5) The policy in favour of balancing the interests of the living and the dead[16]

This element of policy, in conjunction with the consideration mentioned at (6) below, is quite possibly the only rationale for a rule against perpetuities which retains any substantial validity today[17].

(6) The policy in favour of limiting the control of 'the dead hand'[18]

There is indeed a cogent policy of law to the effect that 'the dead hand' should not always prevail. Thus, whereas a man may generally do as he pleases with his property during his lifetime, the same is not necessarily true after his death[19]. It is indeed socially desirable that the wealth of the world should be controlled by its living members and not by the dead. However, it does seem somewhat excessive to attribute to the beneficent operation of the rule against perpetuities any substantial part of the social and technological advancement which may have been made possible by the availability of risk investment[20].

All the considerations rehearsed above have in recent years brought about a profound disaffection from the common law rule against perpetuities[1]. Pressure built up during the 1950s and 1960s for reform of the law, on the ground that the common law rule had outlived its original purpose. In the colourful terms of Professor Leach[2],

> The Rule persists in personifying itself to me as an elderly female clothed in the dress of a bygone period, who obtrudes her personality into current affairs with unpredictable bursts of indecorous energy. Time was when she stood at the centre of family activity, necessary to the family welfare. A new generation with new problems has arisen, yet she persists in treating ancient issues as present realities and in applying her own familiar

13 See J. H. C. Morris and W. B. Leach, op. cit., p. 259.
14 See *Thellusson v Woodford* (1799) 4 Ves 227, (1805) 11 Ves 112.
15 See J. H. C. Morris and W. B. Leach, op. cit., p. 259.
16 See p. 189, ante.
17 See p. 190, ante.
18 See p. 190, ante.
19 See, for instance, *M'Caig v University of Glasgow* 1907 SC 231 at 242, where Lord Kyllachy thought that it would be contrary to public policy that trustees should be directed by a testator to 'turn the income of the estate into money, and throw the money yearly into the sea . . .'
20 See J. H. C. Morris and W. B. Leach, op. cit., p. 16.
1 See W. B. Leach (1952) 68 LQR 35: 'Perpetuities: Staying the Slaughter of the Innocents'; (1952) 65 Harvard LR 721: 'Perpetuities in Perspective: Ending the Rule's Reign of Terror'.
2 (1952) 68 LQR 35 at 39.

solutions. Asserting an authority derived from an earlier day, she insists that a stockade be built round the house to protect it from Indians even though there have been no Indians for decades, the stockade is highly uneconomical, friendly neighbours are rebuffed, and the policeman and fireman are impeded in performing their protective functions.

The process of reaction culminated in the enactment of the Perpetuities and Accumulations Act 1964. It is to this enactment that we must now turn our attention.

5. THE PERPETUITIES AND ACCUMULATIONS ACT 1964

The Perpetuities and Accumulations Act 1964 has vastly modified the operation of the rule against perpetuities in respect of all gifts of property taking effect after 16 July 1964[3]. The statutory rule has introduced an entirely new emphasis in the application of the rule prohibiting perpetuity, thus dramatically reflecting the way in which social and economic conditions have changed since the original formulation of the rule[4]. The principal amendments of the common law rule are the following innovations.

(1) The principle of 'wait and see'

The Perpetuities and Accumulations Act 1964 may be invoked only where a gift has already failed at common law[5]. One of the major criticisms of the common law rule has been that it strikes down gifts on the ground of the merest possibility of a vesting outside the perpetuity period. Gifts have been invalidated by the remorseless application of the rule even where there has been little likelihood of an offence against the rule.

In order to remedy this harsh consequence the 1964 Act introduces a wholly novel provision in the form of a 'wait and see' principle. The Act now allows us to 'wait and see' whether a gift will *in fact* offend the rule against perpetuities: only if it must so offend is the gift finally declared invalid. This principle is contained in section 3(1) of the Act:

> Where, apart from the provisions of this section and sections 4 and 5 of this Act, a disposition would be void on the ground that the interest disposed of might not become vested until too remote a time, the disposition shall be treated, until such time (if any) as it becomes established that the vesting must occur, if at all, after the end of the perpetuity period, as if the disposition were not subject to the rule against perpetuities.

This provision effectively allows us to 'wait and see' whether a gift will vest within the perpetuity period defined by the Act[6]. Only if and when it is

3 The common law rule applies still to gifts which took effect before the commencement date of the 1964 Act.

4 See generally S. J. Bailey (1965) 23 Cambridge LJ 232: 'Perpetuities and the Act of 1964'; J. H. C. Morris and H. W. R. Wade (1964) 80 LQR 486: 'Perpetuities Reform at Last'.

5 Perpetuities and Accumulations Act 1964, s. 3(1). The common law rule is the 'platform' on which the 1964 Act is based (see R. H. Maudsley, op. cit., p. 44).

6 See p. 206, post.

established that vesting must occur, if at all, after the end of that perpetuity period, is the gift in question declared void. In other words, the gift concerned is given every opportunity of vesting within the period. It is not struck down simply because there is a remote possibility that it might vest outside the period. It is struck down only when it is quite clear that vesting within the period is impossible. In this sense, the modern rule against perpetuities provides an entirely new focus on the issue of perpetuity: gifts are invalidated not if they may, but only if they must, offend against the principle of perpetuity. In this respect the mechanical application of the common law rule is alleviated by a much more sensible pragmatism.

(2) The 'wait and see' period

For the purpose of the 'wait and see' provision in the Perpetuities and Accumulations Act 1964, the perpetuity period (or 'wait and see' period) is defined in slightly different terms from those which delineate the perpetuity period at common law. The 'wait and see' period is calculated with reference to the statutory 'lives in being' enumerated in section 3(5) of the Act, the period consisting of those lives plus 21 years[7]. There is a general rider to the effect that the 'lives in being' used for this purpose must pertain to 'individuals in being and ascertainable at the commencement of the perpetuity period[8].' Furthermore, it is provided that reference cannot be made to a generic category of 'lives in being' under section 3(5), if 'the number of persons of that description is such as to render it impracticable to ascertain the date of death of the survivor[9].' The 'lives in being' for the purpose of the statutory rule are the following:

(*a*) the person by whom the disposition was made;
(*b*) a person to whom or in whose favour the disposition was made, that is to say—

(i) in the case of a disposition to a class of persons, any member or potential member of the class;

(ii) in the case of an individual disposition to a person taking only on certain conditions being satisfied, any person as to whom some of the conditions are satisfied and the remainder may in time be satisfied;

(iii) in the case of a special power of appointment exercisable in favour of members of a class, any member or potential member of the class;

(iv) in the case of a special power of appointment exercisable in favour of one person only, that person or, where the object of the power is ascertainable only on certain conditions being satisfied, any person as to whom some of the conditions are satisfied and the remainder may in time be satisfied;

(v) in the case of any power, option or other right, the person on whom the right is conferred;

7 Where there are no statutory 'lives in being' relevant to a gift, the perpetuity period is a period of 21 years (see Perpetuities and Accumulations Act 1964, s. 3(4)(b)).
8 Perpetuities and Accumulations Act 1964, s. 3(4)(a).
9 Perpetuities and Accumulations Act 1964, s. 3(4)(a). See, for instance, *Re Moore* [1901] 1 Ch 936, where an over-ambitious testatrix attempted to use as her perpetuity period 'the longest period allowed by law, that is to say, until the end of the period of 21 years from the death of the last survivor of all the persons who shall be living at my death.' This formula was held to be vitiated by uncertainty.

(*c*) a person having a child or grandchild within sub-paragraphs (i) to (iv) of paragraph (*b*) above, or any of whose children or grandchildren, if subsequently born, would by virtue of his or her descent fall within those sub-paragraphs;
(*d*) any person on the failure or determination of whose prior interest the disposition is limited to take effect[10].

It is clear from this provision that the statutory lives in being include those of the settlor, potential donees[11], and parents and grandparents of potential donees. The lives in being specified by the statute exclude some lives which would have been relevant to the common law rule, e.g., royal lives expressly selected by the settlor as the measuring lives and to which the date of vesting is related[12].

(3) An alternative perpetuity period

The Perpetuities and Accumulations Act 1964 introduced a further significant innovation. Section 1(1) provides that

> where the instrument by which any disposition is made so provides, the perpetuity period applicable to the disposition under the rule against perpetuities, instead of being of any other duration, shall be of a duration equal to such number of years not exceeding eighty as is specified in that behalf in the instrument.

It has thus become possible for a settlor to specify, in substitution for the traditional common law period of 'lives in being' plus 21 years, an alternative perpetuity period of not more than 80 years in duration. This alternative period has the advantage of great simplicity, but requires to be instituted by express provision in the instrument of grant[13]. However, the Act seems to permit the use of the alternative 80-year period in conjunction with the principle of 'wait and see'[14].

(4) Age reduction

The Perpetuities and Accumulations Act 1964 contains other provisions the main import of which is to reformulate the terms of a gift to make those terms conformable to the rule against perpetuities. One of the principal reasons for failure of a gift under the common law rule has tended to be the fact that the gift is contingent upon a person reaching an age in excess of 21 years. One rather obvious method of eliminating the danger of perpetuity in such cases is to cut the age contingency down to 21 years, and this indeed was the technique chosen by the draftsmen of the 1925 property legislation. Section 163 of the Law of Property Act 1925 reduces automatically to 21 years any excessive age

10 See D. E. Allan (1965) 81 LQR 106: 'Perpetuities: Who are the Lives in Being?'
11 Potential donees must, however, be 'individuals in being and ascertainable at the commencement of the perpetuity period' (see Perpetuities and Accumulations Act 1964, s. 3(4)(a)). If this were not required, no perpetuity problem could *ever* arise, since the donee of any gift would be a statutory 'life in being' for the purpose of validating his own gift.
12 See R. H. Maudsley, op. cit., p. 125f.
13 See R. H. Maudsley, op. cit., p. 113f.
14 See however R. H. Maudsley, op. cit., p. 124f.

contingency which would otherwise cause a gift to fail under the common law rule[15].

An even more effective method directed towards the same end is contained in section 4(1) of the 1964 Act:

> Where a disposition is limited by reference to the attainment by any person or persons of a specified age exceeding twenty-one years, and it is apparent at the time the disposition is made or becomes apparent at a subsequent time—
> (*a*) that the disposition would, apart from this section, be void for remoteness, but
> (*b*) that it would not be so void if the specified age had been twenty-one years,
> the disposition shall be treated for all purposes as if, instead of being limited by reference to the age in fact specified, it had been limited by reference to the age nearest to that age which would, if specified instead, have prevented the disposition from being so void.

The result of this provision is that if, at the end of the 'wait and see' period, a contingent beneficiary would still fall short of attaining a specified age in excess of 21 years, the age stipulated in the instrument of gift may be reduced quite artificially in order that the qualification may be performed. Thus, in relation to a gift to 'such of the children of A as attain the age of 30', the age of 30 may be reduced if it subsequently becomes clear that even at the end of the 'wait and see' period vesting is incomplete. In such a case, the age contingency expressed may be reduced to such age between 21 years and 30 years as will enable the offending beneficiary to take a vested interest in the final moment of the 'wait and see' period.

(5) Class reduction

We saw earlier[16] that the operation of the common law class-closing presumption may sometimes quite fortuitously save a gift from the vice of perpetuity by means of an artificial reduction of the class of potential donees who then go on to attempt to satisfy the stipulated contingency. It is, however, still possible that some members of even this reduced class may take a vested interest outside the common law perpetuity period, thereby vitiating the entire gift. Under the 1964 Act, of course, a 'wait and see' provision now operates, with the result that the danger of perpetuity in such a case is effectively postponed until the end of the 'wait and see' period. However, if at this point it appears that some of the members of a class have not yet qualified in terms of the specified contingency, the 1964 Act permits a further measure of class reduction in order to save the gift for those members who have qualified in time. Section 4(4) provides that where

> it is apparent at the time the disposition is made or becomes apparent at a subsequent time that, apart from this subsection, the inclusion of any persons, being potential members of a class or unborn persons who at birth would become members or potential members of the class, would cause the disposition to be treated as void for remoteness,

15 This provision has now been repealed in respect of instruments coming into effect after 15 July 1976 (see Children Act 1975, s. 108(1)(a), Sch. 3).

16 See p. 198, ante.

those persons shall, unless their exclusion would exhaust the class, thenceforth be deemed for all the purposes of the disposition to be excluded from the class[17].

Thus remaining potential donees who have not yet satisfied the contingency in question are arbitrarily excluded from the class in order that the gift be saved for those who have managed to qualify within the 'wait and see' period.

We looked earlier at the case of a gift to 'A for life, with remainder to such of A's grandchildren as qualify at the Bar[18].' The grandchildren of A have the entire 'wait and see' period in which to qualify as barristers (assuming that one is not already qualified at the date of the gift). The class may of course 'close' in the common law sense as soon as the first member of the class takes a share vested in possession (i.e., qualifies as a barrister on or after the death of A). However, whether the class 'closes' at this intermediate point or remains open until the end of the 'wait and see' period, any members within the class who have not qualified by the latter point are simply excluded from the class under section 4(4). Their exclusion is indeed vital for the purpose of the rule against perpetuities, since their inclusion within the class of donees would postpone vesting for the entire class until a point outside the statutory perpetuity period and would invalidate the gift.

(6) Presumptions as to fertility

The Perpetuities and Accumulations Act 1964 also attempts to introduce some much needed realism into the question whether, for the purpose of a determination of perpetuity, a given individual is capable of having a child. Section 2(1) effectively overturns decisions such as that in *Jee v Audley*[19], by providing the following presumptions as to future parenthood:

Where in any proceedings there arises on the rule against perpetuities a question which turns on the ability of a person to have a child at some future time, then—

(*a*) subject to paragraph (*b*) below, it shall be presumed that a male can have a child at the age of fourteen years or over, but not under that age, and that a female can have a child at the age of twelve years or over, but not under that age or over the age of fifty-five years; but

(*b*) in the case of a living person evidence may be given to show that he or she will or will not be able to have a child at the time in question[20].

(7) The problem of the surviving spouse

We saw earlier[1] that a problem of perpetuity arises at common law in relation to a gift of 'Blackacre to A (a bachelor) for life, remainder to any wife he may

17 Age reduction may be combined with class reduction: see Perpetuities and Accumulations Act 1964, s. 4(3).

18 See p. 199, ante.

19 See p. 200, ante.

20 Where a question as to fertility is decided by treating a person as unable to have a child at a particular time, and he or she does so, the High Court may make such order as it thinks fit for placing the persons interested in the property comprised in the disposition, so far as may be just, in the position they would have held if the question had not been so decided. See Perpetuities and Accumulations Act 1964, s. 2(2).

1 See p. 197, ante.

marry for life, and, upon their deaths, remainder to the eldest child of A then living.' The third gift contained in this limitation is void at common law since vesting may occur outside the period of 'lives in being' plus 21 years, as would for instance become inevitable if A's wife were a person unborn at the date of the gift and she were to survive A by more than 21 years.

Such a gift is now validated by virtue of a special provision included in the Perpetuities and Accumulations Act 1964. According to section 5,

> Where a disposition is limited by reference to the time of death of the survivor of a person in being at the commencement of the perpetuity period and any spouse of that person, and that time has not arrived at the end of the perpetuity period, the disposition shall be treated for all purposes, where to do so would save it from being void for remoteness, as if it had instead been limited by reference to the time immediately before the end of that period.

(8) Options and the rule against perpetuities

Options to purchase land have always presented grave potential problems for the purpose of the rule against perpetuities. Section 9(2) of the Perpetuities and Accumulations Act 1964 expressly provides a perpetuity period of 21 years in respect of any disposition which confers an 'option to acquire for valuable consideration any interest in land[2].' The rule against perpetuities has no application at all to the grant of an option to purchase an interest reversionary upon a lease provided that the option in question is exercisable only by the lessee or his successors in title and ceases to be exercisable no later than one year following the determination of the lease[3].

6. THE NET EFFECT OF THE PERPETUITIES AND ACCUMULATIONS ACT 1964

It has been said that the Perpetuities and Accumulations Act 1964 'comes out . . . better . . . than any other Wait and See legislation in the world[4].' Perhaps the only major criticism which might be made of the new statutory rule against perpetuity is that it should have abrogated the old common law rule entirely. Instead the statutory rule comes into operation only where the application of the common law rule invalidates the gift under review. However, the modern law relating to perpetuities fundamentally alters the perspective of the common law rule. Instead of destroying a gift for fear that it may possibly offend against the rule against perpetuities, the law now effectively validates a gift for all those beneficiaries who do in fact contrive to obey the rule. In effect, the Perpetuities and Accumulations Act 1964 simply implies into all gifts made after 1964 the very rider which, as we saw earlier[5], is quite capable (if incorporated expressly)

2 No recourse can be had to the alternative perpetuity period of 80 years (see Perpetuities and Accumulations Act 1964, s. 9(2)).
3 Perpetuities and Accumulations Act 1964, s. 9(1).
4 R. H. Maudsley, op. cit., p. 227.
5 See p. 201, ante.

of saving gifts from the vice of perpetuity at common law. In this sense the rule as modified by statute preserves the ultimate rationale of a rule against perpetuities, by ensuring that society retains some measure of balance between the dispositive control of 'the dead hand' and the dispositive control of the living.

CHAPTER 7

Trusts for sale

Having looked in some detail at the strict settlement, we must examine a device of landholding which is nowadays more important in social terms—the 'trust for sale'. Although both strict settlements and trusts for sale are sometimes known, in generic terms, as 'settlements' of land, there exist between them several broad and fundamental differences.

Of these differences perhaps the most significant is that, whereas in the strict settlement the trustees play only a marginal role, in the trust for sale the trustees occupy a central position as owners of the legal estate in the property. The historical reason for this distinction lies in the fact that the strict settlement operated characteristically as a device of dynastic landholding which was able to achieve its object of retaining land within the family *without* much active intervention from the settlement trustees. However, the trust for sale has an altogether different origin. In its classic 19th century form it provided a means by which a testator could direct trusted friends (i.e., his 'executors') to sell his property after his death and distribute the money proceeds to a number of specified beneficiaries. The duties of these 'trustees' were therefore unequivocal and immediate; they became subject immediately to a duty to convert (i.e., to sell) the trust property, normally within a period of one year from the date of the testator's death (the so-called 'executor's year'). As a legal device, therefore, the trust for sale was more concerned with the 'exchange value' of land than with its 'use value'. The overriding emphasis was on property as capital rather than property as utility[1]. It was this conception of the trust for sale which was adopted in the 1925 legislation in order to fulfil a much broader function in regulating co-ownership of land. However, this modified version of the trust for sale has now become—not least in the residential context—a somewhat inappropriate medium for the legal expression of co-ownership[2]. Nevertheless it is necessary to examine the basic structure and operation of trusts for sale of land.

It is important to remember that a 'trust for sale' of land does in fact exhibit the classic features of the trust concept. As in the case of any trust, the trust for sale separates the functions of administration and enjoyment of property. Administration is vested in the trustees for sale as owners of the legal estate in the land. It is they who exercise the appropriate powers of management and disposition in relation to that estate; it is they who exercise the power of control. Enjoyment, however, is conferred upon the beneficiaries behind the trust for sale, i.e., upon those who hold the equitable interests and on whose behalf the

1 See p.176, ante.
2 See p. 232, post.

trustees are invested with the legal estate. Even so, the trust for sale is more than simply a 'trust' of property: it is a trust *for sale.* Certain essential features have been superimposed upon the basic trust device by the 1925 legislation, with the express object of ensuring that the property held on 'trust' is ultimately converted and its money value distributed in the manner specified by the settlor or otherwise ordained by law.

1. SUCCESSIVE INTERESTS AND CONCURRENT INTERESTS

It is possible to incorporate two quite different modes of beneficial entitlement within the framework of the trust for sale. A trust for sale can provide for a succession of beneficial interests to be held in the land, as for instance where Blackacre is conveyed to trustees for sale on behalf of 'A for life, remainder to B in tail, remainder to C in fee simple.' Alternatively, a trust for sale may provide for simultaneous entitlement in possession on the part of the beneficiaries, as where Blackacre is conveyed to trustees for sale on behalf of 'A, B and C in equal shares.' The latter situation (the 'co-ownership trust for sale') is nowadays by far the more common.

(1) The 'successive interest trust for sale'

The following diagram illustrates the possible lay-out of a 'successive interest' trust for sale:

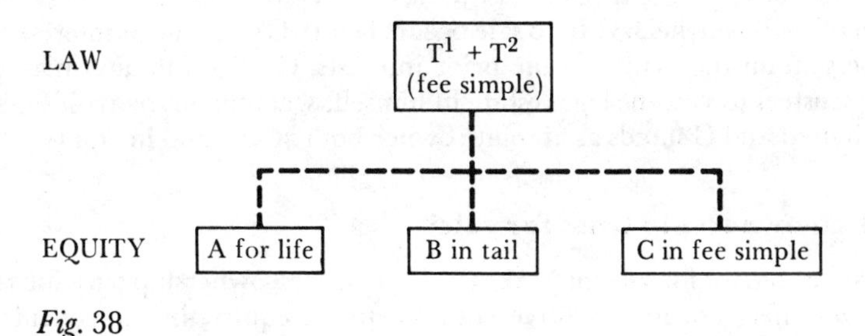

Fig. 38

This use of the trust for sale device produces an effect which is very similar to that of our archetypal model of the strict settlement, in terms of which Blackacre was granted to 'A for life, remainder to B in tail, remainder to C in fee simple.'

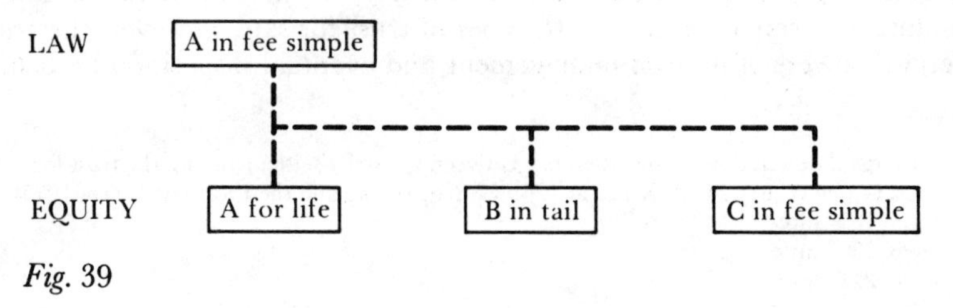

Fig. 39

In both *Figs.* 38 and 39 we have, quite plainly, a series of successive equitable interests in land, one series created behind a trust for sale and the other behind a strict settlement. In reality, the most significant distinction between these two forms of landholding is the identity of the owner of the legal estate[3]. Under the strict settlement (*Fig.* 39) the legal estate in the land and the attendant decision-making powers are vested in the beneficiary who is currently entitled in possession (i.e., A, the tenant for life)[4]. However, in the trust for sale (*Fig.* 38), the trustees (T^1 and T^2) who remained in the wings of the strict settlement have now come into the centre of the stage. They hold the legal estate and it is they who exercise all the decision-making powers with regard to the administration of the land and its eventual disposition. A trust for sale in this form may be preferred to a strict settlement if, for some reason, it is thought desirable that the legal initiative in respect of management and disposition should be entrusted to persons other than the beneficiary in possession. Moreover there are nowadays substantial tax reasons for opting in favour of the more flexible arrangement of the trust for sale; and, as we have already seen[5], the corresponding strict settlement creates more problems in probate terms since special vesting procedures are necessary on the death of each tenant for life.

Under the trust for sale (*Fig.* 38), the trustees manage the property pending sale, allowing the beneficiary in possession at any given time either to reside on the land or to enjoy the rents and profits derived from the land. The trustees also exercise discretion as to the *timing* of sale, in which event the beneficial interests of A, B and C will normally be overreached and translated into the resulting proceeds of sale[6]. In the absence of sale, the legal estate remains vested in the trustees: it is not subject to transfer (as in the case of settled land) in the event of the death of each beneficiary. If no sale occurs before C's beneficial interest falls into possession on the expiry of the prior interests, C (if of full age) may call upon the trustees to vest the legal estate in himself, whereupon the trust for sale has terminated and C stands as absolute owner both at law and in equity.

(2) The 'co-ownership trust for sale'

Alternatively, a trust for sale may take the form of a 'co-ownership trust for sale', which gives effect not to successive entitlements in equity, but to concurrent beneficial ownership. In this case, the interests of the beneficiaries are held simultaneously in possession, whether in specific proportions or otherwise. Whereas in the trust for sale outlined in *Fig.* 38 the beneficial interests (other than that of the final remainderman C) were limited and consecutive, the interests enjoyed by beneficiaries behind a 'co-ownership trust for sale' are absolute and concurrent. In both types of trust for sale, however, the trustees exercise powers of interim management and eventual disposition on behalf of

3 For a good description of the difference between the strict settlement and the trust for sale, see G. A. Grove (1961) 24 MLR 123 at 126: 'Conveyancing and the Property Acts of 1925'.
4 See p. 162, ante.
5 See p. 180f, ante.
6 See p. 227, ante.

the beneficiaries. The beneficiaries have equal rights in the income derived from the land before sale, and usually enjoy specific shares of the capital proceeds of sale if and when sale takes place. The picture looks something like this:

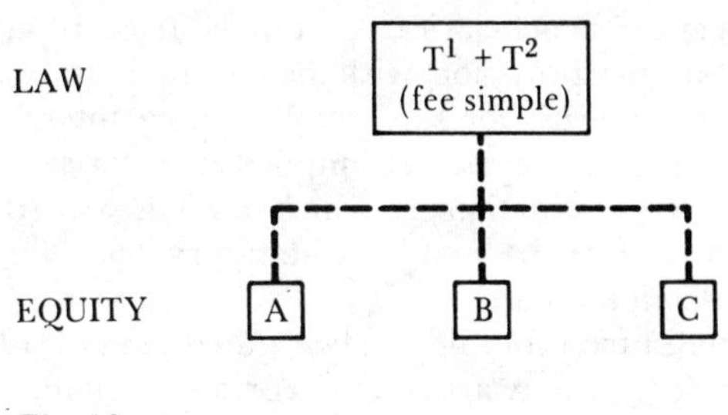

Fig. 40

The co-ownership trust for sale is nowadays very much more common than the successive interest trust for sale. This is due largely to the same reasons which have caused the demise of the strict settlement as a device of landholding[7]. But whether a trust for sale gives effect to successive or concurrent beneficial entitlements, at the heart of its structure is the firm distinction between ownership of the legal estate (which is essentially a 'paper title') and ownership of the equitable interests (which carry beneficial enjoyment). The legal title is concerned with the exercise of powers of management and disposition; the beneficial interests are concerned with money and actual occupation.

There is nothing, of course, to prevent trustees and beneficiaries from being the same people. T^1 and T^2 may hold a legal estate on trust for sale for *themselves* as beneficiaries. But there remains a vital division of function: T^1 and T^2 wear different hats at different times—those of trustee and beneficiary respectively. In the capacity of trustee for sale, each is the owner of the legal estate. In the capacity of beneficiary, each owns an equitable interest. Their various hats must never be confused:

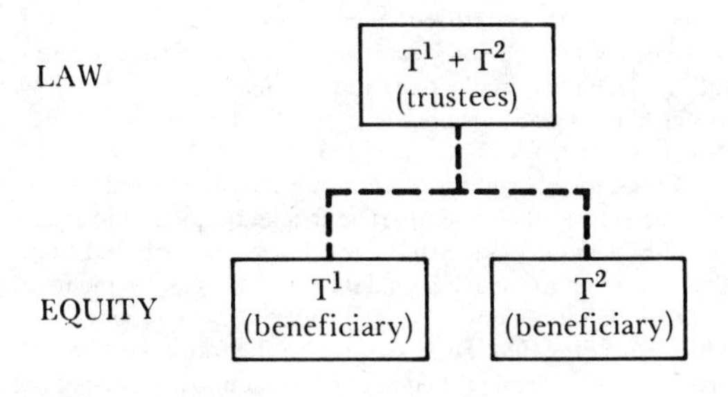

Fig. 41

7 See p. 156f, ante, p. 233, post.

2. EXPRESS AND IMPLIED TRUSTS FOR SALE

Trusts for sale arise either expressly or by implication. An express trust for sale arises where land is specifically vested in persons as trustees to hold 'on trust for sale' on behalf of certain beneficiaries. An implied trust for sale is normally the creation of some statutory provision, with the result that the terms 'implied trust for sale' and 'statutory trust for sale' may be used interchangeably. In the absence of an express trust for sale, an implied trust for sale arises by force of statute in almost every situation in which land is owned concurrently in possession by two or more persons[8]. A statutory trust for sale also occurs automatically on death intestate[9].

A successive interest trust for sale can be created *only expressly*[10]. In contrast, a co-ownership trust for sale may arise *either* expressly *or* by implication of statute. An express trust for sale of the latter variety would be brought about, for instance, by a conveyance of land 'to T^1 and T^2 on trust for sale for themselves in equity.' An implied trust for sale would arise, for instance, where land is conveyed simply 'to A and B.' Statute intervenes here to supply the existence of a trust for sale, more or less as a conveyancing device, with the result that the legal estate in the land is then held by A and B as trustees for sale for themselves in equity[11].

Trusts for sale are today much more significant than strict settlements. Indeed, the latter are now rarely created deliberately, and usually arise only where a settlor has unwisely attempted to confer a life interest by informal means. Unless, in so doing, he has expressly referred to a *trust for sale*, his grant is treated by default as initiating an imperfect strict settlement with all the disadvantages which ensue under the Settled Land Act 1925[12]. There is, however, no statute

8 For certain exceptional cases, see pp. 252, 257, post.

9 Administration of Estates Act 1925, s. 33.

10 In *Fig.* 38, for instance, it is only the express nature of the conveyance of the legal estate to T^1 and T^2 'on trust for sale for' A for life, remainder to B in tail, remainder to C in fee simple which, in this situation, brings about a trust for sale rather than a strict settlement. Merely to grant a legal estate to T^1 and T^2 'on trust for' A for life, remainder to B in tail, and remainder to C in fee simple would in fact result in a strict settlement of the land, thus giving A (*not* T^1 and T^2) the right to call for a vesting of the legal estate. Accordingly in such a case the grant of the legal estate to T^1 and T^2 would be ineffective, and the legal estate would remain in the grantor pending its transfer to the tenant for life, A.

11 See Law of Property Act 1925, s. 36(1), p. 252, post.

12 See p. 154, ante. This somewhat unfortunate result could be avoided if such anomalous grants were capable of being regarded not as imperfect strict settlements but rather as appropriate cases for the implication of a trust for sale. Indeed it has been suggested that much confusion and difficulty could be averted if the existing dual scheme of strict settlements and trusts for sale were replaced by one form of 'settlement' bearing primarily the characteristics of the trust for sale. G. A. Grove, while conceding that it was 'natural for the framers of the 1925 legislation to retain the two principal forms of settlement then in use,' went on to ask: 'Could not a single and simpler scheme be substituted for the present dual one, adopting the best features of each, by providing that wherever land is held in trust for persons in succession or subject to family charges or for the benefit of an infant or of two or more persons beneficially as joint tenants or tenants in common it shall be called settled land, and the legal estate shall be conveyed to or vested in not more than four persons jointly as trustees, such persons to have all the powers which are now described as the Settled Land Act powers? This would at one blow do away with the whole machinery of

entirely devoted to the trust for sale. The principal provisions governing express trusts for sale are found in sections 23–33 of the Law of Property Act 1925. Implied trusts for sale are dealt with in sections 34–36 of the Law of Property Act 1925 and section 36 of the Settled Land Act 1925.

3. THE DEFINITION OF A 'TRUST FOR SALE'

According to section 205(1)(xxix) of the Law of Property Act 1925, a 'trust for sale' in relation to land means

> an immediate binding trust for sale, whether or not exercisable at the request or with the consent of any person, and with or without a power at discretion to postpone the sale.

Care must always be taken to differentiate the trust for sale from the strict settlement, for these two devices of landholding are mutually exclusive[13].

A 'trust for sale' must obviously import a 'trust' or duty imposed upon the trustees. The essence of this trust is the *duty of sale* which is imposed upon all trustees for sale by the very nature of a 'trust for sale'. If a mere *power of sale* has been conferred, then there can be no 'trust for sale'. There exists instead a strict settlement of land, in which case the power of sale belongs, not to the trustees in the first instance, but to the tenant for life[14].

In terms of section 205(1)(xxix), a trust for sale must be an 'immediate' trust for sale. However, the requirement of immediacy attaches not to the sale, but to the trust. The existence of a trust for sale does not necessitate an instant sale of the land. In fact, section 25(1) of the Law of Property Act 1925 provides that 'a power to postpone sale shall, in the case of every trust for sale of land, be implied unless a contrary intention appears'[15]. However, section 205(1)(xxix) does mean that no trust for sale arises until the land is impressed by a duty of sale in the trustees. If the 'trust' to sell arises only with effect from some future point in time, there is meanwhile no 'immediate' trust for sale[16]. Any attempt to postpone the coming into effect of a trust for sale brings the relevant trust within the scope (at least initially) of the Settled Land Act 1925.

In effect, a 'trust for sale' is in most cases a device of landholding which is directed not towards a *sale* but rather towards the *retention* of the land in question—at least for the foreseeable future[17]. In imposing the (at first confusing)

---

special grants limited to settled land, with its attendant body of rules of probate practice, and would render the devolution of the legal estate a simple matter save in a very few cases . . . It would also do away with the difference between ordinary trustees and Settled Land Act trustees; there seems little reason to continue this distinction.' See (1961) 24 MLR 123 at 127.

13 Settled Land Act 1925, s. 1(7).

14 A direction which somewhat ambiguously imposes a 'trust either to retain or to sell the land' is to be construed as a trust to sell the land with power to postpone the sale (Law of Property Act 1925, s. 25(4)). See also Law of Property Act 1925, s. 32(1) and *Re Hanson* [1928] Ch 96.

15 For an instance of 'contrary intention', see *Re Atkins' Will Trusts* [1974] 1 WLR 761.

16 Suppose that land is granted to A for life, then to B and C on trust for sale. In this case there is a strict settlement during the lifetime of A, and the trust becomes an 'immediate trust for sale' only on A's death.

17 See *Re Evers' Trust* [1980] 1 WLR 1327 at 1330 per Ormrod LJ: '[T]he trust for sale has become a very convenient and much used conveyancing technique. Combined with the statutory power

terminology of 'trust for sale' upon various forms of landholding, the Law of Property Act 1925 merely strives towards a simplification of conveyancing. The use of a 'trust for sale' simply ensures that when, at some distant date, the land comes to be sold (i.e., when the trust to sell is eventually 'executed') the conveyancing machinery is already at hand to ensure—once again—facility for the third party purchaser and security for those who own equitable interests. We shall go on to see that protection for both purchaser and beneficiary is provided by the way in which the use of the conveyancing device of the 'trust for sale' enables the purchaser to take an unencumbered title, thus overreaching the beneficial interests which are thenceforth satisfied in terms of the proceeds of sale. However, this eventual result should not blind us to the fact that, in most cases, unless and until a sale takes place the presence of a 'trust for sale' is nothing other than a convenient 'legal fiction'[18].

A trust for sale must also be 'binding'. This means that the trustees for sale must be able, upon sale, to give a conveyance which overreaches all interests affecting the land. Only in this way can a third party take title free of all previous interests. A trust would not, for instance, constitute a 'binding trust for sale' where the land subject to the trust is also the subject of ***prior*** legal or equitable entitlements which the trustees are not competent to overreach[19]. The case law on the meaning of the term 'binding' is confused[20], but happily this aspect of the definition of a 'trust for sale' nowadays rarely causes problems in practice. The interpretation of the word 'binding' has importance in demarcating the point in time at which a grant of land originally in the form of a strict settlement gives way to a trust for sale[1]. But, since strict settlements are now seldom created, the problem of construction is very much less pressing.

A 'trust for sale' may be 'immediate' and 'binding' within section 205(1)(xxix) even though exercisable only at the request or with the consent of a named person or named persons. Thus, if a grantor of land wishes to render that land effectively unsalable in the hands of his grantee, all he need do is convey the land to trustees on trust for sale and specify that sale is subject to the consent of a person or body which is extremely unlikely to agree to any sale[2]. The possibility that the exercise of a trust for sale may thus be comprehensively controlled by requisite and unobtainable consents has brought about the rather strange and perhaps undesirable result that, in some situations, land held on trust for sale is effectively incapable of sale. It is debatable whether the imposition of an

in the trustees to postpone the sale, it can be used to meet a variety of situations, in some of which an actual sale is far from the intentions of the parties at the time when the trust for sale comes into existence.'

18 *Williams & Glyn's Bank Ltd v Boland* [1979] Ch 312 at 336 per Ormrod LJ.

19 Additional overreaching powers appropriate to such a case are available only if the trust for sale is converted into an *ad hoc* trust for sale under section 2(2) of the Law of Property Act 1925. The essence of an *ad hoc* trust for sale is that the trustees are either a trust corporation or persons appointed or approved by the court.

20 See *Re Leigh's Settled Estates* [1926] Ch 852; *Re Parker's Settled Estates* [1928] Ch 247; *Re Norton* [1929] 1 Ch 84. See also M. M. Lewis (1938) 54 LQR 576: 'Settlements of Land'.

1 This issue is, of course, vital in determining whether a third party purchaser should look to the tenant for life or to the trustees for the conveyance of a good legal title.

2 See *Re Inns* [1947] 1 Ch 576; *Re Herklot's Will Trusts* [1964] 2 All ER 66.

unobtainable consent to the execution of a trust for sale is in truth compatible with the trustees' duty to sell[3], but the point has not so far been taken up by the courts. Theoretically the courts have jurisdiction under section 30 of the Law of Property Act 1925[4] to set aside a requisite consent which is not forthcoming, but this jurisdiction has not yet been exercised in any reported decision.

4. THE RESPECTIVE ROLES OF TRUSTEE AND BENEFICIARY

We have seen that, in any form of trust for sale, the trustees hold the legal estate in the land and are invested with powers of management and disposition. The beneficiaries merely benefit. Even if the trustees and beneficiaries happen to be the same persons, their functions are quite distinct.

The powers exercisable by trustees for sale are defined by statute on an express analogy with the powers enjoyed by the tenant for life and settlement trustees under the Settled Land Act 1925[5]. In other words, the trustees for sale are invested with all the powers of management and disposition which would be enjoyed by a tenant for life and settlement trustees under a strict settlement. The ultimate power of disposition held by trustees for sale is also a *duty*—the duty to sell the land held by them on trust for sale[6]. However, the trustees' powers of management and leasing may be delegated revocably and in writing to any beneficiary in possession pending sale of the property (e.g., A in *Fig.* 38)[7]. But

3 There is, in relation to trusts for sale, no express equivalent of section 106 of the Settled Land Act 1925, which makes void any attempt to inhibit or restrict the exercise of a tenant for life's powers of disposition over settled land, p. 179, ante. However, it can be argued that, apart from the strictures necessarily imposed by the requirement of a specified consent to the execution of a trust for sale or by the exercise of the power to postpone sale, the powers of trustees for sale are—like those of a tenant for life—irreducible. It might even be argued that section 106 is impliedly incorporated in the trust for sale provisions of the Law of Property Act by means of the reference in section 28(1) of the Law of Property Act 1925 (footnote 5). See *Cheshire's Modern Law of Real Property* (12th edn. ed. E. H. Burn, London 1976), p. 202; R. E. Megarry and H. W. R. Wade, *The Law of Real Property* (4th edn., London 1975), p. 368f.; R. H. Maudsley and E. H. Burn, *Land Law: Cases and Materials* (4th edn., London 1980), p. 199.

4 See pp. 268, 274, post.

5 See Law of Property Act 1925, s. 28(1). These powers include the powers conferred by section 102 of the Settled Land Act 1925 during a minority, even though no minority in fact exists (see *Re Gray* [1927] 1 Ch 242).

6 The proceeds of sale may then be invested in the purchase of other land which, under section 32(1) of the Law of Property Act 1925, becomes subject in its turn to a trust for sale (see Settled Land Act 1925, s. 73(1)(xi) and *Re Wellsted's Will Trusts* [1949] Ch 296). However, this useful power of investment impliedly conferred by section 28(1) of the Law of Property Act 1925 is liable to one possible restriction. It may be that the trustees' power to invest in land is lost if at any point the trustees do not retain at least some land on trust for sale. By selling *all* the land originally held on trust for sale, the trustees may lose their status as 'trustees for sale' (as defined by section 205(1)(xxix) of the Law of Property Act 1925) and may therefore fall outside the ambit of section 28(1). See *Re Wakeman* [1945] Ch 177 at 181 per Uthwatt J. For this reason, it is sometimes said that it may be prudent for trustees for sale always to retain a small portion of land on trust for sale simply in order to preserve their character as 'trustees for sale'.

7 Law of Property Act 1925, s. 29(1).

this is the only circumstance in which the functions of trustee and beneficiary are even slightly interchangeable. Normally the beneficiary in possession has no powers at all over the legal estate: the powers incidental to the legal estate are powers exercisable by the trustees.

Of course, a trust for sale confers upon the trustees a mixture of powers and duties: a trust for sale imports a duty to sell coupled with a power at discretion to postpone sale. A power is by nature merely permissive: it is of the essence of a duty that its execution is mandatory. It may sometimes happen that the trustees cannot reach unanimity either in the discharge of their duty to sell or in the exercise of their power to postpone sale. In such a case, the duty to sell overrides the power to postpone sale and is normally determinative of the controversy. A trust 'for sale' must prevail (i.e., the land must be sold) unless *all* the trustees agree to exercise the power to postpone sale[8]. Given the primacy of the duty to sell, if a recalcitrant trustee refuses to join his co-trustees in selling land held by them on trust for sale, an application may be made to court in the last resort and the court may make 'such order as it thinks fit'[9].

5. THE DOCTRINE OF CONVERSION

The net income derived from the land held on trust for sale is usually paid to the beneficiary or beneficiaries entitled in possession. Often a beneficiary with an immediate life interest is allowed by the trustees to reside on and occupy the land itself. In view of these facts it might be thought that a beneficiary under a trust for sale holds an equitable interest in the land itself. However, this conclusion is not justified in terms of the orthodoxy which has prevailed until relatively recently. According to the orthodox view of the matter, a beneficiary under a trust for sale of land is regarded at each and every stage as holding not an interest in land but rather an interest in personalty—in this case money—even though the land has not yet been sold. In other words, the interests of the beneficiaries under a trust for sale are deemed to attach not to the land which is the subject of the trust, but to the prospective proceeds of sale which the land represents. The curious mental process which leads to this result is known as 'the doctrine of conversion'.

The doctrine of conversion unfolds itself as follows. Where land is held on trust for sale, the trustees are ipso facto bound by a duty to sell. They are obliged to sell the land unless there is unanimous agreement to postpone sale. Upon sale the trust property manifestly ceases to be realty and becomes instead personalty, i.e., proceeds of sale. It is, however, a maxim of equity that 'Equity looks on that as done which ought to be done.' Equity therefore anticipates the factual result brought about by the discharge of the trustees' duty to sell, and converts the beneficiaries' interests into personalty from the very moment at which a binding

8 See *Re Mayo* [1943] Ch 302. Here, however, Simonds J conceded that the position would be quite different if there were any suggestion of mala fides on the part of the trustee or trustees who were pressing for sale.
9 Law of Property Act 1925, s. 30, p. 274, post.

trust for sale attaches to the land. Hence, even before sale takes place—even if sale *never* takes place—the beneficiaries are treated by the land lawyer as holding interests in money rather than interests in land.

It is perhaps worth noting at this point that the historical purpose of the doctrine of conversion was, and its purpose still is, to ensure clarity and certainty in the devolution of beneficial interests existing behind a trust for sale of land. The doctrine of conversion carries the great advantage that the nature and therefore the devolution of such interests do not fall to be determined by such fortuitous factors as the precise timing of sale by the trustees. Suppose, for instance, that a beneficiary behind a trust for sale disposes of his equitable interest under a will which leaves all his 'real property' to A and all his 'personal property' to B. Were it not for the equitable doctrine of conversion, the devolution of the testator's beneficial interest would turn upon whether the trustees for sale had sold the land by the effective date of the will (i.e., by the date of the testator's death). If the land were sold the day before the testator died, his beneficial interest would pass (as 'personal property') to B; whereas if the land were sold the day after his death, his beneficial interest would pass (as 'real property') to A. It is manifestly unsatisfactory, however, that the testator's beneficial interest should thus fluctuate between realty and personalty in accordance with the timing of sale, and the doctrine of conversion is designed precisely to preclude this kind of uncertainty. Under the doctrine of conversion a beneficial interest behind a trust for sale of land remains at all times—both before and after sale—an interest in money proceeds and, therefore, an interest in personalty[10].

It can be seen from this analysis that the true emphasis of the doctrine of conversion is upon the needs of beneficiaries rather than upon the protection of third party purchasers. That the doctrine should have the effect of conferring any benefit on third parties is entirely fortuitous, since the purpose which the doctrine seeks to serve is simply the orderly and convenient characterisation of interests on the death of a beneficial owner, not the protection of third party purchasers—and certainly not the protection of such purchasers to the detriment of a living beneficiary[11]. Yet in more recent times this has been the consequence of the strict application of the doctrine. The theory of 'conversion' has made it tempting to suggest that a purchaser of land held on trust for sale need never be concerned with the rights of beneficiaries on the ground that those rights have always been detached from the land itself and inhere merely in the prospective proceeds of sale.

Such was the concentration upon the protection of third party purchasers at the time of the 1925 property legislation that the original emphasis of the

10 Care must, however, be taken if the beneficiary under a trust for sale of land wishes to dispose of his equitable interest by means of a home-made will. A testamentary disposition of 'all my real property to my wife, Mary' and of 'all my fishing tackle and other personal property to my old friend, Fred' will result in the testator's beneficial interest behind the trust passing to Fred (not Mary)—a consequence which might surprise the layman and will certainly surprise Mary if the subject of the disposition was the testator's equitable interest in the matrimonial home. See, for instance, *Re Kempthorne* [1930] 1 Ch 268. Compare *Re Newman* [1930] 2 Ch 409.

11 See p. 357, post.

doctrine of conversion has since become distorted and obscured. This process was further accentuated by the tendency—which pervades the enactments of 1925—to confine the significance of property to its value in immediate exchange terms. The concern for the protection of purchasers and the inclination to monetise all value operated in close conjunction. Both directed the primary focus of the property legislation upon the need to ensure unrestricted alienability of title within an efficient property market. This in turn created a need for a legal mechanism which would enable the purchaser of land to take title free from (i.e., to overreach) fragments of benefit already vested in others which might prejudice, or conflict with, his own interest in that land.

The doctrine of conversion seemed to provide just such a mechanism. In *Irani Finance Ltd v Singh*[12] Cross LJ went so far as to assert that the *whole* purpose of the trust for sale is, by virtue of the equitable doctrine of conversion, to enable third party purchasers to buy land free from beneficial incumbrances. He reiterated the orthodox view that the beneficiaries behind a trust for sale of land are

> no doubt . . . interested in the land in the general sense . . . But that is not the same thing as their being owners of the equitable interests in the realty. The whole purpose of the trust for sale is to make sure, by shifting the equitable interests away from the land and into the proceeds of sale, that a purchaser of the land takes free from the equitable interests. To hold these to be equitable interests in the land itself would be to frustrate this purpose. Even to hold that they have equitable interests in the land for a limited period, namely until the land is sold, would . . . be inconsistent with the trust for sale being an 'immediate' trust for sale working an immediate conversion, which is what the Law of Property Act 1925 envisages (see section 205(1)(xxix)).

Of course there have always been occasions when the full rigour of the doctrine of conversion could not be maintained without offence to statutory intention. But such cases are rare. Nevertheless, the Court of Appeal thought in *Cooper v Critchley*[13] that a beneficial interest behind a trust for sale would constitute an interest in 'land' for the purpose of section 40 of the Law of Property Act 1925[14]. Likewise, it was ruled in *Elias v Mitchell*[15] that a beneficiary behind a trust for sale is a 'person interested . . . in . . . land' for the purpose of protecting his beneficial interest as a minor interest by entry of a caution against a registered title.

Such instances have in the past been regarded merely as isolated deviations from the doctrine of conversion. That doctrine, in its traditional formulation, dramatically reinforces the idea of a 'trust to sell' as underlying the legal reality of almost all situations of co-ownership of land[16]. In recent years, however, the doctrine of conversion has become the subject of considerable judicial criticism based not least on the ground that it fails in significant respects to accord with the social reality of co-ownership. The doctrine anticipates the effect of an

12 [1971] Ch 59 at 79.
13 [1955] Ch 431. See (1955) 19 Conv (NS) 148 (F. R. Crane); (1955) 71 LQR 177 (REM); (1955) 14 Cambridge LJ 155 (H. W. R. Wade).
14 See p. 81, ante. According to this provision, a contract for sale of 'any interest in land' is actionable only if contained in writing or evidenced in a written memorandum.
15 [1972] Ch 652. See (1972) 36 Conv (NS) 206 (D. J. Hayton), p. 271, post.
16 See p. 217, ante.

eventual sale by insisting that the interest of a beneficiary behind a trust for sale is at all times an interest in money rather than an interest in land. It is not always easy to maintain this analysis with any conviction where the immediate and primary motivation of the trust for sale is not sale but the retention of land[17]. It is increasingly said, for instance, that the mechanics of a trust for sale are not apt to describe the reality of most matrimonial homes, where the spouses have little interest in sale but are rather more concerned to provide a secure base for themselves and their children. It was essentially for this reason that in 1971 the Law Commission floated the idea of a 'matrimonial home trust' in substitution for the 'trust for sale', on the ground that 'this is a far more appropriate term than "trust for sale" which to the layman seems to imply that the property must be sold'[18]. This led in turn to the Law Commission's later proposal that all matrimonial homes should be co-owned by the spouses either in consequence of an express trust for sale or by virtue of a new statutory regime of co-ownership of the matrimonial home[19]. Such a proposal would, for the first time, have created a special regime for family homes, but no legislation to this effect has yet been enacted[20]. Instead there has been, in the matrimonial homes context, a fairly strong reaction against the traditional understanding of the equitable doctrine of conversion.

This reaction emerged most markedly in the judgments of the Court of Appeal and the House of Lords in *Williams & Glyn's Bank Ltd v Boland*[1]. This case involved conjoined appeals relating to two husbands who, as the sole trustees for sale of registered land, had mortgaged their respective matrimonial homes to a bank for the purpose of raising business loans. The businesses concerned later experienced liquidity problems, and the bank accordingly sought possession of the two matrimonial homes as a realisable security for the loans which the husbands were unable to repay. The appeals raised an important point of law in the context of registered land and are the subject of an extended treatment in Chapter 11[2]. However, for present purposes we can proceed on the basis that the issue of priority between the bank mortgagee and the two wives in *Boland* turned in large degree upon whether the equitable interest of each wife behind the trust for sale of the matrimonial home could be regarded as an interest in land or merely as an interest in proceeds of sale.

Not surprisingly the Court of Appeal declined to apply the received doctrine of conversion in characterising the nature of each wife's beneficial interest. Lord Denning MR asked

What is the nature of this trust? It was suggested to us that it was not a trust of the house itself, but only a trust in the proceeds of sale. That cannot be right. When a married man

17 See, for instance, S. M. Cretney (1971) 34 MLR 441, 443: 'A Technical and Tricky Matter'.
18 See Law Commission Published Working Paper No. 42: *Family Law, Family Property Law* (1971), para. 1.115. See also J. G. Miller (1972) 36 Conv (NS) 99 at 111f.: 'Trusts for Sale and the Matrimonial Home'; I. A. Saunders and A. McGregor (1973) 37 Conv (NS) 270 at 279: 'Disposal of Equitable Interest in Joint Tenancy'.
19 See p. 149, ante; p. 303, post.
20 See p. 151, ante.
1 [1979] Ch 312 CA, [1980] 3 WLR 138, HL.
2 See p. 353, post.

and his wife buy a house, they do it so as to live in it—so that it should be a home for them both and their children—for the foreseeable future. They do not intend to sell it—at any rate not for many years hence. In determining what the nature of the trust is, the court must give effect to the intention of the parties—to be inferred from their words and conduct . . . In nearly all these cases the inexorable inference is that the husband is to hold the legal estate in the house in trust for them both—for both to live in for the foreseeable future. The couple do not have in mind a sale—nor a division of the proceeds of sale—except in the far distance[3].

He concluded that the interest of a beneficiary behind a trust for sale must be regarded, at least before sale takes place, as 'an equitable interest in land'[4].

Ormrod LJ, in giving judgment in the same case, did not go quite so far. He was, however, prepared to accept that the wife/beneficiary's interest behind the trust for sale was a right 'subsisting in reference to registered land' for the purpose of the point at issue[5]. He expressed the view that the rights of such a beneficiary

are not accurately described as an interest in a sum of money, simpliciter . . . In the instant cases the object of the trust was to provide a joint home and the last thing the parties contemplated was that the house would be sold and the cash divided between them. In converting such a relationship into a trust for sale the legislation of 1925 created, in effect, a legal fiction . . . This may have been an inescapable consequence of the method adopted to achieve its primary objective, that is, the simplification of conveyancing. But to press this legal fiction to its logical conclusion and beyond the point which is necessary to achieve the primary objective is not justifiable, particularly when it involves the sacrifice of the interests of a class or classes of person. The consequence is that the interests of persons in the position of the [appellant] wives ought not to be dismissed as a mere interest in the proceeds of sale except where it is essential to the working of the scheme to do so[6].

By eschewing the orthodox doctrine of conversion, the Court of Appeal was able to hold that the bank was bound by the beneficial interests of the appellant wives. The bank in its turn appealed.

When *Williams & Glyn's Bank Ltd v Boland* reached the House of Lords, the appellant bank did not plead the traditional doctrine of conversion in support of its case against each wife/beneficiary. It was considered by counsel that Ormrod LJ had sufficiently disposed of the matter in recognising that the wife/beneficiary's interest was, at the very least, a right 'subsisting in reference to registered land', and it was felt that this conclusion was irresistible as a matter of law. The House of Lords did not therefore address itself squarely to the applicability of the doctrine of conversion to the modern co-ownership trust for sale. It was unanimously held that the equitable interest of each wife/beneficiary took priority over the security received by the bank. Lord Wilberforce, in giving the principal speech in the House, noted obliquely that

3 [1979] Ch 312 at 329.
4 [1979] Ch 312 at 331.
5 The point at issue concerned the proper construction of section 70(1)(g) of the Land Registration Act 1925, p.334, post.
6 [1979] Ch 312 at 336. See (1979) 38 Cambridge LJ 254 (M. J. Prichard).

to describe the interests of spouses in a house jointly bought to be lived in as a matrimonial home as merely an interest in the proceeds of sale, or rents and profits until sale, is just a little unreal . . .[7]

In *Boland* the Court of Appeal and the House of Lords reached an ethically satisfying conclusion on a legal issue of considerable social importance. The decision has wide implications not only for conveyancers and lending institutions in this country but also for millions of married couples. The House of Lords—effectively for socio-political reasons—issued a significant public endorsement of the proprietary rights (and therefore indirectly the elevated personal status) of the married woman in the matrimonial home. However, by accepting that beneficial interests behind a trust for sale could be characterised without further ado as interests 'subsisting in reference' to land, the law lords deflected a more radical examination of the traditional doctrine of conversion. In so doing, the House of Lords failed to confront certain underlying conceptual problems which have for long demanded a much clearer analysis. The speeches in Boland (and in particular that of Lord Scarman) emerged more in the form of an essay in social ethics than as a reasoned dissection of the legal and conceptual issues at stake. Lord Scarman adverted to the way in which the English courts have recently come to recognise the property rights of wives in the matrimonial home[8]. He clearly viewed the point at issue in *Boland* as one which required to be decided in a manner which promoted the 'achievement of social justice'[9].

This approach to the resolution of problems of priority in land law is symptomatic of a more modern view of the law of property[10]. According to this view property entitlements are increasingly defined by the courts so as to reflect the reasonable expectations of litigants and the demands of social justice and conscionable dealing. In *Boland*, however, both the Court of Appeal and the House of Lords neglected to inquire into certain important conceptual issues—and these we shall examine shortly[11]. First, however, we must look at a case which throws into some confusion the jurisprudence which *Boland* so neatly sidestepped.

Cedar Holdings Ltd v Green[12] was decided by the Court of Appeal two days after a differently constituted division of the Court of Appeal had delivered its judgments in *Williams & Glyn's Bank Ltd v Boland*. The Court in *Cedar Holdings* proceeded to take a diametrically opposed view of the applicability of the doctrine of conversion in relation to trusts for sale. The case concerned a matrimonial home which was held by H and W on trust for sale. H and W were thus joint legal and beneficial owners of the house (which was registered land). Following the granting of a divorce between H and W, H feared that W would apply for a property transfer order under the Matrimonial Causes Act 1973 for the purpose of vesting the entire interest in the home in herself. H therefore

7 [1980] 3 WLR 138 at 146. See (1980) 39 Cambridge LJ 243 (M. J. Prichard).
8 See p. 560f, post.
9 [1980] 3 WLR 138 at 148.
10 See p. 488, post.
11 See pp. 259, 383, post.
12 [1979] 3 WLR 31.

procured X to impersonate W in a visit to the plaintiff bank in order to execute a legal charge on the freehold estate in the matrimonial home as security for a loan advanced to H. The bank later took proceedings in order to establish its rights against H.

It was conceded by the bank that the fraudulently executed legal charge could have no operation upon the jointly held legal estate in the matrimonial home. Nor could it affect the equitable interest held by W behind the trust for sale of the land, since she had been uninvolved in H's fraudulent dealings. However, the bank argued that its charge, while plainly ineffective against the legal estate, was nevertheless binding upon the equitable interest of H behind the trust for sale. The bank relied principally on section 63(1) of the Law of Property Act 1925, which provides that

> Every conveyance is effectual to pass all the estate, right, title, interest, claim, and demand which the conveying parties respectively have, in, to, or on the property conveyed or expressed or intended so to be . . .

According to the bank, the charge executed by H constituted a 'conveyance'[13] within the meaning of this section, and therefore was effectual to pass H's equitable interest as part of the totality of his 'interest . . . in . . . the property conveyed.'

The Court of Appeal decided, however, that H's beneficial interest behind the trust for sale did not constitute an 'interest . . . in . . . the property conveyed or expressed or intended so to be . . .' Buckley LJ applied the equitable doctrine of conversion in order to hold that

> a beneficial interest in the proceeds of sale of land held on the statutory trusts is not an interest in that land within the meaning of the section and a conveyance of that land is not effectual to pass a beneficial interest in the proceeds of sale. It follows that . . . in the present case the legal charge executed by [H] was not effectual to charge his beneficial interest in the proceeds of sale of his matrimonial home . . . [H] has no interest in the matrimonial home; his interest is confined to a half share of the proceeds of sale of the house and of any rents and profits until sale. That interest is, in my opinion, an entirely different subject-matter from that which [H] contracted to mortgage[14].

It is clear that the Court of Appeal's application of the doctrine of conversion in *Cedar Holdings Ltd v Green* was entirely inconsistent with the shift away from this doctrine in the context of the matrimonial home. It may well be true that, as Goff LJ hinted, the Court of Appeal was attempting to preserve in H's hands an equitable share in proceeds of sale which W might later attack in property transfer proceedings brought under the Matrimonial Causes Act 1973. Nevertheless the decision in *Cedar Holdings* is grotesquely incompatible with the subsequent decision of the House of Lords in *Williams & Glyn's Bank Ltd v Boland*[15]. The two decisions taken in conjunction compel the following

13 A 'conveyance' is defined for the purpose of the Law of Property Act 1925 as including a mortgage (see Law of Property Act 1925, s. 205(1)(ii)).

14 [1979] 3 WLR 31 at 38f. Goff LJ also based his judgment on the doctrine of conversion—albeit 'not without some hesitation on the way.'

15 See (1980) 43 MLR 225 at 228 (B. Berkovits); (1979) 38 Cambridge LJ 251 (M. J. Prichard); [1979] Conv 372 (F. R. Crane).

conclusions in relation to the beneficial interests behind a trust for sale of a matrimonial home which has been mortgaged to a bank:

(i) In determining the bank's rights against a spouse, that spouse has an interest in money not land (*Cedar Holdings*).
(ii) In determining a spouse's rights against the bank, that spouse has an interest in land not money (*Boland*).

The contradiction is absurd, and in the House of Lords in *Williams & Glyn's Bank Ltd v Boland*[16] Lord Wilberforce said simply that he considered *Cedar Holdings Ltd v Green* 'to have been wrongly decided.'

The present position in relation to the equitable doctrine of conversion is thus a little unclear. There is House of Lords authority for the proposition that the doctrine no longer applies in its traditional form for the purpose of characterising beneficial interests behind a trust for sale of the matrimonial home. It is uncertain, for instance, whether this liberated view of the doctrine extends to other kinds of property (e.g., business or partnership property) held on trust for sale. What is more certain is that the 'much overworked' doctrine of conversion is now tending slowly towards its demise[17]. Michael Prichard has pointed out that the 'fostering of the doctrine of conversion after 1925 introduces a regrettable unreality into land ownership, as more and more homes are held jointly and thus upon trust for sale'[18]. To the argument that the doctrine of conversion is somehow 'absolutely crucial' to the working of the 1925 legislation and to the operation of overreaching, Mr Prichard replies that, in the event of sale,

> the reason why the purchaser takes free from the equitable interests is because a sale under a trust for sale is a performance of the trust, not a breach of it, and the purchaser is therefore a bona fide purchaser for value without notice of any breach of trust which would affect his conscience. The doctrine of conversion evolved to regulate the devolution of beneficial interests, not to protect purchasers, and it could have been allowed to wither without depriving trusts for sale of their overreaching effect.

6. PROTECTION FOR A PURCHASER FROM TRUSTEES FOR SALE

(1) The protection of 'overreaching'

As we saw in the context of settled land[19], one of the major achievements of the property legislation of 1925 was that it tended to make land commerciable without simultaneously destroying the utility of land as a medium of family endowment. Likewise, part of the object of the trust for sale as a conveyancing device is that it should enable a third party purchaser to acquire a good title free of the beneficiaries' interests when eventually the land held on trust for sale is sold. The legal title is therefore rendered freely alienable while the fragments of

16 [1980] 3 WLR 138 at 146.
17 See (1979) 38 Cambridge LJ 23 at 25 (M. J. Prichard).
18 (1979) 38 Cambridge LJ 251 at 253.
19 See p. 165, ante.

benefit in the land are jealously safeguarded. The realisation of this object depends upon a combination of facility for the purchaser and security for the beneficial owners which is achieved by the technical device of 'overreaching'.

Where land is held on an express trust for sale, the details of ownership (both legal and equitable) are often—although not necessarily—contained in two documents. One document is a vesting document or conveyance: it records the details of the legal title vested in the trustees for sale. The other document—in the form of a trust instrument—records the equitable rights behind the trust. Normally a purchaser of the land need concern himself only with the first document, since he knows that the equitable interests will be overreached upon sale if he complies with the relevant statutory requirements. It is the overreaching of the beneficial interests which provides the primary protection for the purchaser, while at the same time affording security to the equitable interests behind the trust, which thereafter take effect in the proceeds of sale.

It is perhaps worth noting parenthetically that the terminology of overreaching is technically inaccurate in the context of the trust for sale. By virtue of the doctrine of conversion—at least in its orthodox application—the beneficiaries' interests consist ab initio of interests in money. It is not strictly true to say that on sale a purchaser 'overreaches' those interests and that those interests are converted into money. In the traditional understanding of the trust for sale of land, the interests in question were always mere interests in money, and there is therefore, in this sense, no subsisting beneficial interest in the land which the purchaser requires to 'overreach'. However, the utility of the misnomer is recognised even in statute, and we shall continue to talk here of the effect of sale in sweeping the equities from the land on to the proceeds of sale by way of overreaching. Section 2(1)(ii) of the Law of Property Act 1925 provides that

> A conveyance to a purchaser of a legal estate in land shall overreach any equitable interest or power affecting that estate, whether or not he has notice thereof, if . . . the conveyance is made by trustees for sale and the equitable interest or power is at the date of the conveyance capable of being overreached by such trustees . . . and the statutory requirements respecting the payment of capital money arising under a disposition upon trust for sale are complied with.

It is vital to realise that the Law of Property Act 1925 thus places three fundamentally important conditions upon the overreaching of interests behind a trust for sale of land.

(a) *The conveyance must be 'made by trustees for sale'*[20]

'Trustees for sale' are defined by section 205(1)(xxix) of the Law of Property Act 1925 in terms of 'persons . . . holding land on trust for sale', and a 'trust for sale' is further defined as an 'immediate binding trust for sale'[1]. It is, of course,

20 For the purpose of the Law of Property Act 1925, the term 'conveyance' is defined as including, unless the context otherwise requires, 'a mortgage, charge, lease, assent, vesting declaration, vesting instrument, disclaimer, release and every other assurance of property or of an interest therein by any instrument, except a will . . .' (Law of Property Act 1925, s. 205(1)(ii)).

1 See p. 217, ante.

this requirement that an overreaching conveyance be made by 'trustees for sale' which makes it imperative to identify the precise moment at which a strict settlement escapes from the scope of the Settled Land Act 1925 and becomes instead a trust for sale[2].

We shall examine later the consequences which flow if a purchaser of land held on trust for sale fails to take his conveyance from 'trustees for sale' (e.g., where he takes his conveyance from a single trustee for sale)[3]. It is quite clear, however, from section 2(1)(ii) of the Law of Property Act 1925 that such a purchaser cannot statutorily overreach the equitable interests behind the trust for sale.

(b) *The equitable interests must be 'capable of being overreached'*

The equitable interests which are 'capable of being overreached' by a purchaser of land held on trust for sale are in general 'family equitable interests'[4]. A sale of land held on trust for sale cannot overreach 'commercial equitable interests', which will continue to affect the land if (but only if) protected by the appropriate form of registration[5]. Apart from the case of registrable commercial equitable interests, the only type of equitable interest which is incapable of being overreached by an ordinary sale by trustees for sale is an equity created prior to a trust for sale[6]. Such an equitable interest arises only rarely nowadays, but can be overreached by using the machinery of an *ad hoc* trust for sale under section 2(2) of the Law of Property Act 1925[7].

(c) *There must be compliance with 'the statutory requirements respecting the payment of capital money arising under a disposition upon trust for sale'*

There are strict statutory requirements respecting the payment of capital money which arises from a disposition of land held on trust for sale. According to section 27(2) of the Law of Property Act 1925,

> the proceeds of sale or other capital money shall not be paid to or applied by the direction of fewer than two persons as trustees for sale . . .[8]

2 If a purchaser takes his conveyance from *soi disant* 'trustees for sale', and the land turns out still to have been the subject of a strict settlement, then the purchaser does not overreach the beneficial interests pursuant to section 2(1)(ii) of the Law of Property Act 1925, because he has not bought from genuine 'trustees for sale'. Nor does he obtain immunity from the equities behind the settlement by virtue of section 2(1)(i), since he has not bought from the person having power under the Settled Land Act 1925 to sell the settled land, i.e., the tenant for life. It has been suggested that, in cases of doubt as to whether a settlement is a strict settlement or a trust for sale, the purchaser should take his conveyance from both the beneficiary currently entitled in possession (qua tenant for life) and the trustees (qua trustees for sale). See R. E. Megarry and H. W. R. Wade, *The Law of Real Property* (4th edn., London 1975), p. 362.

3 See p. 286, post.

4 See p. 69, ante.

5 See p. 69, ante.

6 There is, in this context, no equivalent to section 72(3) of the Settled Land Act 1925, p. 183, ante. See *In Re Ryder and Steadman's Contract* [1927] 2 Ch 62 at 82f. per Sargant LJ.

7 See p. 218, ante.

8 As substituted by the Law of Property (Amendment) Act 1926, Schedule.

The requirement of payment to two trustees is mandatory in the sense that it overrides any contrary provision in the instrument (if any) creating the trust for sale[9]. Payment to fewer than two trustees prevents the equitable interests behind the trust for sale from being overreached. This is a rigid principle and admits of scarcely any exceptions. The two exceptions permitted allow payment to be made to a trust corporation or to a sole personal representative[10].

If the three conditions of overreaching are satisfied, the purchaser of land held on trust for sale overreaches the beneficial interests behind the trust. Under section 27(1) of the Law of Property Act 1925,

> A purchaser of a legal estate from trustees for sale shall not be concerned with the trusts affecting the proceeds of sale of land subject to a trust for sale . . . or affecting the rents and profits of the land until sale, whether or not those trusts are declared by the same instrument by which the trust for sale is created.

In other words, the equitable interests behind the trust now take effect (in reality as well as in theory) in the capital moneys arising from the disposition. The purchaser becomes the sole owner of the land both at law and in equity: he takes the land free of the interests of the beneficiaries.

Under section 14(1) of the Trustee Act 1925, a receipt in writing in respect of the purchase moneys operates as a 'sufficient discharge' to the purchaser, and effectively exonerates him from seeing to the application of the proceeds of sale by the trustees or from being 'answerable for any loss or misapplication thereof.' The overall result of section 14(1) of the Trustee 1925 and section 27(1) of the Law of Property Act 1925 is that the purchaser who fulfils the three conditions of overreaching takes the legal estate entirely free both of the beneficial interests and of the terms of the trust.

(2) Other forms of protection for the purchaser

Although overreaching is the primary form of protection conferred upon the purchaser of land held on trust for sale, there are several additional provisions which operate in favour of the purchaser.

(a) *Consents*

Where the execution of a trust is made the subject of the consent of two or more persons, the consent of any two of such persons is deemed sufficient in favour of the purchaser[11].

(b) *Consultation*

The purchaser is 'not concerned to see' that the trustees for sale have duly discharged any duty which they may have to consult their beneficiaries in

9 Law of Property Act 1925, s. 27(2).
10 There is no provision for the payment of purchase moneys into court.
11 Law of Property Act 1925, s. 26(1), p. 218f, ante.

accordance with the provisions of section 26(3) of the Law of Property Act 1925[12].

(c) *Postponement of sale*

The purchaser is not 'concerned in any case with any directions respecting the postponement of a sale' contained in any instrument creative of the trust for sale[13].

(d) *Currency of the trust for sale*

In order to activate all the statutory protections conferred upon the purchaser of land held on trust for sale, that trust for sale is 'deemed to be subsisting until the land has been conveyed to or under the direction of the persons interested in the proceeds of sale'[14].

In all these ways the Law of Property Act 1925 attempts to promote facility for the third party purchaser of land held on trust for sale by assuring him of valuable protection in the event of transfer of the legal estate.

12 Law of Property Act 1925, s. 26(3), p. 266, post.
13 Law of Property Act 1925, s. 25(2), p. 217, ante.
14 Law of Property Act 1925, s. 23.

CHAPTER 8

Co-ownership

In purely social terms, the trust for sale is nowadays infinitely more significant than the strict settlement. One reason why this should be so is the fact that the strict settlement was devised as a form of landholding designed to satisfy the aspirations of a class of landed gentry which no longer exists. The strict settlement aimed broadly at the inter-generational transfer of wealth within the family in an age when wealth was synonymous with land. It provided a medium of landholding which gave effect to the living arrangements ordained by a patriarchal figure—a paterfamilias. The interests created under a strict settlement were, in the classic case, determined by status and sex. Status was determinative in the sense that the settled land interests were graded according to status within the family structure. Sex was relevant inasmuch as the male of the species was infinitely to be preferred to the female.

The demise of the strict settlement in favour of the trust for sale is, in many ways, symptomatic of certain fundamental changes in social norms. Our society is no longer regulated to the same degree by status and gender. There is, for instance, little doubt that status has been displaced by contract as the conceptual basis of marital relationships. In former times, the relation of husband and wife was strictly defined in terms of the incidents of a lifelong status. Nowadays the continuance and quality of the spousal relationship are governed by the fact that (given our liberal divorce laws) marriage has become a form of permissive cohabitation, terminable at the will of either or both of the parties. Marriage has become a relationship of consent in the truest sense. Since most people are born into a family, this development influences our most important living arrangements—those which relate to the family home—with obvious implications for our law of real property.

Coupled with this movement from status-dependent relationships to purely voluntary co-operative relationships has been the recognition of a new egalitarian ideal. This has been particularly evident in respect of the relationship between male and female, between husband and wife. Thus we no longer accept the sex-based lines of demarcation which, in real property terms, classed married women along with infants, idiots, traitors, felons and aliens, under the general heading of 'disabilities'[1]. The emphasis in our living arrangements is nowadays very much more upon the sharing of property interests by persons situated in a relation of equality—a relation which is not constrained by the incidents of status but which springs from mutual consent and retains vitality only so long

1 For the residual vigour of this approach, see however R. E. Megarry and H. W. R. Wade, *The Law of Real Property* (4th edn., London 1975), Chapter 15.

as that consent endures. The social pattern described here is far removed from that of a former age which saw the grant of patriarchal largesse epitomised in the strict settlement. Concurrent ownership of the absolute interest in land—rather than the successive entitlement to limited interests conferred by the strict settlement—has become the appropriate medium for the tangible expression of this new social pattern. The vertical power structure embodied in the strict settlement of the 19th century has been displaced by the horizontal power relationship preferred in the democratic, egalitarian, industrial and largely urban society of the 20th century.

It is here that our look at the reality of the modern trust for sale must begin, because the existence of concurrent interests in real property necessarily brings about the existence of a trust for sale. Since 1925, it has been the position that co-ownership in possession of any interest in land—whether legal or equitable—must inevitably take effect behind a trust for sale[2]. Moreover, a trust for sale arises wherever concurrent interests fall into possession[3]. Thus, insofar as the almost universal social desire to cohabit in family form is reflected in the phenomenon of co-ownership of land, the trust for sale provides perhaps the major technical device through which that desire finds legal expression. We must now examine in greater detail the legal structure of co-ownership of land in order to learn more about the form of landholding which affords a base for a large portion of our social and economic interaction.

1. TYPES OF CO-OWNERSHIP

English law has known four types of co-ownership. They are respectively (1) joint tenancy, (2) tenancy in common, (3) coparcenary, and (4) tenancy by entireties. The last two forms of co-ownership are for all practical purposes archaic. Coparcenary was a co-ownership which bore characteristics of both joint tenancy and tenancy in common; it can now arise only in certain highly anomalous situations[4]. The tenancy by entireties was a form of unseverable joint tenancy which applied only to husband and wife and bespoke the degree of matrimonial symbiosis implicit in the canon law belief that the spouses were one person at law[5]. All tenancies by entireties were abolished in 1926[6]. Our attention will henceforth be devoted entirely to joint tenancy and tenancy in common.

2 To this rule there is but one exception—the case of two or more persons who are jointly entitled for *life*. Here, of course, there exists not a trust for sale but a strict settlement under the Settled Land Act 1925, p. 162, ante.

3 Suppose, for instance, that Blackacre is limited to A for life, remainder to B and C equally in fee simple. There is here a strict settlement of the land during the lifetime of A (see Settled Land Act 1925, s. 1(1)(i)). However, on A's death that settlement terminates and is replaced by an immediate binding trust for sale—because the concurrent interests of B and C have now fallen into possession, p. 217, ante.

4 See R. E. Megarry and H. W. R. Wade, op. cit., p. 429ff.

5 Severance of joint tenancies is discussed later, p. 306, post.

6 All tenancies by entireties which remained outstanding in 1925 were automatically converted into joint tenancies on 1 January 1926 (Law of Property Act 1925, Sch. 1, Part VI).

2. JOINT TENANCY

It was once acutely observed by Dixon J in the High Court of Australia that joint tenancy is 'a form of ownership bearing many traces of the scholasticism of the times in which its principles were developed'[7]. Indeed, the essence of joint tenancy consists in the dogma that each and every joint tenant is 'wholly entitled to the whole' of the land[8]. No joint tenant holds any specific share in the property himself, but each is (together with the other joint tenant or tenants) invested with the absolute interest in the land[9]. In Bracton's expressive language, each joint tenant *totum tenet et nihil tenet*[10]: each holds everything and yet holds nothing. Joint tenancy is thus an amorphous kind of co-ownership in which the entire estate or interest in property—rather than any defined proportion or share in that property—is vested simultaneously in each and all of the co-owners[11]. In fact, any reference to landholding in specific 'shares' (e.g., A as to two-thirds and B as to one-third) is sufficient to establish that A and B co-own not as joint tenants, but rather as tenants in common[12].

The distinguishing characteristics of joint tenancy are two in number. First, joint tenants operate between themselves a 'right of survivorship'. Second, the existence of joint tenancy always presupposes the presence of the 'four unities'.

(1) The right of survivorship (ius accrescendi)

It was Blackstone who, over two hundred years ago, so elegantly described the operation of the doctrine of 'survivorship'. He wrote that

7 *Wright v Gibbons* (1949) 78 CLR 313 at 330.

8 In this context, of course, the term 'tenant' has nothing to do with the landlord–tenant relationship: it merely signifies 'owner'.

9 In the words of Dixon J, 'in contemplation of law joint tenants are jointly seised for the whole estate they take in land and no one of them has a distinct or separate title, interest or possession' (*Wright v Gibbons* (1949) 78 CLR 313 at 329).

10 'Et sic totum tenet et nihil tenet scilicet totum in communi et nihil separatim per se' (Bracton, fo 430 (Woodbine's edn.), Vol. 4, 336; Co Litt, 186a).

11 'A gift of lands to two or more persons in joint tenancy is such a gift as imparts to them, with respect to all other persons than themselves, the properties of one single owner' (see Joshua Williams, *Principles of the Law of Real Property* (23rd edn. by T. C. Williams, London 1920), p. 143).

12 Even to say that A and B hold land in half-shares is, in strict terms, to indicate that A and B are tenants in common. Once again, it is Blackstone who expresses the truth most clearly: 'Joint-tenants . . . have not, one of them a seisin of one-half or moiety, and the other of the other moiety; neither can be exclusively seised of one acre, and his companion of another; but each has an undivided moiety of the whole, and not the whole of an undivided moiety' (*Commentaries on the Laws of England* (Facsimile edn., Chicago and London 1979) Vol. 2, p. 182). Any ambivalence as to the nature of co-ownership in equal or half-shares may be attributed to the fact that upon severance joint tenancy is automatically converted into tenancy in common in equal shares, with the result that any joint tenancy is potentially a tenancy in common in equal shares, p. 306, post. It was with this possibility in mind that Coke, while conceding that joint tenants are wholly seised of the whole, was nevertheless careful to point out that 'yet to divers purposes each of them hath but a right to a moietie' (Co Litt, p. 186a). Thus, for purposes of alienation each joint tenant is conceived as entitled to dispose of an aliquot share or to grant a lease or life interest in his equal 'share'. However, as we shall discover, p. 309, post, such forms of alienation automatically bring about either a total or partial severance of the joint tenancy.

when two or more persons are seised of a joint estate . . . the entire tenancy upon the decease of any of them remains to the survivors, and at length to the last survivor . . . The interest of two joint-tenants is not only equal or similar, but also is one and the same. One has not originally a distinct moiety from the other . . . but . . . each . . . has a concurrent interest in the whole; and therefore, on the death of his companion, the sole interest in the whole remains to the survivor[13].

The right of survivorship (*ius accrescendi*) may be illustrated in the following way. Suppose that the fee simple estate in Blackacre is vested in three joint tenants, A, B and C. If C later dies, the estate remains vested in A and B as the surviving joint tenants, and C simply drops out of the picture. No 'share' in Blackacre devolves with C's estate because, as a joint tenant, C had no 'share' as such in the land. He had no fragment of ownership which was capable of disposition on his death, since together with A and B he was 'wholly entitled to the whole.' By virtue of the same argument, when C dies A and B are already entitled as joint tenants to the entire fee simple estate in Blackacre, and no further vesting in them as survivors is required. No interest passes to either of them on C's death; the entire interest in the land merely 'survives' to them as the remaining joint tenants. Similarly, if and when B dies, the right of survivorship operates once more: B drops out of the picture, leaving A as the sole owner of the fee simple estate in Blackacre. Throughout this whole process, A's ownership has been enlarged only to the extent that he is himself no longer subject to the hazards of survivorship. This enlargement, such as it is, comes about by reason of the *ius accrescendi*.

Joint tenancy, with its right of survivorship, may at first sight appear somewhat capricious, but the undifferentiated co-ownership of joint tenancy is ideal for some purposes. We shall soon discover that since 1925 co-ownership of a legal estate in land (e.g., the fee simple absolute in possession) must necessarily take the form of joint tenancy[14]. The co-owners of the legal estate (i.e., the trustees) automatically hold as joint tenants. This fact has great importance both for the internal administration of the trust and for the conduct of transactions with third parties in respect of the trust property. It would, for instance, be highly inconvenient if there had to be a new vesting of the trust property every time one of the trustees died. It is however of the essence of joint tenancy that, on the death of one trustee, the surviving trustees are *already* invested with the entire interest in the property and no further vesting in their names is required[15].

Similarly, we have seen before[16] that a purchaser from joint tenants need investigate only one title—the title held by each and all of the joint tenants—with the result that co-ownership by way of joint tenancy not only facilitates the internal management of the trust, but also promotes the free alienation of land. Thus joint tenancy serves admirably the needs which arise in connection with the administration and disposition of the legal title to property. Since the legal

13 Op. cit., Vol. 2, p. 183f.

14 See p. 240, post.

15 New trustees may be appointed without the necessity of re-conveyance of the trust property by reliance upon the vesting provision contained in the Trustee Act 1925, s. 40(1).

16 See p. 71, ante.

title is only a 'paper title', entitling its owners merely to exercise fiduciary powers of management and disposition, the caprice of survivorship is usually rendered quite harmless in reality, since it in no way affects the equitable (i.e., beneficial) ownership of property. It is of course beneficial ownership which determines entitlements to the prospective proceeds of sale of the co-owned land[17].

There is therefore a unique and intimate union between joint tenants. Moreover the outward symbol of that union—the right of survivorship—takes precedence over any contrary testamentary disposition made by a joint tenant. A disposition contained in the will of a joint tenant is ineffective in respect of any land to which his joint tenancy relates, simply because a joint tenant has no specific share or interest which he can pass on his death. When we come later to consider the rules of severance[18], we shall see that another way of expressing this point is found in the proposition that severance of a joint tenancy cannot be effected by will[19].

(2) The 'four unities'

It is axiomatic that the 'four unities' must be present before a joint tenancy can be said to exist. These unities are the unities of possession, interest, title and time. Only unity of possession is required as a precondition of tenancy in common.

(a) *Unity of possession*

Unity of possession means that each joint tenant is as much entitled to possession of every part of the land as the other joint tenant or tenants: he cannot physically demarcate part of the co-owned land as his to the exclusion of his brethren. This unity of possession is occasionally displaced by statutory intervention[20].

(b) *Unity of interest*

Unity of interest follows from the proposition that each joint tenant is 'wholly entitled to the whole'. The interest held by each joint tenant is therefore the same in extent, nature and duration[1]. Joint tenancy cannot exist between persons holding interests of different natures or duration, e.g., between a freeholder and a leaseholder, an owner in possession and an owner in remainder, an owner of a fee simple and an owner of a life interest[2]. The unity of interest enjoyed by joint tenants means that a purchaser from joint tenants need

17 See p. 215, ante.
18 See p. 306, post.
19 Severance is the name given to the conversion of joint tenancy into tenancy in common. We shall see later that certain acts or events cause the amorphous co-ownership of the whole signified by joint tenancy to crystallise into distinct shares for each of the co-owners as tenants in common.
20 See, for instance, Domestic Violence and Matrimonial Proceedings Act 1976, ss. 1(1), (2), 4(1); *Davis v Johnson* [1979] AC 264, 317.
1 All rents and profits derived from the co-owned land must be divided between the joint tenants.
2 See W. Blackstone, op. cit., Vol. 2, p. 181.

investigate only *one* title. It also brings about the consequence that the full legal estate in jointly owned property cannot be sold and conveyed to a third party without the participation of all the joint tenants: all must put their signature to the transfer document. A purchaser of a legal estate owned by joint tenants cannot take a good title if he receives a conveyance from only one of the joint tenants, since the purchaser can see on the face of the vendor's title deeds (or the Land Register in the case of registered land[3]) explicit reference to the existence of a joint tenancy. It is indeed the mandatory participation of all the joint tenants in effecting dispositions of the joint property which has led in recent years to the proposal that all matrimonial homes automatically be held by way of joint tenancy between husband and wife[4]. Only in this way can the law ultimately remove the insecurity which affects the wife's position when her husband attempts to sell the home over her head or where he becomes insolvent.

(c) *Unity of title*

Unity of title entails that each joint tenant must derive his title to the land from the same act or document.

(d) *Unity of time*

Unity of time expresses the idea that the interest of each joint tenant must normally vest at the same time[5].

3. TENANCY IN COMMON

Tenancy in common is firmly to be distinguished from joint tenancy. It is frequently said that, unlike joint tenants, tenants in common hold land in 'undivided shares'. The phrase 'undivided shares' may seem a little confusing at first sight, since it appears to conjure up a picture of the amorphous undifferentiated co-ownership which we have just defined as joint tenancy. However, the key to the distinction between joint tenancy and tenancy in common lies in the reference to the word 'shares'. It is only in the tenancy in common that the co-owners hold distinct shares at all. It is only of tenants in common that it can be meaningful to say that A is entitled as to one-third and B as to the remaining two-thirds, or even that A and B are each entitled to a one-half share[6]. The allocation of shares or proportions is not possible as between joint tenants, who are of course 'wholly entitled to the whole'. Tenants in common are however owners of distinct shares, albeit in property which has not yet been divided up physically. It is not possible to point to one parcel (i.e., area) of the co-owned land rather than any other as belonging to a particular tenant

3 See p. 319, post.
4 See p. 149, ante; p. 303, post.
5 See p. 193, ante.
6 See p. 234, ante.

in common. Tenants in common own specific, but undivided, shares in the land[7].

The principal characteristics of tenancy in common are two in number:

(1) There is no right of survivorship

There exists no right of survivorship (*ius accrescendi*) between tenants in common. The size of each tenant in common's share is a fixed proportion which cannot be altered by reason of the death of any other tenant in common. No right of survivorship operates on the death of a tenant in common: his share passes to a third party under the terms of his will or according to the rules of intestate succession[8].

(2) Only unity of possession is required

Only unity of possession is required between tenants in common. Unity of interest is not essential: it is for precisely this reason that it is possible for one tenant in common to hold, say, a one-third share in property while another tenant in common holds a two-thirds share. Nor is unity of title or time required: as we have just seen, it is possible for the share of a tenant in common to be the subject of a subsequent testamentary (or inter vivos) disposition in favour of a third party. However, alone of the 'four unities' unity of possession is an integral component of tenancy in common, for otherwise we should not have co-ownership at all but rather separate ownership. Thus each tenant in common is as much entitled to physical possession of every part of the property as the other tenant or tenants in common[9]. It follows moreover that one tenant in common is not entitled to require the payment of rent by another tenant in common, even though the latter occupies the whole property[10].

4. THE KEY TO CONCURRENT INTERESTS

The vital secret in the understanding of concurrent interests in land law lies in the maintenance of a rigid distinction between ownership *at law* and ownership *in equity*. If this distinction is preserved, it becomes possible to view with some degree of equanimity and comprehension the apparent contradiction that, for

7 For the technical argument that tenants in common own shares not in land but in the prospective proceeds of sale of land, see p. 220, ante.

8 The share of the deceased tenant in common may pass to another tenant in common, but this will happen only if the latter is named as the intended beneficiary in the former's will or is the beneficiary entitled on death intestate.

9 See *Jacobs v Seward* (1872) LR 5 HL 464; *Bull v Bull* [1955] 1 QB 234 at 237; *Jones (A. E.) v Jones (F. W.)* [1977] 1 WLR 438, (1978) 41 MLR 208 (J. Alder).

10 *M'Mahon v Burchell* (1846) 2 Ph 127 at 134 per Lord Cottenham LC; *Henderson v Eason* (1851) 17 QB 701 at 720; *Kennedy v De Trafford* [1897] AC 180. However, if one of the tenants in common lets the co-owned premises to a stranger and receives the rent himself, he becomes liable to account to his fellow tenants in common in respect of any profit made (see *Jones (A. E.) v Jones (F. W.)* [1977] 1 WLR 438 at 442). Moreover, if one of the tenants in common is expelled from

instance, the same persons may be simultaneously joint tenants at law and tenants in common in equity.

It is important to remember that the legal title to land, while of course it binds the whole world, is otherwise relatively unimportant. It comprises merely a 'paper title', indicating those persons who are entrusted with nominal ownership and the appropriate powers of management and disposition. In other words, the legal title is concerned with the internal administration and formal execution of the trust: it invests the trustees with fiduciary (and largely administrative) duties. On the other hand, equitable ownership is concerned with actual beneficial enjoyment—enjoyment either of the residential utility conferred by occupation of the land or of the rents and profits derived from letting the land, and ultimately of course enjoyment of the proceeds resulting from any sale of the land. So, for instance, when we say that A and B are joint tenants *at law* (i.e., joint tenants of the legal estate), we mean that they are jointly invested with the paper title and are jointly charged with the managerial and dispositive functions connected with it. Since they are joint tenants, the right of survivorship operates between them. However, it is a quite different (and not incompatible) proposition to say that, in a particular case, A and B are tenants in common *in equity*, since what we are now saying is that each has a distinct share in the fruits of beneficial enjoyment, that is, a distinct share in essentially the money value of the property. Most importantly, we are saying that when A and B (as joint tenants) convey their legal estate to a third party purchaser in execution of their trust, it is in their respective capacities as beneficial tenants in common that they may each claim a share in the capital proceeds of sale. Of course, we shall see later that it is indeed perfectly possible in some situations for A and B to hold as joint tenants *both* at law *and* in equity[11].

In view of the foregoing we must distinguish clearly between co-ownership at law and co-ownership in equity.

5. CO-OWNERSHIP AT LAW

Historically the common law has always preferred joint tenancy to tenancy in common as the medium of co-ownership, largely because the operation of the right of survivorship tended to restrict the number of persons from whom feudal services might be due[12]. Later joint tenancy came to be preferred simply because conveyancers could more easily investigate the single title held by joint tenants (who in any event operate a rule of survivorship) than if the legal title were fragmented between tenants in common, each of whom could in turn dispose separately of his share. In short, the law favoured the sweeping together of

---

the co-owned property by reason of domestic violence, he or she may be able to claim rent from any tenant in common who retains sole occupation (see *Dennis v McDonald* [1981] 1 WLR 810).

11 See p. 252, post.

12 These feudal services and their incidents, which were owed by an occupier of land to his immediate superior in the tenurial relationship, p. 43f., ante, were of course more effectively secured if due from persons whose number was liable to decrease rather than increase with the passage of time.

interests by means of survivorship and leaned away from tenancy in common. The law, said Holt CJ in 1700, 'loves not fractions of estates, nor to divide and multiply tenures'[13]. The presumption at law was therefore in favour of joint tenancy, and wherever co-ownership existed in relation to a legal estate in land the co-owners were presumed to be joint tenants of that legal estate *except* where (i) one of the 'four unities' was absent, or (ii) 'words of severance' were employed in the grant of the land to the co-owners. Words of severance could be either express or implied, and comprised any language which denoted that the grantees were intended to take distinct and identifiable shares in the land granted, thereby negating the presumption of joint tenancy[14].

These principles regulating co-ownership at law must now be read subject to the significant alterations effected by the 1925 property legislation. We discussed earlier the way in which this legislation intervened to resolve some of the tensions which existed in 1925 between the conflicting objectives of alienability of land and security of endowment[15]. The interest of alienability was promoted by a series of important provisions contained in the Law of Property Act 1925. Prior to this enactment it had been possible for a legal estate to be held in undivided shares, although the presumption of the law was clearly in favour of joint tenancy. The 1925 Act extended the presumption of the law to its logical conclusion by providing that co-ownership at law must now take only the form of joint tenancy and may never take the form of tenancy in common. Section 1(6) of the Law of Property Act 1925 provides unequivocally that

> A legal estate is not capable of subsisting or of being created in an undivided share in land.

Tenancies in common can no longer exist at law, and the effect of the 1925 legislation is to sweep co-ownership in undivided shares into equity[16]. The corollary of the mandatory nature of joint tenancy at law is the provision in section 36(2) of the Law of Property Act 1925 that

> No severance of a joint tenancy of a legal estate, so as to create a tenancy in common in land, shall be permissible.

The cumulative effect of these provisions is to facilitate the purchaser of the legal estate, who no longer faces the risk of investigating title to a fragmented

13 *Fisher v Wigg* (1700) 1 Salk 391 at 392.

14 A list of typical terms of severance is to be found in R. E. Megarry and H. W. R. Wade, op. cit., p. 399. Difficulty is, of course, occasioned by an ambivalent grant of land to 'A and B jointly and severally.' The rule has been clear since *Slingsby's Case* (1587) 5 Co Rep 18b that this grant conferred a joint tenancy if contained in a deed inter vivos, but created a tenancy in common if contained in a will. The assumption here is presumably that, in the latter case, the final utterance of the moribund testator was the utterance which he intended to be definitive. The same dilemma of construction arose more recently in *Joyce v Barker Bros (Builders) Ltd* (1980) Times, 26 February. Here land had been conveyed to a husband and wife 'in fee simple as beneficial joint tenants in common in equal shares.' Vinelott J held that this habendum clause created a joint tenancy in equity rather than a tenancy in common. See [1980] Conv 171 (J. E. Adams).

15 See p. 70f., ante.

16 See Law of Property Act 1925, s. 34(1).

legal estate[17]. His task is further eased by the fact that the maximum number of persons who may be joint tenants of any legal estate is now restricted to four[18].

6. CO-OWNERSHIP IN EQUITY

Equity, in contrast to the common law, has traditionally preferred tenancy in common to joint tenancy as the medium of co-ownership. Tenancy in common represents certainty and fairness in the property relations of co-owners. Each tenant in common holds a fixed beneficial interest immune from the caprice of survivorship. Each share constitutes a tangible quantum of wealth which can serve as the subject matter of family endowment. Thus, whereas the law leaned in favour of joint tenancy largely for reasons of convenience, equity has leaned towards tenancy in common for reasons of fairness.

In consequence equity, as always following the law, was accustomed even before 1925 to treat co-owners as tenants in common in all cases in which they were tenants in common in the eyes of the law. In other words, equity regarded co-owners as tenants in common in all cases where the 'four unities' were not present or where words of severance were expressed or implied. But equity went further, and in three special cases of concurrent entitlement was prepared to presume that—quite irrespective of the position at law—the co-owners were tenants in common in equity. All three cases concerned circumstances in which equity was anxious to avoid the caprice of survivorship, and thus effectively compelled persons who were joint tenants at law to hold in equity as tenants in common:

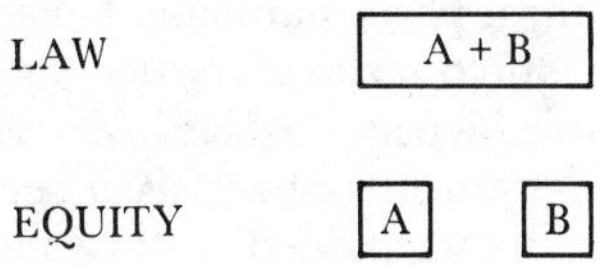

LAW	A + B	
EQUITY	A	B

Fig. 42

These special cases arose in relation to the following persons.

(1) Partners

Where commercial partners acquired title to land for the purpose of their business enterprise, equity presumed that they held the equitable interest in the land as tenants in common. It was thought that the hazards of survivorship were alien to the essence of partnership: *ius accrescendi inter mercatores locum non habet*[19].

17 See pp. 71f., 235, ante.
18 See Trustee Act 1925, s. 34(2); Law of Property Act 1925, s. 34(2), (3).
19 See *Lake v Craddock* (1732) 3 P Wms 158.

(2) Mortgagees

Where two or more persons lent money on the security of property, equity presumed that the mortgagees were tenants in common as between themselves even though they had taken the mortgage as joint tenants vis à vis the mortgagor. The basis of this presumption was the belief that each mortgagee, irrespective of his posture towards the outside world, intended as against his co-mortgagee to 'lend his own and take back his own.'[20]

(3) Purchasers who contribute money in unequal proportions

By far the most important situation in which equity presumed tenancy in common rather than joint tenancy arose where two or more persons contributed money in unequal proportions towards the purchase of property. The presumption of equity was, and still is, that as between persons who advance differing amounts of money the resulting beneficial ownership ought to reflect the disparity in contribution. The rights acquired by the contributors should not be regulated by the crude rule of survivorship.

In order to understand the view thus taken by equity, we must first refer to the 'presumption of resulting trust'.

7. THE PRESUMPTION OF RESULTING TRUST

Scarcely ever is there any doubt as to the legal ownership of land, since the primary purpose of a conveyance is to identify the transferee or transferees of the legal estate in the context of third party purchase. Legal ownership is thus almost always determined by the express terms of the documents of title relating to the land. However, the equitable ownership of transferred land is often left unspecified by the parties to a conveyance. The details of beneficial entitlement after the transfer are frequently not contained in any formal document or writing of any kind, and come into question only if at some later stage—perhaps many years after the conveyance—some dispute arises. At this point it becomes necessary to render explicit that which was previously left unexpressed[1].

It is a cardinal tenet of English law that the equitable ownership of property depends fundamentally upon the intentions of the relevant parties at the date of acquisition of the property[2]. It is true, of course, that the transfer to a single individual of a legal estate in land carries with it prima facie the absolute beneficial interest in that property[3]. But in order to determine the beneficial ownership which was actually intended, the courts may have recourse to parol

20 See *Re Jackson* (1887) 34 Ch D 732, and Law of Property Act 1925, s. 111.
1 For the result which emerges where the conveyance *does* spell out the details of beneficial entitlement, see later, p. 253, post.
2 See *Pettitt v Pettitt* [1970] AC 777 at 813 per Lord Upjohn.
3 See *Vandervell v IRC* [1966] Ch 261 at 287, CA, per Diplock LJ; affd., [1967] 2 AC 291 at 311, HL, per Lord Upjohn. For another view of the matter, see *Comr of Stamp Duties (Queensland) v Livingston* [1965] AC 694 at 712 per Viscount Radcliffe, p. 502, post.

or other evidence based upon inferences from the parties' conduct at the relevant time[4]. Such evidence may often clarify and conclude the question of beneficial ownership. Sometimes, however, it is impossible to elicit or infer the intentions relevant to a prior transaction. In such a case, in the absence of evidence relating to actual intention, the courts determine the issue of beneficial ownership with reference to one or other of the equitable presumptions of intention. According to Lord Diplock in *Pettitt v Pettitt*[5], the presumptions of equity are

> no more than a consensus of judicial opinion disclosed by reported cases as to the most likely inference of fact to be drawn in the absence of any evidence to the contrary.

The 'presumption of resulting trust' is merely one of the residual aids upon which the courts may fall back if beneficial ownership is obscure. A 'resulting trust' is presumed to have been intended where a legal estate in land is purchased in the name of A, but the purchase money has been provided by B. In this situation, A holds the legal estate—but this is merely a paper title and A is simply a nominee. Equity presumes that the legal estate is held by A on a trust which 'results back' to the real purchaser, B[6]. Therefore, although A holds the legal title, the equitable interest in the land belongs to B behind a bare trust[7];

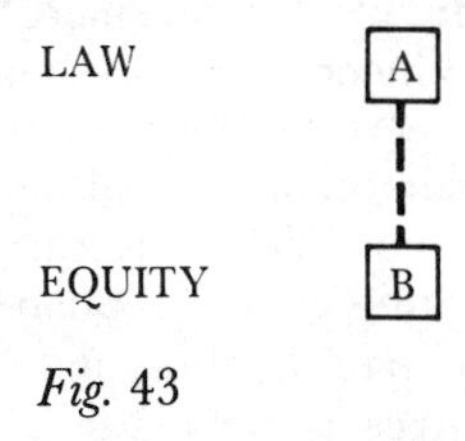

Fig. 43

4 In other words, the relevant intentions may be inferred from conduct even though they have not been the subject of any express communication between the parties. The dogma that beneficial title must depend on intentions which are present *at the date of acquisition* generates some difficulty in the context of property purchased with the aid of mortgage finance. In *Gissing v Gissing* [1971] AC 886 at 906, Lord Diplock adverted to the problem of inferring intention in relation to the beneficial ownership of a matrimonial home effectively purchased over the period of the mortgage term, p. 506, post. He pointed out that it would be 'unreasonably legalistic to treat the relevant transaction involved in the acquisition of a matrimonial home as restricted to the actual conveyance of the fee simple into the name of one or other spouse. Their common intention is more likely to have been concerned with the economic realities of the transaction than with the unfamiliar technicalities of the English law of legal and equitable interests in land. The economic reality which lies behind the conveyance of the fee simple to a purchaser in return for a purchase price the greater part of which is advanced to the purchaser upon a mortgage repayable by instalments over a number of years, is that the new freeholder is purchasing the matrimonial home upon credit and that the purchase price is represented by the instalments by which the mortgage is repaid in addition to the initial payment in cash. The conduct of the spouses in relation to the payment of the mortgage instalments may be no less relevant to their common intention as to the beneficial interests in a matrimonial home acquired in this way than their conduct in relation to the payment of the cash deposit.'

5 [1970] AC 777 at 823.

6 The word 'result' in this context is not used in any sense of causation and consequence, but rather in its root sense of 'leaping back' (Latin, *resultare*). A trust of the legal estate springs back in favour of the real purchaser.

7 Note carefully that the situation discussed here involves a purchase by B in the name of A of property which previously belonged to V, the vendor. This situation must be clearly

The classic exposition of the resulting trust is to be found in *Dyer v Dyer*[8]. Here Eyre CB declared that

the trust of a legal estate, whether freehold, copyhold, or leasehold; whether taken in the names of the purchasers and others jointly, or in the names of others without that of the purchaser; whether in one name or several; whether jointly or successive—results to the man who advances the purchase-money. This is a general proposition, supported by all the cases, and there is nothing to contradict it; and it goes on a strict analogy to the rule of the common law, that where a feoffment is made without consideration, the use results to the feoffor. It is the established doctrine of a court of equity, that this resulting trust may be rebutted by circumstances in evidence.

The resulting trust generated in this way is one consequence of what Woodhouse J has termed 'the solid tug of money'[9]. It is almost certainly no accident that the common law rule about feoffments made without consideration (which in turn provided the model for the equitable presumption of resulting trust) arose at just the point in time when economic relationships between individuals ceased to be governed by the principles of communal solidarity and feudal status which caused the old medieval world to cohere. In contrast the new principles, which drew a sharp distinction between the nominal and the real purchaser, found their rightful place in an emerging exchange economy which came to rest upon the pre-eminence of the cash nexus between man and man. Today when B purchases property in the name of A there is, in the absence of other intention, a clear presumption of resulting trust in favour of B simply because, in our money-conscious society, it is scarcely conceivable that B might have intended to confer a gratuitous benefit upon A.

There is, however, one group of situations in which it might be thought that the presumption of resulting trust is less apposite. These situations occur where A and B are, respectively, child and parent or wife and husband. In the context of such relationships, it is often said, the presumption of resulting trust is rebutted by a 'presumption of advancement' in favour of A, with the consequence that the property acquired is owned by A both at law and in equity[10]. In other words, the presumption of advancement supplies an all-important donative intent in certain stereotyped situations where it would be natural to expect the real purchaser to have intended to 'advance' the interests of some person who comes within the bonds of familial affection[11].

---

distinguished from that in which B voluntarily (i.e., for no consideration) conveys to A a legal estate which already belongs to B. In the latter case, there is no necessary presumption of resulting trust, and A becomes the owner both at law and in equity (see Law of Property Act 1925, s. 60(3)).

8 (1788) 2 Cox Eq Cas 92 at 93.

9 *Hofman v Hofman* [1965] NZLR 795 at 800.

10 It must be remembered, of course, that a child is competent to hold a legal estate in land only if he has attained the age of 18 (see Law of Property Act 1925, s. 1(6)).

11 The presumption of advancement is of course rebuttable, but may not be rebutted by evidence of a fraudulent intent. See, for instance, *Tinker v Tinker* [1970] P 136, where a husband had conveyed the matrimonial home to his wife with the intention of thereby shielding the property from his creditors in the event that his business should later collapse. It was in fact his marriage which subsequently collapsed, and the Court of Appeal declined to allow him to maintain as against his creditors that the house belonged to his wife, but as against his wife that the house still

It is only fair to say, however, that the equitable presumptions of advancement and resulting trust have been the subject of much criticism during recent years, on the ground that they no longer provide the same assistance as previously in determining questions of equitable title[12]. In particular it appears that the presumption of advancement as between husband and wife has lost much of its force in resolving questions of beneficial ownership in relation to the matrimonial home[13]. Recent decisions have suggested that the presumption of advancement, when applied in the marital context, was merely an index of a former social era in which wives enjoyed an inferior status relative to that which they now occupy[14]. In consequence, the ideas which underlay the presumptions of resulting trust and advancement have been re-stated and refined in several new formulations of which perhaps the most significant is that expressed by Lord Diplock in *Gissing v Gissing*[15]. Here he ruled that

A resulting, implied or constructive trust—and it is unnecessary for present purposes to distinguish between these three classes of trust—is created by a transaction between the trustee and the cestui que trust [i.e., beneficiary] in connection with the acquisition by the trustee of a legal estate in land, whenever the trustee has so conducted himself that it would be inequitable to allow him to deny to the cestui que trust a beneficial interest in

---

belonged in equity to him. The presumption of advancement was held to prevail. See also *Gascoigne v Gascoigne* [1918] 1 KB 223; *Re Emery's Investments Trusts* [1959] Ch 410.

12 Some of the most trenchant criticism appears in *Pettitt v Pettitt* [1970] AC 777 at 824, where Lord Diplock noted that 'the most likely inference as to a person's intention in the transactions of his everyday life depends upon the social environment in which he lives and the common habits of thought of those who live in it. The consensus of judicial opinion which gave rise to the presumptions of "advancement" and "resulting trust" in transactions between husband and wife is to be found in cases relating to the propertied classes of the nineteenth century and the first quarter of the twentieth century among whom marriage settlements were common, and it was unusual for the wife to contribute by her earnings to the family income. It was not until after World War II that the courts were required to consider the proprietary rights in family assets of a different social class. The advent of legal aid, the wider employment of married women in industry, commerce and the professions and the emergence of a property-owning, particularly a real-property-mortgaged-to-a-building-society-owning, democracy has compelled the courts to direct their attention to this during the last 20 years. It would, in my view, be an abuse of the legal technique for ascertaining or imputing intention to apply to transactions between the post-war generation of married couples "presumptions" which are based upon inferences of fact which an earlier generation of judges drew as to the most likely intentions of earlier generations of spouses belonging to the propertied classes of a different social era.' However, Lord Upjohn, that great Chancery judge, remained unrepentant about the role of the equitable presumptions. He acknowledged that they had been 'criticised as being out of touch with the realities of today', but maintained that 'when properly understood and properly applied to the circumstances of today . . . they remain as useful as ever in solving questions of title' ([1970] AC 777 at 813).

13 It appears from *Re Figgis* [1969] 1 Ch 123 that the presumption of advancement still applies in relation to a joint bank account held by husband and wife.

14 However, clarity in this matter has not been aided by the fact that, notwithstanding his own judgment in *Tinker v Tinker* [1970] P 136 (see footnote 11), Lord Denning MR declared in *Falconer v Falconer* [1970] 1 WLR 1333 at 1335f., that the presumption of advancement 'found its place in the law in Victorian days when a wife was utterly subordinate to her husband. It has no place, or, at any rate, very little place, in our law today . . . We have decided these cases now for some years without much regard to a presumption of advancement, and I think we should continue to do so.'

15 [1971] AC 886 at 905.

the land acquired. And he will be held so to have conducted himself if by his words or conduct he has induced the cestui que trust to act to his own detriment in the reasonable belief that by so acting he was acquiring a beneficial interest in the land.

We have now reached the point where we can combine the operation of the resulting (or 'constructive') trust with the equitable rule that a tenancy in common arises as between persons who contribute unequally towards the purchase price of property.

8. CO-OPERATIVE PURCHASES OF PROPERTY

Assume that a legal estate in land is purchased in the name of A. The purchase price is contributed in unequal proportions by A and B, who have pooled their financial resources for this purpose. Equity presumes that A and B are tenants in common, by reason of the disparity in their contributions. We have already seen that tenancy in common cannot exist at law: it can take effect only in equity[16]. A and B must therefore be equitable tenants in common, i.e., they are co-owners of the equitable interest in property which at law clearly belongs to A. As tenants in common, A and B are owners of that equitable interest in certain fixed shares or proportions. In the absence of evidence of intention as to the proportions of beneficial ownership, it is presumed that there is a resulting trust of the legal estate in favour of A and B in strict proportion to the relative financial contributions made by them.

The loose and ill-defined arrangement made by A and B for the purpose of purchasing real property is by no means an isolated social phenomenon. It is a not uncommon occurrence for two or more people—and especially for married couples—to pool their money in an indiscriminate manner in order to purchase a house legal title to which is then vested in the name of only one. The possible permutations of circumstance which may arise are seen in the following examples.

Suppose that Jack and Jill get married and buy a house. They purchase a dwelling-house for £30,000. Jack contributes £20,000 from his cash savings and the remainder of the purchase price is composed of a cash contribution of £10,000 from Jill. The house is conveyed into the name of Jack, with the result that the legal estate is manifestly vested in him alone. It never occurs to Jack and Jill to articulate their precise intentions as to the beneficial ownership of the house, nor is there any conduct on their part from which such intentions might be inferred. Jack and Jill simply regard the house in wholly non-legal terms as 'theirs'. But to the land lawyer the consequent ownership of the house will appear as in *Fig.* 44. Jack will be said to hold the legal estate in the land on trust for himself and Jill in the proportions of two to one, the beneficial ownership reflecting the relative extent of their respective direct and quantifiable contributions of money[17].

16 See p. 240, ante.

17 See *Re Rogers' Question* [1948] 1 All ER 328; *Williams & Glyn's Bank Ltd v Boland* [1980] 3 WLR 138 at 141 per Lord Wilberforce: 'Each wife contributed a substantial sum of her own money

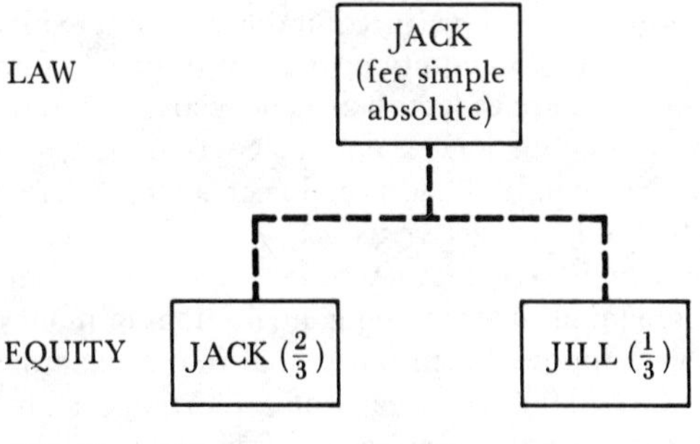

Fig. 44

An exactly similar result would have followed if Jack had not contributed £20,000 in cash, but had instead raised £20,000 by means of a mortgage for the servicing of which he undertook sole responsibility[18]. Again, the same result would occur if Jack and Jill were merely an engaged couple, or were living in de facto cohabitation—a situation normally indistinguishable (for all but theological purposes) from that of de iure marriage. In all of these cases, an equitable tenancy in common in the proportions of two to one would follow from the relative contributions of money made by Jack and Jill, unless by words or conduct at the date of acquisition they had agreed that their beneficial shares should be other than those arising on the purely mathematical basis of the presumed resulting trust[19].

It was at one stage thought that grave complications would be raised in this area by the operation of section 53(1) of the Law of Property Act 1925, a provision which stems historically from the Statute of Frauds 1677. Section 53(1)(b) requires that

> a declaration of trust respecting any land or any interest therein must be manifested and proved by some writing signed by some person who is able to declare such trust or by his will.

Section 53(1)(c) goes even further and requires that

> a disposition of an equitable interest or trust subsisting at the time of the disposition must be in writing signed by the person disposing of the same, or by his agent thereunto lawfully authorised in writing or by will.

These important provisions are inspired by the long recognised need to

---

toward the purchase of the matrimonial home or to paying off a mortgage on it. This, indisputably, made her an equitable tenant in common to the extent of her contribution.'

18 For the view that a mortgage-generated contribution of cash should not in fact be regarded as equivalent to a contribution of free cash, see J. Levin (1972) 35 MLR 547 at 551: 'The Matrimonial Home—Another Round'.

19 It should be noted, however, that if Jill made no initial money contribution at all, even an express oral assurance by Jack that she would be an equitable tenant in common would be entirely ineffective. Such an assurance would 'at best be a mere "voluntary declaration of trust" which would be "unenforceable for want of writing"' (see *Gissing v Gissing* [1971] AC 886 at 905 per Lord Diplock; *Eves v Eves* [1975] 1 WLR 1338 at 1345 per Brightman J).

prevent hidden oral transactions in equitable interests which might defraud those persons truly entitled in equity or make it difficult (if not impossible) for trustees to ascertain who are in fact their beneficiaries[20]. To these requirements of writing there is one major exception. Section 53(2) provides that the documentary requirements of the section do not 'affect the creation or operation of resulting, implied or constructive trusts.'

The difficulty which was at one time contemplated in this connection concerned the problem of supervening contributions of money by an equitable tenant in common. Suppose, for instance, that in our example Jack had raised his contribution of £20,000 by means of a mortgage loan from a building society. Suppose further that some years after the date of acquisition of the property Jill inherited a sum of £5,000 from a relative and proceeded to devote this sum towards a partial diminution of her husband's mortgage debt. Assuming that the capital debt outstanding had remained static until this point (as would be the case with an endowment mortgage[1]), Jill might with some justification claim that her share in the equitable interest in the property had been increased from one-third to one-half. However, such a conclusion was thought untenable in the similar circumstances which came before Bagnall J in *Cowcher v Cowcher*[2]. Bagnall J took the view that the original money contributions of the parties in this situation constituted a 'money consensus' which created a resulting trust for them in exactly the proportions indicated by the relative extent of their respective financial contributions (i.e., two-thirds for Jack and one-third for Jill). Such a trust required no writing under section 53(1) of the Law of Property Act 1925. In Bagnall J's analysis, any attempt to vary the beneficial shares thus fixed at the date of acquisition must be the consequence of some further 'interest consensus' reached by the parties. In other words, the parties must have come to some agreement that, irrespective of the initial equitable proportions arising on the purely mathematical basis of the resulting trust, they should be regarded as holding different shares. According to Bagnall J, however, such an 'interest consensus' could operate only as an express trust or express disposition[3], and would therefore fail for want of the appropriate writing under section 53(1). In *Cowcher v Cowcher*, the wife's equitable share was held to remain a one-third share notwithstanding her substantial supervening contributions of cash[4].

The justice of this approach was subsequently questioned in *Re Densham (A Bankrupt)*[5]. Here Goff J adverted to the distinction drawn by Bagnall J between 'money consensus' and 'interest consensus', and observed that

20 See *Vandervell v IRC* [1967] 2 AC 291 at 311 per Lord Upjohn.
1 See p. 507, post.
2 [1972] 1 WLR 425. See (1972) 35 MLR 547 (J. Levin).
3 The increased share claimed by the wife would effectively involve a later disposition of a one-sixth share in order to bring her entitlement up to a one-half share.
4 In *Cowcher* the wife was allowed to recover the sum of money advanced by her to help her husband (i.e., approximately £1,500) in addition to the value of her one-third equitable share. However, the value of the extra one-sixth share which she was unable to claim as a tenant in common amounted, in days of rampant inflation, to roughly £7,000.
5 [1975] 1 WLR 1519 at 1525.

If I have rightly understood it, then, with respect, I cannot agree. In the vast majority of cases, parties do not direct their minds to treating the money payments as notionally other than they are. What they think about, if they think at all, is ownership. Of course, if the evidence shows there was no agreement, *Gissing v Gissing* [1971] AC 886 makes it plain that one cannot infer or import one, but if the evidence, including conduct, leads ... to the inference that there was an agreement, it will generally be ... an interest consensus. To hold such an agreement unenforceable unless in writing, or a specifically enforceable contract, is, in my opinion, contrary to equitable principles, because once the agreement is found it would be unconscionable for a party to set up the statute and repudiate the agreement. Accordingly ... he or she becomes a constructive trustee of the property so far as necessary to give effect to the agreement.

Thus, in our example, if it could be inferred that Jack and Jill had agreed that Jill's supervening contributions should increase her beneficial interest in the property, it would become unconscionable for Jack to set up the statutory requirement of writing in defence to any claim to a larger share subsequently made by her. The approach adopted in *Re Densham* has been generally preferred to the rather more strict approach evident in *Cowcher*[6].

The examples which we have so far discussed have concerned tenancies in common arising from direct and quantifiable contributions of money towards the purchase of property. Particularly in the context of the matrimonial home it has been accepted that other species of money contribution may be relied upon as raising a tenancy in common in the equitable interest[7]. However, the fundamental difficulty experienced in the ascertainment of beneficial ownership in the matrimonial context results from the fact that the property relations of spouses are governed by the same general principles which govern the property rights of strangers. There is no special regime of matrimonial property law applicable during the subsistence of a marriage[8].

The presumption of resulting trust has its roots in 'the solid tug of money', and any law which recognises financial contribution as the basis of beneficial entitlement must inevitably generate injustice in the family context. The doctrine of resulting trust (even in its refined form in *Gissing v Gissing*) has the effect of working discrimination against wives, for the married woman's financial contributions towards the acquisition of property are usually restricted not only by reason of the sexual imbalance of the labour market, but also because of her fluctuation between periods of gainful employment and active motherhood. Her purely domestic contributions (in looking after the home and caring for children) are not cognisable within the strictures of our law of

6 See, for instance, *Allen v Snyder* [1977] 2 NSWLR 685 at 692 per Glass JA.

7 See, for instance, *Rimmer v Rimmer* [1953] 1 QB 63 (direct unquantifiable contribution of money); *Fribance v Fribance (No. 2)* [1957] 1 WLR 384; *Gissing v Gissing* [1971] AC 886 (indirect contribution of money), p. 561, post. Contributions towards the 'improvement' of property may generate beneficial entitlement as between husband and wife under section 37 of the Matrimonial Proceedings and Property Act 1970. This provision reverses the law as applied in *Pettitt v Pettitt* [1970] AC 777, but would not have affected the result in that case since there the husband's supposed improvements were described as 'ephemeral' (see p. 561, post).

8 See, however, Law Commission, *Third Report on Family Property: The Matrimonial Home (Co-ownership and Occupation Rights) and Household Goods* (Law Com No. 86, June 1978), p. 149, ante.

property[9]. Ironically, it is only when a marriage terminates in divorce or death that such contributions become relevant in determining property rights in the matrimonial assets[10]. In the normal case, the spouses never think in terms of beneficial ownership when using indiscriminately mixed family funds in the purchase of real property during the course of a happy marriage. Their beneficial entitlements are left to be determined later (if at all) according to the unsympathetic principles of the law of property and the law of trusts[11].

Here we see one of the recurring features of our land law—the opposition of what might be termed 'family considerations' and 'money considerations' respectively. Where these two types of consideration conflict, it has hitherto almost invariably been the case that the 'money interest' prevails over the less tangible and less articulate interest of the family as an organic social entity. In the present context, the cash nexus (represented by notions of resulting and constructive trust) prevails over considerations of equality and community which are more apposite to the reality of family life[12].

9. THE IMPOSITION OF A TRUST FOR SALE IN ALL CASES OF CO-OWNERSHIP

It has been seen that the objectives of the property legislation of 1925 were essentially twofold: the achievement of facility for the purchaser of real property coupled with a guarantee of security for the owners of equitable interests in that property. In the context of co-ownership of land, the first objective was furthered by the prohibition of tenancies in common of the legal estate. Both objectives were promoted by the policy, introduced in 1925, according to which a trust for sale was imposed upon all cases of co-ownership.

Section 2(1)(ii) of the Law of Property Act 1925 declares, as a matter of first principle, that a conveyance of a legal estate shall overreach all equitable interests affecting that estate if the conveyance is made by 'trustees for sale'. It was therefore vital, for the purpose of conveyancing simplicity, that all situations of co-ownership should be able to attract the overreaching consequences of a sale of land held on trust for sale. The only way in which the 1925 legislation could secure this desirable result was, of course, by ensuring that all cases of co-ownership of land (whether in relation to a legal estate or in respect of the equitable interest) should necessarily give rise to a trust for sale. This at least was the intention which lay behind the 1925 Act. Thus, if in a case of co-ownership

9 As Otto Kahn-Freund once pointed out, by ignoring the non-financial dimension of the wife's contribution to matrimonial property, the superficially equalitarian treatment of the financial contributions of husband and wife becomes 'as mechanical as the crude idea of "freedom of contract" which insists on treating as "equals" landlord and tenant, employer and employee' (see (1959) 22 MLR 241 at 248: 'Matrimonial Property—Some Recent Developments').

10 See Matrimonial Causes Act 1973, s. 25(1)(f); *Wachtel v Wachtel* [1973] Fam 72 at 93f.; Inheritance (Provision for Family and Dependants) Act 1975, s. 3(2)(b).

11 For an indication that the law of constructive trusts may become more sensitive to the reality of the situation, see p. 479, post.

12 See, for instance, *Gissing v Gissing* [1971] AC 886, p. 477, post.

a trust for sale does not already exist in the express terms of the relevant conveyance, the 1925 Act aims to supply a trust for sale by implication of statute. By and large the Law of Property Act 1925 succeeds in ensuring that a trust for sale arises wherever there is co-ownership either at law or in equity or indeed where there is co-ownership both at law and in equity. In a couple of cases where the legislation fails to provide a trust for sale, the courts have—whether by fair means or foul—filled in the gaps[13].

The imposition of a trust for sale in all cases of co-ownership is, of course, purely a conveyancing device[14]. The use of a trust for sale by implication of statute brings into operation the conveyancing machinery which we have already examined[15]. It enables land held in co-ownership to be dealt with commercially. The existence of a trust for sale ensures that a purchaser of that land need be concerned only with the legal title. He need not concern himself with the equitable interests of the co-owners (whether as joint tenants or as tenants in common), because he knows that those beneficial interests are hidden behind the trust and will be overreached upon sale. Similarly the beneficiaries behind the trust for sale are guaranteed certain forms of protection. The comprehensive nature of the trust for sale brings them within the ambit of the protective provisions expressly conferred in the context of 'trusts for sale' by sections 26–30 of the Law of Property Act 1925[16]. The statutory activation of a trust for sale ensures that upon sale of the land the equitable interests of the beneficiaries are translated, in fact as well as in theory, into equivalent interests in the proceeds of sale[17]. Of course, the beneficiaries are more generally protected throughout by the fact that the owners of the legal estate in the land are bound by strict duties of trusteeship.

In these ways the Law of Property Act 1925 attempts to accommodate the potentially conflicting interests of purchaser and co-owner. We shall go on to see later that, in view of the increased importance of residential utility during the years since 1925, the money-oriented solution reached in the 1925 Act is sometimes far from satisfactory[18]. However, we shall for the moment confine ourselves to examining the way in which a trust for sale emerges in various kinds of situation.

(1) Conveyance to 'A and B'

Suppose that A and B purchase land in fee simple[19]. The conveyance or transfer is simply executed in favour of 'A and B', and there is no available evidence

13 See p. 257, post.
14 See p. 217, ante.
15 See p. 227, ante.
16 See p. 266f., post.
17 One of the supposed purposes of the doctrine of conversion is to ensure that the interests of the beneficiaries survive a sale of the land by adhering at all times to the actual or prospective proceeds of sale p. 222, ante.
18 See p. 260ff., post.
19 Exactly the same principles would apply if A and B purchased a legal term of years absolute (i.e., a long lease).

relating to the intentions of A and B as to beneficial ownership or as to the way in which the purchase money was contributed. There is plainly no express trust for sale.

A and B are clearly co-owners of the legal fee simple absolute in possession, because the conveyance says that they are. Since the only form of co-ownership now permitted at law is joint tenancy, A and B must be joint tenants of the legal estate. In the absence of evidence relating to intention or to money contributions, the equitable ownership is governed by the maxim that 'equity follows the law.' A and B are therefore joint tenants in equity just as they are joint tenants at law[20]. This being the case, a trust for sale arises by implication of statute[1], and A and B are said to hold the legal estate in the land on trust for sale for themselves as beneficial joint tenants. We may illustrate this ownership by the following diagram:

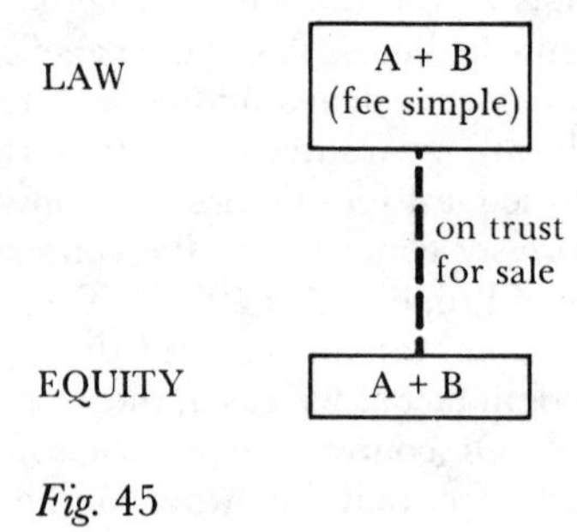

Fig. 45

(2) Conveyance to 'A and B' after purchase with unequal contributions

Suppose that A and B purchase land in fee simple. The conveyance is executed, as before, in favour of 'A and B'. As before, the conveyance makes no reference to equitable ownership, but there is clear evidence that A and B contributed the purchase price in unequal proportions.

Once again, A and B are necessarily joint tenants of the legal estate. In equity, however, they are tenants in common since the situation of unequal contribution is one in which equity—regardless of the position at law—leans in favour of undivided shares. This is in fact one of the cases not caught by the express terms of the Law of Property Act 1925, and there is therefore no clear statutory authority for the imposition of a trust for sale. However, the courts have glossed section 36(1) of that Act in order to imply a statutory trust for sale in the situation of a conveyance to persons whom equity regards as tenants in common[2]. A and B thus hold the legal estate as joint tenants on trust for sale for themselves as beneficial tenants in common in proportion to their relative contributions of money, e.g., in the proportions of two to one (see *Fig.* 46).

20 See *Cowcher v Cowcher* [1972] 1 WLR 425 at 430 per Bagnall J.
1 Law of Property Act 1925, s. 36(1).
2 See *Re Buchanan-Wollaston's Conveyance* [1939] Ch 738 at 744 per Greene MR.

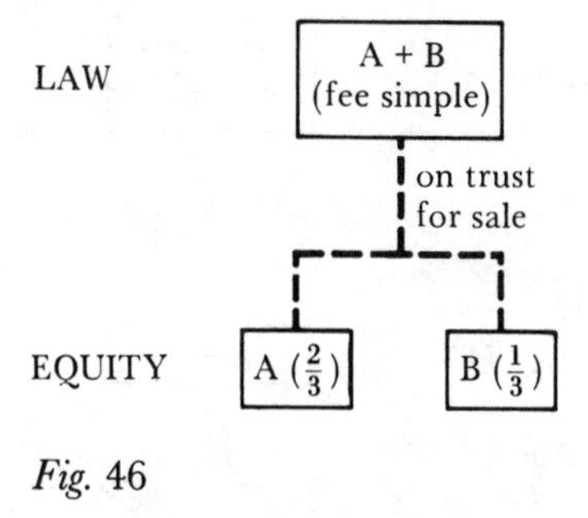

Fig. 46

(3) Conveyance to 'A and B on trust for sale for themselves as joint tenants'

Suppose that A and B purchase land in fee simple. They contribute the purchase price in unequal proportions, but they have the legal estate conveyed to themselves as trustees holding 'on trust for sale for themselves as equitable joint tenants'. In this situation there is clearly a trust for sale of an express character, and we must carefully examine its effect.

By virtue of this form of conveyance, A and B are quite plainly joint tenants of the legal estate. Equity presumes tenancy in common as between unequal contributors of purchase money (as here), but this is *only* a presumption. In the present case, the presumption of equitable tenancy in common is rebutted by the express declaration of trust contained in the conveyance, which unquestionably indicates that A and B are intended to be joint tenants in equity irrespective of the proportions of their respective contributions[3]. The express stipulation of equitable joint tenancy overrides the presumption of equity and

> necessarily concludes the question of title . . . for all time, and in the absence of fraud or mistake at the time of the transaction the parties cannot go behind it at any time thereafter[4].

In our example, A and B are joint tenants of the legal estate, holding on an express trust for sale for themselves as joint tenants in equity[5] (see *Fig.* 47).

The express declaration of beneficial ownership is definitive as between A and B even if, for instance, A provided *all* the purchase money for the acquisition of the property. Both A and B have, as equitable joint tenants, a unilateral right of severance: that is, each may convert the amorphous co-ownership of the whole

3 As Lamm J observed in *Mackowik v Kansas City* (1906) 94 SW 256 at 264, 'presumptions may be looked on as the bats of the law, flitting in the twilight but disappearing in the sunshine of actual facts.'

4 *Pettitt v Pettitt* [1970] AC 777 at 813 per Lord Upjohn. See also *Re John's Assignment Trusts* [1970] 1 WLR 955; *Boydell v Gillespie* (1970) 216 Estates Gazette 1505; *Pink v Lawrence* (1977) 36 P & CR 98 at 101; *Brykiert v Jones* (1981) Times, 16th January.

5 It seems, however, that a declaration of trust may be conclusive only if the joint purchasers both execute (i.e., sign) the conveyance, effectively as settlors. See *Robinson v Robinson* (1976) 241 Estates Gazette 153; J. T. Farrand, *Contract And Conveyance* (3rd edn., London 1980), p. 299.

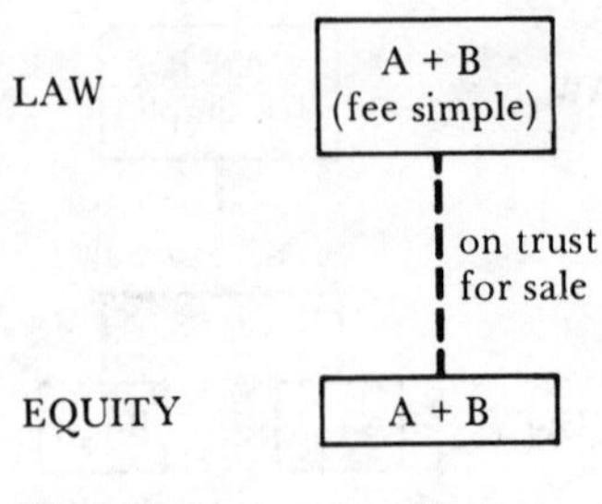

Fig. 47

beneficial interest into co-ownership in undivided shares. Upon severance the share of each would—irrespective of the original contributions of money—comprise a one-half share. This result follows inexorably from the fact that the parties at the outset committed themselves to an equitable joint tenancy. The fact that they may not have understood the precise technical significance of equitable joint tenancy is quite irrelevant[6].

The courts have upheld the conclusiveness of an express trust even where the express trust in question stipulates some other form of equitable co-ownership than joint tenancy. Thus if a legal estate is conveyed to A, B and C upon trust for sale for themselves 'in equal shares as tenants in common', it is irrelevant that A, B and C may have contributed the purchase money in unequal proportions. The express declaration of trust prevails[7].

(4) Conveyance to 'A, B and C each as to a one-third share'

Suppose that land is conveyed to 'A, B and C, each as to a one-third share.' The effect of such a conveyance is laid down in section 34(2) of the Law of Property Act 1925. If A, B and C are all of full age, the conveyance operates

> as if the land had been expressed to be conveyed to the grantees . . . as joint tenants upon the statutory trusts . . . and so as to give effect to the rights of the persons who would have been entitled to the shares had the conveyance operated to create those shares . . .

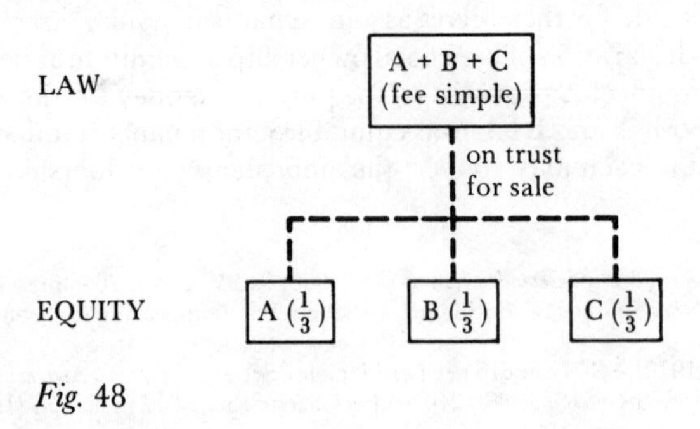

Fig. 48

6 See *Re John's Assignment Trusts* [1970] 1 WLR 955 at 958 per Goff J.
7 See *Brown v Staniek* (1969) 211 Estates Gazette 283.

In other words, the conveyance vests the legal estate in the land in A, B and C as joint tenants upon a statutory trust for sale for themselves as equitable tenants in common in the shares indicated by the conveyance. The legal estate itself cannot be held in undivided shares. Therefore the tenancy in common supposedly created by the conveyance is effective only in equity, under the umbrella of a trust for sale implied by statute (see *Fig.* 48).

(5) Conveyance to 'A, B, C, D and E, each as to a one-fifth share'

Suppose that land is conveyed to 'A, B, C, D and E, each as to a one-fifth share.' The result of this conveyance is also governed by section 34(2) of the Law of Property Act 1925, which (as in example (4) above) gives purely equitable effect to the tenancy in common erroneously intended at law. According to section 34(2), the conveyance operates as if the land had been expressed to be conveyed to the first four grantees named in the conveyance, the legal estate being held by those four as joint tenants upon a statutory trust for sale for all five of the original grantees as equitable tenants in common (see *Fig.* 49).

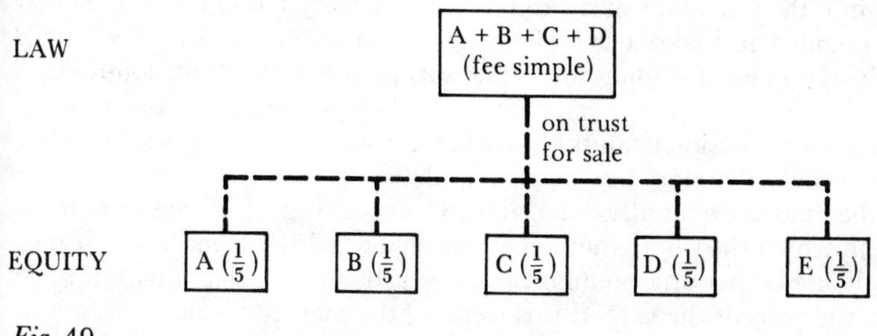

Fig. 49

This result accords with the rule that the number of trustees of a legal estate may never exceed four[8]. It also demonstrates the difference between legal and equitable entitlement. No great injustice is worked against E by reason of his exclusion from the trusteeship of the legal estate, for that trusteeship is concerned with purely administrative, managerial and dispositive functions[9]. E's real interest—that from which he derives actual benefit—is effectively secured by his beneficial ownership as a tenant in common behind the trust for sale imposed by virtue of section 34(2).

Exactly the same results would follow in situations (4) and (5) if the land had not been conveyed by an inter vivos deed but had been instead the subject of a testamentary disposition[10].

8 See p. 241, ante.
9 See, however, the discussion of the decision to sell land held on trust for sale, p. 260, post.
10 Law of Property Act 1925, s. 34(3).

(6) Conveyance to A after purchase with unequal contributions

Cases (1) to (5) above have all involved co-ownership at law. We must now look at one situation in which there can be no question of co-ownership of the legal estate.

Suppose that A and B purchase land in fee simple. They contribute unequal proportions of the purchase price. Suppose moreover that the legal estate is conveyed simply to A, so that he alone is entitled at law. We have already seen that, in the absence of evidence of contrary intention, A and B are regarded as equitable tenants in common in proportion to their respective contributions of money[11]. This, however, is an extremely problematic case of co-ownership, for it would seem at first sight to provide one very significant breach in the general policy of the 1925 legislation that all situations of co-ownership in possession should be covered by a trust for sale of the land. There is here no express trust for sale, since the conveyance simply transfers the legal estate 'to A'. Nor does a trust for sale arise by implication of statute, because the statutes make no reference at all to circumstances of this kind—an omission which has been attributed to simple legislative oversight[12].

The problem arose in *Bull v Bull*[13]. Here a mother and her son contributed unequal proportions of the purchase price of a dwelling-house which was then conveyed into the sole name of the son. It was expressly found that the mother had not intended to make a gift of her contribution to the son. They lived together in the house for some time. The son then married and, following a dispute between the mother and her daughter-in-law, the son brought proceedings for possession against his mother. He argued that she was merely a licensee and could therefore be evicted at will.

When the matter eventually reached the Court of Appeal, it seemed that the only way in which the Court could save the ageing mother from being thrown out of the house by her ungrateful offspring was by finding that a trust for sale existed on the facts of the case. If this were so, the mother would therefore be entitled to the statutory protection given to beneficial co-owners[14]. Although the 1925 legislation does not supply a trust for sale in the circumstances of *Bull v Bull*, Denning LJ glossed the wording of section 36(4) of the Settled Land Act 1925 to produce the desired result that an equitable tenancy in common 'shall . . . only take effect behind a trust for sale.' Such a trust for sale will, if necessary, be implied by statute (see *Fig.* 50).

The Court's decision had the effect of making the mother a beneficiary behind a trust for sale. She could not be arbitrarily evicted from the home which she had helped to buy. The only way in which the son could effectively move his mother

11 See p. 246, ante.
12 See *Williams & Glyn's Bank Ltd v Boland* [1979] Ch 312 at 330 per Lord Denning MR.
13 [1955] 1 QB 234. See (1955) 14 Cambridge LJ 155 at 156 (H. W. R. Wade): (1955) 18 MLR 303 (V. Latham), 408 (H. R. Gray); (1956) 19 MLR 312 (E. A. Forrest).
14 See p. 266ff., post.

from the house was either by arranging a sale of the property (in which case the mother's beneficial interest would be translated into the proceeds of sale) or by buying out her interest with cash. In either event the mother would receive value for her interest[15].

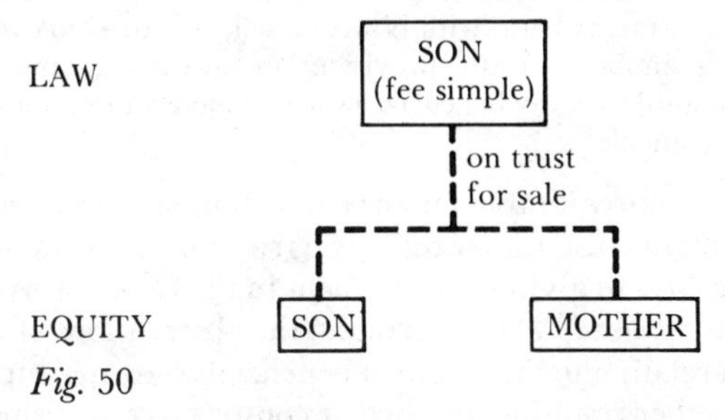

Fig. 50

Although based upon an extremely bold statutory construction[16], ***Bull v Bull*** provides clear authority for the proposition that where a legal estate is purchased in the name of one, using the moneys of two or more, there arises an implied (or statutory) trust for sale of the legal estate on behalf of the contributors as equitable tenants in common in proportion to their contributions. In relation to the practical problem highlighted in the facts in *Bull v Bull*, this result represents a highly convenient solution[17]. For other purposes, however, the implication of a trust for sale may prove to have less desirable consequences[18].

15 See p. 267f., post.

16 Denning LJ appeared to apply a rather strained construction of section 36(4) of the Settled Land Act 1925 in reaching this conclusion. Section 36(4) provides that '[a]n undivided share in land shall not be capable of being created except under a trust instrument or under the Law of Property Act 1925, and shall then only take effect behind a trust for sale.' The circumstances present in *Bull v Bull* involved no trust instrument; nor were they covered by any provision in the Law of Property Act 1925 (hence the resort to the Settled Land Act 1925). However, Denning LJ read s. 36(4) as if it contained no reference to such matters, thus reaching the convenient (if technically unwarranted) conclusion that a trust for sale must exist in every case of equitable tenancy in common. For a discussion of this flawed reasoning, see B. Rudden (1963) 27 Conv (NS) 51: 'The Wife, the Husband and the Conveyancer.' It is not without interest that the Law of Property Act 1922 contained a much clearer indication that all situations of equitable co-ownership were intended to be covered by at least an implied trust for sale. Section 10 of that Act (which was not duplicated in any of the 1925 legislation) was expressly directed at 'removing the difficulties incidental to land being held in undivided shares' and at 'preventing the creation of undivided shares in land, except under a settlement and behind a trust for sale...'

17 It could be said that in *Bull v Bull* the Court of Appeal simply used common sense and a little ingenuity in filling one of the lacunae left in the 1925 legislation (see F. R. Crane (1955) 19 Conv (NS) 146). The result reached in *Bull v Bull* had already been applied—although without reference to section 36(4) of the Settled Land Act 1925—in *Re Rayleigh Weir Stadium* [1954] 1 WLR 786 at 790 per Harman J. Later cases have somewhat blandly assumed the existence of a statutory trust for sale in all situations of equitable tenancy in common of property vested at law in the name of only one—although, and perhaps significantly, these cases have all concerned an abuse of power by the sole legal owner to the prejudice of a vulnerable beneficiary. See *Waller v Waller* [1967] 1 WLR 451 at 453 per Stamp J, (1967) 31 Conv (NS) 140 (F. R. Crane); *Taylor v Taylor* [1968] 1 All ER 843 at 846f. per Danckwerts LJ.

18 Quite apart from the problems raised by the doctrine of conversion, the over-ready implication of a statutory trust for sale brings about the consequence that vast numbers of property owners are elevated, quite unwittingly, to the status of trustee. The conferment of fiduciary status and

Indeed, it has even been questioned whether it is necessary in the *Bull v Bull* situation to invoke the device of the trust for sale at all. Professor F. R. Crane has challenged

the premise that only a trust for sale enables land held in co-ownership to be dealt with commercially ... A straight trust, with power to sell, etc., so as to overreach beneficial interests, and with similar 'curtain' provisions in favour of a purchaser, is equally practicable. Then, until sale, the beneficiaries would have an interest in land—and law and reality would coincide[19].

The possibility that equitable tenancy in common may be quite adequately covered by a 'straight trust' rather than by a trust for sale seems to have occurred to Lord Denning MR in giving his judgment in the Court of Appeal in *Williams & Glyn's Bank Ltd v Boland*[20]. He referred to the observations of Lord Diplock in *Gissing v Gissing*[1], relating to the origin of beneficial co-ownership in a trust of the legal estate—whether resulting, implied or constructive—arising 'whenever the trustee has so conducted himself that it would be inequitable to allow him to deny to the cestui que trust a beneficial interest in the land acquired.' The Master of the Rolls went on in *Boland* to tackle the problem of placing 'this trust concept into the conveyancing structure erected by the property legislation of 1925.' He noted the way in which this legislation supplies a trust for sale in most situations of co-ownership occurring after that date;

No doubt the framers of the statute had in mind the case where the legal estate was vested in *two* persons. They became trustees for sale and could together 'overreach' any equitable interests... But the framers of the statutes did not have in mind the cases where the legal estate is vested in *one* single person. At any rate they did not provide for it. They did not think of the cases where the legal estate is vested in one person on trust for two or more persons jointly as beneficial owners.

It is significant that Lord Denning did not refer to the husband in *Boland* as holding the legal estate on an implied trust for sale for himself and his wife as equitable tenants in common, even though it was agreed by all concerned that both parties in this case had made substantial contributions of money to the purchase of the property in dispute. Instead, he seemed content to treat the relationship between the parties in terms simply of a straight trust with the result that he thought it

---

responsibility will surprise not only the property owner but may well introduce unsuspected complications for third parties with whom he deals. Where, as in *Bull v Bull*, a trust for sale arises by implication of statute, there will be no reference to the trust on the face of the conveyance of the legal estate to the trustee. To any prospective purchaser who examines the trustee's title deeds, the trustee will appear not as a trustee for sale, but as the sole owner at law and, so far as the purchaser can tell, as the sole owner in equity as well. In other words, the trustee will appear to be making title 'as beneficial owner.' This may sometimes raise a conveyancing problem which we shall look at later, see p. 286, post.

19 (1970) 34 Conv (NS) 420 at 421.

20 [1979] Ch 312 at 329ff., p. 233, ante; p. 366, post.

1 [1971] AC 886 at 905. The relevant passage is quoted in full elsewhere in this book, p. 245, ante; p. 478, post.

entirely appropriate to describe them as equitable tenants in common of the land—that is, of the house itself—until sale: and then after sale, in the proceeds of sale. Such a beneficial interest is an equitable interest in land.

In this way Lord Denning avoided the problems posed by the orthodox doctrine of conversion[2]. By appearing to deny the necessity of a trust for sale in the instant situation of beneficial co-ownership[3], he was able to reach a conclusion favourable to the appellant wife in relation to the central issue raised in *Boland's* case[4]. Moreover, Lord Denning's straight trust analysis has the great advantage that it eliminates the awkward question as to the precise location of the beneficial interest in the land during the currency of a 'trust for sale'[5].

Lord Denning's novel views on this aspect of *Boland* were not, however, adopted by his brethren in the Court of Appeal. Although reaching the same overall conclusion on the facts of the case, both Ormrod and Browne LJJ preferred to adopt the trust for sale analysis of beneficial co-ownership in the single legal owner context, while accepting a somewhat more flexible view of the applicability of the doctrine of conversion[6]. Neither considered the possibility of an alternative 'straight trust' solution to the conceptual problem of co-ownership in equity in the single legal owner situation.

Moreover, when the matter finally reached the House of Lords, Lord Wilberforce (who delivered the major speech) likewise did not challenge the orthodox trust for sale analysis of the problem in hand. The speeches of their Lordships are notable for the absence of any exploration either of the true statutory basis for the trust for sale solution or of any conceptual alternative such as that of the 'straight trust'. Lord Wilberforce was happy to follow, somewhat unquestioningly, the lead effectively given twenty-five years earlier in *Bull v Bull*, observing merely that since the enactment of the Law of Property Act 1925

undivided shares in land can only take effect in equity, behind a trust for sale on which the legal owner is to hold the land[7].

It is disappointing that the House of Lords did not address itself to a more fundamental reconsideration of an appropriate regime for co-ownership of land. This is especially so at a time when the orthodox trust for sale analysis, introduced in such cavalier fashion in *Bull v Bull*, now emerges not simply as an overworked device, but as an approach in the family home context which has created more problems than it has solved. Nevertheless, even though it may be regretted that the House of Lords did not enquire more searchingly into the

2 See p. 220, ante.
3 See R. J. Smith (1979) 95 LQR 501: 'Overriding Interests and Wives'.
4 For further discussion of this issue, see later, p. 353, post.
5 See, for instance, the question put by Michael Prichard as to whether 'all beneficial interest in a parcel of land evaporates (*in nubibus*?) once it is held upon trust for sale...' ((1979) 38 Cambridge LJ 251 at 253).
6 [1979] Ch 312 at 333ff. per Ormrod LJ, at 340 per Browne LJ.
7 [1980] 3 WLR 138 at 142. See also Lord Scarman at 148: 'It is conceded that each wife has a beneficial interest in the land, which is her matrimonial home. Each is an equitable tenant in common behind a trust for sale, there being only one trustee, her husband, in whom the legal estate (a freehold) is vested.'

precise source of the trust for sale in the *Bull v Bull* situation, *Williams & Glyn's Bank Ltd v Boland* at last provides clear House of Lords authority for the proposition that a trust for sale arises (by implication) wherever a legal estate in land is vested in one owner following a joint purchase using the moneys of more than one contributor.

We have now covered most of the situations of co-ownership which arise in practice. In all these situations, where there is concurrent entitlement at law or in equity or both at law and in equity, there seems to be a trust for sale of the legal estate. The trust for sale is either express or supplied by statute in the terms of section 35 of the Law of Property Act 1925:

For the purposes of this Act land held upon the 'statutory trusts' shall be held upon the trusts and subject to the provisions following, namely, upon trust to sell the same and to stand possessed of the net proceeds of sale, after payment of costs, and of the net rents and profits until sale after payment of rates, taxes, costs of insurance, repairs, and other outgoings, upon such trusts, and subject to such powers and provisions, as may be requisite for giving effect to the rights of the persons (including an incumbrancer of a former undivided share or whose incumbrance is not secured by a legal mortgage) interested in the land [and the right of a person who, if the land had not been made subject to a trust for sale by virtue of this Act, would have been entitled to an entailed interest in an undivided share in the land, shall be deemed to be a right to a corresponding entailed interest in the net proceeds of sale attributable to that share][8].

10. THE DECISION TO SELL OR OTHERWISE DISPOSE OF CO-OWNED LAND

Peculiar problems surround the decision whether co-owned land should be sold or otherwise disposed of (e.g., by way of mortgage). These difficulties flow partly from the fact that it is intrinsic in this situation that more than one person is concerned. However, the significance of any potential conflict of interest is greatly increased by the fact that land is a uniquely flexible form of property. Land, by its very nature, provides not merely a medium of capital accumulation, investment and exchange; it also has a vital significance in terms of use and enjoyment (or 'occupation utility'). The question whether land should be sold at any given time highlights an underlying tension between the 'exchange value' or investment potential of the land and its 'use value' in terms of continued occupation. Some of the co-owners may wish to sell the land for cash; others may wish to retain it for occupation[9].

It is, of course, of the essence of a trust for sale that the trustees are the persons invested with the decision-making powers of management and disposition. Technically the trustees are obliged to sell the land held on trust unless they unanimously agree to postpone sale. However, this power to postpone sale effectively negates the otherwise mandatory duty to sell, and means that the

8 Added by the Law of Property (Entailed Interests) Act 1932, s. 1(1).
9 See p. 222, ante.

trustees are invested with a large measure of discretion as to whether sale ever takes place[10].

It is important to note that this discretion goes beyond the usual fiduciary concern to ensure prudent 'investment' of the trust capital. Because the subject of the trust is land, it has not merely 'investment' characteristics but also an importance as a base for actual occupation. The trustees have it within their power (at least within the conventional view) to control the allocation of the 'utility' inherent in the land which they hold on trust. In other words, they have within their gift the beneficial interest in the land itself—an interest which, as we shall see, proves fairly elusive in the theory of the trust for sale.

It is for these reasons that the beneficiaries behind a trust for sale may often be vitally concerned to influence the decision-making processes which are in principle the responsibility of the trustees alone. We shall now examine the various ways in which beneficiaries can intercept the decision-making processes in order to ensure that their own individual preferences in the matter of sale are not entirely ignored. We shall approach the issues concerned from four different angles, by asking the following questions:

(1) How can a beneficiary prevent sale by the trustees (of whom he may or may not be one)?
(2) How can a beneficiary compel sale if he is also a trustee?
(3) How can a beneficiary compel sale if he is not a trustee?
(4) How can a beneficiary prevent sale at the behest of a trustee in bankruptcy?

In general, a beneficiary behind the trust will wish to prevent sale if his concern is with the continued enjoyment of occupation (i.e., the 'use value' of the land). He will wish to compel sale if his concern is to extract his capital share from the land (i.e., to realise the 'exchange value' of the land).

(1) How can a beneficiary prevent sale by the trustees (of whom he may or may not be one)?

This question raises immediately a problem concerning the nature of a beneficiary's right to occupy the land before sale occurs. Does a beneficiary have a 'right' of occupation at all? This is a crucial question in the light of the developments which will be outlined in this section. We must look first at the orthodox theory of the trust for sale.

(a) *The orthodox view of the trust for sale*

In order to clarify the nature of the beneficiary's occupational privilege, it is necessary to bear in mind the respective positions of trustee and beneficiary before and after the 1925 property legislation.

10 A power to postpone sale is implied in the case of every trust for sale of land unless the instrument (if any) which creates the trust for sale expressly precludes postponement (Law of Property Act 1925, s. 25(1)).

(i) *Physical occupation—a privilege not a right* There are some rights enjoyed by a trust for sale beneficiary during the period preceding sale which, in the orthodox view, are quite unequivocal[11]. These rights include the right to receive the rents and profits derived from the land under the management of the trustees (e.g., the rents and profits arising from a lease granted by the trustees in favour of a stranger). The trustees have no discretion to withhold such rents and profits from any beneficiary who is entitled 'in possession' (i.e., entitled in the technical sense that there is no prior interest[12]).

In sharp contrast, however, there is considerable authority for the proposition that even a beneficiary 'in possession' has no *right* as such to physical occupation of the land. Even before 1926 beneficiaries with equitable interests behind trusts of land were not entitled to physical possession as of right but only at the discretion of their trustees, duly controlled by the court[13]. This is, after all, entirely consistent with the theory of the trust for sale, for the allocation of physical possession is within the fiduciary discretion of the trustees. According to the conventional theory, the trustees may exercise their powers of management and disposition by granting physical possession to *any* person or persons (other than themselves[14]). Thus they may let the land held on trust to a stranger and pass on the rents and profits obtained to the beneficiaries who are currently entitled 'in possession'. Alternatively, they may permit those beneficiaries themselves to occupy the land in lieu of receiving rents and profits, but their decision to do so is, in the traditional view, a matter of discretion constrained only by their fiduciary duty to act bona fide in the general interest of their trust.

This view of the relationship between trustees and beneficiaries is reflected in the case law after 1925. In *Re Landi*[15], the Court of Appeal was concerned with a legal tenancy in common which was automatically made equitable on the commencement of the Law of Property Act 1925. Sir Wilfred Greene MR pointed out that thereafter the tenants in common acquired the new character of trustees, holding the legal estate on trust for sale for themselves as equitable tenants in common. He was careful to say that

Under the Law of Property Act 1925, [a] fiduciary element unquestionably came into the picture, and it constitutes a trust under which their obligation as trustees is an

11 See S. M. Cretney (1971) 34 MLR 441.

12 See p. 58, ante.

13 See *Re Bagot's Settlement* [1894] 1 Ch 177; *Re Earl of Stamford and Warrington* [1925] Ch 162; (1955) 19 Conv (NS) 146 at 147 (F. R. Crane).

14 It is a fundamental principle of equity that a trustee must never place himself in a position where his self-interest conflicts with his duty to the trust. Such however would be the result if a trustee were allowed to offer himself a lease of the trust property. See *Keech v Sandford* (1726) Sel Cas Ch 61, Cas temp King 61, 2 Eq Cas Abr 741, pl 7 per King LC: 'I very well see, if a trustee, on the refusal to renew, might have a lease to himself, few trust estates would be renewed to cestui que use; though I do not say there is fraud in this case, yet he should rather have let it run out, than to have had the lease to himself. This may seem hard, that the trustee is the only person of all mankind who might not have the lease; but it is very proper that rule should be strictly pursued, and not in the least relaxed; for it is very obvious what would be the consequences of letting trustees have the lease, on refusal to renew to cestui que use.'

15 [1939] Ch 828

obligation to sell the property and divide the proceeds, *and in the meantime their possession is the possession of trustees, because it is in that capacity that they hold the legal title*[16].

As Professor F. R. Crane has stated, *Re Landi* 'cannot . . . be reconciled with the proposition that equitable tenants in common can still claim possession as of right'[17].

This conclusion has a significance for the discussion contained in the following pages, since a fundamental uncertainty about the nature of a beneficiary's right of occupation underlies even the House of Lords' decision in *Williams & Glyn's Bank Ltd v Boland*[18]. In *Boland* the House of Lords accepted that a statutory trust for sale arose on the facts, but never addressed itself explicitly to a question which has long awaited a satisfactory answer—where is the beneficial interest in the *land* during a trust for sale?

Before *Boland* it had generally been assumed, in deference to the doctrine of conversion, that a trust for sale beneficiary held only an interest in personalty, i.e., a right to receive the rents and profits of the land pending sale and a right to a share in the eventual proceeds of sale. The beneficiary, however, had no beneficial interest in the land itself. Where then was the beneficial interest in the land during a trust for sale? This intriguing question had been posed but never fully explored. Michael Prichard noted that

There is something bizarre about the proposition that the legal estate in Blackacre may be held on trust without any beneficial interest in Blackacre existing anywhere or in anyone. Yet this seems to be the case with the very great deal of land that is held upon trust for sale today[19].

Indeed, it is not easy on reflection to 'accept that all beneficial interest in a parcel of land evaporates (*in nubibus*?) once it is held upon trust for sale'[20], presumably condensing only when the land is finally freed from the trust for sale, e.g., by transfer of the legal estate to a third party purchaser.

The vital point here is what is meant by a 'beneficial interest in land'. This holds the key to the problem in *Williams & Glyn's Bank Ltd v Boland* but was never analysed by the courts although it was precisely this 'beneficial interest in land' which formed the subject of the competing claims of the bank and the wife/beneficiaries in that case.

For our present purpose we can say that the 'beneficial interest in land' held on trust for sale includes at least a right to physical occupation of that land. In the orthodox view of the operation of trusts for sale, physical occupation of the land is within the gift of the trustees. The beneficiary has no right to the land itself—which is exactly what the traditional doctrine of conversion confirms. He enjoys occupation of the land only if and for so long as the trustees, in the

16 [1939] Ch 828 at 835 (emphasis supplied). Greene MR also pointed out (at 836) that 'when one tenant in common dies now (I will still call him a tenant in common) his legal personal representatives have no right to go into possession and have no right to collect the rents; that right survives and survives only to the survivor in his capacity as surviving trustee . . .'

17 (1955) 19 Conv (NS) 146 at 147.

18 [1980] 3 WLR 138, p. 224, ante; p. 370, post.

19 (1971) 29 Cambridge LJ 44 at 48.

20 See M. J. Prichard, (1979) 38 Cambridge LJ 251 at 253.

exercise of their fiduciary discretion, decide to allow him physical possession of the property. In other words, in the conventional theory as supported by authority, the 'use value' of land held on trust for sale is at all times effectively within the gift or control of the trustees. It is this idea of 'control' which not only illuminates the matters of doubt raised by the doctrine of conversion but also clarifies the developments which accompany the demise which has begun to affect that doctrine.

(ii) *Two types of 'control'* It is becoming obvious that the key concept in this area is one of 'control'. It is therefore important to analyse the 'control' exercised by the trustees for sale in terms of the orthodox theory. Such trustees clearly enjoy two different kinds of 'control'.

First, like all legal owners, the trustees enjoy a *dispositive control* over *the bare legal estate* (i.e., the 'paper title'). They exercise this control in deciding whether to convey their legal title to a third party (by sale, lease or mortgage).

Second, the trustees enjoy an *allocation control* over *the occupation of the land itself*, in the sense that they have a discretion to allocate actual occupation of that land either to a stranger who pays rent or to one or more of the beneficiaries.

It can be seen that, according to this analysis of the relationship between trustee and beneficiary, both kinds of control are vested in the trustees. The beneficiary has no vote in the allocation of physical possession of the land. He is effectively disenfranchised and enjoys actual occupation only at the discretion of his trustees. Control of both the 'exchange value' and the 'use value' of the land is vested firmly in the hands of the trustees;

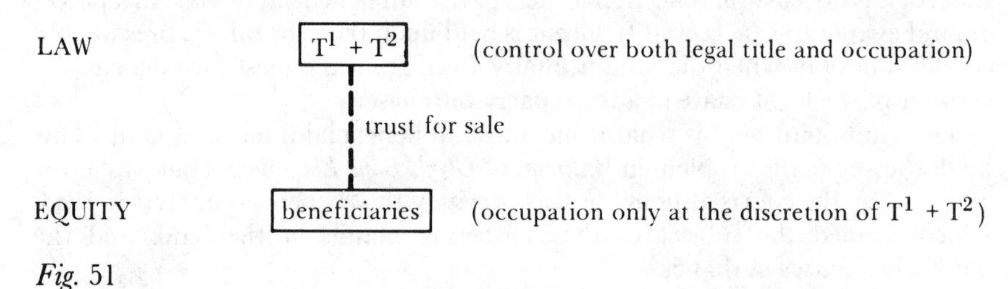

Fig. 51

(b) *The gradual enfranchisement of the trust for sale beneficiary*

We have already seen that the trust for sale beneficiary may not be entirely disinterested in the allocation of physical occupation of the land held on trust. We shall now see that several significant social and economic factors have combined to bring about a partial redistribution of 'control' functions between trustee and beneficiary, with the result that the beneficiary of residential property held on trust for sale is nowadays entitled to some kind of vote in the allocation of actual occupation of the land. It is this process which we describe in terms of the gradual enfranchisement of the trust for sale beneficiary.

There is today a vastly increased emphasis upon residential security—as indeed a heightened consciousness of the need for security is evidenced in other fields by modern legislation providing for employment security, social security and pension security. This is not unconnected with the fact that we live in an age of great insecurity. We are living through times of severe housing shortage, general economic recession and a growing incidence of family breakdown. The universal quest of the ordinary man is not for dispositive power over 'things' but for some degree of security in the enjoyment of 'utility'[1].

There is also nowadays a more general acknowledgement that a married woman enjoys as of right an enhanced social status relative to that of former times when the law was content to regard her merely as some kind of simpering domestic idiot. This recognition is a particularly important factor in the development which we trace, since most trusts for sale relate to the matrimonial home and many beneficiaries are therefore wives who have contributed financially to the purchase of those homes[2]. It is inevitable that the opprobrium of sex-based discrimination should attach to any distribution of control functions within a trust for sale which effectively isolates *all* control in the hands of the trustee (who is more likely to be a husband) and effectively disenfranchises the wife.

In consequence of these (and many other) factors, the judicial temper has turned remarkably in favour of providing protection for the interests of those in actual occupation of land. This protection was, of course, present in the enactments of 1925[3], but tended to be somewhat overshadowed by the heavy emphasis placed by the 1925 legislation upon alienability of title and the 'solid tug of money.' However, money is not a particularly valuable asset in days of inflation. For many people it is often much more important to have the security of bricks and mortar around them. In the years following World War II, therefore, the courts have slowly begun to elevate the 'use value' of property over its 'exchange' or 'capital' value, thereby recognising that entitlement to the unhindered *enjoyment* of residential property is frequently more significant than entitlement to the *cash value* of that property on the open market.

In terms of this analysis, the right to enjoy secure accommodation in a house or flat, free from the interventions of third parties, has itself become the equivalent of a new species of property right. This right is essentially a right of residential protection. It comprises a right to 'security of tenure' of a kind not dissimilar to the 'status of irremovability' conferred upon protected and statutory tenants under the Rent Act[4], and as such it is not easily assimilated within existing proprietary interests in land[5]. Nevertheless, the development of our law of property during the past 30 years has thrown up many instances in which existing legal mechanisms have been adapted in order to give effect to the general social interest in protecting persons in actual occupation of land[6].

1 See p. 504, post.
2 See p. 249, ante.
3 See, e.g., Law of Property Act 1925, s. 14, p. 117, ante; Land Registration Act 1925, s. 70(1)(g), p. 334, post.
4 See p. 416ff., post.
5 See for instance the abhorrence of the 'monstrum horrendum, informe, ingens' expressed by Evershed MR in *Marcroft Wagons Ltd v Smith* [1951] 2 KB 496 at 501, p. 434, post; and reiterated by Megarry J in *Wroth v Tyler* [1974] Ch 30 at 64, p. 147, ante.
6 See p. 50, ante.

For our present purpose, it is important to note that once the occupation aspect of property is elevated to a position of primary significance, the right which becomes critical to the occupier is the right to control the allocation of physical possession of the land. We have seen that, in the traditional view of the trust for sale, this right was firmly vested in the trustees for sale, who could within their discretion deal as they wished with the legal estate, to the prejudice of what might broadly be termed the 'occupation aspirations' of their beneficiaries. We shall now see that a series of developments during recent years has enabled beneficiaries to intercept the decision-making processes of their trustees at various critical points, in order to ensure that their own preferences as to the allocation of utility in the land are not entirely ignored. These developments have in effect conferred upon trust for sale beneficiaries something in the nature of a power of veto over dealings by trustees which threaten to prejudice their own enjoyment of the land.

We saw some time ago that the trustees' discretion in respect of sale may be curtailed or even negated by a requisite (and perhaps unobtainable) consent to sale expressly vested in one or more of the beneficiaries behind the trust[7]. However, this element of control is available to a beneficiary only if expressly conferred by the instrument which creates the trust for sale. Other elements of such control have been made available—albeit by piecemeal and incomplete stages—in the following respects.

(i) *Appointment of a second trustee* Where a single trustee for sale (as in *Bull v Bull*[8]) proposes to sell the land held on trust, it is open to any person interested in equity to apply to the court for an injunction restraining sale until at least one other trustee has been appointed[9]. Of course the technical possibility of obtaining an injunction of this kind is of little use to a beneficiary who is unaware of an impending sale, and even an injunction will delay sale only temporarily since the single trustee is free to appoint one of his cronies as co-trustee to join with him in giving a good conveyance of the legal estate[10].

(ii) *Duty of consultation* The Law of Property Act 1925 contains a special provision for consultation in relation to trusts for sale which arise by implication of statute[11]. Section 26(3) provides that

Trustees for sale shall so far as practicable consult the persons of full age for the time being beneficially interested in possession in the rents and profits of the land until sale, and shall, so far as consistent with the general interest of the trust, give effect to the wishes

7 See p. 218, ante.
8 [1955] 1 QB 234, p. 256, ante.
9 See *Waller v Waller* [1967] 1 WLR 451; (1967) 31 Conv (NS) 140 (F. R. Crane).
10 See the Law Commission's proposal of 'trusteeship rights' in the matrimonial home, p. 374, post.
11 This provision has no application to express trusts for sale, thereby providing support for Stephen Cretney's argument that in the Law of Property Act 1925 Parliament itself recognised 'the need to distinguish between cases where the trust for sale should be regarded as machinery, on the one hand, and those where it has been expressly chosen, when its logical consequences e.g., the conversion of the equitable interests may be implemented' ((1971) 34 MLR 441 at 442: 'A Technical and Tricky Matter').

of such persons, or in the case of dispute, of the majority (according to the value of their combined interests) of such persons . . .

If the trustees attempt to sell land without first discharging this duty of consultation, they may be restrained by injunction from completing the transaction[12]. However, this statutory duty of consultation is only a duty to listen coupled with a privilege to say 'no'. There is no duty to listen and obey, except where the wishes expressed are those of the majority shareholder(s) in equity and those wishes are also 'consistent with the general interest of the trust'. In *Bull v Bull*, Denning LJ accepted that the son could have forced a sale of the property against the wishes of his mother if he so desired: all he needed to do was to appoint a second trustee for sale to act with him. The two trustees

would no doubt have to consider the mother's wishes, but as the son appears to have made the greater contribution, he could in theory override her wishes about a sale: see section 26(3) of the Law of Property Act 1925[13].

However, Denning LJ pointed to a 'practical difficulty', which is dealt with under the next heading.

(iii) *Implied consent of the beneficiary in possession* In *Bull v Bull* Denning LJ conceded that even if the single trustee for sale complied with the matters here referred to in (i) and (ii) above, the trustees for sale would still experience a 'practical difficulty' in that 'so long as the [mother/beneficiary] is there, they could not sell with vacant possession'[14]. It is important to re-trace the route by which Denning LJ arrived at this conclusion.

Denning LJ observed first that the 'rights of equitable tenants in common as between themselves' had never yet been defined, but pointed out that there was 'plenty of authority' about the rights of legal owners in common dating from before the enactment of the 1925 property legislation. He then recited the rights of legal tenants in common before 1925, indicating (quite correctly) that the law had always regarded such owners as being 'entitled to the possession of the land and to the use and enjoyment of it in a proper manner. Neither can turn out the other.' He then stated

Such being the rights of legal tenants in common, I think that the rights of equitable tenants in common are the same, save only for such differences as are necessarily consequent on the interest being equitable and not legal. It is well known that equity follows the law . . .

Denning LJ thus concluded that, although all tenancies in common must since 1925 be equitable only (taking effect behind a trust for sale[15]), nevertheless

until a sale takes place these equitable tenants in common have the same right to enjoy the land as legal tenants used to have . . . [T]herefore . . . when there are two equitable

12 See *Waller v Waller* [1967] 1 WLR 451.

13 [1955] 1 QB 234 at 238. For a scathing note on *Bull v Bull*, see (1955) 14 Cambridge LJ 157f. (H. W. R. Wade): 'What is the effect, one may wonder, of a provision in an Act of Parliament which operates only "in theory"?'.

14 [1955] 1 QB 234 at 238.

15 See p. 257, ante.

tenants in common, then, until the place is sold, each of them is concurrently entitled with the other to the possession of the land and to the use and enjoyment of it in a proper manner; and . . . neither of them is entitled to turn out the other[16].

It can be seen that Denning LJ defined the beneficiary's position with regard to occupation in a manner quite inconsistent with that adopted earlier by the Court of Appeal in *Re Landi*[17]. By ignoring the implications of imposing a trust for sale here (e.g., the implication that all control and initiative are vested in the trustees as a matter of principle), Denning LJ constructed for the beneficiary a *right of occupation* of the land. More accurately, he constructed on behalf of the beneficiary in possession a certain 'status of irremovability'. He was therefore able to derive from his earlier argument a somewhat dubious proposition of law:

The mother here is in possession and in actual occupation as equitable co-owner and by virtue of that interest she could not be turned out by the trustees except with her consent[18].

In other words, Denning LJ appeared to suggest in *Bull v Bull* that a beneficiary in possession behind a trust for sale enjoys an implied right of consent to sale which must be obtained before the trustees can properly dispose of the property[19]. If the mother refused to consent to sale, thereby disabling the trustees from giving vacant possession to the purchaser, Denning LJ thought that the only recourse available to the trustees would be an application under section 30 of the Law of Property Act 1925 that the court dispense with the consent thus withheld. Denning LJ anticipated that the court

would only make such an order if it was satisfied that it was right and proper to do so and on such terms as to alternative accommodation as it thought fit to impose[20].

This 'unnecessary coda' to the judgment in *Bull v Bull* has been criticised on the ground that it 'elevates the wishes of a beneficiary to the status of a "requisite consent"'[1]. It does even more than this, for it confers upon the beneficiary in possession a negative control (or power of veto) over dealings by the trustees. This result is irreconcilable with the former theory that a beneficiary enjoys possession (if at all) only at the discretion of his trustees[2].

Denning LJ's dubious proposition of law has had a somewhat chequered history since *Bull v Bull* was decided in 1955. It was later pleaded before the Court of Appeal in *Barclay v Barclay*[3]. Here a testator had left his bungalow on

16 [1955] 1 QB 234 at 237f.

17 [1939] Ch 828, p. 262, ante. This decision was not cited before the Court of Appeal in *Bull v Bull*.

18 [1955] 1 QB 234 at 238.

19 See (1955) 14 Cambridge LJ 157 (H. W. R. Wade): 'Why it should be in the power of a beneficiary with a minor interest to impede the execution of a trust for sale is something of a mystery.' See also (1955) 18 MLR 303 (V. Latham).

20 [1955] 1 QB 234 at 239.

1 See M. J. Prichard (1971) 29 Cambridge LJ 44 at 45.

2 Professor Crane, after reviewing the authorities, has submitted that 'beneficiaries are not entitled to possession as of right, though the trustee should give it in proper cases, especially where section 26(3) of the Law of Property Act applies' ((1955) 19 Conv (NS) 146 at 147). See also (1970) 34 Conv (NS) 420 (F. R. Crane); (1979) 95 LQR 501 at 503 (R. J. Smith).

3 [1970] 2 QB 677. See (1970) 86 LQR 443 (P. V. Baker); (1971) 29 Cambridge LJ 44 (M. J. Prichard).

trust for sale, the proceeds of sale to be divided after his death between five members of his family. After the testator's death, the majority of the beneficiaries clearly wished the property to be sold in order that each might obtain his aliquot share of the wealth comprised in the bungalow. However one of the beneficiaries, a son of the testator who had been allowed to occupy the property following the break-up of his own marriage, was still living in the bungalow. He greatly preferred to retain on his own behalf the utility which he enjoyed in the property rather than receive a one-fifth share in the capital which would be released by a sale. He therefore resisted sale, alleging that, as a beneficiary in possession behind a trust for sale, he had by implication a requisite consent which he declined to give.

It was plainly inequitable on the facts of *Barclay* that a tenant in common as to a mere one-fifth share should be able to frustrate the realisation of the aliquot shares of his brethren. However, the Court of Appeal (presided over on this occasion by none other than Lord Denning MR) was faced with the difficult task of providing a respectable ground of distinction between the instant case and the not dissimilar situation which had arisen in *Bull v Bull*. The Master of the Rolls thought that *Bull* was 'quite distinguishable' in that there 'the prime object of the trust was that the parties should occupy the house together'[4]. The present case was, in his judgment, 'very different', since in *Barclay* the 'prime object of the trust was that the bungalow should be sold.'

In his judgment in *Barclay v Barclay*, Lord Denning thus appeared to suggest that the applicability of the doctrine of conversion depends upon whether the 'prime object' of the trust for sale is residence or sale. In *Bull*, where the 'prime object' had been joint residential occupation by the son and his mother, the mother had a beneficial interest in the *land*, at least to the extent that sale with vacant possession required her consent. To this degree, in Lord Denning's analysis, the doctrine of conversion was displaced. But, held Lord Denning, where the 'prime object' is sale of the property and division of the proceeds (as for instance in accordance with the testamentary direction for sale and distribution in *Barclay*), the beneficiaries have from the very outset not interests in land but interests in money. In such a case there can be no question of obtaining a requisite consent from a beneficiary who happens to be in possession (in order that sale be effected), since the doctrine of conversion applies here in its full rigour[5].

We have already seen how the displacement of the doctrine of conversion goes hand in hand with the conferment upon the trust for sale beneficiary of an

4 [1970] 2 QB 677 at 684. See also Edmund Davies LJ at 684 and Megaw LJ at 685.

5 This casuistry is supported by Stephen Cretney: 'If the clear intention is that a dwelling-house should be occupied by the joint purchasers it is absurd to deny them, because of conveyancing machinery, any sufficient interest in the house: *Bull v Bull*; if, on the other hand, there is an express trust for sale (not created on the purchase of the property), and it is clear that the intention was that the property be sold and the proceeds divided, it is equally absurd to claim that any single beneficiary is entitled to frustrate this object by retaining possession as against the trustee: *Barclay v Barclay*' ((1971) 34 MLR 441 at 443). However, it has been pointed out that this reasoning 'comes perilously close to drawing a line between express and statutory trusts for sale' (see M. J. Prichard (1971) 29 Cambridge LJ 44 at 46).

interest in the land itself[6]. This interest, in Lord Denning's analysis, takes the form of a degree of control over dealings which is sufficient to guarantee the residential occupier a virtual status of irremovability. It could be predicted that this analysis would not appeal to property lawyers of a more orthodox mould, and it was for this reason that Lord Denning's approach to the doctrine of conversion was subjected to heavy criticism in *Irani Finance Ltd v Singh*[7]. Here a differently constituted Court of Appeal categorically rejected the idea that any helpful distinction might be drawn between differing kinds of 'prime object' in a trust for sale. Cross LJ expressed the view that

The whole purpose of the trust for sale is to make sure, by shifting the equitable interests away from the land and into the proceeds of sale, that a purchaser of the land takes free from the equitable interests. To hold these to be equitable interests in the land itself would be to frustrate this purpose. Even to hold that they have equitable interests in the land for a limited period, namely until the land is sold, would . . . be inconsistent with the trust for sale being an 'immediate' trust for sale working an immediate conversion, which is what the Law of Property Act 1925 envisages[8].

In the view put forward here, the applicability of the doctrine of conversion does not vary between an express trust for sale (as in *Barclay*) and a machinery trust for sale which is implied (as in *Bull*) simply in order to give effect to beneficial co-ownership. In neither case does a beneficiary have rights in land: his rights attach only to the proceeds of sale of the land.

The decision of the Court of Appeal in *Irani Finance Ltd v Singh* marked, however, only a temporary setback to the new idea that a trust for sale beneficiary may have a power of veto over dealings by the trustees to the prejudice of his occupation. A further development has taken place which carries even further the process which Denning LJ began 25 years ago in *Bull v Bull*.

(iv) *The overriding status of the actual occupier* The balance of power between trustee and beneficiary in the single legal owner situation (i.e., the *Bull v Bull* situation) has been profoundly affected by the decision of the Court of Appeal and House of Lords in *Williams & Glyn's Bank Ltd v Boland*[9]. This case concerned a question of priority between a bank and two wives who were beneficiaries behind a statutory trust for sale of their respective matrimonial homes[10]. The bank sued for possession of the two matrimonial homes, and the issue at stake was the continued occupation of the wives in those properties. The wives claimed that their beneficial interests were protected as 'overriding interests' under the Land Registration Act 1925, by virtue of being 'rights' belonging to persons 'in actual occupation of the land'[11]. It was integral to this defence that the wives

6 See p. 223f., ante.
7 [1971] Ch 59.
8 [1971] Ch 59 at 80, p. 222, ante.
9 [1979] Ch 312, CA; affd. [1980] 3 WLR 138, HL.
10 See p. 223, ante; p. 357, post.
11 See Land Registration Act 1925, s. 70(1)(g), p. 334, post.

should be able to show that their equitable interests behind the respective trusts were interests 'subsisting in reference' to land[12].

Two members of the Court of Appeal were prepared to accept the wives' equitable interests quite straightforwardly as interests 'subsisting in reference' to land in the required sense[13]. However, Lord Denning MR went much further and declared that the interest of each wife comprised 'an equitable interest in land'[14]. He reaffirmed the casuistry of *Barclay v Barclay*[15], and found 'most compelling' the anti-conversion dicta in *Cooper v Critchley*[16] and *Elias v Mitchell*[17]. Correspondingly, Lord Denning professed to find the observations of Cross LJ in *Irani Finance Ltd v Singh* 'less compelling'. On this basis, the Court of Appeal held the equitable interest of each wife to be an 'overriding interest' for the purpose of the Land Registration Act 1925 and therefore binding on the bank.

In the House of Lords in *Williams & Glyn's Bank Ltd v Boland*[18], Lord Wilberforce had no difficulty in accepting the wives' interests as 'interests subsisting in reference to the land.' The House of Lords unanimously decided that the wives had 'rights' within the meaning of the Land Registration Act 1925 which therefore took priority over the mortgages taken by the bank. There was, however, some uncertainty in the House as to which precise right of each wife was to be rendered 'overriding' by virtue of her 'actual occupation'. Lord Scarman declared boldly that

It is conceded that each wife has a beneficial interest in the land, which is her matrimonial home. Each is an equitable tenant in common behind a trust for sale, there being only one trustee, her husband, in whom the legal estate (a freehold) is vested. Each, therefore, enjoys by reason of her interest, a present right of occupation as well as a right to a share in the proceeds of sale, if and when the house is sold: *Bull v Bull* [1955] 1 QB 234[19].

Lord Scarman then proceeded to hold that the wives had been 'in actual occupation' of the land at all material times, and that overriding status was statutorily conferred on such 'rights' as they had 'subsisting in reference' to that land:

The critically important right of the wife, so far as these appeals are concerned, is the right of occupation of the land . . . The bank fails in each case to obtain what it seeks, an order for possession of the matrimonial home, because the wife is in actual occupation and has herself a right of occupation[20].

Lord Wilberforce was much more hesitant in defining the nature of the wives' occupation privilege in the matrimonial home. He referred to sections 23 to 31 of the Law of Property Act 1925 and observed

12 See p. 223, ante; p. 357, post.
13 See p. 224, ante; p. 358, post.
14 [1979] Ch 312 at 331, p. 224, ante.
15 [1970] 2 QB 677 at 684, p. 268f., ante.
16 [1955] Ch 431 at 438, p. 222, ante.
17 [1972] Ch 652, p. 222, ante.
18 [1980] 3 WLR 138 at 146.
19 [1980] 3 WLR 138 at 148f.
20 [1980] 3 WLR 138 at 150. One thing is clear. The 'right of occupation' to which Lord Scarman referred could not possibly have been any right of occupation granted by the Matrimonial Homes Act 1967. See Matrimonial Homes Act 1967, s. 2(7), p. 338, post.

The right of occupation of the land pending sale is not explicitly dealt with in these sections and the position as to it is obscure. Before the Act the position was that owners of undivided shares (which could exist at law) had concurrent rights of occupation. In *Bull v Bull* [1955] 1 QB 234, it was held by the Court of Appeal, applying *Re Warren* [1932] 1 Ch 42, that the conversion of these legal estates into equitable interests by the Law of Property Act 1925 should not affect the mutual rights of the owners. Denning LJ, in a judgment which I find most illuminating, there held, at p. 238 in a factual situation similar to that of the instant cases, that 'when there are two equitable tenants in common, then, until the place is sold, each of them is entitled concurrently with the other to the possession of the land and to the use and enjoyment of it in a proper manner.' And he referred to section 14 of the Law of Property Act 1925 which provides that the Act 'shall not prejudicially affect the interest of any person in possession or in actual occupation of land to which he may be entitled in right of such possession or occupation.'[1]

Despite his having doubts on the point, Lord Wilberforce eventually conceded that

to describe the interests of spouses in a house jointly bought to be lived in as a matrimonial home as merely an interest in the proceeds of sale, or rents and profits until sale, is just a little unreal . . .[2]

The implications of *Williams & Glyn's Bank Ltd v Boland* are significant indeed. By holding that a beneficiary behind a statutory trust for sale may have an 'overriding interest' binding upon third parties by virtue of 'actual occupation', the House of Lords has cut back considerably the power of a single trustee for sale to deal effectively with his legal estate. Although the decision was concerned with a question of priority in registered land, the conclusion reached must inevitably govern the resolution of the same issue in unregistered land[3]. It seems that the House of Lords has recognised that at least some beneficiaries behind a trust for sale of land have an interest in the land itself, to the extent of having rights to the utility in the land which override the interests of third parties.

It might be said that in *Williams & Glyn's Bank Ltd v Boland* the House of Lords re-located the long lost *beneficial interest in land* which had been misplaced by the overworked doctrine of conversion. With the demise of that doctrine, at least in respect of residential property, the beneficiary in possession under a trust for sale is effectively given a power of veto over dealings by his trustee in the single legal owner situation[4]. This development thus confers upon the beneficiary a franchise denied him under the orthodox theory of the trust for sale, for he is now given an important element of 'control' over the allocation of enjoyment of the land.

In this sense *Boland* introduces a new degree of 'democracy' into the trust for sale, in recognition of the priority accorded to the particular social interest in issue—the protection of the residential security of the spouse in the matrimonial home. Moreover, the House of Lords professed to take the view that its decision was not based upon some supposed special status for the matrimonial home or upon the especial vulnerability of the married woman[5]. It may therefore be

1 [1980] 3 WLR 138 at 145.
2 [1980] 3 WLR 138 at 146.
3 See p. 301, post.
4 See p. 266, ante.
5 See p. 376, post.

anticipated that the 'democratisation' of the trust for sale will extend to other kinds of residential property which are covered by a machinery trust for sale for reasons merely of conveyancing simplicity.

If this surmise is justified, then it will be true to say that there has been a limited, but important, redistribution of 'control' functions within the single legal owner trust for sale. The hidden significance of this development can be assessed only if one imagines the number of residential properties vested in the name of one legal owner which were purchased or improved or extended[6] with the aid of another party, with the result that a statutory trust for sale came into being. In all such situations, the beneficiary unrepresented on the title is given a paramountly important right to defend his actual enjoyment and occupation. He has a power of veto over dealings by the single trustee, in the sense that he can oppose his own occupation against any interest taken by a third party and thereby effectively frustrate prejudicial transactions effected by his trustee in relation to the legal title.

(2) How can a beneficiary compel sale if he is also a trustee?

There are, of course, occasions when it is in the interest of a beneficiary (or indeed some interested third party) to press for the *execution* of a trust for sale of land. It may be that one of the beneficiaries wishes that the property should be sold in order that his own beneficial share in the proceeds of sale can be realised. If the beneficiary who desires sale is himself one of the trustees for sale, he may be able to persuade the other trustee or trustees to join with him in selling the trust property. However, the question of sale is a potential source of difficulty (especially where the trust property is residential property) because it may bring to the fore a conflict of interest in respect of that property, some of the trustees wishing to retain the investment represented by the property held on trust, others wishing that sale should take place. If the property concerned is a matrimonial home, the conflict of interest commonly presents itself in the form of disagreement between a spouse/trustee who is anxious to realise his capital investment in the home and the other spouse/trustee who is equally anxious that the property should be retained as a residence for herself and the children of the family.

In dealing with conflicting claims in respect of the execution of a trust for sale, the courts have developed a jurisprudence which throws much light upon the origin and purpose of the co-ownership trust for sale.

(a) *The primary rule*

We have already seen that a trust for sale imports a *duty* to sell, which must be discharged unless the trustees for sale unanimously exercise their power to postpone sale[7]. Thus, in the first instance, if even one of a number of trustees wishes to execute the trust, the other trustees can be directed to join with him in

6 See p. 302, post.
7 See p. 220, ante.

giving a conveyance of the property. It was held by Simonds J in *Re Mayo*[8] that disagreement among the trustees should be resolved in favour of fulfilling the nominal purpose of the trust for sale. The trust for sale will prevail in the absence of mala fides in the trustee who presses for sale[9].

The rule adumbrated in *Re Mayo* does not always dispose of the problem of disagreement between trustees for sale. It still sometimes happens that, even though the fiduciary duty to sell is primary and even though a majority of the beneficiaries wishes that sale should occur, one of the trustees adamantly refuses to join in effecting sale to a third party. The conveyance cannot be given at law since the signature of all the trustees is required. In these circumstances, those who press for sale must make an application to the court under section 30 of the Law of Property Act 1925 for an order directing the recalcitrant trustee to co-operate in giving a conveyance of the land. This section confers upon the court a discretion which is somewhat wider than the reference to 'consent' which we have already examined[10].

(b) *The exercise of discretion under section 30 of the Law of Property Act 1925*

Section 30 of the Law of Property Act 1925 provides that

> If the trustees refuse to sell or to exercise any of the powers conferred by either of the last two sections, or any requisite consent cannot be obtained, any person interested may apply to the court for a vesting or other order for giving effect to the proposed transaction or for an order directing the trustees for sale to give effect thereto, and the Court may make such order as it thinks fit.

This section is aimed at assisting a party who wishes to compel the execution of a trust for sale in furtherance of the prime object of that trust, i.e., sale of the land held on trust for sale. However, section 30 ultimately confers a discretion on the court to 'make such order as it thinks fit', and the terms in which the court should address this exercise of discretion were spelt out in *Re Buchanan-Wollaston's Conveyance*[11]. Here Sir Wilfred Greene MR indicated that

> the court of equity, when asked to enforce the trust for sale, . . . must look into all the circumstances of the case and consider whether or not, at the particular moment and in the particular circumstances when the application is made to it, it is right and proper that such an order shall be made. In considering a question of that kind . . . the Court is bound to . . . ask itself the question whether or not the person applying for execution of the trust for sale is a person whose voice should be allowed to prevail.

It is clear that the test to be applied under section 30 is not 'what is reasonable[12].' As Devlin LJ pointed out in *Jones v Challenger*[13], it is often entirely

8 [1943] Ch 302 at 304.

9 See *Re Buchanan-Wollaston's Conveyance* [1939] Ch 738 at 748, where reference was made to the argument of the plaintiff trustee to the effect that the trustees had indeed determined the question of sale by vote, in the sense of that 'vote being a vote at a meeting which he and he alone attended, although the respondents were invited to come.'

10 See p. 268, ante.

11 [1939] Ch 738 at 747.

12 See *Jones v Challenger* [1961] 1 QB 176 at 180, 184 per Devlin LJ; *Re Turner* (*A Bankrupt*) [1974] 1 WLR 1556 at 1558 per Goff J.

13 [1961] 1 QB 176 at 184.

reasonable both that one of the trustees should wish to continue to live in a house and that another trustee should want to realise his beneficial share in cash. The exercise of discretion pursuant to section 30 must be governed by criteria other than some supposed consideration of 'reasonableness'. It is against this background that the courts have developed a doctrine of 'secondary or collateral objects' underlying a trust for sale which may, in some circumstances, displace the primacy of the duty of sale.

(c) *Circumstances displacing the primacy of the duty to sell*

In terms of the orthodox approach to the trust for sale of land, the prime object of such a trust is the 'conversion of the property into a form in which [all] parties can enjoy their rights equally.' It is this consideration which lies behind the insistence in *Re Mayo* that the trust to sell must prevail in the absence of mala fides. However, as Devlin LJ was later to say in *Jones v Challenger*[14], 'this simple principle cannot prevail where the trust itself or the circumstances in which it was made show that there was a secondary or collateral object besides that of sale.' It is here that difficulty enters, because it is increasingly recognised today that

> the trust for sale has become a very convenient and much used conveyancing technique. Combined with the statutory power in the trustees to postpone the sale, it can be used to meet a variety of situations, in some of which an actual sale is far from the intentions of the parties at the time when the trust for sale comes into existence[15].

In *Jones v Challenger*[16], Devlin LJ reviewed the way in which the court's exercise of discretion under section 30 has been influenced by the fact that the conveyancing device of the trust for sale may serve a multiplicity of secondary purposes. He noted that

> If it be not mala fides, it is at any rate wrong and inequitable for one of the parties to the trust to invoke the letter of the trust in order to defeat one of its purposes, whether that purpose be written or unwritten, and the court will not permit it ... There is ... something akin to mala fides if one trustee tries to defeat a collateral object in the trust by arbitrarily insisting on the duty of sale. He should have good grounds for doing so and, therefore, the court will inquire whether, in all the circumstances, it is right and proper to order the sale.

We must examine some of the kinds of circumstance which have been regarded as disclosing a collateral object or underlying purpose of sufficient importance to justify the displacement of the 'prime object' of sale. We shall see that the jurisprudence expressed in the case law provides an interesting indication of the relative priority of the interests which commonly come into conflict in this area.

14 [1961] 1 QB 176 at 181. Devlin LJ pointed out that *Re Mayo* had been 'a simple uncomplicated case of a trust for sale of freehold property, where the beneficiaries were brother and sister, and where there was no suggestion that either of them were intended to or even wished to occupy the property.'

15 *Re Evers' Trust* [1980] 1 WLR 1327 at 1330 per Ormrod LJ.

16 [1961] 1 QB 176 at 181, 183.

(i) *Contract not to sell without the consent of all the trustees* There is authority for the view that the court, in exercising jurisdiction under section 30, may not think it 'right and proper' to order sale where the trustees have already covenanted inter se not to sell without the concurrence of all the trustees.

In *Re Buchanan-Wollaston's Conveyance*[17], four owners, who each had separate but neighbouring properties overlooking the sea, combined to buy a piece of land which they desired to keep as an open space in order to preserve their common sea view. The land was conveyed to them as joint tenants, and they therefore held the legal estate as trustees for sale on trust for themselves in the proportions of their respective financial contributions towards the purchase of the property[18]. The parties then entered into a deed of covenant by which they mutually undertook not to part or deal with the land except with the unanimous consent of all parties or by majority vote. One of the trustees subsequently sold his own property and thus wished, notwithstanding the opposition of the other trustees, to withdraw his investment from the jointly held open land. He brought proceedings under section 30 for a court order directing the other trustees to join with him in selling that property and realising the proceeds. Farwell J refused at first instance to order sale of the land, observing that this was not an 'ordinary case of a beneficiary seeking to compel a trustee to carry out his duties as trustee.' The present application had been made by a party who 'was putting forward a claim to equitable assistance merely to enable him thereby to escape from his contractual obligations.' To facilitate this course of action 'would be to disregard the well established rule of equity that he who seeks equity must do equity[19].' Farwell J's decision was upheld by the Court of Appeal, Sir Wilfred Greene MR agreeing on behalf of that Court that the plaintiff 'could not . . . ask the Court to act in a way inconsistent with his own contractual obligations[20].'

Thus, if the trustees for sale have contractually displaced the primacy of the duty to sell, the court will not so exercise discretion under section 30 as to facilitate a breach of contract. Sale will not be ordered while the underlying purpose of the trust for sale still subsists[1].

(ii) *The provision of a family home* The principles outlined in *Re Buchanan-Wollaston's Conveyance* have been applied in other cases where a trust for sale has come into being expressly or impliedly in order to give effect to co-ownership of a matrimonial home. In such cases, even if the orthodox view is accepted that the 'prime object' of the trust is sale[2], the trust clearly has a secondary or collateral

17 [1939] Ch 217, 739.
18 See p. 252, ante.
19 [1939] Ch 217 at 223f.
20 [1939] Ch 738 at 745.
1 In *Re Buchanan-Wollaston's Conveyance* [1939] Ch 738 at 747f., Sir Wilfred Greene, while refusing to order sale in the circumstances present in that case, added the qualification that sale might be ordered under section 30 under different circumstances: 'Circumstances may change. If all the parties died, and all their houses were sold, I apprehend, for example, that the Court, if asked to enforce a statutory trust for sale, would not be disposed to listen to arguments against such a sale adduced by people who had no real interest in keeping this land unsold.'
2 See p. 269, ante.

purpose of providing a home for joint occupation by a family. It has been held that sale of the matrimonial home will not normally be ordered under section 30 so long as this purpose subsists[3]. However, if the underlying object of the trust for sale (i.e., the provision of a matrimonial home) at any stage becomes incapable of fulfilment, it seems that 'very special circumstances need to be shown to induce the court not to order a sale[4].' Thus the court has in the past exercised its discretion in favour of sale where the initial purpose of a trust for sale of the matrimonial home has been frustrated by reason of the divorce of the parties who held on trust for sale[5]. Likewise, it has been considered that the underlying purpose of the trust is spent, when, by reason of the separation of the legal owners, the marriage is dead in fact though not at law[6].

This approach is based upon the reasoning that the purpose of the trust has failed if the relationship of the trustees breaks down and there no longer exists a marriage in relation to which the property is required as a 'matrimonial' home. In such a case the primacy of the duty to sell is restored—at least according to the view expressed in the older cases. In the words of Devlin LJ in *Jones v Challenger*[7], it is not 'inequitable' in this event for one of the spouses to want to realise his investment. According to Devlin LJ, if the 'prime object' of the trust is to have any weight, 'the preservation of the house as a home for one of them singly is not an object at all.'

More recently, however, it has come to be questioned whether the underlying object of a trust for sale of the matrimonial home is indeed truly spent when the marriage of the trustees breaks down. It may well be that one of the spouses continues to require the former matrimonial home as accommodation for herself and the children of the family. There has emerged a marked divergence in the courts' view of this issue. According to one view, the presence of minor children of the marriage prolongs the secondary or collateral purpose of the trust for sale beyond the termination of the mutual relationship of the trustees. Thus, in *Rawlings v Rawlings*[8], Salmon LJ opined that the court would not execute the trust where there were young children:

> One of the purposes of the trust would no doubt have been to provide a home for them, and whilst that purpose still existed a sale would not generally be ordered[9].

3 See *Jones v Challenger* [1961] 1 QB 176 at 183 per Devlin LJ: '. . . [W]here property is acquired by husband and wife for the purpose of providing a matrimonial home, neither party has a right to demand the sale while that purpose still exists; that might defeat the object behind the trust, and the court must do what is right and proper in all the circumstances.'

4 *Re Holliday (A Bankrupt)* [1980] 3 All ER 385 at 391 per Goff LJ.

5 See *Jones v Challenger* [1961] 1 QB 176.

6 See *Rawlings v Rawlings* [1964] P 398. See, however, the vigorous dissent by Willmer LJ: 'The wife has, on the face of it, already done the husband one grievous wrong by deserting him. I do not think that the discretion of the court ought now to be exercised in such a way as will enable her to do him another grievous wrong by turning him out of his home' ([1964] P 398 at 414). See also the approach adopted by Lord Denning MR in *Bedson v Bedson* [1965] 2 QB 666 at 680; *Jackson v Jackson* [1971] 1 WLR 1539 at 1543.

7 [1961] 1 QB 176 at 184.

8 [1964] P 398 at 419.

9 See the much more startling (and surely inaccurate) statement of Lawton LJ in *Burke v Burke*

This view has not gone unchallenged. In *Burke v Burke*[10], the Court of Appeal was not prepared to attach such significance to the presence of children in the former matrimonial home. Buckley LJ referred to the view taken by Salmon LJ in *Rawlings v Rawlings*:

[I]f you had property held by two persons in undivided shares, one of whom was in occupation of the property and the other was claiming a sale, and the one who was in occupation had some infirm and aged relative living with him or her who might have to be rehoused somehow and whom there was great difficulty in rehousing, the court would not order a sale instanter in such a way as to cause great difficulty in making proper arrangements to rehouse that person. But the interests of the children in the present case, it seems to me, with due respect to Salmon LJ are interests which are only incidentally to be taken into consideration in that sort of way. They are proper to be taken into consideration so far as they affect the equities in the matter as between the two persons entitled to the beneficial interests in the property. But it is not, I think, right to treat this case as though the husband was obliged to make provision for his children by agreeing to retain the property unsold. To do so is ... to confuse with a problem relating to property considerations which are relevant to maintenance. Those are two different things[11].

Burke v Burke was not itself concerned with an application under section 30 of the Law of Property Act 1925[12], but the appropriateness of the views expressed by Buckley LJ was later called into question in *Williams v Williams*[13]. Here a trustee for sale applied under section 30 for an order directing the sale of the former jointly owned matrimonial home. Although the two trustees for sale had been divorced, the plaintiff's ex-wife continued to live in the property with the children of the marriage. The plaintiff sought a sale and equal division of the proceeds, in order that he could extract his capital investment from the house and apply it for other purposes. The Court of Appeal reversed the judgment of Foster J at first instance, and declined to order a sale which would have had the effect of evicting the plaintiff's ex-wife and children.

Lord Denning MR took this opportunity to distinguish between 'the old approach' (as applied in *Jones v Challenger* and *Burke v Burke*) and a 'modern view', which he proceeded to expound. Referring to Buckley LJ's approach in *Burke v Burke* as 'now out-dated', Lord Denning indicated that the exercise of discretion under section 30 had been cross-fertilised by the family code which now operates in the reallocation of property on divorce[14]:

When judges are dealing with the matrimonial home, they nowadays have great regard to the fact that the house is bought as a home in which the family is to be brought up. It

---

[1974] 1 WLR 1063 at 1068: 'If the circumstances are such that the parents buy a house in which to accommodate themselves and any children of the marriage, for my part I cannot see why the children should not be beneficiaries under any implied trust which may come into existence on the purchase of the home; and if that is the position on the evidence in any particular case, then it may well be that the position of the children has to be considered.'

10 [1974] 1 WLR 1063.

11 [1974] 1 WLR 1063 at 1067.

12 It was instead an application under s. 17 of the Married Women's Property Act 1882.

13 [1976] Ch 278.

14 See p. 563ff., post.

is not treated as property to be sold, nor as an investment to be realised for cash. That was emphasised by this court in the recent case of *Browne v Pritchard*. The court, in executing the trust, should regard the primary object as being to provide a home and not a sale. Steps should be taken to preserve it as a home for the remaining partner and children, but giving the outgoing partner such compensation, by way of a charge or being bought out, as is reasonable in the circumstances ... Foster J [did] not give proper effect to the modern view, which is to have regard to the needs of the family as a whole before a sale is ordered... The truth is that the approach to these cases has been transformed since the Matrimonial Proceedings and Property Act 1970 and the Matrimonial Causes Act 1973, which have given the power to the court, after a divorce, to order the transfer of property. In exercising any discretion under section 30 of the 1925 Act, those Acts must be taken into account[15].

Thus in *Williams v Williams* Lord Denning strongly emphasised the importance of the 'use value' rather than the 'capital value' of such property as the matrimonial home. The decision reflected the way in which the bleak and inflexible rules of property law have been increasingly coloured during recent years by considerations which are much more sympathetic to the realities of family life. In preferring the residential security of the ex-wife and children above the achievement of capital liquidity for the ex-husband, the Court of Appeal's judgments marked a significant development in the courts' sensitivity to the balance which exists in this area between property considerations and family considerations.

The case law on the family home continues to disclose this underlying tension between, on the one hand, a predominantly commercialist view of the trust for sale as a device whose highest fulfilment is indeed sale and, on the other hand, a more 'utility-oriented' view of the trust for sale as a machinery device whose prime object is the provision of a family home for joint occupation. In *Jones v Jones*[16], the Court of Appeal, led by Lord Denning MR, declined to order sale of the disputed property at the behest of a trustee, on the ground that such an order would 'defeat the very purpose of the acquisition, namely that [the beneficiary currently in possession] would be able to be there for his life and remain in it as his home.' In *Re Holliday (A Bankrupt)*[17], however, Goff LJ reiterated the more commercialist view of the matrimonial home trust for sale,

15 [1976] Ch 278 at 285f. In *Browne v Pritchard* [1975] 1 WLR 1366 at 1371, in the context of property adjustment under the Matrimonial Causes Act 1973, Ormrod LJ had referred thus to the argument that there the wife would be 'kept out of her money' if the court did not order immediate sale of the former matrimonial home and division of the proceeds: 'That is, in my view, a complete misapprehension. She is not being kept out of her money. If the marriage had not broken down ... she would never have touched a penny of the value of the house, because investment in a home is the least liquid investment that one can possibly make. It cannot be converted into cash while the children are at home and often not until one spouse dies unless it is possible to move into much smaller and cheaper accommodation.' For further reference to the courts' powers pursuant to the Matrimonial Causes Act 1973, see later, p. 568, post.

16 [1977] 1 WLR 438 at 442. Since rent cannot be charged of a resident tenant in common by a non-resident tenant in common, p. 238, ante, it has been pointed out that the court's refusal to order sale is sometimes tantamount to the making of a maintenance order against the latter. See J. Martin [1980] Conv 361 at 376.

17 [1980] 3 All ER 385 at 393, p. 284, post.

preferring the approach taken by Buckley LJ in *Burke v Burke* to that expressed by Salmon LJ in *Rawlings v Rawlings.* In Goff LJ's view, the secondary or collateral purpose of a matrimonial home trust for sale ended on divorce or marital breakdown, but the existence of children remained 'a factor incidentally to be taken into account so far as they affect the equities in the matter as between the persons entitled to the beneficial interests in the property.' However, the preservation of the house as a home for the children could 'be no more an object than its preservation as a home for the spouse.'

The family approach has emerged once more, however, in the decision of the Court of Appeal in *Re Evers' Trust*[18]. The circumstances of this case illustrate the increasing frequency with which the courts are being faced with what are essentially 'security claims' after the breakdown of family relationships (whether de iure or de facto)[19]. Here a couple had lived together as man and wife for several years, purchasing a home in joint names largely with the aid of a joint mortgage loan. When the parties later separated, the woman and three children (including two from an earlier union) remained in the house. The man sought a court order for sale under section 30, but the Court of Appeal refused to make such an order on the facts of the case. Ormrod LJ leant towards the family-oriented view of section 30 as revealed in the judgment of Lord Denning MR in *Williams v Williams*[20], remarking that Lord Denning's approach

> has considerable advantages in these 'family' cases. It enables the court to deal with substance (that is, reality) rather than form (that is, convenience of conveyancing); it brings the exercise of discretion under this section, so far as possible, into line with the exercise of the discretion given by section 24 of the Matrimonial Causes Act 1973[1].

Thus, while the 'usual practice' of the courts in section 30 applications has been to order a sale and division of the proceeds, thereby 'giving effect to the express purpose of the trust', Ormrod LJ agreed that the court must in every case have regard to the 'underlying purpose' of the trust in question[2]. In the present case, the interests of children, both legitimate and illegitimate, were to be considered, and it was moreover clear that the underlying purpose of the trust for sale had been to provide a home for the couple and their three children 'for the indefinite future[3].' The Court of Appeal, in declining to order sale under section 30, took into account that the man had a secure home now with his own mother and had no present need to realise his investment[4], while the woman was

18 [1980] 1 WLR 1327. See [1981] Conv 79 (A. Sydenham).

19 Pointing out that this was the first occasion on which the Court of Appeal had been faced with a section 30 application in respect of property jointly titled in an unmarried couple, Ormrod LJ said: 'This is a situation which is occurring much more frequently now than in the past and is a social development of considerable importance with which the courts are now likely to have to deal from time to time' ([1980] 1 WLR 1327 at 1330).

20 Ormrod LJ also expressed the view that the dictum of Salmon LJ in *Rawlings v Rawlings* 'appears . . . to be more in line with the judgments of this court in the *Buchanan-Wollaston* case and in *Jones v Challenger.*'

1 [1980] 1 WLR 1327 at 1332f., p. 563, post.

2 [1980] 1 WLR 1327 at 1330.

3 [1980] 1 WLR 1327 at 1333.

4 'It is an excellent one, combining complete security with considerable capital appreciation in money terms' ([1980] 1 WLR 1327 at 1334 per Ormrod LJ).

prepared to accept full responsibility for the outstanding mortgage liability and would have found it extremely difficult to rehouse herself if the property had been sold[5]. The Court therefore postponed any question of sale, but indicated that sale might become appropriate at some future stage if circumstances changed, as, for instance, if the woman remarried or it became financially possible for her to buy the man out.

(3) How can a beneficiary compel sale if he is not a trustee?

If a beneficiary is not himself one of the trustees of the legal estate in the land held on trust for sale, his ability to compel a sale of that title is severely limited. If the trust is a statutory trust for sale, he may be able to claim the benefit of section 26(3) of the Law of Property Act 1925[6] if he owns the largest share in the equitable interest. Under this provision, the trustees are obliged 'so far as consistent with the general interest of the trust' to give effect to the wishes of such a person.

Failing this, the only way in which the beneficiary can compel sale is by persuading his fellow beneficiaries to join with him in invoking the rule in *Saunders v Vautier*[7], under which the beneficiaries of a trust, if all of full age and sound mind, may by common consent direct their trustees to deal with the trust property in the manner specified by them. However, the difficulties which confront the beneficiary who looks to the rule in *Saunders v Vautier* are not inconsiderable. The rule is inapplicable if one of the beneficiaries is a minor, and is of no help in any case in which unanimity cannot be obtained between the beneficiaries. It is almost of the essence of the situation under discussion that the problem in hand arises precisely because there is disagreement as to what should be done with the land held on trust for sale.

(4) How can a beneficiary prevent sale at the behest of a trustee in bankruptcy?

It is not unknown that bankruptcy can follow in the aftermath of marriage breakdown. It is a truth of general application that a man cannot support two families at once. In a society which does not practise the extended family form but which is nevertheless prepared to practise successive polygamy it is virtually inevitable that some men who attempt to support two families will be unable to discharge this burden[8]. Often, in such cases, the only capital asset which is available to meet the claims of the man's creditors is the jointly owned former matrimonial home in which the man's first wife and family are still living. The application for a court order for sale under section 30 of the Law of Property Act 1925 may well be initiated, not by either of the spouses (since both may

5 [1980] 1 WLR 1327 at 1334.
6 See p. 266, ante.
7 (1841) Cr & Ph 240.
8 It may even be that bankruptcy provides a means of defeating the first wife's claims for property adjustment. See, e.g., *Re Holliday (A Bankrupt)* [1980] 3 All ER 385.

desperately wish to retain the former matrimonial home), but by the man's trustee in bankruptcy[9].

In the law of bankruptcy, a trustee in bankruptcy steps into the shoes of the insolvent debtor and is statutorily bound to realise any assets to which the debtor is beneficially entitled and to apply the proceeds in satisfaction of the claims of the creditors. Where the debtor is beneficially entitled to a share in a jointly owned matrimonial home, it was held by Goff J in *Re Solomon (A Bankrupt)*[10] that the trustee in bankruptcy of one of the spouses (usually, of course, the husband) is a 'person interested' within the meaning of section 30 and may therefore apply to the court for an order for sale of the matrimonial home. In the event of such an application, it is irrelevant that neither of the spouses wishes that sale should occur.

An application brought in these circumstances by a trustee in bankruptcy raises a number of 'conflicting legal and moral claims' which require to be weighed in the balance[11]. On the one hand, there are the claims of the creditors asserted through the trustee in bankruptcy, and on the other hand there are the competing claims of a wife and children (or sometimes even an entire family) to residential security at a time of peculiar crisis. The case law in this area reveals that in almost every instance this difficult question of priority has been resolved in favour of the trustee in bankruptcy, and that the courts have been ready to exercise the section 30 discretion in favour of sale at his behest even though the matrimonial home may still be required for the debtor's wife and children. Here again the 'money interest'—that of the husband's creditors as represented by his trustee in bankruptcy—prevails over the 'family interest' implicit in the need to provide a roof over the heads of the wife and children. Once again, the commercialist principle of the *Gesellschaft* (i.e., the 'solid tug of money') exerts overwhelming force.

The courts have nevertheless insisted that, even though a trustee in bankruptcy brings a section 30 application, the matter is still one of discretion for the court[12]. In *Re Turner (A Bankrupt)*[13] Goff J made it clear that there is no presumption (whether rebuttable or irrebuttable) in favour of the trustee in bankruptcy. In each case, the question before the court is simply concerned with 'whose voice in equity ought to prevail.' It is impossible, however, to find a single case in which the voice of the trustee in bankruptcy has not prevailed in equity[14]. Discretion has been exercised uniformly in favour of ordering sale of the matrimonial home in order that the debtor's share of the proceeds be applied in satisfaction of his debts[15]. It seems to have been of extreme relevance to the

9 See J. G. Miller (1975) 119 Sol Jo 582: 'Creditors and the Matrimonial Home'.
10 [1967] Ch 573 at 586.
11 See *Re Holliday (A Bankrupt)* [1980] 3 All ER 385 at 395 per Buckley LJ.
12 *Re Turner (A Bankrupt)* [1974] 1 WLR 1556 at 1558; *Re Holliday (A Bankrupt)* [1980] 3 All ER 385 at 395.
13 [1974] 1 WLR 1556 at 1558.
14 The case law tends to have a self-fulfilling quality: '. . . no case of the many referred to yet has thrown up the case where [the trustee in bankruptcy's] voice was not allowed to prevail' (see *Re Bailey (A Bankrupt)* [1977] 1 WLR 278 at 283 per Walton J).
15 See *Re Densham (A Bankrupt)* [1975] 1 WLR 1519 at 1531 per Goff J; *Bird v Syme-Thomson* [1979] 1 WLR 440 at 445 per Templeman J.

courts' exercise of discretion in this matter that a trustee in bankruptcy is *bound by statute* to realise the debtor's assets[16].

A good illustration of the commercialist bias of the courts in section 30 applications brought by a trustee in bankruptcy is provided by *Re Bailey (A Bankrupt)*[17]. Here the two trustees for sale of a matrimonial home had been divorced and the ex-husband had gone bankrupt. His ex-wife was still living in the property with a 16 year old son of the marriage, and she asked that sale of the matrimonial home should be postponed for two years in order that the son might complete his studies at the local school and take his GCE 'A level' examinations. The court declined to postpone sale for this purpose. Megarry V-C distinguished the family-based approach of the Court of Appeal in *Williams v Williams*[18] on the ground that that case 'was not a bankruptcy case, but a husband and wife case[19].' In other words, Megarry V-C considered that the intervention of the trustee in bankruptcy materially altered the nature of the exercise under section 30. In his view, the 'husband and wife' cases were irrelevant for the present purpose since they 'were not cases in which matters of commercial obligation arose, as in the case of bankruptcy.' Moreover, thought Megarry V-C, 'bankruptcy has, in relation to the matrimonial home, its own claim to protection.' Here the claims of the ex-wife and child were not sufficiently weighty to counter-balance the third party considerations which were expressed by the trustee in bankruptcy[20].

Walton J concurred in this decision, preferring to incline towards what he called 'the purely property aspect of the matter'.[1] He pointed out that, in deciding between the competing interests in this case, the maxim *pacta sunt servanda*, 'although somewhat out of fashion, must be borne in mind. A person must discharge his liabilities before there is any room for being generous. One's debts must be paid, and paid promptly . . .' Walton J indicated that there might be special circumstances of bankruptcy where the court 'would hesitate long before making an immediate order for sale'[2], but that those circumstances were not present in this case. Some impression of the *Gesellschaft* flavour of his judgment can be gleaned from his concluding observation that the statutory preference given to the claims of creditors[3]

16 See Bankruptcy Act 1914, ss. 48ff.; *Re Turner (A Bankrupt)* [1974] 1 WLR 1556 at 1558; *Re Densham (A Bankrupt)* [1975] 1 WLR 1519 at 1531. It has been suggested that if the third party who applies under section 30 for an order for sale of the matrimonial home is not a trustee in bankruptcy, but merely a mortgagee, different considerations therefore apply. Unlike a trustee in bankruptcy, a mortgagee has no statutory *duty* as such to realise the mortgagor's assets, and it may be that sale would less readily be ordered at the behest of such a third party. See R. J. Smith (1979) 95 LQR 501 at 506; J. Martin [1980] Conv 361 at 376ff.

17 [1977] 1 WLR 278.

18 [1976] Ch 278, p. 278, ante.

19 [1977] 1 WLR 278 at 281.

20 Megarry V-C thought it improbable that the sale of the matrimonial home would affect the son's educational prospects other than very slightly.

1 [1977] 1 WLR 278 at 283.

2 The circumstances postulated included the case where, for example, a house had been specially adapted to suit the needs of a handicapped child.

3 Here Walton J was referring to Matrimonial Homes Act 1967, s. 2(5), p. 147, ante; Matrimonial Causes Act 1973, s. 39, p. 572, post.

[makes] it perfectly clear that the voice of the trustee in bankruptcy, reminding the debtor of the obligation to pay one's debts, should prevail as compared with one's obligations to maintain one's wife and family. This may be yet another case where the sins of the father have to be visited on the children, but that is the way in which the world is constructed, and one must be just before one is generous[4].

It remains to be seen whether the later decision of the Court of Appeal in *Re Holliday (A Bankrupt)*[5] is an aberration from, or merely a confirmation of, the solid preference expressed throughout the case law for the claims of creditors as asserted through the trustee in bankruptcy. Here an ex-wife was still living in the former matrimonial home with three young children. Her ex-husband was adjudicated bankrupt on his own petition, but the extent of his outstanding liabilities was fairly small (in the region of £6,000). In view of all the circumstances the Court of Appeal declined to order an *immediate* sale of the property, in which there was currently an equity of £27,000. While agreeing that the ex-husband's creditors had an 'unassailable right' to be paid out of the assets of the bankrupt, Buckley LJ stated that nevertheless

when one of those assets is an undivided share in land in respect of which the debtor's right to an immediate sale is not an absolute right, that is an asset in the bankruptcy which is liable to be affected by the interest of any other party interested in that land, and if there are reasons which seem to the court to be good reasons for saying that the trust for sale of the land should not be immediately enforced, then that is an asset of the bankruptcy which is not immediately available because it cannot be immediately realised for the benefit of the creditors[6].

The court took the view that the ex-wife had 'strong and justifiable grounds' for saying that an immediate sale would be 'unfair' to her. In reaching this conclusion, the Court had regard to the debtor's conduct in leaving his wife for another woman while she remained 'saddled with the burden of providing a proper home for her children' and without other resources with which to do so. Thus the voice of the trustee in bankruptcy was not allowed to prevail, at least in the sense that the Court declined to order an immediate sale[7]. However, the trustee's voice was not ignored entirely, since the Court granted a merely temporary concession to the extreme hardship in which the ex-wife found herself. The Court postponed sale for five years (by which time the two eldest children would be over 17 years of age), while reserving the power to enforce the trust for sale on the application of any interested party should circumstances change in the meantime.

It is fairly inevitable that the broadly commercialist view adopted by the courts in these matters will prevail until the enactment of some type of 'homestead legislation' in the form of a new regime of co-ownership of the matrimonial home[8]. Such legislation is in force, for instance, in New Zealand,

4 [1977] 1 WLR 278 at 284.
5 [1980] 3 All ER 385. See [1981] Conv 79 (A. Sydenham); (1981) 97 LQR 200 (C. Hand).
6 [1980] 3 All ER 385 at 397.
7 It may be significant that Goff LJ died before the final judgments were delivered in *Re Holliday*.
8 See p. 149, ante; p. 303, post.

where under the Joint Family Homes Act 1964 it is possible for spouses to register their home as a 'joint family home'[9]. Upon registration the spouses become legal and beneficial joint tenants[10], and while the joint family home settlement remains registered the interests of the husband and wife are unaffected by bankruptcy or assignment for the benefit of creditors. Creditors of one or other spouse may oppose the registration[11], but otherwise creditors may secure the cancellation of the registration only on the terms laid down in the 1964 Act[12]. It is clear that these terms confer on the court a discretion to cancel the registration[13], and that this discretion will not be exercised in favour of sale by reason merely of bankruptcy[14]. Even if the court decides that the joint family home must, in a particular case, be sold up to meet the claims of creditors, the proceeds of sale remain to a level specified by statute immune from third party claims[15], with the result that the family salvages something in the calamity of insolvency.

The priorities expressed in the Joint Family Homes Act 1964 are quite different from those which prevail in the exercise of discretion under section 30 of the Law of Property Act 1925 in cases of bankruptcy. The New Zealand legislation is an imaginative attempt to strike a new balance between the legitimate demands of creditors and the protection of the principal family asset. It was enacted with the express object of promoting the stability and permanence of family life as a higher social interest than that represented by commercial security for the creditor[16]. As Wilson J said in *Official Assignee of Pannell v Pannell*[17],

> The policy of the Joint Family Homes Act 1964 which I distil from reading it as a whole is that, except in special circumstances, a joint family home settled under the Act shall be preserved for the benefit of the registered proprietors and their family. The special circumstances which justify an order for the sale of a joint family home will necessarily vary with each case but I think that the greater the hardship to the registered proprietors and their family the weightier must be the countervailing circumstances necessary to be proved in order to justify making an order for sale.

9 Joint Family Homes Act 1964, s. 5. Registration is entirely voluntary.
10 Joint Family Homes Act 1964, s. 9(1)(b).
11 Joint Family Homes Act 1964, s. 6(1).
12 Joint Family Homes Act 1964, ss. 16–20.
13 Joint Family Homes Act 1964, s. 16(1).
14 See *Official Assignee of Pannell v Pannell* [1966] NZLR 324 at 325. In this case, Wilson J did not consider the very considerable total of the bankrupt's debts and the large number of his creditors to be 'sufficient, without more, to warrant . . . an order for sale . . .' It seems that the court is, in such cases, looking for evidence for instance of 'unconscientious dealings by the debtor with his creditors and his expenditure of money which should have been used in payment of his debts in making capital improvements to the settled property' ([1966] NZLR 324 at 326).
15 In the event of the cancellation of a joint family home registration on the ground of bankruptcy, $15,000 must be set aside for the beneficiaries of the joint family home settlement, notwithstanding that this defeats pro tanto the claims of the creditors. See Joint Family Homes Act 1964, s. 16(1)(a), as amended by Regulation No. 65 of 1978 promulgated by the Governor General of New Zealand.
16 See Vol. 292, *New Zealand Parliamentary Debates*, 3493.
17 [1966] NZLR 324 at 326.

11. PROTECTION FOR THE PURCHASER OF LAND HELD ON TRUST FOR SALE

We have already seen that the primary protection available to the purchaser of land held on trust for sale lies in the device of overreaching[18]. Where overreaching occurs, the beneficial interests behind the trust for sale are automatically confirmed as the equivalent interests in the proceeds of sale and thus need not concern the purchaser at all.

We also discovered that the beneficial interests are overreached in this way only if three conditions are fulfilled[19]. The sale must be effected by 'trustees for sale'; the equitable interests must be capable of being overreached; and the purchase moneys must usually be paid to at least two trustees for sale. The purchaser is absolutely safe if he knows of the existence of the trust for sale and complies with those conditions. In cases (1) to (5) inclusive, which we examined earlier[20], the purchaser will be aware of the existence of a trust for sale simply because the fact of co-ownership will be apparent from the very face of the document or documents of title. He will therefore know that overreaching is dependent upon his compliance with the three conditions outlined above, and he will know, most importantly, that he must pay the purchase money to at least two trustees.

The one case which represents a potential trap for the purchaser is case (6)[1].

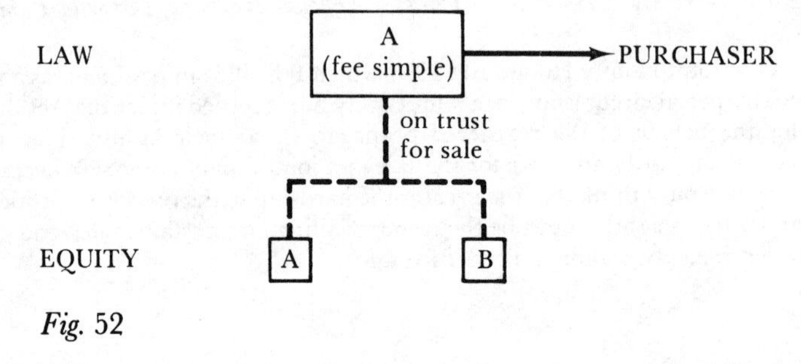

Fig. 52

This is the situation in which a legal estate is vested in the name of A alone, the purchase moneys for this acquisition having been provided in unequal proportions by A and B. A trust for sale arises here by implication of statute[2]. It is possible therefore that a third party purchaser of the land thus held on trust for sale will be unaware that the vendor, A, is in fact a trustee for sale. Since the trust for sale in these circumstances is implied by statute, it does not appear on the title deeds produced by A. The purchaser will assume—not unreasonably—that A is selling as 'beneficial owner', i.e., as owner of the entire legal and

18 See p. 227, ante.
19 See p. 228ff., ante.
20 See pp. 251–255, ante.
1 See p. 256, ante.
2 See *Bull v Bull* [1955] 1 QB 234; *Williams & Glyn's Bank Ltd v Boland* [1980] 3 WLR 138, pp. 257, 259, ante.

equitable interest, free from any trust or settlement. It might even come as a surprise to A himself to be told that he is not the absolute owner at law and in equity! Nevertheless it will be the case that A is merely a trustee for sale and that there is a co-ownership in equity which is effectively concealed behind the paper title vested in the vendor.

Since in this situation the purchaser is quite unaware of the existence of a trust for sale, he will obviously pay the purchase money to A and take a conveyance of the legal estate from A alone. Two difficult problems arise if the land is unregistered land[3]:

(i) Can a single trustee for sale effect a valid disposition at law?
(ii) Does a purchaser from a single trustee take free of the beneficial interests behind the trust for sale?

We must examine these questions in turn, and then see the conclusions indicated by the relevant case law.

(1) Can a single trustee for sale effect a valid disposition of the legal estate?

This first question concerns the validity of any purported conveyance made by A in favour of a third party purchaser[4]. Is a single trustee for sale competent to deal with the legal estate without appointing another trustee? The overreaching (and consequently the protection) of the equitable interests behind the trust for sale requires that the purchase moneys be paid to at least two trustees for sale[5].

There are judicial dicta which indicate that, as a matter of policy, it may be undesirable that a single trustee for sale should be able to give a good conveyance of a legal estate. In *Bull v Bull*[6], Denning LJ said quite clearly that

> The son is the legal owner and he holds . . . on the statutory trusts for sale. He cannot at the present moment sell the house because he cannot give a valid receipt for the proceeds. It needs two trustees to give a receipt; see section 14 of the Trustee Act, 1925[7].

In *Waller v Waller*[8], Stamp J observed that

> it is the policy of the law for obvious reasons . . . not to allow a single trustee to sell land which he is holding on trust for sale, and in the proceeds of sale of which other persons are interested in equity . . .

Stamp J went on to say that a single trustee for sale could not therefore

3 We shall examine later the problems which present themselves if the land is registered land, p. 353, post.
4 For an excellent discussion of this issue, see B. Rudden (1963) 27 Conv (NS) 51 at 55ff.: 'The Wife, the Husband and the Conveyancer'.
5 Law of Property Act 1925, ss. 2(1)(ii), 27(2).
6 [1955] 1 QB 234 at 238.
7 Under s. 14(2) of the Trustee Act 1925, a sole trustee cannot give a 'valid receipt' for proceeds of sale paid to him. This provision could, at least in theory, make it difficult for a purchaser subsequently to prove that he was a 'purchaser for value'—a point which may be crucial later (p. 292, post).
8 [1967] 1 WLR 451 at 453. Compare, however, *Tunstall v Tunstall* [1953] 1 WLR 770 at 771 per Lord Goddard CJ.

have sold the property and given a good receipt for the proceeds without first appointing an additional trustee (see the Trustee Act 1925, s. 14(2))[9].

If, following these dicta, it were the case that a single trustee for sale is incompetent to deal with the legal title himself, then, in our example, A's conveyance to the purchaser would be rendered void and ineffective. The purchaser would be thrown back upon a contractual remedy: A contracted to convey a legal estate and has not done so.

It is perhaps worth remembering that the corresponding situation in relation to the strict settlement is that in which a purchaser buys land not knowing that it is settled land. Quite innocently he fails to pay the purchase money to two trustees of the settlement. Under these circumstances there is a strong statutory indication that the conveyance to the purchaser is void at law[10], on the ground that an irregular disposition which is precluded from overreaching the beneficial interests behind the settlement should not be allowed to take effect. It could be argued that section 27(2) of the Law of Property Act 1925 indirectly produces the same result in relation to the purchaser who does not realise that the land which he proposes to buy is held by the vendor on trust for sale. Section 27(2) requires that the capital money arising under a disposition of land held on trust for sale be paid to at least two persons as trustees for sale[11], but goes on to provide in express terms that

> this subsection does not . . . except where capital money arises on the transaction, render it necessary to have more than one trustee.

This provision could be construed as bearing the positive implication that it is indeed necessary to have more than one trustee for sale in relation to those transactions (such as sale and mortgage) on which capital money *is* paid over[12], and that in the absence of at least two trustees any transaction effected must be void at law. However, it is difficult to base so firm a conclusion upon a mere implication from statute. As Professor Bernard Rudden once pointed out, in order to achieve this result in the comparable settled land situation, Parliament obviously felt it necessary to make the express provision contained in section 18(1) of the Settled Land Act 1925[13].

Before we discover the answer to the question which we have just discussed, let us pose the second (and not unrelated) question which arises in this context.

9 See also *Taylor v Taylor (1968)* [1968] 1 WLR 378 at 382 per Danckwerts LJ: '[T]he husband is the owner in law of the property. The effect is that there is a trust for sale, and that the husband can sell as trustee for sale; and indeed the only thing existing in his way in completing the sale . . . is that he will require to appoint a second trustee, so that the two trustees can receive the purchase money and give a good discharge to the purchaser; and the fact that it is in the hands of two trustees is a safeguard to the wife against the husband putting the whole of the proceeds of sale in the bank, or something of that sort, and not giving the wife her share.'

10 See Settled Land Act 1925, s. 18(1)(a); *Weston v Henshaw* [1950] Ch 510, p. 171, ante.

11 See p. 229, ante.

12 See M. J. Prichard (1979) 38 Cambridge LJ 23 at 26, p. 291, post. See also S. M. Clayton [1981] Conv 19: 'Void Mortgages?'

13 (1963) 27 Conv (NS) 51 at 56.

(2) Does a purchaser from a single trustee take free of the beneficial interests behind the trust for sale?

This question is relevant only upon the assumption that a disposition by a single trustee for sale is good at law, for the focus is now placed on the fate of the equitable interests hidden behind the statutory trust for sale. Even if a single trustee is indeed competent to give an effective conveyance of the legal estate—and this would appear to be contrary to some of the arguments mustered above—the purchaser will still have failed, through no fault of his own, to observe the statutory requirements relating to the payment of purchase money. Being unaware of the existence of a trust for sale, he will have paid the money to only one trustee. Quite clearly, in these circumstances no overreaching of the beneficial interests can possibly occur under section 2(1)(ii) of the Law of Property Act 1925. The purchaser has not taken a conveyance from 'trustees for sale' in the plural, as is required by that provision. Is he therefore bound by the equitable interests which have not been overreached? If he is bound by those interests, he will merely have stepped into the shoes of the vendor as a single trustee for sale and he will thereafter hold the legal estate on behalf of himself and any beneficiary whose interest was not overreached.

Now there must be thousands of conveyances completed each year by vendors who are in fact single trustees for sale although neither they nor their purchasers realise this fact. There must be thousands of cases in which purchasers quite innocently pay their purchase money otherwise than in accordance with the conditions of overreaching. The statutory protection afforded the purchaser of land held on trust for sale thus falls to the ground, since no overreaching takes place under the Law of Property Act 1925.

In almost all of these cases, however, the failure to comply with the statutory policy requiring dealings by two trustees makes no difference at all. The single trustee receives the purchase money himself and simply re-invests the proceeds of sale in real property on the same terms as before[14]. The statutory trust for sale of which nobody is aware subsists in the new property. This must occur countless times in the family context, yet nobody is any the wiser. What the parties do not know generally cannot hurt them. Problems arise in reality only if the disposition by the single trustee for sale is in some way dishonest or if he becomes insolvent. Both dishonesty and insolvency tend to afflict the trustees who feature in the case law.

(3) The case law

Caunce v Caunce[15] is a decision worthy of close attention because many of the fundamental principles of unregistered conveyancing emerge both from what

14 The Law Commission has proposed, within the context of a new regime of statutory co-ownership of the matrimonial home, that each spouse should have rights to 'ensure that the other spouse's share of the proceeds of sale of a former home are [sic] used in the acquisition of a new one' (see Law Com No. 86, paras. 1.365ff.). The rights proposed by the Commission in respect of the replacement home were spelt out in the abortive Matrimonial Homes (Co-ownership) Bill 1980, clause 26.

15 [1969] 1 WLR 286. See (1969) 33 Conv (NS) 205 (F. R. Crane).

was said expressly in the judgment and from what was left unsaid. *Caunce* throws much light not only upon the validity of a single trustee's dealing with the legal estate, but also upon the fate of the beneficial interests behind a statutory trust for sale in the event of such a transaction. The case thus provides much valuable guidance which is not found in the Law of Property Act 1925.

In *Caunce v Caunce*, a husband and wife (hereafter referred to as H and W respectively) purchased a house in unregistered land, contributing the purchase moneys unequally. The property was to have been conveyed to H and W as joint tenants at law, but H wrongfully and in breach of the parties' agreement procured that the property should be conveyed to him alone. On the basis of these facts there existed of course a statutory trust for sale of the legal estate, H holding as a single trustee on behalf of H and W as equitable tenants in common in proportion to their contributions of money[16]. Some time after the purchase of the house, which was the parties' matrimonial home, H, acting without the knowledge or acquiescence of W, charged the property by way of legal mortgage in favour of Lloyds Bank Ltd in order to secure a loan of some £1,200. It is inferable that H intended, by means of this mortgage, to extract a portion of the capital value of the house in order to disappear and make a new life with another woman. *Cherchez la femme*! is a principle which illuminates in the area of land law no less than in other areas of life the mainspring of human action and behaviour. In *Caunce* H had gone bankrupt and at the time of the hearing was, in the euphemism applied by the judge, 'in default of appearance'.

Now, in order to understand *Caunce v Caunce*, it is vital to realise that a mortgagee of a legal estate in land stands in the same position as if he had obtained a legal estate itself[17]. The issue in *Caunce* is therefore comparable with that which would have arisen if H had simply sold and conveyed the legal fee simple to a third party purchaser. *Caunce* thus represents an important extension of the *Bull v Bull* situation, for it introduces a third party dimension:

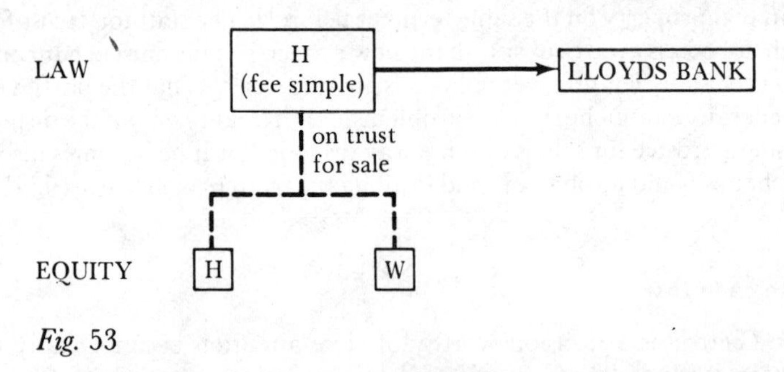

Fig. 53

The contest in *Caunce* concerned two innocent parties, both duped by reason of the dishonesty of a third person. The issue arose effectively between W and Lloyds Bank Ltd, H now being bankrupt. When the facts came to light, the bank

16 H's initial contribution to the purchase price of the house was raised by means of a building society loan for which he was himself responsible.

17 See Law of Property Act 1925, s. 87(1); *Caunce v Caunce* [1969] 1 WLR 286 at 289, p. 533, post.

was aghast to discover that it had lent money on the security of property which (unknown to it) was held on trust for sale. W, on her part, was quite horrified to learn that the house was now mortgaged to the hilt. The issue was simply whether the bank, ranking as a third party purchaser, took priority over the equitable interest which undoubtedly belonged to W behind the statutory trust for sale. In other words, there arose here the old conflict between the owner of an equitable interest and a third party purchaser of a legal estate.

The entire issue in *Caunce* could have been resolved quite easily in favour of W by holding that the mortgage given to the bank by H was void on the ground that a single trustee for sale cannot deal effectively with the legal estate unless he appoints another trustee. Stamp J did not adopt this solution. Instead, he glossed over the absence of a second trustee, appearing to assume that a disposition by a de facto legal owner—albeit a single trustee for sale—is effective at law[18]. This assumption, although possibly in conflict with earlier dicta and even statutory authority[19], reflected however a cogent argument of public policy, since a contrary holding (i.e., that a single trustee's dealings are void) would of course place a third party purchaser in grave jeopardy. The purchaser from an apparently single vendor would in every case be subjected to a quite intolerable burden of enquiry, for in order to take a good legal title he would have to satisfy himself of the non-existence of a trust for sale. How could a purchaser ever prove this negative in relation to a vendor whom he has never seen before and who may well in years past have been the recipient of money contributions creative of an implied trust for sale? The acceptance sub silentio in *Caunce* that a single trustee can deal effectively in respect of a legal estate held on statutory trust for sale simply marks the social and economic importance of the principle that the innocent purchaser of land must be protected[20].

The court in *Caunce* then had to resolve the secondary question as to the effect of the mortgage transaction on W's equitable interest behind the statutory trust for sale. We established long ago[1] that equitable interests in unregistered land are *either* 'commercial' interests protectible by registration of the appropriate land charge *or* 'family' interests protectible in consequence of statutory overreaching.

In *Caunce*, however, W's beneficial interest behind the implied trust for sale

18 See D. G. Barnsley, *Conveyancing Law and Practice* (London 1973), p. 287f.; J. F. Garner, (1969) 33 Conv (NS) 240 at 242f.

19 Michael Prichard has adverted to the fact that, in later cases in registered land, the argument has been put forward that the mortgagee cannot obtain a valid legal title from the husband in this situation since he is a single trustee. 'In the context of unregistered land this argument has some force, and Stamp J's judgment in *Caunce v Caunce* may rightly be criticised for its complete failure to notice the existence of a trust for sale and therefore to deal with the Law of Property Act 1925, ss. 2(1)(ii) and 27(2) and the Trustee Act 1925, s. 14(2). Even in unregistered land the argument can be countered, but in registered land it can have no force at all: the requirement of two trustees for sale is achieved by the entry of a restriction (or caution) on the proprietorship register, and in the absence of such an entry the sole proprietor has the unfettered statutory powers of disposition, so that upon registration the transferee is, by virtue of the Land Registration Act, unassailable' (see (1979) 38 Cambridge LJ 23 at 26).

20 See p. 174, ante; p. 362, post.

1 See p. 72ff., ante.

could not have been protected by registration of any kind of land charge pursuant to the provisions of the Land Charges Act. Nor could W have registered a Class F land charge in respect of statutory 'rights of occupation' in the matrimonial home, since the Matrimonial Homes Act 1967 had not yet been extended to confer such rights upon beneficial co-owners[2]. W did not therefore qualify for the protection normally appropriate for the holders of 'commercial' equitable interests in unregistered land.

On the other hand, however, W could not claim that her beneficial interest had been statutorily overreached and thus translated into an equivalent interest in the capital proceeds arising under the disposition of mortgage effected by H. Those proceeds had not been paid in accordance with the conditions laid down in the Law of Property Act 1925 in respect of overreaching transactions, since the bank had—albeit innocently—advanced the loan money not to two trustees for sale, but to a single trustee[3]. W was therefore unable to argue that her beneficial interest was protected in the manner normally appropriate to 'family' equitable interests in unregistered land.

This being so, Stamp J took the view that the issue of priority between the bank and W turned upon a residual application of the equitable doctrine of notice[4]. Was the bank in the position of a bona fide purchaser of a legal estate for value without notice (actual, constructive or imputed) of W's beneficial interest? In the circumstances, the only doubt centred around the question of constructive notice. Plainly the bank had not had actual notice: if it had had actual notice, it would never have entered into the transaction with H. When it advanced the loan moneys it had no idea that it was dealing with a trustee for sale.

The judgment in *Caunce* was therefore concerned entirely with W's rather desperate attempts to fix the bank with constructive notice of her equitable interest concealed behind the implied trust for sale. She argued, for instance, that the bank was fixed with constructive notice by reason of the fact that her financial contribution towards the purchase of the disputed property had been withdrawn by her from an account at the very same branch of the very same bank which was, five years later, to advance the mortgage moneys to H. The bank, she contended, should have realised that her substantial withdrawals of cash arose in connection with the purchase of the matrimonial home in H's

2 See Matrimonial Homes Act 1967, s. 1(9), as introduced by Matrimonial Proceedings and Property Act 1970, s. 38, p. 144f., ante.

3 See Law of Property Act 1925, s. 27(2).

4 [1969] 1 WLR 286 at 289. See J. F. Garner (1969) 33 Conv (NS) 240: 'A Single Trustee for Sale'. That the issue in this situation becomes ultimately a question of notice has since been confirmed by the Court of Appeal in *Williams & Glyn's Bank Ltd v Boland* [1979] Ch 312 at 330 per Lord Denning MR. Ormrod LJ said (at 334) that implied trusts for sale of the *Caunce* variety 'do not fit easily into the scheme of the Law of Property Act 1925 . . . It certainly seems to leave owners of equitable interests in property under such circumstances with little protection against purchasers for value from the legal proprietor. They do not have the protection of section 2(1)(ii) which requires the purchase money to be paid to two trustees, because there is only a single trustee. The result is that unless it can be shown in the case of unregistered land that the purchaser took with notice, actual or constructive, . . . they are left to their remedies, for what they are worth, against the single trustee.'

name and that she was therefore a tenant in common in the equitable ownership in that property.

Stamp J rejected this argument in forthright terms, refusing to accept that the bank came under any duty of enquiry such as that proposed by W. To hold otherwise, thought Stamp J, would 'be to place on the bank an intolerable burden and would stretch the doctrine of constructive notice to a point beyond its proper limits[5].' He did not

> find the suggestion that a bank mortgagee should, at its peril, be bound to conduct an enquiry into the financial relations between husband and wife before it can advance money on security of property vested in the husband, at all an attractive one . . . [I]n this day and age husbands and wives ought to be able to bank at the same bank without having their accounts analysed by the bank in order to find out whether one of them is deceiving the other. The exercise which, it is submitted, ought to have been conducted in the present case would, it seems to me, have been more appropriate to a police enquiry or that of a detective agency than to a bank manager who no doubt often arranges advances daily in the ordinary course of business. And one may ask the rhetorical question, 'At what point are such enquiries to end?' Such enquiries, perhaps, lie within a small compass in the case of a country branch of a bank but would assume a most complicated and difficult character when embarked on in a bank which carries many thousands of accounts. Is the bank, being uncertain how the borrower can have found the money, to search not only his wife's account but also, perhaps, his father's account?[6]

W then contended that her own occupation of the matrimonial home at the time of the mortgage transaction was sufficient to fix the bank with constructive notice of any interest which she might have. However, Stamp J rejected this argument too, on the ground that W's cohabitation with H (who at this point had not yet absconded) had been 'wholly consistent with the sole title offered by the husband to the bank[7].' W had not been 'in apparent occupation or possession' since she had been present in the matrimonial home 'ostensibly because she was the husband's wife . . .' In other words, Stamp J implied, the bank was perfectly entitled to conclude that W was in occupation simply because she was married to the apparent owner, H. It is not unusual, even in these days, that a wife should actually live with her husband, and there was in the fact of joint occupation nothing so remarkable as reasonably to cause the bank to suspect that W was in residence not merely qua dutiful wife but also qua beneficial owner[8].

The bank therefore took priority over the beneficial interest of W. We shall return later to the general issue of joint occupation of a family home and its significance under the doctrine of notice[9]. However, we must first note several important implications which flow from the judgment of Stamp J in *Caunce*.

(4) The larger implications of Caunce v Caunce

The decision of Stamp J in *Caunce v Caunce* is redolent with implications for the

5 [1969] 1 WLR 286 at 291.
6 [1969] 1 WLR 286 at 292.
7 [1969] 1 WLR 286 at 293.
8 See B. Rudden (1963) 27 Conv (NS) 51 at 57ff.
9 See p. 299, post.

way in which property lawyers look at issues of priority in land law. The judgment of Stamp J—from which no appeal was ever made—conceals a number of important premises which are but obliquely expressed in the conclusions which that judge reached.

The judgment in *Caunce v Caunce* constitutes a typical expression of the hard-headed conveyancer's view of a key issue of priority in the land law context. As such, *Caunce v Caunce*, together with the social and economic assumptions upon which it builds, belongs to the ideological world of the *Gesellschaft*, to which reference has already been made[10]. The decision reflects the characteristic preference which the *Gesellschaft* displays in favour of facility for purchasers rather than in favour of security for those who own fragments of benefit. It elevates the 'exchange value' of property as distinct from the 'use value' of that property, by giving expression at every point to the importance of facilitating transactions in land, of reducing the burdens placed on purchasers and of protecting innocent third parties from the claims of undetected (and equally innocent) beneficial incumbrancers. It gives effect to the traditional view of the property lawyer that 'where the ethics are equal the purchaser should prevail, for the policy of the law is to favour alienability and clean titles[11].'

This emphasis upon ensuring the free alienability of title found expression in two ways in the judgment of Stamp J. First, he relied heavily upon the familiar dictum uttered by Lord Upjohn in *National Provincial Bank Ltd v Hastings Car Mart Ltd*[12] to the effect that

> It has been the policy of the law for over a hundred years to simplify and facilitate transactions in real property. It is of great importance that persons should be able freely and easily to raise money on the security of their property[13].

It was this consideration which, in large measure persuaded Stamp J to conclude that the bank was under no duty of enquiry into the details of the wife's bank account for the purpose of ascertaining whether she had provided part of the purchase price of the house titled in the name of her husband. To add the burden of this kind of enquiry to the already heavy duties imposed upon institutional lenders would be counter-productive and here emerges an important lesson from *Caunce v Caunce*. In *Caunce*, the bank won and the wife lost—a forceful demonstration of the useful rule of thumb that banks seldom lose cases!

A cogent element of policy underlies this rule of thumb. It is unlikely that banks or other lending institutions would be so ready to lend money on the security of real property if the law imposed added risks upon the entirely innocent mortgagee[14]. The bulk of housing finance in this country is provided by banks, building societies and local authorities[15], and there is little doubt that the availability of credit for the purpose of financing home-ownership would be

10 See p. 16f., ante.
11 H. W. R. Wade (1956) 14 Cambridge LJ 216 at 219: 'Land Charge Registration Reviewed'.
12 [1965] AC 1175 at 1233f., p. 54, ante.
13 [1969] 1 WLR 286 at 292.
14 Ante, 54; post, 376f.
15 See p. 509, post.

adversely affected by the imposition of onerous legal liability upon the lender[16]. It was this persuasive policy consideration—never made wholly explicit in the judgment in *Caunce*—which caused Stamp J to relegate the wife to a purely nominal remedy *in personam* (for breach of trust) against her absent and insolvent husband.

Precisely the same policy consideration influenced Stamp J to decline to extend the doctrine of constructive notice against the interests of the bank in *Caunce*. It is widely acknowledged that

> in a society accepting free alienability of proprietary rights, there is a general interest in an efficient market. This requires that a purchaser should be able to ascertain easily and cheaply the existence and scope of the incumbrance on any land[17].

The corollary of this view is that a purchaser of land should not be held bound by constructive notice of any incumbrance which is not easily detectable. Any other approach would destroy the object of facility for purchasers which underlies the commercial ethic of the exchange economy. Doubtless with this consideration in mind, Stamp J cited with approval the passage in *Hunt v Luck*[18], where Farwell J pointed quite firmly to the fact that the

> doctrine of constructive notice, imputing as it does knowledge which the person affected does not actually possess, is one which the courts of late years have been unwilling to extend[19].

The *Gesellschaft* character of the judgment in *Caunce v Caunce* was evidenced in two further ways. The first relates to the view adopted by Stamp J in relation to the wife's response to her husband's dishonest dealing with the legal estate in the matrimonial home. The *Gesellschaft* accentuates and rewards the role of rational calculation and purposive economic deliberation in the conduct of human (and particularly commercial) affairs. The *Gesellschaft* represents a world of self-determining individuals each of whom jealously safeguards and promotes his own interests in competition with everybody else. Indeed, perhaps the most distinctive feature of the *Gesellschaft* is its expectation that all will act in the aggressive pursuit of self-interest and its confidence that the process of unrestrained competition and unregulated exchange will conduce inevitably to the common good[20].

This being so, it is not surprising that Stamp J was not particularly impressed by the way in which the wife in *Caunce* had allowed matters to get out of hand. H and W had agreed initially that the matrimonial home should be conveyed into joint names, but H had wrongfully procured a conveyance into his name alone. It seems that W quickly became aware of H's wrongful action, but did not seek to have the property re-conveyed into joint names. In view of W's passivity, Stamp J was even less inclined to extend the doctrine of constructive notice so

16 See *Multiservice Bookbinding Ltd v Marden* [1979] Ch 84 at 105, where in a different context Browne-Wilkinson J made the point that it 'would surely not be in the public interest' that the 'availability of loan capital' should be diminished.
17 G. Woodman (1980) 96 LQR 336 at 340.
18 [1901] 1 Ch 45 at 48, p. 56, ante.
19 [1969] 1 WLR 286 at 291f.
20 See p. 126, ante.

as to fasten liability upon the bank. He refused to hold the bank subject to any duty of enquiry in relation to a wife who 'knew almost at the outset that the property was in the sole name of the husband and had taken no step to assert her rights[1].' The view clearly expressed here is a strong reluctance (as is typical of the *Gesellschaft* framework of values) to help someone who manifestly cannot help herself. The fact that a wife may—perhaps unwisely and indeed foolishly—have trusted her husband is entirely discounted. In the world of the *Gesellschaft* there is no place for emotion, loyalty or the more integrative aspects of human behaviour. The *Gesellschaft* is an impersonal, contract-based society which is heavily responsive to the mercenary incentives of the world of the exchange economy.

A further (and not unrelated) *Gesellschaft* feature of the judgment in *Caunce v Caunce* is apparent in the way in which Stamp J dealt with one of the arguments which W advanced in the hope of fixing the bank with constructive notice of her equitable interest behind the implied statutory trust for sale. In the forefront of W's argument was the point that

> today when so many matrimonial homes are purchased out of moneys provided in part by the wife, a purchaser ... who finds the matrimonial home vested in one of these spouses, more particularly in this case a husband, is put on enquiry whether the other spouse has an equitable interest in the property and .. if he does not enquire of the other spouse whether such an interest is claimed, he takes subject to the interest[2].

To this argument Stamp J was predictably unsympathetic. He observed that 'as a bare proposition of law no authority has been cited for that proposition', and held that 'in view of the disinclination of the courts to extend the doctrine of constructive notice (see *Hunt v Luck*)' he was not prepared to accept it. He pointed out that

> counsel for the bank ... has called attention to the fact that this is a conveyancing question, and I accept the point ... that in such a matter the practice of conveyancers carries great weight. I have never heard it suggested, and no textbook or judicial utterance has been cited which suggests, that where one finds a vendor and his wife living together on the property a prudent solicitor acting for the purchaser ought to enquire of the wife whether she claims an interest in the house. Counsel for the bank also points out ... how unworkable and undesirable it would be if the law required such an enquiry—an enquiry, let me add, which would be as embarrassing to the enquirer as it would be, in my view, intolerable to the wife and the husband. Counsel for the bank put it well when ... he said that it is not in the public interest that bank mortgagees should be snoopers and busybodies in relation to wholly normal transactions of mortgages[3].

The judgment in *Caunce v Caunce* belongs to the days in which it was virtually conclusive of any issue of priority in land law to declare the question to be essentially a problem of conveyancing or banking practice. The importance of ensuring facility for third party purchasers or of preserving security for a commercial interest outweighed any argument which could be advanced in favour of residential protection for the family. As happens consistently under

1 [1969] 1 WLR 286 at 290.
2 [1969] 1 WLR 286 at 289.
3 [1969] 1 WLR 286 at 294.

the regime of bourgeois individualism extolled by the *Gesellschaft*, the money interest was allowed in *Caunce v Caunce* to prevail over the interest of the family as a social entity.

In such matters, however, developments occur apace, and it may well be that the value judgments expressed in *Caunce v Caunce* are no longer valid in the 1980s. We shall discover that it is now almost certain that a purchaser *cannot* afford to ignore the possibility that both spouses enjoy some beneficial interest in the matrimonial home[4].

(5) The limitations of Caunce v Caunce

Caunce v Caunce thus establishes that the purchaser of unregistered land who pays the capital moneys arising under any disposition to only one trustee for sale takes the legal estate free from the beneficial interests behind any statutory trust for sale affecting the land if, at the time of the disposition, he had no notice (actual or constructive) of the existence of the trust. It is, however, vitally important to realise that the decision in *Caunce* is subject to certain limitations.

(a) *No application to express trusts for sale*

It is quite clear that the ruling in *Caunce v Caunce* has no application whatsoever to *express* trusts for sale of the matrimonial home. If a matrimonial home is expressly vested in one or more persons 'on trust for sale', it is impossible for any third party to disclaim notice of the trust affecting the property. In the case of property so clearly held on trust for sale, the purchaser must take his conveyance from, and pay the purchase money to, at least two trustees. If he finds that he is dealing with a single trustee for sale, he must demand the appointment of a second trustee. The purchaser's protection lies in his ability to claim that he has statutorily overreached the beneficial interests behind the trust for sale, and he will be unable to claim this protection unless he has paid the purchase money arising in the manner required by statute. If the purchaser continues to deal with merely a single trustee for sale, in the face of an express trust for sale, he will not overreach the equities behind the trust but will take subject to them. And if he does not deal with all of the existing trustees for sale (i.e., where the legal title is already vested in two or more joint tenants), he will not even receive a good conveyance *at law*, since an effective disposition of a jointly held legal title requires the active participation of all the joint tenants[5].

(b) *No application to a wife in sole occupation of the matrimonial home*

In *Caunce v Caunce*, Stamp J pointed out very firmly that on the facts of the case W had been living with H in the matrimonial home at the time of the mortgage transactions effected by H. He concluded, as we have seen, that her presence on the property was in no way inconsistent with the sole title offered by the

4 See p. 367, post.
5 See p. 237, ante.

mortgagor to the bank. In such a case, the vendor/mortgagor being in possession, the presence of his wife

> implies nothing to negative the title offered. It is otherwise if the vendor is not in occupation and one finds another party whose presence demands an explanation and whose presence one ignores at one's peril[6].

It would seem then that the ruling in *Caunce v Caunce* has no relevance to the situation where the vendor/mortgagor is not himself in occupation at the date of the disposition in question, since then the presence on the property of another person who turns out to be a beneficial co-owner would indeed be inconsistent with the sole title offered. If, in such a case, the purchaser pays the capital moneys arising to an absent single legal owner, he presumably takes the legal title subject to all equitable interests (other than that of the vendor) which subsisted behind the implied trust for sale.

(6) Class F land charges and the Caunce v Caunce situation

In dealing with the judgment of Stamp J in *Caunce v Caunce*, we noted that W could not have been expected to register a Class F land charge in respect of statutory 'rights of occupation' under the Matrimonial Homes Act 1967[7]. No question was raised in *Caunce* as to the possibility of such a registration, simply because at the time of that decision in 1969 the Matrimonial Homes Act 1967 had not yet been extended to confer 'rights of occupation' upon a beneficial co-owner behind a trust for sale. It was for this reason that, in the absence of an overreaching disposition by H, the issue of priority between W and the bank turned on the application of the traditional doctrine of notice.

The scope of the Matrimonial Homes Act 1967 was extended in 1970, however, partly in response to the decision in *Caunce* which relegated the interest of the wife/beneficiary in the matrimonial home and gave priority instead to the bank mortgagee[8]. The result of this legislative amendment is that in the *Caunce* situation today W would be entitled to register her statutory 'rights of occupation' as a Class F land charge. How would the availability of this new form of protection affect the resolution of the *Caunce* problem?

It is one of the ironies of legislative progress that the amendment of the Matrimonial Homes Act in 1970 almost certainly puts the wife in *Caunce* in no

6 [1969] 1 WLR 286 at 294.
7 See p. 144, ante.
8 Matrimonial Proceedings and Property Act 1970, s. 38, introducing Matrimonial Homes Act 1967, s. 1(9), p. 144, ante. See Law Commission, *Report on Financial Provision in Matrimonial Proceedings* (Law Com No. 25, July 1969), para. 60: '. . . our foregoing recommendation regarding registration of a right of occupation under the 1967 Act will help to clarify the position and will, we think, preserve a proper balance between purchasers and mortgagees on the one hand and the spouse on the other. If the property concerned is the matrimonial home the spouse will be able to protect his or her right of occupation by registration with the result that there will not be a sale or mortgage without his or her consent. If the property concerned is not the matrimonial home or if, though it is the matrimonial home, there has been no registration, the purchaser or mortgagee will be protected so long as he acts in good faith and will not be put on notice of the rights of the other spouse.'

better a position today than she enjoyed before that amendment was introduced. In all probability, the wife will never have heard of a Class F land charge, and her statutory 'rights of occupation' will therefore be void against a third party for want of registration[9]. However, a wife/beneficiary's statutory 'rights of occupation' in the matrimonial home are quite distinct from her beneficial interest in the home itself. The 'rights of occupation' are conferred upon her by statute in virtue of her beneficial co-ownership behind the implied trust for sale. In other words, her 'rights of occupation' are derived from, and are parasitic upon, her beneficial interest as an equitable tenant in common[10]. Thus, although she cannot rely as against a third party purchaser upon her statutory 'rights of occupation' (since they are void for non-registration), she can nevertheless stake her claim to protection against the third party purchaser upon the basis of her equitable interest behind the trust. However, this is simply to reduce the issue of priority once more to the question posed in *Caunce v Caunce*, for that issue will still rest ultimately upon whether the purchaser, in transacting with a single trustee for sale, was fixed with actual or constructive notice of the wife's beneficial interest.

(7) Joint occupation and the issue of constructive notice

Since it now seems clear that priority as between beneficiary and purchaser from a single statutory trustee for sale of unregistered land depends ultimately upon the doctrine of notice, it becomes paramountly important to know how that doctrine will operate in the context of joint or multiple occupation of the property held on the statutory trusts.

In *Caunce v Caunce*[11], Stamp J held that the mere presence of a wife/beneficiary in joint occupation of the matrimonial home with the husband/vendor was in itself insufficient to fix a third party with constructive notice of her beneficial interest behind the statutory trust for sale. The wife's presence on the property was perfectly explicable—from the point of view of the purchaser—on the basis of her relationship with the husband/vendor. Joint occupation in a family context did not carry any necessary implication for third parties to the effect that the wife was beneficially entitled. Her presence in the matrimonial home was 'wholly consistent with the sole title offered' by her husband.

This approach was, of course, enough to dispose of the claim made by the wife in *Caunce* to priority over the mortgage taken by the bank. Significantly, however, Stamp J went further and opined that there might well be other persons whose joint occupation of the land with the vendor/mortgagor would in itself be insufficient to fix a purchaser with constructive notice of such rights as they might have behind a statutory trust for sale. In the judgment of Stamp J,

> where the vendor or mortgagor is himself in possession and occupation of the property, the purchaser or the mortgagee is not affected with notice of the equitable interests of any

9 Land Charges Act 1972, s. 4(8); see *Williams & Glyn's Bank Ltd v Boland* [1979] Ch 312 at 328 per Lord Denning MR, p. 148f., ante.
10 See p. 145, ante.
11 [1969] 1 WLR 286 at 293.

other person who may be resident there, and whose presence is wholly consistent with the title offered. If one buys with vacant possession on completion and one knows or finds out that the vendor is himself in possession and occupation of the property, one is, . . . by reason of one's failure to make further enquiries on the premises, no more fixed with notice of the equitable interest of the vendor's wife who is living there with him than one would be affected with notice of the equitable interest of any other person who might also be resident on the premises, e.g., the vendor's father, his Uncle Harry or his Aunt Matilda, any of whom, be it observed, might have contributed money towards the purchase of the property. The reason is that the vendor being in possession, the presence of his wife or guest or lodger implies nothing to negative the title offered[12].

Stamp J seemed here to imply that there may be many categories of person whose joint occupation of property is perfectly explicable on the basis of family relationship, and whose presence is not sufficiently remarkable to put a purchaser on enquiry as to the possibility of their beneficial entitlement. The observations made by Stamp J tend heavily, of course, towards increased protection for the purchaser from a single trustee for sale at the expense of the beneficiaries behind that trust, even though they be in actual occupation of the land. It is chiefly in this respect that the dicta in *Caunce* have been subjected to considerable criticism in more recent cases.

Hodgson v Marks[13] concerned the proper construction of 'actual occupation' for the purpose of section 70(1)(g) of the Land Registration Act 1925[14]. In delivering the judgment of the Court of Appeal, Russell LJ adverted to *Caunce v Caunce*, and remarked that he could not accept a 'general proposition that enquiry need not be made of any person on the premises if the proposed vendor himself appears to be in occupation.' Insofar as 'some phrases in the judgment' of Stamp J might have appeared to lay down such a proposition, Russell LJ was unwilling to agree, although he said that it was not necessary to the decision in *Hodgson v Marks* to 'pronounce on the decision in *Caunce v Caunce*.' In *Caunce*'s case, the occupation of the wife 'may have been rightly taken to be not her occupation but that of her husband[15].' No strict rule could be laid down, but Russell LJ added slightly ominously that the issue 'must depend on the circumstances, and a wise purchaser or lender will take no risks.'

The clear implication arising from these dicta is that there may well be occasions when the mere presence of a wife, parent, relative (or indeed common law wife) is incompatible with the sole title proffered by the vendor/trustee, and that joint occupation by such persons may, as a matter of law, fix a third party in the unregistered land context with constructive notice of the beneficial interests behind a statutory trust for sale. However, everything will depend upon the facts of each case, always bearing in mind the courts' known reluctance to extend the scope of constructive notice[16].

Similar doubts were expressed in *Williams & Glyn's Bank Ltd v Boland*[17] as to

12 [1969] 1 WLR 286 at 293f.
13 [1971] Ch 892, p. 339, post.
14 See p. 334, post.
15 [1971] Ch 892 at 935.
16 See *Hunt v Luck* [1901] 1 Ch 45 (Farwell J); affd. [1902] 1 Ch 428, CA, p. 295, ante.
17 [1979] Ch 312, CA; affd. [1980] 3 WLR 138, HL, p. 270, ante; p. 353, post.

whether the duty of enquiry incumbent upon a purchaser is really as restricted in scope as Stamp J's judgment in *Caunce v Caunce* seemed to indicate. Although *Boland* again concerned issues in registered land, Lord Denning MR took the general view that 'anyone who lends money on the security of a matrimonial home nowadays ought to realise that the wife may have a share in it[18].' Ormrod LJ noted the doubt expressed in *Hodgson v Marks* as to the correctness of Stamp J's reasoning in *Caunce*. He thought it unnecessary for the purpose of *Boland* to decide 'whether a purchaser in 1979 of an ordinary house, occupied by a couple, is or is not affected with notice of the wife's equitable rights if he makes no inquiry of her.' However, it is significant that Ormrod LJ went on to observe that

> It is sufficient to say from experience in another division of this court that the changes in attitude towards the property rights of wives as a result of the Matrimonial Proceedings and Property Act 1970 seem so marked and so widespread that if *Caunce v Caunce* had to be decided today the result might have been different[19].

The House of Lords in *Boland* likewise declined to overrule *Caunce*, on the ground that *Caunce* had been concerned with unregistered land. However, Lord Wilberforce stated his agreement with the disapproval expressed of *Caunce* in the judgment of Russell LJ in *Hodgson v Marks*[20]. Lord Scarman indicated even more strongly that he was 'by no means certain that *Caunce v Caunce* was correctly decided[1].' Furthermore, the entire tenor of the House of Lords' decision tended to suggest that there are persons whose joint occupation with a vendor, although not apparent from the title, will bind a purchaser on the basis, in registered land, of 'actual occupation', and, in unregistered land, of constructive notice of their rights. Lord Wilberforce, in particular, seemed to envisage that the persons falling within this category might well include not merely a wife/beneficiary (as in *Boland* itself), but also 'other members of the [vendor's] family or even outside it[2].'

In the final analysis it remains unclear which kinds of beneficiary behind a statutory trust for sale are capable of fixing a third party with constructive notice by reason merely of their joint occupation of unregistered land. The strong implication flowing from the obiter dicta in *Williams & Glyn's Bank Ltd v Boland* is that the presence of a de iure wife will be sufficient for this purpose. Although *Boland* was concerned with registered land, it is scarcely conceivable that the courts would apply the doctrine of constructive notice in unregistered land to produce different results on so important an issue from those arrived at in the construction of 'actual occupation' in the registered land context in *Boland*.

Whether the same will apply to joint occupation by other members of a domestic *ménage* (e.g., relatives, children, de facto wives or even—for that

18 [1979] Ch 312 at 332.
19 [1979] Ch 312 at 335. See also the discussion of the Matrimonial Proceedings and Property Act 1970—now consolidated in the Matrimonial Causes Act 1973, p. 563, post.
20 [1980] 3 WLR 138 at 144.
1 [1980] 3 WLR 138 at 149.
2 [1980] 3 WLR 138 at 147, p. 376f., post.

matter—homosexual partners) is less clear[3]. It is perhaps not without significance that, in addressing himself to equivalent problems in the registered land context, in *Boland*, Ormrod LJ observed that the arguments bearing upon the issue would be 'exactly the same if [the beneficial co-owners] were not married or were of the same sex as the legal proprietors[4].' In other words, the marriage relationship which was present in *Boland* was actually 'incidental', since the appellant wives relied 'not upon their position as married women, but upon their property rights as ordinary citizens.' When it is asked whose presence in jointly occupied property is sufficient to fix third parties with constructive notice, the real answer is that occupation will be protected in the case of those persons whose residential security is generally recognised as having a claim to social (and therefore legal) priority. It is ultimately a social calculus which decides the issue. Social arguments mould the law, by defining the categories of persons whose residential protection has become a matter of overriding social interest. The decision of the House of Lords in *Williams & Glyn's Bank Ltd v Boland* was, at its roots, a statement of social ethics about the importance of protecting the occupation of the married woman in the matrimonial home. It can be anticipated that the courts will similarly endorse the claims to residential security presented by such joint occupiers as the de facto wife, Uncle Harry, Aunt Matilda, and the ageing parent—all of whom have acquired beneficiary status behind implied trusts by virtue of small contributions to the purchase, extension or improvement of the vendor's house. (The numbers of old people are expected to increase during the 1980s and 1990s, and the phenomenon of multiple occupation may well acquire a new significance as the extended family re-groups in order to pool resources in the face of the economic adversity, housing shortage and scarcity of fuel predicted for those years.) But will the same protection be accorded to homosexual cohabitees or the participants in a freewheeling commune located somewhere in suburbia?

It is at such points that it becomes most clearly apparent that the law of property is but a complex index of changing perceptions and evaluations of social relationship. The law of property is concerned ultimately not with property but with people and their interactions. It mirrors fairly accurately the way in which a community defines its culture and values. The law of property has as much to say about the social rules regulating family or domestic relationships as will ever be found in the area of law known traditionally as 'family law'. In the world of social reality, it is for instance vastly more significant that various types of family structure or domestic relationship be recognised for the purpose of fixing a purchaser with constructive notice of beneficial rights than that those forms of familial organisation receive some abstract approval as officially endorsed or publicly legitimated modes of social relation. In other words, the 'real law' about de facto relationships or kinship networks or homosexual partnerships is sometimes to be found not in books on family law, but deeply secreted in the interstices of the law relating to trusts for

3 See J. Martin [1980] Conv 361 at 371f.: 'Section 70(1)(g) and the Vendor's Spouse'.

4 [1979] Ch 312 at 333. See also a similar statement in the House of Lords by Lord Wilberforce ([1980] 3 WLR 138 at 141).

sale or the law relating to residential tenancies. Black-letter law but thinly conceals an instructive world of social insights.

(8) The Law Commission's proposals

We have already seen that the Law Commission has proposed its own remedy for the problems disclosed in the single legal owner trust for sale. In the view taken by the Law Commission, it should be open to a beneficiary behind such a trust of the matrimonial home to protect his interest against third parties by registering a Class G land charge[5]. Such a registration would ensure that the land held on trust for sale could not be disposed of without the consent of the registering beneficiary. The Law Commission believed that the imposition of such a 'consent requirement' would effectively confer upon the registering spouse a 'right of control'. The registration of a Class G charge would moreover amount to the registration of that spouse's beneficial interest under the trust for sale[6]. Thereafter it would not be open to any third party to disclaim notice of that beneficial interest, and the only way in which the third party could overreach the beneficial interest would be by compliance with the 'two trustee rule[7],' i.e., by paying the capital moneys arising to at least two trustees and thereby acquiring the benefit of the statutory overreaching provisions of the Law of Property Act 1925[8]. Thus, by providing the facility of registration, the Law Commission hoped to overcome the 'main shortcoming' of the 'two trustee rule', which it identified as the fact that the rule 'does not apply at all unless the purchaser has notice . . . of the trust[9].'

We have already noted that one of the principal drawbacks in the Law Commission's complicated proposals is precisely the point that protection for the beneficiary requires a positive act of registration[10]. It is, however, interesting that the Law Commission also dealt more specifically with the actual problem which arose in *Caunce v Caunce*—the problem not of an 'acquisition mortgage' but of a 'further advance' made by a lender on the security of the matrimonial home perhaps many years after the acquisition of that home.

The Law Commission observed that the form of protection which it proposed generally for the beneficiary in relation to dealings by a single trustee for sale could not apply effectively in this instance. The consent requirement of a spouse/beneficiary could be safeguarded by registration of a Class G charge, but the Law Commission agreed that where a single trustee sought a further advance

5 See p. 150, ante.
6 See *Third Report on Family Property: The Matrimonial Home (Co-ownership and Occupation Rights) and Household Goods* (Law Com No. 86, June 1978), paras. 1.318ff.
7 Ibid., para. 1.320.
8 See Law of Property Act 1925, ss. 2(1)(ii), 27(2).
9 Law Com. No. 86, para. 1.251. The Law Commission's Report was issued in 1978 before the matter in *Williams & Glyn's Bank Ltd v Boland* went to the Court of Appeal and House of Lords. It is interesting that the Law Commission stated with reference to *Caunce v Caunce* that 'on balance we incline to the view that the mere presence of a wife is probably not enough, under the present law, to put a purchaser upon enquiry.' (Law Com No. 86, para. 1.252).
10 See p. 151, ante.

secured on the matrimonial home the registration mechanism would prove unwieldy. If, for instance, a single trustee obtained overdraft facilities from a bank on the security of his matrimonial home, 'the bank could not reasonably be required to make a search [of the register] every time a cheque was presented[11].'

The Law Commission therefore suggested that in the case of a further advance the lender should be affected by failure to obtain the consent of the spouse/beneficiary if *either* that spouse's consent had been required for the original mortgage and had been duly obtained *or* notice in writing was served on the lender by that spouse stating that his consent was required[12]. Furthermore, the Law Commission proposed that a lender should, in making a further advance in breach of the 'two trustee rule', be affected by the beneficial interest of a spouse if the lender had 'effective notice' of that spouse's interest. 'Effective notice' could arise *either* on the ground that the original mortgage itself had failed to overreach the beneficial interest in question or the lender had knowledge that the original mortgage had been granted by two or more persons, *or* on the ground of a written notice served on the lender by the spouse/beneficiary stating that the mortgaged property was held on trust[13]. Thus, if a lender had 'effective notice' of a spouse's beneficial interest, and nonetheless paid the advance in breach of the 'two trustee rule', the mortgage, in so far as it secured the advance, would not in the Law Commission's view overreach the interest in question[14].

It is a fact of legislative history that the Law Commission's proposals came to nothing when the Matrimonial Homes (Co-ownership) Bill 1980 failed to secure its passage through Parliament.

12. TERMINATION OF CO-OWNERSHIP

We have in this chapter dealt at some length with the creation and operation of co-ownership of land. We must now look at the ways in which co-ownership (whether in the form of joint tenancy or tenancy in common) comes to an end. Co-ownership may be terminated altogether by the following means:

(1) Partition

The unity of possession which is essential to both joint tenancy and tenancy in common is destroyed if the co-owned land is physically divided up or partitioned among the individual co-owners. Under section 28(3) of the Law of Property Act 1925, trustees for sale are now given power to effect a partition with the consent of their beneficiaries and to convey to each his separate portion of the realty. If the trustees or any of the beneficiaries refuse to consent to a partition, it is open to any person interested to approach the court under section 30 of the

11 Law Com No. 86, para. 1.351.
12 Ibid., paras. 1.352f.
13 Ibid., paras. 1.359ff.
14 Ibid., para. 1.362.

Law of Property Act 1925, in which case the court may make 'such order as it thinks fit[15].' After partition takes place, there can be no co-ownership: there is merely separate ownership of the individual parcels of land which once formed the co-owned realty.

(2) Union of the property in one joint tenant

Co-ownership clearly ends if one joint tenant releases his joint interest to the only other joint tenant[16]. The same effect follows if one of two joint tenants dies without having effected a severance in equity[17]. The entire interest at law and in equity survives to the remaining joint tenant. The trust for sale which previously gave effect to the co-ownership terminates, and the interest held by the survivor becomes realty rather than personalty[18]. Moreover, it is expressly provided by section 36(2) of the Law of Property Act 1925 that

> Nothing in this Act affects the right of a survivor of joint tenants, who is solely and beneficially interested, to deal with his legal estate as if it were not held on trust for sale.

There is, however, a practical difficulty here. The survivor is faced with the problem that if he should ever try to sell the property, his purchaser will require clear proof that the deceased joint tenant did not sever in equity before his death. The fact of a pre-existing joint tenancy will, of course, be obvious from the face of the vendor's title deeds, and the vendor is thus put effectively on proof of a negative.

The survivor could always circumvent the difficulty in which he finds himself by appointing another trustee to act with him in giving an overreaching conveyance to the purchaser. However, legislation has intervened to spare the surviving joint tenant both the inconvenience of such a step and the possibility that he might otherwise be required to discharge a quite impossible onus of proof in respect of suspected severance by the deceased joint tenant. Under section 1(1) of the Law of Property (Joint Tenants) Act 1964, the surviving joint tenant is deemed to be solely and beneficially entitled if he conveys as 'beneficial owner' or if the conveyance contains a statement that he is so interested. The 1964 Act has no application to registered land[19], and is moreover ineffective in relation to unregistered land if a memorandum of severance has already been attached to the title deeds[20]. In all other cases, however, it is safe for a purchaser to rely upon the presumption brought into being by the Act.

15 See p. 274, ante.
16 In strict terms, a joint tenant has no interest with which he can deal unilaterally at law. However, the Law of Property Act 1925 permits a joint tenant to 'release' his interest (see Law of Property Act 1925, s. 36(2)), and even makes provision for him to 'convey' it to another joint tenant (see Law of Property Act 1925, s. 72(4)).
17 For the meaning of 'severance' see p. 306, post.
18 *Re Cook* [1948] Ch 212.
19 Law of Property (Joint Tenants) Act 1964, s. 3.
20 Law of Property (Joint Tenants) Act 1964, s. 1(1)(a). On the 1964 Act, see (1964) 28 Conv (NS) 329; (1966) 30 Conv (NS) 27 (P. Jackson).

(3) Conveyance of the property to a single third party

Co-ownership of any kind clearly ends if the co-owners convey their land to a single third party. That third party takes the land free of the trusts if he pays the purchase moneys to two trustees. Of course, conveyance of the land to more than one purchaser will create a new trust for sale, as will conveyance to a single purchaser where two or more persons contribute the purchase moneys[1].

13. SEVERANCE

Severance is simply the term given to one specific method by which joint tenancy may be brought to an end. It connotes the conversion of joint tenancy into tenancy in common[2]. Certain acts or events cause the undifferentiated co-ownership of joint tenancy to crystallise into co-ownership in distinct undivided shares.

Historically the common law has been quite willing to mitigate the hazards of survivorship by allowing severance to occur fairly easily. For the purpose of common law severance the consent of the other joint tenant or joint tenants is not required, and severance may in this sense be quite unilateral. The only restriction upon the availability of severance is the rule that severance can be effected only inter vivos: there can be no severance by will.

Before 1926 there used to be a form of joint tenancy between husband and wife known as 'tenancy by entireties'. This form of co-ownership was effectively an unseverable joint tenancy which reflected the indivisible unity of husband and wife. Tenancies by entireties were abolished on 1 January 1926, being converted automatically into joint tenancies[3]. There has, however, been a more recent attempt to impose restrictions on the availability of severance in relation to property jointly owned by husband and wife. In *Bedson v Bedson*[4], a deserting wife sought a court order for the sale of the jointly owned matrimonial home. The Court of Appeal refused to order sale. Lord Denning MR, whose sympathies in the matter lay clearly with the husband, argued that neither spouse could sever the equitable interest unilaterally:

> So long as the house is in the possession of the husband and wife as joint tenants or one of them, there can be no severance of their equitable interests . . . Neither of them can sell his or her equitable interest separately. If he or she could do so, it would mean that the purchaser could insist on going into possession himself—with the other spouse there—which is absurd. It would mean also that one of them could, of his own head, destroy the right of survivorship which was the essence of the joint tenancy. That cannot be right[5].

In coming to this conclusion, Lord Denning purported to rely on section 36(1), (3) of the Law of Property Act 1925, although those provisions appear to

1 See *Bull v Bull* [1955] 1 QB 234, p. 256, ante.
2 See p. 234ff., ante.
3 Law of Property Act 1925, Sch. 1, Part VI.
4 [1965] 2 QB 666.
5 [1965] 2 QB 666 at 678.

be irrelevant to the proposition put forward[6]. His view was in accord with statements made in other cases which imply that a beneficiary in possession of land has a *right* of occupation or at least a right not to have that occupation prejudiced by the intervention of any third party[7]. However, Lord Denning's novel proposition as to the severability of joint tenancy between husband and wife provoked an outspoken disagreement within the Court of Appeal in *Bedson v Bedson.* Russell LJ professed himself

> unable to accept the legal proposition of Lord Denning MR ... The proposition is, I think, without the slightest foundation in law or in equity. If anything, it appears to be an attempt to revive to some extent the long defunct tenancy by entireties ...[8]

By far the better view nowadays is that Lord Denning's statement in *Bedson v Bedson* is heretical and that there are no restrictions upon unilateral severance of the equitable interest in a matrimonial home[9]. As Russell LJ said in *Bedson v Bedson*[10], it is 'inherent in the nature of the beneficial interest created that either joint tenant may sever at any time inter vivos.'

Since the commencement of the Law of Property Act 1925, joint tenancy has been capable of severance only in equity. Under section 36(2) of the Law of Property Act 1925,

> No severance of a joint tenancy of a legal estate, so as to create a tenancy in common in land, shall be permissible, whether by operation of law or otherwise, but this subsection does not affect the ... right to sever a joint tenancy in an equitable interest whether or not the legal estate is vested in the joint tenants:

Section 36(2) goes on to provide two major means of effecting severance in equity:

> where a legal estate (not being settled land) is vested in joint tenants beneficially, and any tenant desires to sever the joint tenancy in equity, he shall give to the other joint tenants a notice in writing of such desire or do such other acts or things as would, in the case of personal estate, have been effectual to sever the tenancy in equity, and thereupon under the trust for sale affecting the land the net proceeds of sale, and the net rents and profits until sale, shall be held upon the trusts which would have been requisite for giving effect to the beneficial interests if there had been an actual severance.

We must look at these methods of severance in turn.

(1) Severance by written notice

Although doubt has been expressed on the point[11], it is generally agreed that section 36(2) of the 1925 Act has radically altered the law of severance by introducing an entirely new method of severance as regards land—that of

6 See *Re Draper's Conveyance* [1969] 1 Ch 486 at 493 per Plowman J.
7 See p. 267f., ante. See also I. A. Saunders and A. McGregor (1973) 37 Conv (NS) 270 at 272: 'Disposal of Equitable Interest in Joint Tenancy'.
8 [1965] 2 QB 666 at 690.
9 See *Re Draper's Conveyance* [1969] 1 Ch 486 at 494; (1966) 82 LQR 29 (REM).
10 [1965] 2 QB 666 at 689.
11 See p. 311, post.

notice in writing given by one joint tenant to the other joint tenant or tenants. This is a convenient method of severance, but is subject to several limitations. It has no application to settled land, and moreover excludes those cases in which the names on the legal title are not identical to the beneficiaries behind the trust (e.g., where A, B and C hold the legal estate on trust for sale for A, B, C and D, or where T^1 and T^2 hold the legal estate on trust for sale for A, B and C). In such cases it seems that severance may be effected only by other means than that of written notice[12]. It appears, however, that the phrase 'notice in writing' is sufficiently wide to cover any writ or originating summons by which proceedings are commenced for a determination of the rights of joint tenants inter se[13]. In *Re Draper's Conveyance*[14], a wife applied by summons under the Married Women's Property Act 1882[15] for an order for sale of the jointly owned matrimonial home and equal distribution of the proceeds of sale. Her husband died shortly after the court had made an order for sale, and the question arose whether the wife was beneficially entitled to the entire proceeds of sale by reason of the right of survivorship. Plowman J held that the issue of the summons had, however, severed the joint tenancy with the result that the wife now held the legal estate (as sole surviving trustee) on trust for herself and her husband's estate in equal shares[16].

(2) Other methods of severance

Section 36(2) makes it clear that severance can be effected in equity by such 'acts or things as would, in the case of personal estate, have been effectual to sever the tenancy in equity' before 1926. The classic authority on the pre-1926 forms of severance in personalty (which, of course, included the equitable interests of beneficiaries under a trust for sale) was provided by Page Wood V-C in *Williams v Hensman*[17]. Here Page Wood V-C laid down three categories of circumstance resulting in severance:

> A joint tenancy may be severed in three ways: in the first place, an act of any one of the persons interested operating upon his own share may create a severance as to that share . . . Secondly, a joint tenancy may be severed by mutual agreement. And, in the third place, there may be a severance by any course of dealing sufficient to intimate that the interests of all were mutually treated as constituting a tenancy in common. Where the severance depends on an inference of this kind without any express act of severance, it will not suffice to rely on an intention, with respect to the particular share, declared only behind the backs of the other persons interested. You must find in this class of cases a course of dealing by which the shares of all the parties to the contest have been effected . . .

We shall examine these categories in turn.

12 See R. E. Megarry and H. W. R. Wade, op. cit., p. 409.
13 See *Burgess v Rawnsley* [1975] Ch 429 at 447 per Sir John Pennycuick. See, however, *Re Wilks* [1891] 3 Ch 59.
14 [1969] 1 Ch 486. See (1968) 84 LQR 462 (P. V. Baker).
15 See p. 559, post.
16 [1969] 1 Ch 486 at 494.
17 (1861) 1 John & H 546 at 557.

(a) *Act of a joint tenant 'operating upon his own share'*

Joint tenancy is severed if one of the 'four unities' is destroyed[18]. A clear case is provided where one joint tenant alienates his interest to a third party. Here the alienee would not enjoy unity of title with the other joint tenants; nor would the alienor have had an 'interest' to alienate if he had not already exercised his unilateral right of severance[19].

Take the following example. A, B and C are joint tenants at law and in equity (i.e., situation (i) below).

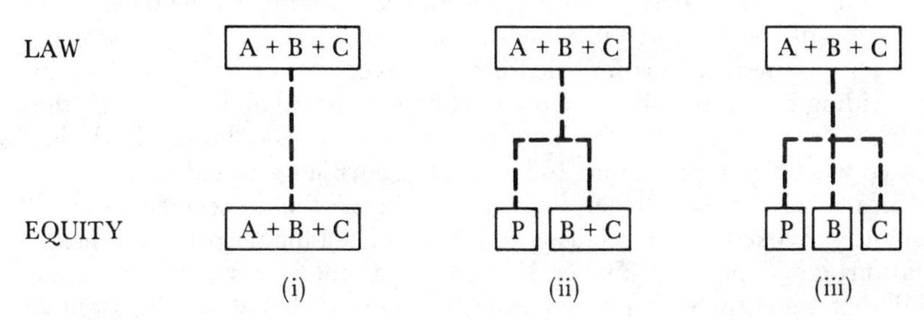

Fig. 54

Suppose that A sells his 'interest' to P. A thereby destroys the pre-existing unity of title and thereby severs the joint tenancy. This severance affects only the equitable ownership, since there can never be a tenancy in common of the legal estate[20]. The result (as reflected in situation (ii) above) is that A, B and C remain as trustees, holding the legal estate on trust for sale for P (as a tenant in common as to a one-third share in equity) and B and C (as joint tenants of the remaining two-thirds). The right of survivorship applies to B and C unless either severs, in which case A, B and C still hold the legal estate on trust for sale for P, B and C as tenants in common each as to a one-third share in equity (i.e., situation (iii) above)[1].

It would make no difference to the steps outlined above if, instead of selling his interest to P, A had merely concluded a specifically enforceable contract to sell. Once again, equity looks on as done that which ought to be done, and the contract would operate in equity to transfer A's equitable interest to P under the doctrine in *Walsh v Lonsdale*[2]. The effect would be identical to that of an actual sale[3].

The 'four unities' can also be destroyed by merger, e.g., where A, B and C are joint tenants for life, with remainder to D in fee simple, and A later buys D's

18 See p. 236, ante.
19 In cases falling within this category severance can indeed be quite unilateral. See, for instance, *Cedar Holdings Ltd v Green* [1979] 3 WLR 31, p. 225, ante; (1979) 38 Cambridge LJ 251 (M. J. Prichard).
20 See p. 240, ante.
1 See *Bedson v Bedson* [1965] 2 QB 666 at 689 per Russell LJ.
2 (1882) 21 Ch D 9, p. 398, post.
3 See *Burgess v Rawnsley* [1975] Ch 429 at 443 per Browne LJ.

remainder. Such a transaction would destroy unity of interest between A, B and C, with the result that A would become a tenant in common while B and C remained joint tenants for life.

(b) *Mutual agreement*

The operation of the second limb or rule in the categories laid down by Page Wood V-C was illustrated in *Burgess v Rawnsley*[4]. Here two parties, H and R, met at a 'scripture rally' in Trafalgar Square. Being old and lonely, they became friendly and later H invited the woman, R, to join with him in the purchase of the reversion of the property in which he was then living. They bought the house in joint names on trust for sale for themselves as beneficial joint tenants, each providing half of the purchase price. H had contemplated that R would in due course marry him, but this hope turned out to be unfounded. H then negotiated with R to buy her out, and a county court judge found as a fact that R had orally agreed to sell her share in the house for a specified price. R subsequently revoked that agreement and demanded a higher price, but before negotiations could proceed further H died. R, as the sole surviving trustee, claimed that the beneficial interest now belonged to her alone by right of survivorship. H's estate maintained that it was entitled to a half-share in equity.

The Court of Appeal held that H had indeed severed the beneficial joint tenancy before his death and that his estate was therefore entitled to a half-share in any proceeds of sale of the property. Both Browne LJ and Sir John Pennycuick based their conclusion on the ground that severance had been effected by the agreement which the county court judge had found on the somewhat unsatisfactory evidence before him[5]. Sir John Pennycuick held that, for the purpose of establishing 'mutual agreement' within 'rule 2 of Page Wood V-C', it was not necessary that the agreement disclosed by the facts should have been carried through to performance, or even that the agreement should have been specifically enforceable[6]. In the words of Sir John Pennycuick,

> The significance of an agreement is not that it binds the parties; but that it serves as an indication of a common intention to sever, something which it was indisputably within their power to do. It will be observed that Page Wood V-C in his rule 2 makes no mention of specific enforceability. Contrast this position where severance is claimed under his rule 1 by reason of alienation by one joint tenant in favour of a third party. We were referred to a sentence in *Megarry and Wade, The Law of Real Property*, 3rd edn., p. 418, where, under the heading of 'Alienation in equity,' it is said:
>
> 'In equity, . . . a specifically enforceable contract to alienate creates an equitable interest in the property even though the legal act of alienation has not taken place.'
>
> That statement has, I think, no application to an agreement between the two joint tenants themselves[7].

4 [1975] Ch 429. See (1976) 35 Cambridge LJ 20 (D. J. Hayton); (1975) 39 Conv (NS) 433 (F. R. Crane); (1977) 41 Conv (NS) 243 (S. M. Bandali); (1976) 40 Conv (NS) 77 (J. F. Garner).

5 'The evidence upon which that finding was based appears to be rather weak . . .' ([1975] Ch 429 at 445 per Sir John Pennycuick).

6 Being purely verbal in nature, the agreement (if there was one) was unenforceable by virtue of section 40 of the Law of Property Act 1925, p. 81f., ante.

7 [1975] Ch 429 at 446.

(c) *Mutual conduct*

In *Burgess v Rawnsley*, Lord Denning MR seemed to rest his judgment in favour of H's estate on the ground either of 'mutual agreement' or of 'mutual conduct.' In his opinion,

> Even if there was not any firm agreement but only a course of dealing, it clearly evinced an intention by both parties that the property should henceforth be held in common and not jointly[8].

Lord Denning referred to the judgment of Page Wood V-C in *Williams v Hensman*, and pointed out that

> In that passage Page Wood V-C distinguished between severance 'by mutual agreement' and severance by a 'course of dealing.' That shows that a 'course of dealing' need not amount to an agreement, expressed or implied, for severance. It is sufficient if there is a course of dealing in which one party makes clear to the other that he desires that their shares should no longer be held jointly but be held in common. I emphasise that it must be made clear to the other party. That is implicit in the sentence in which Page Wood V-C says:
>
> > 'it will not suffice to rely on an intention, with respect to the particular share, declared only behind the backs of the other persons interested.'
>
> Similarly it is sufficient if both parties enter on a course of dealing which evinces an intention by both of them that their shares shall henceforth be held in common and not jointly[9].

The other members of the Court of Appeal did not, however, agree either with Lord Denning's elaboration of the idea of a 'course of dealing' or with his application of Page Wood V-C's third category to the facts of *Burgess v Rawnsley.* Both Browne LJ and Sir John Pennycuick doubted whether there was sufficiently clearly established a 'course of dealing' to bring that third category of severing circumstances into play[10]. While agreeing that Page Wood V-C's third category was not 'a mere sub-heading of rule 2', Sir John Pennycuick indicated the nature of his reservations:

> I do not doubt myself that where one tenant negotiates with another for some rearrangement of interest, it may be possible to infer from the particular facts a common intention to sever even though the negotiations break down. Whether such an inference can be drawn must I think depend upon the particular facts. In the present case the negotiations between [H] and [R], if they can be properly described as negotiations at all, fall, it seems to me, far short of warranting an inference. One could not ascribe to joint tenants an intention to sever merely because one offers to buy out the other for £X and the other makes a counter-offer of £Y[11].

8 [1975] Ch 429 at 440.
9 [1975] Ch 429 at 439.
10 [1975] Ch 429 at 444 per Browne LJ, 447 per Sir John Pennycuick. See also *Greenfield v Greenfield* (1979) 38 P & CR 570.
11 [1975] Ch 429 at 447.

Sir John Pennycuick was quite ready to concede that the 'policy of the law as it stands today . . . is to facilitate severance at the instance of either party', but neither he nor any other member of the Court was prepared to hold that severance could be effected either by an uncommunicated declaration by one joint tenant or indeed by a mere verbal notice by one joint tenant to the other tenant or tenants[12].

12 [1975] Ch 429 at 444 per Browne LJ, 448 per Sir John Pennycuick.

CHAPTER 9

A review of equitable interests in unregistered land

It is clear at this point that our view of equitable interests in unregistered land must now become slightly more subtle. So far we have been content to accept that such interests are capable of simple separation into two sub-sets[1]:

(i) 'commercial' equitable interests—which are registrable as land charges;

(ii) 'family' equitable interests—which are protected on sale by the consequences of overreaching.

It appears now that the subdivision must be not two-fold but three-fold. In a twilight zone beyond the major categories of registrable and overreachable interests there lies a third category of equitable rights in unregistered land:

(iii) equitable interests which are neither registrable nor overreached, whose impact upon a third party purchaser of a legal estate turns on the doctrine of notice in its traditional formulation.

We encountered one such interest in *E. R. Ives Investment Ltd v High*[2], and were confronted by another example in *Caunce v Caunce*[3]. Yet another instance arose in *Shiloh Spinners Ltd v Harding*[4], where Lord Wilberforce was prepared to accept that

> there may well be rights, of an equitable character, outside the provisions as to registration and which are incapable of being overreached.

These rights are few and anomalous, but they present some of the most difficult issues dealt with in the area of unregistered land[5]. Collectively they constitute the nightmare of the conveyancer, since they comprise unregistrable, non-overreachable and sometimes virtually undiscoverable equitable interests which may yet bind the purchaser of land on the basis of constructive notice.

If we implement this three-fold division of equitable interests in unregistered land, we can then adopt the following approach wherever the owner of an equitable interest in unregistered land is confronted by a third party who has purchased a legal estate in that land. In addressing ourselves to the solution of this classic problem of land law[6], we can ask:

1 See p. 69, ante.
2 [1967] 2 QB 379, p. 140, ante.
3 [1969] 1 WLR 286, p. 289, ante.
4 [1973] AC 691 at 721, p. 414, post.
5 For other examples, see *Poster v Slough Estates Ltd* [1969] 1 Ch 495 (equitable right of an owner to remove a hired fixture in the event of breach of the contract of hire); *McCarthy and Stone Ltd v Julian S. Hodge & Co Ltd* [1971] 1 WLR 1547 (unprotected land charge which remains effective despite non-registration); *Crabb v Arun District Council* [1976] Ch 179 (equitable proprietary and estoppel interests, p. 497, post). See also (1973) 37 Conv (NS) 134 (F. R. Crane).
6 See p. 54, ante.

(1) Could the owner of the equitable interest have protected himself against the third party by means of a land charge registration?

If the owner of the equitable interest had rights which were capable of registration as a land charge, then

(a) if those rights were duly registered they bind the purchaser[7]

(b) if those rights were not duly registered they become void as against the purchaser for want of registration—even though the purchaser had actual express knowledge of the rights at the time of the conveyance to him[8].

If, however, the equitable interest in question does not become void for want of registration as a land charge, then we must ask:

(2) Was the equitable interest overreachable by the disposition to the third party?

The transactions in land which are capable of enjoying overreaching effect are detailed in section 2(1) of the Law of Property Act 1925. Such transactions are essentially conveyances[9] to a purchaser of a legal estate in land which are made (i) under the powers conferred by the Settled Land Act 1925, (ii) by trustees for sale, (iii) by a mortgagee or personal representative in the exercise of his paramount powers, or (iv) under an order of the court.

It can therefore be seen that some dispositions of a legal estate in land (e.g., a conveyance by a bare trustee[10]) are inherently non-overreaching, for the purely artificial reason that they are not included within the statutory list of transactions which are capable of overreaching effect. If, however, an equitable interest is in principle overreachable according to section 2(1) of the Law of Property Act 1925, then

(a) if the statutory conditions of overreaching were complied with[11], the equitable interest is overreached by the purchaser and is henceforth satisfied out of the proceeds of the disposition;

7 Law of Property Act 1925, s. 198(1), p. 113, ante.

8 Land Charges Act 1972, s. 4, p. 114, ante. See *Midland Bank Trust Co Ltd v Green* [1981] 2 WLR 28. Note, however, that not all unprotected land charges become void by reason of non-registration. An unregistered estate contract would remain valid, for instance, as against a purchaser of an equitable interest in the land (see Land Charges Act 1972, s. 4(6); *McCarthy and Stone Ltd v Hodge* [1971] 1 WLR 1547).

9 A 'conveyance' is defined for the purpose of the Law of Property Act 1925 as *including* a mortgage, charge and lease of property (see Law of Property Act 1925, s. 205(1)(ii)).

10 See pp. 160, 182, ante. See *Hodgson v Marks* [1971] Ch 892, p. 339, post.

11 See Settled Land Act 1925, ss. 18(1), 72(2), p. 171, ante; Law of Property Act 1925, s. 27(2), p. 229, ante.

(b) if the statutory conditions of overreaching were not observed (as in *Caunce v Caunce* where there was no payment to two trustees[12]), the purchaser does not statutorily overreach the equitable interest.

If for any reason the equitable interest in question is not overreached—either because it is inherently non-overreachable or because the statutory conditions were not fulfilled, the issue of priority must turn upon the answer given to the final question:

(3) Is the third party against whom that equitable interest is opposed a bona fide purchaser of a legal estate for value without notice?

The question of priority is ultimately determined by applying the traditional doctrine of notice:

(a) if the third party ranks as 'Equity's Darling', he takes the legal estate free of the equitable interest (as in *Caunce*);

(b) if the third party does not rank as a bona fide purchaser of a legal estate for value without notice, he is bound by the equitable interest.

Before 1926 this application of the equitable doctrine of notice would have provided the complete answer to any question arising between the owner of an equitable interest and the purchaser of a legal estate in unregistered land. But since 1925 the classical doctrine of notice has been overlaid by two devices aimed at the protection of the equitable owner, and this is why we must ask questions (1) and (2) above before we reach the question of notice (3). One of these protective devices (i.e., land charge registration) renders notice inescapable; the other (i.e., overreaching) renders notice irrelevant[13]. Taken in conjunction, however, the questions posed in (1), (2) and (3) above must disclose the fate of *any* equitable interest in unregistered land the legal estate in which is purchased by a third party. Given that the entire field of equitable interests in unregistered land may now be divided into three major categories, our three interrogatories simply serve to exhaust all the logical possibilities affecting the

12 See p. 290, ante. It should be noted, incidentally, that if in the *Caunce v Caunce* situation, H had appointed one of his cronies as co-trustee in order to give a disposition in relation to the legal estate and receive capital moneys from a third party, W's equitable interest behind the trust for sale would have been overreached by that disposition. This would be the case even though it meant that W's rights became operative in respect of a fund of money which, in view of H's dishonesty, for all practical purposes no longer existed. Technically, W's only remedy in such a case would be an action in damages against H and his co-trustee for an undoubted breach of trust—small comfort where H has disappeared or has become insolvent.

13 See p. 73f, ante.

issue of priority between equitable owner and purchaser. If we apply some set theory for a moment, the *set of equitable interests in unregistered land* can be represented in terms of *three sub-sets,* to each of which one of our interrogatories is appropriate:

SUB-SET 1	SUB-SET 2	SUB-SET 3
'COMMERCIAL' EQUITABLE INTERESTS	'FAMILY' EQUITABLE INTERESTS	RESIDUAL CATEGORY OF UNREGISTRABLE NON-OVERREACHABLE INTERESTS
(protected by land charge registration)	(protected by the effect of over-reaching)	(protected under the doctrine of notice)
QUESTION (1)	QUESTION (2)	QUESTION (3)

Fig. 55

The three-fold formula which we have elaborated here may be applied to the solution of *any* problem of priority arising in relation to unregistered land between the owner of an equitable interest and a purchaser of a legal estate in that land. The formula is therefore one of general utility.

PART III

Registration of title

CHAPTER 10

The mechanics of registered conveyancing

So far in this book, we have devoted most of our attention to the principles which govern land where title is unregistered. It is now time to examine the principles which affect land where title is registered.

The system of registered land law in its modern form dates from the enactment of the Land Registration Act 1925. This system is administered by the Land Registry in accordance with the terms of the 1925 Act and in conformity with the Land Registration Rules prescribed pursuant to that legislation[1]. The basic difference between the systems of registered and unregistered land is the fact that under the latter system the purchaser must, on each occasion of purchase, undertake a fresh investigation of the title to be purchased. He must satisfy himself as to the validity of the title offered by investigating the documents of title (i.e., the 'title deeds') covering at least the last 15 years[2]. The basis of this practice is the pragmatic assumption that such investigation will reveal all the pertinent details relating to the land which he proposes to buy. By and large, this assumption is quite correct, but the principal defect in the system of unregistered conveyancing is precisely the fact that the cumbersome investigation of title must be carried out on every occasion of purchase, irrespective of the length of time which has elapsed since the last transfer and investigation of title. The process of land transfer is thus self-perpetuating, repetitive, protracted and costly[3].

1 Whether a particular property falls to be dealt with under the provisions of the Land Registration Act 1925 depends upon whether that property is situated within an area currently designated as an area of compulsory registration of title. The areas currently designated include most large urban areas, and it has been estimated that about 75 per cent of all conveyancing in England and Wales is registered conveyancing (see D. J. Hayton, *Registered Land* (3rd edn., London 1981), p. 1f.). The old system of unregistered land is gradually being displaced as from time to time further areas are officially designated as districts henceforth to be governed by the Land Registration Act. It was at one stage anticipated that unregistered land conveyancing would soon be superseded by registration of title, but it now appears that the administrative difficulties involved in the extension of the registered land system may prevent the realisation of this objective in the near future.

2 See p. 127, ante. The Chief Land Registrar, in giving evidence to the Royal Commission on Legal Services, expressed the hope that the whole of England and Wales would be subject to compulsory registration 'by about 1985'. See Report of the Royal Commission on Legal Services Cmnd 7648, October 1979, Vol. 1, para. 21.6.

3 In *Williams & Glyn's Bank Ltd v Boland* [1980] 3 WLR 138 at 149, Lord Scarman described the process of unregistered conveyancing as the 'wearisome and intricate task of examining title ...' For an excoriating account of the 'ritual dance' of conveyancers, see M. Joseph, *The Conveyancing Fraud* (London 1976), p. 30ff.

By contrast, the objective which underlies the scheme of registration of title contained in the Land Registration Act 1925 is that the legal title to a plot of land should be investigated only once—by the Land Registrar. All the details pertinent to the ownership and enjoyment of that land (other than matters which may be discovered only on physical inspection of the land) are then recorded on a central register—the Land Register. These details go far beyond the one isolated category of interest—the commercial equitable interest—which is centrally recorded in the context of unregistered land[4]. Registration of title involves the registration of almost every kind of interest in the land in question—whether legal or equitable, family or commercial. The aim of the registered land scheme is that the Land Register should accurately reflect the totality of estates and interests created with reference to any land falling within the area of registration. The register is then kept accurate by regular up-dating of the information contained in it: there is a requirement that all subsequent transactions affecting the registered land be recorded on the register as a condition precedent to their efficacy. The intended result is that, at any given time, a prospective purchaser of registered land should be able to verify, by a simple examination of the register, the exact nature of any interests in or over the land which he proposes to buy.

1. THE BASIC FEATURES OF REGISTRATION OF TITLE

The scheme of registration of title described above in outline represented for many years an aspiration of law reformers. The Royal Commission on Land Registration which reported in 1857 sought means for bringing about 'such a system of registration as will enable owners to deal with land in as simple and easy a manner . . . as they can now deal with movable chattels or stock[5].' It has for long been quite clear that the law of conveyancing can serve the interests of the community only if it provides a secure, efficient and inexpensive mode of land transfer—an objective which becomes increasingly important in a highly mobile and industrialised society.

The archetypal system of registration of title was introduced during the last century in the Torrens Title legislation enacted in Australia and New Zealand[6]. This legislation provided in many respects a model for the English enactments which culminated in the Land Registration Act 1925. It has been said that the fundamental features of a system of registration of title, whether in the form of

4 It is perhaps appropriate at this point to utter some cautionary words about the need rigidly to distinguish between *registration of title* and *registration of land charges.* Never must the two forms of registration be confused: they operate within entirely different contexts. Almost paradoxically, at first sight, registration of land charges in the Land Charges Register occurs in relation to *unregistered land.* Of course, commercial equitable interests are also registrable where they arise in *registered land,* but in the latter case they are protected as 'minor interests', and are recorded in a quite different register (the Land Register) as an integral part of a much more general process of registration.

5 *Report of the Royal Commission on Land Registration,* quoted by T. B. F. Ruoff and R. B. Roper, *Law and Practice of Registered Conveyancing* (4th edn., London 1979), p. 4.

6 The Torrens scheme was first adopted in the Real Property Act 1858 (South Australia).

Torrens legislation or in the form of the Land Registration Act 1925, are three in number[7]. *First*, as we have already seen, the register is intended to operate as a 'mirror', reflecting accurately and incontrovertibly the totality of estates and interests affecting the registered land (the 'mirror principle'). *Second*, trusts affecting the registered land are kept off the title, with the result that the purchaser of that land may safely transact in the assurance that the interests behind any trust will be overreached on sale (the 'curtain principle'). *Third*, the state itself guarantees the accuracy of the registered title, in the sense that an indemnity is payable from public funds if a registered proprietor is deprived of his title or is otherwise prejudiced by the operation of the registration scheme (the 'insurance principle').

During the course of this chapter we shall examine the extent to which the objectives of title registration are achieved in the provisions of the Land Registration Act 1925[8]. It will be seen that registration of title has not eliminated all problems in the context of land transfer. Difficulties remain, not least in relation to the extent of the true divergence between the principles which govern registered land and those which govern unregistered land.

For many purposes it is true to say that the system of registered title contained in the Land Registration Act 1925 utilises existing concepts of unregistered land conveyancing and simply provides more streamlined conveyancing machinery[9]. There is, however, an important sense in which it is beginning to be realised that registration of title may achieve more than merely procedural changes in the law relating to land. It is possible that the law governing registered land will come in time to be recognised as a body of rules and concepts which is *substantively* quite different from the principles which regulate unregistered land[10]. It may be

7 T. B. F. Ruoff, *An Englishman Looks at the Torrens System* (Sydney, Melbourne and Brisbane 1957), p. 8.

8 On the system of registration contained in the Land Registration Act 1925, see generally T. B. F. Ruoff and R. B. Roper, op. cit.; T. B. F. Ruoff, (1969) 32 MLR 121: 'The Protection of the Purchaser of Land under English Law'.

9 It has been suggested, somewhat mordantly, that the Land Registration Act 1925 'seems to be an example of the British genius for compromise. During the middle of the last century, a group of men had the idea of altering the conveyancing system, so that a layman could buy and sell a house as easily as he could buy and sell anything else. Another group opposed them. At the beginning of this century a compromise was finally worked out: instead of a *completely efficient* Land Registry, which would make solicitors superfluous, a *semi-efficient* Land Registry would be set up, which would cut out *half* the solicitor's work, while still allowing them to do the other half, but at substantially reduced costs. . . . The only effect of setting up the Land Registry has been to make the solicitors' job easier. A final irony is that whereas the Land Registry benefits only solicitors, it is their customers who pay for it. Each time a registered house changes hands, the purchaser has to pay a land registry fee' (see M. Joseph, op. cit., p. 137f.). There seems, incidentally, to be little foundation for the hope that registered land transactions can be carried out more easily or more cheaply than those in unregistered land. In *Property & Reversionary Investment Corporation Ltd v Secretary of State for the Environment* [1975] 1 WLR 1504 at 1507, Donaldson J recognised it as 'common ground that nowadays, when in unregistered land short title can be made, there is little, if any, saving in time or effort in dealing with a registered title.' It may be for this reason that the abolition in 1973 of solicitors' scale fees for conveyancing did not result in the intended downward levelling of unregistered conveyancing charges with the traditionally lower charges for registered conveyancing.

10 A significant step in this direction was taken by the decision of the House of Lords in *Williams & Glyn's Bank Ltd v Boland* [1980] 3 WLR 138.

that the classic concepts of unregistered land (e.g., the distinction between legal and equitable rights and the equitable doctrine of notice) will be rendered redundant by the steadily expanding scheme of registered title. Under a system of registered title the only relevant distinction is that between 'major' and 'minor' interests; that is, between rights equivalent to absolute ownership of land (which are registered 'substantively') and all other kinds of interest which diminish or qualify that ownership. Interests of the latter variety are registered, as it were, 'adjectivally', by subsidiary 'entry' on the register against the substantively registered title.

This indeed is the pattern on which the Land Registration Act 1925 is modelled. Yet one of the greatest difficulties experienced in the application of this Act concerns the tendency of the courts from time to time to resurrect traditional concepts of unregistered land conveyancing[11].

2. THE REGISTER

The Land Register is controlled by the Chief Land Registrar[12]. The Register is maintained both centrally at the Land Registry in London and regionally at ten district land registries. The Registrar and his staff are invested with a limited quasi-judicial capacity to determine questions or difficulties arising in relation to registration matters[13]. There is a right of appeal to the Chancery Division of the High Court from decisions reached by the Registrar[14].

The Register records details pertinent to each individual title maintained at the Land Registry. The individual title is identified by the title number assigned to the plot of land concerned, thus reinforcing the point that the Land Registration Act 1925 directs that registration be effected against an area of land identified numerically rather than against the name of the current estate owner (as is the case in relation to the registration of land charges[15]).

The register of each individual title is subdivided into a 'Property Register', a 'Proprietorship Register', and a 'Charges Register'. The Property Register relevant to a particular title records the advantageous features of the land in question: it describes the land by reference to a filed map, and notes such matters as easements, rights and privileges over other land which enure to the benefit of the land comprised in the title number. The Proprietorship Register indicates the name and address of the current registered proprietor, and denotes whether the title enjoyed by that proprietor is 'absolute', 'good leasehold', 'qualified' or 'possessory'[16]. The Proprietorship Register also records any restrictions, cautions or inhibitions which affect or diminish the right of the registered proprietor to dispose of the land. The Charges Register records all the disadvantageous

11 See p. 328, post.
12 Land Registration Act 1925, s. 126(1).
13 Land Registration Rules 1925, r. 298(1).
14 Land Registration Rules 1925, r. 299.
15 See p. 131, ante.
16 See p. 324f, post.

features of ownership of the land in question. Here are entered notices of charges or incumbrances which adversely affect the land.

The three subdivisions of the register are correlated on one index card, a copy of which is issued to the current registered proprietor and is known as the 'land certificate'[17]. This certificate provides each registered proprietor with his immediate evidence of title.

The Land Register is not open to public inspection[18]—a point which is not without political significance since the preclusion of access to the Register ultimately frustrates any attempt to compile an accurate record of the allocation of land ownership in this country. However, the registered proprietor may (and indeed in specified circumstances must) supply an intending purchaser with the necessary authorisation to inspect the register of the individual title concerned[19].

3. THE CLASSIFICATION OF INTERESTS IN REGISTERED LAND

The interests in land which require to be dealt with in terms of the Land Registration Act 1925 are in essence the same kinds of interest which arise in the context of unregistered land, and the only difference is one of terminology[20]. The range of possible interests in registered land includes 'registrable interests', 'minor interests', 'overriding interests' and 'registered charges'.

4. REGISTRABLE INTERESTS

Registrable interests are those interests in registered land which are indicated in the 1925 Act as being capable of substantive registration, i.e., capable of registration in their own right under an individual title number. Under section 2(1) of the Land Registration Act 1925, the only interests which are thus capable of substantive registration are those estates in land which are 'capable of existing as legal estates'. Therefore registrable interests include the legal fee simple absolute in possession, and a person holding such an interest in land may apply to be registered as proprietor with an absolute title or with a possessory title[1]. In addition, registrable interests include terms of years absolute of which more than 21 years remain unexpired[2]. This brings about the result that the landlord–tenant relationship may well produce *two* registrable interests, both of which require substantive registration under different title numbers and both of which are evidenced in separate land certificates. The tenant is required to

17 Land Registration Act 1925, s. 63(1). The certificate is, however, retained in the Land Registry if and so long as the property concerned is subject to an outstanding mortgage or 'charge' (Land Registration Act 1925, s. 65).
18 Land Registration Act 1925, s. 112.
19 Land Registration Act 1925, s. 110(1).
20 See generally D. Jackson (1972) 88 LQR 93: 'Registration of Land Interests—the English Version'.
1 Land Registration Act 1925, s. 4.
2 Land Registration Act 1925, s. 8(1)(a).

register his term of years absolute quite independently of the substantive registration effected by the landlord in respect of his fee simple absolute in possession[3].

The existence of a legal easement benefiting land which is the subject of a substantive registration should be recorded on the Property Register of the relevant registered estate[4].

In unregistered conveyancing the transfer of a legal estate (whether freehold or leasehold) is completed by the deed of transfer (i.e., the conveyance). The same is not true of registered conveyancing. Although the same process of contract and conveyance occurs when dealing with registered title, the transfer of a legal estate to a purchaser is effectual and complete only when the transferee is entered upon the Land Register as the new proprietor of the estate conveyed[5]. Thus the efficacy of transactions in relation to the legal estate is made to depend upon entry of the appropriate record in the Land Register[6]. The conveyance of a legal estate becomes 'void' if not entered upon the Register within a period of two months[7].

When the Land Registry receives an application for substantive registration of an estate in registered land, the quality of title to be accorded to the new registered proprietor must be graded within the four possible classes of title, and the class of title enjoyed is indicated in the relevant Proprietorship Register. Registration with *absolute title* invests the applicant with the full legal estate, subject only to overriding interests and minor interests protected by entry on the register[8]. Absolute title is granted in the case of almost all freehold applications for registration, but is granted less often to those who seek a substantive registration of a leasehold interest. In the latter case, a leasehold can be registered with absolute title only if the Land Registrar is in a position to approve the title to any superior freehold or leasehold interest[9]. This in turn means that an

3 The existence of the leasehold interest must, however, be noted upon the Charges Register of the superior title.
4 Land Registration Rules 1925, r. 257.
5 Land Registration Act 1925, s. 19(1). For reference to the 'statutory magic' of registration, see T. B. F. Ruoff and R. B. Roper, op. cit., p. 64.
6 This requirement of entry in the Register begins to operate only with the first transfer which occurs after the date on which the relevant district has been designated as an area of compulsory registration. Thus many years may elapse before the first registered transfer in respect of a piece of land within an area of compulsory registration. However, the requirement of registration as a condition of effective transfer applies not only to that first transfer but also to all subsequent transactions in relation to that legal estate.
7 Land Registration Act 1925, s. 123(1). It is, of course, possible that the intended transferee may go into 'actual occupation' of the land by virtue of a transaction which should have been (but has not in fact been) registered. Under section 70(1)(g) of the Land Registration Act 1925, such a person currently enjoys the protection of an 'overriding interest' in respect of his unregistered transfer (p. 334, post.) However, the Law Commission has recommended that section 70(1)(g) should be amended to ensure that no interest which is capable of substantive registration can nevertheless constitute an overriding interest in the absence of such registration. See Law Commission, Published Working Paper No. 37: *Land Registration (Second Paper)* (July 1971), para. 14.
8 Land Registration Act 1925, s. 5.
9 Land Registration Act 1925, s. 8(1), proviso (i).

applicant for leasehold registration with absolute title must deduce title to the Registrar's satisfaction, not only in relation to his own leasehold, but also in relation to any superior title. Most lessees are effectively unable to do this, simply because a tenant is not normally entitled to call for and investigate superior titles[10].

The result is that most leasehold applications for substantive registration under the Land Registration Act 1925 are accorded the status of *good leasehold title*. The registered proprietor with good leasehold title is in exactly the same position as the recipient of an absolute title, except to the extent that the good leasehold title is held subject to any estate, right or interest which affects the superior title or titles[11].

When an applicant for registration bases his application not upon documentary evidence of title but upon a period of adverse possession of land, it is open to the Land Registrar to grant a *possessory title*. This possessory title is, however, subject to all adverse interests affecting the land which may later be shown to have existed at the date of registration[12].

In extremely rare cases the Registrar grants only a *qualified title* to an applicant for registration. Such cases arise, for instance, where the applicant can establish title only in respect of a limited period or where there are other fundamental doubts as to the subject matter of the registration. A qualified title is subject to any adverse interests which later emerge as having been in existence at the date of registration[13].

It has been suggested that the legal estate in registered land has now become so heavily regulated by statutory incidents under the Land Registration Act 1925 that it has indeed become a new kind of statutory or registered estate which replaces or abrogates the common law estate[14]. This view has aroused much controversy[15] and, if correct, would add credence to the theory that the principles of registered land are evolving into a quite distinct law of property which recognises only the distinction between 'major' interests (i.e., substantively registered titles) and 'minor' interests (i.e., everything else)[16].

5. MINOR INTERESTS

A second category of interest in registered land is the category of minor interests. This category comprises a residual class of interests, in the sense that it includes

10 See Law of Property Act 1925, s. 44.
11 Land Registration Act 1925, s. 10.
12 Land Registration Act 1925, ss. 6, 11. It is not uncommon for an initially possessory title to be converted to an absolute or good leasehold title by a subsequent determination on the part of the Land Registrar (see Land Registration Act 1925, s. 77).
13 Land Registration Act 1925, ss. 7, 12.
14 See *Chowood Ltd v Lyall* (No. 2) [1930] 2 Ch 156 at 163 per Lord Hanworth MR.
15 See H. Potter, *Principles and Practice of Conveyancing under the Land Registration Act 1925* (London 1934), p. 30; R. C. Connell, (1947) 11 Conv (NS) 183 at 232: 'The Registered Estate'. Compare A. D. Hargreaves, (1949) 12 MLR 139 at 205, 477. See also J. T. Farrand, *Contract and Conveyance* (3rd edn., London 1980), p. 31; D. C. Jackson (1972) 88 LQR 93; D. G. Barnsley, op. cit., p. 30ff.
16 See p. 322, ante.

most interests which do not otherwise qualify as registrable interests or as overriding interests[17]. Minor interests thus include both family and commercial equitable interests[18]. Such interests qualify for protection not by means of substantive registration but by the subsidiary means of 'entry' on the register.

Family equitable interests (i.e., beneficial interests arising under a strict settlement or behind a trust for sale) may be protected as minor interests in registered land by the entry of a 'restriction' upon the relevant Proprietorship Register[19]. The presence of a restriction on the register plainly indicates that any disposition or transaction in relation to that land can be effected only in a restricted manner. In the case of family equitable interests thus entered upon the register, the essence of the restriction is that any transfer of the legal estate can be effected only through a conveyance under which the purchase moneys are paid to at least two trustees. In this way, it is ensured that the only transactions which can ever occur are those which inevitably have the effect of overreaching the beneficial interests which were the subject of the entry and translating them into equivalent interests in the proceeds of sale.

Commercial equitable interests in registered land[20] are capable of entry as minor interests on the Land Register by way either of a 'notice' entered upon the Charges Register[1] or of a 'caution' entered upon the Proprietorship Register[2]. Protection for minor interests of a commercial character may more rarely be obtained by entry of a restriction or an 'inhibition' on the Proprietorship Register[3]. Normally, however, commercial equitable interests are protected by notice or caution, the principal distinction between these two forms of protection being the fact that the former requires the co-operation of the registered proprietor who must consent to make his land certificate available for the entry of the notice[4]. A caution may be entered unilaterally, but generally represents a more temporary form of protection of some contentious matter[5].

17 See Land Registration Act 1925, s. 3(xv).
18 See p. 69f, ante.
19 Land Registration Act 1925, s. 58(1). In the normal case, a restriction may be entered only by the registered proprietor, but there is now provision for restrictions to be entered by other persons if the registered proprietor is willing to produce the land certificate (see Land Registration Act 1925, s. 58(5); Land Registration Rules 1925, r. 236).
20 These are the equivalent of those interests in unregistered land which are capable of protection by registration of a land charge in the Land Charges Register, p. 111, ante.
1 Land Registration Act 1925, s. 49(1).
2 Land Registration Act 1925, ss. 53–56. A 'caution' may take the form of either a 'caution against first registration' (s. 53) or a 'caution against dealings' (s. 54). The effect of lodging a caution in either case is that no registration or dealing can be effected by the registrar until a notice has been served on the cautioner giving him an opportunity to object. He has a specified number of days within which to substantiate his claim before the registrar (ss. 53(2), 55(1)).
3 Land Registration Act 1925, s. 57.
4 Land Registration Act 1925, s. 64(1)(c).
5 It will have been seen that the means of protection for minor interests are not always mutually exclusive: minor interests may often be protectible by any of several kinds of entry on the register (see *Re White Rose Cottage* [1965] Ch 940). The Law Commission has proposed a rationalisation of this area which would draw a clear distinction between entries on the register which are contentious and those which are not. In the Law Commission's view, an interest which is not disputed by the registered proprietor should always be protected by notice or (where

It is open to the purchaser of registered land to requisition an official search of the Land Register for the purpose of discovering the existence of minor interests entered against the title with which he is concerned[6]. The recipient of an official search certificate acquires a 15 day priority period during which he may safely apply for the registration of his transfer[7]. However, if the official search fails (because of some error in the Registry) to reveal a registered or protected interest belonging to a third party, it seems that the purchaser—albeit entirely innocent—takes the land subject to the prior interest[8].

6. THE EFFECT OF FAILURE TO PROTECT A MINOR INTEREST BY ENTRY ON THE REGISTER

One of the fundamental objectives of a system of registered title must be to ensure that the register remains an accurate record of the interests affecting registered land. It is therefore important that there should be a strong incentive towards protection of minor interests by means of the appropriate entry on the register. This incentive is injected into the Land Registration Act 1925 by a couple of provisions whose clear import is to deny effect to unprotected minor interests when the land affected is transferred to a third party. Under section 20(1), a disposition for valuable consideration of a legal estate in registered land (whether freehold or leasehold) has the effect of conferring that estate upon the transferee or grantee subject only to 'the incumbrances and other entries, if any, appearing on the register . . . and . . . to the overriding interests, if any, affecting the estate transferred or created . . .' The estate transferred or created is declared to be

> free from all other estates and interests whatsoever . . . and the disposition shall operate in like manner as if the registered transferor or grantor were (subject to any entry to the contrary in the register) entitled to the registered land in fee simple in possession for his own benefit.

The policy expressed in this provision appears even more clearly in section 59(6), which declares that, with several exceptions,

> a purchaser acquiring title under a registered disposition shall not be concerned with any . . . document, matter, or claim (not being an overriding interest . . .) which is not protected by a caution, or other entry on the register, whether he has or has not notice thereof, express, implied, or constructive.

---

appropriate) by restriction, whereas a disputed interest should always be protected by caution. See Law Commission, Published Working Paper No. 67: *Land Registration (Fourth Paper)* (April 1976), para. 57f.

6 Land Registration (Official Searches) Rules 1978, r. 3(1).

7 Land Registration (Official Searches) Rules 1978, rr. 2(2), 5, 6(3), 7. In other words, the purchaser acquires priority over any minor interests which may be entered on the register during that intervening period.

8 *Parkash v Irani Finance Ltd* [1970] Ch 101. Compare the effect in unregistered land of Land Charges Act 1972, s. 10(4), p. 127, ante, a provision which has no equivalent in the registered land context.

These provisions make it clear that the position of unprotected minor interests in registered land is intended to be exactly analogous to that which obtains in respect of unprotected land charges in unregistered land. In the latter context, an unregistered charge is wholly ineffectual even as against a subsequent purchaser who has actual knowledge of the existence of the unregistered interest[9]. An unprotected minor interest in registered land binds neither a 'transferee' within section 20(1) nor a 'purchaser' within section 59(6), irrespective of the state of his mind[10]. As Plowman J observed in *Parkash v Irani Finance Ltd*[11], 'one of the essential features of registration of title is to substitute a system of registration of rights for the doctrine of notice[12].' Once again, the objective plainly intended in the legislation is that certainty should prevail over short-term justice in matters of conflict between purchasers and the owners of equitable interests[13].

In view of this clear policy, it is noteworthy that the law relating to minor interests has been thrown into some confusion by the decision in *Peffer v Rigg*[14]. Here, P and D^1 had married two sisters; they therefore shared one relative in common—a mother-in-law, M. Partly in order to accommodate M during her old age, P and D^1 joined together in the purchase of a house. They contributed money in equal proportions towards the purchase of a property with registered title, and the property was transferred into the sole name of D^1. There arose on these facts an implied trust for sale, D^1 holding the legal title as registered proprietor on behalf of himself and P as equitable tenants in common. The circumstances of this purchase were known by the entire family of M, and indeed the implied trust was later confirmed expressly in a formal deed of trust drawn up by P and D^1. Later, however, D^1's marriage to D^2 broke down and ended in divorce. As part of the divorce settlement, D^1 purported to transfer the legal estate in the house to D^2, M by this stage having died. D^1 purported to transfer the 'whole' of the property 'as beneficial owner', in consideration of the payment of £1 by D^2. In property terms, the position was this:

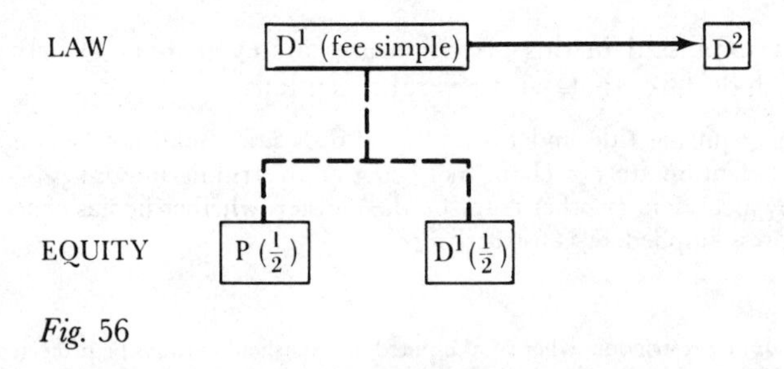

Fig. 56

9 See *Midland Bank Trust Co Ltd v Green* [1981] 2 WLR 28, p. 119, ante.
10 See *Strand Securities Ltd v Caswell* [1965] Ch 373 at 390; *Miles v Bull* (No. 2) [1969] 3 All ER 1585 at 1590; *De Lusignan v Johnson* (1973) 230 Estates Gazette 499.
11 [1970] Ch 101 at 108.
12 See also *Williams & Glyn's Bank Ltd v Boland* [1980] 3 WLR 138 at 142 per Lord Wilberforce.
13 See p. 116, ante.
14 [1977] 1 WLR 285.

D^2 subsequently contended that the transfer invested her, as the new registered proprietor, with the legal estate in fee simple free of P's minor interest as a beneficiary behind the trust for sale. It was plain on the facts that P had neglected to protect that minor interest appropriately by the entry of a restriction against the title previously held by D^1. D^2 argued therefore that P's beneficial interest had become ineffective against her by reason of sections 20(1), 59(6) of the Land Registration Act 1925.

It was, of course, equally plain on the facts that D^2 had at all times been perfectly well aware of the existence of the trust in favour of P, the entire question of M's accommodation having been discussed and resolved *en famille.* Nevertheless, D^2 was able to invoke weighty authority in support of the proposition that an unprotected minor interest is ineffective against a subsequent purchaser or transferee irrespective of notice[15].

Graham J held, however, that D^2 held the transferred title on trust for herself and P as equitable tenants in common notwithstanding the provisions contained in the Land Registration Act 1925, sections 20(1), 59(6). Graham J took the tentative view that D^2 could not claim the immunity from unprotected minor interests conferred by section 20(1) since the transfer had been described by the parties themselves as involving only a 'nominal' consideration. Section 20(1) requires that there be a transfer for 'valuable consideration', a phrase which for the purposes of the Act 'does not include a nominal consideration in money[16].' Under section 20(4), unprotected minor interests remain binding upon the transferee where a disposition is made 'without valuable consideration'. However, D^2 had also taken over a mortgage commitment in respect of the property under the terms of the divorce settlement, and it can be argued that this obligation surely placed the transfer within the realm of transactions for valuable consideration.

In any event, Graham J went on to provide supplementary grounds for his judgment in favour of P. He relied upon the statutory definition of 'purchaser'[17] for the view that unprotected minor interests become ineffective under section 59(6) only against a purchaser 'in good faith'. He then ruled that D^2 could not claim to be a purchaser in good faith for this purpose, because she 'knew quite well' that D^1 held the property on trust:

> [A purchaser] cannot in my judgment be in good faith if he has in fact notice of something which affects his title as in the present case[18].

Graham J found yet another basis for his decision in the doctrine of constructive trusts[19], pointing out that D^2

15 There was incidentally no question that P could claim the protection of an overriding interest by reason of 'actual occupation', not least because he had never lived in the house in question.

16 Land Registration Act 1925, s. 3(xxxi).

17 For the purpose of the Land Registration Act 1925, 'purchaser' is defined as 'a purchaser in good faith for valuable consideration and includes a lessee, mortgagee, or other person who for valuable consideration acquires any interest in land or in any charge on land' (see Land Registration Act 1925, s. 3(xxi)).

18 [1977] 1 WLR 285 at 294.

19 See p. 476, post.

knew . . . that the property was trust property when the transfer was made to her, and therefore she took the property on a constructive trust in accordance with general equitable principles . . . This is a new trust imposed by equity and is distinct from the trust which bound [D[1]].

The decision in *Peffer v Rigg* is remarkable in the sense that, if applied broadly, the reasoning contained in the judgment would drive the proverbial coach and four through the Land Registration Act 1925. The ruling appears to have the effect that an unprotected minor interest remains binding upon a purchaser with express actual notice, notwithstanding the clear wording of section 59(6) and the weight of the existing case law. Yet, as Cross J pointed out in *Strand Securities Ltd v Caswell*[20], it is

vital to the working of the land registration system that notice of something which is not on the register of title should not affect a transferee unless it is an overriding interest.

The decision in *Peffer v Rigg* has incurred much criticism[1]. It may be that Graham J allowed an ethical view of the instant facts to prevail over the strict wording of the statute in order (as he himself said) to avoid

the unreasonable result of permitting a transferee purchaser to take advantage of the Act, and divest himself of knowledge of defects in his own title, and secure to himself a flawless title which he ought not in justice to be allowed to obtain.

In any event the ruling is a somewhat surprising revitalisation of the doctrine of notice in the context of registered land. Certainly never before has it been regarded as 'bad faith' for a purchaser to take advantage of the folly of those who fail to effect the appropriate registration in protection of their interests[2]. In *De Lusignan v Johnson*[3] Brightman J expressly indicated that to allege 'bad faith' in this situation 'would be stretching the language.' He ruled that

bad faith, in the sense of acquiring a legal estate for valuable consideration with notice of the existence or possible existence of an unregistered land charge, was as irrelevant under section 20 of the Land Registration Act as it was under section [4] of the Land Charges Act. Fraud was of course a different matter, and would give rise to its own remedies[4].

20 [1965] Ch 373 at 390.

1 'In other words, a purchaser with notice cannot rely on the registered title. This proposition is most unsatisfactory' (see J. T. Farrand, op. cit., p. 156). See also (1977) 41 Conv (NS) 207 (F. R. Crane); [1978] Conv 52 (J. Martin); (1977) 93 LQR 341 (R. J. Smith); (1977) 40 MLR 602 (S. Anderson); (1977) 36 CLJ 227 (D. J. Hayton); D. C. Jackson (1978) 94 LQR 239 at 240ff., 252: 'Security of Title in Registered Land'.

2 A guideline in this respect has always been found in the dictum of Lord Cozens-Hardy MR in *Re Monolithic Building Co* [1915] 1 Ch 643 at 663, that 'it is not fraud to take advantage of legal rights . . .'

3 (1973) 230 Estates Gazette 499. This case concerned the disputed priority of an unprotected estate contract relating to registered land against a subsequent disposition (in the form of a charge of the property).

4 Compare the view taken in relation to unregistered land in *Hollington Bros Ltd v Rhodes* [1951] 2 TLR 691, p. 115, ante; *Midland Bank Trust Co Ltd v Green* [1981] 2 WLR 28, p. 119, ante. In *Orakpo v Manson Investments Ltd* [1977] 1 WLR 347 at 360, Buckley LJ declined to accept that section 20(1) of the Land Registration Act 1925 should be read 'in a modified manner, so as not

As Brightman J suggested in this case, there is indeed a distinction between sharp dealing (i.e., the *Peffer v Rigg* situation) and the case of clear fraud. This distinction must surely turn upon the primary motive underlying the disputed transfer. In *Peffer v Rigg*, D^1's primary motive in conveying the property to D^2 was not to defraud P but rather to provide his former wife with a home in the aftermath of their divorce. Nor was D^2 guilty of bad faith in the sense relevant here, albeit that her motives were not entirely pure. However, in cases of manifestly dishonest dealing by a transferor, it has always been clear that the courts may exercise an *in personam* jurisdiction to prevent a statute from being pleaded as an instrument of fraud. In *Jones v Lipman*[5], for instance, Russell J held that an unprotected estate contract remained binding upon, and specifically enforceable against, the transferee of a registered title. Here the transferee was a limited company which, on closer inspection, turned out to be merely the alter ego of the transferor who earlier had granted the estate contract to the aggrieved third party, the present plaintiff. In Russell J's view, the defendant company 'is the creature of the first defendant [the transferor], a device and a sham, a mask which he holds before his face in an attempt to avoid recognition by the eye of equity[6].'

Peffer v Rigg may well come to be regarded as a decision restricted to its own facts. Nevertheless the judgment indicates once more the frequent tension between considerations of justice and certainty in land law[7], and provides a further dramatic illustration of the intrusion of unregistered land principles into the supposedly quite different context of registered title.

7. OVERRIDING INTERESTS

Overriding interests comprise a third major category of interest in registered land, being defined as including

> all the incumbrances, interests, rights, and powers not entered on the register but subject to which registered dispositions are by this Act to take effect[8].

Most of the interests which fall within this 'intermediate or hybrid class'[9] are enumerated in section 70(1) of the Land Registration Act 1925. Overriding interests represent a highly problematic area within the law of registered title.

The essence of an 'overriding interest' under the Land Registration Act 1925 is that certain kinds of interest in land are made to bind a third party purchaser

---

to free a registered proprietor from liabilities or incumbrances to the creation of which he has himself been privy.'

5 [1962] 1 WLR 832.

6 [1962] 1 WLR 832 at 836. For a similar treatment of fraud in relation to unregistered land, see *Midland Bank Trust Co Ltd v Green* [1980] Ch 590, CA, p. 121, ante. In *Whittingham v Whittingham* [1979] Fam 9 at 12, Balcombe J indicated that 'lack of "good faith" . . . requires something akin to fraud: at the very least it connotes a lack of honesty.' See also *Frazer v Walker* [1967] AC 569 at 585 per Lord Wilberforce.

7 See p. 116, ante.

8 Land Registration Act 1925, s. 3(xvi).

9 *Williams & Glyn's Bank Ltd v Boland* [1980] 3 WLR 138 at 141 per Lord Wilberforce.

automatically, even though they relate to matters which would not normally be shown on title deeds or disclosed in abstracts of title. Since such matters would not therefore become apparent upon an inspection of the documentary title (whether carried out by an intending purchaser or by the Land Registrar), they are matters in relation to which it is not possible to compile a trustworthy record on the register of the relevant title. As to such matters, persons dealing with registered land must seek information outside the register in the same manner and from the same sources as would persons dealing with unregistered land. In other words, a purchaser of registered land must obtain information about the possible presence of overriding interests by means of physical inspection of the land itself and of enquiries made of persons living there. Overriding interests are, in the main, supposed to be rights which would become obvious to any purchaser who bothered to go and look at the property which he proposed to buy.

Overriding interests, as defined in the statute, are interests which bind the purchaser of registered land notwithstanding that they are not recorded on the face of the register and notwithstanding that the purchaser may have no actual knowledge of their existence. They are quite literally 'overriding'. Cumulatively, they represent a group of interests in registered land which have been singled out either as having such distinct social importance or as involving such technical conveyancing difficulty as to merit a protection which derives not from the force of the register but from the force of statute.

Herein lies the difficulty. The existence of overriding interests in registered land fundamentally distorts the mirror image of the register, since the register can no longer be relied upon as a comprehensive record of the totality of interests in and affecting registered land. Another factor which exacerbates this difficulty is the circumstance that, in spite of the original (and vaguely comforting) theory that overriding interests will always be apparent upon physical inspection of the land, it is now becoming clear that several categories of overriding interest may well remain undiscovered even by a purchaser who carefully inspects both land and title. In addition, recent decisions have tended to increase rather than restrict the number of rights which may claim protected status as overriding interests, as we shall go on to see. The ultimate irony is that a purchaser who is innocently ensnared by a virtually undiscoverable overriding interest does not qualify for statutory compensation if the register is rectified to his prejudice in recognition of that overriding interest[10].

At this stage, two ancillary points might be made. *First*, we shall soon see that some interests in registered land may enjoy a dual status under the scheme of registered title in the sense that they may be protected *either* as minor interests *or* as overriding interests. It should, however, be noted that if an overriding interest is at any stage protected by entry on the register as a minor interest, it

10 The quite logical rationale for this rule is founded in the legal (though not social or commercial) reality that the purchaser has not technically suffered loss. The land which he has bought was at all material times subject to the overriding interest in question. The only new feature in the factual situation is that now, for the first time, the purchaser knows about the qualification upon his title. Thus runs the unsympathetic argument: no loss, no compensation. Rectification merely regularises a pre-existing position (see *Re Chowood's Registered Land* [1933] Ch 574).

ceases ipso facto to be an overriding interest and must thereafter be dealt with purely as a minor interest[11].

Second, it is open to the Registrar, upon receiving satisfactory proof of an overriding interest, to enter it on the register[12], whereupon it ranks merely as a minor interest. Likewise, the Registrar has discretion in appropriate cases to enter upon the register a notice indicating that the land is free from specified overriding interests[13]. However, the powers vested in the Registrar only partially mitigate the problems inherent in the existence of overriding interests which do not reach the stage of being recorded on the register[14].

8. THE CATEGORIES OF OVERRIDING INTEREST

Most of the categories of overriding interest in registered land are laid down in section 70(1) of the Land Registration Act 1925[15]. Foremost among the rights thus referred to are 'rights acquired or in the course of being acquired under the Limitation Acts'[16], the 'rights of every person in actual occupation of the land or in receipt of the rents and profits thereof'[17] and 'leases for any term or interest not exceeding 21 years, granted at a rent without taking a fine'[18]. Of these the most important rights are the 'rights of every person in actual occupation', and we shall look in some detail at this class. Meanwhile, the following observations should be noted[19].

(1) Section 70(1)(f)

The operation of section 70(1)(f) was illustrated in *Bridges v Mees*[20]. Here P contracted to purchase from V the fee simple estate in an area of registered land. He paid the full purchase price and entered into occupation, but never obtained from V a transfer of the registered title and never protected his estate contract by entering a minor interest on the register. When nearly 20 years later V transferred the fee simple not to P but to D instead, P was able to argue successfully before Harman J that his contractual rights were protected under

11 Land Registration Act 1925, s. 3(xvi).
12 Land Registration Act 1925, s. 70(3).
13 Land Registration Rules 1925, r. 197.
14 So grave is the danger that a purchaser of registered land may be trapped unwittingly by an overriding interest in the land purchased that many conveyancing solicitors commonly—and most unconscionably—attempt to divert responsibility for the discovery of overriding interests to the client-purchaser himself. Illusory indeed may be the protection which a layman imagines he buys when he employs a solicitor to convey registered land into his name!
15 See also Land Registration Rules 1925, r. 258.
16 Land Registration Act 1925, s. 70(1)(f).
17 Land Registration Act 1925, s. 70(1)(g).
18 Land Registration Act 1925, s. 70(1)(k).
19 For the avoidance of doubt, it may be said that it appears generally accepted now that equitable easements over registered land do not qualify as overriding interests under section 70(1)(a) of the Land Registration Act 1925. See T. B. F. Ruoff and R. B. Roper, op. cit., p. 97f.; D. G. Barnsley, op. cit., p. 44; D. J. Hayton, *Registered Land* (3rd edn., London 1981), p. 83f.
20 [1957] Ch 475.

section 70(1)(f)—and also for that matter under section 70(1)(g)—by reason of his adverse possession. D, although registered as the new proprietor, was therefore bound by P's overriding interest.

(2) Section 70(1)(k)

Similar protection is conferred by section 70(1)(k) upon tenants who hold leasehold interests not exceeding 21 years[1]. However, this provision covers only legal terms of years: equitable leases are excluded from protection[2], as are leases obtained on payment of a fine or premium (i.e., a capital sum as distinct from periodic rent)[3].

9. THE OPERATION OF SECTION 70(1)(g)

The most dramatic category of overriding interest is without doubt the category referred to in section 70(1)(g) as comprising

> the rights of every person in actual occupation of the land or in receipt of the rents and profits thereof, save where enquiry is made of such person and the rights are not disclosed[4].

The object of this fundamentally important provision was described by Lord Denning MR in *Strand Securities Ltd v Caswell*[5] as being to

> protect a person in actual occupation of the land from having his rights lost in the welter of registration. He can stay there and do nothing. Yet he will be protected. No one can

1 It has been suggested by some that a lease which is not noted on the register ought not to be an overriding interest at all unless the tenant is in actual occupation and his existence is therefore discoverable on physical inspection of the property. However, the Law Commission has rejected this view in principle: 'Many short tenancies are informal and where they relate to dwelling-houses and flats are often granted without the tenant being legally represented. We cannot think that it would be regarded as reasonable that a monthly tenant or even a tenant of a flat for, say, three years, who has not yet moved in, would have to register notice of this tenancy against the reversionary title at the Land Registry to protect himself against a purchaser of the reversion . . . Where there is a conflict we think that the law should incline in favour of the tenant. By not requiring occupation, the existing paragraph (k) does this and we agree with it' (Law Commission, Published Working Paper No. 37: *Land Registration (Second Paper)* (July 1971), para. 89).

2 See *City Permanent Building Society v Miller* [1952] Ch 840. However, equitable leases may sometimes acquire protection under section 70(1)(g) by reason of the 'actual occupation' of the equitable tenant, p. 338, post, note 20.

3 The Law Commission has proposed that *all* leases for terms not exceeding 21 years should be overriding interests whether or not obtained on payment of a fine or premium. See Law Commission, Published Working Papers No. 32, *Land Registration (First Paper)* (September 1970), para. 46, No. 37 (supra), para. 88.

4 The concept of 'actual possession' appears first in this context in the judgment of Lord Loughborough LC in *Taylor v Stibbert* (1794) 2 Ves Jun 437 at 440. For the first use of the phrase 'actual occupation', see *Barnhart v Greenshields* (1853) Moo PCC 18 at 34. The idea of 'actual occupation' first appears in statutory form in the list of 'overriding interests' contained in Law of Property Act 1922, Sch. 16, Part I, para. 5(3)(i), amending Land Transfer Act 1875, s. 18.

5 [1965] Ch 958 at 979f.

buy the land over his head and thereby take away or diminish his rights. It is up to every purchaser before he buys to make enquiry on the premises. If he fails to do so it is at his own risk[6].

Section 70(1)(g) was thus intended to benefit lay persons who own interests in registered land (perhaps of short duration) and to whom it might not occur that protective entry on the register is required in the event of a transfer of the registered title. In such cases, it was considered that it might well be unfair to demand positive protective action in circumstances where the very fact of actual occupation of the land would signal to all prudent purchasers both the possible existence of undocumented interests affecting the land and the necessity of further enquiry[7].

In examining section 70(1)(g), several preliminary points need to be made. *First*, the date on which an overriding interest crystallises by reason of 'actual occupation' is the date on which the transferee of the registered title is registered as the new proprietor of the estate in question[8]. The 'rights'—whatever they may be—of any person in 'actual occupation' of the land on this crucial day become overriding.

Second, once an overriding interest has thus crystallised on the date of registration, that interest remains enforceable against the transferee notwithstanding that the owner of the overriding interest ceases thereafter to occupy the land[9]. In other words, once the overriding interest materialises by virtue of actual occupation on the relevant date, its bindingness on the transferee thereafter does not depend on continued actual occupation.

Third, a derivative interest (e.g., a lease) which is subsequently carved out of an overriding interest enjoys the shelter of that overriding interest against any claim to possession brought by a transferee of the registered freehold title. For instance, in *Marks v Attallah*[10] E held an estate in fee simple as registered proprietor on a bare trust for H. On the assumption[11] that H had an overriding interest vis à vis M (a transferee of the freehold from E), Ungoed-Thomas J was prepared to hold that M was also bound by the lease granted to T after the effective date of registration of the transfer (see *Fig.* 57):

6 It has been said that section 70(1)(g) is 'an important safety valve in the registration system.' See R. J. Smith (1979) 95 LQR 501 at 505: 'Overriding Interests and Wives'.

7 See p. 332, ante.

8 *Re Boyle's Claim* [1961] 1 WLR 339. In order to pre-empt questions which might ultimately turn upon the precise day on which the registry staff actually processed an application for registration, the date of registration is deemed to be the date on which the application for registration was delivered at the registry (Land Registration Rules 1925, r. 83(2), as substituted by Land Registration Rules 1978, r. 8). This means that the vital date, for the purpose of the operation of section 70(1)(g), occurs *after* conveyance. If anyone is in actual occupation of the land on the deemed date of registration, then any property right owned by such an occupier becomes overriding under section 70(1)(g).

9 *London and Cheshire Insurance Co Ltd v Laplagrene Property Co Ltd* [1971] Ch 499.

10 (1966) 110 Sol Jo 709.

11 This assumption was tested and confirmed when the issue was later presented before the Court of Appeal in *Hodgson v Marks* [1971] Ch 892, p. 339, post.

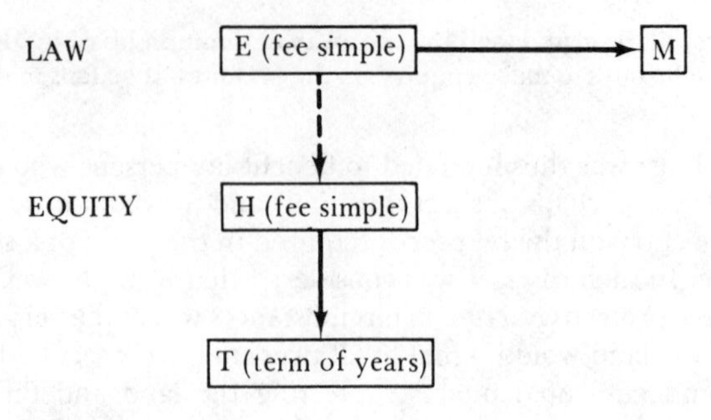

Fig. 57

Fourth, section 70(1)(g) applies in its terms to afford protection to the rights of any person who, at the relevant date, is 'in receipt of the rents and profits' derived from the land even though that person is not 'in actual occupation of the land.' Thus section 70(1)(g) protects the rights of a non-resident landlord as well as those of his tenant. The landlord is protected by virtue of his receipt of rents and profits, the tenant by virtue of his actual occupation. However, if the relationship is not based upon a lease but takes the form of a rent-free occupation licence granted by a non-resident licensor, neither the licensor nor the licensee is protected under section 70(1)(g)[12].

10. THE NATURE OF THE 'RIGHTS' PROTECTED BY SECTION 70(1)(g)

In order to understand the operation of section 70(1)(g), it is vital to recognise that this provision affords overriding status to 'the rights' of every person in actual occupation of the land or in receipt of the rents and profits thereof. What thus becomes 'overriding' is not necessarily the occupation of the person who claims rights under cover of section 70(1)(g), but rather those very rights themselves. In other words, occupation of the land is not per se the right referred to in section 70(1)(g); it is merely the trigger which activates the statutory protection of *any rights* belonging to the actual occupier—whatever those rights may be[13].

The range of 'rights' capable of protection under section 70(1)(g) is, however, subject to certain qualifications implicit in other provisions of the Land Registration Act 1925. For instance, section 20(1) refers to overriding interests as interests 'affecting the estate transferred or created'. Likewise, section 70(1) speaks of overriding interests as interests 'subsisting in reference' to 'registered land'. On the basis of these passing references, it is commonly maintained that

12 See *Strand Securities Ltd v Caswell* [1965] Ch 958. The licensor is not protected because he is not 'in actual occupation' nor is he 'in receipt of the rents and profits'. The licensee is not protected either, but for a different reason—he enjoys only a bare licence, and bare licences are not proprietary interests and do not therefore enter the threshold of section 70(1)(g).

13 The particular right protected under section 70(1)(g) may well be entirely unrelated to occupation of the land. It may, for instance, be an option to purchase the land (see *Webb v Pollmount Ltd* [1966] Ch 584).

section 70(1)(g) embraces only rights in land, i.e., rights which are proprietary rather than merely personal in character[14].

This restriction on the scope of section 70(1)(g) was adverted to in *National Provincial Bank Ltd v Hastings Car Mart Ltd*[15] by Russell LJ, who thought that

> section 70 in all its parts is dealing with rights in reference to land which have the quality of being capable of enduring through different ownerships of land, according to normal conceptions of title to real property.

This view of section 70(1)(g) was subsequently confirmed by the House of Lords in the same case[16], Lord Wilberforce emphasising that the

> whole frame of section 70 . . . shows that it is made against a background of interests or rights whose nature and whose transmissible character is known, or ascertainable, aliunde, i.e., under other statutes or under the common law.

Thus, in order to ascertain what 'rights' come within the ambit of section 70(1)(g),

> one must look outside the Land Registration Act and see what rights affect purchasers under the general law. To suppose that the subsection makes any right, of howsoever a personal character, which a person in occupation may have, an overriding interest by which a purchaser is bound, would involve two consequences: first that this Act is, in this respect, bringing about a substantive change in real property law by making personal rights bind purchasers; second, that there is a difference *as to the nature of the rights by which a purchaser may be bound* between registered and unregistered land; for purely personal rights . . . cannot affect purchasers of unregistered land even with notice. One may have to accept that there is a difference between unregistered and registered land as regards what kind of notice binds a purchaser, or what kind of inquiries a purchaser has to make. But there is no warrant in the terms of this paragraph or elsewhere in the Act for supposing that the nature of the rights which are to bind a purchaser is to be different, excluding personal rights in one case, including them in another[17].

The orthodox view of the scope of section 70(1)(g) is, therefore, that this provision refers only to rights of actual occupiers which have a proprietary character[18]. The category of overriding interests gathered under this head would include such rights as an option to purchase a legal estate[19], an equitable

14 This view of the status of personal rights in registered land would, of course, be wholly consistent with the orthodox doctrine which holds that such rights have no effect upon a third party purchaser in the corresponding context of unregistered land.

15 [1964] Ch 665 at 696.

16 [1965] AC 1175 at 1261.

17 A difference in the kind of notice which binds purchasers of unregistered and registered land respectively arises automatically from the fact that section 70(1)(g) renders 'overriding' the rights of any person 'in receipt of the rents and profits' of the land. It is quite clear that a purchaser of unregistered land occupied by a tenant is *not* thereby fixed with constructive notice of the landlord's rights (see *Hunt v Luck* [1901] 1 Ch 45, [1902] 1 Ch 428). The Law Commission has expressed the view that it is no longer necessary for the rights of persons 'in receipt of the rents and profits' of land to be protected under section 70(1)(g). See Published Working Paper No. 37, para. 63.

18 It is significant that proprietary character has hitherto been defined by the courts largely in terms of commerciability (i.e., 'transmissibility') and durability in the context of third party transfer (i.e., 'being capable of enduring through different ownerships of land'), p. 503, post.

19 *Webb v Pollmount Ltd* [1966] Ch 584.

lease or tenancy[20], the rights of a beneficiary behind a bare trust[1] or trust for sale[2], the right to an unpaid vendor's lien[3], the Rent Act entitlements of protected tenants[4], the equitable proprietary rights of an estoppel licensee[5], the right of a tenant to deduct from future rent the cost of repairs which his landlord has wrongfully failed to effect[6], and the right to have a registered title rectified under the Land Registration Act 1925[7]. All such rights conform sufficiently to the traditional characteristics of a proprietary interest in land to be capable of 'subsisting in reference' to registered land for the purpose of section 70(1)(g).

Correspondingly, it is quite consistent that section 70(1)(g) should exclude from its ambit essentially personal rights such as the 'deserted wife's equity' which was once thought to prevail in the matrimonial context. It should be remembered that the point in issue in *National Provincial Bank Ltd v Hastings Car Mart Ltd*[8] was precisely the question whether section 70(1)(g) extended to the 'deserted wife's equity.' The House of Lords had no doubt that the 'deserted wife's equity' was a purely personal right effective only against the other spouse. It could not, in view of its nature and origin, rank under the general law as a right *in rem*, and since it lacked an essential proprietary character it fell outside the scope of section 70(1)(g). The conclusion thus reached by the House of Lords is now preserved in the Matrimonial Homes Act 1967, in relation to the statutory 'rights of occupation' in the matrimonial home of which the 'deserted wife's equity' was the forerunner. Section 2(7) of the 1967 Act expressly provides that

> a spouse's rights of occupation shall not be an overriding interest . . . affecting the dwelling house notwithstanding that the spouse is in actual occupation of the dwelling house[9].

It was not, of course, surprising that in the Court of Appeal in *National Provincial Bank Ltd v Hastings Car Mart Ltd*[10] Lord Denning MR had expressed the view that a 'deserted wife's equity' to remain in occupation of registered land was indeed capable of ranking as an overriding interest under section 70(1)(g). He was even prepared to accord similar protection to other kinds of 'equity' which are not normally regarded as being truly proprietary rights in land. Among these interests Lord Denning numbered the rights of a contractual licensee in occupation[11]. It may well be that Lord Denning's liberal approach to

20 *Grace Rymer Investments Ltd v Waite* [1958] Ch 831.
1 *Hodgson v Marks* [1971] Ch 892.
2 *Williams & Glyn's Bank Ltd v Boland* [1980] 3 WLR 138.
3 *London and Cheshire Insurance Co Ltd v Laplagrene Property Co Ltd* [1971] Ch 499.
4 *National Provincial Bank Ltd v Hastings Car Mart Ltd* [1964] Ch 665 at 689 per Lord Denning MR.
5 Ibid.
6 *Lee-Parker v Izzett* [1971] 1 WLR 1688, p. 403, post.
7 *In re Brickwall Farm* (1981) Times, 10th April, p. 350 post.
8 [1965] AC 1175, p. 144 ante.
9 Of course, if those rights of occupation are protected as a minor interest in registered land by the entry of a notice or caution—as indeed they may be—they would automatically fall to be considered as a minor interest rather than as an overriding interest, p. 333, ante.
10 [1964] Ch 665 at 689.
11 The orthodox rule is that the rights of a contractual licensee bind only the licensor, and that third party purchasers are never affected by a contractual licence even though they purchase with express notice of the licensee's rights (see *Clore v Theatrical Properties Ltd and Westby & Co Ltd* [1936] 3 All ER 483 p. 499, post). However, Lord Denning's liberal view that section 70(1)(g)

contractual licences previews the future development of this area of law, but for the time being it is at least highly doubtful whether such rights as the contractual licence can properly be said to comprise 'rights' in registered land within the ambit of section 70(1)(g)[12]. As we have already noted, to take any other view is to give life and substance to that most dreadful nightmare of conveyancers—the unregistrable, non-overreachable, undiscoverable interest in land[13].

There are two categories of right in respect of which no doubt arises under section 70(1)(g). It is expressly provided by section 86(2) of the Land Registration Act 1925 that the equitable interests of beneficiaries under a strict settlement of land 'take effect as minor interests and not otherwise.' Thus, there is no possibility that such interests may ever claim dual status as overriding interests under section 70(1)(g). Likewise, it is made clear in section 5(5) of the Leasehold Reform Act 1967 that the right of a qualifying tenant to purchase the freehold reversion on a long lease can never constitute an overriding interest in registered land[14].

We shall look later in somewhat greater detail at the question whether the right of a beneficiary behind a trust for sale is capable of inclusion within section 70(1)(g). The House of Lords has given an affirmative answer to this question in *Williams & Glyn's Bank Ltd v Boland*[15], but the issue will be seen to have ramifications which extend far beyond the scope of that case[16].

11. THE NATURE OF 'ACTUAL OCCUPATION' FOR THE PURPOSE OF SECTION 70(1)(g)

Section 70(1)(g) affords protection to the rights of every person 'in actual occupation' of the land sold to a third party purchaser. The meaning of 'actual occupation' for this purpose must be sought in the case law.

This question of construction arose significantly for the first time in *Hodgson v Marks*[17]. Here, H had been the owner of her house in fee simple. After the death of her second husband, she took in E as her lodger and soon came to regard him as a man of substance. She entrusted him with the management of her affairs, and at his suggestion executed a voluntary transfer to him of the legal estate in the house. E was registered as the proprietor, the parties having reached a verbal understanding that the transfer was simply nominal and that H should remain the real owner of the property. H and E continued to live together in the

---

embraces even such equities as those enjoyed by a contractual licensee is in clear accord with his diligent efforts over the years to elevate the status of contractual licences so that they should receive the same protection under the general law as that which is accorded to equitable proprietary interests (see, e.g., *Errington v Errington and Woods* [1952] 1 KB 290; *Binions v Evans* [1972] Ch 359).

12 See the caution expressed in *National Provincial Bank Ltd v Hastings Car Mart Ltd* [1965] AC 1175 at 1239f. per Lord Upjohn, 1251 per Lord Wilberforce.

13 See p. 313, ante.

14 See p. 404, ante.

15 [1980] 3 WLR 138.

16 See p. 376, post.

17 [1971] Ch 892.

house after the transfer. However, E later sold and transferred the legal estate to M without the knowledge or concurrence of H. E then died, and the present litigation concerned the claim now made by H that her rights were protected against M by virtue of section 70(1)(g).

It was accepted both by Ungoed-Thomas J at first instance and by the Court of Appeal that before the transfer by E to M, E had held the registered title on a bare trust for H. It was found that H had not intended to make a gift of the property to E, and that the original transfer had therefore brought about a resulting trust of the legal estate in favour of H[18]. The major question now in dispute was whether H could assert her rights as beneficiary behind the bare or resulting trust against the new registered proprietor, M:

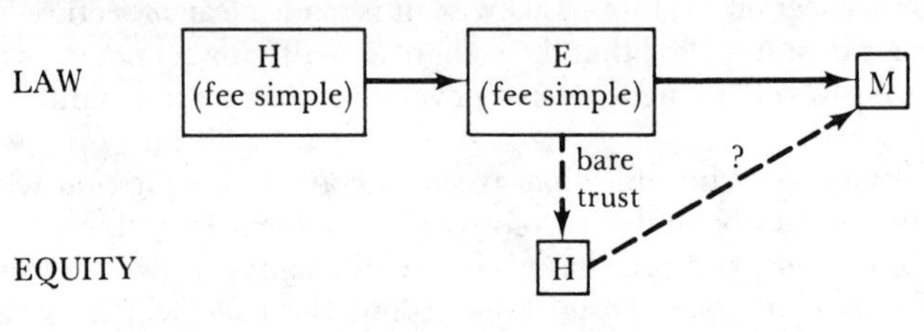

Fig. 58

At the actual time when M presented his transfer document for registration[19], H was indeed in residence in the property in question. But was she 'in actual occupation' for the purpose of section 70(1)(g)? Ungoed-Thomas J answered this question in the negative, with the result that H's claim for protection failed. Ungoed-Thomas J expressed the view that section 70(1)(g) was deliberately enacted as the statutory equivalent in the area of registered land of the well known doctrine of notice which protects the rights of persons in occupation of unregistered land[20]. He thus construed 'actual occupation' in the present context as connoting 'actual and apparent occupation . . . occupation by act recognisable as such', since any other construction, by subjecting a purchaser to the rights of occupiers irrespective altogether of notice, would mean that section 70(1)(g) had become 'not a form of notice at all, but its negation[1]'.

On the present facts, it appeared that M had known of the existence of H when he contracted to purchase the property from E: he had seen H coming up the garden path on one occasion when he visited the property prior to the transfer. He had assumed, however, that H was E's wife and that as such she had no beneficial interest in the property[2]. There was even some evidence to suggest that E had dishonestly attempted to implant such an impression in M's mind.

18 H could not now be precluded from asserting the existence of such a trust vis à vis E, since resulting trusts are excepted from the requirement of writing normally imposed by section 53(1) of the Law of Property Act 1925 (see Law of Property Act 1925, section 53(2)), p. 247f, ante.
19 See p. 335, ante.
20 See *Hunt v Luck* [1902] 1 Ch 428.
1 [1971] Ch 892 at 915. See (1971) 35 Conv (NS) 255 (I. Leeming); (1972) 88 LQR 14 (J. L. Barton); (1973) 36 MLR 25 (R. H. Maudsley).
2 This assumption was still current at the time of *Hodgson v Marks* but by the 1980s was no longer a safe one. See *Williams & Glyn's Bank Ltd v Boland* [1979] Ch 312, [1980] 3 WLR 138.

Nevertheless Ungoed-Thomas J held that H had not been 'in actual occupation' for the purpose of section 70(1)(g), in the sense that it would not have been apparent to a purchaser from the mere fact of her presence on the property that she was beneficially entitled[3].

The Court of Appeal in *Hodgson v Marks* reversed the decision of Ungoed-Thomas J, ruling that H's beneficial interest behind the bare trust ranked as an overriding interest under section 70(1)(g). Russell LJ, while declining to 'lay down a code or catalogue of situations in which a person other than the vendor should be held to be . . . in actual occupation of registered land for the purpose of section 70(1)(g)', had no doubt that, on the present facts, H had indeed been 'in actual occupation' of the property. The Court of Appeal thus construed the phrase 'actual occupation' literally, as connoting a mere physical presence on the part of persons other than the vendor. Russell LJ pointed out that

> it is a principle of law (and of the Land Registration Act 1925) that a person in occupation is protected in his rights by that occupation, unless, of course, the rights are such that they require registration if they are to be protected. A purchaser must pay heed to anyone in occupation if he is to be sure of getting a good title . . . Moreover, I do not consider that it is correct in law to say that any rights of a person who is in occupation will be overridden whenever the vendor is, or appears to be, also in occupation . . . It must depend on the circumstances, and a wise purchaser or lender will take no risks. Indeed, however wise he may be he may have no ready opportunity of finding out; but, nevertheless, the law will protect the occupier[4].

Thus it seems in the aftermath of *Hodgson v Marks* that 'actual occupation' in the sense of section 70(1)(g) is to be determined as a matter of physical fact. As Lord Denning MR held in *Williams & Glyn's Bank Ltd v Boland*[5], '"actual occupation" is matter of fact not matter of law.' This approach was upheld by the House of Lords in the same case, Lord Wilberforce observing that

> the only solution which is consistent with the Act . . . and with common sense is to read the paragraph for what it says. Occupation, existing as a fact, may protect rights if the person in occupation has rights[6].

Likewise, Lord Scarman declined to read the Land Registration Act 1925

> as requiring the courts to give the words 'actual occupation' in section 70(1)(g) the special meaning for which the appellants contend, namely an occupation, which by its nature necessarily puts a would-be purchaser (or mortgagee) upon notice of a claim adverse to the registered owner. On the contrary, I expect to find—as I do find—that the statute has substituted a plain factual situation for the uncertainties of notice, actual or constructive, as the determinant of an overriding interest[7].

However, the result of the case law may be that (as in *Hodgson v Marks* and arguably in *Williams & Glyn's Bank Ltd v Boland*) it becomes exceedingly

3 Compare *Caunce v Caunce* [1969] 1 WLR 286, p. 289ff, ante.
4 [1971] Ch 892 at 932.
5 [1979] Ch 312 at 332.
6 [1980] 3 WLR 138 at 143: 'These words are ordinary words of plain English, and should, in my opinion, be interpreted as such.'
7 [1980] 3 WLR 138 at 149.

difficult—if not in some cases quite impossible—for a purchaser to detect the existence of certain kinds of overriding interest affecting the land which he proposes to buy[8].

12. ENQUIRY UNDER SECTION 70(1)(g)

Pursuant to section 70(1)(g), the rights of every person in actual occupation constitute an overriding interest in registered land 'save where enquiry is made of such person and the rights are not disclosed.' Clearly, it was not the intendment of the legislature that an actual occupier should be able to entrench his rights as an overriding interest if he dishonestly conceals their existence from an intending purchaser.

Yet it is important to read the proviso to section 70(1)(g) with some care. In order to take the land free of overriding interests, a purchaser must make enquiry of the person whose rights would otherwise comprise an overriding interest. In *Hodgson v Marks*[9], M may have made some enquiry as to the precise status or entitlement of H, but since he directed his enquiry towards E only, that enquiry was utterly irrelevant for the purpose of complying with section 70(1)(g). In order to guarantee immunity from the overriding interest, M would have had to make enquiry of H herself—and this he did not do. In the words of Russell LJ, 'reliance on the untrue ipse dixit of the vendor will not suffice[10].' As we have already seen, the requirement of enquiry under section 70(1)(g) imposes in some cases an extremely heavy onus of enquiry upon the purchaser, since he must make enquiry of persons whose actual occupation may not be at all apparent[11]. However, as Russell LJ stressed, the law will protect the occupier of registered land irrespective of the difficulty facing the purchaser[12].

13. THE DUAL STATUS OF MINOR INTEREST AND OVERRIDING INTEREST

Most schemes for the registration of land interests operate ultimately on the basis of two simple rules. *First,* if a registrable interest has in fact been duly registered, it is binding on all third party purchasers regardless of whether they have inspected the register. *Second,* a registrable right becomes void and unenforceable against a third party purchaser if it is not entered on the register. In the latter case it matters not that the purchaser has actual knowledge of the unregistered interest from another source.

8 See p. 376f, post.
9 [1971] Ch 892.
10 [1971] Ch 892 at 932.
11 The onus placed upon the purchaser becomes even greater in situations of multiple occupation. We will shortly discuss more fully the problems of 'actual occupation' and the duty of 'enquiry' relevant to the situation where a spouse claims an overriding interest behind a trust for sale of the matrimonial home, p. 353ff, post.
12 See p. 341, ante.

These straightforward principles apply both in the context of registration of land charges[13] and in the context of registration of title[14]. The underlying motive is readily understandable—the rules are clear-cut and admit of easy application. The public medium of registration serves as an effective form of notice. Moreover, the statutory sanction of voidness in the event of non-registration ensures that the register—whether it be the register of land charges or the Land Register—contains an accurate, current and comprehensive record of the interests affecting the land in question.

It is against this background of principle that it appears particularly strange that the Land Registration Act 1925 permits an area of overlap between minor interests and overriding interests in registered land[15]. It seems to be possible for certain kinds of equitable interest relating to registered land to claim a dual protected status vis à vis transferees of the legal estate *either* on the ground that they have been duly protected by entry as minor interests on the register *or* on the quite different ground that they have not been so protected but nevertheless enjoy the immunity given to overriding interests by section 70(1) of the Land Registration Act 1925. In other words, it is possible that a failure to protect a minor interest by entry on the register—far from incurring the penalty of voidness—may indeed have the paradoxical effect of reinforcing that interest as an overriding interest[16]. It is strange that a scheme of registration can so operate that interests which are left unprotected qua minor interest are then, in default of such protection, upheld qua overriding interest[17]. A scheme directed towards securing registration of interests should firmly attach disadvantage rather than advantage to a negligent failure to register.

Notwithstanding such considerations, the House of Lords decided in *Williams & Glyn's Bank Ltd v Boland*[18] that some interests in registered land do indeed enjoy the dual protection of minor interest and overriding interest. The appellant Bank had argued that the categories of minor interest and overriding interest are mutually exclusive[19]. Lord Wilberforce professed to find this argument 'formidable', but pointed to previous decisions in which potentially minor interests had been regarded as overriding interests, e.g., *Bridges v Mees*[20] and *Hodgson v Marks*[1]. He observed[2]

These decisions . . . provide an answer to the argument that there is a firm dividing line, or an unbridgeable gulf, between minor interests and overriding interests, and, on the

13 See Law of Property Act 1925, ss. 198(1), 199(1)(i); Land Charges Act 1972, s. 4, p. 114, ante.
14 See Land Registration Act 1925, ss. 20(1), 59(6), but compare *Peffer v Rigg* [1977] 1 WLR 285, p. 328, ante.
15 That there may be an overlap is clearly contemplated by Law Commission, Published Working Paper No. 37, paras. 18ff.
16 An overriding interest is, by definition, one which does not appear as a minor interest on the face of the register, p. 331, ante.
17 See Law Commission, Published Working Paper No. 37, paras. 14, 19ff.
18 [1980] 3 WLR 138.
19 Some support for this contention may indeed be found in Land Registration Act 1925, ss. 86(2), 101.
20 [1957] Ch 475, p. 333, ante.
1 [1971] Ch 892, p. 339, ante.
2 [1980] 3 WLR 138 at 146.

contrary, confirm that the fact of occupation enables protection of the latter to extend to what without it would be the former.

Likewise, Lord Scarman agreed with the appellants

that overriding interests and minor interests are, as categories, exclusive of each other. But there is no logical difficulty in the association of a minor interest with another factor (i.e. actual occupation) being, qua association, an overriding interest[3].

The overall consequence is that, in the area of registered land, we can adopt a two-fold formula in dealing with that central question of land law, i.e., the question whether the owner of an equitable interest takes priority over a transferee of the legal estate[4]. In determining this issue of priority, it is necessary to ask two questions only:

(i) *Did the owner of that equitable interest have any right capable of protection by entry as a minor interest on the register?* If the answer is in the affirmative and that right has been duly entered as a minor interest, that entry of course prevails against the transferee[5]. If that right has not been so protected, there is some—albeit dubious—authority for the view that an unprotected minor interest is binding on a transferee who has actual express knowledge of the existence of the right in question[6]. However, the better view is that (apart from cases of clear fraud) a transferee is unaffected by an unprotected minor interest 'whether he has or has not notice thereof, express, implied or constructive[7].' If, on this view, an unprotected minor interest thus becomes ineffective qua minor interest as against a transferee, then we must ask a second question:

(ii) *Can the owner of that equitable interest nevertheless qualify for the statutory immunity afforded overriding interests?* If the answer to this question is in the affirmative, then even an unprotected minor interest may be saved as an overriding interest and may therefore bind a transferee of the legal title. Statutory immunity may well be available, for instance, on the ground that the owner of the equitable interest is 'in actual occupation' of the registered land or is 'in receipt of the rents and profits' of such land[8].

The result is that the owner of an equitable interest in registered land who claims priority over a transferee of the legal estate may have 'two bites at the cherry'. He may, in some circumstances, base his argument either upon the ground that he has duly protected his minor interest or, in default of securing such protection, upon the ground that the equitable interest in question qualifies as an overriding interest binding the transferee. We must examine the extent to which this 'heads I win, tails you lose' argument is applicable in the resolution

3 [1980] 3 WLR 138 at 150.
4 It will be remembered that, in relation to the equivalent question in the area of unregistered land, it is possible to construct a three-fold formula which must eventually resolve the issue, p. 313ff, ante.
5 Land Registration Act 1925, s. 20(1).
6 See *Peffer v Rigg* [1977] 1 WLR 285.
7 Land Registration Act 1925, s. 59(6).
8 Land Registration Act 1925, s. 70(1)(g). See p. 334, ante.

of the classic questions of unregistered land law when those questions are transposed into registered land terms.

(1) The unprotected estate contract (Hollington Brothers Ltd v Rhodes)

Hollington Brothers Ltd v Rhodes[9] provides clear authority for the proposition that, in unregistered land, an unregistered estate contract is void against a purchaser of a legal estate for money or money's worth even though the purchaser has acquired actual knowledge of the estate contract from another source than the register. Thus on the actual facts which underlay *Hollington Brothers Ltd v Rhodes* the purchaser of the legal estate won[10].

If *Hollington Brothers Ltd v Rhodes* were recast in terms of registered land, the result would be determined in the following manner. Using the nomenclature adopted when we earlier considered this case[11], T should have protected his estate contract as a minor interest in registered land through the entry of a notice or caution on the Land Register. Since he did not do so, his unprotected estate contract (equitable lease) must be ineffective against the transferee P, regardless of the state of P's mind. However, T's estate contract may still be binding on and enforceable against P on the ground that, given that T was 'in actual occupation' of the premises in question, the estate contract constituted an overriding interest under section 70(1)(g) of the Land Registration Act 1925. In this case, the result in law based upon the facts of *Hollington Brothers Ltd v Rhodes* would differ substantively according to whether the problem arose in registered or unregistered land. In the registered land context, T would win; in the unregistered land context, T would lose!

(2) The unwitting purchaser of settled land (Weston v Henshaw)

In *Weston v Henshaw*[12], it was held that section 18(1)(a) of the Settled Land Act 1925 rendered 'void' an unauthorised disposition in relation to the legal estate in unregistered settled land where a mortgagee, being totally unaware of the existence of the settlement, paid the capital moneys arising otherwise than to the trustees of the settlement. In other words, in the unregistered land context, the purchaser/mortgagee lost[13].

The particular form of fraud which occurred in *Weston v Henshaw* almost certainly could not occur if the land concerned were registered land, simply because a transferee or chargee would inspect not documents of title produced by the transferor or mortgagor but rather the register of title. In any event, however, the protection of beneficial interests under a strict settlement must be

9 [1951] 2 TLR 691 (p. 115, ante). See also *Midland Bank Trust Co Ltd v Green* [1981] 2 WLR 28.
10 See, however, the argument outlined earlier, p. 117, ante, which indicates that the result should perhaps have gone the other way.
11 See p. 115, ante.
12 [1950] Ch 510, p. 172, ante. See R. H. Maudsley (1973) 36 MLR 25 at 28.
13 Compare, however, *Re Morgan's Lease* [1972] Ch 1, p. 173, ante.

procured by entry of those beneficial interests as minor interests on the register[14]. If no appropriate entry is made, then the beneficial interests under the settlement become ineffective against a subsequent purchaser[15]. In this case the unprotected settled land interests *cannot* be salvaged as overriding interests (e.g., under section 70(1)(g) of the Land Registration Act 1925), because of the express preclusion contained in section 86(2) of the 1925 Act[16]. Section 86(2) makes it clear that settled land interests 'take effect as minor interests and not otherwise', thus foreclosing any possibility that settled land beneficiaries may claim dual protected status for their interests as *either* minor interests *or* overriding interests[17]. Parliament in 1925 appears to have been peculiarly sensitive to the anomalous nature of a potential overlap and thus took special steps to prevent the occurrence of such an overlap. It is unfortunate from the point of view of technical efficiency and consistency that the potential overlap between minor and overriding interests was not pre-empted in other areas.

(3) The unwitting purchaser of land held on trust for sale (Caunce v Caunce)

The translation of the priority issue in *Caunce v Caunce*[18] into terms of registered land raises extremely complex questions which are the subject of an extended discussion contained in the next chapter[19].

14. THE FUTURE OF OVERRIDING INTERESTS

It is quite clear that the expanding universe of overriding interests within section 70(1) of the Land Registration Act 1925 has begun to present problems for those concerned with the law and practice of land transactions. Even if this was not clear before the decision of the House of Lords in *Williams & Glyn's Bank Ltd v Boland*[20], it is compellingly apparent in the aftermath of that ruling that some reform of the law of overriding interests is now long overdue. The existence of a wide and ill-defined category of overriding interests represents not merely a disincentive to the protection of registrable interests but also a gross violation of the 'mirror principle' relating to registered land[1].

With these considerations in mind, the Law Commission has proposed certain amendments to the law of overriding interests. The Law Commission takes as its starting point the view

> that, in the interests of certainty and of simplifying conveyancing, the class of right which may bind a purchaser otherwise than as the result of an entry in the register should be as narrow as possible[2].

14 See p. 326, ante.
15 Land Registration Act 1925, s. 59(6).
16 See p. 339, ante.
17 See F. R. Crane (1958) 22 Conv (NS) 14 at 23f.: 'Equitable Interests in Registered Land'.
18 [1969] 1 WLR 286, p. 289ff, ante.
19 See p. 353, post.
20 [1980] 3 WLR 138.
1 See p. 321, ante.
2 Published Working Paper No. 37: *Land Registration (Second Paper)* (July 1971), para. 34.

The Law Commission has therefore suggested that the classes of overriding interests should be re-drawn to exclude all interests which are capable themselves of either substantive registration[3] or protection as minor interests[4]. Furthermore, the Law Commission has suggested an amended version of section 70(1)(g) which would confer overriding status upon

> contractual rights to occupy the land or any part thereof of every person who at the date of the relevant disposition is in actual and apparent occupation of the land, save where enquiry is made of such person and such rights are not disclosed[5].

The modified version of section 70(1)(g) would protect only contractual occupation rights[6]. It would exclude beneficial interests behind a trust (whether a trust for sale or bare trust), the Law Commission's view being that interests of this kind would be better protected if the court had wider powers in the field of rectification and indemnity[7]. It is significant that the Law Commission would make the date of the relevant disposition rather than the date of registration the determinative date[8]. The Commission made it clear that the new requirement of actual *and apparent* occupation was intended

> to convey the sense that the occupation must be apparent from such enquiries and inspections as ought reasonably to have been made by a purchaser in the circumstances of each particular case[9].

There has as yet been no implementation of the Law Commission's proposals to reduce the numbers of overriding interests and to amend section 70(1)(g). Indeed, the Commission's modification of section 70(1)(g) has been criticised by some[10] as effecting an unjustifiable substantive alteration in the traditional principles of land law, by elevating purely contractual occupation rights (e.g., the licence enjoyed by a lodger) to the status of proprietary rights in land. However, such a change has already been foreshadowed by the courts[11], and if

3 Ibid., para. 14, p. 324, ante.
4 Ibid., para. 20, p. 343, ante.
5 Ibid., para. 73.
6 'We have in mind that only rights of occupation arising under contract including (if the other conditions of the paragraph are satisfied) the contractual rights of a lodger or person sharing accommodation should be protected, but not, for example, the rights of occupation of the matrimonial home which arise by operation of law' (ibid., para. 74). The class of contractual occupation right envisaged by the Law Commission would include the right which was disputed in *Binions v Evans* [1972] Ch 359, p. 490, post, but not, for instance, the rights of a tenant holding over under the Rent Act. Rights of the latter kind are expressly granted by statute, not by contract, and the Law Commission considered that the statutory tenant should not therefore come within the reformulated section 70(1)(g). However, the Law Commission did suggest that the rights of the statutory tenant should be protected under a new and specific head of overriding interest by being so described in the statute which creates the right (ibid., para. 72).
7 Ibid., para. 69. See Published Working Paper No. 45, paras. 71ff., p. 348, post.
8 See p. 335, ante.
9 Published Working Paper No. 37, para. 75.
10 See D. G. Barnsley, op. cit., p. 54f.; D. Jackson (1972) 88 LQR 93 at 114f.
11 In *National Provincial Bank Ltd v Hastings Car Mart Ltd* [1964] Ch 665 at 699, Russell LJ said that 'in the case of contractual licences, their elevation for the purposes of title to a status equivalent to an estate or interest in land might be thought desirable, at least in the case of licences to occupy', but added that such a substantive change in the law would be 'a matter for legislation'.

accomplished by legislation would constitute a most desirable recognition of the vastly increased significance of rights of occupation and residential security.

15. REGISTERED CHARGES[12]

Registered land may be mortgaged by way of 'registered charge'. Such a charge

> shall, unless made or taking effect by demise or subdemise, and subject to any provision to the contrary contained in the charge, take effect as a charge by way of legal mortgage[13].

A registered charge is therefore a legal interest which is capable of creation and disposition by means only of a 'registered disposition'[14]. It can never qualify as a registrable interest, minor interest or overriding interest, and becomes fully effective only when the chargee is entered as the 'proprietor' of the charge on the relevant register of title[15]. The chargee is then issued with a charge certificate, and while the charge remains in effect in relation to the registered land the relevant land certificate of the chargor is deposited in the Land Registry as security against further dealings by the estate owner[16]. Subject to any contrary indication on the register, registered charges on the same land rank as between themselves according to the order in which they are entered on the register, and not according to the order in which they are created[17].

16. RECTIFICATION AND INDEMNITY[18]

(1) Grounds of rectification

It is of fundamental significance in the statutory scheme of registered title under the Land Registration Act 1925 that no title is ever quite absolute. Even a proprietor who has been registered with a supposedly 'absolute title'[19] is liable to have the register of title rectified to his prejudice in certain specified

---

See also [1965] AC 1175 at 1251 per Lord Wilberforce. Lord Denning MR has, of course, decided cases for a long time now on the basis that contractual occupation licences are already—without the benefit of enabling legislation—proprietary interests in land, p. 498, post.

12 See Chapter 15 on mortgages, p. 506, post.

13 Land Registration Act 1925, s. 27(1).

14 See Land Registration Act 1925, ss. 3(xxii), 18(4), 21(4).

15 Land Registration Act 1925, s. 26(1).

16 Land Registration Act 1925, s. 65.

17 Land Registration Act 1925, s. 29. On the priorities of equitable mortgages of registered land, see Land Registration Act 1925, s. 106(2), (3); *Abigail v Lapin* [1934] AC 491; *Barclays Bank Ltd v Taylor* [1974] Ch 137. See also R. J. Smith (1977) 93 LQR 541: 'The Priority of Competing Minor Interests in Registered Land'.

18 See Law Commission, Published Working Paper No. 45: *Land Registration (Third Paper)* (July 1972); S. M. Cretney and G. Dworkin (1968) 84 LQR 528: 'Rectification and Indemnity: Illusion and Reality'; D. C. Jackson (1978) 94 LQR 239: 'Security of Title in Registered Land'.

19 See p. 324, ante.

circumstances. These circumstances are enumerated in section 82(1) of the Land Registration Act 1925. They include cases where rectification is required in order to enter upon the register a subsisting overriding interest[20], or to enter an interest wrongly omitted by the registrar on first registration[1], or where the court or the registrar is satisfied that an existing entry in the register has been 'obtained by fraud[2],' or even where 'by reason of any error or omission in the register, or by reason of any entry made under a mistake, it may be deemed just to rectify the register[3].' It is of interest that in *Peffer v Rigg*[4], Graham J granted rectification of D[2]'s title under section 82(1), although he did not specify the particular head under which he did so. It is possible that the circumstances present in that case might have qualified under section 82(1)(d) as an instance of entry 'obtained by fraud[5].'

Some doubt has been cast upon the grounds of rectification by remarks made in the Court of Appeal in *Orakpo v Manson Investments Ltd*[6]. Here P had executed a number of legal charges on his properties in favour of D as security for loans made to him by D. D registered those charges against P's title in each case, but it was subsequently held that the charges were unenforceable under section 6 of the Moneylenders Act 1927 and were not therefore proper entries on the register. However, D argued successfully that it was entitled, by subrogation, to unpaid vendor's liens in respect of the disputed transactions. Although the case was ultimately decided on other grounds by the House of Lords[7], it is significant that two of the judges in the Court of Appeal expressed the court's discretion to rectify the register in wider terms than had hitherto been usual. Buckley LJ stated somewhat bluntly that

> if the present entries on the register do not reflect the true position, the register is open to rectification[8].

He pointed out that the legal charges executed by P pursuant to the loan agreements required cancellation (which itself would necessitate rectification), but saw no reason to preclude D from seeking entry on the register, by way of further rectification, of suitable notices, cautions or restrictions to protect its subrogated rights.

Buckley LJ considered that section 82(1)(a) and (h) might be applicable to the circumstances of the present case. With particular reference to the latter ground of rectification, Buckley LJ indicated that

> if there is an omission in the register of some entry which ought to be there for the

20 Land Registration Act 1925, s. 82(1)(a). See *Chowood Ltd v Lyall* (No. 2) [1930] 2 Ch 156.
1 Land Registration Act 1925, s. 82(1)(b). See *Calgary and Edmonton Land Co Ltd v Discount Bank (Overseas) Ltd* [1971] 1 WLR 81.
2 Land Registration Act 1925, s. 82(1)(d). See *Re Leighton's Conveyance* [1936] 1 All ER 667.
3 Land Registration Act 1925, s. 82(1)(h). See *Re Dance's Way, West Town, Hayling Island* [1962] Ch 490.
4 [1977] 1 WLR 285 at 294f., p. 328, ante.
5 See (1977) 36 Cambridge LJ 227 at 231 (D. J. Hayton).
6 [1977] 1 WLR 347. See (1977) 41 Conv (NS) 210 (F. R. Crane).
7 [1978] AC 95. See (1977) 41 Conv (NS) 354 (F. R. Crane).
8 [1977] 1 WLR 347 at 360.

protection of [D], it seems to me that they can apply for rectification of the register to effect the necessary entry to protect them[9].

Goff LJ was likewise of opinion that D would 'clearly be entitled to have the register rectified under section 82 of the 1925 Act'[10], but did not state any specific head under section 82(1) as being applicable.

The eventual decision in *Orakpo v Manson Investments Ltd* was reached on other grounds, but if the observations made in the Court of Appeal are indicative of the future approach of the courts, it may be that the courts are beginning to arrogate to themselves a significantly wider discretion in matters of rectification than has hitherto been recognised.

(2) The effect of rectification

When the register is rectified by the removal of the name of the existing proprietor and the substitution of another person's name, the consequence is to vest the legal title in the new registered proprietor[11]. The former proprietor is thereafter divested of title, although it may be open to him to seek an indemnity in respect of any loss suffered by him by reason of the rectification. It is provided in section 82(2) of the Land Registration Act 1925 that

> The register may be rectified under this section, notwithstanding that the rectification may affect any estates, rights, charges, or interests acquired or protected by registration, or by any entry on the register, or otherwise.

This provision appears to authorise orders for rectification which can be effective not merely to rectify the title in question, but also to operate adversely against the interests of third parties which are already duly protected by entry on the register or which are protected in any event as overriding interests. However, section 82(2) has not been accorded this extensive interpretation. In *Freer v Unwins Ltd*[12], a register of title was rectified by order of the Chief Land Registrar, by entering notice of restrictive covenants affecting the land which had been omitted at the time of first registration. D was the assignee of a leasehold interest in the land which had been granted prior to the rectification and which was itself an overriding interest. D had knowledge of the existence of the restrictive covenants but knew also that those covenants had not been protected by entry on the register. When P brought proceedings to enforce the restrictive covenants against D, Walton J held that D was not bound by them. According to Walton J, D's lease must, in accordance with section 19(2) of the Land Registration Act 1925, be deemed to have taken effect as if it were a registered disposition immediately on its being granted. Under section 20(1), therefore, it took effect subject to any entries appearing on the register at that date and subject to overriding interests (if any), but free from all other estates

9 [1977] 1 WLR 347 at 361.
10 [1977] 1 WLR 347 at 370.
11 Land Registration Act 1925, s. 69(1). The right to rectification may itself constitute an overriding interest. See *In re Brickwall Farm* (1981) Times, 10th April.
12 [1976] Ch 288. See (1976) 35 Cambridge LJ 211 (D. J. Hayton).

and interests[13]. The lease assigned to D was accordingly unaffected by the subsequent entry on the register of the restrictive covenant relating to the freehold title[14]. The decision in *Freer v Unwins Ltd* thus provides a surprising instance of rectification in derogation of the rights of a freeholder but without prejudice to the rights of a leaseholder in the same land.

(3) Restrictions upon rectification

Certain restrictions are imposed upon the right to secure rectification. Under section 82(3) of the Land Registration Act 1925,

> The register shall not be rectified, except for the purpose of giving effect to an overriding interest or an order of the court, so as to affect the title of the proprietor who is in possession . . .

Apart from the exceptional cases of the overriding interest and the order of the court, there are two further exceptions to the general rule that the register may not be rectified to the prejudice of the proprietor 'in possession'. These additional exceptions arise in cases where 'the proprietor has caused or substantially contributed by fraud or lack of proper care' to the error or omission in respect of which rectification is sought[15], and where 'for any other reason, in any particular case, it is considered that it would be unjust not to rectify the register against him[16].' Again in *Peffer v Rigg*[17], Graham J expressed the view that rectification could be ordered against D^2, notwithstanding that she was a proprietor 'in possession', on the ground of one or other exception within section 82(3). He did not, however, indicate which exceptional case applied.

(4) Indemnity

Subject to contrary statutory provisions, 'any person suffering loss by reason of any rectification of the register . . . shall be entitled to be indemnified[18].' In

13 See p. 327, ante.
14 If the lessee had been held bound by the restrictive covenants in question, it would have received compensation under the provisions for statutory indemnity, and this would have appeared to be a good ground for holding the defendant to be subject to the unprotected covenants. However, this pragmatic approach was not adopted, and the actual decision in *Freer v Unwins Ltd* simply highlights an even more fundamental question: why was the title rectified in the first place? Walton J considered the Registrar's decision in favour of rectification 'a very great surprise' ([1976] Ch 288 at 295), presumably because the general scheme of the Land Registration Act 1925 is that a transferee (such as the original lessee) takes his interest in the registered land free from all third party rights other than those duly protected by entry on the register and, of course, overriding interests (see Land Registration Act 1925, s. 20 (1)). See also T. B. F. Ruoff and R. B. Roper, op. cit., p. 793f.; (1980) 39 Cambridge LJ 380f. (D. J. Hayton).
15 Land Registration Act 1925, s. 82(3)(a), as substituted by Administration of Justice Act 1977, s. 24(b). See *Re 139 High Street, Deptford* [1951] Ch 884; *Claridge v Tingey, Re Sea View Gardens* [1967] 1 WLR 134.
16 Land Registration Act 1925, s. 82(3)(c). See *Epps v Esso Petroleum Co Ltd* [1973] 1 WLR 1071; (1974) 33 Cambridge LJ 60 (S. N. Palk).
17 [1977] 1 WLR 285, p. 328, ante.
18 Land Registration Act 1925, s. 83(1).

addition, where an 'error or omission' has occurred in the register but the register is not rectified, any person suffering loss by reason of that error or omission shall likewise be entitled to be indemnified[19].

These provisions are supposedly the basis of the claim that the scheme of registered title operates on the premise of a state-guaranteed title which is reinforced by automatic compensation in the event that the guarantee fails. The right to receive an indemnity in cases of prejudice is not, however, as unqualified as might at first sight appear. We have already noted that, in the vital case of a subsisting overriding interest, the transferee of the registered title is ineligible for compensation, on the ground that technically he has suffered no 'loss'[20]. The right to indemnity is expressly withheld in other circumstances specified in the Land Registration Act 1925, such as the case where an applicant for the statutory indemnity 'has caused or substantially contributed' to the loss in respect of which he claims compensation 'by fraud or lack of proper care'[1]. However, where a right to receive compensation is recognised, the indemnity is paid by the Chief Land Registrar out of moneys provided by Parliament. An interesting, but somewhat cynical, note on which to conclude this review of the system of registered title is the fact that, out of an annual fee income of many millions of pounds[2], the average amount of compensation paid out each year totals only a few thousand pounds[3].

19 Land Registration Act 1925, s. 83(2).
20 See *Re Chowood's Registered Land* [1933] Ch 574, p. 332, ante.
1 Land Registration Act 1925, s. 83(5)(a), as substituted by Land Registration and Land Charges Act 1971, s. 3(1).
2 See *Report of the Chief Land Registrar* (London 1976), pp. 10, 14.
3 See T. B. F. Ruoff and R. B. Roper, op. cit., p. 805f.

CHAPTER 11

Registered land and the single trustee for sale

In this chapter we consider a crucial issue of priority which has arisen recently in the area of registered land. The issue concerned here is the problem which arose in the context of unregistered land in *Caunce v Caunce*[1].

1. THE CAUNCE v CAUNCE PROBLEM

It was decided in *Caunce v Caunce* that, in unregistered land, the equitable doctrine of notice determines priority between a beneficiary behind an implied trust for sale and a mortgagee who does not realise that the land is subject to a trust. In *Caunce v Caunce* Stamp J ruled that the mere presence of a wife/beneficiary in the matrimonial home at the time of a mortgage transaction effected by her husband is in itself insufficient to fix the mortgagee with constructive notice of her beneficial interest. The joint occupation of the wife in the matrimonial home in that case was considered to be 'wholly consistent with the sole title offered' to the bank by the husband. It was not in itself so remarkable as reasonably to cause the bank to leap to the conclusion that the wife's presence might be attributable not simply to her matrimonial status but to some beneficial co-ownership in the home.

Thus in *Caunce v Caunce* the bank won: banks very seldom lose cases. We noted earlier[2] that important policy considerations—derived essentially from the significance of the cash nexus in a capitalist exchange economy—provide the unspoken rationale for this decision. The 'solid tug of money'[3], coupled with a pragmatic desire not to inhibit lending institutions from financing home ownership and entrepreneurial endeavour, usually exerts an hypnotic influence over the determination of priorities in this area.

It is less easy to predicate the legal result when the problem of *Caunce v Caunce* is translated into terms of registered land. The questions raised in this context are complex, and the difficulty is aggravated by the statutory interposition of spousal rights of occupation in the matrimonial home by means of amending legislation in 1970—the year after *Caunce* was decided[4].

Suppose that the legal title in a house situated in registered land is transferred

1 [1969] 1 WLR 286, p. 289ff., ante.
2 See p. 294, ante.
3 See *Hofman v Hofman* [1965] NZLR 795 at 800 per Woodhouse J, p. 244, ante.
4 See Matrimonial Homes Act 1967, s. 1(9), as added by Matrimonial Proceedings and Property Act 1970, s. 38, p. 145, ante.

to a married man, H, and that H is duly registered as the new proprietor. Suppose further that the purchase moneys for the acquisition by H were provided in unequal proportions by H and his wife, W. In the absence of evidence of contrary intention, this circumstance will mean that the legal estate is held by H on an implied trust for sale for H and W as equitable tenants in common[5].

Suppose now that H, the registered proprietor, transfers or mortgages the legal estate to a third party, P, who is in his turn duly registered as the current registered proprietor or chargee[6]. The situation described here may be depicted thus:

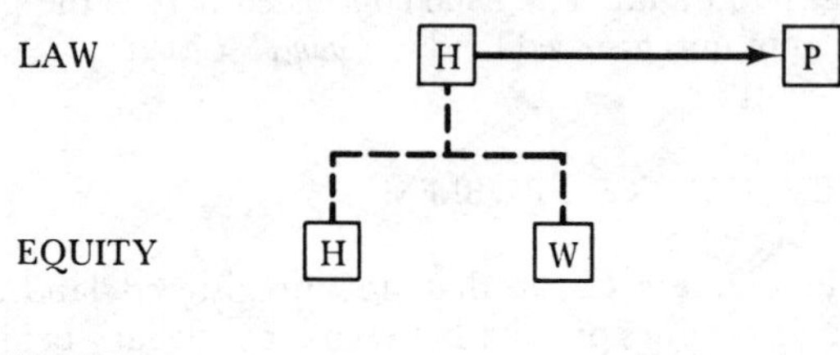

Fig. 59

If the events described above occur with the concurrence of W, no problem will arise even though it may be that P (being unaware of the existence of a trust for sale) pays the capital money to one trustee only, i.e., to H. Given a state of concord between H and W, H will probably use or invest the capital moneys for family purposes in any event. However, if H transfers or mortgages the legal estate to P without the knowledge or agreement of W, extremely difficult questions of priority arise between P (as transferee or chargee) and W (as beneficiary behind the implied or statutory trust for sale). These questions are even more complicated if H becomes insolvent and the matrimonial home represents the only substantial asset available for the purpose of meeting his several financial liabilities. We must now examine how these issues may be resolved.

If we apply the two-fold formula which was elaborated in Chapter 9[7] we must first ask:

(1) Did W have any interest capable of protection as a minor interest?

Here the answer is clearly in the affirmative. W had not merely one interest

5 See p. 257, ante.

6 Exactly the same problems arise regardless of whether H's legal estate is transferred or merely mortgaged, since a mortgagee (or 'chargee' in registered land parlance) is statutorily invested with the same degree of protection as he would have acquired if he had been a purchaser of a legal estate (see Law of Property Act 1925, s. 87(1), p. 290, ante).

7 See p. 313, ante.

which was capable of protection by entry of a minor interest on the register: she had two interests which were thus protectible. Those two interests were:

(a) *W's beneficial interest as tenant in common behind the statutory trust for sale*

W's beneficial interest behind the trust for sale implied by statute qualifies for protection as a minor interest in registered land by virtue of the definition of 'minor interests' contained in section 3(xv) of the Land Registration Act 1925. The appropriate form of protection in respect of such a minor interest is the entry of either a 'restriction' or a 'caution'[8], an entry which would in either case indicate quite clearly to a third party that the capital moneys arising must be paid to at least two trustees for sale.

(b) *W's spousal 'rights of occupation' in the matrimonial home*

W's spousal 'rights of occupation' in the matrimonial home are conferred by section 1(9) of the Matrimonial Homes Act 1967 and are derived from the fact of her co-ownership of the beneficial interest in the matrimonial home[9]. However, although the statutory 'rights of occupation' are parasitic upon W's beneficial interest as tenant in common behind the trust for sale, they are utterly distinct from that beneficial interest and must therefore be dealt with quite separately when we resolve the various priorities as between W and P. W's statutory 'rights of occupation' are capable of protection as a minor interest by the entry of a 'notice' or 'caution' on the register[10].

Continuing the application of our two-fold formula, we must now ask whether W made any protective entry on the register of H's title in respect of either of these categories of protectible interest. Of course, if W had in fact entered either interest as a minor interest on the register at any time before H's transaction with the third party, P, the interest thus protected would clearly bind P[11]. It would be irrelevant whether P had actually inspected the register, since the entry in due form would be conclusive against him. If, however, W had neglected to make the appropriate entry on the register in respect of either her beneficial interest or her statutory rights of occupation, the unprotected rights would become ineffective against P[12]. This result should follow inexorably, regardless of whether P had notice of the interest in question[13]. It might be said at this point that, as a matter of social reality, there is every likelihood that a wife who is a co-owner behind an implied trust for sale of the matrimonial home will be totally unaware of the need to protect herself by formal entry on the face of the register. Indeed she may even be unaware that she has rights in the first place, or that these rights are capable of protection[14].

8 See *Elias v Mitchell* [1972] Ch 652, p. 222, ante.
9 See p. 144f., ante.
10 Matrimonial Homes Act 1967, s. 2(7), p. 326, ante.
11 Land Registration Act 1925, s. 20(1), p. 327, ante.
12 Land Registration Act 1925, s. 59(6), p. 327, ante.
13 See, however, *Peffer v Rigg* [1977] 1 WLR 285, p. 328, ante.
14 See *Williams & Glyn's Bank Ltd v Boland* [1979] Ch 312 at 328 per Lord Denning MR, p. 148, ante.

To the rule in section 59(6) of the Land Registration Act 1925 that unprotected minor interests are ineffective against a purchaser for valuable consideration, there is only one exception. This exception, which is incorporated in the very wording of section 59(6), relates to the possibility that the unprotected interest may rank as an overriding interest, and may thus be binding on the purchaser. This possibility is the subject of the second limb in our two-fold formula. We must ask:

(2) Does either of W's protectible interests qualify as an overriding interest?

It is upon this question that intense interest focuses where W has failed to enter her protectible interests on the register in the appropriate manner. One half of the answer to this question is clear beyond any doubt, and may therefore be disposed of immediately and conclusively. It has already been mentioned that a spouse's statutory rights of occupation in the matrimonial home can never claim dual status as an overriding interest in registered land. There is in section 2(7) of the Matrimonial Homes Act 1967 an extremely clear and unambiguous prohibition of this possibility[15].

Since this is so, the issue of priority between W and P is ultimately refined to the question whether W's equitable interest behind the statutory trust for sale is capable of being regarded as an overriding interest, e.g., by reason of her occupation of the home at the relevant date[16]. Upon the answer to this question rests W's fate vis à vis the third party transferee or chargee, P. The following diagram illustrates how the present issue of priority between W and P has come finally to focus upon this question when W fails to take the appropriate protective action:

W's INTEREST	PROTECTED AS MINOR INTEREST ?	PROTECTED AS OVERRIDING INTEREST ?
(i) beneficial interest	no (LRA 1925, s.59(6))	maybe (LRA 1925, s.70 (1) (g))
(ii) statutory rights of occupation	no (LRA 1925, s.59(6))	no (MHA 1967, s.2(7))

Fig. 60

2. IS W'S BENEFICIAL INTEREST A 'RIGHT' FOR THE PURPOSE OF SECTION 70(1)(g)?

We have already noted the generally accepted view that only proprietary rights in land (as distinct from rights in other property and personal rights in land) can come within the protective scope of section 70(1)(g) of the Land Registration

15 See p. 338, ante.
16 See Land Registration Act 1925, s. 70(1)(g).

Act 1925[17]. In dealing with the issue of priority between a transferee/chargee and a beneficiary behind an implied trust for sale, a problem is raised immediately by the doctrine of conversion.

(1) The doctrine of conversion

By virtue of the equitable doctrine of conversion, the interest of a beneficiary behind a trust for sale is at all times considered to be an interest not in land but in the proceeds of sale of land[18]. On this basis, therefore, it would seem that a beneficiary's equitable interest behind a trust for sale of land can *never* rank as an overriding interest. Indeed, it has even been argued that this implication of the doctrine of conversion has always so clearly precluded such equitable interests from qualifying as overriding interests that an express prohibition—similar to section 86(2) of the Land Registration Act 1925 relating to beneficial interests in settled land (to which, of course, the doctrine of conversion has no application)—is rendered quite superfluous[19].

The point in issue here came before the Court of Appeal in *Williams & Glyn's Bank Ltd v Boland*[20], a case which consolidated appeals brought by two wives whose respective husbands, each acting as a single statutory trustee for sale, had charged the matrimonial home to the plaintiff bank in order to raise loans for the purposes of their various business enterprises. Both wives had been living in the matrimonial home at the date of the charge to the bank, but the bank made no enquiry as to the possibility that either might be beneficially entitled. It was common ground, however, that both wives had a beneficial interest behind an implied trust for sale of the matrimonial home (see *Fig.* 61).

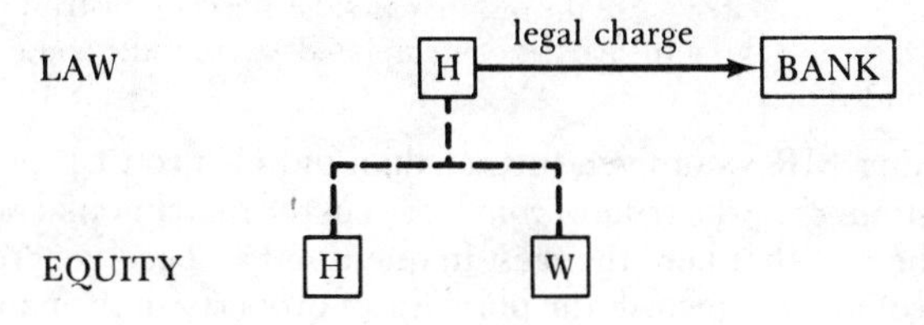

Fig. 61

When the husbands' respective businesses went into liquidation, the bank claimed possession of the charged properties, only to find that adverse interests were claimed in each matrimonial home by the wife concerned. There was no doubt when the matter reached the Court of Appeal that, unless the appellant wives could protect their beneficial interests behind the respective statutory trusts as 'overriding interests', the bank must succeed, since it was quite clear that neither wife had protected any interest of any kind by entry of a minor interest in the register.

17 See p. 336, ante.
18 See p. 220, ante.
19 See D. J. Hayton (1969) 33 Conv (NS) 254 at 263: 'Overriding Rights of Occupiers of Matrimonial Homes'; but compare now D. J. Hayton, *Registered Land* (3rd edn., London 1981), p. 97f. See also R. J. Smith (1979) 95 LQR 501 at 502: 'Overriding Interests and Wives'.
20 [1979] Ch 312. See [1979] Conv 377 (F. R. Crane); (1979) 42 MLR 567 (W. T. Murphy); (1979) 95 LQR 501 (R. J. Smith); (1979) 129 NLJ 700 (H. W. Wilkinson).

The Court of Appeal, presided over by Lord Denning MR, unanimously allowed the appeal by the wives. The Court of Appeal reversed the decision of Templeman J at first instance, and ruled that the bank was not entitled to possession as against the wives. In holding the wives' beneficial interests to be protected under section 70(1)(g) of the Land Registration Act 1925 by virtue of their 'actual occupation' of the respective matrimonial homes, the Court had to grapple first with the difficulties generated in this context by the doctrine of conversion.

Ormrod LJ pointed out that an orthodox application of the doctrine of conversion

> converted the interests of the wives into interests in the proceeds of sale and deprived them of an interest in the land. From the point of view of the wives this is an unforeseen and highly disadvantageous mutation[1].

In the event, Ormrod LJ concluded that, because of the fictitious nature of the 'trust for sale' in the matrimonial home context, the doctrine of conversion should not be applied so rigorously as to do 'violence to the rights of holders of equitable interests in the property[2].' In his view, section 70(1) of the Land Registration Act 1925, which refers to 'rights subsisting in reference' to registered land, was

> apt to include the interests of a co-owner or equitable tenant in common whose rights are not fully described . . . as an interest in the proceeds of sale[3].

In the judgment of Ormrod LJ,

> the rights of an equitable tenant in common are not accurately described as an interest in a sum of money, simpliciter . . . In the instant cases the object of the trust was to provide a joint home and the last thing the parties contemplated was that the house should be sold and the cash divided between them[4].

Lord Denning MR went even further than did Ormrod LJ in rejecting the normal operation of the doctrine of conversion in the matrimonial home context. Pointing to the fact that here the trust in question had been generated by joint contributions of money towards the purchase of property in the name of a single owner, the Master of the Rolls ruled that

> it is entirely appropriate to describe [husband and wife] as equitable tenants in common of the land—that is, of the house itself—until sale: and then after sale, in the proceeds of sale. Such a beneficial interest is an equitable interest in land[5].

Lord Denning thus rejected the doctrine of conversion—at least in the matrimonial home context—notwithstanding the difficulties presented by dicta in previous cases[6]. His view of the interests held by the appellant wives as equitable interests in land laid the legal and intellectual foundation for his

1 [1979] Ch 312 at 333.
2 [1979] Ch 312 at 337.
3 [1979] Ch 312 at 337.
4 [1979] Ch 312 at 336.
5 [1979] Ch 312 at 331.
6 See p. 222ff., ante.

eventual conclusion that those wives had 'rights' which became overriding by reason of their 'actual occupation' of the properties in dispute. Taken in conjunction with the views expressed by the other members of the Court of Appeal, Lord Denning's approach at least seemed to confirm that the interest of a beneficiary behind a trust for sale of registered land is sufficiently closely related to that land to come within the protective ambit of section 70(1)(g).

This indeed was the view taken of the matter by the House of Lords. The doctrine of conversion was not argued in its full force before the House, which was content to accept that the interest of a beneficiary behind a trust for sale is at the very least an interest 'subsisting in reference' to land for the purpose of section 70(1)(g). As Lord Wilberforce pointed out,

> to describe the interests of spouses in a house jointly bought to be lived in as a matrimonial home as merely an interest in proceeds of sale, or rents and profits until sale, is just a little unreal[7].

The inescapable conclusion, made explicit in the decision of the House of Lords in *Williams & Glyn's Bank Ltd v Boland*, is that, in relation to beneficial interests under a trust for sale, there is indeed a potential overlap between the categories of minor interest and overriding interest. A trust for sale beneficiary may therefore claim a dual status for his equitable interest. It becomes a minor interest if he protects it by entry on the relevant register of title; it may, in the absence of such protection, nevertheless rank as an overriding interest precisely because it has not been entered on the register. It may be thought slightly odd that the apparent consequence of the beneficiary's default should be a statutory reinforcement of his rights—but this is the effect of the House of Lords' decision.

(2) Implications flowing from the Matrimonial Homes Act 1967

There has been resistance on other grounds to the idea that a trust for sale interest which is unprotected as a minor interest should nevertheless survive in the form of an overriding interest. It was thought by some that the equitable doctrine of conversion operated to prevent such a result, but the reformulation of that doctrine in *Williams & Glyn's Bank Ltd v Boland* has now deprived that argument of its former vigour. However, the same resistance to the dual status of trust for sale interests has been expressed on grounds connected with the Matrimonial Homes Act 1967.

At first instance in *Williams & Glyn's Bank Ltd v Boland*[8], Templeman J held that a wife/beneficiary could not claim the further option of an overriding interest under the Land Registration Act 1925. He pointed out that the previous cases in which a beneficiary behind a trust had been held to have an overriding interest were cases involving a 'bare trust' rather than a trust for sale[9], where therefore it had not been open to the beneficiary in question to a claim a minor

7 [1980] 3 WLR 138 at 146, p. 225, ante. See A. E. Boyle [1981] Conv 108: 'Trusts for Sale and the Doctrine of Conversion'.
8 (1978) 36 P & CR 448.
9 See *Bridges v Mees* [1957] Ch 475; *Hodgson v Marks* [1971] Ch 892, p. 339, ante.

interest[10]. In the context of a trust for sale, however, Templeman J considered that it would be quite absurd if a wife/beneficiary were able to claim an overriding interest even though she had not entered a minor interest on the register in respect of *either* her beneficial interest *or* the statutory 'rights of occupation' derived from that interest under the Matrimonial Homes Act 1967[11]. In his view, it

> would really make that Act a nonsense provided that the spouse of the legal owner could say *or allege* at any time that he or she had contributed to the purchase price. The position which would result from that . . . would be quite intolerable[12].

In terms of this view, it would indeed be plainly wrong that a fictitious allegation of money contribution by a spouse should avert the consequence of failure to protect the statutory 'rights of occupation' by the appropriate entry on the register. Often the only evidence of the existence of a statutory trust for sale in the matrimonial home context is a vague, unsubstantiated, self-serving and possibly even collusive claim of financial contribution towards a purchase of the property many years before. It is significant that, whereas the Court of Appeal and House of Lords were prepared to accept the allegations of joint financial contribution by the respective spouses[13], Templeman J was careful at every point to say merely that the wife in question 'claimed' to have made the cash contributions which supposedly generated a statutory trust for sale of the matrimonial home. The husbands in *Williams & Glyn's Bank Ltd v Boland* were both insolvent at the date of hearing. There was clearly a fear in Templeman J's mind that a collusive fabrication of joint contribution might enable those husbands to save their respective matrimonial homes from the hands of the creditors under cover of fictitious beneficial entitlements now claimed as overriding interests on behalf of their wives.

The apprehension implicit in Templeman J's judgment was apparently not felt by the Court of Appeal or the House of Lords. The Court of Appeal expressed the view that the Matrimonial Homes Act 1967 had 'no relevance' in the instant appeals[14]. Lord Wilberforce stated that the appeals did 'not involve any question of matrimonial law, or of the rights of married women or of women as such[15].' We shall have more to say about this later[16], but for the moment it is sufficient to note that the Court of Appeal and the House of Lords were content to regard beneficial interests behind statutory trusts for sale as coming within the scope of section 70(1)(g) of the Land Registration Act 1925. This conclusion allowed those Courts to proceed to the second vital question relating to the applicability of section 70(1)(g)—the question whether the appellant wives were 'in actual occupation' of the land for the purpose of that provision.

10 Templeman J seemed to think that a beneficiary behind a bare trust cannot protect his interest as a minor interest. See, however, the different view expressed by Lord Wilberforce in the House of Lords ([1980] 3 WLR 138 at 146).
11 See p. 144, ante.
12 (1978) 36 P & CR 448 at 454 (emphasis supplied).
13 See [1979] Ch 312 at 327; [1980] 3 WLR 138 at 141.
14 [1979] Ch 312 at 343 per Browne LJ.
15 [1980] 3 WLR 138 at 141.
16 See p. 376, post.

3. DOES JOINT OCCUPATION BY W AMOUNT TO 'ACTUAL OCCUPATION' WITHIN SECTION 70(1)(g)?

We have already examined the nature of 'actual occupation' for the purpose of section 70(1)(g) of the Land Registration Act 1925[17]. However, additional problems are posed by the question whether a wife/beneficiary can be said to be 'in actual occupation' for the purpose of claiming an overriding interest.

(1) The problem of consistency between registered and unregistered land

The first problem stems from an understandable reluctance on the part of land lawyers to concede that different degrees of occupation by a beneficiary are required for the purpose of

(a) fixing a purchaser with constructive notice of that beneficiary's interest in unregistered land, and

(b) constituting 'actual occupation' of registered land within the terms of section 70(1)(g) of the Land Registration Act 1925.

It would be highly undesirable if the regimes of registered and unregistered land were to diverge in this respect.

In *Hodgson v Marks*[18], Russell LJ was clearly aware of the problem and was therefore, for the purpose of that decision, 'prepared ... to assume (without necessarily accepting)' that the nature of the occupation in both cases was the same. However, in *National Provincial Bank Ltd v Hastings Car Mart Ltd*[19], Lord Wilberforce seemed willing to concede that there might be a discrepancy at this point between the principles governing registered and unregistered land, a possibility which Lord Denning MR in the Court of Appeal had in fact regarded as 'inevitable'[20].

If it is true that there is an exact equivalence between the degrees of occupation required as between registered and unregistered land, an initial difficulty emerges from Stamp J's ruling in *Caunce v Caunce*[1] that a wife's joint occupation of the matrimonial home does *not* fix a purchaser from her husband with constructive notice of any equitable interest which she might have behind a statutory trust for sale. Her presence on the property was held to be wholly consistent with the sole title offered by the vendor/husband. However, on the assumption that parity exists between the registered and unregistered regimes, the conclusion reached in *Caunce v Caunce* becomes even less credible when translated into registered land terms. What we are now asked to believe is that a woman who is physically resident in a matrimonial home, who lives, cooks, washes clothes and rears children in that same matrimonial home, is not 'in actual occupation' of it. The man in the street would seriously—and with good

17 See p. 339, ante.
18 [1971] Ch 892 at 932.
19 [1965] AC 1175 at 1261, p. 337, ante.
20 [1964] Ch 665 at 689.
1 [1969] 1 WLR 286, p. 289, ante.

reason—question both the lawyer's sanity and integrity if it ever became generally known that lawyers as a breed were capable of giving mental assent to such nonsense.

(2) The problem of sex-based discrimination

A second problem is raised by the general question whether joint occupation by a wife/beneficiary amounts to 'actual occupation' for the purpose of section 70(1)(g). The answer given to this question must be contingent, at least to some degree, upon one's perception of the relative social and economic status of husband and wife. The way is therefore opened for a sex-biased conclusion as to the relative significance of the married woman's presence and function in the matrimonial home.

(3) The problem of the conveyancing implications

A third problem relates quite simply to the fact that if joint occupation by a particular class of beneficial owner behind an implied trust for sale is regarded as 'actual occupation' for the purpose of determining the presence of overriding interests, the onus of enquiry thereby imposed upon the third party purchaser is increased—and perhaps very heavily increased. The purchaser can no longer rely on an apparently unencumbered title offered him at law: he must take special steps in order to ascertain whether there are persons in actual occupation of the property other than the vendor who claim rights sustained by section 70(1)(g). He must make enquiry of all persons living on the property who might conceivably satisfy the description of the various classes of beneficial owner who have 'rights' capable of protection as overriding interests.

If his investigations successfully locate potentially overriding interests, he at least knows where he stands. If he makes enquiry of persons who fall within section 70(1)(g) but is deceived by them, he is safe because 'the rights are not disclosed.' But if the purchaser's enquiry simply draws a blank—or if he makes no enquiry at all—then his position is extremely hazardous: he is bound by any overriding interest which exists at the relevant date[2]. It is easily seen how this onerous duty of enquiry militates against the vigorous policy preference expressed in English land law in favour of protection for the innocent purchaser[3]. Such a policy can never be promoted by the extension of a rule which effectively demands that a purchaser should at his own risk prove a negative—that is, satisfy himself that no overriding interests exist.

In this context, one further difficulty adds to the problems of enquiry imposed on a purchaser if it is held that a wife/beneficiary's joint occupation amounts to 'actual occupation' of the matrimonial home for the purpose of section 70(1)(g). If an intending purchaser from a male vendor diligently makes enquiry on the premises, he may have to pose two questions, one of which is embarrassing, the other difficult to answer. He may have to inquire into the marital status of any

2 See p. 335, ante.
3 For a forthright statement of this policy in a slightly different context, see *Whittingham v Whittingham* [1979] Fam 9 at 16f.

woman he finds on the property, and he may thereafter obtain no clear answer to his second query, which relates to the possible beneficial entitlement of such a person. It was precisely this kind of difficulty which helped to doom the doctrine of the 'deserted wife's equity' which flourished during the 1950s and 1960s[4]. If the first difficulty is relieved by extending the scope of enquiry to include not only de iure wives but also de facto wives, this merely makes it even more artificial to exclude from the ambit of enquiry such persons as members of a wider kinship group (i.e., 'Uncle Harry' and 'Aunt Matilda') and members of unorthodox domestic relationships (e.g., homosexual partners, participants in a polygamous marriage or members of a *ménage à trois*)—all of whom may own beneficial interests behind informally created statutory trusts for sale[5].

All of these problems bear upon the question whether a wife/beneficiary's joint occupation of registered land should rank as 'actual occupation' for the purpose of establishing an overriding interest under section 70(1)(g). We must now look at the case law in order to examine the way in which the courts have handled the issues in dispute.

4. THE CASE LAW

The issue of priority between a spouse/beneficiary and a transferee or chargee of registered land held by a single statutory trustee for sale is a matter of considerable social and economic importance[6]. The case law relating to this question discloses a particularly stark confrontation between the claims of social justice (i.e., as represented here by the 'family consideration') and the practical realities of an uncompromising mercantilist world (as represented by the 'commercial consideration'). These widely diverging policy interests each provide the intellectual premise for fundamentally discrepant sets of solutions to the problems which we have just discussed. The 'family consideration' argues in favour of security for the beneficiary in occupation, and the 'commercial consideration' in favour of utility for the purchaser. The two competing premises reflect markedly differing perceptions of social relationship and economic responsibility.

(1) Gemeinschaft and Gesellschaft

Secreted within the interstices of the technical legal debate which follows here is the familiar antithesis of *Gemeinschaft* and *Gesellschaft*[7]. The terms *Gemeinschaft*

4 See p. 143, ante. For reference to the undesirability of imposing on a purchaser or mortgagee a duty to make this kind of enquiry, see *National Provincial Bank Ltd v Hastings Car Mart Ltd* [1964] Ch 665 at 700f. per Russell LJ, [1965] AC 1175 at 1233f. per Lord Upjohn, at 1248f. per Lord Wilberforce; *Whittingham v Whittingham* [1979] Fam 9 at 17ff. per Balcombe J.

5 See p. 301f., ante.

6 When *Williams & Glyn's Bank Ltd v Boland* [1980] 3 WLR 138 was argued before the House of Lords, counsel for the bank referred to what the Deputy Secretary of the Building Societies Association had described as 'a fairly educated guess' that of the 6 million mortgages outstanding in this country, 1 million are in the name of a sole borrower.

7 See p. 14ff., ante.

and *Gesellschaft*, when used as tools of social inquiry, connote two ideal types of social relation which have probably never existed in a pure or perfect form but which nevertheless reflect fundamentally divergent perceptions of the proper mode of relation between man and man in society at large. Although the terminology of *Gemeinschaft* and *Gesellschaft* has passed into general social theory as a kind of descriptive shorthand, it will prove useful and interesting for our present purpose as land lawyers simply because it epitomises precisely the policy motivations which underlie the case law which we are about to consider. It may therefore be helpful briefly to recapitulate the meaning of these two terms.

Gemeinschaft reflects a vision of man as a participant in a vast social family—a vision which finds its nearest expression in the economy of the organic medieval agrarian household. Here the relation between man and man is mediated by principles of love and duty, and priorities are ordered in accordance with the accumulated and inscrutable wisdom of religious teaching, folkways and community mores. *Gesellschaft* reflects, on the other hand, a vision of an atomistic world of self-determining individuals—a mode of relation most closely expressed in the age of free market and laissez faire philosophy around the turn of the present century.

Whereas the *Gemeinschaft* is founded upon the 'consonance of duties', the *Gesellschaft* recognises only the 'insolence of rights'[8]. Whereas men in the *Gemeinschaft* world are measured with reference to some ultimate value of human dignity and integrity, men in the *Gesellschaft* world are measured only against the universal medium of money. The *Gemeinschaft* is essentially a family-oriented, status-dependent form of association which operates on principles of affection, compassion, loyalty and voluntarily assumed obligation. The *Gesellschaft* reflects an impersonal, contract-based society which operates largely if not exclusively in response to the mercenary incentives of the world of the exchange economy. While the *Gemeinschaft* is founded upon emotion, intuitive perception and community-based solidarity as the mainsprings of human interaction, the *Gesellschaft* is characterised by rational calculation, purposive economic deliberation and more or less uncontrolled competition. The *Gemeinschaft* is based upon a community of 'blood and soil', and reflects an essentially religious ideology; the *Gesellschaft* is bourgeois and primarily secular. Whereas the *Gemeinschaft* is integrative in its vision of man and his social relations, the *Gesellschaft* is divisive and alienating, for it contains the classic features of a capitalist industrial society.

The polarities expressed in the ideas of *Gemeinschaft* and *Gesellschaft* are, of course, no longer reflected in the society in which we live—if indeed they ever were—but strangely enough these very different perceptions of the way in which man relates to man symbolise the tensions underlying the narrow legal issue as to whether a wife/beneficiary in joint occupation of the matrimonial home can be said to be 'in actual occupation' for the purpose of claiming an overriding interest.

8 See B. de Jouvenel, *Sovereignty* (Cambridge 1957), p. 202.

(2) The Gesellschaft perspective

The social ethics of the *Gesellschaft* found expression, for instance, in the judgment of Templeman J in *Bird v Syme-Thomson*[9]. Here the issue of priority arose between a wife/beneficiary and the chargees of a leasehold flat held on statutory trust for sale by her husband as sole registered proprietor. Templeman J held that the wife/beneficiary (who had provided part of the purchase money for the acquisition of the flat) could not successfully claim an overriding interest under section 70(1)(g). In his view, the *Caunce v Caunce* solution should be adopted in registered land, thus bringing registered land into agreement with the position obtaining in unregistered land. In other words,

> when a mortgagor is in actual occupation of the matrimonial home, it cannot be said that his wife also is in actual occupation[10].

Indeed, Templeman J went so far as to say that

> when husband and wife are in occupation of premises and the legal title is in one of them, actual occupation for the purposes of section 70 belongs to that one and the other is not in actual occupation but only there as a shadow of occupation of the owner[11].

Templeman J emphasised that any other solution would impose an excessively onerous burden of enquiry upon the purchaser/chargee, for

> it would be necessary to find out not only whether there was a wife there, as mortgagees had to do in the old days of the deserted wife's equity, not only whether the wife had registered her equity under the provisions of the Act which made that possible, but also whether she claimed any interest in the proceeds of sale of the house by virtue of a contribution to the purchase price or otherwise.

Significantly, he thought that the 'same inquiry would need to be made from every person who was found in the house, including a son or daughter over the age of 18 years.' Thus, in *Bird v Syme-Thomson*, preference was given to facility and protection for the purchaser at the expense of security for the beneficial co-owner of the matrimonial home.

When essentially the same factual situation arose in *Williams & Glyn's Bank Ltd v Boland*[12], Templeman J at first instance again applied Stamp J's reasoning in *Caunce v Caunce* in order to hold that 'actual occupation' did not include occupation by a spouse of the legal owner. In view of the extensive burden of enquiry which would be imposed upon prospective purchasers by any contrary view of the matter, Templeman J considered it 'neither necessary nor desirable to construe "actual occupation" so as to have such a wide and almost catastrophic effect[13].'

9 [1979] 1 WLR 440. See (1979) 38 Cambridge LJ 23 (M. J. Prichard); [1979] Conv 72 (F. R. Crane).
10 [1979] 1 WLR 440 at 444.
11 [1979] 1 WLR 440 at 444.
12 (1978) 36 P & CR 448.
13 (1978) 36 P & CR 448 at 454. It has been pointed out that Templeman J is a judge with lengthy experience of conveyancing practice at the Chancery Bar and was a member of the Royal Commission on Legal Services whose Report (Cmnd. 7648, 1979) was very much concerned

The judgments delivered by Templeman J in *Bird v Syme-Thomson* and *Williams & Glyn's Bank Ltd v Boland* both reflect the world of the *Gesellschaft* in which those who lend money expect to be repaid in full even if that means that wives and families must be evicted from their homes. This view is aptly expressed in the adage that 'an Englishman's home is his bank manager's castle!' A quite different approach was adopted by the Court of Appeal in *Williams & Glyn's Bank Ltd v Boland*, and it is interesting to observe the points of departure.

(3) The Gemeinschaft perspective

In *Williams & Glyn's Bank Ltd v Boland*[14] the Court of Appeal decided unanimously that the appellant wives were 'in actual occupation' of the respective matrimonial homes and therefore had overriding interests which enjoyed priority over the charges taken by the bank. Lord Denning MR said:

> Most wives now are joint owners of the matrimonial home—in law or in equity—with their husbands . . . Visit the home and you will find that she is in personal occupation of it just as much as he is. She eats there and sleeps there just as he does. She is in control of all that goes on there—just as much as he. In no respect whatever does the nature of her occupation differ from his . . .[15]

Ormrod LJ likewise pointed to the fact that the

> wives in this case were living on the land; the houses were their homes which they were sharing with their husbands. It would be difficult to imagine clearer examples of 'actual occupation' in the ordinary sense[16].

The view expressed in *Caunce v Caunce* that the presence of a wife should be restrictively construed as merely a form of vicarious occupation by her husband was condemned by Ormrod LJ as a view which

> seems to re-introduce technical concepts of occupation which the use of the word 'actual' in its ordinary sense is intended to exclude[17].

The Court of Appeal thus found fault with the way in which Templeman J, in following the lead given in *Caunce v Caunce*, had dismissed the wife's occupation in *Bird v Syme-Thomson* as 'a shadow of occupation of the owner.' Lord Denning rejected such sentiments as archaic, representing the law 'a hundred years ago when the law regarded husband and wife as one: and the husband as that one[18].' Browne LJ felt that 'today it is unrealistic and anachronistic to talk about a wife's occupation being only a "shadow" of her husband's occupation[19].' Ormrod LJ voiced the objection that the notion of vicarious occupation through a wife 'resurrects the outmoded concept of the head of the family[20].'

---

with the conveyancing process. See S. Freeman (1980) 43 MLR 692 at 693: 'Wives, Conveyancers and Justice'.

14 [1979] Ch 312. See (1979) 38 Cambridge LJ 254 (M. J. Prichard).

15 [1979] Ch 312 at 332.

16 [1979] Ch 312 at 338.

17 [1979] Ch 312 at 339.

18 [1979] Ch 312 at 332.

19 [1979] Ch 312 at 343.

20 [1979] Ch 312 at 338.

By deciding that the appellant wives had been 'in actual occupation' for the purpose of section 70(1)(g), all three judges in the Court of Appeal expressed their preference for the policy interest which seeks to preserve the integrity of the family home on behalf of the family members. All three judges correspondingly took the view that the bank had overstated the argument of facility for the purchaser/chargee. Lord Denning saw no reason why the Court's decision

> should cause any difficulty to conveyancers. Nor should it impair the proper conduct of businesses. Anyone who lends money on the security of a matrimonial home nowadays ought to realise that the wife may have a share in it. He ought to make sure that the wife agrees to it, or to go to the house and make inquiries of her. It seems to me utterly wrong that a lender should turn a blind eye to the wife's interest or the possibility of it—and afterwards seek to turn her and the family out—on the plea that he did not know that she was in actual occupation[1].

Likewise, Ormrod LJ minimised the conveyancing difficulties which had been heavily stressed by the bank. He agreed that such difficulties 'must be taken seriously', but observed that

> one cannot help noticing a tendency to express them in unusually strong language. The judge in this case used the word 'chaos' to describe the consequences which would follow if the appellants were right. But one wonders whether equitable tenants in common, in actual occupation at the same time as the vendor, really are to be found in significant numbers outside the purely domestic sphere. Within that sphere, on the other hand, co-ownership is becoming increasingly popular. Building societies and other institutions which finance house purchase are familiar with it and, if necessary, can protect themselves by requiring the spouse of the purchaser to join in the purchase and mortgage. The people who, on the whole, seem more likely to be affected are those who advance money on the security of domestic property either in the form of overdrafts or other loans, and those legal proprietors who wish to raise money on their homes. In these days the word 'chaos' is a strong word to describe the plight of such persons who have only got to get the consent of the co-owner, or forgo a transaction gravely prejudicial to the co-owner. So, with some trepidation, I venture to doubt whether the success of the wives will really have such catastrophic consequences. If, on the other hand, they fail the result will certainly be catastrophic for them and many like them[2].

1 [1979] Ch 312 at 332. See also *Brikom Investments Ltd v Carr* [1979] QB 467 at 484, where, in a quite different context, the Court of Appeal faced the objection that its decision 'would cause chaos and confusion amongst conveyancers. No one buying property would know where he stood.' To this the reply of Lord Denning MR was robust: 'I am not disturbed by those forebodings. I prefer to see that justice is done; and let the conveyancers look after themselves.'

2 [1979] Ch 312 at 339. One ironic footnote is perhaps in point here. It may not have escaped the attention of the Court of Appeal that Williams & Glyn's Bank had rather publicly prided itself on the service which it gives to its customers. A series of advertisements in the national press in 1979 had contained such puffs as 'Williams & Glyn's knows there is no such person as an average customer' (Guardian, 26th March 1979). In view of the fact that the husbands in *Boland*'s case were both small businessmen who had gone bankrupt when Williams & Glyn's Bank called in their respective loans, it was particularly unfortunate that Williams & Glyn's had announced (Guardian, 12th July 1979) that 'Williams & Glyn's believes businesses should make their bank managers work harder for them . . . Call in and see your local Williams & Glyn's manager soon. You've got nothing to lose . . .' Of some relevance to the legal issue concerning the Bank's duty of enquiry in *Boland*'s case was the Bank's assurance (Guardian, 8th May 1979) that 'Williams

The decision of the Court of Appeal in *Williams & Glyn's Bank Ltd v Boland* thus marks a vigorous policy preference in favour of priority for the 'family interest' and a corresponding—and indeed almost dismissive—relegation of the 'commercial interest'. The *Gemeinschaft* character of the Court's decision was most clearly articulated in Lord Denning's judgment, which emerged almost as a latter-day Parable of the Debtors. (After all, a bank can be a debtor too—its relationship with its own depositors is based upon a contract of loan in which the customer is the creditor.) Lord Denning described the facts of the instant case in emotive language; he spoke pejoratively of the fact that 'the bank now come down on' the respective husbands for the sums lent to them on the security of the matrimonial home. In a passage which expressed an almost medieval abhorrence of the practice of usury[3], he fastened upon the bank an overriding moral obligation reflective of precisely the broad network of social relationship and economic responsibility idealised in the classical description of the *Gemeinschaft*:

If a bank is to do its duty, in the society in which we live, it should recognise the integrity of the matrimonial home. It should not destroy it by disregarding the wife's interest in it—simply to ensure that it is paid the husband's debt in full—with the high interest rate now prevailing[4].

Lord Denning accurately perceived the ultimate conflict of values presented by this case when he concluded:

We should not give monied might priority over social justice ... [E]ach of the wives ... is entitled to be protected in her occupation of the matrimonial home. The bank is not entitled to throw these families out into the street—simply to get the last penny of the husband's debt[5].

Lord Denning's judgment in *Williams & Glyn's Bank Ltd v Boland* provides one of the most remarkable statements in recent times of the social philosophy of the *Gemeinschaft.* The tenor of that judgment is entirely consistent with Lord Denning's lifelong—and often single-handed—judicial crusade against oppressive bargaining and the exploitation of superior economic strength. One of the most deeply unifying themes of Lord Denning's jurisprudence has been the retrospective adjustment of 'inequality of bargaining power'[6]. Few situations so palpably involve a disparity of bargaining power as an application by an ordinary citizen for a loan of money from a bank or building society. Few situations invest financial institutions with quite so much power to determine individual destinies and to control the quality of life enjoyed by ordinary people

---

& Glyn's believes small businesses deserve all the help a bank can give ... we encourage managers to visit customers on their home ground ... That's a higher degree of commitment than many banks undertake. But then Williams & Glyn's Bank is a rather different kind of bank ...'

3 See p. 514, post.

4 [1979] Ch 312 at 332f.

5 [1979] Ch 312 at 333. Compare Lord Denning MR in *Hanlon v Law Society* [1981] AC 124 at 150, where the Master of the Rolls questioned whether the Law Society was to 'be like the hard-hearted mortgagees of the 19th century, foreclosing and obtaining possession, turning out the innocent and grinding the faces of the poor?'

6 See *Lloyds Bank Ltd v Bundy* [1975] QB 326 at 339.

as does the exercise of a discretion to grant or withhold such a loan. The aspirations and ambitions of people's lives are here at stake.

The *Gemeinschaft* philosophy recognises quite openly the existence—indeed the inevitability—of vertical power relations within society. After all, the *Gemeinschaft* is fundamentally a status-based society. It is, however, overlaid with a transcending social or religious obligation—and in the *Gemeinschaft* this distinction has no significance—to refrain from abuse of the power conferred by status[7]. In the *Gemeinschaft*, this duty is paramount, and its proper discharge serves an infinitely important human purpose—that of preserving the integrative and harmonious component in social interaction. The *Gemeinschaft* recognises that ultimately there exists a higher social interest than can be achieved by means merely of the strict and legalistic regulation of commercial intercourse. It perceives that ultimately people matter more than the repayment of debts. This philosophy, when translated into the modern context of conflicting claims brought by families and financial institutions, provides the moral base for the view expressed—typically by Lord Denning—in *National Provincial Bank Ltd v Hastings Car Mart Ltd*[8]:

> On the one hand there is the bank who desire to recoup themselves all that is owing to them. On the other hand there is the wife with four children, receiving nothing from her husband, and on National Assistance. Of all the creditors of the husband, she has the most crying claim of all. It is a case where I would fain temper justice with mercy. Justice to the bank, with mercy to the wife.

The *Gemeinschaft* inverts the values of the *Gesellschaft*. In the *Gemeinschaft* the meek shall indeed inherit the earth, the mighty are indeed put down from their seats, and only the merciful shall in fact obtain mercy.

The values expressed in the Court of Appeal's judgments in *Williams & Glyn's Bank Ltd v Boland* are, therefore, entirely inconsistent with the *Gesellschaft* principles which inform and infuse the law of property. It is a fundamental assumption of the law of property that initial disparities in the distribution of social and economic power should be adjusted only through the normal operation of market forces, i.e., by means of a process in which all exchange is deemed to have been commercially motivated and all contracts are presumed to have been freely negotiated. Hence the overwhelming emphasis in land law upon the simple mechanics of contract and conveyance: the morality of the exchange thereby effected lies completely outside the field of inquiry. Hence too the priority given in almost every case of conflict to the interest of certainty in preference to the interest of 'justice'. The fundamental ethos of the law of property is the *Gesellschaft* ideal of a world of bourgeois individualism in which all are deemed equal and competent to contract freely for the purpose of personal gain. The aggressive pursuit of self-interest must, 'as if guided by an invisible hand', conduce to the common good. This being so, the only justifiable motive of the law relating to land is 'to simplify and facilitate transactions in

7 The idea is superbly captured in Chaucer's lines: 'I woot wel ther is degree above degree, as reson is; and skile it is, that men do hir devoir ther-as it is due; but certes, extorcions and despit of youre underlinges is dampnable' (*The Parson's Tale*, §66), p. 514, post.

8 [1964] Ch 665 at 691.

real property[9].' The only purpose of the law of property is to provide clarity and procedural efficiency in the combined operation of bargain and exchange. Almost as a matter of definition, the transaction concluded has no moral dimension: the only social ethic of the *Gesellschaft* is the freedom to compete and exploit.

5. THE HOUSE OF LORDS' DECISION IN WILLIAMS & GLYN'S BANK LTD v BOLAND

In *Williams & Glyn's Bank Ltd v Boland*[10] the House of Lords decisively rejected the claim by the appellant bank to possession of the matrimonial homes in which the respondent wives held beneficial interests behind a statutory trust for sale. The House held that the wives were persons 'in actual occupation' of registered land for the purpose of section 70(1)(g) of the Land Registration Act 1925, and therefore took priority over the mortgages obtained by the bank, which had made no enquiry of the wives themselves. We shall now examine what the House of Lords said, with particular reference to the three special problems posed by the general issue of joint occupation by a wife/beneficiary in a matrimonial home vested at law in the sole name of her husband[11].

(1) The problem of consistency between registered and unregistered land

In *Boland* Lord Wilberforce traced the historical derivation of the concept of 'actual occupation'[12], and indicated that there is a difference between the code which applies to registered land and that which applies to unregistered land. To be sure, there are marked similarities between the two codes, not least in the sense that section 70(1)(g) duplicates for registered land 'the well-known rule protecting the rights of persons in occupation' of unregistered land[13]. Here, however, the analogy is not with the equitable doctrine of notice (whether actual or constructive), but with the rule now contained in section 14 of the Law of Property Act 1925[14], which partially safeguards the interests of 'any person in possession or in actual occupation' of unregistered land. Thus, in the words of Lord Wilberforce,

> the law as to notice as it may affect purchasers of unregistered land . . . has no application even by analogy to registered land. Whether a particular right is an overriding interest,

9 *National Provincial Bank Ltd v Hastings Car Mart Ltd* [1965] AC 1175 at 1233 per Lord Upjohn, p. 54, ante.
10 [1980] 3 WLR 138. See (1980) 39 Cambridge LJ 243 (M. J. Prichard); (1980) 43 MLR 692 (S. Freeman); [1980] Conv 361 (J. Martin); (1981) 97 LQR 12 (R. J. Smith).
11 See p. 361ff, ante.
12 See p. 334, ante.
13 *National Provincial Bank Ltd v Hastings Car Mart Ltd* [1964] Ch 665 at 689 per Lord Denning MR, cited with approval by Lord Wilberforce at [1965] AC 1175 at 1259, and in *Williams & Glyn's Bank Ltd v Boland* [1980] 3 WLR 138 at 143.
14 See p. 117, ante.

and whether it affects a purchaser, is to be decided upon the terms of section 70, and other relevant provisions of the Land Registration Act 1925, and upon nothing else[15].

Lord Wilberforce underlined the inevitable divergence between the systems of registered and unregistered land, observing that

the purpose, in each system, is the same, namely, to safeguard the rights of persons in occupation, but the method used differs. In the case of unregistered land, the purchaser's obligation depends upon what he has notice of—notice actual or constructive. In the case of registered land, it is the fact of occupation that matters. If there is actual occupation, and the occupier has rights, the purchaser takes subject to them. If not, he does not. No further element is material[16].

Lord Wilberforce thus countered decisively any impulse to read the traditional doctrine of notice into the plain provision in section 70(1)(g) which accords overriding status to those 'in actual occupation'[17]. His view of the matter was endorsed by Lord Scarman, who pointed out that by the Land Registration Act 1925

the wearisome and intricate task of examining title, and with it the doctrine of notice, have been replaced by a statutory system of registration (where the Act applies), subject to the overriding interests set out in section 70(1). These interests take effect under the section without registration and whether or not a purchaser has notice of them . . . [T]he statute has substituted a plain factual situation for the uncertainties of notice, actual or constructive, as the determinant of an overriding interest[18].

This being so, it is not surprising that Lord Scarman indicated that little assistance in the interpretation of section 70(1)(g) could be derived from cases in the unregistered land context such as *Caunce v Caunce*[19]. He joined Lord Wilberforce in rejecting any specialised meaning in the phrase 'actual occupation' which might imply that the occupation pleaded must be in some sense adverse to that of the registered owner. In the judgment of Lord Wilberforce,

Given occupation, i.e. presence on the land, I do not think that the word 'actual' was

15 [1980] 3 WLR 138 at 142.
16 [1980] 3 WLR 138 at 143.
17 The House of Lords even rejected an attempt to import the equitable doctrine of notice into section 70(1)(g) via the provision in section 74 of the Land Registration Act 1925 that '[s]ubject to the provisions of this Act as to settled land, neither the registrar nor any person dealing with a registered estate or charge shall be affected with notice of a trust express implied or constructive, and references to trusts shall, so far as possible, be excluded from the register.' The argument put by the bank was that if the overriding interest sought to be protected is, under the general law, only binding on a purchaser by virtue of notice, section 74 has the effect of denying the protection. Lord Wilberforce was, however, firmly of opinion that section 74 has no such effect. He said that the purpose of section 74 is rather 'to make clear . . . that the doctrine of notice has no application to registered conveyancing, and accordingly to establish, as an administration measure, that entries may not be made in the register which would only be appropriate if that doctrine were applicable. It cannot have the effect of cutting down the general application of section 70(1)' ([1980] 3 WLR 138 at 146). See also Browne LJ in the Court of Appeal ([1979] Ch 312 at 343]; (1979) 38 Cambridge LJ 254 at 256 (M. J. Prichard).
18 [1980] 3 WLR 138 at 149.
19 [1969] 1 WLR 286.

intended to introduce any additional qualification, certainly not to suggest that possession must be 'adverse': it merely emphasises that what is required is physical presence, not some entitlement in law ... Occupation, existing as a fact, may protect rights if the person in occupation has rights. On this part of the case I have no difficulty in concluding that a spouse, living in a house, has an actual occupation capable of conferring protection, as an overriding interest, upon rights of that spouse[20].

As we shall see, the approach adopted by the House of Lords may well mean that the occupation of a beneficiary behind a trust for sale may be such as to constitute 'actual occupation' within the terms of section 70(1)(g) of the Land Registration Act 1925, but may not fix a purchaser with constructive notice in the equivalent unregistered land context. In *Boland*, neither the Court of Appeal nor the House of Lords actually overruled *Caunce v Caunce*. Ormrod LJ merely observed that if *Caunce v Caunce* 'had to be decided today the result might have been different[1].' In the House of Lords, Lord Scarman was 'by no means certain that *Caunce v Caunce* was correctly decided,' but found it 'unnecessary to express a final opinion upon the point' since the case in hand concerned only registered land[2]. Thus, while the argument remains for preserving consistency between the systems of registered and unregistered conveyancing, it is not quite obvious that this goal is realised by the decision in *Boland*.

(2) The problem of sex-based discrimination

The House of Lords in *Boland* joined the Court of Appeal in roundly condemning any tendency to construe the statutory phrase 'actual occupation' in such a way as to discriminate against the married woman. Lord Wilberforce stated firmly that

the appeals do not ... involve any question of matrimonial law, or of the rights of married women or of women as such. Exactly the same issue could arise if the roles of husband and wife were reversed, or if the persons interested in the house were not married to each other. The solution must be derived from a consideration in the light of current social conditions of the Land Registration Act 1925 and other property statutes[3].

He adverted to the argument

that the wife's 'occupation was nothing but the shadow of the husband's'—a version I suppose of the doctrine of unity of husband and wife. This expression ... somewhat faded from the arguments in the present case and appears to me to be heavily obsolete[4].

Lord Wilberforce then proceeded to deal with the suggestion that the occupation relevant within section 70(1)(g) must be 'apparently inconsistent with the title of the vendor' and that this requirement excluded the wife of a husband-vendor on the ground that her apparent occupation 'would be satisfactorily accounted for by his.' He found the suggestion quite 'unacceptable', observing that

20 [1980] 3 WLR 138 at 143f.
1 [1979] Ch 312 at 335.
2 [1980] 3 WLR 138 at 149.
3 [1980] 3 WLR 138 at 141.
4 [1980] 3 WLR 138 at 144.

Consistency, or inconsistency, involves the absence, or presence, of an independent right to occupy, though I must observe that 'inconsistency' in this context is an inappropriate word. But how can either quality be predicated of a wife, simply qua wife? A wife may, and everyone knows this, have rights of her own; particularly, many wives have a share in a matrimonial home. How can it be said that the presence of a wife in the house, as occupier, is consistent or inconsistent with the husband's rights until one knows what rights she has? And if she has rights, why, just because she is a wife (or in the converse case, just because the occupier is the husband), should these rights be denied protection under the paragraph? ... I have no difficulty in concluding that a spouse, living in a house, has an actual occupation capable of conferring protection, as an overriding interest, upon rights of that spouse[5].

(3) The problem of the conveyancing implications

The House of Lords also had words to say about the conveyancing implications of the *Boland* case which had so alarmed Templeman J at first instance. In recognising beneficial interests behind a trust for sale as potentially overriding interests, the House of Lords vastly widened the category of overriding interests. Third parties are now liable to be bound by perhaps scarcely discoverable interests in registered land. However, the House of Lords was confident of the ability of conveyancers to handle the new dimension of necessary enquiry. Lord Wilberforce acknowledged that the decision of the House might 'add to the burdens of purchasers, and involve them in enquiries which in some cases may be troublesome.' He noted, nevertheless, that

What is involved is a departure from an easy-going practice of dispensing with enquiries as to occupation beyond that of the vendor and accepting the risks of doing so. To substitute for this a practice of more careful enquiry as to the fact of occupation, and if necessary, as to the rights of occupiers can not ... be considered as unacceptable except at the price of overlooking the widespread development of shared interests of ownership ... I cannot believe that Parliament intended this ...[6]

An even more robust unconcern for the protests of conveyancers emerged in the judgment of Lord Scarman:

Nor must the courts flinch when assailed by arguments to the effect that the protection of [the wife's] interest will create difficulties in banking or conveyancing practice. The difficulties are, I believe, exaggerated: but bankers, and solicitors, exist to provide the service which the public needs. They can—as they have successfully done in the past—adjust their practice, if it be socially required[7].

We shall look more closely in following pages at the precise nature of the banking and conveyancing implications of *Boland.*

6. DID THE HOUSE OF LORDS ACHIEVE SOCIAL JUSTICE?

The basic premises of the decision of the House of Lords in *Williams & Glyn's Bank Ltd v Boland* are inconsistent with the underlying tenets of the law and

5 [1980] 3 WLR 138 at 144.
6 [1980] 3 WLR 138 at 147.
7 [1980] 3 WLR 138 at 148.

practice of English conveyancing. However, it is probably true to say that the decision was motivated more deeply by social rather than legal considerations[8]. Lord Scarman saw the task of the Court in the following terms:

While the technical task faced by the courts, and now facing the House, is the construction to be put upon a sub-clause in a subsection of a conveyancing statute, it is our duty, when tackling it, to give the provisions, if we properly can, a meaning which will work for, rather than against, rights conferred by Parliament, or recognised by judicial decision, as being necessary for the achievement of social justice[9].

Lord Scarman was here making reference to the remarkable way in which the law has, during the last 30 years, come to acknowledge an informal regime of co-ownership of the matrimonial home[10]. For him, the paramount nature of the requirements of social justice demanded that in the *Boland* case

The courts may not . . . put aside, as irrelevant, the undoubted fact that, if the two wives succeed, the protection of the beneficial interest which English law now recognises that a married woman has in the matrimonial home will be strengthened whereas, if they lose, this interest can be weakened, and even destroyed, by an unscrupulous husband[11].

It is, however, open to question whether the *Boland* decision did in fact achieve social justice. Many would argue that, while mercy may have been extended to the wives, it is highly doubtful whether justice was done to the bank. It may be replied that the House of Lords effectively traded off justice for the bank in favour of a higher social interest—that of greater security for the married woman in her occupation of the matrimonial home. But even this initially comforting thought may have no substance. The 'unscrupulous husband' can easily evade the protection conferred upon his wife in the *Boland* situation by appointing a crony as his second trustee for the purpose of making an overreaching disposition in favour of a third party (i.e., purchaser or mortgagee)[12].

In any event the *Boland* decision raises as many moral problems as it purports to solve. Were the wives in *Boland* as innocent and as helpless as the judgments delivered in the Court of Appeal and the House of Lords seemed to suggest? They were not quite helpless—at least in the technical sense that the law had at all material times provided a prophylactic for the situation of which they

8 See p. 302, ante.
9 [1980] 3 WLR 138 at 148.
10 See pp. 249, ante; 560, post.
11 [1980] 3 WLR 138 at 148.
12 See p. 266, ante. A disposition effected by two trustees would, even in the absence of consultation with the wife/beneficiary, overreach her equitable interest, although such a disposition would of course constitute a breach of trust in respect of which the wife/beneficiary would have a nominal remedy in damages. See (1980) 43 MLR 692 at 695 (S. Freeman). Compare, however, C. Sydenham, [1980] Conv 427: 'Overreaching and the Ratio of Boland's Case'. The Law Commission has proposed that a beneficial owner of the matrimonial home should have statutory 'trusteeship rights'. These rights would include a right to prevent other persons becoming trustees of the matrimonial home without the consent of the spouse/beneficiary, and a right for the spouse/beneficiary himself or herself to apply to the court to be appointed a trustee. See Law Commission, *Third Report on Family Property: The Matrimonial Home (Co-ownership and Occupation Rights) and Household Goods* (Law Com No. 86, June 1978), paras. 1.295ff.

subsequently complained. It was open to them to enter both their alleged beneficial entitlements and their statutory 'rights of occupation' in the register of title to the respective matrimonial homes[13]. Nor perhaps were the wives quite so innocent as might at first appear. They were not involved in matrimonial battles with their respective husbands, but rather it was the case that each husband was seeking grimly to hang on to the family home by opposing against the bank his wife's equitable interest behind a statutory trust for sale.

Even assuming that each wife did in fact have a beneficial entitlement—and for this we have only the vague (and possibly collusive) evidence of the spouses themselves on which to rely—the outcome in *Boland* raises even more fundamental problems of social ethics. The essence of the wives' case was, not that they had been unaware that their husbands had mortgaged the matrimonial home to the bank for business purposes, but that the bank had never made any enquiry as to their own possible beneficial entitlement. Had the business enterprises for which the secured loans were obtained gone on to enjoy prosperity, the wives would no doubt have shared indirectly in that prosperity, in the sense that they would have participated with their spouses in an elevated standard of living. Marriage is an economic partnership in which the life-fortunes of the spouses are inextricably bound together. A wife commits her economic destiny to that of her husband no less irrevocably when he is a businessman than when he is a wage-earner, and the fortuity of business success and failure affects one spouse as much as the other[14]. There is a powerful—some would say overwhelming—argument in support of the proposition that the risks inherent in the pursuit of a business enterprise are not fairly susceptible of a narrower allocation than the benefits conferred by that enterprise if it succeeds. It is questionable whether the wives in *Boland* should have been allowed to enjoy the prospects of their husbands' business prosperity, while remaining immune to the shared misfortune of their adversity.

It should, of course, be noticed that the arguments rehearsed in the last two paragraphs are the brutal commercially-oriented arguments which count for so much in the world of the *Gesellschaft*. In terms of this perspective, people are viewed (and judged) as self-determining agents governed by rational calculation and by purposive economic deliberation[15]. It may ultimately be a little harsh to judge the wives in *Boland* in precisely these terms. However, the *Boland* decision—if it does nothing else—casts in sharp relief the moral question whether it is justifiable even with the consent of both spouses to exploit the family home as a commercial security for a loan earmarked for entrepreneurial purposes[16]. Such a manoeuvre extracts an 'exchange value' from an asset which comprises essentially a 'use value' in terms of residential occupation[17]. This form of dealing is always to be viewed with suspicion. There is a strong moral argument in favour of saying that the matrimonial home should be mortgaged only where

13 See p. 142ff., ante.
14 See K. J. Gray, *Reallocation of Property on Divorce* (Abingdon 1977), p. 188.
15 See p. 364, ante.
16 See p. 508, post.
17 See p. 260, ante.

the loan thereby obtained advances the interest of residential occupation (e.g., by enabling the house to be bought in the first place or by facilitating the construction of an extension for occupation by an ageing parent). It is more questionable whether the family base should be used as security for a business loan. However, the issues are not clear. It may be possible, for instance, to claim that the jobs established or safeguarded by a business loan indirectly promote the residential interests of numerous employees by providing them with an income base for the purpose of acquiring their own homes. Only one thing is clear, and it is this. So long as the private entrepreneur survives in this country, any bank which lends him money will demand adequate security, and it may well be that the only practicable security which he can offer is the security of his own matrimonial home.

The House of Lords' decision in *Boland* glosses over these and many other matters and, in so doing, has laid itself open to criticism as 'disturbingly superficial, and wholly inadequate as an evaluation of the competing interests involved[18].'

7. THE LONG-TERM IMPLICATIONS OF WILLIAMS & GLYN'S BANK LTD v BOLAND

The decision of the House of Lords in *Williams & Glyn's Bank Ltd v Boland* has important long-term implications which we must examine.

(1) Implications for conveyancing and banking practice

It is possible that the House of Lords may not have fully appreciated the conveyancing and banking implications of its decision, in spite of its confident expectation that those implications would cause little difficulty in practice. The fundamental problem left in the aftermath of *Boland* is that it is now uncertain which categories of person in joint occupation with a vendor will be held to be 'in actual occupation of the land' for the purpose of claiming overriding interests under section 70(1)(g) of the Land Registration Act 1925.

In the Court of Appeal in *Boland*, Browne LJ had thought that 'whether ... other people living in a house ... are "in actual occupation" must depend on the facts of each case[19].' Ormrod LJ pointed out that the appellant wives were 'relying not upon their position as married women, but upon their property rights as ordinary citizens[20].' He thought that it was purely 'incidental' that in both cases the wives were married to the persons in whom the legal estate was vested. In his view, the relevant arguments would be 'exactly the same if they were not married or were of the same sex as the legal proprietors.' The inference here seemed to be that joint occupation in a residential setting by a fairly wide range of adults (e.g., 'Uncle Harry', 'Aunt Matilda', members of de facto

18 (1980) 43 MLR 692 at 696 (S. Freeman).
19 [1979] Ch 312 at 343.
20 [1979] Ch 312 at 333.

domestic relationships, polygamous spouses, partners in unorthodox social groupings, and the like) may well constitute 'actual occupation' for the purpose of section 70(1)(g). The position of such persons in the law of registered land would not appear to be distinguishable from that of the de iure wives in *Boland*, with the obvious qualification that it is only in relation to de iure wives that there arises the further complication of protectable 'rights of occupation' under the Matrimonial Homes Act 1967.

The House of Lords confirmed the proliferation of relevant joint occupation beyond the simple situation of husband and wife. Lord Wilberforce pointed out that section 70(1)(g) potentially protected the 'interests of spouses, and indeed, in theory, of other members of the family or even outside it[1].' He made it clear that overriding interests could well arise in 'the case of a man living with a mistress, or of a man and a woman—or for that matter two persons of the same sex—living in a house in separate or partially shared rooms[2].' This approach means that there are potentially large numbers of people who, if in joint occupation of registered land with a vendor/mortgagor, may effectively have a power of veto over dealings with the registered title. Such persons will enjoy this right of control upon proving beneficial entitlement behind even an implied trust for sale, and, as we have seen, such entitlement may have informal and unexpected origins[3].

It is possible to gain some impression of the range of persons involved here by considering the categories of people who may quite easily in the past have made some financial contribution to the acquisition, extension[4], or improvement[5] of residential property. These categories include not merely a spouse (de iure or de facto), but embrace such persons as parents, in-laws, adult children, invalid maiden aunts and other assorted relatives, old cronies and platonic friends[6], homosexual partners, and perhaps many others[7]. The 'rights'—whatever they may be—of such persons in 'actual occupation' will override any interest taken by a third party whether he knows of them or not, and this is where the problem begins. The onus is placed unambiguously upon the third party (e.g., a purchaser, bank or building society) to ascertain whether *any* person 'in actual

1 [1980] 3 WLR 138 at 147.
2 [1980] 3 WLR 138 at 144.
3 See pp. 273, 302, ante.
4 See *Hussey v Palmer* [1972] 1 WLR 1286, p. 481, post.
5 A contribution towards the installation of central heating may be sufficient to generate beneficial entitlement. See *Re Nicholson* [1974] 1 WLR 476, p. 249, ante.
6 See, for instance, *Carega Properties SA v Sharratt* [1979] 1 WLR 928, p. 442, post.
7 During the course of argument in *Boland*, the House of Lords mooted the problems which would occur in relation to such situations as those, for instance, of four young girls sharing a flat the lease of which was vested in only one (see *Savage v Dunningham* [1974] Ch 181), and of the family farm run by a partnership consisting of the brothers of the family. Even greater difficulties arise in relation to any beneficial interest owned by a child of the vendor/mortgagor. In *Bird v Syme-Thomson* [1979] 1 WLR 440 at 444, Templeman J thought that the vendor/mortgagor's adult children would be unable to claim the benefit of section 70(1)(g). It has been observed that one difficulty 'which might arise in the (admittedly unlikely) event of a child having an overriding interest, is the question whether the rule that the rights are not overriding if there is a failure to disclose them in reply to inquiries should apply to a person who might not comprehend the inquiry' (J. Martin, [1980] Conv 361 at 372: 'Section 70(1)(g) and the Vendor's Spouse').

occupation' claims any proprietary interest in the land[8]. The nature of the enquiry imposed on the third party will extend to a careful inspection of the property in order to discover how many people live there[9]. Moreover, enquiry must be made into the nature of the relationship between the joint occupiers whose presence is disclosed by inspection. It is vital that the purchaser/mortgagee should be able to distinguish between the vendor/mortgagor's wife or mistress (who may have beneficial interests in the property) and his lodger or au pair (who almost certainly are not so entitled). The difference in terms of external appearance may not be particularly great or obvious. Yet the risk is now clearly that of the third party and he (or it) must ascertain the true position.

It has been said that the House of Lords had 'no perception of the magnitude of the consequences' of its decision in *Boland*[10]. The appellant bank requested the House in the strongest terms possible[11] that simplicity be secured by narrowing rather than widening the categories of interests within section 70(1)(g). Counsel for the bank expressed the view that the banking world desired and needed 'a workable system', and that this goal would be made quite impossible if third parties were required to make comprehensive, distasteful and embarrassing enquiries in every case. Yet the House decided against the bank, and the reaction from the banking world has been predictably fierce. The chief legal adviser to Lloyds Bank condemned the *Boland* decision as requiring that

> the purchaser or lender should not only question the sole owner of a house as to who lives with him and in what capacity, which will be embarrassing enough, but also search the house to see if he is telling the truth since, if he is not, an undisclosed wife or mistress could destroy the value of his security. Inevitably the cost of house purchase will rise as will the difficulty of borrowing upon the security of house property[12].

It seems fairly clear then that the *Boland* decision has profound implications

8 The problem experienced by the purchaser/mortgagee is greatly accentuated by the fact that, in order to be safe, he must make enquiry of every person on the premises. He cannot short-circuit the process by asking the vendor/mortgagor whether there are others in occupation who claim proprietary interests in the land. Enquiry in this form is not enough for the purpose of s. 70(1)(g), since under this paragraph the enquiry must be made of the person who claims the overriding interest. As Russell LJ said in *Hodgson v Marks* [1971] Ch 892 at 932, 'reliance on the untrue ipse dixit of the vendor will not suffice', p. 342, ante.

9 In *Boland* the Law Lords actively contemplated during the course of argument that a duty might be placed upon a purchaser/mortgagee to search through the bedrooms in a house in order to see who slept with whom, and to rummage through wardrobes in order to determine the gender of the occupiers! Such a process of search is reminiscent of the form of enquiry which Stamp J so firmly condemned in *Caunce v Caunce* [1969] 1 WLR 286 at 292. There Stamp J referred to techniques which 'would ... have been more appropriate to a police enquiry or that of a detective agency than to a bank manager ... [I]t is not in the public interest that bank mortgagees should be snoopers and busybodies in relation to wholly normal transactions of mortgages.'

10 (1980) 43 MLR 692 at 696 (S. Freeman).

11 In his final submission to the House of Lords, counsel for the bank (D. J. Nicholls QC) announced that the bank was so anxious to obtain a declaratory ruling from the House in support of 'a workable system' for bankers and conveyancers that, in the event of a judgment favourable to the bank, the bank would undertake not to pursue any order for possession against the two respondent wives!

12 Derek Wheatley, Legal Adviser, Lloyds Bank Head Office, in a letter to the Times, 24th June 1980.

for house purchase and housing finance[13]. It has been suggested that a simple solution to the problems exposed in *Boland* could take the form of a printed questionnaire sent automatically by a third party to the spouse or any sole vendor/mortgagor, for the purpose of ascertaining whether he or she claims any overriding interest in the property[14]. Such an enquiry would not, however, relieve third parties from the task of discovering whether any other persons are in joint occupation of the land and claim interests protected by section 70(1)(g). It may be that a prudent purchaser will require written waivers from each member of the vendor's household who may conceivably be able to establish a proprietary right in respect of the property[15]. Alternatively, a third party such as a bank or building society may insist upon title to the matrimonial home being vested in the joint names of husband and wife[16]. In any event, the Law Commission's solution of the *Boland* problem seems peculiarly inappropriate. The Law Commission, it will be recalled[17], proposed that the interests of wives in the *Boland* situation should be protected by further recourse to the machinery of registration—an expedient scarcely likely to succeed in its objective since the root of the *Boland* problem consists precisely in the failure of the wives to enter minor interests in the relevant register of title.

(2) The implications for the ascertainment of beneficial ownership

In *Williams & Glyn's Bank Ltd v Boland* it was conceded as 'common ground' before the Court of Appeal that the appellant wives were beneficially entitled in the matrimonial homes which belonged at law to their husbands[18]. It was ultimately this beneficial interest which each wife was able successfully to oppose against the bank as an overriding interest within section 70(1)(g) of the Land Registration Act 1925. It is therefore inferable that in future proceedings of this kind the first challenge of the party claiming possession of the property will be as to whether the party resisting possession is indeed entitled in equity. It may be a very different story if, for instance, a wife is required positively to establish

13 See R. J. Smith (1979) 95 LQR 501: 'In practice, the problem is most likely to arise in the context of mortgages, for the wife's continued possession (with the husband) is compatible with the transaction and she may well be ignorant of the mortgage. In a sale or lease, normally either the wife will acquiesce or her objections will halt the transaction before registration.'

14 See R. J. Smith (1979) 95 LQR 501 at 505. It has been mooted that new pre-contract enquiries of the vendor will be formulated, for example asking the names of all persons residing on the premises in order that enquiries may be addressed to them (see J. Martin [1980] Conv 361 at 369).

15 See S. Freeman (1980) 43 MLR 692 at 694: 'This will inevitably result, not only in a proliferation of paper, but also in the need to make detailed and potentially embarrassing inquiries as to precisely who is going to live in the house. Furthermore, the purchaser's solicitor may be put in a position of professional difficulty: should he not, for example, advise the purchaser's wife that she should be separately represented before signing any waiver?'

16 See M. J. Prichard, (1979) 38 Cambridge LJ 254 at 257: '[I]f the decision leads banks, building societies and other purchasers to insist upon the title to the matrimonial home being properly vested in both spouses, it will do more good than harm; for they are better placed to insist than she is.' See, however, J. T. Farrand [1980] Conv 315ff.; J. Martin [1980] Conv 361 at 370.

17 See p. 303, ante.

18 [1979] Ch 312 at 327.

the origin and quantum of her alleged beneficial entitlement in the matrimonial home[19]. Moreover, a heightened degree of stringency will be exacted in matters of proof if the proceedings in hand are proceedings brought by the husband's trustee in bankruptcy seeking an order for sale of the property under section 30 of the Law of Property Act 1925[20].

(3) The implications for proceedings connected with bankruptcy

It must be borne in mind that the mere fact that a beneficiary takes priority over a mortgagee in the circumstances of *Boland*'s case does not mean that that beneficiary's occupation of the disputed property is necessarily secure for all time. It is commonly the case in the *Boland* situation that the husband/vendor becomes insolvent, and this may entail certain important consequences for his wife notwithstanding that she has successfully claimed an overriding interest.

Under the Bankruptcy Act 1914, a 'settlement' of property by one spouse upon the other is voidable at the behest of the settlor's trustee in bankruptcy within two years of the date of the settlement[1]. In some cases, interspousal dispositions may be reviewed at any time within ten years of the date of the settlement[2]. This brings about the consequence that a beneficial interest established by one spouse may be recovered by the other spouse's trustee in bankruptcy, even though that interest ranks as an overriding interest under the Land Registration Act 1925. A limited exception to this right of recovery is made in the case of a settlement in favour of a spouse who has purchased the transferred interest 'in good faith and for valuable consideration[3].' Thus, if a wife claims an equitable interest in the matrimonial home by way of gift from her husband or an equitable interest beyond that justified by the extent of her money contribution, that interest may be recovered by his trustee in bankruptcy in the event of his insolvency.

Furthermore, even if a wife/beneficiary manages to resist the recovery of her beneficial interest by her husband's trustee in bankruptcy under the Bankruptcy Act 1914, she may not be able to resist a sale of the property and the compulsory conversion of her equitable entitlement into an aliquot share in the proceeds of that sale. The equitable share of the husband vests in his trustee in bankruptcy, who will normally press for an order for sale of the property under section 30 of

19 For an account of the difficulties involved here, see pp. 249, ante; 477, 561, post.
20 See M. J. Prichard (1980) 39 Cambridge LJ 243 at 244; S. Freeman (1980) 43 MLR 692 at 694f.
1 Bankruptcy Act 1914, s. 42(1). A 'settlement' includes for this purpose any transfer or conveyance of a proprietary interest (see Bankruptcy Act 1914, s. 42(4)).
2 A settlement is voidable if the settlor becomes insolvent within ten years of the date of the settlement, unless it can be proved that he was able at that date to pay all his debts without the aid of the property comprised in the settlement and that there was an immediate transfer of the property in question to the trustee of the settlement.
3 Bankruptcy Act 1914, s. 42(1). In order to guarantee immunity from recovery by the trustee in bankruptcy, the consideration must be capable of being regarded 'in a commercial sense' as valuable consideration. See *Re Densham (A Bankrupt)* [1975] 1 WLR 1519 at 1529. Here Goff J gave with one hand and took away with the other, in the sense that the beneficial interest which the wife successfully claimed by way of constructive trust was immediately recovered as a void 'settlement' by the husband's trustee in bankruptcy.

the Law of Property Act 1925, in order that the value of the bankrupt's share be realised in satisfaction of the claims of his creditors. Under section 30, the court has discretion to 'make such order as it thinks fit', but, as we have seen[4], this discretion is almost invariably exercised in favour of ordering sale in cases of insolvency—even though this may mean terminating the occupation of the bankrupt's wife and family[5].

(4) Implications for land law priorities

As Lord Roskill observed astutely during the hearing in *Williams & Glyn's Bank Ltd v Boland*, the fundamental question underlying the case related quite simply to the extent to which a lender of money should as a matter of policy be required to take the risk of a defect in the borrower's title in property offered as security. The notion of 'risk' was to play an important part in the decision reached by the House of Lords. At the end of the day the House ruled in favour of increasing rather than decreasing the risk inevitably assumed by anyone who lends money in any kind of mortgage transaction. An interesting, and indeed perhaps decisive, point was made by Lord Wilberforce in dealing with the conveyancing consequences which had so troubled Templeman J at first instance. Lord Wilberforce agreed with the objections voiced at first instance

> to the extent that whereas the object of a land registration system is to reduce the risks to purchasers from anything not on the register, to extend (if it be an extension) the area of risk so as to include possible interests of spouses, and indeed, in theory, of other members of the family or even outside it, may add to the burdens of purchasers, and involve them in enquiries which in some cases may be troublesome[6].

However, Lord Wilberforce immediately followed this admission by stating:

> But conceded, as it must be, that the Act . . . gives protection to occupation, the extension of the risk area follows necessarily from the extension, beyond the paterfamilias, of rights of ownership, itself following from the diffusion of property and earning capacity. What is involved is a departure from an easy-going practice of dispensing with enquiries as to occupation beyond that of the vendor and accepting the risks of doing so.

Lord Wilberforce thus effectively attributed the emergence of the key issue in *Boland* to the advent of the 'property-owning democracy' in the years following the Second World War[7]. He made particular reference to the new social pattern of co-ownership of the matrimonial home, and pointed out that the imposition upon purchasers of a duty of careful enquiry as to the entitlements of occupiers could not be considered as 'unacceptable except at the price of overlooking the

4 See p. 281, ante.
5 It was significant that in *Bird v Syme-Thomson* [1979] 1 WLR 440 at 444, Templeman J stated that even if he had allowed the wife/beneficiary there to take priority over her husband's mortgagee, he would still have ordered a sale of the property under section 30 of the Law of Property Act 1925. The wife/beneficiary was entitled to only 20 per cent of the equity, the other 80 per cent belonging to her husband—or rather, as Templeman J pointed out—to her husband's trustee in bankruptcy.
6 [1980] 3 WLR 138 at 147.
7 See pp. 10, ante; 509, post.

widespread development of shared interests of ownership[8].' In these circumstances, the House of Lords made a policy decision to allocate an ever greater portion of the risk inherent in credit transactions to the lender of the money.

In this sense, the House of Lords was operating as a loss distributor and the decision in *Boland* should be seen as an integral component of the law relating to the adjustment of pecuniary damage. Just as the law of torts has substantially become an exercise in determining which party is better able to carry a loss which has occurred, so—it seems in *Boland*'s case—the law of land may likewise entail a discretionary exercise in loss-shifting. For a mixture of socio-political reasons connected with the importance of protecting the rights of the married woman, the House of Lords decided that the risk inherent in the *Boland* transactions should be borne by the bank[9]. Not only was this decision an exercise in loss-shifting; it provided also a means of loss-spreading. Insofar as the bank in *Boland* undertook risk and suffered consequent loss by virtue of the House of Lords' decision, the bank's liability was diffused. Banks commonly carry a very effective form of insurance which is designed with the partial object of distributing an adventitious loss among all the participants in the hazardous activity of buying and selling money—they charge interest on the capital which they lend. It was Lord Denning MR in the Court of Appeal who rather wickedly referred to the fact that the bank was supported by an informal means of insurance against loss:

> If a bank is to do its duty, in the society in which we live, it should recognise the integrity of the matrimonial home. It should not destroy it by disregarding the wife's interest in it—simply to ensure that it is paid the husband's debt in full—with the high interest rate now prevailing[10].

As in so many areas of the law of torts, the presence of an insurance mechanism operating in favour of one or other party has modified the traditional legal rules governing liability. *Boland* provides one instance of this pattern in the somewhat surprising context of land law. If the *Boland* decision indicates a more enduring

8 [1980] 3 WLR 138 at 147. Lord Wilberforce did concede, however, that 'it may be true that in 1925 [Parliament] did not foresee the full extent of this development.'

9 See p. 302, ante. See J. Martin [1980] Conv 361 at 383: 'The probability of the vendor's or mortgagor's spouse having an interest in the property is so great that the purchaser or mortgagee should be expected to take it into account. Just as in the case of the Matrimonial Homes Act, it is unrealistic to expect the wife to register a caution or restriction to protect her interest. She may well not be aware even of the existence of her rights, still less how to protect them . . . [T]here is no way of protecting her interest by registration in unregistered land. Is she to be expected to insist on the appointment of a second trustee? The purchaser or mortgagee, on the other hand, is normally receiving legal advice and, in the case of a mortgagee, is often a commercial undertaking. Such persons are usually in a better position to protect themselves, and to suffer the loss if they fail, than the vendor's spouse.' It has even been suggested that ultimately the purchaser's solution for the *Boland* problem may have to lie in some form of insurance indemnity against 'undiscoverable rights' (see C. Sydenham [1980] Conv 427 at 432). Such a proposal even more clearly confirms this area of land law as merely a branch of the law of liability insurance.

10 [1979] Ch 312 at 332f., p. 368, ante.

practice on the part of the courts in dealing with land law issues, it may point the way to what Professor Alice Tay once called

> a bureaucratic-administrative, regulatory and even confiscatory resources-allocation concern, in which the state stands above property owners, as the representative of a general 'socio-political' interest. The focus in social regulation and resources allocations is on *activities*, on the *use* made of property and its effect on other people, other activities, the national economy and the availability of resources. Such regulations, for all their piecemeal and *ad hoc* character, do tend to build up into a body of law governing a whole social province or function . . .[11]

In *Boland* the House of Lords took an important step towards formulating something which we have never had before in this country—a regime of family property. It also added another important development to the emerging 'law of households' which we can see emerging slowly out of the mists of the law of landlord and tenant[12], the law of social security and other largely forgotten areas of social legislation. Nevertheless, the argument remains that the legislative function in these matters is properly that of Parliament and not the courts.

(5) Implications for beneficial rights behind a trust for sale

For socio-political reasons, the House of Lords in *Williams & Glyn's Bank Ltd v Boland* allowed technical considerations of land law to be set aside in order that effect be given to the 'occupation interest' of a wife/beneficiary. The decision thus allowed the interest of the wife in the 'use value' of the land to prevail over the 'exchange value' which the bank imagined it had acquired by means of the mortgage transaction with her husband.

The House of Lords was still fundamentally unclear as to the nature of the right of occupation enjoyed by a beneficiary behind a trust for sale of land. Lord Scarman declared confidently that each wife concerned in *Boland* was

> an equitable tenant in common behind a trust for sale . . . Each, therefore, enjoys by reason of her interest a present right of occupation as well as a right to a share in the proceeds of sale, if and when the house is sold: *Bull v Bull*[13].

Lord Scarman then observed that this 'right of occupation of the land' was the 'critically important right of the wife, so far as these appeals are concerned,' for 'once it is associated with actual occupation, the association is an overriding interest.' These propositions seemed to ignore the fact that it is far from well established that a trust for sale beneficiary has any *right* at all to occupy the land. Lord Wilberforce was much more cautious on this point, preferring simply to say that the 'right of occupation of the land pending sale is not explicitly dealt with' in the Law of Property Act 1925 'and the position as to it is obscure[14].' It

11 'Law, the citizen and the state', in E. Kamenka, R. Brown and A. E.-S. Tay (ed.), *Law and Society—The Crisis in Legal Ideals* (London 1978), p. 13, p. 19, ante.
12 See P. Tennant (1980) 39 Cambridge LJ 31: 'Cohabitation and the Rent Act'.
13 [1980] 3 WLR 138 at 148f.
14 [1980] 3 WLR 138 at 145, p. 272, ante.

is scarcely credible that on an issue so basic to the instant dispute there should have been so little incisive conceptual analysis.

Notwithstanding the continuing uncertainty in *Boland* as to the nature of the beneficiary's occupational privilege, some points can be made with a degree of assurance. The decision in *Boland* marks an important development in the jurisprudence of the trust for sale of land. The ruling recognised the paramount significance of a beneficiary's interest in residential security in the family home. It effectively 'democratised' the trust for sale, by putting in the hands of beneficiaries in actual occupation a virtual power of veto over dealings with the registered title held by a single trustee[15]. It conferred upon the beneficiary in possession a right of dispositive control similar to that which Denning LJ had sought to uphold in *Bull v Bull*[16]. The decision thus highlighted once again the emerging importance of the 'control' aspects of property in the modern world. It is the 'control' aspects of property which have become pivotal as the emphasis in the law of property shifts slowly but surely away from achieving the unrestricted commerciability of title towards guaranteeing the protection of rights of enjoyment[17]. In the interests of enhanced residential security, the 'new property' elevates not the 'exchange' or 'capital' value of land but rather the 'use' value which is most effectively realised in actual enjoyment[18].

(6) A portent of future developments

Before leaving *Williams & Glyn's Bank Ltd v Boland*, there is one other factor which must be mentioned. The judgment of the House of Lords in *Boland* has caused great controversy in the banking and conveyancing world and there will inevitably be pressure brought to bear upon Parliament to reverse the effect of this decision by legislation. It should be noted that a Bill having precisely this effect failed to secure Parliamentary passage during the 1979–1980 session[19].

In 1978 the Law Commission published its proposals for a regime of statutory co-ownership of the matrimonial home[20]. The irony should not pass unobserved that the Law Commission recommended that legislation should be enacted containing a general provision, for the avoidance of doubt, that beneficial interests behind a trust for sale should be regarded as minor interests only. In the view of the Commission,

no beneficial interest which subsists under a trust for sale (or a settlement within the

15 See p. 272, ante.
16 [1955] 1 QB 234, p. 268, ante. It was conceded during argument before the House of Lords in *Boland* that any written waiver of her rights by either wife/beneficiary would have been conclusive against her.
17 See the Law Commission's recent concentration upon the conferment of a 'right of control' upon a wife/beneficiary behind a trust for sale which gives effect to the Commission's proposed statutory regime of co-ownership of the matrimonial home, pp. 150, 303, ante.
18 See p. 39, ante.
19 See p. 151, ante.
20 See p. 149, ante.

Settled Land Act 1925) should amount to an overriding interest, whether it belongs to a wife or to anyone else[1].

Accordingly, the Commission proposed a provision in the following terms:

For the removal of doubt it is hereby declared that the rights capable of being overriding interests under section 70(1)(g) of the Land Registration Act 1925 . . . do not include—
(a) in the case of land held on trust for sale, interests or powers which are under the Law of Property Act 1925 capable of being overridden by the trustees for sale; or
(b) in the case of settled land, interests or powers which are under the Settled Land Act 1925 and the Law of Property Act 1925 or either of them capable of being overridden by the tenant for life or statutory owner[2].

This provision was contained in the Matrimonial Homes (Co-ownership) Bill which foundered in Parliament during the very session when *Williams & Glyn's Bank Ltd v Boland* was decided by the House of Lords.

We have now looked in great detail at *Williams & Glyn's Bank Ltd v Boland* simply because from it we can learn so much about land law in general and about the mode of thought of land lawyers in particular. Although this chapter has been concerned almost entirely with one single case, such an exercise demonstrates how fertile the careful reading of cases can be.

1 *Third Report on Family Property: The Matrimonial Home (Co-ownership and Occupation Rights) and Household Goods* (Law Com No. 86, June 1978), para. 1.333.

2 Matrimonial Homes (Co-ownership) Bill, clause 24(4). The Law Commission considered that such a provision was made 'particularly desirable by [the] recommendations for statutory co-ownership, because these will increase the number of cases in which a wife not on the legal title has nonetheless a beneficial interest in the property. Our recommendation will therefore avoid a potential source of conveyancing complication and delay, and dispose at the same time of a doubt about the existing law' (Law Com No. 86, para. 1.333).

PART IV

Residential security

CHAPTER 12

Leases

So far in this book we have directed our attention mainly to the legal estate in fee simple absolute in possession[1]. We have considered the way in which commercial equitable rights can be carved out of that legal estate and made to bind third parties[2]. We have also examined the process by which the legal estate in fee simple can be settled in order to give effect to a number of successive or concurrent family equitable interests[3]. Now we look at the other legal estate which may exist in land, the 'term of years absolute' or 'lease'.

The interest in land which we now know as the 'lease', 'demise' or 'tenancy' was originally considered by property lawyers to lie outside the field of the law of real property because the leasehold relationship formed no part of the feudal structure. The right to occupy another's land for a defined period of time was regarded as a mere right *in personam* existing only in contract. Such a right was not regarded as a right *in rem*, i.e., as a right of property[4]. It was only with the development of the action of ejectment in the 15th century that occupation rights of this kind—albeit initially conferred by contract—came to be recognised as constituting a new category of *property* right. Thus, although the lease (the 'term of years absolute') is today recognised as a potential legal estate in land[5], it is still considered as having a somewhat hybrid character, partaking of the nature of both realty and personalty. For this reason the lease is sometimes called a 'chattel real'.

1. THE DEFINITION OF A 'LEASE'

In general terms, a 'lease' is a disposition effected by a 'lessor' (or landlord) which creates in the 'lessee' (or tenant) an interest in land for a fixed period of certain duration. The lease is usually, but not necessarily, granted in consideration of a money rent.

It is an essential characteristic of any 'lease' that the lessee should be given a right to 'exclusive possession' of the demised premises. An occupier upon whom is conferred any lesser right than that of exclusive possession can never under any circumstances claim to be a tenant holding under a lease: in most cases he will be a mere 'licensee'. Moreover, where an occupier has been granted a right of exclusive possession of premises, this fact alone does not necessarily signify

1 See Law of Property Act 1925, s. 1(1)(a).
2 See Chapter 4.
3 See Chapters 5, 7, 8.
4 See A. W. B. Simpson, *An Introduction to the History of the Land Law* (London 1961), p. 68ff.; F. Pollock and F. W. Maitland, *The History of English Law* (London 1968), Vol. II, p. 106ff.
5 Law of Property Act 1925, s. 1(1)(b).

that a lease has been created. Although there is a presumption that such a grant confers a lease, it is still possible that the right conferred is merely a licence—albeit a licence for exclusive occupation[6]. It may therefore be necessary in these circumstances to decide whether the transaction created a lease or merely a licence, the importance of the distinction consisting essentially in the fact that a lease confers an interest or 'stake' in the land (i.e., a right *in rem*), whereas a licence confers merely a personal permission to occupy land—a right *in personam*[7].

In cases of ambivalence the distinction between lease and licence is governed ultimately by the intentions of the parties at the time of the transaction in question. The relevant intentions may be expressed in the document (if any) which records the transaction, or may be left to be gathered from circumstantial evidence or to be inferred from the conduct of the parties. In cases of doubt, the issue whether a particular transaction represents a lease or a licence must be determined by a court. In deciding this question, the court will look to the substance of the disputed transaction and not merely to its external form. The descriptive labels ('lease' or 'licence') applied by the parties themselves are persuasive but not conclusive, and it is open to the court to regard a 'licence' as being in reality a 'lease' (and vice versa)[8]. It has been said[9] that where there is a written document,

> the whole of the document must be looked at; and if, after it has been examined, the right conclusion appears to be that, whatever label may have been attached to it, it in fact conferred and imposed on the grantee in substance the rights and obligations of a tenant, and on the grantor in substance the rights and obligations of a landlord, then it must be given the appropriate effect, that is to say, it must be treated as a tenancy agreement as distinct from a mere licence[10].

Another essential characteristic of any 'lease' is that it must confer an interest in land which is of certain maximum duration: a finite point must be expressed or must be implicit or capable of being rendered certain[11]. Hence, in *Lace v Chantler*[12], no lease was held to exist where a right of occupation had been conferred for the duration of the war. With this qualification, however, a lease may take almost any form. It may be a lease for a fixed term (whether for one year or 3,000 years). It may be a 'periodic tenancy' (e.g., weekly, monthly, yearly). In the latter case, the occupation of the tenant may extend indefinitely,

6 See, for instance, *Booker v Palmer* [1942] 2 All ER 674. The distinction between lease and licence is vital in determining eligibility for residential protection under the Rent Act 1977, p. 421, post.
7 See p. 30f., ante.
8 See *Clore v Theatrical Properties Ltd and Westby & Co Ltd* [1936] 3 All ER 483 (document purporting to be a lease held to create a mere licence); *Addiscombe Garden Estates Ltd v Crabbe* [1958] 1 QB 513 (document purporting to be a mere licence held to create a lease).
9 *Addiscombe Garden Estates Ltd v Crabbe*, supra, at 522 per Jenkins LJ.
10 See also *Marcroft Wagons Ltd v Smith* [1951] 2 KB 496; *Abbeyfield (Harpenden) Society Ltd v Woods* [1968] 1 WLR 374; *Barnes v Barratt* [1970] 2 QB 657; *Shell-Mex and BP Ltd v Manchester Garages Ltd* [1971] 1 WLR 612; *Heslop v Burns* [1974] 1 WLR 1241, p. 422, post.
11 It is necessary, by way of corollary, that the lease must commence at a 'time certain' (see *Harvey v Pratt* [1965] 1 WLR 1025).
12 [1944] KB 368.

but the tenancy nevertheless passes the test of certain maximum duration in the sense that each occupational unit of time, as it is added to the preceding period of occupation, is of strictly defined duration[13]. However, as Russell LJ pointed out in *Re Midland Rly. Co's Agreement*[14],

> If you have an ordinary case of a periodic tenancy (for example, a yearly tenancy), it is plain that in one sense at least it is uncertain at the outset what will be the maximum duration of the term created, which term grows year by year as a single term springing from the original grant. It cannot be predicated that in no circumstances will it exceed, for example, 50 years; there is no previously ascertained maximum duration for the term; its duration will depend upon the time that will elapse before either party gives notice of determination. The simple statement of the law that the maximum duration of a term must be certainly known in advance of its taking effect cannot therefore have direct reference to periodic tenancies.

In order to preserve, in so far as possible, the requirement that a lease be of certain maximum duration, special provisions govern the effect of arrangements which would otherwise fail to qualify. A 'term of years' as defined by statute cannot include a lease for life or a lease which is determinable on anyone's death[15]. Such leases, if granted at a rent or in consideration of a 'fine' (i.e., a premium or initial cash payment), are automatically converted into leases for a 90-year term, as is also any lease which is expressed to be determinable upon the marriage of the lessee[16]. Another lease which represents a problem for want of a clear finite point is the perpetually renewable lease. Such a lease can in theory endure for ever, but is converted automatically by statute into a term of 2,000 years determinable only by the lessee[17].

It should also be noted that statute law declares void any term of years at a rent or granted in consideration of a fine which is limited to take effect more than 21 years after the date of the instrument purporting to create it[18].

The rent payable under the terms of a lease must be certain, in the sense that

13 See *Legg v Strudwick* (1709) 2 Salk 414.

14 [1971] Ch 725 at 732. See [1971] CLJ 198 (D. MacIntyre); compare *Centaploy Ltd v Matlodge Ltd* [1974] Ch 1; (1973) 89 LQR 457.

15 Law of Property Act 1925, s. 205(1)(xxvii).

16 Law of Property Act 1925, s. 149(6). In these cases, the statutory 90-year term may be determined upon the prior death or prior marriage (as the case may be) of the person specified.

17 Law of Property Act 1922, s. 145, and Sch. 15, para. 1. See *Parkus v Greenwood* [1950] Ch 644; *Caerphilly Concrete Products Ltd v Owen* [1972] 1 WLR 372. There is a tendency for the courts to lean against construing a lease as a perpetually renewable lease in the absence of an unequivocal covenant to this effect. Before a lease can be held to have been converted statutorily into a 2,000-year term, it must be found that the lease contained an express covenant or obligation for perpetual renewal. It is not enough, for instance, that a seven-year lease should contain a clause providing that if the tenant was desirous of taking a new lease and gave notice, the landlord would grant 'a new lease' for a further term of seven years 'at a rent to be agreed', and that 'such new lease' should contain a like covenant for renewal for a further seven years. See *Marjorie Burnett Ltd v Barclay* (1980) Times, 19th December.

18 Law of Property Act 1925, s. 149(3). However, this provision does not affect the validity of a *contract* to create a lease at some future time which, when created, will take effect immediately or within 21 years of the date of that instrument (Perpetuities and Accumulations Act 1964, s. 9(2)). See *Re Strand and Savoy Properties Ltd* [1960] Ch 582, (1960) 76 LQR 352 (REM); *Weg Motors Ltd v Hales* [1962] Ch 49.

it must be capable of being calculated with certainty at the time when payment is due[19].

2. CREATION OF LEASES

The creation of most kinds of lease has for a long time been subject to certain statutory requirements of formality. A leasehold interest in land is, at least potentially, a legal estate, and therefore the creation or assignment of such an interest necessarily takes the form of a disposition or 'conveyance' of an estate in the land. The owner of an estate in fee simple absolute 'conveys' a term of years to a third party in almost the same way as that in which he would 'convey' his own fee simple estate. Thus the creation and disposition of both freehold and leasehold are alike subject to fairly stringent rules relating to formality, since the subject of the transaction is in both instances a legal estate in land.

The statutory requirements of formality in respect of the creation or transfer of leasehold interests are contained in an uncoordinated series of provisions in the Law of Property Act 1925[20]. The starting point is the proposition that 'all conveyances of land or of any interest therein are void for the purpose of conveying or creating a legal estate unless made by deed[1].' An exception is then made in relation to 'leases or tenancies . . . not required by law to be made in writing[2].' No writing of any kind is required for the creation of 'leases taking effect in possession for a term not exceeding three years . . . at the best rent which can be reasonably obtained without taking a fine[3].' All other interests in land, if not created in writing, have the 'force and effect of interests at will only[4].' The net effect of these provisions is that a legal lease for a period not exceeding three years can be created either orally or in writing. However, a legal lease for a period in excess of three years and an assignment of *any* lease (irrespective of its duration) must be effected by deed.

It follows from these provisions that a legal periodic tenancy may be created without any kind of formality: it may be created simply by verbal grant. Moreover, a periodic tenancy may be created either expressly or impliedly. An express periodic tenancy is one which is granted, for instance, 'from week to week' or 'from month to month.' An implied periodic tenancy arises where a property owner accepts rent paid on a periodic basis by a 'tenant at will[5]' (i.e., one who occupies land with the consent of the owner) or by a tenant under a formally invalid lease[6]. In these cases the precise nature of the tenancy is determined prima facie by the period with reference to which the rent payable

19 *Greater London Council v Connolly* [1970] 2 QB 100.
20 These provisions stem from the Statute of Frauds 1677, ss. 1, 2, and the Real Property Act 1845, s. 3.
1 Law of Property Act 1925, s. 52(1).
2 Law of Property Act 1925, s. 52(2)(d).
3 Law of Property Act 1925, s. 54(2).
4 Law of Property Act 1925, s. 54(1).
5 See p. 395, post.
6 See p. 395, post.

is calculated, not by the frequency with which that rent is actually paid[7]. Where a landlord accepts rent paid on a periodic basis by a 'tenant at sufferance'[8] (i.e., a tenant who holds over at the end of a valid tenancy), that payment may well be construed as giving rise to a weekly tenancy notwithstanding the fact that the original tenancy comprised a fixed term of one year[9].

A yearly periodic tenancy may be terminated, in the absence of contrary agreement between the parties, by the giving of half a year's notice. At common law the period of notice required for the termination of other periodic tenancies is one full period (e.g., one week's notice of termination by either party in the case of a weekly tenancy)[10].

3. THE FLEXIBILITY OF LEASEHOLD ARRANGEMENTS

The extreme flexibility of leasehold arrangements may be demonstrated with reference to the following diagram:

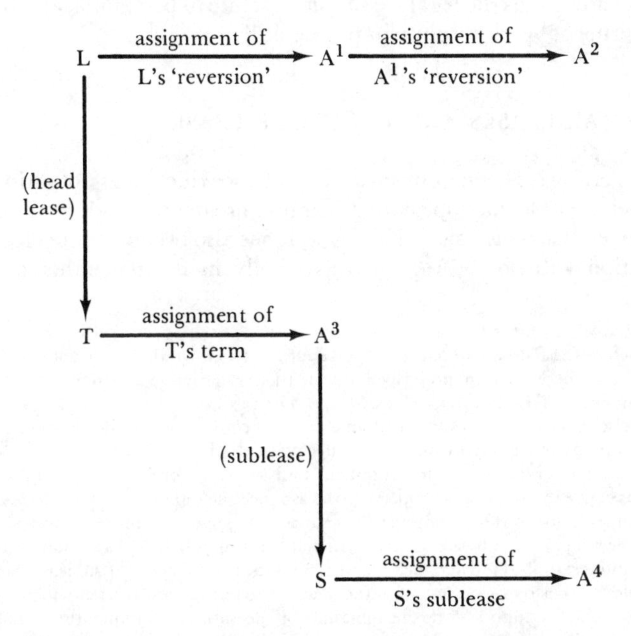

Fig. 62

7 Thus, in the absence of some express description of the precise nature of the tenancy, a tenant whose rent obligation amounts to '£520 per annum payable weekly' is presumed to hold a yearly tenancy, whereas a tenant whose rent obligation amounts to '£10 per week' is presumed to hold a weekly tenancy. See *Ladies' Hosiery & Underwear Ltd v Parker* [1930] 1 Ch 304 at 328f.

8 See p. 395, post.

9 See *Adler v Blackman*; [1952] 2 All ER 41; affd. [1953] 1 QB 146, CA.

10 These rules relating to notice must now be read subject to the overriding statutory provision that in the case of residential premises no notice to quit has any validity if it is given less than four

Assume that L holds an estate in fee simple absolute in possession in a plot of land and that all subsequent leases and assignments are executed by deed. L now grants a term of years absolute to a tenant, T. On granting this lease, L, although still the owner in fee simple, has effectively disabled himself from resuming occupation of the land until the termination of the lease. In the meantime the sum total of his rights in relation to the land is called a 'reversion', i.e., a residue of rights reversionary upon the lease.

L may later assign this 'reversion' to an assignee, A^1, by selling to him his fee simple estate subject to the lease[11]. Thereafter A^1 himself may execute a further assignment of the 'reversion' to A^2, the 'reversion' steadily increasing in value as the lease approaches its expiry. Meanwhile, T may assign (i.e., sell) the unexpired portion of his lease to A^3, who may in turn create a sublease in favour of S.[12] Finally, S may assign the remaining portion of his sublease to A^4, the sublease of course decreasing in value as it nears the expiry of the term granted[13]. At the point of this last assignment, it can be said that the relationship of landlord and tenant exists, first, between A^2 and A^3 and, second, between A^3 and A^4. A^2 now holds the legal fee simple absolute in possession, and both A^3 and A^4 hold terms of years absolute in possession[14].

4. INFORMAL LEASES AND EQUITABLE LEASES

At law it has always been quite clear that a lease which does not satisfy the strict requirements of formal execution cannot create a valid legal estate: the purported legal lease is void[15]. However, it has also become quite clear that such a transaction will not be regarded as wholly ineffectual either at law or in equity.

---

weeks before the date on which it is to take effect. To be valid, such a notice must also be in writing and must contain prescribed information relating to the tenant's statutory rights (Protection from Eviction Act 1977, s. 5(1), p. 470, post).

11 It is precisely because this assignment amounts to a conveyance of the fee simple estate that it requires (as any other conveyance) to be effected by deed.

12 The essential difference between 'assignment' and 'sublease' consists in the fact that the assignor passes his entire interest in the property to the assignee: he retains no 'estate' or 'reversion' in the land. The assignor thus loses for ever the chance of enjoying the property free of the claims of another occupier. In a sublease, however, the sublessor merely carves a subsidiary interest out of his own interest in the land and meanwhile retains the reversion on the sublease thereby created. The sublessor thus retains an estate in the land in the form of a reversion which will take effect (perhaps only fleetingly) at the termination of the sublease. Frequently a sublessor sublets property for the remainder of his own term minus one day.

13 In order to vest in the assignee a legal term, the assignment must be effected by deed even though the interest assigned may have been validly created without formality (e.g., by purely verbal grant or by unsealed writing).

14 It is apparent from this example that it is possible for the two legal estates (freehold and leasehold) to exist concurrently *in possession*. Of course, it might seem odd at first that a non-resident landlord should be said to be 'in possession' of the land, but 'possession' is defined in section 205(1)(xix) of the Law of Property Act 1925 as including 'receipt of rents and profits or the right to receive the same . . .' Thus, in the relevant sense, A^2, A^3 and A^4 may all be said to be 'in possession' of the land.

15 This result is now confirmed by Law of Property Act 1925, s. 52(1).

The relevant law is best explained with reference to a series of fairly logical steps which the courts have taken in attempting to give some kind of meaning to an essentially invalid lease. Let us assume that L has attempted to confer upon T a seven year lease, but that the grant is contained merely in a written document. In other words, L has not created the lease by deed as required by the Law of Property Act 1925, s. 52(1). Such a transaction is ineffective to convey to T a legal lease for a term of seven years, but may nevertheless bring about the following train of consequences.

(1) Tenancy at will

At law a tenancy at will arises where a tenant under a formally invalid lease enters into possession of the premises which are the subject of the defective lease. A tenancy at will is not a 'tenancy' properly so called, but is merely a type of licence terminable by either party[16]. The existence of a tenancy at will precludes any liability for trespass in the occupier.

Thus, to use our example, if L allows T to enter into possession notwithstanding the formal defect in the lease, T has a tenancy at will. This, however, is to express no more than the tautology that where L permits T to occupy, T has a licence to occupy.

(2) Periodic tenancy by implication

Where a tenant at will offers, and the landlord accepts, payment of any rent in virtue of that tenant's occupation, the tenancy at will is converted automatically into an implied periodic tenancy. The tenant is then presumed to hold a yearly or other periodic tenancy, depending on the period with reference to which the rent is paid. In most cases the periodic tenancy implied by reason of entry into possession and payment of rent will be a legal yearly tenancy, in the sense that as soon as the tenant at will 'expressly agrees to pay any part of the annual rent thereby reserved, his tenancy at will changes into a tenancy from year to year upon the terms of the intended lease, so far as they are applicable to and not inconsistent with a yearly tenancy[17].'

If we apply these rules to L and T, we find that if T enters into possession (on the basis of an ineffective seven-year legal lease) and he then offers a periodic rent to L which L accepts, T becomes a yearly tenant of L. Such a tenancy requires no formality in the matter of creation, and is therefore, irrespective of its mode of creation, a legal tenancy. What is the result if, by deed, L assigns his

16 See *Clayton v Blakey* (1798) 8 Term Rep 3; *Dougal v McCarthy* [1893] 1 QB 736. A tenancy at will is to be distinguished from a 'tenancy at sufferance', under which the occupier is in possession without either the agreement or the disagreement of the property owner. A tenant at will is, however, regarded as 'being in possession by his own will and at the will, express or implied, of his landlord . . . a tenant by their mutual agreement . . . A tenancy at will . . . has been properly described as a personal relation between the landlord and his tenant . . .' (*Wheeler v Mercer* [1957] AC 416 at 426 per Viscount Simonds).

17 *Woodfall's Law of Landlord and Tenant* (28th edn., London 1978), Vol. 1, para. 1-0631. See *Martin v Smith* (1874) LR 9 Exch 50.

own interest in the property (i.e., his freehold reversion) to a third party purchaser, A¹?

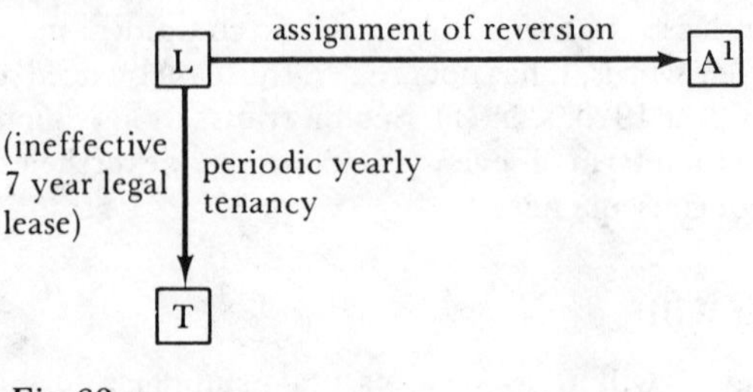

Fig. 63

Clearly the answer here turns upon the fact that T's periodic tenancy is a legal tenancy. It is therefore binding upon A¹ unless and until A¹ terminates the tenancy in the appropriate manner by giving T (normally) half a year's notice to quit the property. To the extent that A¹ accepts any periodic payment of rent offered by T, the periodic tenancy will continue.

(3) Contract to create a lease

We have just seen that an invalid legal lease for seven years may be partially saved as a legal yearly tenancy and may thereby enjoy some limited effect as a legal transaction. There is, however, another quite different way in which the invalid seven-year term may have some effect both at law and in equity.

There is in the hearts of lawyers a quite understandable reluctance to concede that a transaction which has been deliberately and voluntarily concluded by persons of full age and sound mind is forever doomed to nullity in law by reason of a failure to comply with some simple requirement of formal execution. Moreover, since the omission in the matter of form is very likely the consequence of negligent default by some fellow lawyer, an elementary principle of trade union solidarity comes into play. Assistance must be rendered to brothers in difficulty, especially where the difficulty is of their own making. Thus it is quite frequently the case that where a conveyance of a legal estate is, for some technical reason, deprived of legal effect (i.e., the conveyance is void as a conveyance), the transaction is nevertheless regarded at law and in equity as a *contract* for valuable consideration to convey the relevant legal estate at some later stage when the technical impediment has been removed[18]. In other words, a transaction which was intended to operate by way of conveyance is given a limited effect in contract: that which should have acted *in rem* acts in this instance merely *in personam.*

This approach, when translated into terms of the present problem, brings about the result that an invalid attempt to create a legal lease is treated both at law and in equity as a contract to create a lease. In other words, by means of a

18 Compare, for instance, Settled Land Act 1925, ss. 13, 27(1), pp. 168f., ante.

now well established fiction, the ineffective conveyance of a legal estate to T is deemed to constitute an agreement to create a legal estate, and thus L becomes subject to a contractual obligation to convey a seven-year lease to T by deed[19].

The next step in this logical sequence turns upon the difference between the remedies offered at law and in equity in respect of breach of contract.

(4) Remedies for breach of a contract to create a lease

L's ineffective grant of a legal seven-year lease to T is regarded at law as a contract to convey a seven-year lease to T by deed. The common law remedy for any failure by L so to convey the intended legal estate consists in the award of money damages to T as compensation for breach of contract. However, the ineffective legal transaction is also regarded in equity as a contract for a lease, and the remedy offered by equity in respect of breach of contract goes further than the traditional common law remedy of compensatory damages. A contract for the transfer of an interest in land is a contract of which equity will normally grant specific performance[20]. Since the subject matter of the contract for a lease is unique and irreplaceable, equity takes the view that the loss suffered by the tenant by reason of non-performance of the contract is not compensable in money terms. The only adequate remedy for breach of that contract is an order that the landlord do that which he promised to do, i.e., convey a legal estate by deed[1].

Thus, returning to our example, T enjoys by virtue of his contract for a lease the right to invoke the equitable jurisdiction of the court in order to enforce the contract by means of a decree directing specific performance. Such a decree will normally be forthcoming unless T has forfeited the sympathy of equity through the commission of unconscionable or inequitable conduct[2]. But short of this possibility, the contract to create a lease in favour of T must normally eventuate in the conveyance of that leasehold estate to him—either in voluntary fulfilment of the contract or in pursuance of a decree of specific performance. The legal inevitability of performance of the contract at the instance of T now secures the

19 This contract carries several implications. One is that T has, by virtue of the agreement to create a legal estate in his favour, an estate contract which is registrable as a Class C(iv) land charge in unregistered land and protectible as a minor interest in registered land, pp. 135, 326, ante. Another implication is that the contractual relationship between L and T is governed by section 40 of the Law of Property Act 1925, p. 81, ante. Neither L nor T may bring any action on their contract for a lease unless that contract is sufficiently evidenced in writing or supported by part performance. However, given that section 40 is satisfied, and provided too that valuable consideration moves from T to L, the contract for a seven-year lease between L and T is actionable both at law and in equity.

20 See p. 84f., ante.

1 Being an equitable remedy, the award of a decree of specific performance is entirely within the discretion of the court, but the decree will usually be made in respect of a contract relating to land except where the party invoking the exercise of discretion has forfeited his claim to the assistance of equity, e.g., by partaking in unconscionable conduct. 'He who comes into equity must come with clean hands.'

2 See, for instance, *Coatsworth v Johnson* (1886) 55 LJQB 220, where the tenant had already broken some of the terms of the agreement for a lease.

last link in the long chain of the present argument for, as we have already seen[3], 'equity looks on that as done which ought to be done.'

(5) The anticipatory effect of equity

The rules of equity are founded upon rudimentary notions of ethical behaviour and fair play. One of the most elementary rules of fair play in any social interaction is the rule that contractual commitments ought to be honoured: *pacta sunt servanda.* Thus where L is under a contractual obligation to convey a lease for seven years to T by deed, there is an overwhelming expectation that L will perform his contract. And if he does not do so voluntarily, the equitable remedy of specific performance will ensure that his obligation is fulfilled compulsorily[4]. Since the performance of L's contractual obligation is thus rendered virtually inevitable, equity is prepared to anticipate the due performance of that contractual obligation: 'equity looks on that as done which ought to be done.' In other words, equity is prepared to adjudge the rights and obligations of L and T on the fictitious basis that the undertakings contained in an as yet unexecuted contract have already been performed. Thus, in our example, the respective rights and duties of L and T are determined in equity as though L had *already* conveyed a seven-year legal lease to T.

This fiction cannot, of course, extend to the point of saying that T is actually invested with a legal lease, for there has been no formal conveyance. But it does enable us to say that T has an *equitable* lease. He is regarded in equity as holding the land on a seven-year lease which contains terms identical to those originally contained in the abortive grant of a seven-year legal lease[5].

Summary

The conclusion of the long and fairly involved argument recited above is that an informal lease created not by deed but by mere writing is not wholly without effect, even though the term purportedly created is in excess of three years. If the tenant enters into occupation and pays rent to the landlord, he will be regarded as holding on a legal periodic (usually yearly) tenancy. Moreover, if the transaction between landlord and tenant is specifically enforceable as a contract for a lease, the tenant will be treated as holding an equitable tenancy on precisely the terms contained in the formally defective lease.

(6) Resolution of the conflict between law and equity

A slight difficulty occurs where there is conflict in a particular case between the terms of a tenancy as implied from the fact of possession and payment of rent and the terms of a tenancy which, on the same facts, is regarded as an equitable lease. Such a conflict was the subject of the significant judgment of the Court of

3 See pp. 85, 220, ante.
4 See, however, *Johnson v Agnew* [1980] AC 367 in relation to the situation where there is non-compliance with a decree of specific performance.
5 *Parker v Taswell* (1858) 2 De G & J 559. The duration of the equitable lease is exactly the same as the intended duration of the original defective legal lease (i.e., seven years). Likewise, the other terms and conditions of T's equitable lease are exactly the same.

Appeal in *Walsh v Lonsdale*[6]. Here D granted P a seven-year lease in writing, one of the terms of the tenancy being that P should pay each year's rent in advance. No lease under seal was executed, but P entered into possession and proceeded for a period to pay rent in arrear, thereby becoming a yearly periodic tenant at law. D then demanded a year's rent in advance and, on P's refusal to pay rent in advance, distrained for it (by seizing P's goods). P then brought the present action, seeking damages for trespass and a decree of specific performance in relation to the informal lease. There arose on these facts a clear conflict between P's yearly tenancy (under which as a matter of law rent was payable only in arrear) and the equitable seven-year lease which P also enjoyed by virtue of *Parker v Taswell*[7] (according to the terms of which rent was payable in advance). The liability of D in trespass obviously turned upon whether the legal yearly tenancy or the equitable seven-year tenancy was conclusive of the respective rights and duties of the parties.

In an historic judgment, the Court of Appeal decided that, in consequence of the Judicature Acts 1873–1875, any conflict between the rules of law and equity must be resolved by an application of the rules of equity[8]. D's act in distraining upon the goods of P had therefore been quite lawful since D's rights were established by the terms of the equitable seven-year lease, which had made it clear that rent was payable yearly in advance. According to Jessel MR[9],

> there are not two estates as there were formerly, one estate at common law by reason of the payment of rent from year to year, and an estate in equity under the agreement. There is only one Court, and the equity rules prevail in it. The tenant holds under an agreement for a lease. He holds, therefore, under the same terms in equity as if a lease had been granted, it being a case in which both parties admit that relief is capable of being given by specific performance. That being so, he cannot complain of the exercise by the landlord of the same rights as the landlord would have had if a lease had been granted.

It is thus perfectly plain from the terms of Jessel MR's judgment that a tenant who enters into possession under a specifically enforceable contract for a lease holds not a legal periodic tenancy from year to year but rather an equitable tenancy on the same terms as those contained in the abortive informal grant. However, this principle is wholly inapplicable to the case where, for some reason or other, a contract for a lease is not capable of specific performance. In the latter situation, the respective obligations of the parties are governed by the terms of the legal periodic tenancy implied from the tenant's entry into possession and payment of rent. An equitable tenancy cannot co-exist with a legal periodic tenancy, and the doctrine founded upon the equitable jurisdiction to order specific performance effectively ensures that the terms of the equitable tenancy prevail where (and only where) the remedy of specific performance is available.

The doctrine of *Walsh v Lonsdale* has come to apply to a wide range of

6 (1882) 21 Ch D 9.
7 See p. 398, ante.
8 Supreme Court of Judicature Act 1873, s. 25(11); see now Supreme Court of Judicature (Consolidation) Act 1925, s. 44, p. 23, ante.
9 (1882) 21 Ch D 9 at 14f.

supposedly legal transactions which are vitiated by non-compliance with some legal formality. The doctrine establishes a principle of general application to such transactions as the grant of easements, profits and mortgages, and has the effect that informal grants in any of these cases are construed as contracts which, if capable of specific performance, are regarded as grants of equitable interests of the relevant kind.

5. IS A CONTRACT FOR A LEASE AS GOOD AS A LEASE?

The effect of the ruling in *Walsh v Lonsdale* is, in most cases, to convert a formally defective lease or a mere contract for a lease into a perfectly valid equitable lease on exactly the same terms. In view of this result, it is often said that an agreement for a lease is as good as a lease itself[10]. This statement is true for many purposes, but is subject to a number of important qualifications which we must now examine. Thus, although the tenant under a contract for a lease may well have no interest in seeking specific performance of the contract (and indeed many such contracts *never* eventuate in the conveyance of a leasehold estate), a contract for a lease falls short of a legal lease in certain significant respects.

(1) T is dependent on the availability of specific performance

When T enters into possession under an informal grant and pays periodic rent, his status as an equitable tenant is, as we have seen, dependent upon the willingness of the court to grant the discretionary remedy of specific performance. If T's contract for a lease is a contract in relation to which the court cannot or will not grant specific performance, T's position is very different from that which would obtain if a legal lease had been granted in the first place. T will be thrown back upon a mere action for damages against L for breach of contract, and in the meantime T's rights will be simply those (much less secure) rights which exist by virtue of the periodic tenancy implied at law.

10 The illusion that an agreement for a lease is the equivalent of a lease itself is perpetuated most vigorously by the profession of estate agents. Estate agents are legally entitled (as indeed is every citizen in the community) to draw up a contract for the disposition of an interest in land. However, it is a criminal offence for any legally unqualified person to draw up or prepare a deed of conveyance, transfer or charge in relation to any interest in land unless that person 'proves that the act was not done for or in expectation of any fee, gain or reward' (Solicitors Act 1974, section 22(1)). Since the idea of doing something for nothing is thought by many to be almost a precise inversion of the estate agent's professional interest in life, he is effectively excluded from that lucrative form of white-collar crime known as conveyancing. The legal profession's claim for monopolistic control of all land transactions (whether by way of conveyance *or contract*) received the enthusiastic support of the Royal Commission on Legal Services (see *Final Report of the Royal Commission on Legal Services* (Cmnd 7648, October 1979), Vol. 1, para. 21.61). Indeed, in its anxiety to uphold the present conveyancing monopoly enjoyed by solicitors, the Royal Commission fell deep into the trap of the misplaced negative. There is a certain wry amusement to be derived from para. 21.4 of the *Final Report*, in which the Royal Commission seems to go on record as advocating the imposition of criminal liability upon the entire profession of conveyancing solicitors under section 22(1) of the Solicitors Act 1974!

(2) There is no 'privity of estate' under a contract for a lease

We shall discover shortly that certain leasehold covenants may be binding upon even the assignees of the original lessor and lessee where there exists 'privity of estate'[11]. This term will be explained later, but it is sufficient for the moment to note that 'privity of estate' can arise only where the original lease is correctly granted as a legal lease and where subsequent assignments by either lessor or lessee are formally executed by deed. No 'privity of estate' can obtain in relation to a contract for a lease, for the simple reason that there exists no 'estate' in respect of which anyone can be privy. The net result is that the leasehold covenants entered into by the original lessee under a contract for a lease may not be enforceable against his assignees—an illustration of the general rule that the benefit but not the burden of a contract is assignable. This is one important respect in which, from the point of view of the lessor, a contract for a lease is certainly not as good as a lease.

(3) T cannot derive the benefit of section 62 of the Law of Property Act 1925

It should be noted in passing that the important 'general words' provision contained in section 62 of the Law of Property Act 1925 is activated only by a deed of conveyance—although it is immaterial whether the conveyance is of a freehold or leasehold estate[12]. Section 62 cannot therefore be invoked by a tenant under a contract for a lease[13], with the result that no easements can be implied in favour of such a tenant on the basis of the 'general words.'[14]

(4) Under a contract for a lease T is insecure against third parties

Perhaps the most important deficiency of a contract for a lease consists in the fact that the tenant is exceedingly insecure vis à vis third party purchasers from the landlord. If the contract is capable of specific performance, the tenant, T, is regarded as holding an equitable lease. Such an interest, if held in unregistered land, ought to be registered as a Class C(iv) land charge against the name of the landlord, L[15]. If not so registered, T's interest becomes void against any purchaser of a legal estate from L for money or money's worth, irrespective of the purchaser's state of mind[16]. If for some reason a contract for a lease relating

11 See p. 410, post.
12 See p. 595, post. For the definition of 'conveyance', see Law of Property Act 1925, s. 205(1)(ii), p. 228, ante.
13 *Borman v Griffith* [1930] 1 Ch 493.
14 For the position in relation to a legal lease, see *International Tea Stores Co v Hobbs* [1903] 2 Ch 165.
15 See p. 135, ante.
16 See *Midland Bank Trust Co Ltd v Green* [1981] 2 WLR 28, p. 119, ante.

to unregistered land is not specifically enforceable, T has at best merely a legal periodic tenancy which, although binding on the third party purchaser, may be terminated by the appropriate notice to quit at the end of the relevant period.

If, however, a specifically enforceable contract for a lease relates to registered land, then T has an equitable interest which should be protected as a 'minor interest'[17]. Such an interest, if not duly protected, is ineffective against a third party purchaser from L, subject only to the possibility that it may become an 'overriding interest' binding on the purchaser by reason of 'actual occupation' by T[18]. If, conversely, T's contract for a lease relates to registered land but is not capable of specific performance, his position rests upon the legal periodic tenancy implied from possession and payment of rent, and that tenancy may be terminated by an appropriate notice to quit served by the purchaser.

Thus, although a contract for a lease may often appear, as between the immediate parties, to be the equivalent of a legal lease, grave defects are revealed when the third party dimension is introduced.

6. THE RESPECTIVE RIGHTS AND DUTIES OF LANDLORD AND TENANT

(1) Legal lease

On the grant of a legal lease, in the absence of express terms to the contrary, a number of rights and duties are implied by law in the landlord-tenant relationship[19]. The leasehold covenants thus impliedly given by a lessor include a covenant to permit the lessee 'quiet enjoyment' of the premises let[20], and an obligation not to derogate from grant[1].

There is in general no implied guarantee by a lessor as to the fitness for habitation of the premises which are let: the broad rule is *caveat emptor*. However, in certain exceptional situations an implied undertaking in this regard is imposed upon the lessor. Most important, there is in the lease of any furnished house an implied condition as to the fitness of the property for human habitation at the commencement of the tenancy[2]. Moreover, in the lease of a house at a low rent, there is (notwithstanding any contrary provision) an implied condition that 'the house will be kept by the landlord during the tenancy fit for human

17 See p. 326, ante.
18 See p. 337, ante.
19 See Law Commission, *Report on Obligations of Landlords and Tenants* (Law Com No. 67, June 1975).
20 This covenant entitles the tenant to freedom from any physical interference with his enjoyment of the premises. See also Protection from Eviction Act 1977, s. 1(3), p. 470, post; *Perera v Vandiyar* [1953] 1 All ER 1109.
1 See *Harmer v Jumbil (Nigeria) Tin Areas Ltd* [1921] 1 Ch 200 at 225, where Younger LJ described the rule against derogation from grant as 'a principle which merely embodies in a legal maxim a rule of common honesty.' In other words, a grantor may not grant land to another on terms which effectively negative the utility of the grant. Compare, however, *Port v Griffith* [1938] 1 All ER 295.
2 See *Smith v Marrable* (1843) 11 M & W 5.

habitation[3].' In a lease of a dwelling-house for a period less than seven years, there is an additional implied covenant by the lessor to keep in repair the structure and exterior of the property and to keep in working order installations for the supply of water, gas and electricity, and installations for sanitation and for space heating or water heating[4].

A lessor is also liable in certain circumstances to take reasonable care to ensure the safety of persons who might reasonably be expected to be affected by defects in the premises let[5]. This statutory duty cannot be avoided by express stipulation in the lease[6], but is owed only in relation to defects which come within the ambit of the lessor's obligation to repair or maintain, and arises only where the lessor knows or should have known of the existence of the defect. There is also an implied duty at common law on the part of the lessor of a high-rise block of flats 'not only to keep the lifts and stairs reasonably safe, but also to keep them reasonably fit for use by the tenants and their visitors[7].'

Defective Premises Act.

In the absence of contrary stipulation in the lease there are implied on the part of the lessee covenants to pay rent and rates. The lessee is under an implied obligation not to commit waste and to use the premises in a 'tenant-like manner[8].' The lessee is also obliged to allow the lessor to enter the premises in order to view the state of repair in all cases where the lessor bears responsibility in respect of repairs.

(2) Equitable lease

The respective rights and duties usually implied into a contract for a lease are similar to those which are imposed by implication of law upon the parties to a legal lease. The landlord is, however, subject only to a covenant to afford quiet enjoyment to the tenant, and moreover enjoys the benefit of an implied proviso for re-entry of the premises in the event of non-payment of rent by the tenant[9]. The covenants implied on the part of the tenant are much the same as those imposed upon a lessee under a legal lease[10], but the tenant enjoys in return the benefit of the protective provisions of the Housing Acts 1957 and 1961 in relation to the condition and fitness for habitation of the premises.

3 Housing Act 1957, s. 6(2). See *Summers v Salford Corpn* [1943] AC 283, p. 468, post.
4 Housing Act 1961, ss. 32, 33. Where a landlord fails to discharge any duty to repair, the tenant is entitled at common law, on giving the landlord notice of the disrepair, to have the necessary works done and to deduct the proper cost of those repairs from future payments of rent. See *Lee-Parker v Izzet* [1971] 1 WLR 1688; *Asco Developments Ltd and Newman v Lowes, Lewis and Gordon* (1978) LAG Bulletin 293; A. Arden (1979) LAG Bulletin 210.
5 Defective Premises Act 1972, s. 4.
6 Defective Premises Act 1972, s. 6(3).
7 *Liverpool City Council v Irwin* [1977] AC 239.
8 See *Warren v Keen* [1954] 1 QB 15.
9 This proviso is not implied in a legal lease, p. 406, post.
10 It was decided in *Flexman v Corbett* [1930] 1 Ch 672, that the list of 'usual covenants' implied into an equitable lease is neither fixed nor closed. The definition of 'usual covenants' turns on the circumstances of each case, and is influenced by the practice of conveyancers in the relevant district and by the character of the property concerned. See also *Chester v Buckingham Travel Ltd* [1981] 1 WLR 96.

7. TWO STATUTORY SCHEMES WHICH SUPPLEMENT THE LAW OF LEASEHOLDS

We must at this point refer briefly to two quite distinct statutory schemes which impinge upon the rights and duties of the parties in the landlord-tenant relationship.

(1) The Leasehold Reform Act 1967

The principal object of the Leasehold Reform Act 1967 is to confer upon tenants holding long leases at a low rent[11] the right to purchase the freehold reversion at the price which their property would obtain on the open market. The legislation applies only to premises which consist of a house (as distinct from a flat), and the property in question must not have a rateable value in excess of the statutorily designated limits[12]. The property must have been held on a 'long tenancy'[13], and a tenant who wishes to exercise his statutory right must have occupied the house as his only or main residence during the past five years or for periods together totalling five years during the past ten years[14].

In order to exercise his right to purchase the freehold reversion of the demised premises, the tenant must serve upon his landlord a written notice in the prescribed form[15]. The price to be paid is determined on the basis of the value which the property would currently command on the open market, given the assumption that the property is to remain encumbered by the existing lease for a further period of 50 years[16]. Such purchase of the freehold reversion is commonly known as 'leasehold enfranchisement[17].'

The underlying motive of the Leasehold Reform Act 1967 is that, since the real purchase price of a long lease is paid by the tenant at the commencement of the lease in the form of a 'premium' or capital sum, no great harm is done to the landlord by the enfranchisement of the lease. He has already extracted a fair capital value from the property, and any continuing income which he receives is at best an entirely nominal ground rent. There is indeed much to be said for

11 On the definition of 'low' rent for the purpose of enfranchisement, see Leasehold Reform Act 1967, s. 4(1); *Manson v Duke of Westminster* [1981] 2 WLR 428.

12 These limits are sufficiently widely drawn to embrace almost all residential properties.

13 A 'long tenancy' is a term which when granted was in excess of 21 years (Leasehold Reform Act 1967, s. 3(1)).

14 Leasehold Reform Act 1967, s. 1(1)(b). See *Poland v Earl Cadogan* [1980] 3 All ER 544.

15 Such a notice may be served at any time during the lease, and is registrable against the landlord as a Class C(iv) land charge in unregistered land and protectible as a minor interest in registered land. The tenant's right to purchase the freehold cannot, however, constitute an 'overriding interest' within section 70(1)(g) of the Land Registration Act 1925 (see Leasehold Reform Act 1967, s. 5(5), p. 339, ante.

16 Leasehold Reform Act 1967, s. 9, as amended by the Housing Act 1969, s. 82, and the Leasehold Reform Act 1979, s. 1. Thus the operative value is effectively the present value of the right to take possession in 50 years' time. See also *Jones v Wrotham Park Settled Estates* [1980] AC 74.

17 An alternative to 'enfranchisement' is open to the tenant under a long lease who qualifies within the 1967 Act. He may opt not for enfranchisement but for a 50 year extension of his existing lease on terms which correspond to those already contained in that lease (Leasehold Reform Act 1967, ss. 14, 15).

the view that a tenant who holds, for instance, a residential lease for a largely unexpired term of 99 years should be recognised as being effectively the absolute owner of the property. If this view is accepted, then the Leasehold Reform Act 1967 performs a valuable function in enabling the position to be thus rationalised[18]. However, the 1967 Act has been heavily criticised by some as having 'expropriated the reversioner without compensation[19].' The basis of this objection rests upon the argument that, especially as a long lease approaches its conclusion, it is unfair to deprive the landlord of the value of the steadily appreciating asset which he holds in the form of the freehold reversion by conferring upon the tenant a right to purchase that reversion at what may often be an almost derisory price.

(2) The Rent Act 1977 and the Housing Act 1980

Of even greater significance for residential tenants than the Leasehold Reform Act 1967 is the operation of the vast network of protective provisions contained in the Rent Act 1977 and the Housing Act 1980. These two enactments profoundly modify the law of landlord and tenant as discussed in this chapter, by superimposing on that law a statutory code which seeks to guarantee the residential tenant some degree of security of tenure and restriction of rents.

The protective code in respect of private sector tenants is contained principally in the Rent Act 1977; the provisions relevant to public sector tenants are to be found in the Housing Act 1980. Both sets of provisions form the subject of the next chapter[20]. It is sufficient here simply to make the point that the respective rights and obligations of lessor and lessee must always be read subject to the relevant code regulating the status of residential tenants.

8. REMEDIES FOR BREACH OF LEASEHOLD COVENANTS

The remedies available to a lessor in respect of his tenant's breach of the covenants contained (either expressly or impliedly) in the lease are of differing kinds. They include:

(1) Distress for rent in arrears

Although sometimes described as an obsolete remedy, distress is not infrequently used, especially by local authorities, for the purpose of recovering arrears of rent from a defaulting tenant. Distress is essentially the seizure and selling up of goods found on the demised premises, the proceeds of sale being used to recoup

18 The whole issue of leasehold enfranchisement has taken on a new dimension with the enactment of the Housing Act 1980. This legislation enables public sector tenants (i.e., council tenants holding periodic tenancies of local authority owned properties) to purchase the freehold reversion in their dwelling-houses, provided that certain qualifying conditions are met, p. 463, post.

19 R. E. Megarry and H. W. R. Wade, *The Law of Real Property* (4th edn., London 1975), p. 1149.

20 See p. 415, post.

the rent owed to the landlord[1]. Distress may not be levied between sunset and sunrise, and there are certain restrictions on the kinds of goods upon which the landlord may lawfully distrain. No distress may be levied upon clothes, bedding or tools of trade to the value of £50[2]. Also exempted are perishables (e.g., food), fixtures and things 'in actual use[3].'

Distress is a remedy applicable only in respect of non-payment of rent.

(2) Action for arrears of rent

The effect of the Limitation Act is that a maximum of six years' arrears of rent may be recovered in an action brought by a landlord in respect of a tenant's non-payment of rent[4]. There is, however, no prescriptive right to freedom from the obligation to pay rent[5].

(3) Action for breach of covenant other than a covenant relating to payment of rent

Damages may be awarded by the court where a landlord proves breach by the tenant of any covenant other than a covenant respecting payment of rent[6].

(4) Re-entry and forfeiture of the lease

The right to 're-enter' the demised premises and secure forfeiture of the lease is the most draconian weapon in the armoury of the landlord. Often the landlord's only real concern, when faced with a defaulting tenant, is to ensure his eviction from the property. It is at this point that the principles enunciated in this chapter must be most carefully read in conjunction with the code relating to residential tenancies discussed in Chapter 13[7].

The right of the landlord to demand forfeiture of a lease exists only where the lease contains an *express* proviso for forfeiture or where the lease is phrased in such a way that the performance of the lessee's obligations is rendered a condition upon which the future subsistence of the lease depends. A right of re-entry (i.e., to resume possession and secure forfeiture of the lease) must be reserved expressly in the conveyance of the lease: it cannot be implied[8]. An

1 See p. 455, post.
2 Law of Distress Amendment Act 1888, s. 4; County Courts Act 1959, s. 124.
3 Things 'in actual use' include articles which are immune from seizure simply on the ground that a breach of the peace would otherwise almost necessarily occur. It is not certain how far the exemption extends, but it seems that a tenant can effectively resist attempts at distress simply by switching on any kind of electrical apparatus in his home before the landlord or bailiff arrives to carry out the distress (e.g., television set, radio, refrigerator, washing machine, cooker). See A. Arden (1978) LAG Bulletin 57: 'Distress for Rent'.
4 Limitation Act 1980, s. 19.
5 A prescriptive right is one which comes into being by reason simply of the effluxion of time.
6 There may also be an action in tort for the commission of waste.
7 See p. 415ff., post.
8 A right of re-entry is implied only in a contract for a lease, and even then only in respect of non-payment of rent, p. 403, ante.

express right of re-entry, if exercisable in respect of a legal lease, is itself a legal interest in the demised land[9].

There is a general statutory restriction upon re-entry without due process of law. Unless a tenant goes voluntarily out of possession, where any premises are 'let as a dwelling on a lease which is subject to a right of re-entry or forfeiture, it shall not be lawful to enforce that right otherwise than by proceedings in the court while any person is lawfully residing in the premises or part of them[10].' The protection against forcible eviction contained in this provision is symptomatic of the respect traditionally shown by the common law for the security of residential occupation. The Protection from Eviction Act 1977 is a modern expression of a general distaste for violent eviction which has its roots in the medieval concept of seisin[11].

There exist other statutory restrictions and qualifications upon the right of a landlord to terminate a lease in accordance with an express proviso for re-entry[12]. In a case of forfeiture for non-payment of rent, a tenant has a right to 'relief from forfeiture' if he pays the arrears of rent in advance of court proceedings for possession of the premises[13]. Alternatively, he may ask the court to exercise discretion in his favour if he is able to pay the arrears of rent within six months of re-entry by the landlord[14]. In the case of forfeiture for breaches of covenant other than the covenant to pay rent, the landlord must first serve a statutory notice upon the tenant, specifying the particular breach complained of, requiring the tenant to remedy the breach (if indeed the breach is capable of remedy[15]), and in any case requiring the tenant to make compensation in money for the breach[16]. If after serving such a notice the landlord proceeds to enforce his right of re-entry by court proceedings, the tenant may ask the court to grant relief from forfeiture, but must do so before actual re-entry takes place[17].

Forfeiture of a head lease necessarily destroys any sublease created out of that

9 As such it binds the world and is enforceable against *any* occupier of the demised premises. See *Shiloh Spinners Ltd v Harding* [1973] AC 691 at 717 per Lord Wilberforce, p. 413, post.
10 Protection from Eviction Act 1977, s. 2.
11 See p. 50, ante, p. 469, post.
12 See generally *Shiloh Spinners Ltd v Harding* [1973] AC 691 at 722 per Lord Wilberforce.
13 See, however, *Standard Pattern Co Ltd v Ivey* [1962] Ch 432, where Wilberforce J limited the tenant's right to cases in which at least six months' rent is in arrear.
14 The provisions relating to relief from forfeiture for non-payment of rent are contained in Common Law Procedure Act 1852, ss. 210–212, and County Courts Act 1959, s. 191. See *Gill v Lewis* [1956] 2 QB 1; *Belgravia Insurance Co Ltd v Meah* [1964] 1 QB 436.
15 On the question whether a particular breach is capable of remedy, see *Rugby School (Governors) v Tannahill* [1935] 1 KB 87; *Glass v Kencakes Ltd* [1966] 1 QB 611 (covenants against immoral user of property). However, compare now *Scala House and District Property Co Ltd v Forbes* [1974] QB 575 at 588, where the Court of Appeal expressed the view that there can be no 'remedy' in respect of either a covenant not to sublet or assign or a user covenant (e.g., a covenant which prohibits illegal or immoral user), even where the prohibited user has ceased before the service of the statutory notice. See (1973) 89 LQR 460 (P. V. Baker); (1974) 33 Cambridge LJ 54 (D. J. Hayton). See also *GMS Syndicate Ltd v Gary Elliott* [1981] 2 WLR 478.
16 Law of Property Act 1925, s. 146(1).
17 Law of Property Act 1925, s. 146(2).

head lease[18]. Relief against forfeiture is never available to a person in adverse possession of property (i.e., a squatter)[19].

(5) Injunction

It is possible in some circumstances for a landlord to seek the discretionary remedy of the injunction for the purpose of restraining breaches of certain covenants of the lease[20].

9. THE ENFORCEABILITY OF LEASEHOLD COVENANTS IN A LEGAL LEASE

In concluding this chapter on the law of leaseholds we must examine the rules which govern the enforceability of leasehold covenants. The enforceability of these covenants presents little problem as between the original parties to the lease, but may become much more problematic when assignment or subletting occurs. Moreover, the rules differ slightly in accordance with whether the head lease is legal or equitable.

We shall look at a network of leasehold relationships in order to determine whether, and if so on what basis, the covenants contained in a head lease may be

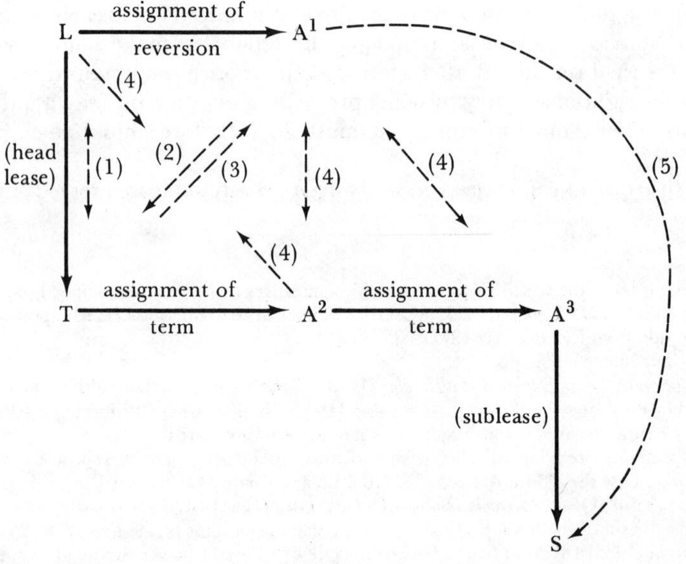

Fig. 64

18 *Great Western Rly Co v Smith* (1876) 2 Ch D 235 at 253. A subtenant may, however, seek relief from forfeiture on his own behalf in the discretion of the court (see Law of Property Act 1925, s. 146(4), and *Chatham Empire Theatre (1955) Ltd v Ultrans Ltd* [1961] 1 WLR 817).

19 *Tickner v Buzzacott* [1965] Ch 426, p. 102, ante.

20 This remedy is closely linked with the development of the law relating to restrictive covenants, pp. 411, 614ff., post.

enforced between the parties involved. We shall assume first that the head lease is legal and was made by deed and that all assignments are effected by deed. In *Fig.* 64, L assigns the reversion to A¹; T then assigns his term of years to A², who in turn assigns to A³, who finally sublets to S.

(1) Liability as between L and T

Before any assignment the relationship of L and T is quite simply analysed as a matter of contract. Privity of contract exists between L and T, and each is liable to the other on all the covenants of the lease.

So clearly is T's liability founded on contract that even an assignment of his term to A² does not relieve T of responsibility for the due performance of his leasehold obligations. T remains liable on his covenants throughout the entire lease[1]. Thus, if A² (or A³) defaults on any of the leasehold covenants, T is ultimately liable on the ground that he initially contracted that those covenants would be performed for the duration of the lease[2]. In effect, T is rendered an insurer of the lease, in the sense that he can be made answerable for *any* breach which occurs[3]. T has, of course, a right of indemnity against the defaulting assignee in respect of any liability which he has had to discharge personally[4]. This right of indemnity arises both by way of quasi-contract[5] and by way of an implied statutory right of indemnity[6].

(2) The liability of T towards A¹

The liability of T towards A¹ rests upon a statutory base. Under section 141(1) of the Law of Property Act 1925, the assignment of the reversion by L in favour of A¹ passes to A¹ the benefit of all the covenants undertaken by T in so far as those covenants have 'reference to the subject matter' of the lease. This last qualification implies that the covenants in question must 'touch and concern' the

1 There is only one exception to the rule of continuing liability despite assignment by T. The lessee under a perpetually renewable lease does not remain liable after assignment of his term (Law of Property Act 1922, Sch. 15, para. 11).
2 See, for instance, *Warnford Investments Ltd v Duckworth* [1979] Ch 127.
3 A heavy onus of care is thereby imposed upon T to select only a reliable and creditworthy assignee, although in most cases L will have made assurance doubly sure by including in the lease a covenant prohibiting any assignment or subletting without his prior consent.
4 If T is made to account for the default not of A² but of A³, T's right of indemnity is available against A³ directly. In most cases, however, T's right of indemnity against the defaulting assignee is afflicted by one enormous fallacy. L will invoke T's enduring liability on the original leasehold covenants in the event of breach by a subsequent assignee only where it has proved impossible to recover from the defaulter himself. If L has been unable to recover damages or arrears of rent from the assignee in default, for instance because that assignee is insolvent, there is for T only an illusory comfort in the assurance that he has a right to be indemnified by that assignee. T can no more successfully enforce his right of indemnity against a man of straw than L could recover in respect of the primary liability for breach of covenant. See, e.g., *Warnford Investments Ltd v Duckworth*, supra, where L sued T precisely because T's assignee had become insolvent.
5 See *Moule v Garrett* (1872) LR 7 Exch 101.
6 Law of Property Act 1925, s. 77.

demised premises, i.e., must affect the lessor qua lessor and the lessee qua lessee[7]. A covenant of purely personal significance between landlord and tenant does not 'touch and concern' the demised premises or (in the modern statutory formulation) have 'reference to the subject matter' of the lease, and is therefore incapable of conferring benefit upon the assignee of the landlord's reversion[8]. When L assigns his freehold reversion to A^1, A^1 acquires the right to sue in respect of breaches of covenant whensoever committed: he may sue even in respect of breaches prior to the date of assignment[9].

(3) The liability of A^1 towards T

The liability of A^1 towards T also rests upon a statutory basis. Under section 142(1) of the Law of Property Act 1925, the burden of all the leasehold obligations initially undertaken by L passes by assignment of the reversion to A^1, in so far as those obligations have 'reference to the subject matter' of the lease.

(4) The liability of L and A^2, A^1 and A^2, A^1 and A^3

Once we pass beyond the leasehold relationships which are regulated by privity of contract and its statutory extension[10], the rules governing the enforceability of leasehold obligations are simply stated. First, only those leasehold covenants which 'touch and concern' the demised premises are capable of enforcement. Second, no covenant can be enforced unless there exists 'privity of estate' between plaintiff and defendant.

The first requirement has already been discussed[11]. The second requirement is more problematic. 'Privity of estate' is a wider concept than that comprised in 'privity of contract.' 'Privity of estate' embraces all persons within the framework of leasehold relationships who stand vis à vis each other in the position of landlord and tenant. In *Fig.* 64, 'privity of estate' thus includes all those who can trace their leasehold status directly to the 'estate' comprised within the head lease, e.g., A^1, A^2 and A^3. Each of these persons can trace his position to one or other side of the notional feudal divide (or 'estate') which separates landlord from tenant and places them in a relationship of tenure. All are therefore 'privy' to that 'estate'[12].

7 See *Spencer's* Case (1583) 5 Co Rep 16a; *Clegg v Hands* (1890) 44 Ch D 503; *Lewin v American and Colonial Distributors Ltd* [1945] Ch 225.

8 See *Congleton Corpn v Pattison* (1808) 10 East 130; *Thomas v Hayward* (1869) LR 4 Exch 311; *Dewar v Goodman* [1909] AC 72. It is usually not difficult to distinguish between those covenants which 'touch and concern' the land and those which do not. A covenant for the payment of rent clearly does impinge upon the status of the parties as respectively landlord and tenant, while a covenant by a tenant to cut his landlord's hair every quarter equally clearly does not so impinge.

9 L loses the right henceforth to sue in respect of such breaches: the assignment of the reversion therefore has the effect of assigning even the right to sue for breaches of covenant (see *Re King* [1963] Ch 459; *Arlesford Trading Co Ltd v Servansingh* [1971] 1 WLR 1080).

10 Law of Property Act 1925, ss. 141, 142.

11 See p. 409, ante.

12 It is essential to note, however, that S is not in this sense 'privy' to the estate comprised in the head

The idea that leasehold covenants can 'run with the land' so as to affect assignees was first clearly enunciated in the historic ruling of the Court of King's Bench in *Spencer*'s case[13]. Thus, in *Fig.* 64, those leasehold covenants which 'touch and concern' the demised land are enforceable as between L and A^2 (where L has not yet assigned his reversion), between A^1 and A^2, and between A^1 and A^3[14].

(5) The liability of S towards A^1

We must now look at the liability of S towards A^1 (or indeed, for that matter, towards L if L has not yet assigned the reversion). Here it is quite clear that A^1 and S are not privy to the same estate. Thus even those covenants which 'touch and concern' the land are incapable of enforcement by direct action between A^1 and S: one of the two vital preconditions of enforcement has not been satisfied[15]. A^1 cannot, for instance, successfully sue S to recover arrears of rent, since A^1's redress lies primarily in an action against S's immediate superior, A^3, with whom A^1 does enjoy a relationship of privity of estate.

Having established that no direct action may be brought by A^1 against S for a recovery of a monetary nature, it must be pointed out that A^1 is not precluded from remedies of other kinds. First, it may be possible for A^1 to obtain an injunction restraining S from the breach of restrictive covenants contained in the head lease, notwithstanding that S is not privy to that head lease. This possibility finds its roots in the decision of Lord Cottenham LC in *Tulk v Moxhay*[16], which effectively converted restrictive covenants into a species of proprietary interest capable of running with the land and binding any purchaser other than a purchaser of a legal estate for value without notice[17]. This means, in the leasehold context, that a restrictive covenant contained in a head lease (e.g., a covenant to use premises for residential or domestic purposes only) can be enforced by injunction against *any* occupier who takes possession of the land with notice of the existence of that covenant.

The classic case on this point is *Hall v Ewin*[18]. This case relates a delightful, quintessentially Victorian melodrama concerning residential life in the Edgware Road in London towards the end of the last century. Here the plaintiff and defendant (P and D respectively) were distanced by a lease, a sublease and an assignment (see *Fig.* 65). There was a covenant in the head lease prohibiting the tenant from carrying on 'any noisome or offensive trade, business or employment'

lease. S's relationship of privity obtains not in respect of the head lease but in respect of the sublease to which he is an immediate party. He cannot trace his position directly (or, in diagrammatic terms, horizontally) to the 'estate' granted by the head lease and cannot therefore claim privity to that head lease.

13 (1583) 5 Co Rep 16a.

14 However, unlike the original tenant (who bears a non-assignable liability for the duration of the lease), assignees are liable only in respect of those breaches committed while they are in possession of the land (see *Paul v Nurse* (1828) 8 B & C 486).

15 See p. 410, ante.

16 (1848) 2 Ph 774.

17 See p. 614, post.

18 (1888) 37 Ch D 74.

in the demised premises. D sublet the premises (which comprised a substantial residential property and adjoining garden) to M, whose sublease contained a restrictive covenant identical to that in the head lease.

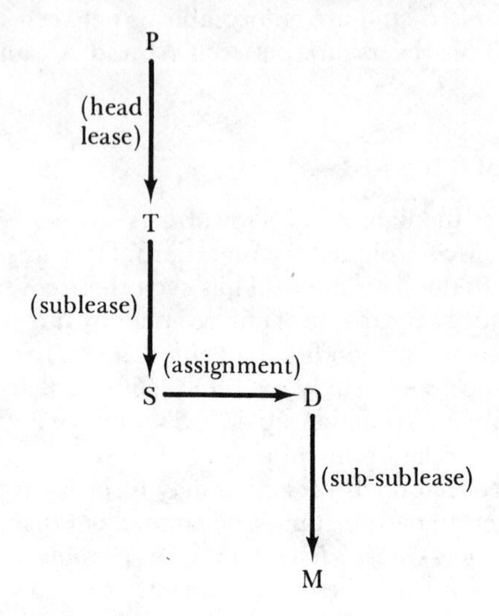

Fig. 65

In 1886, M purchased some lions (imported no doubt at prodigious expense to M and not inconsiderable discomfort to the lions), and proceeded to open an 'exhibition of wild beasts' upon the premises. It appears from the law report that M 'exhibited pictures outside the house, and employed black men to parade in front of it with a gong and trumpet, so that the neighbours complained of the nuisance[19].' The Court of Appeal ruled that no injunction could be awarded to P restraining D from breach of the restrictive covenant contained in the head lease, for the fairly obvious reason that it was not D but D's tenant, M, whose actions were in violation of that covenant. However, the Court of Appeal endorsed the decision of Kekewich J at first instance granting an injunction against M (against which decision M did not appeal), obviously regarding the matter as governed by the rule in *Tulk v Moxhay*.

Hall v Ewin thus stands as authority for the proposition that a restrictive covenant contained in a head lease can be enforced by way of injunction, outside the area demarcated by privity of estate, against any occupier who takes possession of the demised premises with notice of that covenant[20].

Returning to *Fig.* 64[1], the other means by which A^1 can effectively enforce

19 There seems to have been no obvious explanation for M's activities other than the dubious financial gain to be made from exhibiting the rather sad and somewhat improbable spectacle of lions pacing around a back-garden in Paddington. But this, after all, was the Golden Age of impresarios and entrepreneurs, of laissez faire individualism and private commercial initiative!

20 Leasehold restrictive covenants can *never* be registered as a Class D(ii) land charge (see Land Charges Act 1972, s. 2(5), p. 138, ante.

1 See p. 408, ante.

the covenants of the head lease against S is by reliance upon any express proviso for forfeiture which may be contained in that head lease. A right of re-entry expressly reserved for the landlord in a legal lease is itself a legal interest which binds the world irrespective of notice[2]. It enables the landlord to seek forfeiture against *any* occupier of the demised premises, without regard to whether that occupier falls within the ambit of 'privity of contract' or 'privity of estate.' A right of re-entry may thus be exercised by A[1] against S even in respect of covenants for breach of which S cannot technically be liable[3].

We must now examine whether any of the enforcement relationships depicted in *Fig.* 64 differs if the head lease is not executed by deed and is therefore equitable.

10. THE ENFORCEABILITY OF LEASEHOLD COVENANTS IN AN EQUITABLE LEASE

(1) Liability as between L and T

Here the result is not different if the transaction concluded by L and T is not a legal lease but merely a specifically enforceable contract for a lease. L and T are still bound, perhaps now even more obviously, by contract.

(2) and (3) Liability as between A[1] and T

Here the existence of a mere contract for a lease produces no difference in the rules governing questions of liability between A[1] and T. The terms of sections 141, 142 of the Law of Property Act 1925 are equally applicable to legal leases and contracts for a lease[4].

(4) Liability as between assignees

It is here that the major difference emerges between a legal lease (which is made by deed) and an equitable lease (which is not made by deed). Where the head lease takes the form of a contract for a lease, there can be no privity of estate between L and T, for the simple reason that there exists no 'estate' to which anyone can be 'privy'[5]. One of the two essential conditions for the enforcement of leasehold obligations between assignees is therefore absent[6]. The issue of liability between the assignees now falls to be determined by the elementary rule of contract law that the benefit but not the burden of a contract can be assigned. Thus although the benefit of the lessor's covenants in an agreement for a lease passes on an assignment of the reversion[7], the burden of the lessee's covenants

2 See p. 65, ante.
3 See *Shiloh Spinners Ltd v Harding* [1973] AC 691 at 717 per Lord Wilberforce.
4 See *Rickett v Green* [1910] 1 KB 253.
5 See p. 401, ante.
6 See p. 410, ante.
7 See *Manchester Brewery Co v Coombs* [1901] 2 Ch 608.

does not pass on an assignment of the lessee's term of years[8]. This brings about the odd result in *Fig.* 64 that, where L and T have merely a specifically enforceable contract for a lease (or indeed where any of the subsequent assignments is informal), neither A^2 nor A^3 can be sued directly for arrears of rent. It seems that the plaintiff's action must be brought against T, who bears a continuing contractual liability, and who may therefore have to claim an indemnity on his own behalf against the defaulting assignee.

Several avenues of escape from this profoundly inconvenient result have been suggested. These include the qualified proposal that a liability on the part of an assignee of an equitable lease may be constructed on the basis of an implied contract or periodic tenancy rooted in possession of the premises and payment of rent[9]. Other suggestions include the much more radical theory that the difference between legal and equitable leases has been eliminated by the 'fusion of law and equity' in the Judicature Act 1873–1875[10]. In this area, however, little is clear.

(5) The liability of S towards A

Here the general rule indicated before still obtains: A^1 cannot succeed in any action brought directly against S for a money remedy under a specifically enforceable contract for a lease. However, the possibility of obtaining injunctive relief in respect of breaches of restrictive covenants remains an active option for A^1 because injunctive relief is an intrinsically equitable remedy and, as such, is entirely appropriate in the context of an equitable lease.

Moreover, a right of re-entry is implied on behalf of the lessor in an equitable lease. When attached to an equitable lease, such a right is, of course, merely equitable. It will, however, prevail over S, whose interest is also equitable and who cannot therefore claim immunity as a bona fide purchaser of a legal estate without notice[11].

In conclusion it might be said that the only real difference between the enforceability of leasehold covenants in a legal lease made by deed and those in an equitable lease not made by deed concerns the liability of an assignee of the original tenant's term of years. Such an assignee is made liable on the original tenant's covenants where the lease is legal but not where the lease is equitable. The same result flows from the introduction of any other equitable link in an otherwise legal chain of leasehold relationships (e.g., if an assignment of any kind is effected by informal means rather than by deed).

8 See *Purchase v Lichfield Brewery Co* [1915] 1 KB 184.
9 See R. J. Smith (1978) 37 Cambridge LJ 98: 'The Running of Covenants in Equitable Leases and Equitable Assignments of Legal Leases.'
10 See *Boyer v Warbey* [1953] 1 QB 234 at 245f. per Denning LJ.
11 An equitable right of entry is not protectible by registration of a land charge (see *Shiloh Spinners Ltd v Harding* [1973] AC 691). The effect of such an interest on third parties is governed simply by the orthodox equitable doctrine of notice. The equitable right of entry (or re-entry) thus provides yet another example of that rare category of equitable interest in unregistered land which is neither registrable nor overreachable and whose fate depends upon an application of the traditional (i.e., pre-1925) doctrine of notice, pp. 140, 313, ante.

CHAPTER 13

Housing law

The last chapter outlined the basic rules which govern the creation and enforcement of leasehold obligations in English law. It is the concern of the present chapter to refer to the ways in which, in the context of residential accommodation, these basic rules must be read subject to the paramountly important protective code contained in the housing legislation currently in force. We shall look first at the protective code as it affects tenants in the private sector: these provisions are contained for the most part in the Rent Act 1977. Then we shall examine the code as it bears upon tenants in the public sector: these provisions are to be found in the Housing Act 1980. Finally, we shall advert to several general statutory provisions which are intended to achieve greater security for residential occupiers.

PRIVATE SECTOR TENANTS

1. THE HISTORY AND SOCIAL PHILOSOPHY OF THE RENT ACTS

The Rent Acts have existed in this country for over 60 years. The first Rent Act—the Increase of Rent and Mortgage Interest (War Restrictions) Act 1915—was introduced as a supposedly temporary measure during the emergency of war time. Passed originally in response to agitation by munitions workers who protested at proposals that their rents should be raised[1], the legislation has since arrogated to itself a life and substance never contemplated by its framers. The Rent Acts are now broadly intended to impose some measure of social control in the private sector over the relationship between property owners and residential occupiers, in order to prevent exploitation of the latter by the former. The imposition of such control clearly restricts freedom of contract in the housing market and has had the effect of inhibiting the exercise by private landlords of formerly sacrosanct rights of property. Approximately 13 per cent of all dwellings in England and Wales come potentially within the ambit of the Rent Act[2].

The history of the Rent Act legislation has, of course, been marked by fluctuations of political and economic policy. Extensions of the Rent Act have in general occurred during periods of Labour administration[3]. Restrictions of the legislation have in general been instituted by Conservative administrations.

1 See M. Partington *Landlord and Tenant* (2nd edn., London 1980), p. 152ff.; P. H. Pettit, *Private Sector Tenancies* (London 1981), 3f.; R. E. Megarry, *The Rent Acts* (10th edn., London 1967), Vol. 1, p. 1ff.

2 Central Statistical Office, *Social Trends No. 11* (London 1981), p. 145 (Table 9.4).

3 See, for instance, the Rent Acts 1965, 1968, 1974.

The most recent legislation in this area, the Housing Act 1980, provides no exception to this distinct pattern. Although the Housing Act 1980 extends many of the traditional features of Rent Act protection to public sector tenants (who comprise roughly 30 per cent of the householders of England and Wales[4]), it also introduces many important qualifications upon the rights currently enjoyed by private sector tenants under the Rent Act[5].

Yet, if the extent of statutory protection of residential tenancies is subject to the changing tides of political fortune, it may well be that some judges are becoming increasingly willing to endorse the protective policy embodied in the Rent Act legislation. In *Davis v Johnson*[6], Lord Scarman declared that he found

> nothing illogical or surprising in Parliament legislating to override a property right, if it be thought to be socially necessary ... [T]he restriction or suspension for a time of property rights is a familiar aspect of much of our social legislation; the Rent Acts are a striking example.

The same judge pointed out in *Horford Investments Ltd v Lambert*[7] that the

> policy of the Rent Acts was and is to protect the tenant in his home, whether the threat be to extort a premium for the grant or renewal of his tenancy, to increase his rent, or to evict him ... The Rent Acts have throughout their history constituted an interference with contract and property rights for a specific purpose—the redress of the balance of advantage enjoyed in a world of housing shortage by the landlord over those who have to rent their homes.

The Rent Act seeks to attain its objective by assuring the private tenant both a certain 'status of irremovability' and a guarantee that only a 'fair rent' will be asked as the price of his security of tenure. It is obvious that security of tenure and rent restriction thus constitute an indivisible form of protection for the tenant. The two measures are plainly interdependent, since one blade alone of the double-edged sword of the Rent Act would provide merely illusory protection for the tenant against the rapacious private landlord[8].

The overall effect of the Rent Act is therefore, in many cases, to confirm at fair rents the existence of tenancies in dwelling-houses which (irrespective of their contractually agreed duration) are not terminable within the lifetime of the original tenant or indeed during the lifetime of some of the members of his family. To this extent the social interest in residential security for the family has been allowed to override the claim of the property owner to dispose freely of his land in accordance with the nominal terms of the lease. Indeed, it is widely recognised nowadays that 'a good and secure home is essential to successful family life'[9].

The corollary of this recognition, when realised in practical terms in the Rent

4 *Social Trends No. 11*, supra, p. 145 (Table 9.4).
5 See p. 449, post.
6 [1979] AC 264 at 348.
7 [1976] Ch 39 at 52. Declared Denning LJ in *Feyereisel v Turnidge* [1952] 2 QB 29 at 37, 'the guiding light through the darkness of the Rent Acts is to remember that they confer personal security on a tenant in respect of his home.'
8 See R. E. Megarry, op. cit., Vol. 1, p. 14.
9 *Report of the Committee on One-Parent Families* (Cmnd 5629, July 1974), Vol. 1, para. 6.1.

Act, is the gradual metamorphosis of the legal position of the protected residential tenant. The tenant's mere right to enjoy possession for a limited period has now been extended—often indefinitely—by force of statute, with the consequence that it begins much more closely to resemble some qualified claim of ownership. The Rent Act may seem at first sight to provide only for a temporary restriction or suspension of the property rights belonging to the landlord. In reality, however, the legislation confers upon eligible residential tenants certain 'social rights of property' which prevail over strict legal entitlements as defined in the orthodox law of property or as fixed by contract between landlord and tenant.

Yet in this very proposition there may lie a source of potential confusion whose excision is necessary for any deep understanding of the law of property. We noted long ago[10] that there is a certain unreality in any search for 'the' owner of any particular 'thing'. The law of property is concerned not with things but with relationships. As Professor Ackerman said[11],

> property law discusses the relationships that arise *between people* with respect to things. More precisely, the law of property considers the way rights to use things may be parceled out amongst a host of competing resource users. Each resource user is conceived as holding a bundle of rights vis à vis other potential users ... Hence, it risks serious confusion to identify any single individual as *the* owner of any particular thing.

Thus it is fundamental to our task, as we embark on an examination of the Rent Act, to rid our minds of the false dichotomy between the 'ownership' supposedly retained by the landlord and the 'mere' use or possession enjoyed by the residential tenant. The history of the Rent Acts has comprised essentially various kinds of inter-change between the bundles of user claims enjoyed by landlord and tenant respectively, the inter-change in every case being premised ultimately upon some allegedly overriding principle of social justice. The law relating to residential tenancies is fundamentally concerned with human dignity and decency. Its primary objective is the provision of a secure domestic base for a wide range of family and other social interactions and a temporary base for the relatively large numbers of people on the move between jobs and between marriages. The legislation represents a response to that sad but timeless capacity of man to exploit the economic necessity of his fellow man when the demand for a particular resource—here housing—is not met by an adequate supply. Ultimately the Rent Act is concerned with a problem of distributive justice—the allocation of one of the elementary 'goods' of life, i.e., the enjoyment of adequate housing and living conditions. The legislation seeks to achieve its social objective through a partial displacement of the normal market forces which would otherwise dominate the allocation of the primary economic resource of housing stock.

The operation of the Rent Act is, of course, controversial simply because it seems to deprive 'the' property owner of much of the utility which he imagined he had by virtue of being 'the' property owner. The statute is doubly

10 See p. 4, ante.
11 *Private Property and the Constitution* (New Haven and London 1977), p. 26f.

controversial because it intervenes within a primarily commercial relationship in order to impose standards of social morality. The Rent Act legislation subverts the basic rule in property law of *caveat emptor* and reflects a viewpoint which, when expressed in an extreme form, holds it to be immoral for one person to own another's home for personal profit.

It is, however, important to notice that the effects of such legislation as the Rent Act are consistent with contemporary trends in the jurisprudence of property. We noted before the argument advanced by Professor C. B. Macpherson that whereas the concept of a property right has traditionally comprised a *right to exclude* all others from the use or enjoyment of something, the newly emerging idea of property consists essentially of a *right not to be excluded* from the use or enjoyment of something[12]. Thus the idea of property is being

> broadened . . . to include . . . a right to a kind of society or set of power relations which will enable the individual to live a fully human life.

This analysis is in accord with Charles Reich's now classic plea for a recognition of 'the new property' as the basis for 'a Homestead Act for rootless twentieth century man[13].'

If this analysis is correct, it indicates an intellectual shift at the core of the property notion away from the idea of a private right to exclude from personally owned resources towards the idea of a public right of access to socially valued resources. Coinciding with this shift is the advent of the welfare state—an institution which for many purposes has taken over the allocative function of the market in relation to the 'goods' of life. It is not difficult to locate the role of Rent Act legislation within this general pattern of development.

Some writers, like Macpherson, see the entire evolutionary process in this area as securing the right of the citizen to 'that kind of society which is instrumental to a full and free life', and therefore to 'a set of power relations that permits a full life of enjoyment and development of one's human capacities.' Others have not viewed the current trend with such favour. Kamenka and Tay, for instance, have measured the 'decline in respect for private property' partly in terms of 'the demand for *access* as independent of ownership and as something that ought to be maintainable against it'[14]. Alice Tay has, in particular, pointed to the dangers implicit in the contemporary movement towards

> a bureaucratic-administrative, regulatory and even confiscatory resources-allocation concern, in which the state stands above property owners as the representative of a general 'socio-political' interest[15].

Irrespective of one's ideological standpoint, there is little doubt that there is currently in progress something in the nature of a redefinition of the general

12 'Capitalism and the Changing Concept of Property', in E. Kamenka and R. S. Neale (ed.), *Feudalism, Capitalism and Beyond* (Canberra 1975), p. 116ff.

13 (1964) 73 Yale LJ 733 at 787: 'The New Property'.

14 'Beyond Bourgeois Individualism: the Contemporary Crisis in Law and Legal Ideology', in E. Kamenka and R. S. Neale (ed.), op. cit., p. 133.

15 'Law, the citizen and the state', in E. Kamenka, R. Brown and A. E.-S. Tay (ed.), *Law and Society* (London 1978), p. 13.

concept of property. This redefinition emerges in the Rent Act in the form of a legally protected status of irremovability vested in the residential tenant. This status of irremovability cannot be classified easily within the framework of existing proprietary rights in land. In a very real sense, the right to live in a house or flat free from the threat of arbitrary eviction, free from the exploitative and oppressive impact of normal market forces, has itself become a new form of property right[16]. Entitlement to the 'use value' of residential property has in this context become more significant than entitlement to its 'exchange' or 'capital value' as a disposable asset on the freehold property market.

The property right which emerges from the application of the Rent Act is defined in terms of a status—the status enjoyed by the 'protected tenant'. We must now look at this status and its incidents, but before we do so it is interesting to note that a key concept in the Rent Act is indeed the idea of *status.* The whole point of the Rent Act is that the rights of the tenant are defined in terms of a status rather than by contract—a feature which nowadays is not uncharacteristic of social legislation in a collectivist world. This fact represents a partial reversal of Henry Sumner Maine's famous dictum of 1861 that 'the movement of the progressive societies has hitherto been a movement *from Status to Contract*'[17].

Maine's dictum and its eventual rejection across large areas of social legislation were adverted to by the House of Lords in *Johnson v Moreton*[18]. The issue at stake in this case was whether an agricultural tenant could validly contract out of protection conferred upon him by statute. The House of Lords decided unanimously that the tenant could not by agreement deprive himself of the benefit of statutory provisions which were designed to afford him a certain security of tenure. Although in this book we are not concerned with the legislation which applies to agricultural tenants[19], the observations of Lord Simon of Glaisdale in *Johnson v Moreton*[20] have a relevance which is much wider than the immediate context in which he spoke:

The appellants rely on the principle of law expressed in the maxim *Quilibet potest renunciare juri pro se introducto* ('Anyone may, at his pleasure, renounce the benefit of a stipulation or other right introduced entirely in his own favour'): see *Broom's Legal Maxims*, 10th edn. (1939).

The maxim exemplifies Maine's famous observation (*Ancient Law* (1861), 1st edn. (Chapter 5)) that the movement of progressive societies had thitherto been a movement

16 See C. Hand [1980] Conv 351: 'The Statutory Tenancy: An Unrecognised Proprietary Interest?'.

17 It is significant that the recent abrasion inflicted by the Housing Act 1980 upon the social philosophy of the Rent Act takes the form of a provision which, by means of a fiction of freedom of contract in the housing market, effectively enables private landlords to let property on a 'shorthold tenancy' which guarantees the tenant 'fair rent' protection but not long-term security of tenure, p. 449, post. The relative extent of protection for the residential tenant can almost always be measured in accordance with the oscillation of the pendulum of time between 'status' and 'contract' as the basis of the tenant's entitlement to residential security for himself and his family.

18 [1980] AC 37. See N. D. M. Parry [1980] Conv 117: 'Contracting out of a Statute'.

19 See Agricultural Holdings Act 1948 and Rent (Agriculture) Act 1976.

20 [1980] AC 37 at 65ff.

from status to contract—that is, from on the one hand societies where legal relationships between persons arise from their membership of classes to which the law ascribes peculiar rights and obligations, capacities and incapacities, to on the other hand societies where those relationships arise from private agreements between the parties which will be enforced by the law. It was natural for Maine, writing in the middle of the 19th century, to discern such a movement. The laisser-faire laisser-aller ideology was dominant. Human felicity, it was argued, was best promoted by leaving every person to seek his own advantage in competition with his fellows. A free market would ensure that the individual's effort was directed to anticipating and satisfying with maximum efficiency the wants of his fellows. The most powerful motive force in the universe—man's pursuit of his own interest—would thus be harnessed to drive a whole society forward. 'Man's selfishness is God's providence,' they said.

The general development of the law, as so often, reflected the dominant ideology. Freedom and sanctity of contract tended to be considered as pre-eminent legal values. It is unnecessary to expatiate after Dicey's classic study: it is sufficient to note, for example, Equity's increasing reluctance to relieve against contractual forfeitures (cf. *Sanders v Pope* (1806) 12 Ves Jun 282 with *Hill v Barclay* (1811) 18 Ves Jun 56 and the latter's evolution to produce *Barrow v Isaacs & Son* [1891] 1 QB 417), and Jessel MR's representative pronouncement in *Printing and Numerical Registering Co v Sampson* (1875) LR 19 Eq 462 at 465:

> '. . . if there is one thing which more than another public policy requires it is that men of full age and competent understanding shall have the utmost liberty of contracting, and that their contracts when entered into freely and voluntarily shall be held sacred and shall be enforced by courts of justice.'

But well within the lifetimes of Maine and Jessel the ideology which lay behind their juristic views was questioned. By some it was directly attacked: society's objective should be not wealth but welfare (with the implication that the pursuit and achievement of wealth were destructive of welfare), which was best promoted by the direct intervention of the organs of the state and could not be left to the bargain of the marketplace. 'Competition' came to have the cliché 'cut-throat' attached to it. Others, more subtly, argued that, for the laisser-faire system to work felicitously as claimed, there must be a genuinely free, open and abundant market in which there is equality of bargaining power—equality of knowledge of the market and of staying-power in holding out for a bargain: this called for at least a limited intervention by the state to prevent or counteract rigging of the market by monopolies or oligopolies and to redress inequalities of bargaining power. And consonantly, even in the 19th century, the law began to back-pedal. The maxim Quilibet, etc., was held to be inapplicable to a matter in which the public had an interest (*Graham v Ingleby* (1848) 1 Exch 651, per Pollock CB at p. 655, per Parke B at pp. 656–657, per Alderson B at p. 657 '. . . an individual cannot waive a matter in which the public have an interest,' Platt B concurring: and see also *Halesowen Presswork & Assemblies Ltd v National Westminster Bank Ltd* [1972] AC 785, 808): it was apparently no longer accepted by the law that freedom and sanctity of contract were conclusive of the public interest.

There was one economic and social relationship where it was claimed that there were palpably lacking the prerequisites for the beneficent operation of laisser-faire—that of landlord and tenant. The market was limited and sluggish: the supply of land could not expand immediately and flexibly in response to demand, and even humble dwellings took more time to erect than those in want of them could spare. Generally, a man became a tenant rather than an owner-occupier because his circumstances compelled him to live hand-to-mouth; the landlord's purse was generally longer and his command of knowledge and counsel far greater than the tenant's. In short, it was held, the constriction of the market and the inequality of bargaining power enabled the landlord to dictate contractual terms which did not necessarily operate to the general benefit of society. It was to counteract this descried constriction of the market and to redress this descried inequality of bargaining power that the law—specifically, in the shape of legislation—came to intervene repeatedly to modify freedom of contract between landlord and tenant. Since Maine the movement of many 'progressive' societies has been reversed. The holding of a statutory or a protected tenancy is rather a status than a pure creature of contract.

2. THE DEFINITION OF A 'PROTECTED TENANCY' WITHIN THE RENT ACT 1977

So stringent are the implications of protected status under the Rent Act that the courts have traditionally tended to interpret the legislation restrictively and therefore adversely to the interests of the residential occupier. The gates of the Rent Act do not open wide to all comers. Those who seek the full protection of the statute must show that they qualify in terms of section 1 of the Rent Act 1977. This deceptively simple provision has in the past engendered so much difficulty that it now deserves special consideration. The most difficult question under the Rent Act relates to the question of eligibility. It is an altogether easier task to outline the provisions which apply once a tenancy is shown to fall within the protective dragnet of the legislation.

Section 1 of the Rent Act 1977 defines a 'protected tenancy' as

> a tenancy under which a dwelling-house (which may be a house or part of a house) is let as a separate dwelling.

This definition is subject to exceptions both express and implied, but the situations thus excluded from full protected status under the Rent Act may nevertheless qualify for the lesser degree of protection given by the Act to restricted contracts[1].

In order to secure full protected status under the Rent Act, it is clear that the following conditions must be met.

(1) There must be a 'tenancy' and not a mere 'licence' or other arrangement

The fundamentally important distinction between a 'tenancy' and a 'licence' has always been somewhat elusive. A tenancy confers upon the tenant a right of exclusive occupation for a certain period of time; a licence confers merely a personal permission to be present on the premises[2]. It is plain from the express words of section 1 of the Rent Act 1977 that full protected status can be acquired

1 A 'restricted contract' is defined as 'a contract whereby one person grants to another person, in consideration of a rent which includes payment for the use of furniture or for services, the right to occupy a dwelling as a residence' (Rent Act 1977, s. 19(2), p. 455, post).

2 See p. 474, ante.

only where there is a tenancy and never where there is a licence[3]. The kinds of tenancy eligible for full statutory protection are fairly unrestricted: they include periodic and fixed term tenancies, equitable tenancies, tenancies by estoppel and, by virtue of section 152(1) of the Rent Act 1977, subtenancies.

It may therefore be vital in any given case to identify whether a residential occupier is a tenant or a licensee. The distinction is made no easier by the fact that the criterion of 'exclusive occupation' is far from conclusive of the issue. An occupier who enjoys exclusive occupation may well be found to be in reality a mere licensee[4]. All that can be said is that there can never be a tenancy unless the occupier has a right to exclusive possession. However, where the occupier has such a right, there may be *either* a tenancy *or* a licence, depending on the circumstances. In assessing the status of a letting of a single bed-sitting room in *Marchant v Charters*[5], Lord Denning MR indicated that the difference between a tenancy and a licence turns ultimately upon

> the nature and quality of the occupancy. Was it intended that the occupier should have a stake in the room or did he have only permission for himself personally to occupy the room, whether under a contract or not, in which case he is a licensee?

The difference between tenancy and licence thus depends upon the intention formed by the parties at the time of the transaction. The law looks to the inner substance of the transaction rather than to its external form[6].

It used to be thought that once a right to exclusive occupation had been established, the courts would declare the presence of a licence in the residential context only in cases involving an element of grace and favour on the part of the property owner. In *Facchini v Bryson*[7], Denning LJ identified as the unifying feature of the licence cases the fact that

> there has been something in the circumstances, such as a family arrangement, an act of friendship or generosity, or such like to negative any intention to create a tenancy[8].

However, one of the most alarming developments in the modern law of residential lettings is the apparent willingness of the courts to uphold licences in

3 A licence may, however, qualify for the limited protection given to restricted contracts, p. 455, post. In rare instances, a licence may provide the occupier with greater protection for some purposes than does the Rent Act. See, e.g., *Hardwick v Johnson* [1978] 1 WLR 683, (p. 488, post); *Appah v Parncliffe Investments Ltd* [1964] 1 WLR 1064.
4 See *Luganda v Service Hotels Ltd* [1969] 2 Ch 209.
5 [1977] 1 WLR 1181 at 1185.
6 See p. 390, ante.
7 [1952] 1 TLR 1386 at 1389. Certainly the presence of some therapeutic or charitable motive helps to explain why, until very recently, the courts have upheld the existence of mere licences in the case of residents of a YWCA hostel (*R v South Middlesex Rent Tribunal, ex parte Beswick* (1976) 32 P & CR 67), an old people's home (*Abbeyfield (Harpenden) Society Ltd v Woods* [1968] 1 WLR 374) and a rehabilitative hostel for former alcoholics (*Trustees of the Alcoholic Recovery Project v Farrell* (1976) LAG Bulletin 259). It was, of course, an act of generosity which underlay the classic case of *Marcroft Wagons Ltd v Smith* [1951] 2 KB 496. See also *Heslop v Burns* [1974] 1 WLR 1241 at 1252, where Scarman LJ based his finding of a licence upon the fact that the case involved 'something very akin to a family arrangement'.
8 Where an employer grants a right of occupation to his employee, the difference between tenancy and licence may turn upon whether undue influence was brought to bear upon the employee to

cases falling outside these fairly restrictive categories of situation. It may be that this is a judicial response to the general need to increase the overall supply of private rented accommodation in the large cities.

It has been argued most vigorously by some that the operation of the Rent Act is ultimately counterproductive, in that it strangulates the supply of residential lettings by inhibiting those who, but for the strictures imposed by the Rent Act, would be willing to release accommodation on to the market for short-term and easily recoverable occupation. The success of this argument is now clearly apparent in the new mandatory ground for possession introduced by the Housing Act 1980 in respect of the private 'shorthold tenancy'. A trade-off between a statutory policy of protection and the practical realities of the marketplace may be inevitable within a mixed economy. Herein lies one of the cruxes of the Rent Act question: should a little wrong be allowed in order that a greater good ensue? The pragmatic raw data of the market preclude any ready expression of the ethics of Rent Act protection in simple terms of black and white. The moral issues presented by the housing market—and more generally by the allocation of any valued resource in short supply—are far from easy. The relevant considerations are, as always, conditional and interactive rather than absolute and independent.

Symptomatic of the more recent (and less liberal) approach of the courts towards residential lettings is the decision of the Court of Appeal in *Somma v Hazlehurst and Savelli*[9]. Here Cumming-Bruce LJ declared that he could see

> no reason why an ordinary landlord not in any of these special categories [enumerated in *Facchini v Bryson*] should not be able to grant a licence to occupy an ordinary house.

In this case, the Court of Appeal held that a 'non-exclusive occupation agreement' phrased in terms of a mere licence fell outside the ambit of Rent Act protection. The decision has been severely criticised on the ground that it effectively permits prospective landlords to contract out of the Rent Act by concealing a protected tenancy under the cloak of a licence. It is, of course, trite law that there can be no contractual displacement of the provisions of the Rent Act[10], but the ruling in *Somma*'s case seems to indicate that the courts may not be overly astute to strike down indirect means of securing the same objective. It is

---

accept the employer's characterisation of the arrangement as a 'licence'. In *Matthew v Bobbins* (1980) 41 P & CR 1, Lord Denning MR recognised that in the nineteenth century a master might have been seen as occupying a 'dominant position' with the result that undue pressure might result in this situation. However, the Master of the Rolls thought that, in the light of the modern employment protection legislation, it was by no means clear that masters are today in a dominant position over their servants, and on this basis declined to set aside a 'licence' which an employee had been induced to accept. This decision is reminiscent of the even more disturbing decision of the Court of Appeal in *Foster v Robinson* [1951] 1 KB 149, where it does indeed seem that an employer induced an old and sick employee to accept a rent-free 'licence' for life in exchange for Rent Act protection. The employee lived only another three years, and the effect of his agreement was to deprive his daughter of the possibility of succeeding to a statutory tenancy. The employer, by forgoing the annual rent of £6·50, effectively bought his freedom from the Rent Act at minimal cost.

9 [1978] 1 WLR 1014, p. 429, post.

10 See R. E. Megarry, op. cit., Vol. 1, p. 18; *Brown v Draper* [1944] KB 309 at 313; *Baxter v Eckersley*

true that in *Somma*'s case Cumming-Bruce LJ observed that the courts would still be prepared to detect the case of 'an agreement for a lease masquerading as a licence'[11], but it was nevertheless quite clear that the courts would not intervene merely on the ground that they disapproved of the bargain concluded between owner and occupier[12].

It may well be that the boundary between legitimate avoidance and illicit evasion[13] of the Rent Act is slowly shifting in response to a desire to stimulate rather than fetter the supply of rented accommodation. But if this is the case, then the developments typified in *Somma*'s case have inflicted serious harm upon the social philosophy expressed in the Rent Act. That decision may well signify a more general retrenching of judicial opinion in favour of the entrepreneurial interest as opposed to the interest of the residential tenant. In *Aldrington Garages Ltd v Fielder*[14], Geoffrey Lane LJ (as he then was) went so far as to say that

> if the parties succeed in producing an agreement which, in all the circumstances of the case, is in fact a licence and not a tenancy they should not be prevented from that course by the courts bending over backwards to ensure that landlords do not manage to avoid the provisions of the Rent Acts. There is no reason why, if it is possible and properly done, agreements should not be entered into which do not fall within the Rent Acts, and the mere fact that those agreements may result in enhanced profits for the owners does

---

[1950] 1 KB 480 at 485. Compare *Maclay v Dixon* [1944] 1 All ER 22; *Foster v Robinson* [1951] 1 KB 149. See also, in relation to the Agricultural Holdings Act 1948, *Johnson v Moreton* [1980] AC 37, p. 419, ante.

11 For cases in which the court has declared a transaction to be an evasive sham, see *Samrose Properties Ltd v Gibbard* [1958] 1 WLR 235; *Elmdene Estates Ltd v White* [1960] AC 528. See generally A. Nichol (1981) 44 MLR 21: 'Outflanking Protective Legislation—Shams and Beyond'.

12 It is interesting to note that the courts have adopted a much more interventionist stance in relation to a not dissimilar question in the field of employment law, i.e., whether, and if so to what extent, an agreement for work may be labelled a 'contract for services' even though it bears many of the characteristics of a 'contract of service'. The primary relevance of the distinction between the 'employee' and the 'self-employed person' is, of course, that only the former is eligible for the statutory protection (e.g., in respect of unfair dismissal, redundancy and unemployment benefit) afforded by the employment legislation (see Employment Protection (Consolidation) Act 1978, ss. 54ff., 81ff.; Social Security Act 1975, ss. 14ff.'). In *Young & Woods Ltd v West* [1980] IRLR 201 at 207, the Court of Appeal held that a worker who had been designated as 'self-employed' was nevertheless entitled to bring a complaint of unfair dismissal. Stephenson LJ saw 'the dangers . . . of employers anxious to escape from their statutory liabilities . . . offering this choice to persons whom they intend to employ . . . and pressing them to take that employment—it may be even insisting upon their taking that employment—on the terms that it shall not be called that employment at all, but shall be called a contract for services with a self-employed person . . . I do not find anything . . . which clearly indicates that, where the agreement to treat a man as self-employed is made as openly as it was in this case, the person called self-employed is forced to accept that position, whatever the reality of the matter, when he comes to try to persuade an Industrial Tribunal to hear a complaint of unfair dismissal. That seems to me to presuppose some kind of estoppel against invoking the statute equivalent to, or closely analogous to, a power to contract out of the Act; and to give effect to it would . . . be plainly wrong.'

13 On the distinction between 'avoidance' and 'evasion', see R. E. Megarry, op. cit., Vol. 1, p. 19f. The ambivalent middleground between 'avoidance' and 'evasion' in the comparable area of tax law has recently been termed 'avoision'! (see A. Seldon (ed.), *Tax Avoision* (London 1979), p. 4).

14 (1978) 37 P & CR 461 at 468 at 470.

not necessarily mean that the agreements should be construed as tenancies rather than as licences . . . [T]here seems to me to be nothing wrong in trying to escape the provisions of those Acts or, indeed, trying to increase one's profits if one can legitimately do so[15].

Yet it may be thought that this is to take a slightly unrealistic view of the relative bargaining power of the potential occupier vis à vis the property owner. It is certainly true that the recent willingness of the courts to uphold so-called licences on the basis of a theory of freedom of contract is a retrogressive step which has done much to prejudice the residential protection offered by the Rent Act. It was Denning LJ who once pointed out that if the courts are not astute to look behind the labels given to transactions of this sort,

we should make a hole in the Rent Acts through which could be driven—I will not in these days say a coach and four—but an articulated vehicle[16].

It is of course possible to use other kinds of legal device than the licence for the purpose of ensuring that occupation does not attract Rent Act protection[17]. The courts have power to stigmatise such arrangements as mere shams intended to evade the Rent Act[18], but no conspicuous use has been made of this power in recent cases[19]. In any event, the nominal label attached to any evasive device will be conclusive until successfully challenged in court, and many occupiers will be deterred by one reason or another from undertaking such a challenge.

(2) The tenancy must relate to a 'dwelling-house'

Section 1 of the Rent Act 1977 makes it quite clear that the subject of a 'protected tenancy' must be a 'dwelling-house'. It is equally clear that for the purpose of the Act a 'dwelling-house' may comprise 'either a house or part of a

15 See also *Shell-Mex and BP Ltd v Manchester Garages Ltd* [1971] 1 WLR 612 at 619 per Buckley LJ.
16 *Facchini v Bryson* [1952] 1 TLR 1386 at 1389. See generally P. Robson and P. Watchman [1980] Conv 27: 'The Hidden Wealth of Licences'.
17 See *Report of the Committee on the Rent Acts* (Cmnd 4609, 1971), p. 112ff. Ready examples of evasive devices are provided by an agreement for rent-free letting coupled with hire of furniture at exorbitant rates; an agreement for rent-free occupation coupled with the provision of onerous services by the occupier for the property owner or coupled with an obligation upon the occupier to make large donations to a third party (e.g., a church, society or charity); an agreement for rent-free occupation coupled with an obligation on the occupier to pay household bills and expenses; and an agreement for 'rental purchase' or 'deferred purchase' or other device which effectively conceals the relationship of landlord and tenant behind an arrangement for instalment purchase. See also B. M. Hoggett (1972) 36 Conv (NS) 325: 'Houses on the Never-Never: Some Legal Aspects of Rental Purchase'. The Housing Act 1980 does, however, introduce one welcome form of statutory relief for occupiers under a 'rental purchase agreement' (as defined in Housing Act 1980, s. 88(4)). Where court possession proceedings are brought against such occupiers, the court may now adjourn the proceedings, or stay or suspend the execution of any possession order, or postpone the date for possession (see Housing Act 1980, s. 88(1)). This discretion is similar to, but subtly different from, the powers conferred upon the court under Rent Act 1977, s. 100, as amended by Housing Act 1980, s. 75(1), (2), p. 446, post. The court need not, for instance, impose conditions under section 88 as to continued payments.
18 As Geoffrey Lane LJ said in *Aldrington Garages Ltd v Fielder* (1978) 37 P & CR 461 at 469, 'in Rent Act cases the court has to be especially wary and especially careful to see that the wool is not being pulled over its eyes . . .'
19 See, however, *Martin v Davies* (1952) 42 TC 114n.

house.' Whether a building or a component part of a building thus qualifies as a 'dwelling-house' is ultimately a question of fact. Almost any building which has been constructed or adapted for residential occupation constitutes a 'dwelling-house', although it has been said that 'if the agreement is to let a barn, the tenant even though he lives there cannot be heard to say that it is let as a dwelling-house[20]'. Usually, however, full protection under the Rent Act may apply to a letting of an entire house, or to a letting of a self-contained flat, or to a letting of a single bed-sitting room or even non-adjacent rooms within a house[1]. Even a letting of two or more rooms in separate houses could be construed as relating in aggregate to a single 'dwelling-house'[2].

(3) The rent payable must be expressed in definite monetary terms

The courts have ruled that to 'let' a dwelling-house within the meaning of section 1 of the Rent Act 1977, there must be a tenancy under which a definite sum of money is payable as rent. The implications of the Rent Act for rent restriction and control would have no meaning if in any given case the rent to be paid were quantified in any other manner. Thus there can be no letting within the protection of the Rent Act if the tenant's obligation is expressed in terms of the performance of services or in terms of other payment in kind[3]. Even if a tenant pays money to his landlord, such payment is not necessarily rent. The tenancy will fall outside the Rent Act if the payment is made in respect of the hire of furniture or in respect of general household expenditure (e.g., rates, electricity bills) in rent-free accommodation, unless, of course, the court declares such an arrangement to be an unconvincing disguise for what is in reality a protected tenancy.

(4) The dwelling-house must be let 'as a separate dwelling'

Statutory protection under section 1 of the Rent Act 1977 extends only to those dwelling-houses which are let 'as a separate dwelling'. It is of cardinal importance that the element of purpose referred to in this phrase should be construed in the light of the actual terms of the tenancy in question and not from subsequent events[4]. The decisive factor is the original purpose of the letting rather than the actual user of the premises by the tenant.

It is clear that a tenancy may qualify as a 'protected tenancy' notwithstanding that the tenant never dwells in the premises at any time, as for instance where he sublets to a single subtenant[5]. However, if a non-resident tenant sublets a

20 *Epsom Grand Stand Association Ltd v Clarke* (1919) WN 170 at 171 per Bankes LJ. See *Horsford v Carnill* (1951) 157 Estates Gazette 243, 158 Estates Gazette 287, where it was argued that a cave might constitute a 'dwelling-house'.

1 See *Curl v Angelo* [1948] 2 All ER 189.

2 *Whitty v Scott-Russell* [1950] 2 KB 32. See also R. E. Megarry, op. cit., Vol. 1, p. 50.

3 See *Barnes v Barratt* [1970] 2 QB 657; compare *Montague v Browning* [1954] 1 WLR 1039.

4 See *Wolfe v Hogan* [1949] 2 KB 194 at 204f.; *Horford Investments Ltd v Lambert* [1976] Ch 39 at 52; R. E. Megarry, op. cit., Vol. 1, p. 67f.

5 *Horford Investments Ltd v Lambert*, supra, at 51 per Scarman LJ. The subtenant may also have a protected tenancy within the Rent Act (see Rent Act 1977, s. 152 (1)).

dwelling-house to more than one subtenant, he loses the protection of the Rent Act in respect of his own tenancy, since in this case the dwelling-house has not been let to him 'as a separate dwelling' but rather as a *number* of separate dwellings[6]. This at least is the case where the dwelling-house in question is already adapted for or converted to multiple residential occupation at the beginning of the non-residential tenancy. The Rent Act does not promote

> a policy for the protection of an entrepreneur . . . whose interest is exclusively commercial, that is to say, to obtain from his tenants a greater rental income than the rent he has contracted to pay his landlord[7].

Further difficulties arise under the Rent Act in respect of sharing arrangements in a dwelling-house[8]. The most important point in this connection is that there can be no protected tenancy under the Act if the person who grants the tenancy also occupies a dwelling-house in the same building[9]. Thus the resident landlord is excepted from the full rigour of the Act[10]. We shall look later in detail at the 'resident landlord' exception, but before we do so we must examine other difficulties which arise from the requirement that a protected tenancy must relate to the letting of a dwelling-house 'as a separate dwelling.' The following are the most important situations which demand consideration.

(a) *Multiple lettings by a non-resident landlord, where the tenants share some accommodation but each retains exclusive occupation of at least some separate accommodation*

If the landlord does not reside on the premises but merely lets to persons in multiple occupation, each living unit is regarded as having been 'let as a separate dwelling' for the purpose of the Act, notwithstanding that the tenants enjoy the right to share certain accommodation such as a kitchen, bathroom or lavatory. Each tenant thus qualifies for full protection under section 1 of the Rent Act 1977, provided that he has exclusive occupation of at least some accommodation[11].

(b) *Letting by a non-resident landlord to persons as joint tenants*

Exclusive possession of an entire house, flat or other living unit may be granted

6 *Horford Investments Ltd v Lambert*, supra; *St Catherine's College, Oxford v Dorling* [1980] 1 WLR 66 at 70f. See also *Regalian Securities Ltd v Ramsden* [1981] 1 WLR 611 at 616 per Lord Roskill.

7 Just though this result undoubtedly is, it does however raise the problem that a non-resident tenant *does* acquire protected status under the Rent Act where at the commencement of his tenancy the dwelling-house is not yet adapted or converted to multiple residential occupation (see *Horford Investments Ltd v Lambert*, supra, at 48 per Russell LJ). Thus a non-resident tenant may in effect acquire Rent Act protection for his entrepreneurial activity by the simple expedient of ensuring that the conversion of his dwelling-house into multiple units of habitation does not occur until after the commencement of his own tenancy. As always, the determining factor is the original purpose of the letting as expressed in the terms of the tenancy rather than the actual purpose of the letting as revealed by subsequent user.

8 See R. M. Aldridge (1974) 118 Sol Jo 3: 'Flat Sharing'; J. E. Adams (1976) 120 Sol Jo 125: 'Rent Act Problems of Sharing and Multi-occupation'.

9 Rent Act 1977, s. 12.

10 See p. 432, post.

11 See Rent Act 1977, s. 22(1).

to a number of persons as joint tenants. Although the Rent Act surprisingly omits any reference to the phenomenon of joint tenancy[12], it is clear that joint tenants are to be regarded as one person in law for the purpose of determining whether property has been let 'as a separate dwelling.' Thus, in principle, joint tenants are together eligible for full protected status under section 1 of the Rent Act 1977[13].

(c) *Letting to a resident tenant who grants contractual licences to a number of occupiers, where all persons concerned retain exclusive occupation of some accommodation but share other facilities*

It may sometimes occur that a tenancy of a dwelling-house is granted to an individual who in his turn grants contractual occupation licences to a number of persons, the result being that both the tenant and his licensees share some parts of the house. Although the licensees are clearly excluded from Rent Act protection, the original tenant may nevertheless enjoy full protected status. The dwelling-house has been let to him 'as a separate dwelling' within section 1 of the Rent Act 1977 notwithstanding that he shares some parts of the premises (e.g., a kitchen, bathroom or lavatory) with others[14].

(d) *Non-exclusive occupation agreements*[15]

To be distinguished from (b) above, where joint tenants clearly enjoy full protection under the Rent Act, is the case of the 'non-exclusive occupation agreement'[16]. Such agreements have recently acquired prominence as a common form of residential letting device. A non-exclusive occupation agreement is simply a variation on the theme of the occupation licence which, as we have seen[17], falls outside the scope of full Rent Act protection.

A non-exclusive occupation agreement typically provides for multiple occupation of living accommodation in a manner not dissimilar to joint tenancy but with the crucial difference that no one occupier is allowed to enjoy exclusive occupation of any part of the premises. Without exclusive possession, there can be no tenancy, and thus none of the occupiers is eligible for full protection under the Rent Act[18]. In consequence, the landlord effectively evades all statutory

12 See *Howson v Buxton* (1929) 139 LT 504 at 506 per Scrutton LJ: 'I have looked through the Act carefully, and think there is a good deal to be said for the view that the legislature had not definitely present to its mind the fact that there might be joint tenants, and that it has continually used the phrase "tenant" without any nice consideration of what would happen if there were more than one tenant.' See also J. Martin [1978] Conv 436: 'Joint Landlords and Tenants: Some Problems'.

13 For other problems posed by joint tenancies under the Rent Act, see pp. 435, 448, post.

14 See *Baker v Turner* [1950] AC 401 at 417 per Lord Porter; *Rogers v Hyde* [1951] 2 KB 923 at 932 per Lord Asquith.

15 See A. Arden (1978) LAG Bulletin 92, 138, 265.

16 See p. 423, ante.

17 See p. 421, ante.

18 Nor do any of the occupiers qualify for the protection given to restricted contracts, since the clear implication of section 19(6) of the Rent Act 1977 is that an occupier under a restricted contract must also enjoy exclusive occupation of at least some part of the premises.

control in the matter of rent restriction and security of tenure: the premises have not been let as a 'separate' dwelling for anyone. Yet the distinction between joint tenancy and this situation of 'total sharing' (sometimes called letting on a per capita rent basis) is elusive and ambiguous: the very unity of possession which must be present if there is to be a joint tenancy at all may be construed as rebutting the exclusiveness of occupation which is essential for the creation of a tenancy.

The courts do have jurisdiction to declare that a non-exclusive occupation agreement is in reality an elaborate disguise for a protected tenancy under the Rent Act[19]. However, as was demonstrated by the Court of Appeal's judgment in *Somma v Hazlehurst and Savelli*[20], the courts have frequently shown themselves reluctant to condemn a multiple occupation agreement as a sham.

In *Somma's* case, an unmarried man and woman had both entered into non-exclusive occupation agreements with a landlady in respect of a double bed-sitting room. Both agreements were phrased in terms of a 'licence.' In both agreements the landlady expressly declared herself unwilling to grant either occupier exclusive possession of the room; furthermore, she reserved herself the right to use the room in common with the occupiers and to nominate a replacement in the event that one of the occupiers should leave. The man and woman were both employed, and thus paid rent separately to the landlady (although she gave them a single receipt). Somewhat surprisingly, the Court of Appeal declined to treat the couple as being the unit which they undoubtedly constituted, holding instead that both had quite separate and distinct licences in accordance with their original agreements. It followed that neither was therefore eligible for any form of protection under the Rent Act[1].

The significance of *Somma's* case lies in the fact that it seems to provide landlords with a foolproof means of evading the Rent Act through the granting of largely fictitious 'licences' for non-exclusive multiple occupation. Indeed, the effect of *Somma's* case is that the Rent Act is wholly inapplicable if a landlord merely reserves himself a right (never of course exercised) to use accommodation in common with even a single occupier. This simple fiction is enough to destroy the exclusiveness of possession which is the sine qua non of either a protected tenancy under section 1 or a restricted contract under section 19[2].

There is, incidentally, an interesting comparison to be drawn between *Somma*

19 See, for instance, *Walsh v Griffiths-Jones and Durant* [1978] 2 All ER 1002; *Demuren and Adefope v Seal Estates Ltd* (1978) 249 Estates Gazette 440; *O'Malley v Seymour* (1979) 250 Estates Gazette 1083.

20 [1978] 1 WLR 1014.

1 It appeared to weigh heavily with the Court that the occupiers' rent obligations were calculated quite separately, although it was clear that neither occupier would have entered into an agreement alone and that the couple agreed to the terms offered only because they were in urgent need of accommodation. Joint tenants are, of course, jointly and severally liable for rent, although this consideration did not preclude a finding of joint tenancy in *Walsh v Griffiths-Jones and Durant*, supra. See A. Arden (1978) LAG Bulletin 265: 'Joint Tenants and Separate Payment of Rent'.

2 See K. J. Gray (1979) 38 Cambridge LJ 38: 'Lease or Licence to evade the Rent Act?'; M. Partington (1979) 42 MLR 331: 'Non-exclusive Occupation Agreements'; P. Robson and P. Watchman [1980] Conv 27; A. Arden (1978) LAG Bulletin 138; (1979) LAG Bulletin 87: 'Defending Rent Act Evasions'.

v Hazlehurst and Savelli and *Walsh v Griffiths-Jones and Durant*[3]. The factual situations in both cases were virtually identical. In the former case, a non-exclusive occupation agreement was upheld and enforced by the Court of Appeal notwithstanding that the agreement in question illustrated the very mischief against which the Rent Act is directed and notwithstanding that the Court of Appeal's judgment threatens to subvert the entire protective purpose of that statute[4]. In the latter case, a non-exclusive occupation agreement was declared to be a sham: the occupiers were held to be joint tenants rather than licensees, and as such were entitled to the full protection of the Rent Act. It is a little difficult to explain the vastly differing conclusions reached by two courts in relation to essentially the same facts[5].

Before we leave the requirement that a protected tenancy relate to a dwelling-house let 'as a separate dwelling', we must examine briefly the issue of mixed user of property. In general, the Rent Act is concerned only with the occupation of residential premises. The occupation of business premises is governed by Part II of the Landlord and Tenant Act 1954. Difficulties arise if residential premises are used for the purpose of a business conducted by the tenant. The fact that part of a dwelling-house is used for a business purpose, where the premises would otherwise be subject to a protected tenancy, is enough to disqualify that letting from full statutory protection, unless the tenant's business activities are merely incidental to the residential occupation and do not comprise a significant purpose of his occupation taken as a whole[6]. The relevant degree of commercial user of residential premises is always a question of fact in each individual case, but the protection of the Rent Act apparently extends to a tenant who takes in a few lodgers at minimal rents without reaping any substantial commercial advantage from such activity[7].

3. EXPRESS EXCLUSION FROM THE SCOPE OF A 'PROTECTED TENANCY'

We have until now looked at the implied exceptions to full protected status

3 [1978] 2 All ER 1002.

4 A proposal to confer full Rent Act protection on licences, 'notwithstanding that the occupier may not have exclusive possession of his accommodation', was rejected at the committee stage of the House of Commons' consideration of the Housing Bill 1980. See *Parliamentary Debates, House of Commons, Official Report* (Standing Committee F), Cols. 2317ff. (22 April 1980).

5 One possible distinction may be the fact that *Walsh* concerned two young graduates of Trinity College, Cambridge, who having shared rooms at Cambridge were sharing accommodation in London. The legal realist might well suggest that the courts look perhaps more kindly upon a couple of young Trinity graduates, bristling with sincerity at the threshold of their new careers in the metropolis, than upon a man and woman who merely prefer to live in sin! If there is any truth at all in this rationalisation, it simply illustrates the fact that the implicit value orientations of judges emerge more clearly in the area of landlord and tenant law than in perhaps any other area. Nowhere else are political and policy preferences so effectively secured or less effectively concealed.

6 See Rent Act 1977, s. 24(3); *Cheryl Investments Ltd v Saldanha, Royal Life Saving Society v Page* [1978] 1 WLR 1329.

7 See *Lewis v Weldcrest Ltd* [1978] 1 WLR 1107. It would be otherwise, however, if the tenant let a large number of rooms in a spacious house for the purpose of obtaining considerable profit:

under the Rent Act 1977. It is now time to examine the situations which are excluded from such protection by the express words of the Act.

A tenancy cannot be a protected tenancy if the dwelling-house in question either has or (at any relevant time) has had too high a rateable value[8]. The intention behind this exclusion is to take luxury accommodation outside the scope of the legislation, for almost all other accommodation falls within the stipulated rateable limits. There can be no protected tenancy if the tenant pays no rent at all or pays an annual rent which is less than two-thirds of the relevant rateable value[9].

No protected tenancy can arise where a dwelling-house is let together with (and for a purpose subsidiary to) other land[10]. Nor can a protected tenancy be created if a dwelling-house forms part of an agricultural holding[11], comprises premises licensed for the sale of alcohol[12], or is the subject of a letting by the Crown or by a government department[13]. Also excluded from the scope of the protected tenancy is any letting by a local authority, the Commission for the New Towns, a development corporation, housing association or housing co-operative[14]. No protected tenancy can be claimed where a letting is made to a student by a specified educational institution[15].

There remain three other cases of exclusion from protected status under the Rent Act, and at these we must look rather more closely.

(1) Holiday lettings

There can be no protected tenancy if the purpose of the tenancy is to confer on the tenant the right to occupy the dwelling-house for a holiday[16]. Whether a letting is a holiday letting is always an issue of fact, but the 'holiday lettings' exemption has generated a quite remarkable expansion of the tourist industry in the most unlikely areas of large cities! Although a landlord's description of a letting as being for the purpose of a 'holiday' is not per se conclusive, the courts have not been particularly astute to examine whether such a description simply conceals cases which in reality should qualify for Rent Act protection[17].

---

such a tenancy would fall to be considered not under the residential code contained in the Rent Act but under the business code contained in the Landlord and Tenant Act 1954.

8 Rent Act 1977, s. 4(1).

9 Rent Act 1977, s. 5.

10 Rent Act 1977, ss. 6, 26(1).

11 Rent Act 1977, s. 10.

12 Rent Act 1977, s. 11.

13 Rent Act 1977, s. 13(1) as amended by Housing Act 1980, s. 73(1).

14 Rent Act 1977, ss. 14–16. However, most public or quasi-public tenancies falling within these excluded categories receive statutory protection as 'secure tenancies' under the Housing Act 1980, s. 28ff., p. 460, post.

15 Rent Act 1977, s. 8.

16 Rent Act 1977, s. 9.

17 See, for instance, *Buchmann v May* [1978] 2 All ER 993. A proposal that section 9 should apply 'only where the dwelling-house has been approved by the local authority as a short-term dwelling' was rejected at committee stage in the House of Commons' consideration of the Housing Bill 1980. See *Parliamentary Debates, House of Commons, Official Report* (Standing Committee F), Cols. 2317ff. (22 April 1980). See also *R v Rent Officer of the London Borough of Camden, ex parte Plant* (1981) LAG Bulletin 67.

(2) Inclusion of board or attendance

A tenancy is not a protected tenancy if under the tenancy the dwelling-house is 'bona fide let at a rent which includes payments in respect of board or attendance'[18]. In strict legal terms, what matters here is the tenant's contractual entitlement at the commencement of the tenancy: it is irrelevant that in actual fact he does not receive the board or attendance to which he is entitled. The provision of *any* board is sufficient to displace the protected tenancy. There is no statutory definition of 'board', but 'in practice, the dividing line appears to fall between the early morning cup of tea on the one hand and "bed and breakfast" on the other'[19]. There is nothing to prevent the 'board' comprising simply pre-packaged food or uncooked food[20], and the relative ease with which this particular Rent Act immunity may be obtained by landlords remains one of the weakest features of the legislation[1].

The provision of 'attendance', however, will rule a tenancy out as a protected tenancy only if

> the amount of rent which is fairly attributable to attendance, having regard to the value of the attendance to the tenant, forms a substantial part of the whole rent[2].

What is 'substantial' is clearly a question of fact to be determined on a commonsense basis, and 'attendance' is generally taken to indicate service personal to the tenant provided by the landlord[3].

(3) The 'resident landlord' exception

Perhaps the most important express exclusion from full protected status under the Rent Act concerns tenancies where the landlord resides on the premises. The 'resident landlord' exception was introduced by the Rent Act 1974 in order to replace the immunity previously conferred upon furnished tenancies, and

18 Rent Act 1977, s. 7(1).

19 R. E. Megarry, op. cit., Vol. 1, p. 141. In *Wilkes v Goodwin* [1923] 2 KB 86 at 93, Bankes LJ thought that a tenancy would be excluded from the Rent Act by any amount of board 'which is not ruled out of consideration by the application of the rule *de minimis non curat lex*'. In the same case (at 110) Younger LJ expressed the view that 'board' involves 'the conception of a provision by the landlord of such food as in the case of any particular tenancy would ordinarily be consumed at daily meals and would be obtained and prepared by a tenant for himself, if it were not provided by somebody else'. See also *Palser v Grinling* [1948] AC 291; *R v Battersea, etc, Rent Tribunal, ex parte Parikh* [1957] 1 WLR 410.

20 In a Scots case, *Holiday Flat Co v Kuczera* 1978 SLT 47 (Sh Ct), it was thought that 'it would probably be pedantic (particularly since the British entry into the European Economic Community) to deny the continental breakfast the status of a meal sufficient to constitute board.'

1 In its consideration of the Housing Bill 1980, the House of Commons rejected at committee stage an amendment to the Rent Act 1977 which would have precluded the application of section 7 to any tenancy granted after the commencement of the Housing Act 1980. See *Parliamentary Debates, House of Commons, Official Report* (Standing Committee F), Cols. 2317ff. (22 April 1980).

2 Rent Act 1977, s. 7(2).

3 See *Palser v Grinling* [1948] AC 291 at 310 at 317f. per Viscount Simon. The term 'attendance' does not, for instance, include the provision of a communal hot water supply or the maintenance of the communal areas and facilities in a block of flats. For guidance as to what is 'substantial', see *Woodward v Docherty* [1974] 1 WLR 966 at 970 per Scarman LJ.

applies only to tenancies granted on or after 14th August 1974. Section 12 of the Rent Act 1977[4] provides that the exception comes into operation only if three conditions are satisfied. *First*, the tenancy in question must relate to a dwelling-house which forms part only of a building which is not itself a purpose-built block of flats[5]. *Second*, the tenancy must have been granted by a person who, at the time of the grant, occupied as his residence another dwelling-house which also forms 'part of the same building.' *Third*, the interest of the landlord must, throughout the period since the grant of the tenancy, have belonged to a person who resided continuously in that other dwelling-house[6]. The purpose of the 'resident landlord' exception is plainly to permit a property owner to let off a couple of rooms in his house without thereby incurring the full rigour of the Rent Act[7].

The 'resident landlord' exception may sometimes raise technical points of statutory construction. For instance, it may be difficult to determine whether the landlord's dwelling-house and the tenant's dwelling-house constitute parts of the same building. It has been said that section 12 is aimed at

> the mischief of that sort of social embarrassment arising out of close proximity—close proximity which the landlord had accepted in the belief that he could bring it to an end at any time allowed by the contract of tenancy[8].

Much would therefore seem to turn upon whether the dwelling-houses in question have separate external access, with the result that section 12 would not apply if a landlord and tenant lived, for example, in adjacent terraced houses or semi-detached houses with separate entrances.

Another difficulty may sometimes concern whether the landlord is truly 'resident'. The test of residence has been put broadly on a par with the test of residence which applies for the purpose of determining eligibility for a statutory tenancy[9]. The landlord must be able to show substantial use as a home if he is to take advantage of section 12. Occasional or token residence is not sufficient, and the only kind of residence by proxy which is even capable of preserving the 'resident landlord' immunity is perhaps residence by the landlord's wife.

4. 'PROTECTED' AND 'STATUTORY' TENANCIES

Provided that a tenancy of a dwelling-house does not fall within any of the express or implied exceptions considered above, it will constitute a 'protected tenancy' for the purpose of the Rent Act so long as there is a continuing

4 As amended by Housing Act 1980, s. 65(1).

5 Section 12(1) of the Housing Act 1977 has been amended to make it clear that the 'resident landlord' exception applies even in relation to a purpose-built block of flats if a resident of one of those flats sublets to a person who occupies one of the rooms in his flat (see Housing Act 1980, s. 65(1)).

6 Certain minor exceptions are allowed: see Rent Act 1977, Sch. 2, para. 1, as amended by Housing Act 1980, s. 65(2), (3), (4), (5); *Landau v Sloane* [1981] 2 WLR 349.

7 The occupation may, however, constitute a 'restricted contract', p. 455, post.

8 *Bardrick v Haycock* (1976) 31 P & CR 420 at 424 per Scarman LJ.

9 See Rent Act 1977, Sch. 2, para. 5, p. 434, post.

contractual relationship between landlord and tenant. The duration of that contractual relationship is fixed by the terms of the tenancy agreement. When the contractual tenancy comes to an end, that tenancy may nevertheless continue in existence, not as a 'protected tenancy' but as a 'statutory tenancy'. In other words, it is possible that an expired protected tenancy may in some circumstances receive almost literally a new lease of life in the form of a 'statutory tenancy' which enjoys substantially the same protection under the Rent Act as did the former protected tenancy. So valuable is this protection that the courts have recognised that often the possession of a statutory tenancy is 'one of the most significant rights of property' which an individual may hold[10].

In effect, a statutory tenancy is not a tenancy in the strict sense, but merely confers upon the occupier a statutorily protected 'status of irremovability.' In *Marcroft Wagons Ltd v Smith*[11], Evershed MR observed that

> a new 'monstrum horrendum, informe, ingens', has come into our ken—the conception of a statutory tenancy—the conception that a person may have such a right of exclusive possession of property as will entitle him to bring an action for trespass against the owner of that property but which confers no interest whatever in the land: such a person is unable to dispose of the land by grant or by testamentary disposition. It is, as has been said, a statutory right of irremovability[12].

When a 'protected' tenant becomes a 'statutory' tenant, he holds on exactly the same terms as before, so far as is consistent with the Rent Act[13]. The basic conditions of eligibility for a statutory tenancy are laid down in section 2(1)(a) of the Rent Act 1977. This provision makes it clear that if, immediately before the termination of a protected tenancy, a person was the protected tenant of the dwelling-house in question, that person shall become the statutory tenant 'if and so long as he occupies the dwelling-house as his residence.' Thus no statutory tenancy can be claimed by a tenant who sublets the entire dwelling-house or who cannot show substantial use of the property as a home[14]. However, the test of occupation may be satisfied if the property is substantially used as 'a' home for the tenant, and not necessarily as his only home. Absence from the dwelling-house is not fatal to a claim of continued residence if there remains a *corpus* of possession (e.g., in the form of the belongings of the statutory tenant) coupled

10 See *Mafo v Adams* [1970] 1 QB 548 at 557 per Widgery LJ.
11 [1951] 2 KB 496 at 501. See also *Keeves v Dean* [1924] 1 KB 685 at 694 per Scrutton LJ; *Jessamine Investment Co v Schwartz* [1977] 2 WLR 145 at 153 per Sir John Pennycuick.
12 This description of the statutory tenancy points to precisely those features which are today characteristic of the 'new property', which comprises rights of an essentially intangible, non-disposable, non-survivable and largely personal nature, p. 11, 39ff., ante.
13 Rent Act 1977, s. 3(1).
14 See *Skinner v Geary* [1931] 2 KB 546 at 564, where Scrutton LJ declared that one object of the Rent Restriction Acts 'was to provide as many houses as possible at a moderate rent. A man who does not live in a house and never intends to do so is . . . withdrawing from circulation that house which was intended for occupation by other people.' A very similar rationale for the legislation was expressed in *Brown v Brash and Ambrose* [1948] 2 KB 247 at 254. Here Asquith LJ again reflected a view of housing as essentially a social and economic resource requiring careful distribution. He pointed to the 'clear policy of the Acts, which is to keep a roof over the tenant's or someone's head, not over an unoccupied shell, and to economise rather than sterilise housing accommodation.' See also *Beck v Scholz* [1953] 1 QB 570; *Walker v Ogilvy* [1975] EGD 322.

with an *animus revertendi* (i.e., an intention on his part to return at some future date). In *Bevington v Crawford*[15], a tenant who was absent abroad for all but two or three months of each year was held by the Court of Appeal to be a statutory tenant since he appeared to have a genuine intention when practicable to revert to using the property as his home. Similarly, a statutory tenancy could be claimed in respect of a London flat where the tenant lives most days of the week in his house in the country. However it has been decided that a limited company cannot 'reside' in a dwelling-house personally and cannot therefore claim a statutory tenancy[16]. Thus a landlord may effectively evade the Rent Act by making it a condition of any letting that the intending occupiers purchase an 'off-the-peg' company and thereby adopt a corporate form.

Continued residence may be established vicariously through the presence of relatives of the statutory tenant, provided that the tenant has an intention to return[17]. It has also been held that if two persons are joint tenants under a protected tenancy and one ceases to occupy the dwelling-house before that tenancy determines, the remaining joint tenant will become the statutory tenant if he is still in occupation when the protected tenancy does end[18].

A statutory tenancy enjoys broadly the same protection under the Rent Act which applies to a protected tenancy. Moreover, a statutory tenancy is capable of transmission to another person or persons in specified circumstances.

(1) Transmission on death

If a protected or statutory tenant dies, the tenancy may pass to another person who then becomes a 'statutory tenant by succession', enjoying precisely the same protection under the Rent Act. The persons eligible to succeed to a statutory tenancy are laid down in the Rent Act 1977, Schedule 1, as amended by the Housing Act 1980.

(a) *Statutory succession*

If the original tenant under a protected or statutory tenancy dies leaving a 'surviving spouse' who was 'residing in the dwelling-house immediately before the death of the original tenant', that person now becomes the statutory tenant 'if and so long as he or she occupies the dwelling-house as his or her residence'[19]. The term 'surviving spouse' does not include a de facto spouse or a divorced spouse.

If nobody qualifies as the statutory tenant by virtue of this provision, then the statutory tenancy devolves upon any person who was 'a member of the original tenant's family' and who was residing with the deceased at the time of and for the period of six months immediately preceding his death[20]. Such a person

15 (1974) 232 Estates Gazette 191. It appeared that the tenant in this case spent most of the year in Cannes, but Lord Denning MR pointed out that the wealth of the tenant was irrelevant to the applicability of the Rent Act. See also *Gofor Investments Ltd v Roberts* (1975) 119 Sol Jo 320.
16 *Firstcross Ltd v East West (Export/Import) Ltd* (1981) 41 P & CR 145.
17 See *Colin Smith Music Ltd v Ridge* [1975] 1 WLR 463.
18 *Lloyd v Sadler* [1978] QB 774. See J. Martin [1978] Conv 436.
19 Rent Act 1977, Sch. 1, para. 2, as substituted by Housing Act 1980, s. 76(1).
20 Rent Act 1977, Sch. 1, para. 3.

becomes the statutory tenant 'if and so long as he occupies the dwelling-house as his residence.' If more than one person qualifies under this definition, the county court may be asked to allocate the statutory tenancy to one or other claimant in the exercise of its discretion and in default of agreement between the parties concerned[1].

In cases which satisfy the conditions for the devolution of statutory tenancies, there may also be a second succession to the surviving spouse or member of the family of the first successor if immediately before his death the first successor was still a statutory tenant and if the same conditions are fulfilled as applied to the first succession[2]. A person who becomes a statutory tenant by succession continues to be regarded as such even if he enters into a new contractual tenancy of the dwelling-house[3].

The rules concerning the devolution of statutory tenancies on death ensure that in many cases the granting of a residential tenancy in a dwelling-house can amount in effect to a disposition of utility in relation to that property for the duration of several generations. In this sense the Rent Act has introduced a new and quite remarkable form of homestead property right designed to secure the family interest. To this considerable extent, the Rent Act legislation is thus fundamentally opposed to the prevailing ethos of the general law of property, which rests almost entirely upon premises of a forthrightly commercial character. It has indeed been said that 'the world of the family represents the "integry"—the 'last holdout' against the world of the cash-nexus brought into being by the industrial revolution'[4].

(b) *The definition of familial nexus*

It is possible, in the circumstances outlined above, that a statutory tenancy may devolve upon 'a member of the original tenant's family'. It has sometimes proved difficult to determine whether a given person qualifies as 'a member of the original tenant's family.' The construction of this phrase is heavily coloured by social and moral perceptions of the legitimacy of certain kinds of relationship, and one of the pressing questions of the 1980s will be whether the Rent Act provisions for statutory succession will be applied to cover various emerging kinds of de facto relationship. The attempts made so far by the courts to elucidate the idea of familial nexus have engendered controversy, but a close study of the cases decided in this area reveals something in the nature of a social history of the family over the last 30 years. The decisions reached by the courts are significant primarily because they represent important statements of the boundaries of kinship socially and legally recognised in our community.

(i) *The test of familial nexus* There is in the Rent Act 1977 no definition of 'a member of the original tenant's family.' It is by now notorious that the test to be

1 See *Trayfoot v Lock* [1957] 1 WLR 351; *Williams v Williams* [1970] 1 WLR 1350.
2 Rent Act 1977, Sch. 1, paras. 6, 7, as amended by Housing Act 1980, s. 76(2).
3 Rent Act 1977, Sch. 1, para. 10.
4 See K. J. Gray, *Reallocation of Property on Divorce* (Abingdon 1977), p. 69; J. Bernard, *The Future of Marriage* (Harmondsworth 1976), p. 269.

applied in determining the question of definition is that of 'the ordinary man'. Cohen LJ formulated the question thus in *Brock v Wollams*[5]:

> Would an ordinary man, addressing his mind to the question whether [X] was a member of the family or not, have answered 'yes' or 'no'?

Furthermore, it is clear that the word 'family' is used here 'to borrow the words used of the soldier in King Henry V, in a sense "base, common, and popular"'[6]. There is also authority for the view that, in reaching his conclusion, the 'ordinary man' is to be placed not in 1920 (when Parliament first used the phrase which lies at the crux of this discussion), but at the date of the death of the original tenant[7]. He is also to be placed 'in possession of the evidence which the judge had before he gives his answer'[8]. Within these confines, the 'ordinary man' is called upon to declare whether, in the context of any given relationship, there exists

> at least a broadly recognisable de facto familial nexus. This may be capable of being found and recognised as such by the ordinary man—where the link would be strictly familial had there been a marriage, or where the link is through adoption of a minor, de jure or de facto, or where the link is 'step-', or where the link is 'in-law' or by marriage'[9].

The 'ordinary man' of course can speak only through the medium of the judge before whom is brought the question of statutory construction under the Rent Act, and as Viscount Dilhorne observed in *Carega Properties SA v Sharratt*[10], 'the answer to the question is not likely to extract any more than the judge's personal view'. It is highly arguable that the 'ordinary man approach' provides respectable cover for what may be purely subjective judicial pronouncements on the kinds of social grouping that are to be recognised as a 'family'[11].

It has been said that, in deciding whether a person qualifies as 'a member of the original tenant's family', two elements have to be considered—relationship and conduct[12]. The list of 'members' of a 'family' is not yet closed: the categories have not so far been fully or finally defined[13]. We shall now examine the case law to ascertain which relationships are clearly within the Act and which are clearly excluded.

(ii) *Relationships clearly within the Act* There is no doubt that the phrase 'member of the original tenant's family' includes certain members of a de iure family. It has been said that

5 [1949] 2 KB 388 at 395.
6 *Langdon v Horton* [1951] 1 KB 666 at 669 per Evershed MR.
7 *Watson v Lucas* [1980] 1 WLR 1493 at 1497 per Stephenson LJ. For criticism of this extraordinary canon of statutory construction (first applied by the Court of Appeal in *Dyson Holdings Ltd v Fox* [1976] QB 503), see *Helby v Rafferty* [1979] 1 WLR 13 at 16 per Stamp LJ, 23 per Roskill LJ, 25 per Cumming-Bruce LJ.
8 Ibid.
9 *Ross v Collins* [1964] 1 WLR 425 at 432 per Russell LJ, approved in *Carega Properties SA v Sharratt* [1979] 1 WLR 928 at 931 per Lord Diplock.
10 [1979] 1 WLR 928 at 932.
11 See (1980) 39 Cambridge LJ 31 at 34 (P. Tennant).
12 *Joram Developments Ltd v Sharratt* [1979] 1 WLR 3 at 10 per Browne LJ.
13 Ibid., at 11 per Browne LJ.

membership of the family is in general confined to those related by marriage, to children (and the tenant's brothers and sisters are children of his parents), and to relationships where one person is in loco parentis to another[14].

However, mere relationship is not always sufficient to establish membership of a family for Rent Act purposes. In *Langdon v Horton*[15], the Court of Appeal refused Rent Act protection to two elderly ladies who had for 30 years lived with their cousin in a house which she held on a statutory tenancy. It was ruled that mere consanguinity was not enough to establish membership of the tenant's family, and that where the motive for cohabitation is provided by reasons of convenience the statutory requirement is not satisfied.

(iii) *The de facto marriage relationship* Difficult as these questions may be in the context of a de iure family, even more difficult questions arise in connection with de facto family relationships. It was thought during the 1950s that the phrase 'member of the original tenant's family' had no application to a de facto spouse, on the ground that any contrary view would 'presuppose an intention of Parliament to reward immorality with irremovability'[16]. In *Gammans v Ekins*[17], an unmarried man and woman had lived together for a number of years before the death of the woman, at which point the man claimed to succeed to the woman's statutory tenancy. The Court of Appeal denied his claim on grounds of public policy. Asquith LJ employed a double-edged argument, pointing out that

Either the relationship was platonic or it was not . . . [I]f their relations were platonic, I can see no principle on which it could be said that these two were members of the same family, which would not require the court to predicate the same of two old cronies of the same sex innocently sharing a flat. If, on the other hand, the relationship involves sexual relations, it seems to me anomalous that a person can acquire a 'status of irremovability' by living or having lived in sin, even if the liaison has not been a mere casual encounter but protracted in time and conclusive in character. But I would decide the case on a simpler view. To say of two people masquerading, as these two were, as husband and wife (there being no children to complicate the picture) that they were members of the same family, seems to be an abuse of the English language[18].

Evershed MR confessed to having experienced 'greater difficulty' in reaching a conclusion in this case, but was comforted by his belief that

It may not be a bad thing that by this decision it is shown that, in the Christian society in which we live, one, at any rate, of the privileges which may be derived from marriage is not equally enjoyed by those who are living together as man and wife but who are not married[19].

14 R. E. Megarry, op. cit., Vol. 1, p. 215. See, e.g., *Salter v Lask* [1925] 1 KB 584 (husband); *Price v Gould* (1930) 143 LT 333 (brother and sister); *Jones v Whitehill* [1950] 2 KB 204 (niece by marriage); *Stewart v Higgins* [1951] EGD 353 (brother-in-law and sister-in-law); *Collier v Stoneman* [1957] 1 WLR 1108 (grandchild); *Brock v Wollams* [1949] 2 KB 388 (informally adopted child).
15 [1951] 1 KB 666.
16 *Watson v Lucas* [1980] 1 WLR 1493 at 1497 per Stephenson LJ.
17 [1950] 2 KB 328.
18 [1950] 2 KB 328 at 331.
19 [1950] 2 KB 328 at 334.

In *Gammans v Ekins*, the unmarried couple did not have children, but the Court of Appeal left open the question whether the presence of children could bring a de facto family within the scope of the succession provisions of the Rent Act[20]. This issue was finally clarified in *Hawes v Evenden*[1], where the Court of Appeal answered that question in the affirmative. In more recent cases, therefore, the attention of the courts has focused upon the status of childless de facto relationships.

In *Dyson Holdings Ltd v Fox*[2], the defendant had lived with a protected tenant for 21 years before his death. In the words of Lord Denning MR, 'in every respect they were man and wife save that they had not gone through a ceremony of marriage.' The Court of Appeal, in a decision which has proved highly controversial, held that the woman succeeded to the man's statutory tenancy. Lord Denning led the court in overruling *Gammans v Ekins* on the ground that 'owing to the lapse of time, and the changing social conditions, the previous decision is not in accord with modern thinking'[3]. In the view of James LJ,

> The popular meaning given to the word 'family' is not fixed once and for all time. I have no doubt that with the passage of years it has changed. The cases reveal that it is not restricted to blood relationships and those created by the marriage ceremony. It can include de facto as well as de iure relationships[4].

Bridge LJ, concurring, noted that 'between 1950 and 1975 there has been a complete revolution in society's attitude to unmarried partnerships', and that the social stigma which once attached to them 'has almost, if not entirely, disappeared'[5].

At this point it seemed as if the courts were becoming fairly amenable to the idea of treating most stable de facto marriages as coming within the ambit of the Rent Act. However, in *Dyson Holdings Ltd v Fox*[6] James LJ had been careful to state that 'relationships of a casual or intermittent character and those bearing indications of impermanence would not come within the popular concept of a family unit.' This note of caution was borne out in *Helby v Rafferty*[7]. Here the Court of Appeal denied status as a tenant by succession to a man who had cohabited with a statutory tenant for five years before her death. There was evidence in this case that the couple had deliberately remained unmarried, and that the woman had been a lady of some independence who had not wished to assume the overt character of a wife. In the view taken by the Court of Appeal the relationship apparent here did not have the permanence and stability necessary to justify the conclusion that the surviving cohabitee was a 'member of the original tenant's family' within the meaning of the Rent Act 1977.

20 [1950] 2 KB 328 at 332f. per Jenkins LJ, 334 per Evershed MR.
1 [1953] 1 WLR 1169.
2 [1976] QB 503. See D. C. Bradley (1976) 39 MLR 222: 'Meaning of "Family": Changing Morality and Changing Justice'.
3 [1976] QB 503 at 509.
4 [1976] QB 503 at 511.
5 [1976] QB 503 at 512.
6 [1976] QB 503 at 511.
7 [1979] 1 WLR 13.

In coming to this decision the Court of Appeal expressed grave disquiet as to the way in which the earlier and differently constituted Court of Appeal in *Dyson Holdings Ltd v Fox* had purported to overrule *Gammans v Ekins*[8]. It is now clear, however, that the Court of Appeal is not prepared, in the absence of definitive guidance from the House of Lords, to return to the construction adopted in *Gammans v Ekins*. In *Watson v Lucas*[9], Stephenson LJ indicated that to 'go back to *Gammans v Ekins* would be to introduce impermanence and instability into our own decisions.'

In *Watson v Lucas* the Court of Appeal decided by a majority to uphold the devolution of a statutory tenancy upon a man who had for almost 20 years lived with a woman in a childless de facto union. Throughout this entire period he had been legally married to another woman who had left him several years before he began to cohabit with the deceased statutory tenant. The majority in the Court of Appeal declined to hold that his marital status was incompatible with his being a 'member' of the statutory tenant's family. The majority was not dissuaded from this conclusion by evidence that the parties in this case had retained their separate names throughout the relationship and had not striven to hold themselves out as a married couple. Stephenson LJ felt 'bound to move with the times'. He declared that

> Holding this man to be a member of this woman's family will not promote the support of marriage or the reduction of illicit unions . . . but though those objects might have influenced the judges who decided *Gammans v Ekins* . . . they had lost their relevance to the interpretation of this provision of the Rent Acts a quarter of a century later . . . [A] judge, putting himself in the place of the ordinary man, can consider an association which has every outward appearance of marriage, except the false pretence of being married, as not constituting a family. If it looks like a marriage in the old and perhaps obsolete sense of a lifelong union, with nothing casual or temporary about it, it is a family until the House of Lords declares . . . that the case of *Dyson Holdings Ltd v Fox* was wrongly decided . . . The time has gone by when the courts can hold such a union not to be 'familial' simply because the parties to it do not pretend to be married in due form of law[10].

All the members of the Court of Appeal in *Watson v Lucas* expressed the view, however, that the construction of the phrase 'member of the original tenant's family' should not be extended *beyond* the boundaries indicated in *Dyson Holdings Ltd v Fox*[11]. This makes it fairly plain that the statutory phrase does not embrace broader household relationships. But within those boundaries the Court of Appeal gave some indication of what may perhaps be a significant shift in the criteria to be applied by the courts in the future. The majority of the Court took the view that the formal features of any relationship were significant only to the extent that they gave guidance as to the degree of mutual commitment present in the union. Stephenson LJ agreed, for instance, that a subsisting marital status

8 The Court of Appeal made it clear that it was accepting, although distinguishing, *Dyson Holdings Ltd v Fox*, only on the ground that the Court of Appeal is (according to the better view) bound by its own decisions. See [1979] 1 WLR 13 at 17 per Stamp LJ, 23 per Roskill LJ, 25 per Cumming-Bruce LJ.

9 [1980] 1 WLR 1493 at 1498. See [1981] Conv 78 (A. Sydenham).

10 [1980] 1 WLR 1493 at 1500f. See the dissent of Oliver LJ at 1502ff.

11 [1980] 1 WLR 1493 at 1501, 1506.

or the retention of a separate name were 'important factors' which might in some cases (as in *Helby v Rafferty*) be conclusive. In the present case, however, the decision of the man (who was a Roman Catholic) not to seek a divorce from his own wife was

> not an absolute impediment to membership of another woman's family, but a factor to be weighed with all others including their decision to keep their own names in every part of their life together but one ... These two factors ... are of far too little weight to contradict the evidence that this was a lasting, indeed a lifelong association, more permanent and stable than many marriages including [the man's] own[12].

(iv) *Other relationships* In *Gammans v Ekins*[13] Asquith LJ stated firmly that a familial nexus would not exist, in the sense required by the Rent Act, between 'two old cronies of the same sex innocently sharing a flat.' Indeed Jenkins LJ went so far in the same case as to suggest that 'an alarming vista would ... be opened up' if the succession provisions of the Rent Act were allowed to extend to such persons[14]. Likewise, in *Brock v Wollams*[15], Cohen LJ indicated that it could not have been the intention of Parliament to provide Rent Act protection for such members of the original tenant's 'household' as his 'servants and lodgers.'

A more difficult situation required to be dealt with by the Court of Appeal in *Ross v Collins*[16]. Here a woman claimed to succeed to the statutory tenancy enjoyed by a man with whom she had lived for a substantial period. She had been nearly forty years younger than him and had looked after him dutifully, regarding him as 'a sort of elder relative, partly as ... father, partly as ... elder brother.' Although the conduct of the couple had clearly been of a familial nature, the Court of Appeal regarded the absence of kinship as precluding this platonic liaison from constituting the necessary familial nexus. In the words of Russell LJ

> two strangers cannot ... ever establish artificially ... a familial nexus by acting as brothers or as sisters, even if they call each other such and consider their relationship to be tantamount to that. Nor ... can an adult man and woman who establish a platonic relationship establish a familial nexus by acting as a devoted brother and sister or father and daughter would act, even if they address each other as such, and even if they refer to each other as such and regard their association as tantamount to such. Nor ... would they indeed be recognised as familial links by the ordinary man[17].

It could scarcely be expected that *Ross v Collins* would be the final word on this issue in an age which tolerates diversified social relationships and in which traditional family forms have been exposed to unprecedented challenge. The construction of the phrase 'member of the original tenant's family' involves the cultural definition of the concept of kinship and social bonding within an increasingly impersonal community.

12 [1980] 1 WLR 1493 at 1500.
13 [1950] 2 KB 328 at 331.
14 [1950] 2 KB 328 at 333.
15 [1949] 2 KB 388 at 394.
16 [1964] 1 WLR 425.
17 [1964] 1 WLR 425 at 432.

In *Carega Properties SA v Sharratt*[18] the courts were again confronted by the claim that the Rent Act should recognise new and unconventional forms of social grouping. In this case, an unrelated man and woman (separated in age by more than half a century) lived together for 18 years in a platonic association which was 'wholly admirable and of the highest standard'[19]. The woman was the statutory tenant of the flat in which they lived. The couple referred to each other as 'Aunt Nora' and 'Bunny' respectively, and they shared a life of intellectual and cultural intimacy. The House of Lords decided that, when the statutory tenant eventually died at the age of 94, the tenancy could not devolve upon her faithful and much younger male companion. The House of Lords, following *Ross v Collins*, refused to recognise that changing social conditions had enlarged the meaning of the word 'family' so that it now signified 'household'.

It is very likely that during the course of the 1980s the House of Lords will be called upon to reconsider the term 'family' in order to accord with changing social and moral perceptions. If the term 'family' is confirmed in the meaning which it bore under the social conditions of the 1920s[20], that meaning may in fact be closer to 'household' than to the modern concept of the nuclear family[1]. Alternatively, the House of Lords will have to face the implications of a changing meaning of 'family'. So far, the courts, as in *Carega Properties SA v Sharratt*, have demanded something more than the mere performance of domestic functions. By attaching significance to the sexual nature of a relationship, the courts have gradually been forced to concede that a permanent heterosexual union—notwithstanding its lack of legal structure—may be taken to constitute a 'family'. What then of the permanent homosexual relationship? It is arguable that if two homosexual friends could avail themselves of Rent Act protection, there could then be no justification for excluding the 'two old cronies' whose relationship is merely platonic, for they can scarcely be distinguished for having failed to express their relationship in sexual terms[2]. It may well be that, in the light of the more variegated forms of social relationship current today, the only realistic criteria of familial nexus for the purpose of Rent Act succession are related to the degree of mutual commitment and permanence exhibited by the relationship under scrutiny.

18 [1979] 1 WLR 928, on appeal from *Joram Developments Ltd v Sharratt* [1979] 1 WLR 3. See (1980) 39 Cambridge LJ 31 (P. Tennant); (1980) 43 MLR 77 (C. H. Sherrin).

19 [1979] 1 WLR 3 at 5 per Megaw LJ.

20 The phrase 'member of the tenant's family' first appeared in statutory form in the Rent Restriction Act 1920, s. 12(1)(g). There is a clear canon of statutory construction which requires that 'the words of an Act will generally be understood in the sense which they bore when it was passed.' See *Maxwell on Interpretation of Statutes* (12th edn., London 1969), p. 85; *Helby v Rafferty* [1979] 1 WLR 13 at 25f. per Stamp LJ.

1 There is a certain irony in the fact that the statutory tenant in *Carega Properties SA v Sharratt* [1979] 1 WLR 928 had been Lady Salter, the widow of Salter J who, in 1925, had contemplated the clear possibility that the statutory reference to 'family' in the Rent Act legislation might well be 'equivalent to "household" . . .' (see *Salter v Lask* [1925] 1 KB 584 at 587 per Salter J; (1980) 39 Cambridge LJ 31 at 32, 34).

2 See (1980) 39 Cambridge LJ 31 at 34f. (P. Tennant); B. Berkovits, [1981] JSWL 83: 'The Family and the Rent Acts: Reflections on Law and Policy'.

(2) Transmission on desertion or divorce

Occupation by a husband or wife in a dwelling-house let on a protected or statutory tenancy is regarded, for the purpose of the Rent Act, as occupation by the other spouse also[3]. Thus if a husband has a statutory tenancy of a dwelling-house and resides there with his wife, the statutory tenancy will continue even if the husband subsequently deserts, so long as the wife remains in residence. The landlord is not entitled to refuse rent tendered by the wife in such circumstances, since such payment by her 'feeds' the husband's original tenancy[4]. Even if the deserted wife cannot afford to continue to pay the rent, she cannot be removed from possession without a court order, which might well be suspended if she has no alternative accommodation[5]. Furthermore, she may be able to obtain payment of her rent as a component of an entitlement to supplementary benefit[6]. However, none of these protective measures (apart from supplementary benefit) is available in respect of a de facto wife who has been deserted, even though the relationship was of long standing and even though the woman has borne the tenant's children[7].

On divorce, the court granting the decree of dissolution has power to order a transfer of one spouse's interest in a protected tenancy to the other spouse, subject to the transferee taking over all liabilities[8]. Moreover, in the case of a statutory tenant, the court may order that one spouse shall cease to be entitled to live in the dwelling-house and that the other spouse shall be deemed to be henceforth the statutory tenant[9]. A more general power to transfer a tenancy from one spouse to another on divorce is conferred by the Matrimonial Causes Act 1973[10].

3 Matrimonial Homes Act 1967, s. 1(5).
4 Matrimonial Homes Act 1967, s. 1(5). See, however, *Penn v Dunn* [1970] 2 QB 686, where the Court of Appeal held that section 1(5) does not apply in favour of a wife against whose husband a possession order has already been made on the ground of non-payment of rent. The husband's statutory tenancy is terminated by the making of such a possession order, with the result that the wife no longer qualifies within section 1(1) of the 1967 Act as the spouse of a person 'entitled to occupy a dwelling house . . .'
5 There is a danger, however, that a deserted wife may be unaware that her husband has ceased to pay the rent, and she may therefore neglect to tender rent herself. If, in this situation, a possession order is made against the husband, it used to be that the deserted wife thereafter had no locus standi to apply (under Rent Act 1977, s. 100) for a suspension of the order or postponement of the date for possession. In *Penn v Dunn* [1970] 2 QB 686, the Court of Appeal held that the making of the possession order ended the husband's statutory tenancy and, with it, not only his entitlement to occupy but hers as well. See D. A. Nevitt and J. Levin (1973) 36 MLR 345 at 359: 'Social Policy and the Matrimonial Home.' The Law Commission recommended that the law be amended to ensure that a possession order does not destroy a wife's *locus standi* under Rent Act 1977, s. 100. See Law Commission, *Third Report on Family Property: The Matrimonial Home (Co-ownership and Occupation Rights) and Household Goods* (Law Com No. 86, June 1978), paras. 2.42ff. This useful reform has now been enacted in the Housing Act 1980, s. 75(3).
6 See The Supplementary Benefit (Requirements) Regulations 1980 (S.I. 1980/1299), reg. 15.
7 See *Colin Smith Music Ltd v Ridge* [1975] 1 WLR 463.
8 Matrimonial Homes Act 1967, s. 7(2). This power may be exercised irrespective of a prohibition against assignment contained in the tenancy agreement.
9 Matrimonial Homes Act 1967, s. 7(3).
10 See Matrimonial Causes Act 1973, s. 24(1)(a); *Thompson v Thompson* [1976] Fam 25; *Rodewald v Rodewald* [1977] Fam 192.

5. PROTECTION UNDER THE RENT ACT[11]

The foregoing pages of this chapter have given a brief account of the conditions which attach to eligibility for full protection under the Rent Act 1977. The categories of tenancy which at present fall within the ambit of this protection are the 'regulated' protected tenancy and the 'regulated' statutory tenancy[12]. The implications of the Rent Act protection which applies to these tenancies may be gathered under four broad heads: (1) security of tenure, (2) restriction of rents, (3) prohibition of unlawful premiums, and (4) restriction of the landlord's right to levy distress. These heads will now be considered in turn.

(1) Security of tenure

If a tenant qualifies as either a 'protected tenant' or a 'statutory tenant' for full protection under the Rent Act, he automatically acquires a certain security of tenure. If the tenant is not prepared to vacate his dwelling-house voluntarily, his landlord cannot lawfully obtain possession without (i) terminating his contractual tenancy (if such is still in force) and (ii) obtaining a court order for possession, thereby terminating the statutory tenancy which arises ex hypothesi at the end of the contractual tenancy[13]. A court will make a possession order against a protected or statutory tenant only on the grounds specified in the Rent Act 1977[14]. Some of these grounds are discretionary grounds for the recovery of possession; others are mandatory.

(a) *Discretionary grounds for possession under the Rent Act*

It is made clear by the Rent Act 1977 that no order for possession will be made in favour of the landlord *unless*

(i) the court considers it 'reasonable to make such an order'[15], *and*

11 See A. Arden, *Housing: Security and Rent Control* (London 1978).

12 Before the commencement of the Housing Act 1980, protected and statutory tenancies under the Rent Act were, in either case, either 'regulated' tenancies or 'controlled' tenancies, with the result that the Rent Act in effect covered four different kinds of tenancy: (1) regulated protected, (2) regulated statutory, (3) controlled protected, and (4) controlled statutory. The distinction between 'controlled' and 'regulated' tenancies was largely historical. 'Controlled' tenancies were essentially those tenancies which were granted prior to 6 July 1957, and were governed by a different method of rent restriction from that which obtains in respect of 'regulated' tenancies. By 1980, fewer than 2,000 'controlled' tenancies remained in England and Wales, and the preservation of this distinct category of tenancy had become unnecessary and highly inconvenient. The Housing Act 1980, s. 64(1) thus provides for automatic conversion of almost all 'controlled' tenancies into 'regulated' tenancies, with the result that, for all practical purposes, the protected and statutory tenancies covered by the Rent Act may now be taken to be 'regulated' tenancies.

13 Protection for residential occupiers who are not statutorily protected tenants is conferred by the Protection from Eviction Act 1977, s. 3, as amended by the Housing Act 1980, s. 69(1).

14 See A. Arden (1976) LAG Bulletin 280, (1978) LAG Bulletin 10, 186, (1979) LAG Bulletin 11: 'Grounds for Possession'. For a critical study of possession proceedings under the Rent Act, see SHAC, *A Fair Hearing? Possession Hearings in the County Court* (April 1977).

15 See *Cumming v Danson* [1942] 2 All ER 653; *Williamson v Pallant* (1924) 131 LT 474; *Warren v Austen* [1947] 2 All ER 185; *Fisher v Macpherson* 1954 SLT (Sh Ct) 28.

(ii) *either* the court is satisfied that 'suitable alternative accommodation' is available for the tenant or will be available for him when the order takes effect[16],
or the circumstances are such as are specified in any of the Cases in Part I of Schedule 15 of the Rent Act 1977[17].

The Cases contained in Part I of Schedule 15 are as follows:

Case 1 The tenant has failed to pay or tender any rent lawfully due or is in breach of any lawful obligation of the tenancy (express or implied). It has, incidentally, been held that if the terms of a tenancy agreement expressly prohibit use of the premises for an immoral purpose, there is no breach by reason merely of the fact that two persons live together as man and wife[18].

Case 2 The tenant has been guilty of 'nuisance' or 'annoyance' to adjoining occupiers, or has been convicted of using the dwelling-house or allowing the dwelling-house to be used for immoral or illegal purposes. 'Nuisance' and 'annoyance' bear an ordinary non-technical meaning, connoting such activities as would disturb a reasonable occupier of normal sensitivity. It has been held to amount to nuisance or annoyance for a tenant to entertain overnight a visitor of the opposite sex[19]. However, it might be thought today that this represents a somewhat hypersensitive response on the part of the adjoining occupier. Social mores have changed dramatically over the last 25 years[20]. Yet this is simply another illustration of the way in which the 'black letter' law of landlord and tenant interacts with the life styles and values of residential tenants. This area of the law, like so many other areas of 'black letter' law, provides an accurate index of changing social perceptions.

Case 3 The tenant has been guilty of waste, neglect or default thereby causing the condition of the dwelling-house to deteriorate.

Case 4 The tenant's ill-treatment has caused the deterioration of furniture provided for use under the tenancy.

Case 5 The tenant has given notice to quit, and the lordlord has relied on that notice to his prejudice (e.g., by contracting to sell or let the property to a third party).

Case 6 The tenant has assigned or sublet the whole dwelling-house without consent.

16 See Rent Act 1977, s. 98(1)(a), (4), Sch. 15, Part IV, paras. 3–6, as amended by Housing Act 1980, Sch. 25, para. 58. See also *Siddiqui v Rashid* [1980] 1 WLR 1018.
17 Rent Act 1977, s. 98(1)(b), (5) as added by Housing Act 1980, s. 66(3).
18 See *Heglibiston Establishment v Heyman* (1978) LAG Bulletin 35.
19 See *Benton v Chapman* (1953) CLY 3099.
20 See, for instance, *Heglibiston Establishment v Heyman*, supra. It was held by the Court of Appeal in *Legg v Coole and Sheaff* (1978) LAG Bulletin 189, that there is no obligation on a prospective tenant

Case 7 This Case has now been repealed[1].

Case 8 The tenant was a service tenant of the landlord and, that employment having now ceased, the landlord reasonably requires the dwelling-house for occupation as a residence for some person engaged in his whole-time employment. The tenant against whom this case is raised must have been in the landlord's employment at the beginning of the tenancy, but need not have known that the tenancy was intended to be co-terminous with his employment[2].

Case 9 The dwelling-house is 'reasonably required' by the landlord[3] for occupation as a residence for himself or any son or daughter of his over 18 years of age, or his father or mother or his father-in-law or mother-in-law. If there are joint landlords, the dwelling-house must be reasonably required as a residence for both or all[4]. There is a special proviso to Case 9 in the form of a 'greater hardship' test. No possession order may be made under Case 9 if the court is satisfied that,

> having regard to all the circumstances, including the question whether other accommodation is available for the landlord or the tenant, greater hardship would be caused by granting the order than by refusing to grant it[5].

Case 10 The tenant has been charging excessive rent on sublettings.

It is clear that the foregoing Cases deal either with wrongdoing on the part of the tenant or with the requirements of the landlord. The onus rests upon the landlord to prove one or more of the relevant grounds for possession, and even when this onus has been discharged the court[6] still retains discretion to adjourn possession proceedings (or suspend or put back the date of possession under a possession order) for such period or periods or on such terms as it thinks fit[7]. Cases 1 to 10 are indeed discretionary, in the sense that the court will order possession only if it considers such an order to be 'reasonable'. Often the draconian effect of eviction will render it unreasonable to grant a possession order even though the facts fall clearly within one of the Cases.

---

to tell a landlord who does not enquire into the matter that he is not married to the person with whom he intends to live.

1 Housing Act 1980, s. 152(3), Sch. 26.
2 See *Royal Crown Derby Porcelain Co v Russell* [1949] 2 KB 417.
3 See *Richter v Wilson* [1963] 2 QB 426 at 430 per Willmer J.
4 *McIntyre v Hardcastle* [1948] 2 KB 82.
5 Rent Act 1977, Sch. 15, Part III, para. 1.
6 The court concerned with possession proceedings is usually the county court, although, where the value of the property is great, it may be the High Court.
7 Rent Act 1977, s. 100, as amended by Housing Act 1980, s. 75. In granting discretionary relief under s. 100 of the 1977 Act, the court must lay down conditions relating to the payment of rent and arrears (if any), except in cases of 'exceptional hardship' or where such an order would otherwise be 'unreasonable' (see Housing Act 1980, s. 75(2)). The court's powers under Part I of Schedule 15 of the Rent Act 1977 are not subject to the constraints imposed by the Housing Act 1980, s. 89(1) (see Housing Act 1980, s. 89(2)(c)). If the landlord agrees to the arrangement, it

(b) *Mandatory grounds for possession under the Rent Act*

Part II of Schedule 15 of the Rent Act 1977 sets out certain grounds which, if proved, lead *automatically* to the making of a possession order against the tenant[8]. However, these grounds all require that the landlord should have given the tenant written notice before the commencement of the tenancy that he might seek to repossess under the relevant Case. The Cases in Part II of Schedule 15 are as follows:

Case 11[9] The landlord is an 'owner-occupier' who now seeks to recover possession from the tenant on the ground that one of the conditions set out in Part V of Schedule 15, paragraphs (a) and (c) to (f) is satisfied. The conditions contained in Part V are the following:

(*a*) the dwelling-house is required as a residence for the owner or any member of his family who resided with the owner when he last occupied the dwelling-house as a residence;
(*b*) the owner has retired from regular employment and requires the dwelling-house as a residence;
(*c*) the owner has died and the dwelling-house is required as a residence for a member of his family who was residing with him at the time of his death;
(*d*) the owner has died and the dwelling-house is required by a successor in title as his residence or for the purpose of disposing of it with vacant possession;
(*e*) the dwelling-house is subject to a mortgage, made by deed and granted before the tenancy, and the mortgagee—
   (i) is entitled to exercise a power of sale conferred on him by the mortgage or by section 101 of the Law of Property Act 1925; and
   (ii) requires the dwelling-house for the purpose of disposing of it with vacant possession in exercise of that power; and
(*f*) the dwelling-house is not reasonably suitable to the needs of the owner, having regard to his place of work, and he requires it for the purpose of disposing of it with vacant possession and of using the proceeds of that disposal in acquiring, as his residence, a dwelling-house which is more suitable to those needs.

This is perhaps the most problematic of the Cases contained in Part II of Schedule 15. Case 11 is similar to Case 9, but must be distinguished in the following respects. Case 11 provides a mandatory ground of possession: there is no requirement that the court consider it 'reasonable' to make an order for

---

is open to the Department of Health and Social Security to deduct rent payments at source from any entitlement which the tenant may have to supplementary benefit. These amounts, plus a weekly proportion of any arrears, are then paid by the Department to the landlord, on condition that the landlord does not proceed for possession. See Supplementary Benefit (Deduction and Payment to Third Parties) Regulations 1980 (S.I. 1980/983), reg. 3.

8 Rent Act 1977, s. 98(2). In making an order for possession under Part II, the court may not postpone the giving up of possession to a date later than 14 days after the making of that order, unless 'it appears to the court that exceptional hardship would be caused by requiring possession to be given up by that date' (see Housing Act 1980, s. 89(1)). Even where 'exceptional hardship' is present, possession cannot be postponed to a date later than six weeks after the making of the court order.

9 Amended by Housing Act 1980, s. 66(1), Sch. 7.

possession[10]. Case 11 requires that the landlord must himself have occupied the dwelling-house as his residence before letting it to the present tenant. The landlord must have served a written notice on the tenant by the commencement of the tenancy to the effect that possession might be recovered under this Case.

Case 11 is primarily relevant to the owner-occupier who wishes to recover a dwelling-house for residence by himself or by a member of his family. The dwelling-house may be required as a residence for a somewhat wider category of person than under Case 9, in that the phrase 'member of his family' is construed as including de facto relationships on the analogy of eligibility for succession to a statutory tenancy[11]. There is no 'greater hardship' test, and it need not be proved that the dwelling-house is 'reasonably' required as a residence: it is enough that it is 'required'[12]. Moreover, if two or more persons are joint owners of a dwelling-house, the court has jurisdiction to make an order for possession under Case 11 even though the house is required as a residence for only one of the owners[13]. In essence, the main purpose of Case 11 is that

> a landlord who is living in his own house should be free to take up a post in another part of the country or abroad and to let his home to a tenant, secure in the knowledge that when the job is finished and he wants to return home he can, on giving the proper notice, come back and resume life in his own home, without being confronted with all the difficulties which a landlord who seeks possession under [Case 9] has to overcome[14].

Case 12[15] The landlord has let the dwelling-house on a protected tenancy before his retirement and one of the conditions set out in Part V of Schedule 15, paragraphs (b) to (e) is satisfied[16]. This Case is primarily relevant to the situation where the property is required as a retirement home for the landlord or for a member of his family. However, the landlord need not have bought the property 'with a view to occupying it as his residence at such time as he might retire from regular employment'[17].

Case 13 The dwelling-house has been let on an out-of-season letting (e.g., of a holiday home) for a period not exceeding eight months.

Case 14 The dwelling-house is the subject of a vacation letting (not exceeding twelve months) of student lodgings.

Case 15 The dwelling-house is required as a residence for a minister of religion as a place from which to perform the duties of his office.

10 This ground of possession is subject to the powers of the court as specified by Housing Act 1980, s. 89, p. 447, ante.
11 See p. 438, ante.
12 See *Kennealy v Dunne* [1977] QB 837.
13 *Tilling v Whiteman* [1980] AC 1. See K. J. Gray (1980) 39 Cambridge LJ 27: 'The Rent Act: Recovery of Possession by a Joint Lessor'. Compare *Lloyd v Sadler* [1978] QB 774, p. 435, ante.
14 *Kennealy v Dunne* [1977] QB 837 at 849 per Stephenson LJ.
15 As amended by Housing Act 1980, s. 66(2), (4), Sch. 7.
16 See p. 447, ante.
17 This intention was required by Case 12 in its original form in Schedule 15 of the Rent Act 1977, but is now made unnecessary by Housing Act 1980, s. 66(4).

Case 16 The dwelling-house is required for occupation by an agricultural employee.

Case 17 A farmhouse has become redundant on amalgamation under the Agriculture Act 1967, and is now required for occupation by an agricultural employee.

Case 18 This Case relates to other redundant farmhouses.

Case 19 The dwelling-house has been let under a 'protected shorthold tenancy'.

Case 19 has been added by the Housing Act 1980 to the Cases contained in Part II of Schedule 15 of the Rent Act 1977[18]. It provides a mandatory ground for the recovery of possession of property let on a 'protected shorthold tenancy'. Although introduced at the end of a long list of Cases providing grounds for the recovery of possession, Case 19 enjoys a significance which belies its deceptively innocuous position, for it strikes at the very basis of protected status under the Rent Act[19].

A 'protected shorthold tenancy' is defined as a protected tenancy which is granted after the commencement of the Housing Act 1980 'for a term certain of not less than one year nor more than five years', and which satisfies the other conditions specified in the statute[20]. It must be a tenancy which cannot be terminated by the landlord before the expiry of the term except in pursuance of a provision for re-entry or forfeiture for non-payment of rent or breach of any other obligation of the tenancy[1]. The landlord must, not later than the beginning of the tenancy, have given the tenant a valid notice stating that the tenancy is to be a protected shorthold tenancy[2]. A 'fair rent' registration must have been in force in relation to the dwelling-house at the commencement of the tenancy (or application for such made within 28 days of the commencement of the tenancy)[3]. It is also provided that the new 'protected shorthold tenancy' will be capable of termination by the tenant before the expiry of the term certain by means of a written notice of the appropriate length given to the landlord[4].

If a protected shorthold tenant does not voluntarily give up possession at the end of his term certain, the landlord may commence proceedings for possession not later than three months after the expiry of a further written notice indicating

18 Housing Act 1980, s. 55(1).
19 See A. Arden (1980) LAG Bulletin 33: 'A New Rent Act'; (1980) *New Statesman* 50 (11 January 1980): 'Turning the Poor out of Doors'; (1980) LAG Bulletin 266f.
20 Housing Act 1980, s. 52(1).
1 Housing Act 1980, s. 52(1)(a).
2 Housing Act 1980, s. 52(1)(b).
3 Housing Act 1980, s. 52(1)(c). Since a 'fair rent' now takes effect only from the date of registration, p. 453, post, and since the determination of an application may well be delayed by many months, it is quite possible that in relation to a shorthold letting of, say, one year, no 'fair rent' will ever come into force. Such a result would utterly frustrate the intended trade-off between fair rent and security of tenure in respect of shorthold lettings.
4 The appropriate length of notice is one month if the term certain is two years or less, and three months if it is more than two years (Housing Act 1980, s. 53(1)).

to the tenant that possession will be sought under Case 19[5]. As is the case with all protected tenancies under the Rent Act, no shorthold tenant may lawfully be evicted except by order of the court, but there is in the Housing Act 1980 one remarkable provision which reflects the tenor of the new law relating to shorthold tenancies. It appears that if, in proceedings for possession under Case 19, a court is of opinion that 'it is just and equitable to make an order for possession' in relation to a dwelling-house, it 'may treat the tenancy under which the dwelling-house was let as a protected shorthold tenancy', notwithstanding that no notice was given by the landlord at the commencement of the tenancy indicating the existence of a protected shorthold tenancy, and notwithstanding that no 'fair rent' registration has ever been obtained in respect of the property[6]. This provision, if applied, will effectively enable the court to deem many ordinary protected tenancies granted after the commencement of the Housing Act 1980 to be 'protected shorthold tenancies', with the result that, without warning to the tenants in question, those tenancies become subject to the automatic ground of possession contained in Case 19[7].

The introduction of the 'protected shorthold tenancy' was a politically motivated device intended to turn the flank of the protective policy embodied in the Rent Act. At one level, it was doubtless a genuine attempt to entice owners to release more residential property on to the housing market by the promise of easily recoverable possession after short-term occupation[8]. However, the underlying motive behind the shorthold tenancy has been seen by some as consisting of a much more far-reaching political concern to emasculate the social philosophy of the Rent Act legislation, by redressing the balance of bargaining power on the housing market this time in favour of the owner of private property[9]. The innovation of the shorthold tenancy is an implicit repudiation of the idea that residential tenants may acquire 'social rights of property' in their homes.

The concept of the shorthold tenancy is not itself entirely new, having been the subject of several private member's Bills introduced unsuccessfully in

5 This notice must itself be of at least three months in duration. The county court's discretion to postpone the possession order which is made mandatory by Case 19 is limited by the Housing Act 1980. The maximum suspension of any order for possession is for a period of 14 days, extendable in cases of 'exceptional hardship' for a period not exceeding six weeks from the date of the possession order (Housing Act 1980, s. 89(1)).

6 Housing Act 1980, s. 55(2). Compare Rent Act 1977, Sch. 15, Part II, Cases 11 and 12.

7 The provision has been described as 'peculiar and dangerous . . . virtually a loophole within a loophole' (Mr J. Tilley MP). An unsuccessful attempt was made to remove the provision at the committee stage of the House of Commons' consideration of the Housing Bill 1980 (*Parliamentary Debates, House of Commons, Official Report* (Standing Committee F), Cols. 1165ff. (13 March 1980)).

8 However, it can be argued that the last major measure of 'de-control' in the housing area, the Rent Act 1957, was followed not by an increase but rather by a marked decrease in the availability of private residential lettings. See *Social Trends No. 11* (London 1981), p. 144 (Table 9.3); M. Partington, op. cit., 14f.; J. Hillman (1980) 53 New Society 17: 'The shrinking pool of private-rented housing'. The statistical evidence seems to suggest that the removal of Rent Act protection is more closely correlated with re-sale on the open freehold market.

9 The Labour Party is pledged to an early repeal of the shorthold provisions in their present form. See *Parliamentary Debates, House of Commons, Official Report* (Standing Committee F), Col. 1180 (Mr G. Kaufman, Opposition Spokesman on Housing) (18 March 1980).

Parliament by Sir Brandon Rhys Williams MP[10]. However, even these Bills contained certain important forms of protection for the tenant which are ignored in the shorthold tenancy provisions now in force under the Housing Act 1980[11]. Although Case 19 cannot, of course, have any application to protected tenancies granted before the commencement of the 1980 Act, it can be anticipated that few protected tenancies will now be granted except on the terms of a shorthold tenancy (which may be for as short a period as one year)[12]. This result, when taken in conjunction with the right given to public sector tenants to purchase their own homes in fee simple[13], may well reverse the terms of trade on the private rental market decisively in favour of the landlord. Those who cannot afford to buy their own home, who do not for financial reasons qualify for a mortgage loan, who are not eligible for available local authority housing, will be thrown even more helplessly upon the mercy of an increasingly constricted market in private residential lettings.

It is not difficult to see how the introduction of the shorthold tenancy strikes at the basis of Rent Act protection for the residential tenant. The entire purpose of the Rent Act is to mitigate the disparity in bargaining power otherwise evident in a situation of free contracting on the private rental market. This legislative purpose has hitherto been achieved by substituting for the normal operation of market forces a protective scheme which guarantees for the residential tenant certain rights not grounded in contract but founded upon status[14]. This purpose is severely jeopardised by the innovation of the shorthold tenancy, which at least partially relegates the basis of the tenant's protection to the realm of contract. The shorthold tenancy also offends the fundamental premise that the twin tenets of long-term security of tenure and restriction of rents together constitute an indivisible basis for the protected status of the tenant under the Rent Act[15]. Although a shorthold tenant will enjoy security of tenure during his term, he is by definition deprived of long-term security. Thus the shorthold tenancy separates, for the first time since 1920, the twin prongs of Rent Act protection, and, if section 55(2) of the Housing Act 1980 is widely

10 See, for instance, the Housing (Shorthold Tenancies) Bill introduced on 19 May 1976 (*Parliamentary Debates, House of Commons, Official Report* (1975–76), Vol. 911, Col. 1445), and on 30 January 1979 (Ibid. (1978–79), Vol. 961, Col. 1240).

11 Several safeguards were unsuccessfully proposed at the committee stage in the House of Commons' consideration of the Housing Bill 1980 (see *Parliamentary Debates, House of Commons, Official Report* (Standing Committee F), Cols. 1125f. (11, 13 March 1980)). These included amendments which would have ensured (1) that no shorthold tenancy could be granted to a person who was immediately before the grant a protected or statutory tenant; (2) that the relevant dwelling-house should be vacant for a continuous period of at least 6 months immediately preceding the commencement of the Housing Act 1980; (3) that the landlord be required to give a right of 'first refusal' to any sitting shortholder where the landlord wished to create a new shorthold on the termination of an expired shorthold; (4) that the Rent Officer be required to countersign a written shorthold lease, doing so only after satisfying himself that the parties were 'aware of their rights and obligations under shorthold tenure.'

12 There is, of course, the additional possibility that landlords will continue to use non-exclusive occupation agreements, thereby circumventing the Rent Act in its entirety.

13 See p. 463, post.

14 See p. 419, ante.

15 See p. 416, ante.

invoked, the tenant may even lose the benefit conferred by the statutory restriction of rents[16].

Case 20[17] This case relates to lettings granted to members of the regular armed forces of the Crown.

'*Overcrowding*' There is one other situation in which, irrespective of the nature of the tenancy involved, an order for possession will be made virtually automatically. This situation occurs where a dwelling-house is 'overcrowded' within the meaning of the Housing Act 1957 in circumstances which render the occupier guilty of an offence[18]. In such a case, the occupier's immediate landlord can obtain possession under section 101 of the Rent Act 1977, but this provision is restricted in its scope to 'a dwelling-house which consists of premises used as a separate dwelling by members of the working classes or of a type suitable for such use'[19].

(2) Restriction of rents

A second implication of protected status under the Rent Act is that a measure of statutory control is exerted over the rent which may lawfully be charged by the landlord[20].

Both landlord and tenant have a statutory right to apply to the local rent officer for registration of a 'fair rent' in respect of the dwelling which is the subject of the tenancy[1]. Once a fair rent has been registered, the maximum rent recoverable in respect of any contractual period is limited to the registered rent[2]. If the tenant has agreed to pay more, the excess is not recoverable by the landlord. Indeed, if the tenant has actually paid a rent in excess of the registered rent, he may recover that excess from the landlord either directly or by

16 See p. 450, ante.
17 Housing Act 1980, s. 67.
18 Under section 77(1) of the Housing Act 1957, a dwelling-house is deemed to be 'overcrowded' at any time when 'the number of persons sleeping in the house either—(a) is such that any two of those persons, being persons ten years old or more of opposite sexes and not being persons living together as husband and wife, must sleep in the same room; or (b) is, in relation to the number and floor area of the rooms of which the house consists, in excess of the permitted number of persons as defined in the Sixth Schedule to this Act.' In determining the number of persons sleeping in a house, no account is taken of a child under one year old, and a child aged between one and ten is reckoned as 'one-half of a unit' (Housing Act 1957, s. 77(2)). See also *Somma v Hazlehurst and Savelli* [1978] 1 WLR 1014 at 1028f., p. 429, ante.
19 Rent Act 1977, s. 101(2). It has been said in another context that the phrase 'houses intended to be used as dwellings for the working classes' is today 'anachronistic' and liable to be condemned as containing 'a hint of paternalism' (*Chorley Borough Council v Barratt Developments (North West) Ltd* [1979] 3 All ER 634 at 637 at 639 per Blackett-Ord VC). Yet it is surprising that class-biased perceptions of social stratification should be preserved in modern legislation. See also R. G. Lee [1980] Conv 281: 'The Demise of the Working Classes'.
20 See F. A. Hayek, et al., *Verdict on Rent Control* (London 1972); M. Partington, op. cit., p. 239ff.
1 Rent Act 1977, s. 67(1).
2 Rent Act 1977, s. 44(1).

deducting it from any rent still due to the landlord[3]. When the contractual period of the tenancy comes to an end, the tenant need not pay more than the last contractual rent or the relevant registered rent, whichever is the lower[4].

The application for registration of a fair rent is determined in the first instance by the rent officer. If the rent officer's determination is not accepted by the parties, the matter can be referred to a rent assessment committee. As soon as a fair rent is registered, it is effective from the date of registration[5], and must normally remain unaltered for a period of two years[6]. It is, however, possible for the landlord and the tenant to make a joint application for cancellation or alteration of the fair rent, or for either to allege that by reason of a relevant change of circumstance the registered rent no longer represents a fair rent[7].

It is possible to apply for a 'certificate of fair rent' before any letting occurs, simply in order to discover what rent would be considered by the rent officer to represent a fair rent if the premises were subsequently let[8]. The rent indicated in the certificate will determine the amount of any fair rent registrable on an application made within two years of the date of issue of the certificate[9].

In determining the amount of a fair rent, regard must be had to all the circumstances (other than the personal circumstances of the parties), and in particular to the age, character, locality and state of repair of the dwelling-house and the quantity, quality and condition of any furniture provided for use under the tenancy[10]. The rent officer is statutorily directed to disregard any element of 'scarcity value' within a particular 'locality' when determining a fair rent[11]. The motive underlying this direction is plainly that any inherent amenities or advantages possessed by the dwelling-house in question should be reflected in the rent assessed, but that no regard should be had to any element in the market rent which would confer on the landlord a wholly unmeritorious increase in rent simply because of an excess of demand over supply in any 'locality'[12]. It is

3 Rent Act 1977, s. 57. No excess may be recovered more than two years after the date of payment (see Rent Act 1977, s. 57(3), and compare the six year limitation period imposed on the landlord's right to sue for arrears of rent, p. 406, ante).

4 However, if the contractual rent at that point is lower than the rent which is registrable as a fair rent, the landlord may increase the rent to a fair rent by serving notices of increase in the prescribed form, and such increase will normally be phased over a period of one year (Housing Act 1980, s. 60(3)).

5 Housing Act 1980, s. 61(1), amending Rent Act 1977, s. 72. Before the commencement of the Housing Act 1980, registrations were normally back-dated to the date of application, thus conferring a substantial advantage on the tenant.

6 Housing Act 1980, s. 60(1), (3), amending Rent Act 1977, s. 67, Sch. 8. Any permitted increase in rent is phased in over one year. Before the commencement of the Housing Act 1980, registered fair rents were immune from alteration for three years. The changes effected by the Housing Act 1980 are symptomatic not only of the impact of inflation on the real value of rents but also of a new legislative sympathy for the entrepreneurial impulse as applied to the housing market.

7 Rent Act 1977, s. 67(3).

8 Rent Act 1977, s. 69(1).

9 Housing Act 1980, Sch. 25, para. 40, amending Rent Act 1977, s. 69(4).

10 Rent Act 1977, s. 70(1). See also *Mason v Skilling* [1974] 1 WLR 1437; *London Housing and Commercial Properties Ltd v Cowan* [1977] QB 148.

11 Rent Act 1977, s. 70(2).

12 It has been held that the rent officer, in deciding whether there exists an overall scarcity to be discounted, must 'pick a really large area, an area that really gives [him] a fair appreciation of

likewise clear that the means of the individual landlord and tenant are irrelevant to the level of a fair rent, as is any disrepair or defect for which the tenant is responsible or any improvement effected by the tenant himself (unless required by the terms of the tenancy)[13].

It is the duty of the rent officer to prepare and keep up to date a register of all registered rents within the area of his jurisdiction. The register is open to inspection, and in practice provides a means of ensuring that rents applicable in the same locality are broadly comparable. However, one of the most controversial questions in the matter of rent assessment has always been the question whether the determination of a fair rent should be reached having regard to the registered rents of comparable dwellings or having regard to a notional level of return on the landlord's capital investment[14].

(3) Prohibition of unlawful premiums

It is a criminal offence for any person to require or receive a premium or loan as a condition of, or in connection with, the grant, renewal or continuance of a protected tenancy[15]. The court may order the repayment of any illicit premium. The term 'premium' includes any pecuniary consideration received in addition to rent, and may indeed be sufficiently wide to cover any payments required or received otherwise than as rent, e.g., an excessive deposit on the letting[16]. The Rent Act contains a similar prohibition against premiums and loans on the assignment of protected tenancies, although a proper apportionment of outgoings or money spent on alterations and fixtures is permissible[17]. For the purpose of all these provisions, the charging of an excessive price for furniture which the tenant is required to purchase under the terms of his tenancy is regarded as a premium[18].

It is a criminal offence for the landlord to require the payment of rent excessively in advance of the rental period in respect of which the rent is payable[19]. Such requirement of payment in advance is void and unenforceable, and rent for any rental period to which a prohibited requirement relates is

---

the trends of scarcity and their consequences' (*Metropolitan Property Holdings Ltd v Finegold* [1975] 1 WLR 349 at 354 per Lord Widgery CJ). Thus the presence in the immediate vicinity of some amenity (e.g., a school, zoo, theatre or swimming pool) which has not been provided by the landlord cannot be a ground for raising a fair rent.

13 Rent Act 1977, s. 70(3). Perhaps surprisingly, the Court of Appeal held in *Williams v Khan* (1981) Times, 17th February, that the fact that a closing order has been made in respect of a dwelling-house under Housing Act 1957, s. 17, on the ground that it is unfit for human habitation, is not of itself conclusive evidence that the fair rent registrable in respect of the premises should be either nil or nominal. See, however, *Black v Oliver* [1978] QB 870, [1978] Conv 407. See also [1980] Conv 389.

14 See (1979) LAG Bulletin 128: 'Fair Rents and Capital Values'.

15 Rent Act 1977, s. 119.

16 Rent Act 1977, s. 128(1), as substituted by Housing Act 1980, s. 79. An excessive deposit comprises any deposit which exceeds one-sixth of the annual rent (see Housing Act 1980, s. 79(c)).

17 Rent Act 1977, s. 120.

18 Rent Act 1977, s. 123.

19 Rent Act 1977, s. 126.

irrecoverable from the tenant and, if already paid, may be recovered from the landlord.

(4) Restriction of the right to levy distress

Distress is an ancient common law remedy designed to facilitate the recovery of arrears of rent from a defaulting tenant[20]. There is, however, one important restriction on the right to distrain upon the tenant's goods where the tenancy concerned is a protected or statutory tenancy under the Rent Act. No distress for the rent of any dwelling-house let on such a tenancy may be levied except with the leave of a county court[1]. On an application for leave to levy distress, the county court is possessed of the same powers with respect to adjournment, stay, suspension, postponement and otherwise as are conferred by section 100 of the Rent Act 1977 in relation to proceedings for possession of such a dwelling-house[2].

6. RESTRICTED CONTRACTS

We must now deal with the protection given under the Rent Act to 'restricted contracts'[3]. In many respects this protection is similar to, but much less sophisticated and certainly much less effective than, the protection conferred by the Rent Act upon 'protected' and 'statutory' tenancies.

A 'restricted contract' is defined in the Rent Act 1977 as

> a contract . . . whereby one person grants to another person, in consideration of a rent which includes payment for the use of furniture or for services, the right to occupy a dwelling as a residence[4].

A restricted contract may be either a tenancy or a licence, but there is a clear implication in the Rent Act that a restricted contract can never exist unless the occupier is entitled to 'exclusive occupation' of at least some accommodation within a dwelling-house[5]. But where the occupier has such a right, it is irrelevant that he is also entitled to 'the use in common with any other person of other rooms or accommodation in the house.'

Several other situations are expressly brought within the ambit of the 'restricted contract'. A tenancy which is precluded from being a protected tenancy by reason only of the 'resident landlord' exception[6] is declared to constitute a restricted contract 'notwithstanding that the rent may not include payment for the use of furniture or for services'[7]. Similarly, the absence of a rent

20 See p. 405, ante. See also A. Arden (1978) LAG Bulletin 57: 'Distress for Rent'.
1 Rent Act 1977, s. 147(1).
2 See p. 446, ante.
3 Such contracts used to be called 'Part VI contracts, in the terminology of the Rent Act 1968.
4 Rent Act 1977, s. 19(2).
5 See Rent Act 1977, s. 19(6).
6 Rent Act 1977, s. 12, p. 432, ante.
7 Rent Act 1977, s. 20.

component in respect of furniture or services does not preclude the possibility of a restricted contract where the tenant has exclusive occupation of some accommodation, but shares the use of other accommodation in common either with his landlord *or* with his landlord and others[8].

The restricted contract thus defined applies to most contractual occupation licences. Such licences can never, of course, qualify as protected tenancies under the Rent Act simply by reason of the fact that they are 'licences' as opposed to 'tenancies'. However, as always, the contractual licensee, in order to claim even a restricted contract, must show that he is entitled to exclusive occupation of at least some part (e.g., a separate bed-sitting room) of the dwelling-house in question[9].

7. EXPRESS EXCLUSION FROM THE SCOPE OF THE 'RESTRICTED CONTRACT'

Certain residential arrangements are expressly excluded from possible status as a restricted contract. No restricted contract can arise where the relevant dwelling-house has a rateable value in excess of specified statutory limits[10]. Nor can a contract constitute a restricted contract if it creates a regulated tenancy[11]. No restricted contract can exist in relation to a letting by the Crown or by a government department[12], a protected tenancy as defined in the Rent (Agriculture) Act 1976[13], or a tenancy granted by a housing association or housing trust or by the Housing Corporation[14]. Nor can a restricted contract comprise any contract 'for the letting of any premises at a rent which includes payment in respect of board if the value of the board to the lessee forms a substantial proportion of the whole rent'[15].

8. THE EXTENT OF STATUTORY PROTECTION FOR RESTRICTED CONTRACTS

Restricted contracts fall within the jurisdiction of the area rent tribunal, which has power to provide certain forms of protection for occupiers under restricted

8 Rent Act 1977, s. 21. This provision is applicable, however, only where the tenant would have had a 'protected tenancy' but for the element of common user or the presence of a resident landlord (Rent Act 1977, s. 21(c)). In other words, the occupation cannot constitute a restricted contract if it is precluded from being a protected tenancy for some other reason, e.g., that the rateable value of the property lies outside the Rent Act limits.

9 Rent Act 1977, s. 21(a).

10 Rent Act 1977, s. 19(4). The limits designated are such as to rule out only luxury accommodation.

11 Rent Act 1977, s. 19(5)(a). Thus the borderline between the restricted contract and the protected tenancy is strictly preserved.

12 Rent Act 1977, s. 19(5)(b), as amended by Housing Act 1980, s. 73(2).

13 Rent Act 1977, s. 19(5)(d).

14 Rent Act 1977, s. 19(5)(e). The Housing Corporation is a public body which is statutorily empowered to purchase and develop land for lease or sale, and to lend money to and control the operations of housing associations. Its powers were greatly extended by the Housing Act 1974.

15 Rent Act 1977, s. 19(5)(c).

contracts by way of limited security of tenure and rent restriction. We shall now examine the protection available in respect of restricted contracts under the following heads: (1) security of tenure, (2) restriction of rents, and (3) prohibition of unlawful premiums.

(1) Security of tenure

Unfortunately the law governing security of tenure under restricted contracts differs according to whether the contract in question was granted before or after the commencement date of the Housing Act 1980.

(a) *Restricted contracts granted before the commencement of the Housing Act 1980*

Certain complicated provisions govern the law relating to security of tenure under restricted contracts concluded before the commencement of the Housing Act 1980. In general, the occupier under such a contract has in the first instance no security of tenure at all. However, the rent tribunal has power to order a postponement of any notice to quit which is served on the occupier, but this jurisdiction in matters of security of tenure is exercisable only in conjunction with an application to the rent tribunal for registration of a 'reasonable' rent[16].

Thus if after a restricted contract has been referred to a rent tribunal for rent registration, the landlord serves on the occupier a notice to quit the premises, that notice normally cannot take effect before the expiry of a period of six months following the tribunal's determination of the reference[17]. If a notice to quit is served before the occupier has made any application for rent registration, the occupier may refer the restricted contract to a rent tribunal for rent registration at any time *before* the expiry of the notice to quit. In this event, the protective jurisdiction of the rent tribunal will be activated by the reference in respect of rent, with the result that it is open to the tribunal to order a postponement of the effect of the notice to quit for a period of up to six months[18]. Further postponements may be granted in the discretion of the tribunal, although the tribunal may in any case substitute a shorter period than six months.

The protective powers of the rent tribunal are, of course, available in strict terms only where a notice to quit is required in order to terminate the restricted contract in question. No notice to quit is necessary in the case of either a fixed term tenancy or an occupation licence: both come to an end automatically in accordance with their terms.

Even where the rent tribunal's discretion to postpone possession has finally been exhausted, there exists one last protection for the occupier under a restricted contract. It is not lawful for the owner to enforce his right to possession except by proceedings in court[19].

16 See p. 459, post.
17 Rent Act 1977, s. 103(1).
18 Rent Act 1977, s. 104(1). However, even this limited security of tenure is lost if the occupier fails to apply to the tribunal within the period of the notice to quit (see Rent Act 1977, s. 104(1)(c)).
19 Protection from Eviction Act 1977, s. 3(1).

There is one provision in the Rent Act which overrides all the forms of protection which we have just discussed in relation to restricted contracts. A special ground of immediate recovery of possession is available to an owner-occupier who, by virtue of a restricted contract, has granted the right to occupy his dwelling to another person. Such an owner-occupier may recover possession on the expiry of a notice to quit if

> at the time the notice is to take effect, the dwelling is required as a residence for the owner-occupier or any member of his family who resided with him when he last occupied the dwelling as a residence[20].

This right of recovery is, however, constrained by certain conditions. *First*, the 'owner-occupier' must originally have occupied the dwelling in question 'as a residence'. *Second*, he must at or before the commencement of the restricted contract have given to the occupier a notice in writing 'that he is the owner-occupier within the meaning of [section 105].' *Third*, the owner-occupier must not occupy any part of the dwelling-house during the currency of the restricted contract.

(b) *Restricted contracts granted after the commencement of the Housing Act 1980*

The law relating to security of tenure is substantially different in respect of restricted contracts granted after the commencement of the Housing Act 1980. Sections 103 to 106 of the Rent Act 1977 have no application to such contracts[1]. Instead, it is provided that a court may grant a postponement of no longer than three months of any order for possession made in favour of the owner of the property[2]. It therefore becomes much easier for the owner to recover his property, but the limited security of tenure now enjoyed by the occupier under a post-1980 restricted contract is supplemented by the disappearance of the ground of recovery of possession conferred upon an 'owner-occupier' by section 105 of the Rent Act 1977. Moreover, the occupier under a post-1980 restricted contract cannot ultimately be evicted except by court order, even though he is merely a licensee[3].

(2) Restriction of rents

Either the lessor or the lessee under a restricted contract or the local authority

20 Rent Act 1977, s. 105. This provision is effectively the analogue of the mandatory ground for possession in relation to a regulated tenancy under Case 11 of the Rent Act 1977, Sch. 15, Part II, p. 447, ante.
1 Housing Act 1980, s. 69(3).
2 Rent Act 1977, s. 106A(2), (3), as added by Housing Act 1980, s. 69(2). In granting relief under section 106A of the Rent Act 1977, the court must impose conditions as to payment of rent and arrears, except in cases of 'exceptional hardship' or where such an order would otherwise be 'unreasonable' (see Rent Act 1977, s. 106A(4), as added by Housing Act 1980, s. 69(2)). However, the court's powers under section 106A are not subject to the restrictions contained in section 89 of the Housing Act 1980. Section 89 normally limits the court's power to postpone the date for the giving up of possession to a mere 14 days after the date of the court order. See, however, the exception made in the case of restricted contracts (Housing Act 1980, s. 89(2)(d)).
3 Protection from Eviction Act 1977, s. 3(2A), as added by Housing Act 1980, s. 69(1).

may refer the contract in question to a rent tribunal for the determination of a 'reasonable' rent[4]. The tribunal may then fix a 'reasonable' rent after making inquiries and hearing any representations made by either party[5]. The rent fixed is entered in a register of rents maintained by the relevant local authority[6], and may not be the subject of any reference to a rent tribunal during the following three years except where the lessor and lessee apply jointly for a reconsideration of the rent or where, by reason of a change of circumstance, the registered rent is no longer a reasonable rent[7]. In relation to registrations effected after the commencement of the Housing Act 1980, the period of immunity from reconsideration is reduced to two years[8]. It is illegal to require or receive any amount in excess of a registered rent[9], and any excess paid is recoverable by the occupier[10].

(3) Prohibition of unlawful premiums

The provisions of the Rent Act which prohibit certain premiums[11] are extended to apply to similar payments which are required as a condition of the grant, renewal, continuance or assignment of rights conferred by a restricted contract, so long as the rent payable under that contract is registered[12].

B. PUBLIC SECTOR TENANTS

So far we have examined the statutory code which governs residential tenancies in the private sector. We must now consider the law which regulates residential tenancies in what might broadly be termed the public sector. The tenancies included under this heading comprise not only those lettings granted by local authorities but also the quasi-public tenancies granted by such landlords as the Housing Corporation, the Commission for the New Towns, housing associations, housing trusts and housing co-operatives. We shall look at the statutory protection enjoyed under such tenancies with reference to the following features: security of tenure, restriction of rents, and the right to purchase the reversion in the rented property.

1. SECURITY OF TENURE

Certain important provisions relating to security of tenure are conferred on public and quasi-public tenants by the Housing Act 1980. Chapter II of Part I

4 Rent Act 1977, s. 77(1). In practice 'reasonable' rents are almost always higher than 'fair' rents in respect of the same premises.
5 Rent Act 1977, s. 78(2).
6 Rent Act 1977, s. 79(1).
7 Rent Act 1977, s. 80(2).
8 Housing Act 1980, s. 70(1), amending Rent Act 1977, s. 80(2).
9 Rent Act 1977, s. 81(1).
10 Rent Act 1977, s. 81(3).
11 See p. 454, ante.
12 Rent Act 1977, s. 122.

of this Act introduced the concept of the 'secure tenancy' in order to cover such tenancies. The definition of a 'secure tenancy' in many respects mirrors the definition of a 'protected tenancy' under the Rent Act 1977[13], but describes of course an entirely different phenomenon[14].

A tenancy under which 'a dwelling-house is let as a separate dwelling' is a 'secure tenancy' at any time when the conditions described in the Housing Act 1980 as respectively 'the landlord condition' and 'the tenant condition' are satisfied[15]. The essence of 'the landlord condition' is that the dwelling-house should belong to such bodies as a local authority, the Housing Corporation, the Commission for the New Towns, a housing association, housing trust or housing co-operative[16]. The essence of 'the tenant condition' is that the tenant

> is an individual and occupies the dwelling-house as his only or principal home; or, where the tenancy is a joint tenancy, that each of the joint tenants is an individual and at least one of them occupies the dwelling-house as his only or principal home[17].

Certain lettings are expressly excluded from the scope of the 'secure tenancy'. These exceptions are contained largely in Schedule 3 of the Housing Act 1980, and include long leases for a term exceeding 21 years[18], tenancies granted in conjunction with a contract of employment[19], and student lettings[20]. A tenancy granted by a local authority pursuant to the Housing (Homeless Persons) Act 1977 will not normally become a 'secure tenancy' until twelve months after the local authority has notified the applicant for accommodation that it regards him as 'homeless' within the meaning of that Act[1]. It is also provided that a tenancy may be excluded from security for a period of one year if granted to a person requiring temporary accommodation while seeking employment within the district or London Borough[2].

It is a term of every secure tenancy that the tenant may allow any persons to reside as lodgers in the dwelling-house[3]. However, he may not without the written consent of the landlord either sublet or part with possession of part of the

13 See p. 421, ante.
14 See Rent Act 1977, ss. 14–16, p. 431, ante. One very significant distinction between the protected tenancy and the 'secure tenancy' is that the latter term will generally include a 'licence (whether or not granted for a consideration) to occupy the dwelling-house' (Housing Act 1980, s. 48(1)), if the licence otherwise fulfils the conditions required of a 'secure tenancy'.
15 Housing Act 1980, s. 28(1). See generally A. Arden (1980) LAG Bulletin 207.
16 Housing Act 1980, s. 28(2), (4). It had been suggested, before the enactment of the Housing Act 1980, that local authority tenancies might well qualify as restricted contracts under the Rent Act. See *Lambeth London Borough Council v Udechuku* (1980) 41 P & CR 200; J. Davies (1976) LAG Bulletin 158; A. Arden (1980) LAG Bulletin 143. This possibility is now presumably foreclosed by the advent of the 'secure tenancy'; see also Housing Act 1980, Sch. 25, para. 36 (effective 3 October 1980 under the Housing Act 1980 (Commencement No. 1) Order (S.I. 1980/1406)).
17 Housing Act 1980, s. 28(3).
18 Para. 1.
19 Para. 2.
20 Para. 11.
1 Para. 5. The operation of the Housing (Homeless Persons) Act 1977 is described at p. 464, post.
2 Para. 6.
3 Housing Act 1980, s. 35(1).

dwelling-house[4]. A secure tenancy normally ceases to be a secure tenancy where the tenant sublets or assigns the whole of the property[5].

Security of tenure in relation to 'secure tenancies' takes two main forms. First, there is provision for one (and only one[6]) statutory succession on the death of the secure tenant. The succession operates in favour of that tenant's 'spouse'[7], provided that that person 'occupied the dwelling-house as his only or principal home at the time of the tenant's death'[8].

In default of a person qualifying on this ground, the secure tenancy will devolve upon any other 'member of the tenant's family' who has 'occupied the dwelling-house as his only or principal home throughout the period of twelve months ending with the tenant's death'[9]. It is interesting that, for the present purpose, there is for the first time a statutory definition of membership of a family. A person is to be regarded as 'a member' of another's 'family' if he is his spouse, parent, grandparent, child, grandchild, brother, sister, uncle, aunt nephew or niece, of 'if they live together as husband and wife'[10]. This definition provides a useful insight into the way in which we perceive the boundaries of kinship within a modern context of urban living[11].

4 Housing Act 1980, s. 35(2).

5 Housing Act 1980, s. 37(1), (2). An assigned tenancy remains secure, however, if assigned by order of the court under section 24(1)(a) of the Matrimonial Causes Act 1973 or if assigned to a person within the class of qualifying successors under section 30 of the Housing Act 1980 (see Housing Act 1980, s. 37(1)).

6 An amendment designed to produce parity with the private sector by allowing two statutory successions was defeated during the committee stage in the House of Commons' consideration of the Housing Bill 1980. See *Parliamentary Debates, House of Commons, Official Report* (Standing Committee F), Cols. 662ff. (26 February 1980). Compare succession under the Rent Act 1977, p. 436, ante.

7 The House of Commons also rejected an amendment which, if successful, would have given the same right of succession to 'any person living with the tenant as husband and wife' (see ibid., Cols. 675ff.). Such an amendment would have given equal status to the de facto wife, but the Government opposed the amendment on the ground that 'it is no part of the philosophy of this Bill to take a lead on an issue of social policy' (Mr G. Finsberg MP, Under-Secretary of State for the Environment). Compare, however, the insistence of the Opposition that 'in housing matters, one cannot dissociate housing from social policies' (Mr A. Roberts MP, ibid., Col. 682), and that 'quite rightly, every page of the Bill is redolent of social policy' (Mr G. Kaufman MP, ibid., Col. 682).

8 Housing Act 1980, s. 30(1), (2)(a), (3)(a).

9 Housing Act 1980, s. 30(1), (2)(b). A proposal to reduce this period to six months was rejected at committee stage for fear that, in conjunction with the wide definition of 'family', there might be a danger of relatives moving in with elderly tenants in order to qualify for succession to the tenancy. See *Parliamentary Debates, House of Commons, Official Report* (Standing Committee F), Cols. 673ff. (28 March 1980).

10 Housing Act 1980, s. 50(3). For this purpose, any relationship by marriage is treated as a relationship by blood, any relationship of the half blood as a relationship of the whole blood, any stepchild of any person as his own child, and any illegitimate person as the legitimate child of his mother and the reputed father.

11 There was at committee stage in the House of Commons' consideration of the Housing Bill 1980 an attempt to amend what is now section 50(3) by providing that membership of another's family should include 'cohabitants', where a 'cohabitant' was defined as 'such person, man or woman, whom the tenant designates by declaration in writing to be his cohabitant.' The purpose

The second measure of security of tenure conferred by the Housing Act 1980 on 'secure tenants' relates to the circumstances in which possession of a dwelling-house let on a secure tenancy may be recovered. A secure tenancy will not normally be terminable except by court order for possession[12], and the court will not be able to make an order for possession except on the grounds specified in Part I of Schedule 4 of the Housing Act 1980[13]. These grounds fall into three categories. The court will not be able to order possession on grounds 1 to 6 unless the court 'considers it reasonable to make the order'[14]. No order will be made on grounds 7 to 9 unless the court is 'satisfied that suitable accommodation will be available for the tenant when the order takes effect'[15]. No order will be made on grounds 10 to 13 unless the court is satisfied both that it would be 'reasonable' to make the order and that 'suitable accommodation' will be available[16].

All the provisions conferring security of tenure on 'secure tenants' have retrospective effect, and therefore apply even to tenancies created before the commencement of the Housing Act 1980[17].

2. RESTRICTION OF RENTS

In relation to local authority (i.e., council) tenants there exists no formal mechanism for the control of rent levels. An attempt was made in the Housing Finance Act 1972 to institute a 'fair rent' scheme to cover public sector tenants[18],

---

of this amendment (put down by Mr J. Tilley MP at the instance of the Campaign for Homosexual Equality) was to 'ensure that families should include cohabitees of the same sex.' The CHE had argued that homosexual couples contribute no less in financial terms to the costs of providing public housing and that it is therefore 'unjust that, while being obliged to finance the provision of housing services and having the same needs of them, they should be debarred by statute from enjoying equal rights with their fellow citizens.' The proposed amendment was rejected. See *Parliamentary Debates, House of Commons, Official Report* (Standing Committee F), Cols. 675ff., 968 (28 February 1980).

12 Housing Act 1980, s. 32(1). Where a court order for possession is sought in respect of a fixed-term secure tenancy, the provisions of section 146 of the Law of Property Act 1925 (relief against forfeiture) apply, with the exception of section 146(4) of that Act, p. 407, ante. See Housing Act 1980, s. 32(3).

13 Housing Act 1980, s. 34(1). The court has some degree of discretion (similar to that conferred by section 100 of the Rent Act 1977) to adjourn proceedings, to stay or suspend execution of a possession order, and to postpone the date for possession (see Housing Act 1980, s. 87).

14 Housing Act 1980, s. 34(2)(a), (3)(a). These grounds relate to non-payment of rent or other breach of covenant by the tenant (Ground 1), nuisance or annoyance caused by the tenant (Ground 2), deterioration in the condition of the dwelling-house or the landlord's furniture by reason of the tenant's neglect or default (Grounds 3 and 4), false statement by the tenant inducing the grant of the tenancy (Ground 5) and the temporary nature of accommodation (Ground 6).

15 Housing Act 1980, s. 34(2)(b), (3)(b). These grounds relate to overcrowding (Ground 7), intended demolition or reconstruction of the dwelling-house (Ground 8), and the charitable status of the landlord (Ground 9).

16 Housing Act 1980, s. 34(2)(c), (3)(c). These grounds relate to the existence of special needs on the part of other persons (e.g., physically disabled persons) (Grounds 10, 11 and 12), and the excessive nature of any accommodation which has devolved on a secure tenant by succession (Ground 13).

17 Housing Act 1980, s. 47.

18 See Housing Finance Act 1972, s. 49ff.

but since such a scheme would have had the effect in most cases of raising rent levels, the scheme was abandoned in 1975[19]. The current position is that local authorities are vested with a wide power to 'make such reasonable charges . . . as they may determine'.[20] This power must be exercised by local authorities in conjunction with the statutory rent rebate scheme contained in the Housing Finance Act 1972[1].

A 'fair rent' scheme operates in relation to quasi-public tenancies (such as those granted by the Housing Corporation, housing associations and housing trusts) in much the same manner as the 'fair rent' scheme which currently governs protected tenancies[2].

3. THE RIGHT TO PURCHASE THE REVERSION IN RENTED PROPERTY

One further (and highly controversial) feature of the charter of rights supposedly conferred by the Housing Act 1980 on residential tenants in the public sector consists of the right to acquire either the freehold or a long lease in a dwelling-house which is currently the subject of a secure tenancy. The introduction of this right represents an important movement towards what was once called 'the emergence of a property-owning, particularly a real-property-mortgaged-to-a-building-society-owning, democracy'[3].

The Housing Act 1980 confers upon a secure tenant the right (if his dwelling-house is a house) to acquire the freehold in it, and (if his dwelling-house is a flat) to be granted a long lease with respect to it[4]. The right to buy arises only after the tenant has been a secure tenant for a period of not less than three years, although neither the landlord nor the dwelling-house need have been the same during the whole of that period[5]. The secure tenant has the right to buy at the price which the property would achieve on the open market minus a discount ranging from 33 per cent to 50 per cent, depending on the duration of the pre-existing secure tenancy[6]. The prospective purchaser has a statutory right to financial assistance towards his purchase. He is entitled to leave the whole or part of the purchase price outstanding on the security of the dwelling-house or, if the landlord is a housing association, to have the whole or part of that amount advanced to him on the same security by the Housing Corporation[7].

19 See Housing Rents and Subsidies Act 1975, s. 1(1).
20 Housing Act 1957, s. 111(1).
1 See Housing Finance Act 1972, s. 18ff.; Rent Rebate and Rent Allowance Schemes (England and Wales) (No. 2) Regulations 1980 (S.I. 1980/1555).
2 Rent Act 1977, ss. 86ff.
3 *Pettitt v Pettitt* [1970] AC 777 at 824 per Lord Diplock. For further discussion of the 'property-owning democracy', see p. 509, post.
4 Housing Act 1980, s. 1(1). A 'long lease' for this purpose comprises a term of not less than 125 years (Housing Act 1980, s. 16(1)(b)).
5 Housing Act 1980, s. 1(3).
6 Housing Act 1980, s. 7(1). The purchaser is liable, however, to repay that discount in whole or part if he disposes of the dwelling-house within five years of the purchase by further conveyance of the freehold, assignment of a leasehold interest or the granting of a lease for a period exceeding 21 years (Housing Act 1980, s. 8(1), (2), (3)).
7 See Housing Act 1980, s. 1(1)(c).

C. GENERAL PROVISIONS

Having looked at the law relating to private sector and public sector lettings, we must now advert to other protective legislation which is concerned with the provision, terms, quality and secure enjoyment of residential accommodation.

1. THE HOUSING (HOMELESS PERSONS) ACT 1977

The Housing (Homeless Persons) Act 1977 is a highly significant piece of social legislation. Its basic aim is to impose upon the relevant housing authority[8] a clear statutory duty to house homeless families, and to provide distinct guidelines for determining whether a homeless family falls within the responsibility of one local authority rather than another. The mischief against which the Act is directed is the social evil whereby homeless persons are endlessly passed from one local authority to another and often from one department to another within the same local authority[9].

In effect, the 1977 Act imposes on a local authority a duty to provide full and permanent rehousing for homeless families within its area of responsibility. This duty is, however, graded in accordance with a number of criteria, and in some circumstances the duty is of a lesser degree, consisting in reality only of an obligation to furnish a homeless person with 'advice and appropriate assistance' towards securing accommodation. In order to enforce the local authority's ultimate legal obligation to provide permanent housing, a person must show (1) that he is 'homeless', (2) that he has a 'priority need for accommodation' and (3) that he did not become homeless 'intentionally'[10].

The Act contains a definition of homelessness. A person is 'homeless' for the purpose of the Act 'if he has no accommodation'[11]. He is to be regarded as having no accommodation if

> there is no accommodation . . . which he, together with any other person who normally resides with him as a member of his family or in circumstances in which the housing authority consider it reasonable for that person to reside with him . . . is entitled to occupy[12].

A person is regarded as being 'threatened with homelessness' if it is 'likely that he will become homeless within 28 days'[13].

A 'priority need for accommodation' is defined as arising in circumstances where a homeless person has dependent children who are residing with him or is homeless as a result of any emergency such as flood, fire or any other disaster

8 The relevant housing authority is the District Council (in both metropolitan and non-metropolitan authority areas), except in London, where the appropriate authority is the relevant London Borough Council.

9 For a critical examination of the legislation, see P. W. Robson and P. Watchman [1981] JSWL 1, 65: 'The Homeless Persons' Obstacle Race'.

10 Housing (Homeless Persons) Act 1977, s. 4(5).

11 Housing (Homeless Persons) Act 1977, s. 1(1).

12 Housing (Homeless Persons) Act 1977, s. 1(1).

13 Housing (Homeless Persons) Act 1977, s. 1(3).

or is vulnerable as a result of old age, mental illness or physical disability or other special reason[14].

The Act introduces the novel concept of intentional homelessness. For the purpose of the Act, a person becomes 'homeless intentionally' if he

> deliberately does or fails to do anything in consequence of which he ceases to occupy accommodation which is available for his occupation and which it would have been reasonable for him to continue to occupy[15].

However, any act or omission 'in good faith on the part of a person who was unaware of any relevant fact is not to be treated as deliberate . . .'[16].

In relation to a person who can show that he is homeless, has a priority need, and is not intentionally homeless, a local authority is under a 'duty . . . to secure that accommodation becomes available for his occupation'[17]. In relation to a person who, in the same circumstances, is threatened with homelessness, the local authority is under a 'duty . . . to take reasonable steps to secure that accommodation does not cease to be available for his occupation'[18]. The duty of the local authority is further calibrated downwards, becoming a mere duty to render 'advice and appropriate assistance' where a person fails to establish any one or more of the three criteria which activate the full legal duty imposed statutorily upon the local authority[19]. Responsibility as between local authorities in respect of particular homeless persons is allocated largely on the basis of a person's 'local connection' with one or other local authority area[20].

A problem which has arisen in the context of the definition of intentional homelessness concerns whether a housing authority is entitled to refuse to provide accommodation for a family unit one member of which has been found to be intentionally homeless. This question arose in *Lewis v North Devon District Council*[1], where the de facto husband of an applicant under the Housing (Homeless Persons) Act 1977 had become homeless by virtue of the fact that he had voluntarily given up employment which carried with it tied accommodation on a farm. The housing authority took the view that he had thereby rendered himself intentionally homeless but Woolf J held that his de facto spouse was not precluded in principle from making a separate application under the 1977 Act even though the man might indirectly benefit from her eligibility. He expressed the view that Parliament had not intended to treat members of the same family

14 Housing (Homeless Persons) Act 1977, s. 2(1).
15 Housing (Homeless Persons) Act 1977, s. 17(1).
16 Housing (Homeless Persons) Act 1977, s. 17(3).
17 Housing (Homeless Persons) Act 1977, s. 4(5).
18 Housing (Homeless Persons) Act 1977, s. 4(4).
19 Housing (Homeless Persons) Act 1977, s. 4(2). Under section 4(3), this duty may extend to securing accommodation for the applicant 'for such period as [the housing authority] consider will give him a reasonable opportunity of himself securing accommodation for his occupation.' It has been held that a 14 day period allowed by a housing authority as a matter of general policy is insufficient for this purpose (see *Lally v Kensington and Chelsea Royal Borough* (1980) Times, 27th March).
20 Housing (Homeless Persons) Act 1977, s. 5(4). See *R v Bristol City Council, ex parte Browne* [1979] 1 WLR 1437.
1 [1981] 1 All ER 27.

unit as tainted automatically by the misconduct of one member of that unit. However, he also ruled that on the facts of the present case the woman applicant had acquiesced in her cohabitee's decision to terminate his employment, knowing that the accommodation was tied. Woolf J thus made it clear that his construction of the 1977 Act did not mean that a housing authority should close its eyes to the conduct of the other members of the family. On the contrary the fact that the Act required consideration of the family unit as a whole indicated that it would be perfectly proper in the ordinary case for the authority to look at the family as a whole and assume, in the absence of material which indicated the contrary, where the conduct of one member of the family was such that he should be regarded as having become homeless intentionally, that was conduct to which the other members of the family were a party.

It is perhaps the definition of intentional homelessness which has caused the courts most difficulty in construing the Housing (Homeless Persons) Act 1977[2]. Under section 3(1) of the Act, when a person applies to a housing authority for accommodation or for assistance in obtaining accommodation, and the authority has reason to believe that he may be homeless or threatened with homelessness, that authority must make 'appropriate enquiries'. Such enquiries may, of course, establish whether the applicant became homeless 'intentionally', but uncertainty surrounds the extent of the investigation which must be carried out before the housing authority may safely conclude that the applicant did indeed become homeless 'intentionally'. It is clear that, in discharging its duty under the Act, the authority must observe the rules of natural justice, e.g., by allowing both sides of the case to be heard and considered[3]. The authority is not under a 'positive duty to conduct detailed CID-type inquiries' in determining the basis of homelessness[4]. However, where comprehensive enquiries have been made, the result of those enquiries is highly relevant in proceedings brought in connection with the 1977 Act. In *Dyson v Kerrier District Council*[5], it was discovered by the housing authority that the applicant had misrepresented the reasons for her loss of secure accommodation. Here the applicant had deliberately surrendered the tenancy of a council flat and had thereafter taken a short-term tenancy of a house let only on a winter letting. When she was rendered homeless on the termination of this short-term letting, the Court of Appeal held that the housing authority could properly base a finding of intentional homelessness on the facts surrounding the termination of the former (council) tenancy. The applicant was therefore excluded from the scope of the 1977 Act, notwithstanding

2 On the difficulties experienced in the application of the Housing (Homeless Persons) Act 1977, see A. Arden (1979) LAG Bulletin 283, (1980) LAG Bulletin 14, 64, 91, 117, 187, 211, 295.

3 See *Afan Borough Council v Marchant* (1980) LAG Bulletin 15; *Stubbs v Slough Borough Council* (1980) LAG Bulletin 16. The housing authority may be in breach of the 1977 Act if it fails to consider all the *relevant* elements in each case (see, e.g., *Barry v London Borough of Newham* (1980) LAG Bulletin 142). It seems that there will be a violation of the rules of natural justice where a council adopts a general policy of treating as 'intentionally' homeless all persons evicted for rent arrears, instead of considering each case individually (see *Williams v Cynon Valley Council* (1980) LAG Bulletin 16).

4 *Lally v Kensington and Chelsea Royal Borough* (1980) Times, 27th March, per Browne-Wilkinson J.

5 [1980] 1 WLR 1205.

that she was the mother of a young child and had moved to the short-term accommodation in order to live next door to her sister, with whom she had previously shared the council flat[6].

Yet more problems have been raised under the Housing (Homeless Persons) Act 1977 in relation to foreigners who arrive in the United Kingdom without having arranged long-term accommodation. In *De Falco v Crawley Borough Council*[7], two Italian families left secure accommodation in Italy in order to come to live in this country. The Court of Appeal held that, by quitting permanent accommodation abroad, the two families had rendered themselves intentionally homeless in this country[8]. However, it can be argued that in *De Falco* the Court of Appeal failed to take full account of either the relevant EEC Regulations[9] or the Code of Guidance prepared for use in conjunction with the Housing (Homeless Persons) Act 1977[10]. In any event, the later decision of the Court of Appeal in *R v Hillingdon London Borough Council, ex parte Streeting*[11] seems to indicate that there may still be a statutory duty even in respect of persons who arrive in this country without permanent accommodation and who have no 'local connection' with the area of any housing authority in the United Kingdom.

It has been held that a local authority which fails to perform its duty under the Housing (Homeless Persons) Act 1977 can be sued for damages in tort by the aggrieved homeless person[12]. In such an action, however, the plaintiff would be required to discharge a fairly difficult onus of proof, e.g., that he had indeed suffered damage by reason of the local authority's default.

2. THE PUBLIC HEALTH AND HOUSING ACTS

Important protection for residential occupiers is provided by the statutory conferment of certain powers on local authorities to control the quality of

6 See A. Arden (1980) LAG Bulletin 187 at 189: 'Intentional Homelessness'.

7 [1980] QB 460. See (1980) 43 MLR 703 (J. M. Steiner and D. C. Hoath).

8 According to Lord Denning MR, 'the local authority at Crawley are very concerned about these two cases. They have Gatwick airport within their area. If any family from the Common Market can fly into Gatwick, stay a month or two with relatives, and then claim to be unintentionally homeless, it would be a most serious matter for their overcrowded borough. They should be able to do better than King Canute. He bade the rising tide at Southampton to come no further. It took no notice. He got his feet wet. I trust the councillors of Crawley will keep theirs dry against this new advancing tide' ([1980] QB 460 at 478).

9 See EEC Regulation No. 1612/68, art. 9(1), which provides that 'a worker who is a national of a member state and who is employed in the territory of another member state shall enjoy all the rights and benefits accorded to national workers in matters of housing.'

10 This Code states that 'in assessing whether a person has become homeless intentionally, it will be relevant to consider the most immediate cause of that homelessness rather than events that may have taken place previously. It would be inappropriate to treat as intentionally homeless a person who gave up accommodation to move in with relatives or friends who then decided after a few months that they could no longer continue to accommodate him' (para. 2.18). The Code is not, of course, a binding statute (see *De Falco v Crawley Borough Council* [1980] QB 460 at 478 per Lord Denning MR), but its terms are highly persuasive.

11 [1980] 1 WLR 1425. See [1981] JSWL 124.

12 See *Thornton v Kirklees Metropolitan Borough Council* [1979] QB 626.

housing. These powers are contained in the Public Health Acts and the Housing Acts, and are designed to ensure that all residential housing meets minimum standards of amenity and adequacy in respect of public health. The legislation applies to all premises irrespective of whether they are owner-occupied or rented[13].

The first ground on which a local authority is empowered to intervene in cases of alleged housing disrepair is related to the concept of 'statutory nuisance'. A 'statutory nuisance' arises where any premises are 'in such a state as to be prejudicial to health or a nuisance'[14]. The situations thus covered include such eventualities as structural defects in houses, blocked drains and lavatories, and disrepair caused by damp. A complaint relating to a statutory nuisance may be made to the local environmental health officer, who has power to serve on the owner of the premises an 'abatement notice' requiring that the condition be remedied[15]. If no appropriate action is taken, the local authority must issue a summons in the magistrates' court either for an order requiring the relevant repair to be effected or, in the last resort, for a 'closing order'[16]. If the local authority fails to institute proceedings for the abatement of a statutory nuisance, it is open to an aggrieved private individual to lay a complaint before the magistrates' court under section 99 of the Public Health Act 1936, whereupon the court may impose a fine on the property owner and order the local authority to abate the nuisance in question.

Various courses are open to a local authority in respect of a dwelling which is unfit for human habitation. The local authority's powers in this respect are conferred by the Housing Acts. It is for the environmental health officer to determine in the first instance whether a house is 'unfit for human habitation'[17]. This phrase is defined as relating to such matters as repair, stability, freedom from damp, natural lighting, ventilation, water supply, drainage and sanitary conveniences, and the presence or absence of facilities for storage, preparation and cooking of food and for the disposal of waste water[18]. If a house is found to be 'unfit for human habitation' but can be repaired at reasonable cost, the local authority has power to serve a notice on the owner requiring him to effect the necessary repairs[19]. If the property is not capable of repair at reasonable cost,

13 See generally T. Hadden, *Housing: Repairs and Improvements* (London 1979).

14 Public Health Act 1936, s. 92.

15 It is no remedy simply to keep the property empty (see *Lambeth London Borough Council v Stubbs* (1980) Times, 15th May).

16 Public Health Act 1936, s. 94.

17 A private individual may request a justice of the peace to require the local authority to determine whether a dwelling-house is 'unfit for human habitation' within the meaning of the Act (Housing Act 1957, s. 157(2)). This is often the most effective means of forcing a local authority to take action in cases of severely substandard housing. According to Tom Hadden (op. cit., p. 67), the section 157 procedure is frequently 'the best and quickest method of securing a closing order and rehousing for the occupants.'

18 Housing Act 1957, s. 4(1). In *Summers v Salford Corpn* [1943] AC 283, the House of Lords held that a house was 'unfit for human habitation' where a bedroom window had jammed because the sash-cord had broken.

19 Housing Act 1957, s. 9. See D. Morgan [1979] Conv 414: 'Unfit Housing: The Issue of Reasonable Cost'.

the local authority may require the owner to cease to use the property for human habitation[20], or may compulsorily purchase the property and repair it for short-term use, or may issue either a 'demolition order' or a 'closing order'[1].

The local authority also has special powers to order repairs and renovations in houses used for the purpose of multiple occupation. More generally, local authorities now have powers under the Housing Act 1974 to undertake slum clearance and rehabilitation of property by declaring a 'housing action area'[2].

3. RENT BOOKS

Where a person is granted a right to occupy any premises as a residence in consideration of a rent which is payable weekly, it is the duty of the landlord to provide a 'rent book or other similar document' for use in respect of the premises[3]. However, no such duty exists if the rent 'includes a payment in respect of board and the value of that board to the tenant forms a substantial proportion of the whole rent'[4]. Any rent book provided in pursuance of the statutory duty must contain such details as the name and address of the landlord, particulars of the rent, details of the statutory rent allowance scheme operated by the local authority, and other prescribed information. It is an offence for a landlord to fail to comply with the statutory requirements relating to the provision of rent books[5], but such failure does not invalidate the tenancy or licence or render the rent unrecoverable[6].

The statutory rules relating to rent books are often ignored by landlords, and there is a strong argument for an extension and reinforcement of those rules in the interest of increased residential security for tenants[7].

4. THE PROTECTION FROM EVICTION ACT 1977

The Protection from Eviction Act 1977 is the modern expression of the timeless social sentiment which abhors the forcible eviction of a man and his family from their home. We noted before[8] that the roots of this general distaste for violent eviction are buried in the 'seisin-possession' concept which has influenced the English law of real property from its earliest days. Regardless of the merits of the case, eviction is not merely the forcible vacation of property. It is the destruction of someone's way of life.

20 Housing Act 1957, s. 16(4).
1 Housing Act 1957, s. 17. See *Williams v Khan* (1981) Times, 17th February, p. 454, ante.
2 Housing Act 1974, s. 36. See T. Hadden, op. cit., p. 130ff.
3 Landlord and Tenant Act 1962, s. 1(1). It is irrelevant for this purpose whether the occupier is a tenant or a mere licensee.
4 Landlord and Tenant Act 1962, s. 1(2).
5 Landlord and Tenant Act 1962, s. 4.
6 *Shaw v Groom* [1970] 2 QB 504.
7 See D. C. Hoath [1978–79] JSWL 3: 'Rent Books: the Law, its Uses and Abuses'.
8 See p. 50, ante.

It is against this background that the Protection from Eviction Act 1977 provides important additional protection for 'residential occupiers'—a term which includes any person 'occupying . . . premises as a residence, whether under a contract or by virtue of any enactment or rule of law'[9]. The term does not therefore include trespassers or casual lodgers. Under section 1 of the Act, a criminal offence is committed if any person unlawfully deprives the residential occupier of his occupation, or attempts so to do, unless that person proves that he believed on reasonable grounds that the residential occupier had ceased to reside in the premises. A criminal offence is likewise committed if any person

> does acts calculated to interfere with the peace or comfort of the residential occupier or members of his household, or persistently withdraws or withholds services reasonably required for the occupation of the premises[10].

However, this head of criminal liability for harassment arises only if that person can be shown to have acted

> with intent to cause the residential occupier . . . (a) to give up the occupation of the premises . . . or (b) to refrain from exercising any right or pursuing any remedy in respect of the premises . . .[11]

A person convicted of any offence under section 1 is liable to a maximum fine of £400 and imprisonment for a maximum period of two years[12].

Further protection is conferred on tenants by section 2 of the Protection from Eviction Act 1977, which provides that

> Where any premises are let as a dwelling on a lease which is subject to a right of re-entry or forfeiture, it shall not be lawful to enforce that right otherwise than by proceedings in the court while any person is lawfully residing in the premises or part of them.

Likewise, if an unprotected tenant remains in residence after the end of his tenancy, it is unlawful for the owner to recover possession of the property except through court order[13].

There is also a provision in the 1977 Act to the effect that where a notice to quit is required, no notice shall be valid (whether given by a landlord or a tenant) unless it is in writing, contains certain prescribed information, and is

9 Protection from Eviction Act 1977, s. 1(1).
10 Protection from Eviction Act 1977, s. 1(3).
11 Ibid. See also *R v Phekoo* (1981) 125 Sol Jo 239.
12 Protection from Eviction Act 1977, s. 1(4). See A. J. Ashworth [1978–79] JSWL 76: 'Protecting the Home through Criminal Law'. The Court of Appeal held in *McCall v Abelesz* [1976] QB 585 that the provision now contained in section 1(3) of the 1977 Act does not create a new statutory cause of action for civil damages in favour of an evicted occupier. However, this does not preclude an aggrieved tenant from suing for damages for trespass, assault and breach of covenant for quiet enjoyment. In *Edwards v Marbyn* (1980) LAG Bulletin 17, a wrongfully evicted tenant was awarded £150 for assault, £50 for inconvenience, £25 special damages, £475 aggravated damages and £300 exemplary damages. The landlord was also fined £200 with £50 costs.
13 Protection from Eviction Act 1977, s. 3(1), (2A), as added by Housing Act 1980, s. 69(1). The Protection from Eviction Act 1977 applies similarly to an occupier under a 'rental purchase agreement' as defined by Housing Act 1980, s. 88(4) (see Housing Act 1980, Sch. 25, para. 61).

given not less than four weeks before the date on which it is to take effect[14]. No notice to quit is, of course, required in the case of a fixed term tenancy or licence. Where, however, a landlord is required to serve a notice to quit upon his tenant, the information prescribed for inclusion in the notice includes statements which assure the occupier that even after the notice to quit has expired the landlord must take possession proceedings in court before the occupier can be lawfully evicted. The occupier must also be informed of the possibility that he may have a protected tenancy or restricted contract, with their respective forms of residential protection, and that he may be able to obtain free legal advice relating to the tenancy or contract[15]. In other words, every effort must be made to ensure that the notice to quit does not have an intimidating impact on the occupier or inhibit his exercise of such rights as he may have at law.

5. TRESPASS AND THE RECOVERY OF POSSESSION FROM A STRANGER

Under the law relating to adverse possession[16], if the owner of property fails to take legal action to secure the eviction of a squatter or trespasser within twelve years of the entry of such a person upon his land, the owner is statutorily barred from recovering possession thereafter, and the intruder acquires a right to remain in possession[17].

This, however, is not to say that the law does not lend assistance to occupiers of land who are dispossessed by trespassers or squatters. A land-owner may invoke a speedy remedy against any person who occupies his land without his consent. The remedies available to the displaced owner and the circumstances in which they may be exercised have already been discussed[18].

14 Protection from Eviction Act 1977, s. 5(1).
15 See Notices to Quit (Prescribed Information) Regulations 1980 (S.I. 1980/1624) (operative 28 November 1980).
16 See p. 93f., ante.
17 Limitation Act 1980, s. 15(1), p. 95, ante.
18 See p. 103, ante.

CHAPTER 14

Licences, equities and constructive trusts

Throughout this book it has been emphasised that the law of property is not really about things: it is about people, their relationships, their values and their mutual obligations. We are now moving in this chapter into an area in which this characteristic of the law of property becomes particularly evident. We shall see, moreover, how certain dramatic developments of doctrine are beginning to accentuate the legal protection given to various forms of residential utility.

It is an intrinsic feature of the property relations of family members that these relations are normally marked by a greater degree of informality and by a lesser degree of specificity than are usually present in the equivalent property relations of strangers. For this simple truth there are many reasons. One reason is undoubtedly that the process of hard bargaining and clear definition of rights is in itself entirely alien to the spirit in which family interaction is normally conducted. Another reason is provided by the fact that, at least until the attainment of adulthood, the younger members of family groups are usually subject to some measure of economic disability. It is therefore more likely that such family members will become the beneficiaries of non-commercial transactions motivated by parental generosity. Yet another, and perhaps more subtle, explanation flows from the fact that the reciprocity which is so keenly sought in the hard-nosed bargaining of strangers is no less effectively secured in the family context—albeit by totally different means. Since family living implies at least some continuity of relationship between family members, the expected reciprocity of family transactions may well take many years to be realised. As William J. Goode has said, the continuity of family relationships

> means that husband and wife, as well as children, enjoy a much longer line of social credit than they would have if they were engaged in random social interaction with strangers. It also means that an individual can give more at one time to a family member, knowing that in the longer run this will not be a loss, for the other person (or someone else) is likely to reciprocate at some point[1].

The net result is that the members of family and kinship groups are often prone to participate in loose, informally based living arrangements which are negotiated—if they are discussed at all—not in clearly defined terms of legal entitlement, but rather in vaguely expressed terms of anticipated mutuality. It is our concern in this chapter to examine some of the law relating to informal 'family arrangements', bearing in mind the increasing frequency and diversity

1 *The Resistance of Family Forces to Industrialisation* in J. M. Eekelaar and S. N. Katz (ed.) *Marriage and Cohabitation in Contemporary Societies* (Toronto 1980), xiv.

of such arrangements in the modern social setting. The law of property ought, almost as a matter of definition, to apply indifferently to all property relationships arising out of cohabitation in a home legally owned by one member of the household, whether that cohabitation be heterosexual, homosexual, platonic, dual or multiple in nature. A not insignificant dimension is added to the law of 'family arrangements' by the problems of sharing accommodation with elderly (and perhaps incapacitated) relatives—a phenomenon which will undoubtedly increase in incidence as the relative proportion of old people in the community rises towards the end of this century and the present housing problem becomes even more acute[2].

It is extremely difficult to analyse the legal effect of informal family arrangements within the traditional categories of property and contract[3]. Indeed, such arrangements are in essence so unlegalistic that for many years the courts declined to attribute to family members any intention thereby to create legally actionable relationships. As Atkin LJ observed on one occasion[4], family arrangements

> are outside the realm of contracts altogether. The common law does not regulate the form of agreements between spouses. Their promises are not sealed with seals and sealing wax. The consideration that really obtains for them is that natural love and affection which counts for so little in these cold Courts ... The parties themselves are advocates, judges, Courts, sheriff's officer and reporter. In respect of these promises each house is a domain into which the King's writ does not seek to run, and to which his officers do not seek to be admitted.

It is no easier to ascribe to informal family arrangements consequences in the law of property, for so often the rights conferred are either wholly lacking in the clarity of definition which, in our law, marks out a right of property, or are otherwise vitiated by the very circumstance of informal creation (i.e., by non-compliance with some requirement of writing or sealed documentation).

For these reasons the law relating to family arrangements is somewhat haphazardly and incoherently gathered within the range of concepts to which we have devoted this chapter. We shall now look at the ways in which the courts have attempted to adapt the concepts of licence, equity and constructive trust in order to deal with the legal implications of loosely based family arrangements.

1. THE TRADITIONAL APPLICATION OF LICENCES, EQUITIES AND CONSTRUCTIVE TRUSTS

Each of the legal concepts which we examine in this chapter has a traditional application which we must use as a starting point in our discussion. In each case, the courts have today extended the orthodox understanding of each concept, in

2 See Central Statistical Office, *Social Trends No. 11* (London 1981), p. 15 (Chart 1.3: 1979-based population projections: by age groups).
3 See J. D. Davies (1979) 8 Sydney LR 578 at 580f.: 'Informal Arrangements Affecting Land'.
4 *Balfour v Balfour* [1919] 2 KB 571 at 579.

order to spell out the legal consequences of informal arrangements for cohabitation.

(1) Licences[5]

We have already noted the distinction between a licence and a lease[6]. The essential difference lies in the fact that a lease confers upon its grantee an estate or interest in the land; a licence does not. In the words of Vaughan CJ[7], a licence

> properly passeth no interest nor alters or transfers property in any thing, but only makes an action lawful, which without it had been unlawful.

In its narrowest application, then, a licence is a purely personal permission to be present upon land—a permission which legitimates what would otherwise be the tort of trespass.

A licence may take the form of a 'bare licence' (e.g., an invitation to a dinner party): a licence of this kind may be revoked at any time by giving reasonable notice[8]. Alternatively, a licence may take the form of a 'licence coupled with a proprietary interest' (e.g., a permission to enter another's land and there abstract something like timber or crops). Such a licence would, under these circumstances, be merely an adjunct to the grant of a proprietary interest (in this case a profit à prendre). A licence coupled with a proprietary interest is irrevocable, provided that the proprietary interest to which it pertains has been validly created by deed or by prescription (i.e., by long user). If this condition is satisfied, the licence effectively enjoys the same legal (and thus perpetual) character which attaches to the proprietary interest. It is therefore not only binding on the licensor and all third party purchasers from him, it is also capable of assignment to third parties[9].

A licence may also take the form of a 'contractual licence' which has been granted for value (e.g., the right to attend a football match as a spectator or to sit in a cinema). However, we shall deal with this type of licence later[10].

(2) Equities

'Equity', in the large sense, is of course the name given to that system of principles which has been devised over the centuries in order to act as a corrective of legal justice. Equity, said Christopher St Germain four hundred years ago, 'is ordained ... to temper and mitigate the rigour of the law[11].' Equity supplements the common law and, in so doing, modifies its effect. It

5 See H. G. Hanbury (1954) 13 Cambridge LJ 201, (1955) 14 Cambridge LJ 47: 'Licences, A Jonah's Gourd'.
6 See pp. 390, 422, ante. See generally I. J. Dawson and R. A. Pearce, *Licences relating to the occupation or use of land* (London 1979).
7 *Thomas v Sorrell* (1673) Vaugh 351.
8 See *Robson v Hallett* [1967] 2 QB 939.
9 *Webb v Paternoster* (1619) Palm 71; *Wood v Manley* (1839) 11 Ad & El 34; *James Jones & Sons Ltd v Earl of Tankerville* [1909] 2 Ch 440.
10 See p. 483ff., post.
11 *Doctor And Student* (17th edn., London 1787), p. 45.

achieves its objective through the granting of various kinds of equitable relief in circumstances where it would be unjust or unconscionable to permit a litigant to insist upon his legal rights to the exclusion or disadvantage of another[12].

For our present purpose the relevant point is that the benefit conferred on a litigant by the granting of equitable relief in derogation of another's strict legal rights is very often itself called 'an equity'. 'An equity' is simply the right to pray in aid the equitable jurisdiction of the court, and, of course, since the Judicature Acts 1873–1875, the administration of the legal and equitable jurisdictions has been fused and vested in all courts of the land. In cases of conflict the rules of equity prevail[13].

In a sense, the clearest example of 'an equity' is the right enjoyed by the beneficiary of a trust. Trusts are not recognised at all at common law, and thus the beneficiary behind a trust is dependent upon the equitable jurisdiction of the court for recognition of the essential feature of any trust, i.e., that legal rights of ownership are not conclusive of the allocation of benefit. The beneficiary benefits only because Equity precludes the legal owner (the trustee) from asserting his common law rights to the exclusion of beneficial enjoyment on the part of the 'cestui que trust'. However, as Upjohn J pointed out in relation to land[14],

> the Court of Equity has been careful to distinguish between two kinds of equities, first, an equity which creates an estate or interest in the land and, secondly, an equity which falls short of that.

The 'equity' enjoyed by the cestui que trust falls within the former category although sometimes regarded as an interest not in land but in proceeds of sale[15].

Equities which come within Upjohn J's latter category are sometimes referred to as 'mere equities', and comprise such claims to equitable relief as for instance the right, within the discretion of the court, to obtain rescission of a land transaction on the ground of undue influence, fraud or mutual mistake. A 'mere equity' is binding upon all persons other than a bona fide purchaser of a legal or equitable interest in the relevant land for value without notice[16]. Thus, if V is induced by fraud on the part of P to convey land to P, V's equity of rescission will be binding upon any subsequent purchaser, X, who buys an equitable interest in that land with notice of V's equity of rescission (see Fig. *66)*.

12 This is not to imply that Equity intervenes in all cases of moral wrong, for over the years the categories of case in which Equity will grant relief have, to a large degree, crystallised in accordance with the established canon of 'equitable maxims'. See *Snell's Principles of Equity* (27th edn. by R. E. Megarry and P. V. Baker, London 1973), p. 27ff.; R. P. Meagher, W. M. C. Gummow and J. R. F. Lehane, *Equity: Doctrines and Remedies* (Sydney, Melbourne, Brisbane and Perth 1975), paras. 302ff. See also the statement of Buckley J in *Re Telescriptor Syndicate* [1903] 2 Ch 174 at 195, that 'This court is not a court of conscience.' See also *Re Diplock* [1948] Ch 465 at 481f.

13 Judicature Act 1873, s. 25(11). See R. P. Meagher, W. M. C. Gummow and J. R. F. Lehane, op. cit., paras. 210ff.

14 *Westminster Bank Ltd v Lee* [1956] Ch 7 at 18.

15 See p. 220ff., ante.

16 See *Phillips v Phillips* (1862) 4 De GF & J 208. See M. Neave and M. Weinberg, (1978) 6 University of Tasmania LR 24, 115: 'The Nature and Function of Equities'.

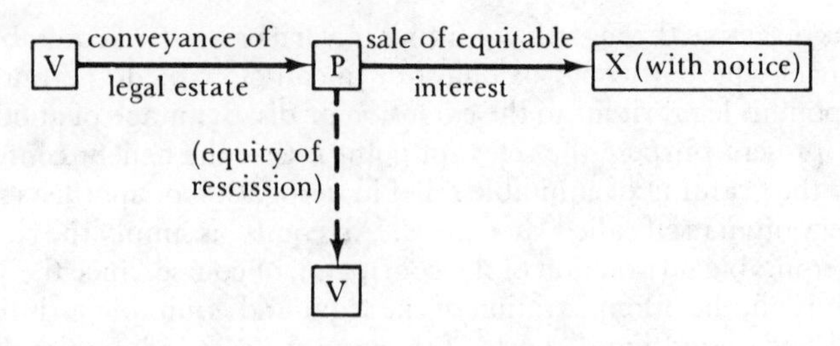

Fig. 66

This rule is simply an application of the equitable doctrine of notice at a point further down that hierarchy of interests which seems at first sight to range from legal interests in land through equitable interests in land to 'mere equities' affecting land. However, we shall go on in due course to see that it is, in many respects, unhelpful and even inaccurate to suppose that a quantum step intervenes between the equitable interest in land and the 'mere equity'. Ultimately both are but graded instances of conceptually the same idea—that the equitable jurisdiction will interpose itself in order to prevent the unconscionable assertion of legal title. Herein lies the key to much that will be said in this chapter.

(3) Constructive trusts

English law has long treated the constructive trust as an analogous institution to the express trust. In this traditional sense a constructive trust is regarded as arising in certain fairly well defined circumstances such as the assumption of trustee duties by a stranger to a trust, the participation by a stranger in a fraud committed by a trustee, and the reception and dealing with trust property by a stranger in a manner inconsistent with the terms of the trust[17]. In all of these situations, the stranger may be made liable in equity *as though he were a trustee.* As Ungoed-Thomas J indicated in *Selangor United Rubber Estates Ltd v Cradock (No. 3)*[18], such a person 'is made liable in equity as trustee by the imposition or construction of the court of equity.' His liability as constructive trustee rests not upon intention (for this is the last result which such a person would wish), but upon the fact that he has undertaken in relation to trust property a fiduciary role which he cannot now in good faith be heard to disavow.

This view of the constructive trust is, however, still constrained by the idea of the trust as an institution. The stranger in the examples referred to is liable on the ground of culpable involvement with an existing trust. We must now take note of a wider concept of constructive trust which originated in North America but which has recently found some acceptance in the English courts.

17 See *Barnes v Addy* (1874) LR 9 Ch App 244; *Soar v Ashwell* [1893] 2 QB 390; *Nelson v Larholt* [1948] 1 KB 339; *Belmont Finance Corpn Ltd v Williams Furniture Ltd* [1979] Ch 250.
18 [1968] 1 WLR 1555 at 1582.

2. THE CONSTRUCTIVE TRUST AS A REMEDIAL DEVICE

The constructive trust, in the American model, is a remedial mechanism[19]. It provides a third head of civil obligation, quite distinct from contract and tort, in which the court subjects a person holding title to property to an equitable duty to convey it or hold it on trust for another, on the ground that the former would be 'unjustly enriched' if he were permitted to retain the property beneficially[20]. The constructive trust in this sense is closely linked with the emergence of the law of restitution as a third major form of civil liability in the common law world[1]. The American constructive trust was once most aptly described by Cardozo J as

> the formula through which the conscience of equity finds expression. When property has been acquired in such circumstances that the holder of the legal title may not in good conscience retain the beneficial interest, equity converts him into a trustee[2].

This wider view of the application of the constructive trust has not been accorded an unqualified reception in English jurisprudence[3]. In *Pettitt v Pettitt*[4], Lord Reid expressed the opinion that the doctrine of unjust enrichment, whilst applicable to money claims, is not necessarily appropriate in relation to real property[5]. Indeed, the House of Lords went on in *Gissing v Gissing*[6] to deny any beneficial entitlement to a wife who, during a marriage of some 25 years' duration, had made indirect financial contributions towards the acquisition of a matrimonial home vested at law solely in her husband's name. Here the applicant had defrayed items of general household expenditure, thereby freeing her husband to devote his income to the discharge of the mortgage commitment which he had undertaken in respect of the home.

In *Gissing* the House of Lords stressed that the beneficial ownership of property is ultimately to be determined by reference to the intentions of the parties to the acquisition[7], and that there is moreover a vital distinction between 'inferring' and 'imputing' those intentions. Thus, although in the absence of other evidence the relevant intentions may be inferred from conduct, the court cannot

19 See *Chase Manhattan Bank NA v Israel-British Bank (London) Ltd* [1981] Ch 105; *Simonds v Simonds* 402 NYS 2d 359 (1978).

20 The American *Restatement of Restitution* provides that 'a person who has been unjustly enriched at the expense of another is required to make restitution to that other' (para. 1). Likewise, where 'a person holding title to property is subject to an equitable duty to convey it to another on the gound that he would be unjustly enriched if he were permitted to retain it, a constructive trust arises' (para. 160). See also A. W. Scott (1955) 71 LQR 39: 'Constructive Trusts'; *Law of Trusts* (3rd edn., Boston and Toronto 1967), Vol. V, p. 3413; D. W. M. Waters, *The Constructive Trust* (London 1964).

1 See R. Goff and G. Jones, *The Law of Restitution* (2nd edn., London 1978).

2 *Beatty v Guggenheim Exploration Co* 225 NY 380 at 386 (1919).

3 In *Re Sharpe (A Bankrupt)* [1980] 1 WLR 219 at 225, Browne-Wilkinson J declared the 'constructive trust as a remedy' to be 'a novel concept in English law.'

4 [1970] AC 777 at 795.

5 See also *Orakpo v Manson Investments Ltd* [1978] AC 95 at 104 per Lord Diplock.

6 [1971] AC 886, p. 561, post.

7 [1971] AC 886 at 902 per Lord Pearson, at 905f. per Lord Diplock.

retrospectively impute to the parties intentions as to beneficial ownership which in fact they never had and for the inference of which their conduct provides no convincing ground[8]. Nor, in the absence of some common intention as to beneficial ownership, will the court 'hold that property is subject to a trust on the ground that that would be fair in all the circumstances[9].' Thus, a *direct* contribution of money towards the acquisition of property is sufficient conduct to raise an inference of intended beneficial co-ownership by way of resulting trust for the contributor[10]. But, in the view taken by the House of Lords, an *indirect* financial contribution (such as that made by the wife in *Gissing*) is incapable of producing the same result except where 'it can be inferred' that such a contribution is 'referable to the acquisition of the house[11]'. Lord Diplock declared, in a passage which has now become a locus classicus in the law of real property:

> A resulting, implied or constructive trust—and it is unnecessary for present purposes to distinguish between these three classes of trust—is created by a transaction between the trustee and the cestui que trust in connection with the acquisition by the trustee of a legal estate in land, whenever the trustee has so conducted himself that it would be inequitable to allow him to deny to the cestui que trust a beneficial interest in the land acquired . . .[12]

Couched in these terms, Lord Diplock's application of trust doctrines begins to resemble the remedial device embodied in the American constructive trust. However, Lord Diplock proceeded immediately to qualify his statement, observing that, in the situation to which he had just adverted, the trustee

> will be held so to have conducted himself if by his words or conduct he has induced the cestui que trust to act to his own detriment in the reasonable belief that by so acting he was acquiring a beneficial interest in the land.

The reasons why the applicant wife in *Gissing* failed to prove the existence of a beneficial co-ownership lay not in any argument that it was 'inequitable' to grant her a beneficial share in the matrimonial home. Her failure rested simply on the fact that she could not convince the court that the parties had ever consciously contemplated her indirect financial contributions in the legalistic terms of inducement to believe that a beneficial entitlement was thereby being acquired. In the absence of evidence supporting the inference of a real and effective common intention, the court was not prepared to do justice between the parties by imputing to them a fictitious and non-existent common intention. The remedy, thought the House of Lords, lay in legislation[13].

The decision of the House of Lords in *Gissing* is, of course, open to severe

8 [1971] AC 886 at 898 per Lord Morris of Borth-y-Gest, at 900 per Viscount Dilhorne, 904 per Lord Diplock. This proposition applies even though, if the parties had actually considered the question of beneficial entitlement inter se, they would almost certainly have agreed on some form of equitable co-ownership.

9 [1971] AC 886 at 900 per Viscount Dilhorne.

10 See p. 246ff., ante. See *Re Rogers' Question* [1948] 1 All ER 328; *Rimmer v Rimmer* [1953] 1 QB 63.

11 [1971] AC 886 at 909 per Lord Diplock.

12 [1971] AC 886 at 905. On the 'apparent amalgamation of resulting and constructive trusts into one congruent class', see *Allen v Snyder* [1977] 2 NSWLR 685 at 698 per Samuels JA.

13 See now, in the context of divorce, Matrimonial Causes Act 1973, s. 25(1)(f).

criticism on the ground of elementary social justice. However, the approach applied in that case was inevitably and necessarily constrained by the fact that behind the equitable presumption of resulting trust there lies the 'solid tug of money[14].' This phrase is but a laconic expression of the pragmatic rule of everyday life that people who pay money expect something in return. The more solid the tug, the more ready will be the presumption of resulting trust. The indirect contribution made by the wife in *Gissing* was not sufficiently 'solid' to raise the required inference of intention, and in one sense the House of Lords was absolutely correct in so holding. The wife in that case (and indeed most wives) would have continued to make her appropriate contribution to the marriage partnership without regard to any anticipation of immediate reward or tangible pay-off—and this for at least two reasons. First, the wife never contemplated that her marriage would break down and thus require that the respective property rights of the parties be crystallised. Second, it is an intrinsic feature of family life that the constructive contributions of family members are motivated not by the mercenary incentives of an exchange economy, but by the higher principles of love and duty.

The application of trust doctrines in *Gissing* is clearly unsympathetic towards the realities of family living, and it is to precisely such realities that the American constructive trust appears most apposite. The 'remedial' constructive trust arises quite independently of the vagaries of intentions which may or may not have been formulated by the parties. It substitutes the broad principle of restitution of unjust enrichment for the sterile and ritualistic preoccupation with phantoms of common intention. Such a doctrine of constructive trust has been invoked by Dickson J in the Supreme Court of Canada to confer a half-share in the matrimonial property upon a wife who had made substantial domestic contributions to the marriage partnership. In the words of Dickson J, the constructive trust

> comprehends the imposition of trust machinery by the Court in order to achieve a result consonant with good conscience. As a matter of principle, the Court will not allow any man unjustly to appropriate to himself the value earned by the labours of another. That principle is not defeated by the existence of a matrimonial relationship between the parties; but, for the principle to succeed, the facts must display an enrichment, a corresponding deprivation, and the absence of any juristic reason—such as a contract or disposition of law—for the enrichment[15].

14 *Hofman v Hofman* [1965] NZLR 795 at 800 per Woodhouse J. See also *Reid v Reid* [1979] 1 NZLR 572 at 582 per Woodhouse J.

15 *Rathwell v Rathwell* (1978) 83 DLR (3d) 289 at 306. See also *Pettkus v Becker* (Decision of the Supreme Court of Canada, 18 December 1980). Here Dickson J again applied the doctrine of the remedial constructive trust, this time in the context of a claim made by a de facto wife. Dickson J noted that 'the principle of unjust enrichment lies at the heart of the constructive trust. "Unjust enrichment" has played a role in Anglo-American legal writing for centuries ... The great advantage of ancient principles of equity is their flexibility: the judiciary is thus able to shape these malleable principles so as to accommodate the changing needs and mores of society, in order to achieve justice. The constructive trust has proven to be a useful tool in the judicial armoury' (Transcript, p. 11). The other judges in the Supreme Court preferred, however, to reach the same conclusion as Dickson J on the basis not of constructive trust but rather of resulting trust.

This articulation of the theory of the constructive trust is interesting because it widens considerably the conditions which activate the imposition of a trust upon the owner of a legal estate. If the trigger for the old presumption of resulting trust was a contribution of money, the trigger for the application of the modern constructive trust may well be a contribution of labour. Indeed, part of the concept of 'the new property'[16] consists precisely in the recognition that a man has a 'property' in his own labour—although this idea is itself far from new[17]. In the remedial constructive trust the 'solid tug of money' has arguably become the 'solid tug of labour', and in this evolution there is a certain justice. In the earliest manifestations of primitive capitalism, the contribution of money which brought into play the presumption of resulting trust may well have signified a past expenditure of the contributor's labour power. Today, in the era of the post-industrial economy and the welfare state—the age of 'welfare capitalism'—it often seems that money and labour are inversely related. Those who have money are frequently those who do not work for it at all!

The remedial constructive trust—marked as it is by its close association with the Protestant work ethic—has found its foremost protagonist in the English courts in the predictable shape of Lord Denning MR. In *Cooke v Head*[18], the Master of the Rolls indicated that

> whenever two parties by their joint efforts acquire property to be used for their joint benefit, the courts may impose or impute a constructive or resulting trust[19].

Cooke v Head involved parties to a de facto relationship, but Lord Denning pointed out that the constructive trust doctrine is applicable to 'husband and wife, to engaged couples, and to man and mistress, and maybe to other relationships too.' In particular, de facto marriage is frequently indistinguishable from de iure marriage, and the Court of Appeal has on many occasions invoked the broad concept of constructive trust in order to do justice between cohabiting couples.

In *Eves v Eves*[20], for instance, a de facto wife claimed to have effected extensive improvements to a house vested at law in the sole name of her partner. The Court of Appeal awarded her one quarter of the beneficial ownership in the property, Lord Denning basing his reasoning on the constructive trust doctrine[1]. He observed that 'a few years ago even equity would not have helped' a claimant in the position of the plaintiff, but noted that

> things have altered now. Equity is not past the age of child bearing. One of her latest progeny is a constructive trust of a new model. Lord Diplock brought it into the world and we have nourished it.

Lord Denning proceeded to quote the very passage from Lord Diplock's speech

16 See pp. 12f., 39ff., ante.
17 See John Locke, *The Second Treatise of Civil Government* (ed. J. W. Gough, Oxford 1946), para. 27.
18 [1972] 1 WLR 518 at 520.
19 Such a trust is, of course, relieved of any requirement of writing under section 53(1) of the Law of Property Act 1925 (see Law of Property Act 1925, s. 53(2)).
20 [1975] 1 WLR 1338.
1 The other judges in the Court of Appeal (Browne LJ and Brightman J) were more cautious and preferred to find a more traditional basis for reaching the same conclusion.

in *Gissing v Gissing* which is reproduced above[2] as marking the beginning of the English reception of the doctrine. It must, however, be said that the Master of the Rolls consistently appears to have concentrated on the first part of Lord Diplock's dictum to the virtual exclusion of the second (and severely limiting) passage[3]. In fact, Lord Diplock's speech when read closely in context provides no support for the proposition that a new head of inequitable conduct is disclosed whenever, in the absence of a contract or relevant common intention, the court considers that it would be fair to cause beneficial ownership to be shared by two or more parties who have acquired property by joint efforts[4]. In *Gissing* precisely this proposition was rejected[5], and in consequence the applicant wife there lost her case.

Lord Denning's application of the remedial constructive trust was seen in its most liberal form perhaps in *Hussey v Palmer*[6]. Here the Master of the Rolls ruled that the constructive trust

> is a trust imposed by law whenever justice and good conscience require it. It is a liberal process, founded upon large principles of equity to be applied in cases where the legal owner cannot conscientiously keep the property for himself alone, but ought to allow another to have the property or the benefit of it or a share in it. The trust may arise at the outset when the property is acquired, or later on, as the circumstances may require. It is an equitable remedy by which the court can enable an aggrieved party to obtain restitution. It is comparable to the legal remedy of money had and received which, as Lord Mansfield said, is 'very beneficial and, therefore, much encouraged' (*Moses v Macferlan* (1760) 2 Burr 1005)[7].

In *Hussey v Palmer*, Lord Denning awarded a beneficial share by way of constructive trust to a mother-in-law who had paid for the construction of an extra bedroom in a house which belonged to her son-in-law. The purpose of the arrangement was to provide accommodation for her in her old age, but the arrangement came to a premature end for reasons of domestic discord. In the nature of things the terms of the arrangement had never been crystallised by the

2 See p. 478, ante.

3 Lord Denning expressly declined to adopt Lord Diplock's notion of 'referable' contributions, p. 561, post. See *Hargrave v Newton* [1971] 1 WLR 1611 at 1613, where Lord Denning found the concept 'very difficult to apply', and thus preferred 'to take the simple test: did the wife make a substantial contribution, direct or indirect, to the acquisition of the house or the repayment of the mortgage or the loan?' See also *Hazell v Hazell* [1972] 1 WLR 301 at 304.

4 See *Allen v Snyder* [1977] 2 NSWLR 685 at 700f., where in the New South Wales Court of Appeal Samuels JA noted that in *Eves v Eves* Lord Denning had 'proclaimed the legitimacy of equity's latest progeny, plucked by Lord Diplock from her capacious womb, and it was named "a constructive trust of a new model." But I would respectfully suggest that Lord Diplock's speech in *Gissing v Gissing* gives no warrant for identifying him as midwife; his Lordship, by exemplifying the trustee's inequitable conduct as the basis of the trust, is expressing no novelty. It would seem that it was the nourishment lavished upon the infant by the English Court of Appeal which produced the novelty. In *Cowcher v Cowcher* Bagnall J said: "This does not mean that equity is past childbearing; simply that its progeny must be legitimate—by precedent out of principle." So the legitimacy of the new model is at least suspect; at best it is a mutant from which further breeding should be discouraged.'

5 [1971] AC 886 at 900 per Viscount Dilhorne, p. 478 , ante.

6 [1972] 1 WLR 1286.

7 [1972] 1 WLR 1286 at 1290. See (1973) 37 Conv (NS) 65 (D. J. Hayton); (1973) 89 LQR 2.

parties, but Lord Denning ruled that, although the old lady had now moved out, it would be 'entirely against conscience that [the son-in-law] should retain the whole house and not allow [the plaintiff] any interest in it[8].'

3. CRITICISMS OF THE REMEDIAL CONSTRUCTIVE TRUST

The application of the remedial constructive trust in the English context is controversial[9]. It is said that to invoke such a constructive trust is to use an argument of last resort. The 'finding' of a constructive trust is an act of intellectual bankruptcy, since it amounts to a judicial confession that no convincing reason can be found in law for giving judgment in favour of a deserving plaintiff. Moreover, the law of constructive trusts is the law of 'palm-tree justice', in which past decisions are worthless as precedent and future decisions are entirely unpredictable[10].

To these objections can be added the weighty argument that the imposition of a remedial constructive trust unfairly prejudices that category of interests which the law of property so jealously protects—the interests of innocent third parties[11]. The interest of a beneficiary behind a constructive trust gains an automatic priority over the creditors of the constructive trustee in the event that the latter becomes insolvent[12]. Furthermore, even if the constructive trustee remains perfectly solvent, third parties who purchase the trust property from him may, in some circumstances, be trapped by constructive notice of the interest of the constructive beneficiary.

In the light of these criticisms it must be conceded that the acceptance in English law of the remedial constructive trust is at present far from complete. However, we can now turn to an examination of the law relating to contractual licences, where the remedial constructive trust is intricately involved in the developments which are current.

8 The result in *Hussey v Palmer* is made all the more remarkable by the fact that Lord Denning recognised the plaintiff mother-in-law as having a proprietary interest by way of trust, notwithstanding that she herself had given evidence in court to the effect that the transaction in question had been a contract of loan. This is not to imply that a trust cannot co-exist on the same facts with a contract of loan (see *Barclay's Bank Ltd v Quistclose Investments Ltd* [1970] AC 567), but the (perhaps intentional) effect of imposing a trust solution in *Hussey v Palmer* may indeed have been to confer upon the plaintiff a proportionate share in the rapidly inflating value of the house rather than the mere contractual right to have the amount of the loan repaid (see T. C. Ridley, (1973) 36 MLR 436 at 439: 'A Family Affair'). Where, however, there is documentary evidence which confirms the status of a transaction as a loan, this is enough to displace the possibility that a contribution of money may have generated a trust (see, e.g., *Re Sharpe (A Bankrupt)* [1980] 1 WLR 219 at 222).

9 See A. J. Oakley (1973) 26 CLP 17: 'Has the constructive trust become a general equitable remedy?'

10 See, for instance, the objections expressed by Martland J in the Supreme Court of Canada in *Pettkus v Becker* (Unreported Decision, 18th December 1980, Transcript, pp. 3, 6).

11 See A. J. Oakley, *Constructive Trusts* (London 1978), p. 4ff.

12 This is but one implication of the statutory rule that the divisible property of a bankrupt shall not comprise 'property held by the bankrupt on trust for any other person' (Bankruptcy Act 1914, s. 38). See Williams and Muir Hunter, *The Law and Practice in Bankruptcy* (19th edn., London 1979), p. 260ff.

4. CONTRACTUAL LICENCES

We shall now look at some of the difficulties which arise in family arrangements involving the grant of an occupation licence under circumstances of explicit or implicit bargain or expectation. Such licences are commonly known as contractual licences, and indeed we have already dealt with some aspects of the law relating to them.

(1) The received doctrine of contractual licences[13]

Fifty years ago the law relating to contractual licences could be summarised without much difficulty. A contractual licence was a personal permission to be present or to carry on some activity on another's land, often for the purpose of business or entertainment. The residential dimension of the contractual licence was only slowly beginning to emerge. The Rent Acts were as yet in their infancy, and the possibility that that legislation could be circumvented through the grant of an occupation licence had not been fully realised.

The received doctrine was that a contractual licence could be effectively revoked by the licensor at any time, notwithstanding that the revocation constituted a breach of contract. The de facto revocation would undoubtedly give the licensee a cause of action in contract, but could not give rise to any liability in tort if, for instance, the licensee were forcibly ejected or barred from the land[14].

It was likewise received doctrine that a contractual licence conferred on the licensee no interest in the land. There was in the minds of lawyers a considerable reluctance to concede that a contractual licence could ever be, in the ordinary sense of legal language, a proprietary interest in land[15]. The orthodox view was very firm that the rights of contractual licensees were at all times rights in contract, not rights in property. The corollary of this view was similarly clear. The rights generated by a contractual licence bound only the licensor and licensee: they could never bind third parties. There is strong authority for the proposition that a contractual licence cannot bind a third party who purchases the land from the licensor even though the purchaser has actual notice of the licence[16].

We shall now see how these positions have been modified by developments over the years. These developments have been stimulated by two factors: the implication of a contractual term and the liberal intervention of equity.

13 See generally H. W. R. Wade (1948) 64 LQR 57: 'What is a Licence?'; R. H. Maudsley (1956) 20 Conv (NS) 281: 'Licence to remain on land (other than a wife's licence)'.

14 See *Wood v Leadbitter* (1845) 13 M & W 838. On the imprecise borderline in this area between property rights and contractual rights, see further J. D. Davies (1979) 8 Sydney LR 578 at 579.

15 As the Chief Justice of Australia tersely remarked on one occasion, 'fifty thousand people who pay to see a football match do not obtain fifty thousand interests in the football ground' (*Cowell v Rosehill Racecourse Co Ltd* (1937) 56 CLR 605 at 616 per Latham CJ).

16 *King v David Allen and Sons Ltd* [1916] 2 AC 54; *Clore v Theatrical Properties Ltd and Westby & Co Ltd* [1936] 3 All ER 483.

(2) The 'implied contract' theory

It is now accepted that in a contractual licence the licence is not a separate entity but is merely one of the manifestations of the contract in which it finds expression. Thus, where a contract contains a permission to occupy land for a specific purpose or duration of time, it is often possible to spell out in the contract an implied negative obligation on the part of the licensor, i.e., an obligation not to revoke the licence before the completion of that purpose or period. Such a term has been implied, for instance, in contractual licences which confer on the licensee a right to watch a theatre performance[17] or to carry out a building operation[18]. This development has facilitated a much more important step in the evolution of the law.

(3) The intervention of equity

The law of contractual licences has been profoundly influenced in recent years by the increasing willingness of the courts to exercise their equitable jurisdiction in order to govern the relationship of the parties to a licence both inter se and with third parties. The intervention of equity in this respect is intimately bound up with the development of the law relating to 'the licence coupled with an equity'.

5. THE 'LICENCE COUPLED WITH AN EQUITY'[19]

In the Court of Appeal in *National Provincial Bank Ltd v Hastings Car Mart Ltd*[20], Lord Denning MR adverted to a long line of cases which establish the legal implications of the phenomenon known as the 'licence coupled with an equity.' The Master of the Rolls drew an analogy between such a licence and the 'licence coupled with a proprietary interest', which has long been recognised as capable of conferring on the licensee an irrevocable right binding on third parties. He explained the 'licence coupled with an equity' in the following terms:

> If the owner of land grants a licence to another to go upon land and occupy it for a specific period or a prescribed purpose, and on the faith of that authority the licensee enters into occupation and does work, or in some other way alters his position to his detriment, then the owner cannot revoke the licence at his will. He cannot revoke the licence so as to defeat the period or purpose for which it was granted. A court of equity will restrain him from so doing. Not only will it restrain him, but it will restrain any successor in title who takes the land with knowledge or notice of the arrangement that has been made[1].

Lord Denning gave two principal examples of the application of this rule:

17 *Hurst v Picture Theatres Ltd* [1915] 1 KB 1 at 10.
18 *Hounslow London Borough Council v Twickenham Garden Developments Ltd* [1971] Ch 233 at 247.
19 See S. Anderson (1979) 42 MLR 203: 'Of Licences and Similar Mysteries'.
20 [1964] Ch 665 at 686.
1 On the doctrine that a licence, once acted upon, is irrevocable, see *Webb v Paternoster* (1619) Palm 71; *Tayler v Waters* (1816) 7 Taunt 374; *Wood v Manley* (1839) 11 Ad & El 34.

(1) the doctrine of 'proprietary estoppel' or estoppel by acquiescence, and
(2) the equitable approach to contractual licences.

(1) The doctrine of 'proprietary estoppel' or estoppel by acquiescence[2]

A distinguished line of authority dating from the last century establishes that if the owner of land requests or even merely allows another to expend money on his land under an expectation created or encouraged by the land-owner that he will be able to remain there, this is enough to 'raise an equity' in the licensee such as will entitle him to stay[3]. Since it would now be inequitable that the owner should assert his legal title to the exclusion of the licensee, that licensee has a 'licence coupled with an equity' which binds both the licensor and his successors in title. By reason of the original acquiescence in the licensee's expenditure, the licensor (and his successors) are estopped from prejudicing the licensee's occupation, and will indeed be restrained from any prejudicial act by means of court injunction. In giving relief to the licensee, the court exercising equitable jurisdiction 'must look at the circumstances in each case to decide in what way the equity can be satisfied[4].'

The doctrine of proprietary estoppel rests upon much the same basis as the doctrine of promissory estoppel which was highlighted in the law of contract in *Central London Property Trust Ltd v High Trees House Ltd*[5]. Indeed, Lord Denning MR has explained both kinds of estoppel as representing

> the first principle upon which all courts of equity proceed, that is, [to] prevent a person from insisting on his strict legal rights—whether arising under a contract or on his title deeds or by statute—when it would be inequitable for him to do so having regard to the dealings which have taken place between the parties[6].

However, proprietary estoppel differs from promissory estoppel in at least two important respects. First, proprietary estoppel may be relied upon as a sword and not merely as a shield, thus conferring upon the licensee a right of action[7]. Second, the equity created by an estoppel based on expenditure and acquiescence is clearly binding on third party purchasers who have notice of the equity[8]. In this sense, it 'seems in essence to confer a substantive equitable right of property which is not registrable as a land charge[9].'

The classic features of proprietary estoppel are illustrated in the way in which the Court of Appeal dealt with the family arrangement involved in *Inwards v Baker*[10]. Here a father allowed his son to build a bungalow on the father's land,

2 See generally R. H. Maudsley (1956) 20 Conv (NS) 281 at 293ff.
3 See, e.g., *Dillwyn v Llewelyn* (1862) 4 De GF & J 517; *Ramsden v Dyson* (1866) LR 1 HL 129.
4 *Plimmer v Mayor of Wellington* (1884) 9 App Cas 699 at 714 per Sir Arthur Hobhouse.
5 [1947] KB 130. See now *Brikom Investments Ltd v Carr* [1979] QB 467 at 482ff.
6 *Crabb v Arun District Council* [1976] Ch 179 at 187f. See (1976) 92 LQR 174 (P. S. Atiyah), 342 (P. J. Millett).
7 See *Pascoe v Turner* [1979] 1 WLR 431 at 436, p. 493, post.
8 See *E. R. Ives Investment Ltd v High* [1967] 2 QB 379, p. 140, ante.
9 *Snell's Principles of Equity*, p. 565.
10 [1965] 2 QB 29. See (1965) 81 LQR 183 (R. H. Maudsley).

the son thereafter going into occupation of the bungalow and remaining there in the expectation and belief, encouraged by his father, that he would be allowed to live there during his lifetime. The father died without making any binding contractual arrangement to this effect, and did not leave the property to his son by will. The Court of Appeal nevertheless refused to allow the trustees under that will to obtain possession against the son, holding that the son had acquired by reason of his expenditure on the land an equity which bound not only the father (while alive) but also his successors in title with notice[11]. In giving equitable relief, the Court took the view that the equity could be satisfied only by 'holding that the defendant can remain there as long as he desires to [use it] as his home[12].'

(2) The equitable approach to contractual licences

The major development in the law relating to contractual licences finds its origin in the same idea of conscience as is embodied in the doctrine of proprietary estoppel. Where a contractual licence contains, either expressly or by implication, a negative obligation binding the licensor not to revoke the licence during the currency of the contract[13], the court, in the exercise of its equitable jurisdiction, will intervene to restrain the licensor from evicting the licensee before the termination of the contract. The court will not assist the licensor to act in breach of his contractual undertaking[14].

The relatively recently discovered capacity of the courts to exercise equitable jurisdiction to restrain the revocation of a contractual licence has, at least in the view of Lord Denning MR, revolutionised the law relating to contractual licences. In *Errington v Errington and Woods*[15], that judge pointed out that the fusion of law and equity, taken in conjunction with the new approach adumbrated in the *Winter Garden* case, had brought about the result that

> a licensor will not be permitted to eject a licensee in breach of a contract to allow him to remain . . . This infusion of equity means that contractual licences now have a force and validity of their own and cannot be revoked in breach of the contract. Neither the licensor nor anyone who claims through him can disregard the contract except a purchaser for value without notice[16].

In other words, Denning LJ (as he then was) regarded the equitable approach

11 It has been pointed out that this decision, in conferring on the son a possessory licence for life, produced the undesirable result both of rendering the land pro tempore unsaleable and of discouraging the son from moving. See F. R. Crane (1967) 31 Conv (NS) 332 at 342: 'Estoppel Interests in Land'.

12 See the criticism of this decision voiced in the judgment of Russell LJ in *Dodsworth v Dodsworth* (1973) 228 Estates Gazette 1115. For other applications of the doctrine of equitable estoppel, see *Ward v Kirkland* [1967] Ch 194 at 235ff.; *E. R. Ives Investment Ltd v High* [1967] 2 QB 379, p. 140, ante; *Siew Soon Wah v Yong Tong Hong* [1973] AC 836; *Re Sharpe (A Bankrupt)* [1980] 1 WLR 219.

13 See p. 484, ante.

14 See *Winter Garden Theatre (London) Ltd v Millennium Productions Ltd* [1948] AC 173 at 191 per Lord Simon, [1946] 1 All ER 678 at 685 per Lord Greene MR. See also Sir R. Evershed (1954) 70 LQR 326 at 331ff.: 'Reflections on the Fusion of Law and Equity after 75 Years'.

15 [1952] 1 KB 290 at 298f.

16 See G. C. Cheshire (1953) 16 MLR 1: 'A New Equitable Interest in Land'.

to licences as having the effect of transforming a purely personal right into what he described in later cases as 'a licence coupled with an equity' and, finally, 'an equitable licence[17].' The protective vigour of the courts in satisfying the 'equity' effectively converts contractual licences into rights of property.

In *Errington* a father, wishing to provide a home for his son who had recently married, purchased a house in his own name on mortgage loan. He promised that if his son and daughter-in-law continued in occupation of the house and paid all the instalments of the mortgage loan, he would then transfer the property to them absolutely. The son and his wife entered into occupation and began to make repayments of the loan to the building society. The father later died, leaving all his property (including the house) to his widow, the present plaintiff. Shortly after his father's death, the son left his wife and went to live with his widowed mother. The daughter-in-law, the defendant in the present proceedings, continued to occupy the house and to make the appropriate repayments to the building society. The plaintiff now brought an action for possession, alleging that the defendant had a mere revocable licence to occupy the house.

The Court of Appeal unanimously rejected the claim for possession and declined to eject the daughter-in-law. Denning LJ found that the father's promise was 'a unilateral contract—a promise of the house in return for their act of paying the instalments. It could not be revoked by him once the couple entered on performance of the act.' This being so, the couple were in Denning LJ's view

> licensees, having a permissive occupation short of a tenancy, but with a contractual right, or at any rate, an equitable right to remain so long as they paid the instalments, which would grow into a good equitable title to the house itself as soon as the mortgage was paid.

The couple thus had a 'licence coupled with an equity', the 'equity' consisting precisely in the fact that the courts would grant equitable relief to prevent their ejection in breach of contract. Denning LJ fully recognised that, at law, they had no right to remain, 'but only in equity, and equitable rights now prevail.'

The effect of *Errington,* if correctly decided, is to reverse the rule in *Wood v Leadbitter* that contractual licences are de facto revocable. That rule is reversed through the judicial recognition of an 'equity' which the courts will jealously protect against all except a purchaser without notice. This is tantamount to ruling that the contractual licence creates a new species of proprietary interest—a conclusion which most land lawyers are reluctant to accept[18]. Nevertheless,

17 See *Hardwick v Johnson* [1978] 1 WLR 683 at 688.

18 Can it really be so easy, asked Professor H. W. R. Wade, 'to cross the chasm which lies between contract and property?' (see (1952) 68 LQR 337 at 348: 'Licences and Third Parties'). To be sure, that chasm has been crossed before—witness the case of the restrictive covenant, p. 615f., post, but the courts have strictly defined the qualities which must be possessed by restrictive covenants before they cross the threshold of the law of property. A restrictive covenant qualifies as a proprietary interest only if it clearly restricts the user of one defined area of land (the 'servient tenement') for the 'benefit' of another defined area of land (the 'dominant tenement'). This imposition of constraints upon the doctrine proceeding from *Tulk v Moxhay* (1848) 2 Ph 774, represented, as Professor Wade pointed out, a 'decisive repudiation of the notion that the mere

Denning LJ's approach in *Errington* has subsequently provided the basis for an extension of the law relating to family and other living arrangements. In each case, the courts have where appropriate applied the concept of the 'licence coupled with an equity'—whether that 'equity' be founded upon estoppel or upon contract—in order to 'give effect to the expectations of the parties when making their arrangement[19].'

6. 'FAMILY ARRANGEMENTS' AND OTHER RESIDENTIAL ARRANGEMENTS

We shall now look at the way in which the concept of the 'licence coupled with an equity' has been used by the courts in order to spell out the legal implications of loose and informal arrangements for family or other residential living[20]. The categories of case which we shall examine are far from being mutually exclusive.

(1) Arrangements involving payment

Errington v Errington and Woods[1] provides a typical example of a contractual licence given on terms of some form of money payment by the licensees. In that case, of course, the payment was not made to the licensor but to a third party (i.e., the building society which had advanced to the licensor the loan necessary for the purchase of the house). However, there arises no relevant distinction where the terms of a family arrangement envisage payment to the licensor.

In *Hardwick v Johnson*[2], the plaintiff was a mother who, in her own name, purchased a house for occupation by her son and daughter-in-law. It was arranged that the couple would pay the mother £7 per week, and it was vaguely supposed by all concerned that the periodic payments would eventually counterbalance the purchase price. It was not clear, however, whether those payments were in respect of rent or represented instead a kind of instalment purchase of the house. Nor were any terms agreed as to an eventual conveyance of the property to the couple, although it was probably anticipated that the house would ultimately be inherited by them. The arrangement broke down when the son left his wife, and the mother purported to terminate the right of the wife to occupy the house.

Lord Denning MR ruled that, in dealing with informal and ill-defined family arrangements of this kind, the court

> has to look at all the circumstances and spell out the legal relationship . . . and will find the terms of that relationship according to what reason and justice require[3].

---

fact that an equitable remedy was available was enough to turn a contract into an interest in land binding purchasers with notice.'

19 *Chandler v Kerley* [1978] 1 WLR 693 at 698 per Lord Scarman.

20 See E. Ellis (1979) 95 LQR 11: 'Contractual and Equitable Licences'; A. A. S. Zuckerman (1980) 96 LQR 248: 'Formality and the Family—Reform and the Status Quo'.

1 [1952] 1 KB 290, p. 486f., ante.

2 [1978] 1 WLR 683.

3 [1978] 1 WLR 683 at 688.

He considered that the present arrangement created a 'personal licence . . . in the nature of an equitable licence.' He therefore held that the licence was not revocable at the will of the mother, and that the court would not order possession in her favour. The Master of the Rolls took the view that the licence, although perhaps revocable in the future under different circumstances, was

> certainly not revocable as against the daughter-in-law, who was still living in the house with her baby, deserted by the son. Looking simply at what is reasonable, it seems to me that the mother could not turn the daughter-in-law and child out, at all events when the daughter-in-law was ready to pay the £7 a week[4].

(2) Promise of a life interest

A not uncommon feature of family arrangements is a loosely worded undertaking by an owner to allow another to occupy his property during his lifetime. However, an informal occupational privilege of this kind, although granted in all innocence, raises horrendous difficulties in connection with the Settled Land Act 1925[5].

In *Bannister v Bannister*[6], the defendant (D) was the sister-in-law of the plaintiff (P). D had conveyed her freehold interest in two cottages to P at a gross undervalue, upon the latter's oral promise that she would be allowed to live in one of the cottages rent-free for the remainder of her life. There was no reference in the conveyance to the promise made by P. When P later sought to evict D on the ground that she was a mere tenant at will, the Court of Appeal decided that the oral agreement between P and D had conferred on D a life interest in the relevant property which was determinable only upon her ceasing to live there. In other words, she was not a mere tenant at will to be evicted at the caprice of P. Interestingly, the Court thought that a life interest of this kind took effect under the Settled Land Act 1925, but did not elaborate on this point. The Court then continued to hold that D's life interest was enforceable against P, notwithstanding the absence of writing. According to Scott LJ, P was bound by a 'constructive trust' to give effect to that interest, on the ground that equity will intervene to counteract fraud on the part of any purchaser who insists on 'the absolute character of the conveyance for the purpose of defeating the beneficial interest which he had agreed the [vendor] should retain[7].'

Bannister is a decision fraught with problems. Apart from the technical impossibility of creating a strict settlement by means of verbal agreement[8], to hold that such an arrangement comes within the ambit of the Settled Land Act 1925 is to confer upon the vendor the somewhat improbable right qua tenant for life to be re-invested immediately with the legal estate and the attendant powers

4 [1978] 1 WLR 683 at 689.
5 See p. 154ff., ante.
6 [1948] 2 All ER 133.
7 [1948] 2 All ER 136. A constructive trust is, of course, immune from any requirement of writing (see Law of Property Act 1925, s. 53(2)). See also *Last v Rosenfeld* [1972] 2 NSWLR 923.
8 See J. A. Hornby (1977) 93 LQR 561: 'Tenancy for Life or Licence?' Compare, however, [1978] Conv 250 at 251, where it is suggested that the court order itself might be the 'instrument' which constitutes the settlement within the Settled Land Act 1925, s. 1(1).

of management and disposition (including, of course, the power of sale)[9]. The latter difficulty has caused subsequent courts to be disinclined to characterise the interest of the occupier in such circumstances as an equitable life interest[10]. Instead, the status of a 'licence coupled with an equity' appears marginally more appropriate.

In *Binions v Evans*[11], the defendant, D, had been allowed by X, the trustees of the estate for which her late husband had worked, to reside in a cottage on the estate rent-free for the remainder of her life. This permission was granted in a written agreement which, inter alia, imposed on D an obligation to maintain the interior of the cottage and keep the garden in good condition. It was provided that D could terminate the arrangement on giving X four weeks' notice. D continued to live in the cottage (which had been her home for some 50 years). X then conveyed the property to the present plaintiffs, P, expressly subject to the rights enjoyed by D. Notwithstanding the fact that P had secured the purchase at a reduced price in view of D's occupation, P took possession proceedings against D, who was by this stage aged 79.

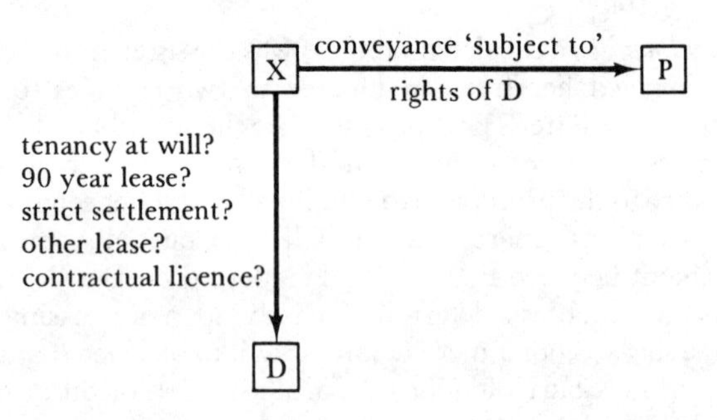

Fig. 67

The success of P's action for possession clearly depended upon the status of the interest held by D. Lord Denning MR in the Court of Appeal took the view that the original written agreement had conferred on D neither a determinable 90 year lease[12], nor any other kind of lease[13], nor a tenancy at will[14]. Nor, said the Master of the Rolls, could D be a tenant for life under the Settled Land Act

9 See also *Re Carne's Settled Estates* [1899] 1 Ch 324; *Re Waleran Settled Estates* [1927] 1 Ch 522; *Re Catling* [1931] 2 Ch 359; *Ayer v Benton* (1967) 204 Estates Gazette 359. See E. H. Scamell [1957] CLP 152 at 160f.: 'The Reform of the Settled Land Act 1925'.

10 See *Dodsworth v Dodsworth* (1973) 228 Estates Gazette 1115, where Russell LJ foresaw that to hold the defendants in that case entitled to a life interest in the disputed property would lead 'by virtue of the provisions of the Settled Land Act to a greater and more extensive interest than was ever contemplated by the plaintiff and the defendants.' The Court of Appeal held that on the facts a reimbursement of the defendants' expenditure on the plaintiff's property was sufficient to satisfy the 'equity' raised by the expenditure. See also *Re Sharpe* (*A Bankrupt*) [1980] 1 WLR 219 at 224.

11 [1972] Ch 359.

12 D's occupation was rent-free (see Law of Property Act 1925, s. 149 (6), p. 391, ante).

13 See *Lace v Chantler* [1944] KB 368, p. 390, ante.

14 The right to determine the agreement was not mutual, p. 395, ante.

1925, for the reasons which are noted above[15]. Instead, ruled Lord Denning, D had been granted a contractual licence to reside in the cottage for the remainder of her life. He held that, in accordance with authority, the courts of equity would not allow the occupier under such a licence to be evicted in disregard of the contract. P, since they bought the property expressly 'subject to' the contractual rights of D, were bound by

> a constructive trust for her benefit: for the simple reason that it would be utterly inequitable for the plaintiffs to turn the defendant out contrary to the stipulation subject to which they took the premises ... In my opinion the defendant, by virtue of the agreement, had an equitable interest in the cottage which the court would protect by granting an injunction against the landlords restraining them from turning her out. When the landlords sold the cottage to a purchaser 'subject to' her rights under the agreement, the purchaser took the cottage on a constructive trust to permit the defendant to reside there during her life, or so long as she might desire. The courts will not allow the purchaser to go back on that trust[16].

The decision in *Binions v Evans* is controversial, not least because Lord Denning held that a contractual licence is binding upon a third party[17]. The ruling is capable of extension to a number of situations involving a contractual licence under which a person is granted the right to occupy land for an indefinite period. In each case, if *Binions v Evans* is correct, the arrangement may give rise to a constructive trust which binds both the owner of the land and successors in title who have notice[18].

Lord Denning's approach in *Binions v Evans* has been followed in Australia. In *Ogilvie v Ryan*[19], a woman, D, left her existing home in order to live with X in a de facto relationship in a house which he bought for this purpose. The terms of the arrangement were that if D kept house and cared for X until he died—he was then aged 82—she would be entitled to live in the home rent-free for so long as she wished. X and D lived together on these terms for a further three years until X died, at which point P, the executor of X's will, took proceedings for possession against D. Holland J held that P was bound by a constructive trust to give effect to the promise made by his predecessor in title, on the ground that it

15 See p. 489, ante. The other two judges in the Court of Appeal, Megaw and Stephenson LJJ, differed on this point in view of the binding authority of *Bannister*, but expressed 'difficulty in seeing precisely how the Settled Land Act of 1925 was applicable' in that case.

16 [1972] Ch 359 at 368f. Lord Denning cited in aid of his view of the constructive trust the authority of *Beatty v Guggenheim Exploration Co* 225 NY 380 at 386 (1919), p. 477, ante and *Gissing v Gissing* [1971] AC 886 at 905 per Lord Diplock, p. 478, ante. It has been questioned whether 'there can be, as an object of a trust, a beneficiary entitled to a licence as distinct from a conventional property interest in equity' (see J. D. Davies (1979) 8 Sydney LR 578 at 579; *Re Potter* [1970] VR 352).

17 See J. Martin (1972) 36 Conv (NS) 266: 'Contractual Licensee or Tenant for Life'; R. J. Smith (1973) 32 Cambridge LJ 123: 'Licences and Constructive Trusts: '"The Law is what it ought to be"'; P. V. Baker (1972) 88 LQR 336: 'Equitable Interests and Constructive Notice Today'; A. J. Oakley (1972) 35 MLR 551: 'The Licensee's Interest'; (1972) 36 Conv (NS) 277 (D. J. Hayton); (1973) 117 Sol Jo 23 (B. W. Harvey).

18 See *DHN Food Distributors Ltd v London Borough of Tower Hamlets* [1976] 1 WLR 852 at 859; (1977) 36 Cambridge LJ 12 (D. J. Hayton).

19 [1976] 2 NSWLR 504. See M. A. Neave, (1977–78) 11 Melbourne ULR 343: 'The Constructive Trust as a Remedial Device'.

would be 'an unconscionable use of the legal title' if P were now to assert it in derogation of an interest conferred by X[20].

(3) Express or implied promise of residential security

The same basic ideas have been used in order to give protection to an occupier who has been promised, whether expressly or impliedly, whether for consideration or voluntarily, that he will enjoy residential security for an indefinite period.

In *Foster v Robinson*[1], the Court of Appeal indicated that a licensee would be protected on the strength of an oral promise of rent-free occupation for life, if such a person, although not giving value for the promise, continued in occupation in reliance upon it. The same approach has been adopted even where the implied promise of residential security does not necessarily extend to security for life. In *Tanner v Tanner*[2], a young mother of twins gave up a Rent Act protected tenancy in order to move into a house owned by her de facto husband, the father of her children. When he later evicted her from that house, the Court of Appeal awarded the woman compensation for the loss of a 'contractual licence.' According to Lord Denning MR, the house had obviously been 'provided for her as a house for herself and the twins for the foreseeable future[3].' Having suffered the detriment of giving up the protected tenancy, she had acquired

a contractual licence—to have accommodation in the house for herself and the children

20 [1976] 2 NSWLR 504 at 518. It has been suggested that justice could have been done in this case (and in similar cases) through an application of the doctrine of equitable estoppel rather than through the invocation of a constructive trust. See J. D. Davies (1979) 8 Sydney LR 578 at 583, who argues that licences should not be converted into equitable interests, 'turning them as if by magic into property rights. I would prefer an injunction to be issued against a third party as a matter of discretion on the basis of the merits as between him and the licensee, and not merely as a repeat of how it would be as between original licensor and licensee. On this basis the extent of the injunction might well be different in the two situations. It is not a question of making an adverse right bind the third parties with notice automatically, but a question of keeping open the possibility that an injunction can be issued against a third party where it is appropriate. It might be possible in this way to ensure that licences are effectively enforced without raising fears of damage to the fabric of the property law.'

1 [1951] 1 KB 149 at 156, p. 423, ante.

2 [1975] 1 WLR 1346.

3 Compare, however, *Chandler v Kerley* [1978] 1 WLR 693. Here D and her ex-husband conveyed the former matrimonial home to P who was at this time D's lover. It was intended that D and the two children of the broken marriage should continue to live there, and P paid a purchase price of £10,000 (which was substantially lower than the probable market value of £15,000). Within six weeks of the purchase, P terminated his relationship with D and brought an action for possession. The Court of Appeal held that D enjoyed a contractual licence terminable upon reasonable notice, which in the circumstances was fixed as a period of 12 calendar months. Significantly the Court of Appeal declined to hold that D had a licence to occupy the house for life. Lord Scarman thought that it would be 'wrong . . . to infer, in the absence of an express promise, that the plaintiff was assuming the burden of housing another man's wife and children indefinitely, and long after his relationship with them had ended.' See A. A. S. Zuckerman (1980) 96 LQR 248 at 257.

so long as they were of school age and the accommodation was reasonably required for her and the children[4].

The court thus regarded the expectations of the parties as having given rise to a residential security which, although terminable in changed circumstances, was none the less protectible in the meantime by injunction or compensable (as here) where the licence had already been wrongfully terminated. Because the man had 'obtained an unjust benefit and should make restitution,' Lord Denning ordered that he pay the woman compensation in the sum of £2,000.

An even more remarkable decision is that of the Court of Appeal (for once not dominated by Lord Denning) in *Pascoe v Turner*[5]. Here P and D lived in a de facto relationship in a house owned by P. When P later moved out in order to live with another woman elsewhere, he informed D orally that she had nothing to worry about as the house and its contents were thenceforth entirely hers. D then effected improvements to the house costing about £230, a figure which amounted to approximately one quarter of her available capital. When P later brought possession proceedings on the basis that D had a mere revocable licence to occupy, the Court of Appeal ruled that the fee simple in the house should be conveyed to D. This rather startling result was reached on the ground of proprietary estoppel[6]. Such an estoppel arose here on the basis of D's (albeit modest) expenditure coupled with P's tacit acquiescence. In deciding the extent of 'the minimum equity' required in order to do justice to D, the Court thought that the only appropriate way in which D's 'equity' could be satisfied in the present circumstances was by perfecting the imperfect oral gift of realty made by P. The court was influenced towards this conclusion by the fact that P was a relatively rich man who had shown himself

determined to pursue his purpose of evicting D from the house by any legal means at his disposal with a ruthless disregard of the obligations binding on conscience. The court must grant a remedy effective to protect her against the future manifestations of his ruthlessness[7].

A mere licence for D was held to be insufficient, not least because it would not enable D to charge the property in order to raise finance for further improvements to the realty which might prove to be necessary. The 'equity' to which the circumstances gave rise could be satisfied only by 'compelling the plaintiff to give effect to his promise and her expectations[8].'

At this point it becomes clear that the jurisprudence of proprietary estoppel

4 [1975] 1 WLR 1346 at 1350. The Court of Appeal has not been so ready in subsequent cases to find the existence of a contractual licence in similar circumstances. See *Horrocks v Forray* [1976] 1 WLR 230 (Megaw, Scarman and Bridge LJJ).
5 [1979] 1 WLR 431.
6 See *Dillwyn v Llewelyn* (1862) 4 De GF & J 517, p. 485, ante.
7 [1979] 1 WLR 431 at 438f. per Cumming-Bruce LJ.
8 *Pascoe v Turner* is remarkable in that the equitable jurisdiction of the court was effectively invoked to bring about a redistribution of assets on the breakdown of a de facto marriage relationship. The manner and extent of the redistribution lay entirely within the discretion of the court, and the common law wife was thereby enabled to circumvent the rule that a de facto spouse cannot claim property adjustment or financial provision from her partner on the demise of their relationship. See B. Sufrin (1979) 42 MLR 574: 'An Equity Richly Satisfied'.

provides an extremely flexible means by which the courts can so fashion discretionary relief as to do justice in the light of the interaction and expectations of the litigants. The development in this area of the law was aptly summarised in *Re Sharpe (A Bankrupt)*[9]. Here, S had acquired a leasehold interest in a shop and maisonette, much of the purchase price of this property being contributed by S's 77 year old aunt, J. In order to raise her contribution to the property, J had sold her existing home and had moved into the maisonette with S and his wife on the understanding that she would be able to stay there for as long as she wished. S later became bankrupt and his trustee in bankruptcy contracted to sell the leasehold premises to a purchaser P with vacant possession. When S's trustee in bankruptcy moved for vacant possession of the property, J argued that she had an interest in the premises. Browne-Wilkinson J declined to hold that she had an equitable interest in the property by way of resulting trust, taking the view that the moneys paid by J had been paid by way of loan[10]. He was, however, prepared to hold that J had acquired 'something less than an aliquot share of the equity in the premises, namely, the right to stay on the premises until the money she provided indirectly to acquire them has been repaid.' He noted that

> This right is based upon the line of recent Court of Appeal decisions which has spelt out irrevocable licences from informal family arrangements, and in some cases characterised such licences as conferring some equity or equitable interest under a constructive trust. I do not think that the principles lying behind these decisions have yet been fully explored and on occasion it seems that such rights are found to exist simply on the ground that to hold otherwise would be a hardship to the plaintiff. It appears that the principle is one akin to or an extension of a proprietary estoppel stemming from Lord Kingsdown's well-known statement of the law in *Ramsden v Dyson* (1866) LR 1 HL 129 at 170. In a strict case of proprietary estoppel the plaintiff has expended his own money on the defendant's property in an expectation encouraged by or known to the defendant that the plaintiff either owns the property or is to have some interest conferred on him. Recent authorities have extended this doctrine and, in my judgment, it is now established that, if the parties have proceeded on a common assumption that the plaintiff is to enjoy a right to reside in a particular property and in reliance on that assumption the plaintiff has expended money or otherwise acted to his detriment, the defendant will not be allowed to go back on that common assumption and the court will imply an irrevocable licence or trust which will give effect to that common assumption[11].

Browne-Wilkinson J thus concluded that the circumstances in which J had lent her money to facilitate the purchase in the name of S plainly gave rise to 'some right' in J. It was relevant that J had

> only loaned the money as part of a wider scheme, an essential feature of which was that she was to make her home in the property to be acquired with the money loaned[12].

9 [1980] 1 WLR 219. See [1980] Conv 207 (J. Martin); (1980) 96 LQR 336 (G. Woodman).

10 The loan analysis of the relationship was made inevitable by the fact that, after S became bankrupt, J (acting on her solicitor's advice) obtained from him a promissory note for £15,700. The parties thereby clearly indicated that the moneys paid by J to S were to be repayable.

11 [1980] 1 WLR 219 at 223.

12 [1980] 1 WLR 219 at 224.

Browne-Wilkinson J ruled that the right thus generated on behalf of J, 'whether it be called a contractual licence or an equitable licence or an interest under a constructive trust', was binding not only upon S but also upon S's trustee in bankruptcy, who simply stepped into the shoes of the debtor. J had a right to live in the property until her loan was repaid, and it followed that the trustee in bankruptcy took the property subject to that right[13].

Although this was sufficient to dispose of the issue between J and S's trustee in bankruptcy, Browne-Wilkinson J observed that P, who was not a party to the proceedings, would not necessarily be bound by such rights as J might have. In fact, Browne-Wilkinson J indicated that 'as a purchaser without express notice' P might well take priority over J in any action for specific performance of his contract.

In reaching this conclusion, Browne-Wilkinson J professed to find the present state of the law in this area

> very confused and difficult to fit in with established equitable principles. I express the hope that in the near future the whole question can receive full consideration in the Court of Appeal, so that, in order to do justice to the many thousands of people who never come into court at all but who wish to know with certainty what their proprietary rights are, the extent to which these irrevocable licences bind third parties may be defined with certainty. Doing justice to the litigant who actually appears in the court by the invention of new principles of law ought not to involve injustice to the other persons who are not litigants before the court but whose rights are fundamentally affected by the new principles[14].

The law relating to family arrangements was not made any more satisfactory by the judgment of the Court of Appeal in *Greasley v Cooke*[15]. Here the defendant, C, claimed a declaration that she had a right to occupy a house rent-free for the rest of her life. She had entered the house at the age of 16 as a living-in maid to the then owner, a widower with four children. She had at first been paid a weekly wage, but after eight years of paid employment had begun to cohabit in

13 Browne-Wilkinson J was unclear as to the precise nature of J's rights. He described them at one point as giving rise to an 'irrevocable licence' and at another as a 'contractual or equitable licence' which conferred 'some interest in the property under a constructive trust' ([1980] 1 WLR 219 at 225f.).

14 [1980] 1 WLR 219 at 226. Browne-Wilkinson J expressed his sympathy for the purchaser in this case, who was in fact in no better position than J. Browne-Wilkinson J pointed out that because of the inability of the trustee in bankruptcy to complete the sale, the purchaser could not open the business he intended, and consequently he and his wife and two children were being forced to live in a small motorised caravan parked on Hampstead Heath. Not every issue of priority involves an old lady being evicted from her home by the bank! See G. Woodman (1980) 96 LQR 336 at 340: 'To generalise ... about those against whom the interest may be initially enforced would ... be unduly simplistic. They are sometimes privileged, but sometimes as socially disadvantaged as the beneficiaries. Nevertheless, we need to identify the class of persons affected, so as to advance beyond the abstraction of "safe conveyancing." We may, perhaps, generalise about those who would be affected by enforcement against third parties ... Thus the class suffering detriment would consist of persons who bought land. There might also be a wider social loss from the brake placed on the market in land. It is submitted that attention should be directed to weighing these conflicting social interests, and considering whose claims should prevail in the distribution of advantages.'

15 [1980] 1 WLR 1306. See [1981] Conv 154 (R. E. Annand).

the house with one of the owner's sons, K. For nearly 30 years C looked after members of the family, including a daughter who suffered from severe mental illness, but received no kind of financial reward for her services during this period. C alleged that she had not asked for any payment because she had been encouraged by members of the family (including G, one of the present plaintiffs) to believe that she could regard the property as her home for the remainder of her life.

When both the original owner and his son, K, had died, the remaining members of the family who had inherited the property brought an action against C for possession. The county court judge declined to recognise that any proprietary estoppel had arisen in favour of C, holding that such a claim must fail on the ground that C had spent no money on the property. His decision was reversed by the Court of Appeal in a judgment which plainly met the justice of the case but may well have extended the doctrine of proprietary estoppel beyond its proper bounds. Lord Denning MR considered that an 'equity' had been raised in C's favour which required to be satisfied. He pointed out that in many of the cases decided on proprietary estoppel there had been expenditure of money. He went on to say

> But that is not a necessary element. I see that in *Snell's Principles of Equity*, 27th edn. (1973), p. 565, it is said: 'A must have incurred expenditure or otherwise have prejudiced himself.' But I do not think that that is necessary. It is sufficient if the party, to whom the assurance is given, acts on the faith of it—in such circumstances that it would be unjust and inequitable for the party making the assurance to go back on it: see *Moorgate Mercantile Co Ltd v Twitchings* [1976] QB 225 and *Crabb v Arun District Council* [1976] Ch 179 at 188. Applying those principles here it can be seen that the assurances given by [K and his brother]—leading her to believe that she would be allowed to stay in the house as long as she wished—raised an equity in her favour. There was no need for her to prove that she acted on the faith of those assurances. It is to be presumed that she did so. There is no need for her to prove that she acted to her detriment or to her prejudice. Suffice it that she stayed on in the house—looking after [K and the invalid daughter]—when otherwise she might have left and got a job elsewhere. The equity having thus been raised in her favour, it is for the courts of equity to decide in what way that equity should be satisfied. In this case it should be by allowing her to stay on in the house as long as she wishes[16].

It remains to be seen whether such a broad doctrine of proprietary estoppel can be sustained for long by the courts[17].

7. CAN AN 'EQUITY' FLUCTUATE?

It is quite clear that the 'equity' enjoyed by a contractual or estoppel licensee is capable of fluctuation. Developments subsequent to the date on which the 'equity' is initially raised may cause the court, in the exercise of its flexible

16 [1980] 1 WLR 1306 at 1311f.

17 Compare *Christian v Christian* (1981) 131 NLJ 43, where a differently constituted Court of Appeal (Lawton and Brightman LJJ and Sir John Ramsey Willis) rejected a claim on the ground of absence of proven 'detriment'.

jurisdiction, either to withhold relief from the licensee or to grant him relief in terms other than those which it would have been inclined to order at an earlier stage. It seems to be accepted that

> when the plaintiff comes to court to enforce his legal rights, the defendant is then entitled to submit that in equity the plaintiff should not be allowed to enforce those rights and that the defendant, raising that equity, must then bring into play all the relevant maxims of equity so that the court is entitled then on the facts to look at all the circumstances and decide what order should be made, if any, to satisfy the equity[18].

This simply indicates that the extent of the 'equity' enjoyed by the licensee in virtue of his rights truly crystallises only at the point of relief.

Thus, in *Tanner v Tanner*[19], Lord Denning MR made it clear that the de facto wife's contractual licence could lawfully have been determined if, by reason of a change of circumstance, the accommodation were no longer reasonably required. In *Crabb v Arun District Council*[20], the Court of Appeal satisfied the 'equity' claimed by ordering the granting of an easement without compensation, even though had the matter been litigated earlier, it would have ordered the party setting up the 'equity' to make compensation for the grant. However, during the time which had elapsed, the party denying the 'equity' had effectively sterilised the user of an industrial estate by his denial of access, and for this the Court was prepared to penalise him.

There is a difficult question as to whether an 'equity' may be prejudiced by subsequent misbehaviour on the part of a licensee. In *Williams v Staite*[1], occupiers under a licence coupled with an equity asserted their licence against the licensor in a threatening and highly unpleasant manner. The Court of Appeal decided that 'excessive user or bad behaviour towards the legal owner cannot bring the equity to an end or forfeit it', although such action might well give rise to a claim in trespass or nuisance. This approach can be justified on the ground that otherwise the position of a third party purchasing from the licensor might depend upon the relative unpleasantness of the licensee at any particular point in time! However, to adhere to this approach is to disregard the maxim that 'he who comes into equity must come with clean hands.'

8. CAN A THIRD PARTY BE BOUND BY A 'LICENCE COUPLED WITH AN EQUITY'?

It is tempting to suggest that, in the aftermath of recent developments in the law relating to licences, the 'licence coupled with an equity' has been elevated by judicial decision to the status of a proprietary interest in land. If such is indeed the case, the corollary must be that various kinds of licence are now capable of binding a third party who purchases the land with notice of the facts which raise the 'equity'.

18 *Williams v Staite* [1979] Ch 291 at 300f. per Cumming-Bruce LJ.
19 [1975] 1 WLR 1346 at 1350, p. 492, ante.
20 [1976] Ch 179.
1 [1979] Ch 291.

The question whether a licence binds third parties has a fundamental significance for property lawyers. For the academic there is the nice point as to the precise location of the borderline between property and contract. For the conveyancer, however, the question assumes an immediate and paramount practical importance. One spectre above all others should haunt the conveyancer in practice—the ghostly apparition of the unregistrable, non-overreachable equitable interest in land. The bindingness of such an interest upon his client depends upon the application of the doctrine of notice where title is unregistered[2], and upon the definition of 'overriding interests' where title is registered[3]. The fear of the conveyancer is that the title taken by his purchaser-client may be rendered effectively worthless if that purchaser is subsequently held to have been trapped by constructive notice or by force of statute in respect of a right which he could have discovered only with great difficulty. Thus in the debate which follows here, there is a lively confrontation between two lines of judicial opinion, one of which expresses an implicit sympathy for the plight of the conveyancing solicitor, and the other a somewhat more robust disregard for the technical problems of conveyancing practice[4].

It is clear that a licence which is coupled with an 'equity' founded upon expenditure, acquiescence and (therefore) estoppel is regarded as having proprietary status. Such a licence binds a third party purchaser with notice[5], for the simple reason that his conscience is no less affected by the 'equity' than was the conscience of his predecessor in title[6]. This result adds, of course, to the category of unregistrable, non-overreachable equitable interests in land, with consequent insecurity and uncertainty for both the licensee and the purchaser[7].

While the bindingness of a licence founded on proprietary estoppel seems fairly plain, the same cannot be said of the question whether contractual licences affect third parties. Lord Denning MR has consistently maintained that such licences can affect third parties, in the sense that a third party will normally be restrained from denying the 'equity' of the occupier in all circumstances except where the third party is a purchaser who takes the land without notice of the 'equity'. In this case his conscience is naturally unencumbered by the rights of the contractual licensee. This approach has been endorsed by Lord Denning on a number of occasions[8].

2 See p. 313ff., ante.
3 See p. 339, ante.
4 For a similar juxtaposition of philosophy, see pp. 367, 373, ante.
5 For a definition of the precise degree of notice required, see R. H. Maudsley (1956) 20 Conv (NS) 281 at 291ff. Here it is suggested that estoppel licensees who do not enjoy exclusive possession are protected against (i) purchasers with actual notice, and (ii) volunteers. However, estoppel licensees who have exclusive possession are protected against *every* person coming to the land except a purchaser for value without notice, actual or constructive, the rule in *Hunt v Luck* being applied. See *Re Sharpe* (*A Bankrupt*) [1980] 1 WLR 219 at 224.
6 See p. 485, ante.
7 It is interesting to note that, in *Pascoe v Turner* [1979] 1 WLR 431 at 493, p. 493, ante, one of the factors which influenced the court to hold the 'equity' satisfied by a conveyance in fee simple was precisely the consideration that 'a licence cannot be registered as a land charge, so that [the occupier] may find herself ousted by a purchaser for value without notice.'
8 See *Errington v Errington and Woods* [1952] 1 KB 290 at 299, p. 487, ante; *National Provincial Bank*

Not the least of the difficulties confronting this approach to contractual licences is the fact that there is weighty authority for the directly contrary view in two previous decisions: that of the House of Lords in *King v David Allen & Sons Ltd*[9] and that of the Court of Appeal itself in *Clore v Theatrical Properties Ltd and Westby & Co Ltd*[10]. The authority of both decisions was gently reaffirmed by the House of Lords in *National Provincial Bank Ltd v Hastings Car Mart Ltd*[11]. However, Lord Denning is not one to be unduly perturbed by contrary precedents[12], and he has therefore ventured to distinguish *King* and *Clore* on two grounds.

(1) Conveyance 'subject to the rights' of the contractual licensee

In *Binions v Evans*[13], it was written into the contract of sale between X and P that the property was sold 'subject to' the rights enjoyed by D. Moreover, P was supplied with a copy of the previous agreement which conferred those rights on D. Lord Denning then observed, in the course of his judgment, that in *King* and *Clore* 'there was no trace of a stipulation, express or implied, that the purchaser should take the property subject to the right of the contractual licensee.' However, in both of those cases it is clear that the third party purchasers took with express actual knowledge of the respective contractual licences. It seems not entirely relevant that such knowledge was not formally incorporated in the contracts of sale or deeds of conveyance by way of some express stipulation that the property in question was sold 'subject to the rights' of the contractual licensee. If conscience is to be treated as determinative, the conscience of the purchaser in either case was already bound by his express actual knowledge. One's conscience is not the more strictly bound by a moral imperative which is delivered twice as distinct from merely once.

(2) Actual occupation of the contractual licensee

A second ground of distinction proffered by Lord Denning consists in his argument that a third party is bound by a licence coupled with an equity only where 'the licensee has been in actual occupation of the land.' Where the licensee is not in actual occupation when the third party takes title, 'the position may be different[14].' This approach is certainly consistent with decisions like *King, Errington* and *Binions v Evans*, providing the basis for Lord Denning's assertion in the last-mentioned case that

---

Ltd v Hastings Car Mart Ltd [1964] Ch 665 at 686, p. 338, ante; *Binions v Evans* [1972] Ch 359 at 368, p. 490, ante; *Tanner v Tanner* [1975] 1 WLR 1346 at 1350, p. 492, ante.

9 [1916] 2 AC 54.

10 [1936] 3 All ER 483, p. 390, ante.

11 [1965] AC 1175 at 1239 per Lord Upjohn, at 1251 per Lord Wilberforce.

12 It was Lord Denning, after all, who declared in *Hill v C. A. Parsons Ltd* [1972] Ch 305 at 316 'the fundamental principle that, whenever a man has a right, the law should give a remedy. The Latin maxim is ubi ius ibi remedium. This principle enables us to step over the trip-wires of previous cases and to bring the law into accord with the needs of today.'

13 [1972] Ch 359, p. 490, ante.

14 *National Provincial Bank Ltd v Hastings Car Mart Ltd* [1964] Ch 665 at 688.

when the licensee is in actual occupation, neither the licensor nor anyone who claims through him can disregard the contract except a purchaser for value without notice[15].

Clore has been distinguished by Lord Denning on the ground that there a licence to exercise 'front of the house' rights in a theatre could 'not properly be said to be actual occupation[16].'

There are, however, two fundamental difficulties in connection with any line of distinction drawn with reference to actual occupation by a contractual licensee. One is the fact that it is simply untrue that the licensee in *Clore* was not in actual occupation[17]. The other objection runs even deeper, and was expressed in Russell LJ's statement in the Court of Appeal in *National Provincial Bank Ltd v Hastings Car Mart Ltd* that he could 'not accept that [*King's* case] depends for its validity on the fact that the licence had not yet been acted upon[18].' Russell LJ pointed out that

the actual occupation is not the right; it is a form of notice of a right; the right must be sought elsewhere. Since in *King's* case there was actual notice of the licence which conferred the right, the question of occupation would not seem to affect the matter[19].

At the end of the day, as Russell LJ indicated, the inexorable truth of the matter is that the real basis for the decisions in *King* and *Clore* was the court's refusal in both cases to accept that a contractual licence is anything other than a private agreement which binds only the immediate parties; it creates no proprietary interest in land. In coming to this conclusion, which certainly represents the orthodox legal view at present, Russell LJ was unmoved by the impact of equitable intervention following *Winter Garden Theatre (London) Ltd v Millennium Productions Ltd*[20]. He confessed that he found it

not easy to see, on authority, how that which has a purely contractual basis between A and B is, though on all hands it is agreed that it is not to be regarded as conferring any estate or interest in property on B, nevertheless to be treated as producing the equivalent result against a purchaser C, simply because an injunction would be granted to restrain A from breaking his contract while he is still in a position to carry it out[1].

This argument must inevitably lead us, in the final section of this chapter, to consider exactly what we mean when we talk of 'property' or of a 'proprietary interest'.

9. THE MEANING OF 'PROPERTY' AND 'EQUITABLE RIGHTS OF PROPERTY'

Throughout this book we have referred to 'property' as connoting not a thing

15 [1972] Ch 359 at 369.
16 *National Provincial Bank Ltd v Hastings Car Mart Ltd* [1964] Ch 665 at 688.
17 This point was taken by Russell LJ in the *National Provincial Bank* case (see [1964] Ch 665 at 698).
18 See R. H. Maudsley (1956) 20 Conv (NS) 281 at 285, for confirmation that the difference between an executory and an executed licence was not relied on in *King's* case and indeed had been regarded as irrelevant for 100 years before that.
19 [1964] Ch 665 at 697.
20 [1948] AC 173, p. 486, ante.
1 [1964] Ch 665 at 698.

but a relationship. This perspective dominates, notwithstanding the fact that we have, for purposes of clarity, used illustrative diagrams which may appear to confer upon property rights a spuriously reified form. The truth is that 'property' is not properly understood in such concrete terms, but rather in terms of socially defined relationships and morally conditioned obligations.

This point is especially true of 'equitable rights of property', and therefore has important implications for the questions which we have just been discussing—whether a contractual licence can bind a third party purchaser with actual notice of that licence. In *National Provincial Bank Ltd v Hastings Car Mart Ltd*[2], Russell LJ answered this question in the negative. On his analysis, a contractual licence creates not a right of 'property' in land but merely a personal right affecting that land. It follows from this premise that, since only proprietary rights have the quality of binding third parties, a contractual licence cannot affect even a third party who takes the land with actual notice.

It can, however, be argued that to approach problems of this kind in terms of a 'property' analysis is to turn the process on its head and to begin with a conclusion. Where an equitable interest in land is protected against third parties, the reality of the matter is not that it is thus protected because it is 'property', but rather that it is 'property' precisely because—ultimately through the equitable intervention of the courts—it is indeed protected[3]. To address the question in terms of a 'property' analysis is to argue at one remove from the legal reality that underlies, and is often to invite obfuscation of the issue.

To say that a person has an equitable interest is not to say that he owns a 'thing' but to indicate that someone owes him an obligation. This idea becomes a little clearer if for the unhelpful term 'beneficiary' we substitute the less modern but more literally expressive term 'cestui que trust'. 'Trusts', said Lindley LJ, 'are equitable obligations to deal with property in a particular way'[4]. As Isaacs J once pointed out[5],

> the right of any *cestui que trust* to have the property dealt with as the trust requires is regarded for the purposes of equity as equivalent to a right in the property itself, but only commensurate with his particular right *in personam*.

As the same judge observed on another occasion[6], 'equitable ownership, as it is called, is always commensurate with the right to relief in a Court of Equity.'

An 'equitable right of property' is therefore simply a right to equitable relief against the assertion by another of legal rights in the same 'thing'[7]. That right

2 [1964] Ch 665 at 697ff.

3 Compare C. B. Macpherson, 'The Meaning of Property', in C. B. Macpherson (ed.), *Property: Mainstream and Critical Positions* (Oxford 1978), 3: 'Property is not thought to be a right because it is an enforceable claim: it is an enforceable claim only because and in so far as the prevailing ethical theory holds that it is a necessary human right.'

4 *Re Williams* [1897] 2 Ch 12 at 18.

5 *Glenn v Federal Comr of Land Tax* (1915) 20 CLR 490 at 503.

6 *Trustees, Executors and Agency Co Ltd v Acting Federal Comr of Taxation* (1917) 23 CLR 576 at 583.

7 See *Chase Manhattan Bank NA v Israel-British Bank (London) Ltd* [1981] Ch 105 at 124 per Goulding J: 'Within the municipal confines of a single legal system, right and remedy are indissolubly connected and correlated, each contributing in historical dialogue to the development of the

to relief is premised upon a perceived obligation binding the legal owner to deal with the property honestly and in good faith. An effective claim to such relief metamorphoses imperceptibly into the kind of right to which, in legal shorthand, we refer as a right of 'property'. As was once said in relation to the equitable rules of tracing, equitable intervention, although

> [s]tarting from a personal equity ... ended, as was so often the case, in creating what were in effect rights of property, though not recognised as such by the common law[8].

Thus, in the creation of an 'equitable right of property', the existence of a moral duty is logically anterior to the recognition of the proprietary right. In the beginning was not a right but a relationship. This is clear from the fact that where there is no relationship there can be no equitable right, as for instance where property is—in lawyers' terms—owned by one person absolutely. In *Comr of Stamp Duties (Queensland) v Livingston*[9], Viscount Radcliffe spoke of the 'fallacy' contained in the assumption that

> for all purposes and at every moment of time the law requires the separate existence of two different kinds of estate or interest in property, the legal and the equitable. There is no need to make this assumption. When the whole right of property is in a person ... there is no need to distinguish between the legal and equitable interest in that property ... Equity in fact calls into existence and protects equitable rights and interests in property only where their recognition has been found to be required in order to give effect to its doctrines.

Whole areas of equitable jurisdiction can be understood only on the basis that an equitable property right is protected not because it has first been characterised as 'property', but because equitable intervention is imperative in order to satisfy the demands of ethical dealing within a given social or commercial relationship. This is particularly true, for example, of the law which protects the integrity of trade marks and regulates the use of confidential information. Holmes J once remarked that

> the word 'property' as applied to trademarks and trade secrets is an unanalysed expression of certain secondary consequences of the primary fact that the law makes some rudimentary requirements of good faith[10].

The same approach can be found at the root of the law relating to restrictive covenants. It is striking that the decision which is generally accepted as marking the conferment of proprietary character upon restrictive covenants is not actually phrased in these terms at all. In *Tulk v Moxhay*[11], Lord Cottenham LC did not hold the restrictive covenant to be binding on the third party purchaser

---

other, and save in very special circumstances it is as idle to ask whether the court vindicates the suitor's substantive right or gives the suitor a procedural remedy, as to ask whether thought is a mental or cerebral process. In fact the court does both things by one and the same act.'

8 *Sinclair v Brougham* [1914] AC 398 at 441f. per Lord Parker of Waddington.

9 [1965] AC 694 at 712.

10 *E.I. Du Pont de Nemours Powder Co v Masland*, 244 US 100 at 102 (1917).

11 (1848) 2 Ph 774, p. 614, post.

on the ground that it was, in some sense, 'property', or because (as he would have expressed the same idea) it 'ran with the land'. Instead, he said expressly that

> the question is not whether the covenant runs with the land, but whether a party shall be permitted to use the land in a manner inconsistent with the contract entered into by his vendor, and with notice of which he purchased. Of course, the price would be affected by the covenant, and nothing could be more inequitable than that the original purchaser should be able to sell the property the next day for a greater price, in consideration of the assignee being allowed to escape from the liability which he had himself undertaken[12].

When the genesis of an equitable interest in land is explained in this way, it becomes increasingly obvious that there is little essential difference between the 'equitable proprietary interest' and many kinds of 'equity' which are, in the traditional view, classified as mere interests *in personam*. Lord Wilberforce expressed the conventional distinction between proprietary and personal rights when he said in *National Provincial Bank Ltd v Hastings Car Mart Ltd*[13] that

> before a right or interest can be admitted into the category of property, or of a right affecting property, it must be definable, identifiable by third parties, capable in its nature of assumption by third parties, and have some degree of permanence or stability.

A contractual licence, in the traditional view, does not conform to these characteristics.

It might be observed that, in so far as Lord Wilberforce's criterion of proprietary character rests upon an indicium of 'permanence or stability', the courts' definition of 'property' is self-fulfilling. However, two other points are peculiarly relevant to the law of contractual licences.

First, it seems strange to exclude the contractual licence from the category of property rights on the ground that the interest of the licensee fails to comply with some supposed criterion of transmissibility, when the only really difficult problem posed by the admission of such licences relates to the effect of a transfer of the interest of the *licensor*. It is the assignment of the latter's interest which is controversial. Contractual licences—particularly in the context of family arrangements—are rarely if ever assigned, largely because the security conferred by the licence is usually envisaged from the outset as being a purely personal and non-transmissible benefit.

Second, the dogma that requires that a property interest be definable and capable both of identification by and transmission to third parties represents an increasingly obsolete approach to the contemporary concept of 'property'. This dogma is pervaded by an image of property as something commerciable—as something which belongs essentially in the world of exchange relationships. This view is not particularly apposite to the kinds of property which enjoy social significance today. In a modern industrial society the traditional concept of a man's wealth has undergone a subtle transformation. His substance is no longer inherently related to the 'ownership' of tangible and freely alienable assets, but is now more readily expressed in terms of intangible, non-assignable, often non-survivable claims of a purely personal nature. And, consistent with the dominant

12 (1848) 2 Ph 774 at 777f.
13 [1965] AC 1175 at 1247f.

need of the present age, the factor which typifies the social desire underlying all such claims is the universal quest not for dispositive power over 'things', but for security in the enjoyment of 'utility'. In other words, the unifying factor is the claim to security in respect of the legal and social bonding of home, work and family. The 'new property' is as profoundly related to the emerging importance of residential security as it is to employment security, pension security, social security and health security[14].

The definition of 'property' is therefore in the middle of a period of scarcely perceptible evolution. In the light of current developments in this regard, it may be wrong arbitrarily to exclude contractual licences from the field of 'property'—not least because in recent times the contractual occupation licence has acquired an unprecedented prominence as a residential device.

It is, moreover, readily understood in other contexts that 'as a practical matter' the granting of injunctive relief, when 'unlimited in point of time,' can be equivalent to a transfer of property order, continuing as long as the other party was living[15]. In the area of Rent Act protection the 'status of irremovability' enjoyed by the protected or statutory tenant is recognised as 'one of the most significant rights of property' which an individual may hold[16].

The courts are only now beginning to acknowledge that, in the matter of residential security, personal rights and property rights are not distinct but interactive[17]. It is worth remembering that the law of licences has been developed in the case law mainly within the context of the ill-fated doctrine of the 'deserted wife's equity'[18]. *National Provincial Bank Ltd v Hastings Car Mart Ltd*[19] was, after all, the decision which conclusively determined that the 'deserted wife's equity' had no capacity to affect a third party. In the Court of Appeal in *Davis v Johnson*[20], Lord Denning MR referred once again to the fact that in the *National Provincial Bank* case 'the personal rights of the deserted wife were not allowed to override the property rights of the husband.' The Master of the Rolls ventured to

> suggest that that concept about rights of property is quite out-of-date. It is true that in the 19th century the law paid quite high regard to rights of property. But this gave rise to such misgivings that in modern times the law has changed course. Social justice requires that personal rights should, in a proper case, be given priority over rights of property.

These sentiments were later to find more than a mere echo in Lord Denning's ruling in *Williams & Glyn's Bank Ltd v Boland*[1] that the court, on the facts of that case, 'should not give monied might priority over social justice'. There is but a relatively short step between such statements and the achievement of a new

14 See p. 39f., ante.
15 *Cantliff v Jenkins* [1978] Fam 47n at 51 per Stamp LJ.
16 See *Mafo v Adams* [1970] 1 QB 548 at 557 per Widgery LJ, p. 434, ante.
17 See Sir R. Evershed (1954) 70 LQR 326 at 331, 341.
18 See p. 143, ante.
19 [1965] AC 1175.
20 [1979] AC 264 at 274.
1 [1979] Ch 312 at 333. The Court of Appeal's decision was unanimously upheld by the House of Lords ([1980] 3 WLR 138, p. 370, ante).

order of 'property' (at least in the residential sphere) in which the distinction between personal rights and proprietary rights is completely eliminated. Indeed, it is highly arguable that the law is already moving towards the recognition of a 'new property', based upon secure enjoyment of the 'goods of life', in which 'personal' and 'proprietary' rights will merge and any distinction will become meaningless.

The immediate context of Lord Denning's remarks in *Davis v Johnson* was, of course, the legislative intervention contained in the Domestic Violence and Matrimonial Proceedings Act 1976[2]. It may be that the elevation of contractual licences to proprietary status (in lawyers' terms) will similarly require statutory intervention[3]. In any event it seems inevitable that new solutions will have to be worked out in relation to the contractual licence. But developments in this area are occurring apace, and serve to demonstrate yet again the shifting nature of the concept of 'property'. It may yet be that the contractual occupation licence will acquire statutory protection against third parties.

2 See p. 236, ante.

3 See *National Provincial Bank Ltd v Hastings Car Mart Ltd* [1964] Ch 665 at 699 per Russell LJ, but compare the observations of Lord Upjohn and Lord Wilberforce respectively, [1965] AC 1175 at 1239, 1251.

CHAPTER 15

Mortgages

1. INTRODUCTION

In this chapter we turn to an examination of the 'mortgage' or 'charge' over real property. Both devices provide the lender of money with a valuable form of security in the property of his borrower. We shall discover, however, that the mortgage or charge is more than merely a legal device intended to provide creditors with security for loans advanced by them. Mortgage finance plays a vitally important part in the realisation of the life chances and aspirations of a large section of the population, and is also intricately connected with the much larger issue of the general availability of credit in the national economy.

We shall therefore look in this chapter at the way in which the mortgage of real property may be used to achieve a wide range of fiscal, commercial and family purposes. We shall ask not simply how, but also why, mortgage transactions are effected.

(1) Definitions

In strict terms, a 'mortgage' is a disposition of some interest in land or other property 'as a security for the payment of a debt or the discharge of some other obligation for which it is given'[1]. The 'mortgagee' (i.e., the lender of money) is thereby placed in the privileged position of being a secured creditor of the 'mortgagor' (i.e., the borrower of money), with the consequence that he enjoys priority over the latter's unsecured creditors if the latter becomes insolvent[2]. Thus, for the purpose of recovering the amount of his loan, the mortgagee enjoys not merely a personal right based upon his contract of loan with the borrower, but also a proprietary right, potentially enforceable against third parties, to realise the value of the mortgaged property. In this sense, mortgage transactions today represent the safest method of lending money on the credit market since ultimately the property offered as security can be sold by the mortgagee and the proceeds of sale applied in repayment of the loan.

In strict terms a 'mortgage' should be distinguished from a 'charge' over property. Whereas a mortgage actually invests the mortgagee with an interest

1 *Santley v Wilde* [1899] 2 Ch 474, per Lindley MR.

2 For a new and controversial means of acquiring priority over creditors in the commercial sphere by means of a contractual 'retention of title' clause, see *Aluminium Industrie Vaassen BV v Romalpa Aluminium Ltd* [1976] 1 WLR 676; *Re Bond Worth Ltd* [1980] Ch 228; *Borden (UK) Ltd v Scottish Timber Products Ltd* [1981] Ch 25.

in the secured property, a charge confers no such interest but merely confers on the 'chargee' certain rights (e.g., in respect of possession and sale) over the property charged as security for the loan[3]. Nevertheless, the practical distinction between mortgages and charges is largely historical, and nowadays the charge may be regarded for most purposes as simply a species of mortgage[4]. The rules discussed in this chapter apply generally both to mortgages and to charges.

The foregoing is a rather bleak legal description of the institution of the mortgage or charge of real property. In order to acquire a keener perception of the role of mortgages, we must inquire into the practical significance of mortgage finance in today's world.

(2) The significance of mortgage finance for the private individual

The institution of the mortgage exerts a profound effect upon ordinary people in a variety of ways. From the point of view of the private individual, his mortgage commitment can indeed become a central concern in his life. By mortgaging real property, he is enabled to acquire a loan of substantial capital which he may then apply for a number of possible purposes. The capital money is normally repayable over a long term (e.g., 25 or 30 years). The repayment may comprise periodic payments of both capital and interest (as in the ordinary 'repayment' or 'instalment' mortgage)[5]. Alternatively, the entire capital sum borrowed may be left outstanding during the mortgage term, the mortgagor meanwhile servicing the loan by paying the periodic interest which accrues on the capital debt (as in the 'endowment mortgage')[6].

A mortgage transaction will almost certainly represent the largest single form of financial indebtedness incurred by the ordinary individual during his lifetime, and the discharge of this obligation will probably rank as his most important financial responsibility. The major benefit offered the borrower of mortgage finance is the opportunity to become an owner-occupier of his dwelling-house in circumstances where he would not otherwise be able to afford to purchase such a property. Many institutional mortgagees (such as building societies, banks, local authorities and insurance companies) are prepared to advance money on the security of a mortgage in order to facilitate home ownership for the private citizen. The individual is thereby enabled simultaneously to buy a house with borrowed money[7] and to offer the home thus purchased as security for the loan

3 See *Weg Motors Ltd v Hales* [1962] Ch 49 at 77 per Donovan LJ.

4 The distinction is finally blurred by the reference in the 1925 legislation to a 'charge by way of legal mortgage'. See Law of Property Act 1925, ss. 1(2)(c), 85(1). See *Grand Junction Co Ltd v Bates* [1954] 2 QB 160 at 168 per Upjohn J; *Regent Oil Co Ltd v J. A. Gregory (Hatch End) Ltd* [1966] Ch 402 at 431 per Harman LJ.

5 During the early years of the mortgage, most of each periodic payment will comprise interest rather than capital, the relative proportions of capital and interest altering during the course of the mortgage term.

6 Under an endowment mortgage, the borrower provides additional security for the capital loan by assigning to the mortgagee a policy of life assurance taken out on the borrower's life. The life assurance is so calculated as to yield a capital sum equivalent to the mortgage debt on the date of its maturing or in the event of the earlier death of the mortgagor.

7 Few mortgagees will, however, lend 100 per cent of the purchase price of property.

advanced to him. The borrower retains the freehold or leasehold estate in the property throughout the period of the mortgage loan, but is usually under an obligation to repay the principal sum and the interest which it bears during the loan term. The mortgagor is ultimately enabled to acquire both a family base and a major capital asset by means of what is essentially an instalment purchase spread over half a lifetime.

The availability of mortgage finance thus has a significant impact upon the life chances of the individual borrower. It may mean for him the difference between owning his own home in a peaceful suburban haven and renting a council house on the local estate or entrusting his fate to the hazards of the private rental market. In turn, the nature of his tenure (whether as owner-occupier or tenant) will be an important status determinant in his life. It may affect his personal life and his marriage prospects. It will certainly affect his creditworthiness for many purposes ranging from the renting of a television set to the buying of goods on hire purchase. The possession of a secure and permanent home base is generally taken to be a good indicator of financial reliability. The nature of his tenure may control the timing both of his marriage and of the arrival of his children, and may well be correlated with the ultimate size of his family. The availability of mortgage finance may ultimately equip him with a source of capital which will help him in his old age. By that time he will probably have acquired an unencumbered estate in land which will either serve as his home or present him with a capital asset which is readily converted into some form of income for his retirement.

The availability of mortgage finance may affect the borrower's life style and family patterns in other ways. Home ownership (even with the aid of borrowed money) provides a means of access to capital during a person's working life. Anyone who has owned a house during the last 15 years would be extremely unlucky not to have accumulated capital of at least £10,000—and in most cases very much more[8]. This capital may not be immediately realisable, but it nevertheless provides an asset against which further money may be borrowed. An increase in the amount of the borrower's mortgage loan may enable him to effect improvements or extensions to his home. These may in turn enable him to realise a number of objectives ranging from the construction of a new sun patio or swimming pool in his back garden to the provision of a self-contained flat for an ageing parent or other relative. Environment and life style significantly interact. If the borrower is a small businessman, new commercial horizons may open up for him if he can use the family home as security for a bank loan earmarked for the creation or extension of a commercial operation. This possibility raises the difficult moral question whether a home-owner should be any more free to offer his family base as security for a loan for entrepreneurial purposes than a landlord to own another's home for the purpose of deriving personal profit[9].

8 See John Stanley MP, Minister for Housing and Construction, Department of the Environment, 'Government Policies on Home Ownership in the 1980s' in SHAC, *Home Ownership in the 1980s* (Policy Paper No. 3, July 1980), p. 6.

9 See p. 418, ante.

It is sometimes said that home ownership with the aid of mortgage finance provides the individual with greater mobility than the occupier who merely rents his home. It must indeed be true that the owner-occupier is more mobile, at least in the geographical sense, than the individual who rents in, say, the public sector. There is, however, an important respect in which it should be noted that the owner-occupier is less mobile. Once installed as a home owner on the strength of a mortgage advance, the borrower becomes subtly tied to his current employment. The legal bonding of employer and employee is no less dictated by the economic necessities of the employee's mortgage commitment than by the advent of modern employment protection legislation. The contemporary prevalence of the building society mortgage has ushered in a new feudal age in which the residential occupier is once again *adscriptus glebae*: he is no longer in a position to afford excessive labour mobility. He himself acquires a vested financial interest in his mortgage, since the capital value of his property is steadily inflating year by year, and he relies increasingly heavily upon his payment of mortgage interest as a means of reducing the marginal rate of taxation to which his income is liable[10].

(3) The 'property-owning democracy'

In a broad sense, then, the law and practice of mortgages play an important role in determining the quality of life of many millions in this country. The availability of mortgage finance has served significantly to promote the ethic of home ownership. As Lord Diplock once observed[11], a range of demographic, economic and social factors has resulted during the last 30 years in 'the emergence of a property-owning, particularly a real-property-mortgaged-to-a-building-society-owning, democracy.' At the beginning of the First World War there were only approximately 750,000 home owners in England, comprising 10 per cent of all households. Today there are estimated to be 9,500,000 home owners[12]. The decade of the 1970s alone saw an increase in owner-occupation from 49 per cent of all households in Great Britain in 1971 to 55 per cent by mid-1979[13]. Of these owner-occupiers, 56 per cent were estimated to be subject to an existing mortgage liability, with the consequence that there are now almost 6 million mortgages on residential properties in Great Britain[14].

The increased participation in the ethic of home ownership has certainly been encouraged by the greater involvement of married women in the labour force

10 Under the Finance Act 1972, s. 75 (as amended by the Finance Act 1974, s. 19), a taxpayer may claim income tax relief to the extent of the interest which is payable on any loan used for the purchase or improvement of land. For an economist's reply to the criticism that home-owners are thus subsidised by other tax-payers, see J. Parry Lewis, *Urban Economics: a set approach* (London 1979), p. 73f.

11 *Pettitt v Pettitt* [1970] AC 777 at 824.

12 John Stanley MP, loc. cit., p. 6.

13 See Office of Population Censuses and Surveys, *General Household Survey 1978* (London 1980), 31 (Table 3.1); Central Statistical Office, *Social Trends No. 11* (London 1981), 145 (Table 9.4).

14 *General Household Survey 1978*, supra, 31 (Table 3.1). It has been estimated that 78 per cent of these mortgages are provided by building societies, 11 per cent by local authorities, 6 per cent by insurance companies and 3 per cent by banks (see Table 3.44).

and by the wider diffusion of earning capacity within the community as a whole. Moreover the nexus of cause and effect in this context is commonly entangled since one of the principal motivations for women to seek employment outside the home is the desire to help their husbands both to qualify for a larger mortgage loan (by showing a greater income base)[15] and to service that loan from current family income.

Whatever the causes which lie behind the extension of owner-occupation, it is quite clear that home ownership has operated during the current century as an immensely powerful engine of wealth creation and wealth distribution. In 1914 the value of personal assets represented by privately owned housing was only £2 billion. By the end of 1977 that figure had increased to £150 billion, a development which—even after making discounts on the ground of inflation—indicates a four-fold increase in the personal assets invested in housing during the last 60 years[16]. The phenomenon of home ownership has plainly brought millions of citizens within the 'propertied classes'. Indeed some would even argue that the explosion of home ownership has done more than any form of taxation to effect the redistribution of private wealth.

(4) The political dimension of mortgages

Mortgage finance enjoys a certain public importance, not least because the ethic of home ownership has a clear political dimension. Home ownership in fee simple, particularly with the aid of mortgage finance, breeds political conservatism[17]—a fact which is not unknown to the political parties themselves[18].

15 Building societies will normally advance loans not exceeding 2½ or 3 times the borrower's gross annual income plus half his wife's gross annual income.

16 John Stanley MP, loc. cit., p. 6.

17 It was Harold Bellman, one of the leading figures in the early building society movement, who in 1927 saw clearly that the 'working man who is merely a tenant has no real anchorage, no permanent abiding place, and in certain circumstances is fair prey for breeders of faction and revolutionaries of every sort and condition. Home-ownership is a civic and national asset. The sense of citizenship is more keenly felt and appreciated, and personal independence opens up many an avenue of wide responsibility and usefulness. The benefits of home-ownership are not merely material, but ethical and moral as well. The man who has something to protect and improve—a stake of some sort in the country—naturally turns his thoughts in the direction of sane, ordered, and perforce economical government. The thrifty man is seldom or never an extremist agitator. To him revolution is anathema; and as in the earliest days Building Societies acted as a stabilising force, so today they stand . . . as a "bulwark against Bolshevism and all that Bolshevism stands for".' See H. Bellman, *The Building Society Movement* (London 1927), p. 53f.

18 A strong desire to promote the ethic of home ownership underlies the scheme introduced in the Conservative Housing Act 1980 for enabling council tenants to purchase their own homes with the aid of mortgage finance provided from public funds controlled by the Housing Corporation, p. 463, ante. Introducing the Housing Bill in the House of Commons, Mr Michael Heseltine (Secretary of State for the Environment) said: 'There is in this country a deeply ingrained desire for home ownership. The Government believe that this spirit should be fostered. It reflects the wishes of the people, ensures the wide spread of wealth through society, encourages a personal desire to improve and modernise one's own home, enables parents to accrue wealth for their children and stimulates the attitudes of independence and self-reliance that are the bedrock of a free society . . . [This Bill] will transform the personal prospects of millions of our citizens, offering to turn them at their wish from tenants to owners. It will establish their rights as individuals above the bureaucracies of the State. It will come to be seen among the finest

The enlightened self-interest of the owner-occupier represents a form of political capital for those who are inclined towards the preservation of the status quo. It should therefore not be forgotten that the ready provision of mortgage facilities can operate to express public endorsement of certain approved patterns of life style and political demeanour. The very institution of the mortgage itself bespeaks a flexibility of choice and self-determination which find their roots in the political philosophy of the right rather than the left. It is, of course, the former influence which has moulded our law of real property, and it should therefore come as no surprise to note that in *National Provincial Bank Ltd v Hastings Car Mart Ltd*[19] Lord Upjohn declared that

> It has been the policy of the law for over a hundred years to simplify and facilitate transactions in real property. It is of great importance that persons should be able freely and easily to raise money on the security of their property.

(5) The 'public interest' in mortgages

Apart from the starkly political dimension of mortgage finance, there is a good case for the maintenance of a 'public interest' in mortgages. The provision of mortgage finance interacts at vital points with our national economy[20], and the more turbulent features of the economic developments of the last decade have posed new problems for the law of mortgage.

The 1970s were characterised by high inflation and exceptional volatility in interest rates. House values soared in relation to retail and share prices, and real property came to be recognised as the safest investment for those who could participate in the expanding market[1]. As more home owners and purchasers sought to take advantage of the increased value of their property, a significant second mortgage market grew up, with borrowers often dealing with 'fringe' institutions and moneylenders. Recourse to such lenders increased the risk that borrowers might be subjected to harsh or unconscionable terms in mortgage transactions. The result was that there developed a need to assert a renewed 'public interest' in the field of credit transactions—for the purpose of protecting borrowers—and this motive was realised in the enactment of the Consumer Credit Act 1974[2].

The property boom of the early 1970s has been followed by a period of marked economic recession. Instances of mortgage default have multiplied, with the rising rate of unemployment, redundancy and bankruptcy. This development has only given even greater emphasis to the need for the courts carefully

---

traditions and philosophies of the Conservative Party' (*Parliamentary Debates, House of Commons, Weekly Hansard*, Issue No. 1156, Cols. 1445, 1460, 15 January 1980). Given this rousing attribution to the Tory credo, it is not surprising that the scheme for the purchase of council homes was so bitterly opposed by the Labour Party.

19 [1965] AC 1175 at 1233f.

20 In 1973, for instance, an interest ceiling of 9½ per cent was imposed by the government in respect of retail bank deposits, with the precise object of preventing an increase in building society interest rates. See A. D. Bain, *The Control of the Money Supply* (Harmondsworth 1980), p. 73.

1 See, for instance, P. Ambrose and B. Colenutt, *The Property Machine* (Harmondsworth 1975).

2 See p. 529, post.

to superintend the process of law in possession actions brought by mortgagees, since often the mortgagee's entry into possession destroys the residential security previously enjoyed by the borrower and his family. We shall see that recent years have witnessed the extension of the courts' jurisdiction to protect the residential occupier from homelessness[3].

2. HOW DIFFERENT ARE THE POSITIONS OF THE MORTGAGOR AND THE TENANT?

In superficial terms it may be thought that the owner-occupier who purchases his home with the aid of mortgage finance is in a wholly different position from the periodic tenant who rents his home. It is true, of course, that the owner-occupier owns the freehold estate in the land. He is eligible for income tax deductions based on any mortgage interest paid by him[4]. He may sell the land and retain any capital gain made by reason of the sale[5]. Likewise he may dispose of the property by will, and by means of certain exemptions in respect of capital transfer tax[6] he will be able to pass on to another generation the substance of the wealth which is tied up in the property. The owner-occupier enjoys ultimate security of tenure because his estate in the land is unlimited. He pays no rent to any other person. He participates fully in the ethic of the 'property-owning democracy' with all the attendant psychological benefits of prestige and irremovability.

At first sight the tenant who merely rents his home enjoys nothing which is comparable with these social and economic advantages. Yet on closer examination the initial dissimilarity between the mortgagor and the periodic tenant is open to question. From the point of view of the occupier, there may be little practical difference between money paid periodically by way of rent and money paid periodically as interest on a mortgage loan. Mortgage interest tax relief may, in some cases, be counterbalanced by the tenant's receipt of a rent and rate rebate[7], or by the rent allowance component in payments of supplementary benefit[8]. The apparently unlimited rights of use and enjoyment which pertain to an owner-occupier are nowadays severely curbed by planning law, building consent regulations and other forms of public and private control of land use. The owner-occupier's title to the capital value of his property in the event of sale may turn out to be a somewhat illusory benefit, since his rights are significantly eroded by the fact that the proceeds of that sale require to be ploughed back into the purchase of a new property in an inflated housing

3 See p. 540, post.
4 See p. 509, ante.
5 A capital gain made on the disposal of a dwelling-house is not chargeable to capital gains tax if the house was the individual's 'only or main residence' throughout the period of ownership (see Finance Act 1965, s. 29).
6 See Finance Act 1975, Sch. 6.
7 See Housing Finance Act 1972, ss. 18ff.; Rent Rebate and Rent Allowance Schemes (England & Wales) (No. 2) Regulations 1980 (S.I. 1980/1555).
8 See Supplementary Benefit (Requirements) Regulations 1980 (S.I. 1980/1299), reg. 16.

market. Even the freedom of testamentary disposition supposedly enjoyed by the owner-occupier is substantially modified by legislation which permits claims to be brought against his estate by certain classes of statutory dependant for whom he has not made reasonable provision[9].

The significance of the owner-occupier's participation in 'the property-owning democracy' may, moreover, be limited quite considerably by the gradual shift which has occurred during the last 10 or 15 years in the ideology of the rented sector. The extension of security of tenure in the private rented sector and the recognition of a 'charter of tenants' rights' in the public rented sector have together gone a long way towards establishing for the residential tenant a more solid base of 'homestead rights' not dissimilar to the housing security enjoyed by the freeholder[10]. This tendency is accentuated as residential housing stock comes increasingly to be regarded not as an essentially commerciable commodity of exchange but primarily as a social resource whose 'allocation' should be governed by considerations of social justice and equity. In terms of this collectivist perspective, what is nowadays regarded as important and valuable is not ownership of the right to dispose, but rather ownership of the right to use and enjoy under living conditions of reasonable security and dignity. It is significant, for instance, that much of the legislation of the last 10 or 15 years in the parallel areas of residential tenancies and residential mortgages has been directed towards protection of the occupier's right not to be evicted from his home arbitrarily or without just cause[11].

Viewed in this light, the difference between the positions of the mortgagor and the periodic tenant may be somewhat more apparent than real. Differences certainly exist, but it was the late Otto Kahn-Freund who so cogently pointed out that

> the social function of the building society mortgage is very closely akin to that of the urban lease. The 'ownership' of a house bought with a building society mortgage (and collateral security) has the economic function of a tenancy combined with the ideological function of property[12].

3. THE BALANCE OF PROTECTION IN MORTGAGE TRANSACTIONS

Two truisms about human experience have influenced the historical development of the law relating to credit transactions. First, those who lend money commercially are more often and more powerfully motivated by the wish to acquire profit than by the desire to render useful service to the community. Second, those who borrow money tend, on the whole, to be necessitous men who lack bargaining power and who are therefore highly vulnerable to harsh or

9 Inheritance (Provision for Family and Dependants) Act 1975.

10 See the reference to the Rent Act legislation bringing about a situation in which we have 'all but reverted to copyhold tenure' in the rented sector (J. S. Colyer (1965) 29 Conv (NS) 429 at 463: 'The Rent Act 1965'.

11 See p. 540, post, p. 416, ante.

12 'Introduction', in K. Renner, *The Institutions of Private Law and Their Social Functions* (London and Boston 1949), p. 35f.

unconscionable dealing. 'Necessitous men', it has been said, 'are not truly speaking, free men[13].'

The starting point for this brief discussion must, of course, be the medieval canon law's abhorrence of usury and the sin of avarice. The initially inflexible rule of the Church prescribed that no man might lawfully charge money for a loan. To do so was not only contrary to Scripture[14]. It was, in the words of R. H. Tawney[15],

> contrary to nature, for it is to live without labour; it is to sell time, which belongs to God, for the advantage of wicked men; it is to rob those who use the money lent, and to whom, since they make it profitable, the profits should belong; it is unjust in itself, for the benefit of the loan to the borrower cannot exceed the value of the principal sum lent him; it is in defiance of sound juristic principles, for when a loan of money is made, the property in the thing lent passes to the borrower, and why should the creditor demand payment from a man who is merely using what is now his own?[16]

As Tawney, perhaps somewhat mischievously, pointed out, 'the true descendant of the doctrines of Aquinas is the labour theory of value. The last of the Schoolmen was Karl Marx[17].'

The practice of usury, however, touched upon another very sensitive nerve within the medieval scheme of economic ethics. This scheme regarded all commercial intercourse as subordinate in importance to the salvation of the soul, and all business life as but one aspect of personal conduct and therefore subject to overriding rules of personal morality. The medieval commercial ethic thus insisted upon the principle of equity in bargaining and correspor.dingly condemned all abuse of superior status or superior bargaining power[18]. Pope Innocent IV himself acknowledged that 'he who borrows is always under stress of necessity[19],' and usury was prohibited not least because it was often the most conspicuous kind of extortion practised against the poor and the needy.

The intellectual and doctrinal assumptions which underlay the proscription of usury were, of course, radically affected by the Protestant Reformation, the arrival of a new age of capitalism and the Calvinist acceptance of the rightness and the inevitability of commercial enterprise. While Luther had condemned even the minor fictions by which the canonists had tried to evade the laws against usury, Calvin declared that the charging of interest was not intrinsically unlawful. Indeed, to charge money as the price of a loan was simply to require the debtor to concede some small part of his profit to the creditor with whose

13 *Vernon v Bethell* (1762) 2 Eden 110 at 113 per Lord Henley.
14 Exodus xxii.25; Luke vi.35.
15 *Religion and the Rise of Capitalism* (Harmondsworth 1938), p. 55.
16 Tawney, in his turn, recounts the tale of the medieval usurer who 'about the year 1240, on entering a church to be married, was crushed by a stone figure falling from the porch, which proved by the grace of God to be a carving of another usurer and his money-bags being carried off by the devil' (op. cit., p. 49).
17 Op. cit., p. 48.
18 'I woot wel ther is degree above degree, as reson is; and skile it is, that men do hir devoir ther-as it is due; but certes, extorcions and despit of youre underlinges is dampnable' (Chaucer, *The Parson's Tale*, §66).
19 *Apparatus Decretalium* (Venice 1491), *Liber Quintus, De Usuris.*

capital assistance the gain had been achieved. The new code of economic ethics perceived a vast distinction between a loan extended to a prosperous merchant for the purpose of his entrepreneurial activities and a loan made to the poor in times of crisis or necessity. Thus, whereas it was undeniably wicked to wring interest from the misfortune of the indigent, it might be equally wrong to deny the creditor a just reward from the manifold profits achieved by the merchant through use of borrowed capital. The Calvinist doctrine held that the exaction of interest was lawful, provided that the rate of interest demanded did not exceed certain stated limits, provided that the creditor did not require an excessive security, and provided always that loans were extended gratis to the poor. The Protestant ethic of thrift, industry and sanctification through one's calling replaced the medieval detestation of usury, first by a qualified tolerance of certain forms of money-lending and finally by the elevation of a new ethic of investment. The lender entered into a community of risk with the borrower, and therefore rightly took his 'fair share of the profits, according to the degree in which God has blessed him by whom the money is used[20].'

When we turn, as we must now do, to the English law of mortgages, we shall see that its approach has likewise been that of cautious regulation of credit transactions related to land. It is in this respect that the jurisdiction of equity has been of pivotal importance in the historical development of the law. At every stage of the evolution of the law of mortgages since the 17th century, equity has intervened on grounds of conscience in the relationship of mortgagor and mortgagee, with the object of preventing any exploitation of the former by the latter. Equity has always been particularly conscious of the possibility that the lender of money might abuse his superior bargaining strength and economic capacity by imposing on the borrower oppressive or unconscionable terms of dealing. The balance of legal protection in the mortgage transaction has therefore tended in favour of the mortgagor rather than the mortgagee.

This protective emphasis is still present in the modern law of mortgages. Of course, it could hardly be claimed that the typical mortgage transaction of today—the granting of a legal charge over the family home—falls neatly within the historic stereotypes of mortgage transaction, either as the merchant's means of raising trading credit or as the last resort of the poor in time of need[1]. The social function of the modern residential mortgage has more to do with family consumption than with the needs of trade or production or even the requirements of a rudimentary and fairly brutal form of social security. The typical mortgage transaction of today is a means of providing residential utility for much of the population. Thus, while the law still strikes down inequitable or unconscionable dealing in the area of credit transactions[2], the impact of legislation on the law

20 W. Ames, *De Conscientia et eius iure vel Casibus, Libri Quinque* (Amsterdam 1630), Book V, p. 289 (Chapter XLIV, xiv, R. 1), *De Contracto Usurario*.

1 In view of this fact, the older authorities on the law of mortgages are often not so readily applicable as before, and therefore require to be read with care.

2 See, for instance, the Consumer Credit Act 1974. This Act, enacted in furtherance of the recommendations made by the *Report of the Committee on Consumer Credit* (the Crowther Report) (Cmnd 4569, March 1971), confers upon the court certain powers to re-open an 'extortionate' credit bargain so as to do justice between the parties (see Consumer Credit Act 1974, s. 137(1)), p. 529, post.

of mortgages has in recent years been more concerned with protection of the residential utility enjoyed by the mortgagor and his family.

This is not to say that in questions of priority as between mortgagor and mortgagee the conclusion is in any way biased towards the interest of the mortgagor. The intervention of statute law has usually been of merely procedural significance. The occupation of a residential mortgagor may be disrupted only, in the last instance, if a court considers that there is no reasonable prospect that he will be able to discharge his liabilities under the mortgage. It is this interposition of a judicial discretion and the requirement of due process of law which ultimately provide a degree of protection for the residential occupier[3].

4. THE CREATION OF LEGAL MORTGAGES

The historical pattern of the English law of mortgages has been to create real securities (i.e., security interests in land) by means of the manipulation of existing estates and interests in the land of the borrower of money. This practice has brought about the consequence that the law of mortgages is heavily marked by fiction. As Maitland said[4], the mortgage transaction is 'one long suppressio veri and suggestio falsi.' Lord Macnaghten declared in *Samuel v Jarrah Timber and Wood Paving Corpn Ltd*[5] that 'no one . . . by the light of nature ever understood an English mortgage of real estate.'

(1) Pre-1926 modes of creation

In order to understand the modern law of mortgages it is necessary to bear in mind the means by which, prior to 1926, a legal mortgage of land could be created. Before the commencement of the 1925 legislation, a legal mortgage of freehold land was effected by a conveyance of the fee simple to the mortgagee, subject to a covenant for re-conveyance on redemption of the mortgage (i.e., on repayment of the loan). A legal mortgage of leasehold land took the form of an assignment to the mortgagee of the residue of the mortgagor's term of years in the land, subject to a proviso for re-assignment by the mortgagee on the repayment of the loan. The creditor's security for the loan was thus in either case the debtor's legal title in the land mortgaged. If the mortgagor failed to redeem the mortgage by the date stipulated for repayment of the capital sum, the mortgagee was entitled at common law to retain his security unencumbered by any further interest vested in the mortgagor.

(2) The mortgagor's equity of redemption

From the seventeenth century onwards, however, equity intervened in a manner which was to make the traditional method of mortgage more than slightly

3 See p. 539, post.
4 *Equity* (London 1936), p. 182.
5 [1904] AC 323 at 326.

fictitious. Although the mortgagee was entitled to enjoy physical possession of the land, equity forced him to account to the mortgagor in respect of any profit derived from that land in excess of the interest due on the contract of loan. Thus there ceased to be any material advantage for the mortgagee in exercising his right to possess the land and the mortgagor was commonly left in possession himself even though he no longer retained the legal title.

Furthermore, although the common law attached drastic consequences to a failure by the mortgagor to repay the capital debt by the date fixed, equity regarded the mortgagor as entitled to redeem the mortgage at any time, even by tendering repayment of the loan *after* that date had passed. The mortgagor could therefore effectively ignore the date on which the debt fell due, knowing that equity would assist him in compelling re-conveyance or re-assignment even in the event of repayment long after that date[6]. Only if the Court of Chancery in the exercise of its equitable jurisdiction considered it reasonable to grant a decree of 'foreclosure' would the mortgagor's equitable rights be terminated and the mortgagee permitted to take a free title to the land. Unless and until such a decree was granted, the sum total of the mortgagor's equitable rights in respect of the mortgaged realty was termed his *equity of redemption.* The equity of redemption simply reflected the view of equity that, irrespective of the strict legal and contractual position, the real owner of the mortgaged land was still the mortgagor—albeit subject to the mortgage granted to his creditor. The inviolability in equity of the borrower's right to redeem the loan thus inverted the legal relationship of the parties to the mortgage transaction, and the mortgagor's 'equity' came to be seen as constituting a proprietary interest in the land which could itself be bought, sold and mortgaged[7].

(3) Post-1925 modes of creation

The developments brought about by the intervention of equity were finally rationalised in the Law of Property Act 1925. Section 85(1) of that Act now provides that a legal mortgage of freehold land may be effected

> either by a demise for a term of years absolute, subject to a provision for cesser on redemption, or by a charge by deed expressed to be by way of legal mortgage.

6 Equity was willing to allow this forbearance in favour of the borrower since the value of the lender's security (i.e., the land) might greatly exceed the sum lent and it therefore seemed inequitable that the mortgagor should forfeit the entire security for failure to repay on the date fixed in the contract of loan. When it became clear that, in view of the stance adopted by equity, the contractual date of redemption was rendered academic, it became customary to fix this date a mere six months after the entry into the contract of loan. It may also be that the fixing of an early (and therefore effectively fictitious) date for repayment under the strict terms of the loan was influenced by the fact that whereas a certain spiritual opprobrium attached to the charging of interest before the loan was due for repayment, the exaction of interest thereafter was regarded by Church doctrine as constituting a wholly legitimate form of 'compensation' (*interesse*) for failure to restore the principal by the date promised. See R. H. Tawney, op. cit., p. 54.

7 See *Casborne v Scarfe* (1738) 2 Jac & W 194. See also A. W. B. Simpson, *An Introduction to the History of the Land Law* (London 1961), p. 226ff.

It is no longer possible to mortgage land by means of a conveyance and re-conveyance of the fee simple[8]. Instead, in the case of freehold land, the mortgagee's security now takes the form of either a long lease of the land[9] (in practice usually a term of 3,000 years) or a charge which, while conferring no proprietary estate upon the mortgagee, is deemed to invest him with 'the same protection, powers and remedies (including the right to take proceedings to obtain possession . . .)' as if such a leasehold interest had been conveyed to him[10]. In the case of leasehold land, a legal mortgage may now be effected only by means of subdemise for a term of years absolute, subject to a provision for cesser on redemption[11], or by 'a charge by deed expressed to be by way of legal mortgage[12]'.

Of these two modes of legal mortgage in respect of either freehold or leasehold land, the charge by way of legal mortgage is nowadays by far the simpler and more commonly used[13]. However, in either case, the result of the 1925 legislation is that the mortgagor manifestly remains in occupation of the land during the mortgage term and, moreover, retains his full legal title throughout. The mortgagee, in closer accordance with the reality of the situation, takes merely a security interest (by way of charge or lease) over the land. The mortgagor still retains his 'equity of redemption', and the effective value of this right is the difference at any given point in time between the market value of the land and the sum of the mortgage debt currently outstanding[14]. Such is the significance of the mortgagor's 'equity of redemption' that the contractual date for repayment of the mortgage loan is rendered entirely academic, and for this reason most mortgage deeds contain a clause which requires repayment of the entire capital sum within a short period (e.g., six months) of the granting of the loan.

The net effect of the provisions contained in the Law of Property Act 1925 is that all transactions which in substance secure a loan of money upon the borrower's real property must inevitably operate by way of mortgage under the terms of the Act. The courts have jurisdiction to determine whether any credit transaction (no matter in what guise presented or obscured) is in reality a

8 Any attempt after 1925 to mortgage a freehold by conveyance of the fee simple necessarily operates as a demise of the land to the mortgagee for a term of 3,000 years (Law of Property Act 1925, s. 85(2)).

9 The real value of the mortgagor's interest in the land is, of course, not so much the (fairly sterile) freehold reversion upon a 3,000 year term, but rather the 'equity of redemption' which he also still retains (i.e., the right to repay the loan and secure the termination of the mortgagee's technical leasehold interest).

10 Law of Property Act 1925, s. 87(1).

11 The subdemise must be for a term which is less by at least one day than the term of years vested in the mortgagor. Thus there is preserved on behalf of the mortgagor both a reversion upon the subdemise and, of course, his own 'equity of redemption'. See Law of Property Act 1925, s. 86(1).

12 Law of Property Act 1925, s. 86(1). Any purported assignment of a leasehold term by way of mortgage after 1925 necessarily operates as a subdemise to the mortgagee for a term of years ten days less than the term supposedly assigned (Law of Property Act 1925, s. 86(2)).

13 See P. B. Fairest, *Mortgages* (2nd edn. London 1980), p. 13.

14 Thus, if a property has a market value of £40,000 and is currently subject to a mortgage debt of £15,000, the value of the mortgagor's equity of redemption is £25,000. The value of that equity will steadily increase as the mortgage debt is gradually discharged.

mortgage transaction. In *Grangeside Properties Ltd v Collingwoods Securities Ltd*[15] Harman LJ referred to

> the ancient law, which has always been that Chancery would treat as a mortgage that which was intended to be a conveyance by way of security between A and B. Once a mortgage, always a mortgage and nothing but a mortgage, has been a principle for centuries . . . It could not be that [the 1925 Act] was intended to sweep away the view of the law which had always been that if the thing was proved to be a mortgage, equity would allow an equity of redemption to redeem on payment of the mortgage money, interest and costs[16].

Thus, in a manner not unlike the way in which the courts test transactions in the rented sector[17], the courts examine the inner substance rather than the external form of credit transactions, in order to ensure that those who borrow money on the security of land actually receive the legal protection promised to mortgagors by statute.

5. THE CREATION OF EQUITABLE MORTGAGES

So far we have discussed only the creation of legal mortgages of real property. It is, of course, possible to effect an equitable mortgage of land. Such a mortgage may arise in three ways.

(1) Mortgage of an equitable interest

The owner of an equitable interest in land, or subsisting in reference to land[18], may effect a mortgage of his interest by assigning that interest to a mortgagee subject to a proviso for re-assignment on redemption. This form of mortgage is necessarily equitable, and unless made by will, must be in writing as required by section 53(1)(c) of the Law of Property Act 1925[19].

(2) Informal mortgage of a legal interest

An equitable mortgage may also arise where the owner of a legal estate in land effects an informal mortgage of his estate by failing to use either of the modes of legal mortgage indicated as appropriate in the Law of Property Act 1925. The consequence of such a transaction is that 'equity looks on that as done which ought to have been done'. The informal mortgage (i.e., the mortgage created by imperfect means) is regarded, under the doctrine in *Walsh v Lonsdale*[20], as having the same effect as a mere agreement to create a legal mortgage of realty. Thus both the imperfect mortgage and the agreement to create a legal mortgage are

15 [1964] 1 WLR 139, 142f., [1964] 1 All ER 143 at 146.
16 See *Seton v Slade* (1802) 7 Ves 265 at 273 per Lord Eldon LC.
17 See p. 422, ante.
18 This qualification makes allowance for the questionable status of the beneficiary behind a trust for sale of land, p. 357ff., ante.
19 See p. 247, ante.
20 See p. 398, ante.

treated as giving rise to an equitable mortgage. However, in the case of an agreement to create a legal mortgage, the further requirements of section 40 of the Law of Property Act 1925 must be satisfied. It must be shown that the agreement was evidenced in writing or that it was supported by a sufficient act of part performance[1].

(3) Equitable mortgage by deposit of title deeds

It has been accepted ever since *Russel v Russel*[2] that an equitable mortgage of land may be effected by a deposit of the title deeds relating to that land coupled with an intention on the part of the owner that the depositee should hold the title deeds as his security for a loan of money. Such a deposit is effectively construed as a sufficient act of part performance to amount to evidence of a contract to create a mortgage. No further formalities are required, although it is usual for the deposit of the title deeds to be accompanied by some written memorandum of the terms of the agreement.

(4) Equitable charge

Although a charge is slightly different in nature from a mortgage, it may be convenient to note here that an equitable charge may arise where land is charged in equity with some obligation such as the repayment of a debt. Thus, in *Matthews v Goodday*[3], Kindersley V-C accepted that a written contract by B, charging his real estate with £500 to A, would not constitute an 'agreement to give a legal mortgage', but would amount to 'a security by which he equitably charged his land with the payment of a sum of money.'

6. PROTECTION FOR THE MORTGAGOR

As we have already seen, much of the historical emphasis of the law relating to mortgages has rested upon the need to protect the interests of the mortgagor against the possibility of harsh or unconscionable dealing. The protective concern of the law focuses upon the mortgagor's equity of redemption which, as was recognised by Lord Hardwicke LC in the classic case of *Casborne v Scarfe*[4], ranks always as a proprietary interest vested in the mortgagor[5]. The protection accorded the mortgagor appears in several forms.

1 See p. 81, ante.
2 (1783) 1 Bro CC 269.
3 (1861) 31 LJ Ch 282.
4 (1738) 1 Atk 603 at 605.
5 The proprietary status of the equity of redemption is so clearly established that it may even be claimed by the Crown as bona vacantia. See, for instance, *Re Sir Thomas Spencer Wells* [1933] Ch 29.

(1) Attempted exclusion of the right to redeem

So jealous was the concern of equity on behalf of the mortgagor that equity developed, and retains to this day, a doctrine that no 'clogs or fetters' should be allowed to be imposed upon the mortgagor's equity of redemption. Any provision in a mortgage transaction which purports to limit, postpone or exclude the mortgagor's equity of redemption is liable to be struck down as void and unenforceable[6]. What is relevant in this context is not the degree of risk that the terms of the mortgage may be oppressive to the mortgagor, but rather the fact that there exists any risk at all. Equity thus directs its sharp gaze upon any provision which might have the effect of negating the value of the equity of redemption belonging to the mortgagor.

The clearest means by which the value of the mortgagor's equity of redemption may be negated is by a mortgage term which purports to exclude altogether the mortgagor's right to redeem. Such a result was threatened (at least in theory) by the mortgage transaction which came before the House of Lords in *Samuel v Jarrah Timber and Wood Paving Corporation Ltd*[7]. Here the mortgagee of a quantity of debenture stock was by the terms of the mortgage given a right to purchase the stock within twelve months of the date of the loan secured by the mortgage. When the mortgagee claimed to exercise this option, the mortgagor sought a declaration that the option thus granted was illegal and void on the ground that it excluded the mortgagor's equity of redemption. The House of Lords granted the declaration, somewhat reluctantly in view of the fact that in this case a 'perfectly fair bargain' had been concluded between two parties 'each of whom was quite sensible of what they were doing.' However, the option was invalidated by reason of the fact that 'at the same time a mortgage arrangement was made between them[8].' Such is the vigilance of equity to ensure that 'a mortgagee can never provide at the time of making the loan for any event or condition on which the equity of redemption shall be discharged . . .[9]'

The great disfavour with which the courts view an option for purchase incorporated within the terms of a mortgage transaction is due to the fact that, as Professor Fairest has explained[10], such an option changes 'the nature of the transaction from a transfer by way of security to what is essentially a potential transfer on sale, at the option of the mortgagee.' There is always a danger that

6 As Professor Paul Fairest has indicated, the doctrine of equity 'runs counter to another hallowed doctrine of the law, that of sanctity of contract.' See Fairest, *Mortgages* (2nd edn. London 1980), p. 25. The intervention of equity in the area of mortgages, in the face of principles of freedom of contract, is therefore even stronger evidence of the concern of equity to preclude unconscionable bargaining. At the same time, however, it must be acknowledged that the equitable doctrine stretched to the limit the courts' willingness to override the otherwise sacred principle *pacta sunt servanda*. See, for instance, the remarks of Lord Macnaghten in *Samuel v Jarrah Timber and Wood Paving Corpn Ltd* [1904] AC 323 at 327, p. 522, post. See also E. E. C. Firth (1895) 11 LQR 144: 'Freedom of Contract in Mortgages.'

7 [1904] AC 323.

8 [1904] AC 323 at 325 per Earl of Halsbury LC. The Lord Chancellor went on to say that 'if a day had intervened between the two parts of the arrangement, the part of the bargain which the appellant claims to be performed would have been perfectly good and capable of being enforced.'

9 [1904] AC 323 at 327 per Lord Macnaghten.

10 Op. cit., p. 26.

this transmutation of the mortgage transaction may have been the result of unfair bargaining by an unscrupulous mortgagee. However, in *Samuel v Jarrah Timber and Wood Paving Corpn Ltd* the House of Lords was clearly reluctant to allow the protective vigilance of equity to be used as 'a means of evading a fair bargain come to between persons dealing at arms' length and negotiating on equal terms.' As Lord Macnaghten pointed out,

> The directors of a trading company in search of financial assistance are certainly in a very different position from that of an impecunious landowner in the toils of a crafty money-lender[11].

The principle of freedom of contract, which was very much part of the commercial ethic of the day, explains not only the House of Lords' diffidence as to the result achieved in the *Jarrah Timber* case but also the willingness of the House to reach a different result on the barely distinguishable facts of *Reeve v Lisle*[12]. Here an option for purchase of part of the secured property was granted to a mortgagee ten days *after* the date of the mortgage transaction. The House of Lords upheld the option as valid since it derived from a transaction which was separate and independent from the original mortgage transaction. The rationale underlying the distinction between *Jarrah Timber* and *Reeve v Lisle* is thus supposedly the idea that the mortgagor, once he has obtained the loan which he seeks, is no longer vulnerable to unconscionable dealing by his mortgagee in respect of a later and quite separate transaction[13].

(2) Postponement of the date of redemption

It is not unknown that a mortgagee, instead of excluding altogether the mortgagor's right to redeem, should merely impose a contractual term in the mortgage transaction which purports to *postpone* the earliest possible date of redemption. Such a term may be used as a means of guaranteeing for the mortgagee a secure investment over a long period at a favourable rate of interest. However, this type of provision may operate so unilaterally in favour of the mortgagee that the courts will hold it to be invalid and unenforceable.

In *Fairclough v Swan Brewery Co Ltd*[14] the mortgagor was contractually precluded from exercising his right of redemption during most of the period of the leasehold term which provided the subject matter of the mortgage. The mortgagor's leasehold estate was for a period of 17½ years, and according to the terms of the mortgage his right to redeem arose at the earliest within only six weeks of the termination of that lease. The Judicial Committee of the Privy Council upheld a claim by the mortgagor to redeem at an earlier date, ruling that 'equity will not permit any device or contrivance being part of the mortgage

11 [1904] AC 323 at 327.
12 [1902] AC 461.
13 For criticism of the supposed logic of the distinction between *Samuel v Jarrah Timber and Wood Paving Corpn Ltd* and *Reeve v Lisle*, see P. B. Fairest, op. cit., p. 27f. Compare, however, *Lewis v Frank Love Ltd* [1961] 1 WLR 261; (1961) 77 LQR 163 (P. V. Baker).
14 [1912] AC 565.

transaction or contemporaneous with it to prevent or impede redemption[15].' In this case the mortgage had been rendered 'for all practical purposes ... irredeemable,' since on redemption the effective value to the mortgagor of an almost expired lease would have been minimal.

Later decisions have not adopted so wide a view of the inequity of postponed redemption. In *Knightsbridge Estates Trust Ltd v Byrne*[16] the Court of Appeal was confronted with a mortgage term which stipulated that the loan advanced should not be repaid before the expiry of 40 years from the granting of the mortgage. The loan had been obtained at an interest rate of 6½ per cent per annum, and when later the mortgagor wished to avail himself of a fall in interest rates by borrowing money elsewhere, he claimed to redeem the mortgage before the expiration of the stipulated period. The Court of Appeal held that the validity of the terms on which the loan had been obtained was not prejudiced by the contractual postponement of the date for redemption. Sir Wilfred Greene MR made it clear that 'equity does not reform mortgage transactions because they are unreasonable.' Equity is concerned, he said, 'to see two things—one that the essential requirements of a mortgage transaction are observed, and the other that oppressive or unconscionable terms are not enforced[17]'. Thus, in the present case, the postponement of the date of redemption could not be challenged on the ground that postponement was permissible only for a 'reasonable' period. The true ground of equitable intervention arose where the contractual right of redemption was rendered 'illusory' by postponement of the right to redeem, as had occurred in *Fairclough v Swan Brewery Co Ltd.* The court declined to intervene in the *Knightsbridge Estates* case, where the mortgagor had bargained at arm's length for a long-term loan of a substantial sum (£300,000) on the most advantageous terms available at the time. The resulting agreement was, in the words of the Master of the Rolls,

> a commercial agreement between two important corporations experienced in such matters, and has none of the features of an oppressive bargain where the borrower is at the mercy of an unscrupulous lender. In transactions of this kind it is notorious that there is competition among the large insurance companies and other bodies having large funds to invest, and we are not prepared to view the agreement made as anything but a proper business transaction[18].

In the view of the Court of Appeal, any other result would have placed 'an unfortunate restriction on the liberty of contract of competent parties who are at arm's length', and would have led to the 'highly inequitable' consequence that whereas the mortgagor would from the outset have had the right to redeem at any time, the mortgagee would have had no right to require repayment of the loan otherwise than by the specified instalments[19].

15 [1912] AC 565 at 570 per Lord Macnaghten.
16 [1939] Ch 441.
17 [1939] Ch 441 at 457.
18 [1939] Ch 441 at 455.
19 The decision of the Court of Appeal was affirmed by the House of Lords, but on the different ground that the mortgage in question constituted a debenture within section 380 of the Companies Act 1929 and was not invalidated on the ground of postponement of the redemption

(3) Collateral advantages subsisting after redemption

It is possible that a mortgage transaction may confer a 'collateral advantage' upon the mortgagee. A 'collateral advantage' is for this purpose the benefit of any term which purports to impose an obligation upon the mortgagor which is 'independent of that for the performance of which the land is charged[20].' Where the mortgagor and mortgagee conduct a common trading concern, it may for instance be advantageous to the mortgagee to require that the mortgagor refrain from any commercial competition prejudicial to the mortgagee's business. A mortgagee such as a petrol company or brewery may, for example, impose upon the mortgagor a condition that the latter shall deal only in the products manufactured or distributed by the mortgagee.

The possibility that a mortgage transaction may thus confer a collateral advantage upon the mortgagee has activated the watchful concern of equity. It is clear that the courts will strike down as void any collateral benefit for a mortgagee which purports to remain in force *after* the redemption of the mortgage[1]. If the law were otherwise, the mortgagor would be in a distinctly less advantageous position after redemption than he was before he granted the mortgage. There is, however, more doubt as to the validity of the collateral benefits conferred upon the mortgagee with respect to the period *preceding* redemption of the mortgage. Such benefits may be valid in so far as they purport to govern the mortgaged property pending redemption[2], but there is today an increasing possibility that the clauses containing these benefits may be suspect on other grounds, e.g., by virtue of the contractual doctrine which strikes at agreements which operate unreasonably 'in restraint of trade[3].' Ultimately the test in any case of the legality of a collateral advantage is that laid down by the House of Lords in *G. and C. Kreglinger v New Patagonia Meat and Cold Storage Co Ltd*[4]. Here Lord Parker of Waddington observed that

> In every case in which a stipulation by a mortgagee for a collateral advantage has, since the repeal of the usury laws, been held invalid, the stipulation has been open to objection, either (1) because it was unconscionable, or (2) because it was in the nature of a penal clause clogging the equity arising on failure to exercise a contractual right to redeem, or (3) because it was in the nature of a condition repugnant as well to the contractual as to the equitable right.

(4) 'Oppressive and unconscionable' terms

The courts have always claimed an overriding equitable jurisdiction to invalidate any term in a mortgage transaction which tends to operate in an

---

date (see [1940] AC 613). However, the House of Lords threw no doubt on the reasoning applied by the Court of Appeal.

20 R. H. Maudsley and E. H. Burn, *Land Law: Cases and Materials* (4th edn., London 1980), p. 616.

1 See *Noakes & Co Ltd v Rice* [1902] AC 24; *Bradley v Carritt* [1903] AC 253.

2 See *Biggs v Hoddinott* [1898] 2 Ch 307; *Santley v Wilde* [1899] 2 Ch 474.

3 See *Esso Petroleum Co Ltd v Harper's Garage (Stourport) Ltd* [1968] AC 269; J. D. Heydon (1969) 85 LQR 229 at 230: 'The Frontiers of the Restraint of Trade Doctrine'.

4 [1914] AC 25 at 56.

'oppressive or unconscionable' manner[5]. This residual power is particularly significant in relation to questions concerning the rate of interest charged by the mortgagee on the loan advanced to the mortgagor.

The modern mortgage transaction is indeed a quite remarkable form of transaction. Most mortgages of residential property are concluded between the owner-occupier and a building society. Such mortgages are, of course, covered by the general law relating to mortgages, but they differ slightly from the ordinary mortgage of realty in that they are affected by certain rules which apply specifically to transactions entered into by building societies[6]. Under the building society mortgage, the mortgagor is required to become a member of the building society which advances him money on loan[7], and the rules of the society are incorporated by implication in any mortgage transaction effected with him[8]. All building societies thus reserve for themselves a right, upon serving notice on the mortgagor, to alter the rate of interest payable on his loan. In other words, the rate of interest payable by the mortgagor is not fixed throughout the period of the loan, but fluctuates in accordance with the rate stipulated from time to time by the society itself.

When viewed in a larger perspective, the open-ended contract thus concluded between the mortgagor and mortgagee is little short of astonishing. The mortgagor agrees to pay *any* rate of interest stipulated by the lender of the money. There may well be some question in theory as to the competence of a mortgagee to contract on this basis. It has been observed that such a unilateral power to vary the interest rate payable, if 'reserved to an individual mortgagee in an ordinary mortgage, would savour of being harsh and unconscionable' and would therefore be liable to be struck down as invalid and unenforceable[9]. However, there has been no litigation concerning the right of building societies to adjust interest rates at their discretion, partly because it is recognised that building societies constitute a special case. It is clear that a building society which tethered itself to a rigid rate of interest in a long-term transaction would be 'hopelessly exposed to the risk of having to pay more to its investors than it was currently receiving from its borrower[10].' Moreover, building society interest rates are in any event subject to an element of quasi-public control, in the sense that the variation of interest rates is now closely related to the general economic strategy of the government of the day.

Nevertheless, it may be significant that most building societies, in framing their powers to adjust mortgage interest rates, afford some protection to their borrowers by offering the alternative facility of redemption within a different or stipulated period without redemption fee or interest in lieu of notice. As Wurtzburg and Mills have said,

5 See *Knightsbridge Estates Trust Ltd v Byrne* [1939] Ch 441 at 457 per Sir Wilfred Greene MR.
6 The principal enactment regulating the operations of building societies is the Building Societies Act 1962. See generally Wurtzburg and Mills, *Building Society Law* (14th edn., ed. J. Mills, London 1976).
7 Building Societies Act 1962, s. 8.
8 See *Rosenberg v Northumberland Building Society* (1889) 22 QBD 373 at 380 per Fry LJ.
9 Wurtzburg and Mills, op. cit., p. 166.
10 Ibid., p. 165.

They have probably been wise to do this, because it is still considered to be open to doubt if an unlimited power simply to vary the interest rate at discretion would be legally valid, whether it was contained in the mortgage itself, or incorporated therein by reference to the rules . . . [I]t is axiomatic that one cannot take over-wide powers, and then uphold a particular exercise of those powers on the ground that the exercise is reasonable[11].

While the protection of the building society mortgagor rests largely upon the responsible exercise of power by the building societies[12] and the underlying element of governmental regulation, no such protection avails the individual who borrows on mortgage from another individual or from a credit company or other fringe financial institution. The protection of such borrowers is dependent upon the vitally important residual power of the courts to declare void any mortgage term which is 'oppressive or unconscionable'.

A dramatic illustration of the courts' powers in this connection occurred in *Cityland and Property (Holdings) Ltd v Dabrah*[13]. Here the plaintiff company had sold a residential property to the defendant, who was the existing occupier. The balance of the purchase price was raised by a loan from the plaintiff secured upon the house in question. The mortgage granted to the plaintiff made no provision for the payment of interest, but required that the defendant pay, by monthly instalments, a sum which exceeded the loan moneys by a figure which was described by the plaintiff as a 'premium'. Moreover, the plaintiff reserved the right to recover on demand the full outstanding balance of the sum payable by the defendant in the event of any default at any time. On the facts it was calculable that the premium payable by the mortgagor represented, over a three year period, an interest rate of 19 per cent per annum. Moreover, the entire capital debt was recoverable immediately in the event of default, and this meant that, taken as a proportion of the capital sum lent, the premium effectively constituted a capitalised interest rate of 57 per cent. Goff J held that the imposition of this rate of interest was in the circumstances 'unfair and unconscionable', and that the mortgagee was entitled to require only a 'reasonable' rate of interest, which he fixed at a rate of 7 per cent per annum. The premium agreed between the parties was unenforceable since it was in effect an unconscionable collateral advantage in favour of the mortgagee[14].

11 Ibid., p. 166.

12 The Payne Committee on the Enforcement of Judgment Debts reported in 1969 that no evidence had been put before it 'to establish or to suggest that the Building Societies impose harsh or unconscionable obligations on their borrowers.' See *Report of the Committee on the Enforcement of Judgment Debts* (Cmnd 3909, 1969), para. 1354.

13 [1968] Ch 166.

14 The plaintiff was, however, granted an order for possession against the defendant. *Cityland and Property (Holdings) Ltd v Dabrah* remains the only well known instance in recent years in which the court has intervened to rewrite a bargain concluded by the parties themselves. At first sight, the approach adopted by Goff J seems to conflict with the insistence by the Court of Appeal in *Knightsbridge Estates Trust Ltd v Byrne* [1939] Ch 441, p. 523, ante, that the relevant test is not one of 'reasonableness' but rather one of 'conscionableness'. It is perhaps noteworthy that the *Knightsbridge Estates* case was not cited before Goff J. As Browne-Wilkinson J observed in *Multiservice Bookbinding Ltd v Marden* [1979] Ch 84 at 110, Goff J appears to have treated the words 'unreasonable' and 'unconscionable' as being interchangeable. However, as Browne-Wilkinson J went on to say, it 'was unnecessary for [Goff J] to distinguish between the two concepts, since on either test the premium was unenforceable.'

It is clear that the approach of the courts in questions as to the conscionableness of a specified interest rate will vary in accordance with the relative bargaining positions of mortgagor and mortgagee. In *Cityland and Property (Holdings) Ltd v Dabrah* there was a plain disparity of bargaining power as between mortgagor and mortgagee, and there was also a suspicion that the mortgagor had agreed to such disadvantageous terms only because, as the existing tenant of the property, he was threatened with homelessness on the expiry of his lease. The courts have for a long time enjoyed a similar jurisdiction under the Moneylenders Acts 1900–1927 to set aside 'harsh and unconscionable' transactions, and disparity of bargaining strength has played an important part in determining the exercise of this discretion[15]. In *Carringtons Ltd v Smith*[16], for instance, a borrower who was 'intelligent and a man of business' was held to be unable to upset an interest rate of 50 per cent on a transaction of loan. In *Wells v Joyce*[17], however, the court was prepared to re-open an unfavourable loan which had been pressed upon a Connemara farmer 'of rustic mind.'

The relevance of bargaining power has recently come to the fore once again in connection with the validity of index-linked rates of loan interest. In days of inflation, it is not unnatural that a lender of money should wish to ensure that he is compensated for any fall in the value of money during the period of the loan. Without such compensation he would receive a sum on redemption which is less valuable in real terms than the loan advanced at the beginning of the transaction. One way in which such a result can be avoided arises through the index-linking of the repayments of capital and interest due under the mortgage.

The legality of the technique of index-linking was challenged in *Multiservice Bookbinding Ltd v Marden*[18]. Here the terms of a mortgage of commercial premises provided that the loan could not be called in by the mortgagee, nor the mortgage redeemed by the mortgagor, within ten years of the date of the grant of the mortgage, and that interest should be payable at 2 per cent above Minimum Lending Rate on the entire capital sum throughout the duration of the loan. Furthermore, the mortgage included a provision which stipulated that any repayment of interest or capital should be increased or decreased in accordance with the alteration in the rate of exchange between the pound sterling and the Swiss franc at the date of payment relative to the rate of exchange prevailing at the commencement of the loan period. The clear object of these provisions was to ensure that the lender was protected against both domestic inflation and any fall in the value of the pound sterling on the international money market. Ten years after the commencement of the loan period, the mortgagor sought to redeem the mortgage on terms to be declared by the court. The mortgagor claimed that the payment clause contained in the mortgage was void and unenforceable on grounds of public policy. During the intervening period, the value of the pound sterling had depreciated relative to the Swiss franc to such an

15 See H. W. Wilkinson (1980) 130 NLJ 749: 'Extortionate Mortgages'.
16 [1906] 1 KB 79.
17 [1905] 2 IR 134.
18 [1979] Ch 84. See (1978) 37 Cambridge LJ 211 (A. J. Oakley); (1978) 128 NLJ 1251 (H. W. Wilkinson); (1979) 42 MLR 338 (W. D. Bishop and B. V. Hindley); [1978] Conv 318 (F. R. Crane).

extent that at the date of redemption the mortgagee would, in return for the original loan of £36,000, have received almost £133,000 by way of payments of capital and interest.

Browne-Wilkinson J gave judgment in favour of the mortgagee, holding that an index-linked money obligation could not be said to be contrary to public policy. He treated the exchange rate provision as a form of index-linking and remarked that

In any economy where there is inflation there are few inducements to make long-term loans expressed in a currency the value of which is being eroded. It is at least possible that, unless lenders can ensure that they are repaid the real value of the money they advanced, and not merely a sum of the same nominal amount but in devalued currency, the availability of loan capital will be much diminished. This would surely not be in the public interest[19].

The mortgagor's challenge on grounds of public policy therefore failed, but the mortgagor went on to claim that the mortgage terms were in any event unenforceable on the ground that they were 'unconscionable' or 'unreasonable'. Browne-Wilkinson J reviewed the case law and concluded that

in order to be freed from the necessity to comply with all the terms of the mortgage, the plaintiffs must show that the bargain, or some of its terms, was unfair and unconscionable: it is not enough to show that, in the eyes of the court, it was unreasonable. In my judgment a bargain cannot be unfair and unconscionable unless one of the parties to it has imposed the objectionable terms in a morally reprehensible manner, that is to say, in a way which affects his conscience. The classic example of an unconscionable bargain is where advantage has been taken of a young, inexperienced or ignorant person to introduce a term which no sensible well-advised person or party would have accepted. But I do not think the categories of unconscionable bargains are limited: the court can and should intervene where a bargain has been procured by unfair means[20].

In the present case, however, Browne-Wilkinson J was not prepared to castigate the terms of the mortgage transaction as 'unconscionable' or 'oppressive', although he did adopt the view that those terms had been 'unreasonable[1]'. The terms had not been 'imposed . . . in a morally reprehensible

19 [1979] Ch 84 at 104. The decision of Browne-Wilkinson J has been welcomed as an expression of judicial approval both for index-linking and for the sanctity of bargains freely entered into by parties of equal bargaining power (see (1978) 37 Cambridge LJ 211 at 213 (A. J. Oakley)). See however R. A. Bowles (1981) 131 NLJ 4: 'Mortgages and Interest Rates: An Economist's View', for the argument that the protection of the mortgagee would have been quite adequately secured by a provision which ensured that his return took some account of deterioration merely in the *domestic* purchasing power of his loan. The point is made here that 'both parties to the mortgage were English and yet it is being claimed that the defendant should be protected from any decline of sterling vis à vis the Swiss franc.' See also H. W. Wilkinson [1978] Conv 346: 'Index-Linked Mortgages'.

20 [1979] Ch 84 at 110.

1 'In particular I consider that it was unreasonable both for the debt to be inflation proofed by reference to the Swiss franc and at the same time to provide for a rate of interest two per cent. above bank rate—a rate which reflects at least in part the unstable state of the pound sterling. On top of this interest on the whole sum was to be paid throughout the term. The defendant made a hard bargain. But the test is not reasonableness . . .' ([1979] Ch 84 at 112 per Browne-Wilkinson J).

manner', in that there had been no great inequality of bargaining power between the parties. The parties had, moreover, received the benefit of independent legal advice. Furthermore, the loan related to commercial premises which had trebled in value during the loan period. Above all, the mortgagee was not 'a professional moneylender' and there was no evidence of 'any sharp practice of any kind' by him. Browne-Wilkinson J declined to treat the 'Swiss franc uplift' element in the capital-repayments as being in any sense a 'premium or collateral advantage.' In his view,

> a lender of money is entitled to insure that he is repaid the real value of his loan and if he introduces a term which so provides, he is not stipulating for anything beyond the repayment of principal[2].

(5) Extortionate credit bargains under the Consumer Credit Act 1974

Further protection for mortgagors is provided by the power now vested in the courts by the Consumer Credit Act 1974 to re-open 'extortionate' credit bargains[3]. The Consumer Credit Act 1974 has no application to agreements under which the credit granted exceeds £5,000[4], or to consumer credit agreements in relation to mortgage transactions entered into by a local authority or building society as creditor[5]. The 1974 Act thus has no relevance to the majority of mortgages of residential property, which are granted in favour of building societies, but nevertheless has an important impact upon transactions in the 'fringe area' controlled by credit companies and non-institutional lenders. Borrowers in this 'fringe area' stand in need of considerable legal protection, since such borrowers are almost by definition the 'poorer risk' borrowers who have been unable to obtain loan facilities from one of the institutional lenders such as a bank or building society[6].

Under the Consumer Credit Act 1974, if a court finds a credit bargain 'extortionate', it may 're-open the credit agreement so as to do justice between the parties[7].' In effect, the court may set aside, in part or whole, any obligation imposed by that bargain upon the debtor or otherwise alter the terms of the credit bargain[8]. In the terms of section 138(1) of the Act, a credit bargain is 'extortionate' if it

(*a*) requires the debtor or a relative of his to make payments (whether unconditionally, or on certain contingencies) which are grossly exorbitant, or
(*b*) otherwise grossly contravenes ordinary principles of fair dealing.

In determining whether a credit bargain is extortionate, the court must have regard to such evidence as is adduced concerning 'interest rates prevailing at the

2 [1979] Ch 84 at 111.
3 See R. M. Goode, *The Consumer Credit Act* (London 1979), paras. 961ff.
4 Consumer Credit Act 1974, s. 8(2). The court has power, however, to 're-open' an 'extortionate' credit bargain under section 137(1), even though the credit extended exceeds the £5,000 limit.
5 Consumer Credit Act 1974, s. 16(1), (2).
6 See R. A. Bowles (1981) 131 NLJ 4.
7 Consumer Credit Act 1974, s. 137(1).
8 Consumer Credit Act 1974, s. 139.

time it was made' and 'any other relevant considerations[9].' The court is particularly directed, in relation to the debtor, to have regard to

(*a*) his age, experience, business capacity and state of health; and
(*b*) the degree to which, at the time of making the credit bargain he was under financial pressure, and the nature of that pressure[10].

In relation to the creditor, the court must have regard to evidence in respect of

(*a*) the degree of risk accepted by him, having regard to the value of any security provided;
(*b*) his relationship to the debtor; and
(*c*) whether or not a colourable cash price was quoted for any goods or services included in the credit bargain[11].

The effect of these provisions on the law of mortgages was expounded in A. Ketley Ltd v Scott[12], the first case to reach the High Court on the construction of sections 137–140 of the 1974 Act. Here Foster J declined to hold that a credit agreement fixing an annual rate of interest equivalent to 48 per cent was 'extortionate' within the meaning of the Act. The defendants had sought a loan from the plaintiff at very short notice in order to complete their contract to purchase a flat in which they lived. They signed a number of documents in great haste, including a legal charge for a loan for three months at 12 per cent interest. One of the defendants had already given a legal charge on the property to secure a bank overdraft, but this fact was not disclosed to the plaintiff in the present transaction.

Foster J, in refusing to grant relief, had regard to the fact that the extraordinary nature and urgency of the transaction justified the imposition of a higher rate of interest than that normally charged by banks and building societies. The defendants had known exactly what they were doing, and had not been subject to real financial pressure. If the loan had not been advanced to them by the plaintiff, they would not have been rendered homeless. They already enjoyed a protected tenancy in respect of the property, and merely wished to purchase the property at what was a temporary bargain price. In view of the high risk accepted by the mortgagee it could not be said that the credit agreement concluded here was extortionate, and in any event Foster J declared that he would have been unwilling to re-open the contract on behalf of a borrower who had deceitfully failed to disclose the existence of a prior charge on the property concerned[13].

7. PROTECTION FOR THE MORTGAGEE

Elsewhere in this book we have noted that important policy considerations underlie the legal protection given to mortgagees. In order that the flow of loan

9 Consumer Credit Act 1974, s. 138(2).
10 Consumer Credit Act 1974, s. 138(2), (3).
11 Consumer Credit Act 1974, s. 138(2), (4).
12 [1981] ICR 241.
13 See H. W. Wilkinson (1980) 130 NLJ 749: 'Extortionate Mortgages'.

finance should be sustained, particularly for the purpose of facilitating home purchase, it is essential that certain safeguards and remedies be maintained on behalf of those who lend money on the security of real property[14]. We must now look at various aspects of the protection accorded to mortgagees.

(1) Investigation of title by the mortgagee

It is customary for an intending mortgagee to investigate the title offered by a would-be mortgagor before taking a mortgage as security for any loan advanced to the latter. Where a building society is the lender of moneys on an 'acquisition mortgage' it often instructs the purchaser's solicitor to investigate title not merely on behalf of the purchaser but also on behalf of the building society itself[15]. In this way the lender seeks to ensure that the title to which the security relates is sound and reliable.

We have already seen that this process of investigation of title may not attain its objective in some circumstances. If the mortgagee is offered a legal security in land which, unknown to him, is already held on trust for sale, he may lose priority to the equitable interests of certain persons in possession or 'in actual occupation' of that land[16]. This danger becomes particularly acute in the context of the matrimonial home, where, as was said by Lord Denning MR in *Williams & Glyn's Bank Ltd v Boland*[17], 'anyone who lends money . . . nowadays ought to realise that the wife may have a share in it.' The only practical solution for the mortgagee in cases of doubt is to ensure that the disposition of mortgage is effected by all the co-owners of the land or that he receives a written disclaimer of entitlement from every person in actual occupation of the land (whether the land be held by way of registered or unregistered title)[18].

However, the problems in this area are not confined to land held on implied trust for sale. Similar difficulties may afflict the mortgagee of land held on a bare trust which is not disclosed by the legal title[19]. Where a mortgagee purports to take an interest in land which, unknown to him, is settled land, the consequence may be even more drastic. In *Weston v Henshaw*[20] it was held that a disposition to a mortgagee was itself rendered 'void' by statute.

14 See pp. 54, 294f., ante.
15 The investigation of title carried out on behalf of the building society is, of course, at the expense of the applicant for a building society loan. The purchaser/mortgagor thus pays the same solicitor twice for doing the same job, once on his own behalf and again on behalf of his building society. It is, however, usual practice for a solicitor to charge a lower fee in respect of the work which he does for the building society, with the result that the purchaser pays roughly one-and-one-half times the cost of the job.
16 See pp. 334, 370, ante.
17 [1979] Ch 312 at 332, p. 367, ante.
18 See p. 379, ante.
19 See *Hodgson v Marks* [1971] Ch 892, p. 339, ante. Here the real loser was the second defendant, the Cheltenham and Gloucester Building Society, which had advanced the purchase moneys to the first defendant, the purchaser. The Court of Appeal was not overly sympathetic towards the building society. Russell LJ observed that 'it is plain that it made no enquiries on the spot save as to repairs; it relied on [the first defendant], who lied to it; and I waste no tears on it.' ([1971] Ch 892 at 932).
20 [1950] Ch 510, p. 172, ante.

The mortgagee may, moreover, be bound by a tenancy agreement granted by the mortgagor before he acquired the legal title which has been offered as security. In *Church of England Building Society v Piskor*[1], the mortgagor had obtained possession of land in advance of the completion of his transaction of purchase. During the interim before completion, he purported to grant periodic tenancies to two tenants who moved in before the date of the conveyance. When the mortgagee later sought possession of the property on the ground of default by the mortgagor, the Court of Appeal held that the rights of the tenants took priority over the mortgage. The tenancies had been mere 'leases by estoppel' during the period before conveyance, since the lessor had not yet acquired the fee simple estate out of which they might be created. However, as soon as the legal estate passed by conveyance to the mortgagor/lessor on completion, those tenancies automatically became legal tenancies. This metamorphosis occurred during the *scintilla temporis* which in theory intervenes between the passing of the legal estate to the mortgagor and the disposition of mortgage in favour of the lender of the purchase moneys. The rights of the tenants thus crystallised as legal rights in the instant when the 'estoppel was fed' by the conveyance of the legal estate[2].

Further difficulties arise for the mortgagee who takes merely an equitable security over the property owned by his mortgagor. Whereas a legal mortgagee may, for instance, ignore contractual rights which should have been protected by registration in the Land Charges Register or Land Register but which were not so protected, an equitable mortgagee is much more vulnerable. Thus an equitable mortgagee of unregistered land may be bound by a prior land charge (even if unregistered), on the basis that 'where the equities are equal, the first in time prevails.' In *McCarthy & Stone Ltd v Julian S. Hodge & Co Ltd*[3], it was held that an unregistered estate contract should take priority over a later equitable mortgagee of the encumbered property, since the latter could not claim the immunity conferred by statute upon a 'purchaser for money or money's worth . . . of a legal estate in the land . . .[4]' The effect of the unregistered estate contract therefore turned on an application of the traditional doctrine of notice, and in this case the equitable mortgagee was considered to be bound by constructive notice[5]. The result would not have been different if the land in question had been held by registered title, since the unprotected contractual rights would have acquired protection as an overriding interest provided that the owner of the estate contract was 'in actual occupation' at the date of the equitable mortgage[6].

1 [1954] Ch 553.
2 A similar result would have followed if title had been registered, since the tenants would have been protected under the Land Registration Act 1925, s. 70(1)(g), (k), pp. 334, 337f., ante. See P. B. Fairest, op. cit., p. 51f. However, if the tenants had had a mere contract for a tenancy, their rights in unregistered land would have depended upon the registration of a Class C (iv) land charge, and in registered land upon the existence of 'actual occupation' for the purpose of the Land Registration Act 1925, s. 70(1)(g), p. 337f., ante.
3 [1971] 1 WLR 1547. See (1972A) 30 Cambridge LJ 34 (P. B. Fairest).
4 Land Charges Act 1972, s. 4(6), p. 114, ante.
5 See p. 313, ante. The equitable mortgagee had, by this stage, acquired a legal mortgage by the exercise of a power of attorney.
6 See p. 337f., ante.

(2) Deposit of title deeds

A legal mortgagee is afforded a substantial safeguard against adverse dealings with the legal title by his mortgagor. Section 85(1) of the Law of Property Act 1925 provides that a first mortgagee has a legal right to retain the title deeds pertaining to the mortgaged property for the duration of the mortgage period. This form of additional security is, of course, applicable only to unregistered land. However, in the context of registered land much the same effect is brought about by section 65 of the Land Registration Act 1925, which requires that the mortgagor's land certificate be deposited in the Land Registry until redemption of the mortgage[7].

It is obvious that a second mortgagee cannot enjoy the security of deposit of the title deeds or the land certificate. However, a second mortgage may be protected as a Class C (i) land charge (if the mortgage is legal)[8], and as a Class C (iii) land charge (if the mortgage takes the form of an equitable charge)[9].

Apart from having the negative effect of preventing prejudicial dealings by the mortgagor, the practice of depositing title deeds with the mortgagee of unregistered land facilitates any later exercise of the mortgagee's power of sale. Should that power become *exercisable*[10], he is already equipped with the necessary documents of title for the purpose of dealing with third parties.

(3) The mortgagee's right to possession

The crucial right of the mortgagee is, for many purposes, the right which he enjoys to enter into possession of the mortgaged land. This right has become controversial in recent times, because it impinges, perhaps more directly than any other remedy available to the mortgagee, upon the residential security of the mortgagor.

(a) *A right or a remedy?*

A legal mortgage confers upon the mortgagee a legal estate in the mortgaged property which carries with it a right to take possession of the land[11]. The mortgagee's right to possession arises as soon as the mortgage is made and is not dependent upon any prior default by the mortgagor. As Harman J graphically pointed out in *Four-Maids Ltd v Dudley Marshall (Properties) Ltd*[12],

7 See p. 348, ante.
8 See p. 134, ante.
9 See p. 135, ante.
10 See p. 545, post.
11 See Law of Property Act 1925, s. 95(4). The legal chargee, who does not of course have any legal estate on which to base his entitlement to possession, is given a corresponding statutory right to possession by section 87(1) of the Law of Property Act 1925. This provision confers upon the legal chargee 'the same protection, powers and remedies (including the right to take proceedings to obtain possession from the occupiers and the persons in receipt of rents and profits, or any of them) as if' he *had* a legal estate, p. 518, ante.
12 [1957] Ch 317 at 320. See (1957) 73 LQR 300 (REM).

The mortgagee may go into possession before the ink is dry on the mortgage unless there is something in the contract, express or by implication, whereby he has contracted himself out of that right[13].

This traditional view has the consequence that the mortgagee is entitled to enter into physical possession of the mortgaged land even though the mortgagor has not defaulted in his payments and even though the date fixed for redemption has not yet passed. Entry into physical possession is impossible only where the land is already subject at the date of the mortgage to a lease which is binding upon the mortgagee. In this situation, the mortgagee is entitled to claim 'possession' in the sense of the right to receive rents and profits[14]. He may therefore direct the tenant to pay his rent henceforth to the mortgagee rather than the mortgagor[15].

The only cases in which the mortgagee is not entitled even to this technical form of possession arise where the terms of the mortgage either expressly or impliedly confer a right of possession on the *mortgagor*. It is not uncommon, for instance, that a building society mortgage should grant the mortgagor an express right of possession until default. It has even been held that a mortgage term which expressly confers a right to possession on the mortgagee in the event of default by the mortgagor constitutes an implied exclusion of any right to possession by the mortgagee before default occurs[16].

It remains the case, however, that the courts are somewhat slow to find that a mortgage impliedly reserves a right of possession to the mortgagor rather than to the mortgagee[17]. In *Western Bank Ltd v Schindler*[18], the defendant mortgagor had borrowed £32,000 from the plaintiff mortgagee on the terms of an endowment mortgage which provided that no payment of capital or interest was contractually due until ten years after the date of the mortgage. Notwithstanding that the mortgagor was guilty of no default, the mortgagee subsequently claimed a right to possession of the property *within* the ten year period, in order to preserve the value of its security. The Court of Appeal unanimously upheld the mortgagee's right to possession even in advance of any default. The Court was unwilling to accept the argument that a contractual term excluding this right should normally be implied 'if and for so long as the terms of the mortgage preclude the mortgagee from making immediate demand for payment or otherwise immediately enforcing his security.'

13 See also *Alliance Perpetual Building Society v Belrum Investments Ltd* [1957] 1 WLR 720 at 722 per Harman J.
14 See Law of Property Act 1925, s. 205(1)(xix).
15 See *Horlock v Smith* (1842) 6 Jur 478.
16 *Birmingham Citizens Permanent Building Society v Caunt* [1962] Ch 883 at 890 per Russell J.
17 See, for instance, *Esso Petroleum Co Ltd v Alstonbridge Properties Ltd* [1975] 1 WLR 1474 at 1484, where Walton J accepted that 'the court will be ready to find an implied term in an instalment mortgage that the mortgagor is to be entitled to remain in possession against the mortgagee until he makes some default in payment of one of the instalments. But there must be something upon which to hang such a conclusion in the mortgage other than the mere fact that it is an instalment mortgage.' See also R. J. Smith [1979] Conv 266 at 268ff.: 'The Mortgagee's Right to Possession—The Modern Law'.
18 [1977] Ch 1. See (1977) 40 MLR 356 (C. Harpum).

Buckley LJ agreed that the fact that a mortgage was an instalment mortgage might make it easier for the court to find such an implied term, but held that even this fact would not in itself be conclusive. In the present case, however, the mortgagee's right to possession was not lightly to be held to have been excluded by implication, since only this right could effectively protect the mortgagee's legitimate interest in ensuring that, on the date fixed for redemption, the property still represented a good security for what would then be a very substantial debt of capital and interest. As Scarman LJ pointed out, the only way in which ultimately the mortgagee could ensure that the mortgaged property was properly managed and maintained, and the value of the security thereby preserved during the period of the loan, was by upholding the mortgagee's right to possession in the absence of a clear contractual exclusion of that right[19].

There is one other, and now somewhat unusual, method by which the mortgagee's right to possession may be excluded. It used to be common practice to insert an *attornment clause* in a deed of mortgage. This clause has the effect of creating a purely nominal lease between the parties to the mortgage, the mortgagor holding as a tenant of the mortgagee[20]. The object of the attornment clause is to make available to the mortgagee the additional remedies open to a lessor for the purpose of obtaining possession against an occupier. However, there is one respect in which the use of an attornment clause significantly qualifies the mortgagee's right to enter into possession of the mortgaged land. Precisely because a notional tenancy is created between mortgagor and mortgagee, the latter is required to terminate the tenancy by serving a notice to quit as a necessary preliminary to any exercise of the right to possession[1]. However, the attornment clause does not confer upon the mortgagor any of the other forms of protection afforded tenants under the Rent Act legislation[2], and the insertion of such a clause in a mortgage is now rare[3].

The foregoing rules represent the strictly legal position concerning the mortgagee's right to possession. It is, however, extremely important to note that the position in reality is very different. Mortgagees rarely insist upon exercising their undoubted right to possession. The entire object of most mortgages is that the *mortgagor* should be entitled to occupy the land which forms the subject matter of the security. There is in general a 'tacit agreement' between the parties to a mortgage that the right to possession should be exercised de facto by the

19 In the words of Scarman LJ (at 17), 'So far from implying a term excluding the common law right, I would expect, as a matter of business efficacy, that the mortgagee would in these circumstances require its retention.'

20 The rent payable under the tenancy created by the attornment clause was commonly a purely nominal rent such as a peppercorn. See R. E. Megarry and H. W. R. Wade, op. cit., p. 917f.

1 *Hinckley and Country Building Society v Henny* [1953] 1 WLR 352.

2 It seems, for instance, that the mortgagor under the attornment clause does not qualify for the protection generally applicable in the area of residential lettings that four weeks' notice to quit is required by law, p. 470f., ante. See *Alliance Building Society v Pinwill* [1958] Ch 788 at 792, where Vaisey J held that the statutory requirement of a minimum period of notice protects only 'a real tenant against a real landlord under a real residential letting.' Compare, however, P. B. Fairest, op. cit., p. 89, and see *Regent Oil Co Ltd v J. A. Gregory (Hatch End) Ltd* [1966] Ch 402.

3 See Wurtzburg and Mills, op. cit., p. 184f.

mortgagor save in the case of default[4]. Indeed, it is not going too far to say that, apart perhaps from the exceptional circumstances typified in *Western Bank Ltd v Schindler*[5], a mortgagee will never nowadays seek possession except where default has already occurred.

Several factors have conduced to bring about this result. As we shall see in due course[6], the exercise of the mortgagee's right to possession has become subject, at least in the residential context, to an important measure of statutory control. It is, moreover, a fact of economic life that most mortgagees are more interested in the receipt of the money payments due under a mortgage than in the exercise of a right to physical possession of the land[7]. In any event, a mortgagee in possession is subject to the particularly stringent control of equity in his dealings with the property. If, while in possession, he intercepts the rents and profits drawn from the land in order to ensure the payment of the interest due to him under the mortgage, he is liable to account strictly to the mortgagor for any income which he thus receives[8]. He may not derive any personal profit beyond that which is stipulated for by the terms of the mortgage. His duties are rendered even more onerous by the fact that he is liable 'on the footing of wilful default.' In consequence he must account to the mortgagor not only in respect of rents and profits actually received, but also in respect of that income which he would have received if he had managed the property with 'due diligence'[9]. Thus, in *White v City of London Brewery Co*[10], a mortgagee who entered into possession and let the mortgaged property as a 'tied' public house (for the benefit of his own brewery business) was held liable to account for the greater rents which he would have received had he let the property as a 'free' house.

The truth of the matter is that, if a mortgagee's concern is to secure the income derived from the mortgaged land, his objective is much better served by the appointment of a receiver[11] than by entry into possession subject to the strict control of equity. The handling of rents and profits by a receiver is not subject to the same rigorous surveillance of equity. In practice, the mortgagee who nowadays exercises his right to possession is not concerned to attach the income drawn from the land, but rather to obtain vacant possession of the property in order that he may sell on the open market and thereby recoup the amount of

4 *Moss v Gallimore* (1779) 1 Doug KB 279 at 283; *Christophers v Sparke* (1820) 2 Jac & W 223 at 235. See B. Rudden (1961) 25 Conv (NS) 278: 'Mortgagee's Right to Possession'.

5 [1977] Ch 1, p. 534, ante. 'Cases where there is a valid need for possession before default would seem very rare.' See R. J. Smith [1979] Conv 266 at 267.

6 Post, p. 541.

7 See, for instance, *Four-Maids Ltd v Dudley Marshall (Properties) Ltd* [1957] Ch 317 at 321, where Harman J made the point that 'Building Societies are not desirous of going into possession, nor would they do business if they were able to go into possession whenever they liked. The whole object of building societies is to maintain the householder in possession of his house so long as he pays the instalments to the society . . .'

8 Alternatively, the mortgagee may pay the entire rent received over to the mortgagor, for 'he cannot be compelled to accept repayment in driblets' (see R. E. Megarry and H. W. R. Wade, op. cit., p. 915; *Nelson v Booth* (1858) 3 De G & J 119; *Wrigley v Gill* [1905] 1 Ch 241). In this case, of course, the mortgagor remains liable in full in respect of any default which he has made.

9 *Chaplin v Young (No. 1)* (1864) 33 Beav 330 at 337f.

10 (1889) 42 Ch D 237.

11 See p. 548, post.

any outstanding loan moneys. Possession is almost invariably sought as a preliminary to the mortgagee's exercise of his power of sale.

It inevitably follows that in practice a mortgagee never seeks possession unless and until there has been default by the mortgagor, because it is only at this point that the mortgagee's power of sale becomes exercisable[12]. In view of the fact that the taking of possession has effectively become 'an adjunct of the power of sale'[13], it has been questioned whether the mortgagee's right to possession ought not to be regarded more as a *remedy* than as a *right*. As a *right* which technically subsists from the date of the mortgage, it is in most cases a misleading fiction. It is arguable that the terminology of *remedy* is distinctly more appropriate, since in reality the right to possession now lies dormant in all situations except that in which the mortgagee's security is threatened by an actual default on the part of his mortgagor.

This approach to the mortgagee's right of possession received some support in the Court of Appeal's judgments in *Quennell v Maltby*[14]. Here the owner of a house in fee simple mortgaged the property to a bank by way of security for his bank overdraft. The mortgage contained a prohibition of any lettings of the property without the consent of the bank. Notwithstanding the terms of the mortgage, the owner let the house to two university students. On the expiry of the contractual period of the letting, the owner wished to sell the property with vacant possession on the open market, but the tenants claimed to be statutory tenants and refused to leave. The owner then unsuccessfully requested the bank to seek possession of the property *qua mortgagee*. He managed, however, to persuade his own wife to pay off the moneys owing to the bank, and in consequence the bank transferred its mortgage over the property to the wife. It was she who brought the present action for possession against the two students, claiming that as the mortgagee of the property she had an absolute right to take possession.

The entire course of dealings involved here smacked heavily of collusion, and it is perhaps not surprising that the Court of Appeal declined to allow the protective effect of the Rent Act to be frustrated by an evasive device. It was plain that the owner would not have been entitled to evict the tenants had he sought possession under the Rent Act. Lord Denning MR pointed out that to allow the owner's wife to achieve in the present proceedings an objective which he could not have achieved in Rent Act proceedings would open the way

> to widespread evasion of the Rent Acts. If the owner of a house wishes to obtain vacant possession, all he has to do is charge it to the bank for a small sum. Then grant a new tenancy without telling the bank. Then get his wife to pay off the bank and take a transfer. Then get the wife to sue for possession[15].

Lord Denning adverted to the fact that the wife's action for possession was not motivated by any desire to enforce the security or to obtain repayment of the loan moneys. She had brought the present action 'simply for an ulterior purpose

12 See p. 545, post.
13 See R. J. Smith [1979] Conv 266.
14 [1979] 1 WLR 318. See (1979) 38 Cambridge LJ 257 (R. A. Pearce).
15 [1979] 1 WLR 318 at 322. On the operation of the Rent Act legislation, see further Chapter 13, p. 415ff., ante.

of getting possession of the house, contrary to the intention of Parliament as expressed in the Rent Acts[16].' This being the case, it was appropriate, in the view adopted by the Master of the Rolls, that equity should step in 'to mitigate the rigour of the law.' However, the method by which Lord Denning proposed that conscience should be satisfied here was sharply at variance with the conventional understanding that a mortgagee, in the absence of contrary contractual provision, may enter into possession at any time after the date of the mortgage. In Lord Denning's judgment,

in modern times equity can step in so as to prevent a mortgagee, or a transferee from him, from getting possession of a house contrary to the justice of the case. A mortgagee will be restrained from getting possession except when it is sought bona fide and reasonably for the purpose of enforcing the security and then only subject to such conditions as the court thinks fit to impose. When the bank itself or a building society lends the money, then it may well be right to allow the mortgagee to obtain possession when the borrower is in default. But so long as the interest is paid and there is nothing outstanding, equity has ample power to restrain any unjust use of the right to possession[17].

In the present case the ulterior object of the transaction had been to enable the owner and his wife to obtain possession of the property 'in order to resell it at a profit.' In these circumstances, held the Court of Appeal, the right to possession should not be enforced.

Although the result attained by the Court of Appeal in *Quennell v Maltby* did admirable justice on the facts of the case[18], the excessively broad sweep of Lord Denning's judgment is inconsistent with authority[19]. Although by relating possession to the bona fide enforcement of the security Lord Denning effectively treated the mortgagee's right to possession as a remedy rather than a right, it cannot be said that this view represents good law at the moment. As Roger Smith has pointed out[20], the approach adopted by the Court of Appeal would, if valid, render completely otiose the protection accorded the mortgagor under the Administration of Justice Acts[1]. The safer view therefore seems to be that the mortgagee's right to possession is still better conceptualised as a right rather than as a remedy.

(b) *Relief for the mortgagor*

The enforcement of the mortgagee's right to possession necessarily brings about

16 [1979] 1 WLR 318 at 323.
17 [1979] 1 WLR 318 at 322f.
18 The result may have been perfectly justified on the alternative basis that the wife was in substance suing as an agent of her husband. See the views expressed by Bridge and Templeman LJJ. ([1979] 1 WLR 318 at 323f.).
19 See, for instance, the classic statement of Grant MR in *Marquis Cholmondeley v Lord Clinton* (1817) 2 Mer 171, 359: 'A court of equity never interferes to prevent the mortgagee from assuming the possession.' See also F. W. Maitland, *Equity* (2nd edn., London 1936), p. 186, where it is pointed out that equity would not interfere with a claim to possession at common law except on terms of payment off of the whole principal, interest and costs, an equity which Maitland described as a 'mock equity', since it required payment in full, and consequently the displacement of the mortgagee from his position as such, the very position which entitled him to possession.
20 [1979] Conv 266 at 268.
1 See p. 541f., post.

drastic consequences, since in the residential context, for instance, it may mean the dispossession of a family from its home. Several forms of relief have therefore been devised on behalf of mortgagors, in a manner not dissimilar to the way in which relief against forfeiture is extended to lessees in certain circumstances[2]. In examining the relief given to mortgagors in the context of proceedings for possession, it should always be borne in mind that to place inhibitions upon the mortgagee's freedom to possess the mortgaged property is indirectly to limit the exercise of his power of sale.

(i) *The court's inherent jurisdiction to grant relief* Before 1936 it was possible for a mortgagee to obtain summarily an order for possession of mortgaged property without the matter being heard before any judge or other officer of the court. Since 1936, however, the Chancery Division of the High Court has assumed jurisdiction to grant orders for possession, and has, furthermore, claimed an inherent discretionary jurisdiction to adjourn proceedings for possession[3]. This jurisdiction is exercisable both in proceedings commenced by writ and in proceedings commenced by originating summons[4]. This equitable jurisdiction, which is in practice exercised by the Masters of the Chancery Division, enables hard-pressed mortgagors to have temporary relief in order that they may resolve their financial difficulties and repay any amounts owing under the mortgage[5]. This discretion used to be exercised quite liberally, one famous Chancery Master describing his function in this context as that of a 'social worker rather than a Judge', in that it is for the Chancery Master to try

> if the matter is not quite hopeless, as in bankruptcy, and any willingness is shown by the defaulter, to enable the borrower to keep his home by paying off his arrears by agreed instalments. If necessary, he uses time and technicality as weapons against a too stony-hearted plaintiff . . .[6]

In recent years, however, the court's inherent jurisdiction to stay proceedings for possession has been exercised more sparingly. In *Birmingham Citizens Permanent Building Society v Caunt*[7], Russell J made it quite clear that the inherent jurisdiction merely empowers the court to adjourn a hearing 'for a short time' in order to 'afford the mortgagor a limited opportunity to find means to pay off the mortgagee or otherwise satisfy him if there was a reasonable prospect of either of those events occurring.' In this case, Russell J indicated that any adjournment would be unlikely to exceed a period of 28 days[8].

This decision did much to restore to the mortgagee the balance of power which some had imagined was removed by the presence of the court's inherent jurisdiction[9]. As Russell J had agreed, in the course of giving judgment,

2 See p. 407, ante.
3 See RSC Ord. 55, r. 5A. The inherent jurisdiction is now exercised under RSC Ord. 88, r. 7.
4 RSC Ord. 88, r. 7; *Redditch Benefit Building Society v Roberts* [1940] Ch 415 at 421.
5 In the celebrated words of Clauson LJ, 'the facts and the circumstances of the case were brought before the court, and in proper cases the wind was tempered to the shorn lamb, time being given for payment and so forth' (see *Redditch Benefit Building Society v Roberts* [1940] Ch 415 at 420).
6 Master Ball (1961) 77 LQR 331 at 351: 'The Chancery Master'.
7 [1962] Ch 883 at 891. See (1962) 78 LQR 171 (REM).
8 [1962] Ch 883 at 908.
9 See *Robertson v Cilia* [1956] 1 WLR 1502; (1957) 73 LQR 18 (REM).

Equity had always interfered with legal rights in order to ensure that the mortgage should not operate otherwise than as it was intended to operate—namely, as security for repayment of money. But there was no principle upon which equity had ever attempted or could ever rightly attempt to interfere with the security *as a security*, or to destroy or suspend or nullify any rights of the mortgagee which were part and parcel of that security. The whole purpose of equity was, by insisting that the transaction was a security for the repayment of money, thereby to shield the mortgagor from attempts in reliance on strict legal rights to turn it into something more. Equity was never and should never be in the hands of the judges a sword to attack any part of the security itself, and the right to possession was an important part of that security, more particularly in the association with the ability to give vacant possession on the exercise of the power of sale[10].

The net effect of this tightening-up of the court's exercise of discretion was to accentuate growing demands for the introduction of a new form of statutory relief for residential mortgagors.

(ii) *The court's statutory power to stay possession proceedings* The principal emphasis of the pressure for reform of the law relating to possession centred around the special status which was thought to attach to mortgages of residential property. It was inevitable that comparison should be made with the protection from eviction conferred upon protected and statutory tenants under the Rent Act legislation[11]. As Harman J had said in *Hughes v Waite*[12],

It used to be recognised that a mortgagee might take possession as a matter of course, and it is only in recent years that the housing shortage and the Rent Restrictions Acts between them have made what seems to be a difficulty on this matter.

The question of a possible statutory extension of the protection given to residential mortgagors was ultimately placed before the Payne Committee on the Enforcement of Judgment Debts. This Committee concluded that the scope of protection should indeed be increased by legislation. The supporting reasons for this conclusion are not without interest. The Committee noted that 'a succession of governments have for some years encouraged the purchase, instead of the renting, of houses by persons of modest means.' It felt therefore that where a mortgagor, because of financial difficulties, falls into arrear with his mortgage instalments,

the courts should be empowered, subject to proper safeguards, to extend to the mortgagor the same protection in relation to the continued occupation of the house as would be given to a tenant of a property of a similar rateable value[13].

10 [1962] Ch 883 at 896.
11 See p. 444f., ante.
12 [1957] 1 WLR 713 at 715.
13 *Report of the Committee on the Enforcement of Judgment Debts* (Cmnd 3909, February 1969), para. 1386(d). The Committee reached its conclusions in the face of strong representations made by the Building Societies Association (see paras. 1379ff.) to the effect that the court's discretion should not be extended. The Committee accepted that the 'responsible building societies have proved themselves to be tolerant and understanding with those of their borrowers who have fallen into arrear with their instalments through misfortune, and not infrequently they enter into reasonable and satisfactory arrangements for the discharge of arrears without initiating or pursuing a claim for possession' (*Report*, para. 1386(b)). However, as the Committee went on to

The Committee thus recognised in effect that the expansion of the 'property-owning democracy' had fixed upon the government of the day a broad social responsibility to assimilate mortgagors within the same kind of protective legislation as that which benefits residential tenants.

The proposal of the Payne Committee was partially realised in the enactment of section 36 of the Administration of Justice Act 1970. This provision confers upon the court a wide power to adjourn possession proceedings or postpone the giving of possession in respect of a 'dwelling-house' for such period or periods 'as the court thinks reasonable[14].' The discretion is exercisable in any claim for possession of residential property in which

it appears to the court that in the event of its exercising the power the mortgagor is likely to be able within a reasonable period to pay any sums due under the mortgage or to remedy a default consisting of a breach of any other obligation arising under or by virtue of the mortgage[15].

Almost immediately it became obvious that section 36(1) contained a severe drafting defect which threatened to destroy the protective import of the provision. In *Halifax Building Society v Clark*[16], the plaintiff building society sought an order for possession against the deserted wife of the mortgagor. Although the beneficial owner of the property was the husband/mortgagor, the wife was, of course, entitled to require the building society to accept any payment tendered by her, since section 1(5) of the Matrimonial Homes Act 1967 provides that payment of any mortgage liability by the spouse of a mortgagor is 'as good as if made or done by the other spouse[17].' The difficulty was, however, that it was impossible for the wife to satisfy the precondition for the exercise of discretion in her favour under section 36 of the 1970 Act. Pennycuick V-C ruled that the defendant must be able to pay 'any sums due under the mortgage' within a reasonable period. Although in the present case, the mortgage instalments in arrear amounted only to £100, the entire capital debt (over £1,400) had become 'due' on the husband's default in accordance with the strict terms of the mortgage. The court was therefore unable to grant the wife relief under section 36, since it was quite obvious that there was no prospect of her raising this larger sum within a reasonable period.

This rather grave defect in the legislation was remedied by the enactment of section 8(1) of the Administration of Justice Act 1973, which redefines the

---

note, 'unfortunately all mortgagees are not responsible building societies . . .' See also *Report of the Committee on One-Parent Families* (Cmnd 5629, July 1974), Vol. 1, para. 6.116ff.

14 Administration of Justice Act 1970, s. 36(2). Under section 36(3), the court may make adjournment conditional upon specified terms relating to the payment of arrears or the remedying of any default.

15 Administration of Justice Act 1970, s. 36(1). The Housing Act 1980, s. 89 introduces certain severe restrictions on the court's exercise of discretion in making possession orders in respect of land, p. 450, ante. In general the court may not postpone possession for more than 14 days from the making of a possession order, but there is an exception from this draconian rule in relation to orders made in an action by a mortgagee for possession (see Housing Act 1980, s. 89(2)(a)).

16 [1973] Ch 307. See (1973) 89 LQR 171 (P. V. Baker); (1973) 36 MLR 550 (P. Jackson); (1973) 37 Conv (NS) 213 (F. R. Crane).

17 See p. 443, ante.

phrase 'any sums due' in section 36(1) of the 1970 Act as referring only to such amounts as the mortgagor would have expected to be required to pay if the mortgage had not contained a default clause which rendered the entire capital debt repayable in the event of the instalments falling into arrear[18]. Section 8(1) thus overturns the decision in *Halifax Building Society v Clark*, and effectively reinstates what was almost certainly the intention of the legislature in framing the provision in the 1970 Act[19]. The court may thus grant an adjournment of possession proceedings if there is a likelihood that the mortgagor will be able during the interim to find not only any mortgage instalments which have fallen into arrear but also any other instalments which may have become due during the period of adjournment[20].

The court's statutory discretion under the Administration of Justice Acts clearly provides some assistance for mortgagors who run into temporary financial difficulties, whether by reason of unemployment, short-time working, redundancy or marital difficulties[1]. The discretion is sufficiently wide to cover not merely instalment mortgages but also any mortgage under which the payment of capital is deferred. There are, however, several respects in which the effect of the recent legislative intervention is limited.

We have already seen that the spouse of the mortgagor has a statutory right to tender payment of mortgage instalments on behalf of the mortgagor[2]. However, this right may not be of much value to a wife who is unaware that her husband's mortgage payments have been allowed to fall into arrear. In *Hastings and Thanet Building Society v Goddard*[3], the Court of Appeal held that there is no statutory justification for requiring that a building society should inform the mortgagor's wife of her husband's default in order that she should have an opportunity to tender payment herself. Russell LJ thought that any contrary view was 'impracticable because a building society can scarcely be expected to keep track of the matrimonial status of its mortgagors[4].' Likewise the Court refused to accept that notice of a mortgagee's possession proceedings should be

18 There is doubt, however, whether section 36 of the Administration of Justice Act 1970 can have any application where mortgage payments have not yet become due. In *Western Bank Ltd v Schindler* [1977] Ch 1, two members of the Court of Appeal (Buckley and Scarman LJJ) thought that section 36 must be applicable irrespective of the absence of actual default, since otherwise a blameless mortgagor would be put in a less advantageous position than a defaulting mortgagor who can rely on section 36. However, Goff LJ was of the view that, on strict construction, section 36 cannot apply where there is no money due or any other default present on the facts. See (1977) 40 MLR 356 (C. Harpum).

19 Even before the enactment of section 8 of the Administration of Justice Act 1973, the problem raised in *Halifax Building Society v Clark* had arisen in *First Middlesbrough Trading and Mortgage Co Ltd v Cunningham* (1974) 28 P & CR 69. Here the Court of Appeal effectively refused to follow the construction of section 36 of the 1970 Act applied in *Halifax Building Society v Clark*. For an argument that the ratio of *Cunningham*'s case may still be wider (and therefore more favourable to the mortgagor) than section 8 of the 1973 Act, see R. J. Smith [1979] Conv 266 at 274f.

20 Administration of Justice Act 1973, s. 8(2).

1 For a consideration of the factors relevant to the exercise of the statutory discretion, see R. J. Smith [1979] Conv 266 at 279f.

2 See p. 541, ante.

3 [1970] 1 WLR 1544. See (1971) 35 Conv (NS) 48 (F. R. Crane).

4 [1970] 1 WLR 1544 at 1548.

served on the mortgagor's spouse (where she was not a joint tenant of the property), since her statutory rights of occupation in the matrimonial home are in no way binding upon the mortgagee. The only right which the spouse may assert against the mortgagee is the right to pay any moneys still owing to him and thereby prevent him from exercising his right to take possession.

The decision of the Court of Appeal in *Hastings and Thanet Building Society v Goddard* has been much criticised[5]. It conduces to a situation in which a deserted wife may discover too late that substantial mortgage arrears have been allowed to accrue, and effectively prevents her from arguing that the court's discretion should be extended in her favour under the Administration of Justice Acts. The Law Commission has proposed that the law be amended so that any wife who has rights under section 1(5) of the Matrimonial Homes Act 1967 should normally be entitled to apply to the court to be joined in any action brought by the mortgagee to enforce his security[6]. Furthermore, the Law Commission has recommended that any mortgagee who seeks to enforce his security in land which comprises a dwelling house should be obliged by law to give notice of his action to a wife who has registered a Class F land charge or its registered land equivalent, thereby enabling her to exercise her right to be joined as a party in the proceedings[7]. The latter proposal imposes the burden of search upon the mortgagee who brings proceedings for possession, but in days of increased emphasis upon residential security this result may not seem entirely unreasonable. A provision implementing these recommendations is now contained in clause 2 of the Matrimonial Homes and Property Bill 1981 currently before Parliament.

The court's discretion under the Administration of Justice Acts is also limited in other respects. In order that the discretion be exercisable, it must appear to the court that the mortgagor is 'likely to be able within a reasonable period to pay any sums due under the mortgage.' There is no scope at all for the exercise of discretion in favour of a mortgagor if he is unable to provide *any* evidence of ability to pay[8]. Simply to ask for time to pay is not enough. Moreover, it may be that the entire discretionary jurisdiction is inapplicable where no sums are yet due under the mortgage, as in *Western Bank Ltd v Schindler*[9].

Where the court decides to exercise discretion in favour of the mortgagor, there are severe restrictions upon the terms on which it may do so. In *Royal Trust Co of Canada v Markham*[10], for instance, the Court of Appeal ruled that it had no jurisdiction to order a suspension of possession proceedings *sine die*. The court

5 See D. A. Nevitt and J. Levin (1973) 36 MLR 345 at 349f.: 'Social Policy and the Matrimonial Home.' The Committee on One-Parent Families expressed the view that 'the courts have seemed to be more concerned with reducing the administrative burdens of building societies than with safeguarding families in their homes . . .' See *Report of the Committee on One-Parent Families* (Cmnd 5629, July 1974), Vol. 1, para. 6.120.

6 *Third Report on Family Property: The Matrimonial Home (Co-ownership and Occupation Rights) and Household Goods* (Law Com No. 86, June 1978), para. 2.25ff.

7 Ibid., para. 2.27ff.

8 *Royal Trust Co. of Canada v Markham* [1975] 1 WLR 1416; *Williams & Glyn's Bank Ltd v Boland* [1980] 3 WLR 138 at 147. See, however, *Centrax Trustees Ltd v Ross* [1979] 2 All ER 952; [1979] Conv 371 (F. R. Crane).

9 [1977] Ch 1, p. 534, ante.

10 [1975] 1 WLR 1416.

must define and fix the period for which the proceedings should be adjourned or any possession order stayed. In any event relief may be granted to the mortgagor only in respect of such period of time as is 'reasonable'. The Payne Committee on the Enforcement of Judgment Debts considered that a period of six months would be sufficient in most cases[11], but the period may well be longer or shorter depending upon the circumstances[12].

There is one provision in the law of social security which may afford the mortgagor or his spouse considerable assistance in putting forward a case for relief under the Administration of Justice Acts. If the applicant for statutory relief is in receipt of supplementary benefit, he may well be able to claim the interest payable on his mortgage as part of his entitlement to supplementary benefit[13]. However, there is a broad principle that supplementary benefit may be used to cover payments of *interest* only rather than *capital*. The official view underlying this principle seems to be the idea that, provided the claimant's accommodation is safeguarded, 'public funds ought not to be used to increase the capital assets' of those on supplementary benefit[14]. In practice, however, the supplementary benefits authorities will give a mortgagee a written guarantee of mortgage interest payments, and will use their discretion indirectly to disregard, in assessing supplementary benefit, certain resources which the claimant may then use for the payment of capital or arrears due under the mortgage[15].

(4) The mortgagee's power of sale

As we have seen, entry into possession by a mortgagee will normally occur in conjunction with an exercise of the mortgagee's power of sale. The obtaining of vacant possession will usually be an essential condition for the securing of a good price in the event of sale.

(a) *When the power of sale arises and becomes exercisable*

A mortgagee has no effective power of sale over the mortgaged property at common law, but such a power is now conferred by statute. Under section 101 of the Law of Property Act 1925, a mortgagee's statutory power of sale *arises* where three conditions are satisfied. *First*, the mortgage in question must be effected by deed[16]. *Second*, the mortgage money must have become due[17], i.e., the legal date for redemption must have passed[18]. Thus, the mortgagee's power of sale arises, for instance, as soon as any instalment of the mortgage repayments

11 *Report* (Cmnd 3909), para. 1388.
12 See R. J. Smith [1979] Conv 266 at 278f.
13 Supplementary Benefit (Requirements) Regulations 1980 (S.I. 1980/1299), reg. 16.
14 See *Report of the Committee on One-Parent Families* (Cmnd 5629, July 1974), Vol. 1, para. 6.126.
15 See David Pearl and Kevin Gray, *Social Welfare Law* (London 1981), p. 89; J. Tunnard and Clare Whately, *Rights Guide for Home Owners* (3rd edn., London 1979), p. 35ff.
16 Law of Property Act 1925, s. 101(1).
17 Law of Property Act 1925, s. 101(1)(i).
18 See pp. 517, ante; 548, post.

falls into arrear[19]. *Third*, the mortgage must contain no expression of contrary intention which would have the effect of precluding a power of sale in the foregoing circumstances[20]. If these conditions are met, the mortgagee may proceed to *exercise* his power of sale, without any application to court, if one or more of three further conditions are fulfilled. These conditions are laid down in section 103 of the Law of Property Act 1925, which provides that

> A mortgagee shall not exercise the power of sale conferred by this Act unless and until—
>
> (i) Notice requiring payment of the mortgage money has been served on the mortgagor or one of two or more mortgagors, and default has been made in payment of the mortgage money, or of part thereof, for three months after such service; or
>
> (ii) Some interest under the mortgage is in arrear and unpaid for two months after becoming due; or
>
> (iii) There has been a breach of some provision contained in the mortgage deed or in this Act, or in an enactment replaced by this Act, and on the part of the mortgagor, or of some person concurring in making the mortgage, to be observed or performed, other than and besides a covenant for payment of the mortgage money or interest thereon.

It is vital to note the important distinction between the point in time at which a power of sale *arises* and that at which it becomes *exercisable*. The mortgagee has no power to sell until the statutory power of sale 'arises'. Any sale by him before this date will simply transfer to the purchaser merely his own rights as mortgagee, and will be ineffective to pass the legal estate.

Certain difficulties occur, however, where the mortgagee's power of sale has *arisen* but has not yet become *exercisable* under the statute. In these circumstances, any sale by the mortgagee will have the effect of vesting a good title in the purchaser but will expose the selling mortgagee to an action in damages brought by the mortgagor[1]. The title transferred to the purchaser is statutorily declared to be unimpeachable, but it is possible that this principle may have no application where at the time of the sale the purchaser is aware of any facts showing that the power of sale is not exercisable or even that there is some impropriety in the sale[2]. There is some authority for the view that

> to uphold the title of a purchaser who had notice of impropriety or irregularity in the exercise of the power of sale would be to convert the provisions of the statute into an instrument of fraud[3].

Thus a purchaser may be prejudicially affected by actual notice, for instance, of the fact that the mortgagor is not at the time of sale in default in his interest payments under the mortgage. However, as Professor Fairest points out, it seems that the purchaser will not be bound by *constructive* notice of such circumstances, although this represents a somewhat anomalous and not entirely justifiable

19 *Payne v Cardiff RDC* [1932] 1 KB 241.
20 Law of Property Act 1925, s. 101(4).
1 Law of Property Act 1925, s. 104(2).
2 *Selwyn v Garfit* (1888) 38 Ch D 273 at 280 per Kay J.
3 *Bailey v Barnes* [1894] 1 Ch 25 at 30 per Stirling J.

departure from the doctrine of notice which normally governs purchasers in general[4].

(b) *The effect of sale by the mortgagee*

Where a power of sale is 'exercisable' according to section 103 of the Law of Property Act 1925, sale by the mortgagee will have the effect of transferring a good title to the purchaser[5]. Moreover, the sale will overreach all equitable interests which are capable of being overreached (e.g., subsequent mortgages and the mortgagor's equity of redemption). All overreachable interests take effect thereafter in the proceeds of the sale[6]. In such a case, the mortgagor can have no complaint against the mortgagee except where it can be shown that the power of sale was exercised in an improper manner[7].

(c) *The price obtained by the mortgagee on sale*

When a mortgagee exercises his statutory power of sale, he becomes subject to certain statutory directions governing the application of the proceeds of sale. Under section 105 of the Law of Property Act 1925, the selling mortgagee becomes a trustee of those proceeds of sale. The proceeds are held by him in trust to be applied by him

(i) in payment of all costs, charges and expenses properly incurred by him in connection with the sale;
(ii) in discharge of the mortgage money and interest due under his mortgage;
(iii) in payment of the residue to the mortgagor.

It is therefore a matter of some concern to the mortgagor that the mortgagee, in exercising his power of sale, should obtain the best price possible in respect of the mortgaged property, since to do otherwise would be to diminish the residue payable to the mortgagor after all other claims have been met. However, it is commonly said that, although the selling mortgagee is a trustee of the proceeds of sale, he is not a trustee of his own power of sale. In other words, he is not under any legal duty to ensure that the mortgaged property is sold for the best price obtainable on the open market. In theory, so long as he acts in good faith, the mortgagee can with impunity sell the property for a sum sufficient to enable him to recover his expenses and the outstanding mortgage moneys, while leaving little or nothing for the mortgagor. This result is, however, plainly inequitable and has been affected by both legislative intervention and judge-made developments.

First, it is provided by section 36 of the Building Societies Act 1962 that a building society is under a legal duty, in exercising any power of sale to take reasonable care to ensure that the sale price is the best which may reasonably be

4 Op. cit., p. 95f.
5 Law of Property Act 1925, s. 88(1). Note, however, the impact of section 19(1) of the Land Registration Act 1925 in the context of registered land.
6 Law of Property Act 1925, s. 2(1)(iii).
7 See Law of Property Act 1925, s. 104(2).

obtained[8]. *Second,* the Court of Appeal held in *Cuckmere Brick Co Ltd v Mutual Finance Ltd*[9] that mortgagees in general are subject to a duty 'to take reasonable care to obtain the true market value of the mortgaged property.' In this case, a mortgagee had sold the mortgaged property by auction but had failed to make reference to an extensive planning permission in respect of the property which permitted the erection of 100 flats. In consequence the land was sold at an undervalue, and the Court of Appeal held that the mortgagee was liable to the mortgagor in damages for breach of the duty which it owed to the latter.

It may not be easy to establish that a mortgagee has fallen short of his duty of care in the matter of sale. In *Cuckmere Brick Co Ltd v Mutual Finance Ltd,* the mortgagee had at least been aware that there was a subsisting planning permission in respect of the mortgaged land, but had carelessly misrepresented the extent of the development permitted. There is, however, no necessary inference of negligence where the mortgagee is completely unaware that a planning permission has been granted in relation to the property[10].

It is still technically inaccurate to describe the selling mortgagee as a 'trustee' of his statutory power of sale. The power is conferred upon him 'for his own benefit to enable him the better to realise his security[11].' It is quite clear, however, that the present position is somewhat more strict than the old common law rule that the mortgagee is entirely free to sell at any price he thinks fit, so long as he acts in good faith. A somewhat higher degree of responsibility is nowadays demanded of the selling mortgagee[12].

(5) Foreclosure

Foreclosure is the most draconian measure open to a mortgagee for the purpose of realising his security in the event of default by the mortgagor. An order for foreclosure effectively abrogates the mortgagor's equity of redemption and leaves the entire value of the mortgaged property in the hands of the mortgagee. Foreclosure is thus directed primarily at recovery of the mortgagee's capital investment.

Unlike the exercise of the power of sale, the remedy of foreclosure is available only upon application to court. A court order for *foreclosure absolute* operates to vest the fee simple estate in the mortgagee, subject only to any legal mortgage which has priority to the mortgage in respect of which the foreclosure is sought[13]. In registered land, the order for foreclosure is completed by the cancellation of the registered charge and the registration of the former chargee as the sole proprietor of the land[14].

Foreclosure proceedings are normally conducted in the High Court. The

8 See *Reliance Permanent Building Society v Harwood-Stamper* [1944] Ch 362.
9 [1971] Ch 949. See (1971) 87 LQR 303.
10 See *Palmer v Barclays Bank Ltd* (1971) 23 P & CR 30.
11 R. E. Megarry and H. W. R. Wade, *The Law of Real Property* (4th edn., London 1975), p. 98f.
12 See P. B. Fairest, op. cit., p. 69ff.
13 Law of Property Act 1925, s. 88(2). Foreclosure likewise vests a leasehold estate in the mortgagee where the subject of the mortgage is a term of years (Law of Property Act 1925, s. 89(2)).
14 Land Registration Act 1925, s. 34(3).

right to foreclose cannot arise until repayment has become due at law[15]. If the court decides to grant an order for foreclosure, it first makes an order for *foreclosure nisi.* This order directs that accounts be taken and provides that unless the mortgagor repays the mortgage moneys due within a period stipulated by the court, the mortgage will be foreclosed. In the event that no payment is made, the court makes an order for *foreclosure absolute*, which has the effect of transferring the fee simple from the mortgagor to the mortgagee. However, during the interim between the order nisi and the order absolute, it is open to the mortgagor or the mortgagee to apply to the court for an order directing sale of the property rather than foreclosure[16]. This alternative form of order may be granted in the discretion of the court, and has the consequence that part of the value of the mortgaged property may thereby be salvaged for the mortgagor. In the case of foreclosure, the entire value of the property is effectively transferred to the mortgagee free of any claim in the mortgagor.

Foreclosure is rarely sought today, and even more rarely granted. It is usually much more convenient for the mortgagee to exercise his statutory power of sale. Moreover, the court's powers to stay proceedings under section 36 of the Administration of Justice Act 1970 have now been extended to actions for foreclosure[17]. The courts have been increasingly reluctant to grant orders for foreclosure, particularly in the context of a rapidly rising property market, simply because foreclosure may effectively transfer to the mortgagee a much more valuable property than the property over which he initially took his security. In such circumstances, foreclosure would confer an increasingly valuable asset upon the mortgagee at what must inevitably be a substantial undervalue.

Even after the court has made an order for foreclosure absolute, it is possible for the mortgagor to request the court to 're-open' the order. The court thus has even further discretion to prevent the final destruction of the mortgagor's equity of redemption[18].

(6) Appointment of a receiver

An alternative remedy to that provided by entry into possession or foreclosure is the appointment of a receiver on behalf of the mortgagee. There is now a statutory power vested in the mortgagee to appoint a receiver in the same circumstances and on the same conditions as those which cause the statutory power of sale to arise and to become exercisable[19]. The appointment of a receiver may be particularly useful if the mortgagee does not presently wish to

15 *Williams v Morgan* [1906] 1 Ch 804. Repayment is due at law either when the legal date for redemption has passed, p. 517, ante, or where the entire mortgage debt is made payable by the terms of the mortgage in the event of any default in respect of interest or principal. See *Keene v Biscoe* (1878) 8 Ch D 201; *Kidderminster Mutual Benefit Building Society v Haddock* [1936] WN 158.

16 Law of Property Act 1925, s. 91(2). See *Twentieth Century Banking Corpn Ltd v Wilkinson* [1977] Ch 99.

17 Administration of Justice Act 1973, s. 8(3).

18 See *Campbell v Holyland* (1877) 7 Ch D 166 at 172ff. per Jessel MR.

19 Law of Property Act 1925, s. 101(1)(iii).

realise his security or otherwise undertake the responsibility of entering into possession of the mortgaged property. The duty of the receiver is to receive all the income derived from the mortgaged land and to ensure that from that income there is payment of all sums due by way of rents, rates, taxes, insurance premiums, repairs and, of course, interest under the mortgage[20].

The receiver must be appointed in writing[1], and is deemed by statute to be the agent of the *mortgagor*[2]. Thus the mortgagor is liable for any acts or defaults of the receiver, even though he has had no hand in his appointment[3].

(7) Action on the mortgagor's personal covenant to repay

It should always be remembered that a further remedy available to a mortgagee lies in an action on the mortgagor's personal covenant to repay the mortgage debt. Most mortgages include such a covenant on the part of the mortgagor. However, it must also be said that most institutional lenders are prepared to assist a hard-pressed borrower in the event of default, and are not over-ready to increase his (perhaps temporary) financial difficulties by bringing an action on the repayment covenant. The limitation period applicable in respect of actions on the personal covenant to repay is normally twelve years[4].

The remedies available to the mortgagee are generally cumulative. It is clear, for instance, that it is open to the mortgagee both to exercise his power of sale and also to sue the mortgagor for the balance of the mortgage debt on the basis of the latter's personal covenant to repay[5]. A mortgagee who has entered into possession may also appoint a receiver[6]. However, foreclosure prevents the mortgagee from pursuing other remedies.

(8) Remedies available to the equitable mortgagee

The remedies available to an equitable mortgagee differ in some important respects from those which are open to a legal mortgagee, largely because the equitable mortgagee takes no legal estate or interest in the land offered as security[7].

(a) *Entry into possession*

Doubt surrounds the question whether an equitable mortgagee has any right to possession of the mortgaged property. In the absence of a right of possession expressly conferred by the mortgage, it is difficult to argue that a right of possession can arise on any other ground, since that right is essentially an

20 Law of Property Act 1925, s. 109(8).
1 Law of Property Act 1925, s. 109(1).
2 Law of Property Act 1925, s. 109(2).
3 Law of Property Act 1925, s. 109(2). See, e.g. *White v Metcalf* [1903] 2 Ch 567.
4 Limitation Act 1980, ss. 5, 8(1), (2).
5 See *Rudge v Richens* (1873) LR 8 CP 358.
6 See *Refuge Assurance Co Ltd v Pearlberg* [1938] Ch 687.
7 See P. B. Fairest, op. cit., p. 108.

incident of the legal estate vested in the legal mortgagee or implied on his behalf by statute[8]. However, it has been suggested that the doctrine in *Walsh v Lonsdale*[9], by drawing an analogy between legal and equitable rights, has the indirect effect of conferring a right of possession upon even the equitable mortgagee[9]. The position is nevertheless far from clear[10].

(b) *Sale*

The statutory power of sale conferred by section 101(1) of the Law of Property Act 1925 is available in respect of any mortgage which has been effected by deed[11]. Thus some equitable mortgagees may be able to exercise the statutory power, but most equitable mortgagees will be excluded from this facility on the ground that their mortgages were effected by purely informal means or were supported by an act of part performance. Such mortgagees may, however, apply to the court under section 91(2) of the Law of Property Act 1925, and the court has a discretion either to order that sale be effected or to vest a legal term of years in the mortgagee, thereby entitling him to exercise the statutory power of sale as a legal mortgagee.

(c) *Foreclosure*

The court has power to order foreclosure of an equitable mortgage or to order a judicial sale in lieu of foreclosure. In the case of an equitable mortgage, however, foreclosure consists of a court order that the mortgagor convey the legal title in the mortgaged property to the mortgagee.

(d) *Appointment of a receiver*

The statutory power to appoint a receiver is available only in respect of mortgages created by deed[12]. In the absence of creation by deed, the court may be asked to appoint a receiver[13].

8 See Law of Property Act 1925, s. 87(1), p. 518, ante.
9 See p. 398, ante. See R. E. Megarry and H. W. R. Wade, op. cit., p. 923. Compare, however, *Cheshire's Modern Law of Real Property* (12th edn., ed. E. H. Burn, London 1976), p. 686. See also (1954) 70 LQR 161 (REM); H. W. R. Wade (1955) 71 LQR 204: 'An Equitable Mortgagee's Right to Possession.'
10 See P. B. Fairest, op. cit., p. 109f.
11 Law of Property Act 1925, s. 101(1), p. 544, ante. The equitable mortgagee, by exercising his power of sale, is able to convey the legal estate. See *Re White Rose Cottage* [1965] Ch 940 at 951.
12 Law of Property Act 1925, s. 101(1)(iii).
13 Supreme Court of Judicature (Consolidation) Act 1925, s. 45; *Shakel v Duke of Marlborough* (1819) 4 Madd 463.

PART V

Matrimonial property

CHAPTER 16

The matrimonial home

Since much of this book has been concerned with the property relations of husband and wife, it may be appropriate to gather together in one chapter some of the major elements of the law of matrimonial property, with particular reference to the law governing the matrimonial home.

The modern law relating to the property rights of husband and wife is firmly premised upon the principle of separate ownership. The fact that two persons are married to each other has no automatic effect on their respective property entitlements. Spouses are, in this context, treated as strangers one to another, and their rights in respect of property are determined according to the bleak and inflexible rules of the general law of property. In other words, English law does not provide for a regime of matrimonial property in the continental sense. There is no special body of principles applicable to married persons, and each spouse remains separate owner of those assets or interests to which he or she has acquired title pursuant to the general law.

The norm of separation of property was introduced into English law through several statutory reforms effected in the late nineteenth and early twentieth centuries. In these reforms, which gradually and haltingly conferred upon the married woman a revolutionary freedom to acquire and dispose of property herself, it was sought to remove one of the lingering consequences of the medieval doctrine of conjugal unity. We shall look in the first part of this chapter at the evolution which brought about the principle of separate property.

1. A BRIEF HISTORY OF MATRIMONIAL PROPERTY LAW

The common law view of the spouses' property relations gave fairly full—though not total—effect to the theory that marriage brought about a merger or union of the legal personalities of husband and wife. This theory was the direct product of the doctrine of 'conjugal unity'.

(1) The doctrine of conjugal unity

The doctrine of conjugal unity was the canon law formulation of the ancient Judaeo-Christian belief that marriage caused husband and wife to become 'one flesh': by marriage husband and wife became one person in the eyes of the law. It is fairly clear now that the figure of conjugal unity was never carried to its logical conclusion in every area of the law, but the idea of fused personality has exercised a profound formative effect upon many of the basic legal norms relating to the family. Only recently has English law begun to loose itself of its influence.

The notion of conjugal unity was derived from a rich biblical metaphor: 'they twain shall be one flesh[1].' Medieval Christendom interpreted this as meaning that matrimony was a 'holy state . . . ordained by Almighty God in Paradise, before the fall of man, signifying . . . that mystical union which is between Christ and His Church[2].' Marriage thus acquired a sacramental meaning, and Church doctrine maintained the dogma that the unity of the spouses was inviolate. Divorce was impossible—even meaningless—since marriage forged an indissoluble link which no earthly power could sever.

Common lawyers soon discovered that the original canon law doctrine provided a perfect subterfuge for domination and oppression. If husband and wife were one, then that one was obviously the husband. As Blackstone said in his classic statement,

> By marriage, the husband and wife are one person in law: that is, the very being or legal existence of the woman is suspended during the marriage, or at least is incorporated and consolidated into that of the husband: under whose wing, protection, and *cover*, she performs every thing; and is therefore called in our law-french a *feme-covert*, *foemina viro co-operta*; is said to be *covert-baron*, or under the protection and influence of her husband, her *baron*, or lord . . .[3]

As was observed by Pollock and Maitland[4], the unity of personality thus envisaged by the common law was not so much a fusion of legal identity and sharing of legal rights, but was more in the nature of a profitable guardianship—the Germanic *Mund*—exercised by the husband over his wife and her property rights. Marriage was, in a sense, a specialised form of social contract, in which the wife surrendered many of her natural rights to her husband in return for the protection afforded within the marital commonwealth. Blackstone was able to argue that 'even the disabilities which the wife lies under are for the most part intended for her protection and benefit. So great a favourite is the female sex of the laws of England[5]!'

The idea of matrimonial symbiosis which lay at the heart of the doctrine of conjugal unity was not consistently applied throughout the entire field of family law, but it did provide the foundation of many basic principles. We have already noted the origin of the theory of indissoluble marriage. From the common law conception of legal unity also flowed the husband's duty to maintain his wife. As Hyde J pointed out in *Manby v Scott*[6], 'she is "bone of his bone, flesh of his flesh", and no man did ever hate his own flesh so far as not to preserve it.' The wife was a mere appendage or extension of the husband's body, which he would of course maintain precisely because it was a part of him. The

1 *Genesis* 2:24; *Matthew* 19:5; *Mark* 10:8.
2 *Manby v Scott* (1663) 1 Mod Rep 124 at 125 per Hyde J.
3 *Commentaries*, Vol. 1, p. 442.
4 *The History of English Law* (2nd edn.), Vol. I, p. 485. See also G. L. Williams (1947) 10 MLR 16: 'The Legal Unity of Husband and Wife.'
5 Op. cit.
6 (1663) 1 Mod Rep 124 at 128.

right to be maintained was not reciprocal: it is only in recent times that legislation has intervened to formulate the maintenance obligation in terms which are sex-neutral[7].

From the doctrine of legal unity evolved the further notion that the husband *owned* the appendage that was his wife: she was a chattel over which he exercised rights approaching dominion. The quasi-proprietary nature of the spousal relationship came to provide the source of many of the historical characteristics of English family law. Thus the husband owned the wife's productive capacity—both in the sense of her domestic services and in the further sense that he enjoyed sole and unimpeachable rights over any children to whom the relationship gave issue[8]. The performance of household services and the provision of comfort and society were the wife's bounden duty in terms of the marital quid pro quo, for marriage could be viewed as a contractual exchange of the husband's support for the wife's services[9]. Almost all the wife's property vested in the husband on marriage, but the wife's disability in this respect was regarded as fully compensated by the enduring maintenance liability fixed upon her consort. The idea that the wife's household management and nurturing of children should receive some visible economic return is of very recent origin[10].

At common law the notion subsisted that the husband had a quasi-proprietary interest in his wife which could be vindicated against third party tortfeasors. Damages lay (and still lie) at the suit of the husband for loss of consortium occasioned by another's negligence. Loss or impairment of consortium could provide a similar head of damage in an action for breach of contract. But no action for loss of consortium can lie at the suit of the wife[11]. Originally at common law the husband had a writ of ravishment or trespass *vi et armis de uxore rapta et abducta* against the seducer of his wife. It later became a male prerogative to sue an adulterer for compensation for 'criminal conversation.' When the civil jurisdiction in divorce was introduced in 1857, the offended husband had a statutory claim against a third party for 'damages' in respect of adultery[12]—a remedy which was abolished only in 1970[13].

(2) The property consequences of the doctrine of conjugal unity

The doctrine of conjugal unity, with its insistence upon the merger of the legal personalities of husband and wife, had profound implications for the property rights of the spouses. In the medieval common law, the husband was regarded as acquiring, on marriage, seisin of all freehold land held at that point by his

7 See, for instance, Matrimonial Causes Act 1973, ss. 23–25, as expounded in *Calderbank v Calderbank* [1976] Fam 93 at 101ff. per Scarman LJ.

8 It is worth remembering that in England it was only in 1973 that the parental rights and authority of father and mother were finally declared to be 'equal and . . . exercisable by either without the other' (Guardianship Act 1973, s. 1(1)).

9 See K. J. Gray, *Reallocation of Property on Divorce* (Abingdon 1977), p. 282.

10 See Matrimonial Causes Act 1973, s. 25(1)(f); Inheritance (Provision for Family and Dependants) Act 1975, s. 3(2)(b).

11 *Best v Samuel Fox & Co Ltd* [1952] AC 716.

12 See P. M. Bromley, *Family Law* (5th edn. London 1976), p. 123.

13 Law Reform (Miscellaneous Provisions) Act 1970, s. 4.

wife, and he was thereafter entitled to receive the rents and profits derived from that property. The same principle applied to freeholds acquired by the wife during the marriage. But the theory of unity did not imply a sharing of property rights between the spouses: the wife received no share during the marriage in any real property acquired by her husband. Moreover, if her husband predeceased her, she automatically resumed her freeholds, but had merely a limited 'right of dower' in his freehold land. In other words, she received a life interest in one third of that land. If she predeceased him, he had in effect a life interest ('right of curtesy') in all of her freeholds. The wife's leasehold land belonged to the husband during the marriage, and he enjoyed an absolute power of disposition inter vivos in respect of such property. However, the husband did not possess an equivalent power in relation to the wife's freeholds vested in him during coverture: these could be alienated only by way of a disposition from husband and wife jointly. On the other hand, the wife's pure personalty vested automatically in the husband on marriage, and in respect of this property he had an absolute power of disposition inter vivos and by will[14].

(3) The emergence of the norm of separation of property

In a manner characteristic of the historical development of English law, the rigour of the medieval common law was mitigated by the intervention of equity. The most significant concession made to the married woman by the principles of equity concerned the institution of the wife's 'separate estate.'

It came to be established towards the end of the sixteenth century that the common law disabilities suffered by the wife in respect of property could be circumvented by a disposition of property (real or personal) to trustees 'to the separate use' of the wife. By means of the device of the separate estate, the married woman was enabled in equity to hold and dispose of the property so settled as if she were a *feme sole*. She was thus freed from the common law fetters regarding enjoyment and alienation. Later it came to be accepted that the same result followed even if property was transferred merely to the wife 'to her separate use', since in this case the husband simply assumed the function of the trustees and held the property on trust for his wife as sole beneficiary. The utility of the married woman's separate estate was subsequently reinforced when, towards the end of the eighteenth century it became possible to impose a 'restraint upon anticipation' upon the property settled to the wife's separate use. This supplementary equitable device effectively disabled the wife from assigning to her husband the beneficial interest in the property subject to the separate use. The restraint upon anticipation therefore protected the married woman from undue pressure which might otherwise have been brought to bear on her in order to secure for the husband beneficial control over the separate estate. The restraint also operated to protect the interest of the wife's kinship group, which stood to succeed to her separate property on her death[15].

The principal defect of the doctrine of the separate estate was nevertheless

14 See P. M. Bromley, op. cit., p. 429ff.

15 See generally Holdsworth, *History of English Law*, Vol. V, p. 310ff.

that the indulgence thus afforded by equity availed only the rich and propertied classes. The effect of the common law in less privileged strata of society was to confirm the husband's ownership of even the wages paid in remuneration of the wife's gainful occupation in industrial work. As increasingly during the nineteenth century the location of economic production moved from the home to some external workplace, the social pressure grew for legal recognition of the married woman's separate ownership of the financial reward for such labour. This recognition came eventually with the enactment of the Married Women's Property Act 1870. This statute followed in the wake of John Stuart Mill's influential essay on 'The Subjection of Women', and the significant role played in the 1870 reform by a newly emerging middle-class pressure group of professional women was apparent in the special reference to the wife's separate ownership of 'money or property ... acquired through the exercise of any literary, artistic, or scientific skill...[16]' The basic norm of separation of property was later affirmed more generally in the Married Women's Property Act 1882, although the conferment of full legal capacity upon the married woman was finally accomplished only with the enactment of the Law Reform (Married Women and Tortfeasors) Act 1935.

The irony implicit in these reforming statutes was that, in attempting to remove injustice from the existing law, the new enactments themselves generated further injustice. By subjecting the spouses to the full rigour of the law of property as applied between strangers, the new law ran counter to the realities of family living. Husband and wife do not live and work as strangers do. On the contrary, they form together an economic unit in which both partners devote their efforts (whether as wage-earners or as homemakers) towards the common weal of the family. Moreover, their co-operative efforts are not governed by the principles of exchange which regulate transactions in the external world: the internal relations of the matrimonial partnership are immune from the rules of the cash nexus. As a matter of social fact, spouses live in an amorphous community of goods, and any attempt to exalt the principle of separate ownership of property has a hollow ring when set against the actuality of married life[17].

Not only is separation of property insensitive to the reality of family relationships: it also implies a substantial offence against the principle of sexual equality. The Married Women's Property Act 1882 contains only a rudimentary concept of sexual equality, in that the norm of separate ownership confirmed in that statute leaves the property rights of husband and wife to be determined alike largely on the basis of money contributions towards the purchase of individual items[18]. The principle of separation, although cast in apparently non-discriminatory terms, emerges from the mould as an instrument of

16 Married Women's Property Act 1870, s. 1.

17 In a survey of public opinion carried out on behalf of the English Law Commission in 1971, it was found that, even where the matrimonial home was vested legally in only one spouse, 87 per cent of the spouses interviewed regarded the property as 'belonging to them both.' See J. E. Todd and L. M. Jones, *Matrimonial Property* (London, 1972), para. 2.1.

18 This is normally the result produced by the presumption of resulting trust which operates in the absence of evidence of the beneficial ownership actually intended by the spouses, p. 560, post.

considerable disadvantage to the married woman, reinforcing rather than removing sex-based inequality. That this should be so results inevitably from the fact that the married woman's *financial* contributions towards the acquisition of property are usually severely restricted not only by reason of the sexual imbalance of the labour market, but also because of her fluctuation between periods of gainful employment and active motherhood. As Otto Kahn-Freund once observed, the idea of equality held out by the 1882 Act was, and still is, 'as mechanical as the crude idea of "freedom of contract" which insists on treating as "equals" landlord and tenant, employer and employee[19].'

The injustice inherent in the principle of separate ownership remained largely unnoticed for many years simply because spouses are generally unconcerned with precise questions of ownership during the subsistence of a happy marriage. Where, as in the vast majority of cases in the past, marriage terminated in the death of one of the parties, the English law of intestacy allowed the survivor extremely generous rights of succession to the few assets of any value normally left by the deceased[20]. This state of affairs, in which strict proprietary entitlements as between the spouses were effectively irrelevant, is now of course no longer viable in the face of a greatly increased tendency for marriage to terminate not in death but in divorce. This is especially the case since the present era of unprecedented resort to divorce has coincided with a hitherto unknown degree of family affluence. The economic problems caused by marital breakdown can no longer be resolved purely in terms of maintenance at subsistence level. It has now become a task for the law to arrange for a fair distribution of not only the revenue resources but also the capital resources built up during the marriage[1].

It is therefore no accident that in England the years following the end of the Second World War witnessed remarkable efforts being made both by the courts and by Parliament to modify the norm of separation of property in order to reflect more accurately the modern idea that marriage is indeed a partnership of equals[2]. We shall now look at the developments which occurred in this area, not only in respect of the determination of the substantive property rights of the spouses, but also in respect of the adjustment of property relations which may be made necessary in the event of divorce.

19 (1959) 22 MLR 241 at 248: 'Matrimonial Property—Some Recent Developments'.

20 Administration of Estates Act 1925, s. 46(1), as now amended by the Family Provision (Intestate Succession) Order 1981 (S.I. 1981/255).

1 See O. Kahn-Freund, 'Matrimonial Property—Where do we go from here?' (Josef Unger Memorial Lecture, University of Birmingham, 29 January 1971); (1971) 4 Human Rights Journal 493: 'Matrimonial Property and Equality before the Law—Some Sceptical Reflections'.

2 In 1955 the Royal Commission on Marriage and Divorce endorsed the belief that 'marriage should be regarded as a partnership in which husband and wife work together as equals, and that the wife's contribution to the joint undertaking in running the home and looking after the children, is just as valuable as that of the husband in providing the home and supporting the family' (*Report of the Royal Commission on Marriage and Divorce* (1951–1955), Cmd 9678, para. 644). See also Sir J. Simon, 'With All My Worldly Goods . . .' (Address to the Holdsworth Club, University of Birmingham, 20 March 1964); (1965) 62 Law Society's Gazette 344 at 345: 'The Seven Pillars of Divorce Reform'; *Hofman v Hofman* [1965] NZLR 795 at 800f. per Woodhouse J.

2. PROPERTY RIGHTS DURING MARRIAGE

We shall now examine the way in which the law of real property governs the ascertainment of the proprietary rights of husband and wife during marriage. Our focus here is upon the substantive entitlements of the spouses, rather than upon their rights to possession and enjoyment[3].

(1) Section 17 of the Married Women's Property Act 1882

When the Married Women's Property Act 1882 freed the law from its medieval origins, it was felt that the new principle of separation of assets would inevitably generate between spouses difficult questions of title and possession to property. To deal with such questions section 17 of the Act allows either party to apply

> by summons or otherwise in a summary way to any judge . . . and the judge . . . may make such order with respect to the property in dispute as he thinks fit . . .

Before the enactment in 1970 of much more far-reaching provisions affecting divorce, it was this section 17 which gave rise to a great deal of the case law concerning the ownership of matrimonial property. Indeed, such was the social pressure that the law should conform to changing perceptions of marriage as a partnership, that during the 1950s and 1960s the Court of Appeal unilaterally sought to carve out of section 17 a virtual presumption of co-ownership of the family assets irrespective of strict entitlements at law and in equity. The leading proponent of this liberal view was the Master of the Rolls, Lord Denning, who took the view that section 17 is sufficiently wide to transcend all rights legal or equitable[4]. It was not until the House of Lords decided *Pettitt v Pettitt*[5] in 1969 that this broad interpretation of section 17 was overruled. It is now clear, however, that section 17 is a procedural provision only[6]. It confers upon the court no discretion to *vary* the spouses' substantive rights of property in order to give effect to a partnership view of marriage. As Lord Morris of Borth-y-Gest indicated, the question for the court in a case of disputed title is 'Whose is this?' and not 'To whom shall this be given[7]?' Their Lordships firmly repudiated any suggestion that the status of marriage implies a common ownership of property between the spouses. The court must under section 17 apply the very same principles of law and equity which it would apply in the resolution of any like dispute over title between strangers[8].

Most of the problems litigated under section 17 have, of course, concerned the ownership of the matrimonial home. Here title may give rise to a dispute in the event of the death or bankruptcy of one of the spouses, or where the parties have

3 Rights to occupation and enjoyment of the matrimonial home have been discussed elsewhere in this book pp. 143ff., 270ff., 290ff., 357ff., ante.
4 *Hine v Hine* [1962] 1 WLR 1124 at 1127f.
5 [1970] AC 777.
6 Section 17 has been extended to afford a limited measure of tracing (Matrimonial Causes (Property and Maintenance) Act 1958, s. 7) and may be invoked by former spouses within a period of three years after a decree of divorce or nullity (Matrimonial Proceedings and Property Act 1970, s. 39).
7 [1970] AC 777 at 798.
8 [1970] AC 777 at 813 per Lord Upjohn.

separated but have not divorced. The beneficial ownership of the matrimonial home is governed essentially by the agreement of the spouses determined at the time of its acquisition[9]. If the conveyance or lease which documents the acquisition of the property expressly stipulates that the property is to be held by the spouses as joint tenants in equity, such a declaration of beneficial ownership is conclusive in the absence of fraud or mistake[10]. It is not, for instance, open to a husband who has paid the entire purchase money for the home subsequently to object to beneficial co-ownership on the ground that his wife has made no monetary contribution or that he has just discovered that she has been unfaithful to him[11].

The documents of title relating to the matrimonial home may, however, be silent as to the beneficial ownership intended by the spouses at the point of acquisition, but parol evidence is admissible in such a case in order to clarify the issue. Alternatively, the court may be able to draw an inference as to the spouses' intentions from their conduct, but it is clear from *Pettitt v Pettitt* that the court will not impute to the spouses an intention which they never had. If there is no evidence of any kind from which the parties' intentions as to beneficial ownership can be discovered, then the court may have recourse to two presumptions of equity in determining the beneficial interest of husband and wife. The first of these presumptions—the presumption of advancement—implies in the absence of contrary evidence a donative intention where a husband vests property in the name of his wife[12]. The presumption of resulting trust may be relied upon, again in the absence of contrary intention, as establishing a trust of property legally vested in one or more persons, where the purchase money involved in the acquisition has been paid by one or more contributors. In such a case, there is a trust for the contributors in strict proportion to their contributions.

The application of these general principles solves most property problems which arise in the context of the matrimonial home. However, substantial difficulties have arisen in the situation where the legal title in the matrimonial home has been put in the name of only one of the spouses, but both spouses have contributed in some way towards the acquisition of the property. Here the result depends upon the types of contribution involved. Where, for instance, the home has been vested in the husband and both spouses have made 'direct' quantifiable contributions of money, it is clear that the beneficial ownership is shared in proportion to those contributions[13]. There is greater difficulty if, in the same

9 [1970] AC 777 at 813 per Lord Upjohn, p. 242, ante.

10 [1970] AC 777 at 813. See also *Re John's Assignment Trusts* [1970] 1 WLR 955.

11 In some circumstances, however, credit may be given in respect of any payment of mortgage interest made by one spouse while the other co-owner voluntarily lived apart. See *Leake v Bruzzi* [1974] 1 WLR 1528; *Shinh v Shinh* [1977] 1 All ER 97.

12 Some doubt was expressed by the House of Lords in *Pettitt* as to the present strength of the presumption of advancement, but Lord Upjohn was firmly of the mind that 'when properly understood and properly applied' the presumption remained 'as useful as ever in solving questions of title.' See [1970] AC 777 at 813, p. 245, ante.

13 *Re Rogers' Question* [1948] 1 All ER 328. A 'direct' contribution of money is a contribution towards, for example, the purchase price of, or cash deposit or mortgage instalments on, the matrimonial home.

situation, the spouses have made 'direct' but unquantifiable contributions, as for example where they have made indiscriminate payments towards the purchase of their home from a fund of pooled earnings. In *Rimmer v Rimmer*[14] the Court of Appeal used an equitable knife to sever the Gordian Knot[15], by applying the maxim 'Equality is equity.' Later, in *Gissing v Gissing*[16], the House of Lords proved to be extremely critical of the excessive reliance which came to be placed upon this maxim, ruling that the principle of equality is appropriate only where it is quite impossible to extricate the contributions of husband and wife one from another.

The law relating to 'indirect' contributions towards the purchase of the matrimonial home is even less satisfactory[17]. It was at first held by the Court of Appeal that beneficial ownership should be shared equally if one spouse contributed 'directly' to the purchase price of the home, being freed to do so by the other spouse's expenditure of money on other items required for the common life of the household and family. The title to family assets, Denning LJ declared, should not depend upon fortuitous questions of family finance, upon how the spouses happened to allocate their earnings and expenditure[18].

The approach of equality of beneficial ownership adopted by the Court was finally overruled by the House of Lords in *Gissing v Gissing*. Here the applicant wife claimed that she had made indirect contributions through payment of the children's school fees and payments for some furniture and the laying of a lawn at the matrimonial home. The House of Lords refused to award her any share in equity, on the ground that there was no evidence from which it could be inferred that her contributions to other expenses of the household had been 'referable to the acquisition of the house[19].' It is, accordingly, only in the rare case that indirect contributions by a wife will generate an equitable interest in the matrimonial property[20]. It is quite clear that no interest will be acquired by reason of domestic contributions made through household management and the care of infant children[1].

(2) Improvements to matrimonial property

Although it is sometimes difficult to maintain a rigorous distinction between contributions towards the acquisition of property and contributions towards the

14 [1953] 1 QB 63.
15 See *National Provincial Bank Ltd v Hastings Car Mart Ltd* [1965] AC 1175 at 1236.
16 [1971] AC 886.
17 See pp. 249, 477, ante.
18 *Fribance v Fribance (No. 2)* [1957] 1 WLR 384 at 387.
19 [1971] AC 886 at 909 per Lord Diplock.
20 Even after the Lords' decision in *Gissing*, Lord Denning MR appeared to apply the older approach in the Court of Appeal: see *Hargrave v Newton* [1971] 1 WLR 1611; *Hazell v Hazell* [1972] 1 WLR 301. However, now that much wider powers are available to the court under what is now the Matrimonial Causes Act 1973, Lord Denning has become slightly less liberal in his treatment of contributions under the Married Women's Property Act 1882. See, for instance, *Kowalczuk v Kowalczuk* [1973] 1 WLR 930.
1 *Button v Button* [1968] 1 WLR 457.

improvement of property, the latter are now governed by a clear statutory provision. Section 37 of the Matrimonial Proceedings and Property Act 1970 was designed to overrule the decision in *Pettitt v Pettitt*[2]. In this case, the House of Lords had declined to recognise that any equitable interest was acquired by a husband who effected improvements in a home owned by his wife, in the absence of some common intention that the performance of improvements should have this effect upon beneficial ownership[3]. Section 37 provides that where a husband or wife 'contributes in money or money's worth to the improvement of real or personal property' belonging beneficially to either or both of the spouses, the spouse so contributing shall, if the contribution is of 'a substantial nature', be treated as having acquired a beneficial share or enlarged beneficial share in the property. The share earned by the improvement is to be determined in the discretion of the court[4], and both the existence and extent of such a share for the improver are subject to any contrary agreement between the spouses.

(3) The path of future reform

It has been seen that during the subsistence of marriage the substantive property rights of the spouses inter se are governed by essentially the same principles which are applied to strangers. In the determination of property rights, some slight account may be taken of the fact that the parties are married to each other, in the sense that this relationship may aid the inference of common intention as to beneficial ownership[5]. However, apart from isolated and haphazard instances of statutory intervention, it still remains untrue that the relationship of marriage per se has any influence upon the spouses' property rights. Separation of assets is still the basic principle, and the primary considerations are still those which govern commercial transactions in the world outside the family. There is as yet no special 'regime of matrimonial property' which permits the property relations of husband and wife to be determined outside the largely unsympathetic rules of the general law of property.

It is likely that the path of future reform of matrimonial property rights will lead in the direction of a new statutory regime of matrimonial assets. The Law Commission has already proposed a form of compulsory co-ownership confined to the matrimonial home[6]. Elsewhere in this book we have examined the details of this scheme of co-ownership, noting its disadvantages and deficiencies[7]. The Bill based on the Law Commission's proposals, the Matrimonial Homes (Co-ownership) Bill, failed to secure parliamentary passage in 1980, but this draft legislation clearly shows the direction of future developments in this area. It will

2 [1970] AC 777.

3 *Pettitt* threw doubt upon the earlier, and much more liberal, approach of the Court of Appeal in the matter of improvements: see *Appleton v Appleton* [1965] 1 WLR 25.

4 On the evaluation of improvements under the 1970 Act, see *Griffiths v Griffiths* [1973] 1 WLR 1454; *Re Nicholson* [1974] 1 WLR 476.

5 See the reference of Lord Upjohn in *Pettitt v Pettitt* [1970] AC 777 at 813 to the possibility that the court may make 'full allowances' in view of the marriage relationship.

6 See *Third Report on Family Property: The Matrimonial Home (Co-ownership and Occupation Rights) and Household Goods* (Law Com No. 86, June 1978).

7 See pp. 149, 303, ante.

only be with the enactment of a regime quite outside the general law of property that 'family considerations' will be more effectively infused into the ascertainment of the property rights of spouses during marriage. Only then will it be true that we have a 'law of matrimonial property' as such.

3. PROPERTY RIGHTS ON DIVORCE

The law governing the property rights of husband and wife in the event of divorce has been utterly revolutionised by the provisions which were enacted in Part I of the Matrimonial Proceedings and Property Act 1970 and which are now contained in Part II of the Matrimonial Causes Act 1973. Pursuant to these provisions, the courts are empowered to afford ancillary relief after divorce by means of orders for 'property adjustment' and 'financial provision.'[8] The law is sex-neutral: the statutory provisions are phrased in terms which do not discriminate between male and female applicants. In *Calderbank v Calderbank*[9] Scarman LJ pointed out that now 'husbands and wives come to the judgment seat in matters of money and property upon a basis of complete equality.' He stressed, however, that it 'does not follow that . . . justice requires an equal division of the assets. The proportion of the division is dependent upon the circumstances.'

(1) The objective of ancillary relief

The overall objective of ancillary relief is expressed in section 25(1) of the Matrimonial Causes Act 1973. The Act does not confer a broad discretion to do justice between the spouses. A specific target is set up. The court is directed so to exercise its powers

> as to place the parties, so far as it is practicable and, having regard to their conduct, just to do so, in the financial position in which they would have been if the marriage had not broken down and each had properly discharged his or her financial obligations and responsibilities towards the other[10].

Two constraints are expressly imposed upon this task of restitution. One concerns conduct, but it has been held by the Court of Appeal in the seminal decision of *Wachtel v Wachtel*[11] that matrimonial misconduct is to be taken into account only in the rare case in which it is 'both obvious and gross' so that it

8 According to section 24(1), 'property adjustment' denotes provision by way of property transfer, settlement of property and the variation of existing settlements upon the parties to the marriage. According to section 23(1), 'financial provision' includes secured and unsecured periodical payments and the payment of a lump sum. Property adjustment and financial provision are not mutually exclusive, but merely offer different means directed towards the same objective spelt out in section 25(1). In particular, the lump sum order, although technically a form of financial provision, may operate in effect as an agent of capital redistribution.

9 [1976] Fam 93 at 103.

10 These words are used mutatis mutandis in relation to orders in favour of children of the family: s. 25(2).

11 [1973] Fam 72 at 90.

would be 'repugnant to anyone's sense of justice' to leave it out of account[12]. Thus it is consistent with the alteration in the conceptual basis of divorce brought about by the Divorce Reform Act 1969 that misconduct will seldom play any part in the economic adjustments necessitated by that event[13].

It is the other qualification upon the court's mandate in section 25(1) which is, of course, the operative one—the limitation inevitably imposed by factors of practicability. Usually it is seldom practicable to place both parties in a divorce proceeding in the financial position occupied prior to the breakdown of the marriage. The court is dealing with parties of limited resources, and it is normally a question of utilising existing resources (both capital and income) in order to salvage for both parties and their children a standard of living for the future which approximates as closely as possible to that which they enjoyed before the divorce. The problem is essentially that of arranging and reorganising limited economic resources so that they serve the needs of not one unit, but henceforth two units, and the wisdom of a Solomon is required of the judge or registrar who must supervise this task. It is the overriding exigency of the situation which controls the exercise of the court's discretion under the 1973 Act[14].

In effect the 1973 Act confers upon the court a special power of appointment over all the economic resources available to either party. The court is given an unlimited reach into those resources in order to preserve, so far as is possible, the pre-divorce standard of living. It has been made quite clear that the court's discretion transcends the strict property entitlements of the spouses as determined at law and in equity[15]. In dealing with the assets of the parties, the court no

12 For instances of 'obvious and gross' misconduct, see *Cuzner v Underdown* [1974] 1 WLR 641; *Armstrong v Armstrong* (1974) 118 Sol Jo 579; *Jones (M.A.) v Jones (W.)* [1976] Fam 8; *West v West* [1978] Fam 1.

13 See, however, *The Matrimonial Jurisdiction of Registrars* (Report issued by the Centre for Socio-Legal Studies, Wolfson College, Oxford, 1977), paras. 2.20ff. Here there is evidence that, in spite of the *Wachtel* ruling, matrimonial misconduct is still regarded by a substantial minority of county court registrars as relevant to questions of ancillary relief on divorce. The reported decisions of the Court of Appeal show that misconduct may be particularly relevant where it has diminished the value or extent of the spouses' assets. See *Martin v Martin* [1976] Fam 335.

14 See *Hanlon v Law Society* [1981] AC 124 at 147, where Lord Denning MR said: 'In the property adjustment order (under ss 23 and 24 of the Matrimonial Causes Act 1973) we have a new concept altogether. The court takes the rights and obligations of the parties all together, and puts the pieces into a mixed bag. Such pieces are the right to occupy the matrimonial home or have a share in it, the obligation to maintain the wife and children, and so forth. The court then takes out the pieces and hands them to the two parties, some to one party and some to the other, so that each can provide for the future with the pieces allotted to him or to her. The court hands them out without paying any too nice a regard to their legal or equitable rights but simply according to what is the fairest provision for the future, for mother and father and the children.' According to Donaldson LJ in the same case ([1981] AC 124 at 160),

'In exercising its powers under s 24 of the 1973 Act the court looks at the whole financial position of the parties jointly and severally during the marriage and at the whole financial position of the parties severally after the breakdown of that marriage. It notionally pools all the assets and redistributes them in such a way as to produce as little change in real terms as possible.'

15 See *Wachtel v Wachtel* [1973] Fam 72 at 92.

longer asks 'Whose is this ?', but rather 'To whom shall this be given?' It follows that section 17 of the Married Women's Property Act 1882 has only residual relevance in claims to property after divorce, and the courts now tend to discourage applications under that section[16].

(2) The 'one-third starting point'

Ground-rules tend to crystallise in the exercise of a judicial discretion over a period of time, and this has proved to be no less true of the law of financial provision and property adjustment. In *Wachtel v Wachtel*[17], the Court of Appeal indicated that in exercising ancillary powers on divorce, the courts should employ a 'one-third starting point'. That is, the courts should ensure that a divorced wife receives (in some form or other) roughly one third of the family's capital assets and one third of the joint earnings of the parties after the divorce.

In *Wachtel v Wachtel*, both parties were in their late forties and there were two children of the family (aged 14 and 11 respectively). Each party retained custody of one child after the divorce. The family's only capital asset was the former matrimonial home, which was owned legally and beneficially by the husband and in which the equity was currently worth approximately £20,000. The husband had a dental practice and his gross earnings were not less than £6,000 per annum. The Court found the wife to have a potential earning capacity of perhaps £750 per annum as a dental nurse, thus giving a combined earning capacity of £6,750. The Court then decided that the direction contained in section 25(1) of the 1973 Act could be carried out only if the divorced wife received a share of both the capital and revenue resources of the parties. The wife was therefore awarded a lump sum of £6,000—approximately one third of the value of the only capital family asset. The Court also awarded her periodical payments of £1,500 per annum—in other words, one third of the combined earning capacities of the parties minus the small income potential imputed to the wife.

The *Wachtel* ruling shows incidentally that the lump sum order, although classified along with periodical payments orders as a form of financial provision, can in reality be used as an agent of capital distribution on divorce. It is no longer possible to maintain a rigid distinction between questions of 'property' and 'maintenance' when a marriage breaks down. In fact, the 1973 Act has abandoned the dependency-related term 'maintenance'[18] in deliberate preference for the 'neutral' term 'financial provision'. Property adjustment and financial provision are not mutually exclusive concepts, but provide merely

16 *Kowalczuk v Kowalczuk* [1973] 1 WLR 930. However, section 17 may still be relevant in applications on divorce if it is necessary to ascertain existing rights for the purely formal purpose of the wording of a property transfer: see *Martin v Martin* [1976] Fam 167 at 180.

17 [1973] Fam 72.

18 See Law Commission, *Report on Financial Provision in Matrimonial Proceedings* (Law Com No. 25, 1969), para. 7; *Trippas v Trippas* [1973] Fam 134 at 144.

different and closely related means directed towards the same end of modifying the parties' economic relationship in the light of their divorce[19].

(3) The criteria governing the court's exercise of discretion

The 'one-third starting point' is, however, only a starting point. Flexibility is of the essence in the financial and property orders made after divorce, and the courts have insisted that precedents are of little value since each case is profoundly anchored in its own facts[20]. The task before the court is usually 'a matter of figures rather than of legal principles[1].' In fact, the *Wachtel* guidelines can only be applied, if at all, with reference to the precise terms of section 25(1) of the 1973 Act.

Section 25(1) directs the court determining ancillary relief to have regard to 'all the circumstances of the case,' and in particular to a number of specific factors. Some of these factors reflect an approach to property and financial adjustment which is *retrospective* in character; some reflect an approach which is *prospective*. The retrospective view is directed towards the past history of the marriage, and postulates a distribution of property between spouses which is based upon accrued entitlements. This view has been called the 'property approach', for it approximates in vital respects to the historic concept of property law. The prospective view of property adjustment has been termed the 'support approach' for it derives essentially from traditional notions of the maintenance obligation within marriage[2].

The factors enumerated in section 25(1) of the Matrimonial Causes Act 1973 as relevant to the court's exercise of discretion are, on analysis, almost all integral to the 'support approach' to marital property rights on divorce. They include the present or foreseeable economic resources of the parties[3], their present or foreseeable needs, obligations and responsibilities[4], the standard of living enjoyed by both parties prior to the breakdown of the marriage[5], the age of each party and the duration of the marriage[6], and any physical or mental disability suffered by either party[7]. Section 25(1) also refers to two factors which are primarily relevant to a 'property approach' to reallocation on divorce, namely the contributions made by each of the parties to the welfare of the family[8], and the value of any prospective benefit which will be lost by reason of the dissolution[9].

19 On the legislative antecedents of the Matrimonial Causes Act 1973, see K. J. Gray, op. cit., p. 305ff.

20 See *Martin v Martin* [1978] Fam 12 at 20 per Ormrod LJ.

1 *Harnett v Harnett* [1974] 1 WLR 219 at 227.

2 See K. J. Gray, op. cit., p. 278ff.; J. M. Eekelaar (1979) 95 LQR 253: 'Some Principles of Financial and Property Adjustment on Divorce'.

3 Section 25(1)(a).

4 Section 25(1)(b).

5 Section 25(1)(c).

6 Section 25(1)(d).

7 Section 25(1)(e).

8 Section 25(1)(f).

9 Section 25(1)(g).

In spite of the close juxtaposition of 'property' and 'support' elements in section 25(1), it is the consideration of *need* which has become the pre-eminent factor in the award of ancillary relief under the 1973 Act. In most cases the needs of families on the breakdown of marriage exceed the resources available for their satisfaction. The reported cases merely provide one example after another of the way in which the courts have attempted so to use their powers as to minister most effectively to the competing claims upon the existing bounty. The task of restitution under section 25(1) has come to rest upon the paramount need to re-house the two units which have emerged from the divorce. As Ormrod J observed in *Wachtel v Wachtel*[10],

> [t]o put [the spouses] into a position which even approximates to their position before the dissolution of the marriage it is essential that each of them should have a home.

The courts have thus directed their efforts towards the provision of a new and viable home environment for each of the parties and their children, giving preference to the party who retains custody of those children.

In *H v H (Family Provision: Remarriage)*[11], the wife had left her husband and four children in the matrimonial home. She later divorced her husband, who was a man of substantial means, and married an equally wealthy second husband. Both parties and their children being thus securely housed, Baker P awarded the wife only a very small share in the former matrimonial home (which was vested in the husband)[12]. Baker P took the view that the wife was in no immediate need and that the award of any share in her first husband's property would in fact 'put her in a better financial position than if the marriage had continued[13].' Such a result would not be in accordance with the court's mandate as expressed in section 25(1).

Likewise, in *Mesher v Mesher and Hall*[14], the Court of Appeal had regard to the fact that both spouses had, as it were, re-paired with new partners and, in both instances, contemplated marriage. The husband was now securely housed in a home which his new partner had recovered in the breakdown of her first marriage, and the wife's new partner had no home with which to provide her and her child, since his former matrimonial home had been transferred to his first wife. The Court of Appeal adopted an eminently pragmatic approach. It decided to treat the newly emerging units as distinct families—which was 'convenient . . . in view of the impending marriages'—and imposed a trust for sale upon the former matrimonial home. Possession of that home was granted to the wife until the child living with her attained the age of 17 or until such other time as the court considered sale to be appropriate.

The courts' concentration on the provision of homes, particularly for parties who have custody of the minor children of the marriage, makes it possible to distinguish in the decided cases a two-fold approach in the disposition of the

10 [1973] Fam 72 at 81.
11 [1975] Fam 9.
12 The wife was awarded a postponed one-twelfth share in the value of the property.
13 [1975] Fam 9 at 16.
14 [1980] 1 All ER 126n.

former matrimonial home on divorce[15]. There has emerged a tendency, where one or other party has custody of children of the family, to regard the immediate question of accommodation as a 'social problem'[16] to be resolved as expeditiously as possible in terms of need. The 'legal problem'—that of ultimate capital disposition—need not necessarily be resolved at the same time, but may be postponed for instance until the children have grown up.

Of course there are circumstances in which it is feasible to harmonise the solution of the 'social' and 'legal' problems. *Wachtel v Wachtel*[17] provided a case in point. Here the former matrimonial home was vested by the court in one spouse absolutely, the other spouse being compensated by the award of an immediate lump sum raised by second mortgage. Such lump sum could provide a deposit for the purchase of a new home[18].

The *Wachtel* approach operates tolerably well where the matrimonial home represents a fairly substantial capital asset. Conditions may be entirely different where the value of the equity in the home is small. In these circumstances, the lump sum which could be raised on the security of the property will be correspondingly small, and to order immediate sale and distribution of the proceeds may well be 'socially disastrous, if not irresponsible[19]' where the house is currently the home of the minor children of the family. Here the solution adopted by the courts has involved a separation of the 'social' and 'legal' issues.

In *Browne v Pritchard*[20], for instance, the equity in the former matrimonial home (which was jointly owned) amounted to less than £6,000. After the divorce the wife had acquired secure accommodation in a council house, and the Court of Appeal held that it would be wrong to make an order requiring the immediate sale of the former home in which the husband was still living with two children. Ormrod LJ pointed out that in the past the courts had been 'primarily concerned with property rights . . . because property rights were the material with which they dealt.' However, since the enactment of a new family code in 1969 and 1970, the position had been entirely changed, with the result that 'property rights are now ancillary to the interests of the family[1].' Ormrod LJ indicated that under the new legislation

> Whenever a court is dealing with families of limited resources, 'needs' are likely to be much more important than resources, when it comes to exercising discretion. In most individuals and most families the most urgent need is a home. It is therefore to the provision of homes for all concerned that the courts should direct their attention in the first place[2].

Likewise Roskill LJ expressed the view, in relation to the matrimonial home, that 'the all-important thing is to consider how that single asset can now best be

15 See K. J. Gray, op. cit., p. 314ff.
16 This was the term used by Roskill LJ in *Browne v Pritchard* [1975] 1 WLR 1366 at 1370.
17 [1973] Fam 72.
18 [1973] Fam 72 at 96 per Lord Denning MR.
19 *Browne v Pritchard* [1975] 1 WLR 1366 at 1371 per Ormrod LJ.
20 [1975] 1 WLR 1366.
1 [1975] 1 WLR 1366 at 1371.
2 [1975] 1 WLR 1366 at 1371.

used as a home[3].' Although the former matrimonial home in this case had been vested in the joint names of the spouses, Ormrod LJ rejected forthrightly the wife's argument that the Court's refusal to order sale would 'keep her out of her money':

> That is, in my view, a complete misapprehension. She is not being kept out of her money. If the marriage had not broken down . . . she would never have touched a penny of the value of the house, because investment in a home is the least liquid investment that one can possibly make. It cannot be converted into cash while the children are at home and often not until one spouse dies unless it is possible to move into much smaller and cheaper accommodation[4].

The Court postponed sale of the home, thus making optimal use of the two living units currently available to the parties. However, the wife was given a charge on the home equivalent to one third of the net proceeds of sale, sale being postponed until after the younger child attained the age of 18. In other words, the 'social' problem was satisfactorily resolved for the moment—the 'legal' problem could be finally resolved at a later date.

In more recent cases the courts have tended to disapprove of postponement of sale *merely* until the point when the children of the family reach the age of 17 or 18. In *Hanlon v Hanlon*[5], as Ormrod LJ pointed out in the Court of Appeal, the family concerned would not 'simply dissolve completely on the 17th birthday of the youngest child.' The wife in this case, as the mother of the family, would doubtless continue to maintain the 'nucleus of the home effectively for a considerable number of years' until all the children had married and settled on their own. Moreover, a sale of the former matrimonial home (in which the wife was still living with the children) would have netted only £2,500 for each of the parties, even if sale were postponed for five years until the youngest child became 17 years of age[6]. The Court of Appeal was unwilling to make any order which might force the wife to leave her home within the foreseeable future, and therefore transferred that home to her absolutely. The husband enjoyed secure accommodation elsewhere and, in order to compensate him for the loss of his interest in the matrimonial home, the Court of Appeal reduced the periodical payments payable by him to a nominal sum.

This approach was taken even further in *Martin v Martin*[7], where there were no children of the family. Here the husband was 43 and his wife 46. The husband had secure accommodation with the party with whom he was now living, and the wife continued to reside in the former matrimonial home. The equity in the home (which belonged at law to the husband) was currently worth £10,000. The Court of Appeal declined to order immediate sale of the property. Stamp LJ said that

3 [1975] 1 WLR 1366 at 1370.
4 [1975] 1 WLR 1366 at 1371.
5 [1978] 1 WLR 592.
6 This was the result which would inevitably flow from the fact that the Law Society has a statutory charge on any property 'recovered or preserved' for a legally assisted litigant (see Legal Aid Act 1974, s. 9(6)). See also *Hanlon v Law Society* [1981] AC 124; (1981) 44 MLR 96 (R. C. A. White).
7 [1978] Fam 12.

It is of primary concern in these cases that on the breakdown of the marriage the parties should, if possible, each have a roof over his or her head. That is perhaps the most important circumstance to be taken into account in applying s 25 of the Matrimonial Causes Act 1973 when the only available asset is the matrimonial home. It is important that each party should have a roof over his or her head whether or not there be children of the marriage[8].

At first instance[9], Purchas J had attached great significance to the fact that, if the marriage had continued, the parties would not in all probability have been able to enjoy the equity comprised in the matrimonial home in the form of a liquid asset until they reached the age of retirement:

At least, therefore, it is likely that for a further 16 or 20 years until the husband retired the inchoate asset represented by the matrimonial home would have been of no practical financial value to either party. In a sense the proceeds of the sale of the matrimonial home in the immediate or not too far distant future would represent an uncovenanted bonus arising out of the breakdown of the marriage from which both parties might benefit, provided that the wife is fortunate enough to find a partner who will provide her with secure and suitable accommodation as the husband has been able to do. Such a course would clearly be just as between the parties and in accordance with the provisions of s 25 of the Matrimonial Causes Act 1973. However, such a sale giving one the bonus unimpaired but the other the bonus impaired by its immediate and necessary application to secure a roof would not, in my judgment, be doing justice between the parties.

Purchas J had therefore ordered that the former matrimonial home should be held by the parties jointly, on trust for the wife's sole use during her lifetime or until her remarriage or voluntary removal from the property (whichever occurred first), and thereafter should be held on trust for sale and the proceeds divided equally. This order was based largely upon the judge's conclusion that

the degree of hardship likely to fall on the wife if she is forcibly removed from the matrimonial home will greatly exceed the hardship inflicted on the husband by being 'kept out of his money' which in this case means little in the context of the continuation of the marriage and the unavailability of the matrimonial home as a liquid asset.'

The Court of Appeal confirmed the order made by Purchas J, Stamp LJ adding his view that

the injustices to the wife of making an order that the house be sold at some specified time in the future might well turn out to be greater than would be the case of an order for sale at the present time. It is at least likely that the wife will be in a far worse position to fend for herself in 10 or 20 years' time than she is at present, and I should have thought that to postpone the sale until some specified date in the future would cause her great hardship when that time arose[10].

Ormrod LJ uttered words of caution in this case in relation to 'the practice which seems to be developing of postponing the sale of matrimonial homes in similar cases to this until after the youngest child has reached the age of 18 . . . and no further.' Ormrod LJ located the origin of this form of court order in

8 [1978] Fam 12 at 16.
9 (1976) Times, 30th November.
10 [1978] Fam 12 at 19.

Mesher v Mesher, and said

But it was never intended to be a general practice. There is no magic in the fact that there are children to be considered. All it means is that the interests of the children take priority in these cases, so that often there can be no question of sale while the children are young. But the situation that will arise when the children reach the age of 18 requires to be carefully considered. Otherwise a great deal of hardship may be stored up in these cases by treating it as a rule of thumb that the matrimonial home should then be sold. It is not a rule of thumb. In some cases it is the only way of dealing with the situation. For example, take a husband who has an onerous mortgage round his neck. He may badly need some capital as soon as it is reasonable to give it to him. In such a case a wife who remains in the matrimonial home with the children may have to endure the hardship of giving up the matrimonial home to relieve the husband's hardship. But that is a matter of weighing each individual case on its merits, of weighing up each side's resources and trying to ensure that neither party is rendered homeless[11].

It is also of interest that Ormrod LJ proffered, as another ground for declining to order sale in this case, the consideration that it would be contrary to public policy to order sale 'in reliance on local authorities to provide housing for people who would thus be enabled to obtain some free capital at the public expense[12].'

Decisions such as those of the Court of Appeal in *Martin v Martin* at least included some allowance for the possibility of sale at some future date. There have, however, been some cases in which the court has decided not merely that distribution of the capital tied up in the family home should be postponed, but that distribution should never take place at all. In *S v S*[13] it was considered that the special needs of a divorced wife with custody of a disabled child were such as to require that the husband's half-share in the former matrimonial home be transferred to the wife absolutely. The wife here was aged 31, and, as Latey J observed

like so many wives when there are children has come off worse as the result of the breakdown of the marriage. It is a sad fact of life that, where there are children, both husband and wife suffer on marriage breakdown, but it is the wife who usually suffers more. The husband continues with his career, goes on establishing himself, increasing his experience and qualification for employment—in a word, his security. With children to care for a wife cannot usually do this. She has not usually embarked on a continuous and progressing career while living with her husband caring for their child or children and running the home. If the marriage breaks down she can only start in any useful way after the children are off her hands and then she starts from scratch in middle life while her husband has started in youth . . . The wife [in the instant case] will be 36 or more before she can begin to forge any real career with prospects of continuity and perhaps some pension rights. The only real security for her future is to be found in this house[14].

Again, the entire interest in the matrimonial home may be vested in the wife as in *Bryant v Bryant*[15], where periodical financial provision is unlikely to be forthcoming from the husband.

11 [1978] Fam 12 at 21. See also *Eshak v Nowojewski*: (1980) Times, 19th November.
12 [1978] Fam 12 at 20.
13 [1976] Fam 18n.
14 [1976] Fam 18n at 23.
15 (1976) Times, 3rd February.

(4) A critique of the 'support approach'

It is quite clear from the foregoing account of the reallocation of the matrimonial home on divorce that the Matrimonial Causes Act 1973 enables the courts to give effect to a 'support approach' in relation to the adjustment of proprietary rights between the spouses. This area of the law demonstrates perhaps more starkly than any other the way in which property rights have come to be defined in accordance with primarily social considerations. The 1973 Act has radically extended the powers of the court to regulate the property consequences of divorce. In effect the courts have been invested with a quite remarkable discretion to transcend established titles of property as between the divorcing spouses in order to minister to the totality of the parties' special needs in the aftermath of marriage breakdown. The arrangements made necessary by divorce are directed by family considerations, in that property rights in this context are now ancillary to the interests of the family. Commercial considerations are largely irrelevant, although it should be noted that, while the courts possess powers to restrain and even set aside transactions by one spouse which are intended to prejudice a claim for financial relief by the other spouse[16], there can be no avoidance of a disposition made to a bona fide third party who has purchased for valuable consideration without notice of the prejudicial intent[17]. Nor does the fact that a settlement or transfer of matrimonial property is made in compliance with a property adjustment order on divorce confer upon that settlement or transfer immunity from review in the event of subsequent insolvency[18].

The new 'support approach' to the adjustment of rights in the matrimonial home on divorce is indeed consistent with the generally emerging emphasis upon rights of use and enjoyment in the law relating to residential property[19]. The perspective adopted by the courts in the implementation of the Matrimonial Causes Act 1973 effectively treats housing as a valuable resource which requires careful allocation between competing claimants. That allocation is carried out under the 1973 Act with reference to a social calculus of *need* as distinct from *entitlement*. More accurately, need generates entitlement, and the courts therefore exercise a special statutory power of appointment over the matrimonial home in accordance with the relative needs of the spouses and their children in the aftermath of family breakdown.

In this way, the economic exigency of the divorce situation has blunted the principle of equality. The criterion of need has pre-empted the claim of entitlement, and this has caused the courts to administer an area of social welfare and housing policy through the medium of supposed obligations of private law. By virtue of the primacy thus attributed to need, the law of economic adjustment on divorce has been transformed into a piece of substitute social security legislation. In effect the economic cost of marriage breakdown (in terms of re-housing former spouses and their children and supplying them with the

16 Matrimonial Causes Act 1973, s. 37.
17 Matrimonial Causes Act 1973, s. 37(4).
18 Matrimonial Causes Act 1973, s. 39.
19 See p. 39, ante.

necessaries of life) is met through the convenient device of a judicial discretion to subvert traditional property rights in a manner quite alien to the historic approach of English property law[20]. In this sense the jurisprudence evolving under the Matrimonial Causes Act 1973 is an interesting reflection of the more general conceptual shift in property law away from the former concentration which saw the meaning of 'property' enshrined in the capital power conferred by 'ownership'. Instead, as we have seen throughout this book, the real significance of property is nowadays much more likely to be found in various forms of entitlement to use or enjoyment.

20 See p. 566, ante. For a critical view of this jurisdiction, see K. J. Gray, op. cit., p. 319ff; Law Commission, *The Financial Consequences of Divorce: The Basic Policy* (Law Com No. 103, Cmnd 8041, October 1980).

PART VI

Control of land use

CHAPTER 17

Easements and profits[1]

Easements and profits comprise some of the most important rights which one landowner may acquire over the land of another. The law relating to profits is of fairly ancient origin[2], but the law of easements has developed in more recent times as a means of enabling the private landowner to plan land use and enhance the enjoyment or utility of his own land. In this chapter we shall deal largely with the law relating to easements and only incidentally with the law of profits.

In Chapter 1 we noted that the law of property is made more complex by the fact that it is possible for a number of people to acquire different, but compatible, rights in or over the same thing. Thus, A may well own a fee simple estate in his land, while his neighbour, B, simultaneously has a legal right to use part of A's land in a certain way or indeed a right to prevent A from using his (i.e., A's) land in a particular way. The rights which may be created between A and B provide the subject matter of the law relating to easements, profits and also covenants[3]. Such rights may well bind A and B as a matter of contract, but for the land lawyer the question inevitably arises whether those rights will bind third parties such as the successors in title of A and B respectively. The rights created by private agreement are usually intended to be not merely contractual, but also proprietary, in the sense that they should affect all who come to the land in question.

Since the concern here is with the borderline of the law of property, it should come as no surprise that the law has traditionally imposed certain stringent requirements as to the definition of the rights which may qualify as easements and profits and as to their mode of creation or acquisition. The marketability of land would be gravely affected if these rules were not fairly clear and fairly rigorously applied. Otherwise titles to land would become encumbered by useless and anti-social user-rights of dubious enforceability, vested in unspecified or unascertainable third parties. The resulting chaos would be gravely prejudicial to the large social interest which pervades our law of property—the interest that property should be freely alienable.

It is therefore our task in this chapter to outline the strict legal rules concerning the creation and acquisition of easements and profits. A consideration of the law of covenants follows in Chapter 18.

1 See generally P. Jackson, *The Law of Easements and Profits* (London 1978).
2 See A. W. B. Simpson, *An Introduction to the History of the Land Law* (London 1961), p. 101ff.
3 See generally *Gale on Easements* (14th edn. London 1972); Preston and Newsom's *Restrictive Covenants affecting Freehold Land* (6th edn. London 1976).

1. DEFINITIONS

An 'easement' has been described as

a right annexed to land to utilise other land of different ownership in a particular manner (not involving the taking of any part of the natural produce of that land or any part of its soil) or to prevent the owner of the other land from utilising his land in a particular manner[4].

An easement is therefore a positive or negative right of user over the land of another. It is essentially a privilege without profit which the owner of one neighbouring tenement (the 'dominant tenement') has over another tenement (the 'servient tenement') by which the servient owner permits (or refrains from) certain activities on his own land for the advantage of the dominant tenement.

It is vital that easements should be distinguished from a number of other rights which may exist over land. These include:

(1) Profits

A *profit* (or, more strictly, profit à prendre) confers a right to take part of the soil or produce of the servient tenement. In this respect profits are to be distinguished from easements, which are essentially privileges without profit. A profit is a right to take either some part of the servient land (e.g., gravel or turf), or something which grows on that land (e.g., grass or crops), or indeed fish or wild animals which are found on the servient owner's land or in his waters.

A profit is further distinguishable from an easement in that a profit may exist '*in gross*'. This means that the owner of the profit need not be the owner of any adjoining or neighbouring land or indeed any land at all[5]. There need not be a 'dominant tenement'. The rules concerning easements are quite different. As we shall see[6], it is an essential condition of an easement that the easement be appurtenant to 'dominant' land.

(2) Licences

A licence grants a permission to do something on or affecting the land of another which would otherwise constitute a trespass[7]. However, licences are distinguishable from easements in the following respects. The categories of conduct which are capable of recognition as easements are relatively limited and are fairly restrictively defined. However, a licence may be used to permit the conduct of almost any kind of activity on the land of the licensor (e.g., an open-air pop

4 *Halsbury's Laws of England* (4th edn., London 1975), Vol. 14, p. 4.

5 A profit 'in gross' is said to be 'unstinted', in the sense that it may be exhaustive of the fruit or produce of the servient land. In other words, the right is unlimited. However, a 'profit appurtenant' (i.e., a profit which is annexed to a nearby dominant tenement) may not be exhaustive, but is limited to the needs of the dominant tenement. See *Bailey v Stephens* (1862) 12 CB NS 91.

6 See p. 580ff., post.

7 For a discussion of the law relating to licences, see Chapter 14, p. 472ff., ante.

festival). Furthermore, an easement cannot exist in gross, but a licence need not be related to the ownership of any dominant tenement. Perhaps most important, an easement creates a proprietary interest which is capable of benefiting and binding third parties. A licence, at least in the orthodox view, does not generate a proprietary interest and is at most of purely contractual effect[8]. It cannot affect third parties.

(3) Restrictive covenants

Restrictive covenants are agreements restrictive of the user of land for the benefit of other land adjoining or in the vicinity. Restrictive covenants are closely related to easements both in terminology and in substance, and indeed it has been said that restrictive covenants are in essence negative easements[9]. Certain differences do, however, exist. Easements are enforceable both at law and in equity. Restrictive covenants are the creature of equity and are enforceable only in equity. Furthermore, easements may be acquired by prescription (i.e., long user)[10], while restrictive covenants may never be acquired in this way[11].

(4) Public rights

Public rights are those rights which are exercisable by anyone, whether he owns land or not, merely by virtue of his being a member of the public. Some public rights resemble profits (e.g., the right to fish in the sea and in all tidal and salt waters). Other public rights are akin to easements (e.g., the right to pass along the public highway). However, public rights of whatsoever kind are distinct from easements, since they do not presuppose the existence of any dominant tenement and are never the subject of specific grant to any individual.

(5) Natural rights

Landowners have certain 'natural rights'. The most important of these natural rights is the right to support for land. In other words, every landowner has a right to have his land supported by his neighbour's land or, as it has perhaps been more accurately expressed[12], a right 'not to have that support removed by his neighbour' (e.g., by mining or excavating operations on his neighbour's land which cause his own land to subside).

A natural right of this kind is distinguishable from an easement in that it comes into being automatically and is not the subject of a grant. Moreover, a natural right is protected by the law of torts[13]. It should also be noted that the

8 See p. 498f., ante.
9 See p. 616, post.
10 See p. 598ff., post.
11 See p. 614ff., post.
12 R. E. Megarry and H. W. R. Wade, *The Law of Real Property* (4th edn., London 1975), p. 814.
13 Violation of a natural right is actionable in the law of nuisance. See, e.g. J. G. Fleming, *The Law of Torts* (5th edn., Sydney, Melbourne, Brisbane, Perth 1977), p. 407f.

natural right of support for land avails the land in its natural state only. It comprises a right of support for land and not for buildings. If the action of a neighbour in demolishing a contiguous and supporting building or wall causes one's house to fall down, there is no remedy in the absence of a duly acquired easement of support[14].

Other forms of natural right may exist. There is a natural right to water where it flows naturally in a defined channel[15]. There is, however, no natural right to 'a single ray of light'[16]. Such a right to light is capable of existence only as an easement.

2. THE ESSENTIAL CHARACTERISTICS OF AN EASEMENT

The essential characteristics of an easement were defined generally by Danckwerts J in *Re Ellenborough Park*[17] in the following terms:

> The essential qualities of an easement are (1) there must be a dominant and a servient tenement; (2) an easement must accommodate the dominant tenement, that is, be connected with its enjoyment and for its benefit; (3) the dominant and servient owners must be different persons; and (4) the right claimed must be capable of forming the subject-matter of a grant.

We must examine these characteristics in turn.

(1) There must be a dominant and a servient tenement

An easement cannot exist 'in gross' but only as appurtenant to a defined area of land[18]. In other words, an easement must be linked with two parcels of land. There must be a 'dominant tenement' in favour of which the easement is created or acquired, and there must be a 'servient tenement' over which the easement is exercised or exercisable.

This requirement of a relationship of dominance and servience was laid down clearly by Cresswell J in *Ackroyd v Smith*[19]. Here the plaintiff and the defendant owned adjoining areas of land. The plaintiff's predecessor in title had granted to an earlier owner of the adjoining land a right to use a road across his land. When this right was subsequently claimed as an easement, Cresswell J held the right to be a mere licence on the ground that a 'right unconnected with the enjoyment or occupation of the land cannot be annexed as an incident to it.' In

14 See *Peyton v The Mayor and Commonalty of London* (1829) 9 B & C 725; *Ray v Fairway Motors (Barnstaple) Ltd* (1968) 20 P & CR 261. However, if a neighbour's activities on his land would have caused the subsidence of land in any event, irrespective of the presence of buildings thereon, the damages recoverable for violation of the natural right of support for land may include damages in respect of any buildings which have been affected. See *Stroyan v Knowles* (1861) 6 H & N 454.

15 See *Swindon Waterworks Co Ltd v Wilts and Berks Canal Navigation Co* (1875) LR 7 HL 697.

16 C. J. Gale, *Law of Easements* (12th edn., London 1950), p. 6.

17 [1956] Ch 131 at 140.

18 See generally M. F. Sturley (1980) 96 LQR 557: 'Easements in Gross'.

19 (1850) 10 CB 164; 138 ER 68.

the present case, the right concerned had been granted to the 'owners and occupiers' of the adjoining land and to 'all persons having occasion to resort thereto.' This right was held to be too ample to qualify as an easement, on the principle that a right of way cannot be granted in gross, and 'no one can have such a way but he who has the land to which it is appendant.' A right granted in gross was, in the view of Cresswell J, 'personal only, and cannot be assigned.'

It is not without interest that Cresswell J expressed the rationale behind this rule in terms of a sentiment which pervades the early law of easements and covenants[20]. He ruled that

> It is not in the power of a vendor to create any rights not connected with the use or enjoyment of the land, and annex them to it: nor can the owner of land render it subject to a new species of burthen, so as to bind it in the hands of an assignee. 'Incidents of a novel kind cannot be devised, and attached to property, at the fancy or caprice of any owner[1].'

Within this statement is contained the implicit concern lest an easement in gross impose 'clogs upon the title' which may render the servient land unmarketable[2].

The various formulations of the rationale underlying the requirement of a dominant tenement are today open to challenge. It has, for instance, been questioned whether a company which runs a helicopter shuttle service should be obliged to make the slightly disingenuous claim that its West End office constitutes the 'dominant tenement' in respect of some distant landing pad over which it exercises rights[3]. It may be that the abolition of the rule which forbids easements in gross would nowadays promote rather than impede maximum utilisation of land. This rule is, of course, sometimes relaxed by statute in order to confer certain rights of use and inspection upon those bodies which operate the public services and utilities needed to maintain supplies which are thought essential for the satisfaction of the needs of a modern industrial society (e.g., electricity, gas, water authorities)[4]. In other words, the requirement of a dominant tenement is abrogated in order to further certain public or community-related purposes. However, it may also be argued that the requirement should also be abrogated in the context of easements directed towards wholly private purposes.

Where an easement is appurtenant to a dominant tenement, it becomes affixed to that tenement in the same way that fixtures become annexed to the realty. In consequence, the easement passes with subsequent conveyances or transfers of the land[5], and may be enjoyed by the occupier for the time being of the dominant land, even if he is a mere lessee of that land[6].

20 See p. 614f., post.
1 (1850) 10 CB 164 at 188, quoting *Keppell v Bailey* (1834) 2 My & K 517 at 540ff. per Lord Brougham LC, p. 615, post.
2 See M. F. Sturley (1980) 96 LQR 557 at 562ff.
3 See M. F. Sturley (1980) 96 LQR 557 at 567f.
4 See R. E. Megarry and H. W. R. Wade, op. cit., p. 827f..
5 Law of Property Act 1925, ss. 62(1), 187(1), p. 595, post. See *Leech v Schweder* (1874) 9 Ch App 463 at 474f.
6 See *Thorpe v Brumfitt* (1873) 8 Ch App 650.

(2) The easement must 'accommodate' the dominant tenement

No right may qualify as an easement unless it can be shown that the right confers benefit upon the dominant tenement and not merely some purely personal advantage upon the dominant owner. The criterion of benefit rests ultimately upon whether the right in question makes the dominant tenement 'a better and more convenient property[7].' In other words, an easement must accommodate not persons but land. It is, however, sufficient for this purpose that a right claimed as an easement should facilitate or benefit some trade or business carried on in the dominant land. In *Moody v Steggles*[8], for instance, Fry J held that the owner of a public house might claim an easement to hang a signboard on the adjoining house.

The classic example provided by the case law of a purely personal advantage which could not be claimed as an easement is the right which was alleged by the plaintiff in *Hill v Tupper*[9]. Here the owner of a canal leased land on the canal bank to the plaintiff and purported to grant him a 'sole and exclusive' right to put pleasure boats on the canal. The plaintiff subsequently contended that he had acquired an easement in respect of the canal which was enforceable against the defendant, the landlord of a nearby inn, who unlawfully interfered with the plaintiff's trade by putting rival boats on the canal. This claim to an easement was not upheld by the court, which took the view that the plaintiff had acquired a mere licence which was, of course, unenforceable except against the licensor.

The ground for this decision was somewhat unclear. Pollock CB observed that a 'new species of incorporeal hereditament cannot be created at the will and pleasure of the owner of property[10].' Martin B held that to admit the right claimed by the plaintiff 'would lead to the creation of an infinite variety of interests in land, and an indefinite increase of possible estates[11].' Such statements appear to be another expression of the policy against imposing 'clogs' on the title which might tend to make that title uncommerciable or inalienable. However, perhaps the most potent factor in the minds of the judges in this case was their clear apprehension that the easement claimed by the plaintiff was not appurtenant to any dominant tenement. Pollock CB cited *Ackroyd v Smith*[12] in support of the proposition that it is impossible to create easements in respect of 'rights unconnected with the use and enjoyment of land.' In the present case, it was scarcely realistic to argue that the plaintiff's contractual rights over the canal were such as to make his occupation of the land on the canal bank more convenient. The area in question included a landing stage, and it was clearly the case that the landing stage facilitated the plaintiff's use of the canal rather than vice versa[13].

7 R. E. Megarry and H. W. R. Wade, op. cit., p. 807.
8 (1879) 12 Ch D 261.
9 (1863) 2 H & C 121.
10 (1863) 2 H & C 121 at 127.
11 (1863) 2 H & C 121 at 128.
12 (1850) 10 CB 164, p. 580, ante.
13 'The result would have been different if the right granted had been to cross and recross the canal to get to and from Hill's land, and Tupper's boats had been so numerous as to interfere with it' (see R. E. Megarry and H. W. R. Wade, op. cit., p. 809).

It may also be that in *Hill v Tupper* the court felt disinclined to allow a *purely* commercial advantage to be claimed as an easement. The plaintiff was seeking in effect to assert a commercial monopoly in respect of the business of putting pleasure boats on the canal in question. There was no sense in which the plaintiff's occupation of the alleged dominant land was enhanced by the easement, because his use of that land was entirely incidental to his entrepreneurial exploitation of the waterway[14]. It is also possible that the judgments in *Hill v Tupper* concealed a distaste for rights which are over-broad. As we shall see[15], it is a characteristic feature of an easement that it must not smack of exclusiveness of possession or control.

In order to support the claim that a given right 'accommodates' the alleged dominant tenement, there is some requirement of propinquity in respect of the servient and dominant tenements. There is no rule that the dominant and servient land must be contiguous[16], but the servient land must at least be sufficiently closely situated to confer a practical benefit upon the dominant land[17]. The test whether the right in question increases the market value of the benefited land is not conclusive. In *Re Ellenborough Park*[18], Evershed MR indicated that there must be some 'sufficient nexus between the enjoyment of the right and the use of [the dominant property].' Thus a right granted to the purchaser of a particular house to use the Zoological Gardens free of charge or to attend Lord's Cricket Ground without payment, although undoubtedly increasing the value of the property conveyed, could not run with the property at law as an easement. Such rights would be 'wholly extraneous to, and independent of, the use of a house as a house, namely as a place in which the householder and his family live and make their home.'

In *Re Ellenborough Park* a number of owners of residential properties had been given a right of common enjoyment of a park or pleasure ground which was enclosed by their houses and which was vested in trustees. Each adjoining owner paid a proportionate part of the cost required to maintain the pleasure ground as a well stocked and carefully ordered garden. The Court of Appeal held that the right granted each purchaser of 'full enjoyment . . . of the pleasure ground' was capable of forming the subject matter of an easement. The Court accepted that the notion of an easement would not encompass a *ius spatiandi*, i.e., a 'privilege of wandering at will over all and every part of another's field or park', which, being an 'indefinite and unregulated privilege', would lack the essential quality of an easement[19]. However, in the view of the Court of Appeal the grant

14 See *Re Ellenborough Park* [1956] Ch 131 at 175, where Evershed MR said, with reference to *Hill v Tupper*, that 'it is clear that what the plaintiff was trying to do was to set up, under the guise of an easement, a monopoly which had no normal connexion with the ordinary use of his land, but which was merely an independent business enterprise. So far from the right claimed sub-serving or accommodating the land, the land was but a convenient incident to the exercise of the right.' See, however, (1956) 14 Cambridge LJ 24 at 25 (R. N. Gooderson).

15 See p. 588, post.

16 See *Re Ellenborough Park* [1956] Ch 131 at 175.

17 *Todrick v Western National Omnibus Co Ltd* [1934] Ch 561. See (1934) 50 LQR 313.

18 [1956] Ch 131 at 174. See (1956) 14 Cambridge LJ 24 (R. N. Gooderson); (1956) 72 LQR 16 (REM).

19 [1956] Ch 131 at 176.

involved in the present case was substantially different. Here there was the required nexus between the right enjoyed and the premises to which the enjoyment was expressed to belong. The park had become the 'communal garden for the benefit and enjoyment of those whose houses adjoined it or were in its close proximity[20]' and as such amply satisfied the 'requirement of connexion with the dominant tenements to which it is appurtenant[1].' Moreover, the Court of Appeal had no doubt that the rights of enjoyment in question in this case conferred benefit upon the adjoining or adjacent houses. There is some authority for the view that a mere right of 'recreation and amusement' can never qualify as an easement[2]. However, Evershed MR was moved to declare that

> No doubt a garden is a pleasure—on high authority, it is the purest of pleasures—but, in our judgment, it is not a right having no quality either of utility or benefit as those words should be understood. The right here in suit is, for reasons already given, one appurtenant to the surrounding houses as such, and constitutes a beneficial attribute of residence in a house as ordinarily understood. Its use for the purposes, not only of exercise and rest but also for such domestic purposes as were suggested in argument—for example, for taking out small children in perambulators or otherwise—is not fairly to be described as one of mere recreation or amusement, and is clearly beneficial to the premises to which it is attached[3].

Throughout our consideration of the law relating to easements, we shall have cause to observe that the definition of the rights which are capable of constituting an easement is heavily coloured by value judgments. These value judgments concern not only the sorts of activity claimed as amounting to an easement, but also the relative degree of merit which is thought to attach to the party making the claim. In *Re Ellenborough Park*, the Court of Appeal had little difficulty in applying the terminology of easements to the civilised user by civilised people of a communal garden situated in an excessively bourgeois location.

(3) The dominant and servient tenements must be owned or occupied by different persons

An easement is by definition a right over somebody else's land. It is therefore impossible that the same person should both own *and occupy* the dominant and servient tenements, since it is a nonsense that a man should have rights against *himself*. It is, however, quite feasible that a tenant should acquire an easement over his landlord's land, since in this situation although there is common ownership of the dominant and servient tenements, there is no common occupation[4].

20 [1956] Ch 131 at 174.
1 [1956] Ch 131 at 175.
2 H. S. Theobald, *The Law of Land* (2nd edn., London 1929), p. 263.
3 [1956] Ch 131 at 179.
4 See *Borman v Griffith* [1930] 1 Ch 493, p. 596, post.

(4) The easement must be capable of forming the subject matter of a grant

It is commonly said that all easements 'lie in grant'. That is, no right can successfully be claimed as an easement which could not have been granted by deed. This requirement imposes certain stringent conditions upon the kinds of right which can constitute an easement, as also upon the circumstances in which a valid easement may be created.

(a) *There must be a capable grantor and a capable grantee*

No easement can be claimed if at the date of creation of the supposed easement the servient land was owned by someone who was legally incompetent to grant an easement (e.g., a statutory or other corporation which has no duly constituted authority to grant easements over its land). Likewise, no easement may be claimed if the alleged dominant owner was at the time legally incompetent to receive such a grant (e.g., a company without power to acquire easements, or a fluctuating body of persons such as 'the inhabitants for the time being' of a named village[5]).

(b) *The right must be sufficiently definite*

In order to qualify as an easement, a right must be sufficiently definite. There is, for instance, no such easement as a right to a prospect or view[6]. Such a right may be acquired only by way of a restrictive covenant which precludes the owner of neighbouring land from building on his land in such a way as to obstruct the view which it is desired to protect. Likewise, there is no such easement as a right to the uninterrupted access of light or air except through defined apertures in a building[7]. There is no easement of indefinite privacy[8].

(c) *The right must be within the general nature of the rights traditionally recognised as easements*

It is commonly said that the list of easements is not closed. As Lord St Leonards observed in *Dyce v Lady James Hay*[9], 'the category of servitudes and easements must alter and expand with the changes that take place in the circumstances of mankind.' However, we have already noted that the courts have often been reluctant to admit new kinds of right to the status of easement. Pollock CB made it clear in *Hill v Tupper*[10] that

5 See R. E. Megarry and H. W. R. Wade, op. cit., p. 813.
6 *William Aldred's Case* (1610) 9 Co Rep 57b at 58b per Wray CJ.
7 See, e.g., *Ough v King* [1967] 1 WLR 1547. The High Court of Australia has, however, recognised the right to the uninterrupted access of light and air as an easement, even though not limited to access through defined apertures. See *Commonwealth v Registrar of Titles (Victoria)* (1918) 24 CLR 348. In England the Court of Appeal has accepted that a greenhouse is 'not to be regarded simply as a garden under glass but as a building with apertures, namely, the glass roof and sides'. See *Allen v Greenwood* [1980] Ch 119 at 129 per Goff LJ.
8 See *Browne v Flower* [1911] 1 Ch 219 at 225 per Parker J.
9 (1852) 1 Macq 305 at 312f.
10 (1863) 2 H & C 121, p. 582, ante.

A new species of incorporeal hereditament cannot be created at the will and pleasure of the owner of property; but he must be content to accept the estate and the right to dispose of it subject to the law as settled by decisions or controlled by Act of Parliament.

In consequence, the courts are not usually willing to establish as easements rights which lie markedly outside the range of rights which have traditionally been recognised as easements. Occasionally a new category of right is admitted within the list of easements. In *Simpson v Godmanchester Corpn*[11], the House of Lords held that an easement could comprise the right to enter on to another's land in order to open and shut sluice gates on a canal. However, in many cases rights claimed as easements have been rejected, not least because the rights claimed are in the nature of negative easements and therefore more appropriately created and protected as restrictive covenants.

In *Phipps v Pears*[12], for instance, the plaintiff sought damages from the defendant on the ground that the latter had demolished his adjoining house thereby exposing the unpointed flank wall of the plaintiff's house to the rigours of the weather[13]. The plaintiff's action was based upon a supposed easement of protection from the weather, but the Court of Appeal denied that any such right could exist as an easement. Lord Denning MR conceded that a right to support from an adjoining building had been long recognised as constituting a possible easement. However, such a right partakes of the nature of both positive and negative easements, in the sense that it comprises not merely a right that one's neighbour should not remove his building but also a right for the protected building to exert a sideways thrust or lean upon the adjoining building. A supposed right to protection from the weather is 'entirely negative'. In Lord Denning's view, such a right is

a right to stop your neighbour pulling down his own house. Seeing that it is a negative easement, it must be looked at with caution. Because the law has been very chary of creating any new negative easements[14].

The Master of the Rolls then explained the reluctance of the courts to recognise new negative easements in the following terms:

The reason underlying these instances is that if such an easement were to be permitted, it would unduly restrict your neighbour in his enjoyment of his own land. It would hamper legitimate development... Likewise here, if we were to stop a man pulling down his house, we would put a brake on desirable improvement. Every man is entitled to pull down his house if he likes. If it exposes your house to the weather, that is your misfortune. It is no wrong on his part. Likewise every man is entitled to cut down his trees if he likes, even if it leaves you without shelter from the wind or shade from the sun[15].

In Lord Denning's view, the only way in which an owner may protect himself

11 [1897] AC 696.
12 [1965] 1 QB 76. See (1964) 22 Cambridge LJ 203 (K. Scott).
13 See Public Health Act 1961, s. 29(5), under which a local authority may require the weatherproofing of surfaces exposed by demolition.
14 [1965] 1 QB 76 at 82f. For a critical view of this rationale, see (1964) 80 LQR 318 (REM); M. A. Peel (1964) 28 Conv (NS) 450 at 451ff.: 'What is an Easement?'
15 [1965] 1 QB 76 at 83.

in such circumstances is by extracting from his neighbour a restrictive covenant that the neighbour will not take action which prejudices the owner's enjoyment of his property[16].

Having entered these qualifications, however, it is fair to point out that the courts have over the years accepted many widely varying kinds of right as constituting easements. An easement may comprise a right to do something on the servient tenement, e.g., to use a right of way, to store goods, to advertise a business. An easement may also comprise a right in the dominant owner to prevent the servient owner from doing certain acts on the servient land which he would otherwise be entitled to perform, although, as we have seen, there is a danger that the court may declare such a right to be both novel and negative and therefore not in the nature of an easement. However, some negative rights have been acknowledged to be easements. In *Ough v King*[17], the Court of Appeal held that there was an easement of access to light flowing through a defined aperture. This right was effectively a right to prevent a neighbour from building on his land in such a way as to obstruct that right to light, and in the circumstances the Court of Appeal upheld an award of damages in favour of the aggrieved dominant owner.

It has even been said that an easement can be granted to do acts affecting the servient land which would otherwise constitute a nuisance. In *Sturges v Bridgman*[18], the defendant claimed to have acquired an easement by reason of long user to generate an excessive amount of noise and vibration in the course of his conduct of the business of a confectioner. The Court of Appeal held that no easement had been acquired on the facts, but acknowledged that an easement to make noise could have been created by long user if during the period of user the noise had amounted to an actionable nuisance in the law of tort and the servient owner had not availed himself of the appropriate remedy.

There is a general rule that an easement must not normally involve the servient owner in the expenditure of money or in any positive action[19]. There is only one situation in which an easement has been held to impose any positive duty upon the servient owner. All other easements require merely that the servient owner either suffer the *dominant owner* to do something on the servient land or refrain from doing something on that land himself which otherwise he would be entitled to do. The exceptional case arises in respect of the obligation to maintain a fence. In *Jones v Price*[20], the Court of Appeal held that a right to require a neighbour to maintain a boundary fence can be validly acquired as an easement. It is doubtful whether such an easement can arise otherwise than by prescription, but the possible existence of this kind of easement is of importance,

16 [1965] 1 QB 76 at 84.
17 [1967] 1 WLR 1547.
18 (1879) 11 Ch D 852. See also *Miller v Jackson* [1977] QB 966 at 978, where Lord Denning MR remarked that 'there is no such easement known to the law as a right to hit cricket balls into your neighbour's land.' Compare, however, (1977) 93 LQR 481 (R. M. Goode).
19 See, e.g., *Regis Property Co Ltd v Redman* [1956] 2 QB 612, where the court declined to accept as an easement a right to the supply of hot water.
20 [1965] 2 QB 618. The duty to fence has been described as being 'in the nature of a spurious easement' (see *Lawrence v Jenkins* (1873) LR 8 QB 274 at 279).

for instance, in determining the respective rights and obligations of holders of grazing rights on open moorland[1].

In concluding this discussion of the categories of right which have been traditionally recognised as capable of creation as easements, it must be said that the courts supposedly apply a rule to the effect that an easement may never comprise a claim to exclusive possession or occupation of the servient land. In *Copeland v Greenhalf*[2], for instance, the defendant was a wheelwright who had for 50 years used a narrow strip of land belonging to the plaintiff for the purpose of storing vehicles awaiting and undergoing repair. Upjohn J held that the prescriptive easement claimed by the defendant was too extensive to constitute an easement in law. In his view, the right claimed went 'wholly outside any normal idea of an easement' since it amounted in effect to 'a claim of joint user of the land by the defendant.' In the words of Upjohn J,

> the defendant is claiming the whole beneficial user of the strip of land on the south-east side of the track there; he can leave as many or as few lorries there as he likes for as long as he likes, he may enter on it by himself, his servants and agents to do repair work thereon. In my judgment, that is not a claim which can be established as an easement. It is virtually a claim to possession of the servient tenement, if necessary to the exclusion of the owner; or, at any rate, to a joint user, and no authority has been cited to me which would justify the conclusion that a right of this wide and undefined nature can be the proper subject-matter of an easement. It seems to me that to succeed, this claim must amount to a successful claim of possession by reason of long adverse possession[3].

The criterion of non-exclusive possession has been frequently applied in testing whether a particular right is capable of being an easement[4]. In *Ward v Kirkland*[5], the plaintiff claimed to have a right to enter an adjoining farmyard in order to maintain the wall of his cottage abutting on that farmyard. Ungoed-Thomas J held that the right claimed was capable of existence as an easement, since the right involved no more than monthly visits to the servient land for the purposes of window-cleaning. The right could not be defeated on the ground that it comprised a user which 'would in effect exclude the defendant from the use of part of the farmyard next to the cottage, or interfere substantially with such use[6].' The right contended for in no way resembled a claim of 'possession or joint possession of part of the defendant's property.' In *Grigsby v Melville*[7], however, Brightman J doubted whether a right of storage in a cellar could constitute an easement in circumstances where the claim amounted to 'an

1 See *Crow v Wood* [1971] 1 QB 77. See also *Egerton v Harding* [1975] QB 62; (1975) 34 Cambridge LJ 34 (C. F. Kolbert).
2 [1952] Ch 488.
3 [1952] Ch 488 at 498.
4 This criterion has been applied in Australia. See *Bursill Enterprises Pty Ltd v Berger Bros Trading Co Pty Ltd* (1971) 45 ALJR 203.
5 [1967] Ch 194.
6 [1967] Ch 194 at 223.
7 [1972] 1 WLR 1355. See (1973) 37 Conv (NS) 60 (D. J. Hayton), where it is suggested that a right to park a car in a particular defined space may be incapable of creation as an easement.

exclusive right of user over the whole of the confined space representing the servient tenement[8].'

It must nevertheless be admitted that the criterion of non-exclusive possession does not seem to have been applied universally throughout the case law[9]. There are instances in which the courts have upheld as easements rights which clearly did constitute exclusive possession or user. It may be that the courts have in fact used the supposed requirement of non-exclusive user as a smokescreen for judicial discretion, invoking the requirement in order to strike down claims felt to be unmeritorious while suppressing the requirement in cases where it has been felt that a remedy should be given. In *Wright v Macadam*[10], for example, the Court of Appeal had no hesitation in recognising as an easement a right claimed by a hard-pressed tenant to store coal in a coal shed provided by her landlord. It may well be that this right extended to exclusive user[11], but it may also be the case that the Court of Appeal did not look particularly kindly upon the fact that the landlord had asserted a right to make an extra charge for use of the coal shed and had pulled down the coal shed before the date of the hearing. Likewise, in *Miller v Emcer Products Ltd*[12], it was held that the right to use a lavatory on another's premises was capable of constituting an easement—although this presumably involved an element of exclusive possession.

3. THE CREATION OF EASEMENTS AND PROFITS

An easement or profit is capable of existing *at law* only if certain conditions are fulfilled. *First*, the easement or profit must be held 'for an interest equivalent to an estate in fee simple absolute in possession or a term of years absolute[13].' *Second*, the easement or profit must be created by statute, by deed or by prescription. In all other cases, any easement or profit must be equitable. There is no exception even in the case of an easement or profit for a period not exceeding three years, since there is no analogy with the rules concerning the informal creation of legal leases[14]. In the absence of statutory or prescriptive creation, an easement or profit granted *informally* for a lesser period than three years must be merely equitable[15]. However, an equitable easement or profit may be created without compliance with any formality at all. An equitable easement or profit may arise

8 Brightman J's decision was upheld by the Court of Appeal ([1974] 1 WLR 80), but without further consideration of the question of exclusive user or possession.

9 There has even been a suggestion that *Copeland v Greenhalf* is 'a decision per incuriam'. See (1973) 32 Cambridge LJ 30 at 33 (J. R. Spencer).

10 [1949] 2 KB 744. See (1950) 66 LQR 302 (REM).

11 In *Grigsby v Melville* [1972] 1 WLR 1355 at 1364, Brightman J noted that the 'precise facts in *Wright v Macadam* in this respect are not wholly clear from the report and it is a little difficult to know whether the tenant had exclusive use of the coal shed or of any defined portion of it. To some extent a problem of this sort may be one of degree.'

12 [1956] Ch 304. See (1956) 72 LQR 172 (REM).

13 Law of Property Act 1925, s. 1(2)(a), p. 61f., ante. The creation of easements is subject to the rule against perpetuities. See *Dunn v Blackdown Properties Ltd* [1961] Ch 433.

14 See p. 392, ante.

15 See *Wood v Leadbitter* (1845) 13 M & W 838 at 843; *Mason v Clarke* [1954] 1 QB 460 at 468, 471 per Denning LJ.

simply on the basis of a written document not under seal[16], or even on the footing of an oral agreement[17], provided in either case that the transaction is a transaction for value or is supported by a sufficient act of part performance.

We must now examine the modes of creation of easements and profits. Here the first distinction which must be drawn is the vital distinction between grant and reservation. Easements and profits may come into existence by means of *either* grant *or* reservation, as can be illustrated by the following diagrams. The difference between grant and reservation turns upon the identity of the party in whose favour the easement or profit is created. In the examples which follow, let us use a right of way as a working basis for our discussion.

Grant arises typically where a landowner (V) disposes of part of his land[18], as in *Fig.* 68, to a stranger (P), on terms that P shall henceforth be entitled to an easement over the land retained by V. In this case the easement concerned is one created in favour of P, the *grantee of the land.*

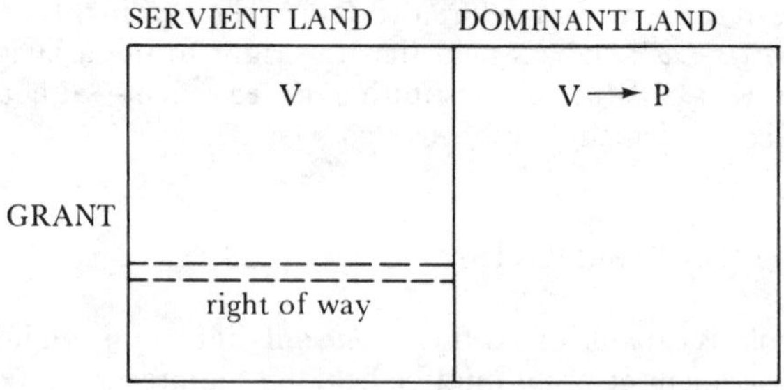

SERVIENT LAND DOMINANT LAND

V V→P

GRANT

right of way

Fig. 68

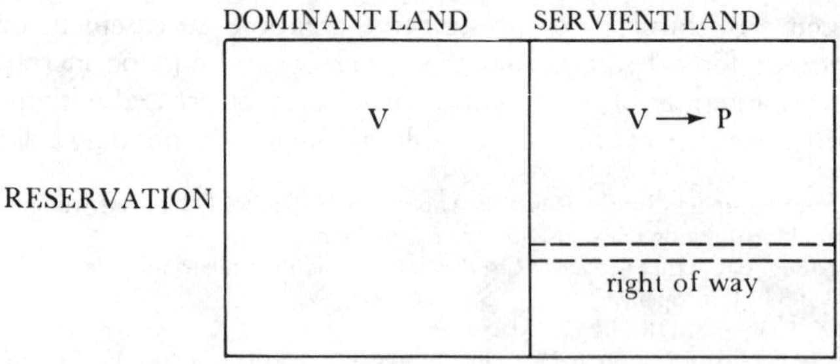

DOMINANT LAND SERVIENT LAND

V V→P

RESERVATION

right of way

Fig. 69

16 See *May v Belleville* [1905] 2 Ch 605; *Frogley v Earl of Lovelace* (1859) John 333. This result is merely yet another application of the doctrine of *Walsh v Lonsdale*, p. 398ff., ante.

17 See *McManus v Cooke* (1887) 35 Ch D 681.

18 Of course, grant need not occur *only* on the disposition of land. It can be effected at any time between freeholders.

Reservation arises where the original landowner (V) disposes of part of his land to P, as in *Fig.* 69, on terms that V shall nevertheless retain an easement over the land purchased by P. In this case the easement concerned is one created in favour of V, the *grantor of the land.*

The rules concerning the creation of rights of easement are made very much easier if this distinction between grant and reservation is borne clearly in mind. The essential difference between grant and reservation turns on whether the right in question is granted to the *grantee* of the land sold or reserved in favour of the *grantor* of that land. In the case of grant, the servient tenement is in the hands of V; in the case of reservation, the servient tenement is that of P.

In analysing any question concerning the creation of easements or profits, the first issue therefore relates to whether the right in question arises by way of grant or by way of reservation. We must look at the modes of grant and reservation respectively.

(1) Grant

Grant of an easement may be brought about by express grant, by implied grant, or by prescription.

(a) *Express grant*

Express grant may in turn arise in two cases—by means of express words of grant and by means of statute.

(i) *Express words of grant* This is the most usual form of grant and, as such, presents relatively few complications. The express words are normally incorporated in the conveyance or transfer of a legal estate in land where it is intended that the purchaser should enjoy certain rights by way of easement over the land retained by the vendor. There is no legal requirement that the grant should make any explicit reference to the dominant tenement or in any other way identify the land benefited by the easement[19]. After 1925 the grant of an easement or profit without words of limitation confers the most ample interest which the grantor of the easement is competent to confer, unless a contrary intention is apparent. Thus an easement granted expressly in a conveyance of the grantor's fee simple estate is effective to grant an easement for an interest equivalent to a fee simple. Likewise, an easement granted in connection with the creation of a leasehold estate is an easement for an interest equivalent to a term of years absolute[20].

19 See R. E. Megarry and H. W. R. Wade, op. cit., p. 807. The court simply examines all the relevant circumstances in order to determine whether there was in fact a dominant tenement benefited by the supposed easement. The rule on this point is different in other common law jurisdictions. In some states of Australia, for instance, no easement is enforceable against a third party unless the instrument which creates the easement clearly indicates both the land to which the benefit is appurtenant and the land which is subject to the burden of the easement. See Conveyancing Act 1919 (New South Wales), s. 88(1); *Maurice Toltz Pty Ltd v Macy's Emporium Pty Ltd* (1969) 91 WN (NSW) 591.

20 See p. 62, ante.

(ii) *Statute* Easements and profits may be granted expressly by statute. Such grants are often made in favour of public utilities for the purpose of the better management or execution of the function with which they are charged. Thus statutorily created easements exist in favour of public utility undertakings in respect of the provision and maintenance of such supplies as gas, water, electricity and sewers[1].

(b) *Implied grant*

There are certain cases in which the grant of an easement will be implied in favour of the purchaser of land. These situations of implied grant fall broadly into four categories.

(i) *Necessity* In certain circumstances the courts are willing to imply the grant of an easement on the ground of necessity. The classic case of necessity in this context is that of the 'land-locked close'. If V sells land to P which has no means of access except across land retained by V, it is clear that the courts will imply on behalf of P an easement of access even though the conveyance or transfer to P makes no express reference to such a right[2]. Indeed it seemed at one stage that the courts would go even further than this. In *Nickerson v Barraclough*[3], it was argued that, in circumstances of the kind now under consideration, V had expressly negatived any right of way in favour of P by the express terms of the conveyance of P's land. When the existence of a possible easement of necessity became a matter of dispute between the successors in title of V and P, Megarry V-C made reference at first instance to 'a rule of public policy which requires that land should not be rendered unusable by being landlocked[4].' He observed that

> There is a rule of public policy that no transaction should, without good reason, be treated as being effectual to deprive any land of a suitable means of access. Alternatively, the point might be put as a matter of construction: any transaction which, without good reason, appears to deprive land of any suitable means of access should, if at all possible, be construed as not producing this result.

In the instant case, Megarry V-C could see no good reason for depriving the land in question of any access to the highway. He regarded his conclusion as being supported by the longstanding rule that a grantor may not 'derogate from his grant[5].' Here the original vendor had sold building land as such and, in the view of Megarry V-C, to negative any means of access to that land in the terms of a conveyance would constitute 'a plain case of derogation[6].'

Megarry V-C's judgment was, however, reversed by the Court of Appeal[7].

1 See J. F. Garner (1956) 20 Conv (NS) 208: 'Statutory "Easements".'
2 *Pinnington v Galland* (1853) 9 Exch 1.
3 [1980] Ch 325. See (1980) 96 LQR 187 (P. Jackson); (1980) 130 NLJ 204 (H. W. Wilkinson).
4 [1980] Ch 325 at 334. See E. H. Bodkin (1973) 89 LQR 87: 'Easements of Necessity and Public Policy'.
5 See p. 594, post.
6 [1980] Ch 325 at 335.
7 [1981] 2 WLR 773.

Brightman LJ ruled that 'the doctrine of way of necessity is not founded upon public policy at all but upon an implication from the circumstances.' The Court held that a way of necessity can exist only in association with a grant of land and rests on the implication, drawn from the circumstances of the case, that unless some way is implied a parcel of land will be inaccessible. Considerations of public policy are relevant therefore only to the extent that the courts may *frustrate* a contract where the underlying intention is contrary to public policy.

Where an easement of necessity is claimed by way of implied grant, it is not fatal to the claim that some of the surrounding land should belong to third parties and not to the original vendor[8]. It is, however, vital that the necessity pleaded by the purchaser or by his successor in title should have existed at the date of the conveyance of the land and not be merely a form of necessity which arose after that date[9].

(ii) *Common intention* Easements may be implied in favour of the grantee of property in order to give effect to a common intention of the grantor and grantee of that property. Such easements may not be essentially different from those mentioned under the last head, in that a common intention to grant a particular easement will normally be found only in cases of necessity[10]. In *Pwllbach Colliery Co Ltd v Woodman*[11], Lord Parker of Waddington stated that the law will readily imply the grant of 'such easements as may be necessary to give effect to the common intention of the parties to a grant of real property, with reference to the manner or purposes in and for which the land granted . . . is to be used.' Lord Parker added, however, that

> it is essential for this purpose that the parties should intend that the subject of the grant . . . should be used in some definite and particular manner. It is not enough that the subject of the grant . . . should be intended to be used in a manner which may or may not involve this definite and particular use.'

This principle was illustrated in *Wong v Beaumont Property Trust Ltd*[12]. Here the defendant's predecessor in title had leased the basement of certain premises to the plaintiff's predecessor in title for the express purpose of use as a restaurant. The plaintiff later bought the remainder of the lease, intending to use the premises as a Chinese restaurant. He covenanted to comply with public health regulations and to eliminate all noxious smells and odours. In fact, unknown to the parties at the date of the assignment of the lease, these obligations could be performed only by the installation of a new ventilation system leading through the upstairs premises retained by the defendant. The Court of Appeal held that the plaintiff was entitled to assert an easement of necessity in respect of the construction of the ventilation duct which alone would enable him to comply both with the terms of the lease and with public health regulations.

8 See *Serff v Acton Local Board* (1886) 31 Ch D 679.
9 See *Midland Rly Co v Miles* (1886) 33 Ch D 632.
10 See, e.g. *Nickerson v Barraclough* [1980] Ch 325 at 336, where Megarry V-C expressed the view that a 'way of necessity' should be 'more accurately referred to as a way implied from the common intention of the parties, based on a necessity apparent from the deeds.'
11 [1915] AC 634 at 646f.
12 [1965] 1 QB 173. See (1964) 80 LQR 322 (REM).

(iii) *Quasi-easements* A third category of implied grant was confirmed by the rule in *Wheeldon v Burrows*[13]. This doctrine is but one specific illustration of the more general rule in English law that a grantor 'may not derogate from his grant.' In other words, he must not grant land to another on terms which effectively negative the utility of the grant for the grantee. This rule against derogation from grant has been described as a 'principle which merely embodies in a legal maxim a rule of common honesty[14].'

The rule in *Wheeldon v Burrows* confers upon the grantee of land (i.e., P in *Fig.* 68[15]) the benefit of any user over land retained by the grantor (i.e., V) which the grantor had found it convenient to exercise on his own behalf during the period when, prior to the conveyance to the grantee, both the land granted and the land now retained were within the common ownership of the grantor. Thus any rights over the tenement now retained by V which V had previously found to be necessary for the proper enjoyment and utilisation of the tenement now granted away will, under the rule in *Wheeldon v Burrows*, pass to the grantee, P. However, since those rights could not have been said to constitute easements before the conveyance to P—for the simple reason that both tenements were under the common ownership and occupation of V[16]—those rights are usually referred to as *quasi-easements*.

There are certain limitations upon the kinds of right which may pass to a grantee under the rule in *Wheeldon v Burrows*. In that case Thesiger LJ expounded the rule in these terms:

> [O]n the grant by the owner of a tenement of part of that tenement as it is then used and enjoyed, there will pass to the grantee all those continuous and apparent easements (by which, of course, I mean *quasi* easements), or, in other words, all those easements which are necessary to the reasonable enjoyment of the property granted, and which have been and are at the time of the grant used by the owners of the entirety for the benefit of the part granted[17].

Although there seems to be some uncertainty, it is probably better to regard the requirement of 'continuous and apparent' user as being merely an alternative to the requirement of necessity, with the result that the rule is satisfied if either of these factors is present in conjunction with an element of user right up until the date of the grant[18]. It has been clear since *Borman v Griffith*[19] that the rule in *Wheeldon v Burrows* applies not only to legal grants (e.g., on the conveyance of an estate in fee simple or term of years), but also to grants which take effect only in equity (e.g., on a contract for a lease[20]).

13 (1879) 12 Ch D 31.
14 *Harmer v Jumbil (Nigeria) Tin Areas Ltd* [1921] 1 Ch 200 at 225 per Younger LJ. See also (1964) 80 LQR 244 (D. W. Elliott).
15 See p. 590, ante.
16 See p. 584, ante.
17 (1879) 12 Ch D 31 at 49. The *rule* in *Wheeldon v Burrows* is to be distinguished from the actual decision in that case, which concerned implied reservation, p. 603, post.
18 See R. E. Megarry and H. W. R. Wade, op. cit., p. 834. See also *Ward v Kirkland* [1967] Ch 194 at 224; (1967) 83 LQR 240 (A. W. B. Simpson).
19 [1930] 1 Ch 493. See (1930) 46 LQR 271 (HP); (1932) 4 Cambridge LJ 219 (KKL).
20 See p. 398, ante.

The conditions laid down by Thesiger LJ for the creation of quasi-easements are not applied with great strictness by the courts. The requirement of 'continuous and apparent' user has been held to be satisfied by any user which is enjoyed over substantial periods of time and which is discoverable or detectable on 'a careful inspection by a person ordinarily conversant with the subject[1].' A worn track provides evidence of 'continuous and apparent' user[2], as indeed does an 'underground drain into which water runs from the eaves of a house[3].'

(iv) *Law of Property Act 1925, s. 62* Another form of implied grant is made possible by the operation of the 'word-saving' provision contained in section 62 of the Law of Property Act 1925[4]. Section 62(1) contains 'general words' which, unless excluded in express terms[5], imply into any conveyance of a legal estate in land a number of rights thenceforth to be enjoyed by the grantee of that estate. Under section 62(1), every conveyance of land

shall be deemed to include and shall by virtue of this Act operate to convey, with the land, all buildings, erections, fixtures, commons, hedges, ditches, fences, ways, waters, watercourses, liberties, privileges, easements, rights, and advantages whatsoever, appertaining or reputed to appertain to the land or any part thereof, or, at the time of conveyance, demised, occupied, or enjoyed with, or reputed or known as part or parcel of or appurtenant to the land or any part thereof.

Section 62(1) is an exceedingly ample provision. It has the effect of passing to any grantee of land the benefit of existing easements and profits which are appurtenant to that land[6]. However, the provision goes even further, and under certain circumstances creates entirely new easements and profits out of many kinds of quasi-easement, right and privilege subsisting at the date of the conveyance which activates section 62(1). It is thus possible that rights which were not easements properly so called before the conveyance may be translated to the status of easement thereafter.

Section 62(1) of the Law of Property Act 1925 is therefore, in many ways, of somewhat wider significance than the rule in *Wheeldon v Burrows.* Although section 62(1) is not competent to convert into easements rights which, by their very nature, are not capable of existing as easements, there is for instance no requirement that the rights to which section 62(1) has reference should be 'continuous and apparent' or 'necessary to the reasonable enjoyment of the land granted[7].' Moreover, section 62(1) seems to provide a mode of implied grant relevant to profits[8], which are not covered by the rule in *Wheeldon v Burrows.*

1 See *Pyer v Carter* (1857) 1 H & N 916 at 922 per Watson B.
2 See *Hansford v Jago* [1921] 1 Ch 322.
3 R. E. Megarry and H. W. R. Wade, op. cit., p. 835.
4 See P. Jackson (1966) 30 Conv (NS) 340: 'Easements and General Words'.
5 Law of Property Act 1925, s. 62(4).
6 See p. 62, ante.
7 In *Goldberg v Edwards* [1950] Ch 247, for instance, the Court of Appeal held that section 62(1) could apply to a way of access through a landlord's house which was clearly not necessary for the tenant in view of the fact that he had a quite separate means of access to the premises which had been let to him. See (1950) 66 LQR 302 (REM). See also *Ward v Kirkland* [1967] Ch 194.
8 See *White v Williams* [1922] 1 KB 727.

There are, however, several important restrictions upon the operation of section 62(1). The provision is activated only by a deed of conveyance of a legal estate in land, although it is immaterial whether that legal estate be a freehold (fee simple) or leasehold (term of years absolute)[9]. Section 62(1) cannot ever be invoked by a tenant under a contract for a lease[10].

An even more severe limitation upon the scope of section 62(1) takes the form of a judge-made rule which drastically restricts the number of situations in which the provision is conceivably relevant. In *Sovmots Investments Ltd v Secretary of State for the Environment*[11], Lord Edmund-Davies confirmed that section 62(1) operates only where there has been some 'diversity of ownership or occupation of the quasi-dominant and quasi-servient tenements prior to the conveyance[12].' This gloss is undoubtedly correct, since without at least some element of prior diversity of ownership or occupation it would be difficult to point to any 'rights' or 'liberties' or 'privileges' which might meaningfully have existed before the conveyance to which section 62(1) relates.

This last restriction has the effect that the primary impact of section 62(1) upon the implied grant of easements is in the context of the landlord-tenant relationship, for it is in precisely such a case that the required diversity of occupation prior to conveyance can be found. Suppose that a landlord, L, owns two adjacent plots of land in fee simple. He himself lives on one plot and leases the other plot to T. Suppose further that during the currency of the lease L permits T to use a means of access and egress which runs across the plot which L occupies. T's user is 'precarious' in the sense that L could, if he so wished, revoke at any time the permission thus granted for T to use this route. In other words, T's user is by grace and favour of L, and not as a matter of entitlement under his lease.

Suppose finally that L then by deed grants T a legal estate in the land which T has occupied heretofore. This grant by deed may take the form of a renewal of the term of years which T has enjoyed in the past, or it may take the form of a conveyance to T of the freehold reversion in the property formerly held by T on lease (see *Fig.* 70).

In either case the conveyance to T will have the effect of vesting in T a legal estate (whether freehold or leasehold) coupled with a right by way of easement to continue against L the user which had previously been merely precarious[13].

9 'Conveyance' is defined in Law of Property Act 1925, s. 205(1)(ii), p. 228, ante.
10 See *Borman v Griffith* [1930] 1 Ch 493.
11 [1979] AC 144 at 176, following *Long v Gowlett* [1923] 2 Ch 177 at 200 per Sargant J. See H. W. Wilkinson (1977) 127 NLJ 695: 'Centre Point Problems.'
12 See C. Harpum (1977) 41 Conv (NS) 415: 'Easements and Centre Point: Old Problems Resolved in a Novel Setting'; [1979] Conv 113: '*Long v Gowlett*: A Strong Fortress.' Compare P. Smith [1978] Conv 449: 'Centre Point: Faulty Towers with Shaky Foundations.'
13 See *International Tea Stores Co v Hobbs* [1903] 2 Ch 165; compare, however, *Green v Ashco Horticulturist Ltd* [1966] 2 All ER 232, where Cross J held that the intermittent consensual privilege enjoyed by a tenant in respect of access through his landlord's premises was not such a user as could have been the subject of a grant of a legal right, and for this reason section 62(1) was inapplicable. In this case there was evidence that the user was extremely precarious in the sense that the access in question had been made available to the tenant only at times when the landlord did not require the access for his own purposes. See also *Wright v Macadam* [1949] 2 KB 744, where the Court of Appeal applied section 62(1) on the renewal of a term of years.

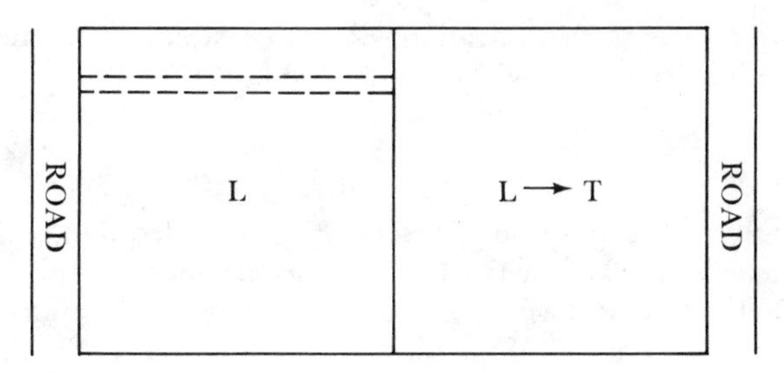

Fig. 70

Such is the direct result of the fact that section 62(1) of the Law of Property Act 1925 implies into the conveyance from L to T all such users as previously comprised 'privileges ... appertaining ... to the land.' What was merely a licence before the conveyance has been converted into an easement. Moreover, since T's new easement has been incorporated by implication within a deed of conveyance, it is clothed with legal character and binds any successor in title of L.

Section 62(1) thus provides a means whereby a purely precarious user may be elevated into a legal easement upon the conveyance of a legal estate to a tenant, thus giving him a right of indefinite enjoyment[14]. The operation of section 62(1) turns, however, upon the fact that prior to the conveyance there was diversity of occupation in respect of the two tenements. There is, incidentally, no reason why precisely the same effect should not occur in relation to a conveyance made in favour of someone who already occupies the quasi-dominant tenement, not by virtue of a lease, but by virtue of a mere licence to occupy. The requirement of prior diversity of occupation would be equally satisfied in such a case, and the operation of section 62(1) would be attracted by any conveyance of a legal estate (whether freehold or leasehold) to the licensee.

The only way in which the far-reaching implication of section 62(1) can be averted is by means of an expression of contrary intention[15]. Thus, if the conveyance to T in the example above had expressly excluded from the scope of the grant any liberties or privileges previously enjoyed by T, the conveyance would have been ineffective to pass those liberties or privileges by way of easement. The court retains an equitable jurisdiction to rectify any conveyance which mistakenly transfers to a grantee more rights than were intended in the contract for sale. Thus, in *Clark v Barnes*[16], the court rectified a conveyance which had failed to exclude as against the purchaser the user of a right of way over other land retained by the vendor. The equitable jurisdiction was available to rectify the vendor's omission to exclude the effect of section 62(1), even though the purchaser maintained that he had contracted to purchase the land on the assumption that the right of way in question was included in the conveyance.

14 See *Goldberg v Edwards* [1950] Ch 247.
15 Law of Property Act 1925, s. 62(4).
16 [1929] 2 Ch 368.

However, the remedy of rectification will not be extended in order to assist any vendor who has acted otherwise than in good faith[17].

(c) *Prescription*

A third method of acquisition of easements is provided by the law relating to prescription. This area of the law has become extremely complex over the years and in 1966 the Law Reform Committee by a majority recommended the total abolition of the concept of prescriptive acquisition[18]. No reform has yet occurred, however, and the matter awaits clarification at the hands of the Law Commission, which is currently preparing a major revision of the law relating to rights appurtenant to land.

We have already seen that there is a strong policy bias in the English law of property towards recognising the legitimacy of a user which has been exercised de facto over long periods of time[19]. It is this consideration which underlies the law of limitation and adverse possession, and it is the importance of long user which also affords the basis for prescriptive acquisition. Prescription provides the legal ground on which the courts may uphold as lawful the long user of any right in the nature of an easement. Although there may be no evidence of any actual grant, the law of prescription spells an often fictitious grant out of the fact of prolonged enjoyment of rights over the land of another. As Fry J said in *Moody v Steggles*[20], it is 'the habit, and . . . the duty, of the court, so far as it lawfully can, to clothe the fact with the right.' However, the process of prescription must be distinguished from the process of limitation and adverse possession, because the latter merely extinguishes existing titles whereas prescription has the effect of generating new rights. Limitation has a negative and extinctive effect, whereas prescription is positive and acquisitive in its mode of operation[1].

(i) *General principles of prescriptive acquisition* The basis of prescriptive acquisition is not merely long user per se. In order that a claim of prescription should succeed, it is necessary that there should have been a history of continuous user *as of right*. It is only against the background of assumed entitlement that the courts can go so far as to imply the existence of the grant from which the lawful exercise of an easement is deemed to have derived.

17 See R. E. Megarry and H. W. R. Wade, op. cit., p. 841.
18 *14th Report of the Law Reform Committee* (Cmnd 3100, 1966), para. 32. A minority of the Committee recommended the retention of a prescription period of 12 years' user in respect of easements. See (1967) 30 MLR 189 (H. W. Wilkinson). Among the main considerations leading to the proposal that the prescriptive acquisition of easements be abolished was the argument that 'there is little, if any, moral justification for the acquisition of easements by prescription, a process which either involves an intention to get something for nothing or, where there is no intention to acquire any right, is purely accidental.'
19 See pp. 49, 93ff., ante.
20 (1879) 12 Ch D 261 at 265.
1 See M. J. Goodman (1968) 32 Conv (NS) 270: 'Adverse Possession or Prescription? Problems of Conflict'.

The nature of the user which must be shown as the basis of a prescriptive claim has traditionally been described in terms of the Roman law concept of prescriptive acquisition. It is commonly said that the user must be *nec vi, nec clam, nec precario*[2]. That is, the user must have been exercised without force, without secrecy and without permission. It is clear that forcible user will vitiate any claim of entitlement as of right. The notion of forcible user for this purpose includes not merely a violent exercise of the user, but also any insistence upon a particular user in the face of continuing protest from the supposedly servient owner[3].

Nor must the user be surreptitious or in any way concealed. In *Union Lighterage Co v London Graving Dock Co*[4], for instance, the Court of Appeal declined to accept that a prescriptive claim had been established by a defendant who fixed the side of a dock to the soil of a wharf by means of underground rods which remained undetected for more than 20 years. Romer LJ held that a prescriptive right to an easement over another's land could be acquired only 'when the enjoyment has been open—that is to say, of such a character that an ordinary owner of the land, diligent in the protection of his interests, would have, or must be taken to have, a reasonable opportunity of becoming aware of that enjoyment[5].'

Any user which is exercised under licence is incapable of supporting a claim of prescriptive acquisition. The element of permission inherent in such user is destructive of any claim that the user was a matter of entitlement[6]. However, whereas user by way of permission or licence precludes any prescriptive claim, the entire law of prescription rests upon some notion of *acquiescence*, i.e., an acquiescence by the servient owner in the exercise by a dominant owner of rights which are acknowledged to be a matter of entitlement in favour of the latter. In *Dalton v Angus & Co*[7], Fry J took the view that, in this sense, acquiescence necessarily presupposes on the part of the servient owner '(1) a knowledge of the acts done; (2) a power in him to stop the acts or to sue in respect of them; and (3) an abstinence on his part from the exercise of such power.' In *Dalton v Angus & Co*, the House of Lords held that the plaintiff had acquired a right of support for his building by reason of 20 years' enjoyment, and could therefore sue the defendant in respect of the damage caused by the removal of the lateral support provided by the latter's adjoining house[8]. It is, in practice, difficult to see how such a prescriptive claim could have been frustrated by the adjoining owner otherwise than by demolishing his building within the prescription period of 20 years. At common law, however, a servient owner could always frustrate the

2 See *Solomon v Mystery of Vintners* (1859) 4 H & N 585 at 602.
3 *Dalton v Angus & Co* (1881) 6 App Cas 740 at 786 per Bowen J.
4 [1902] 2 Ch 557.
5 [1902] 2 Ch 557 at 571.
6 The practice of periodic payment by the claimant is not required in order to bar his claim, but tends to provide evidence that permission for the exercise of the user was regularly sought and renewed. See R. E. Megarry and H. W. R. Wade, op. cit., p. 843; *Gardner v Hodgson's Kingston Brewery Co Ltd* [1903] AC 229. On the question of knowledge by an agent, see *Diment v N. H. Foot Ltd* [1974] 1 WLR 1427.
7 (1881) 6 App Cas 740 at 773f.
8 As to the importance of a 20-year period of user, see later, p. 601, post.

prescriptive acquisition of a right of access to light by erecting a 'spite fence' to obstruct the light. Nowadays the servient owner can achieve the same objective under the Rights of Light Act 1959 by registering a notional 'spite fence' in the local land charges register[9].

A further feature of the general law of prescription consists in the fact that prescription is traditionally based upon user in fee simple. The user alleged must be user 'by or on behalf of a fee simple owner against a fee simple owner[10].' There can therefore be no prescriptive acquisition at common law of an easement or profit for life or for a term of years[11], and any claim to prescriptive acquisition at common law must inevitably fall to the ground if the user began against an occupier of the servient land who was not entitled in fee simple (e.g., a tenant for life or a tenant for years)[12].

(ii) *Grounds of prescriptive acquisition* At common law prescription depends upon the idea that long user is evidence of past grant. In other words, the fact of a long user is deemed to provide evidence that the easement or profit now claimed was once duly granted in proper form. Thus any easement established by prescription is necessarily legal. The theory of prescriptive acquisition is, however, heavily marked by legal fiction.

At common law it was presumed that a long user stemmed originally from a valid grant if that user had continued from time immemorial. Thus prescription was established only where a user had continued 'from time whereof the memory of men runneth not to the contrary[13],' a date which was somewhat arbitrarily fixed as 1189[14]. Any user which predated this point in time could provide an unimpeachable basis for a claim of prescriptive acquisition. With the passage of time, it came to be presumed by the courts of common law that if a user as of right for more than 20 years could be shown at any point, that user must have commenced before 1189. This fiction was a necessary aid to the common law for it 'reduced to reasonable proportions a burden of proof which in theory was absurdly onerous[15].' However, even this presumption of user since 1189 was apt to be frustrated if it could be shown that a particular user could not possibly have been exercised or enjoyed at all times since 1189. Thus an easement of access to light could not be claimed in respect of a building which had clearly been constructed only since 1189[16]. In such a case the presumption of user dating back to 1189 was effectively rebutted.

9 See Rights of Light Act 1959, s. 2.
10 See R. E. Megarry and H. W. R. Wade, op. cit., p. 844.
11 *Wheaton v Maple & Co* [1893] 3 Ch 48 at 63 per Lindley LJ; *Kilgour v Gaddes* [1904] 1 KB 457 at 460 per Collins MR.
12 Some of the problems connected with tenure by limited owners are eased by the provisions of the Prescription Act 1832. Moreover, in *Pugh v Savage* [1970] 2 QB 373, the Court of Appeal took the view that a user which commenced against a fee simple owner is not prejudiced if the land in question is subsequently occupied by a tenant during the period required for prescription.
13 *Coke upon Littleton* (19th edn., London 1832), p. 170.
14 Statute of Westminster I, 1275, c. 39.
15 See R. E. Megarry and H. W. R. Wade, op. cit., p. 847.
16 See *Bury v Pope* (1588) Cro Eliz 118; *Duke of Norfolk v Arbuthnot* (1880) 5 CPD 390.

In order to remedy the deficiencies of presumed user since 1189, the courts then developed the doctrine of the 'lost modern grant.'[17] This doctrine conceded that user dating back to 1189 could not be proved. It therefore allowed prescriptive claims to be made on the basis of a fiction that 20 years' user provided evidence of a 'modern grant' (i.e., a grant by deed at some date after 1189) which had since been misplaced and lost[18]. The doctrine of 'lost modern grant' was upheld by the House of Lords in *Dalton v Angus & Co*[19], the only conditions for its application being proof of 20 years' enjoyment as of right, coupled with the existence of a possible grantor at some time during this period of user[20].

Proof of continuous user as of right for a period of 20 years is therefore usually sufficient to found a claim of prescriptive acquisition nowadays[1]. Some of the difficulties of the common law are dealt with in the Prescription Act 1832, but this statute has been justly described as 'one of the worst drafted Acts on the Statute Book[2].' In respect of easements other than easements of light, the 1832 Act provides that user as of right and without interruption for 20 years cannot be defeated by evidence that such user commenced after 1189[3]. An easement enjoyed for 40 years as of right and without interruption is deemed to be 'absolute and indefeasible', unless enjoyed by written consent[4]. The periods of time pleaded in support of a prescriptive claim under the statute must be the periods 'next before some suit or action' in which the claim is challenged. There is a further provision to the effect that no act of obstruction is deemed to be an interruption until it has been submitted to or acquiesced in for one year after the party interrupted had notice both of the interruption and of the person making it[5].

Slightly different statutory rules apply to the prescriptive acquisition of easements of light. Under the Prescription Act 1832, the actual enjoyment of access to light for a period of 20 years without interruption renders that access 'absolute and indefeasible' unless it was enjoyed merely by reason of written consent or agreement[6].

The Prescription Act 1832 also provides that a profit which has been enjoyed as of right and without interruption for 30 years 'next before some suit or action'

17 In *Dalton v Angus & Co* (1877) 3 QBD 85 at 94, Lush J made his classic reference to the 'revolting fiction' of the lost modern grant.
18 See R. E. Megarry and H. W. R. Wade, op. cit., p. 848ff.
19 (1881) 6 App Cas 740.
20 It may even be the case that the presumption of a lost modern grant cannot be rebutted by evidence that no grant was in fact ever made. See R. E. Megarry and H. W. R. Wade, op. cit., p. 849.
1 See *Tehidy Minerals Ltd v Norman* [1971] 2 QB 528.
2 *14th Report of the Law Reform Committee* (Cmnd 3100, 1966), para. 40.
3 Prescription Act 1832, s. 2.
4 Prescription Act 1832, s. 1.
5 Prescription Act 1832, s. 4.
6 Prescription Act 1832, s. 3. There is no requirement here that the user should have been 'as of right'. See *Colls v Home and Colonial Stores Ltd* [1904] AC 179; *Allen v Greenwood* [1980] Ch 119; [1979] Conv 298 (F. R. Crane).

cannot be defeated by proof that the profit arose only after 1189[7]. Moreover, a period of 60 years' user on the same terms makes the prescriptive claim to the profit 'absolute and indefeasible[8].'

(2) Reservation

We have now dealt with the creation of easements and profits by grant. We must now turn to the creation of similar rights by reservation[9].

Reservation is the converse of grant, and occurs where a landowner reserves for himself easements or profits over a portion of his land which he conveys to a third party. The technique of reservation is nowadays much simpler than it used to be before the enactment of the property legislation of 1925. Once again, reservation may be either express or implied.

(a) *Express reservation*

If a vendor wishes to retain any right in the nature of an easement or profit in respect of land which he conveys to a purchaser, it is open to him to do so by express words contained in the deed of conveyance or document of transfer. Such words are effective to reserve the rights in question for the vendor by virtue of section 65(1) of the Law of Property Act 1925, which provides that

> A reservation of a legal estate shall operate at law without any execution of the conveyance by the grantee of the legal estate out of which the reservation is made, or any regrant by him, so as to create the legal estate reserved, and so as to vest the same in possession in the person (whether being the grantor or not) for whose benefit the reservation is made.

The precise extent of a reservation is ultimately a matter of construction for the court in the light of the general principle that the terms of a grant are, in cases of doubt or ambivalence, to be construed *against* the grantor. In the past the courts were accustomed to regard the reservation of an easement as constituting in law a 'regrant' of that easement by the purchaser of the servient tenement, with the consequence that the *contra proferentem* rule of construction operated *not* in favour of the servient owner but in favour of the party who had in effect reserved the easement for himself (i.e., the dominant owner). It was thought that the balance of advantage conferred by this rule of construction would be reversed by the provision in section 65(1) that a reservation after 1925 shall now 'operate at law without . . . any regrant'. However, the balance of authority is still in favour of the proposition that an express reservation of an easement or profit is to be construed against the servient owner and in favour of the dominant tenant[10].

7 Prescription Act 1832, s. 1.
8 Ibid.
9 See p. 590f., ante.
10 See *Johnstone v Holdway* [1963] 1 QB 601; (1963) 79 LQR 182 (REM); *St Edmundsbury and Ipswich Diocesan Board of Finance v Clark (No. 2)* [1975] 1 WLR 468. Compare *Cordell v Second Clanfield Properties Ltd* [1969] 2 Ch 9.

(b) *Implied reservation*

It is a rule of general application that if a vendor wishes to reserve any rights over land granted away, he must do so expressly. In *Wheeldon v Burrows*[11], a vendor claimed a right of access to light as impliedly reserved in his conveyance of land to a purchaser. This claim was denied by the Court of Appeal on the ground that reservation can arise only by reason of express stipulation in the terms of the conveyance. To this rule it appears that there are only two exceptions.

(i) *Necessity* The implication of a reservation of necessity is rare. The only circumstances in which such an implied reservation will be accepted by the courts arises where a vendor conveys all the land which surrounds the land which he retains, in circumstances in which the only possible access to the land retained lies across the land conveyed. An easement of access will be implied in such a case, since without such a reservation the vendor's land would be rendered unusable[12]. It is not sufficient that the easement claimed should be necessary to the reasonable enjoyment of the land retained: it is essential that, without the easement, the vendor's land should be completely sterilised. In *Ray v Hazeldine*[13], for instance, Kekewich J held that no easement could be impliedly reserved where the vendor retained an adjoining property which permitted a means of access. In order that an easement of necessity should arise by implied reservation, it is vital that the vendor's land should have become completely landlocked.

(ii) *Common intention* In rare circumstances an easement will be implied into a conveyance on behalf of the vendor in order to effectuate some common intention which was left unexpressed by that conveyance[14]. However, a heavy onus of proof rests upon the vendor who wishes to show that a reservation was mutually intended[15].

4. EXTINGUISHMENT OF EASEMENTS AND PROFITS

There is no statutory provision for the discharge or modification of easements or profits which have become redundant or obstructive with the effluxion of time[16]. There are, however, several ways in which easements and profits may be extinguished at common law.

(1) Unity of possession and ownership

It follows from the characteristics attributed to easements and profits that any

11 (1879) 12 Ch D 31.
12 See p. 592, ante. See also *Titchmarsh v Royston Water Co Ltd* (1899) 81 LT 673; *Barry v Hasseldine* [1952] Ch 835.
13 [1904] 2 Ch 17.
14 *Pwllbach Colliery Co v Woodman* [1915] AC 634, p. 593, ante.
15 See *Re Webb's Lease* [1951] Ch 808 at 820 per Evershed MR.
16 Compare Law of Property Act 1925, s. 84, p. 634, post.

right of this nature must be extinguished automatically if at any time the dominant and servient tenements pass into the common ownership and possession of the same person[17].

(2) Release

Release may be express or implied.

(a) *Express release*

The dominant owner may release his rights expressly. Such release must be contained in a deed in the case of a legal easement or profit[18]. However, in the case of release of an equitable easement or profit, it is sufficient if the dominant owner releases his rights by means of an informal agreement which is supported by consideration given by the servient owner or which is attended by circumstances in which it would be inequitable to revive the rights thereby abrogated[19].

(b) *Implied release*

An easement or profit may be released impliedly in cases of abandonment of the exercise of the right coupled with a clear intention to release the right in question[20]. The requisite intention to abandon is usually presumed after 20 years' non-user of an easement or profit[1], but this presumption may be set aside if the non-user is explicable on some other basis[2]. Furthermore, alterations to, or demolition of, a structure situated on the dominant tenement (e.g., a mill which enjoys an easement of water[3]) may provide the required evidence of an intention to abandon user.

17 See *Tyrringham's Case* (1584) 4 Co Rep 36b at 38a; *Buckby v Coles* (1814) 5 Taunt 311.
18 *Lovell v Smith* (1857) 3 CB NS 120 at 127.
19 See *Davies v Marshall* (1861) 10 CB NS 697 at 710.
20 *Swan v Sinclair* [1924] 1 Ch 254.
1 *Moore v Rawson* (1824) 3 B & C 332 at 339. Compare, however, *Cook v Bath Corpn* (1868) LR 6 Eq 177.
2 See, e.g., *James v Stevenson* [1893] AC 162.
3 See *Liggins v Inge* (1831) 7 Bing 682 at 693.

CHAPTER 18

Covenants and the planning of land use

Another common means by which landowners have attempted to control the use of land is found in the law relating to covenants. In the context of real property a 'covenant' is an agreement under seal in which one party (the 'covenantor') promises another party (the 'covenantee') that he will or will not engage in some specified activity in relation to a defined area of land. A covenant is therefore an agreement which creates an obligation and which is contained in a deed. Such an agreement has legal efficacy because the seal imports consideration and averts the strict question of whether consideration has been provided for the promise given by the covenantor. The covenant is therefore clearly enforceable between covenantor and covenantee as a form of contract.

Covenants enjoy a position of importance in the law of real property because they provide a way in which certain obligations relating to land use can be made to 'run with the land' so as to benefit and burden not merely the original covenanting parties but also their successors in title. By operating outside the realm of contract, covenants may effectively impose controls over the use of land which bind all parties into whose hands the land may come at any future time.

The basic principles governing the creation and enforcement of covenants respecting land were formulated during a period when government agencies played little part in planning the use and development of the community's land resources. It was, accordingly, both natural and inevitable that the law should facilitate and enforce agreements by which private landowners sought to regulate the use of land by private treaty. In this chapter we shall examine the legal principles which give effect to *private* covenants in respect of *freehold land*[1]. The device of the covenant provides an important facility for the private planning of land use. Although this facility has more recently been socialised on a more general basis in the form of planning legislation, the law of covenants still retains a significance for land lawyers. Increasingly complex schemes have been introduced in order to make private covenants even more widely enforceable as between freeholders not least because the existence of valid and enforceable covenants affecting land may make that land much more valuable on the open market. The existence of a comprehensive scheme of restrictive covenants binding all purchasers may greatly enhance the market attraction of a particular site or area of development, in that purchasers are thereby assured

1 Covenants relating to leasehold land were discussed in Chapter 12, p. 402ff., ante.

that local amenities or the desirable characteristics of the neighbourhood will be preserved indefinitely in the future.

Covenants may take the form of either *positive* covenants or *negative* covenants. A positive covenant is one which imposes on the covenantor an obligation to perform some specified activity in relation to a defined piece of land. A positive covenant may, for instance, stipulate that a neighbour shall maintain the covenantee's boundary fence in good repair. A negative covenant, however, is a covenant which restricts disadvantageous developments on other land in the vicinity of the covenantee's property. A negative (or 'restrictive') covenant may, for example, preclude the covenantor from using his own land for the purpose of conducting trade or business. Such a covenant clearly promotes the amenity enjoyed by the covenantee on his land, by curtailing the potential scope of the activities conducted on the covenantor's land. The negative covenant may enable the covenantee to live in pleasant surroundings untroubled by the presence of nearby factories belching smoke or by neighbours who insist upon using their homes as a base for private commercial enterprise.

As we have already noted, a covenant is enforceable as a contract—but only between the original covenantor and covenantee. However, if the legal analysis of covenants stopped at this point, private agreements concluded between covenantor and covenantee would have no enduring impact upon third parties. The doctrine of privity of contract ensures that only the contracting parties may claim the benefit or be required to suffer the burden of contractual terms. It is, however, of vital importance that the benefit and burden created by a private covenant should be capable of transmission to third parties. Otherwise any covenantor might well free himself of his obligations under the covenant by the simple expedient of a collusive sale of his land to a friend who immediately reconveys to him. It is essential, for both ethical and commercial reasons that the benefit and burden of a covenant should run with the land to which they relate, no matter into whose hands the land may subsequently pass.

This result is to a large extent achieved by the law governing covenants in respect of freehold land. However, there is a certain public interest that the law of covenants should be clear, and for this reason the law lays down strict rules for determining the circumstances in which covenants are not merely to have contractual force but also to impose benefits and burdens upon third parties. It is important that these rules should tend to be restrictive rather than over-broad. If covenants of *any* kind, however loose or ill-defined, were to bind third parties, this would have the effect of making the encumbered land effectively unmarketable. No purchaser would wish to buy land under circumstances where its future use had already been fettered by trivial or obscure covenants governing the activities which are permissible on that land. As Professor H. W. R. Wade has said,

> It is for good reason that the policy of the law has preserved the frontier between contract and property. If there were no frontier, there would be no limit to the new incidents of property which could be invented. But rights which can bind third parties ought to be of a limited and familiar kind; for otherwise purchasers might have to investigate an infinite variety of incumbrances, and would often have no means of knowing the real effect of some fancy or imaginative transaction to which they were strangers. Therefore

the law has striven to draw lines of demarcation round the special interests which, exceptionally, may be created by contract or covenant[2].

Both law and equity thus provide strict rules relating to the enforceability of covenants, and it is these rules which we must now trace.

1. COVENANTS AT LAW

The rules relating to covenants at law are of ancient origin. It has been clear from early times that at law a covenantor need not own any estate in land. The law will nevertheless enforce his covenant under certain circumstances, whether that covenant be positive or negative. These propositions were established by *The Prior's* case[3] in 1368, where it was held that a positive covenant to sing divine service in a chapel might be enforced at law even though the covenantor had no estate in land which could be burdened by the obligation. The reasoning adopted in *The Prior's* case has been applied in more recent times. In *Smith and Snipes Hall Farm Ltd v River Douglas Catchment Board*[4], the Court of Appeal enforced, on the same basis, the defendant's positive covenant to repair and maintain the floodbanks of a river. However, there is a requirement at law that the *covenantee* must hold some estate in land to which the benefit of the covenant may accrue[5].

Difficulties have arisen in recent years concerning the scope of the benefit conferred by covenants at law. It is clear that, on purely contractual principles, a covenant may confer benefit upon any party who is expressly named as the covenantee in the deed of covenant. At common law there was for many years a strict rule that no person could sue on a deed made inter partes[6] unless he was *named* in that deed as a party[7]. This rule has now been modified by section 56(1) of the Law of Property Act 1925, which provides that

> A person may take an immediate or other interest in land or other property, or the benefit of any condition, right of entry, covenant or agreement over or respecting land or other property, although he may not be named as a party to the conveyance or other instrument.

It was at one time thought that section 56(1) abrogated the entire doctrine of privity of contract[8], but the rather ambivalent utterances of the House of Lords

2 (1952) 68 LQR 337 at 347f.: 'Licences and Third Parties'.
3 (1368) YB 42 Edw III, pl. 14, fol. 3A.
4 [1949] 2 KB 500. See (1949) 12 MLR 498 (A. K. R. Kiralfy).
5 If the covenantee parts with the land benefited by the covenant before any breach of the covenant occurs, he can recover only nominal damages in any action brought against the covenantor, since the real loss is likely to have fallen upon the person to whom he has conveyed the land. See R. E. Megarry and H. W. R. Wade, op. cit., p. 744.
6 A deed made inter partes is to be distinguished from a *deed poll*, i.e., a deed executed unilaterally by one party.
7 See *Lord Southampton v Brown* (1827) 6 B & C 718.
8 See, e.g., *Smith and Snipes Hall Farm Ltd v River Douglas Catchment Board* [1949] 2 KB 500 at 514ff. per Denning LJ; *Beswick v Beswick* [1966] Ch 538 at 556f. per Lord Denning MR.

in *Beswick v Beswick*[9] indicate on balance that this is not so. The better view appears to be that section 56(1) merely removes the old rule that only a party expressly *named* in a deed might properly claim to be a beneficiary of the covenant. Thus, if A covenants with B to confer a benefit upon C, C is still disabled from enforcing the covenant, since he is excluded from doing so by the rules of privity of contract. However, if C is *named* in the covenant as a covenantee, as for instance where A covenants expressly with B *and C* to confer benefit upon C, C is automatically entitled to sue in the event of breach, precisely because he is now one of the contracting parties. Now, after 1925, it is no longer essential that the beneficiary of the covenant be *named* in the covenant. It is sufficient that he is designated as a covenantee under a *generic* description.

It is possible that this restrictive construction of section 56(1) of the Law of Property Act 1925 may not have refuted entirely the idea that a third party may sue for the benefit of a contract[10]. However, the restrictive construction is sufficiently effective to enable a covenantor to covenant with a named party (e.g., the vendor of land) 'and also with the owners for the time being of adjoining plots of land' in such a way that not only the named party but also those other owners who have been referred to merely generically may sue to enforce the benefit of the covenant on their own behalf *as covenantees.* The only limitation upon this principle is the requirement that those named generically as covenantees must, if they are to come within the ambit of section 56(1), be existing and identifiable individuals at the date of the covenant[11]. Thus section 56(1) does not enable a covenant to confer benefit directly upon *future* purchasers of plots of land. A covenant which purports to be made with a named owner of land 'and with his successors in title' does not bring the successors in title within the scope of section 56(1). In such a case, only the named individual can rank as a covenantee of the promise.

(1) Transmission of the benefit of a covenant

With the foregoing qualifications, a covenant is clearly enforceable in contract by the original covenantee[12]. However, greater difficulty is posed by the possibility that the benefit[13] of the covenant may have been transmitted at law to a third party. The common law lays down fairly strict conditions as to the

9 [1968] AC 58. See (1967) 30 MLR 687 (G. Treitel); *White v Bijou Mansions Ltd* [1937] Ch 610 at 624.

10 Although the House of Lords in *Beswick v Beswick* rejected the idea that section 56(1) enables a non-party to enforce a contract made for his benefit, a majority in the House was of the view that section 56(1) is inapplicable because it is confined to real property. Only two of the judges explicitly rejected Lord Denning's view of section 56(1) (see [1968] AC 58 at 94 per Lord Pearce, at 106 per Lord Upjohn). It may therefore be that 'the Court of Appeal's revolutionary doctrine' is still operative as regards real property. See R. E. Megarry and H. W. R. Wade, op. cit., p. 746.

11 See *Westhoughton UDC v Wigan Coal & Iron Co Ltd* [1919] 1 Ch 159; *Re Ecclesiastical Comrs for England's Conveyance* [1936] Ch 430.

12 This is true except where the covenantee has already assigned the benefit of the covenant to some other party. For a similar principle in the context of leaseholds, see Chapter 12, p. 410, ante.

13 For an explanation of this use of the term 'benefit' and the corresponding term 'burden', see earlier, p. 61, ante.

passing of the benefit[14]. In order that the benefit of a covenant should run with the covenantee's land at law, it must be shown that:

(a) *The covenant 'touches and concerns' the land*

It must be shown that the covenant was entered into for the benefit of the land owned by the covenantee and not merely for his personal benefit. The test of whether a covenant 'touches and concerns' the land is essentially the same as that which is applied in the context of leasehold covenants, with the obvious qualification that the land in question here is of course the land of the covenantee rather than any land of the covenantor. It is in fact irrelevant whether the covenantor has any land to be burdened[15]. It must, in effect, be shown that there is some connection between the covenant and the covenantee's land in a sense equivalent to that required by the equitable rules of annexation[16]. As Tucker LJ held in *Smith and Snipes Hall Farm Ltd v River Douglas Catchment Board*[17], a covenant which 'touches and concerns' the covenantee's land

> must either affect the land as regards mode of occupation, or it must be such as per se, and not merely from collateral circumstances, affects the value of the land.

Tucker LJ also ruled that the required connection between the covenant and the land concerned need not appear expressly in the terms of the covenant but may be proved by extrinsic evidence: '*Id certum est quod certum reddi potest*[18]'.

(b) *The covenantee has a legal estate in the land benefited*

A covenant can run with the land at law only if made with a covenantee who has a legal estate in the land benefited. No benefit can pass at law where the original covenantee has a merely equitable interest in his land.

(c) *The assignee of the land has a legal estate in the land benefited*

There used to be a rule at common law that any third party who sought to claim at law the benefit of a covenant relating to land must show that he had the *same* legal estate in that land as the original covenantee. In other words, if the original covenantee was an owner in fee simple, the benefit of the covenant could pass only to a third party who similarly owned the land in fee simple[19]. However, this requirement was not imposed in *The Prior's* case[20], and constituted a somewhat doubtful feature of the common law rules on the passing of the benefit.

14 See E. H. Scamell (1954) 18 Conv (NS) 546: 'Positive Covenants in Conveyances of the Fee Simple.'
15 See p. 607, ante.
16 See p. 622ff., post.
17 [1949] 2 KB 500 at 506.
18 [1949] 2 KB 500 at 508.
19 See, e.g., *Westhoughton UDC v Wigan Coal & Iron Co Ltd* [1919] 1 Ch 159.
20 (1368) YB 42 Edw III, pl. 14, fol. 3A.

The rule that a covenant was enforceable only by an assignee of the same legal estate was finally removed by section 78(1) of the Law of Property Act 1925. This provision makes it clear that

A covenant relating to any land of the covenantee shall be deemed to be made with the covenantee and his successors in title and the persons deriving title under him or them, and shall have effect as if such successors and other persons were expressed.

For the purposes of this subsection in connexion with covenants restrictive of the user of land 'successors in title' shall be deemed to include the owners and occupiers for the time being of the land of the covenantee intended to be benefited.

It was thought at first that this provision was merely a 'word-saving' provision designed for the benefit of conveyancers. However, in *Smith and Snipes Hall Farm Ltd v River Douglas Catchment Board*[1], the Court of Appeal took the view that section 78(1) abrogated the common law requirement[2]. Here the original covenantee had later sold the benefited land to P^1, who in his turn leased the land to P^2. The Court allowed an action for damages for breach of covenant on the suit of both P^1 (the owner in fee simple) and P^2 (who held merely a term of years). Section 78(1) rendered the covenant in question enforceable on behalf of not only the original covenantee but all successors in title and all persons deriving title from such successors.

(d) *It was intended that the benefit should run with the land owned by the covenantee at the date of the covenant*

As indicated by Tucker LJ in *Smith and Snipes Hall Farm Ltd v River Douglas Catchment Board*[3], it must be shown that 'it was the intention of the parties that the benefit [of the covenant] should run with the land.' In that case, the deed in question showed that the object of the covenant was 'to improve the drainage of land liable to flooding and prevent future flooding.'

If these conditions are satisfied, the benefit of a covenant (whether positive or negative) may pass at law to a third party who takes an estate in the benefited land. The legal rules for the transmission of benefit have, in the main, existed since the earliest days of the common law. Equity was later to formulate its own rules for the passing of the benefit of covenants, and did so on the assumption that it was following the rules laid down by the common law[4]. However, the common law rules continue to apply in cases which are not covered under the rules developed by equity, as for instance where the covenantor has no land upon which the burden of the covenant can be imposed.

It should be noted that there is special statutory provision for the most important covenants relating to land—those relating to title. Various covenants for title (e.g., by a person who purports to convey as 'beneficial owner') are laid

1 [1949] 2 KB 500.
2 See, however, D. W. Elliott (1956) 20 Conv (NS) 43 at 53: 'The Effect of Section 56(1) of the Law of Property Act 1925.' *Smith and Snipes Hall Farm Ltd v River Douglas Catchment Board* was followed in *Williams v Unit Construction Co Ltd* (1955) 19 Conv (NS) 262.
3 [1949] 2 KB 500 at 506.
4 See p. 622, post.

down in section 76 of the Law of Property Act 1925. Section 76(6) expressly provides that

> The benefit of a covenant implied as aforesaid shall be annexed and incident to, and shall go with, the estate or interest of the implied covenantee, and shall be capable of being enforced by every person in whom that estate or interest is, for the whole or any part thereof, from time to time vested.

There is a further statutory provision facilitating the transmission at law of the benefit of a covenant. The benefit of a covenant which is not exclusively personal may be assigned as a chose in action under section 136 of the Law of Property Act 1925. In order to be effective at law, this form of assignment requires to be in writing, and express written notice of the assignment must be served upon the covenantor[5].

(2) **Transmission of the burden of a covenant**

The burden of a covenant *cannot* pass at law in such a way as to become directly enforceable against assigns or successors in title of the original covenantor. It is a clear rule of law that the burden of a covenant between freeholders cannot run with the land. This rule is consonant with the general principle that the benefit, but never the burden, of a contract can be assigned to a third party. In *Austerberry v Oldham Corpn*[6], Lindley LJ declared that he was

> not prepared to say that any covenant which imposes a burden upon land does run with the land, unless the covenant does, upon the true construction of the deed containing the covenant, amount to either a grant of an easement, or a rentcharge, or some estate or interest in the land. A mere covenant to repair, or to do something of that kind, does not seem to me, I confess, to run with the land in such a way as to bind those who may acquire it[7].

It was this unwillingness of the courts to hold covenants enforceable at law against the successors in title of the covenantor which made it necessary for equity to provide a means by which at least restrictive covenants could be made to run with the land[8]. Although the principle of *Austerberry v Oldham Corpn* was formulated in order that land should remain unfettered for future generations, the implications of that decision are nowadays a matter of substantial regret. Professor H. W. R. Wade has pointed out, for instance, that the principle 'impedes transactions in land which have become socially desirable[9].' The anxiety of judges in the 19th century to limit the kinds of incumbrance which might be imposed upon the freehold estate is not particularly apposite under the vastly changed conditions of modern life where most people live in large cities. The property law of the 19th century was highly individualistic and made little provision for 'freeholders living like battery hens in urban developments' where

5 See R. E. Megarry and H. W. R. Wade, op. cit., p. 743.
6 (1885) 29 Ch D 750.
7 (1885) 29 Ch D 750 at 781. See also *Jones v Price* [1965] 2 QB 618.
8 See p. 614, post.
9 (1972B) 31 Cambridge LJ 157: 'Covenants—"A Broad and Reasonable View"'.

much of the land area may consist of amenities which belong to none personally but which are socially necessary for all. In the words of Professor Wade, the rule which makes the burden of freehold covenants untransmissible is inappropriate today in view of

> the tendency of an overcrowded population to live in 'developments' where they are more and more dependent upon shared amenities such as roads, stairways and gardens, and where lapses by individual owners from the general standards of repair and maintenance will affect the amenity and value and even perhaps the physical stability of neighbouring homes. The law has failed to provide any mechanism by which the necessary obligations can be made to run satisfactorily with freehold land[10].

The common law principle is so profoundly inconvenient that various devices have been used to circumvent the common law rule and achieve by indirect means a result which is impossible by direct means[11]. These devices include the following:

(a) *Chain of covenants*

Although the burden of a freehold covenant cannot be made to run with the covenantor's land, this result can be achieved indirectly by instituting a chain of indemnity covenants, and indeed it is usually in the interests of the covenantor to extract an indemnity covenant from any subsequent purchaser of his land. The covenantor remains liable on the terms of the original covenant but, in the event of a violation by the subsequent purchaser, is able to sue on the indemnity covenant in order to recover any damages which he may have been required to pay to the covenantee (or to *his* successors in title). The chain of indemnity covenants may extend indefinitely, each succeeding purchaser of the covenantor's land entering into a covenant to indemnify his predecessor in title in respect of any future breaches.

In practice, however, the utility of the chain of covenants is lessened or even destroyed by reason of the death or disappearance of the original covenantor or because the chain of indemnities is interrupted. A further disadvantage with the device of indemnity covenants is the fact that even if the chain of covenants remains intact, the only remedy available to the covenantor is an action in damages, whereas the remedy which he really wants is an injunction or order of specific performance.

(b) *Conversion of leasehold into freehold*

There are two statutory means by which a long lease may be converted into a freehold estate. Under section 153 of the Law of Property Act 1925, a long lease[12] may be enlarged into a freehold if certain conditions are fulfilled. If this

10 (1972B) 31 Cambridge LJ 157 at 158. For reference to solutions to this problem in other jurisdictions, see R. E. Megarry and H. W. R. Wade, op. cit., p. 755.

11 See A. M. Prichard (1973) 37 Conv (NS) 194: 'Making Positive Covenants Run'.

12 A long lease is defined for this purpose as a lease which was originally created for at least 300 years of which not less than 200 years are unexpired, which involves the payment of no rent or money value, and which is not liable to be determined by re-entry for condition broken (see Law of Property Act 1925, s. 153(1), (2)).

occurs, the freehold becomes subject 'to all the same covenants . . . as the term would have been subject to if it had not been so enlarged[13].' This device may be significant in the present context since the freehold is then governed by the principle which applies to leasehold covenants, i.e., the principle that the burden of covenants may run with the estate[14]. A similar result is brought about by the enfranchisement of a long lease under the Leasehold Reform Act 1967[15].

(c) *The doctrine of 'mutual benefit and burden'*

Once again, the burden of a freehold covenant may pass indirectly to a successor in title of the covenantor by virtue of the doctrine of 'mutual benefit and burden[16].' This doctrine was discussed earlier in this book[17].

(d) *Right of entry*

It is possible to reserve a right of entry in respect of land, on terms that the right of entry becomes exercisable on events which amount to a violation of a positive covenant[18]. Such a right of entry, if duly created, becomes a legal interest in the land and thus runs with the burdened land so as to affect the successors in title of the covenantor. The right is, however, subject to the rule against perpetuities[19].

(3) Reform

It is generally recognised that the unenforceability of covenants against the covenantor's successors at law is a deficiency which deserves remedy. In 1965 the Wilberforce Committee recognised that 'the time has come for statutory intervention . . . to introduce legal order and consistency into the present (inevitably) haphazard techniques of multi-unit property development[20].' The Committee acknowledged that many positive covenants in respect of property in this country are quite unenforceable in practice because of the unsatisfactory nature of the rules relating to the burden of those covenants. The Committee therefore recommended that, subject to certain conditions, the assignability and enforcement of positive covenants 'should, as far as possible, be assimilated to

13 Law of Property Act 1925, s. 153(8).
14 See p. 410, ante.
15 Leasehold Reform Act 1967, s. 8(3), p. 404, ante.
16 See *Halsall v Brizell* [1957] Ch 169; (1957) 73 LQR 154 (REM); (1957) 21 Conv (NS) 160 (F. R. Crane); (1957) 15 Cambridge LJ 35 (H. W. R. Wade); *E.R. Ives Investment Ltd v High* [1967] 2 QB 379; *Tito v Waddell (No. 2)* [1977] Ch 106 at 289ff. per Megarry V-C, who held (at 303) that the doctrine covers not merely successors in title but also anybody 'whose connection with the transaction creating the benefit and burden is sufficient to show that he has some claim to the benefit whether or not he has a valid title to it.' See also (1977) 41 Conv (NS) 432 (F. R. Crane).
17 See p. 141, ante.
18 See *Shiloh Spinners Ltd v Harding* [1973] AC 691 at 717, p. 413, ante. It is, of course, possible that relief may be granted against forfeiture.
19 See S. M. Tolson (1950) 14 Conv (NS) 350 at 354ff.: '"Land" Without Earth: Freehold Flats in English Law.'
20 *Report of the Committee on Positive Covenants Affecting Land* (Cmnd 2719, 1965), para. 9.

that of negative covenants' and that, subject to certain necessary qualifications, 'in the case of positive covenants as in that of negative covenants the burden should run with the land encumbered, and the benefit should run with the land advantaged[1].' No legislation has yet been enacted to implement these proposals.

2. COVENANTS IN EQUITY

One of the most revolutionary contributions made by equity in the area of property comprises the development during the 19th century of special equitable rules governing covenants between freeholders. This body of rules was of great importance in regulating the urban and industrial development of England in an age before the advent of planning legislation. The mid-19th century was a period of significant expansion, when the tension was greatest between the desire to keep land unfettered by private covenant (and therefore profitable for industrial development) and the conflicting desire to curb the effects of commercial and urban growth (by preserving residential amenity for the private householder). These conflicting policies were reflected in the case law of the period. In *Keppell v Bailey*[2], Lord Brougham refused to allow that 'incidents of a novel kind can be devised and attached to land at the fancy and caprice of the owner.' He thus declined to enforce the burden of a covenant against a successor in title of the original covenantor, taking the view that such a burden, if enforced, would fetter the use and development of the land in perpetuity[3]. However, the emphasis had altered by the time *Tulk v Moxhay*[4] came to be decided by the courts in 1847. The decision of Lord Cottenham in this case is usually taken as marking the inception of a major development in the equitable rules concerning freehold covenants[5]. Until this date it had been thought that equity would not permit the use of land to be sterilised by the imposition of permanently binding covenants between freeholders.

In *Tulk v Moxhay*, the plaintiff had sold a vacant piece of land in Leicester Square to E, who covenanted on behalf of himself, his heirs and his assigns that he would keep and maintain that land 'in an open state, uncovered with any buildings, in neat and ornamental order.' The land sold subsequently passed by conveyance into the hands of the defendant. The defendant's conveyance had not contained any such covenant as that spelt out in the original conveyance from the plaintiff, but it was common ground that he had had notice of the restrictive covenant imposed in respect of the open land. When the defendant attempted to build on the open land in defiance of the covenant, the plaintiff

1 Ibid., para. 10. See H. W. R. Wade (1972B) 31 Cambridge LJ 157.
2 (1834) 2 My & K 517; 39 ER 1042.
3 (1834) 2 My & K 517 at 540ff.
4 (1848) 2 Ph 774; 41 ER 1143.
5 It has been pointed out that the decision reached in *Tulk v Moxhay* had been anticipated in two poorly reported cases decided by Sir Lancelot Shadwell, *Whatman v Gibson* (1838) 9 Sim 196, and *Mann v Stephens* (1846) 15 Sim 377. See A. W. B. Simpson, *An Introduction to the History of the Land Law* (London 1961), p. 240.

sought an injunction to prevent him from doing so. Lord Cottenham LC upheld a decision at first instance granting the plaintiff the relief required.

Lord Cottenham took an entirely different view from that adopted earlier by Lord Brougham in *Keppell v Bailey*. In the present case, Lord Cottenham held that an injunction should be granted restraining the defendant from acting in violation of the restrictive covenant, not because the burden of such a covenant might run either at law or in equity, but rather because equity asserts a stern view on matters of conscience. In the words of the Lord Chancellor, the question

> is, not whether the covenant runs with the land, but whether a party shall be permitted to use the land in a manner inconsistent with the contract entered into by his vendor, and with notice of which he purchased. Of course, the price would be affected by the covenant, and nothing could be more inequitable than that the original purchaser should be able to sell the property the next day for a greater price, in consideration of the assignee being allowed to escape from the liability which he had himself undertaken.
>
> That the question does not depend upon whether the covenant runs with the land is evident from this, that if there was a mere agreement and no covenant, this Court would enforce it against a party purchasing with notice of it; for if an equity is attached to the property by the owner, no one purchasing with notice of that equity can stand in a different situation from the party from whom he purchased[6].

The decision in *Tulk v Moxhay* was broadly based. Equity was prepared to intervene in restraint of any unconscionable conduct in respect of a contractual undertaking of which the wrongdoer—although not himself a contracting party—nevertheless had notice. The argument which prevailed before Lord Cottenham LC was capable of wide application. Indeed, the view adopted in *Tulk v Moxhay*, far from leading to a sterilisation of land use, could even be seen as promoting the interest of commerciability of land. As Lord Cottenham clearly recognised, unless restrictive covenants could be enforced against the covenantor's successors, 'it would be impossible for an owner of land to sell part of it without incurring the risk of rendering what he retains worthless[7].' The ruling in *Tulk v Moxhay* was, accordingly, applied with enthusiasm during the years which followed that decision. The ruling was applied to both positive and negative covenants; it was applied on behalf of litigants who held no estate in the land benefited by the covenant; it was even applied outside the realm of real property[8].

The doctrine in *Tulk v Moxhay* thus had a dramatic effect upon both the law of contract and the law of property. The covenantee was widely regarded as having not merely a contractual interest in the performance of the covenant made with him, but also a *proprietary* interest in the land of the covenantor. Moreover, the covenantee's proprietary interest could run with the land of the covenantor, so as to bind all those into whose hands that land came, until eventually the covenantor's land was conveyed to a bona fide purchaser of a legal estate for value without notice of the covenant. The covenantee was thus given a contractual right to control activities on the land of the covenantor, and,

6 (1848) 2 Ph 774 at 777.
7 (1848) 2 Ph 774 at 777.
8 See A. W. B. Simpson, op. cit., p. 241.

by virtue of the equitable doctrine, that contractual right enlarged into—and arrogated to itself the status of—a *proprietary right in land.*

It was inevitable that, with the passage of time, the broad doctrine of *Tulk v Moxhay* should be somewhat modified. Aware of the potential scope of doctrine, the courts had begun even during the closing decades of the 19th century to limit its application. The courts started to define the precise qualities which must be possessed by covenants before they can rank as equitable interests in the land of the covenantor[9]. In *London and South. Western Rly Co v Gomm*[10], Jessel MR was already re-interpreting the doctrine in *Tulk v Moxhay* as 'either an extension in equity of the doctrine of *Spencer's* case to another line of cases, or else an extension in equity of the doctrine of negative easements.' Thus the new doctrine had its 'wings clipped[11].' Covenants began to be enforced against third parties on the same conditions as attached to the enforcement of easements, with the result that equity imposed such extra requirements as that there be a servient and a dominant tenement[12]. We must now examine more closely the limitations thus imposed by equity upon the category of covenants capable of enforcement against successors in title.

(1) Characteristics of enforceable covenants

As the doctrine in *Tulk v Moxhay* was slowly refined, it became clear that certain requirements must be satisfied in respect of a covenant relating to land before that covenant can be enforced in equity otherwise than between the original parties.

(a) *The covenant must be restrictive or negative*

If the application of *Tulk v Moxhay* was to be limited by analogy with the doctrine of negative easements, the first limiting factor to emerge was a rule that equity would take cognisance of only those covenants which are negative or restrictive in nature. In *Haywood v Brunswick Permanent Benefit Building Society*[13], the Court of Appeal held that equity had no jurisdiction to enforce against an assignee from the covenantor a positive covenant to build and repair. In the view of Brett LJ, equity would henceforth enforce only those covenants 'restricting the mode of using the land[14].' Thus, from this point onwards, the burden of a positive covenant became unenforceable, either at law or in equity, against successors of the original covenantor. Furthermore, since the purview of

9 See H. W. R. Wade (1952) 68 LQR 337 at 348.

10 (1882) 20 Ch D 562 at 583. See also *Re Nisbet and Potts' Contract* [1905] 1 Ch 391 at 397 per Farwell J; *Reid v Bickerstaff* [1909] 2 Ch 305 at 320 per Cozens-Hardy MR.

11 See H. W. Challis, *Law of Real Property* (3rd edn., London 1911), p. 185.

12 See, e.g., *Newton Abbot Co-operative Society Ltd v Williamson and Treadgold Ltd* [1952] Ch 286 at 293 per Upjohn J.

13 (1881) 8 QBD 403.

14 (1881) 8 QBD 403 at 408. In Brett LJ's view, 'if we enlarged the rule as it is now contended, we should be making a new equity, which we cannot do.'

equity is now confined to restrictive covenants, the remedy given by equity in respect of enforceable restrictive covenants is the remedy of injunction.

The test of a *restrictive* covenant is always a test of substance. A covenant phrased in a positive manner may nevertheless constitute a restrictive covenant, as would be the case, for instance, with a covenant 'to use the property for residential purposes only.' Conversely, a covenant 'not to let the property fall into disrepair' is, on closer examination, a positive covenant to repair. A rule of thumb commonly used to test the nature of a covenant of dubious status is the question whether the covenant requires the expenditure of money for its performance. If the covenantor is required 'to put his hand into his pocket,' the covenant cannot be negative in nature[15].

Restrictive covenants are widely used for the purpose of preserving the residential character of a district or neighbourhood. Restrictive covenants commonly require the covenantor to refrain from conducting any trade or business on his land or to refrain from building within a certain distance from the frontage of his property or even to refrain from erecting any construction at all on his land.

(b) *The covenant must accommodate a dominant tenement*

In conformity with the theory that the equitable rules about restrictive covenants merely extend the rules relating to negative easements, it has come to be accepted that equity will take cognisance only of those covenants which concern two separate plots of land. In other words, there must be a servient tenement and a dominant tenement[16]. The covenantee must own an estate in the dominant tenement and the covenantor an estate in the servient tenement. Furthermore it must be shown that the covenant was made for the protection and benefit of the land retained by the covenantee[17].

In *London County Council v Allen*[18], the Court of Appeal held that the plaintiff

15 See *Haywood v Brunswick Permanent Benefit Building Society* (1881) 8 QBD 403 at 409 per Cotton LJ.
16 See p. 580, ante.
17 See *Formby v Barker* [1903] 2 Ch 539 at 552 per Vaughan Williams LJ. It used to be said, in the hallowed terminology of the law of covenants, that the restrictive covenant must 'touch and concern' the land of the covenantee (see, e.g., *Rogers v Hosegood* [1900] 2 Ch 388 at 395; *Re Ballard's Conveyance* [1937] Ch 473 at 480f.). However, as David Hayton has pointed out, the courts have moved away from the concept of covenants which 'touch and concern' the covenantee's land, in favour of the requirement that the restrictive covenant must 'benefit' the covenantee's land. See D. J. Hayton (1971) 87 LQR 539 at 544: 'Restrictive Covenants as Property Interests'. In this sense, a 'benefit' must be 'something affecting either the value of the land or the method of its occupation or enjoyment' (*Re Gadd's Land Transfer* [1966] Ch 56 at 66 per Buckley J). It has been held that a covenant which forbids a covenantor to compete with a business conducted on the covenantee's land 'touches and concerns' or 'benefits' the land in the required sense (*Newton Abbot Co-operative Society Ltd v Williamson and Treadgold Ltd* [1952] Ch 286). See, however, L. H. Elphinstone (1952) 68 LQR 353 at 362: 'Assignment of the Benefit of Covenants affecting Land'; D. J. Hayton (1971) 87 LQR 539 at 544f. It is always worthwhile to remember the point made by Ungoed-Thomas J in *Stilwell v Blackman* [1968] Ch 508 at 524f.: 'The protection of land, qua land, does not have any rational or, indeed, any human significance, apart from its enjoyment by human beings, and the protection of land is for its enjoyment by human beings.'
18 [1914] 3 KB 642. See D. J. Hayton (1971) 87 LQR 539 at 542f.

was unable to enforce a restrictive covenant against the covenantor's successor, on the ground that the plaintiff was not in possession of, or interested in, any land for the benefit of which the covenant had been taken[19]. Furthermore, the party who seeks to enforce the restrictive covenant must show an interest in some land which is proximate to the servient tenement. As was indicated by Pollock MR in *Kelly v Barrett*[20], 'land at Clapham would be too remote and unable to carry a right to enforce . . . covenants in respect of . . . land at Hampstead.'

Certain difficulties have afflicted the question whether a particular restrictive covenant benefits or protects an alleged dominant tenement. In *Re Ballard's Conveyance*[1], a restrictive covenant had been made in favour of a covenantee who retained approximately 1,700 acres of land. Clauson J held that the covenant was not enforceable at the behest of the covenantee's successor in title, since it could not reasonably be maintained that the covenant in question conferred benefit upon the entirety of such an extensive dominant tenement as that claimed by the successor. While conceding that a breach of the covenant might well affect a portion of the successor's land in the vicinity of the covenantor's property, Clauson J was of opinion that 'far the largest part of this area of 1,700 acres could not possibly be affected by any breach of any of the stipulations[2]'. Nor in his view did the court have jurisdiction to 'sever' the covenant and treat it as relevant to part only of the area of 1,700 acres. This strict view has, however, been relaxed somewhat in more recent cases. In *Wrotham Park Estate Co Ltd v Parkside Homes Ltd*[3], Brightman J stated that

There can be obvious cases where a restrictive covenant clearly is, or clearly is not, of benefit to an estate. Between these two extremes there is inevitably an area where the benefit to the estate is a matter of personal opinion, where responsible and reasonable persons can have divergent views sincerely and reasonably held. In my judgment, in such cases, it is not for the court to pronounce which is the correct view. I think that the court can only decide whether a particular view is one which can reasonably be held.

The courts thus tend nowadays to presume that a covenant confers benefit upon the alleged dominant tenement unless it can be shown that such a view cannot reasonably be held. In other words, it seems that the validity of a restrictive covenant will be upheld 'so long as an estate owner may reasonably take the view that the restriction remains of value to his estate.' The restriction will not be discarded 'merely because others may reasonably argue that the restriction is spent[4].'

The requirement that the covenantee must have an interest in a 'dominant

19 The result reached in this case has now been reversed by statute. See also *Tophams Ltd v Earl of Sefton* [1967] 1 AC 50 at 81 per Lord Wilberforce.
20 [1924] 2 Ch 379 at 404.
1 [1937] Ch 473. See G. R. Y. Radcliffe (1941) 57 LQR 203 at 210f.: 'Some Problems Relating to the Law of Restrictive Covenants'.
2 [1937] Ch 473 at 480f.
3 [1974] 1 WLR 798 at 808. See (1974) 33 Cambridge LJ 214 (C. T. Emery); *Lord Northbourne v Johnston & Son* [1922] 2 Ch 309.
4 [1974] 1 WLR 798 at 808. See G. H. Newsom [1974] JPL 130 at 133: 'Restrictive Covenants–2'.

tenement' means, of course, that if the covenantee parts with all the land for the benefit of which the restrictive covenant was taken, he ceases to be able to enforce the covenant except against the original covenantor[5].

There are certain exceptional cases in which the requirement of dominant and servient tenements is modified or even entirely abrogated. It has been clear since *Hall v Ewin*[6] that a lessor's reversion is a sufficient interest in realty to constitute a dominant tenement for the purpose of the rule that a restrictive covenant must confer benefit upon somebody's land. Likewise a mortgagee's interest in mortgaged land is a sufficiently 'real' interest to enable the mortgagee to enforce a restrictive covenant affecting the land[7]. In consequence of the ruling in *London County Council v Allen*[8], various bodies such as local authorities and the National Trust have now been given specific statutory powers to enforce restrictive covenants even though they are not possessed of any dominant land to serve as a base for enforcement in the conventional sense[9]. Finally, as we shall see later, a common vendor under a building scheme or scheme of development is permitted to enforce restrictive covenants against the purchaser of the last plot within the scheme, even though at this point the vendor no longer retains any dominant land[10].

(c) *The covenant must have been intended to run with the covenantor's land*

A restrictive covenant may be phrased in such a way that it binds only the covenantor[11]. In all other cases, however, it is presumed that the burden of a restrictive covenant is intended to run with the land of the covenantor. This is the effect of section 79 of the Law of Property Act 1925, which provides that

(1) A covenant relating to any land of a covenantor or capable of being bound by him, shall, unless a contrary intention is expressed, be deemed to be made by the covenantor on behalf of himself his successors in title and the persons deriving title under him or them, and, subject as aforesaid, shall have effect as if such successors and other persons were expressed . . .
(2) For the purposes of this section in connexion with covenants restrictive of the user of land 'successors in title' shall be deemed to include the owners and occupiers for the time being of such land.

Section 79 has reference, of course, only to restrictive covenants entered into on or after 1 January 1926[12].

5 See *Chambers v Randall* [1923] 1 Ch 149 at 157f. per Sargant J; *Formby v Barker* [1903] 2 Ch 539 at 551f.; *Miles v Easter* [1933] Ch 611 at 631.
6 (1888) 37 Ch D 74, p. 411, ante; *Regent Oil Co Ltd v J. A. Gregory (Hatch End) Ltd* [1966] Ch 402 at 433 per Harman LJ.
7 See *Regent Oil Co Ltd v J. A. Gregory (Hatch End) Ltd* [1966] Ch 402 at 433, p. 535, ante.
8 [1914] 3 KB 642, p. 617, ante.
9 See, e.g., Housing Act 1957, s. 151; National Trust Act 1937, s. 8; Town and Country Planning Act 1971, s. 52(2).
10 See p. 631, post.
11 See *Re Royal Victoria Pavilion, Ramsgate* [1961] Ch 581.
12 Law of Property Act 1925, s. 79(3).

(2) General principles of enforceability of restrictive covenants between non-parties to the covenant

In order that a restrictive covenant be enforceable between parties other than the original covenantor and covenantee, it is necessary to show first that the covenant in question conforms to the characteristics which equity demands of any 'restrictive covenant'. These characteristics we have already examined. However, it is also essential that the party who seeks to enforce the restrictive covenant should be able to establish both that he is entitled to the *benefit* of the covenant and that the person against whom he seeks enforcement is subject to the *burden* of the covenant[13]. If he can prove only one of these requirements, his action must fail. Successful enforcement depends upon an appropriate transmission of both the benefit and the burden originally taken by covenantee and covenantor respectively. In other words, in the following diagram it is essential that P should be able to claim that

(i) the benefit of the restrictive covenant has been duly transmitted to him, *and*
(ii) the burden of the restrictive covenant has been duly transmitted to D.

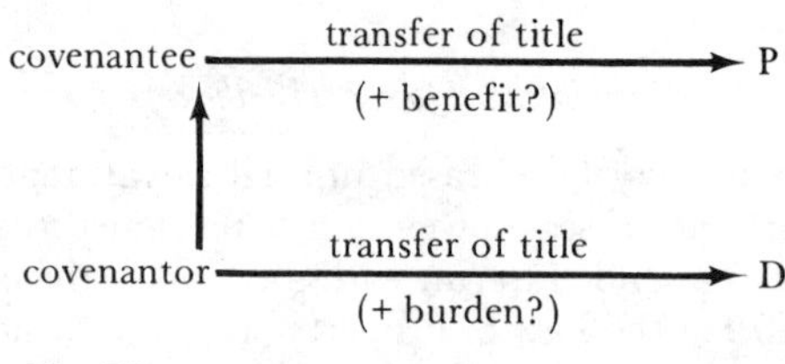

Fig. 71

(3) Transmission of the burden of the restrictive covenant

In consequence of the doctrine proceeding from *Tulk v Moxhay*[14], the restrictive covenant has become an equitable interest in the covenantor's land. As is the case with all equitable interests in land, it binds all persons except a bona fide purchaser of a legal estate for value without notice[15]. It cannot, therefore, be enforced against one who purchases a legal estate in the covenantor's land for value without notice of the covenant[16], or against *any* successor of such a person[17]. In this sense, the restrictive covenant is fully subject to the orthodox doctrine of notice, and the transmission of the burden of such a covenant to a transferee of the covenantor's freehold is, in principle, governed by the operation of that doctrine.

This at least was the position before the enactment of the property legislation

13 See p. 61, ante.
14 (1848) 2 Ph 774, p. 614, ante.
15 See p. 55f., ante.
16 A restrictive covenant does, however, bind an adverse occupier of the servient land, precisely because he is not a *purchaser*. See *Re Nisbet and Potts' Contract* [1906] 1 Ch 386, p. 102, ante.
17 See *Wilkes v Spooner* [1911] 2 KB 473, p. 57, ante.

of 1925. However, this legislation effected major alterations both in the law of restrictive covenants and, more generally, in the application of the doctrine of notice. A restrictive covenant made after 1925 now constitutes a land charge of Class D (ii)[18]. The transmission of the burden of such a restrictive covenant now depends upon whether that covenant has been registered in the Land Charges Register (in the case of unregistered land)[19] or has been duly protected as a minor interest (in the case of registered land) by entry of a notice or caution in the Land Register[20]. In *Fig.* 71, P will be able to enforce the restrictive covenant against D, the covenantor's successor in title, only if the covenantee had protected the land charge by the appropriate means at some time before the covenantor transferred his freehold title to D. If he had protected the interest, by registration or entry, D will be bound; if not, D will take the freehold free of the burden of the covenant, and P will be unable to enforce the covenant against him[1].

It should be remembered that certain categories of restrictive covenant remain unaffected by the provisions of the Land Charges Act 1972. *First*, a restrictive covenant between a lessor and a lessee can never constitute a protectible Class D (ii) land charge. Such a covenant is governed by the rules which regulate the enforceability of leasehold covenants[2]. If the restrictive covenant—albeit contained in a lease—relates to land not comprised within that lease, the position is governed by the equitable doctrine of notice[3]. *Second*, a restrictive covenant entered into by freeholders *before* 1 January 1926 is still fully subject to the equitable doctrine of notice.

(4) Transmission of the benefit of the restrictive covenant[4]

In order that the benefit of a restrictive covenant be transmitted in equity to a successor in title of the covenantee, it is necessary not only that the covenant should 'touch and concern' or 'benefit' some land of the covenantee, but also that the benefit be transmitted in one or more of the modes prescribed by equity[5]. These modes of transmission have tended, historically, to be formulated in very strict terms, since it was thought that the imposition of a requirement of formality would assist in establishing the benefit of the restrictive covenant as appurtenant to the alleged dominant tenement and, therefore, as capable of passing with it to a third party.

Nowadays, however, there is a strong contrary tendency on the part of the courts to relax the strict requirements of equity, by allowing the appurtenant

18 See p. 138, ante.
19 See p. 113 ante.
20 See p. 328, ante.
1 See p. 114, ante.
2 See p. 408, ante.
3 See *Dartstone Ltd v Cleveland Petroleum Co Ltd* [1969] 3 All ER 668, p. 138, ante.
4 See S. J. Bailey (1938) 6 Cambridge LJ 339: 'The Benefit of a Restrictive Covenant.'
5 It was held, however, in *Rogers v Hosegood* [1900] 2 Ch 388, that the plaintiff could claim that the benefit of a restrictive covenant had passed at law, even though the burden of that covenant had passed only by virtue of equitable rules of transmissibility, p. 622, post.

quality of a covenant to be determined with reference to the intentions of the covenanting parties rather than in accordance with stipulated requirements of form. As Professor H. W. R. Wade has pointed out, 'the tendency is thus to assimilate the law of covenants to the law of easements, where no formalities are required for establishing the right as appurtenant to the dominant tenement[6]. This gradual movement away from technicality and heavy formalism has certainly done much to simplify the law of restrictive covenants. However, the trend of recent developments in this area is inevitably vulnerable to the conveyancer's objection that the law now

> detracts from the vital characteristics of all property interests viz. definability, ascertainability, and stability, and ... the uncertainty thereby created casts doubt on many titles, thus inhibiting the marketability and the development of land[7].

If the benefit of a restrictive covenant is to pass to a successor in title of the covenantee (e.g., to P in *Fig.* 71), it must be shown that that benefit was effectively *annexed* to the covenantee's land, or was expressly *assigned* to the successor, or has become enforceable by reason of the presence of a *building scheme* or *scheme of development*.

It is sometimes said that the equitable rules for the transmission of the benefit of restrictive covenants are merely an elucidation of the common law rules governing the passing of the benefit of covenants[8]. Indeed, it is still possible that the *benefit* of a restrictive covenant may be held to pass at law if the conditions for transmission at law are fulfilled, and this may be so even though successful enforcement of the covenant ultimately depends upon the transmission of the burden in accordance with *equitable* principles[9]. However, there are certain circumstances in which the benefit of a restrictive covenant can be claimed only by virtue of the equitable rules concerning transmission, and these cases are essentially situations in which the common law rules are not satisfied. There can be no passing of the benefit at law if, for instance, either the covenantee or his successor has merely an equitable interest in land[10], or if the servient tenement has itself been assigned or transferred to a successor in title against whom enforcement depends upon the doctrine in *Tulk v Moxhay*[11]. In such circumstances, the transmission of the benefit of a restrictive covenant rests entirely upon the operation of the equitable rules.

(a) *Annexation*

Annexation is the metaphorical 'nailing' of the benefit of a restrictive covenant

6 (1972B) 31 Cambridge LJ 157 at 163, p. 591, ante.
7 D. J. Hayton (1971) 87 LQR 539.
8 'Since 1875 it ought to make no practical difference whether the benefit passes under the rules of law or of equity, since the same court can enforce both ... Equity merely followed the law. But more complicated rules have developed which are now assumed to apply in all actions ... so making the law follow equity ... It is ... questionable whether [the rules of equity] entirely displace the rules of law, which are altogether simpler. This part of the subject has therefore become difficult' (R. E. Megarry and H. W. R. Wade, op. cit., p. 761).
9 See, e.g., *Rogers v Hosegood* [1900] 2 Ch 388, p. 621, ante.
10 See *Fairclough v Marshall* (1878) 4 Ex D 37.
11 See *Miles v Easter* [1933] Ch 611 at 630 per Romer LJ.

to a clearly defined area of land belonging to the covenantee, in such a way that the benefit passes with any subsequent transfer of the covenantee's interest in that land. Annexation has traditionally comprised a formal recognition that both covenantor and covenantee intend that the benefit should run with the land so as to avail future owners of that land. Once that intention has been manifested, the benefit of the covenant is notionally fastened upon, or annexed to, the covenantee's land, with the result that the benefit passes to all successive owners, tenants and occupiers of the land irrespective of knowledge or notice[12]. In recent years, however, the formality required for annexation has tended to be relaxed by the courts, with the result that it is now possible to distinguish three different types of annexation.

(i) *Express annexation* Express annexation is the oldest and least controversial form of annexation. In a case of express annexation, the deed which contains the restrictive covenant includes some clear expression of intention that the benefit of the covenant should run with the land to which the covenant is appurtenant. In other words, a formula of annexation is embedded in the very document which brings the restrictive covenant into being.

It is always a question of construction whether the benefit of any restrictive covenant is in fact intended to run with a defined piece of land. It is generally accepted that the benefit is effectively annexed to a particular piece of land if that land is sufficiently defined in the instrument containing the covenant *and* the covenant is expressed to be made for the benefit of the land or to be made 'for the benefit of the [owner] in his capacity of owner of a particular property[13].' In either case, an intention is clearly evinced that the benefit of the covenant should not be personal to the covenantee, but should enure to the advantage of future owners of the covenantee's land.

One of the classic formulae of annexation was that with which the Court of Appeal had to deal in *Rogers v Hosegood*[14]. Here the parties had expressed their 'intent that the covenant may enure to the benefit of the vendors [i.e., the covenantees] their successors and assigns and others claiming under them to all or any of their lands adjoining[15].' On the other hand, in *Renals v Cowlishaw*[16], it

12 In the words of Collins LJ in *Rogers v Hosegood* [1900] 2 Ch 388 at 407, annexation is effective to make the benefit of a covenant run, 'not because the conscience of either party is affected, but because the purchaser has bought something which inhered in or was annexed to the land bought.' It is for this reason, of course, that 'the purchaser's ignorance of the existence of the covenant does not defeat the presumption [that the benefit passes on a sale of the land]' ([1900] 2 Ch 388 at 408).

13 *Osborne v Bradley* [1903] 2 Ch 446 at 450 per Farwell J. See also *Drake v Gray* [1936] Ch 451 at 466, where Greene LJ stated that there are 'two familiar methods of indicating in a covenant of this kind the land in respect of which the benefit is to enure. One is to describe the character in which the covenantee receives the covenant. That is the form which is adopted here, a covenant with so and so, owners or owner for the time being of whatever the land may be. Another method is to state by means of an appropriate declaration that the covenant is taken "for the benefit of" whatever the lands may be.'

14 [1900] 2 Ch 388.

15 It seems to be a matter of no great importance that this formula of annexation defines the benefited tenement in only general terms. It is, however, of vital importance that some reference be made to *land*. See R. E. Megarry and H. W. R. Wade, op. cit., p. 762.

16 (1878) 9 Ch D 125; affd. (1879) 11 Ch D 866, CA.

was held that no effective annexation had been brought about by a covenant made with 'the vendors their heirs executors administrators and assigns', since no reference was made in this covenant to the land which was intended to receive the benefit. Annexation is essentially a conferment of benefit upon *land* not upon *persons*.

There is, of course, a traditional requirement that the alleged dominant tenement must, in any given case, be capable of deriving a realistic benefit from the restrictive covenant which pertains to it. It was held in *Re Ballard's Conveyance*[17] that there was no effective annexation where a restrictive covenant purported to confer benefit upon the *whole* of an excessively large dominant tenement. In such a case, although the original covenantee could always sue on his covenant, his successors in title would be precluded from claiming the benefit of that covenant by way of annexation. However, we have seen that the strictness of the equitable rule in this context has now been substantially relaxed in the light of the decision of Brightman J in *Wrotham Park Estate Co Ltd v Parkside Homes Ltd*[18]. In any event, the unwillingness of the court in *Re Ballard's Conveyance* to sever the benefit and treat it as specific only to a portion of the alleged dominant tenement may be remedied by another means. It has been clear since *Marquess of Zetland v Driver*[19] that none of the problems raised by *Re Ballard's Conveyance* can have any substance if the benefit of the relevant restrictive covenant has been annexed, not to the undifferentiated whole of a large dominant tenement, but to 'each and every part' of that tenement. In such a case, the covenantee's successors are entitled to claim the benefit of the covenant in respect of any part of a large dominant tenement which is particularly adversely affected by any breach of the covenant, provided always that the successor has a proprietary interest in the portion of land in respect of which he claims the benefit.

The fine distinctions drawn in the case law on express annexation have led to the creation of what is acknowledged to be a 'somewhat muddy corner of legal history[20].' Most instances of express annexation effected since *Marquess of Zetland v Driver* have made clear reference to 'each and every part' of the covenantee's land or have used words of similar import. The result of such annexation is that any subsequent purchaser from the covenantee may claim the benefit of the covenant as annexed to the subject matter of *his* purchase even though he may have purchased only a part of the original dominant tenement. In other words subsequent fragmentation of the dominant tenement will not prevent the covenant from being enforceable at the behest of successors in title of the original covenantee.

Difficulties have arisen, however, where fragmentation occurs in respect of a dominant tenement which received the benefit of a restrictive covenant by

17 [1937] Ch 473, p. 618, ante.
18 [1974] 1 WLR 798, p. 618, ante.
19 [1939] Ch 1. In this case the Marquess of Zetland succeeded in depriving the citizens of Redcar in Yorkshire of the facility of 'an eating-house for the consumption of fried fish and other food' ([1939] Ch 1 at 3).
20 See *Griffiths v Band* (1974) 29 P & CR 243 at 246 per Goulding J.

means of an 'integral' rather than 'distributive' annexation[1]. That is, certain logical problems are raised by an annexation to the whole of a dominant tenement as distinct from an annexation to 'each and every part' of that tenement—problems which afflict not the original covenantee (who can always sue) but rather his successors in title. In *Russell v Archdale*[2], for instance, Buckley J suggested that a subsequent purchaser of part only of the dominant tenement could not claim a benefit annexed originally to the whole of that tenement[3]. Furthermore, a successor in title of the covenantee may himself be disabled from claiming a benefit originally annexed to the undifferentiated whole if he later sells even a small portion of that whole to a third party[3]. When applied to this situation, the logic of *Russell v Archdale* would seem to deprive the vendor of the right to rely thereafter upon the annexed benefit, since even he now no longer retains the entire dominant tenement to which that benefit was annexed[4].

The introduction of these technical difficulties seemed likely for a time to threaten good sense and to elevate arid formalism in the law of restrictive covenants[5]. However, some of the gathering problems were assuaged by the decision in *Wrotham Park Estate Co Ltd v Parkside Homes Ltd*[6]. Here Brightman J held that a successor in title—albeit that he has sold away a part of the dominant tenement—may nevertheless claim the benefit if he can show that he retains 'in substance' the dominant tenement for the benefit of which the covenant was unqualifiedly taken.

This decision reflected a more general relaxation of the rules relating to restrictive covenants during the 1970s, although it still fell short of the simplification achieved in other jurisdictions by means of statutory intervention[7].

1 See D. J. Hayton (1971) 87 LQR 539 at 562.

2 [1964] Ch 38. See (1962) 78 LQR 334, 482 (REM). See also *Re Arcade Hotel Pty Ltd* [1962] VR 274 (Full Court of the Supreme Court of Victoria).

3 See also *Stilwell v Blackman* [1968] Ch 508. As in *Russell v Archdale*, the point here was obiter because there was on the facts a valid *assignment* of the benefit of the restrictive covenant in question. See P. V. Baker (1968) 84 LQR 22: 'The Benefit of Restrictive Covenants'. Compare *Re Selwyn's Conveyance* [1967] Ch 674; (1968) 31 MLR 459 (J. W. Harris).

4 It has been pointed out that this conclusion, if correct, brings about strange results. It seems to follow, for instance, that a purchaser of the whole of the dominant land would lose his right to claim the annexed benefit if 'he sold ... perhaps compulsorily a small strip of land for road widening.' See Hanbury, *Modern Equity* (9th edn., London 1969), p. 611. See also D. J. Hayton (1971) 87 LQR 539 at 562ff.

5 The technical principles adumbrated in *Russell v Archdale* and *Stilwell v Blackman* have no counterpart in the law relating to assignment, p. 630, post, or, for that matter, in the law of easements.

6 [1974] 1 WLR 798 at 806. See (1974) 33 Cambridge LJ 214 at 215 (C. T. Emery).

7 See, for instance, s. 79A of the Property Law Act 1958 (No. 6344) of Victoria, as inserted by the Transfer of Land (Restrictive Covenants) Act 1964 (No. 7130) in response to the ruling in *Re Arcade Hotel Pty Ltd* [1962] VR 274. Section 79A provides that when the benefit of any restrictive covenant 'purports to be annexed ... to other land the benefit shall unless it is expressly provided to the contrary be deemed to be and always to have been annexed to the whole and to each and every part of such other land capable of benefiting from such restriction.' This reform vindicates the dissenting judgment of Sholl J in *Re Arcade Hotel Pty Ltd* [1962] VR 274 at 291. See also *Re Miscamble's Application* [1966] VR 596 at 598ff. A similar reform of English statute law has been proposed by the Law Commission. See *Report on Restrictive Covenants* (Law Com. No. 11, 1967), proposition 4(b).

However, as we shall see shortly, statute law has now been recognised in England too as providing a solution for these problems[8].

(ii) *Implied annexation* A more controversial form of annexation is provided by the possibility of implied annexation[9]. It has been said that annexation, although not expressed in the deed containing the restrictive covenant, may nevertheless have been so obviously intended by the covenanting parties that to ignore it would be 'not only an injustice but a departure from common sense[10].' Even in *Rogers v Hosegood*[11] Collins LJ, delivering the judgment of the Court of Appeal, held that annexation merely requires some 'indication in the original conveyance, *or in the circumstances attending it*, that the burden of the restrictive covenant is imposed for the benefit of the land reserved.' Thus, it is argued, annexation of the benefit of a restrictive covenant may be implied from the circumstances surrounding a deed of covenant, where it is clear that the covenant had reference to a defined piece of land and that the parties themselves intended that the benefit should attach to the land rather than to the covenantee personally[12].

(iii) *Statutory annexation* One of the more dramatic developments of recent years in the area of restrictive covenants is the way in which the courts have at last begun to have recourse to what have been in this context long dormant provisions of the Law of Property Act 1925[13]. Section 78(1) of that Act provides that

> A covenant relating to any land of the covenantee shall be deemed to be made with the covenantee and his successors in title and the persons deriving title under him or them, and shall have effect as if such successors and other persons were expressed. For the purposes of this subsection in connexion with covenants restrictive of the user of land 'successors in title' shall be deemed to include the owners and occupiers for the time being of the land of the covenantee intended to be benefited.

At first sight, section 78(1) appears to provide, in statutory language, a formula of annexation no less efficacious than the classic formula which was upheld in *Rogers v Hosegood*[14]. Yet to the obvious puzzlement of many

8 See p. 627, post.
9 For the view that implied annexation is possible, see R. E. Megarry and H. W. R. Wade, op. cit., p. 763f.; H. W. R. Wade (1972B) 31 Cambridge LJ 157 at 169f. The doctrine of implied annexation is, however, criticised by D. J. Hayton (1971) 87 LQR 539; P. V. Baker (1968) 84 LQR 22 at 30.
10 *Marten v Flight Refuelling Ltd* [1962] Ch 115 at 133 per Wilberforce J. See (1962) 26 Conv (NS) 298 (J. F. Garner).
11 [1900] 2 Ch 388 at 404 (emphasis added).
12 It has been suggested that schemes of development, p. 631ff., post, are merely an instance of annexation by implication from surrounding circumstances (see R. E. Megarry and H. W. R. Wade, op. cit., p. 764).
13 See, for instance, the suggestion that section 62 of the Law of Property Act 1925 may be sufficient to enable the benefit of a restrictive covenant to pass on a conveyance of the dominant land. See R. E. Megarry and H. W. R. Wade, op. cit., p. 765; H. W. R. Wade (1972B) 31 Cambridge LJ 157 at 175; D. J. Hayton (1971) 87 LQR 539 at 567, 570.
14 See p. 623, ante.

commentators[15], section 78(1) was never regarded as supplying a general statutory implication of the necessary words of annexation. The provision could, arguably without offence to legislative intention, have been treated as implying a statutory formula of annexation in every deed containing a restrictive covenant which is clearly intended to confer a benefit upon a defined area of land. However, for many years the orthodox view of section 78(1) has been that it provides merely 'word-saving' facility, in that it operates only when a valid annexation has *already* been established without reliance on the subsection, but then operates in such a way as to render it unnecessary to name the covenantee's successors in title[16].

The spell has now been broken, however, by the decision of the Court of Appeal in *Federated Homes Ltd v Mill Lodge Properties Ltd*[17]. The restrictive covenant in issue in this case was clearly enforceable by the covenantee's successor in title on the ground of a valid chain of express assignments[18], but the Court nevertheless dealt with the consequences of the annexation which had supposedly occurred in respect of the covenant. This restrictive covenant contained a reference to 'any adjoining or adjacent property retained by' the covenantee. One parcel of the covenantee's adjoining lands was subsequently transferred to the present plaintiff, and the question arose whether the benefit of the restrictive covenant could be claimed by the plaintiff on the basis of a valid annexation. The Court was of the opinion that it could be so claimed. Brightman LJ rejected a narrow interpretation which treated section 78(1) as 'merely a statutory shorthand for reducing the length of legal documents'. Such an interpretation seemed to him 'to fly in the face of the wording of the section[19].' He held that in the present case 'the benefit of [the] covenant was annexed to the retained land, and . . . this is a consequence of section 78 . . .[20]' In Brightman LJ's view, the actual wording of the restrictive covenant had been sufficient to intimate that the covenant was one 'relating to . . . land of the covenantee' within the sense of section 78(1). The remainder of section 78(1) was therefore activated by this conclusion, with the result that the statute supplied the words necessary to complete the required formula of annexation:

If, as the language of section 78 implies, a covenant relating to land which is restrictive of the user thereof is enforceable at the suit of (1) a successor in title of the covenantee, (2) a person deriving title under the covenantee or under his successors in title, and (3) the owner or occupier of the land intended to be benefited by the covenant, it must, in my

15 'Why the decided cases make no reference to this legislation is a mystery . . . why . . . should counsel never argue the point, judges never mention it, and textbooks not discuss it?' (H. W. R. Wade (1972B) 31 Cambridge LJ 157 at 171ff.). See also R. E. Megarry and H. W. R. Wade, op. cit., p. 765; G. R. Y. Radcliffe (1941) 57 LQR 203 at 205.
16 See, for instance, D. J. Hayton (1971) 87 LQR 539 at 554.
17 [1980] 1 WLR 594. See (1980) 43 MLR 445 (D. J. Hayton); [1980] JPL 371 (G. H. Newsom); (1980) 130 NLJ 531 (T. Bailey).
18 See p. 629f., post.
19 [1980] 1 WLR 594 at 604. In *Tophams Ltd v Earl of Sefton* [1967] 1 AC 50 at 72, Lord Upjohn had dismissed section 79, the companion section of section 78, as having purely 'word-saving significance.' In *Federated Homes*, however, Brightman LJ at 606 simply dismissed section 79 as a provision which 'involves quite different considerations and . . . not . . . a helpful analogy.'
20 [1980] 1 WLR 594 at 603.

view, follow that the covenant runs with the land, because ex hypothesi every successor in title to the land, every derivative proprietor of the land and every other owner and occupier has a right by statute to the covenant. In other words, if the condition precedent of section 78 is satisfied—that is to say, there exists a covenant which touches and concerns the land of the covenantee—that covenant runs with the land for the benefit of his successors in title, persons deriving title under him or them and other owners and occupiers[1].

The Court of Appeal thus concluded that 'section 78 of the Law of Property Act 1925 caused the benefit of the restrictive covenant in question to run with the . . . land and therefore to be annexed to it[2].'

This decision has proved to be highly controversial. It has been pointed out that if section 78 of the Law of Property Act 1925 indeed imposes an automatic annexation effect, the result is to render otiose the entire device of express assignment as an alternative means of transmitting the benefit of restrictive covenants[3]. The effect of the decision of the Court of Appeal has also been criticised on the ground that, for the purpose of determining a question of annexation, which 'is not a question of words but of intention', paramount significance has been attached to statutory words which are 'neutral as to intention'[4]. Unlike section 79(1)[5], the provision contained in section 78(1) makes no allowance for the expression of 'a contrary intention' by the parties to the covenant. If the decision in *Federated Homes Ltd v Mill Lodge Properties Ltd* is correct, it would seem that section 78(1) has the extraordinary effect of creating an automatic annexation quite irrespective of the intentions of covenantor and covenantee. It is such considerations as these which have caused the leading authority on the law of restrictive covenants to express the opinion that 'it really seems almost impossible that the view of Brightman LJ can be correct[6].'

Although it was not strictly necessary for the Court of Appeal's decision, Brightman LJ took the opportunity in *Federated Homes Ltd v Mill Lodge Properties Ltd* to clarify a further aspect of the law of restrictive covenants which has become increasingly difficult in recent years. He completed the simplifying process begun in *Wrotham Park Estate Co Ltd v Parkside Homes Ltd*[7], by striking down in definitive terms the complicated jurisprudence which has developed concerning annexations to the whole as distinct from the constituent parts of a dominant tenement. It seems that the difficulties which have so beguiled the

1 [1980] 1 WLR 594 at 605. Brightman LJ professed to find support for his view of the impact of section 78 in *Smith and Snipes Hall Farm Ltd v River Douglas Catchment Board* [1949] 2 KB 500, and *Williams v Unit Construction Co Ltd* (1955) 19 Conv (NS) 262, p. 610, ante. See, however, G. H. Newsom (1981) 97 LQR 32 at 44ff.: 'Universal Annexation?'.

2 [1980] 1 WLR 594 at 607.

3 (1980) 43 MLR 445 at 446.

4 See G. H. Newsom (1981) 97 LQR 32 at 34.

5 See p. 619, ante.

6 G. H. Newsom (1981) 97 LQR 32 at 48. Mr Newsom points out that the decision of the Court of Appeal effectively destroys the 'whole basis' of titles in land which have been made and accepted under the protection of title insurance granted by insurance companies on the premise that certain restrictive covenants are unlikely to be enforceable: 'This is revolution indeed.'

7 See p. 625, ante.

courts in this context are now swept away by Brightman LJ's declaration that he found

> the idea of the annexation of a covenant to the whole of the land but not to a part of it a difficult conception fully to grasp. I can understand that a covenantee may expressly or by necessary implication retain the benefit of a covenant wholly under his own control, so that the benefit will not pass unless the covenantee chooses to assign; but I would have thought, if the benefit of a covenant is, on a proper construction of a document, annexed to the land, prima facie it is annexed to every part thereof, unless the contrary clearly appears[8].

Although even this element in the Court of Appeal's judgments has been criticised as inconsistent with earlier authorities[9], it may be that the ghost of the 'integral' but not 'distributive' annexation has finally disappeared never to return.

(b) *Assignment*

A second method of transmitting the benefit of a restrictive covenant in equity is provided, in the conventional view, by the device of express assignment of that benefit[10]. Thus, even though a successor in title of the covenantee cannot rest his claim for enforcement upon the ground of effective annexation, he may be able to show that the benefit of the covenant has been expressly assigned to him. However, as we have just seen, it may be that the broad view of annexation adopted by the Court of Appeal in *Federated Homes Ltd v Mill Lodge Properties Ltd*[11] has made the law of assignment virtually redundant.

If the device of assignment has any place in our law, it should be noted that it differs from the device of annexation in the following respects. *First*, annexation and assignment are directed at quite different targets. Annexation involves the attachment of benefit to *land*; assignment involves the conferment of benefit upon *persons*. *Second*, annexation and assignment occur (if at all) at different times. Annexation is effected at the date of the making of the restrictive covenant. Assignment is effected on subsequent transfers, perhaps many years later, of the covenantee's title to later purchasers of the dominant land. *Third*, annexation and assignment have quite different effects. Annexation has the effect of fastening the benefit of a restrictive covenant upon the dominant land for ever, with the result that the benefit passes automatically with that land on any subsequent transfer of title. Assignment is, at least according to one view,

8 [1980] 1 WLR 594 at 606. Megaw LJ agreed at 608. See also *Re Arcade Hotel Pty Ltd* [1962] VR 274 at 291, where Scholl J anticipated the Court of Appeal's construction by 18 years: 'Is there then some particular virtue in the addition of the words "or any part thereof" to the description of the benefited land? . . . why should the benefit of the covenant not be understood to be distributed over the benefited land, in the same way as the burden over the burdened land? I can see no logical reason why not; and as a mere matter of language I can see no such reason.'

9 Compare *Miles v Easter* [1933] Ch 611 at 628 per Romer LJ. See G. H. Newsom (1981) 97 LQR 32 at 48f.

10 See L. H. Elphinstone (1952) 68 LQR 353: 'Assignment of the Benefit of Covenants affecting Land.'

11 See p. 627, ante.

efficacious only in respect of the immediate assignee, with the result that the benefit of the restrictive covenant requires to be assigned afresh with every subsequent transfer of title in the dominant land[12]. *Fourth*, the consequences of fragmentation of the dominant land may differ for the purpose of annexation and assignment respectively[13]. We have seen that it has been thought until recently that a benefit unqualifiedly annexed to the whole of a dominant tenement could not be claimed by a successor in title of merely a portion of that land. There has never been any corresponding limitation in respect of assignment of a benefit, even if that benefit was originally annexed to the entirety of a dominant tenement[14]. Fragmentation of the dominant land has no prejudicial impact upon assignment since assignment is an essentially personal transaction which involves the transmission of a benefit from one individual to another.

Assignment is usually effected by means of express words of assignment inserted into the document of transfer executed by the covenantee in favour of his successor in title or executed by that successor in favour of a later purchaser. Certain specific conditions must be fulfilled in order that assignment be effective, but in general terms the essential requirement is that assignor and assignee express some agreement that the benefit shall pass to the latter.

(i) *The covenant must have been taken for the protection or benefit of land owned by the covenantee at the date of the covenant* It was held in *Miles v Easter*[15] that the assignee of the benefit of a restrictive covenant must be able to show that the covenant was originally taken for the benefit or protection of land owned by the covenantee at the date of the covenant. If this were not so, the covenant would be a 'covenant in gross', and would be unenforceable except as between covenantor and covenantee.

It is permissible to prove this requirement by showing that the circumstances surrounding the making of the covenant clearly establish that the covenant was intended to benefit the covenantee's land. In *Newton Abbot Co-operative Society Ltd v Williamson and Treadgold Ltd*[16], Upjohn J was prepared to accept that the requirement of intended benefit was met by a covenant which precluded the covenantor from conducting trade in competition with the business carried on

12 See *Re Pinewood Estate, Farnborough* [1958] Ch 280; C. H. S. Preston and G. H. Newsom, op. cit., p. 35. There is, however, weighty support for the alternative view that assignment effects a 'delayed annexation'. See *Renals v Cowlishaw* (1878) 9 Ch D 125 at 130f.; *Rogers v Hosegood* [1900] 2 Ch 388 at 408; (1957) 15 Cambridge LJ 146 (H. W. R. Wade); P. V. Baker (1968) 84 LQR 22 at 31f.: 'The Benefit of Restrictive Covenants'; S. J. Bailey (1938) 6 Cambridge LJ 339 at 360f.: 'The Benefit of a Restrictive Covenant'; H. W. R. Wade (1972B) 31 Cambridge LJ 157 at 166.

13 See p. 624f., ante.

14 See, for instance, the cases where assignment was held to be effective under circumstances in which supposedly annexation would not have passed the benefit to the plaintiff: *Russell v Archdale* [1964] Ch 38; *Stilwell v Blackman* [1968] Ch 508, p. 625, ante.

15 [1933] Ch 611 at 625 per Bennett J. See (1933) 49 LQR 483 (H. A. Hollond). This case is otherwise known as *Re Union of London and Smith's Bank Ltd's Conveyance.*

16 [1952] Ch 286 at 293f.

by the covenantee on his nearby premises. It was quite clear here that the covenant had been taken for the protection of the covenantee's land.

(ii) *The assignment must be contemporaneous with the transfer of the dominant land* If the assignee of the benefit of a restrictive covenant seeks to enforce that benefit against the original covenantor, he need prove only that the benefit has been duly assigned to him as a chose in action[17]. However, if he seeks to enforce the covenant against a successor in title to the servient land, he must show that the benefit was assigned to him contemporaneously with the transfer of the title in the dominant land. In other words, he must establish that the assignment was part of the transaction of transfer[18]. If the benefit of a restrictive covenant becomes separated from the dominant land, it ceases to be operative[19].

(iii) *The dominant tenement must be ascertainable* It was held by Romer LJ in *Miles v Easter*[20] that the land benefited by the restrictive covenant which the assignee seeks to enforce must be 'ascertainable' or 'certain'. As Romer LJ indicated, it is impossible to ascertain the existence and location of the dominant land for this purpose unless these are 'indicated in the conveyance or have been otherwise shown with reasonable certainty.' It is clear, however, that the dominant land will be regarded as sufficiently identified if it is ascertainable with reference to extrinsic evidence[1].

It is possible that assignment and annexation may operate concurrently to transmit the benefit of a restrictive covenant to a successor in title of the covenantee[2]. Assignment and annexation are not, in this sense, mutually exclusive[3].

(c) *Scheme of development*

A third method of transmitting the benefit of restrictive covenants in equity is provided by the 'scheme of development' or 'building scheme.'[4]

It is not unusual for a developer of property in an expanding urban location to sub-divide a large area of land into plots with the intention of selling those

17 See R. E. Megarry and H. W. R. Wade, op. cit., p. 766.

18 See *Miles v Easter* [1933] Ch 611 at 632; *Newton Abbot Co-operative Society Ltd v Williamson and Treadgold Ltd* [1952] Ch 286 at 294. See also L. Elphinstone (1952) 68 LQR 353.

19 See *Miles v Easter* [1933] Ch 611 at 632, where Romer LJ explained the assignability of a covenant as being necessary to enable the covenantee to 'dispose of his property to advantage.' This protection is not, however, necessary if he has already managed to sell the dominant land to a third party without simultaneously assigning the benefit.

20 [1933] Ch 611 at 631.

1 See, e.g., *Newton Abbot Co-operative Society Ltd v Williamson and Treadgold Ltd* [1952] Ch 286 at 295ff., where Upjohn J considered that he was entitled to 'look at the attendant circumstances to see if the land to be benefited is shown "otherwise" with reasonable certainty.' See, however, D. J. Hayton (1971) 87 LQR 539 at 568ff.

2 See p. 625, ante.

3 See D. J. Hayton (1971) 87 LQR 539 at 567.

4 According to Megarry J in *Brunner v Greenslade* [1971] Ch 993 at 999, '"scheme of development" . . . is the genus; "building scheme" a species.'

plots to individual purchasers. In order to preserve the value of each plot and the residential amenity of the whole area, the vendor commonly extracts certain restrictive covenants from each purchaser in turn. The object of the exercise is plainly to institute a scheme of mutually enforceable restrictive covenants which will be valid not only for the individual purchasers vis à vis each other but also as between all successors in title of the original covenantors. This aim, if realised, would have the effect of creating a 'local law' for the maintenance of the character of the neighbourhood for all time to come.

A scheme of this kind is known as a *building scheme* or *scheme of development*, and as such is subject to distinct equitable rules governing the enforceability of the restrictive covenants thereby created between the freeholders who purchase property comprised within the scheme. The transmission of the burden of the restrictive covenants entered into by the original purchasers of the individual plots depends, of course, upon due registration of the land charges thus brought into being[5]. However, the transmission of the benefit taken initially by the covenantee—the property developer—turns on the equitable recognition of a scheme of development. If a scheme of development is present in any given circumstances, equity takes the view that the restrictive covenants appurtenant to each and every plot of land comprised within the scheme can be enforced by all who currently own land covered by the scheme. This result follows in equity irrespective of whether the party seeking to enforce a covenant is an original covenantor or a successor in title, and irrespective of the date of purchase by either of the parties in any enforcement action. The scheme of development thus has a quite special equitable character which makes it immune from the normal rules governing the enforceability of restrictive covenants. The scheme of development 'crystallises' on the disposition of the first plot sold within the scheme, and all land comprised within the scheme is automatically bound by the terms of the scheme[6].

The equitable consequence of a finding that there exists a scheme of development is, of course, a vast simplification of the difficulties which would otherwise assail the analysis of the enforceability of the mutual covenants of those who participate in such a scheme. However, the courts initially imposed severely restrictive preconditions for the establishment of a valid scheme of development.

The constituent elements of the scheme of development were described in classic terms in *Elliston v Reacher*[7]. Here Parker J laid down strict requirements in relation to any enforcement of the covenants comprised within such a scheme. It must be proved (1) that both the plaintiff and defendant derive title from one common vendor, (2) that the common vendor laid out the estate in defined plots in advance of the sales of the plots now owned by plaintiff and defendant respectively, (3) that the restrictions imposed by the common vendor were intended to be for the benefit of all of the plots within the scheme, and (4) that

5 *Emmet on Title* (17th edn., London 1978), p. 624f. See, however, D. G. Barnsley, *Conveyancing Law and Practice* (London 1973), p. 340; (1928) 78 LJ 39 (JML).
6 *Brunner v Greenslade* [1971] Ch 993 at 1003.
7 [1908] 2 Ch 374 at 384. See generally D. J. Hayton (1971) 87 LQR 539 at 546ff.

the plaintiff and defendant (or their predecessors in title) purchased their respective plots on the footing that the restrictions imposed were mutually enforceable by the owners of all the plots within the scheme. It was further stipulated by the Court of Appeal in *Reid v Bickerstaff*[8] that the area to which the scheme of development extends must be clearly defined.

So ferocious were the conditions thus laid down for the existence of a scheme of development that between 1908 and 1965 it seems that such a scheme was upheld in only two reported cases[9]. More recently, however, the courts have relaxed the requirements demanded of an enforceable scheme of development, by having regard to the equitable principles regulating schemes of development in the era which preceded *Elliston v Reacher*[10]. In the late 19th century, for instance, it was much more generally recognised that the authentic basis for the enforcement of schemes of development was the idea of community of interest. As Lord Macnaghten said in *Spicer v Martin*[11], 'community of interest necessarily . . . requires and imports reciprocity of obligation.' The intended mutuality of the covenants created within the scheme of development was seen as generating a 'local law' for the area covered by the scheme[12]. This mutuality attracted the protection of a jurisdiction founded upon notions of conscience, for it gave rise to 'an equity which is created by circumstances and is independent of contractual obligation[13].'

As Megarry J was later to observe in *Brunner v Greenslade*[14], when this broader perspective of equity is adopted 'the major theoretical difficulties based on the law of covenant seem . . . to disappear.' The courts have accordingly tended to return to the authentic root of equitable obligation which underlies the scheme of development. In *Re Dolphin's Conveyance*[15], the court was presented with a scheme which was defective in terms of the traditional requirements of a scheme of development as laid down in *Elliston v Reacher.* The scheme lacked a single common vendor, and the vendors had not, prior to the relevant sales, laid out the estate or any defined portion of it in pre-determined lots. Stamp J nevertheless held that there was a valid scheme of development in existence[16]. He noted that in the present case

> what was intended, as well by the vendors as the several purchasers, was to lay down what has been referred to as a local law for the estate for the common benefit of all the several purchasers of it. The purpose of the covenant by the vendors was to enable each

8 [1909] 2 Ch 305 at 319.

9 See *Newman v Real Estate Debenture Corpn Ltd* [1940] 1 All ER 131; *Bell v Norman C. Ashton Ltd* (1956) 7 P & CR 359; C. H. S. Preston and G. H. Newsom, *Restrictive Covenants Affecting Freehold Land* (6th edn., London 1976), p. 54.

10 'I accordingly think that in this case I am fabricating no new equity, but merely emphasising an established equity' (see *Brunner v Greenslade* [1971] Ch 993 at 1005 per Megarry J).

11 (1888) 14 App Cas 12 at 25.

12 See *Reid v Bickerstaff* [1909] 2 Ch 305 at 319 per Cozens-Hardy MR.

13 *Lawrence v South County Freeholds Ltd* [1939] Ch 656 at 682 per Simonds J.

14 [1971] Ch 993 at 1005.

15 [1970] Ch 654. See (1970) 86 LQR 445 (P. V. Baker); (1970) 117 Sol Jo 798 (G. H. Newsom).

16 See also *Baxter v Four Oaks Properties Ltd* [1965] Ch 816.

purchaser to have, as against the other purchasers, in one way or another, the benefit of the restrictions to which he had made himself subject[17].

After reviewing the case law he ruled that

There is not ... a dichotomy between the cases where effect has been given to the common intention inferred from the existence of the concomitants of a building scheme and those where effect has been given to the intention evidenced by the existence of a deed of covenant. Each class of case, in my judgment, depends upon a wider principle. Here the equity ... arises not by the effect of an implication derived from the existence of the four points specified by Parker J in *Elliston v Reacher* [1908] 2 Ch 374 at 384, or by the implication derived from the existence of a deed of mutual covenant, but by the existence of the common interest and the common intention actually expressed in the conveyances themselves[18].

Thus, by elevating the requirement of common intention and its ethical implications, the courts have been able to re-fashion the scheme of development so that it once more becomes a useful and workable device in the enforcement of restrictive covenants[19]. The modern scheme of development appears to be broadly based upon obligations of reciprocity and conscience. It has been said that ultimately there are but two requirements which are universally insisted upon. They are *first*, that the area of the scheme be defined[20]; and *second*, that the purchasers from the person who creates the scheme should purchase 'on the footing that all purchasers shall be mutually bound by, and mutually entitled to enforce, a defined set of restrictions[1].' If these two requirements are fulfilled, it seems to matter not greatly that the other requirements elucidated by Parker J in *Elliston v Reacher* are not satisfied.

(5) **Discharge of restrictive covenants**

The existence of a restrictive covenant affecting a particular piece of land clearly fetters to some extent the kinds of activity which may be conducted on that land. It may sometimes be undesirable that this inhibition upon land use should continue indefinitely. It may be in the interests of social utility that the restrictions imposed by the covenant should be abrogated or otherwise modified.

It is for this reason that section 84(1) of the Law of Property Act 1925 confers a discretionary power upon the Lands Tribunal to discharge or modify any restrictive covenant (with or without compensation) on a number of grounds[2].

17 [1970] Ch 654 at 662.

18 [1970] Ch 654 at 664, citing *Nottingham Patent Brick and Tile Co v Butler* (1885) 15 QBD 261 at 268 per Wills J.

19 See *Texaco Antilles Ltd v Kernochan* [1973] AC 609.

20 See, e.g., the failure of the scheme of development put forward in *Lund v Taylor* (1975) 31 P & CR 167.

1 In determining the intentions of the original and subsequent purchasers, the court will have regard to as many of the relevant instruments of conveyance as possible. See C. H. S. Preston and G. H. Newsom, op. cit., p. 52.

2 The court has jurisdiction under section 84(2) of the Law of Property Act 1925 to declare whether given land is affected by a restrictive covenant. See generally C. H. S. Preston and G. H. Newsom, op. cit., p. 189ff.

These grounds include cases where, by reason of changes in the character of the property concerned or the neighbourhood or otherwise, the restriction is deemed 'obsolete'[3]; cases in which the continued existence of the restriction 'would impede some reasonable user of the land for public or private purposes'[4]; cases where the persons entitled to the benefit of the restriction have agreed expressly or by implication to its discharge or modification[5]; and cases in which the proposed discharge or modification 'will not injure' the persons entitled to the benefit of the restriction[6].

(6) Reform of the law of restrictive covenants

The Law Commission is at present preparing a report on the reform of positive and negative covenants[7]. The shape of future reform in this area is, however, already apparent from the proposals contained in the Law Commission's report in 1967 on the law of restrictive covenants[8]. Here the Law Commission recommended the creation of a new interest in land, to be called a 'land obligation', for the purpose of regulating matters currently dealt with by means of covenants as to user[9]. Land obligations will be capable of creation in respect of freehold and leasehold interests in land. They will be imposed on specified land for the benefit of other specified land so that the burden and benefit will run automatically with the land until released, modified, discharged or terminated (in the case of an obligation affecting leasehold land) by the effluxion of time. In the Law Commission's view, the land obligation will be enforceable only by and against the persons 'currently concerned with the land as owners of interests in it or occupiers of it.' Thus, in effect, land obligations will 'in nature and attributes be more akin to easements than to covenants[10].'

Although the Law Commission's proposals were confined to the law of restrictive covenants, the 'substance' of its proposals was felt to be applicable 'in principle' to positive covenants also[11]. It is likely that the developments of the future will bring about a common code relating to covenants, based upon the recommendations made not only by the Law Commission but also by the Wilberforce Committee which reported in 1965[12].

3 Law of Property Act 1925, s. 84(1)(a).
4 Law of Property Act 1925, s. 84(1)(aa), as inserted by Law of Property Act 1969, s. 28.
5 Law of Property Act 1925, s. 84(1)(b).
6 Law of Property Act 1925, s. 84(1)(c).
7 See *13th Annual Report 1977–1978* (Law Com No. 92), para. 2.30.
8 *Report on Restrictive Covenants* (Law Com No. 11, 1967).
9 Ibid., para. 27.
10 Ibid., para. 27.
11 Ibid., para. 30.
12 See p. 613, ante.

3. PLANNING LAW AND COMPULSORY PURCHASE

It has already been mentioned that much of the law relating to control of land use has been brought within the public domain by modern legislation. The field of planning law and compulsory purchase is now governed by an extremely wide range of statute law and delegated legislation. This area lies outside the scope of this book, and readers are referred to some of the leading works on the subject[13].

13 See P. McAuslan, *Land, Law and Planning* (London 1975); *The Ideologies of Planning Law* (Oxford 1980); K. Davies, *Law of Compulsory Purchase and Compensation* (London 1978); J. Alder, *Development Control* (London 1979); J. M. Simmie, *Citizens in Conflict* (London 1974).

Index